David Kendall is editor of *The Mammoth Book of Best War Comics*. He is an award-winning consultant in developing literacy, and runs workshops to open up the world of books to a wider audience. He lives in Shropshire.

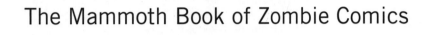
The Mammoth Book of Zombie Comics

Also available

The Mammoth Book of 20th Century Science Fiction
The Mammoth Book of Best British Mysteries
The Mammoth Book of Best Horror Comics
The Mammoth Book of the Best of Best New SF
The Mammoth Book of Best New Erotica 7
The Mammoth Book of Best New Manga 2
The Mammoth Book of Best New SF 20
The Mammoth Book of Best War Comics
The Mammoth Book of Bikers
The Mammoth Book of Boys' Own Stuff
The Mammoth Book of Brain Workouts
The Mammoth Book of Celebrity Murders
The Mammoth Book of Comic Fantasy
The Mammoth Book of Comic Quotes
The Mammoth Book of Cover-Ups
The Mammoth Book of CSI
The Mammoth book of the Deep
The Mammoth Book of Dirty, Sick, X-Rated & Politically Incorrect Jokes
The Mammoth Book of Dickensian Whodunnits
The Mammoth Book of Egyptian Whodunnits
The Mammoth Book of Erotic Online Diaries
The Mammoth Book of Erotic Women
The Mammoth Book of Extreme Fantasy
The Mammoth Book of Funniest Cartoons of All Time
The Mammoth Book of Hard Men
The Mammoth Book of Historical Whodunnits
The Mammoth Book of Illustrated True Crime
The Mammoth Book of Inside the Elite Forces
The Mammoth Book of International Erotica
The Mammoth Book of Jack the Ripper
The Mammoth Book of Jacobean Whodunnits
The Mammoth Book of Killers at Large
The Mammoth Book of King Arthur
The Mammoth Book of Lesbian Erotica
The Mammoth Book of Maneaters
The Mammoth Book of Modern Ghost Stories
The Mammoth Book of Monsters
The Mammoth Book of Mountain Disasters
The Mammoth Book of New Gay Erotica
The Mammoth Book of New Terror
The Mammoth Book of On the Road
The Mammoth Book of Pirates
The Mammoth Book of Poker
The Mammoth Book of Prophecies
The Mammoth Book of Roaring Twenties Whodunnits
The Mammoth Book of Sex, Drugs and Rock 'N' Roll
The Mammoth Book of Short Spy Novels
The Mammoth Book of Sorcerers' Tales
The Mammoth Book of True Crime
The Mammoth Book of True War Stories
The Mammoth Book of Unsolved Crimes
The Mammoth Book of Vintage Whodunnits
The Mammoth Book of Women Who Kill

The Mammoth Book of

Edited by David Kendall

ROBINSON

Constable & Robinson Ltd
3 The Lanchesters
162 Fulham Palace Road
London W6 9ER
www.constablerobinson.com

First published in the UK by Robinson,
an imprint of Constable & Robinson, 2008

A copy of the British Library Cataloguing in Publication
Data is available from the British Library

UK ISBN 978-1-84529-714-5

  3 5 7 9 10 8 6 4 2

PEFC
PEFC/16-33-111
CATG-PEFC-052
www.pefc.org

Printed and bound in the EU

Contents

Introduction – The Rise of the Foot Soldier

Everybody loves zombies these days. They are the rock 'n' roll of horror monsters: raw gore, bloody, and funny. There is none of the elegant posturing of vampires. Zombies are the masses with little need for individualization. Their function is as shock troops to drag down civilization, or what remains of it, through savagery and numbers. Zombies are the frontline grunts, the faceless hundreds that crawl and stagger into oblivion. In a zombie story, at least a part of the audience is rooting for the zombies.

If it's true that monsters reflect our fears and desires, what does the zombie give us? A vision of a time when muscle and bone can no longer be kept under control? It's not just the flesh that we lose; it's our minds, social conventions, and language. Zombies are stripped down to a core hunger, uncaring of what they've lost. There is the occasional melancholic zombie story, of course, and these are often some of the best. Here the image is of the cursed hero who must struggle to free himself from his fate. But most of the time zombies are uncaring of their fate, and many revel in it.

Despite their black magic/voodoo heritage, the zombie belongs firmly to modern times. It shuffled its way into strange travel books and pulp short stories at the beginning of the twentieth century; but it was film that created the zombie's iconic status. For a while they were the hired extras that would be raised up to stagger like town drunks to drag the hero or heroine to the ground. And then came the 1960s and zombies went rotten, and through mindless weighty numbers, became the main agents of terror.

The dead rise, rot, and eat. It's the rotting bit that sets the zombie apart from other horror monsters. Vampires are dead too but generally look pretty good on it. Zombies by contrast inspire awe and delight in their lack of beauty and their complete disregard for the safety of their flesh. It was probably Michael Jackson's "Thriller" that mainstreamed the idea that zombies could be fun as well as terrifying. This strand of black humour can be seen in many zombie comics.

Throughout the 1980s zombie comics kept zombies alive pushing the ideas further and further with often peculiar and gross results.

This anthology pulls in many of the best zombie comics from the last twenty years. There are zombies from different parts of the world, there are zombies that talk, and there are zombies that pull people's heads off. The dead sometimes have our disgust and sometimes our sympathy but they always get our attention.

IDW
no.1
$6.99
HORRORCIDE
STEVE NILES

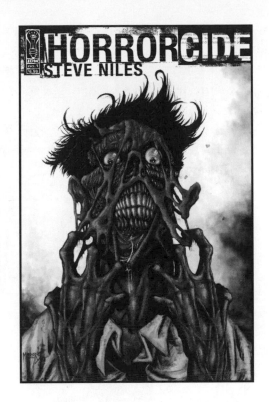

Making Amends (2004)

Creators: Steve Niles (script), Josh Medors (art)

These days zombies have little purpose other than to satisfy their cravings for flesh/brains, but more traditional back-from-the-dead stories were often based around revenge. Here, Niles gives that idea a modern twist.

Steve Niles is one of the writers credited with bringing horror comics back to prominence, with titles such as "30 Days of Night", and "Criminal Macabre".

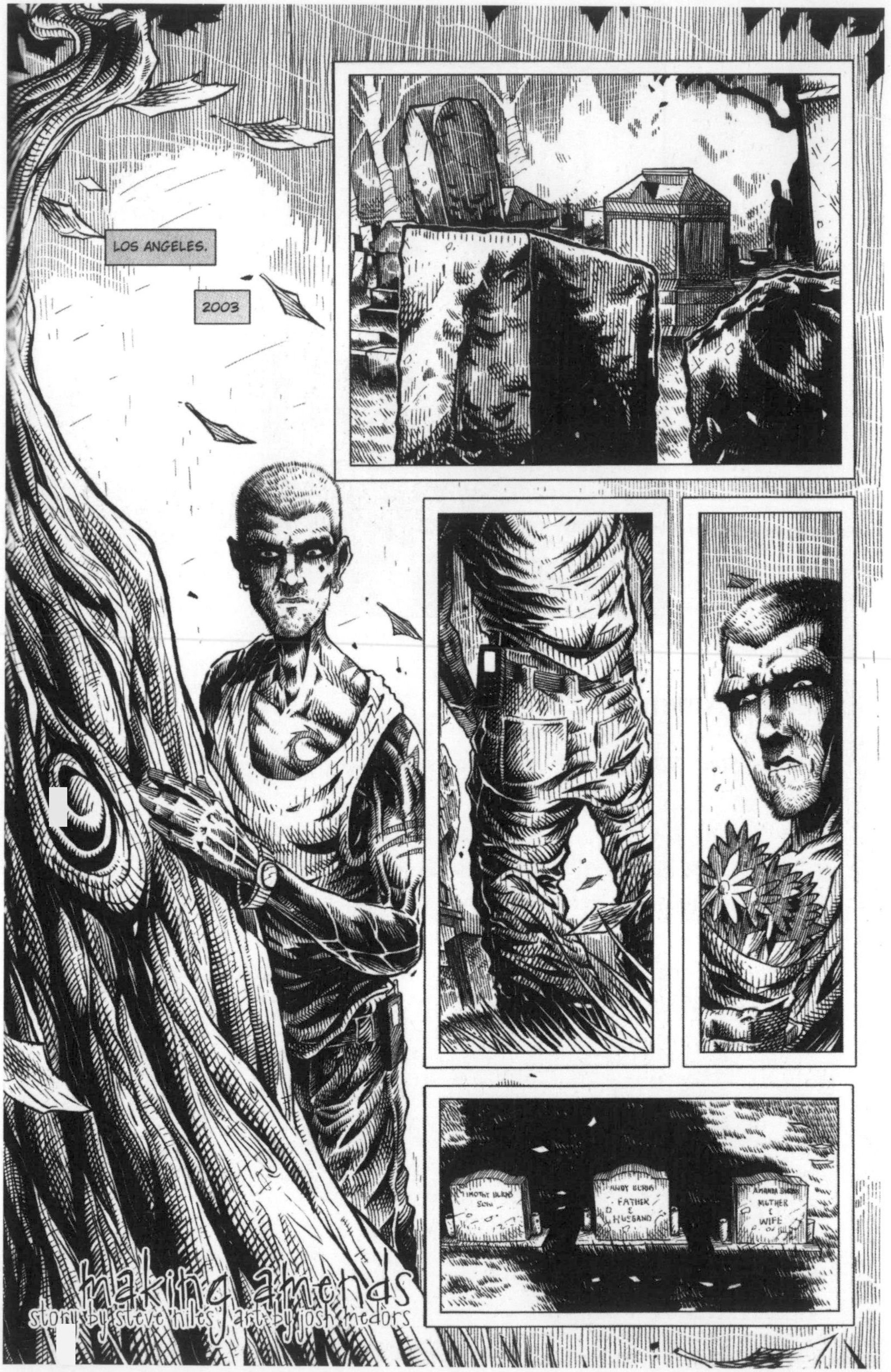
LOS ANGELES.
2003
SON
FATHER & HUSBAND
MOTHER & WIFE
making amends
story by steve niles / art by josh medors

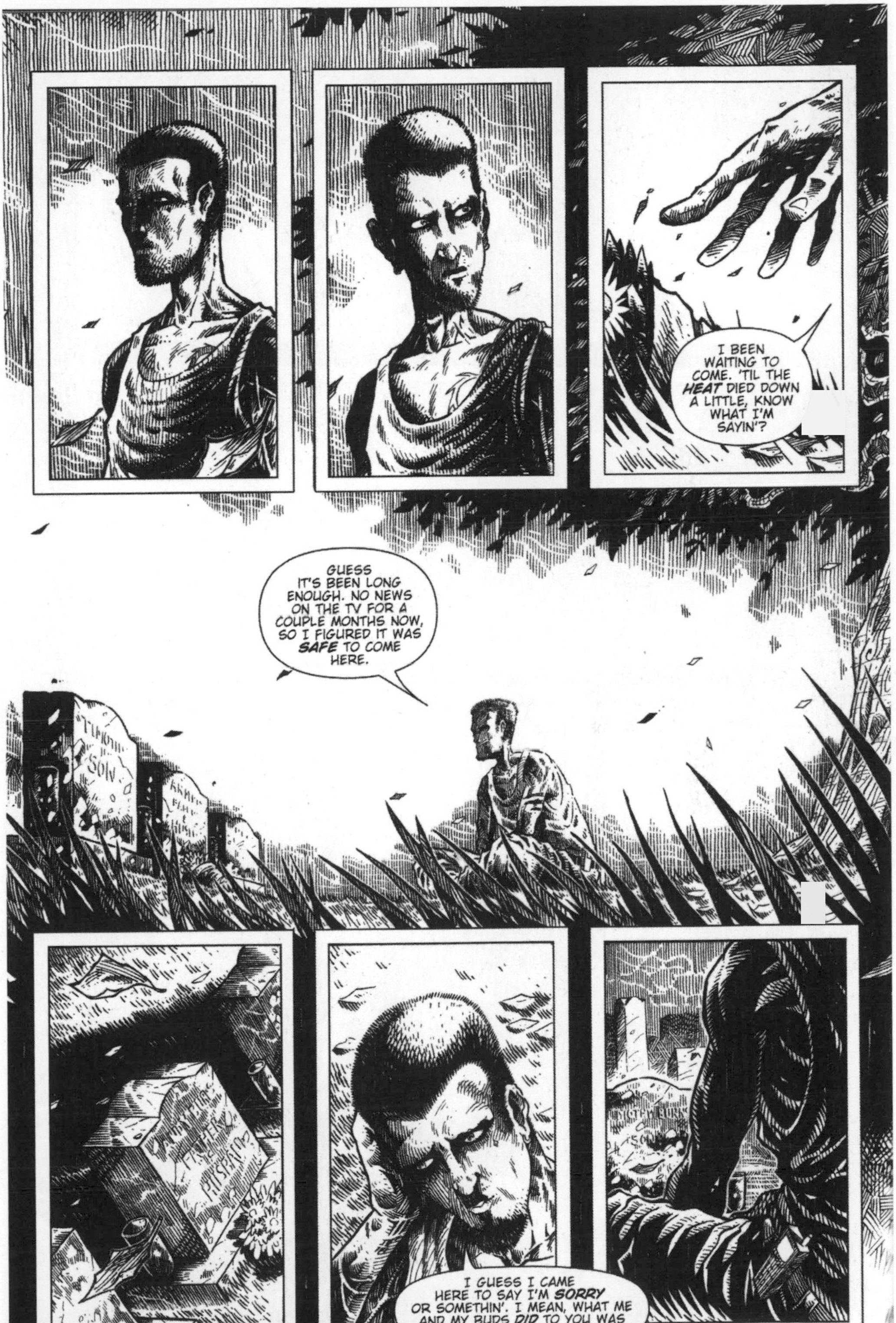
I BEEN WAITING TO COME. 'TIL THE HEAT DIED DOWN A LITTLE, KNOW WHAT I'M SAYIN'?
GUESS IT'S BEEN LONG ENOUGH. NO NEWS ON THE TV FOR A COUPLE MONTHS NOW, SO I FIGURED IT WAS SAFE TO COME HERE.
I GUESS I CAME HERE TO SAY I'M SORRY OR SOMETHIN'. I MEAN, WHAT ME AND MY BUDS DID TO YOU WAS PRETTY FUCKED UP.

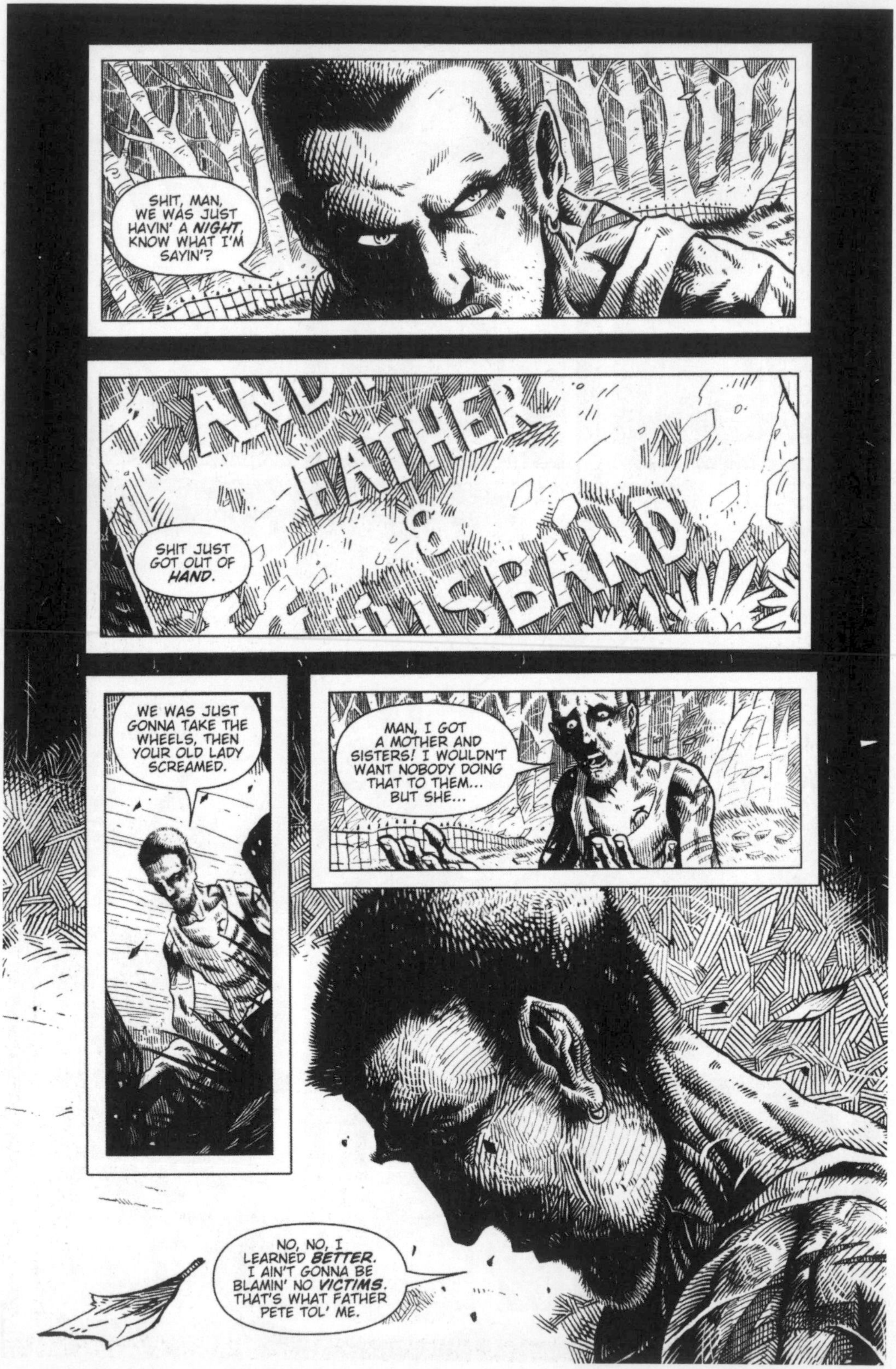
SHIT, MAN, WE WAS JUST HAVIN' A NIGHT, KNOW WHAT I'M SAYIN'?
FATHER
SHIT JUST GOT OUT OF HAND.
WE WAS JUST GONNA TAKE THE WHEELS, THEN YOUR OLD LADY SCREAMED.
MAN, I GOT A MOTHER AND SISTERS! I WOULDN'T WANT NOBODY DOING THAT TO THEM... BUT SHE...
NO, NO, I LEARNED BETTER. I AIN'T GONNA BE BLAMIN' NO VICTIMS. THAT'S WHAT FATHER PETE TOL' ME.

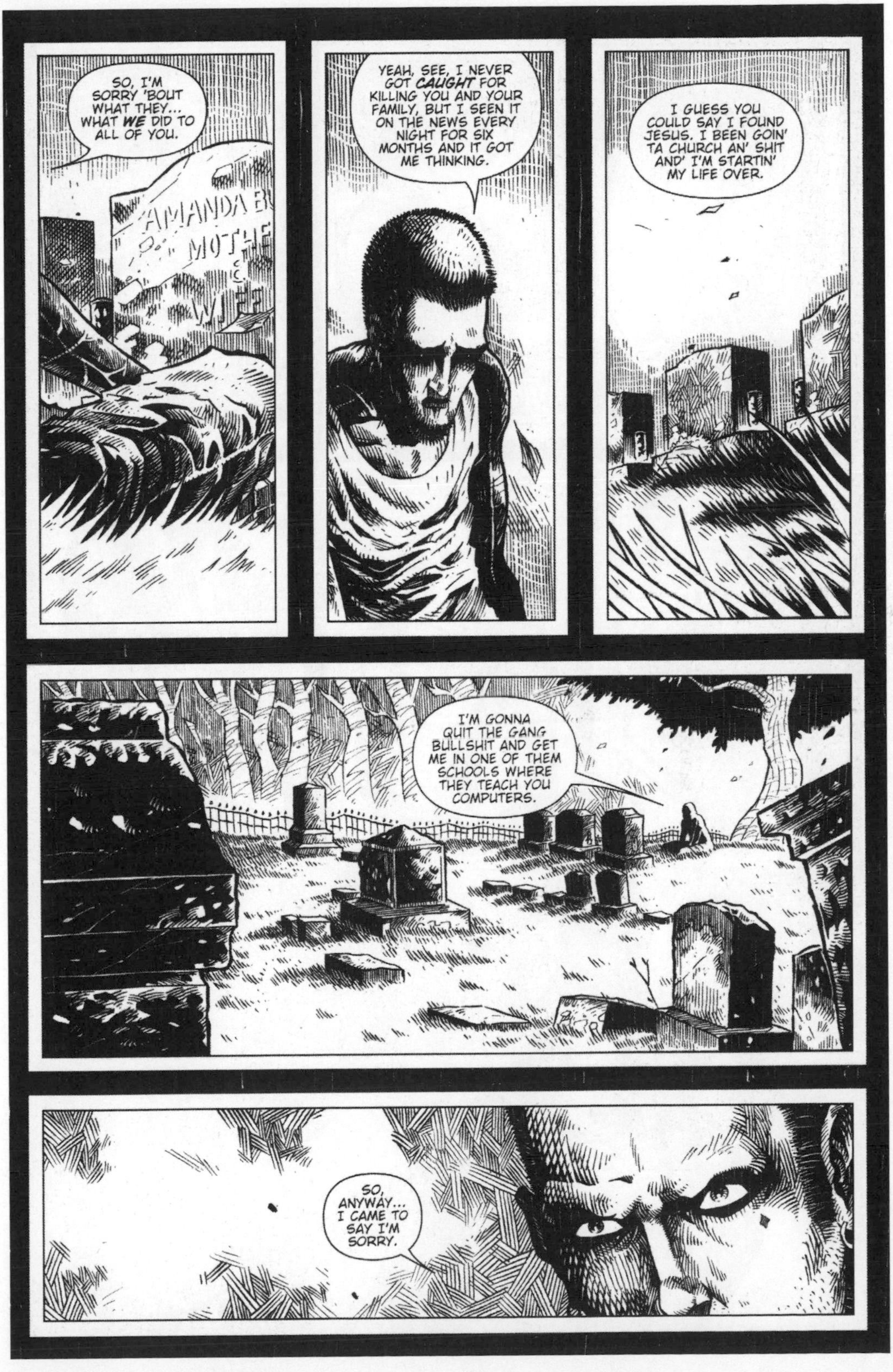
SO, I'M SORRY 'BOUT WHAT THEY... WHAT WE DID TO ALL OF YOU.
AMANDA B
MOTHE
WIF
YEAH, SEE, I NEVER GOT CAUGHT FOR KILLING YOU AND YOUR FAMILY, BUT I SEEN IT ON THE NEWS EVERY NIGHT FOR SIX MONTHS AND IT GOT ME THINKING.
I GUESS YOU COULD SAY I FOUND JESUS. I BEEN GOIN' TA CHURCH AN' SHIT AND' I'M STARTIN' MY LIFE OVER.
I'M GONNA QUIT THE GANG BULLSHIT AND GET ME IN ONE OF THEM SCHOOLS WHERE THEY TEACH YOU COMPUTERS.
SO, ANYWAY... I CAME TO SAY I'M SORRY.

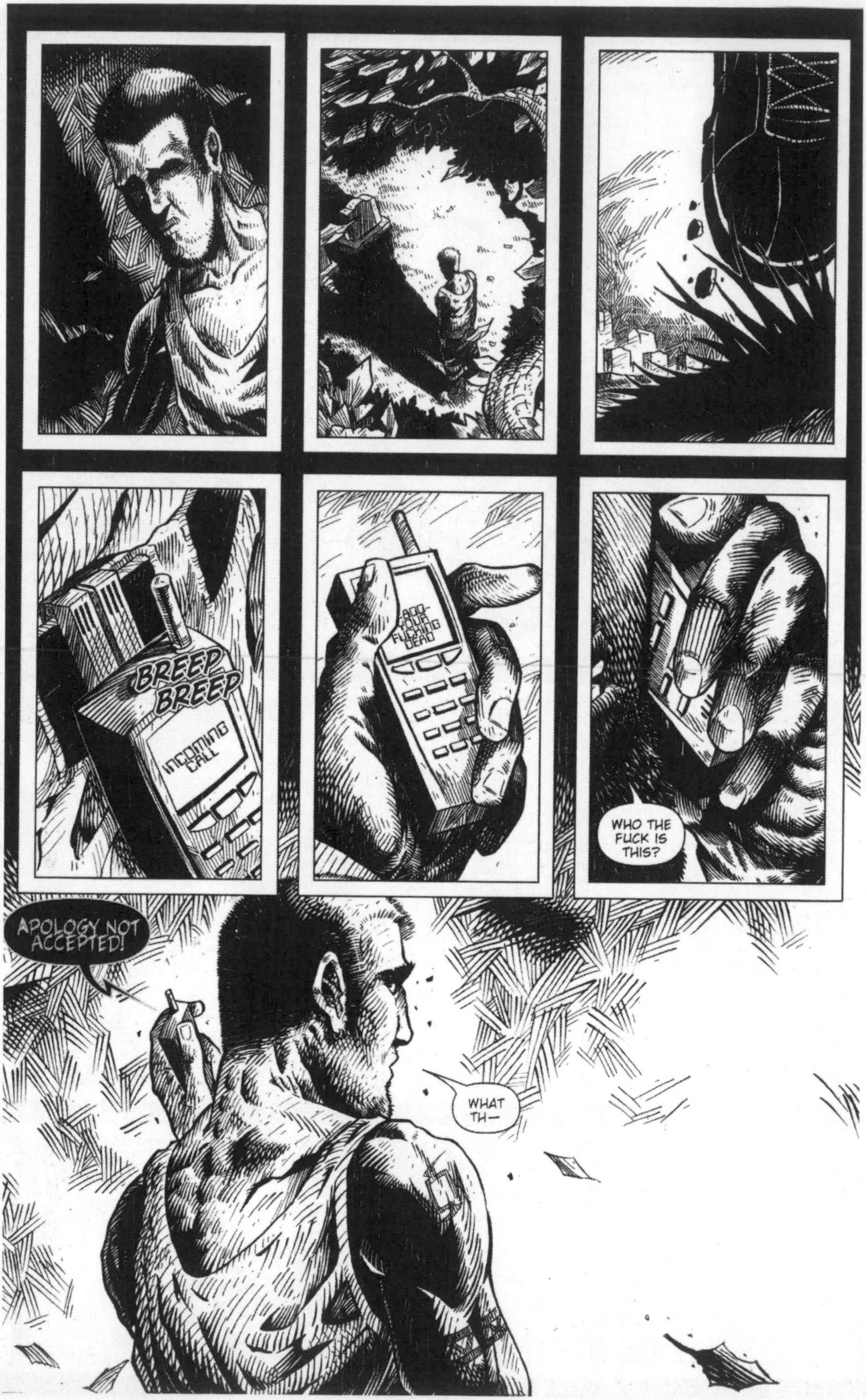
BREEP BREEP
INCOMING CALL
BOO- YOUR FUCKING DEAD
WHO THE FUCK IS THIS?
APOLOGY NOT ACCEPTED!
WHAT TH—

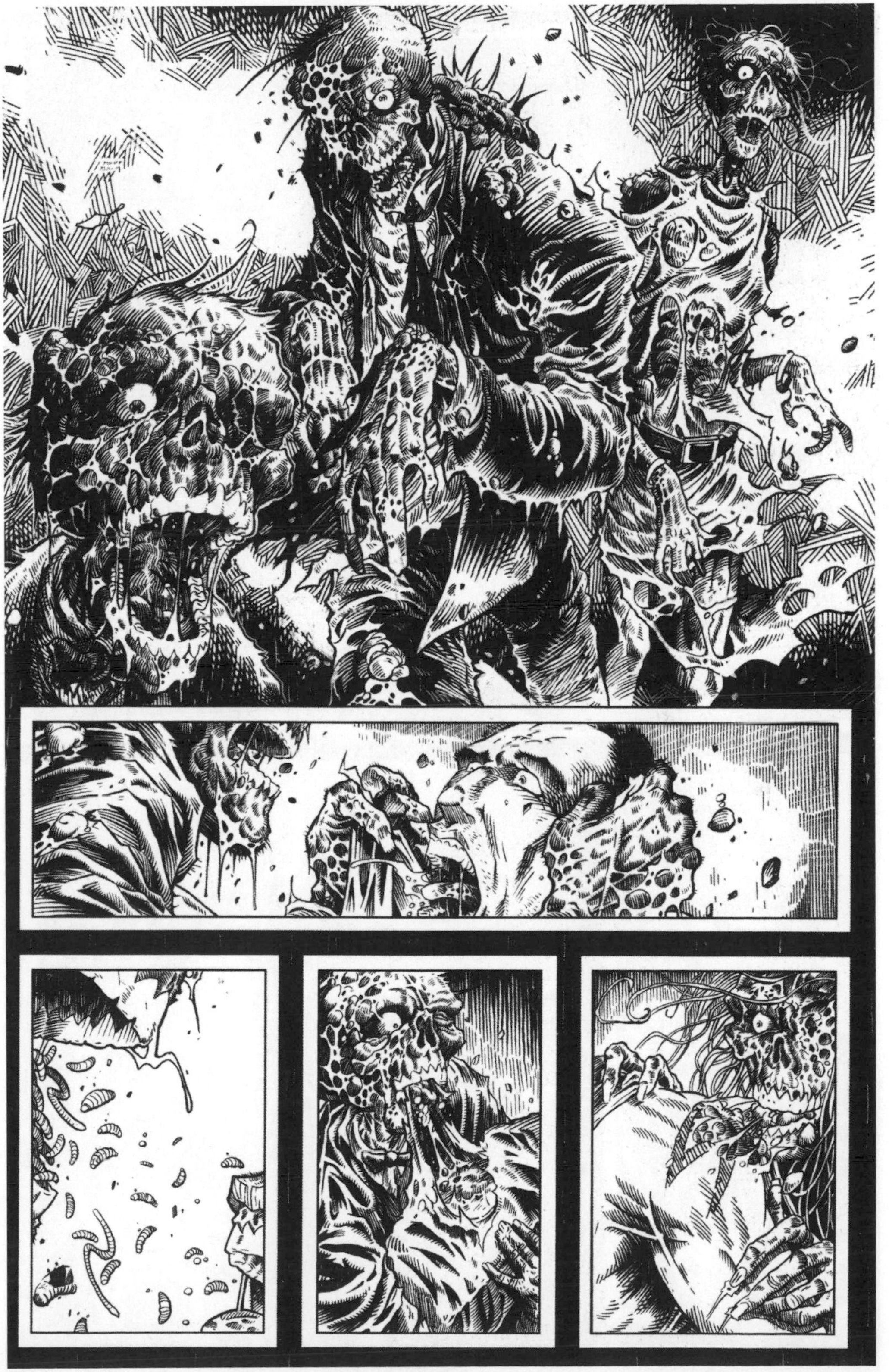

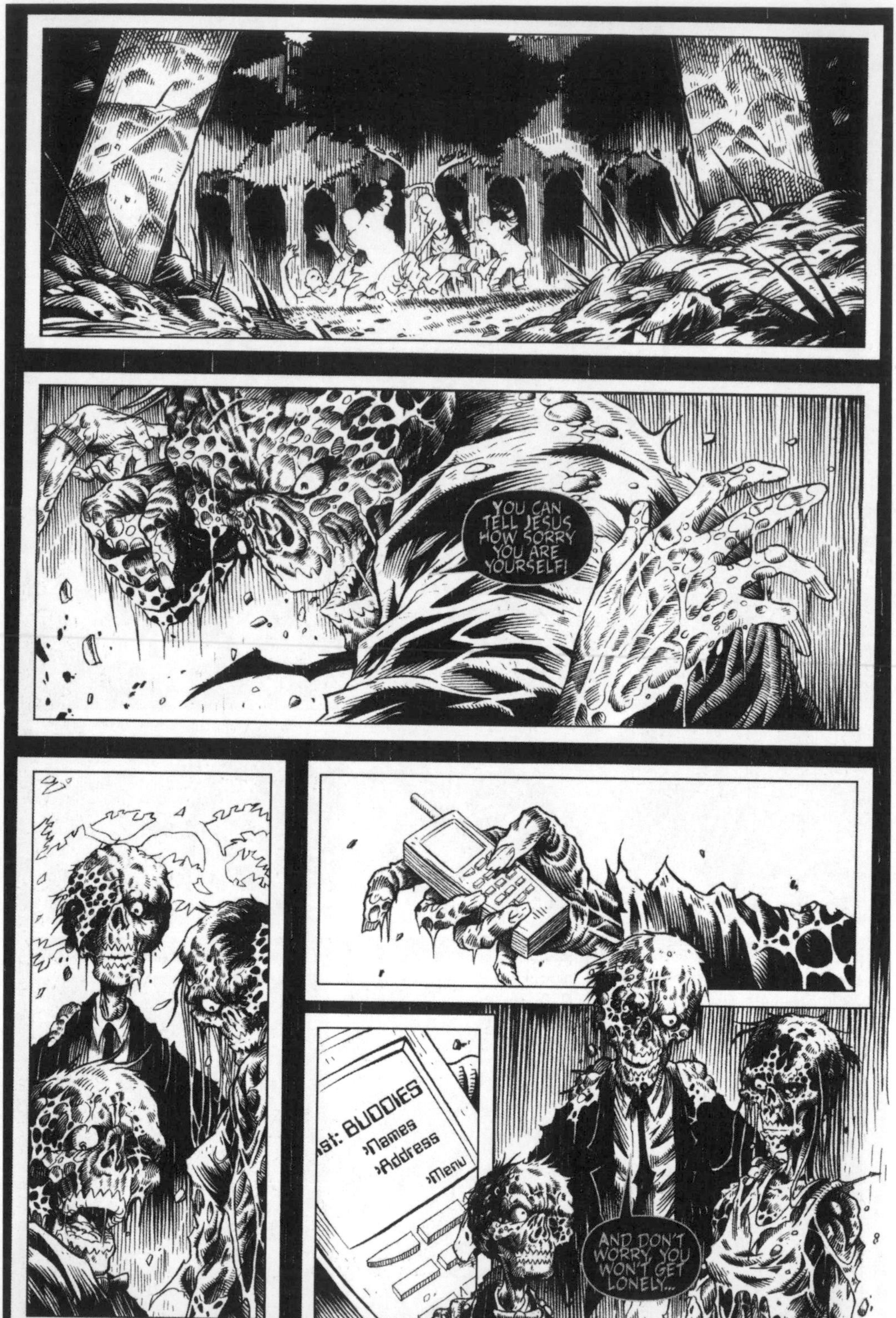
YOU CAN TELL JESUS HOW SORRY YOU ARE YOURSELF!
BUDDIES
›Names
›Address
›Menu
AND DON'T WORRY, YOU WON'T GET LONELY...

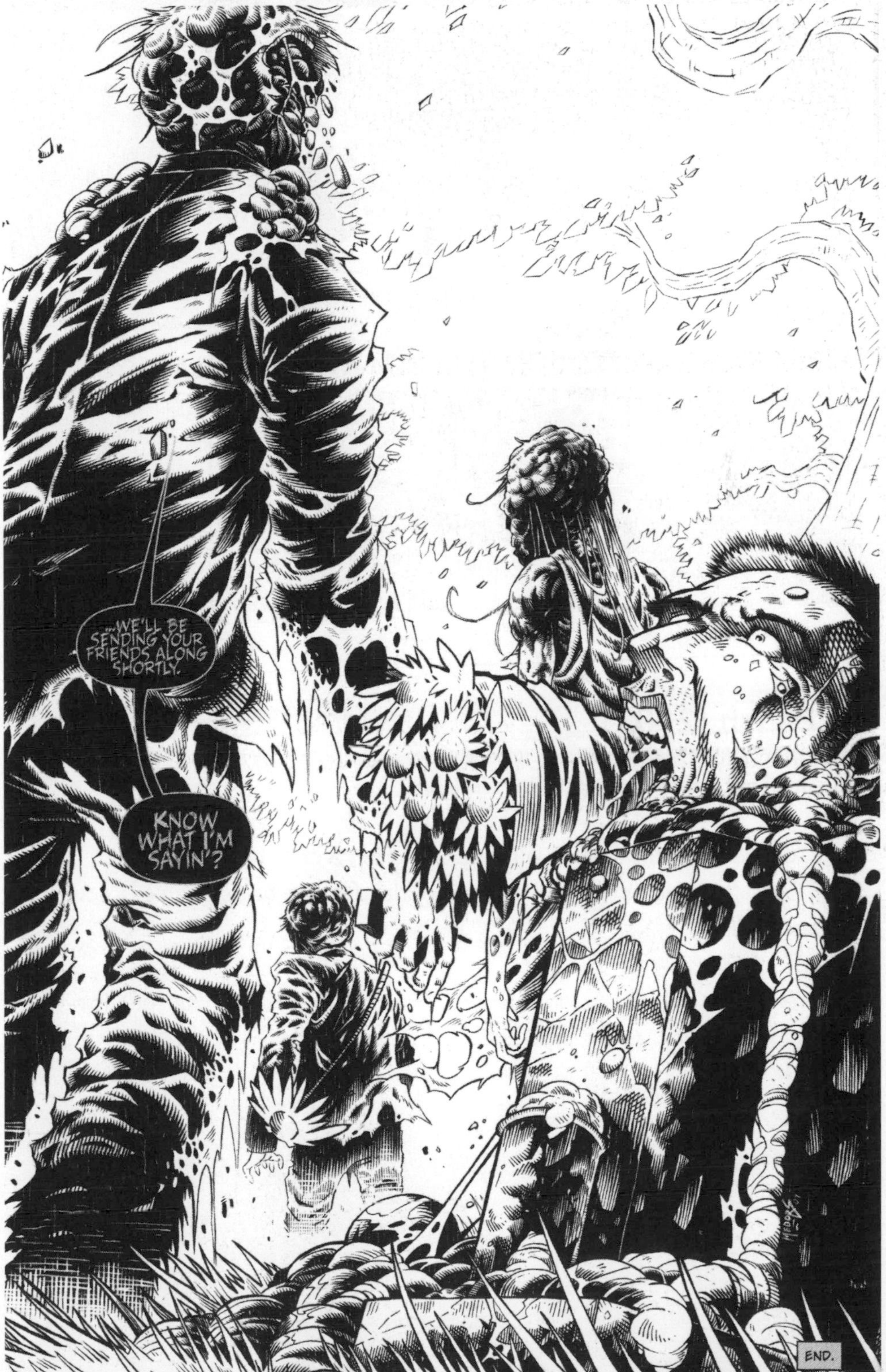
...WE'LL BE SENDING YOUR FRIENDS ALONG SHORTLY.
KNOW WHAT I'M SAYIN'?
END.

Pariah (2007)

Creators: Jon Ayre (script), One Neck (art)

Most people want to fit in with the crowd but a crowd of zombies?
"Pariah" is a powerful short story about the dread of being unable to connect
with others.

Works by One Neck (Iain Laurie) have appeared in various publications
including *The List, Kitchen Sink,* and *Small Axe.*

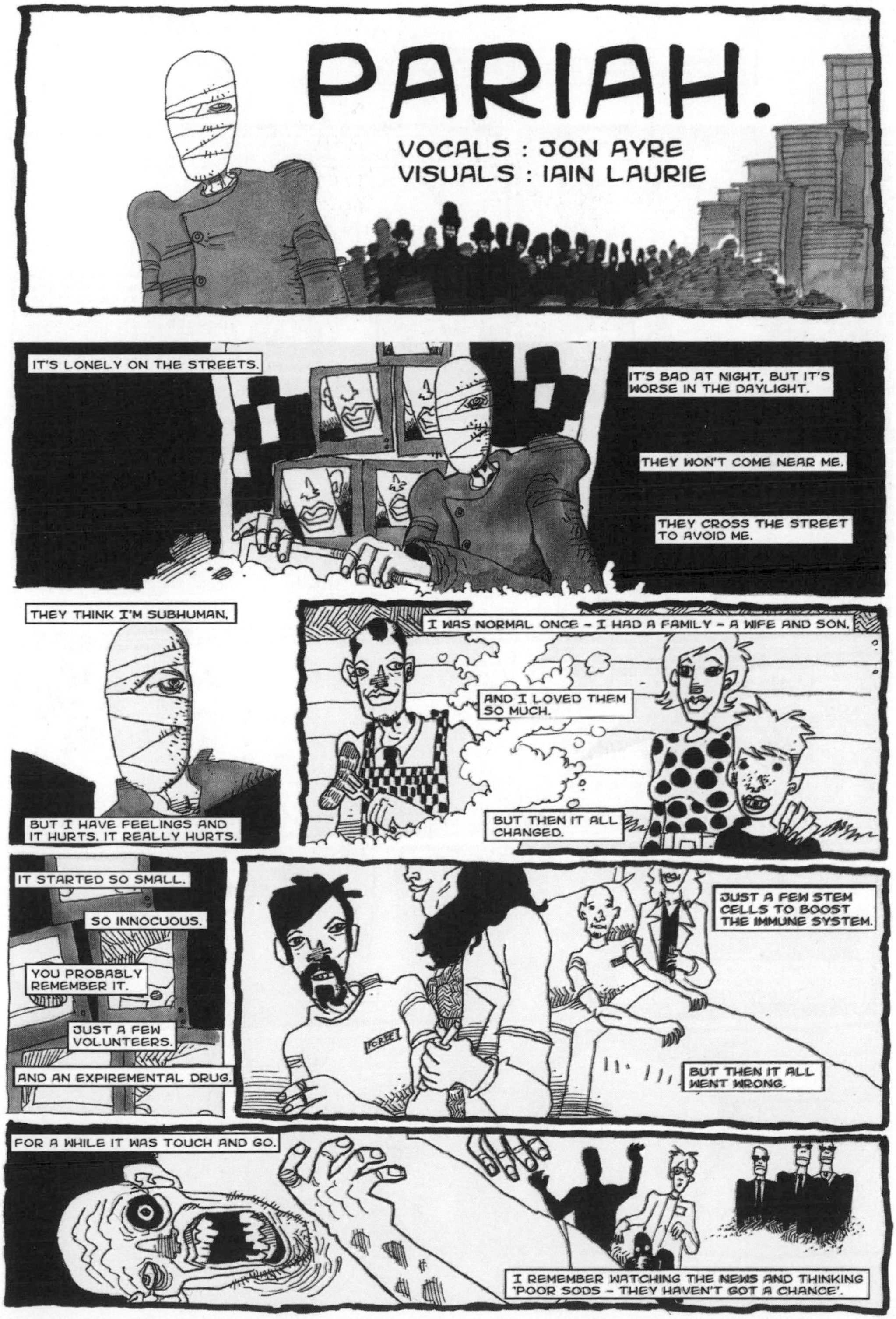
PARIAH.
VOCALS : JON AYRE
VISUALS : IAIN LAURIE
IT'S LONELY ON THE STREETS.
IT'S BAD AT NIGHT, BUT IT'S WORSE IN THE DAYLIGHT.
THEY WON'T COME NEAR ME.
THEY CROSS THE STREET TO AVOID ME.
THEY THINK I'M SUBHUMAN.
BUT I HAVE FEELINGS AND IT HURTS. IT REALLY HURTS.
I WAS NORMAL ONCE – I HAD A FAMILY – A WIFE AND SON.
AND I LOVED THEM SO MUCH.
BUT THEN IT ALL CHANGED.
IT STARTED SO SMALL.
SO INNOCUOUS.
YOU PROBABLY REMEMBER IT.
JUST A FEW VOLUNTEERS.
AND AN EXPIREMENTAL DRUG.
JUST A FEW STEM CELLS TO BOOST THE IMMUNE SYSTEM.
BUT THEN IT ALL WENT WRONG.
FOR A WHILE IT WAS TOUCH AND GO.
I REMEMBER WATCHING THE NEWS AND THINKING 'POOR SODS – THEY HAVEN'T GOT A CHANCE'.

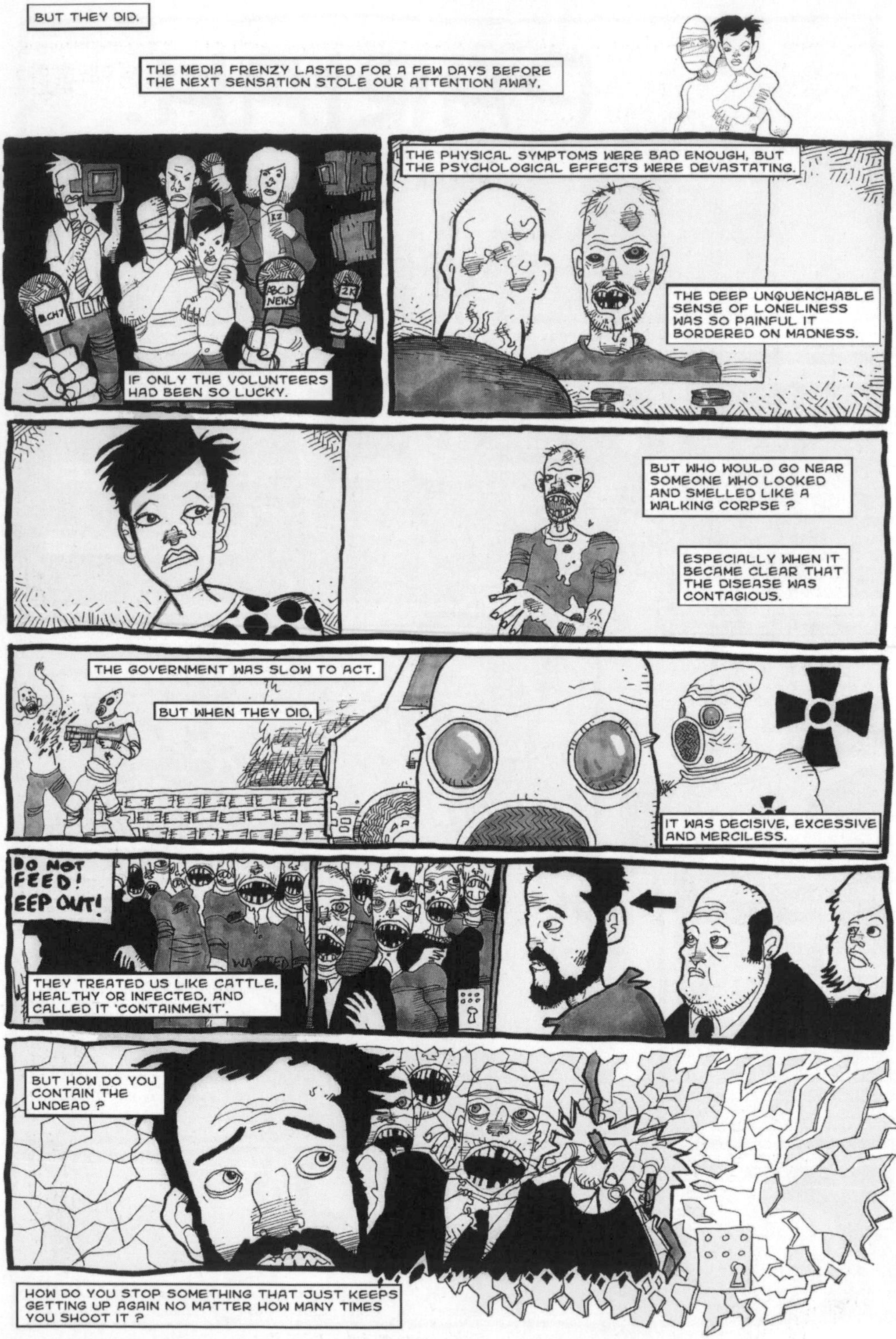
BUT THEY DID.
THE MEDIA FRENZY LASTED FOR A FEW DAYS BEFORE THE NEXT SENSATION STOLE OUR ATTENTION AWAY.
ABCD NEWS
IF ONLY THE VOLUNTEERS HAD BEEN SO LUCKY.
THE PHYSICAL SYMPTOMS WERE BAD ENOUGH, BUT THE PSYCHOLOGICAL EFFECTS WERE DEVASTATING.
THE DEEP UNQUENCHABLE SENSE OF LONELINESS WAS SO PAINFUL IT BORDERED ON MADNESS.
BUT WHO WOULD GO NEAR SOMEONE WHO LOOKED AND SMELLED LIKE A WALKING CORPSE ?
ESPECIALLY WHEN IT BECAME CLEAR THAT THE DISEASE WAS CONTAGIOUS.
THE GOVERNMENT WAS SLOW TO ACT.
BUT WHEN THEY DID,
IT WAS DECISIVE, EXCESSIVE AND MERCILESS.
DO NOT FEED! EEP OUT!
WASTED
THEY TREATED US LIKE CATTLE, HEALTHY OR INFECTED, AND CALLED IT 'CONTAINMENT'.
BUT HOW DO YOU CONTAIN THE UNDEAD ?
HOW DO YOU STOP SOMETHING THAT JUST KEEPS GETTING UP AGAIN NO MATTER HOW MANY TIMES YOU SHOOT IT ?

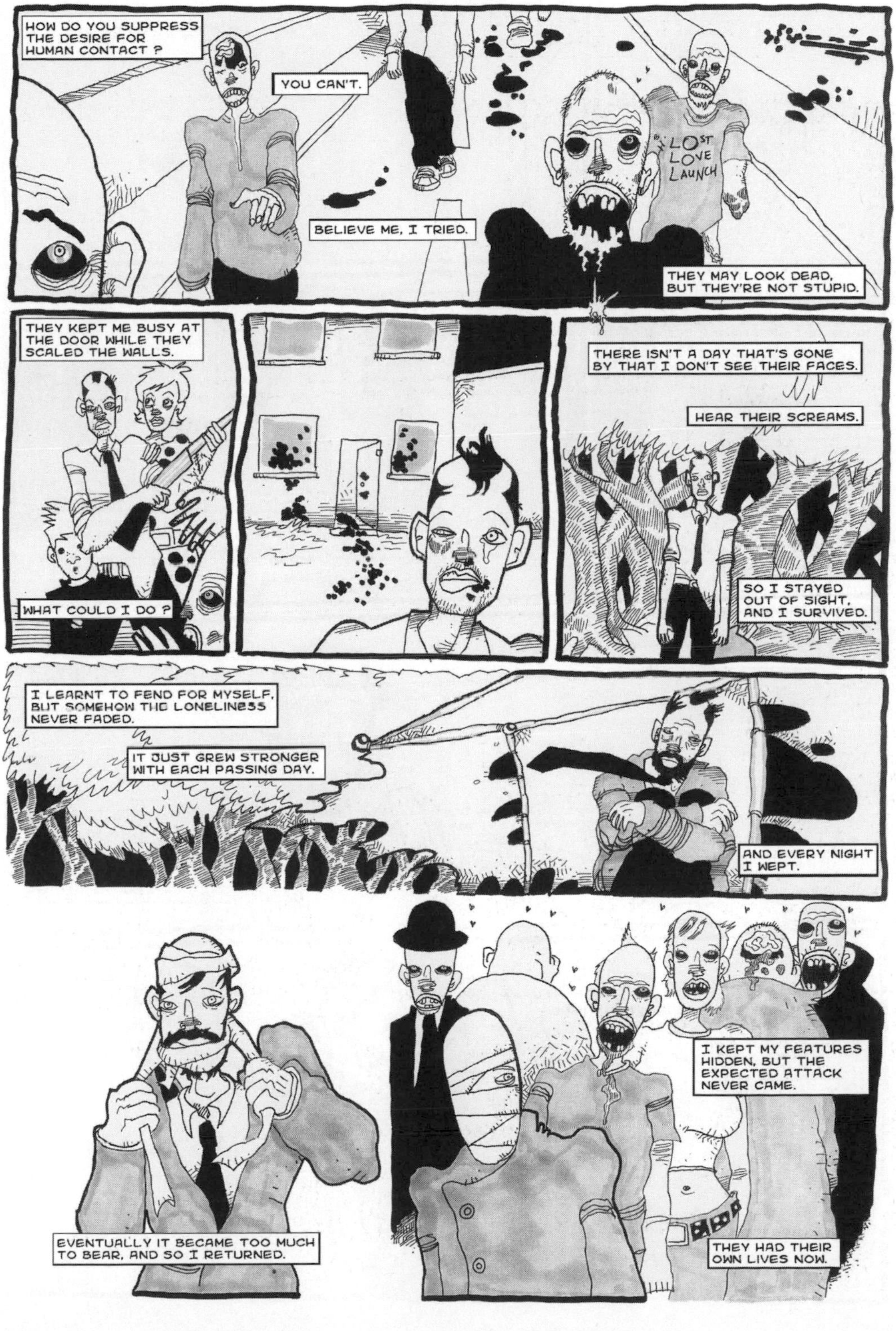
HOW DO YOU SUPPRESS THE DESIRE FOR HUMAN CONTACT ?
YOU CAN'T.
BELIEVE ME, I TRIED.
LOST LOVE LAUNCH
THEY MAY LOOK DEAD, BUT THEY'RE NOT STUPID.
THEY KEPT ME BUSY AT THE DOOR WHILE THEY SCALED THE WALLS.
WHAT COULD I DO ?
THERE ISN'T A DAY THAT'S GONE BY THAT I DON'T SEE THEIR FACES.
HEAR THEIR SCREAMS.
SO I STAYED OUT OF SIGHT, AND I SURVIVED.
I LEARNT TO FEND FOR MYSELF, BUT SOMEHOW THE LONELINESS NEVER FADED.
IT JUST GREW STRONGER WITH EACH PASSING DAY.
AND EVERY NIGHT I WEPT.
EVENTUALLY IT BECAME TOO MUCH TO BEAR, AND SO I RETURNED.
I KEPT MY FEATURES HIDDEN, BUT THE EXPECTED ATTACK NEVER CAME.
THEY HAD THEIR OWN LIVES NOW.

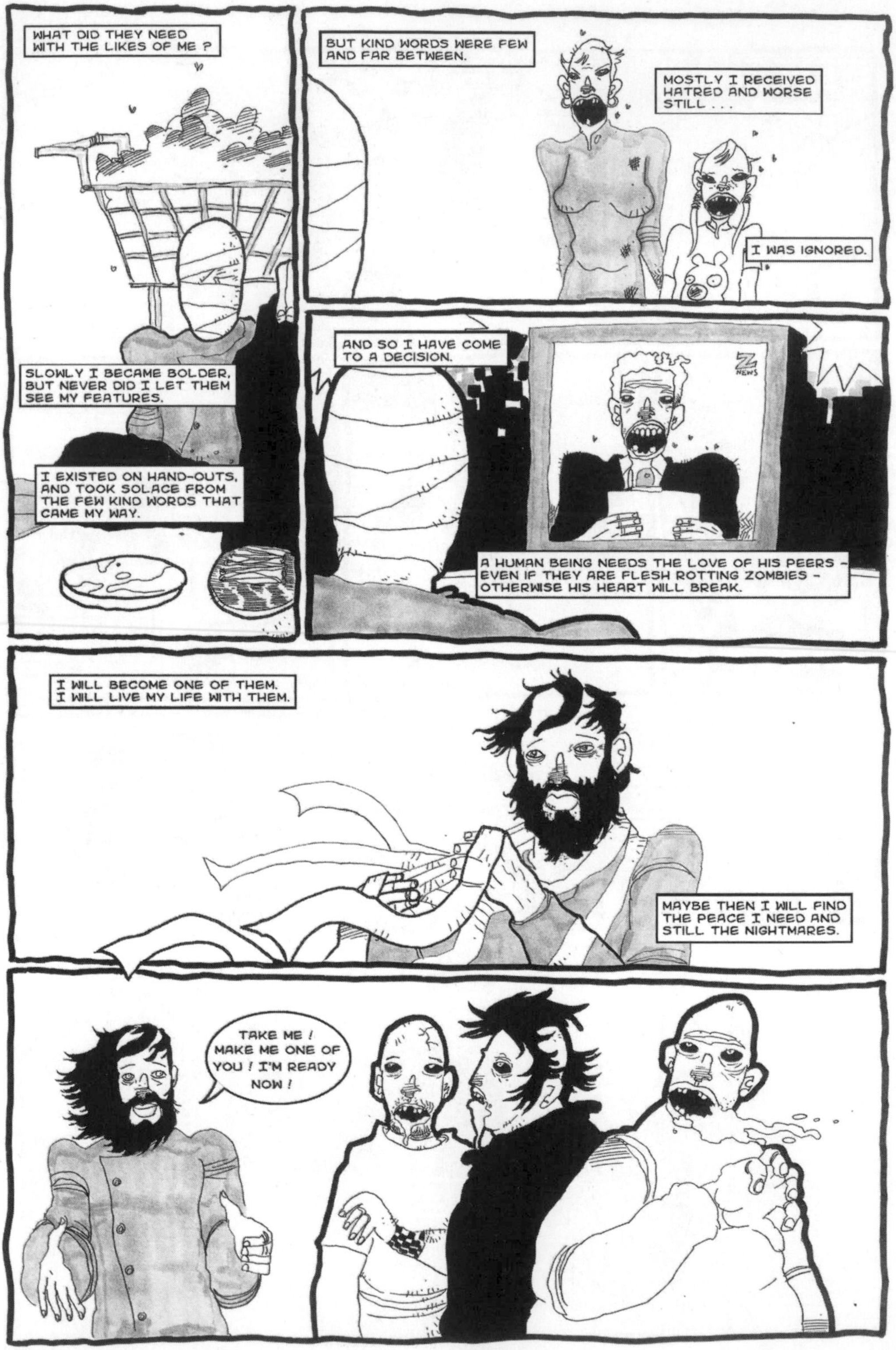
WHAT DID THEY NEED WITH THE LIKES OF ME ?
SLOWLY I BECAME BOLDER, BUT NEVER DID I LET THEM SEE MY FEATURES.
I EXISTED ON HAND-OUTS, AND TOOK SOLACE FROM THE FEW KIND WORDS THAT CAME MY WAY.
BUT KIND WORDS WERE FEW AND FAR BETWEEN.
MOSTLY I RECEIVED HATRED AND WORSE STILL . . .
I WAS IGNORED.
AND SO I HAVE COME TO A DECISION.
Z NEWS
A HUMAN BEING NEEDS THE LOVE OF HIS PEERS - EVEN IF THEY ARE FLESH ROTTING ZOMBIES - OTHERWISE HIS HEART WILL BREAK.
I WILL BECOME ONE OF THEM. I WILL LIVE MY LIFE WITH THEM.
MAYBE THEN I WILL FIND THE PEACE I NEED AND STILL THE NIGHTMARES.
TAKE ME ! MAKE ME ONE OF YOU ! I'M READY NOW !

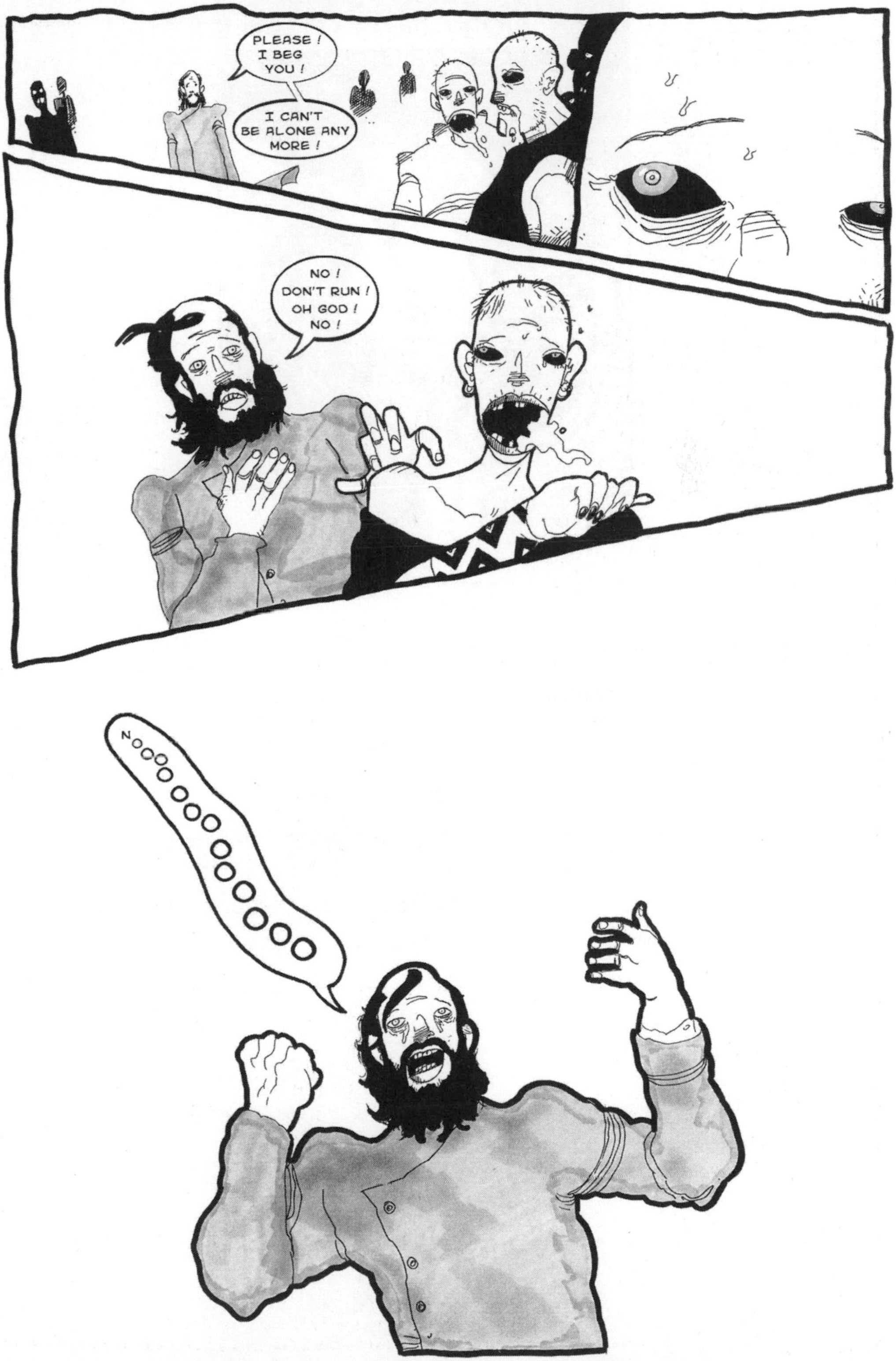
PLEASE ! I BEG YOU !
I CAN'T BE ALONE ANY MORE !
NO ! DON'T RUN ! OH GOD ! NO !
NOOOOOOOOOOOOO

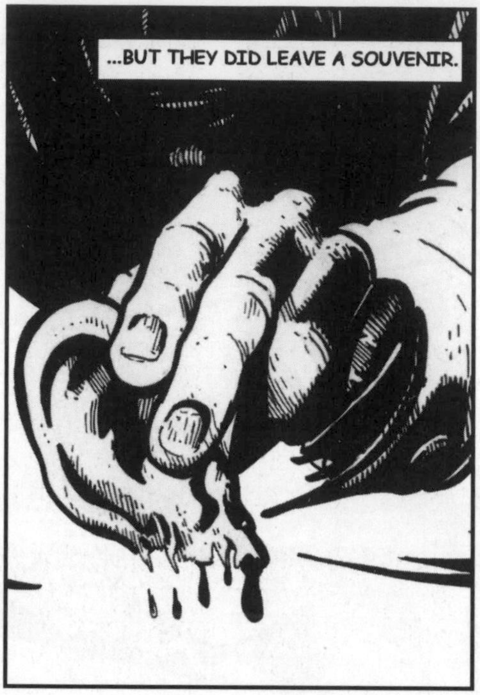
...BUT THEY DID LEAVE A SOUVENIR.

In Sickness (2008)

Creators: Jon Ayre and Stephen Hill

The short horror story is tricky to pull off. Everybody is waiting for the shock ending so they often miss the work supporting the whole idea. "In Sickness" repays a second reading to see how the effect is created. Jon Ayre's work has appeared in several of the themed anthologies from Accent UK.

SLEEP COMES HARD THESE DAYS.

THE SLIGHTEST DISTURBANCE.

THE RAIN AGAINST THE WINDOWS.
THE GATE RATTLING IN THE WIND.

ONCE SAFE SOUNDS,
MADE HARSH BY TIME.

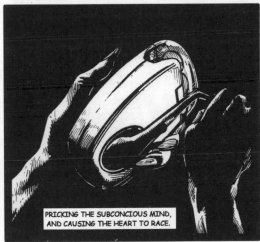

PRICKING THE SUBCONCIOUS MIND,
AND CAUSING THE HEART TO RACE.

AND THEN THERE'S THE NIGHTMARES...

AAARRGGHH!!!

In Sickness...

Story: Jon H Ayre
Art: Stephen Hills

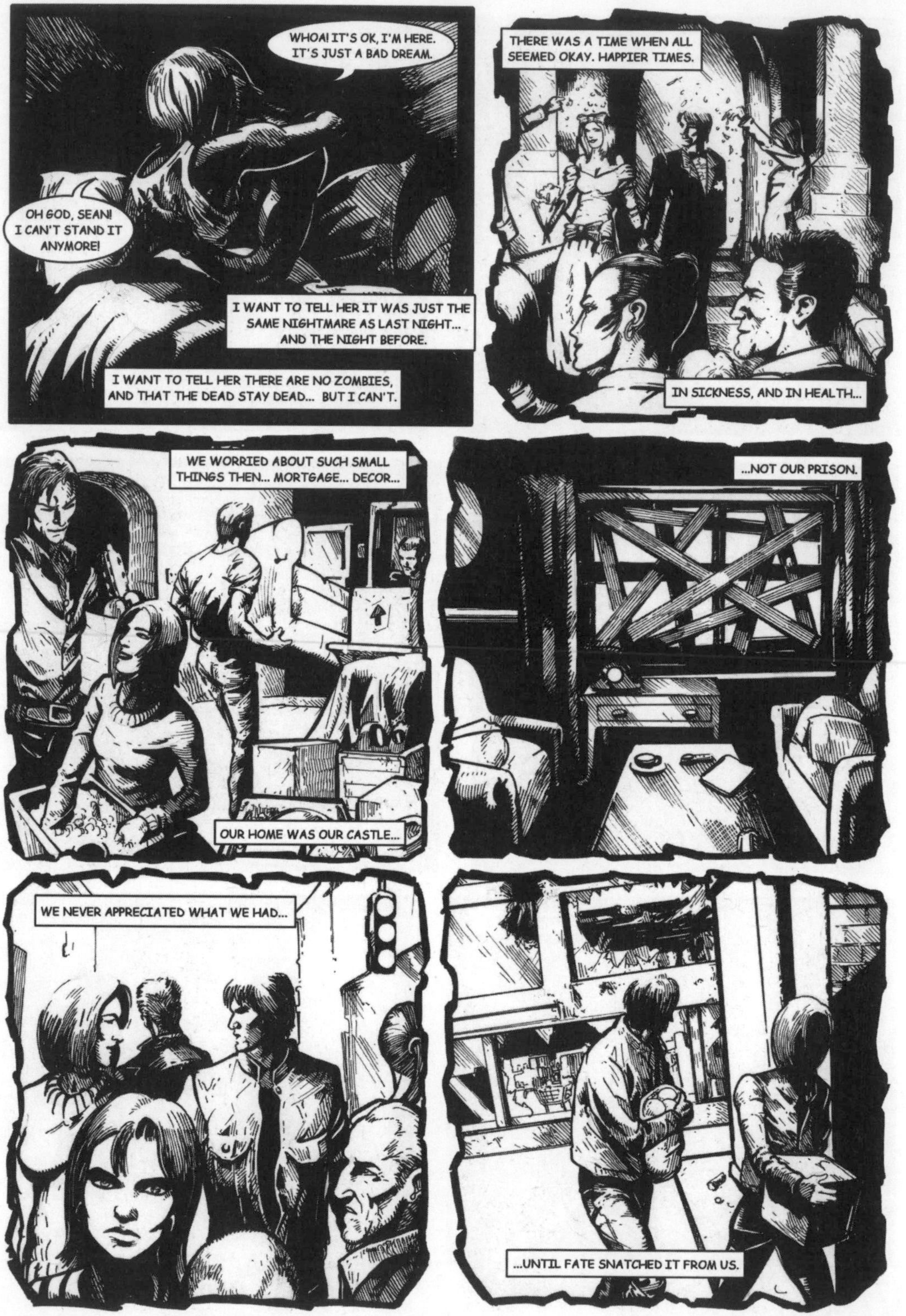
WHOA! IT'S OK, I'M HERE. IT'S JUST A BAD DREAM.
OH GOD, SEAN! I CAN'T STAND IT ANYMORE!
I WANT TO TELL HER IT WAS JUST THE SAME NIGHTMARE AS LAST NIGHT... AND THE NIGHT BEFORE.
I WANT TO TELL HER THERE ARE NO ZOMBIES, AND THAT THE DEAD STAY DEAD... BUT I CAN'T.
THERE WAS A TIME WHEN ALL SEEMED OKAY. HAPPIER TIMES.
IN SICKNESS, AND IN HEALTH...
WE WORRIED ABOUT SUCH SMALL THINGS THEN... MORTGAGE... DECOR...
OUR HOME WAS OUR CASTLE...
...NOT OUR PRISON.
WE NEVER APPRECIATED WHAT WE HAD...
...UNTIL FATE SNATCHED IT FROM US.

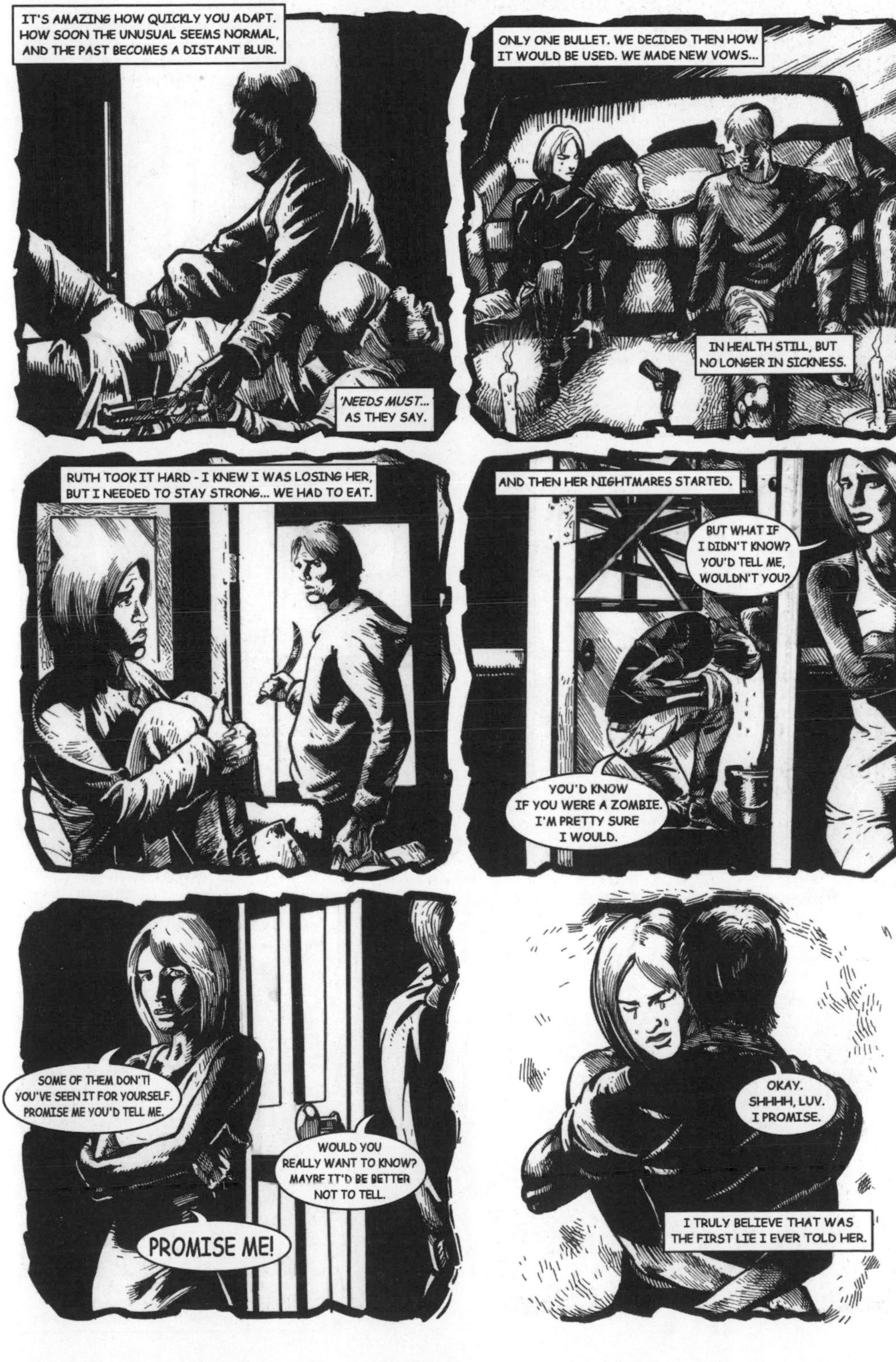
IT'S AMAZING HOW QUICKLY YOU ADAPT. HOW SOON THE UNUSUAL SEEMS NORMAL, AND THE PAST BECOMES A DISTANT BLUR.
'NEEDS MUST... AS THEY SAY.
ONLY ONE BULLET. WE DECIDED THEN HOW IT WOULD BE USED. WE MADE NEW VOWS...
IN HEALTH STILL, BUT NO LONGER IN SICKNESS.
RUTH TOOK IT HARD - I KNEW I WAS LOSING HER, BUT I NEEDED TO STAY STRONG... WE HAD TO EAT.
AND THEN HER NIGHTMARES STARTED.
BUT WHAT IF I DIDN'T KNOW? YOU'D TELL ME, WOULDN'T YOU?
YOU'D KNOW IF YOU WERE A ZOMBIE. I'M PRETTY SURE I WOULD.
SOME OF THEM DON'T! YOU'VE SEEN IT FOR YOURSELF. PROMISE ME YOU'D TELL ME.
WOULD YOU REALLY WANT TO KNOW? MAYBE IT'D BE BETTER NOT TO TELL.
PROMISE ME!
OKAY. SHHHH, LUV. I PROMISE.
I TRULY BELIEVE THAT WAS THE FIRST LIE I EVER TOLD HER.

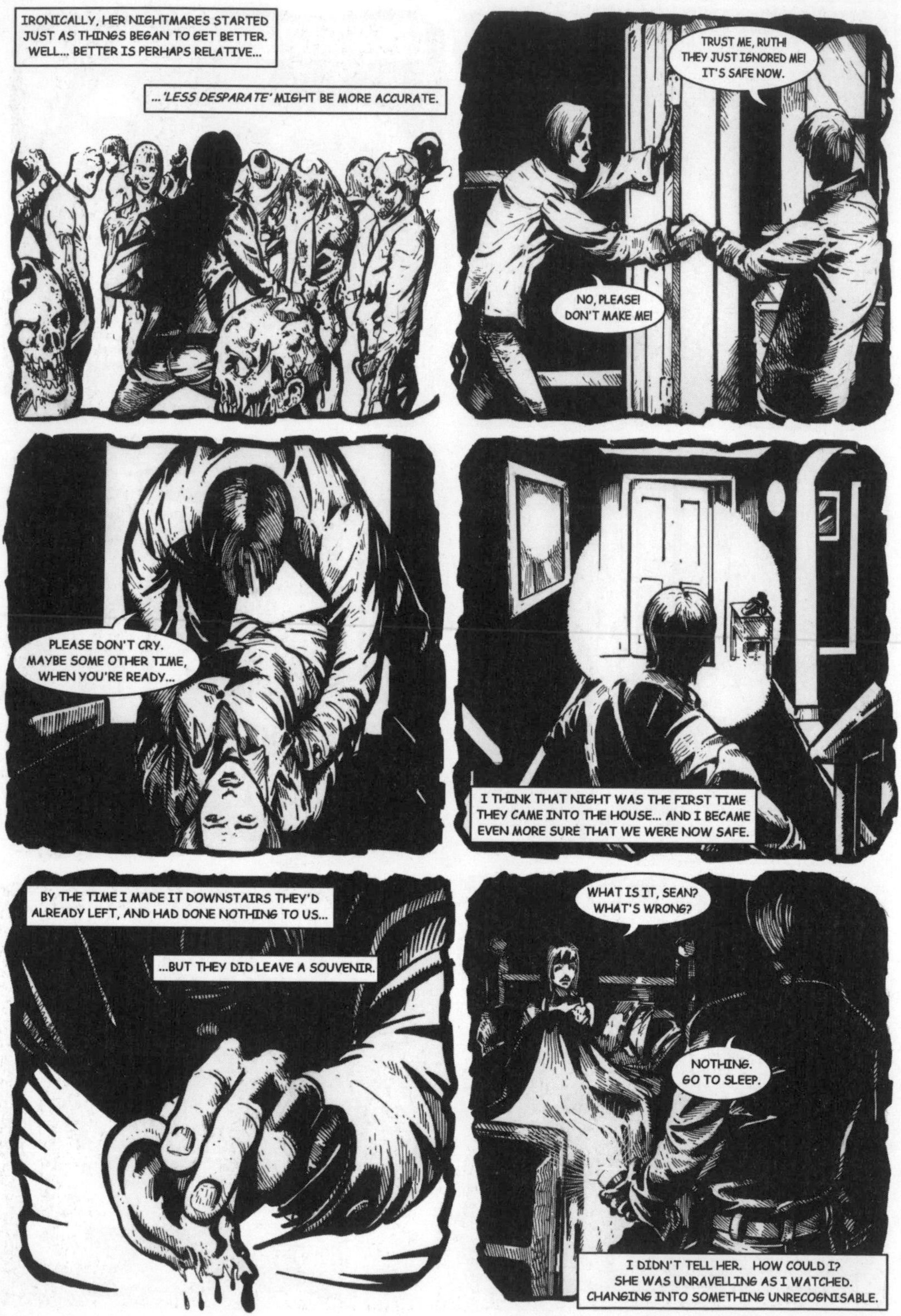
IRONICALLY, HER NIGHTMARES STARTED JUST AS THINGS BEGAN TO GET BETTER. WELL... BETTER IS PERHAPS RELATIVE...
...'LESS DESPARATE' MIGHT BE MORE ACCURATE.
TRUST ME, RUTH! THEY JUST IGNORED ME! IT'S SAFE NOW.
NO, PLEASE! DON'T MAKE ME!
PLEASE DON'T CRY. MAYBE SOME OTHER TIME, WHEN YOU'RE READY...
I THINK THAT NIGHT WAS THE FIRST TIME THEY CAME INTO THE HOUSE... AND I BECAME EVEN MORE SURE THAT WE WERE NOW SAFE.
BY THE TIME I MADE IT DOWNSTAIRS THEY'D ALREADY LEFT, AND HAD DONE NOTHING TO US...
...BUT THEY DID LEAVE A SOUVENIR.
WHAT IS IT, SEAN? WHAT'S WRONG?
NOTHING. GO TO SLEEP.
I DIDN'T TELL HER. HOW COULD I? SHE WAS UNRAVELLING AS I WATCHED. CHANGING INTO SOMETHING UNRECOGNISABLE.

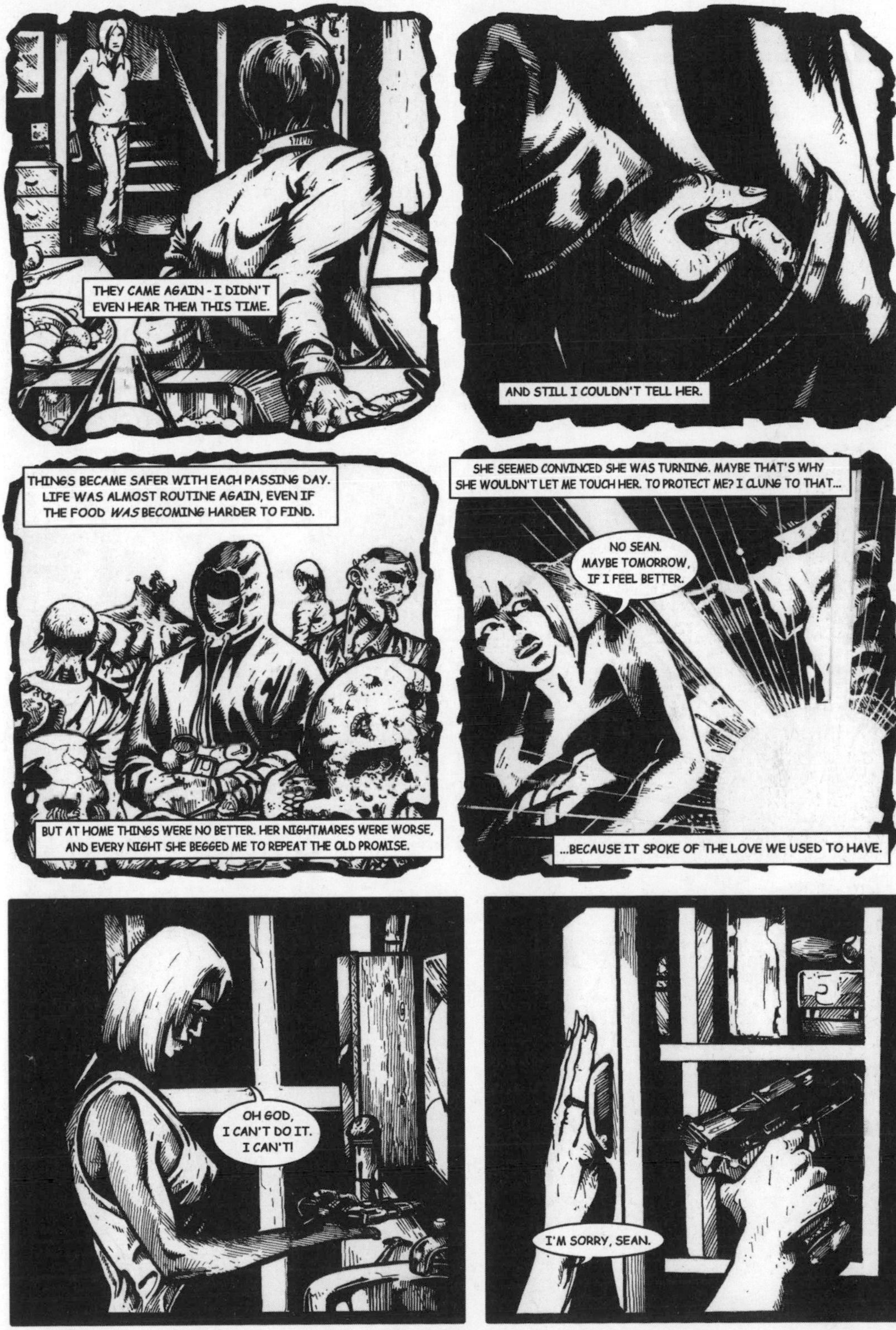
THEY CAME AGAIN - I DIDN'T EVEN HEAR THEM THIS TIME.
AND STILL I COULDN'T TELL HER.
THINGS BECAME SAFER WITH EACH PASSING DAY. LIFE WAS ALMOST ROUTINE AGAIN, EVEN IF THE FOOD *WAS* BECOMING HARDER TO FIND.
BUT AT HOME THINGS WERE NO BETTER. HER NIGHTMARES WERE WORSE, AND EVERY NIGHT SHE BEGGED ME TO REPEAT THE OLD PROMISE.
SHE SEEMED CONVINCED SHE WAS TURNING. MAYBE THAT'S WHY SHE WOULDN'T LET ME TOUCH HER. TO PROTECT ME? I CLUNG TO THAT...
NO SEAN. MAYBE TOMORROW, IF I FEEL BETTER.
...BECAUSE IT SPOKE OF THE LOVE WE USED TO HAVE.
OH GOD, I CAN'T DO IT. I CAN'T!
I'M SORRY, SEAN.

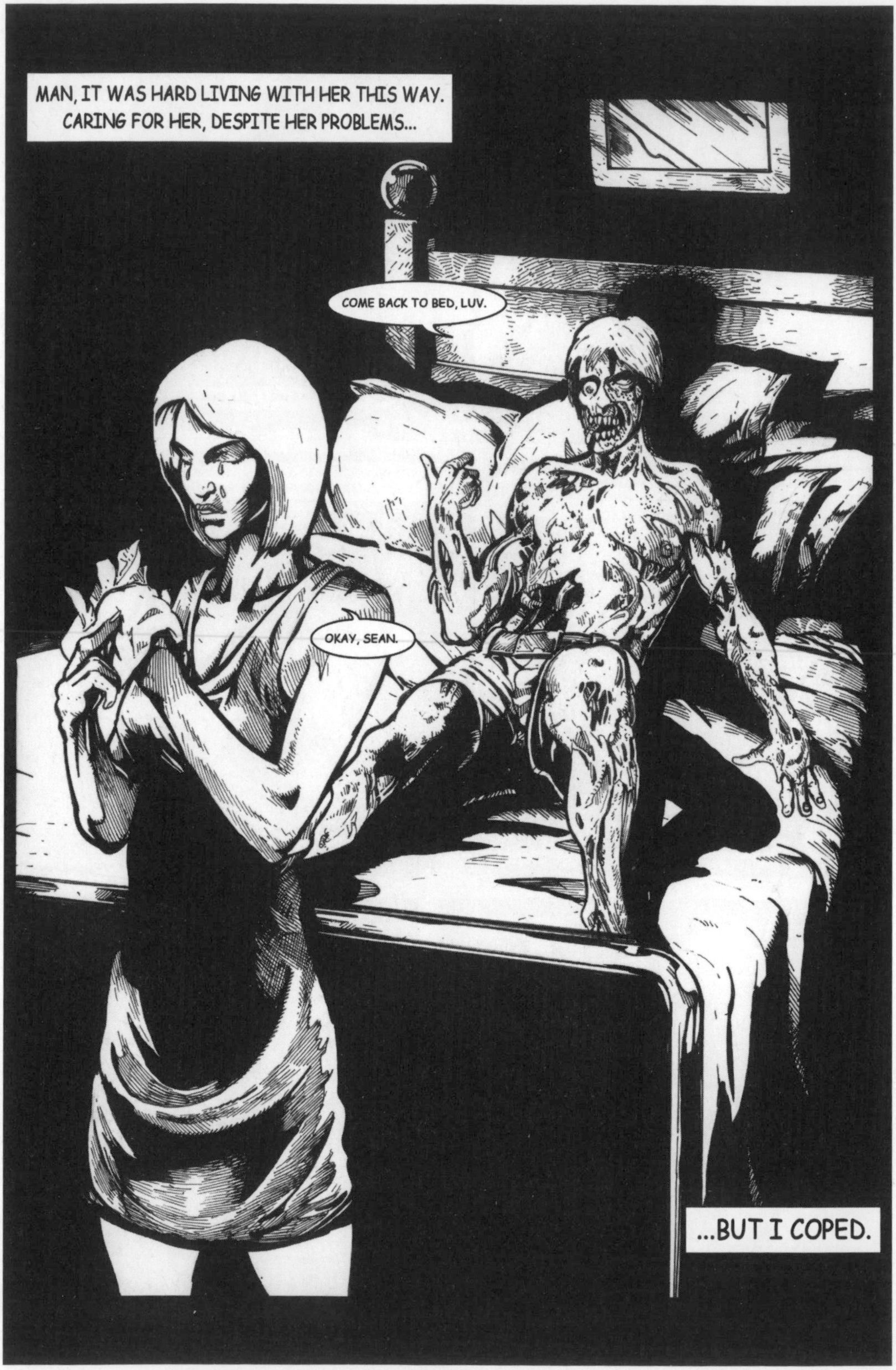
MAN, IT WAS HARD LIVING WITH HER THIS WAY. CARING FOR HER, DESPITE HER PROBLEMS...
COME BACK TO BED, LUV.
OKAY, SEAN.
...BUT I COPED.

Necrotic: Dead Flesh On a Living Body (2001)

Creators: Buddy Scalera and M. Swank (script), Pat Quinn (art)

Ah, the mummy. One of the original twentieth-century monsters but sadly rarely used. Like the zombie, the mummy is dead flesh reanimated, but the original intention of the process was to protect the body for the afterlife. Like all the best monster stories, "Necrotic" is a love story – albeit one with a strong yuck factor.

Buddy Scalera's work has appeared in Marvel Comics including *Deadpool*, *Agent X,* and others. He is the creator of the comic *7 Days to Fame*, and *Visual Reference for Comic Artists.*

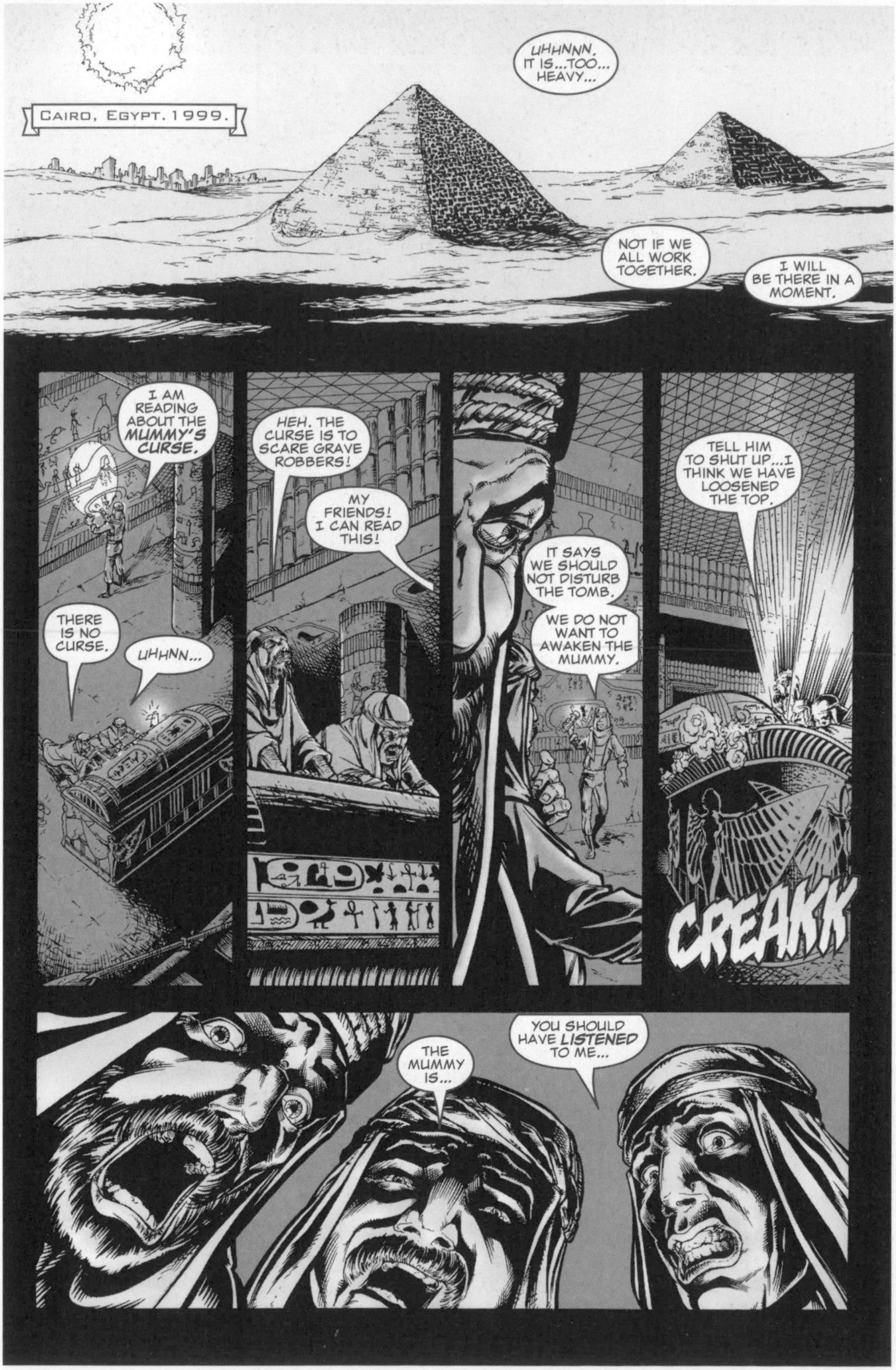
UHHNNN, IT IS...TOO... HEAVY...
CAIRO, EGYPT. 1999.
NOT IF WE ALL WORK TOGETHER.
I WILL BE THERE IN A MOMENT.
I AM READING ABOUT THE MUMMY'S CURSE.
THERE IS NO CURSE.
UHHNN...
HEH. THE CURSE IS TO SCARE GRAVE ROBBERS!
MY FRIENDS! I CAN READ THIS!
IT SAYS WE SHOULD NOT DISTURB THE TOMB.
WE DO NOT WANT TO AWAKEN THE MUMMY.
TELL HIM TO SHUT UP...I THINK WE HAVE LOOSENED THE TOP.
CREAKK
THE MUMMY IS...
YOU SHOULD HAVE LISTENED TO ME...

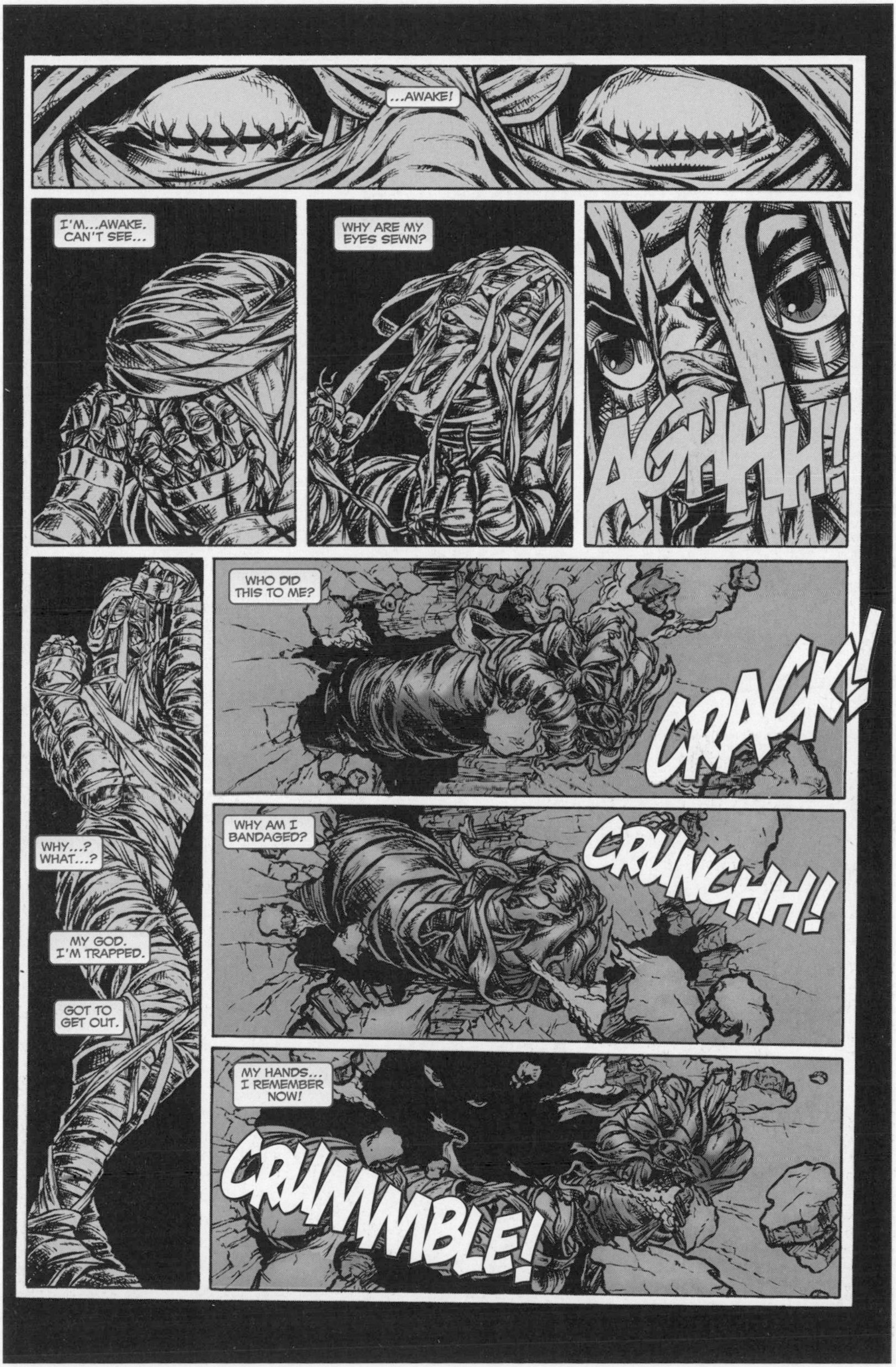
...AWAKE!
I'M...AWAKE. CAN'T SEE...
WHY ARE MY EYES SEWN?
AGHHH!
WHY...? WHAT...?
MY GOD. I'M TRAPPED.
GOT TO GET OUT.
WHO DID THIS TO ME?
CRACK!
WHY AM I BANDAGED?
CRUNCHH!
MY HANDS... I REMEMBER NOW!
CRUMMBLE!

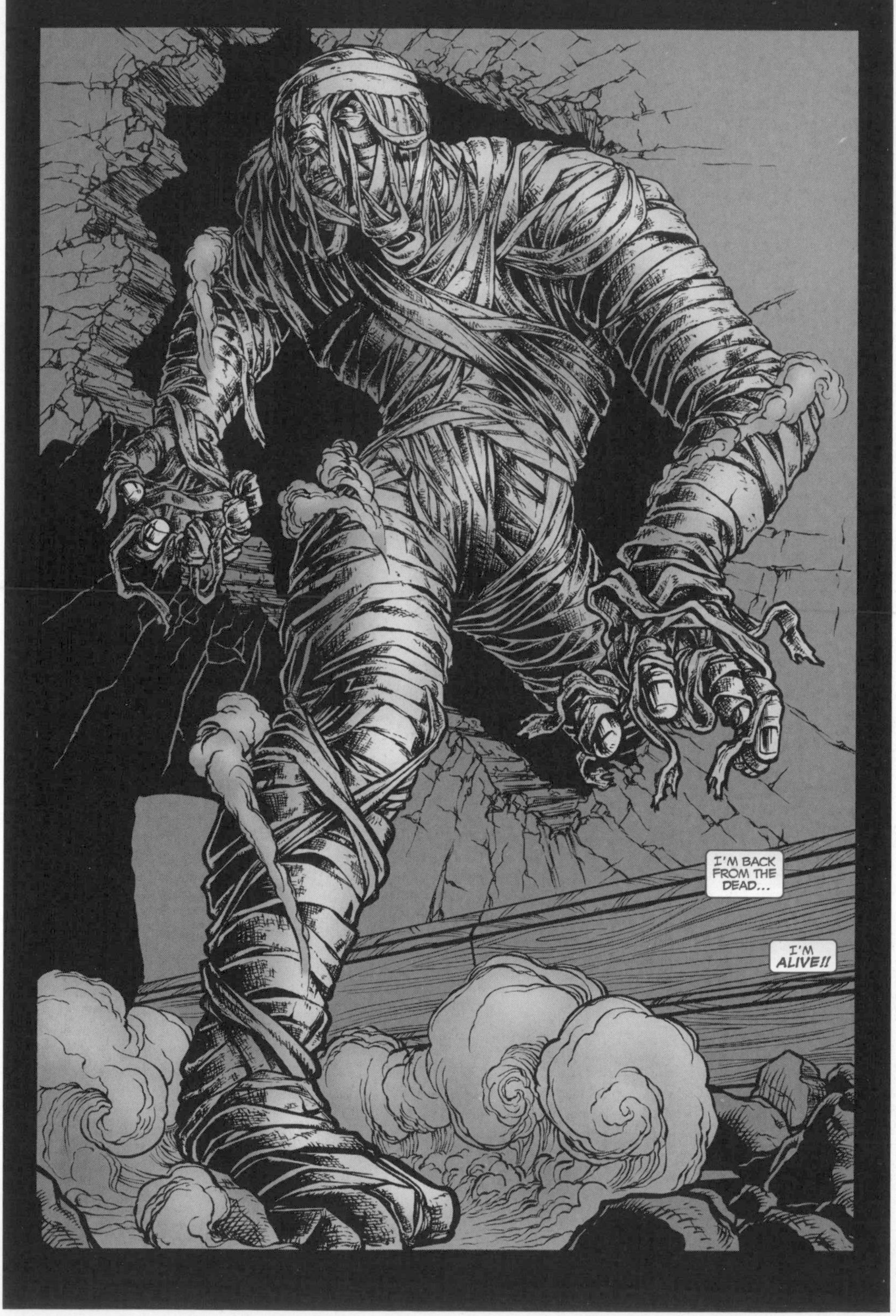
I'M BACK FROM THE DEAD...
I'M ALIVE!!

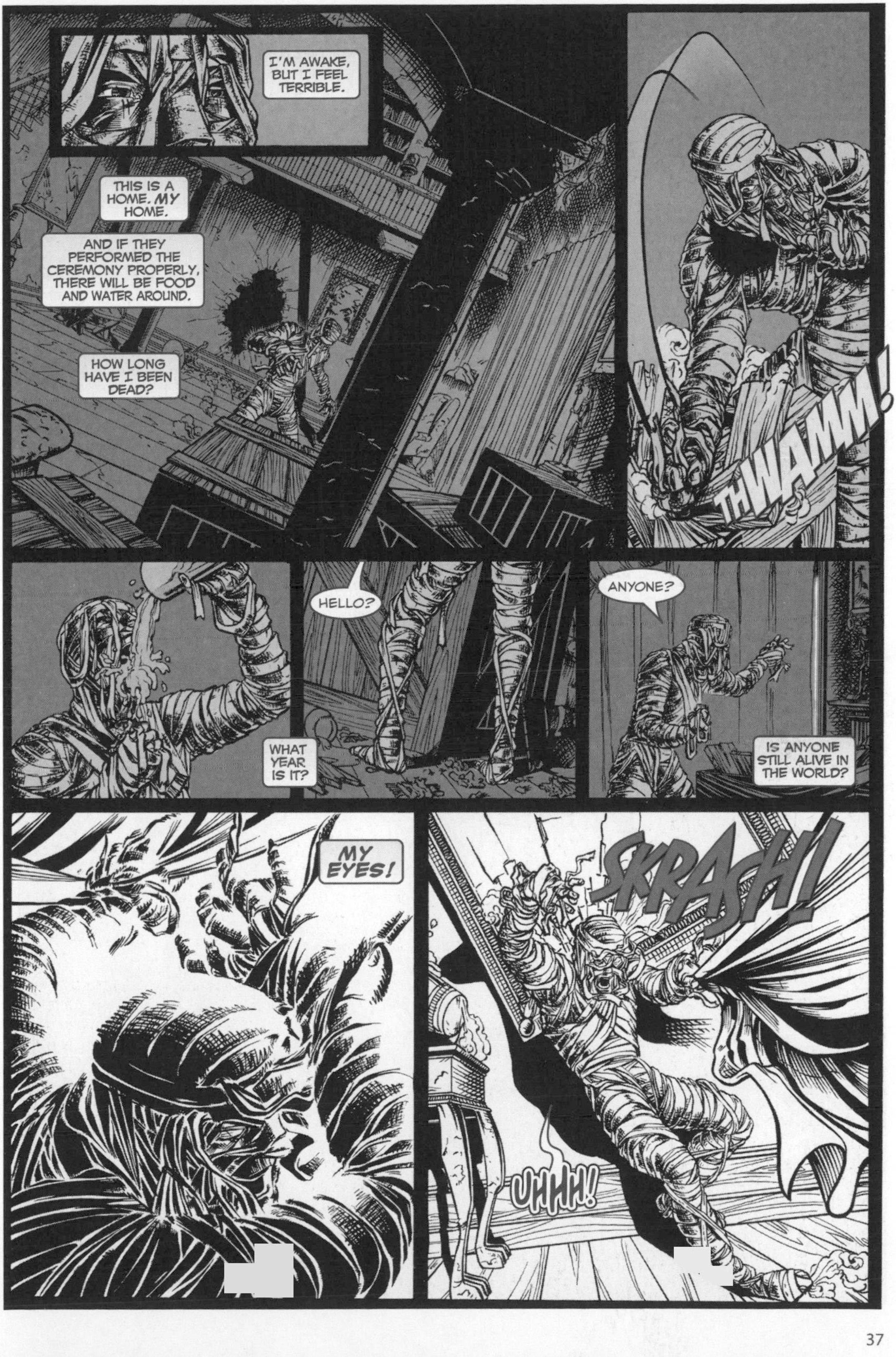
I'M AWAKE, BUT I FEEL TERRIBLE.
THIS IS A HOME. MY HOME.
AND IF THEY PERFORMED THE CEREMONY PROPERLY, THERE WILL BE FOOD AND WATER AROUND.
HOW LONG HAVE I BEEN DEAD?
THWAMM!
HELLO?
WHAT YEAR IS IT?
ANYONE?
IS ANYONE STILL ALIVE IN THE WORLD?
MY EYES!
SKRASH!
UHHH!

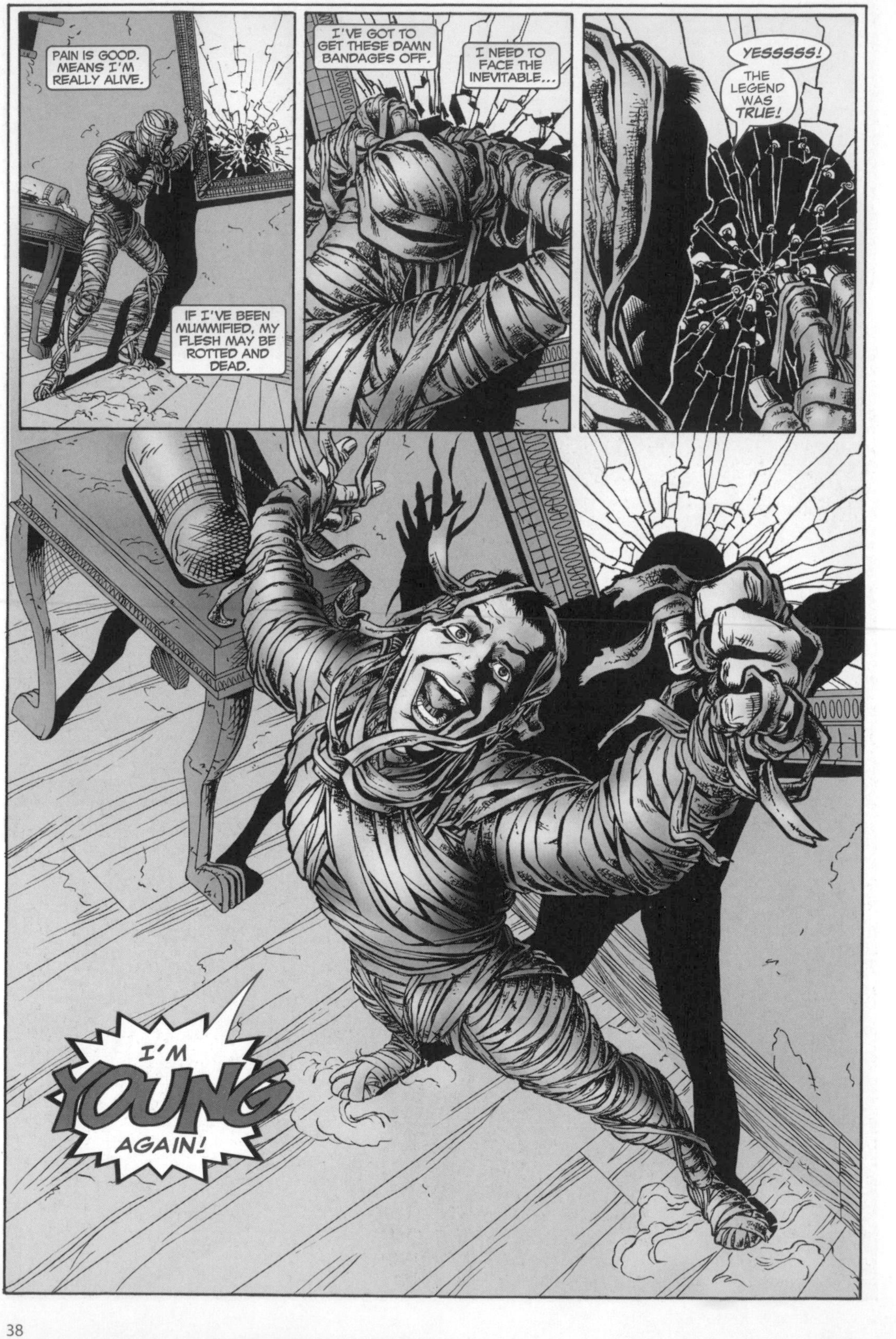
PAIN IS GOOD. MEANS I'M REALLY ALIVE.
IF I'VE BEEN MUMMIFIED, MY FLESH MAY BE ROTTED AND DEAD.
I'VE GOT TO GET THESE DAMN BANDAGES OFF.
I NEED TO FACE THE INEVITABLE...
YESSSSS!
THE LEGEND WAS TRUE!
I'M YOUNG AGAIN!

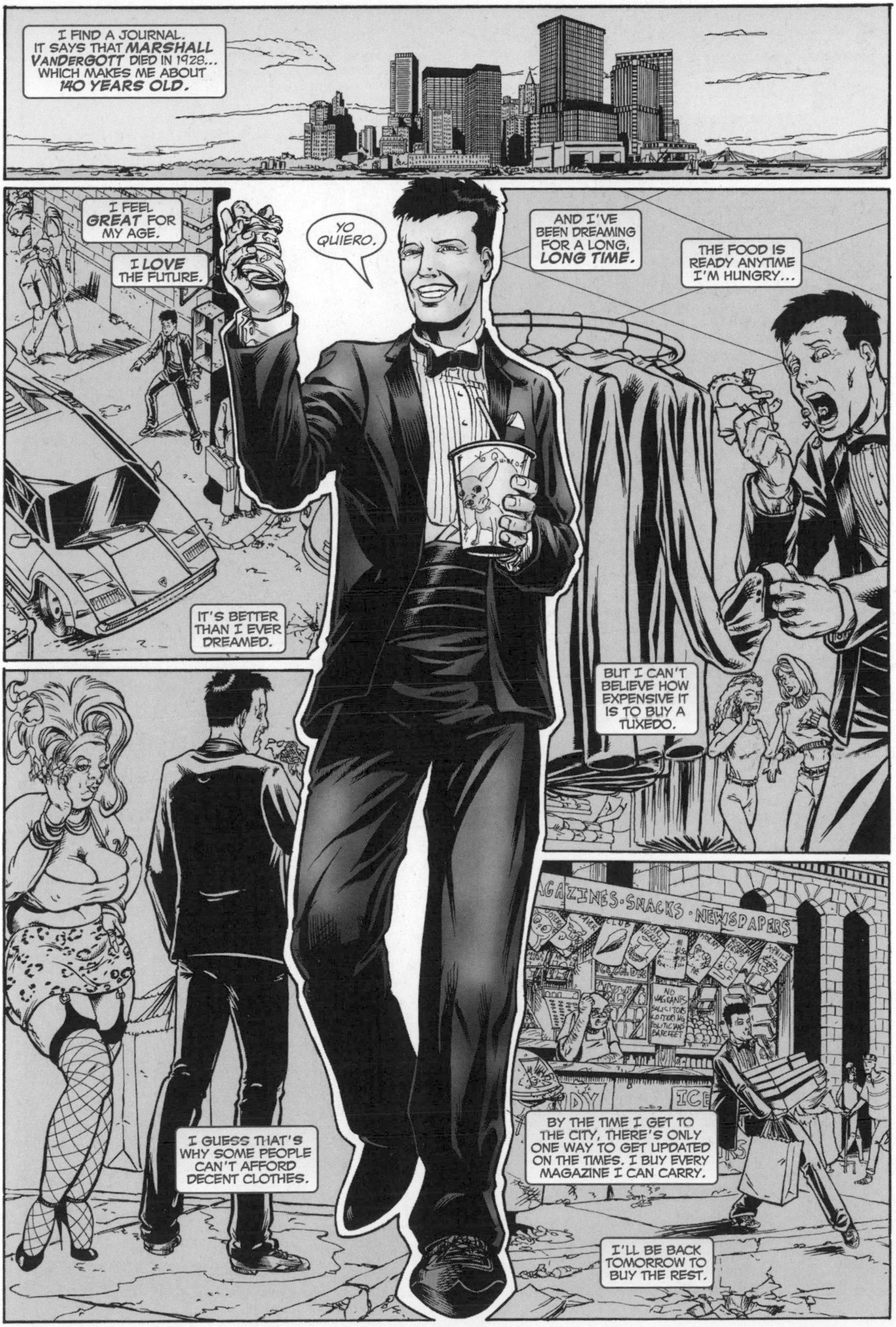
I FIND A JOURNAL. IT SAYS THAT MARSHALL VANDERGOTT DIED IN 1928... WHICH MAKES ME ABOUT 140 YEARS OLD.
I FEEL GREAT FOR MY AGE.
I LOVE THE FUTURE.
IT'S BETTER THAN I EVER DREAMED.
YO QUIERO.
AND I'VE BEEN DREAMING FOR A LONG, LONG TIME.
THE FOOD IS READY ANYTIME I'M HUNGRY...
BUT I CAN'T BELIEVE HOW EXPENSIVE IT IS TO BUY A TUXEDO.
I GUESS THAT'S WHY SOME PEOPLE CAN'T AFFORD DECENT CLOTHES.
SNACKS · NEWSPAPERS
BY THE TIME I GET TO THE CITY, THERE'S ONLY ONE WAY TO GET UPDATED ON THE TIMES. I BUY EVERY MAGAZINE I CAN CARRY.
I'LL BE BACK TOMORROW TO BUY THE REST.

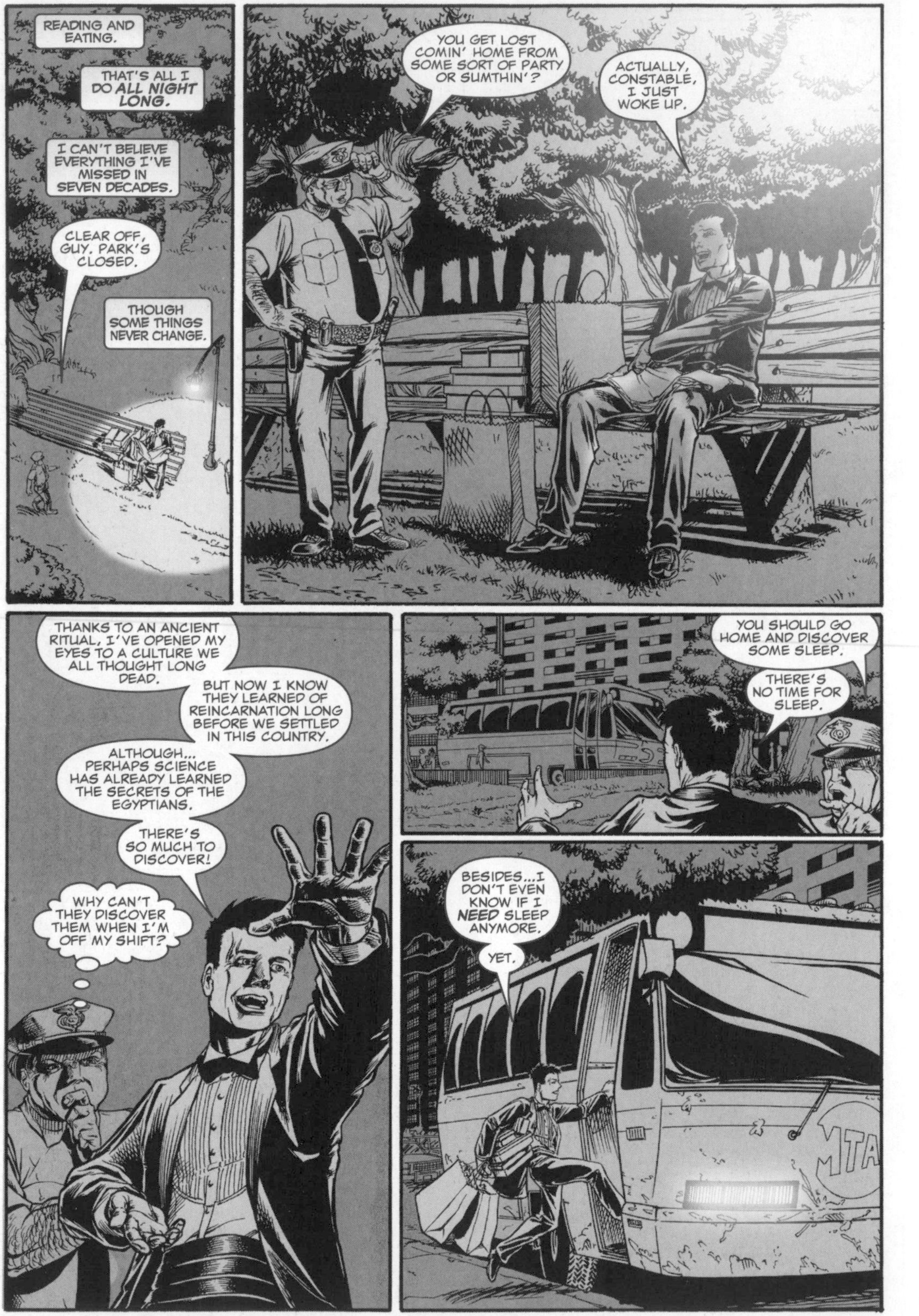
READING AND EATING.
THAT'S ALL I DO ALL NIGHT LONG.
I CAN'T BELIEVE EVERYTHING I'VE MISSED IN SEVEN DECADES.
CLEAR OFF, GUY. PARK'S CLOSED.
THOUGH SOME THINGS NEVER CHANGE.
YOU GET LOST COMIN' HOME FROM SOME SORT OF PARTY OR SUMTHIN'?
ACTUALLY, CONSTABLE, I JUST WOKE UP.
THANKS TO AN ANCIENT RITUAL, I'VE OPENED MY EYES TO A CULTURE WE ALL THOUGHT LONG DEAD.
BUT NOW I KNOW THEY LEARNED OF REINCARNATION LONG BEFORE WE SETTLED IN THIS COUNTRY.
ALTHOUGH... PERHAPS SCIENCE HAS ALREADY LEARNED THE SECRETS OF THE EGYPTIANS.
THERE'S SO MUCH TO DISCOVER!
WHY CAN'T THEY DISCOVER THEM WHEN I'M OFF MY SHIFT?
YOU SHOULD GO HOME AND DISCOVER SOME SLEEP.
THERE'S NO TIME FOR SLEEP.
BESIDES...I DON'T EVEN KNOW IF I NEED SLEEP ANYMORE.
YET.
MTA

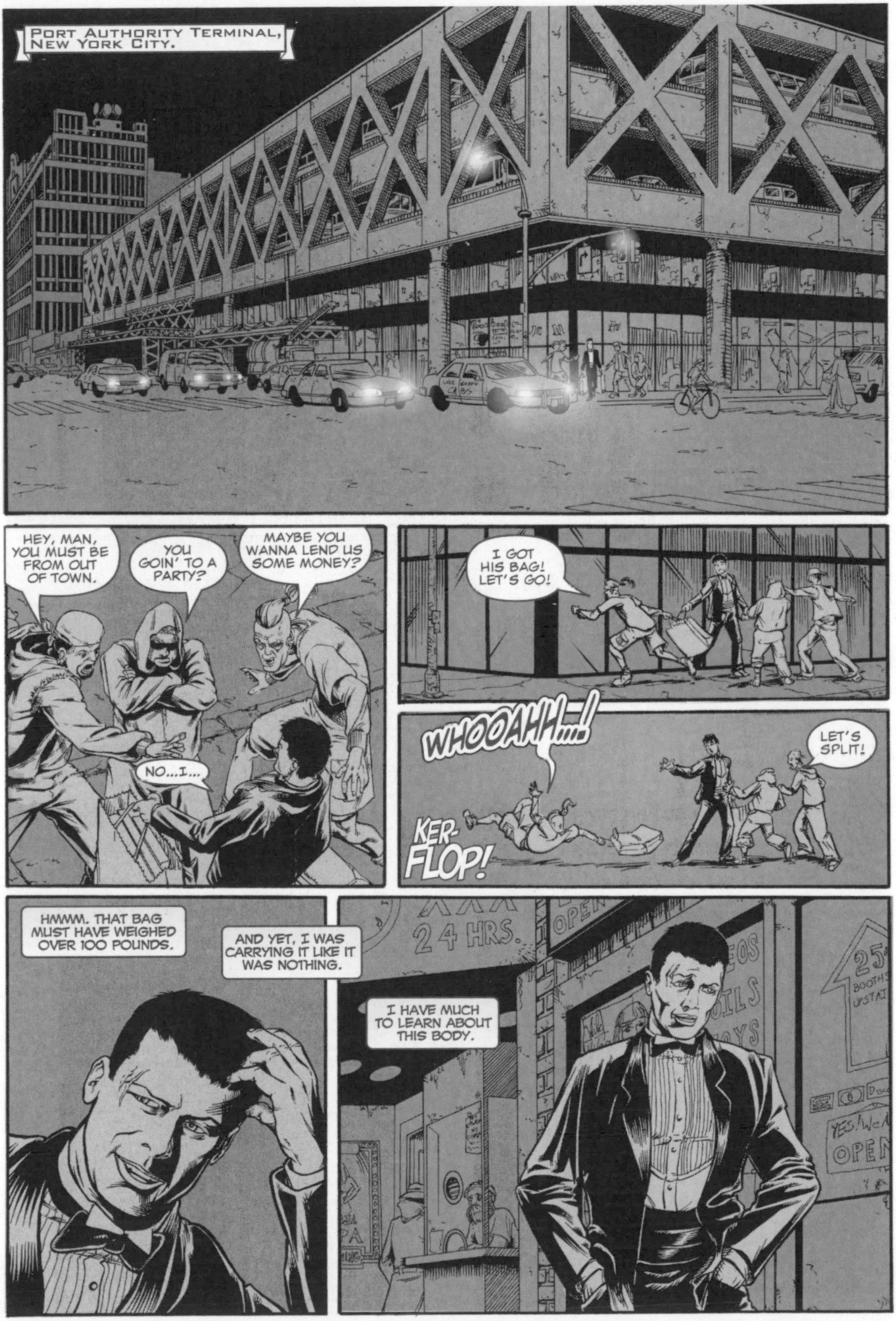
PORT AUTHORITY TERMINAL, NEW YORK CITY.
HEY, MAN, YOU MUST BE FROM OUT OF TOWN.
YOU GOIN' TO A PARTY?
MAYBE YOU WANNA LEND US SOME MONEY?
NO...I...
I GOT HIS BAG! LET'S GO!
WHOOAHH...!
LET'S SPLIT!
KER-FLOP!
HMMM. THAT BAG MUST HAVE WEIGHED OVER 100 POUNDS.
AND YET, I WAS CARRYING IT LIKE IT WAS NOTHING.
24 HRS.
I HAVE MUCH TO LEARN ABOUT THIS BODY.

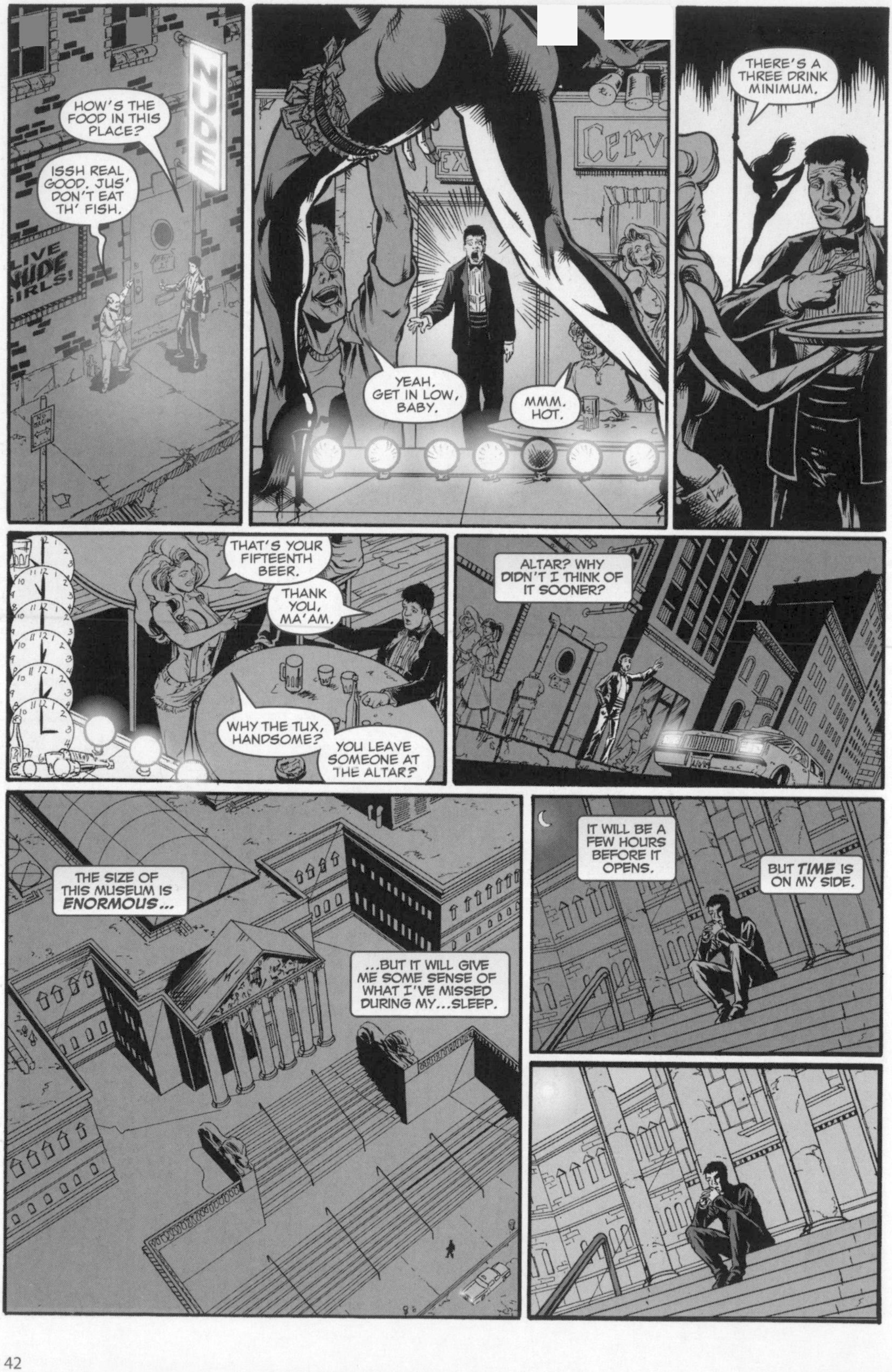
NUDE
HOW'S THE FOOD IN THIS PLACE?
ISSH REAL GOOD. JUS' DON'T EAT TH' FISH.
LIVE NUDE GIRLS!
YEAH. GET IN LOW, BABY.
MMM. HOT.
THERE'S A THREE DRINK MINIMUM.
THAT'S YOUR FIFTEENTH BEER.
THANK YOU, MA'AM.
WHY THE TUX, HANDSOME?
YOU LEAVE SOMEONE AT THE ALTAR?
ALTAR? WHY DIDN'T I THINK OF IT SOONER?
THE SIZE OF THIS MUSEUM IS *ENORMOUS*...
...BUT IT WILL GIVE ME SOME SENSE OF WHAT I'VE MISSED DURING MY...SLEEP.
IT WILL BE A FEW HOURS BEFORE IT OPENS.
BUT *TIME* IS ON MY SIDE.

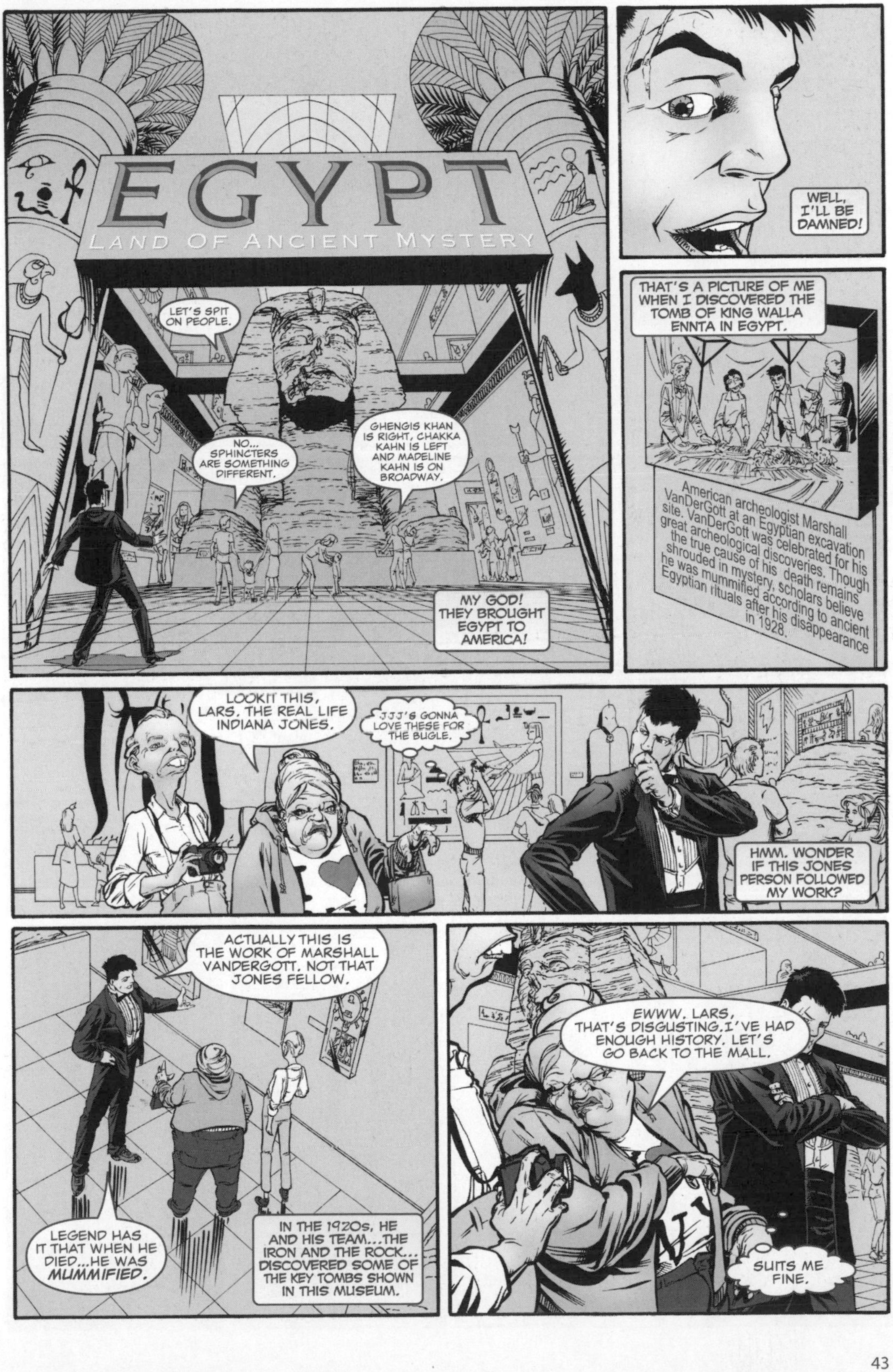
EGYPT
LAND OF ANCIENT MYSTERY
LET'S SPIT ON PEOPLE.
NO... SPHINCTERS ARE SOMETHING DIFFERENT.
GHENGIS KHAN IS RIGHT, CHAKKA KAHN IS LEFT AND MADELINE KAHN IS ON BROADWAY.
MY GOD! THEY BROUGHT EGYPT TO AMERICA!
WELL, I'LL BE DAMNED!
THAT'S A PICTURE OF ME WHEN I DISCOVERED THE TOMB OF KING WALLA ENNTA IN EGYPT.
American archeologist Marshall VanDerGott at an Egyptian excavation site. VanDerGott was celebrated for his great archeological discoveries. Though the true cause of his death remains shrouded in mystery, scholars believe he was mummified according to ancient Egyptian rituals after his disappearance in 1928.
LOOKIT THIS, LARS. THE REAL LIFE INDIANA JONES.
JJJ'S GONNA LOVE THESE FOR THE BUGLE.
HMM. WONDER IF THIS JONES PERSON FOLLOWED MY WORK?
ACTUALLY THIS IS THE WORK OF MARSHALL VANDERGOTT. NOT THAT JONES FELLOW.
LEGEND HAS IT THAT WHEN HE DIED...HE WAS MUMMIFIED.
IN THE 1920s, HE AND HIS TEAM...THE IRON AND THE ROCK...DISCOVERED SOME OF THE KEY TOMBS SHOWN IN THIS MUSEUM.
EWWW. LARS, THAT'S DISGUSTING. I'VE HAD ENOUGH HISTORY. LET'S GO BACK TO THE MALL.
SUITS ME FINE.

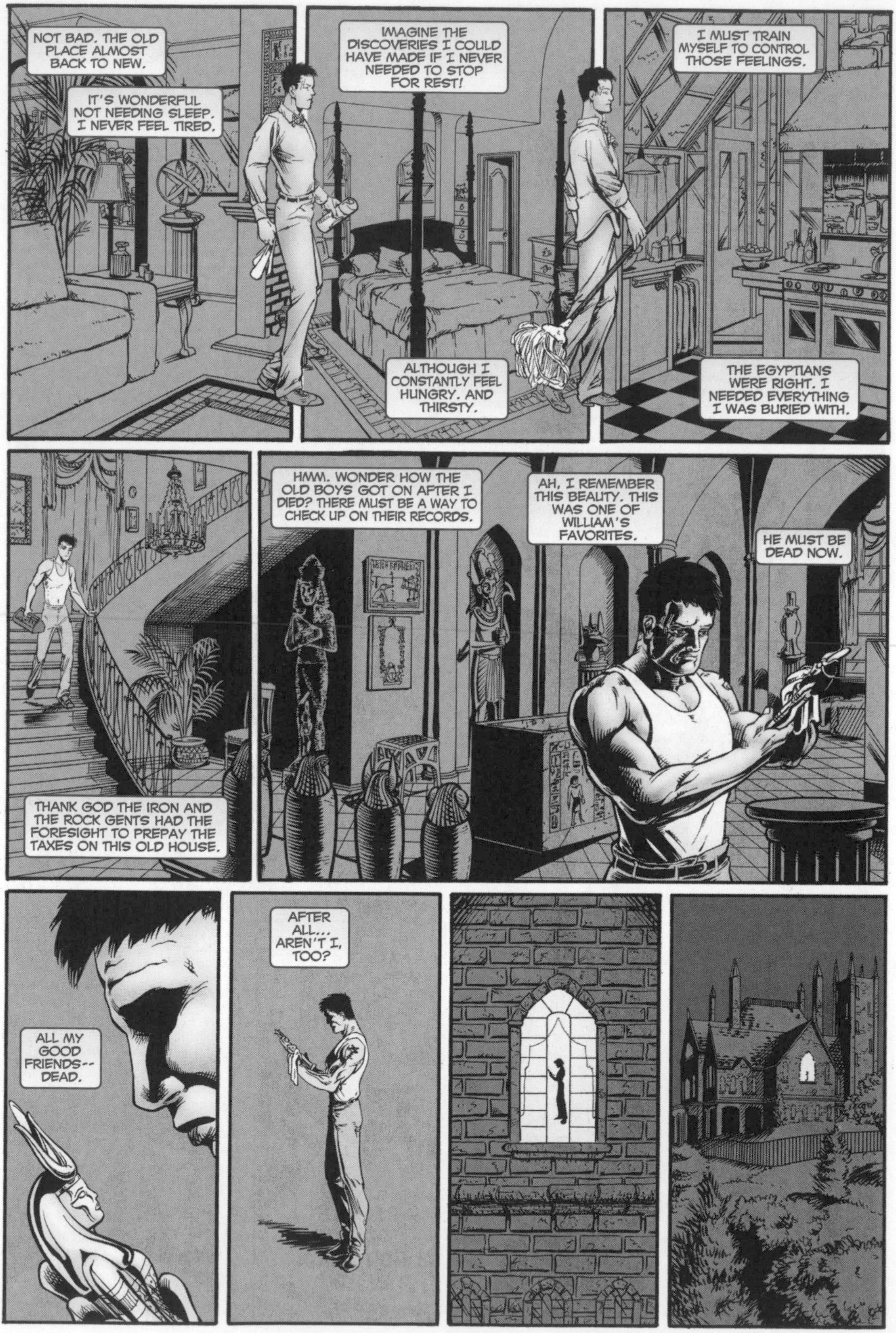
NOT BAD. THE OLD PLACE ALMOST BACK TO NEW.
IT'S WONDERFUL NOT NEEDING SLEEP. I NEVER FEEL TIRED.
IMAGINE THE DISCOVERIES I COULD HAVE MADE IF I NEVER NEEDED TO STOP FOR REST!
ALTHOUGH I CONSTANTLY FEEL HUNGRY. AND THIRSTY.
I MUST TRAIN MYSELF TO CONTROL THOSE FEELINGS.
THE EGYPTIANS WERE RIGHT. I NEEDED EVERYTHING I WAS BURIED WITH.
THANK GOD THE IRON AND THE ROCK GENTS HAD THE FORESIGHT TO PREPAY THE TAXES ON THIS OLD HOUSE.
HMM. WONDER HOW THE OLD BOYS GOT ON AFTER I DIED? THERE MUST BE A WAY TO CHECK UP ON THEIR RECORDS.
AH, I REMEMBER THIS BEAUTY. THIS WAS ONE OF WILLIAM'S FAVORITES.
HE MUST BE DEAD NOW.
ALL MY GOOD FRIENDS--DEAD.
AFTER ALL... AREN'T I, TOO?

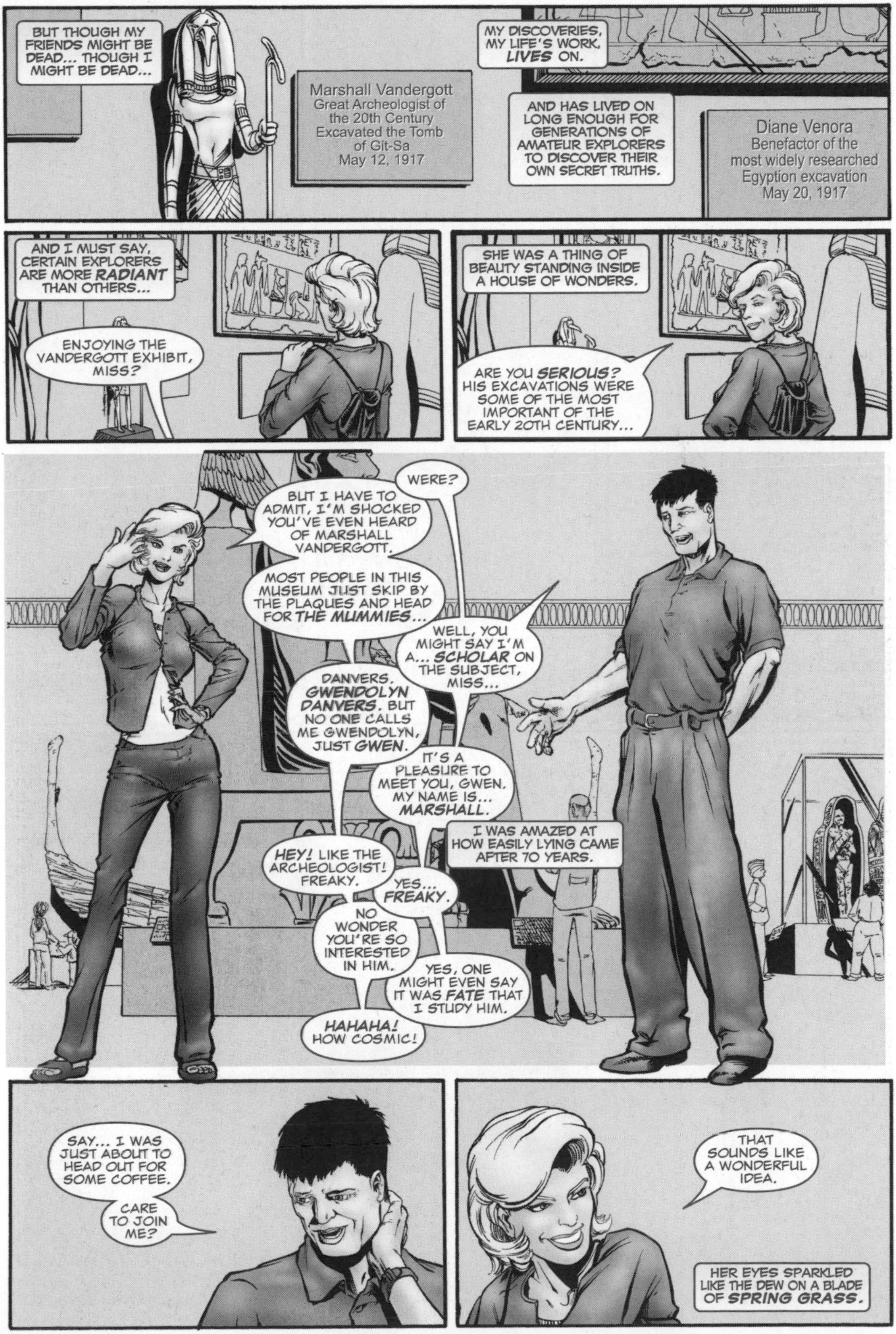
BUT THOUGH MY FRIENDS MIGHT BE DEAD... THOUGH I MIGHT BE DEAD...
Marshall Vandergott Great Archeologist of the 20th Century Excavated the Tomb of Git-Sa May 12, 1917
MY DISCOVERIES, MY LIFE'S WORK, LIVES ON.
AND HAS LIVED ON LONG ENOUGH FOR GENERATIONS OF AMATEUR EXPLORERS TO DISCOVER THEIR OWN SECRET TRUTHS.
Diane Venora Benefactor of the most widely researched Egyption excavation May 20, 1917
AND I MUST SAY, CERTAIN EXPLORERS ARE MORE RADIANT THAN OTHERS...
ENJOYING THE VANDERGOTT EXHIBIT, MISS?
SHE WAS A THING OF BEAUTY STANDING INSIDE A HOUSE OF WONDERS.
ARE YOU SERIOUS? HIS EXCAVATIONS WERE SOME OF THE MOST IMPORTANT OF THE EARLY 20TH CENTURY...
WERE?
BUT I HAVE TO ADMIT, I'M SHOCKED YOU'VE EVEN HEARD OF MARSHALL VANDERGOTT.
MOST PEOPLE IN THIS MUSEUM JUST SKIP BY THE PLAQUES AND HEAD FOR THE MUMMIES...
WELL, YOU MIGHT SAY I'M A... SCHOLAR ON THE SUBJECT, MISS...
DANVERS. GWENDOLYN DANVERS. BUT NO ONE CALLS ME GWENDOLYN, JUST GWEN.
IT'S A PLEASURE TO MEET YOU, GWEN. MY NAME IS... MARSHALL.
I WAS AMAZED AT HOW EASILY LYING CAME AFTER 70 YEARS.
HEY! LIKE THE ARCHEOLOGIST! FREAKY.
YES... FREAKY.
NO WONDER YOU'RE SO INTERESTED IN HIM.
YES, ONE MIGHT EVEN SAY IT WAS FATE THAT I STUDY HIM.
HAHAHA! HOW COSMIC!
SAY... I WAS JUST ABOUT TO HEAD OUT FOR SOME COFFEE.
CARE TO JOIN ME?
THAT SOUNDS LIKE A WONDERFUL IDEA.
HER EYES SPARKLED LIKE THE DEW ON A BLADE OF SPRING GRASS.

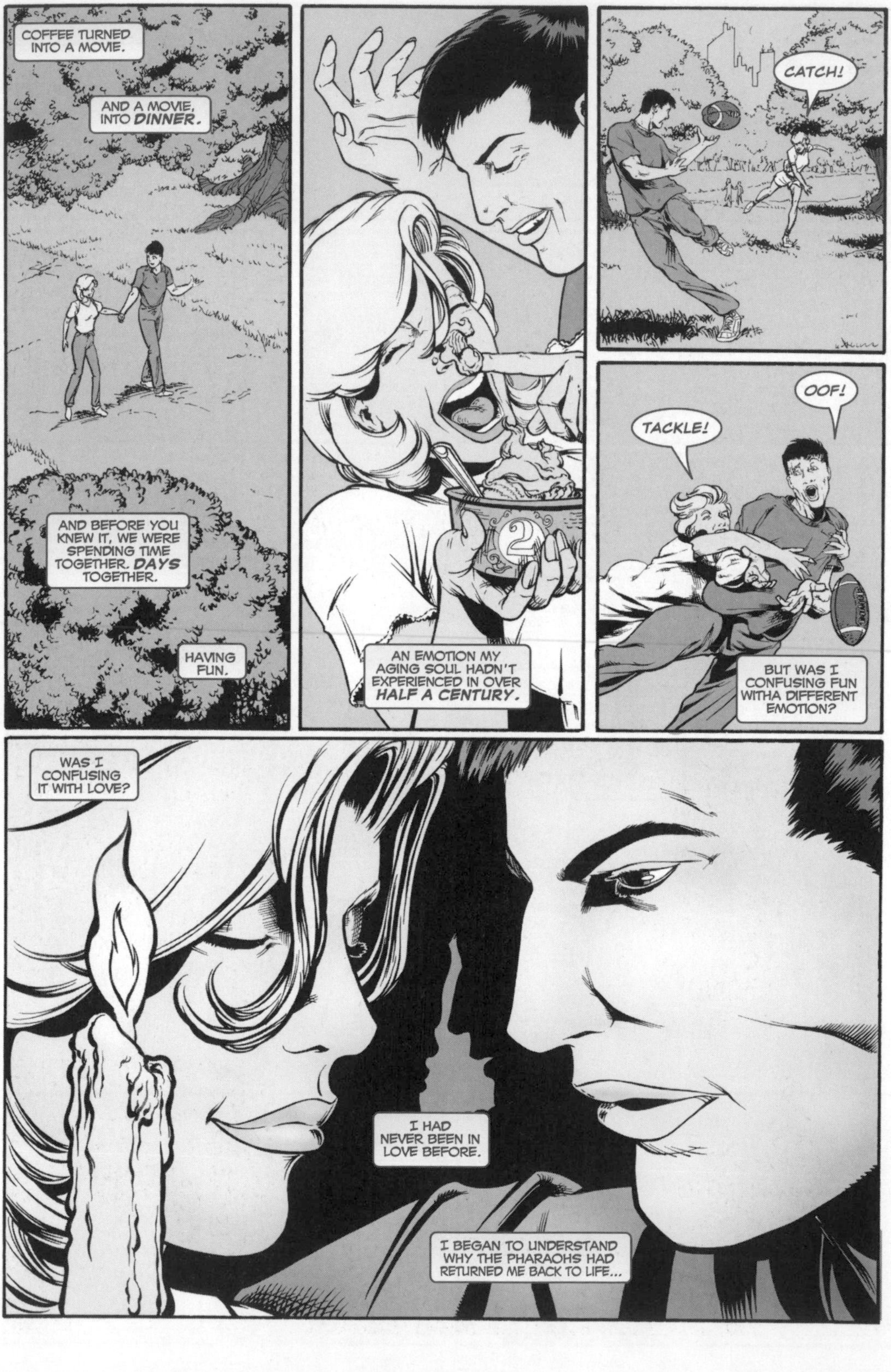
COFFEE TURNED INTO A MOVIE.
AND A MOVIE, INTO DINNER.
AND BEFORE YOU KNEW IT, WE WERE SPENDING TIME TOGETHER. DAYS TOGETHER.
HAVING FUN.
AN EMOTION MY AGING SOUL HADN'T EXPERIENCED IN OVER HALF A CENTURY.
CATCH!
TACKLE!
OOF!
BUT WAS I CONFUSING FUN WITHA DIFFERENT EMOTION?
WAS I CONFUSING IT WITH LOVE?
I HAD NEVER BEEN IN LOVE BEFORE.
I BEGAN TO UNDERSTAND WHY THE PHARAOHS HAD RETURNED ME BACK TO LIFE...

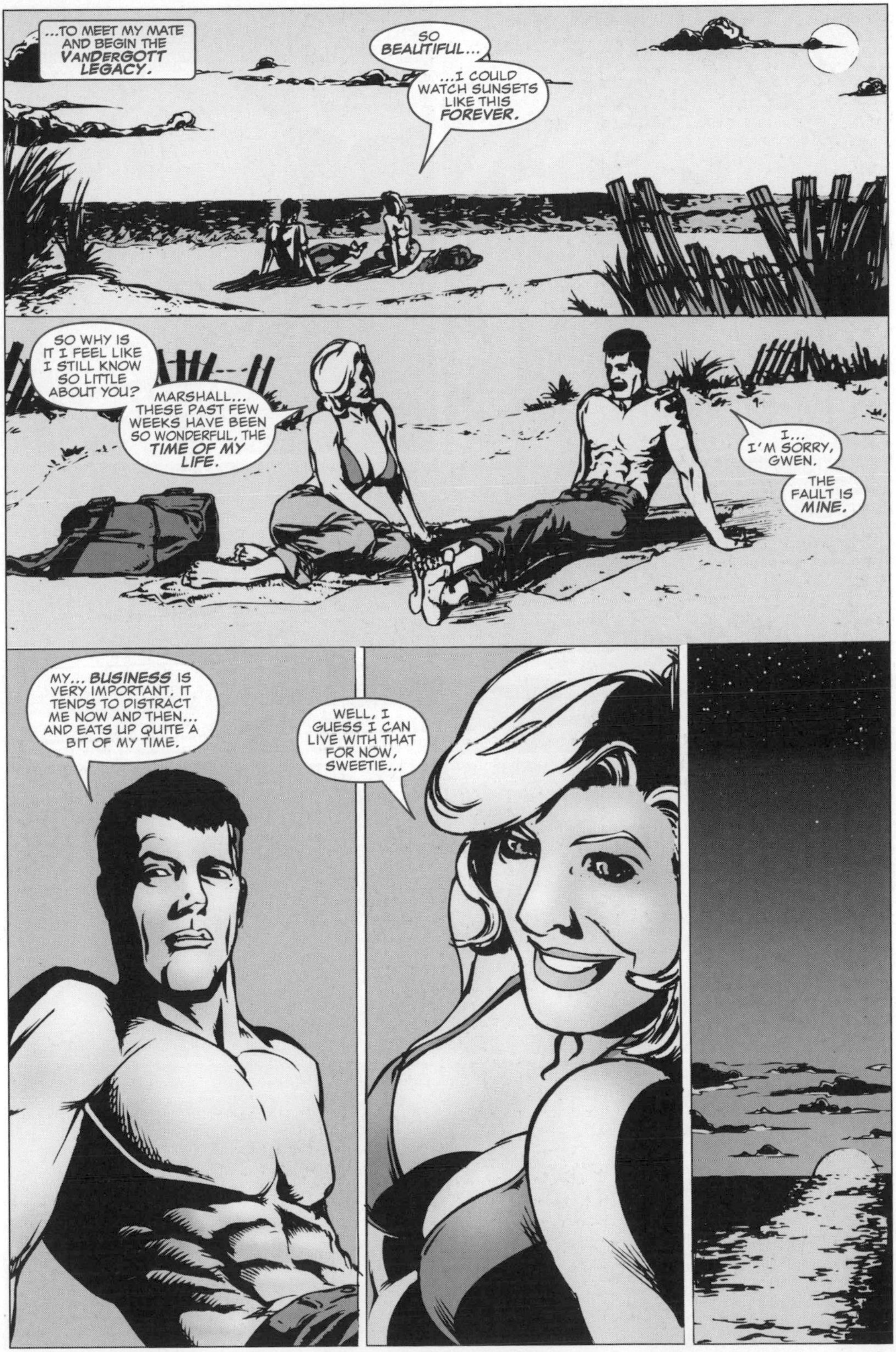
...TO MEET MY MATE AND BEGIN THE VANDERGOTT LEGACY.
SO BEAUTIFUL...
...I COULD WATCH SUNSETS LIKE THIS FOREVER.
MARSHALL... THESE PAST FEW WEEKS HAVE BEEN SO WONDERFUL, THE TIME OF MY LIFE.
SO WHY IS IT I FEEL LIKE I STILL KNOW SO LITTLE ABOUT YOU?
I... I'M SORRY, GWEN.
THE FAULT IS MINE.
MY... BUSINESS IS VERY IMPORTANT. IT TENDS TO DISTRACT ME NOW AND THEN... AND EATS UP QUITE A BIT OF MY TIME.
WELL, I GUESS I CAN LIVE WITH THAT FOR NOW, SWEETIE...

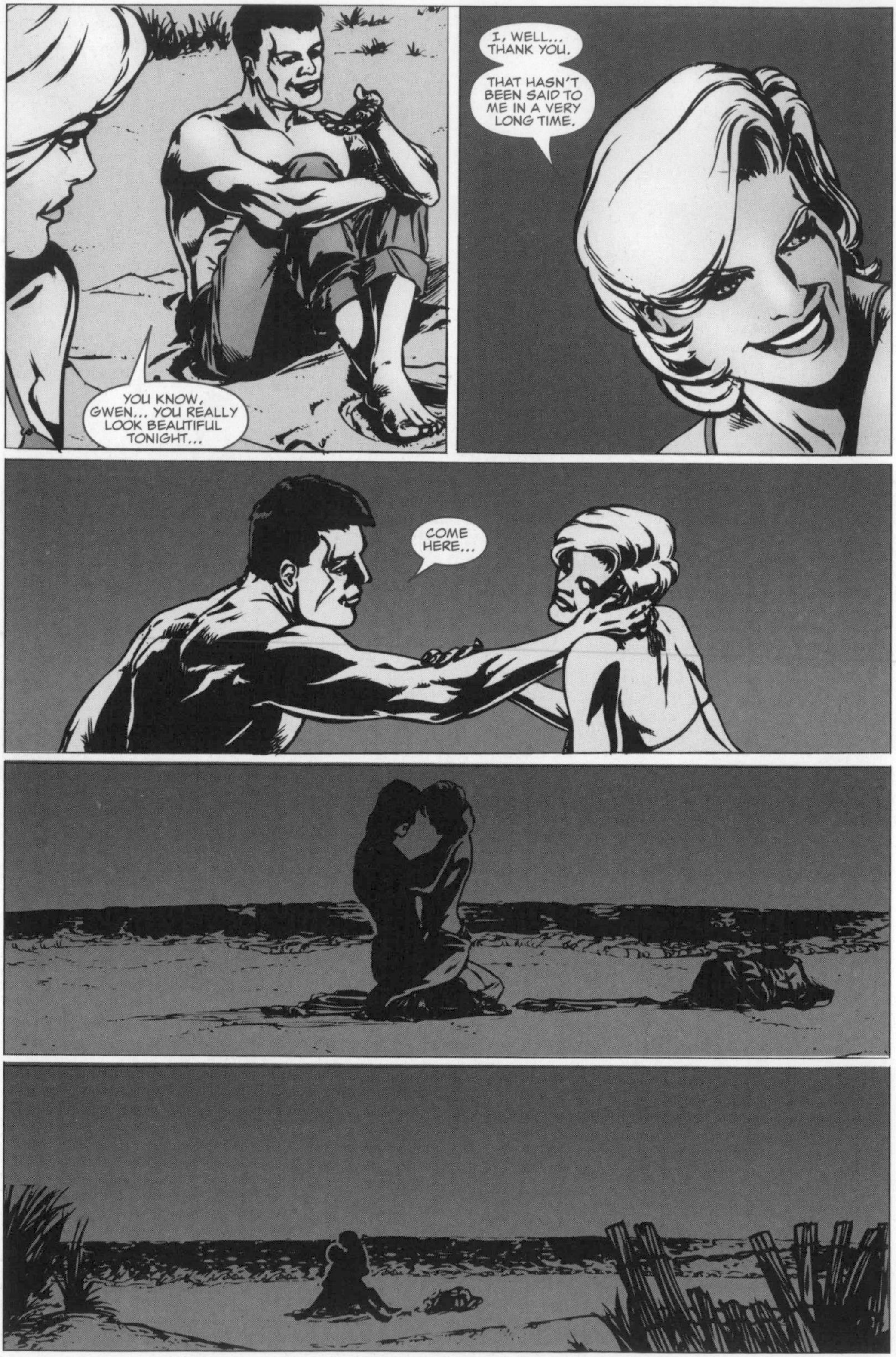
YOU KNOW, GWEN... YOU REALLY LOOK BEAUTIFUL TONIGHT...
I, WELL... THANK YOU.
THAT HASN'T BEEN SAID TO ME IN A VERY LONG TIME.
COME HERE...

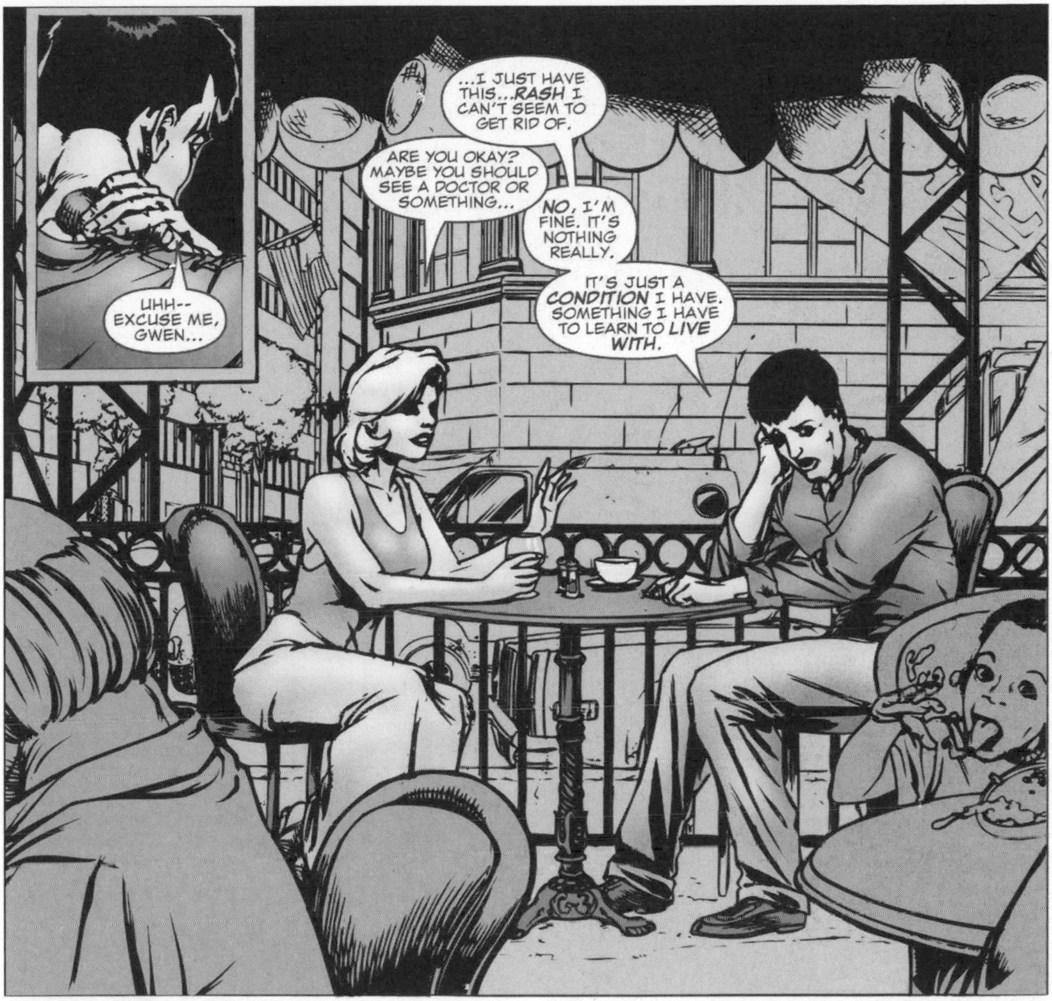
UHH-- EXCUSE ME, GWEN...
...I JUST HAVE THIS...RASH I CAN'T SEEM TO GET RID OF.
ARE YOU OKAY? MAYBE YOU SHOULD SEE A DOCTOR OR SOMETHING...
NO, I'M FINE. IT'S NOTHING REALLY.
IT'S JUST A CONDITION I HAVE. SOMETHING I HAVE TO LEARN TO LIVE WITH.

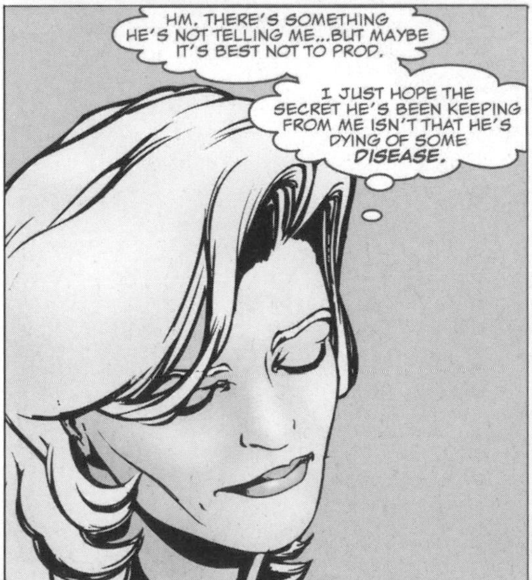
HM. THERE'S SOMETHING HE'S NOT TELLING ME...BUT MAYBE IT'S BEST NOT TO PROD.
I JUST HOPE THE SECRET HE'S BEEN KEEPING FROM ME ISN'T THAT HE'S DYING OF SOME DISEASE.

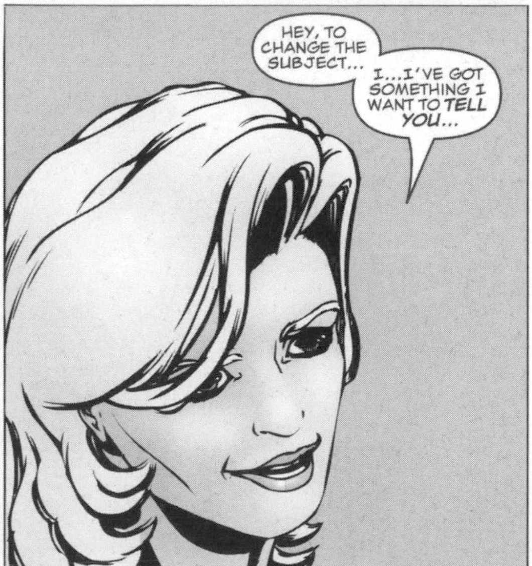
HEY, TO CHANGE THE SUBJECT...
I...I'VE GOT SOMETHING I WANT TO TELL YOU...

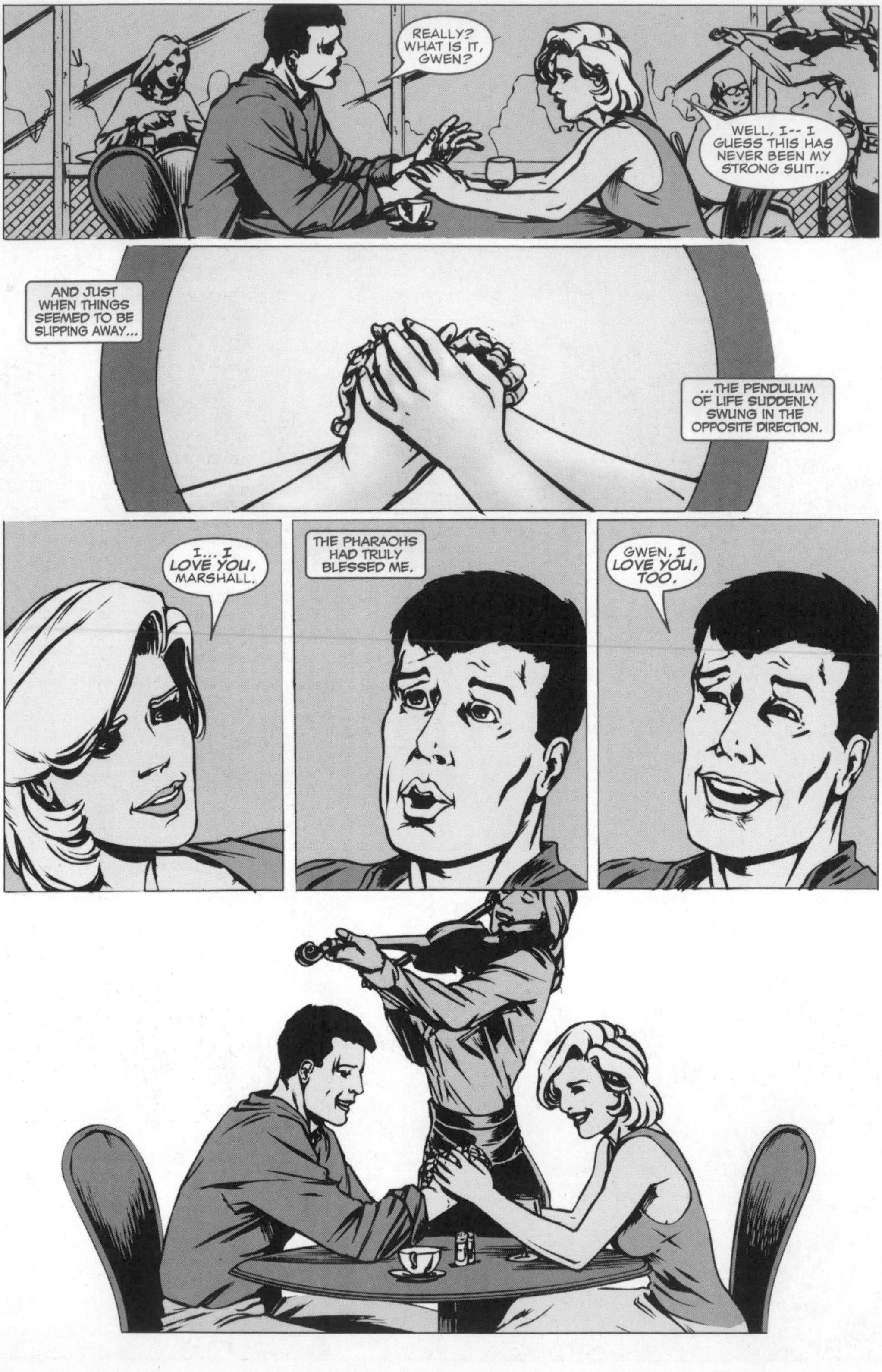
REALLY? WHAT IS IT, GWEN?
WELL, I-- I GUESS THIS HAS NEVER BEEN MY STRONG SUIT...
AND JUST WHEN THINGS SEEMED TO BE SLIPPING AWAY...
...THE PENDULUM OF LIFE SUDDENLY SWUNG IN THE OPPOSITE DIRECTION.
I... I LOVE YOU, MARSHALL.
THE PHARAOHS HAD TRULY BLESSED ME.
GWEN, I LOVE YOU, TOO.

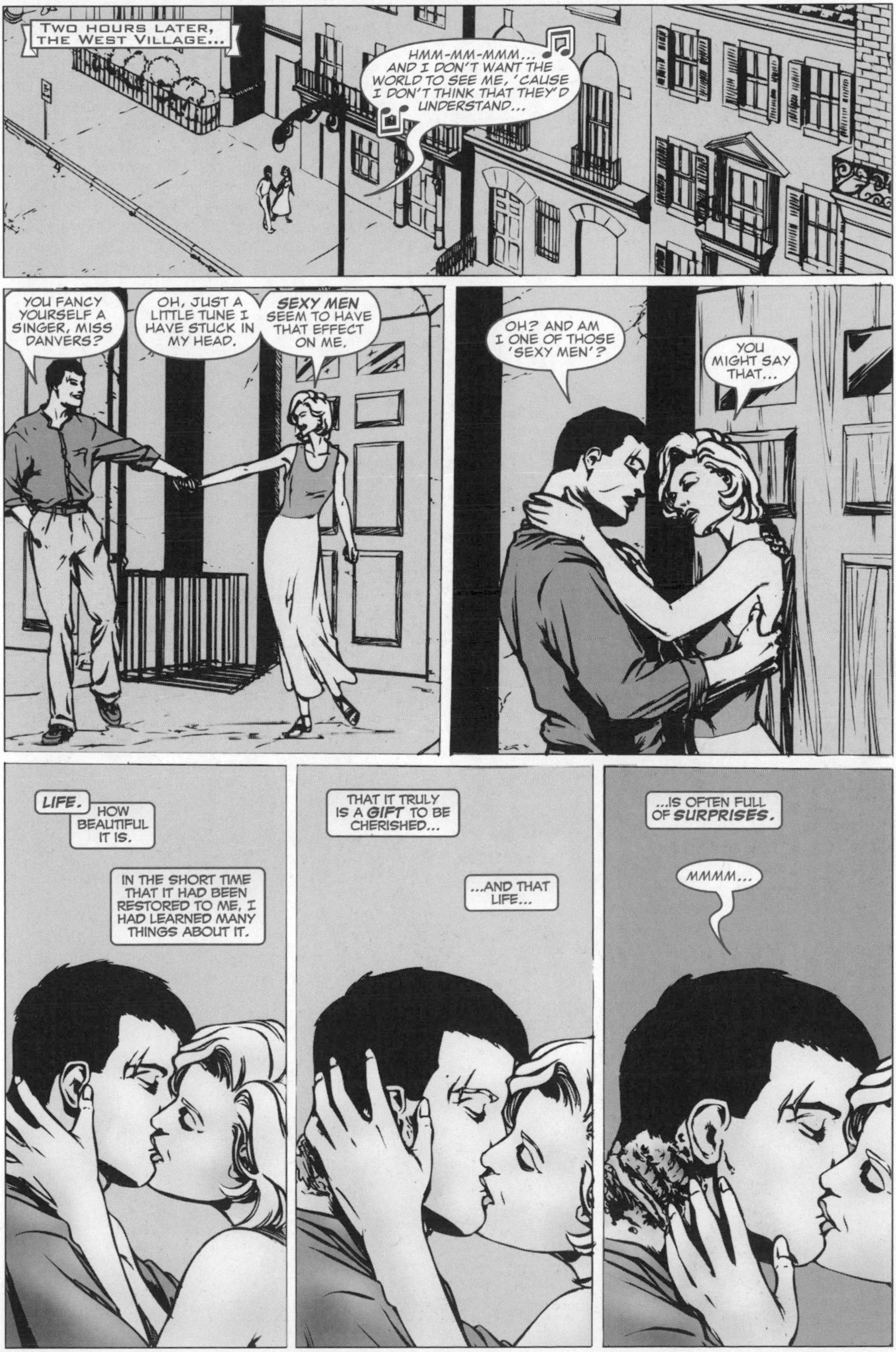
TWO HOURS LATER, THE WEST VILLAGE...
HMM-MM-MMM... AND I DON'T WANT THE WORLD TO SEE ME, 'CAUSE I DON'T THINK THAT THEY'D UNDERSTAND...
YOU FANCY YOURSELF A SINGER, MISS DANVERS?
OH, JUST A LITTLE TUNE I HAVE STUCK IN MY HEAD.
SEXY MEN SEEM TO HAVE THAT EFFECT ON ME.
OH? AND AM I ONE OF THOSE 'SEXY MEN'?
YOU MIGHT SAY THAT...
LIFE. HOW BEAUTIFUL IT IS.
IN THE SHORT TIME THAT IT HAD BEEN RESTORED TO ME, I HAD LEARNED MANY THINGS ABOUT IT.
THAT IT TRULY IS A GIFT TO BE CHERISHED...
...AND THAT LIFE...
...IS OFTEN FULL OF SURPRISES.
MMMM...

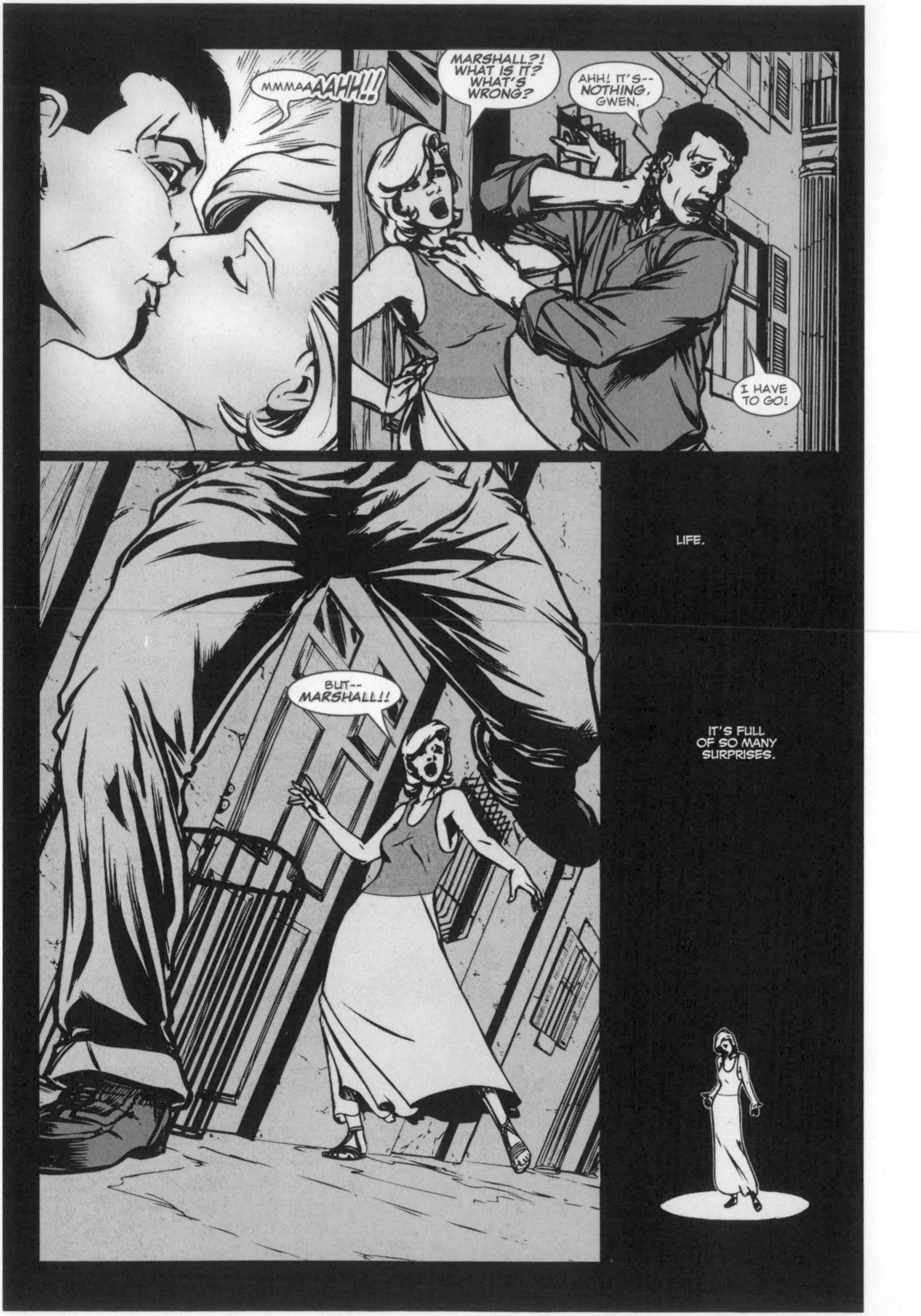
MMMAAAAHH!!
MARSHALL?! WHAT IS IT? WHAT'S WRONG?
AHH! IT'S-- NOTHING, GWEN.
I HAVE TO GO!
BUT-- MARSHALL!!
LIFE.
IT'S FULL OF SO MANY SURPRISES.

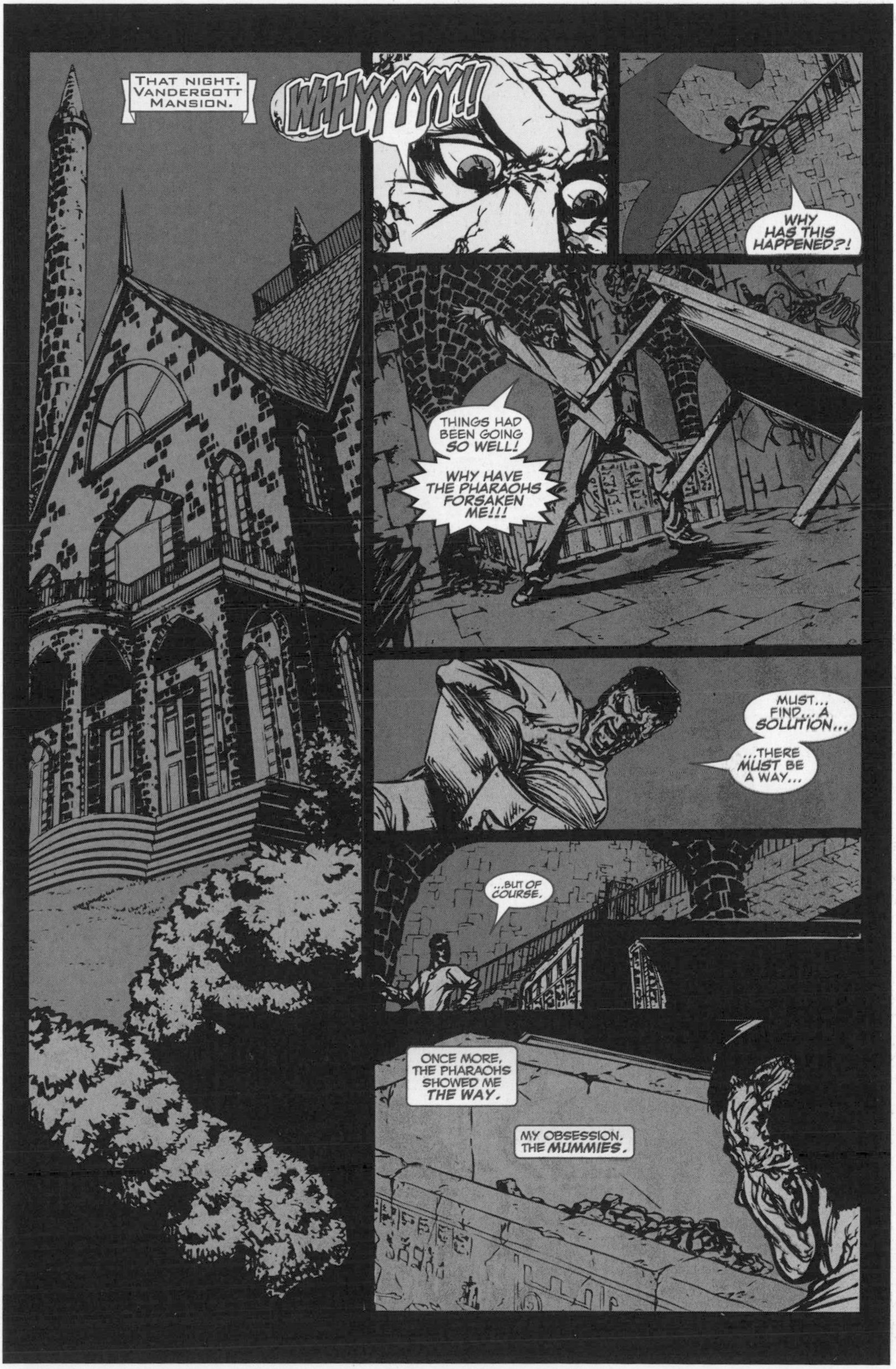
THAT NIGHT. VANDERGOTT MANSION.
WHHYYYYY!!
WHY HAS THIS HAPPENED?!
THINGS HAD BEEN GOING SO WELL!
WHY HAVE THE PHARAOHS FORSAKEN ME!!!
MUST... FIND... A SOLUTION...
...THERE MUST BE A WAY...
...BUT OF COURSE.
ONCE MORE, THE PHARAOHS SHOWED ME THE WAY.
MY OBSESSION. THE MUMMIES.

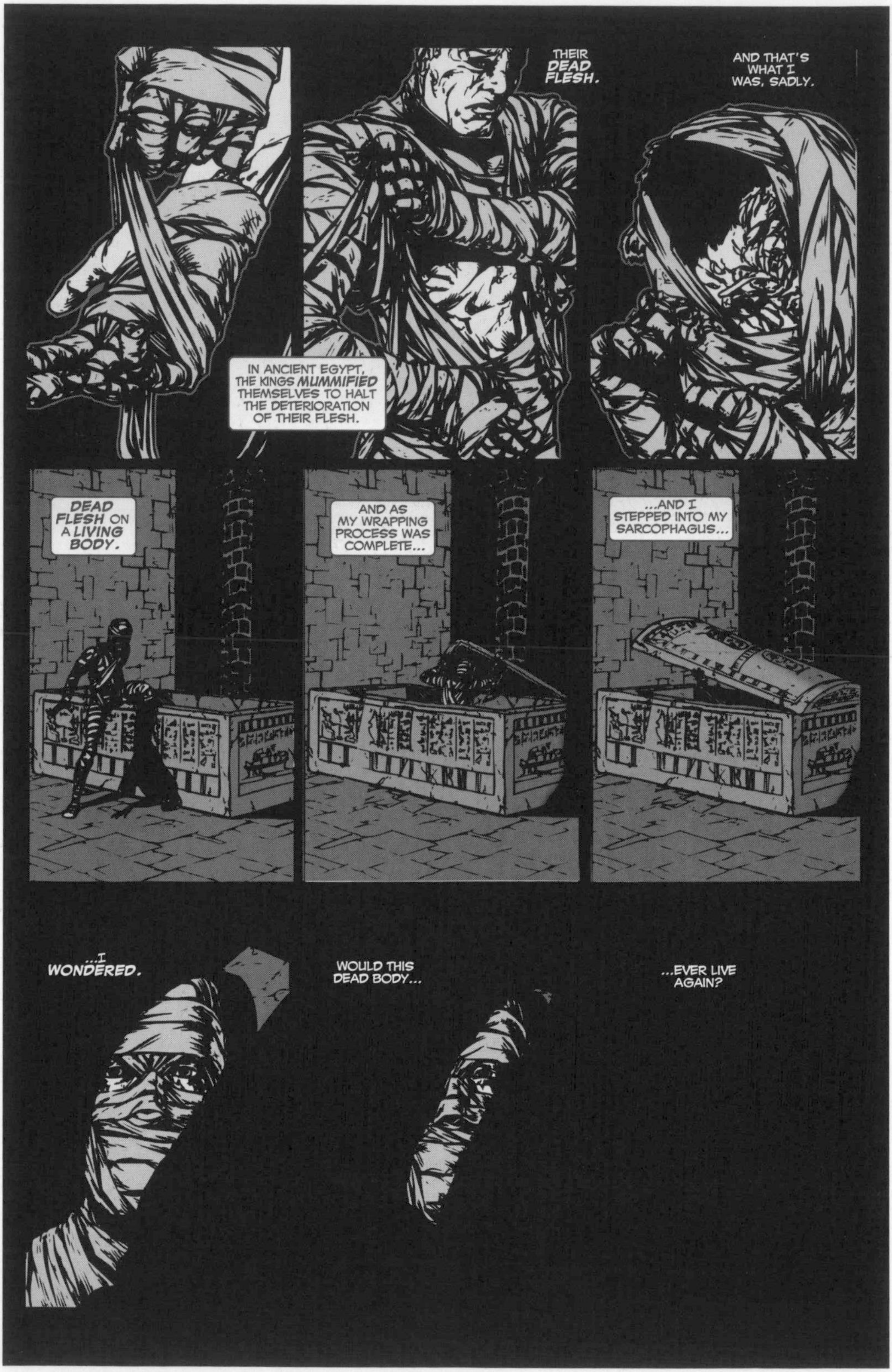
THEIR DEAD FLESH.
IN ANCIENT EGYPT, THE KINGS MUMMIFIED THEMSELVES TO HALT THE DETERIORATION OF THEIR FLESH.
AND THAT'S WHAT I WAS, SADLY.
DEAD FLESH ON A LIVING BODY.
AND AS MY WRAPPING PROCESS WAS COMPLETE...
...AND I STEPPED INTO MY SARCOPHAGUS...
...I WONDERED.
WOULD THIS DEAD BODY...
...EVER LIVE AGAIN?

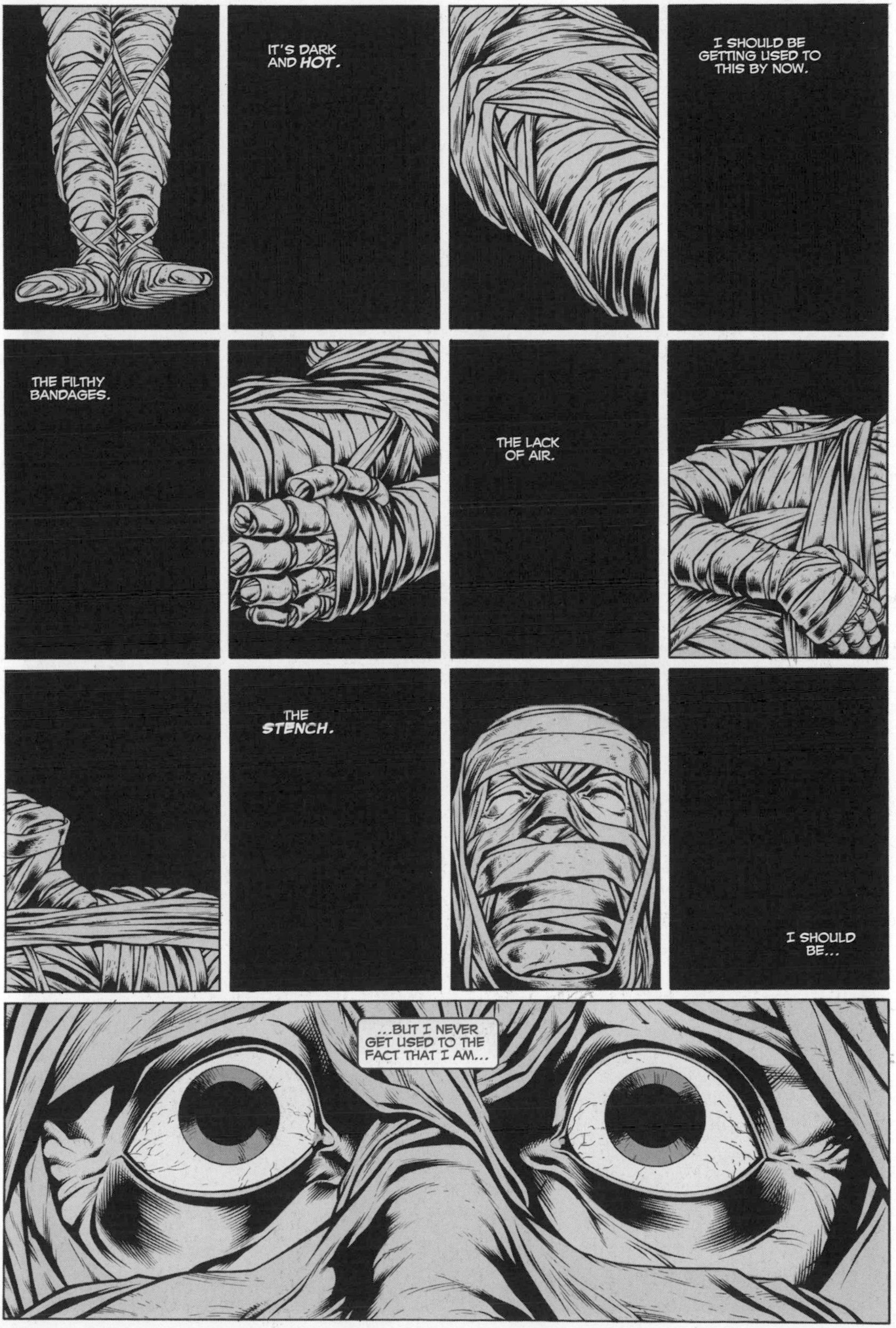
IT'S DARK AND HOT.
I SHOULD BE GETTING USED TO THIS BY NOW.
THE FILTHY BANDAGES.
THE LACK OF AIR.
THE STENCH.
I SHOULD BE...
...BUT I NEVER GET USED TO THE FACT THAT I AM...

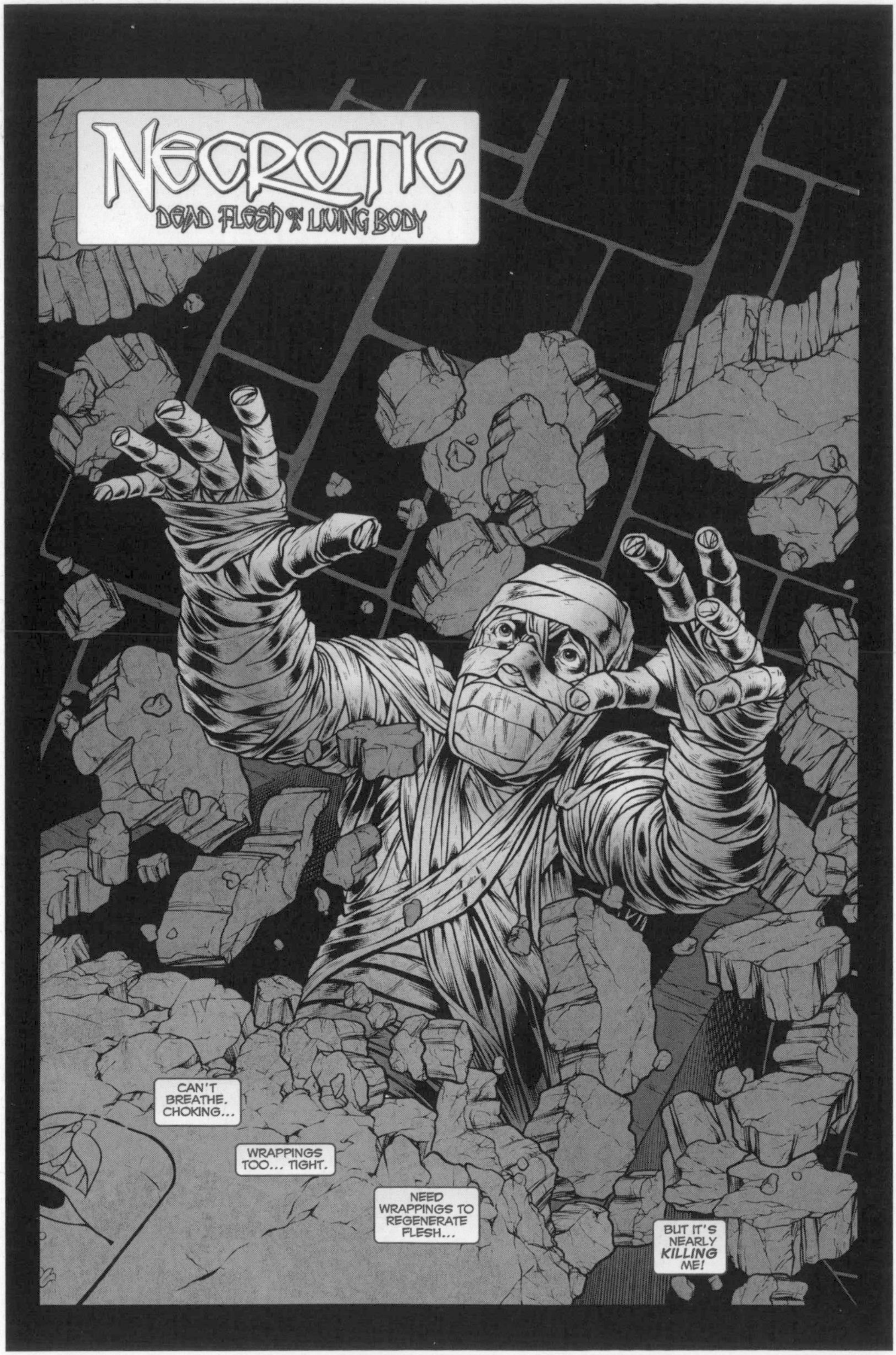
NECROTIC
DEAD FLESH ON LIVING BODY
CAN'T BREATHE. CHOKING...
WRAPPINGS TOO... TIGHT.
NEED WRAPPINGS TO REGENERATE FLESH...
BUT IT'S NEARLY KILLING ME!

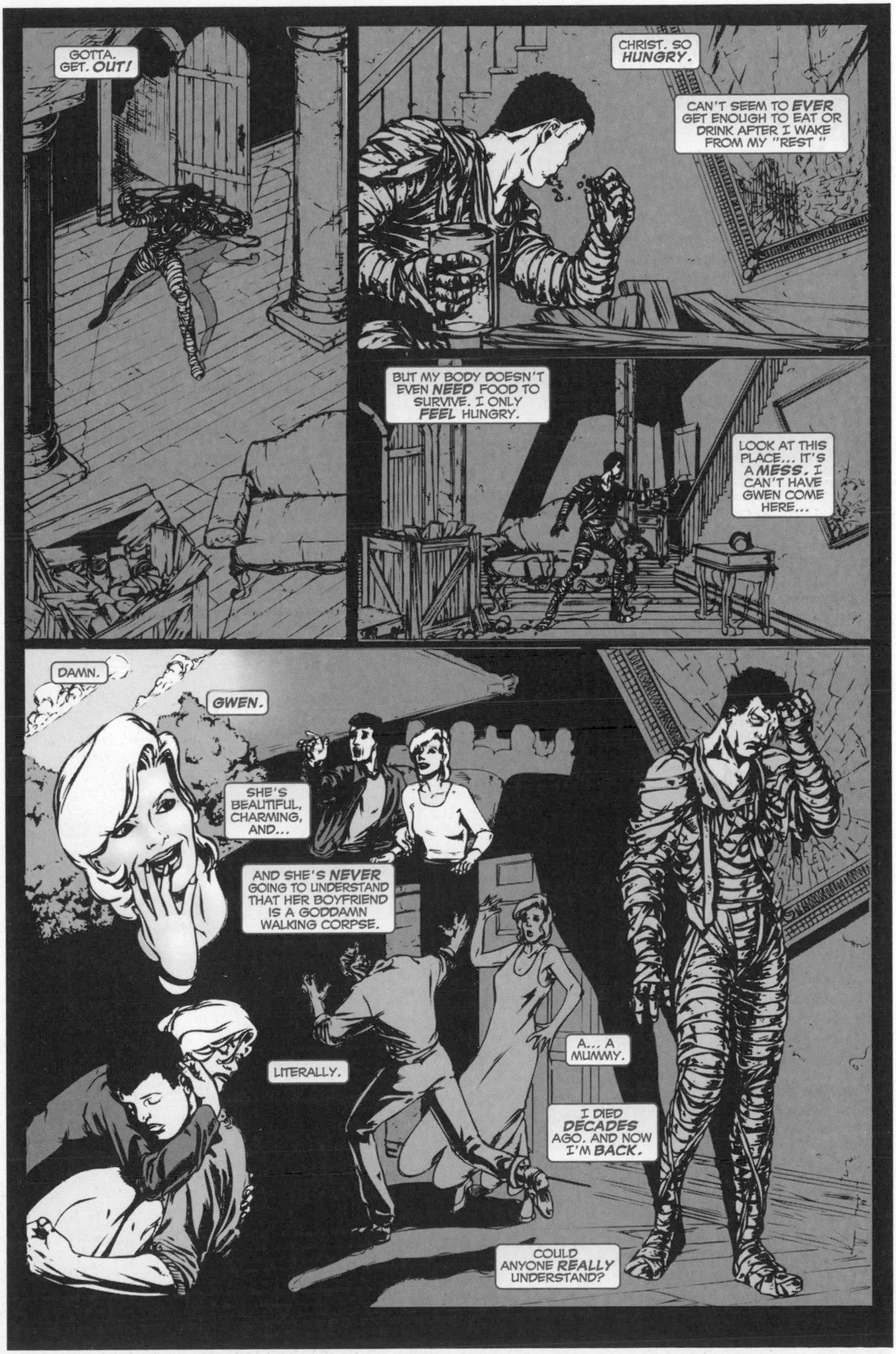
GOTTA. GET. OUT!
CHRIST. SO HUNGRY.
CAN'T SEEM TO EVER GET ENOUGH TO EAT OR DRINK AFTER I WAKE FROM MY "REST"
BUT MY BODY DOESN'T EVEN NEED FOOD TO SURVIVE. I ONLY FEEL HUNGRY.
LOOK AT THIS PLACE... IT'S A MESS. I CAN'T HAVE GWEN COME HERE...
DAMN.
GWEN.
SHE'S BEAUTIFUL, CHARMING, AND...
AND SHE'S NEVER GOING TO UNDERSTAND THAT HER BOYFRIEND IS A GODDAMN WALKING CORPSE.
LITERALLY.
A... A MUMMY.
I DIED DECADES AGO. AND NOW I'M BACK.
COULD ANYONE REALLY UNDERSTAND?

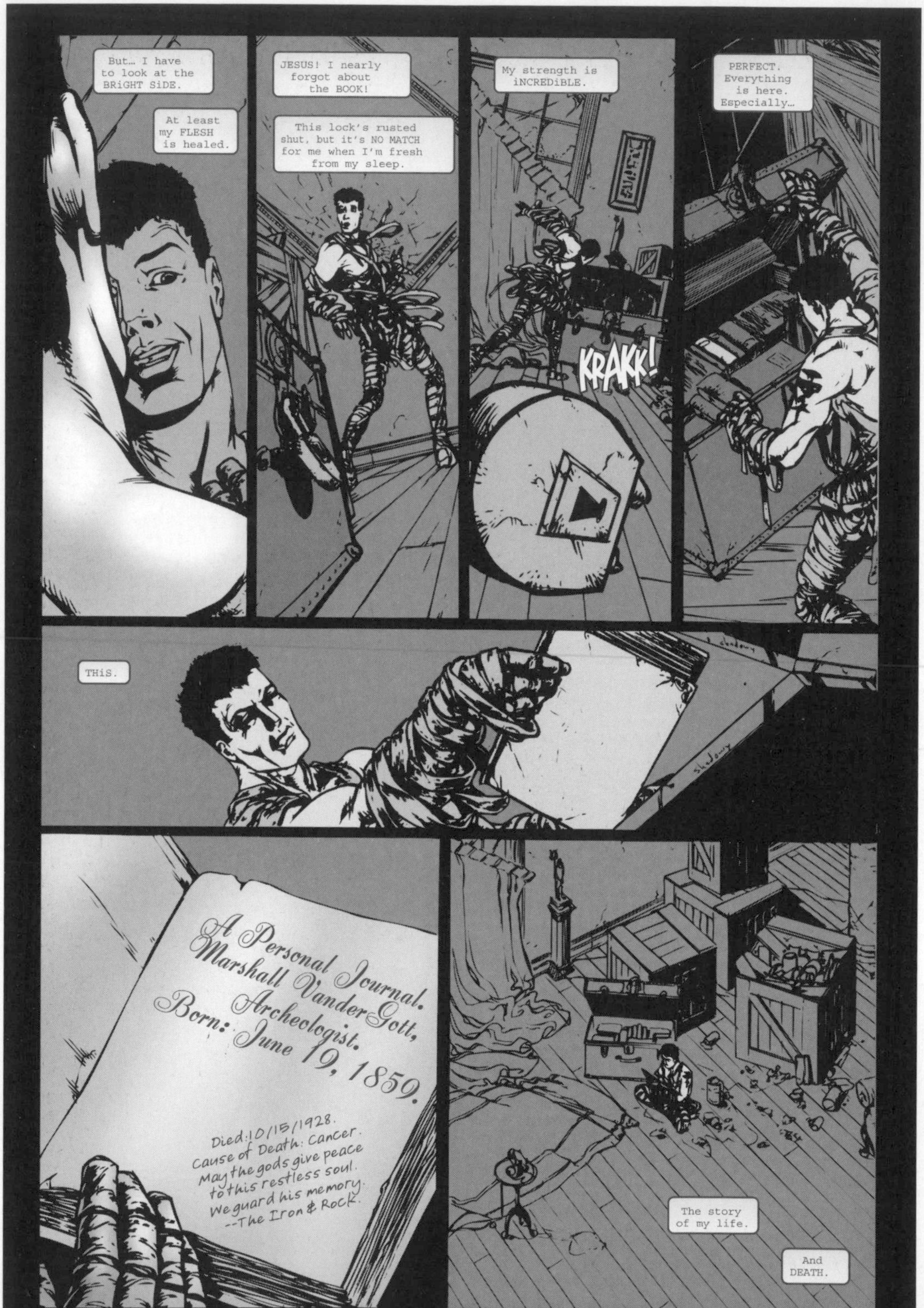
But… I have to look at the BRiGHT SiDE.
At least my FLESH is healed.
JESUS! I nearly forgot about the BOOK!
This lock's rusted shut, but it's NO MATCH for me when I'm fresh from my sleep.
My strength is iNCREDiBLE.
KRAKK!
PERFECT. Everything is here. Especially…
THiS.
A Personal Journal.
Marshall VanderGott,
Archeologist.
Born: June 19, 1859.
Died: 10/15/1928.
Cause of Death: Cancer.
May the gods give peace to this restless soul.
We guard his memory.
--The Iron & Rock.
The story of my life.
And DEATH.

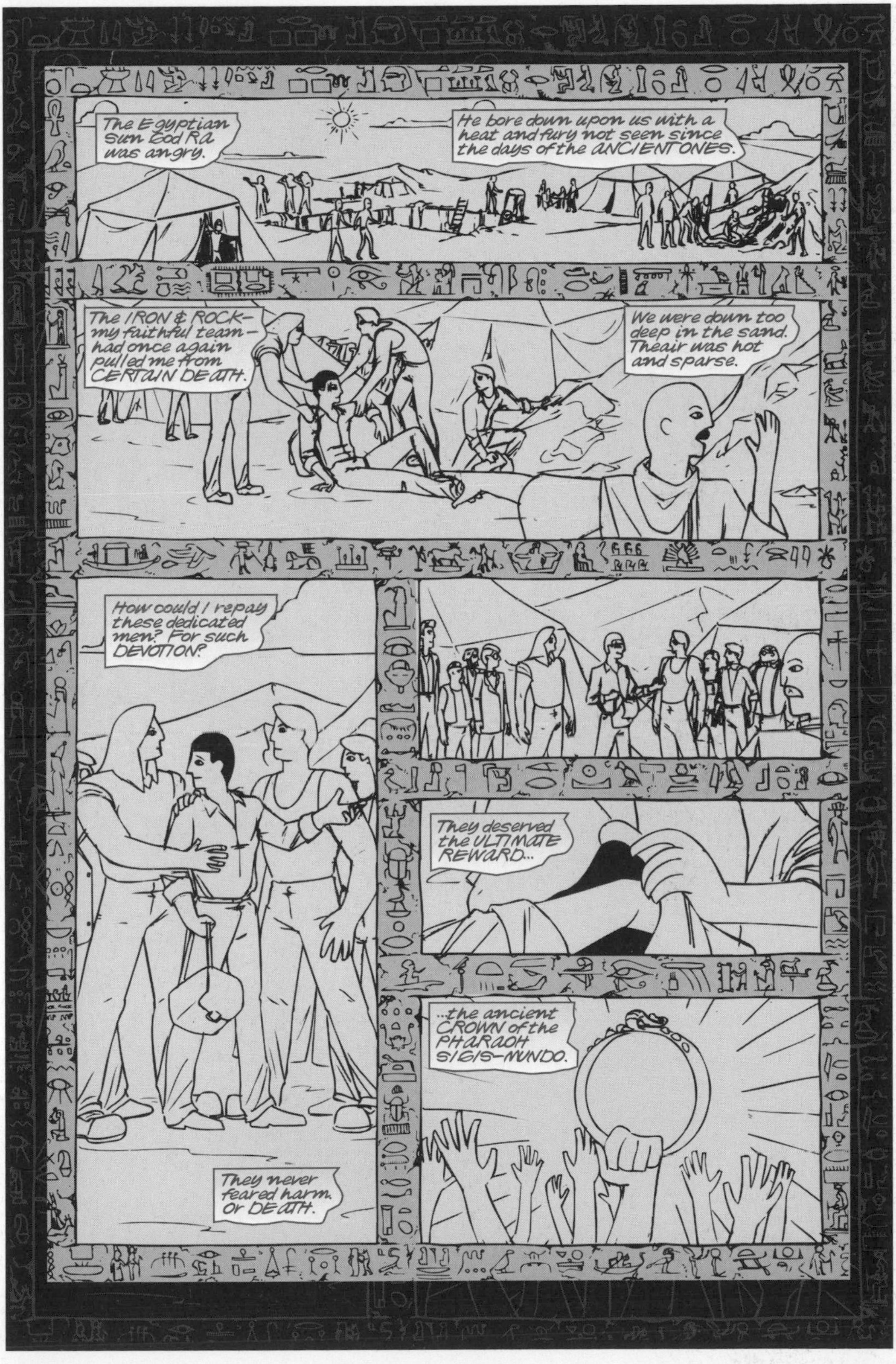
The Egyptian Sun God Ra was angry.
He bore down upon us with a heat and fury not seen since the days of the ANCIENT ONES.
The IRON & ROCK- my faithful team- had once again pulled me from CERTAIN DEATH.
We were down too deep in the sand. The air was hot and sparse.
How could I repay these dedicated men? For such DEVOTION?
They never feared harm. Or DEATH.
They deserved the ULTIMATE REWARD...
...the ancient CROWN of the PHARAOH SIGIS-MUNDO.

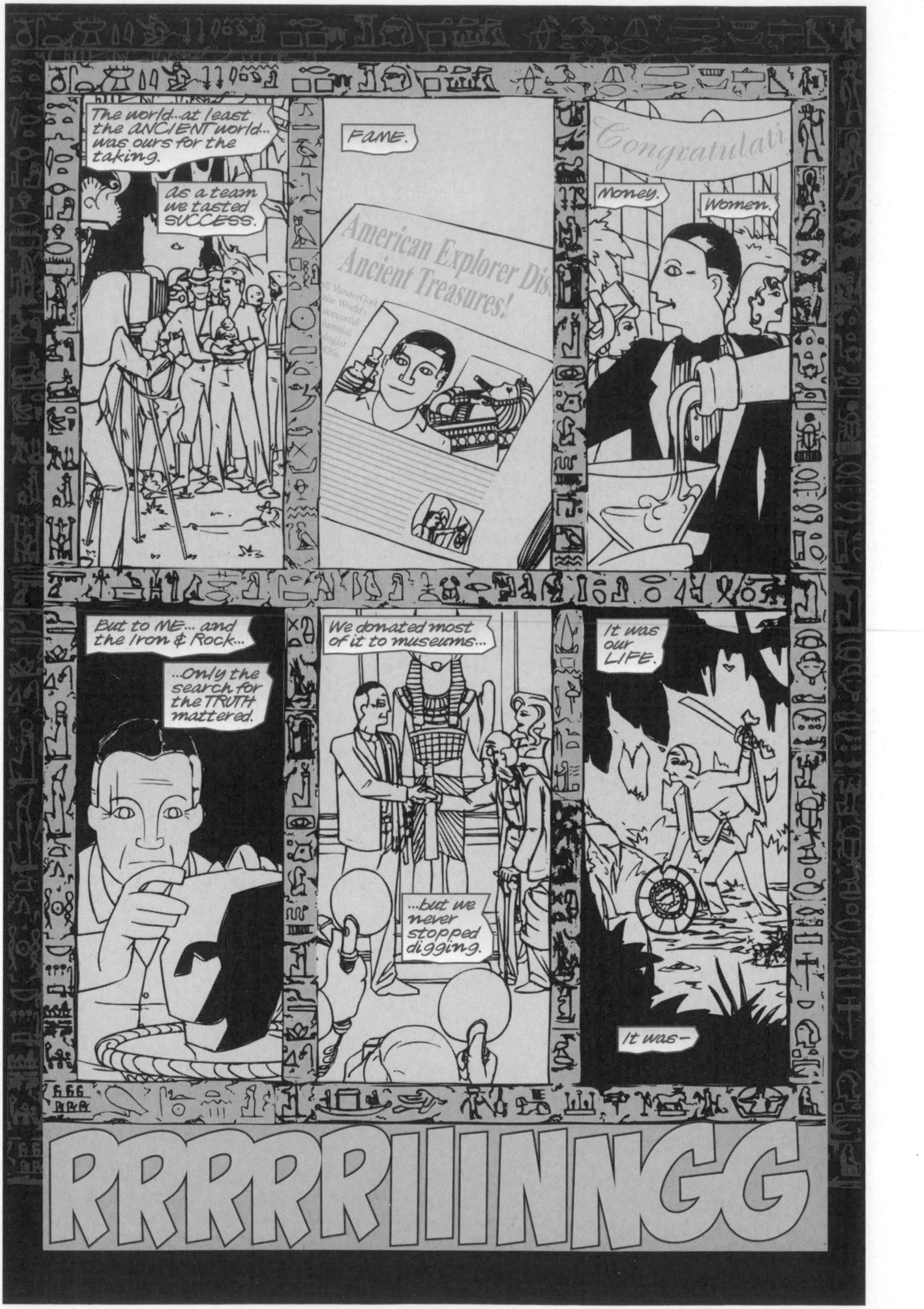

The world...at least the ANCIENT world... was ours for the taking.
As a team we tasted SUCCESS.
FAME.
American Explorer Dis
Ancient Treasures!
Congratulati
Money.
Women.
But to ME... and the Iron & Rock...
...Only the search for the TRUTH mattered.
We donated most of it to museums...
...but we never stopped digging.
It was our LIFE.
It was—
RRRRRIIINNGG

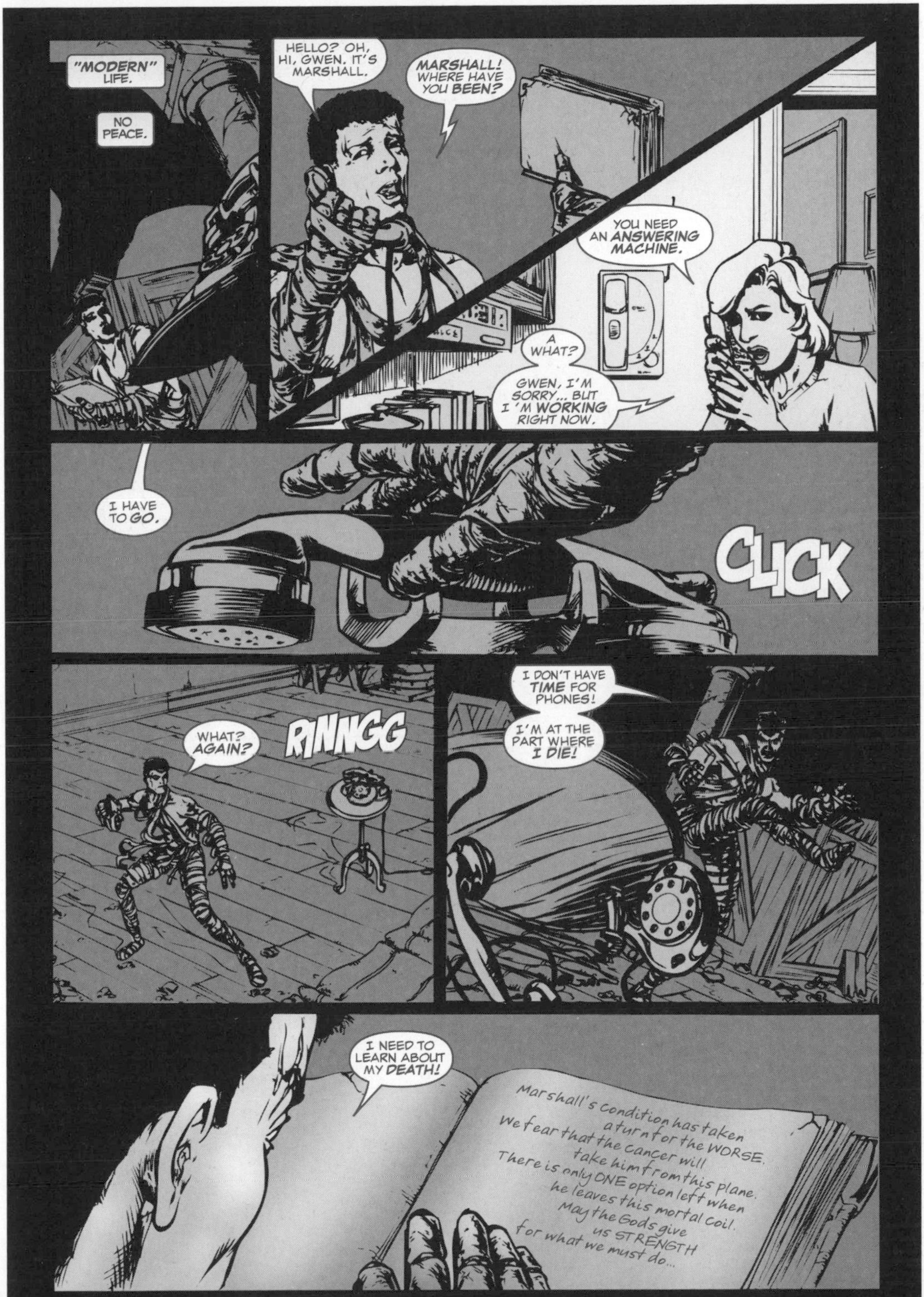
"MODERN" LIFE.
NO PEACE.
HELLO? OH, HI, GWEN. IT'S MARSHALL.
MARSHALL! WHERE HAVE YOU BEEN?
YOU NEED AN ANSWERING MACHINE.
A WHAT?
GWEN, I'M SORRY... BUT I'M WORKING RIGHT NOW.
I HAVE TO GO.
CLICK
WHAT? AGAIN?
RINNGG
I DON'T HAVE TIME FOR PHONES!
I'M AT THE PART WHERE I DIE!
I NEED TO LEARN ABOUT MY DEATH!
Marshall's condition has taken a turn for the WORSE. We fear that the cancer will take him from this plane. There is only ONE option left when he leaves this mortal coil. May the Gods give us STRENGTH for what we must do...

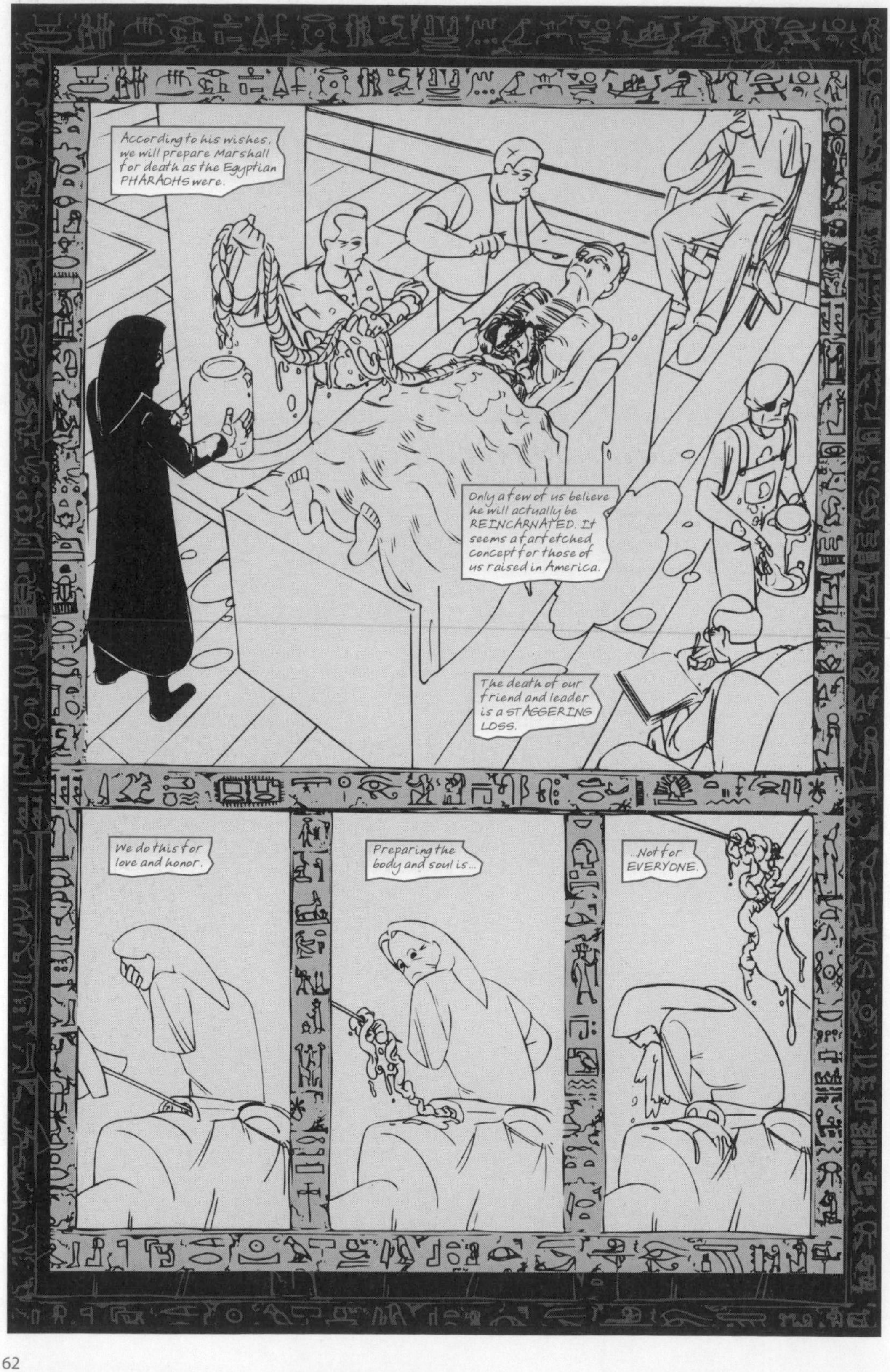
According to his wishes, we will prepare Marshall for death as the Egyptian PHARAOHS were.
Only a few of us believe he will actually be REINCARNATED. It seems a far fetched concept for those of us raised in America.
The death of our friend and leader is a STAGGERING LOSS.
We do this for love and honor.
Preparing the body and soul is...
...Not for EVERYONE.

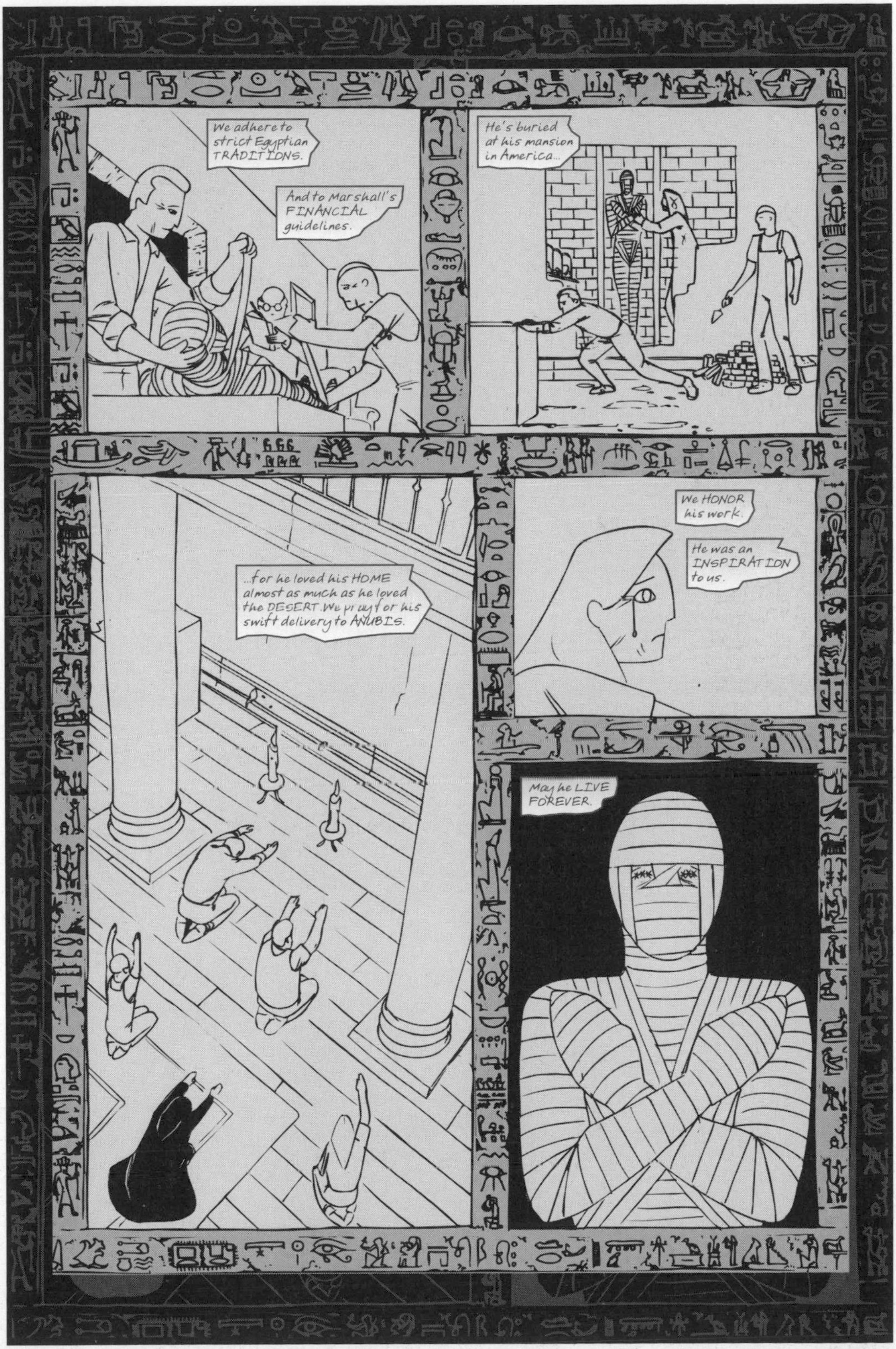
We adhere to strict Egyptian TRADITIONS.
And to Marshall's FINANCIAL guidelines.
He's buried at his mansion in America...
...for he loved his HOME almost as much as he loved the DESERT. We pray for his swift delivery to ANUBIS.
We HONOR his work.
He was an INSPIRATION to us.
May he LIVE FOREVER.

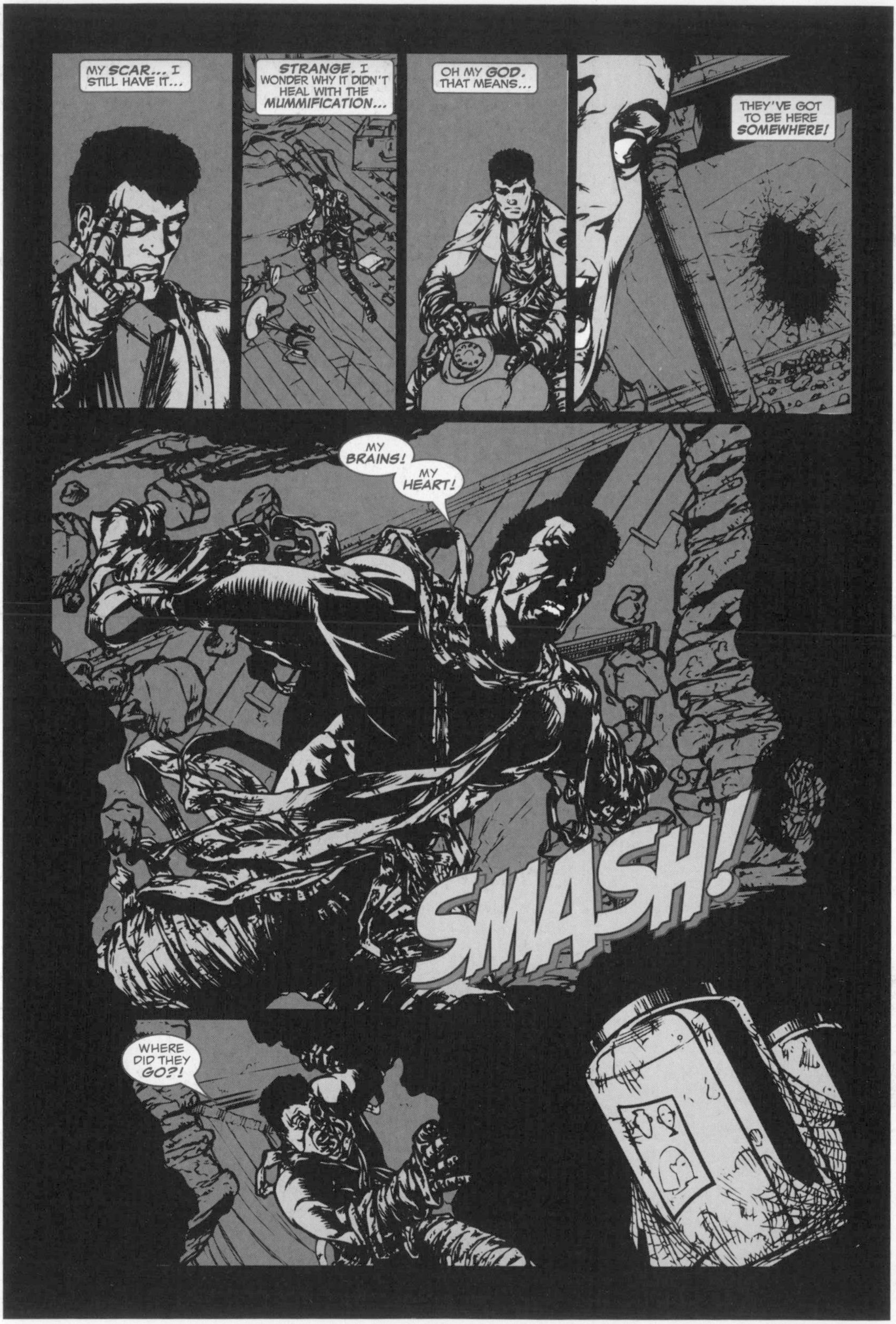
MY SCAR... I STILL HAVE IT...
STRANGE. I WONDER WHY IT DIDN'T HEAL WITH THE MUMMIFICATION...
OH MY GOD. THAT MEANS...
THEY'VE GOT TO BE HERE SOMEWHERE!
MY BRAINS!
MY HEART!
SMASH!
WHERE DID THEY GO?!

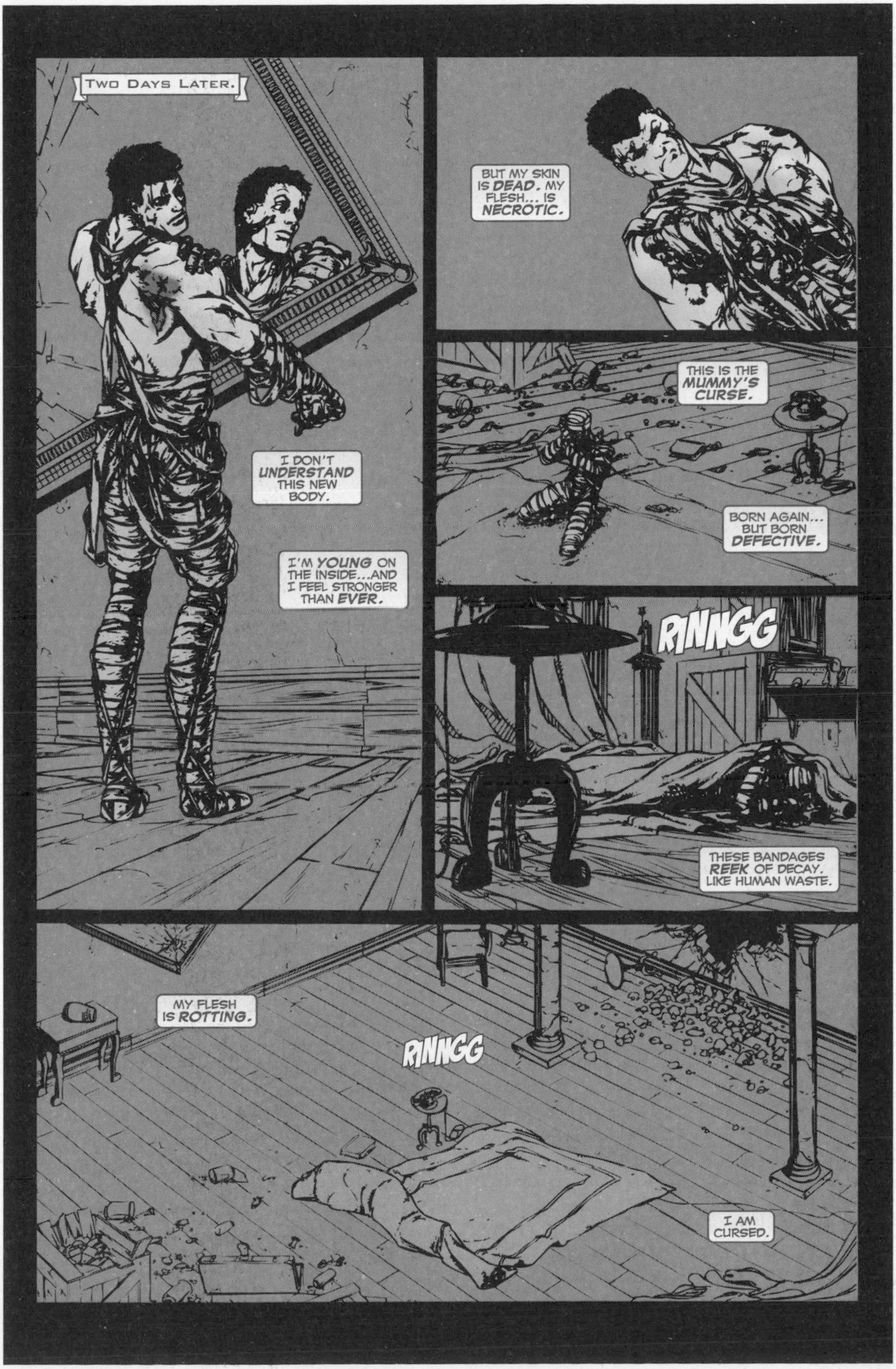
TWO DAYS LATER.
I DON'T UNDERSTAND THIS NEW BODY.
I'M YOUNG ON THE INSIDE...AND I FEEL STRONGER THAN EVER.
BUT MY SKIN IS DEAD. MY FLESH... IS NECROTIC.
THIS IS THE MUMMY'S CURSE.
BORN AGAIN... BUT BORN DEFECTIVE.
RINNGG
THESE BANDAGES REEK OF DECAY. LIKE HUMAN WASTE.
MY FLESH IS ROTTING.
RINNGG
I AM CURSED.

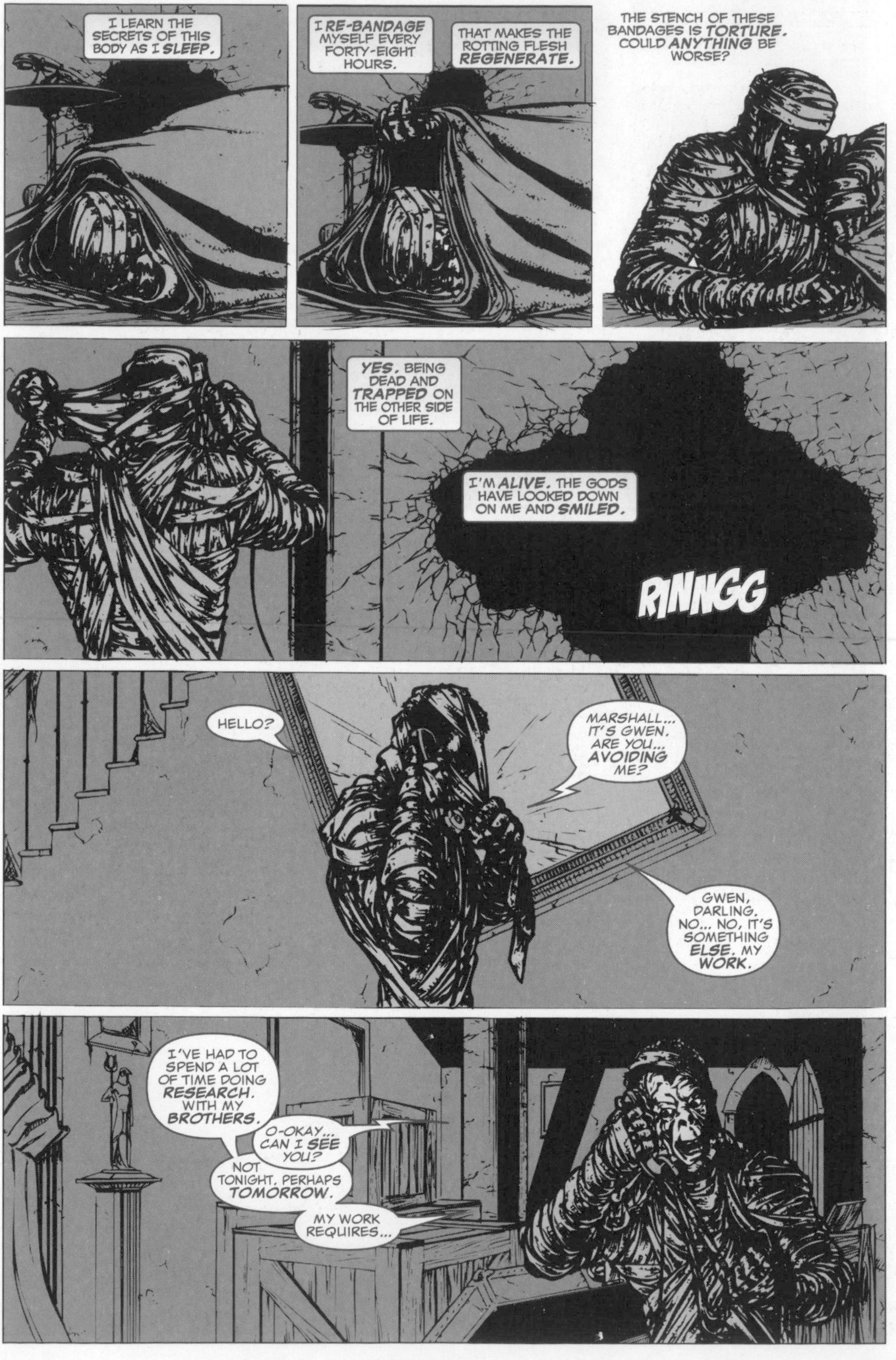
I LEARN THE SECRETS OF THIS BODY AS I SLEEP.
I RE-BANDAGE MYSELF EVERY FORTY-EIGHT HOURS.
THAT MAKES THE ROTTING FLESH REGENERATE.
THE STENCH OF THESE BANDAGES IS TORTURE. COULD ANYTHING BE WORSE?
YES. BEING DEAD AND TRAPPED ON THE OTHER SIDE OF LIFE.
I'M ALIVE. THE GODS HAVE LOOKED DOWN ON ME AND SMILED.
RINNGG
HELLO?
MARSHALL... IT'S GWEN. ARE YOU... AVOIDING ME?
GWEN, DARLING. NO... NO, IT'S SOMETHING ELSE. MY WORK.
I'VE HAD TO SPEND A LOT OF TIME DOING RESEARCH. WITH MY BROTHERS.
O-OKAY... CAN I SEE YOU?
NOT TONIGHT, PERHAPS TOMORROW.
MY WORK REQUIRES...

"...A LITTLE MORE *TIME*"

...SO MY SISTER SAID, "I'LL BE GONE FOR A FEW WEEKS, WHY DON'T YOU STAY AT MY *APARTMENT*!"

THIS PLACE IS *AMAZING*, GWEN.

I WANT YOU TO MEET HER.

YES, THAT WOULD BE PLEASURABLE.

"THAT WOULD BE PLEASURABLE"?! HAHAHA!

WHAT--?

OH, YOU'RE SO *CUTE*! YOU TALK LIKE AN OLD *HOLLYWOOD* MOVIE!

IT'S LIKE YOU'RE FROM *1920S* OR SOMETHING!

UHH... WELLLL... IN MY OF MY WORK, I SPEAK WITH MANY *OLD* PEOPLE.

RIGHT, *MYSTERY MAN*, LET'S SEE THOSE *BUNS* ON THE *DIVING BOARD*!

THAT I CAN *DO*.

ACTUALLY, I CAN DO *MUCH MORE* THAN GWEN COULD EVER IMAGINE.

I WONDER WHAT THIS WATER WILL DO TO MY *SKIN*? WILL IT *ROT OFF*? WILL IT *BUBBLE UP* AND *DISINTEGRATE* IN THE POOL?

THERE'S ONLY *ONE WAY* TO FIND OUT.

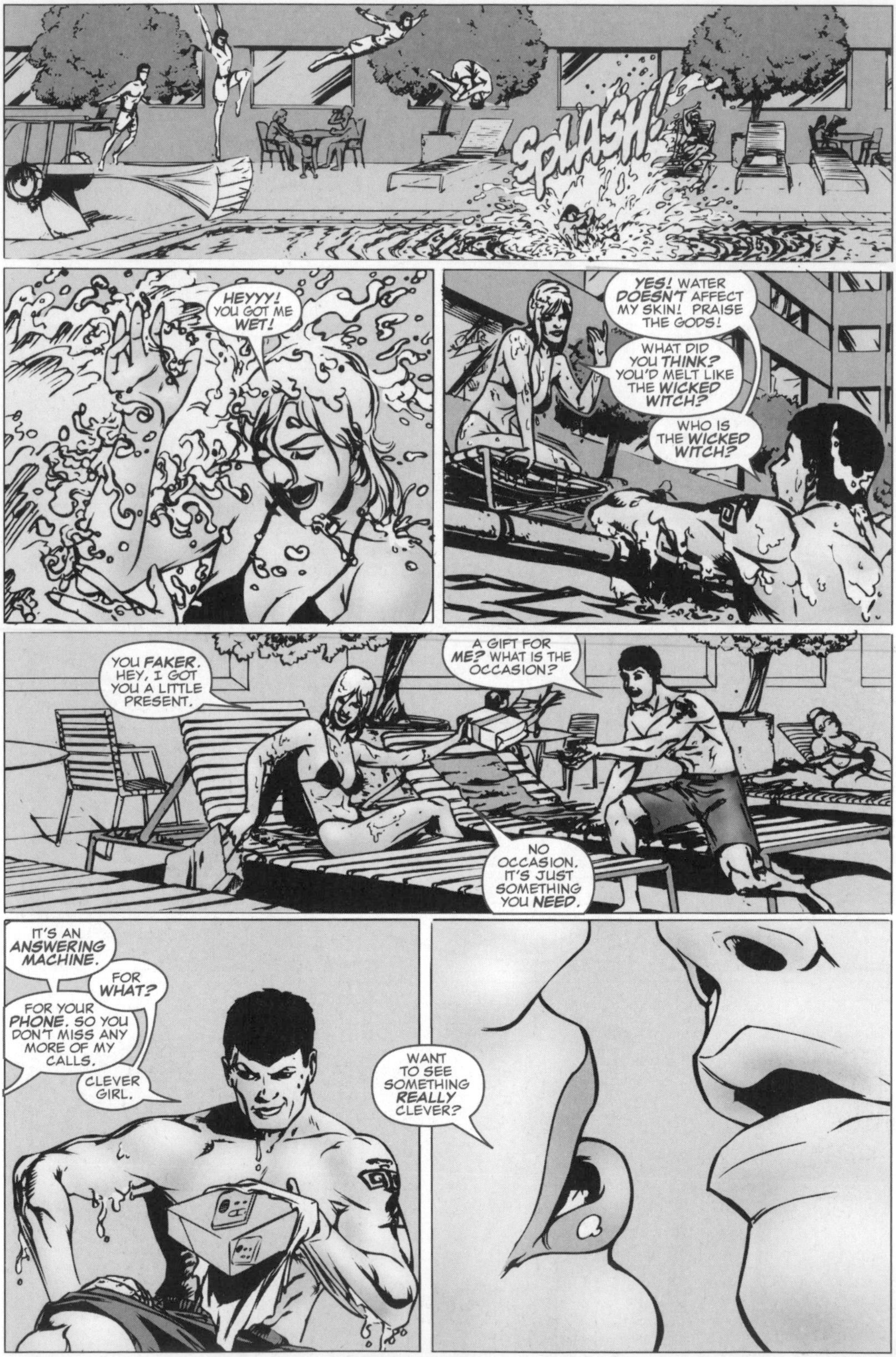
SPLASH!!
HEYYY! YOU GOT ME WET!
YES! WATER DOESN'T AFFECT MY SKIN! PRAISE THE GODS!
WHAT DID YOU THINK? YOU'D MELT LIKE THE WICKED WITCH?
WHO IS THE WICKED WITCH?
YOU FAKER. HEY, I GOT YOU A LITTLE PRESENT.
A GIFT FOR ME? WHAT IS THE OCCASION?
NO OCCASION. IT'S JUST SOMETHING YOU NEED.
IT'S AN ANSWERING MACHINE.
FOR WHAT?
FOR YOUR PHONE. SO YOU DON'T MISS ANY MORE OF MY CALLS.
CLEVER GIRL.
WANT TO SEE SOMETHING REALLY CLEVER?

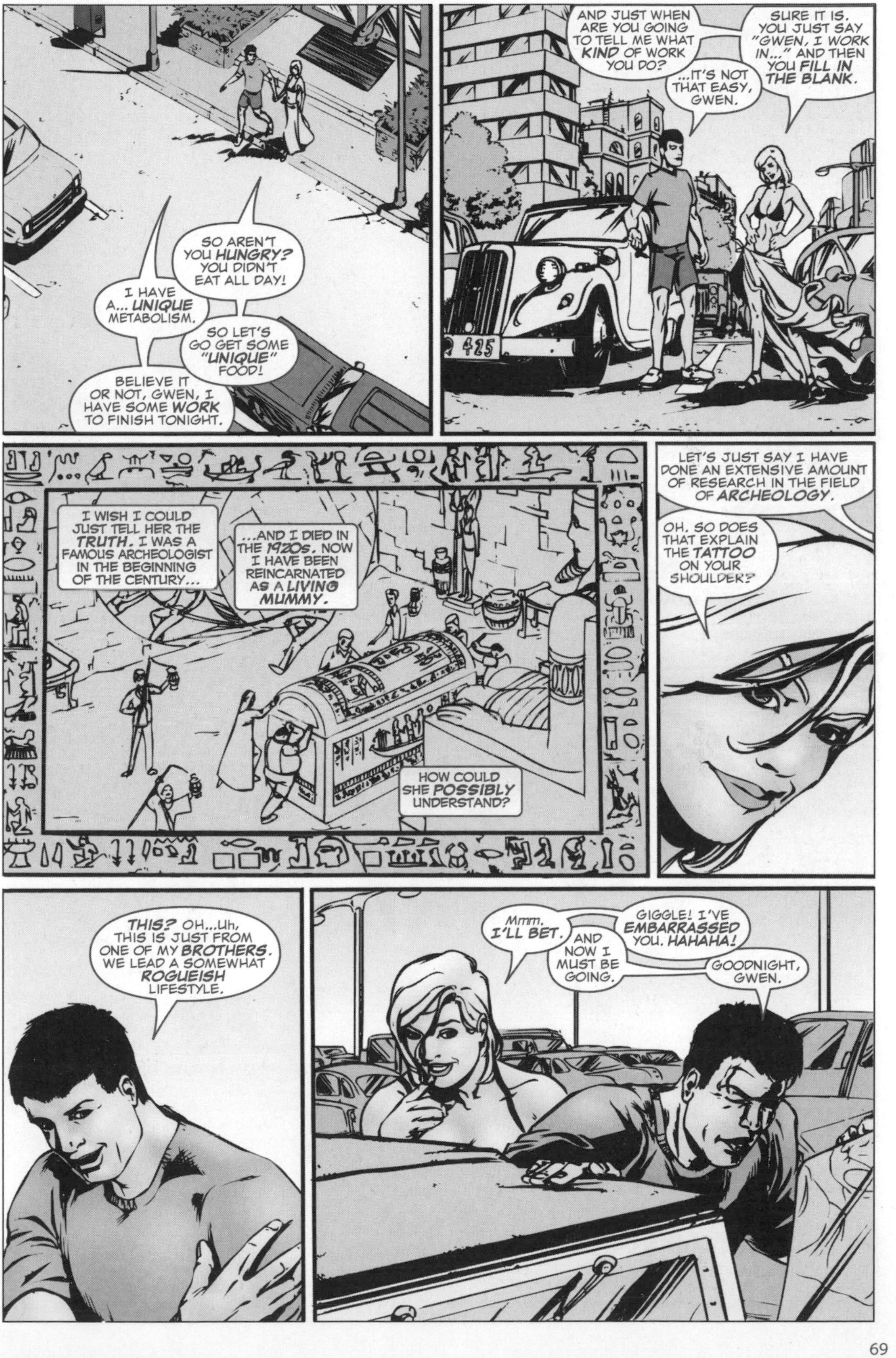
SO AREN'T YOU HUNGRY? YOU DIDN'T EAT ALL DAY!
I HAVE A... UNIQUE METABOLISM.
SO LET'S GO GET SOME "UNIQUE" FOOD!
BELIEVE IT OR NOT, GWEN, I HAVE SOME WORK TO FINISH TONIGHT.
AND JUST WHEN ARE YOU GOING TO TELL ME WHAT KIND OF WORK YOU DO?
...IT'S NOT THAT EASY, GWEN.
SURE IT IS. YOU JUST SAY "GWEN, I WORK IN..." AND THEN YOU FILL IN THE BLANK.
I WISH I COULD JUST TELL HER THE TRUTH. I WAS A FAMOUS ARCHEOLOGIST IN THE BEGINNING OF THE CENTURY...
...AND I DIED IN THE 1920s. NOW I HAVE BEEN REINCARNATED AS A LIVING MUMMY.
HOW COULD SHE POSSIBLY UNDERSTAND?
LET'S JUST SAY I HAVE DONE AN EXTENSIVE AMOUNT OF RESEARCH IN THE FIELD OF ARCHEOLOGY.
OH. SO DOES THAT EXPLAIN THE TATTOO ON YOUR SHOULDER?
THIS? OH...Uh, THIS IS JUST FROM ONE OF MY BROTHERS. WE LEAD A SOMEWHAT ROGUEISH LIFESTYLE.
Mmm. I'LL BET.
GIGGLE! I'VE EMBARRASSED YOU. HAHAHA!
AND NOW I MUST BE GOING.
GOODNIGHT, GWEN.

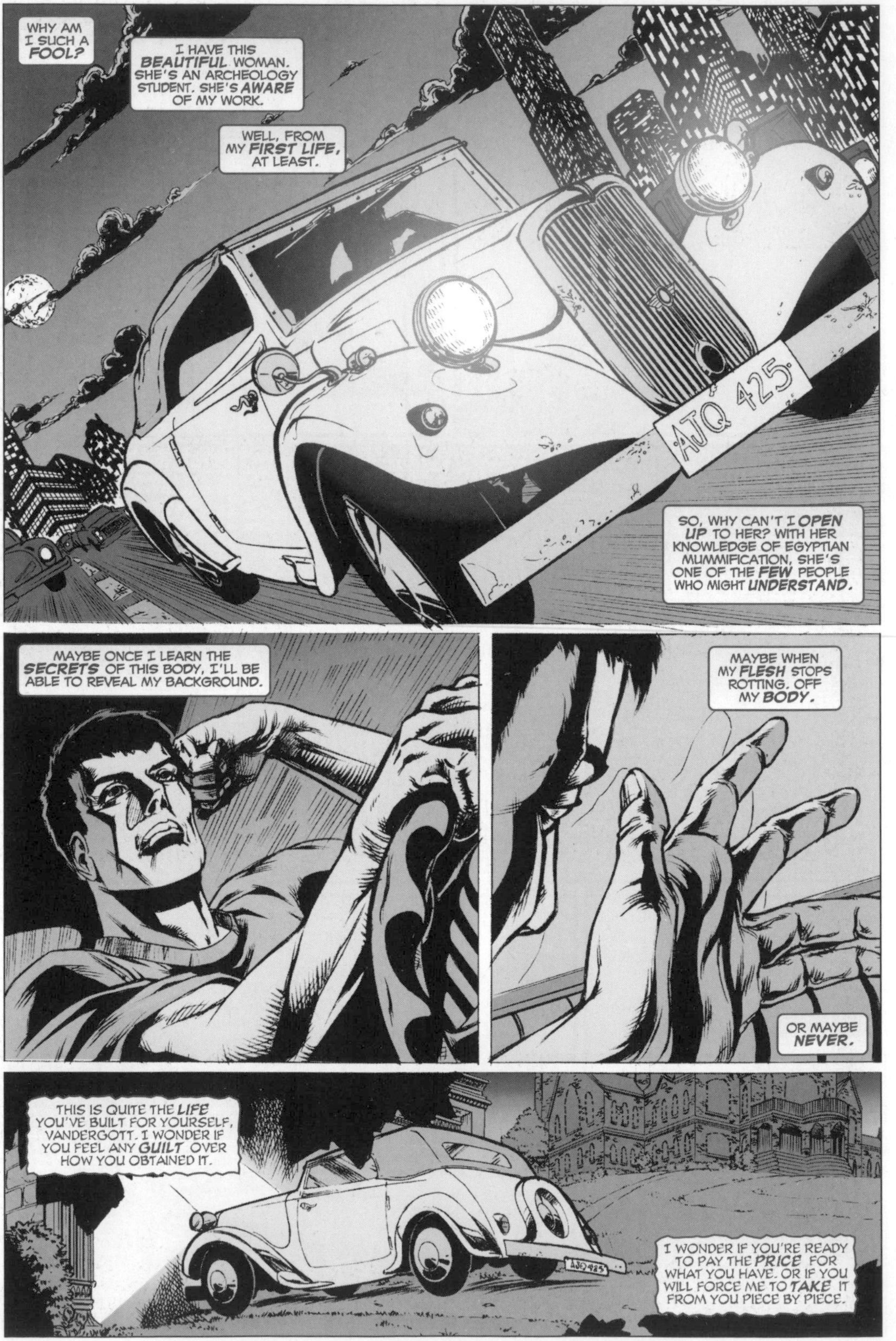
WHY AM I SUCH A FOOL?
I HAVE THIS BEAUTIFUL WOMAN. SHE'S AN ARCHEOLOGY STUDENT. SHE'S AWARE OF MY WORK.
WELL, FROM MY FIRST LIFE, AT LEAST.
AJQ 425
SO, WHY CAN'T I OPEN UP TO HER? WITH HER KNOWLEDGE OF EGYPTIAN MUMMIFICATION, SHE'S ONE OF THE FEW PEOPLE WHO MIGHT UNDERSTAND.
MAYBE ONCE I LEARN THE SECRETS OF THIS BODY, I'LL BE ABLE TO REVEAL MY BACKGROUND.
MAYBE WHEN MY FLESH STOPS ROTTING. OFF MY BODY.
OR MAYBE NEVER.
THIS IS QUITE THE LIFE YOU'VE BUILT FOR YOURSELF, VANDERGOTT. I WONDER IF YOU FEEL ANY GUILT OVER HOW YOU OBTAINED IT.
I WONDER IF YOU'RE READY TO PAY THE PRICE FOR WHAT YOU HAVE. OR IF YOU WILL FORCE ME TO TAKE IT FROM YOU PIECE BY PIECE.

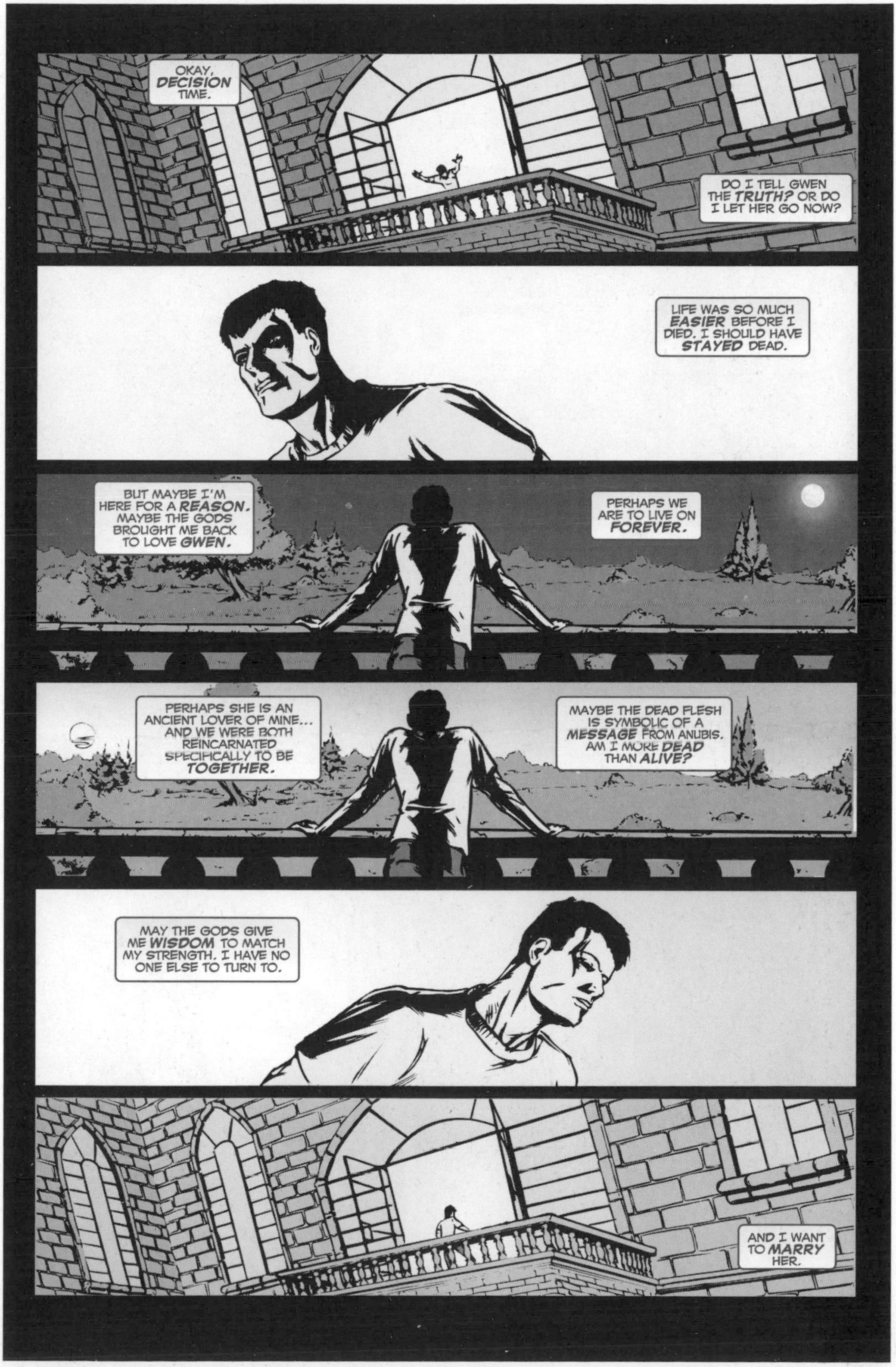
OKAY, DECISION TIME.
DO I TELL GWEN THE TRUTH? OR DO I LET HER GO NOW?
LIFE WAS SO MUCH EASIER BEFORE I DIED. I SHOULD HAVE STAYED DEAD.
BUT MAYBE I'M HERE FOR A REASON. MAYBE THE GODS BROUGHT ME BACK TO LOVE GWEN.
PERHAPS WE ARE TO LIVE ON FOREVER.
PERHAPS SHE IS AN ANCIENT LOVER OF MINE... AND WE WERE BOTH REINCARNATED SPECIFICALLY TO BE TOGETHER.
MAYBE THE DEAD FLESH IS SYMBOLIC OF A MESSAGE FROM ANUBIS. AM I MORE DEAD THAN ALIVE?
MAY THE GODS GIVE ME WISDOM TO MATCH MY STRENGTH. I HAVE NO ONE ELSE TO TURN TO.
AND I WANT TO MARRY HER.

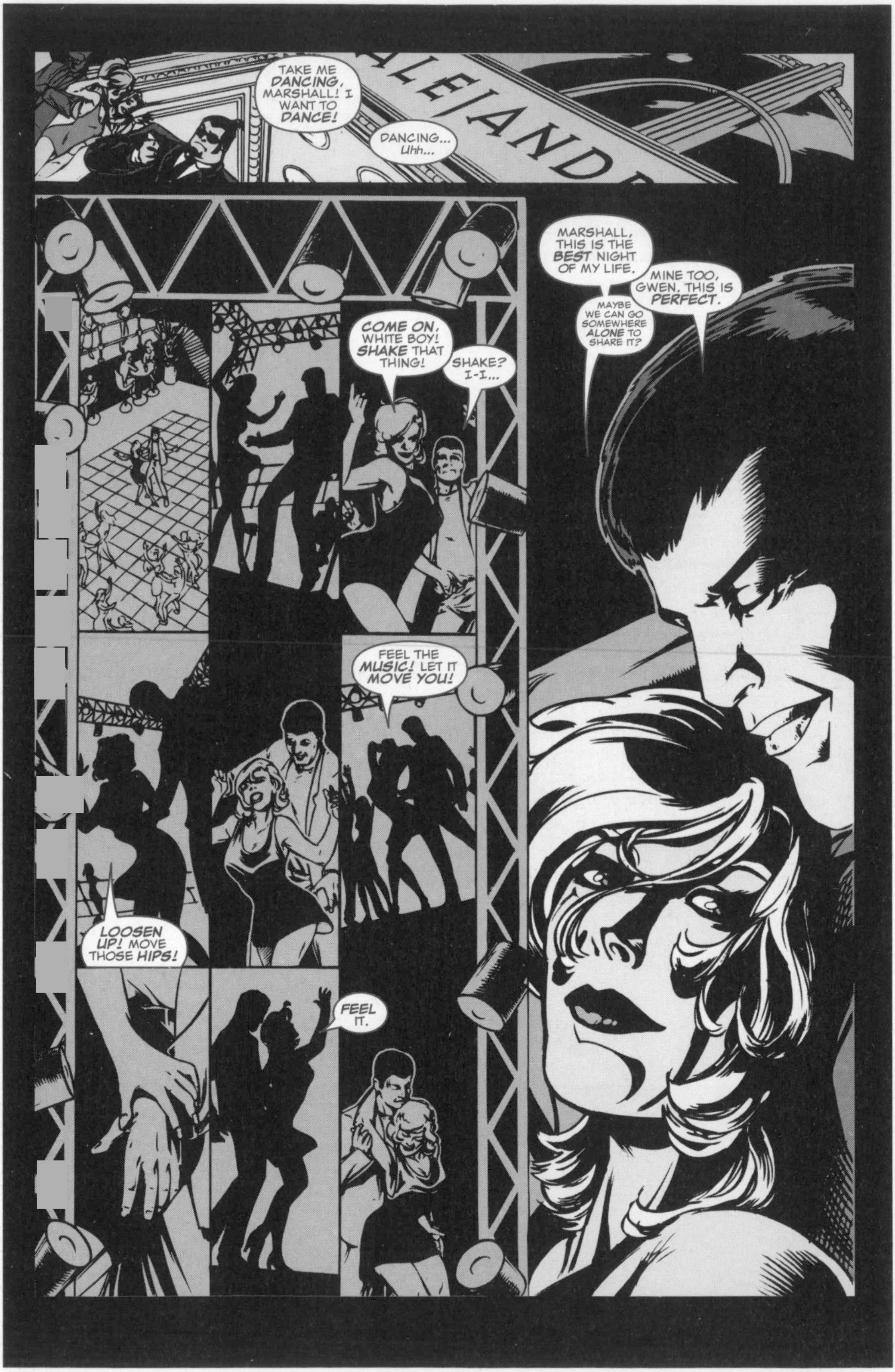
TAKE ME DANCING, MARSHALL! I WANT TO DANCE!
DANCING... Uhh...
COME ON, WHITE BOY! SHAKE THAT THING!
SHAKE? I-I...
LOOSEN UP! MOVE THOSE HIPS!
FEEL THE MUSIC! LET IT MOVE YOU!
FEEL IT.
MARSHALL, THIS IS THE BEST NIGHT OF MY LIFE.
MINE TOO, GWEN. THIS IS PERFECT.
MAYBE WE CAN GO SOMEWHERE ALONE TO SHARE IT?

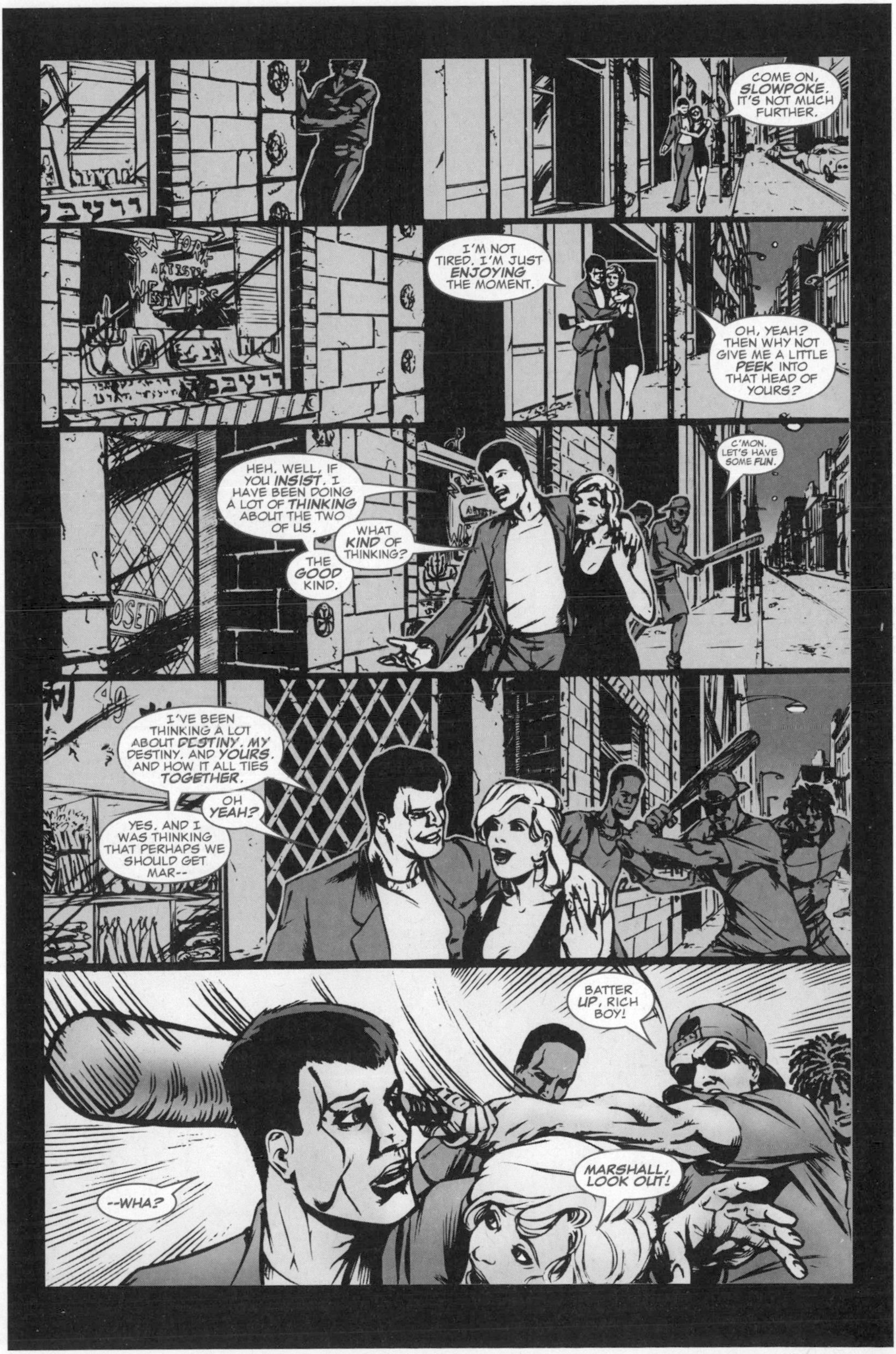
COME ON, SLOWPOKE. IT'S NOT MUCH FURTHER.
I'M NOT TIRED. I'M JUST ENJOYING THE MOMENT.
OH, YEAH? THEN WHY NOT GIVE ME A LITTLE PEEK INTO THAT HEAD OF YOURS?
HEH. WELL, IF YOU INSIST. I HAVE BEEN DOING A LOT OF THINKING ABOUT THE TWO OF US.
WHAT KIND OF THINKING?
THE GOOD KIND.
C'MON. LET'S HAVE SOME FUN.
I'VE BEEN THINKING A LOT ABOUT DESTINY. MY DESTINY. AND YOURS. AND HOW IT ALL TIES TOGETHER.
OH YEAH?
YES. AND I WAS THINKING THAT PERHAPS WE SHOULD GET MAR--
BATTER UP, RICH BOY!
MARSHALL, LOOK OUT!
--WHA?

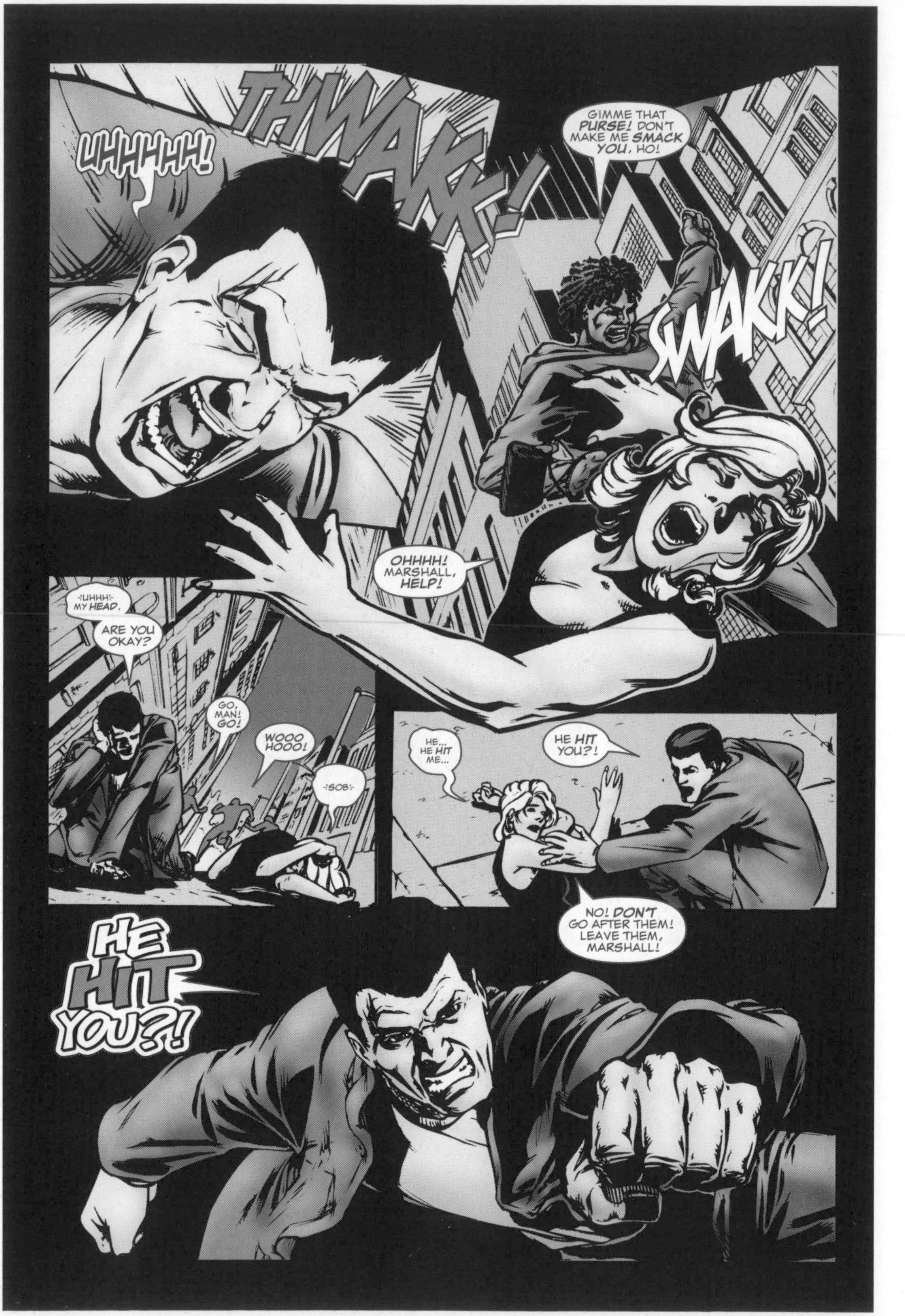

UHHHHH!
THWAKK!
GIMME THAT PURSE! DON'T MAKE ME SMACK YOU, HO!
SWAKK!
OHHHH! MARSHALL, HELP!
-UHHH- MY HEAD.
ARE YOU OKAY?
GO, MAN! GO!
WOOO HOOO!
-SOB-
HE... HE HIT ME...
HE HIT YOU?!
NO! DON'T GO AFTER THEM! LEAVE THEM, MARSHALL!
HE HIT YOU?!

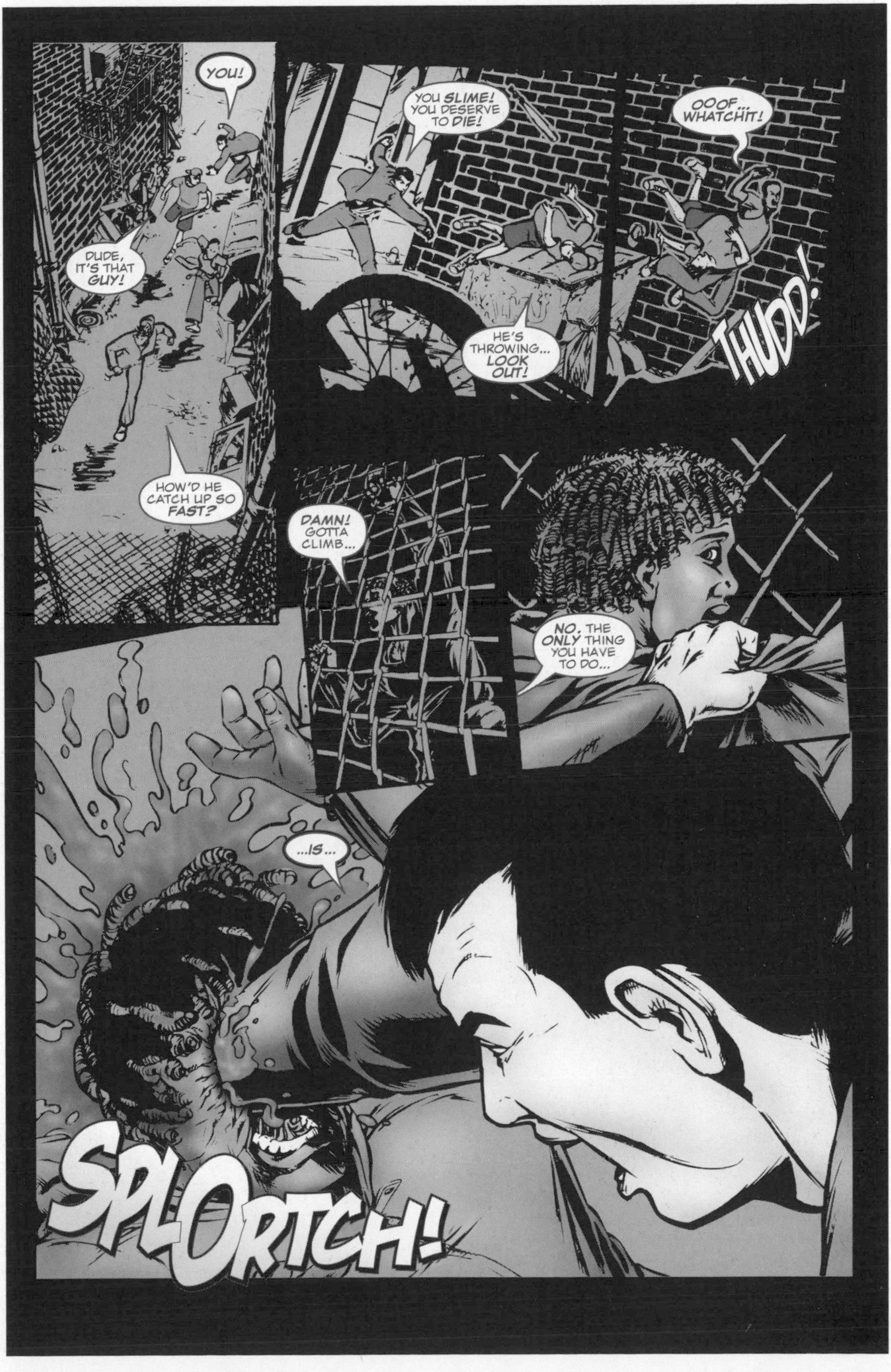
YOU!
DUDE, IT'S THAT GUY!
HOW'D HE CATCH UP SO FAST?
YOU SLIME! YOU DESERVE TO DIE!
HE'S THROWING... LOOK OUT!
OOOF... WHATCHIT!
THUDD!
DAMN! GOTTA CLIMB...
NO. THE ONLY THING YOU HAVE TO DO...
...IS...
SPLORTCH!

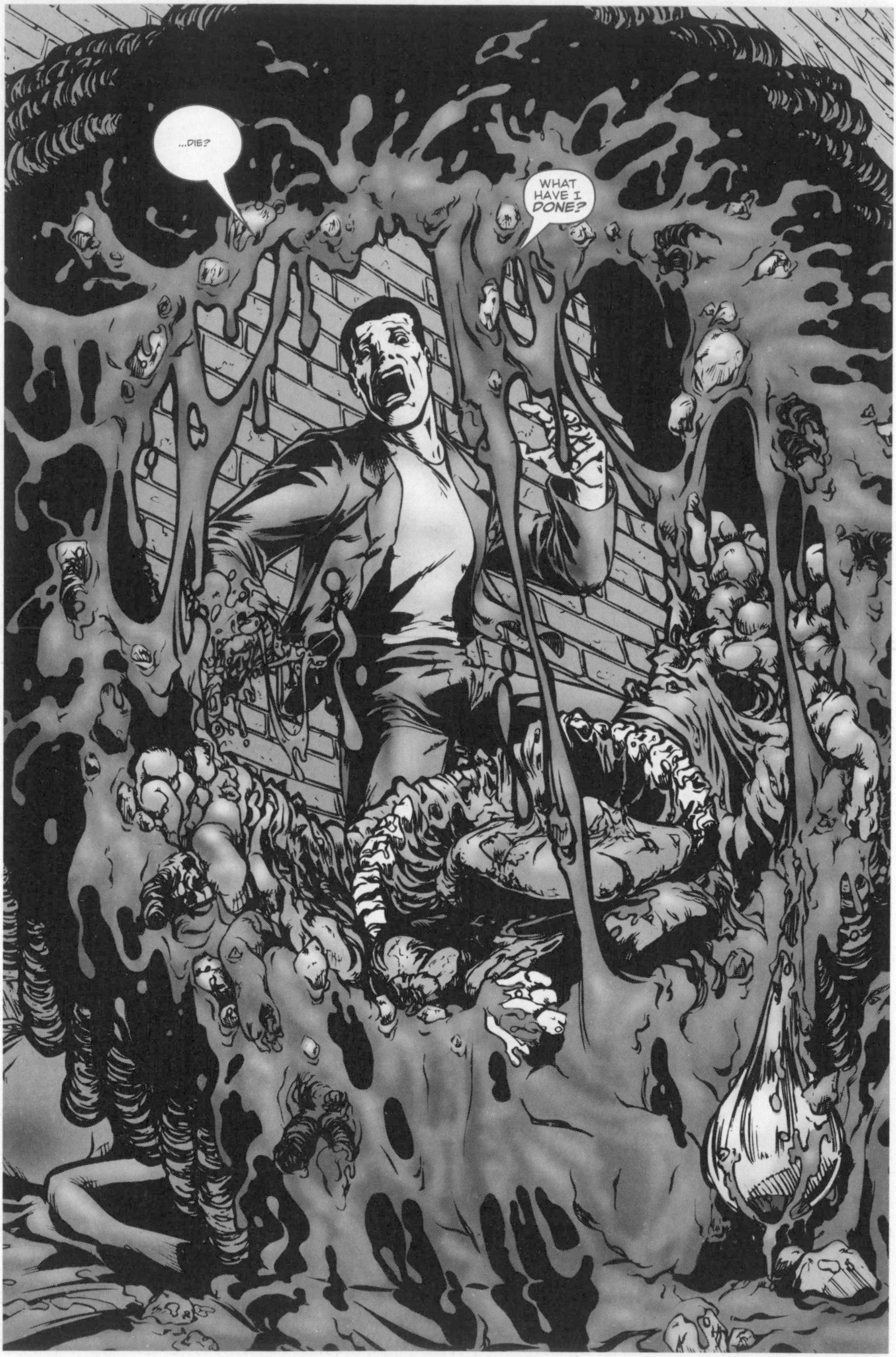
...DIE?
WHAT HAVE I DONE?

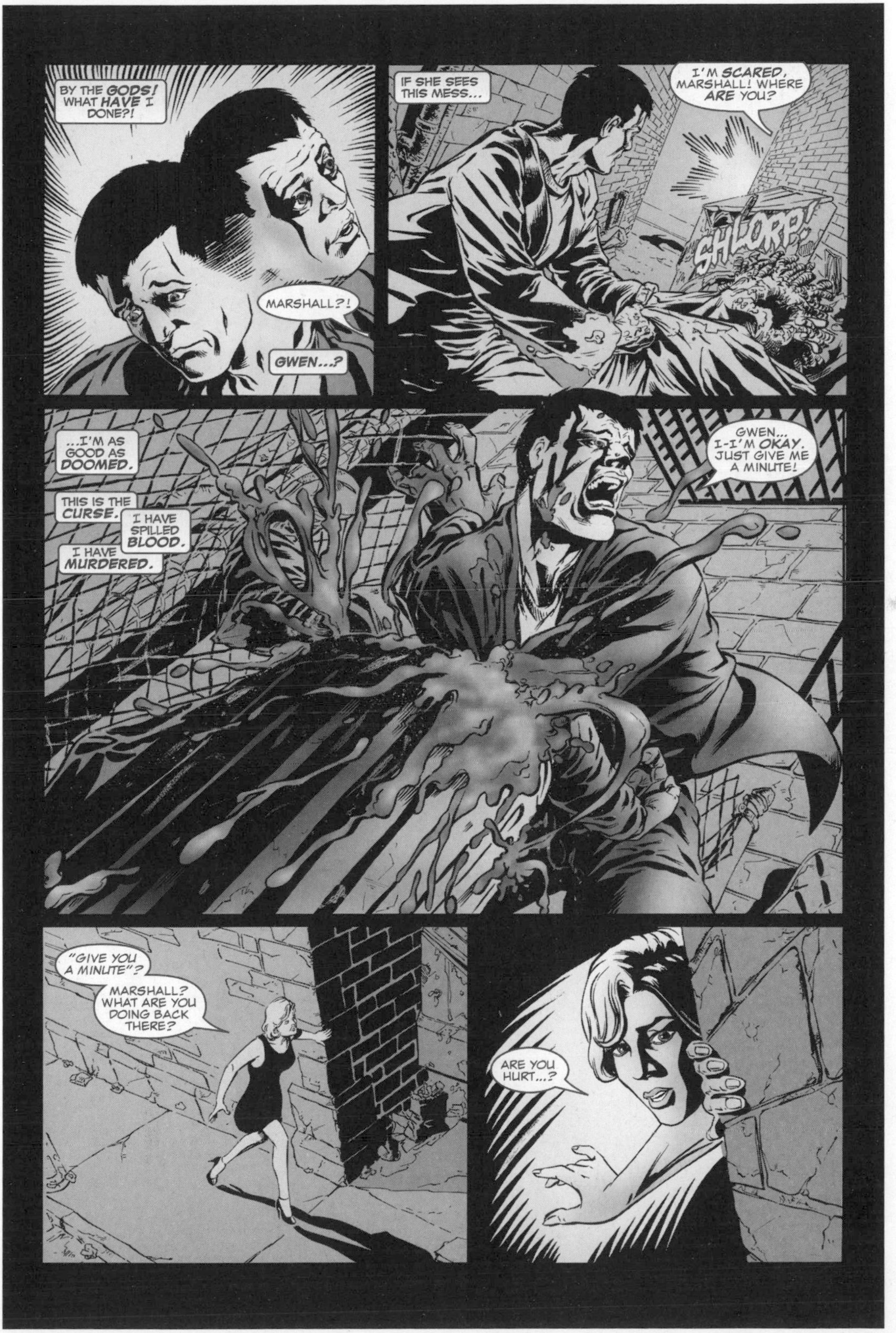
BY THE GODS! WHAT HAVE I DONE?!
MARSHALL?!
GWEN...?
IF SHE SEES THIS MESS...
I'M SCARED, MARSHALL! WHERE ARE YOU?
SHLORP!
...I'M AS GOOD AS DOOMED.
THIS IS THE CURSE.
I HAVE SPILLED BLOOD.
I HAVE MURDERED.
GWEN... I-I'M OKAY. JUST GIVE ME A MINUTE!
"GIVE YOU A MINUTE"?
MARSHALL? WHAT ARE YOU DOING BACK THERE?
ARE YOU HURT...?

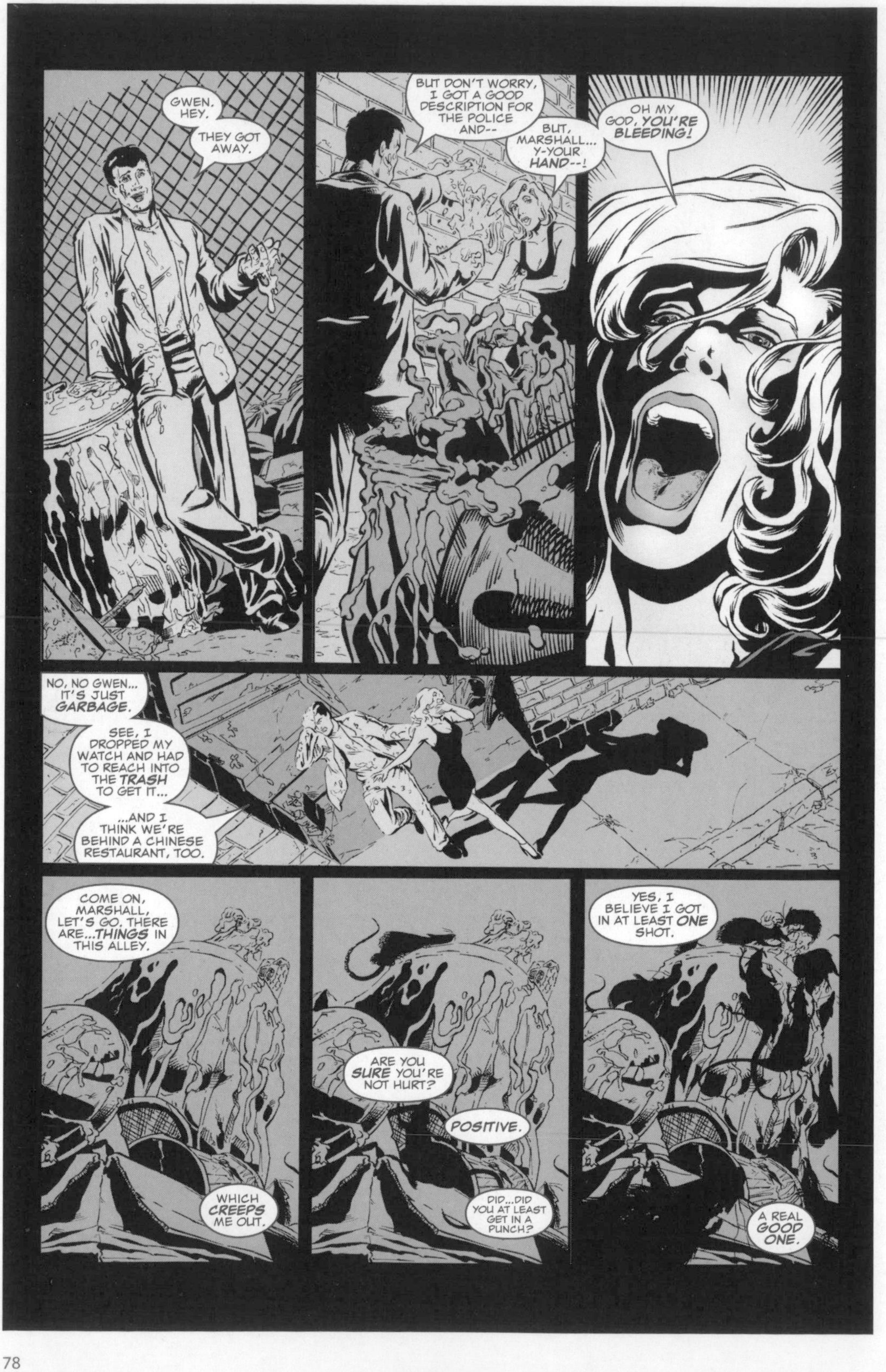
GWEN. HEY.
THEY GOT AWAY.
BUT DON'T WORRY, I GOT A GOOD DESCRIPTION FOR THE POLICE AND--
BUT, MARSHALL... Y-YOUR HAND--!
OH MY GOD, YOU'RE BLEEDING!
NO, NO GWEN... IT'S JUST GARBAGE.
SEE, I DROPPED MY WATCH AND HAD TO REACH INTO THE TRASH TO GET IT...
...AND I THINK WE'RE BEHIND A CHINESE RESTAURANT, TOO.
COME ON, MARSHALL, LET'S GO. THERE ARE...THINGS IN THIS ALLEY.
WHICH CREEPS ME OUT.
ARE YOU SURE YOU'RE NOT HURT?
POSITIVE.
DID...DID YOU AT LEAST GET IN A PUNCH?
YES, I BELIEVE I GOT IN AT LEAST ONE SHOT.
A REAL GOOD ONE.

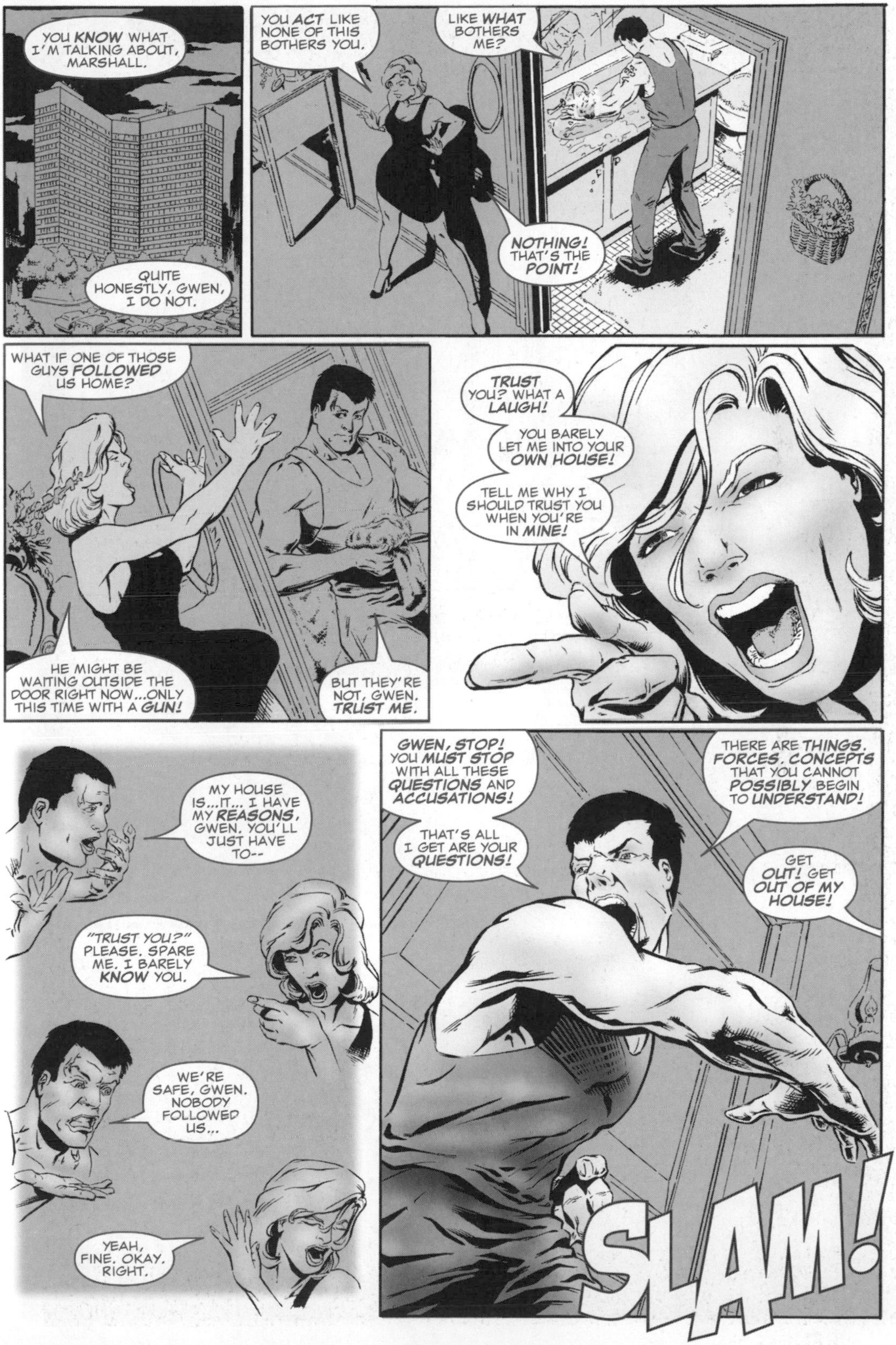
YOU KNOW WHAT I'M TALKING ABOUT, MARSHALL.
QUITE HONESTLY, GWEN, I DO NOT.
YOU ACT LIKE NONE OF THIS BOTHERS YOU.
LIKE WHAT BOTHERS ME?
NOTHING! THAT'S THE POINT!
WHAT IF ONE OF THOSE GUYS FOLLOWED US HOME?
HE MIGHT BE WAITING OUTSIDE THE DOOR RIGHT NOW...ONLY THIS TIME WITH A GUN!
BUT THEY'RE NOT, GWEN. TRUST ME.
TRUST YOU? WHAT A LAUGH!
YOU BARELY LET ME INTO YOUR OWN HOUSE!
TELL ME WHY I SHOULD TRUST YOU WHEN YOU'RE IN MINE!
MY HOUSE IS...IT... I HAVE MY REASONS, GWEN. YOU'LL JUST HAVE TO--
"TRUST YOU?" PLEASE. SPARE ME. I BARELY KNOW YOU.
WE'RE SAFE, GWEN. NOBODY FOLLOWED US...
YEAH, FINE. OKAY. RIGHT.
GWEN, STOP! YOU MUST STOP WITH ALL THESE QUESTIONS AND ACCUSATIONS!
THAT'S ALL I GET ARE YOUR QUESTIONS!
THERE ARE THINGS. FORCES. CONCEPTS THAT YOU CANNOT POSSIBLY BEGIN TO UNDERSTAND!
GET OUT! GET OUT OF MY HOUSE!
SLAM!

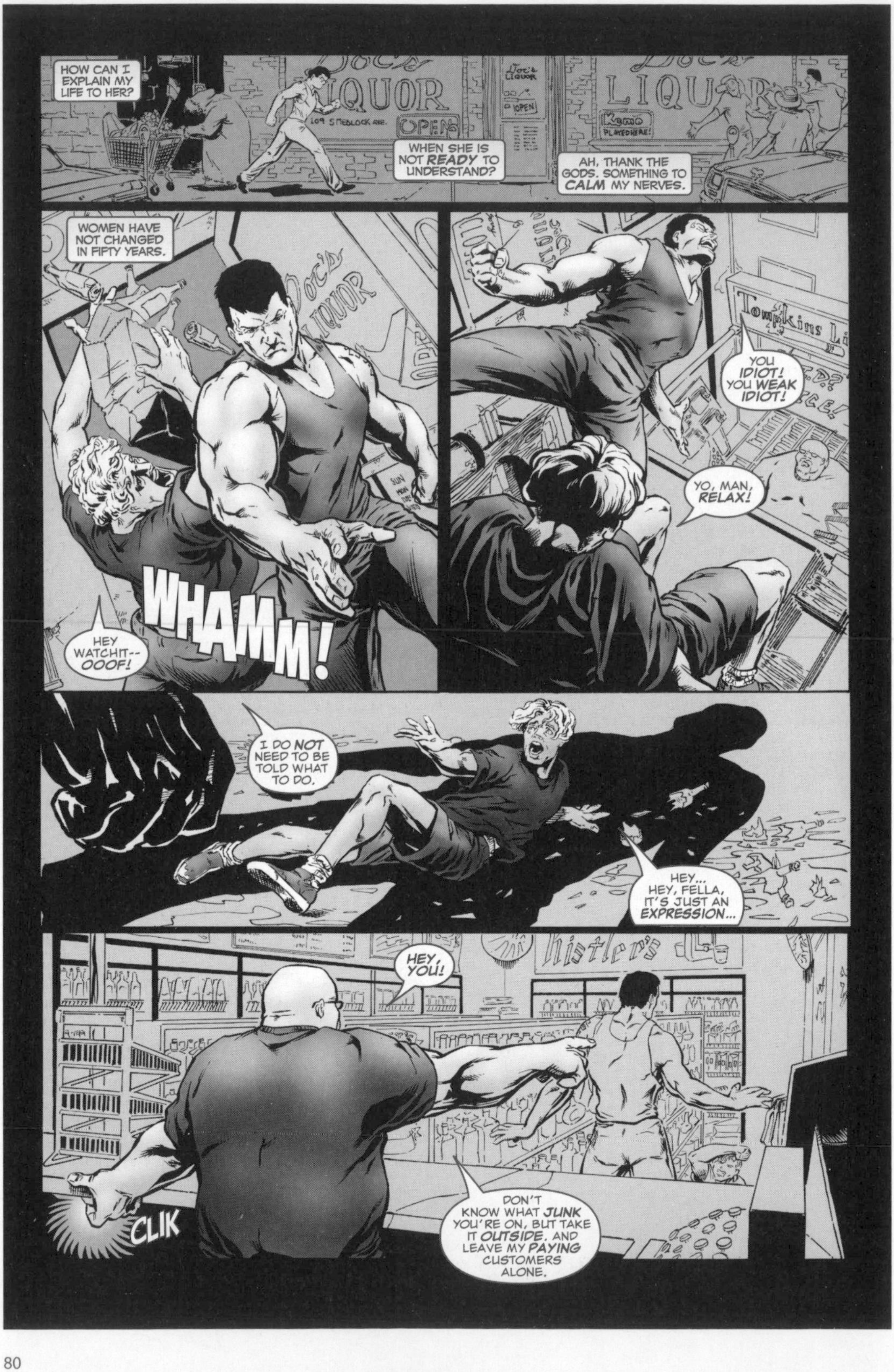
HOW CAN I EXPLAIN MY LIFE TO HER?
Doc's LIQUOR
109 SMEDLOCK AVE.
OPEN
WHEN SHE IS NOT READY TO UNDERSTAND?
Doc's LIQUOR
LIQUOR
AH, THANK THE GODS. SOMETHING TO CALM MY NERVES.
WOMEN HAVE NOT CHANGED IN FIFTY YEARS.
Doc's LIQUOR
WHAMM!
HEY WATCHIT-- OOOF!
Tompkins Li
YOU IDIOT! YOU WEAK IDIOT!
YO, MAN, RELAX!
I DO NOT NEED TO BE TOLD WHAT TO DO.
HEY... HEY, FELLA, IT'S JUST AN EXPRESSION...
HEY, YOU!
DON'T KNOW WHAT JUNK YOU'RE ON, BUT TAKE IT OUTSIDE. AND LEAVE MY PAYING CUSTOMERS ALONE.
CLIK

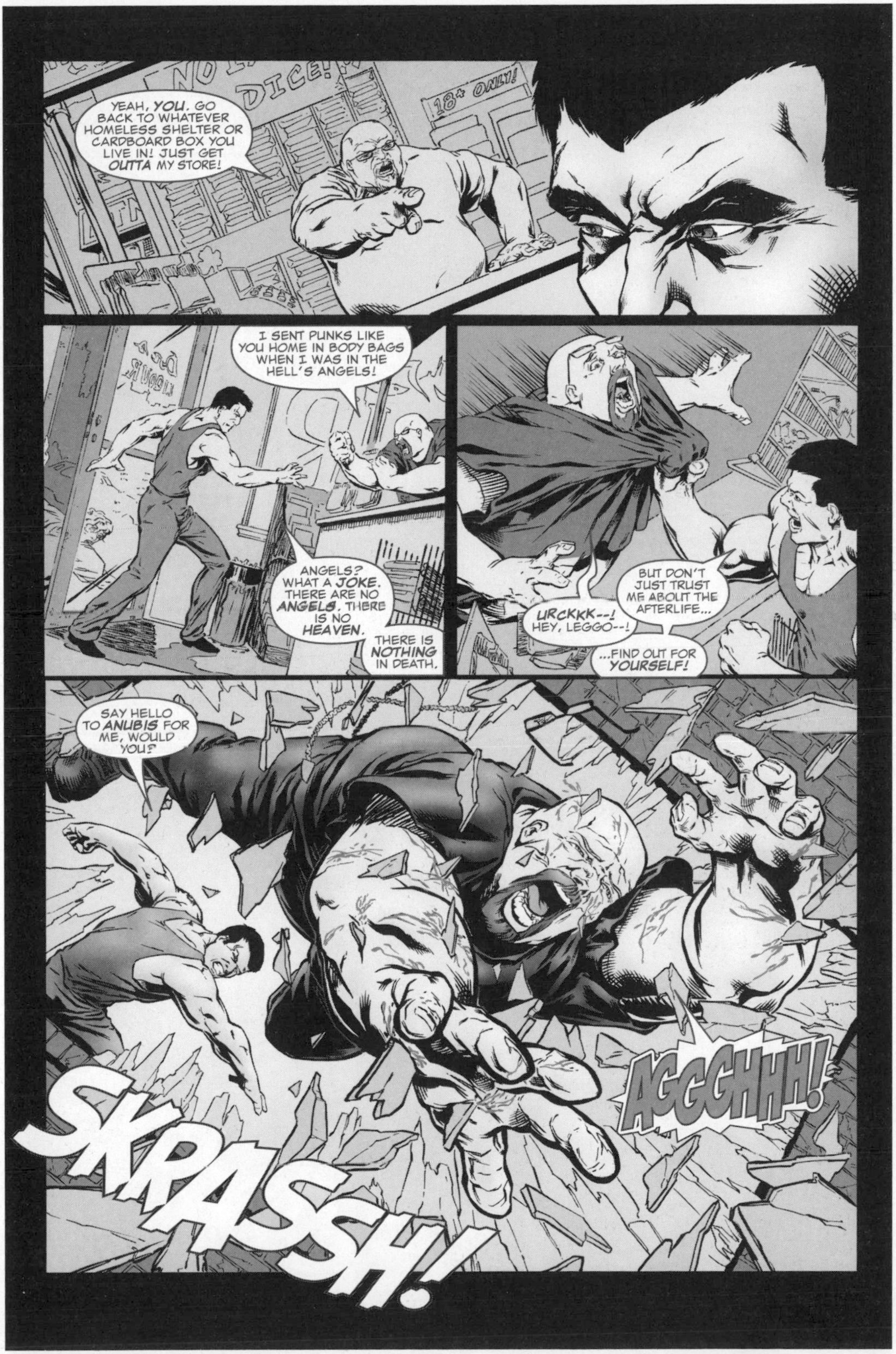
DICE!
18+ ONLY!
YEAH, YOU. GO BACK TO WHATEVER HOMELESS SHELTER OR CARDBOARD BOX YOU LIVE IN! JUST GET OUTTA MY STORE!
I SENT PUNKS LIKE YOU HOME IN BODY BAGS WHEN I WAS IN THE HELL'S ANGELS!
ANGELS? WHAT A JOKE. THERE ARE NO ANGELS. THERE IS NO HEAVEN.
THERE IS NOTHING IN DEATH.
BUT DON'T JUST TRUST ME ABOUT THE AFTERLIFE...
URCKKK--! HEY, LEGGO--!
...FIND OUT FOR YOURSELF!
SAY HELLO TO ANUBIS FOR ME, WOULD YOU?
AGGGHHH!
SKRASSH!

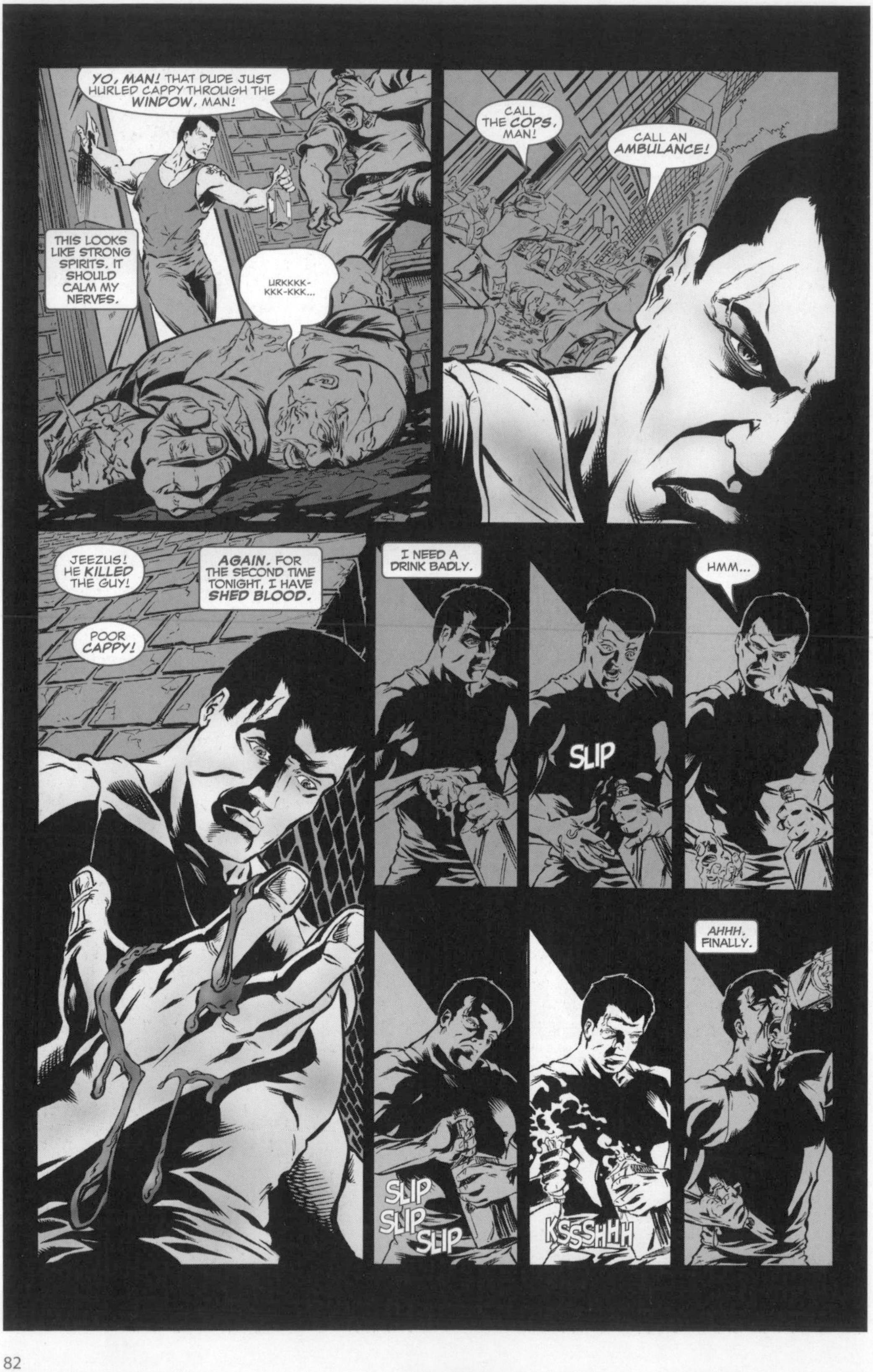
YO, MAN! THAT DUDE JUST HURLED CAPPY THROUGH THE WINDOW, MAN!
THIS LOOKS LIKE STRONG SPIRITS. IT SHOULD CALM MY NERVES.
URKKKK-KKK-KKK...
CALL THE COPS, MAN!
CALL AN AMBULANCE!
JEEZUS! HE KILLED THE GUY!
AGAIN. FOR THE SECOND TIME TONIGHT, I HAVE SHED BLOOD.
POOR CAPPY!
I NEED A DRINK BADLY.
SLIP
HMM...
SLIP SLIP SLIP
KSSSHHH
AHHH. FINALLY.

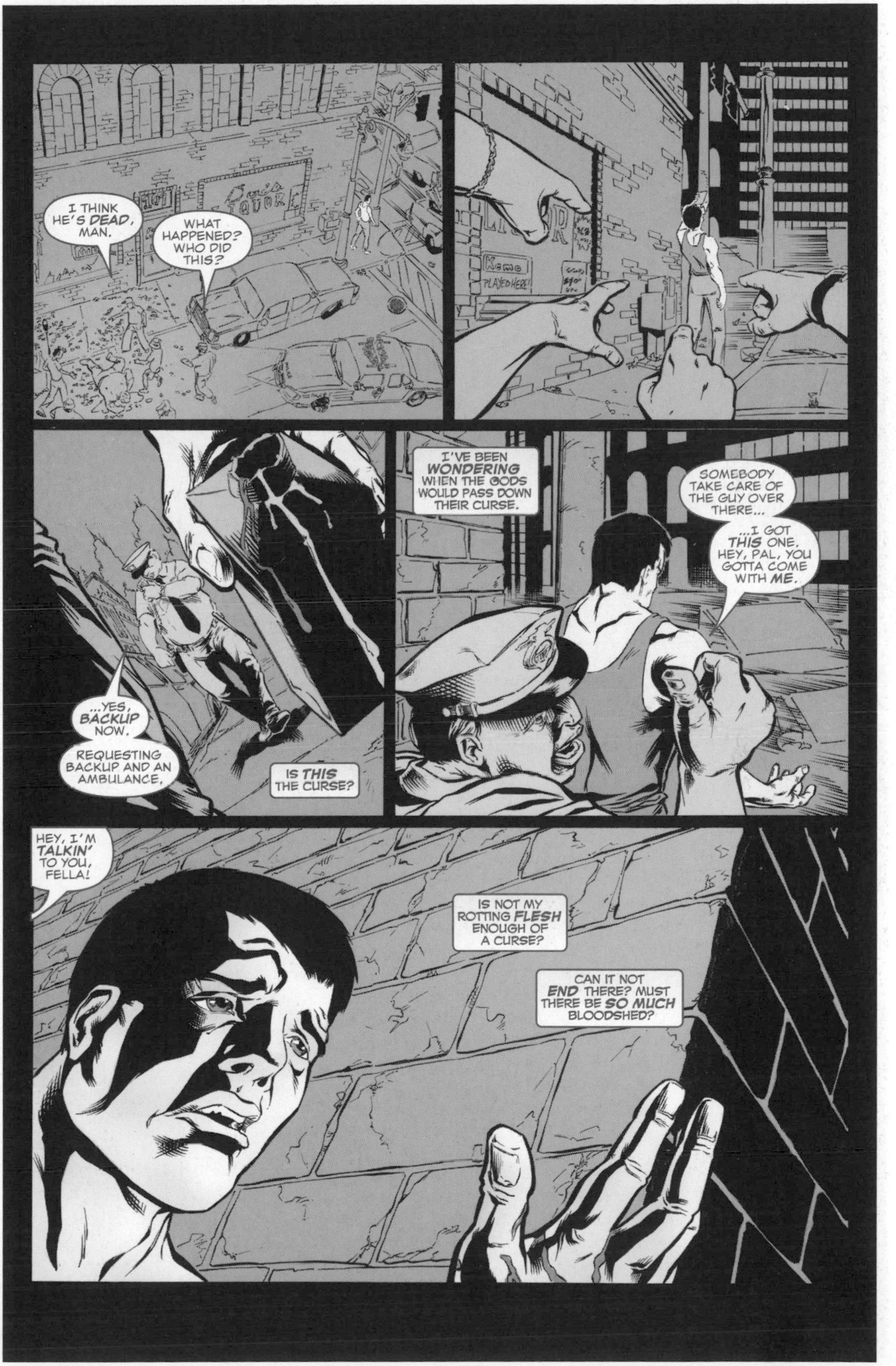
I THINK HE'S DEAD, MAN.
WHAT HAPPENED? WHO DID THIS?
...YES, BACKUP NOW.
REQUESTING BACKUP AND AN AMBULANCE.
IS THIS THE CURSE?
I'VE BEEN WONDERING WHEN THE GODS WOULD PASS DOWN THEIR CURSE.
SOMEBODY TAKE CARE OF THE GUY OVER THERE...
...I GOT THIS ONE. HEY, PAL, YOU GOTTA COME WITH ME.
HEY, I'M TALKIN' TO YOU, FELLA!
IS NOT MY ROTTING FLESH ENOUGH OF A CURSE?
CAN IT NOT END THERE? MUST THERE BE SO MUCH BLOODSHED?

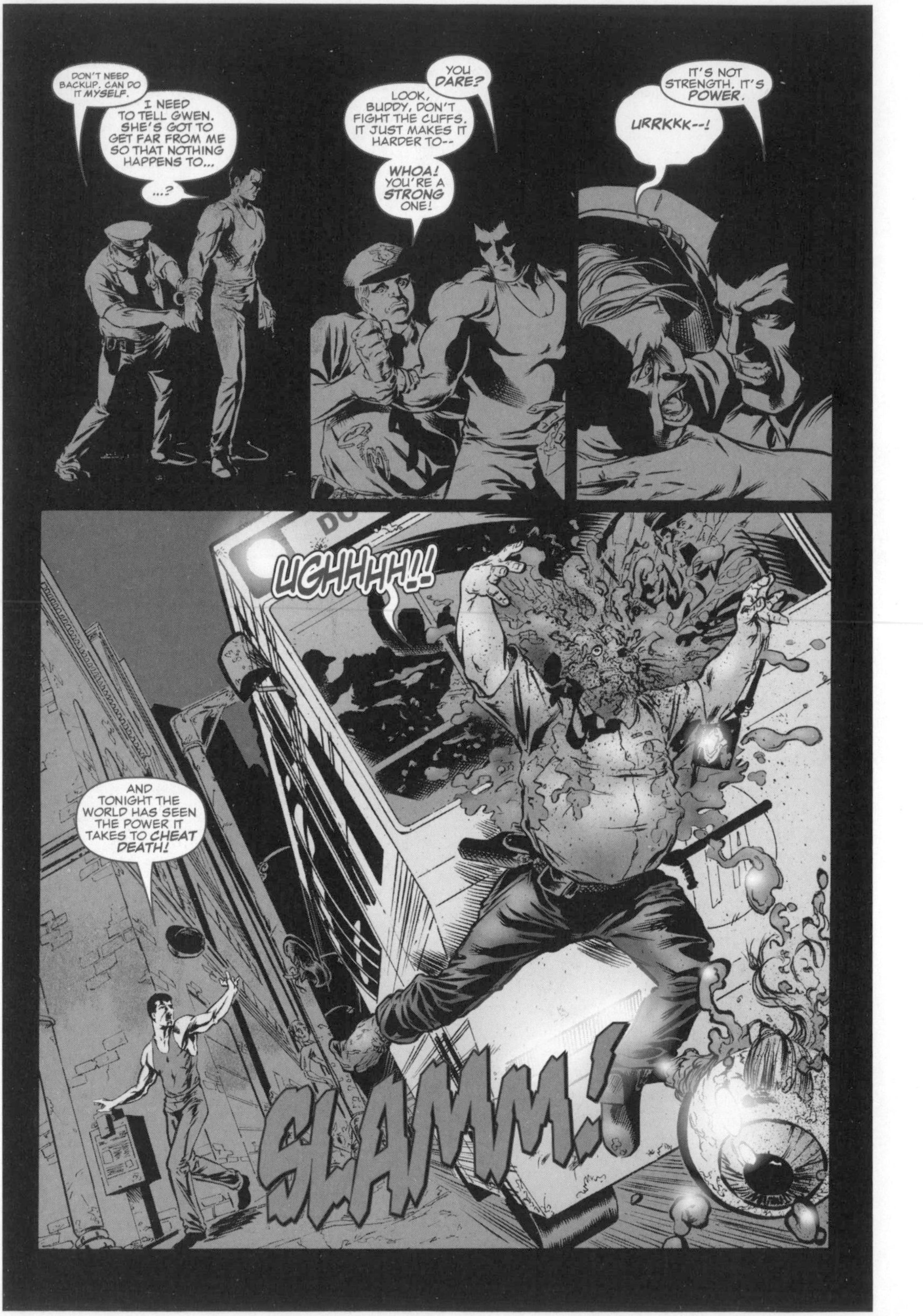
DON'T NEED BACKUP. CAN DO IT MYSELF.
I NEED TO TELL GWEN. SHE'S GOT TO GET FAR FROM ME SO THAT NOTHING HAPPENS TO...
...?
YOU DARE?
LOOK, BUDDY, DON'T FIGHT THE CUFFS. IT JUST MAKES IT HARDER TO--
WHOA! YOU'RE A STRONG ONE!
IT'S NOT STRENGTH. IT'S POWER.
URRKKK--!
UGHHHH!!
AND TONIGHT THE WORLD HAS SEEN THE POWER IT TAKES TO CHEAT DEATH!
SLAMM!

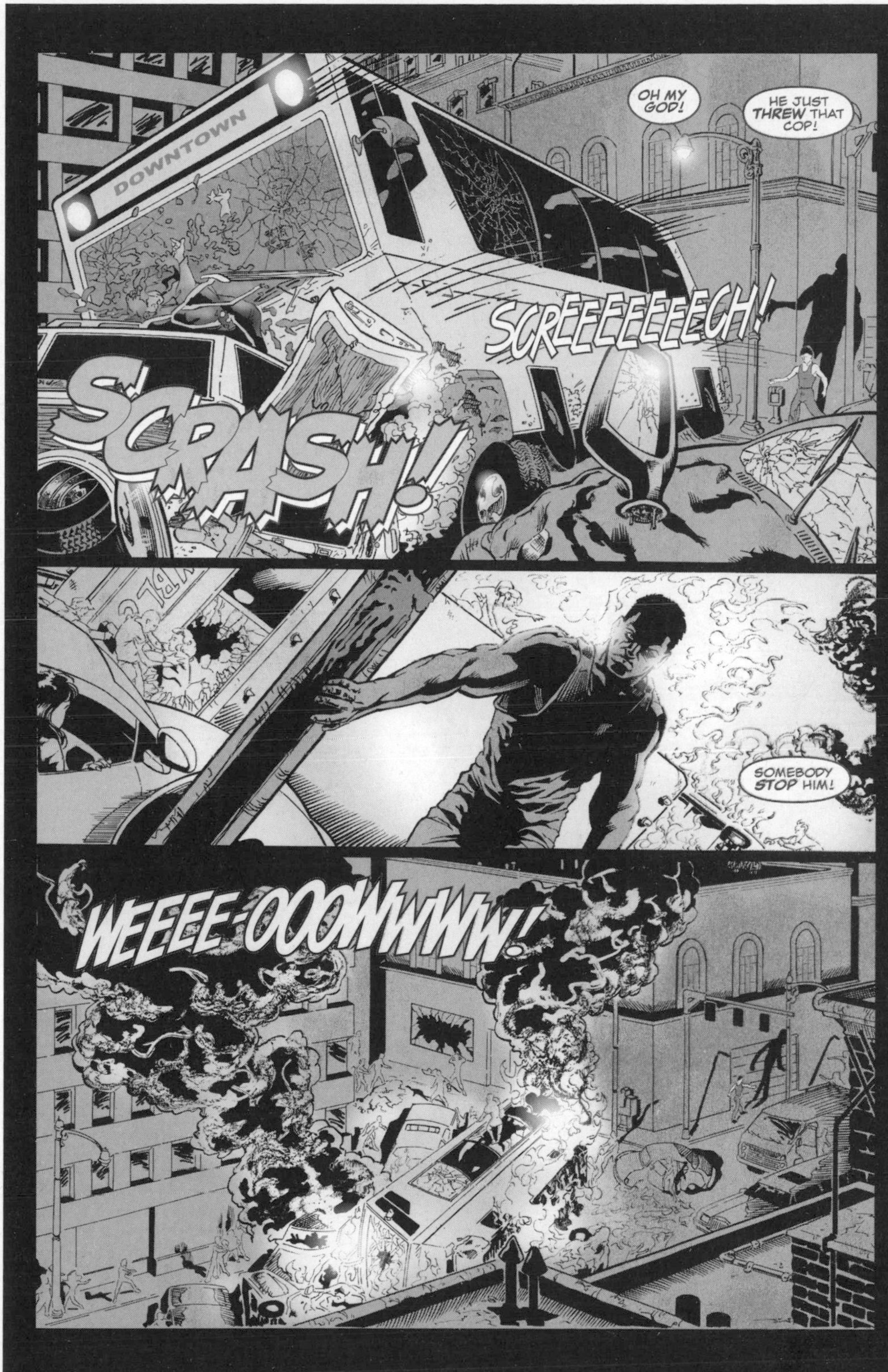
OH MY GOD!
HE JUST THREW THAT COP!
SCREEEEEEEECH!
SCRASH!
SOMEBODY STOP HIM!
WEEEE-OOOWWWW!

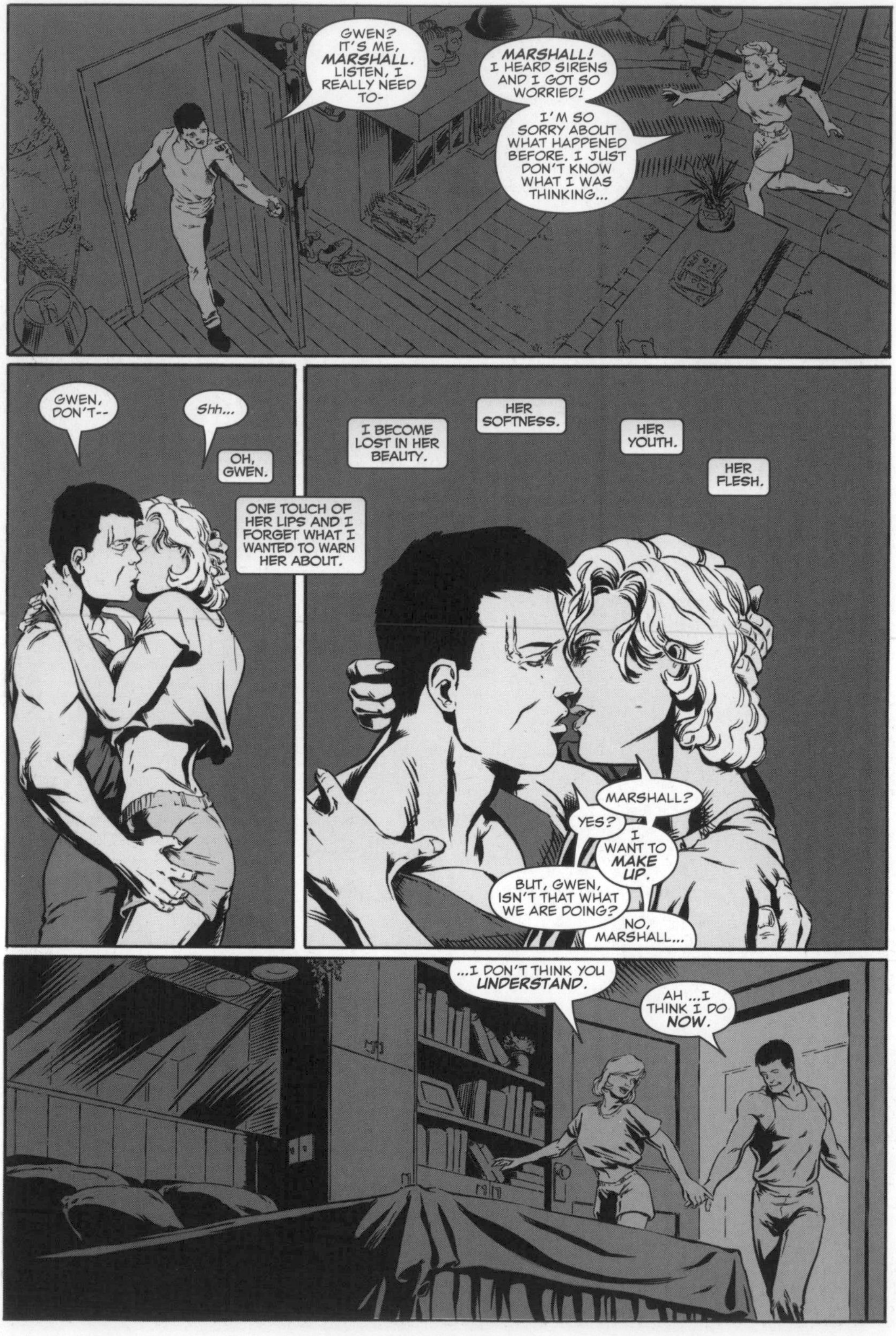
GWEN? IT'S ME, MARSHALL. LISTEN, I REALLY NEED TO-
MARSHALL! I HEARD SIRENS AND I GOT SO WORRIED!
I'M SO SORRY ABOUT WHAT HAPPENED BEFORE. I JUST DON'T KNOW WHAT I WAS THINKING...
GWEN, DON'T--
Shh...
OH, GWEN.
ONE TOUCH OF HER LIPS AND I FORGET WHAT I WANTED TO WARN HER ABOUT.
I BECOME LOST IN HER BEAUTY.
HER SOFTNESS.
HER YOUTH.
HER FLESH.
MARSHALL?
YES?
I WANT TO MAKE UP.
BUT, GWEN, ISN'T THAT WHAT WE ARE DOING?
NO, MARSHALL...
...I DON'T THINK YOU UNDERSTAND.
AH ...I THINK I DO NOW.

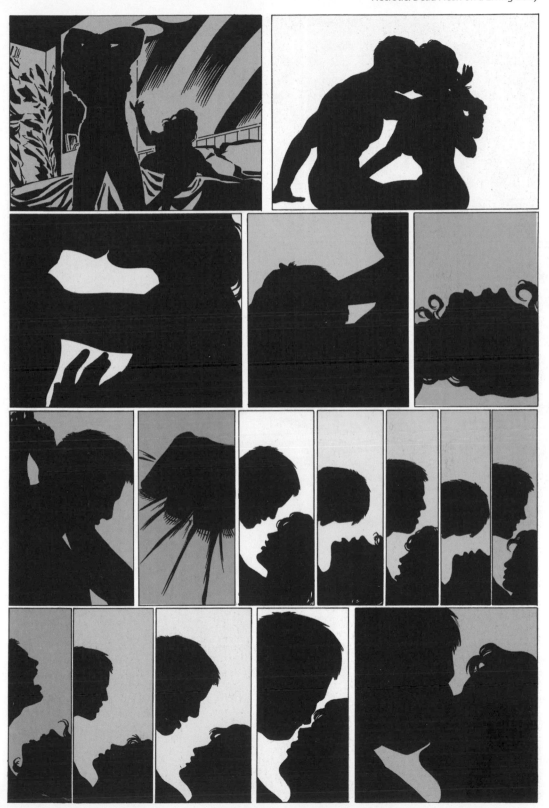

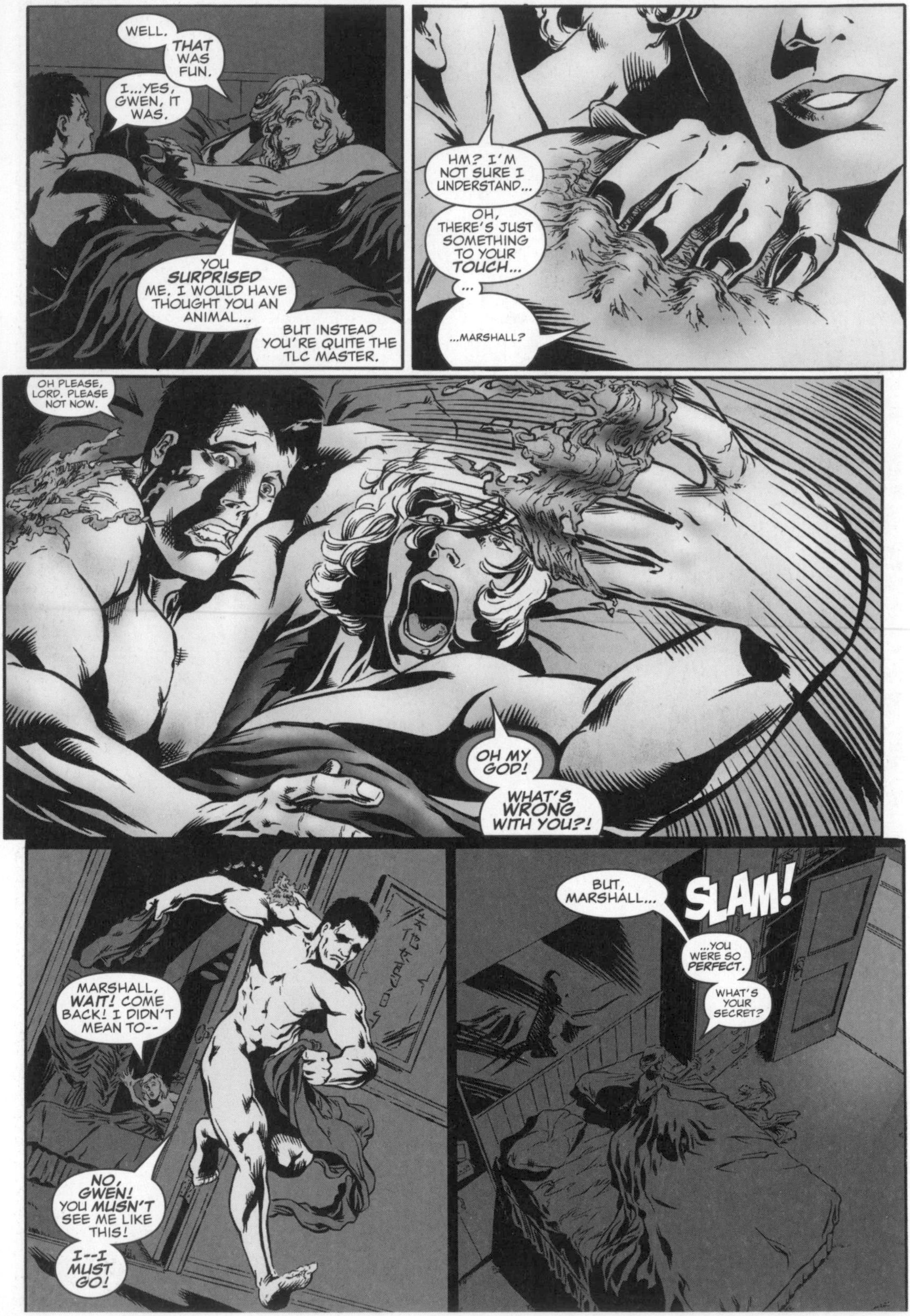
WELL.
THAT WAS FUN.
I...YES, GWEN, IT WAS.
YOU SURPRISED ME. I WOULD HAVE THOUGHT YOU AN ANIMAL...
BUT INSTEAD YOU'RE QUITE THE TLC MASTER.
HM? I'M NOT SURE I UNDERSTAND...
OH, THERE'S JUST SOMETHING TO YOUR TOUCH...
...
...MARSHALL?
OH PLEASE, LORD. PLEASE NOT NOW.
OH MY GOD!
WHAT'S WRONG WITH YOU?!
MARSHALL, WAIT! COME BACK! I DIDN'T MEAN TO--
NO, GWEN! YOU MUSN'T SEE ME LIKE THIS!
I--I MUST GO!
BUT, MARSHALL...
SLAM!
...YOU WERE SO PERFECT.
WHAT'S YOUR SECRET?

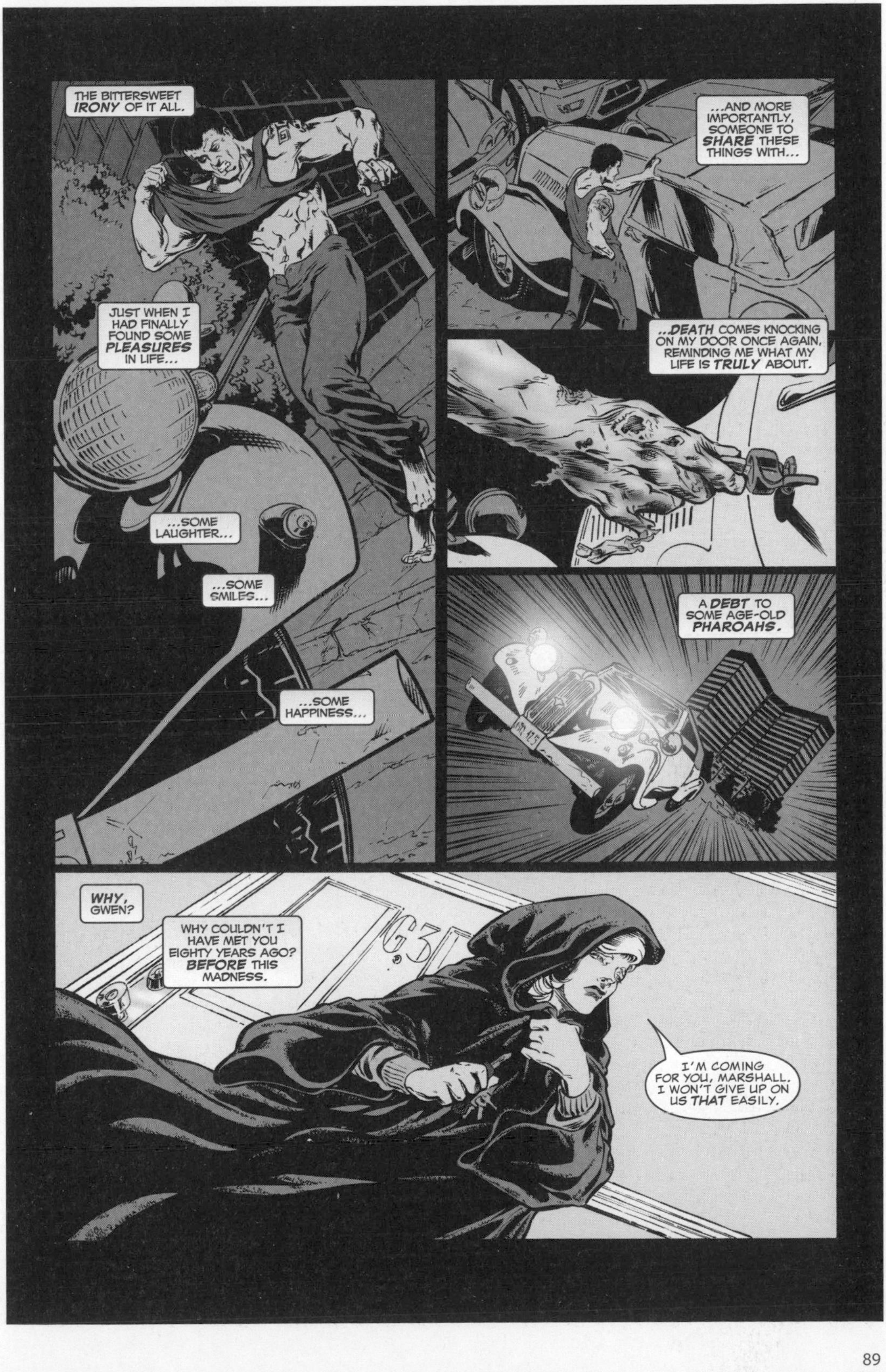
THE BITTERSWEET IRONY OF IT ALL.
JUST WHEN I HAD FINALLY FOUND SOME PLEASURES IN LIFE...
...SOME LAUGHTER...
...SOME SMILES...
...SOME HAPPINESS...
...AND MORE IMPORTANTLY, SOMEONE TO SHARE THESE THINGS WITH...
...DEATH COMES KNOCKING ON MY DOOR ONCE AGAIN, REMINDING ME WHAT MY LIFE IS TRULY ABOUT.
A DEBT TO SOME AGE-OLD PHAROAHS.
WHY, GWEN?
WHY COULDN'T I HAVE MET YOU EIGHTY YEARS AGO? BEFORE THIS MADNESS.
I'M COMING FOR YOU, MARSHALL. I WON'T GIVE UP ON US THAT EASILY.

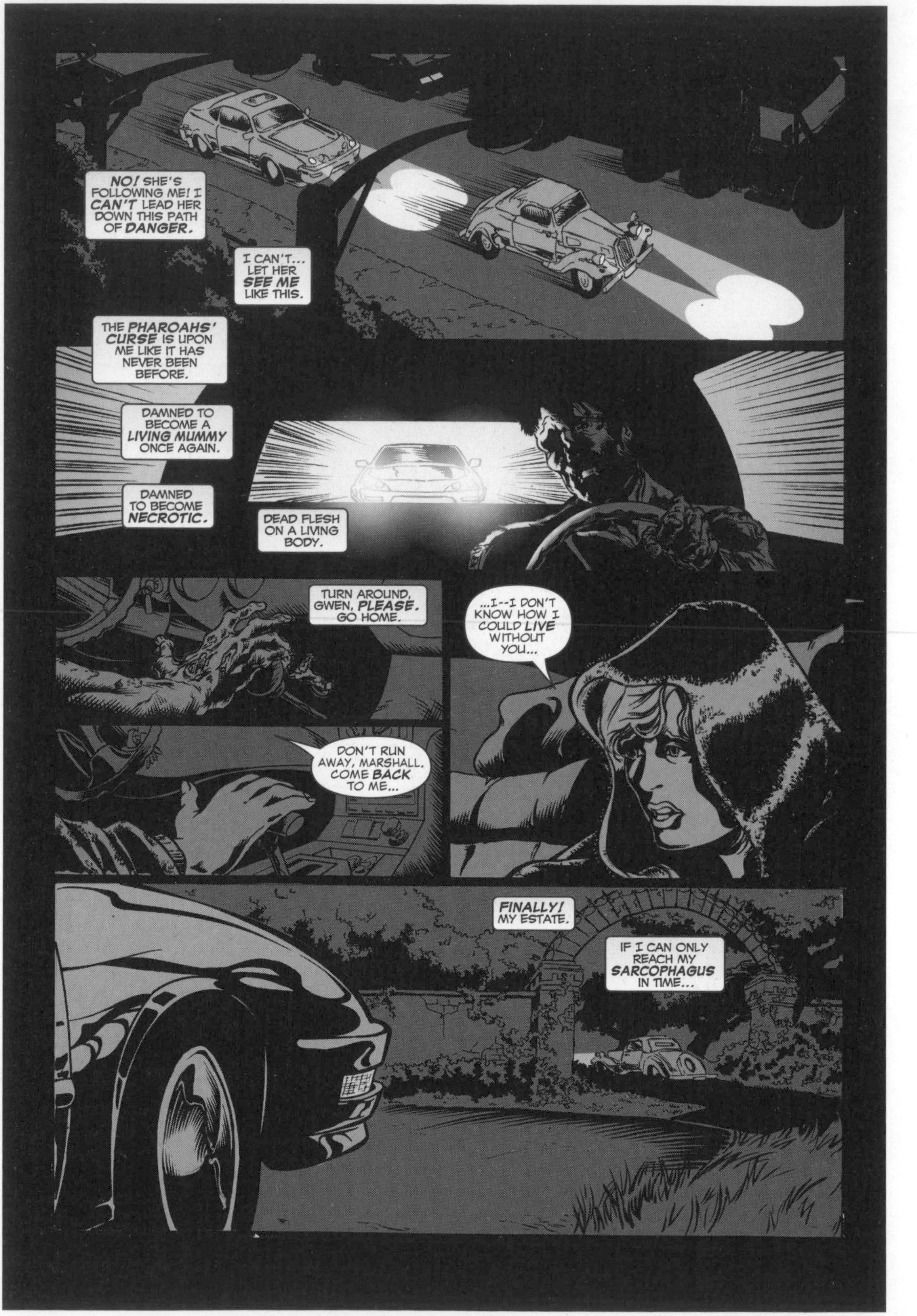
NO! SHE'S FOLLOWING ME! I CAN'T LEAD HER DOWN THIS PATH OF DANGER.
I CAN'T... LET HER SEE ME LIKE THIS.
THE PHAROAHS' CURSE IS UPON ME LIKE IT HAS NEVER BEEN BEFORE.
DAMNED TO BECOME A LIVING MUMMY ONCE AGAIN.
DAMNED TO BECOME NECROTIC.
DEAD FLESH ON A LIVING BODY.
TURN AROUND, GWEN, PLEASE. GO HOME.
...I--I DON'T KNOW HOW I COULD LIVE WITHOUT YOU...
DON'T RUN AWAY, MARSHALL. COME BACK TO ME...
FINALLY! MY ESTATE.
IF I CAN ONLY REACH MY SARCOPHAGUS IN TIME...

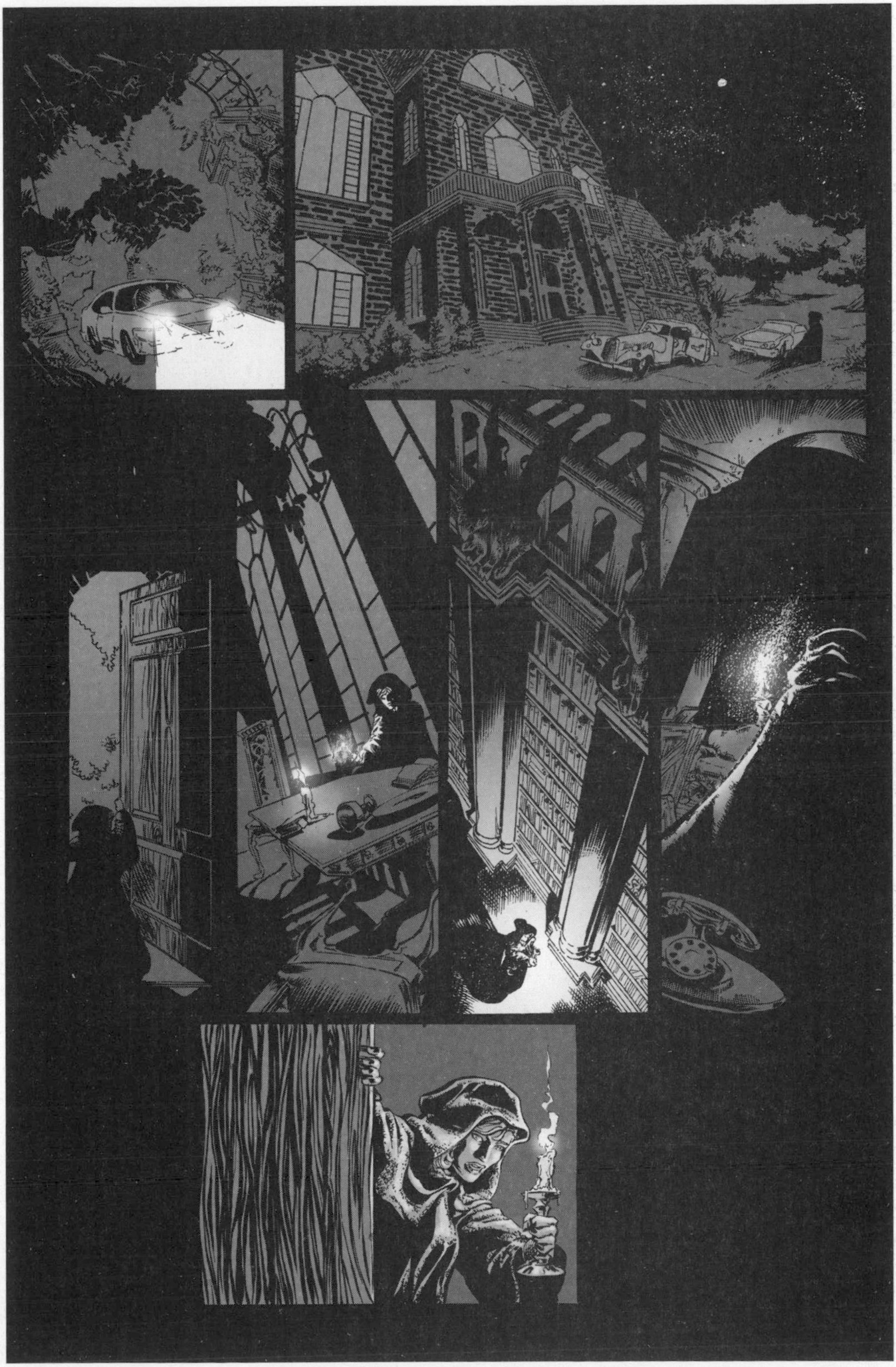

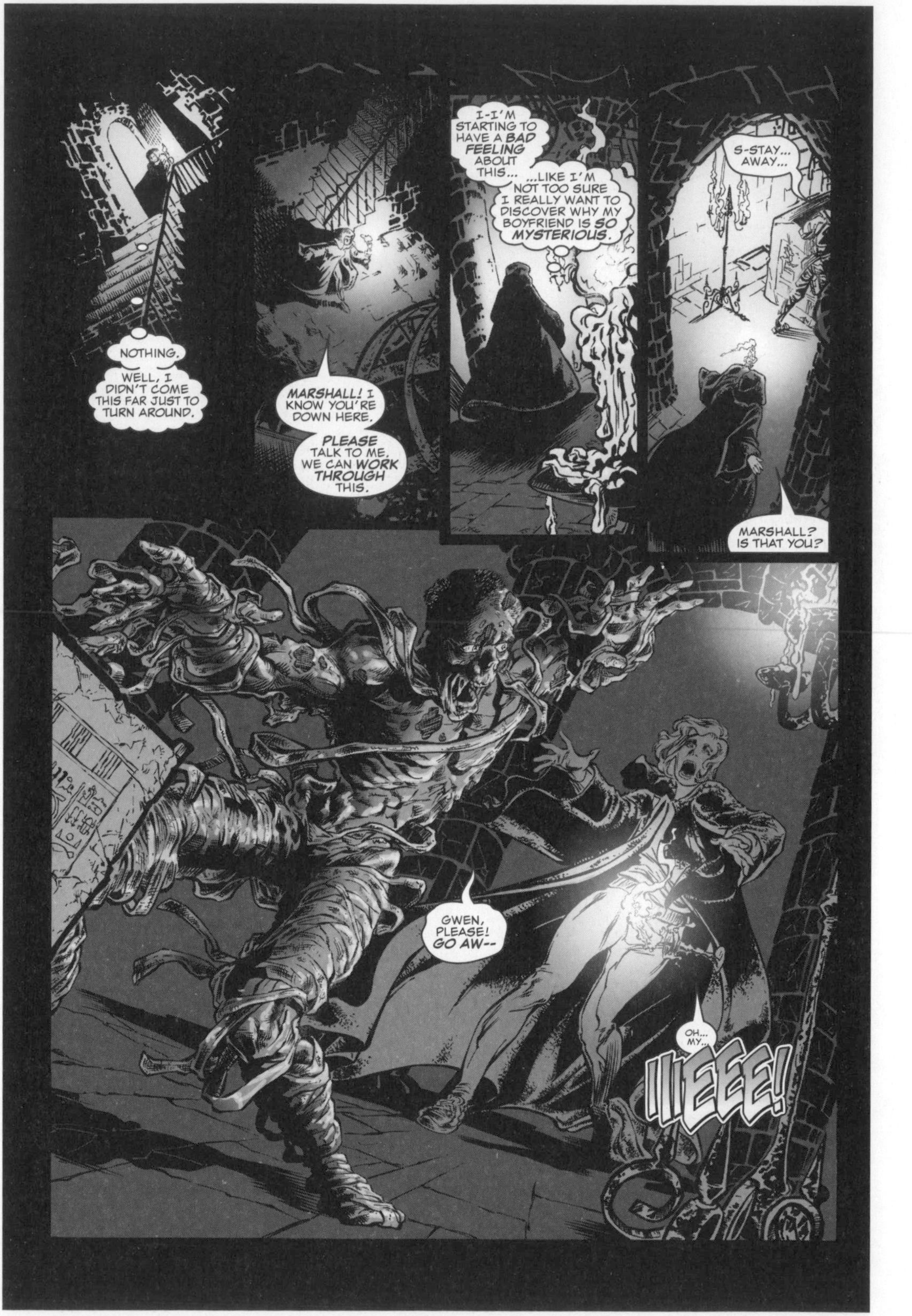

NOTHING.
WELL, I DIDN'T COME THIS FAR JUST TO TURN AROUND.
MARSHALL! I KNOW YOU'RE DOWN HERE.
PLEASE TALK TO ME. WE CAN WORK THROUGH THIS.
I-I'M STARTING TO HAVE A BAD FEELING ABOUT THIS...
...LIKE I'M NOT TOO SURE I REALLY WANT TO DISCOVER WHY MY BOYFRIEND IS SO MYSTERIOUS.
S-STAY... AWAY...
MARSHALL? IS THAT YOU?
GWEN, PLEASE! GO AW--
OH... MY...
IIIEEE!

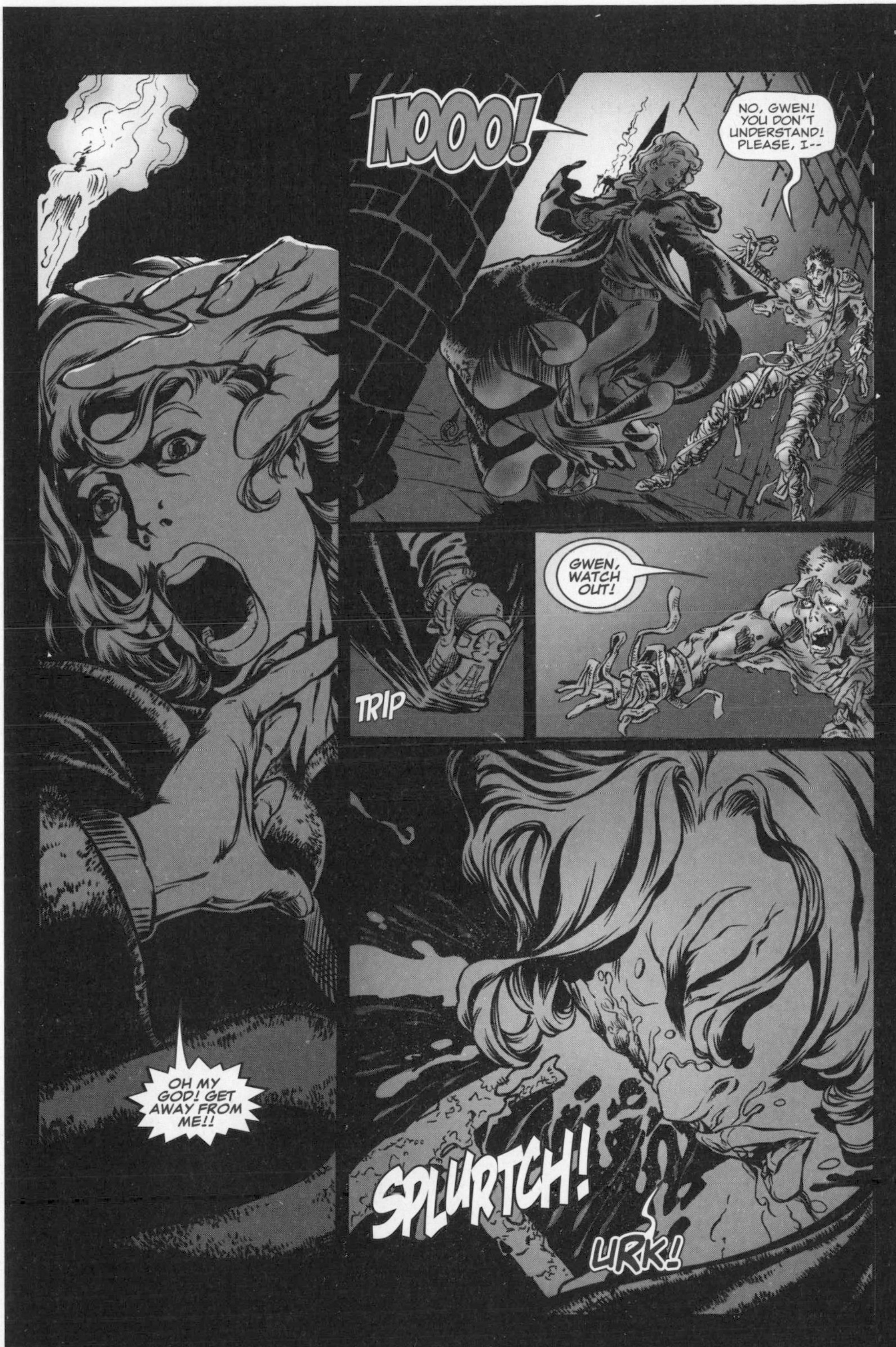
OH MY GOD! GET AWAY FROM ME!!
NOOO!
NO, GWEN! YOU DON'T UNDERSTAND! PLEASE, I--
TRIP
GWEN, WATCH OUT!
SPLURTCH!
URK!

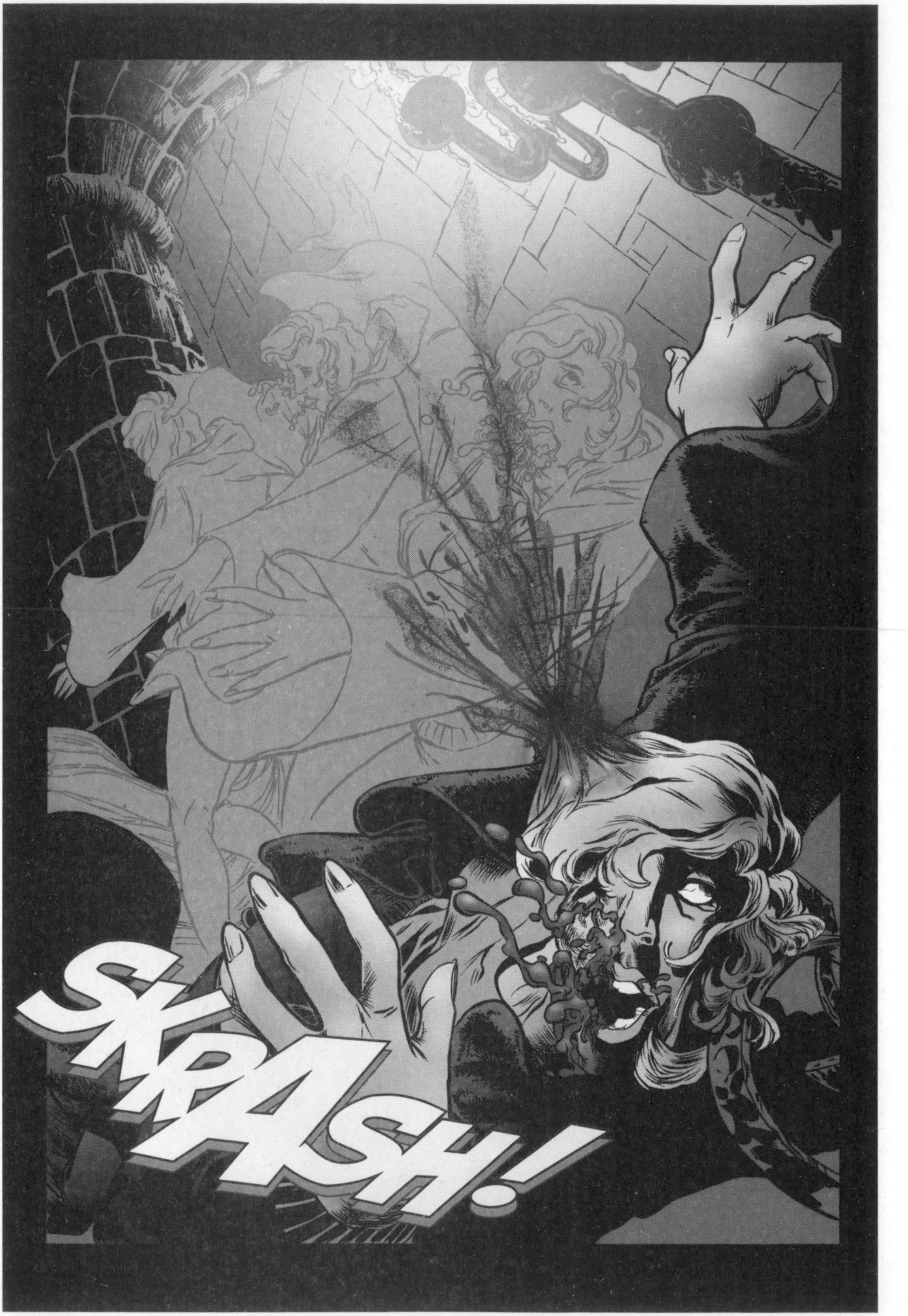
SKRASH!

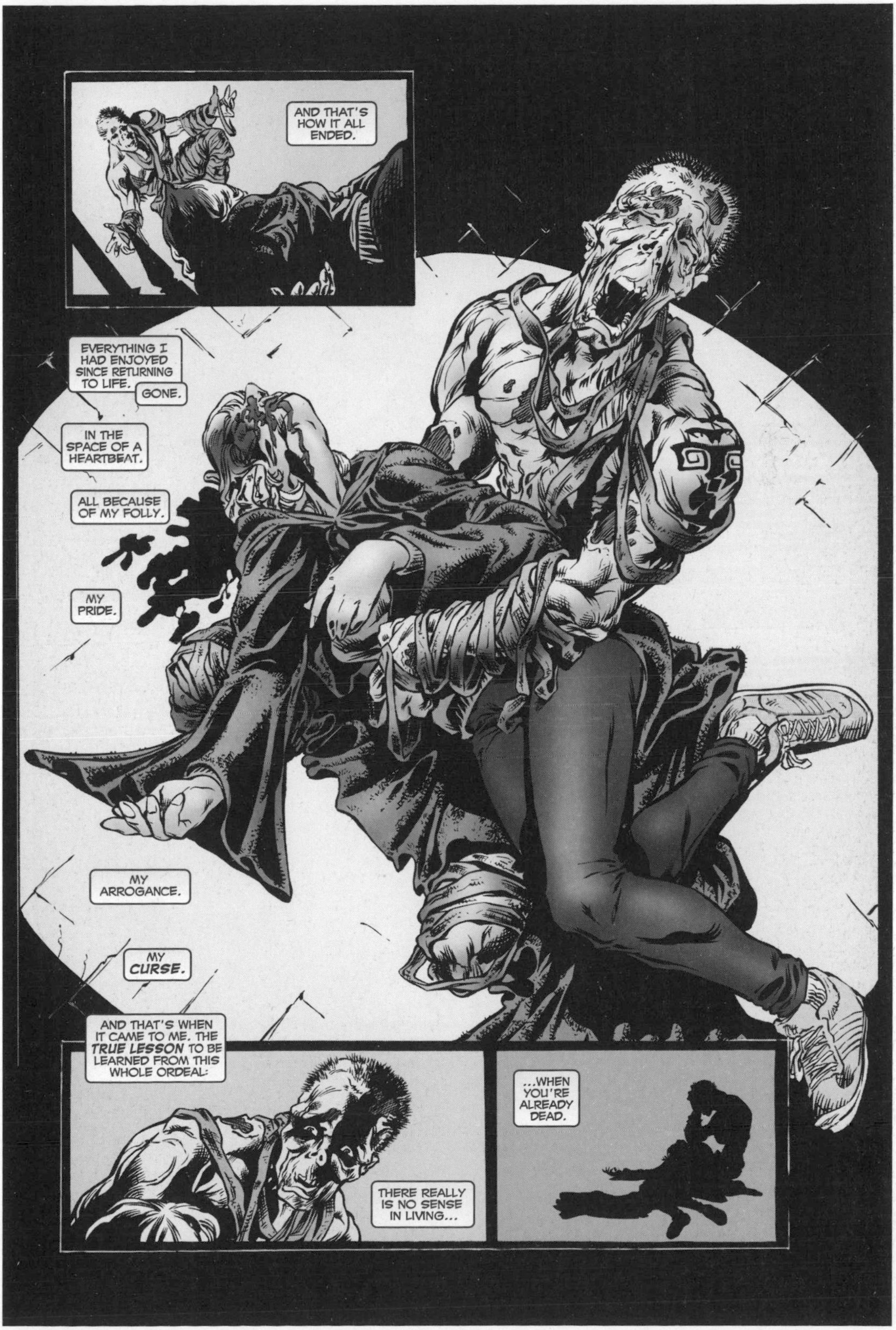
AND THAT'S HOW IT ALL ENDED.
EVERYTHING I HAD ENJOYED SINCE RETURNING TO LIFE.
GONE.
IN THE SPACE OF A HEARTBEAT.
ALL BECAUSE OF MY FOLLY.
MY PRIDE.
MY ARROGANCE.
MY CURSE.
AND THAT'S WHEN IT CAME TO ME. THE TRUE LESSON TO BE LEARNED FROM THIS WHOLE ORDEAL:
THERE REALLY IS NO SENSE IN LIVING...
...WHEN YOU'RE ALREADY DEAD.

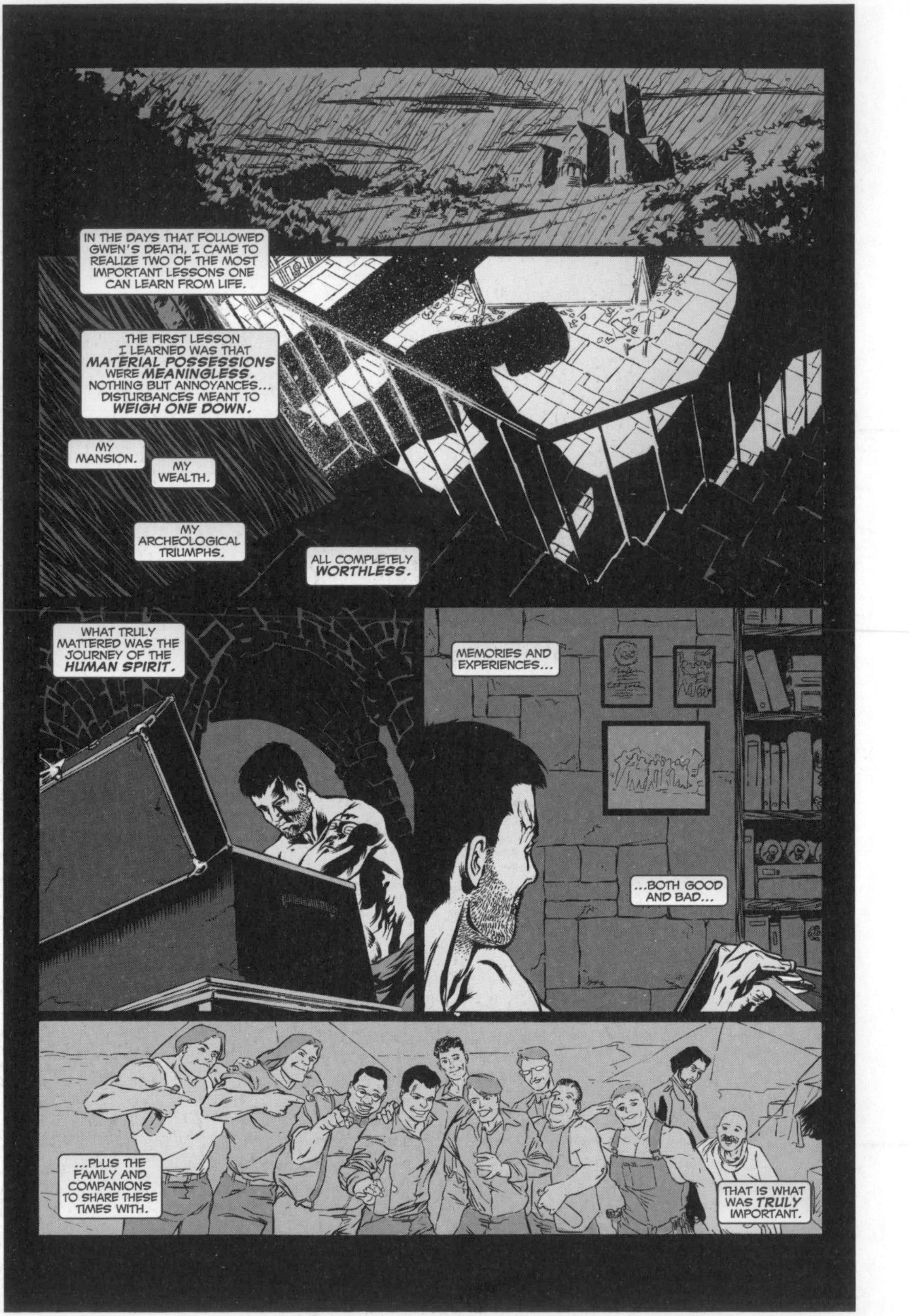
IN THE DAYS THAT FOLLOWED GWEN'S DEATH, I CAME TO REALIZE TWO OF THE MOST IMPORTANT LESSONS ONE CAN LEARN FROM LIFE.
THE FIRST LESSON I LEARNED WAS THAT MATERIAL POSSESSIONS WERE MEANINGLESS. NOTHING BUT ANNOYANCES... DISTURBANCES MEANT TO WEIGH ONE DOWN.
MY MANSION.
MY WEALTH.
MY ARCHEOLOGICAL TRIUMPHS.
ALL COMPLETELY WORTHLESS.
WHAT TRULY MATTERED WAS THE JOURNEY OF THE HUMAN SPIRIT.
MEMORIES AND EXPERIENCES...
...BOTH GOOD AND BAD...
...PLUS THE FAMILY AND COMPANIONS TO SHARE THESE TIMES WITH.
THAT IS WHAT WAS TRULY IMPORTANT.

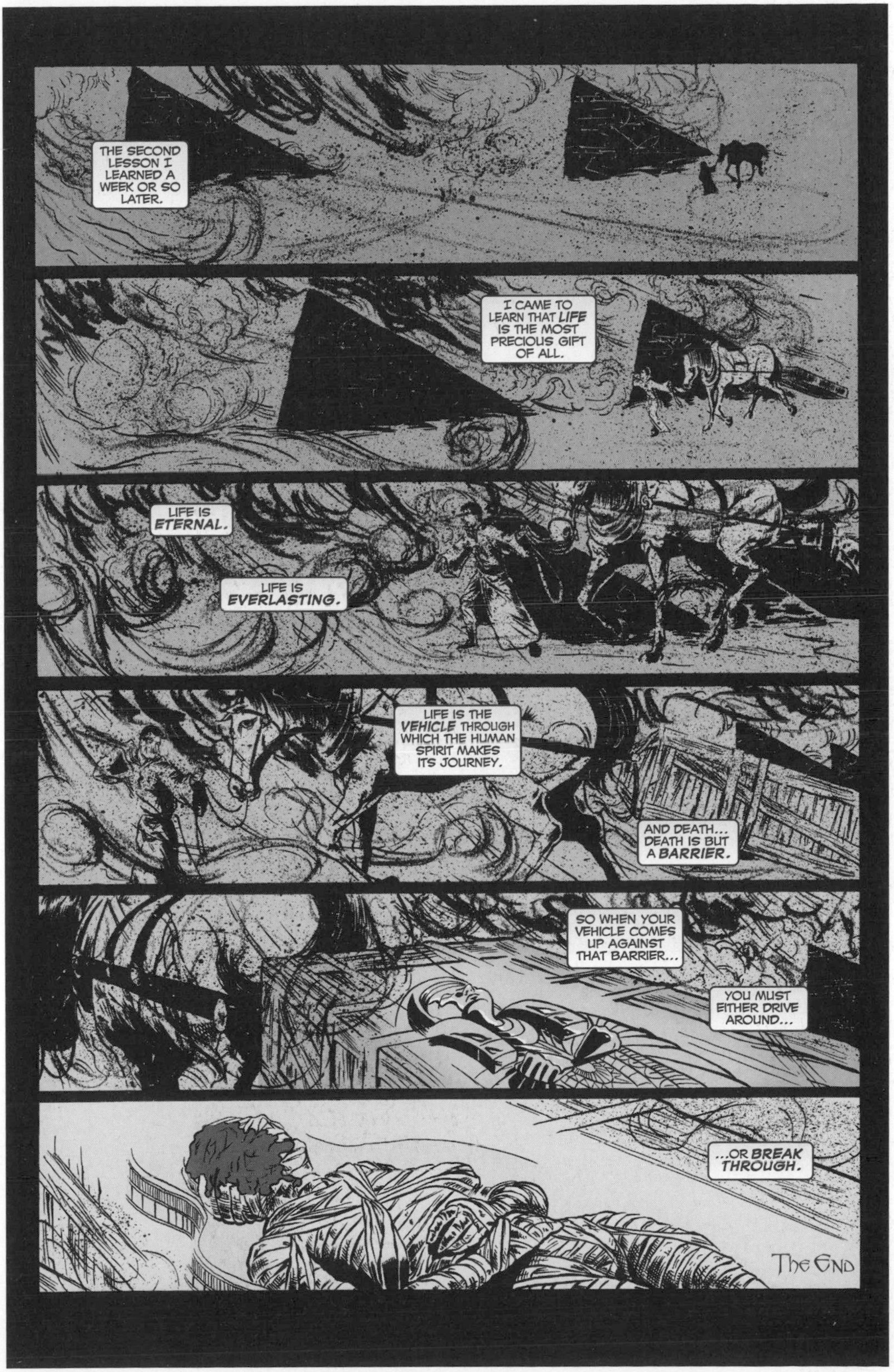
THE SECOND LESSON I LEARNED A WEEK OR SO LATER.
I CAME TO LEARN THAT LIFE IS THE MOST PRECIOUS GIFT OF ALL.
LIFE IS ETERNAL.
LIFE IS EVERLASTING.
LIFE IS THE VEHICLE THROUGH WHICH THE HUMAN SPIRIT MAKES ITS JOURNEY.
AND DEATH... DEATH IS BUT A BARRIER.
SO WHEN YOUR VEHICLE COMES UP AGAINST THAT BARRIER...
YOU MUST EITHER DRIVE AROUND...
...OR BREAK THROUGH.
The End

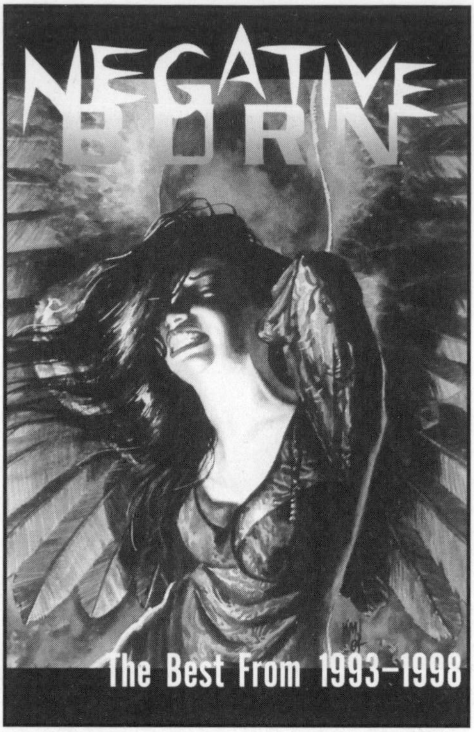
NEGATIVE BURN
The Best From 1993–1998

The Immortals (2005)

Creators: Darko Macan (script) and Edvin Biukovic (art)

Here Darko Macan blends three horror tropes – the haunted painting, the returning dead, and the cursed family – into a fun short EC-style shocker.

Croatian-born Macan and Biukovic collaborated on several stories, all of which are highly rated by readers and collectors alike. Sadly, this collaboration ended with Biukovic's sudden death in 1999. Macan continues to works as a writer, illustrator, and editor of comics.

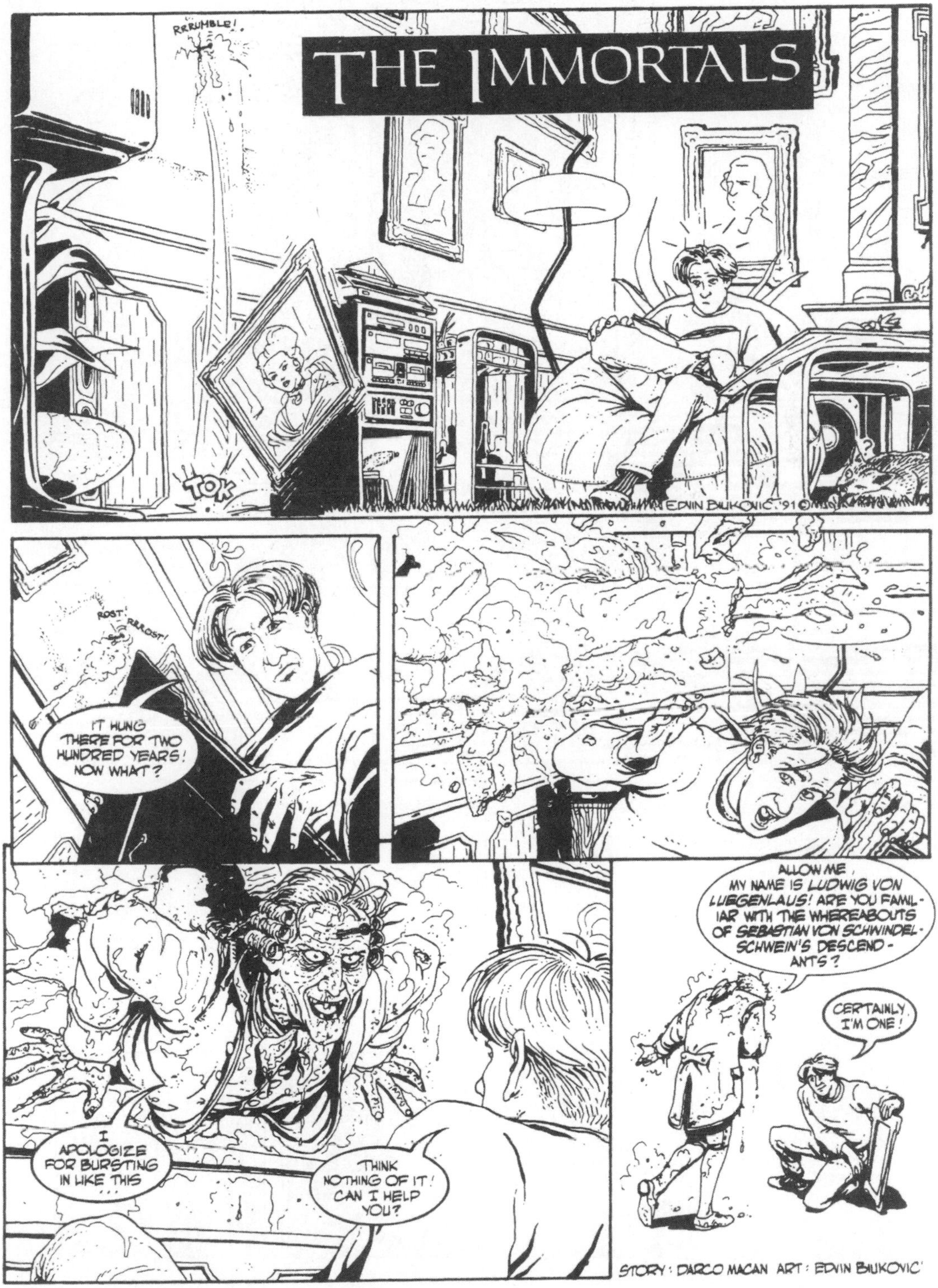
THE IMMORTALS
RRRUMBLE!
TOK
EDVIN BIUKOVIC '91©
ROST! RRROST!
IT HUNG THERE FOR TWO HUNDRED YEARS! NOW WHAT?
I APOLOGIZE FOR BURSTING IN LIKE THIS ...
THINK NOTHING OF IT! CAN I HELP YOU?
ALLOW ME, MY NAME IS LUDWIG VON LUEGENLAUS! ARE YOU FAMILIAR WITH THE WHEREABOUTS OF SEBASTIAN VON SCHWINDELSCHWEIN'S DESCENDANTS?
CERTAINLY I'M ONE!
STORY: DARCO MACAN ART: EDVIN BIUKOVIC'

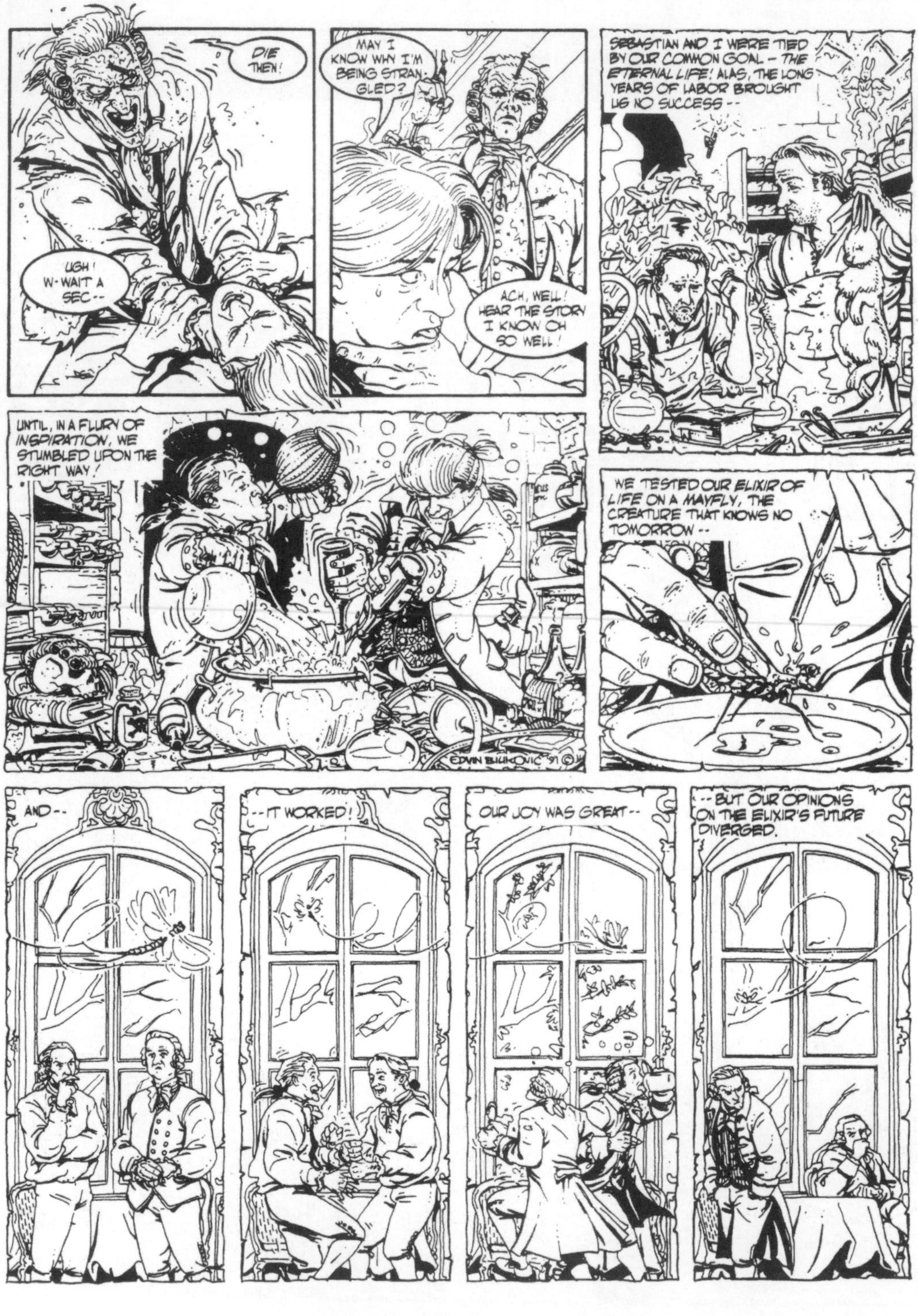
DIE THEN!
UGH! W-WAIT A SEC--
MAY I KNOW WHY I'M BEING STRANGLED?
ACH, WELL! HEAR THE STORY I KNOW OH SO WELL!
SEBASTIAN AND I WERE TIED BY OUR COMMON GOAL - THE ETERNAL LIFE! ALAS, THE LONG YEARS OF LABOR BROUGHT US NO SUCCESS--
UNTIL, IN A FLURY OF INSPIRATION, WE STUMBLED UPON THE RIGHT WAY!
EDVIN BIUKOVIC '97
WE TESTED OUR ELIXIR OF LIFE ON A MAYFLY, THE CREATURE THAT KNOWS NO TOMORROW--
AND--
--IT WORKED!
OUR JOY WAS GREAT--
--BUT OUR OPINIONS ON THE ELIXIR'S FUTURE DIVERGED.

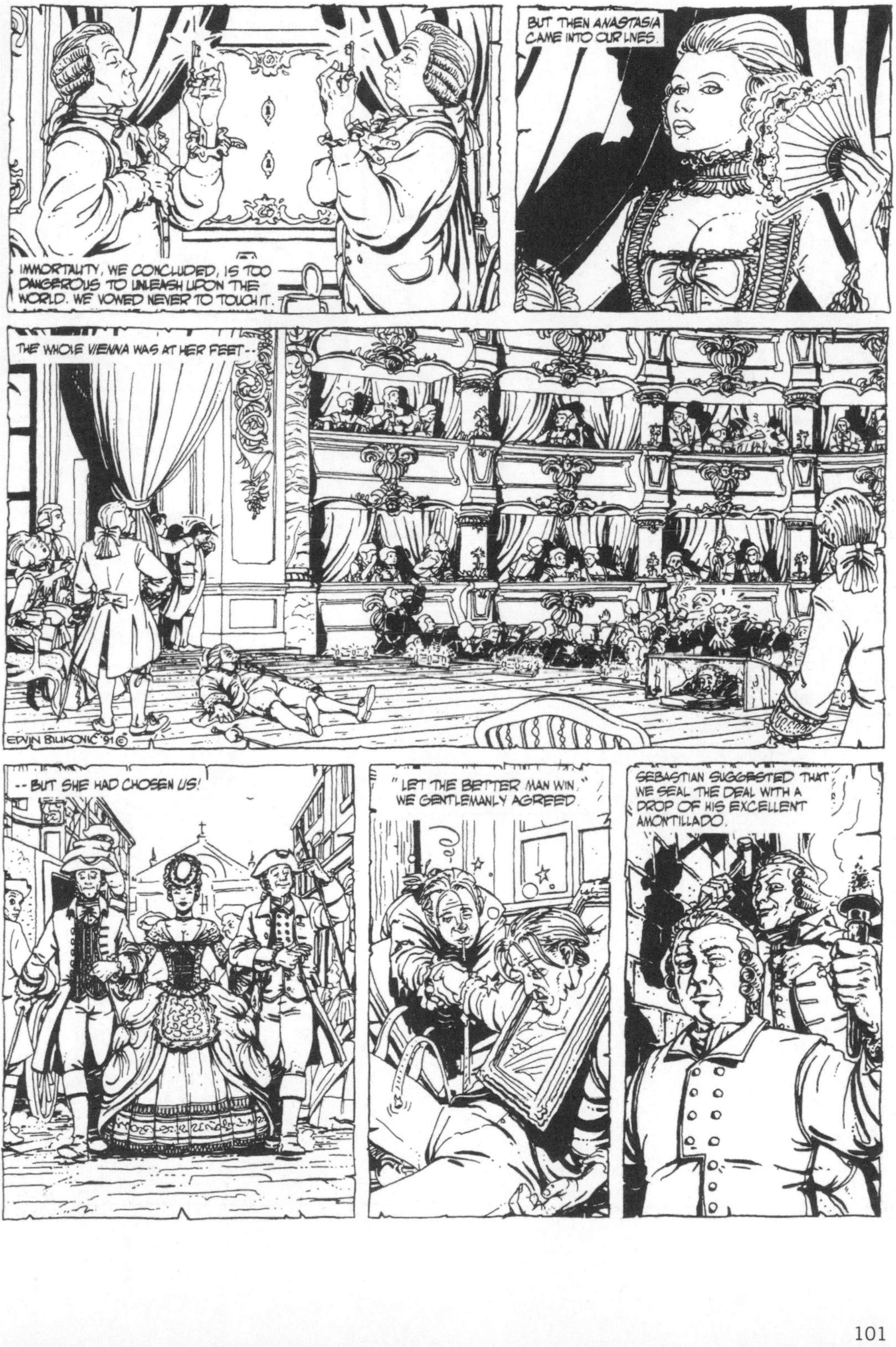
IMMORTALITY, WE CONCLUDED, IS TOO DANGEROUS TO UNLEASH UPON THE WORLD. WE VOWED NEVER TO TOUCH IT.
BUT THEN ANASTASIA CAME INTO OUR LIVES.
THE WHOLE VIENNA WAS AT HER FEET--
EDVIN BIUKOVIĆ '91 ©
--BUT SHE HAD CHOSEN US!
"LET THE BETTER MAN WIN," WE GENTLEMANLY AGREED.
SEBASTIAN SUGGESTED THAT WE SEAL THE DEAL WITH A DROP OF HIS EXCELLENT AMONTILLADO.

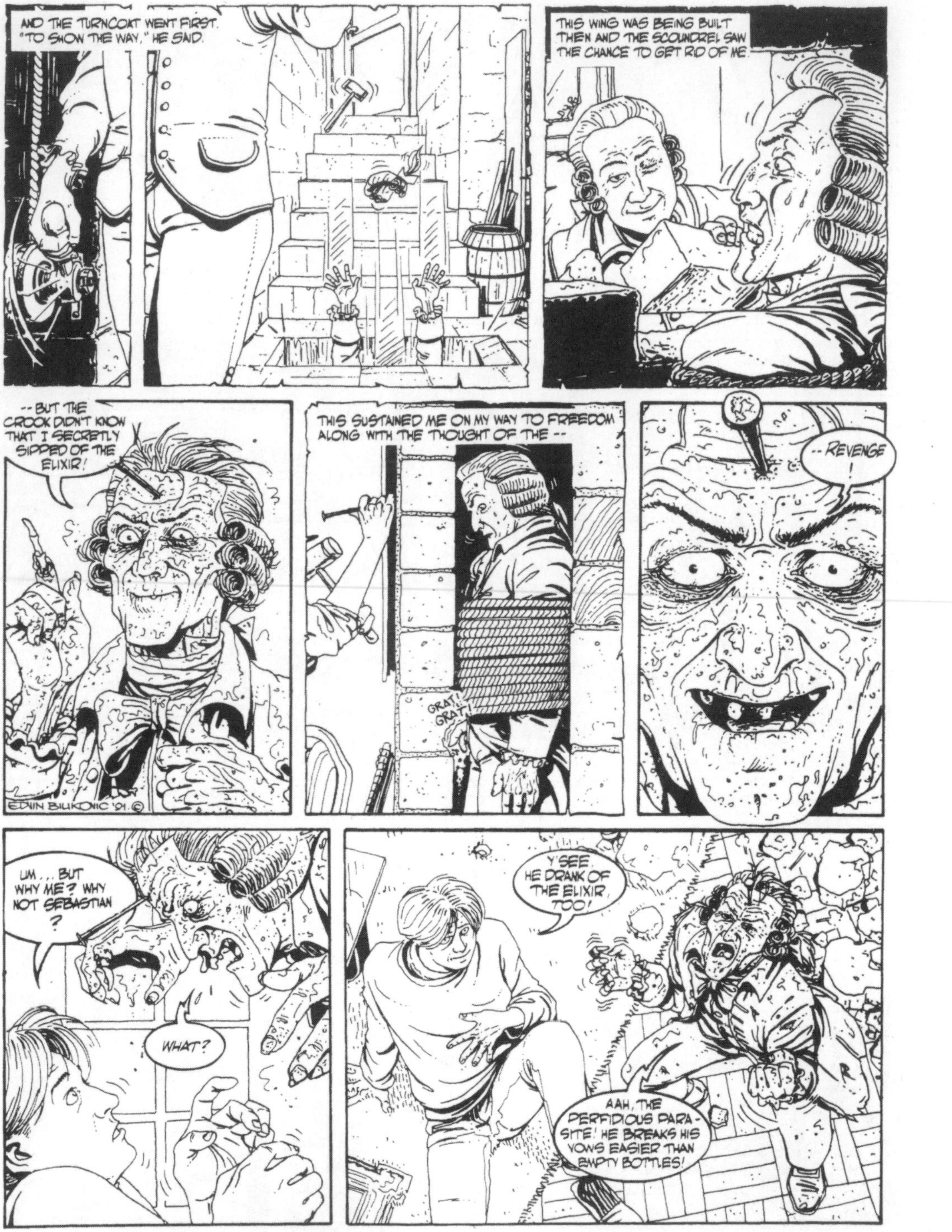
AND THE TURNCOAT WENT FIRST. "TO SHOW THE WAY," HE SAID.
THIS WING WAS BEING BUILT THEN AND THE SCOUNDREL SAW THE CHANCE TO GET RID OF ME.
--BUT THE CROOK DIDN'T KNOW THAT I SECRETLY SIPPED OF THE ELIXIR!
EDVIN BIUKOVIC '91 ©
THIS SUSTAINED ME ON MY WAY TO FREEDOM ALONG WITH THE THOUGHT OF THE --
GRAT! GRAT!
--REVENGE!
UM... BUT WHY ME? WHY NOT SEBASTIAN?
WHAT?
Y'SEE, HE DRANK OF THE ELIXIR, TOO!
AAH, THE PERFIDIOUS PARASITE! HE BREAKS HIS VOWS EASIER THAN EMPTY BOTTLES!

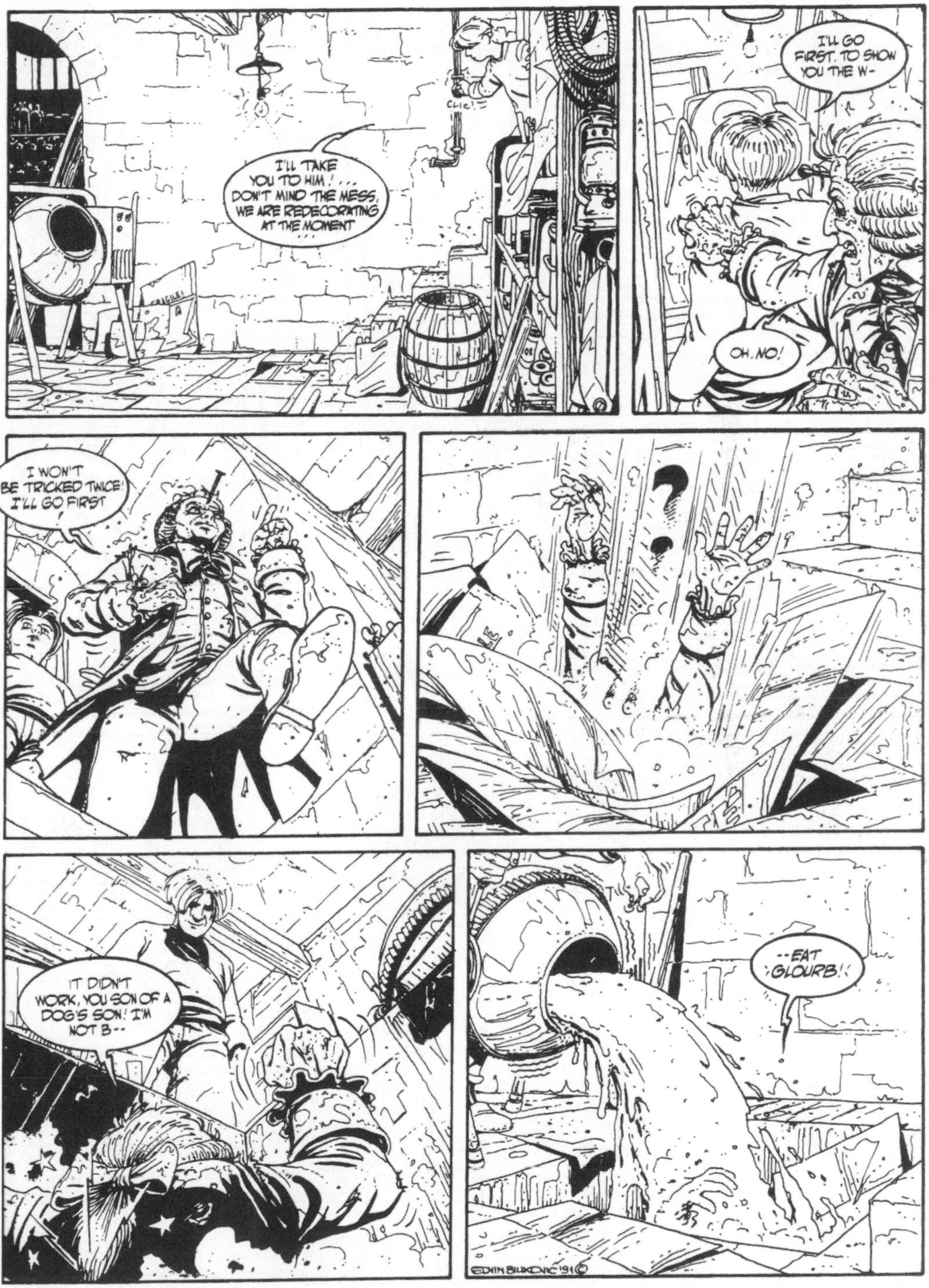
CLIC!
I'LL TAKE YOU TO HIM! ... DON'T MIND THE MESS, WE ARE REDECORATING AT THE MOMENT ...
FRAGILE!
I'LL GO FIRST, TO SHOW YOU THE W-
OH, NO!
I WON'T BE TRICKED TWICE! I'LL GO FIRST!
?
IT DIDN'T WORK, YOU SON OF A DOG'S SON! I'M NOT B--
--EAT GLOURB!
EDVIN BILIKOVIC '91 ©

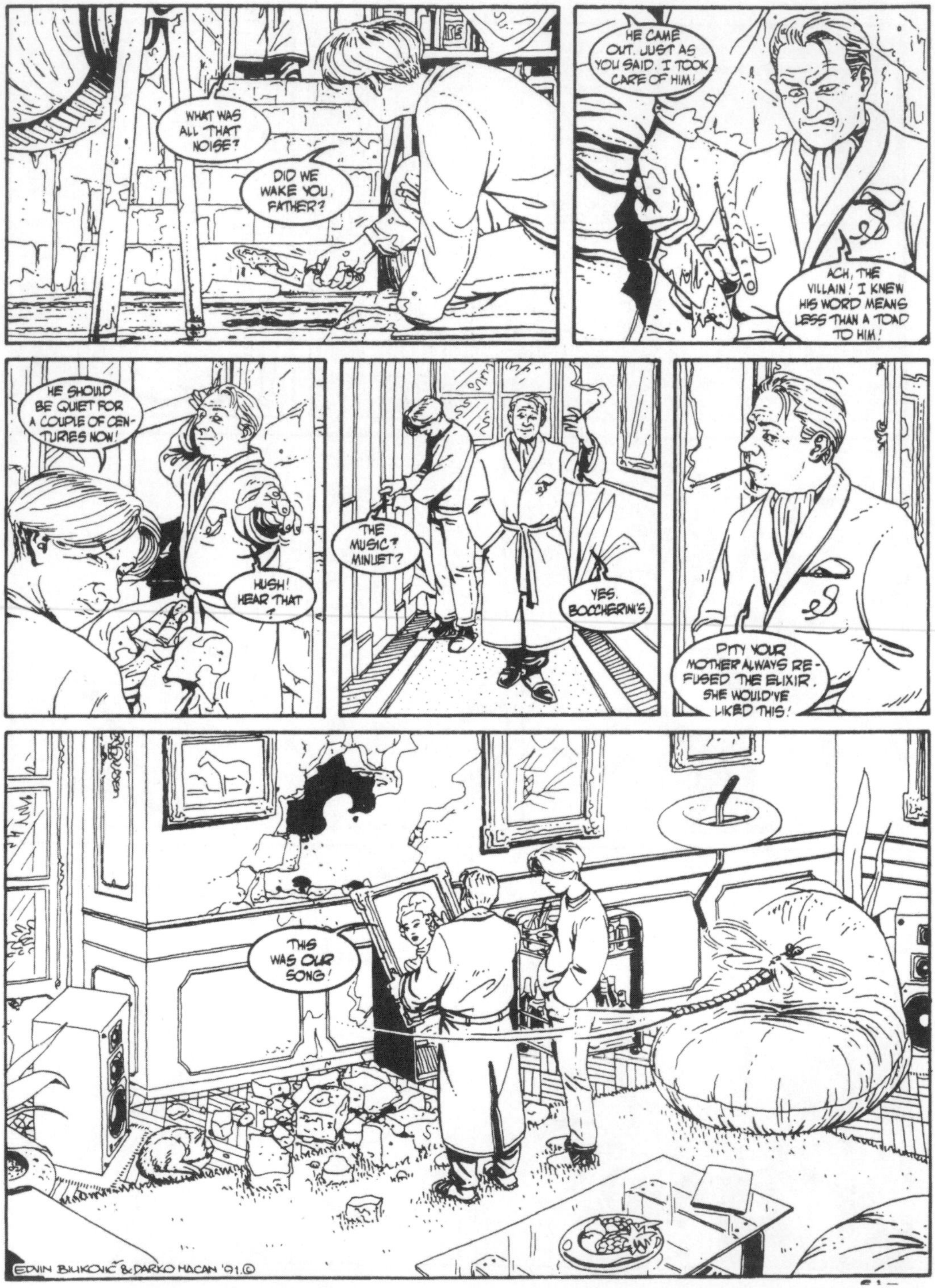
WHAT WAS ALL THAT NOISE?
DID WE WAKE YOU, FATHER?
HE CAME OUT, JUST AS YOU SAID. I TOOK CARE OF HIM!
ACH, THE VILLAIN! I KNEW HIS WORD MEANS LESS THAN A TOAD TO HIM!
HE SHOULD BE QUIET FOR A COUPLE OF CENTURIES NOW!
HUSH! HEAR THAT?
THE MUSIC? MINUET?
YES. BOCCHERINI'S.
PITY YOUR MOTHER ALWAYS REFUSED THE ELIXIR. SHE WOULD'VE LIKED THIS!
THIS WAS OUR SONG!
EDVIN BILIKOVIC & DARKO MACAN '91.©

Flight From Earth (2005)

Creators: Oleg Kozyrev (script) and Roman Surzhenko (art)

It's not often zombies get into space, and this story gives us some idea why. Roman Surzhenko is a Russian creator of comics generally drawn in traditional realistic style. He is probably best known for his work on the graphic novel 1612 based on the movie of the same name. Oleg Kozyrev works in animation, TV and comics and collaborated with Surzhenko on the sf series *The Border Tales*.

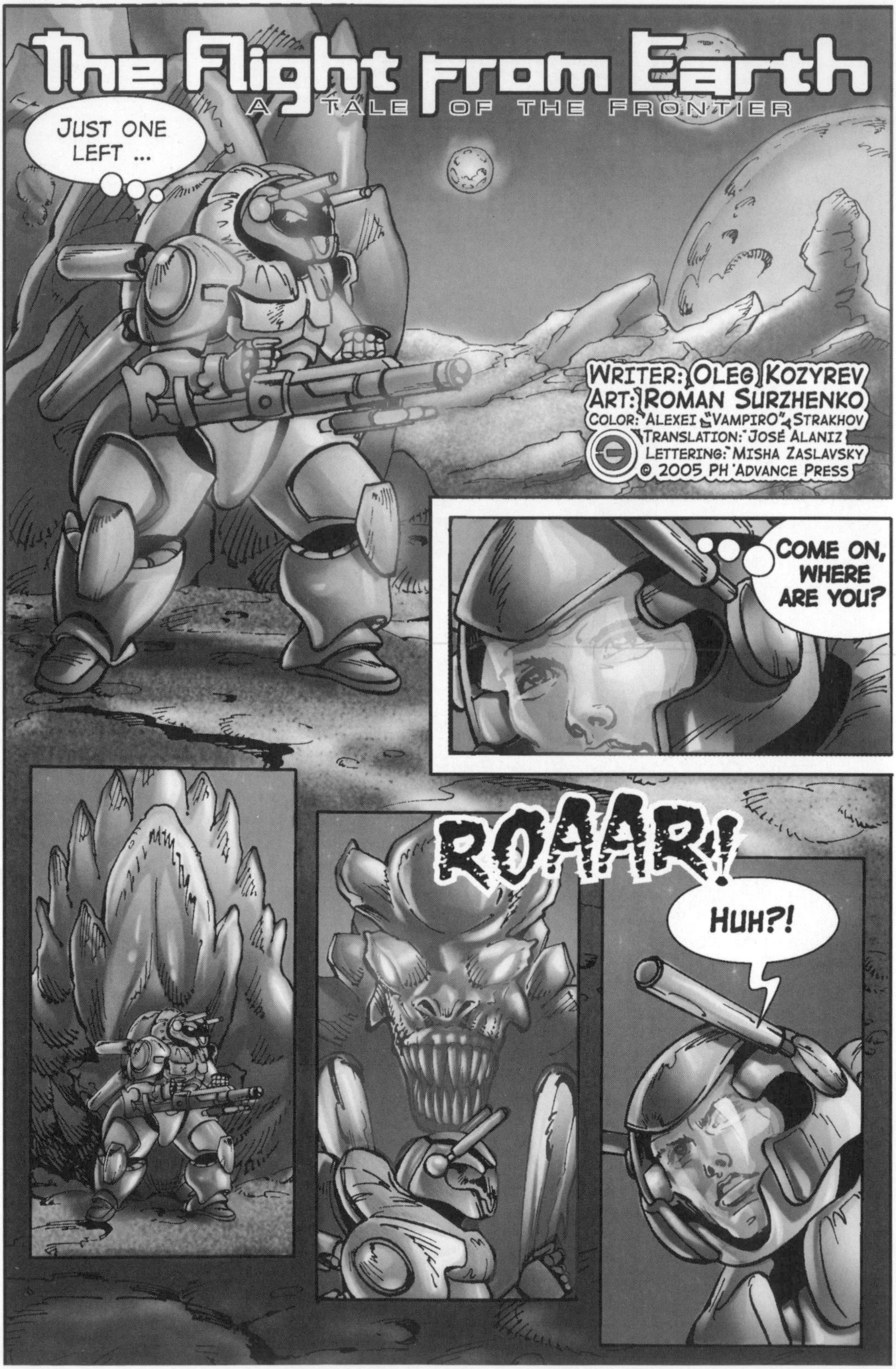
The Flight from Earth
A TALE OF THE FRONTIER
JUST ONE LEFT ...
WRITER: OLEG KOZYREV
ART: ROMAN SURZHENKO
COLOR: ALEXEI "VAMPIRO" STRAKHOV
TRANSLATION: JOSÉ ALANIZ
LETTERING: MISHA ZASLAVSKY
© 2005 PH ADVANCE PRESS
COME ON, WHERE ARE YOU?
ROAAR!
HUH?!

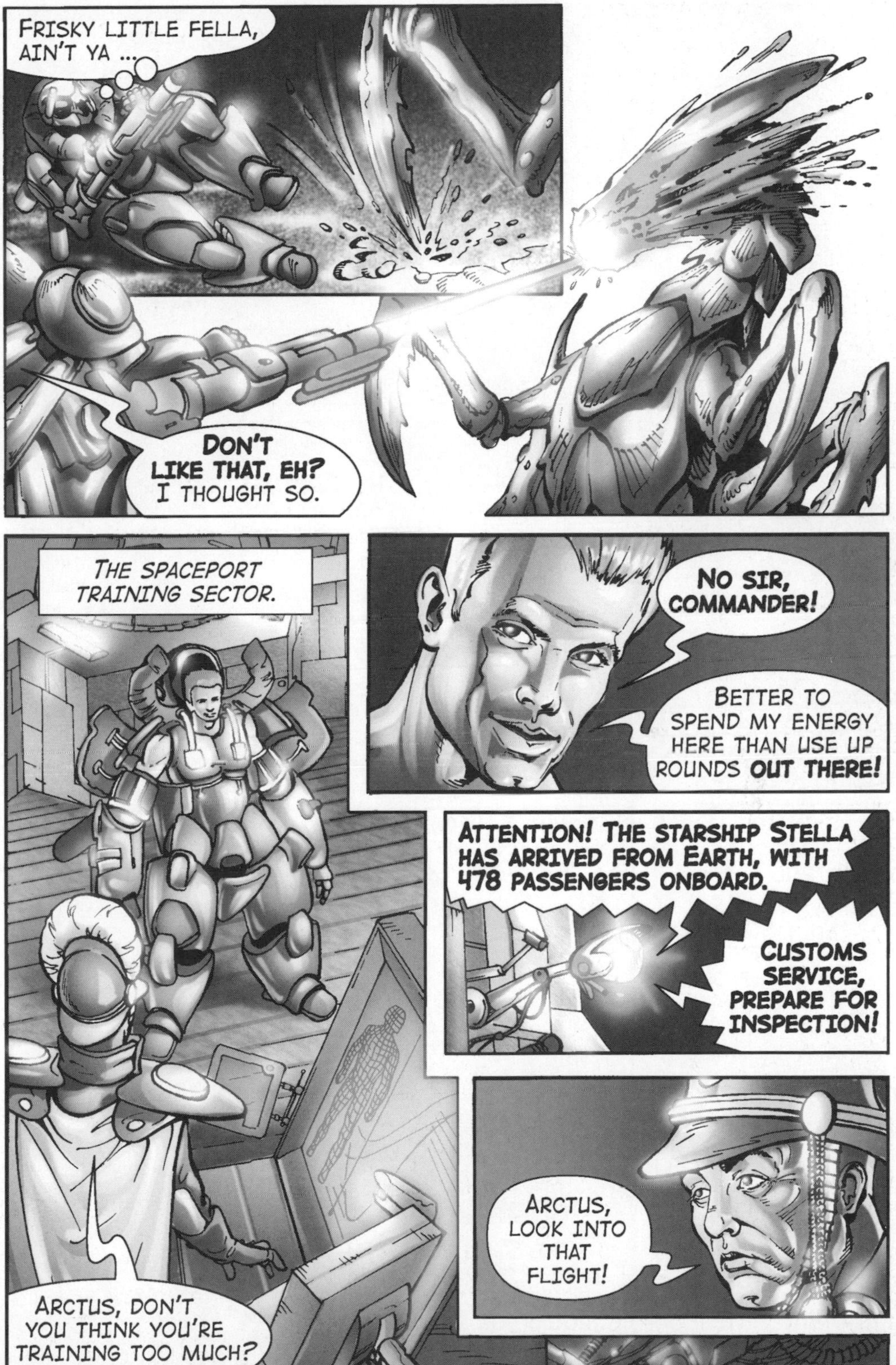
FRISKY LITTLE FELLA, AIN'T YA ...
DON'T LIKE THAT, EH? I THOUGHT SO.
THE SPACEPORT TRAINING SECTOR.
ARCTUS, DON'T YOU THINK YOU'RE TRAINING TOO MUCH?
NO SIR, COMMANDER!
BETTER TO SPEND MY ENERGY HERE THAN USE UP ROUNDS OUT THERE!
ATTENTION! THE STARSHIP STELLA HAS ARRIVED FROM EARTH, WITH 478 PASSENGERS ONBOARD.
CUSTOMS SERVICE, PREPARE FOR INSPECTION!
ARCTUS, LOOK INTO THAT FLIGHT!

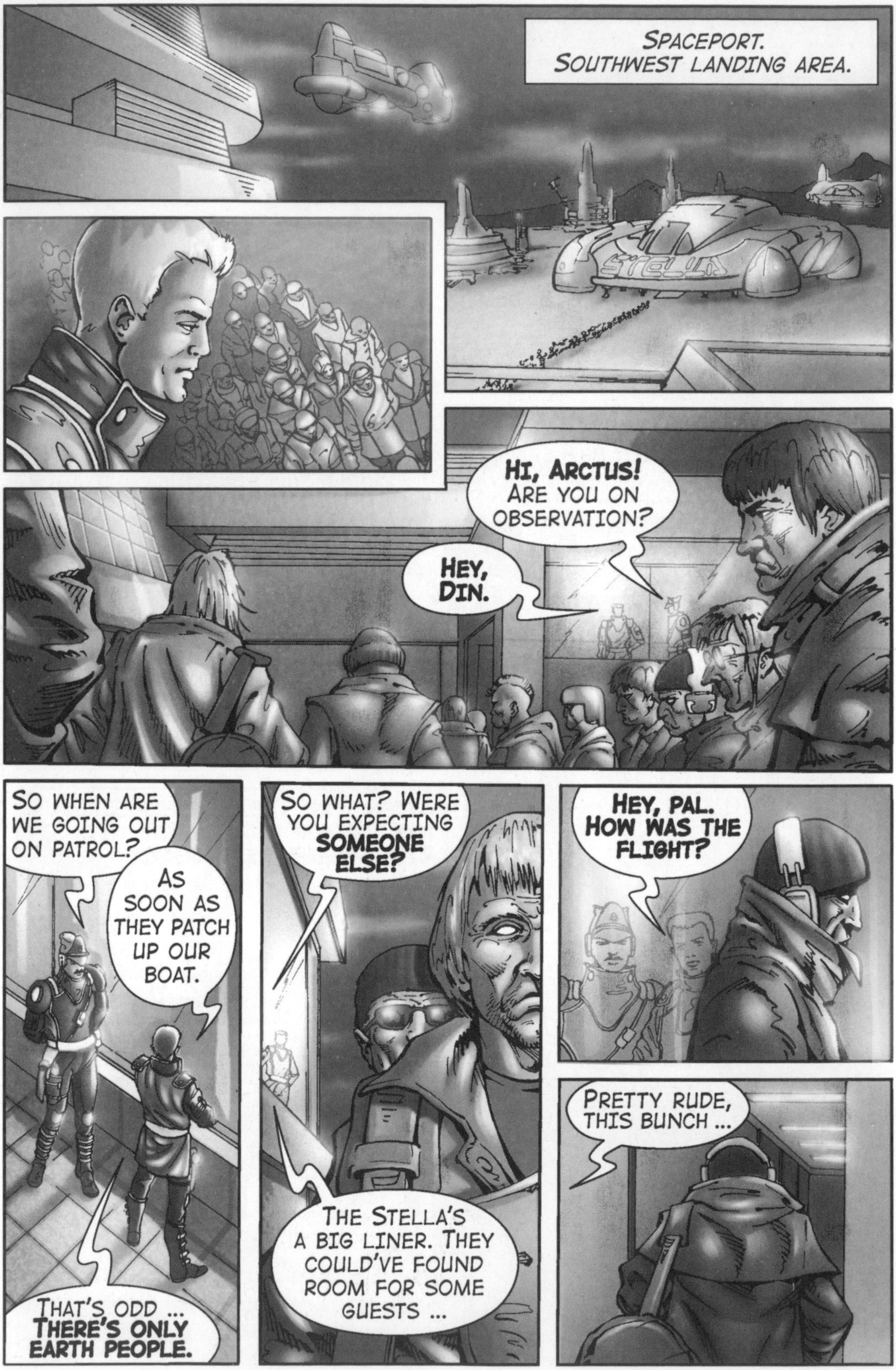
SPACEPORT.
SOUTHWEST LANDING AREA.
STELLA
HI, ARCTUS! ARE YOU ON OBSERVATION?
HEY, DIN.
SO WHEN ARE WE GOING OUT ON PATROL?
AS SOON AS THEY PATCH UP OUR BOAT.
THAT'S ODD ... THERE'S ONLY EARTH PEOPLE.
SO WHAT? WERE YOU EXPECTING SOMEONE ELSE?
THE STELLA'S A BIG LINER. THEY COULD'VE FOUND ROOM FOR SOME GUESTS ...
HEY, PAL. HOW WAS THE FLIGHT?
PRETTY RUDE, THIS BUNCH ...

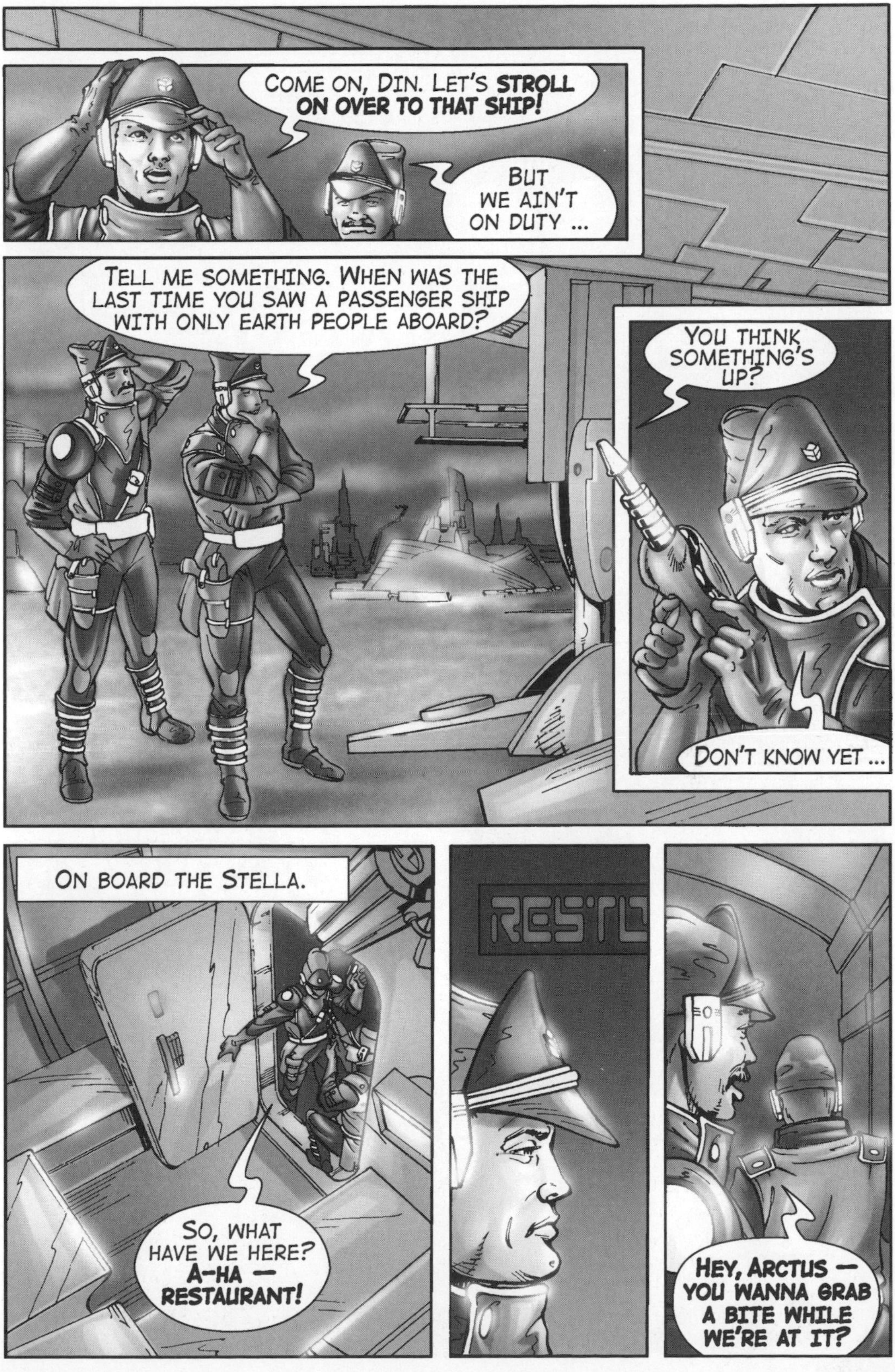
COME ON, DIN. LET'S **STROLL ON OVER TO THAT SHIP!**
BUT WE AIN'T ON DUTY ...
TELL ME SOMETHING. WHEN WAS THE LAST TIME YOU SAW A PASSENGER SHIP WITH ONLY EARTH PEOPLE ABOARD?
YOU THINK SOMETHING'S UP?
DON'T KNOW YET ...
ON BOARD THE STELLA.
SO, WHAT HAVE WE HERE? **A-HA — RESTAURANT!**
HEY, ARCTUS — YOU WANNA GRAB A BITE WHILE WE'RE AT IT?

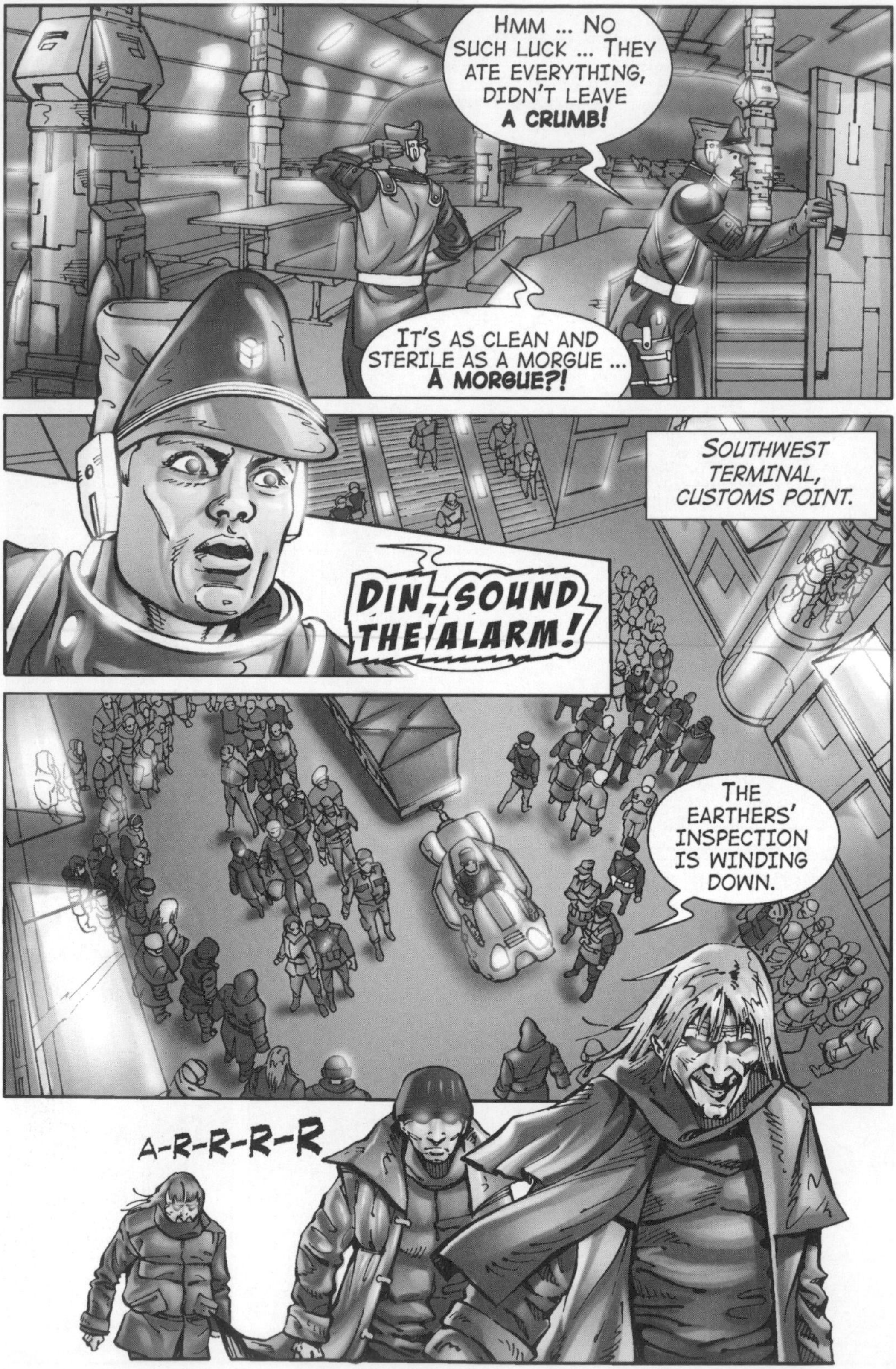
HMM ... NO SUCH LUCK ... THEY ATE EVERYTHING, DIDN'T LEAVE A CRUMB!
IT'S AS CLEAN AND STERILE AS A MORGUE ... A MORGUE?!
DIN, SOUND THE ALARM!
SOUTHWEST TERMINAL, CUSTOMS POINT.
THE EARTHERS' INSPECTION IS WINDING DOWN.
A-R-R-R-R

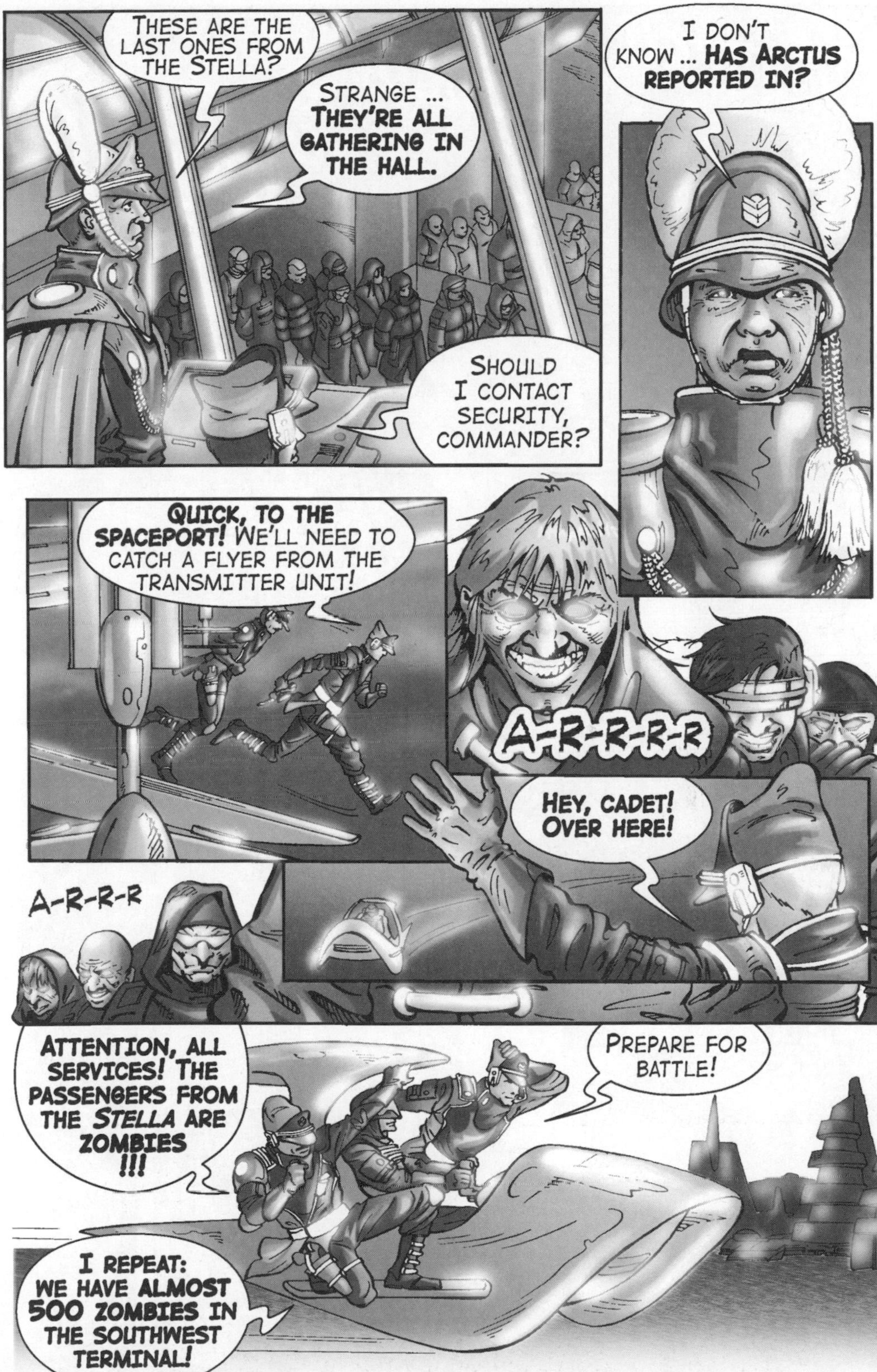
THESE ARE THE LAST ONES FROM THE STELLA?
STRANGE ... THEY'RE ALL GATHERING IN THE HALL.
SHOULD I CONTACT SECURITY, COMMANDER?
I DON'T KNOW ... HAS ARCTUS REPORTED IN?
QUICK, TO THE SPACEPORT! WE'LL NEED TO CATCH A FLYER FROM THE TRANSMITTER UNIT!
A-R-R-R-R
HEY, CADET! OVER HERE!
A-R-R-R
ATTENTION, ALL SERVICES! THE PASSENGERS FROM THE *STELLA* ARE ZOMBIES !!!
PREPARE FOR BATTLE!
I REPEAT: WE HAVE ALMOST 500 ZOMBIES IN THE SOUTHWEST TERMINAL!

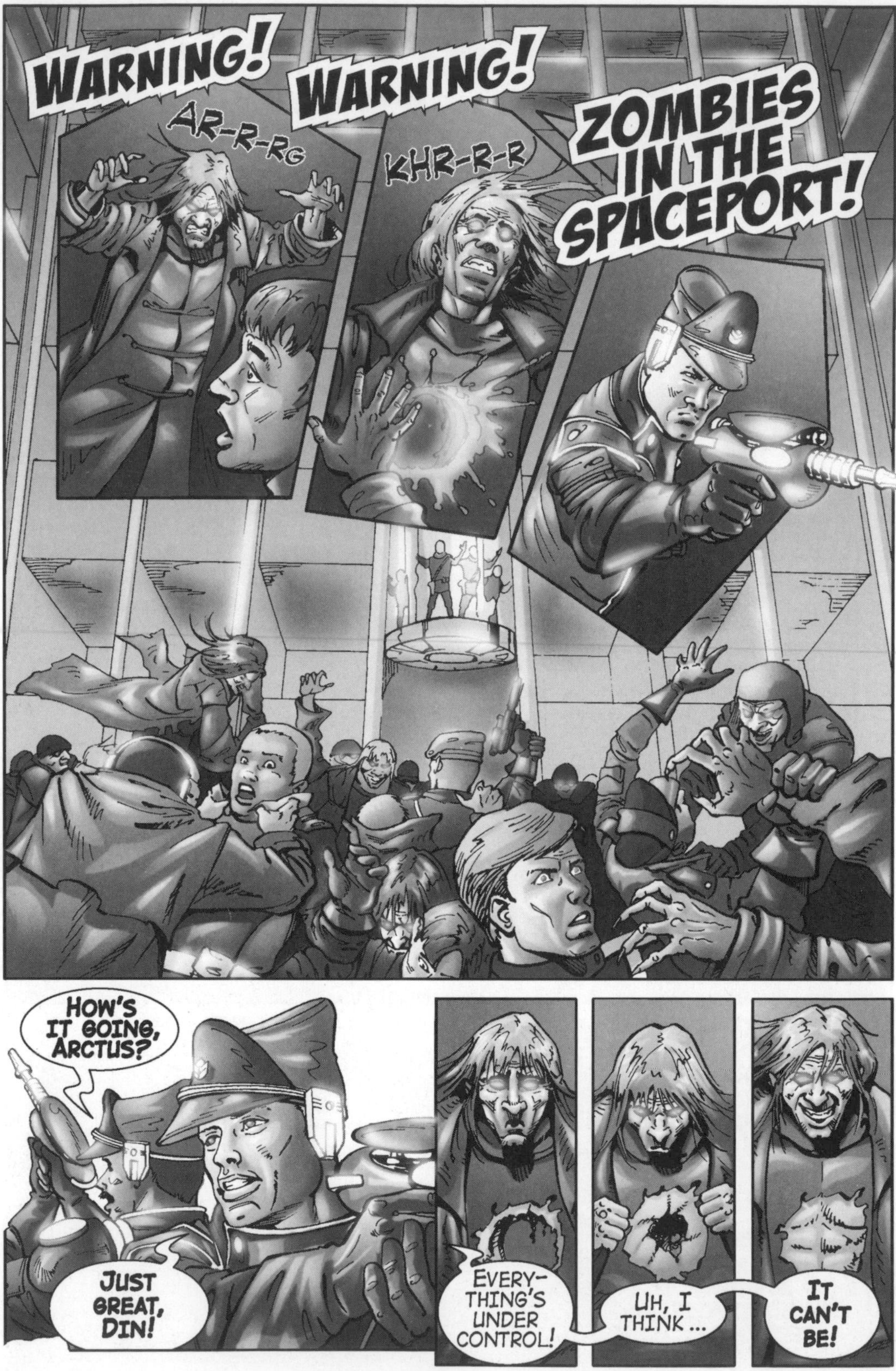
WARNING!
WARNING!
AR-R-RG
KHR-R-R
ZOMBIES IN THE SPACEPORT!
HOW'S IT GOING, ARCTUS?
JUST GREAT, DIN!
EVERY-THING'S UNDER CONTROL!
UH, I THINK ...
IT CAN'T BE!

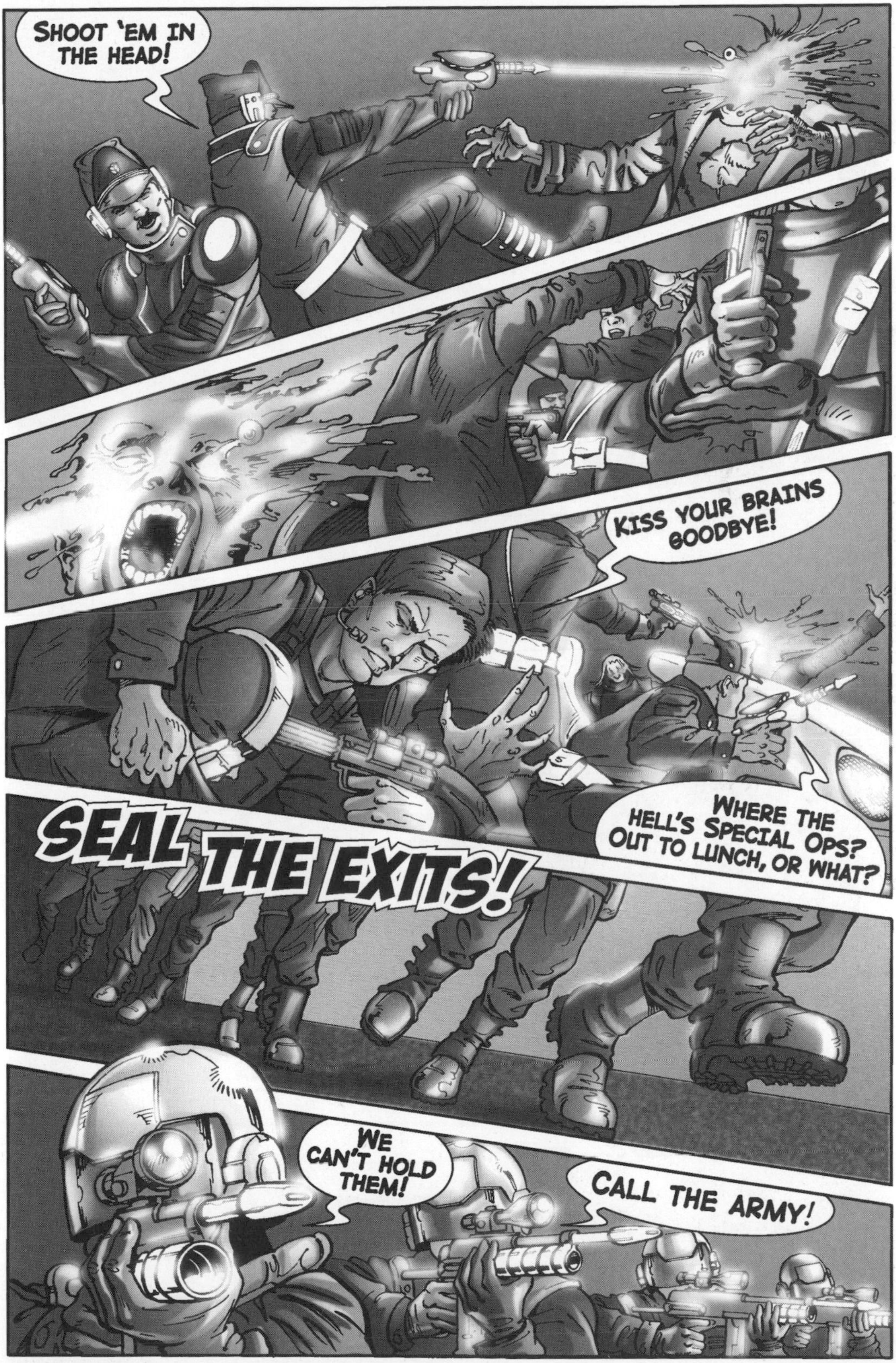
SHOOT 'EM IN THE HEAD!
KISS YOUR BRAINS GOODBYE!
SEAL THE EXITS!
WHERE THE HELL'S SPECIAL OPS? OUT TO LUNCH, OR WHAT?
WE CAN'T HOLD THEM!
CALL THE ARMY!

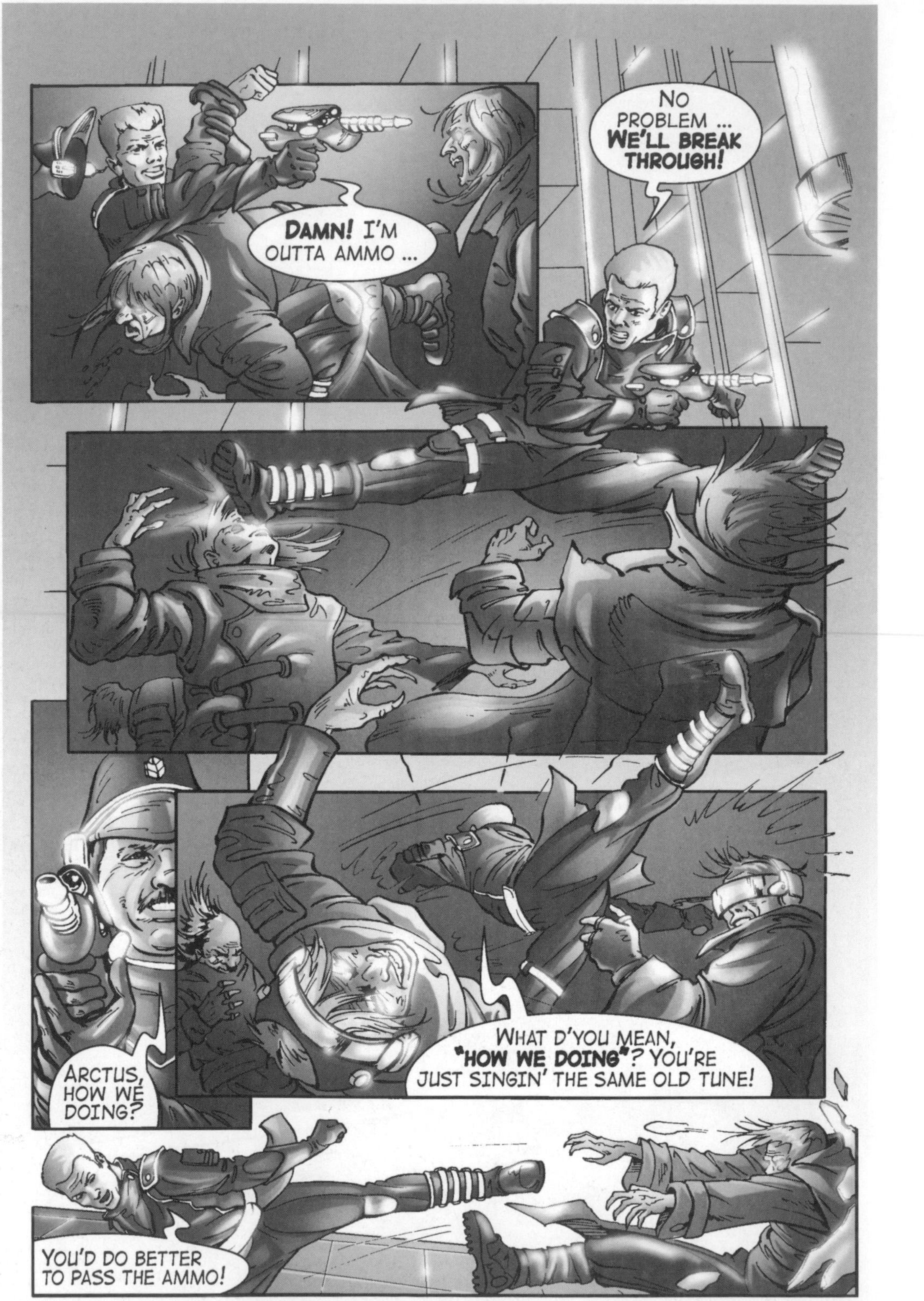
DAMN! I'M OUTTA AMMO ...
NO PROBLEM ... WE'LL BREAK THROUGH!
ARCTUS, HOW WE DOING?
WHAT D'YOU MEAN, "HOW WE DOING"? YOU'RE JUST SINGIN' THE SAME OLD TUNE!
YOU'D DO BETTER TO PASS THE AMMO!

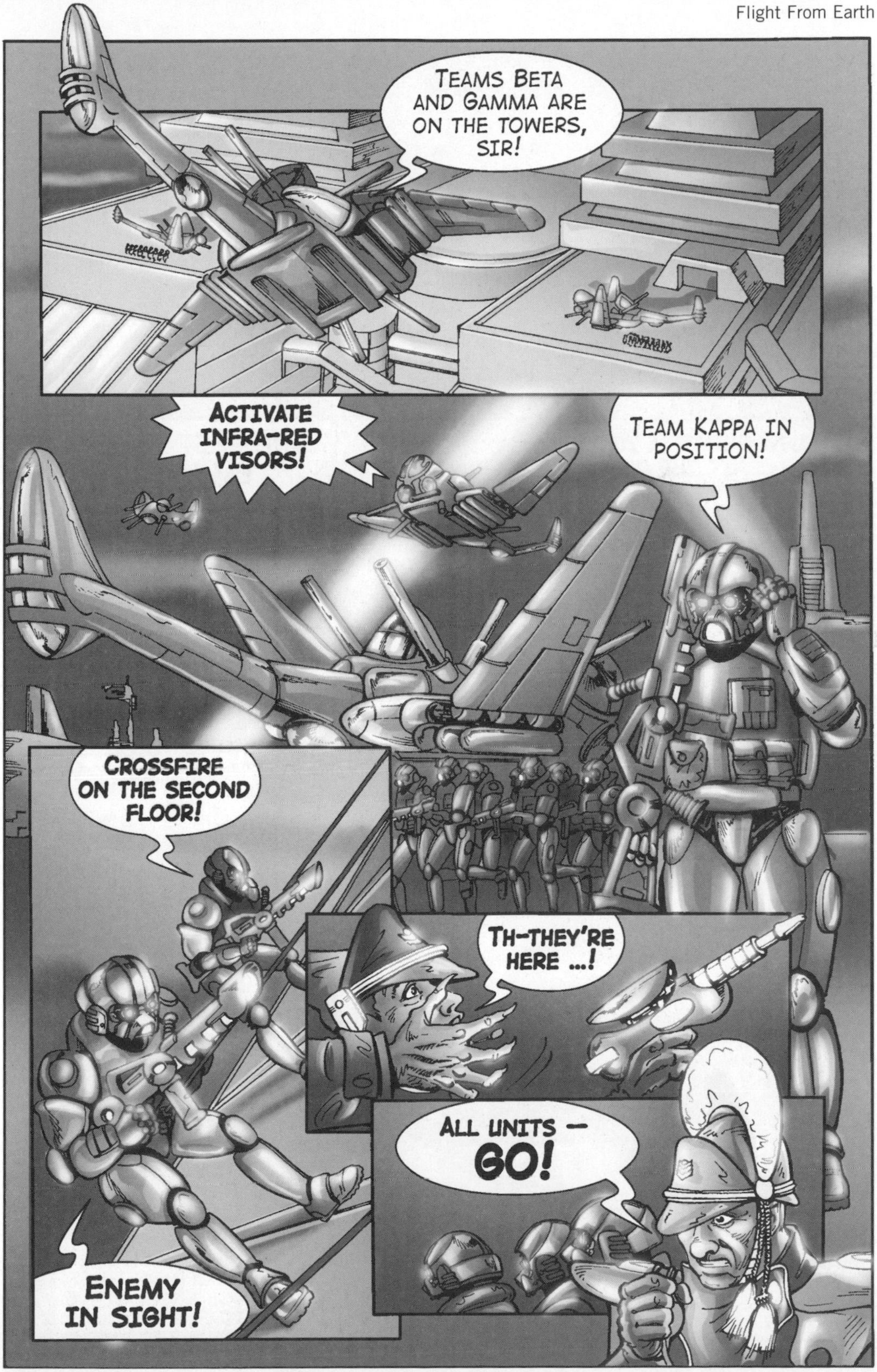
TEAMS BETA AND GAMMA ARE ON THE TOWERS, SIR!
ACTIVATE INFRA-RED VISORS!
TEAM KAPPA IN POSITION!
CROSSFIRE ON THE SECOND FLOOR!
ENEMY IN SIGHT!
TH-THEY'RE HERE ...!
ALL UNITS — GO!

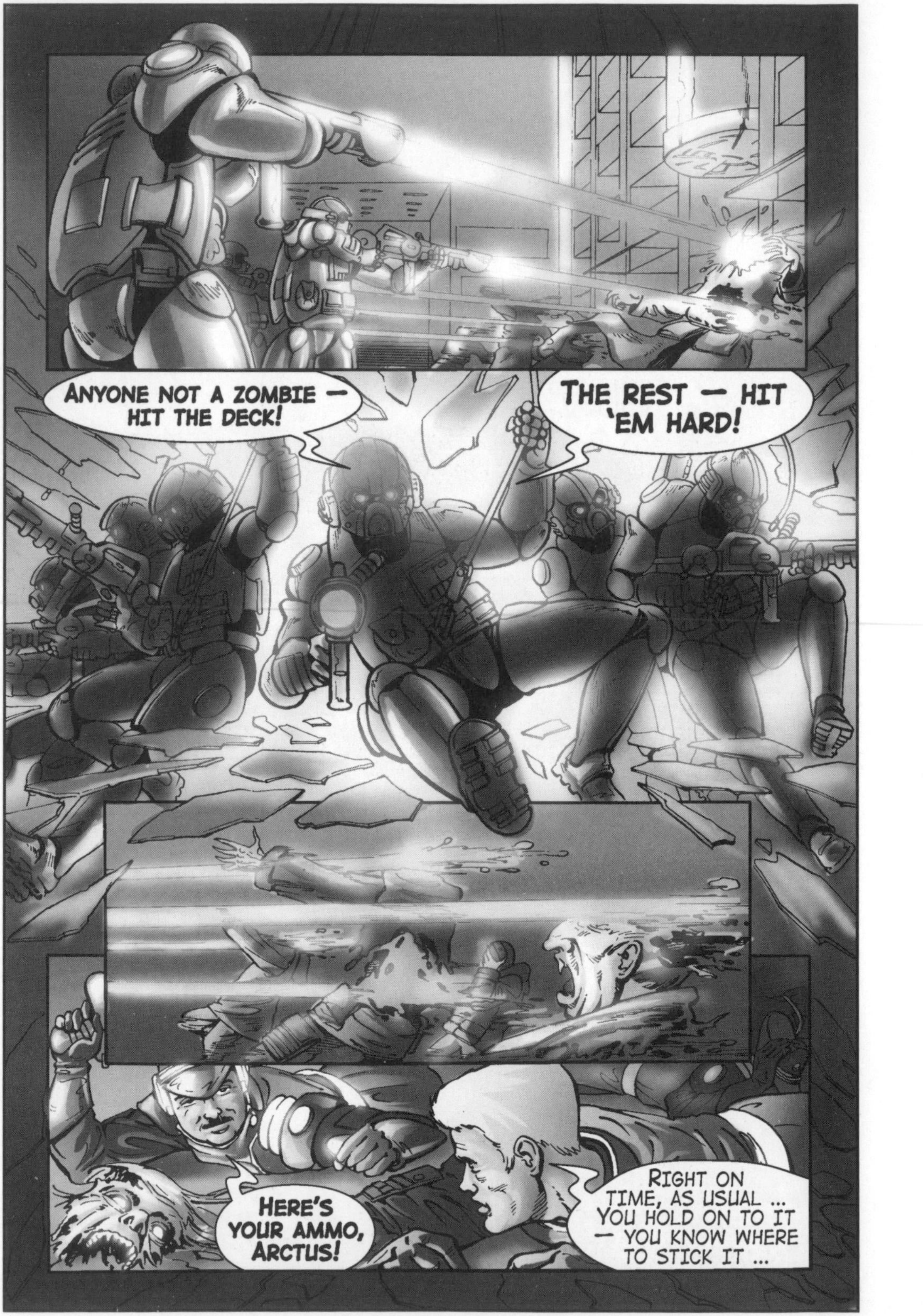
ANYONE NOT A ZOMBIE — HIT THE DECK!
THE REST — HIT 'EM HARD!
HERE'S YOUR AMMO, ARCTUS!
RIGHT ON TIME, AS USUAL ... YOU HOLD ON TO IT — YOU KNOW WHERE TO STICK IT ...

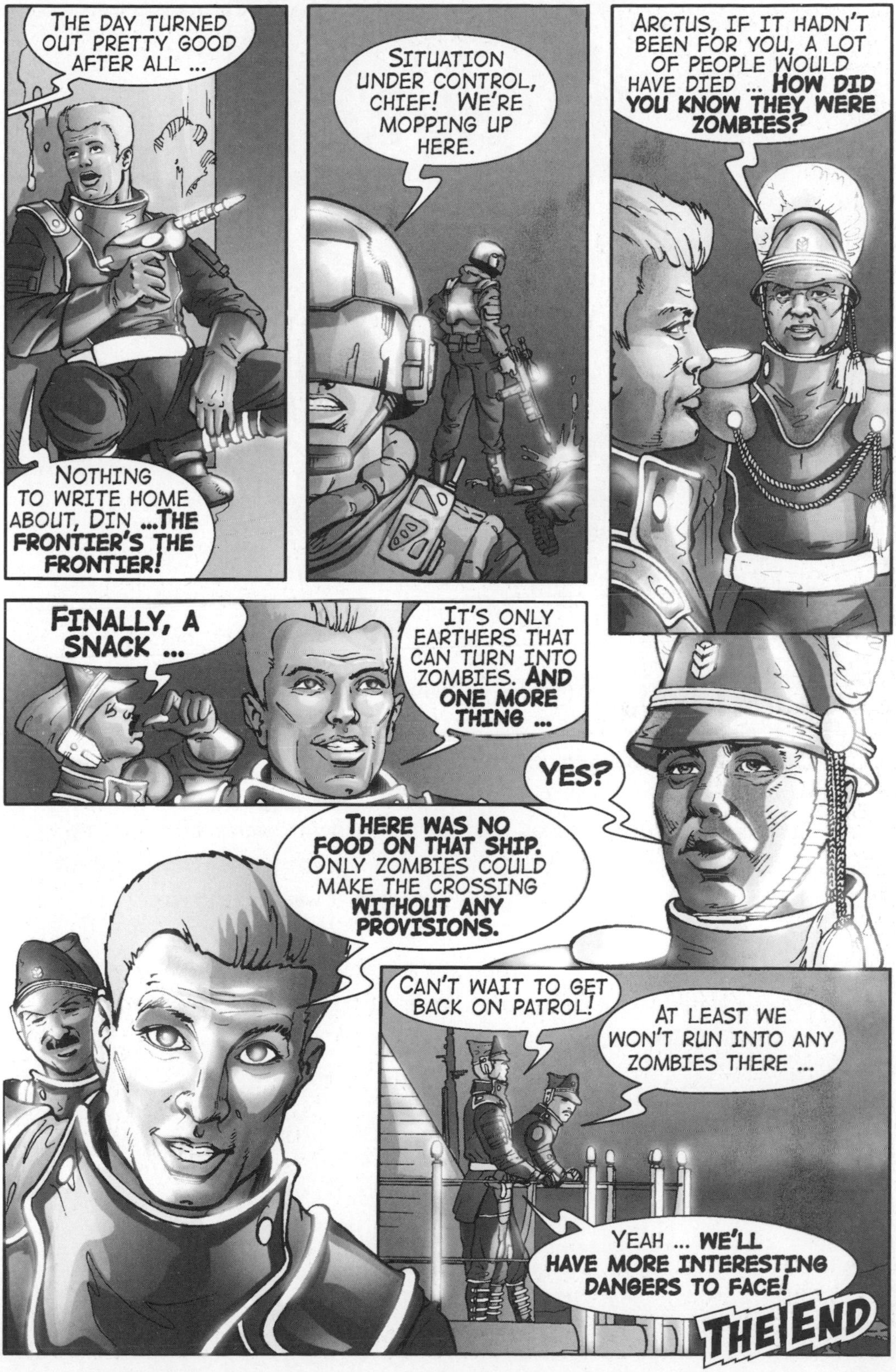
THE DAY TURNED OUT PRETTY GOOD AFTER ALL ...
NOTHING TO WRITE HOME ABOUT, DIN ...THE FRONTIER'S THE FRONTIER!
SITUATION UNDER CONTROL, CHIEF! WE'RE MOPPING UP HERE.
ARCTUS, IF IT HADN'T BEEN FOR YOU, A LOT OF PEOPLE WOULD HAVE DIED ... HOW DID YOU KNOW THEY WERE ZOMBIES?
FINALLY, A SNACK ...
IT'S ONLY EARTHERS THAT CAN TURN INTO ZOMBIES. AND ONE MORE THING ...
YES?
THERE WAS NO FOOD ON THAT SHIP. ONLY ZOMBIES COULD MAKE THE CROSSING WITHOUT ANY PROVISIONS.
CAN'T WAIT TO GET BACK ON PATROL!
AT LEAST WE WON'T RUN INTO ANY ZOMBIES THERE ...
YEAH ... WE'LL HAVE MORE INTERESTING DANGERS TO FACE!
THE END

Amy (1988)

Creators: Mark Bloodworth (script), Vincent Locke (art)

Back in the 1980s zombies roamed independent comics with impunity. Writers and artists delighted in giving readers the shocks they craved. "Amy" is a great horror story but one that you might not want to read twice.

Vincent Locke began with *Deadworld* and went on to work on *American Freak*, *Batman*, and *A History of Violence*. He has also created album covers for Cannibal Corpse.

DEADTALES

"AMY" Script-Mark Bloodworth Pencils-Paul Daily
Inks+Letters-Vincent Locke

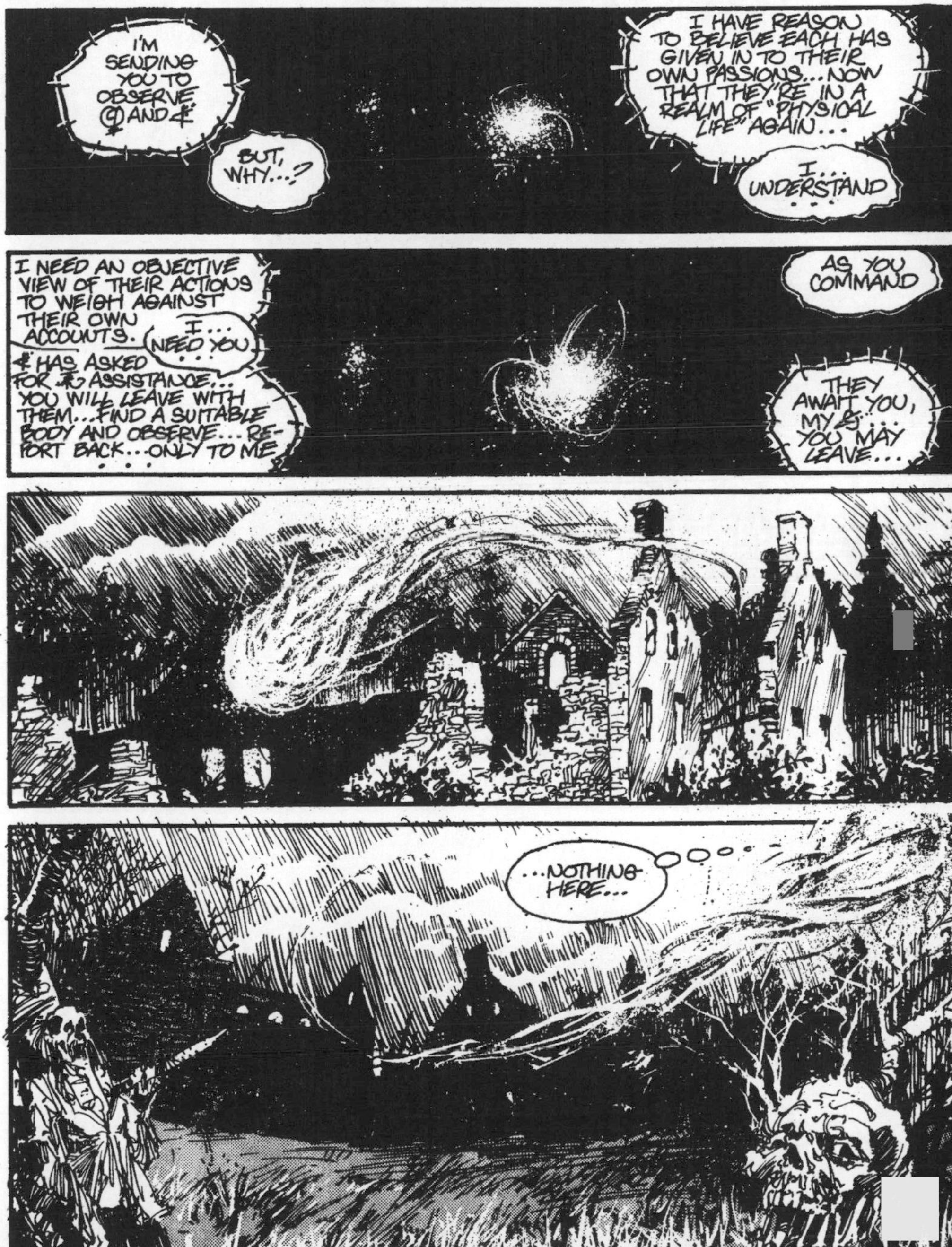
I'M SENDING YOU TO OBSERVE AND
BUT, WHY...?
I HAVE REASON TO BELIEVE EACH HAS GIVEN IN TO THEIR OWN PASSIONS...NOW THAT THEY'RE IN A REALM OF "PHYSICAL LIFE" AGAIN...
I... UNDERSTAND...
I NEED AN OBJECTIVE VIEW OF THEIR ACTIONS TO WEIGH AGAINST THEIR OWN ACCOUNTS.
I... NEED YOU...
HAS ASKED FOR ASSISTANCE... YOU WILL LEAVE WITH THEM...FIND A SUITABLE BODY AND OBSERVE... REPORT BACK...ONLY TO ME...
AS YOU COMMAND
THEY AWAIT YOU, MY... YOU MAY LEAVE...
...NOTHING HERE...

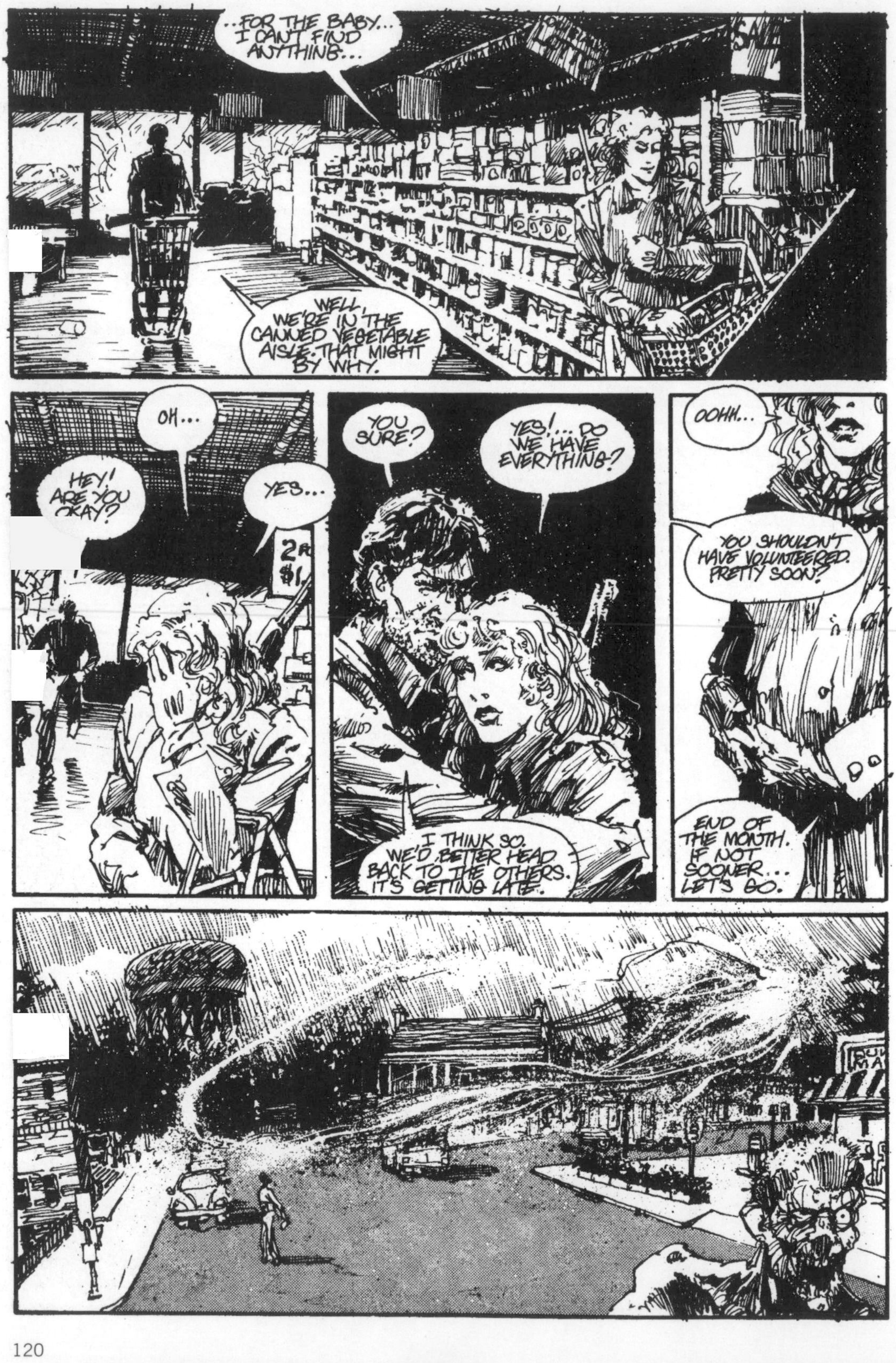
...FOR THE BABY... I CAN'T FIND ANYTHING...
WELL, WE'RE IN THE CANNED VEGETABLE AISLE. THAT MIGHT BY WHY.
OH...
HEY! ARE YOU OKAY?
YES...
YOU SURE?
YES!... DO WE HAVE EVERYTHING?
I THINK SO. WE'D BETTER HEAD BACK TO THE OTHERS. IT'S GETTING LATE.
OOHH...
YOU SHOULDN'T HAVE VOLUNTEERED. PRETTY SOON?
END OF THE MONTH. IF NOT SOONER... LET'S GO.

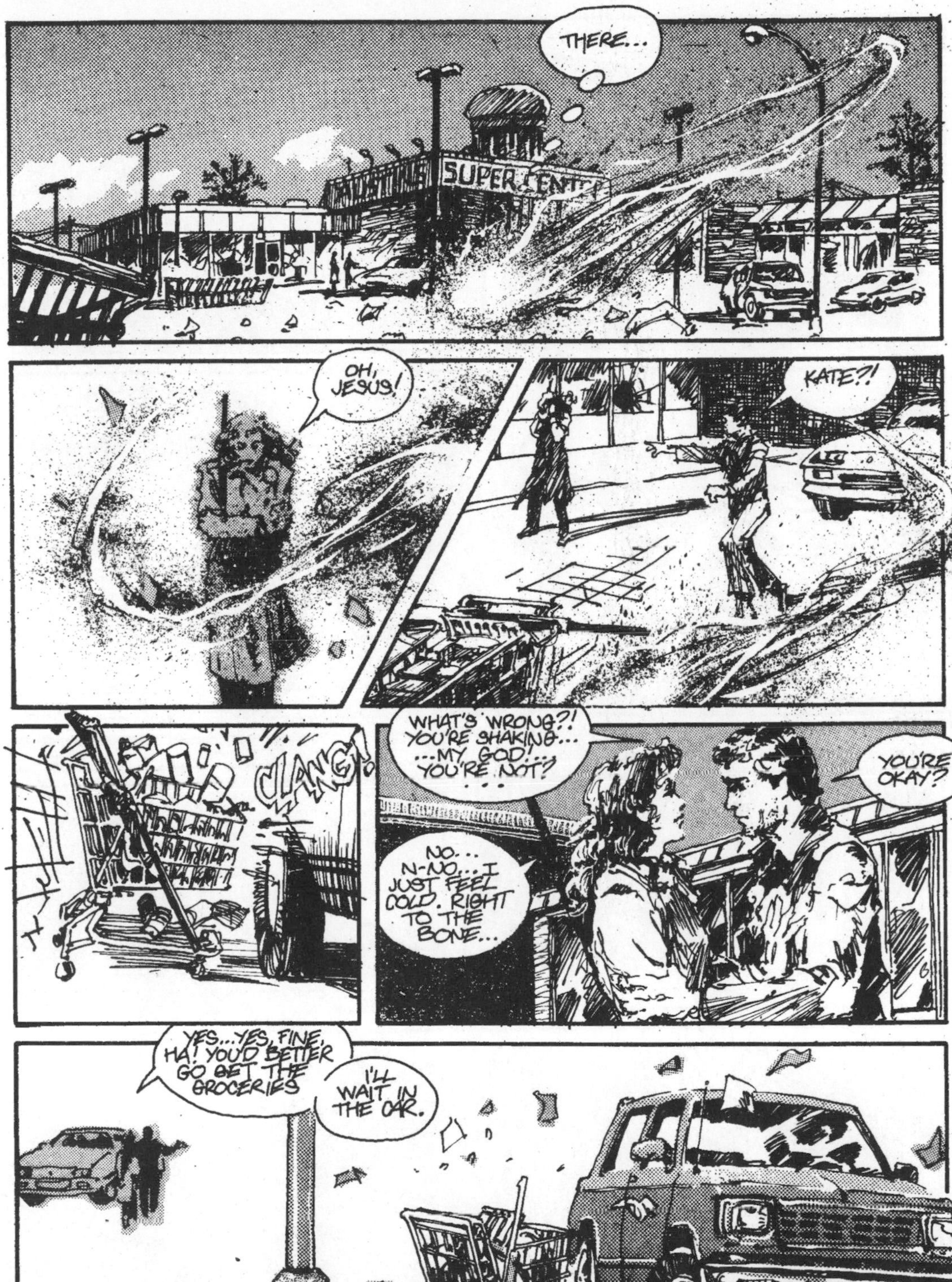
THERE...
OH, JESUS!
KATE?!
CLANG!
WHAT'S WRONG?! YOU'RE SHAKING... ...MY GOD! ...YOU'RE NOT? ...
YOU'RE OKAY?
NO... N-NO... I JUST FEEL COLD. RIGHT TO THE BONE...
YES...YES, FINE. HA! YOU'D BETTER GO GET THE GROCERIES
I'LL WAIT IN THE CAR.

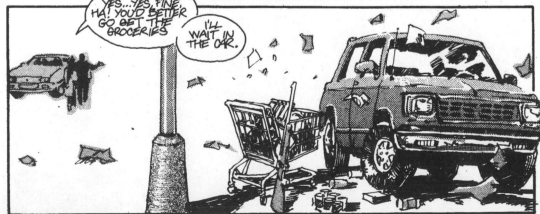

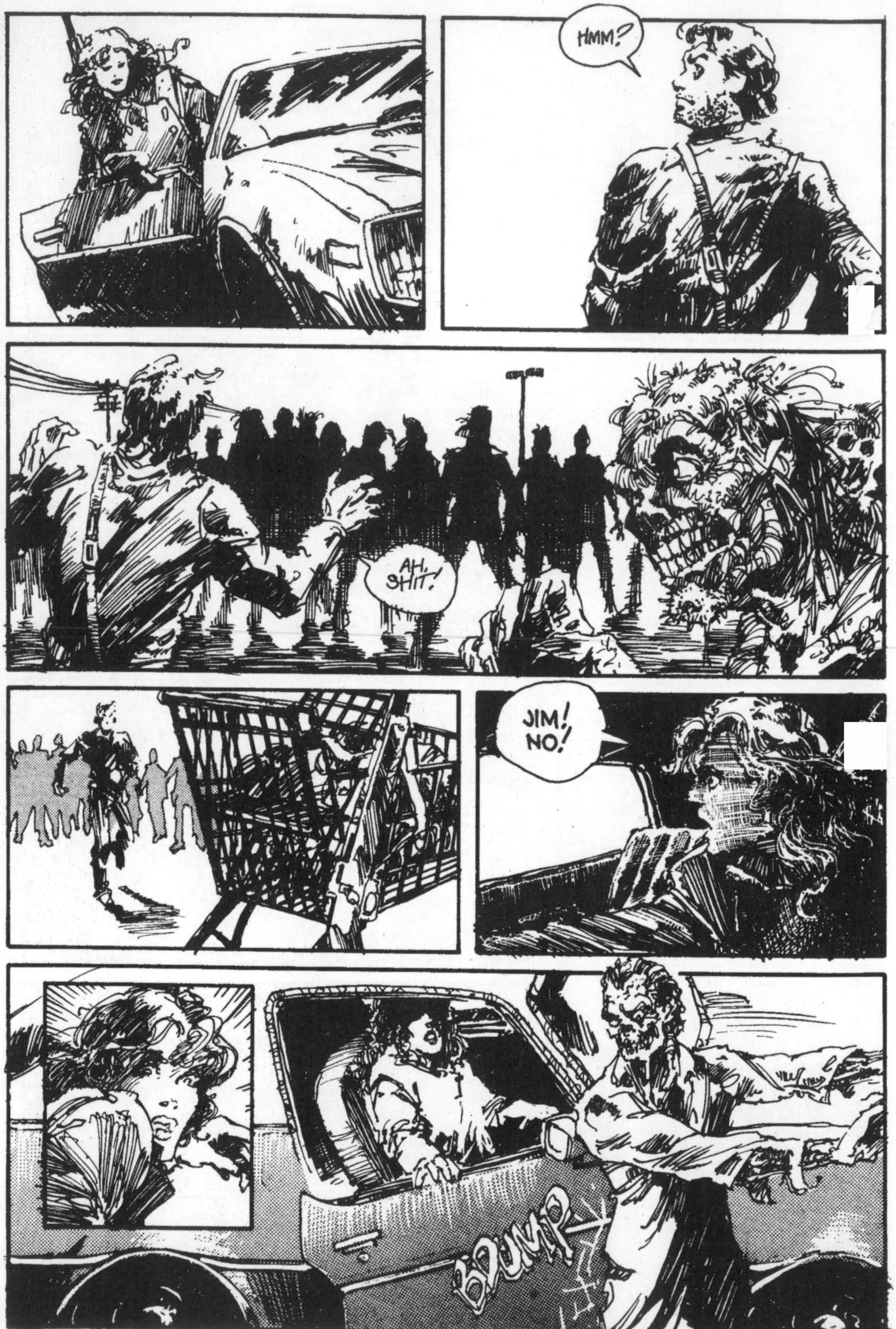
HMM?
AH, SHIT!
JIM! NO!
BDUMP

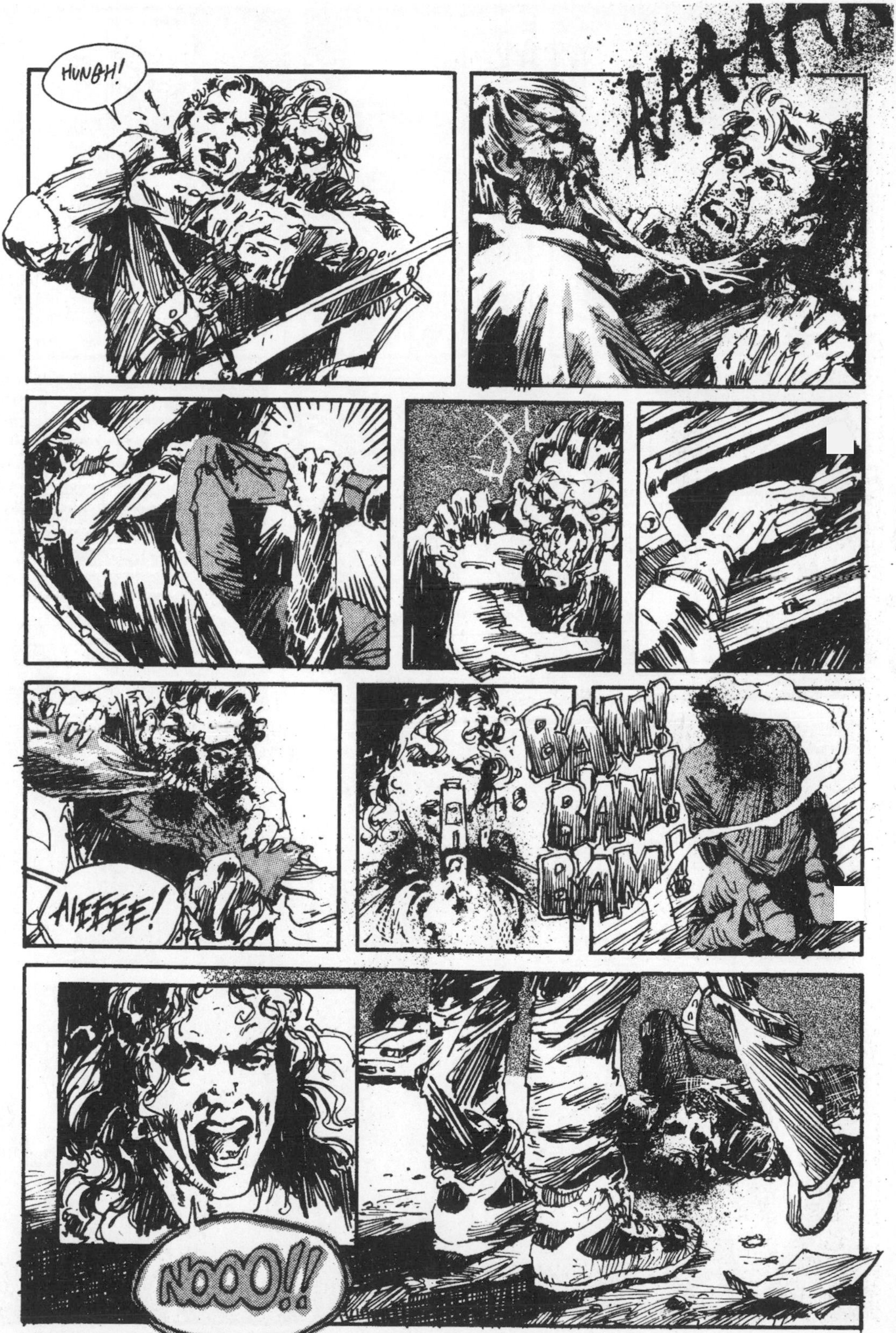
HUNGH!
AAAAR
AIEEEE!
BAM! BAM! BAM! BAM!
NOOO!!

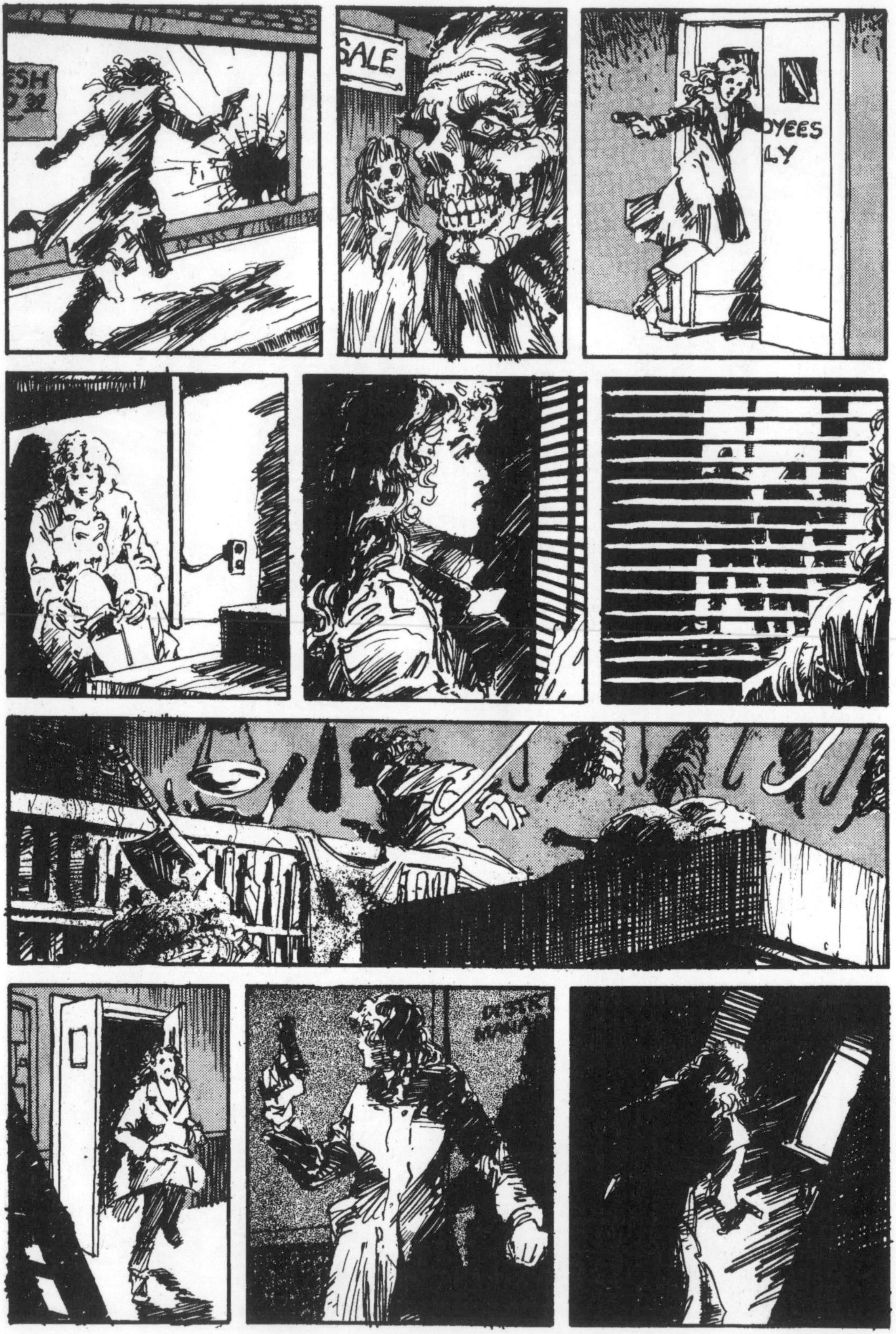
ESH
SALE
OYEES
LY

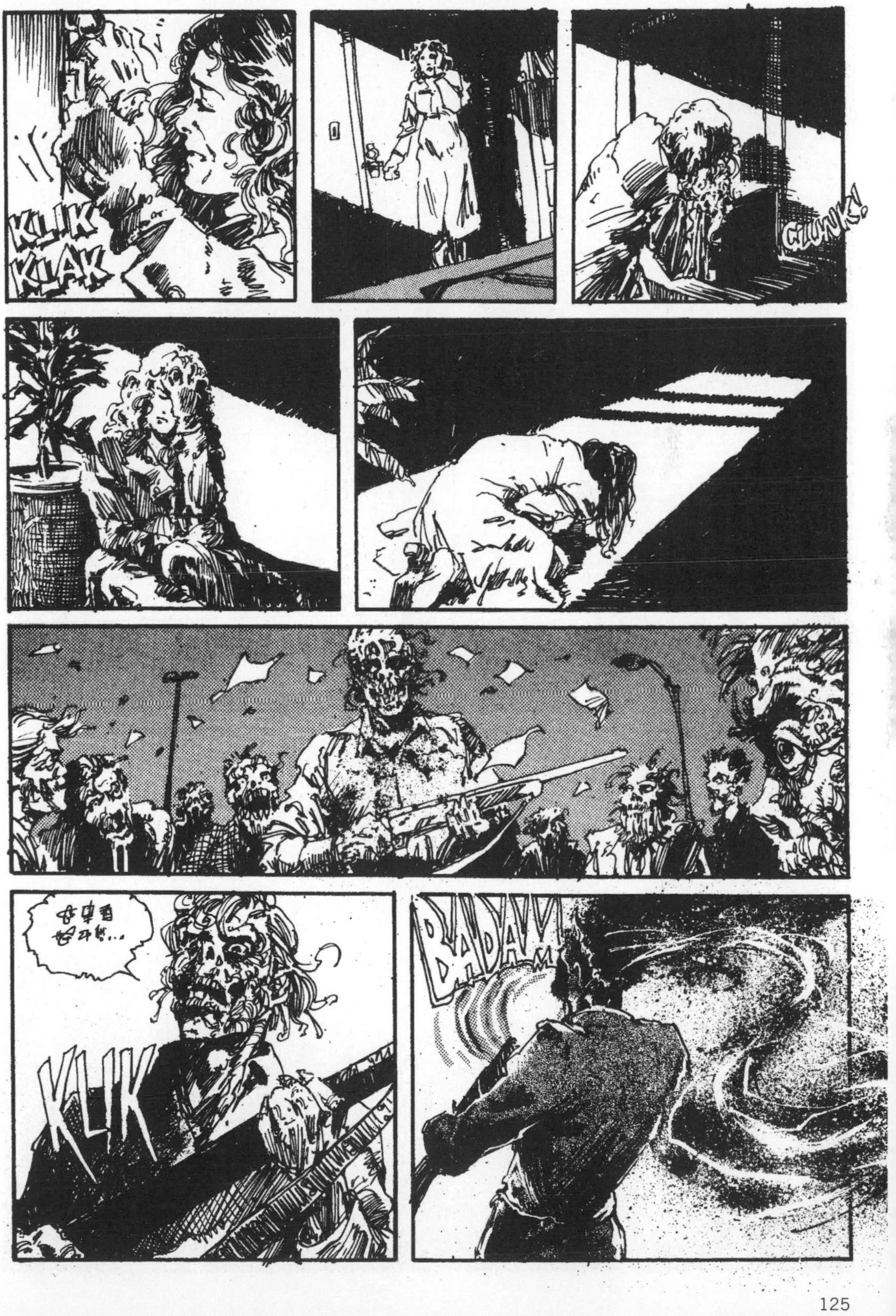
KLIK
KLAK
CLUNK!
KLIK
BADAM

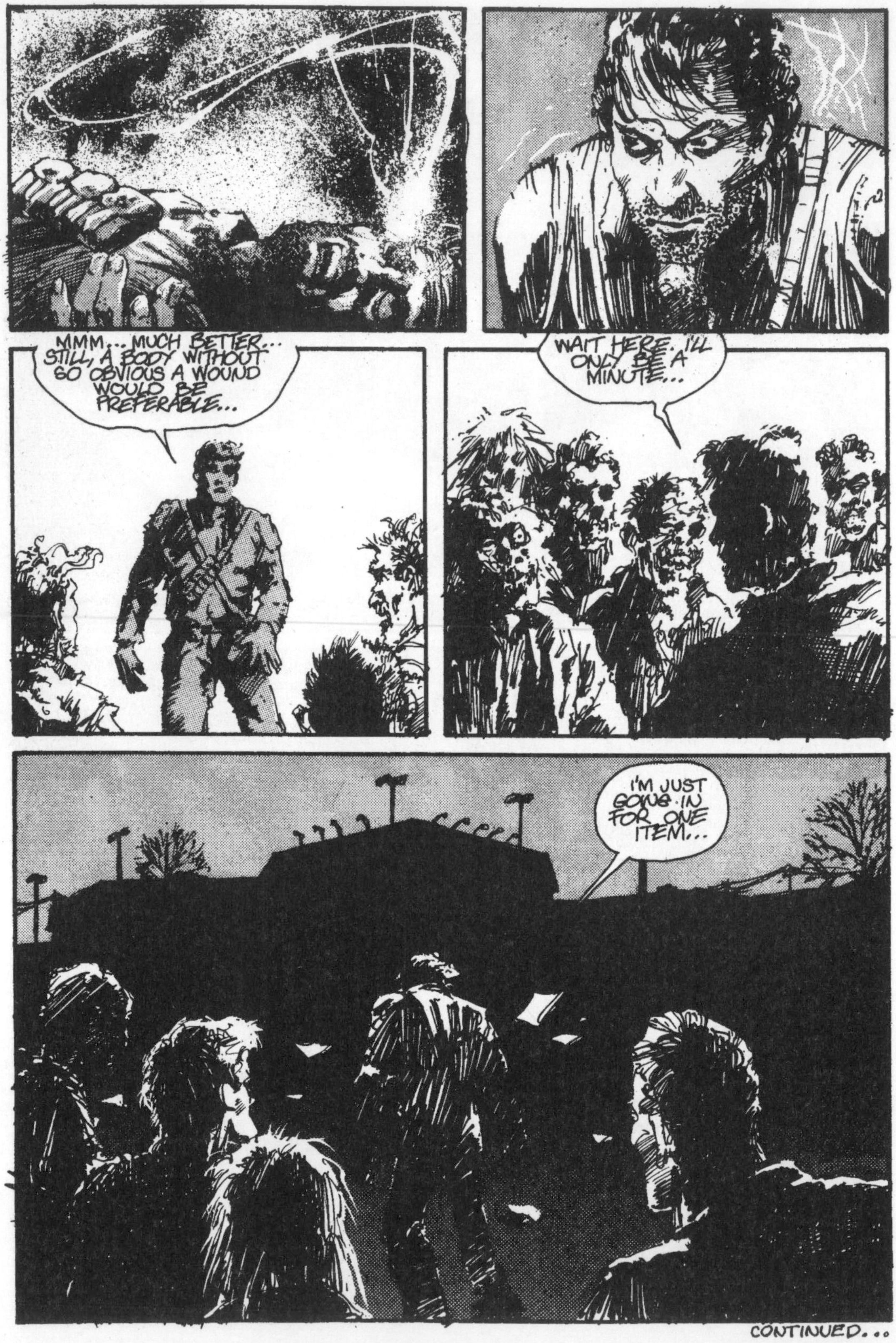
MMM... MUCH BETTER... STILL, A BODY WITHOUT SO OBVIOUS A WOUND WOULD BE PREFERABLE...
WAIT HERE. I'LL ONLY BE A MINUTE...
I'M JUST GOING IN FOR ONE ITEM...

CONTINUED...

DEADTALES

"AMY" Script-Mark Bloodworth Pencils-Paul Daly
Inks+Letters-Vincent Locke

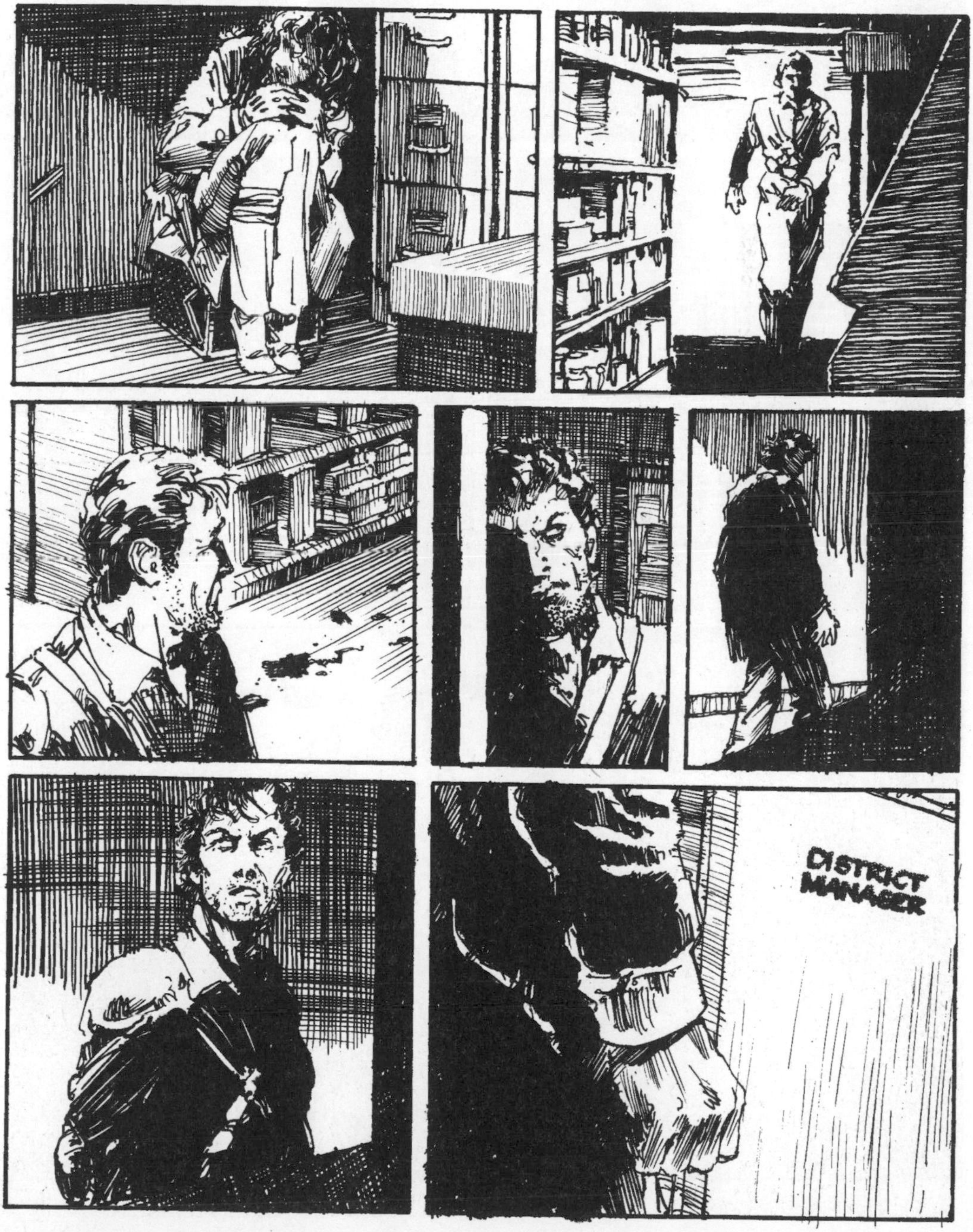
DISTRICT
MANAGER

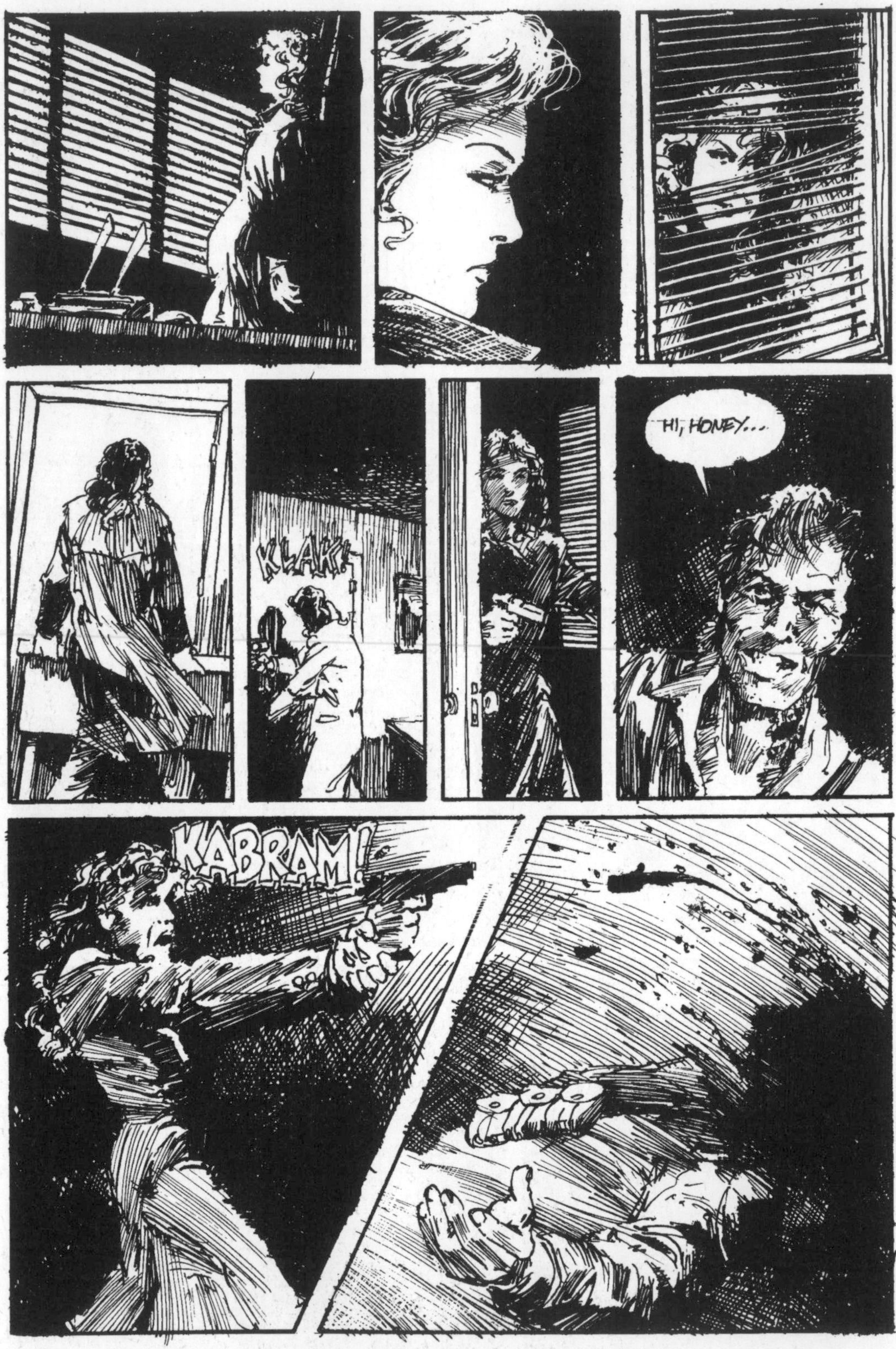
KLAK!
HI, HONEY...
KABRAM!

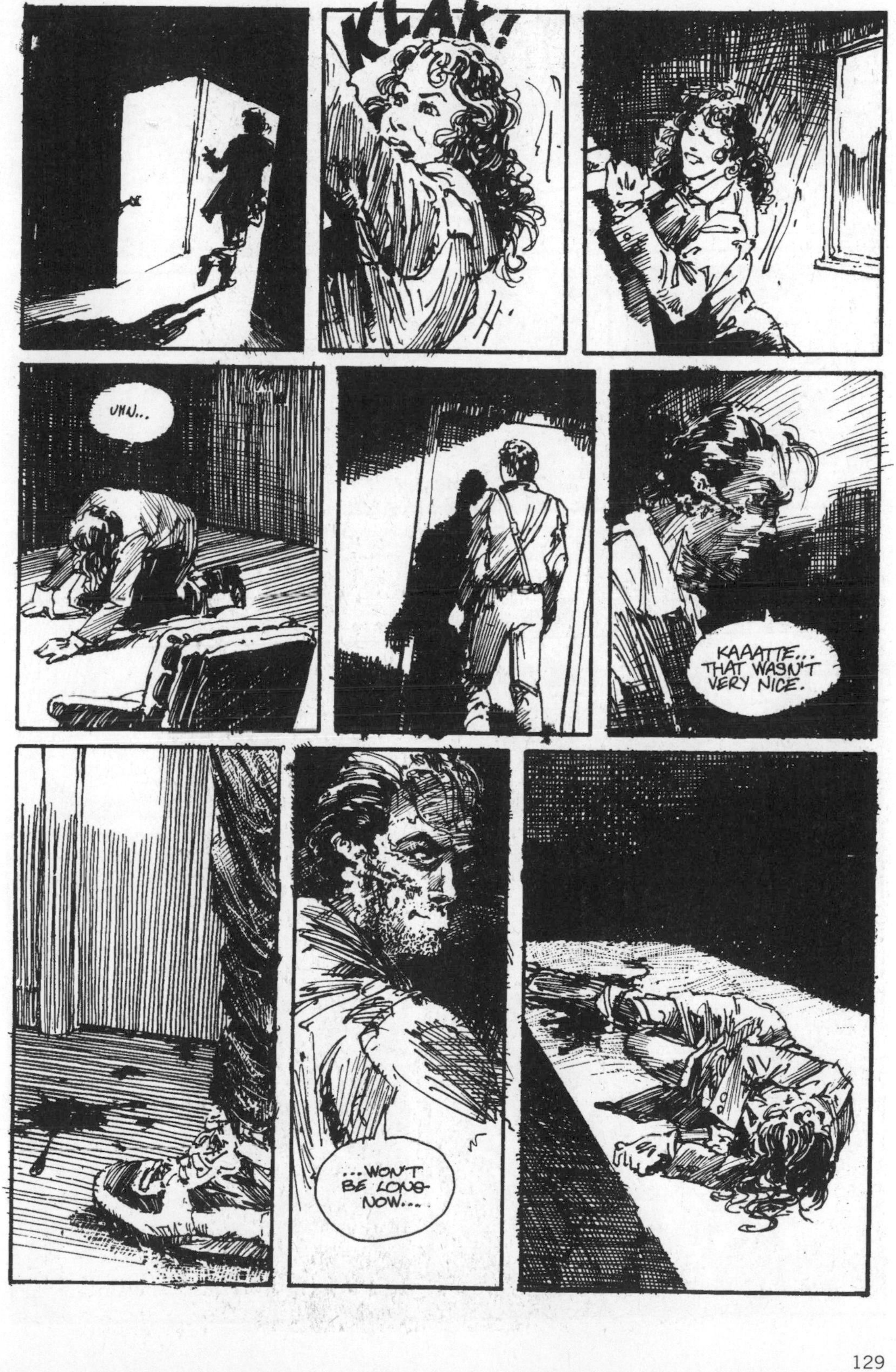
KLAK!
UMN...
KAAATTE... THAT WASN'T VERY NICE.
...WON'T BE LONG NOW...

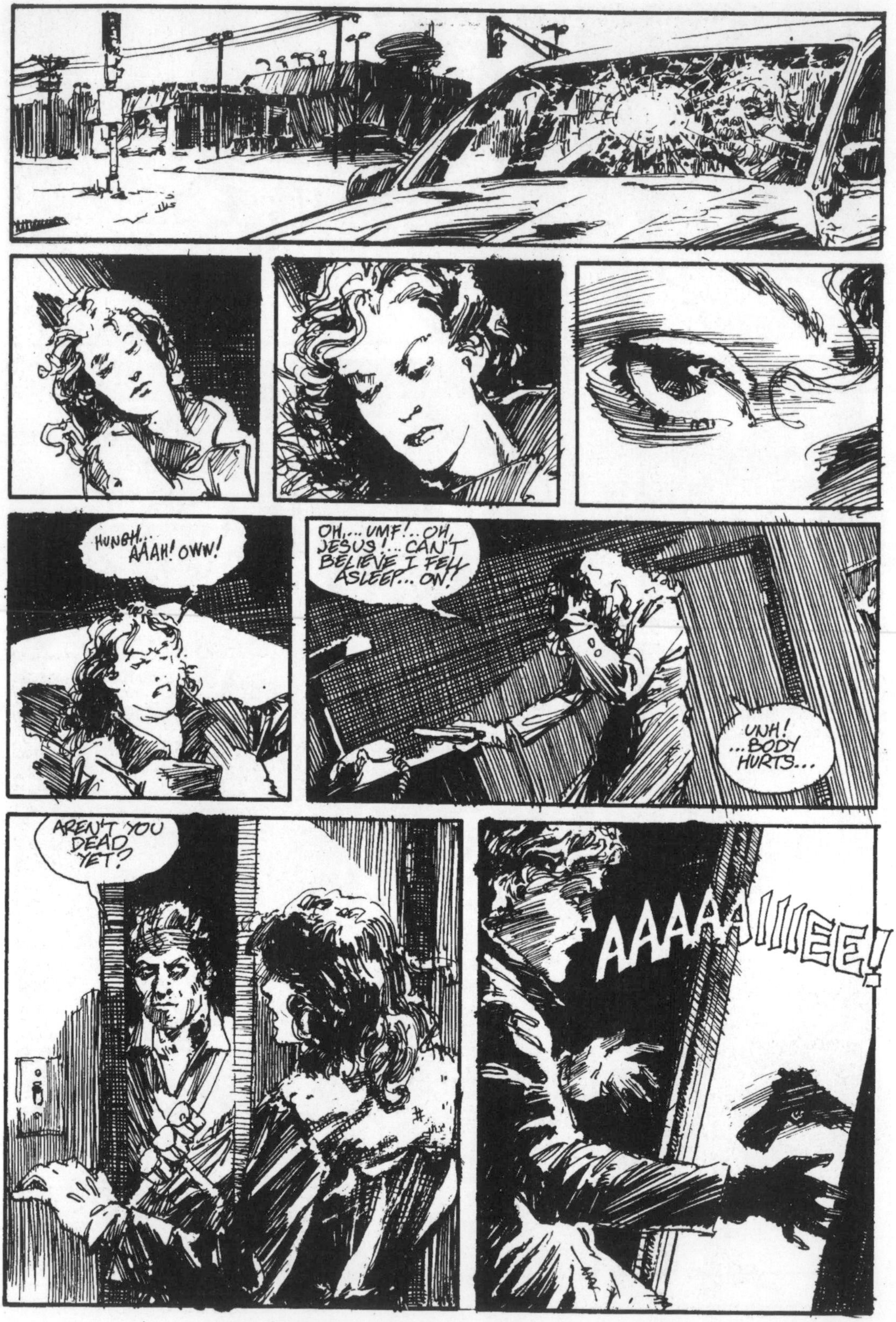
HUNGH... AAAH! OWW!
OH,... UMF!... OH, JESUS!... CAN'T BELIEVE I FELL ASLEEP... ON!
UNH! ...BODY HURTS...
AREN'T YOU DEAD YET?
AAAAAIIIEE!

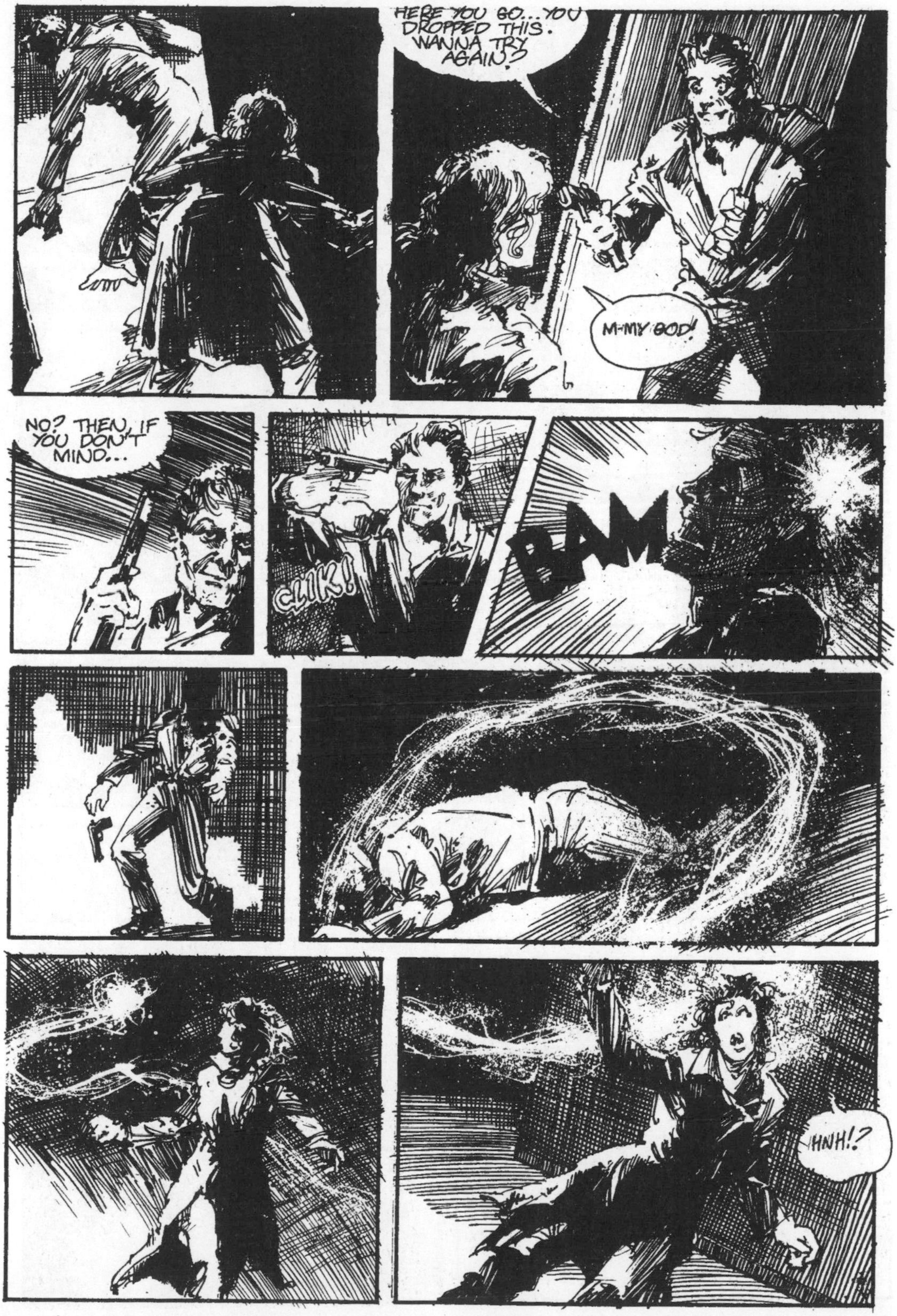
HERE YOU GO... YOU DROPPED THIS. WANNA TRY AGAIN?
M-MY GOD!
NO? THEN, IF YOU DON'T MIND...
CLIK!
BAM
HNH!?

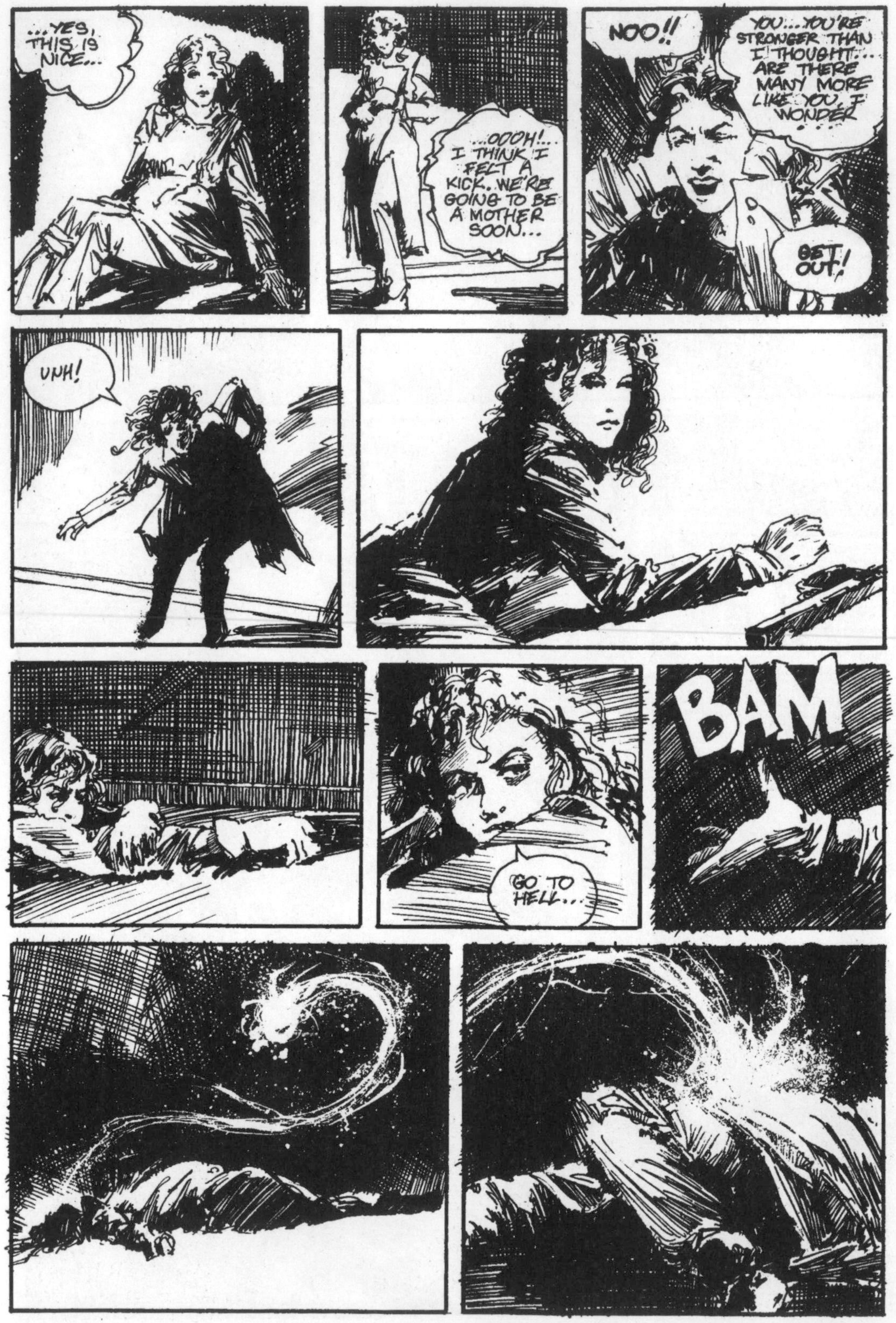
...YES, THIS IS NICE...
...OOOH!... I THINK I FELT A KICK. WE'RE GOING TO BE A MOTHER SOON...
NOO!!
YOU... YOU'RE STRONGER THAN I THOUGHT... ARE THERE MANY MORE LIKE YOU, I WONDER
GET OUT!
UNH!
GO TO HELL...
BAM

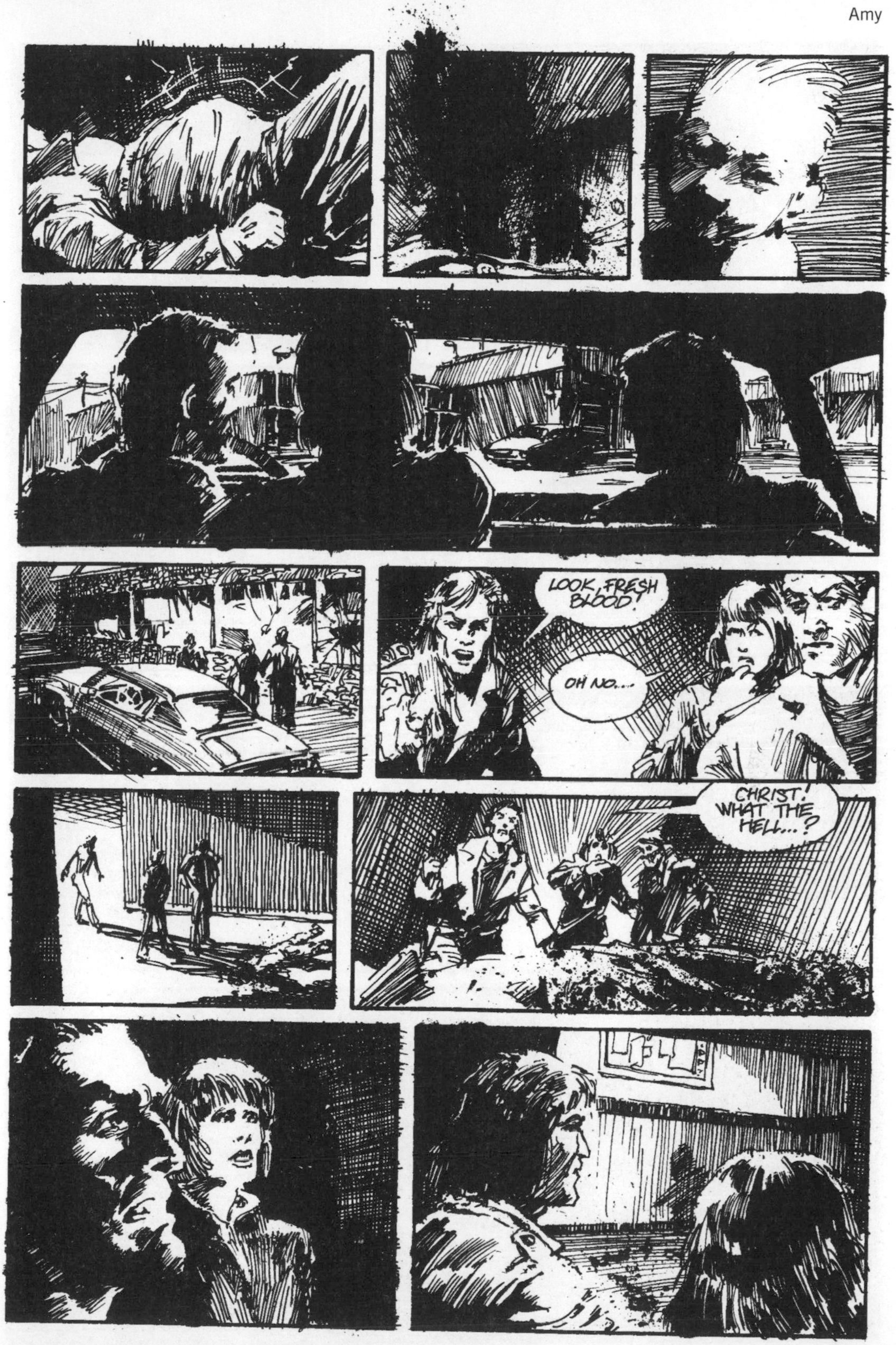
LOOK, FRESH BLOOD!
OH NO....
CHRIST! WHAT THE HELL...?

JESUS!

SHE WAS GOING TO CALL IT EITHER ANDREW OR AMY...

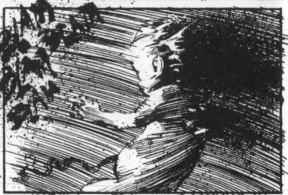

AMY...

Black Sabbath (1986)

Creators: Stuart Kerr (script), Vincent Locke (art)

Black Sabbath was the first time Vincent Locke illustrated a *Deadworld* story. In it, a little window-shopping proves to be dangerous in a world that has been trashed by hungry zombies.

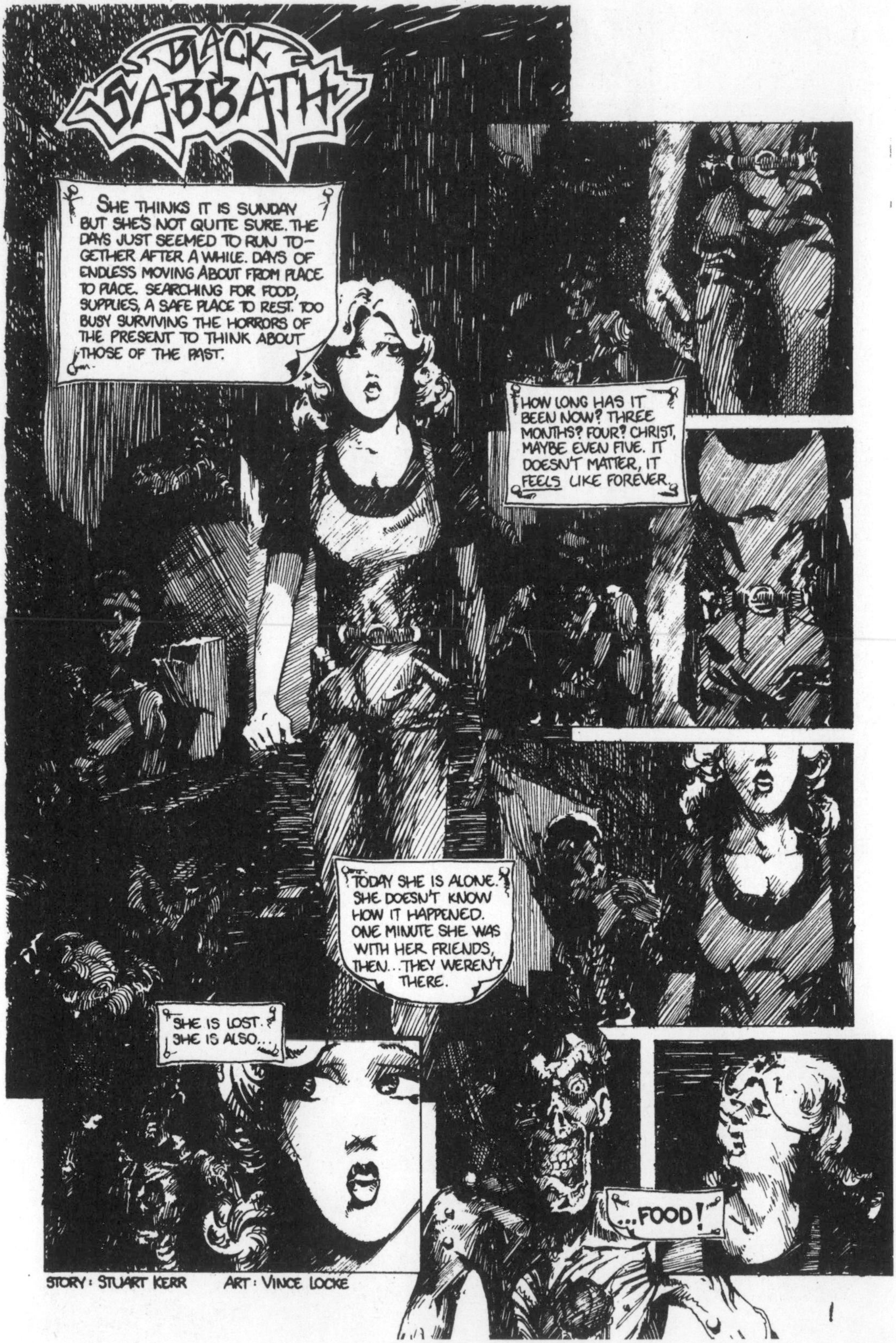
BLACK SABBATH
SHE THINKS IT IS SUNDAY BUT SHE'S NOT QUITE SURE. THE DAYS JUST SEEMED TO RUN TOGETHER AFTER A WHILE. DAYS OF ENDLESS MOVING ABOUT FROM PLACE TO PLACE. SEARCHING FOR FOOD, SUPPLIES, A SAFE PLACE TO REST. TOO BUSY SURVIVING THE HORRORS OF THE PRESENT TO THINK ABOUT THOSE OF THE PAST.
HOW LONG HAS IT BEEN NOW? THREE MONTHS? FOUR? CHRIST, MAYBE EVEN FIVE. IT DOESN'T MATTER, IT FEELS LIKE FOREVER.
TODAY SHE IS ALONE. SHE DOESN'T KNOW HOW IT HAPPENED. ONE MINUTE SHE WAS WITH HER FRIENDS, THEN... THEY WEREN'T THERE.
SHE IS LOST. SHE IS ALSO...
...FOOD!
STORY: STUART KERR ART: VINCE LOCKE

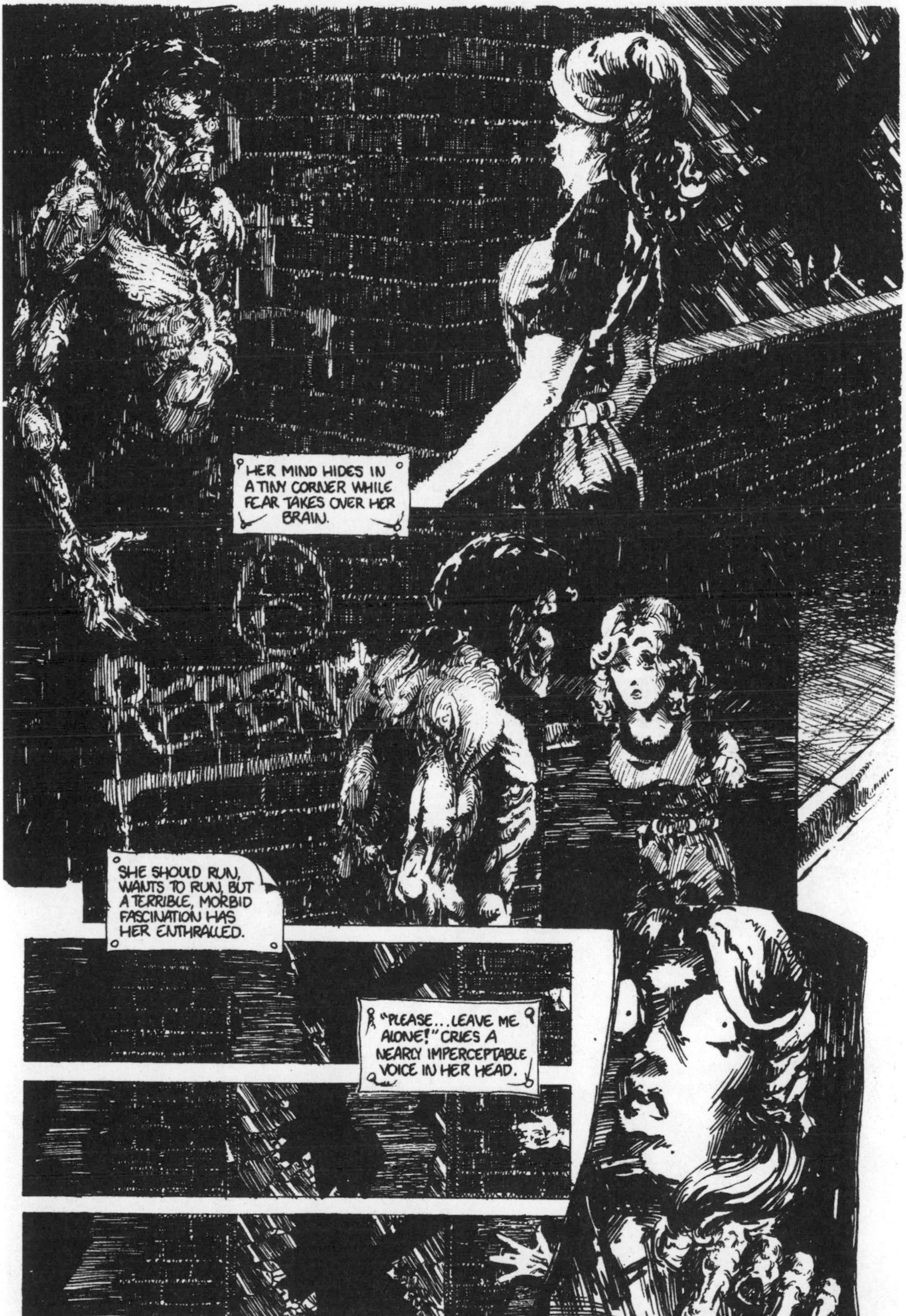
HER MIND HIDES IN A TINY CORNER WHILE FEAR TAKES OVER HER BRAIN.
SHE SHOULD RUN, WANTS TO RUN, BUT A TERRIBLE, MORBID FASCINATION HAS HER ENTHRALLED.
"PLEASE.... LEAVE ME ALONE!" CRIES A NEARLY IMPERCEPTABLE VOICE IN HER HEAD.

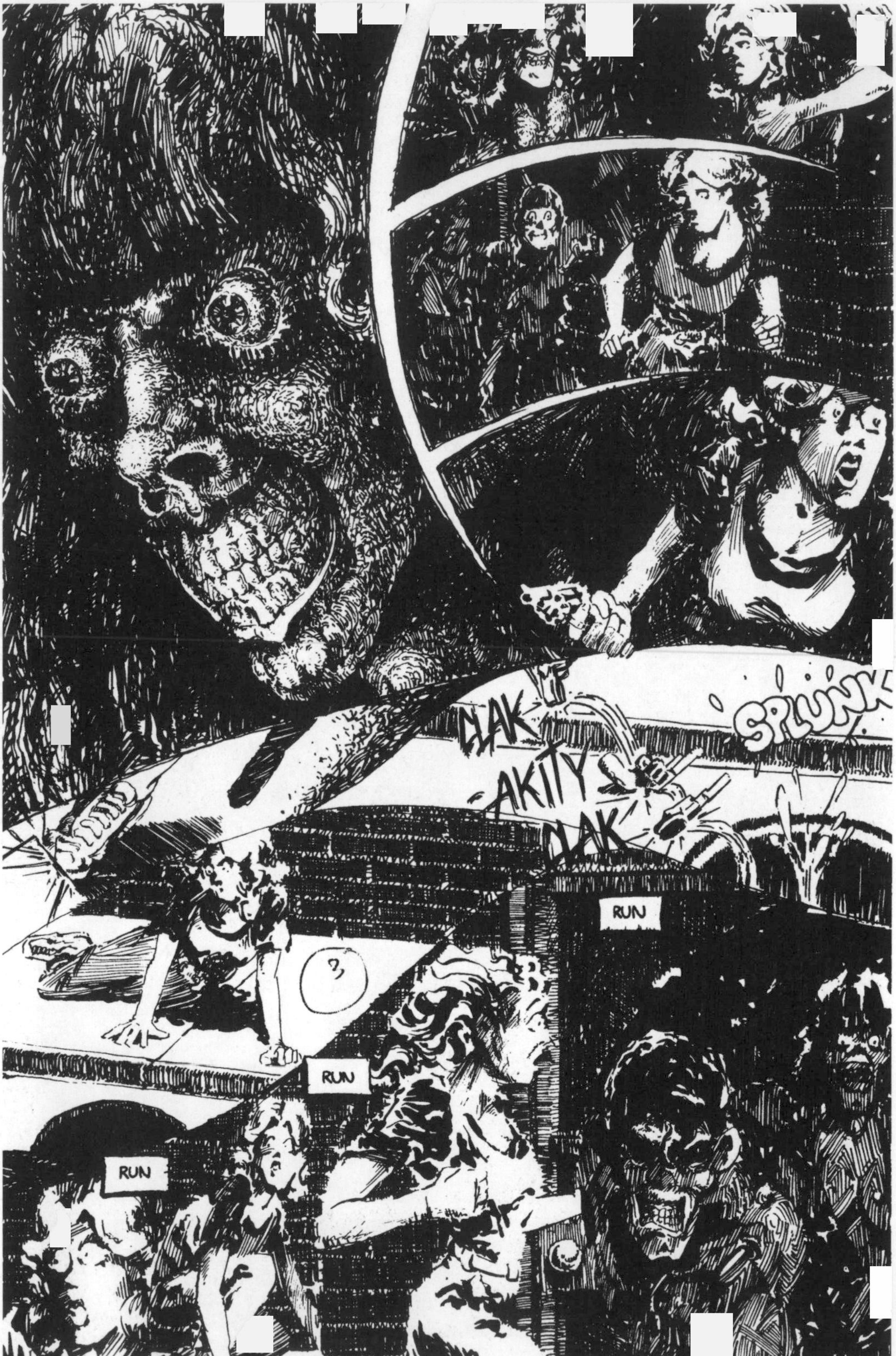
CLAK
AKITY
NAK
SPLUNK
RUN
RUN
RUN

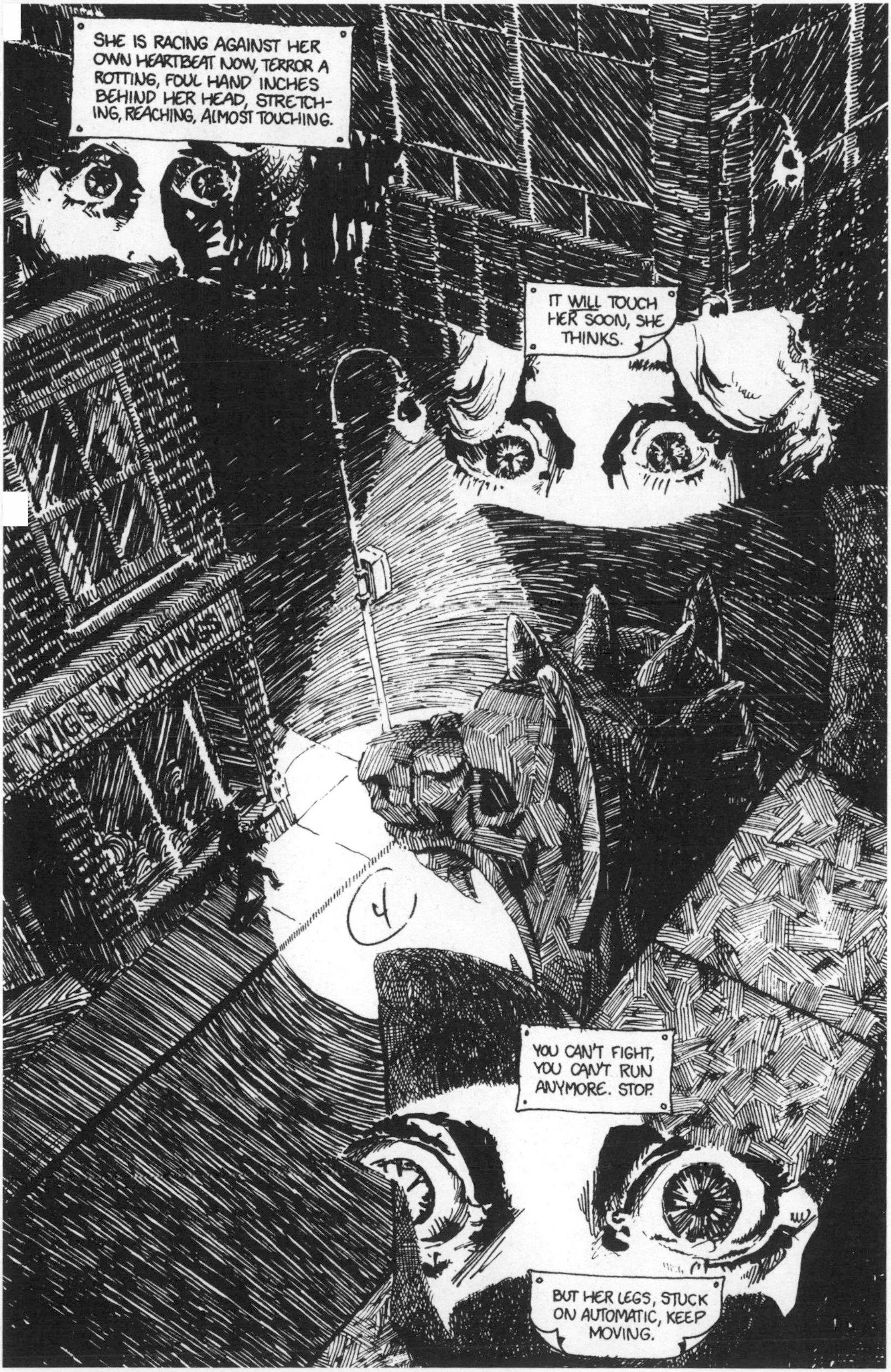
SHE IS RACING AGAINST HER OWN HEARTBEAT NOW, TERROR A ROTTING, FOUL HAND INCHES BEHIND HER HEAD, STRETCHING, REACHING, ALMOST TOUCHING.
IT WILL TOUCH HER SOON, SHE THINKS.
YOU CAN'T FIGHT, YOU CAN'T RUN ANYMORE. STOP.
BUT HER LEGS, STUCK ON AUTOMATIC, KEEP MOVING.

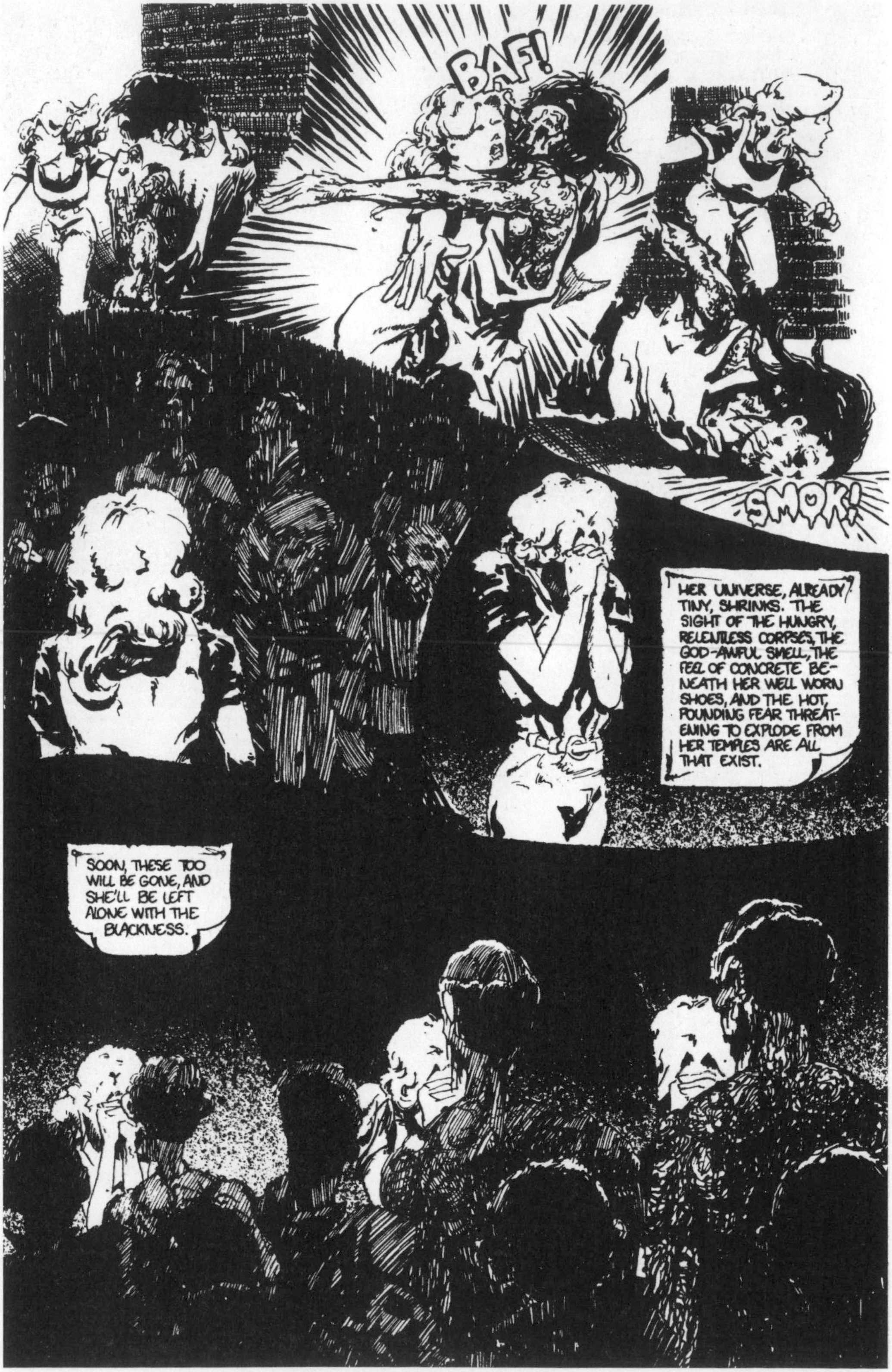
BAF!
SMOK!
HER UNIVERSE, ALREADY TINY, SHRINKS. THE SIGHT OF THE HUNGRY, RELENTLESS CORPSES, THE GOD-AWFUL SMELL, THE FEEL OF CONCRETE BE-NEATH HER WELL WORN SHOES, AND THE HOT, POUNDING FEAR THREAT-ENING TO EXPLODE FROM HER TEMPLES ARE ALL THAT EXIST.
SOON, THESE TOO WILL BE GONE, AND SHE'LL BE LEFT ALONE WITH THE BLACKNESS.

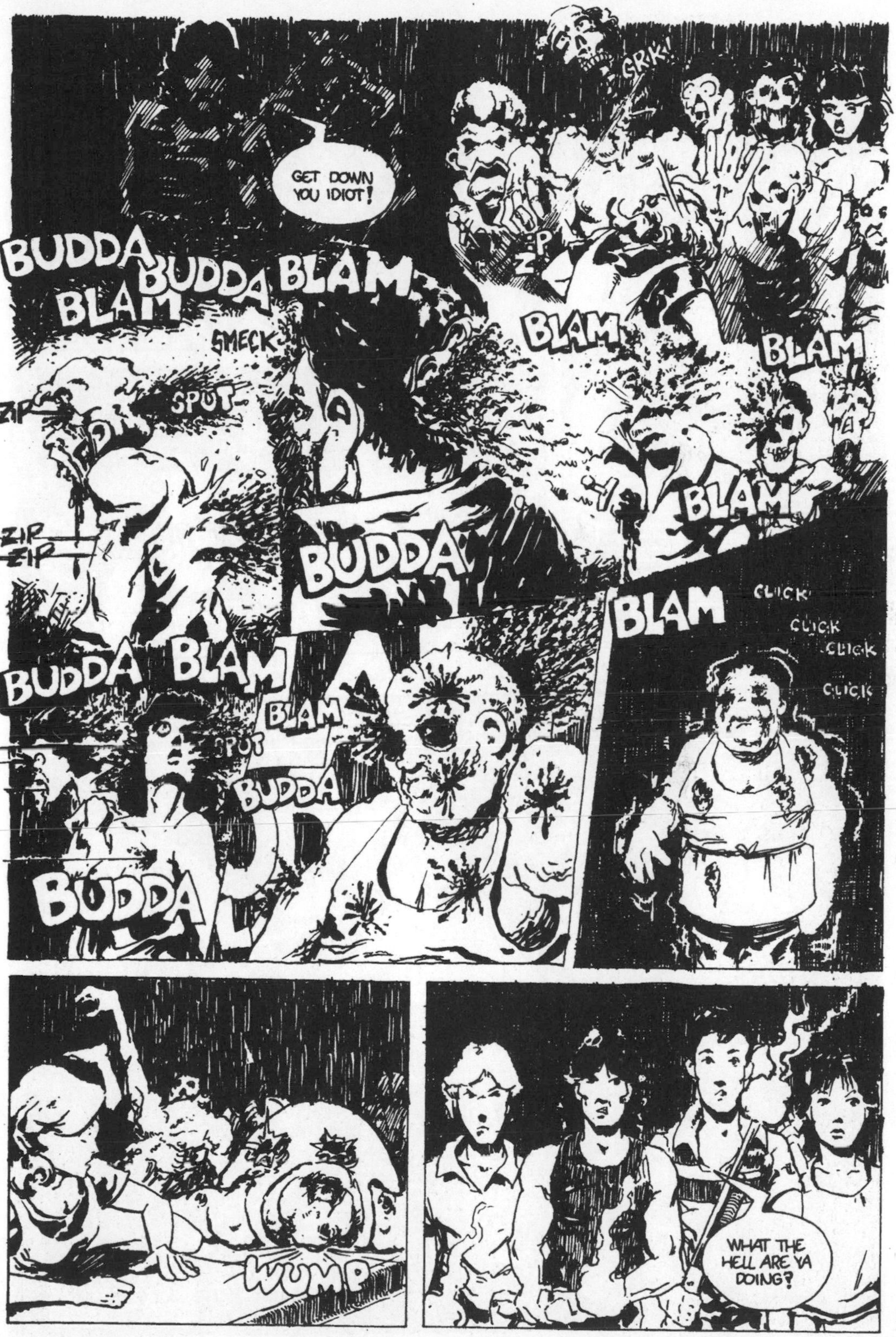
GRK!
GET DOWN YOU IDIOT!
BUDDA BUDDA BLAM BLAM
SMECK
ZIP
SPUT
BLAM
BLAM
BLAM
ZIP ZIP
BUDDA
BUDDA BLAM
BLAM
SPUT
BUDDA
BUDDA
BLAM
CLICK
CLICK
CLICK
CLICK
WUMP
WHAT THE HELL ARE YA DOING?

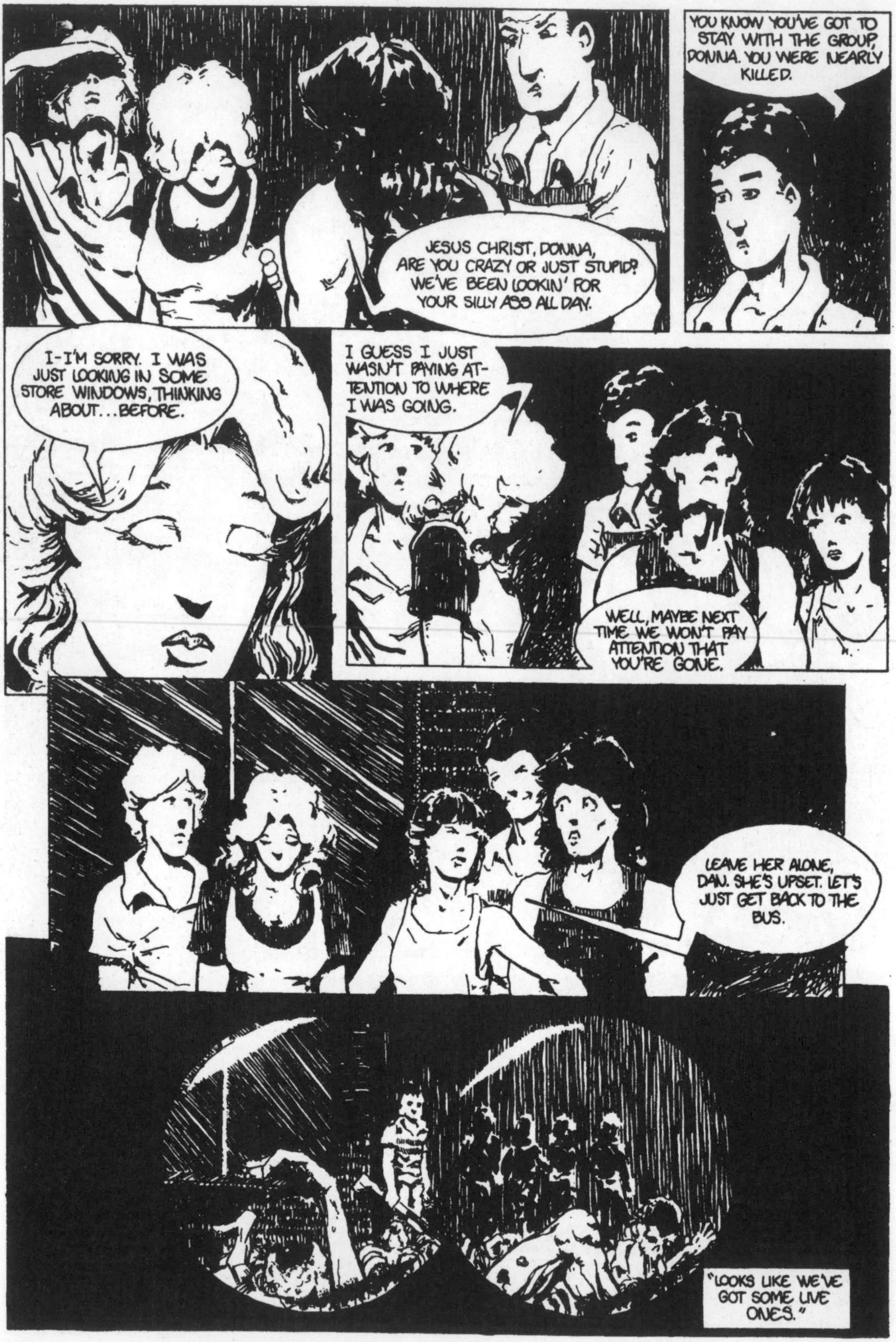
JESUS CHRIST, DONNA, ARE YOU CRAZY OR JUST STUPID? WE'VE BEEN LOOKIN' FOR YOUR SILLY ASS ALL DAY.
YOU KNOW YOU'VE GOT TO STAY WITH THE GROUP, DONNA. YOU WERE NEARLY KILLED.
I-I'M SORRY. I WAS JUST LOOKING IN SOME STORE WINDOWS, THINKING ABOUT... BEFORE.
I GUESS I JUST WASN'T PAYING ATTENTION TO WHERE I WAS GOING.
WELL, MAYBE NEXT TIME WE WON'T PAY ATTENTION THAT YOU'RE GONE.
LEAVE HER ALONE, DAN. SHE'S UPSET. LET'S JUST GET BACK TO THE BUS.
"LOOKS LIKE WE'VE GOT SOME LIVE ONES."

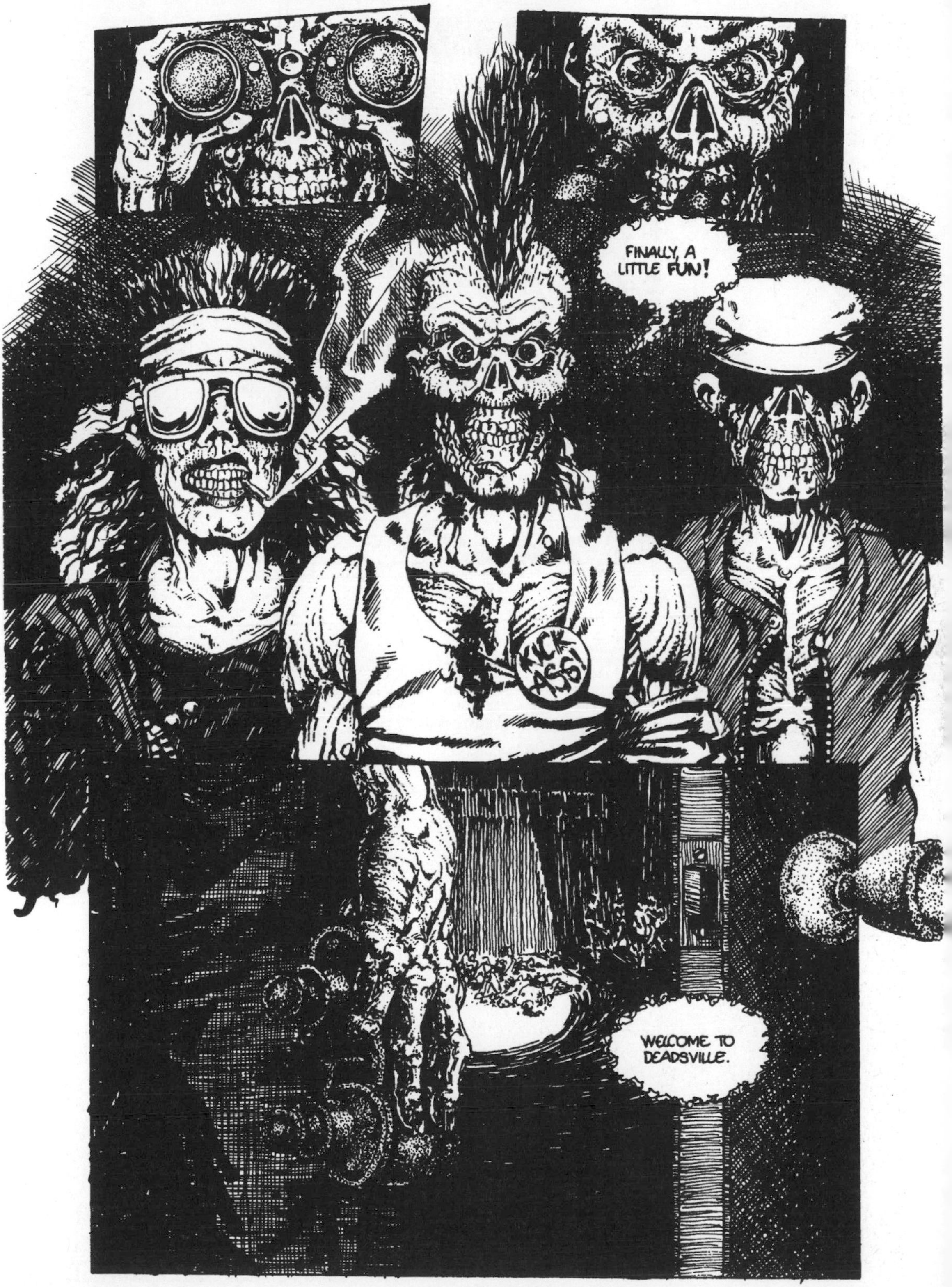
FINALLY, A LITTLE FUN!
KICK ASS!
WELCOME TO DEADSVILLE.

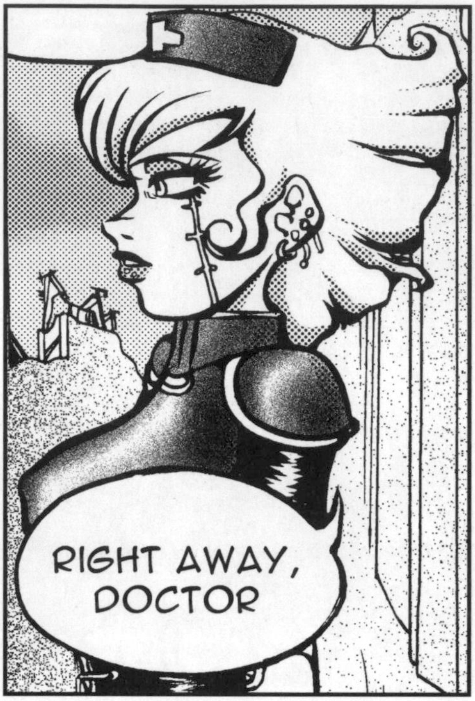
RIGHT AWAY, DOCTOR

M*A*Z*H (2008)

Creators: Andrew Davies (script), Laura Watton (art)

M*A*Z*H injects humour without becoming completely slapstick. This is just another mad interlude in a post-apocalyptic world where a strange doctor brings help to the injured in an unusual way.

Laura Watton is one of the founder members of Sweatdrop Studios and has been a freelance illustrator since 1994. Laura's artwork has appeared in books from Ilex Press, Collins, AC & Black and Tokyopop.

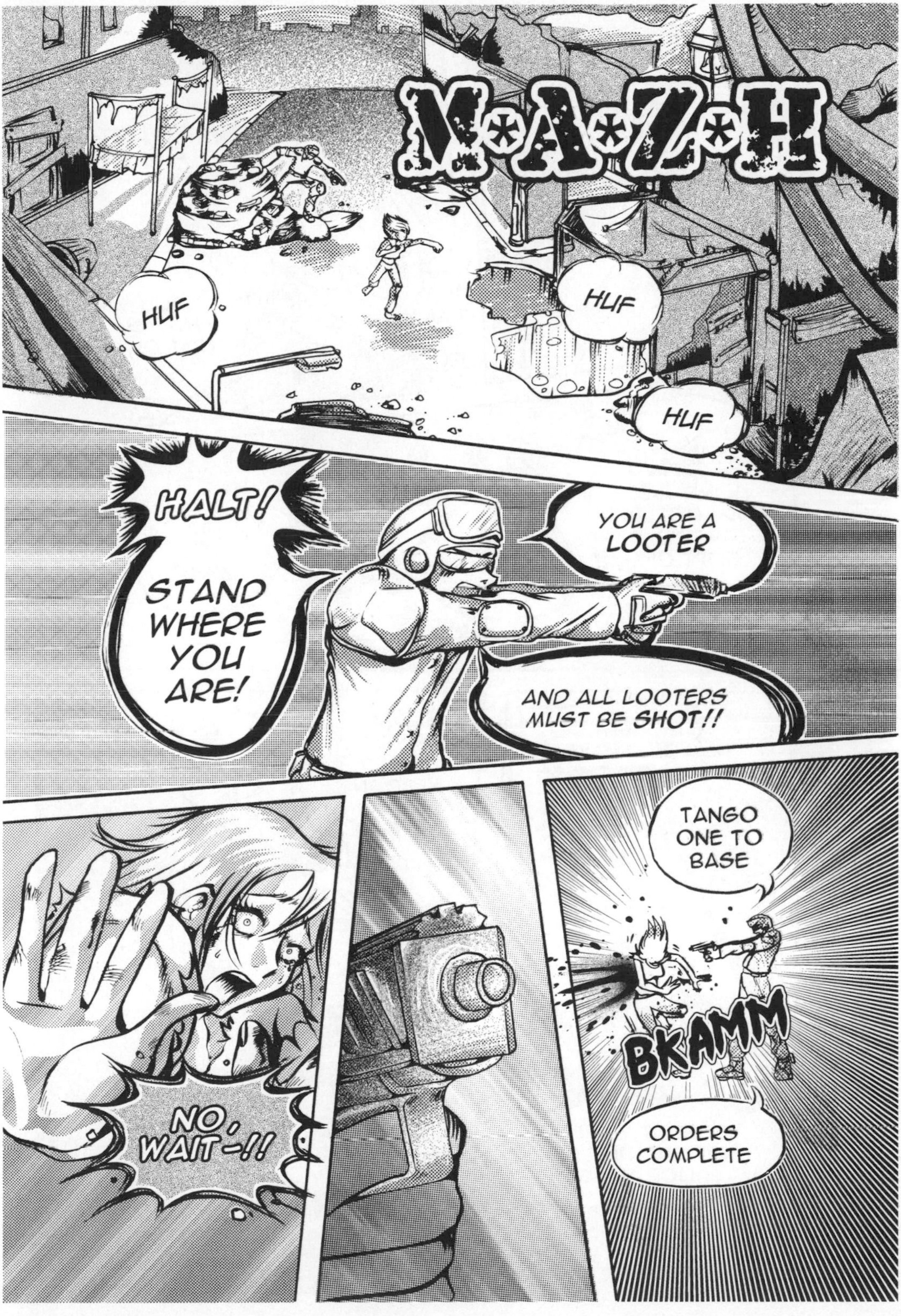
M*A*Z*H
HUF
HUF
HUF
HALT!
STAND WHERE YOU ARE!
YOU ARE A LOOTER
AND ALL LOOTERS MUST BE SHOT!!
NO, WAIT-!!
TANGO ONE TO BASE
BKAMM
ORDERS COMPLETE

WELL, *THAT'S* NOT ON

EXECUTING SOMEONE FOR LOOTING IN THIS SORT OF AREA...

...JUST *NOT* RIGHT

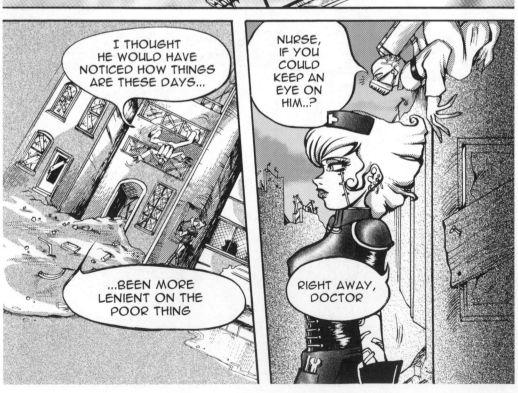

I THOUGHT HE WOULD HAVE NOTICED HOW THINGS ARE THESE DAYS...

...BEEN MORE LENIENT ON THE POOR THING

NURSE, IF YOU COULD KEEP AN EYE ON HIM..?

RIGHT AWAY, DOCTOR

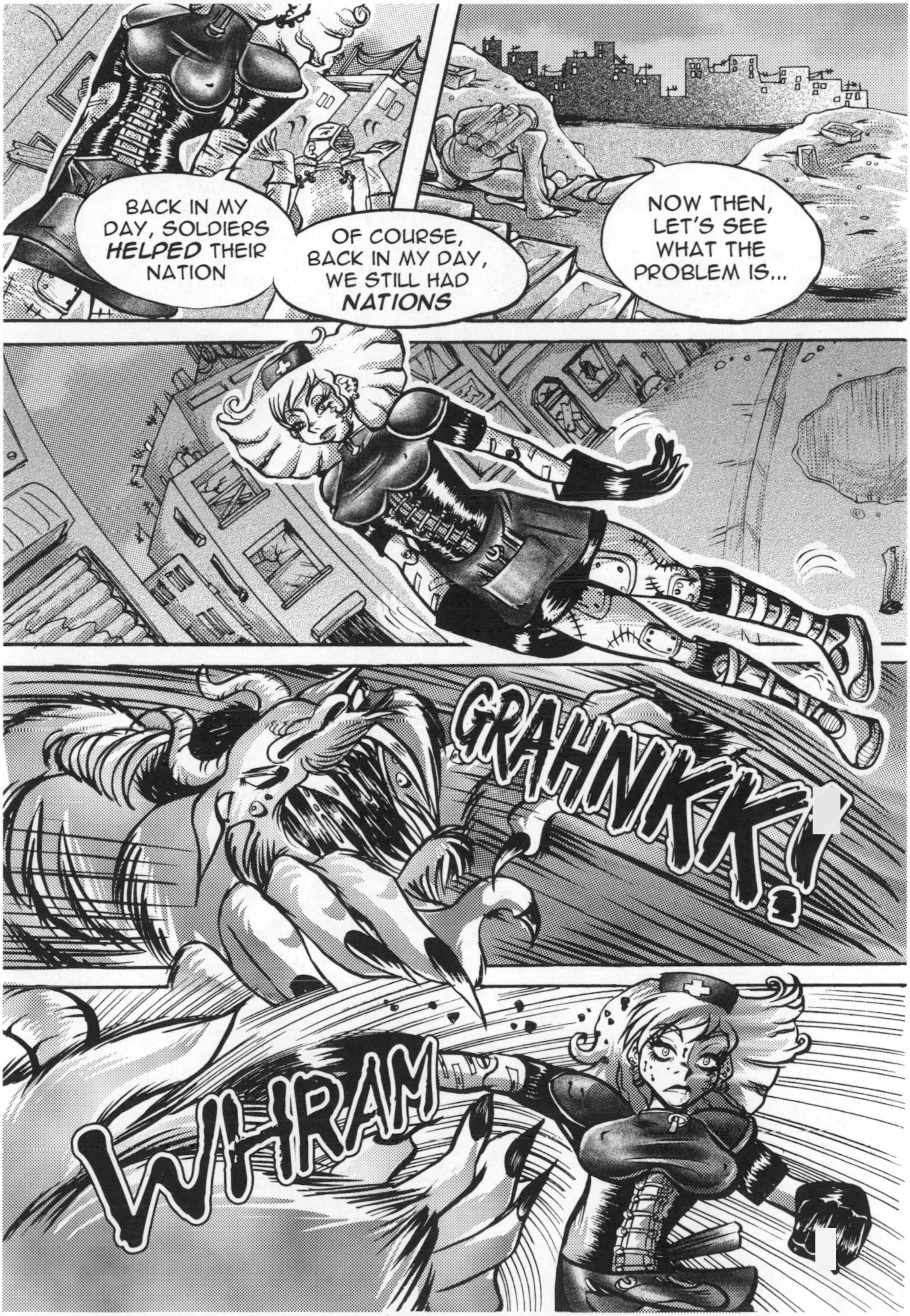

BACK IN MY DAY, SOLDIERS HELPED THEIR NATION
OF COURSE, BACK IN MY DAY, WE STILL HAD NATIONS
NOW THEN, LET'S SEE WHAT THE PROBLEM IS...
GRAHNKKK!
WHRAM

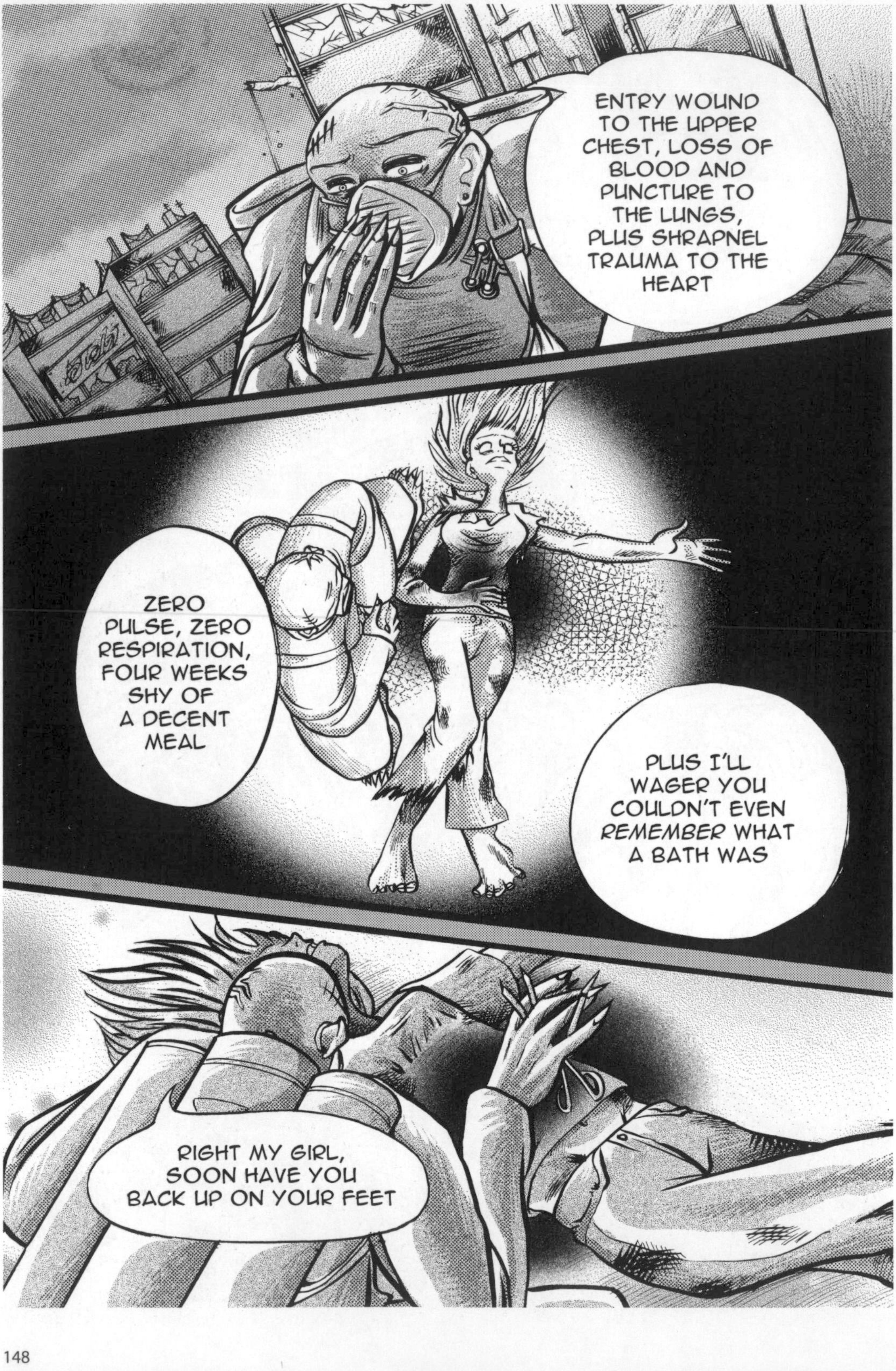
ENTRY WOUND TO THE UPPER CHEST, LOSS OF BLOOD AND PUNCTURE TO THE LUNGS, PLUS SHRAPNEL TRAUMA TO THE HEART
ZERO PULSE, ZERO RESPIRATION, FOUR WEEKS SHY OF A DECENT MEAL
PLUS I'LL WAGER YOU COULDN'T EVEN *REMEMBER* WHAT A BATH WAS
RIGHT MY GIRL, SOON HAVE YOU BACK UP ON YOUR FEET

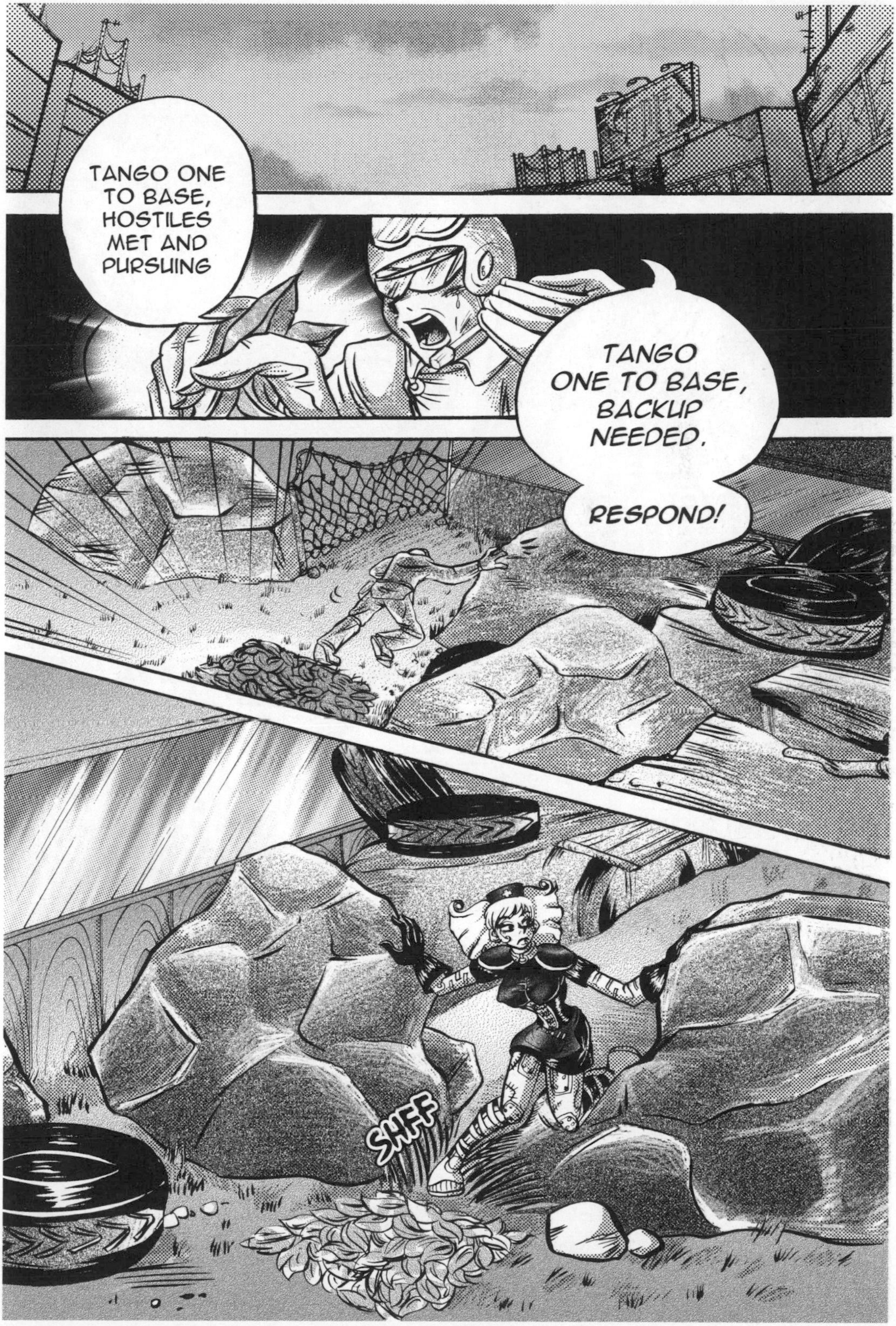
TANGO ONE TO BASE, HOSTILES MET AND PURSUING
TANGO ONE TO BASE, BACKUP NEEDED.
RESPOND!
SHFF

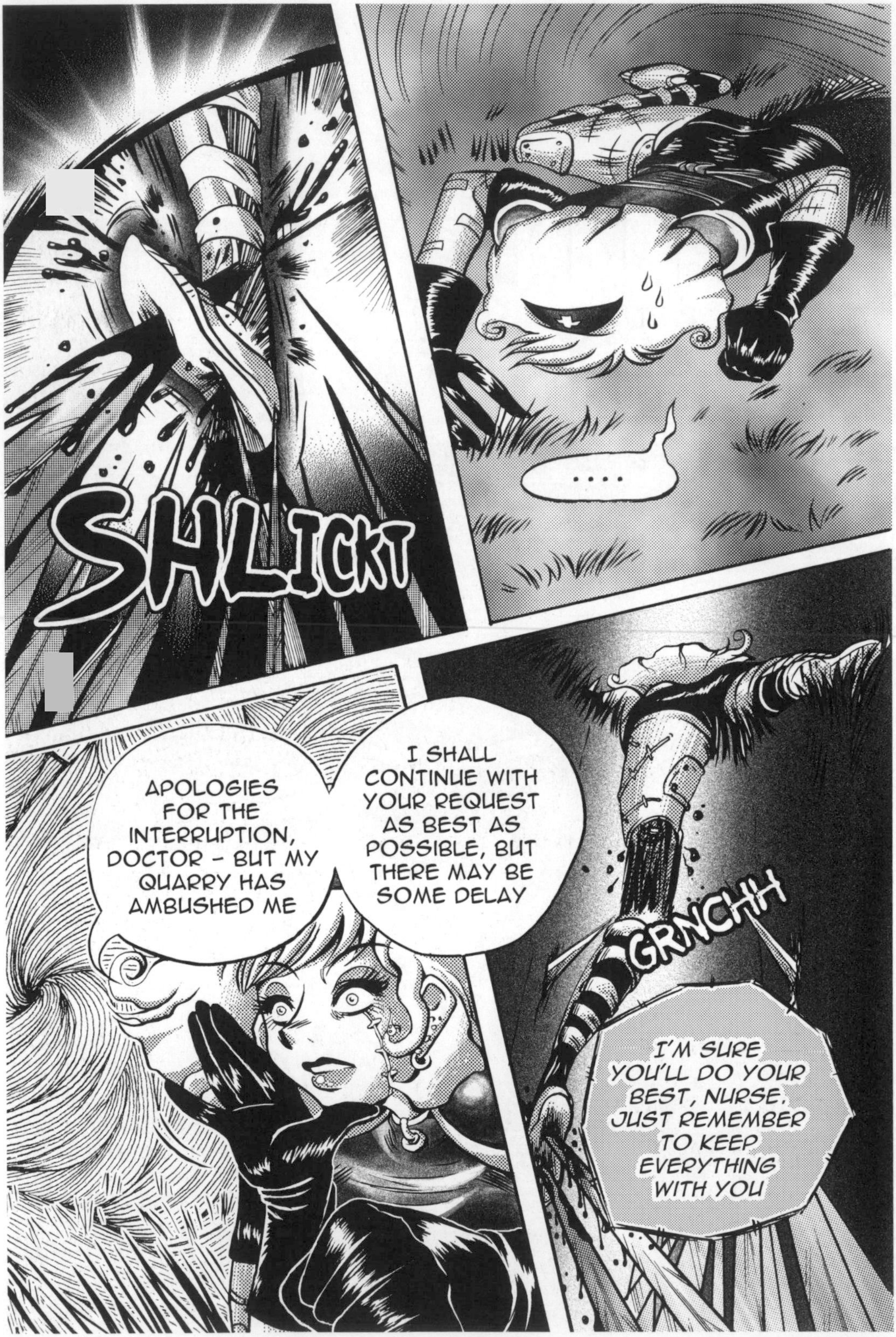
SHLICKT
....
APOLOGIES FOR THE INTERRUPTION, DOCTOR - BUT MY QUARRY HAS AMBUSHED ME
I SHALL CONTINUE WITH YOUR REQUEST AS BEST AS POSSIBLE, BUT THERE MAY BE SOME DELAY
GRNCHH
I'M SURE YOU'LL DO YOUR BEST, NURSE. JUST REMEMBER TO KEEP EVERYTHING WITH YOU

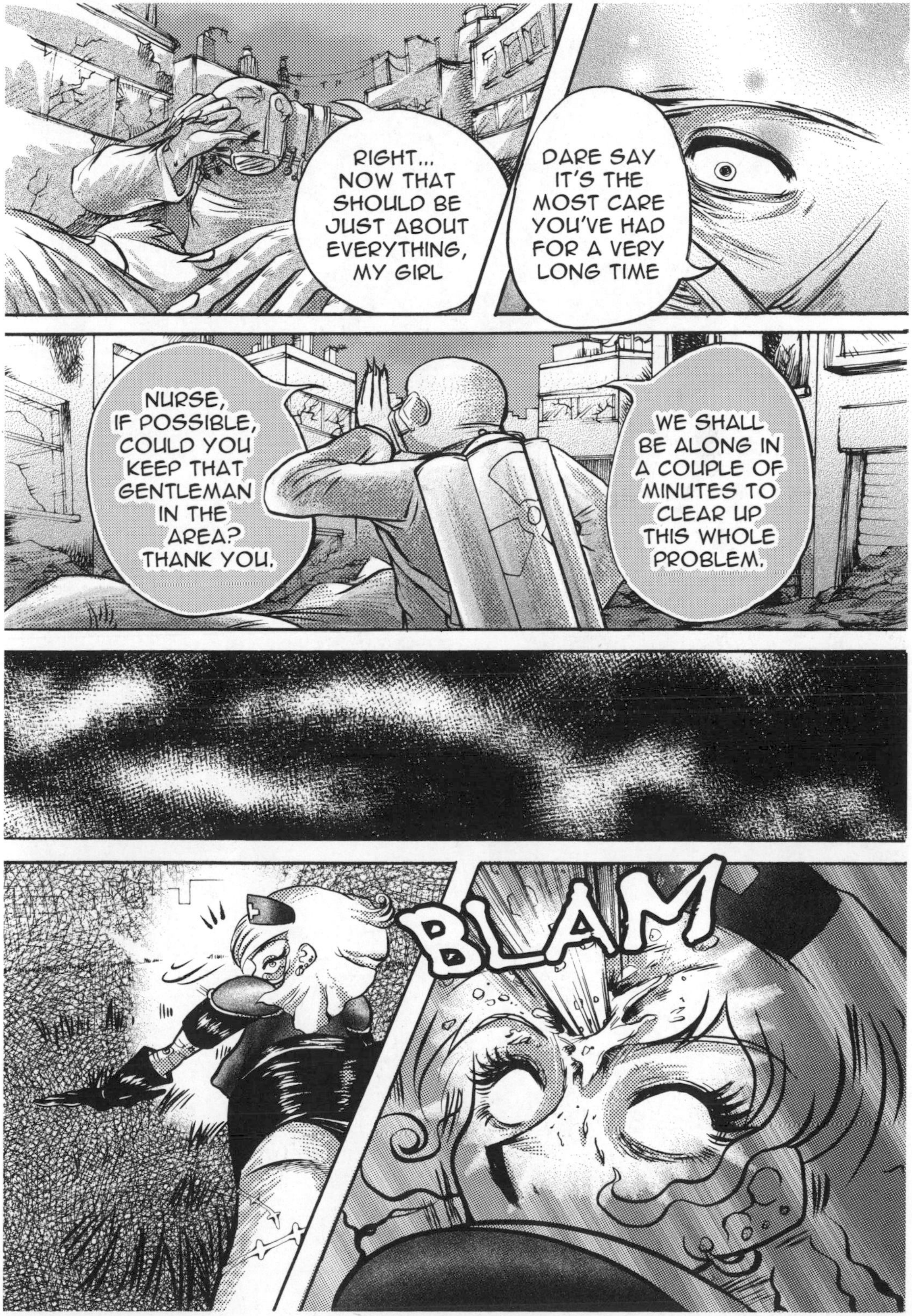
RIGHT... NOW THAT SHOULD BE JUST ABOUT EVERYTHING, MY GIRL
DARE SAY IT'S THE MOST CARE YOU'VE HAD FOR A VERY LONG TIME
NURSE, IF POSSIBLE, COULD YOU KEEP THAT GENTLEMAN IN THE AREA? THANK YOU.
WE SHALL BE ALONG IN A COUPLE OF MINUTES TO CLEAR UP THIS WHOLE PROBLEM.
BLAM

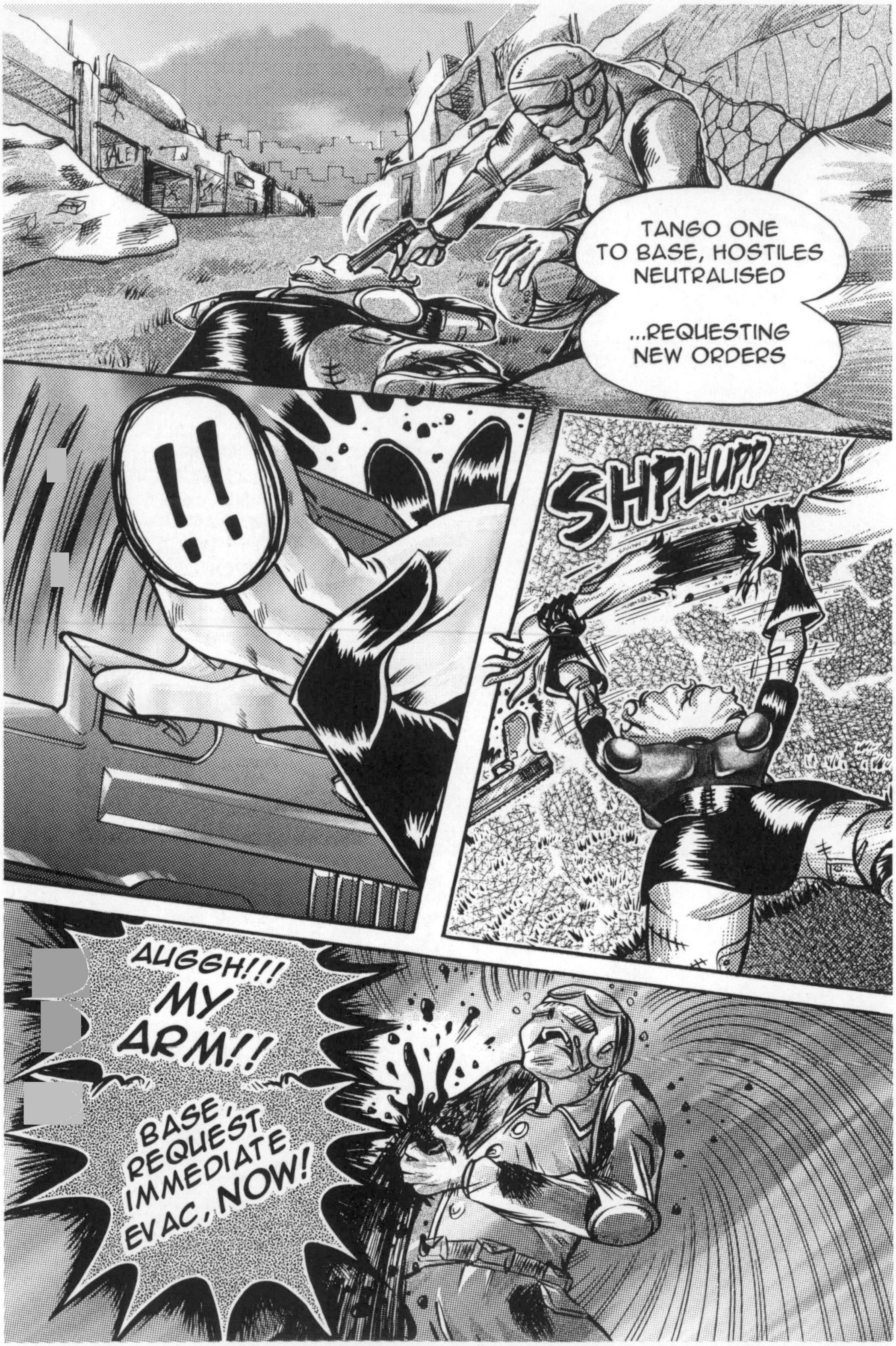
TANGO ONE TO BASE, HOSTILES NEUTRALISED
...REQUESTING NEW ORDERS
!!
SHPLUPP
AUGGH!!! MY ARM!!
BASE, REQUEST IMMEDIATE EVAC, NOW!

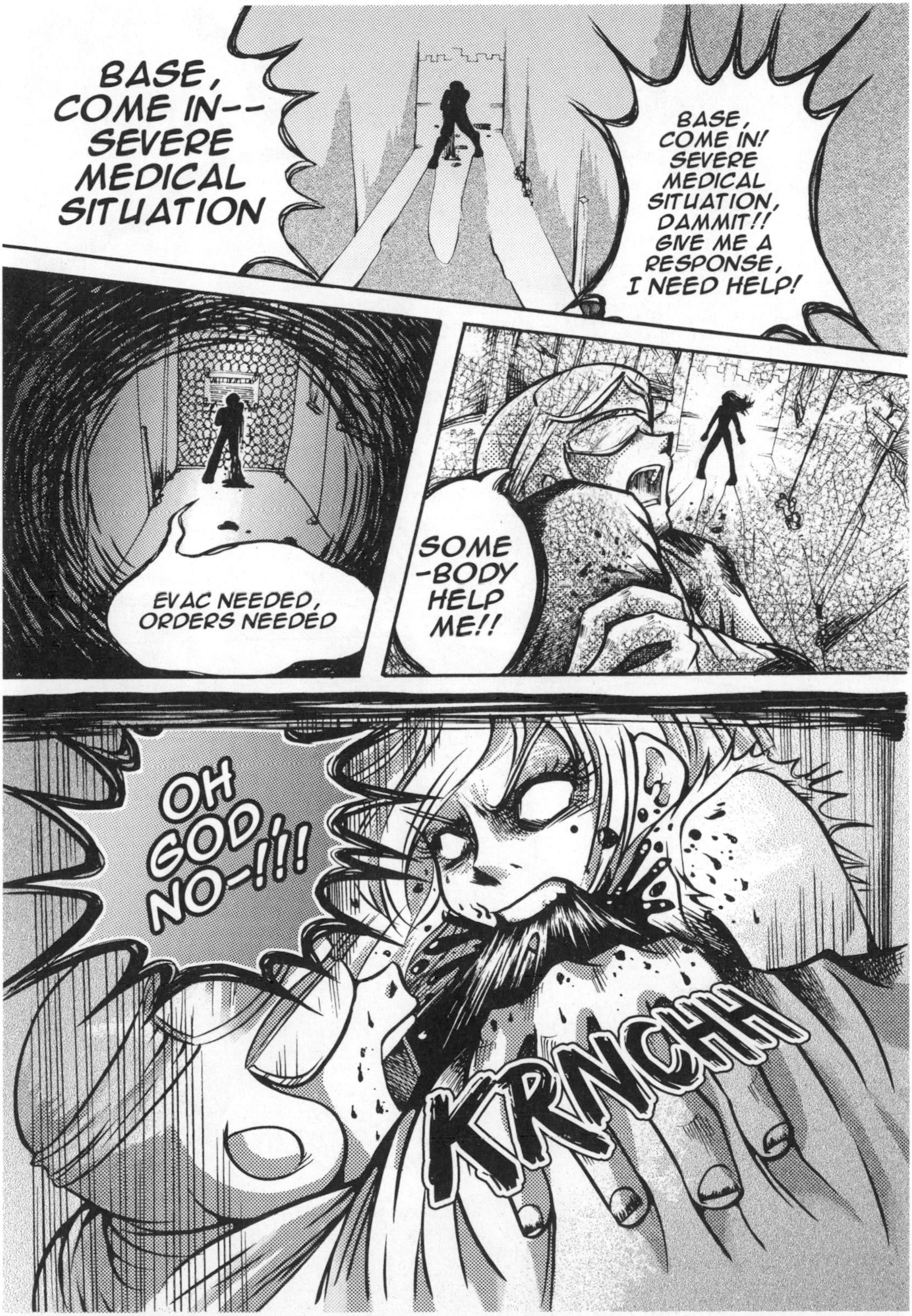
BASE, COME IN-- SEVERE MEDICAL SITUATION
BASE, COME IN! SEVERE MEDICAL SITUATION, DAMMIT!! GIVE ME A RESPONSE, I NEED HELP!
EVAC NEEDED, ORDERS NEEDED
SOME-BODY HELP ME!!
OH GOD NO-!!!
KRNCHH

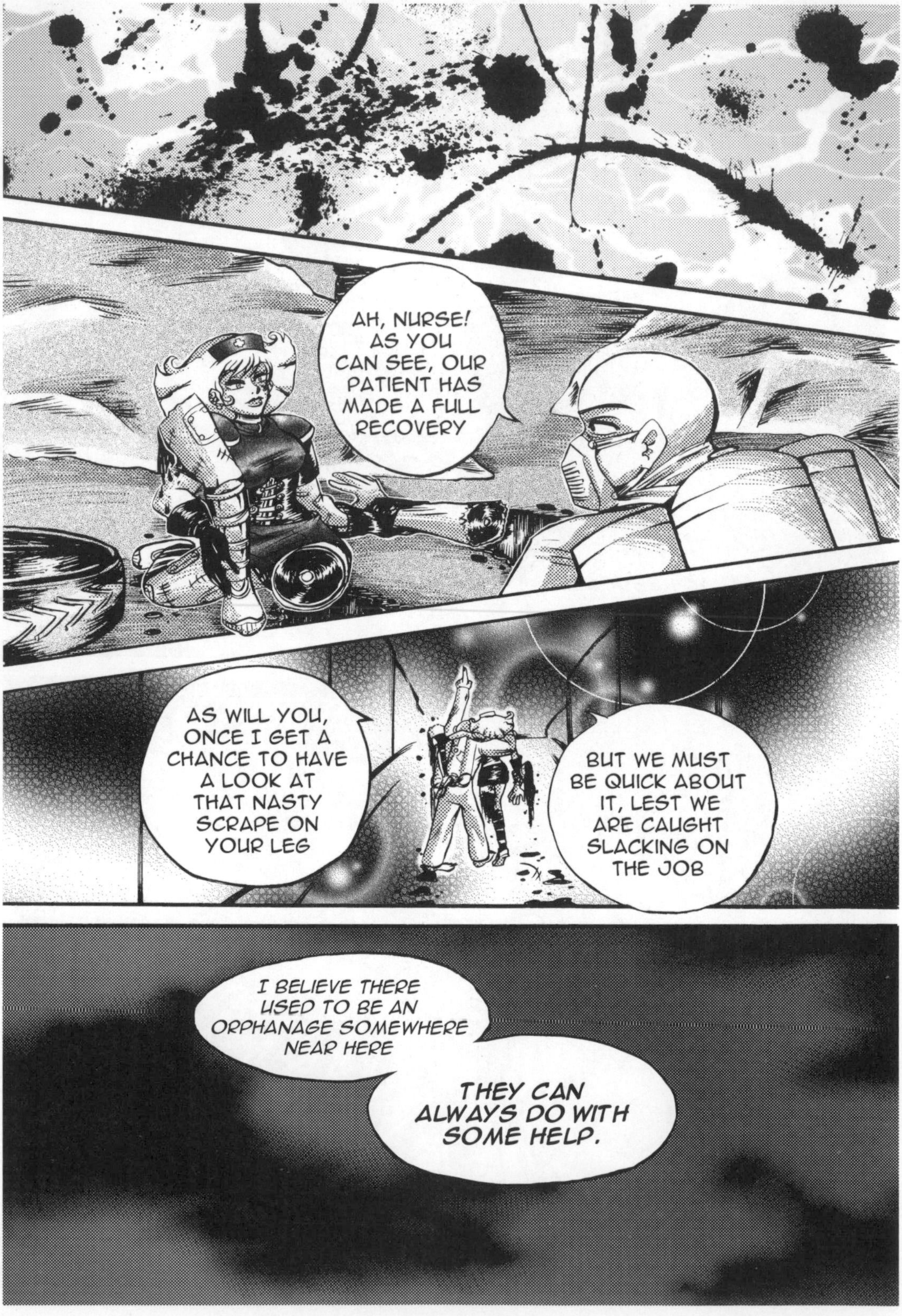
AH, NURSE! AS YOU CAN SEE, OUR PATIENT HAS MADE A FULL RECOVERY
AS WILL YOU, ONCE I GET A CHANCE TO HAVE A LOOK AT THAT NASTY SCRAPE ON YOUR LEG
BUT WE MUST BE QUICK ABOUT IT, LEST WE ARE CAUGHT SLACKING ON THE JOB
I BELIEVE THERE USED TO BE AN ORPHANAGE SOMEWHERE NEAR HERE
THEY CAN ALWAYS DO WITH SOME HELP.

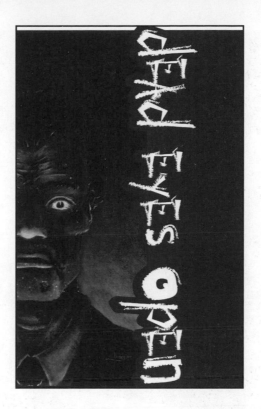

Dead Eyes Open (2005)

Creators: Matthew Shepherd (script), Roy Boney Jr (art)

Sometimes a zombie story comes along that dares to be different. The zombies here are fully fleshed out characters, and the story has a depth of feeling that puts the horror and violence to strong effect.

"Dead Eyes Open" was Shepherd and Boney's first published story. Previously Boney had published the web comic *Plugin Boy*. "Dead Eyes Open" itself came out of a failed internet project *DEADIES*.

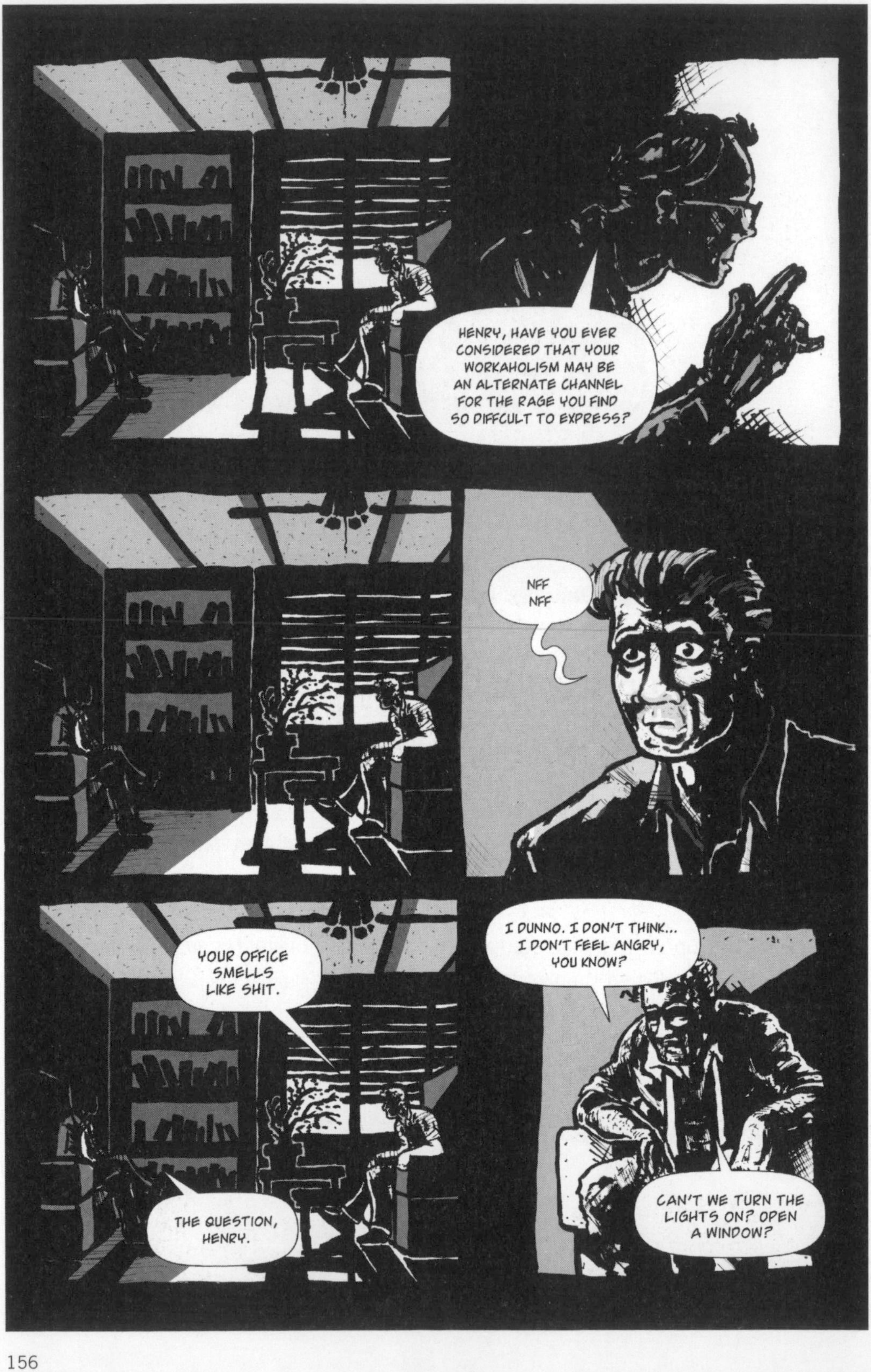
HENRY, HAVE YOU EVER CONSIDERED THAT YOUR WORKAHOLISM MAY BE AN ALTERNATE CHANNEL FOR THE RAGE YOU FIND SO DIFFCULT TO EXPRESS?
NFF NFF
YOUR OFFICE SMELLS LIKE SHIT.
THE QUESTION, HENRY.
I DUNNO. I DON'T THINK... I DON'T FEEL ANGRY, YOU KNOW?
CAN'T WE TURN THE LIGHTS ON? OPEN A WINDOW?

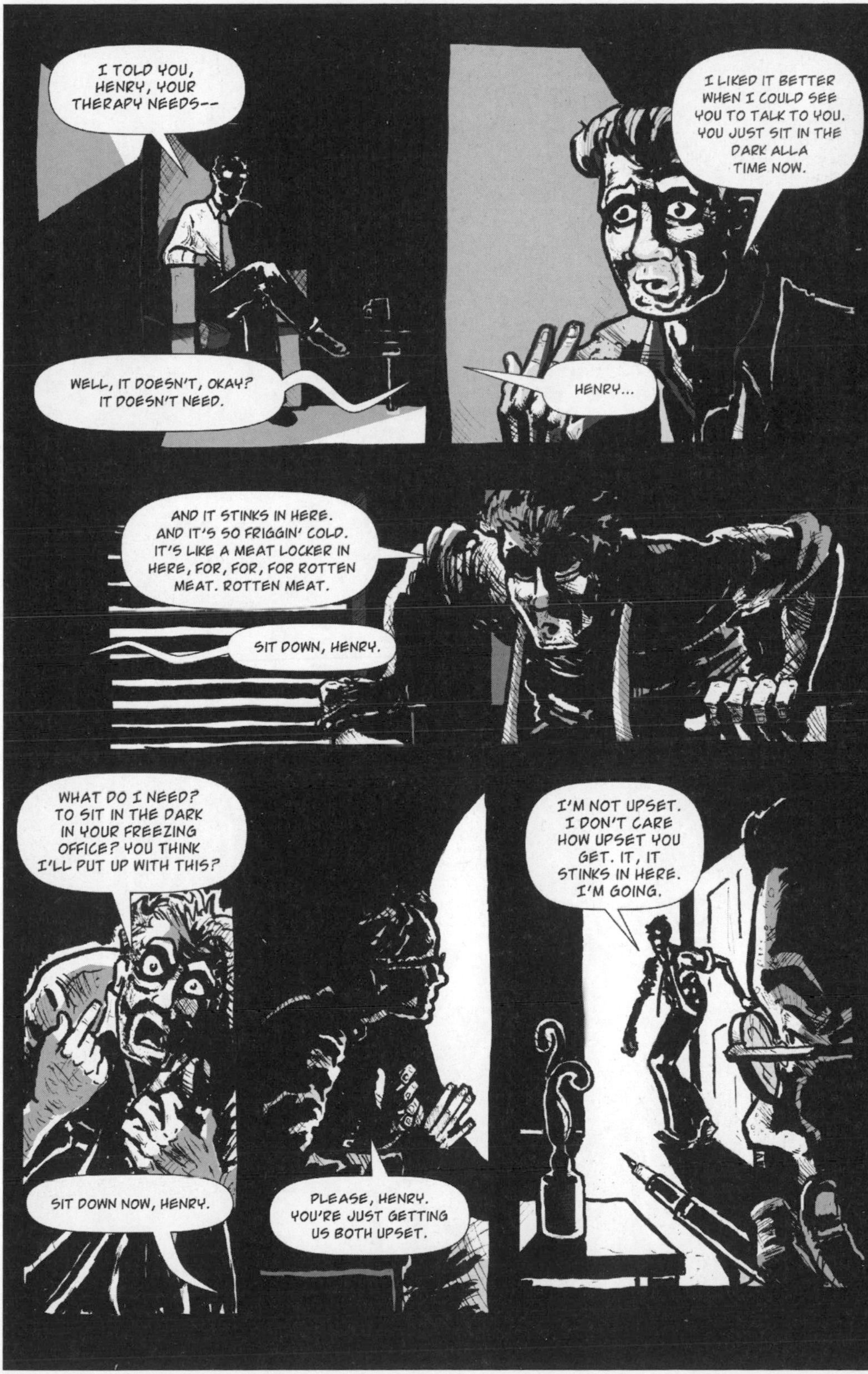
I TOLD YOU, HENRY, YOUR THERAPY NEEDS--
WELL, IT DOESN'T, OKAY? IT DOESN'T NEED.
I LIKED IT BETTER WHEN I COULD SEE YOU TO TALK TO YOU. YOU JUST SIT IN THE DARK ALLA TIME NOW.
HENRY...
AND IT STINKS IN HERE. AND IT'S SO FRIGGIN' COLD. IT'S LIKE A MEAT LOCKER IN HERE, FOR, FOR, FOR ROTTEN MEAT. ROTTEN MEAT.
SIT DOWN, HENRY.
WHAT DO I NEED? TO SIT IN THE DARK IN YOUR FREEZING OFFICE? YOU THINK I'LL PUT UP WITH THIS?
SIT DOWN NOW, HENRY.
PLEASE, HENRY. YOU'RE JUST GETTING US BOTH UPSET.
I'M NOT UPSET. I DON'T CARE HOW UPSET YOU GET. IT, IT STINKS IN HERE. I'M GOING.

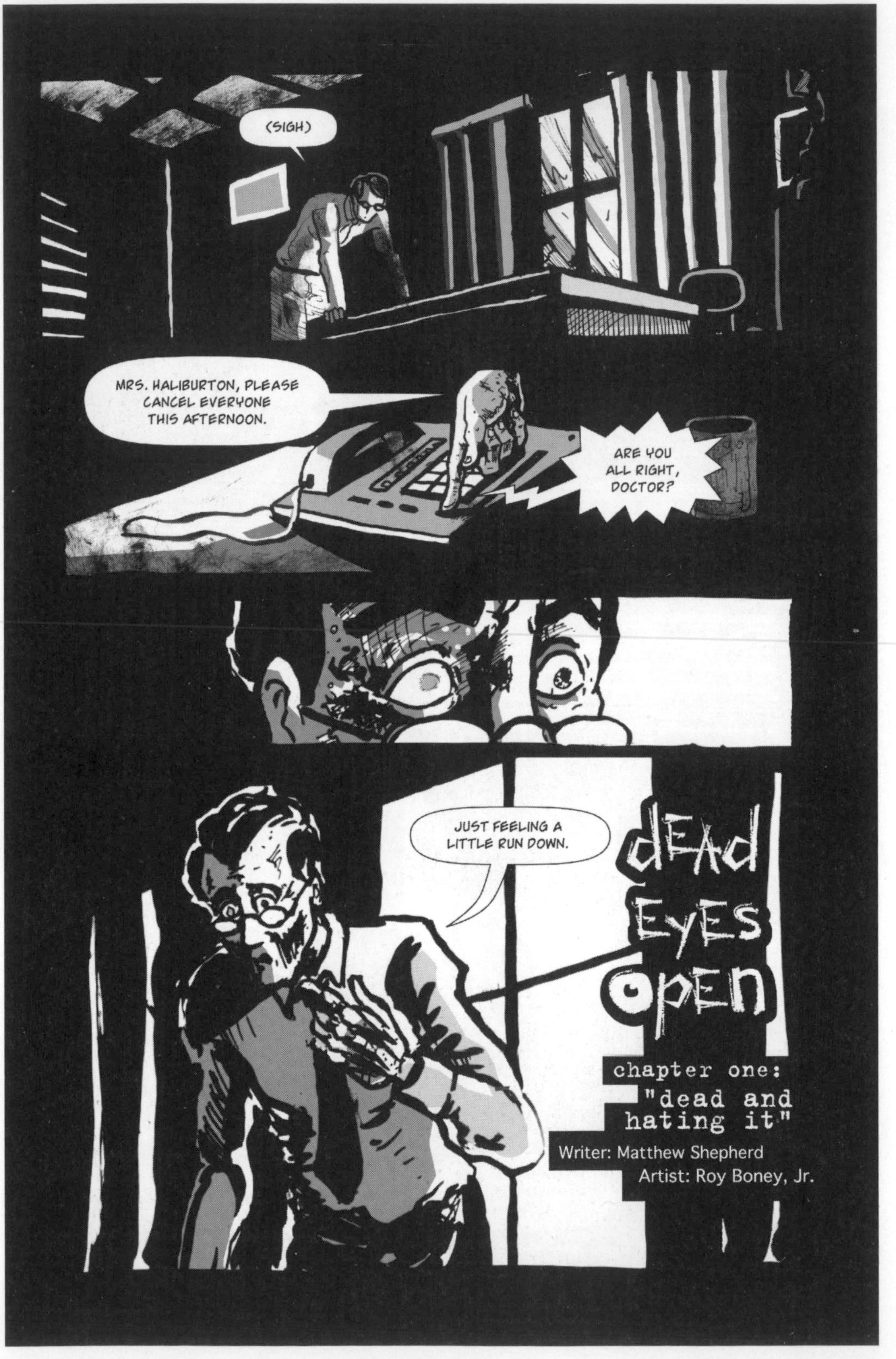
(SIGH)
MRS. HALIBURTON, PLEASE CANCEL EVERYONE THIS AFTERNOON.
ARE YOU ALL RIGHT, DOCTOR?
JUST FEELING A LITTLE RUN DOWN.
dEAd EyES opEN
chapter one: "dead and hating it"
Writer: Matthew Shepherd
Artist: Roy Boney, Jr.

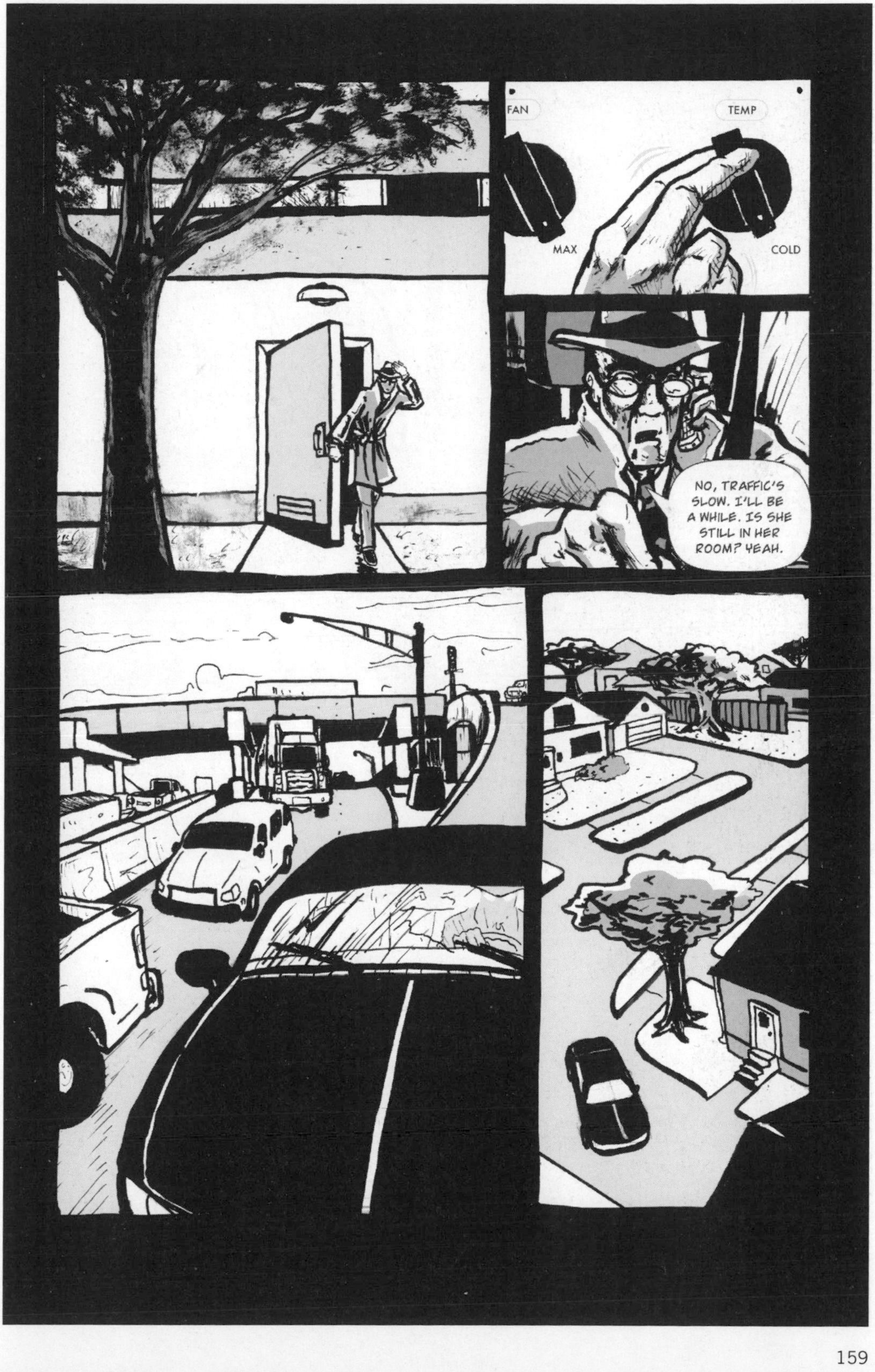
FAN
TEMP
MAX
COLD
NO, TRAFFIC'S SLOW. I'LL BE A WHILE. IS SHE STILL IN HER ROOM? YEAH.

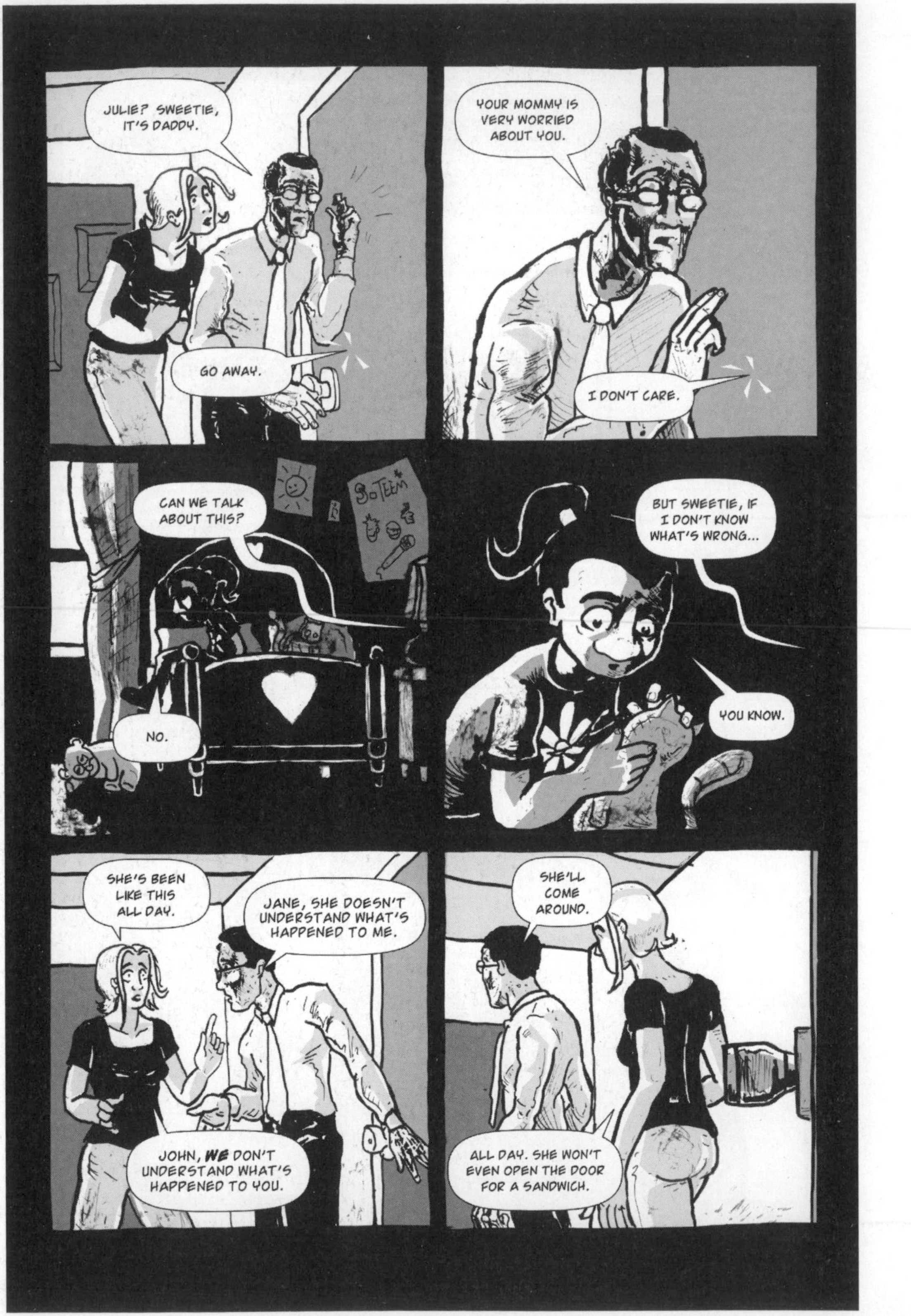
JULIE? SWEETIE, IT'S DADDY.
GO AWAY.
YOUR MOMMY IS VERY WORRIED ABOUT YOU.
I DON'T CARE.
CAN WE TALK ABOUT THIS?
NO.
BUT SWEETIE, IF I DON'T KNOW WHAT'S WRONG...
YOU KNOW.
SHE'S BEEN LIKE THIS ALL DAY.
JANE, SHE DOESN'T UNDERSTAND WHAT'S HAPPENED TO ME.
JOHN, WE DON'T UNDERSTAND WHAT'S HAPPENED TO YOU.
SHE'LL COME AROUND.
ALL DAY. SHE WON'T EVEN OPEN THE DOOR FOR A SANDWICH.

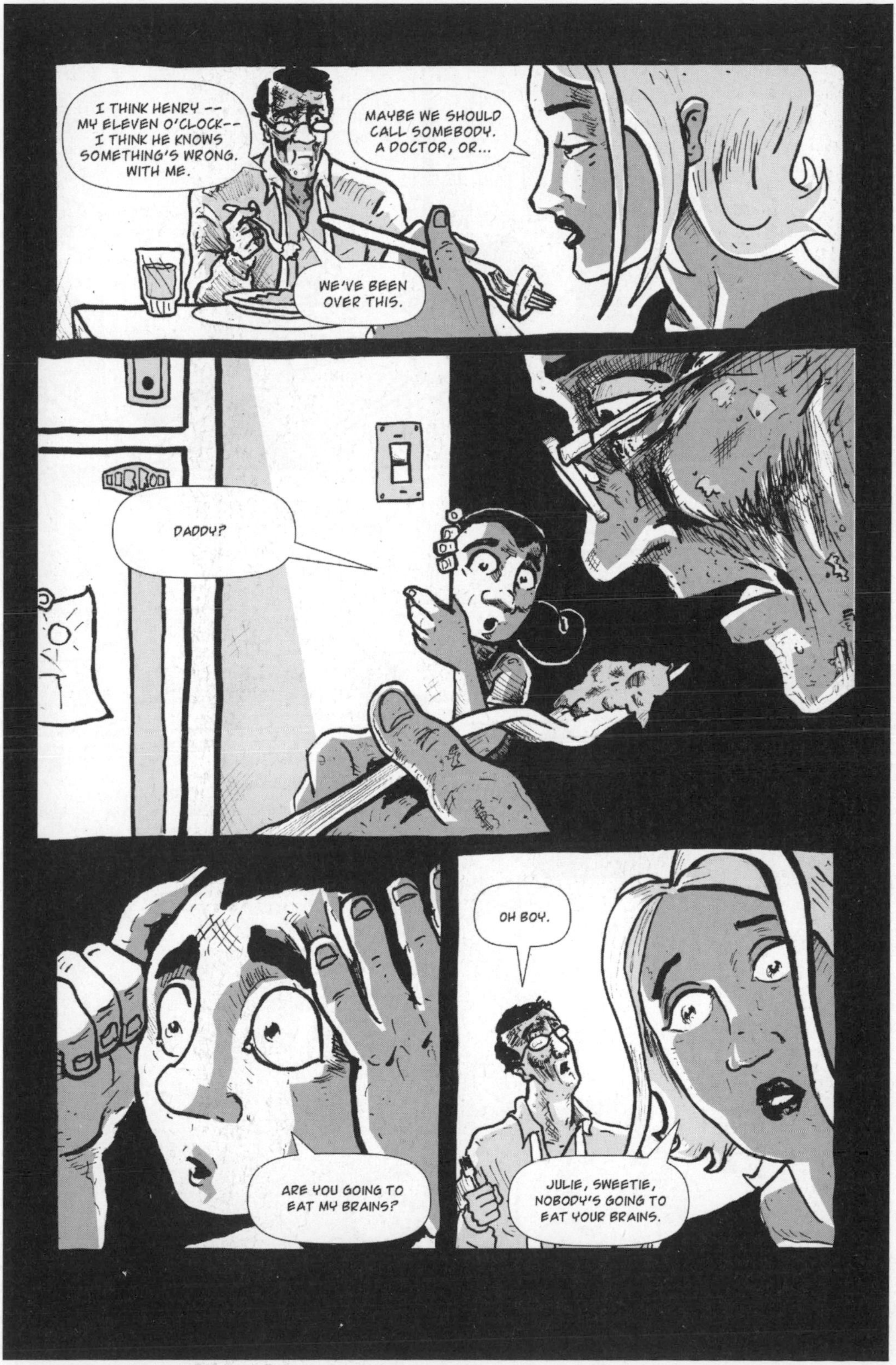
I THINK HENRY -- MY ELEVEN O'CLOCK-- I THINK HE KNOWS SOMETHING'S WRONG. WITH ME.
MAYBE WE SHOULD CALL SOMEBODY. A DOCTOR, OR...
WE'VE BEEN OVER THIS.
DADDY?
OH BOY.
ARE YOU GOING TO EAT MY BRAINS?
JULIE, SWEETIE, NOBODY'S GOING TO EAT YOUR BRAINS.

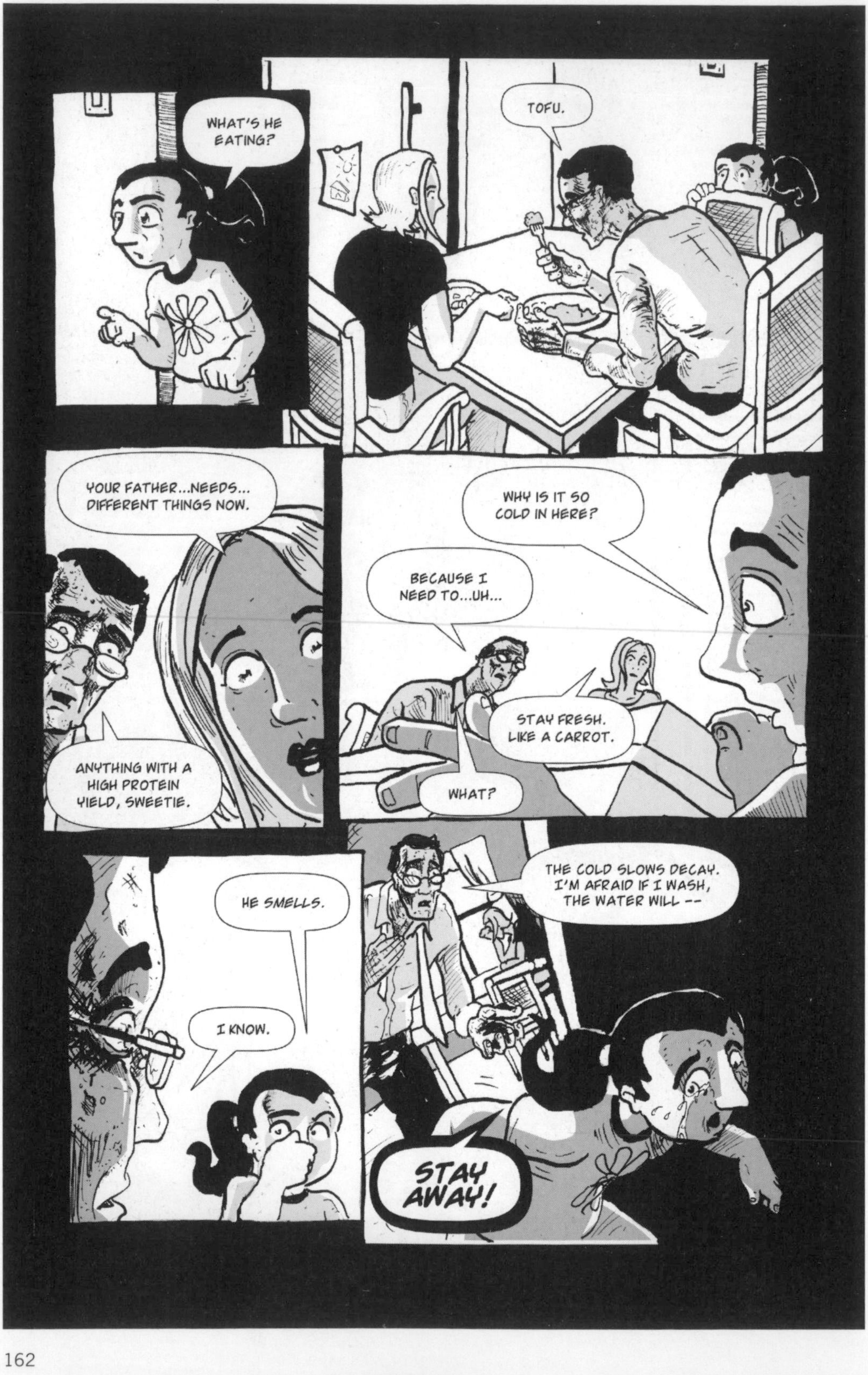
WHAT'S HE EATING?
TOFU.
YOUR FATHER...NEEDS... DIFFERENT THINGS NOW.
ANYTHING WITH A HIGH PROTEIN YIELD, SWEETIE.
WHY IS IT SO COLD IN HERE?
BECAUSE I NEED TO...UH...
STAY FRESH. LIKE A CARROT.
WHAT?
HE SMELLS.
I KNOW.
THE COLD SLOWS DECAY. I'M AFRAID IF I WASH, THE WATER WILL --
STAY AWAY!

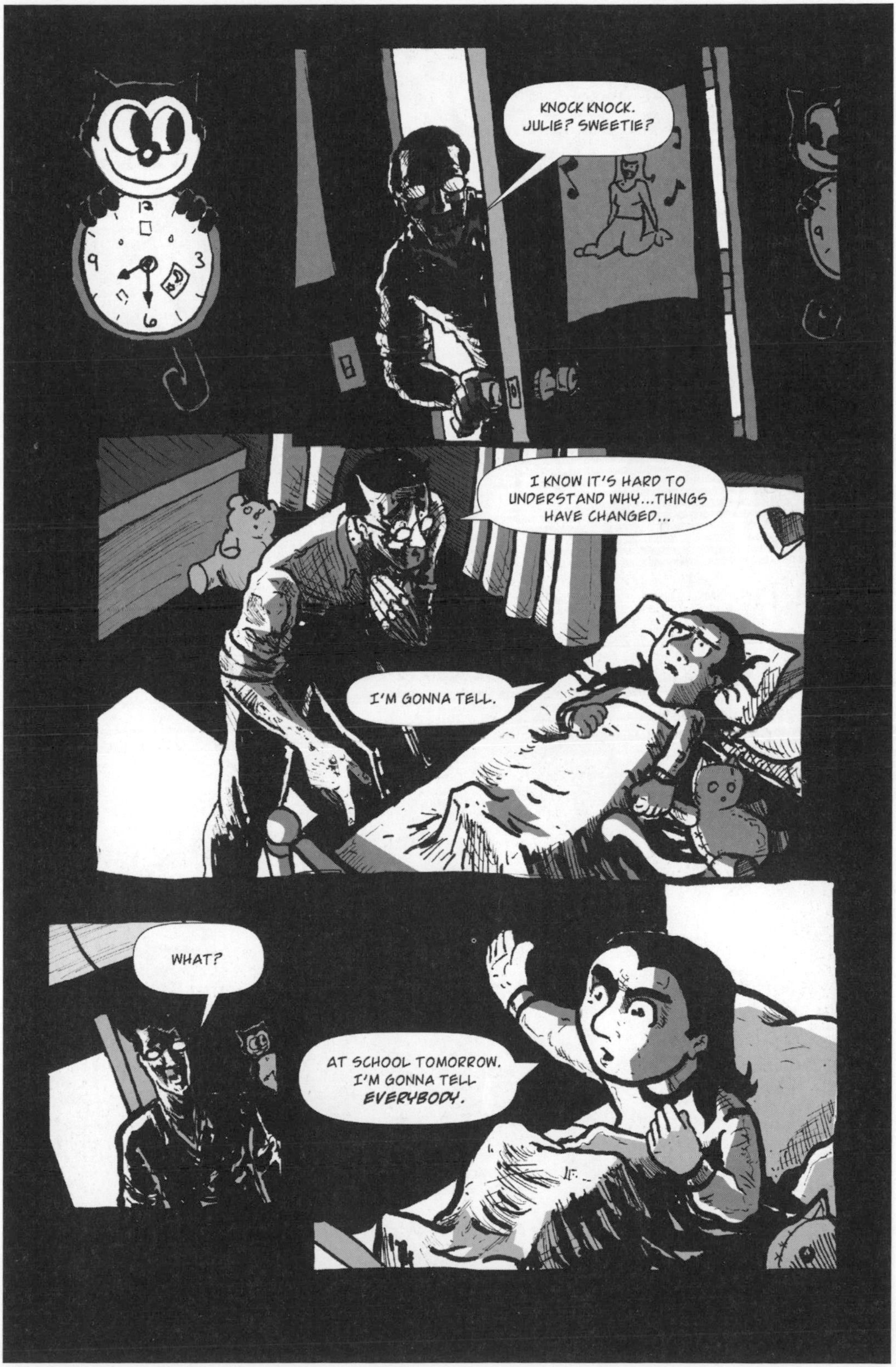
KNOCK KNOCK. JULIE? SWEETIE?
I KNOW IT'S HARD TO UNDERSTAND WHY...THINGS HAVE CHANGED...
I'M GONNA TELL.
WHAT?
AT SCHOOL TOMORROW. I'M GONNA TELL *EVERYBODY*.

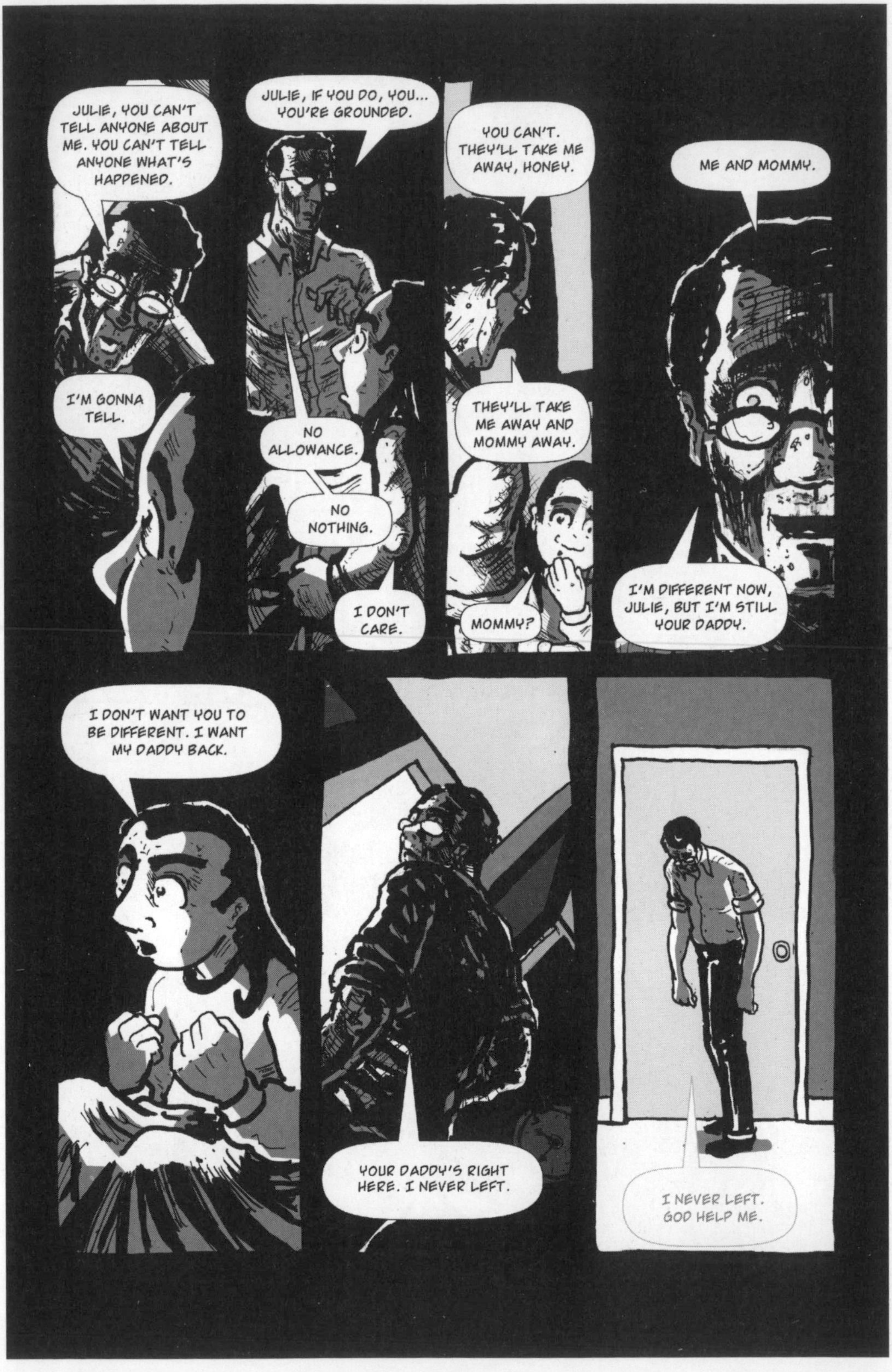
JULIE, YOU CAN'T TELL ANYONE ABOUT ME. YOU CAN'T TELL ANYONE WHAT'S HAPPENED.
I'M GONNA TELL.
JULIE, IF YOU DO, YOU... YOU'RE GROUNDED.
NO ALLOWANCE.
NO NOTHING.
I DON'T CARE.
YOU CAN'T. THEY'LL TAKE ME AWAY, HONEY.
THEY'LL TAKE ME AWAY AND MOMMY AWAY.
MOMMY?
ME AND MOMMY.
I'M DIFFERENT NOW, JULIE, BUT I'M STILL YOUR DADDY.
I DON'T WANT YOU TO BE DIFFERENT. I WANT MY DADDY BACK.
YOUR DADDY'S RIGHT HERE. I NEVER LEFT.
I NEVER LEFT. GOD HELP ME.

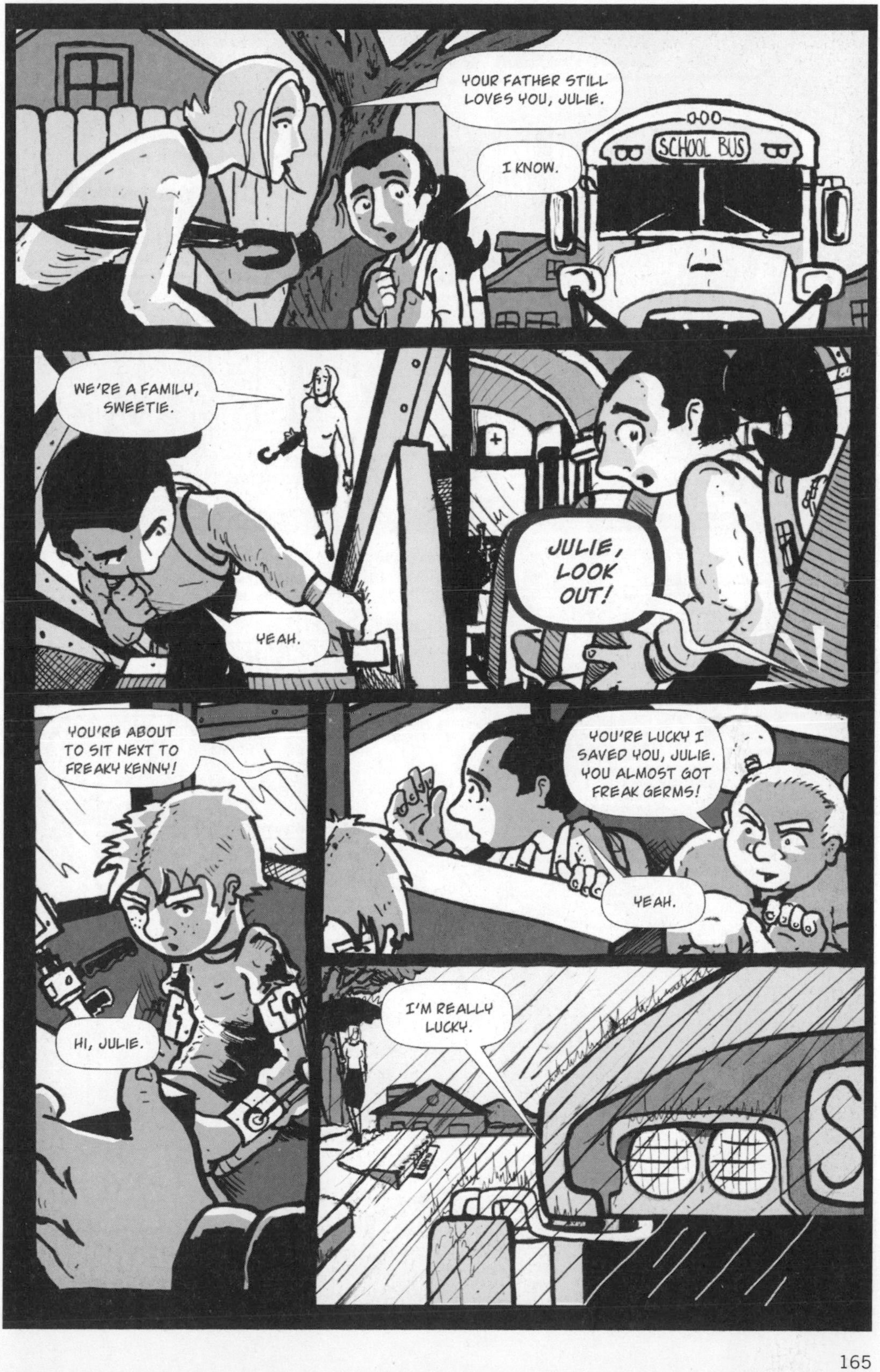
YOUR FATHER STILL LOVES YOU, JULIE.
I KNOW.
SCHOOL BUS
WE'RE A FAMILY, SWEETIE.
YEAH.
JULIE, LOOK OUT!
YOU'RE ABOUT TO SIT NEXT TO FREAKY KENNY!
HI, JULIE.
YOU'RE LUCKY I SAVED YOU, JULIE. YOU ALMOST GOT FREAK GERMS!
YEAH.
I'M REALLY LUCKY.

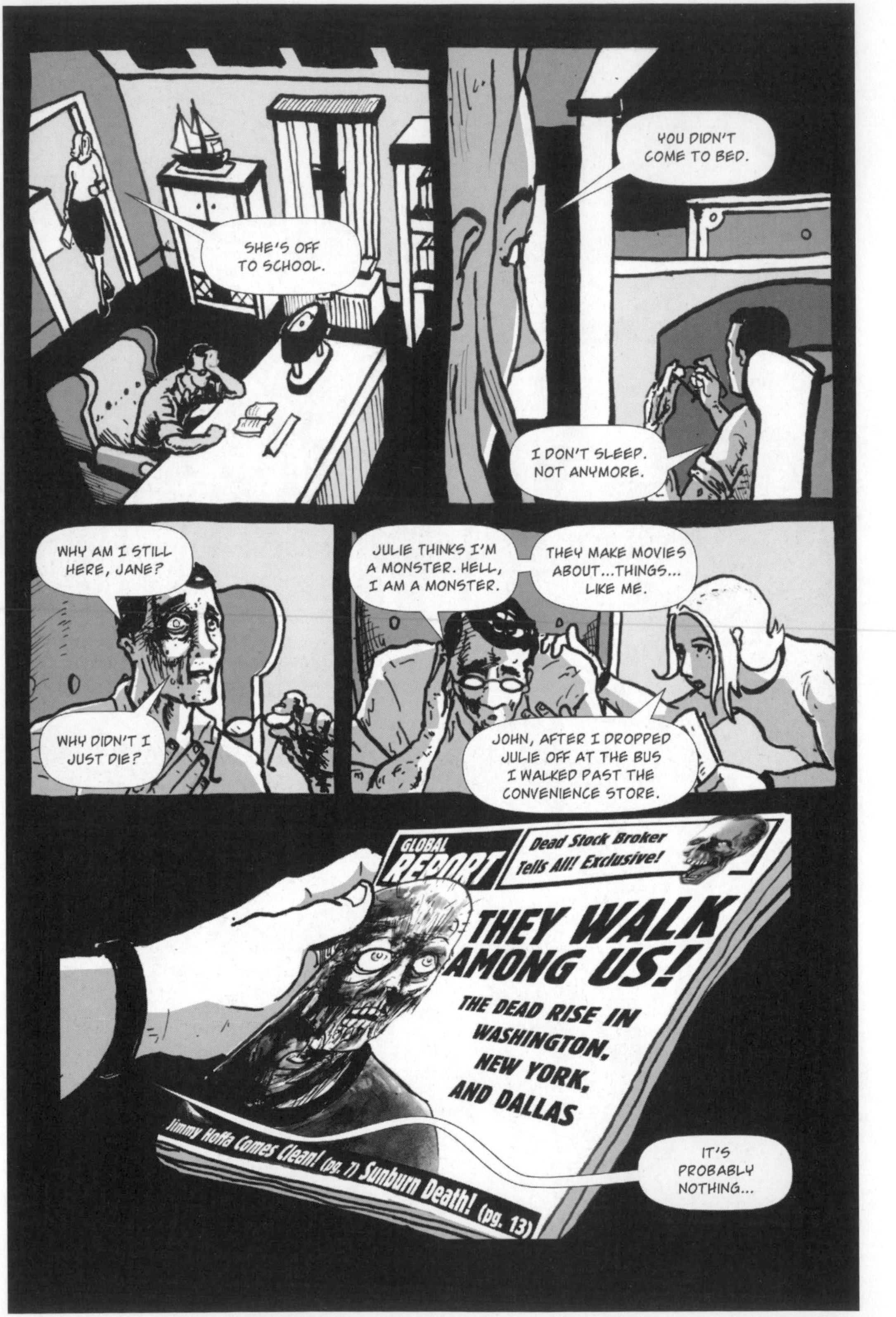
SHE'S OFF TO SCHOOL.
YOU DIDN'T COME TO BED.
I DON'T SLEEP. NOT ANYMORE.
WHY AM I STILL HERE, JANE?
WHY DIDN'T I JUST DIE?
JULIE THINKS I'M A MONSTER. HELL, I AM A MONSTER.
THEY MAKE MOVIES ABOUT...THINGS... LIKE ME.
JOHN, AFTER I DROPPED JULIE OFF AT THE BUS I WALKED PAST THE CONVENIENCE STORE.
GLOBAL REPORT
Dead Stock Broker Tells All! Exclusive!
THEY WALK AMONG US!
THE DEAD RISE IN WASHINGTON, NEW YORK, AND DALLAS
Jimmy Hoffa Comes Clean! (pg. 7) Sunburn Death! (pg. 13)
IT'S PROBABLY NOTHING...

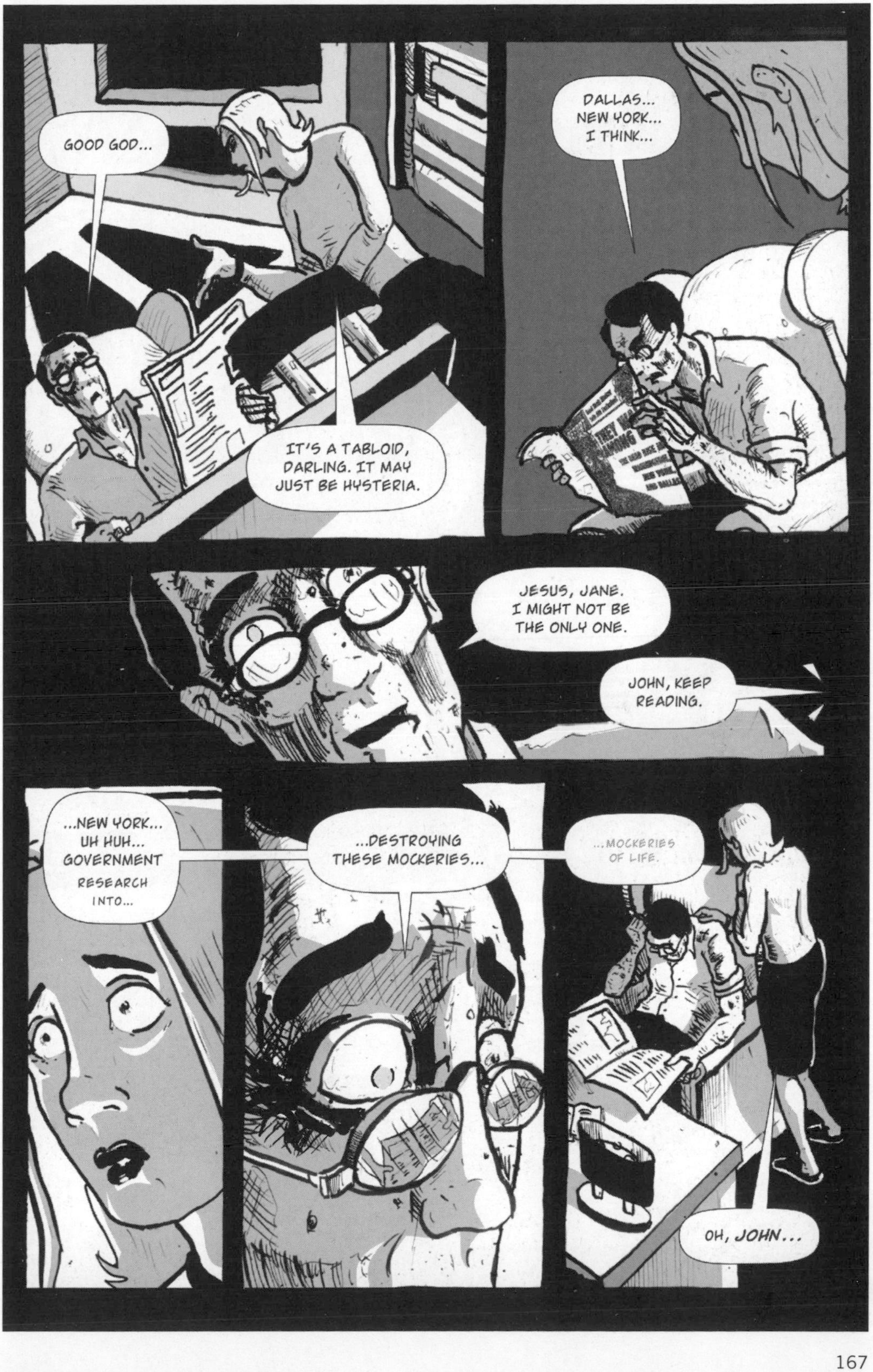
GOOD GOD...
IT'S A TABLOID, DARLING. IT MAY JUST BE HYSTERIA.
DALLAS... NEW YORK... I THINK...
JESUS, JANE. I MIGHT NOT BE THE ONLY ONE.
JOHN, KEEP READING.
...NEW YORK... UH HUH... GOVERNMENT RESEARCH INTO...
...DESTROYING THESE MOCKERIES...
...MOCKERIES OF LIFE.
OH, JOHN...

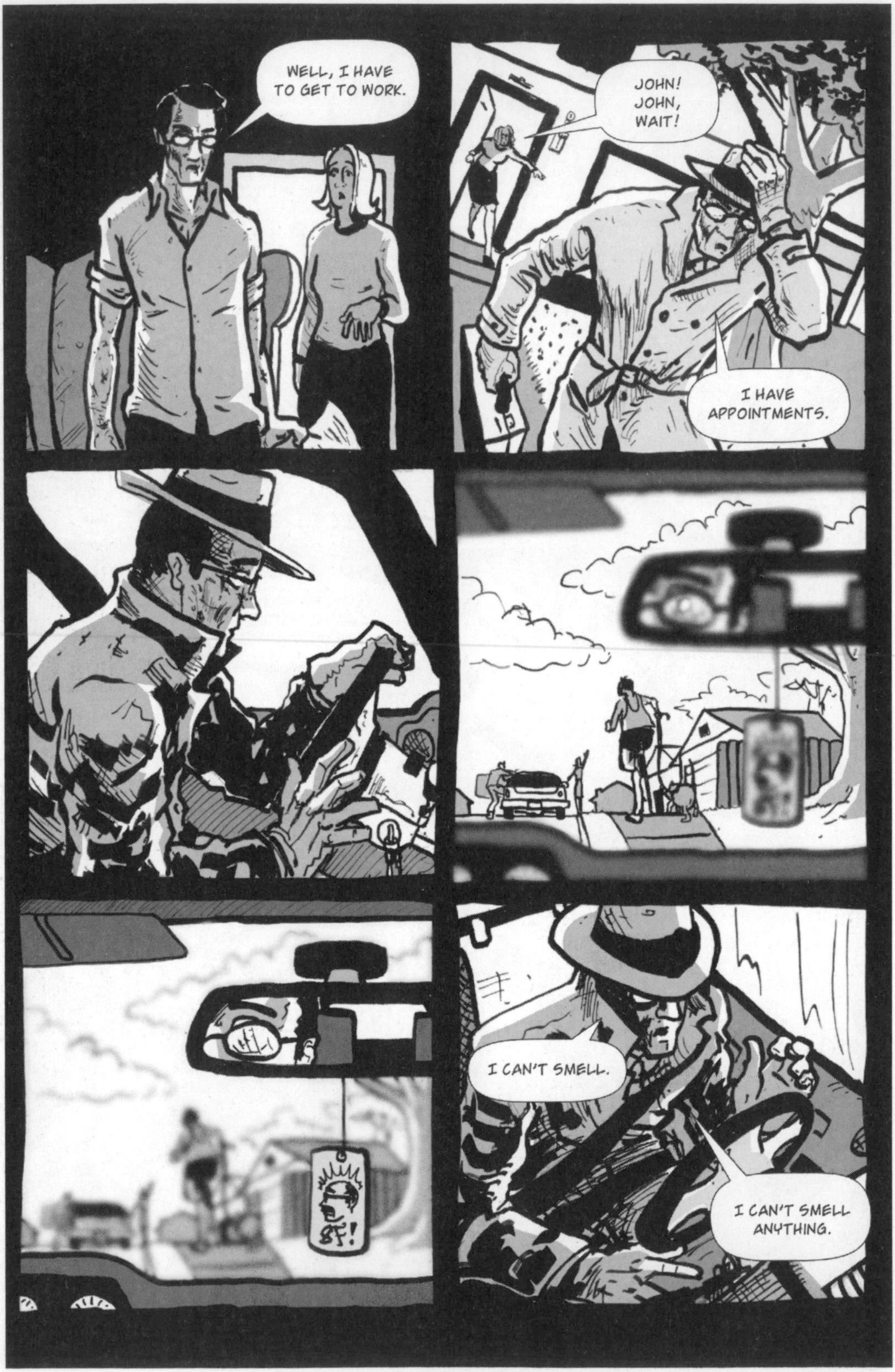
WELL, I HAVE TO GET TO WORK.
JOHN! JOHN, WAIT!
I HAVE APPOINTMENTS.
SF!
I CAN'T SMELL.
I CAN'T SMELL ANYTHING.

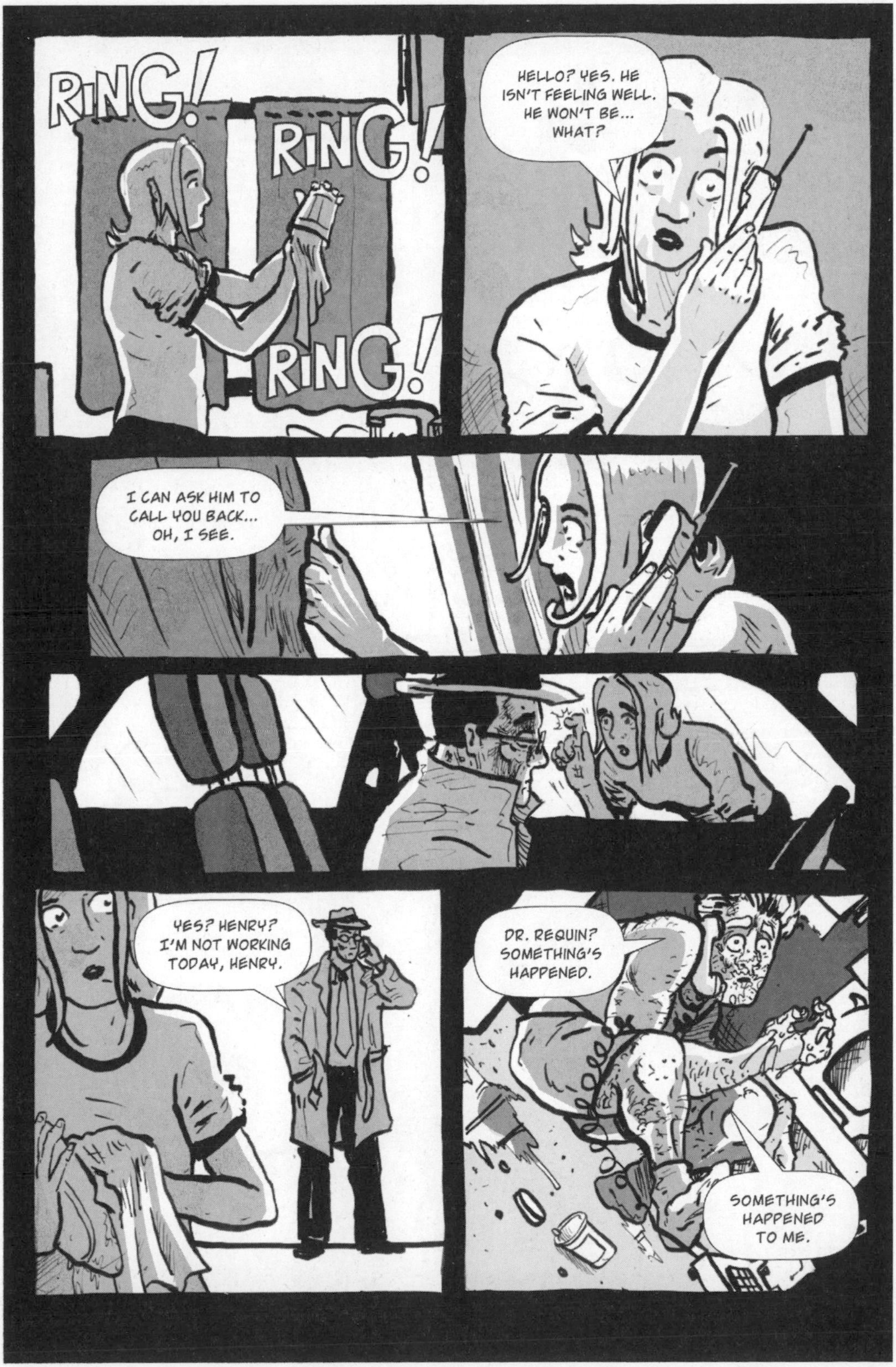
RING!
RING!
RING!
HELLO? YES. HE ISN'T FEELING WELL. HE WON'T BE... WHAT?
I CAN ASK HIM TO CALL YOU BACK... OH, I SEE.
YES? HENRY? I'M NOT WORKING TODAY, HENRY.
DR. REQUIN? SOMETHING'S HAPPENED.
SOMETHING'S HAPPENED TO ME.

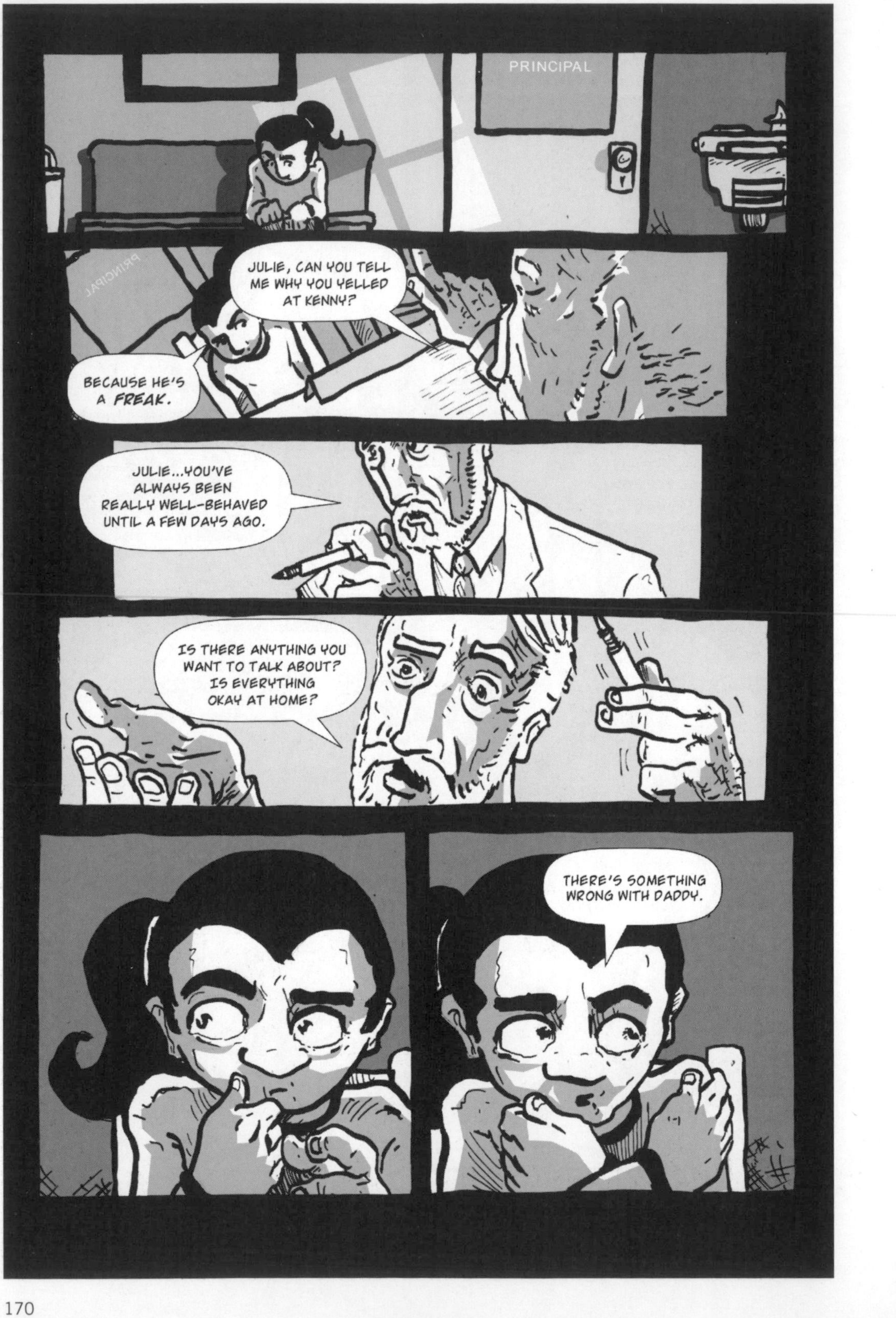
PRINCIPAL
PRINCIPAL
JULIE, CAN YOU TELL ME WHY YOU YELLED AT KENNY?
BECAUSE HE'S A FREAK.
JULIE...YOU'VE ALWAYS BEEN REALLY WELL-BEHAVED UNTIL A FEW DAYS AGO.
IS THERE ANYTHING YOU WANT TO TALK ABOUT? IS EVERYTHING OKAY AT HOME?
THERE'S SOMETHING WRONG WITH DADDY.

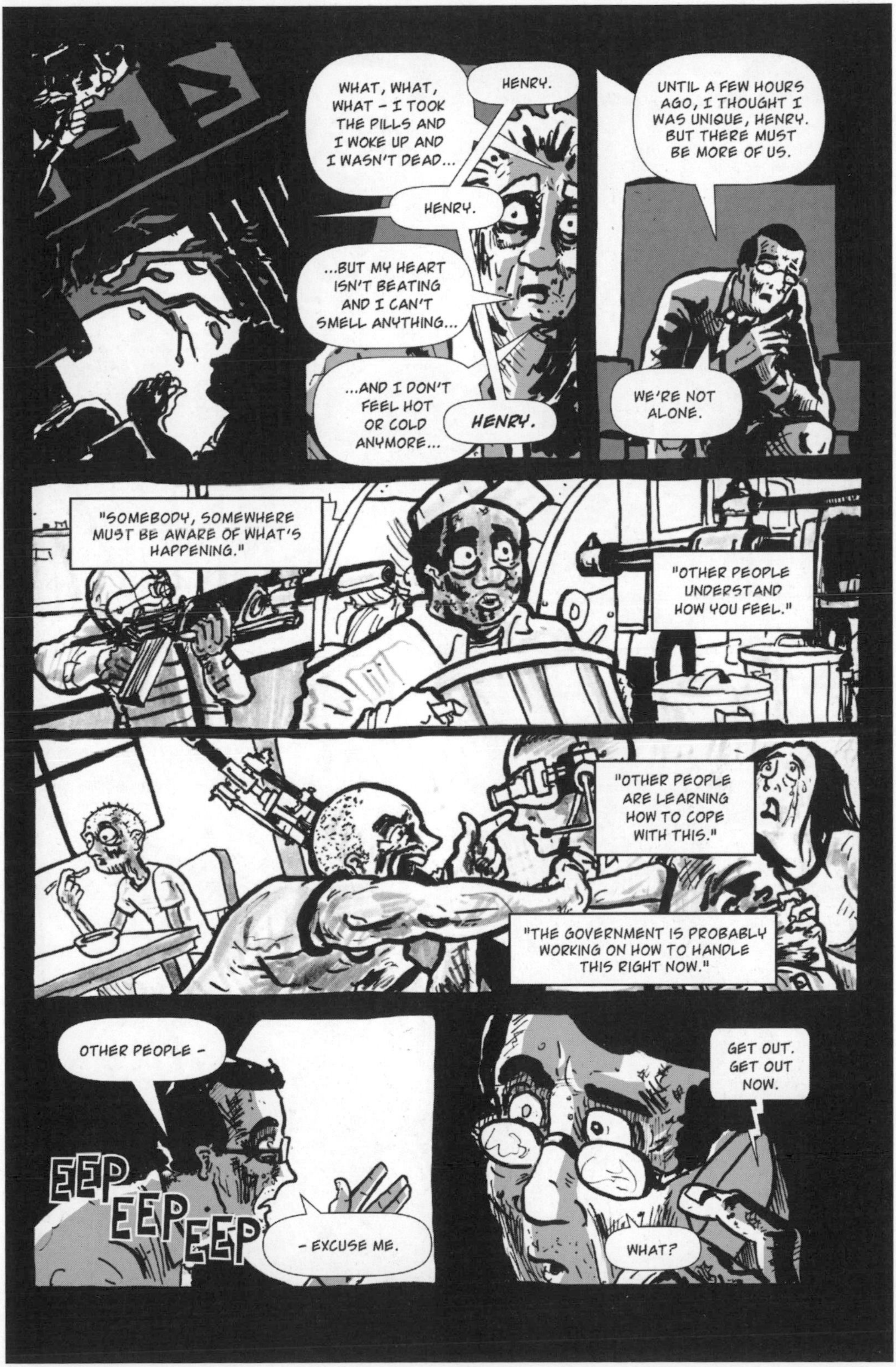
WHAT, WHAT, WHAT - I TOOK THE PILLS AND I WOKE UP AND I WASN'T DEAD...
HENRY.
HENRY.
...BUT MY HEART ISN'T BEATING AND I CAN'T SMELL ANYTHING...
...AND I DON'T FEEL HOT OR COLD ANYMORE...
HENRY.
UNTIL A FEW HOURS AGO, I THOUGHT I WAS UNIQUE, HENRY. BUT THERE MUST BE MORE OF US.
WE'RE NOT ALONE.
"SOMEBODY, SOMEWHERE MUST BE AWARE OF WHAT'S HAPPENING."
"OTHER PEOPLE UNDERSTAND HOW YOU FEEL."
"OTHER PEOPLE ARE LEARNING HOW TO COPE WITH THIS."
"THE GOVERNMENT IS PROBABLY WORKING ON HOW TO HANDLE THIS RIGHT NOW."
OTHER PEOPLE -
EEP EEP EEP
- EXCUSE ME.
GET OUT. GET OUT NOW.
WHAT?

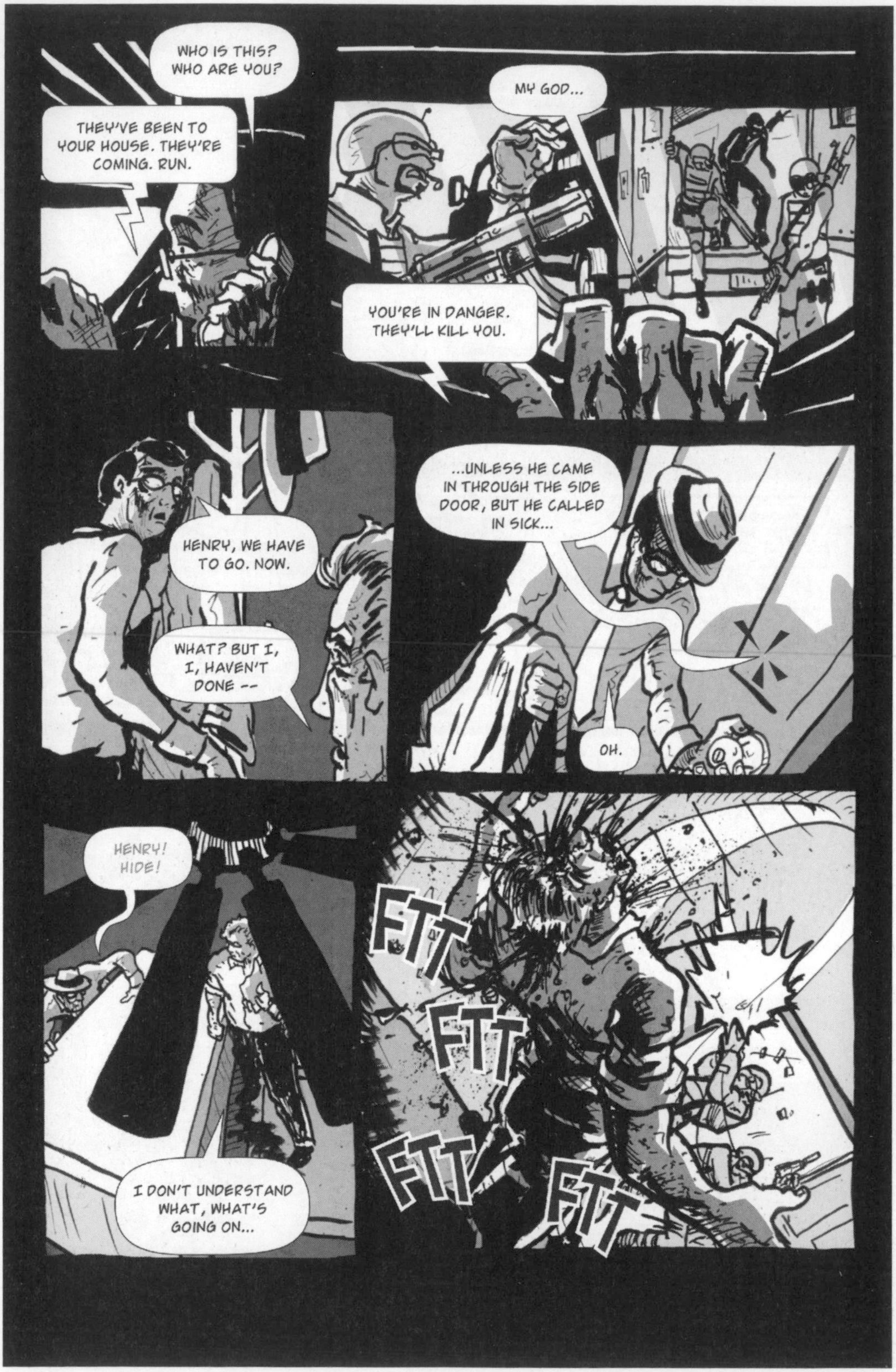
WHO IS THIS? WHO ARE YOU?
THEY'VE BEEN TO YOUR HOUSE. THEY'RE COMING. RUN.
MY GOD...
YOU'RE IN DANGER. THEY'LL KILL YOU.
HENRY, WE HAVE TO GO. NOW.
WHAT? BUT I, I, HAVEN'T DONE --
...UNLESS HE CAME IN THROUGH THE SIDE DOOR, BUT HE CALLED IN SICK...
OH.
HENRY! HIDE!
I DON'T UNDERSTAND WHAT, WHAT'S GOING ON...
FTT
FTT
FTT
FTT

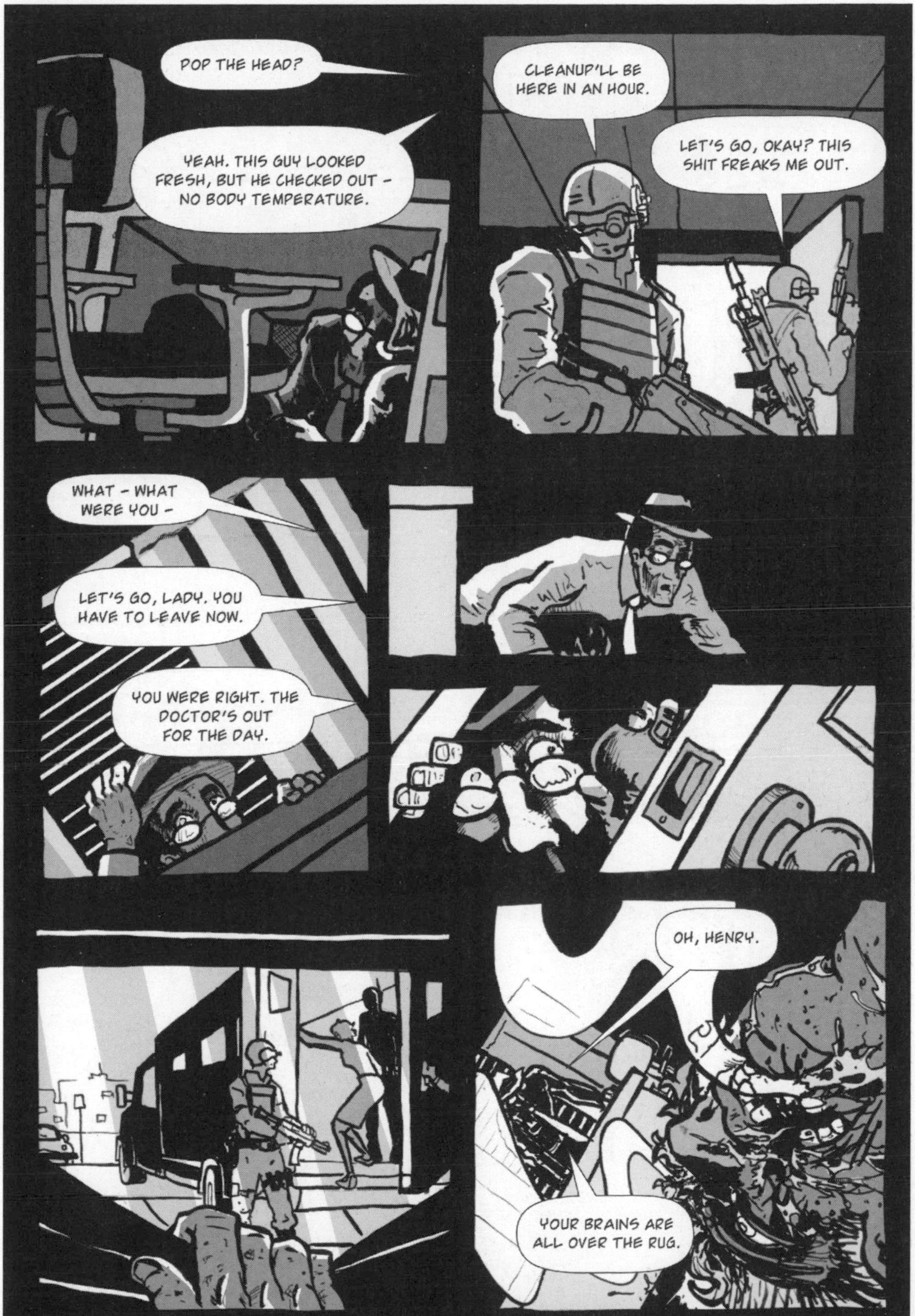
POP THE HEAD?
YEAH. THIS GUY LOOKED FRESH, BUT HE CHECKED OUT - NO BODY TEMPERATURE.
CLEANUP'LL BE HERE IN AN HOUR.
LET'S GO, OKAY? THIS SHIT FREAKS ME OUT.
WHAT - WHAT WERE YOU -
LET'S GO, LADY. YOU HAVE TO LEAVE NOW.
YOU WERE RIGHT. THE DOCTOR'S OUT FOR THE DAY.
OH, HENRY.
YOUR BRAINS ARE ALL OVER THE RUG.

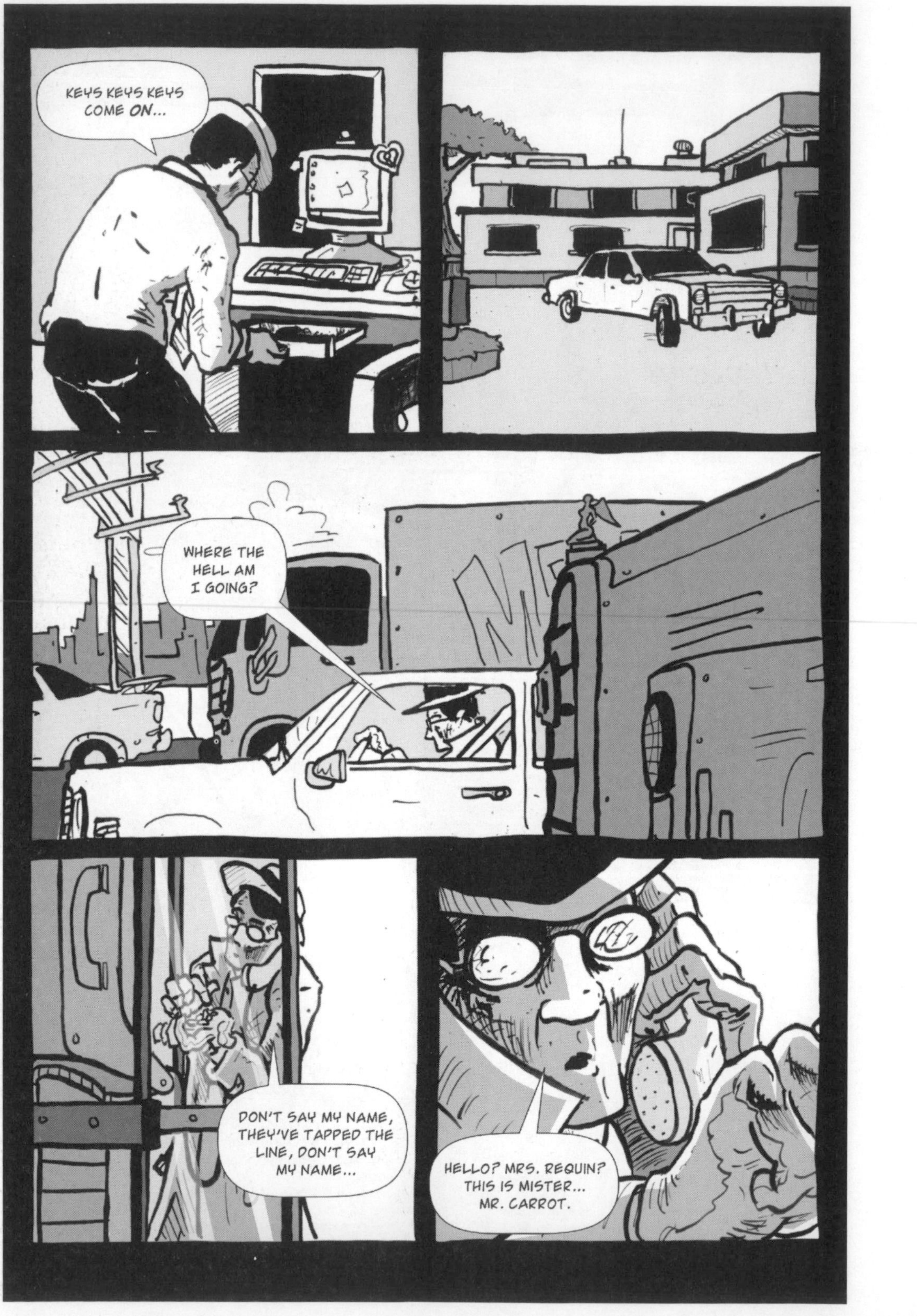
KEYS KEYS KEYS COME ON...
WHERE THE HELL AM I GOING?
DON'T SAY MY NAME, THEY'VE TAPPED THE LINE, DON'T SAY MY NAME...
HELLO? MRS. REQUIN? THIS IS MISTER... MR. CARROT.

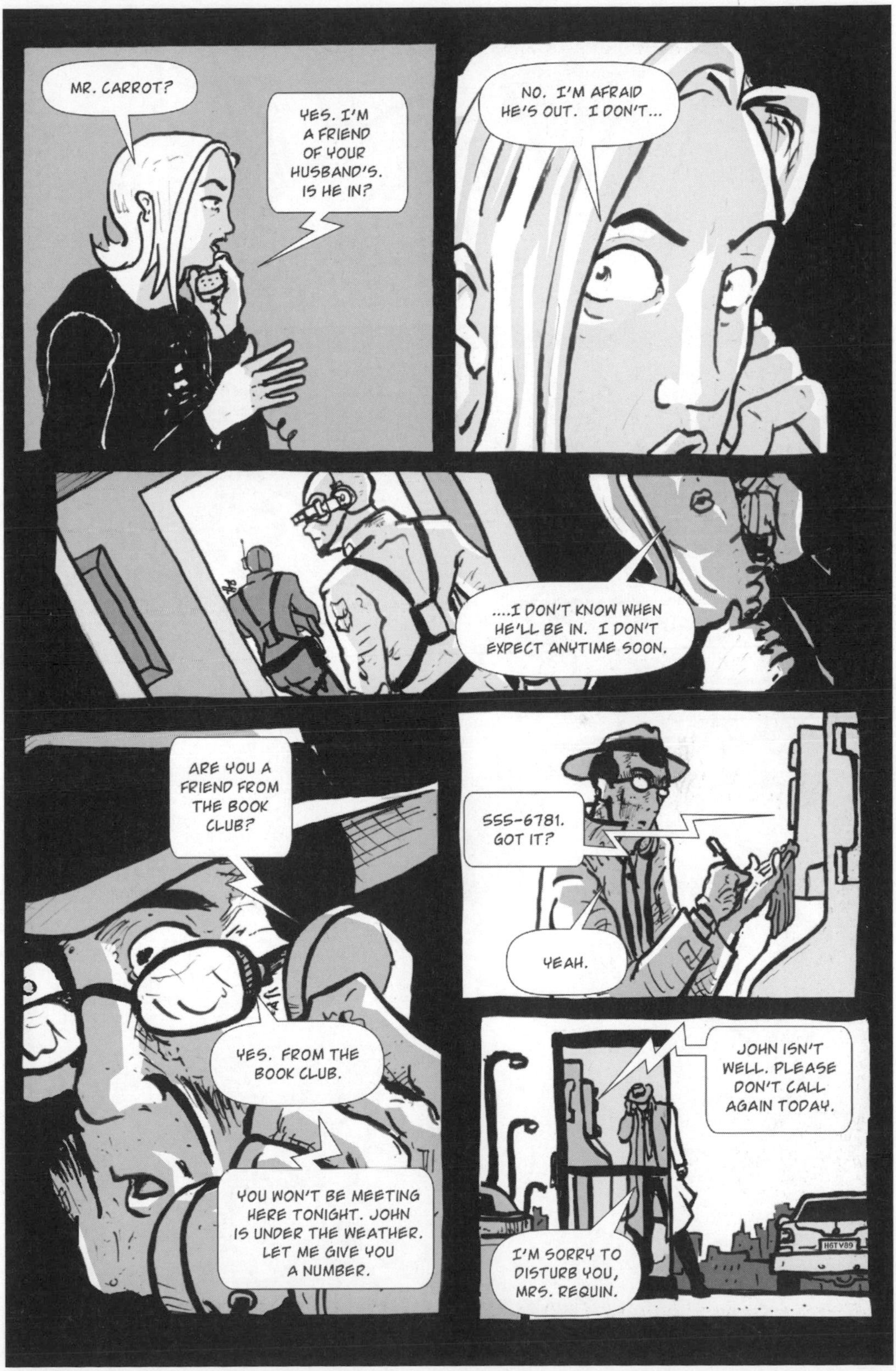
MR. CARROT?
YES. I'M A FRIEND OF YOUR HUSBAND'S. IS HE IN?
NO. I'M AFRAID HE'S OUT. I DON'T...
....I DON'T KNOW WHEN HE'LL BE IN. I DON'T EXPECT ANYTIME SOON.
ARE YOU A FRIEND FROM THE BOOK CLUB?
YES. FROM THE BOOK CLUB.
YOU WON'T BE MEETING HERE TONIGHT. JOHN IS UNDER THE WEATHER. LET ME GIVE YOU A NUMBER.
555-6781. GOT IT?
YEAH.
JOHN ISN'T WELL. PLEASE DON'T CALL AGAIN TODAY.
I'M SORRY TO DISTURB YOU, MRS. REQUIN.

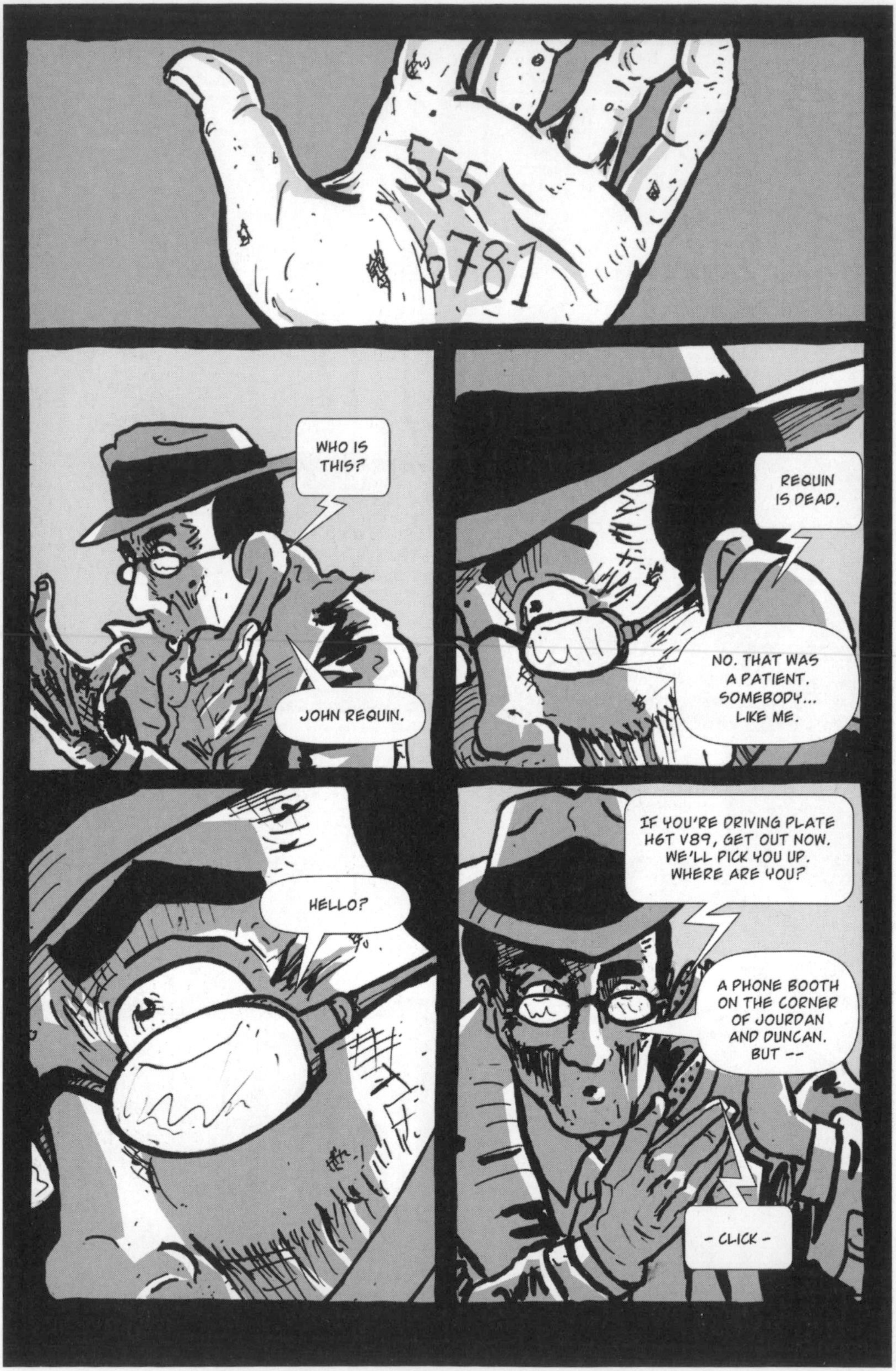
555
6781
WHO IS THIS?
JOHN REQUIN.
REQUIN IS DEAD.
NO. THAT WAS A PATIENT. SOMEBODY... LIKE ME.
HELLO?
IF YOU'RE DRIVING PLATE H6T V89, GET OUT NOW. WE'LL PICK YOU UP. WHERE ARE YOU?
A PHONE BOOTH ON THE CORNER OF JOURDAN AND DUNCAN. BUT --
- CLICK -

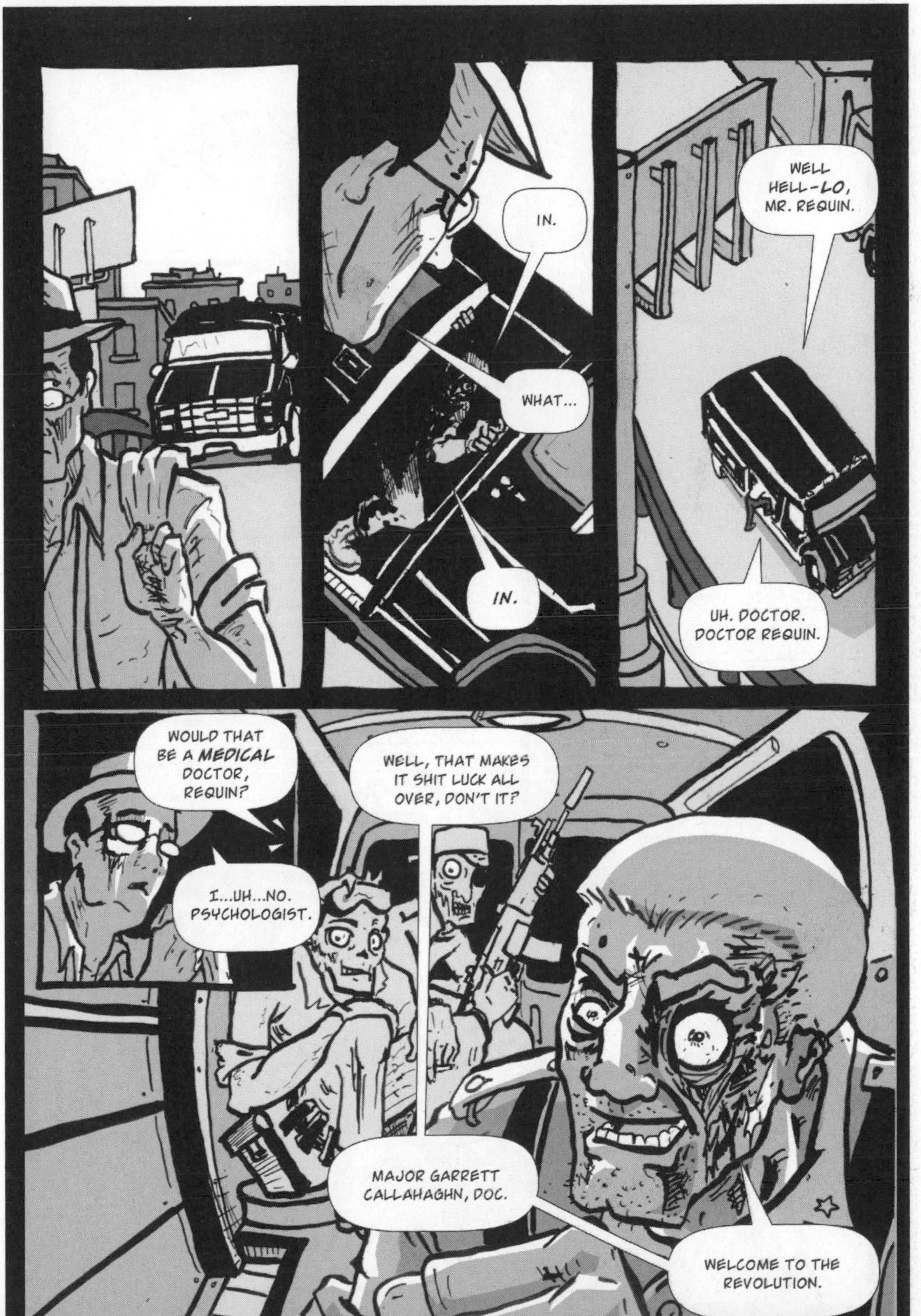
IN.
WHAT...
IN.
WELL HELL-LO, MR. REQUIN.
UH. DOCTOR. DOCTOR REQUIN.
WOULD THAT BE A MEDICAL DOCTOR, REQUIN?
I...UH...NO. PSYCHOLOGIST.
WELL, THAT MAKES IT SHIT LUCK ALL OVER, DON'T IT?
MAJOR GARRETT CALLAHAGHN, DOC.
WELCOME TO THE REVOLUTION.

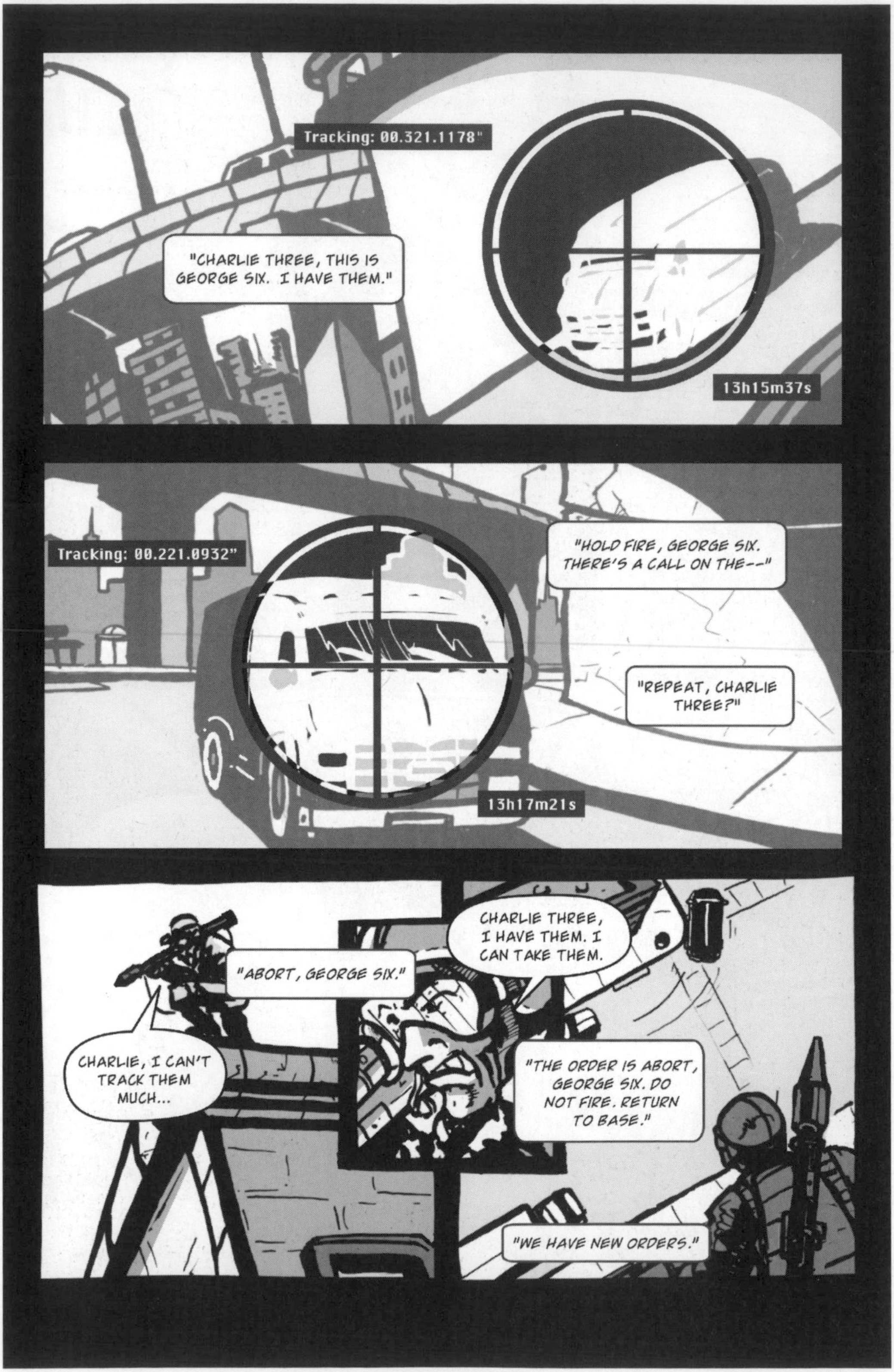
Tracking: 00.321.1178"
"CHARLIE THREE, THIS IS GEORGE SIX. I HAVE THEM."
13h15m37s
Tracking: 00.221.0932"
"HOLD FIRE, GEORGE SIX. THERE'S A CALL ON THE--"
"REPEAT, CHARLIE THREE?"
13h17m21s
"ABORT, GEORGE SIX."
CHARLIE THREE, I HAVE THEM. I CAN TAKE THEM.
CHARLIE, I CAN'T TRACK THEM MUCH...
"THE ORDER IS ABORT, GEORGE SIX. DO NOT FIRE. RETURN TO BASE."
"WE HAVE NEW ORDERS."

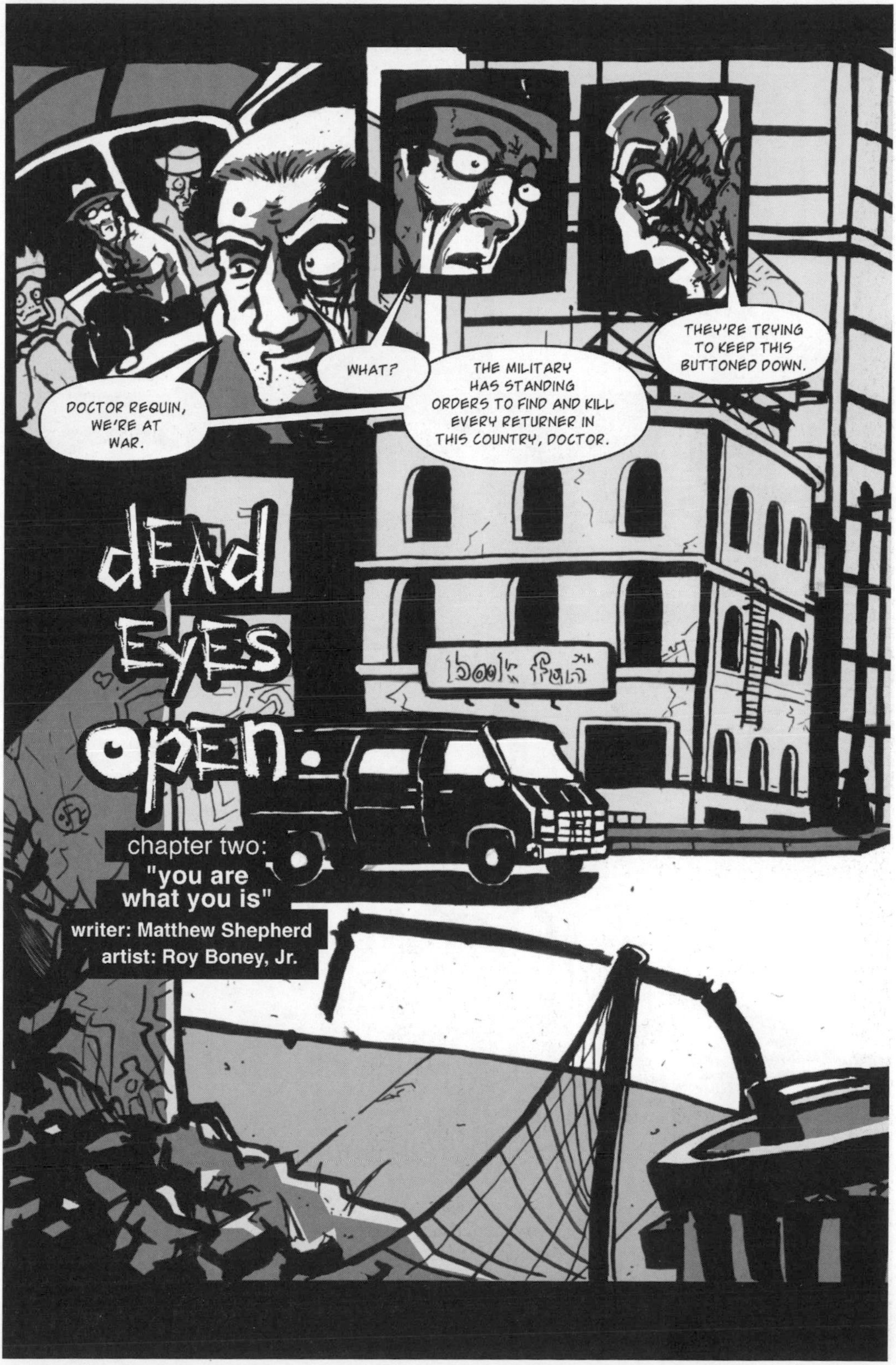
DOCTOR REQUIN, WE'RE AT WAR.
WHAT?
THE MILITARY HAS STANDING ORDERS TO FIND AND KILL EVERY RETURNER IN THIS COUNTRY, DOCTOR.
THEY'RE TRYING TO KEEP THIS BUTTONED DOWN.
dead Eyes open.
chapter two:
"you are what you is"
writer: Matthew Shepherd
artist: Roy Boney, Jr.

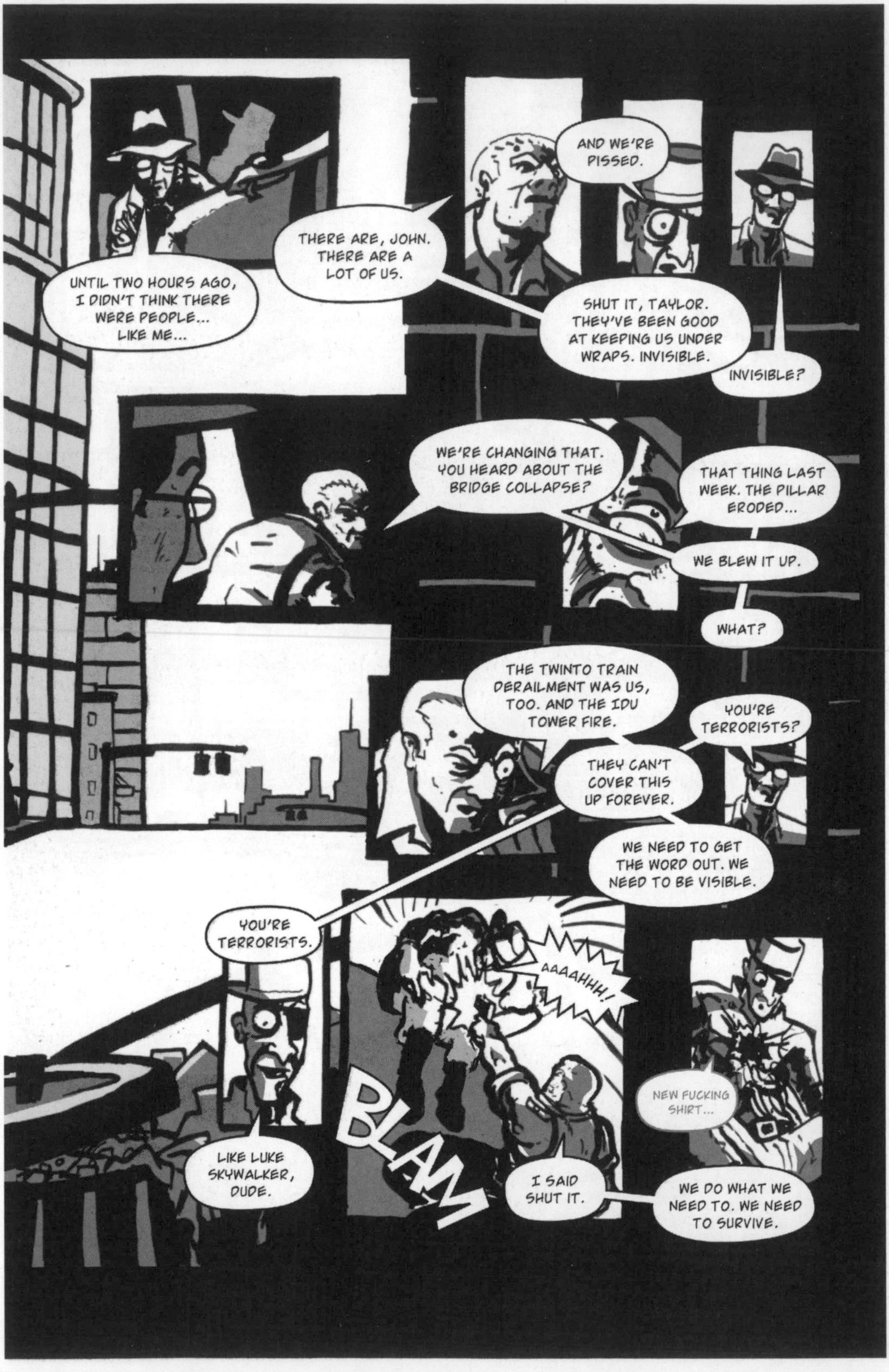
UNTIL TWO HOURS AGO, I DIDN'T THINK THERE WERE PEOPLE... LIKE ME...
THERE ARE, JOHN. THERE ARE A LOT OF US.
AND WE'RE PISSED.
SHUT IT, TAYLOR. THEY'VE BEEN GOOD AT KEEPING US UNDER WRAPS. INVISIBLE.
INVISIBLE?
WE'RE CHANGING THAT. YOU HEARD ABOUT THE BRIDGE COLLAPSE?
THAT THING LAST WEEK. THE PILLAR ERODED...
WE BLEW IT UP.
WHAT?
THE TWINTO TRAIN DERAILMENT WAS US, TOO. AND THE IDU TOWER FIRE.
YOU'RE TERRORISTS?
THEY CAN'T COVER THIS UP FOREVER.
WE NEED TO GET THE WORD OUT. WE NEED TO BE VISIBLE.
YOU'RE TERRORISTS.
LIKE LUKE SKYWALKER, DUDE.
AAAAAHHH!
BLAM
I SAID SHUT IT.
NEW FUCKING SHIRT...
WE DO WHAT WE NEED TO. WE NEED TO SURVIVE.

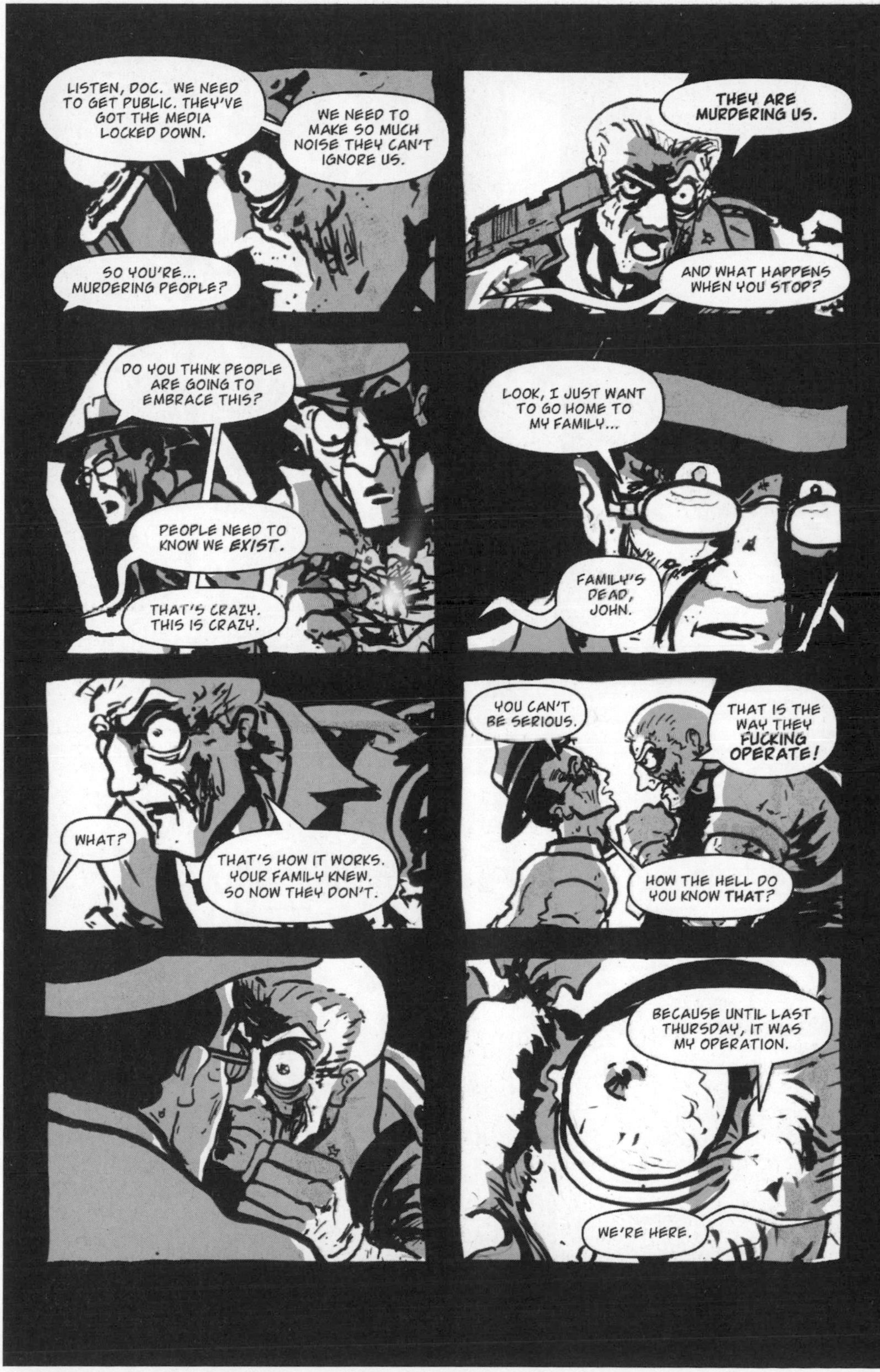
LISTEN, DOC. WE NEED TO GET PUBLIC. THEY'VE GOT THE MEDIA LOCKED DOWN.
WE NEED TO MAKE SO MUCH NOISE THEY CAN'T IGNORE US.
SO YOU'RE... MURDERING PEOPLE?
THEY ARE MURDERING US.
AND WHAT HAPPENS WHEN YOU STOP?
DO YOU THINK PEOPLE ARE GOING TO EMBRACE THIS?
PEOPLE NEED TO KNOW WE EXIST.
THAT'S CRAZY. THIS IS CRAZY.
LOOK, I JUST WANT TO GO HOME TO MY FAMILY...
FAMILY'S DEAD, JOHN.
WHAT?
THAT'S HOW IT WORKS. YOUR FAMILY KNEW. SO NOW THEY DON'T.
YOU CAN'T BE SERIOUS.
THAT IS THE WAY THEY FUCKING OPERATE!
HOW THE HELL DO YOU KNOW THAT?
BECAUSE UNTIL LAST THURSDAY, IT WAS MY OPERATION.
WE'RE HERE.

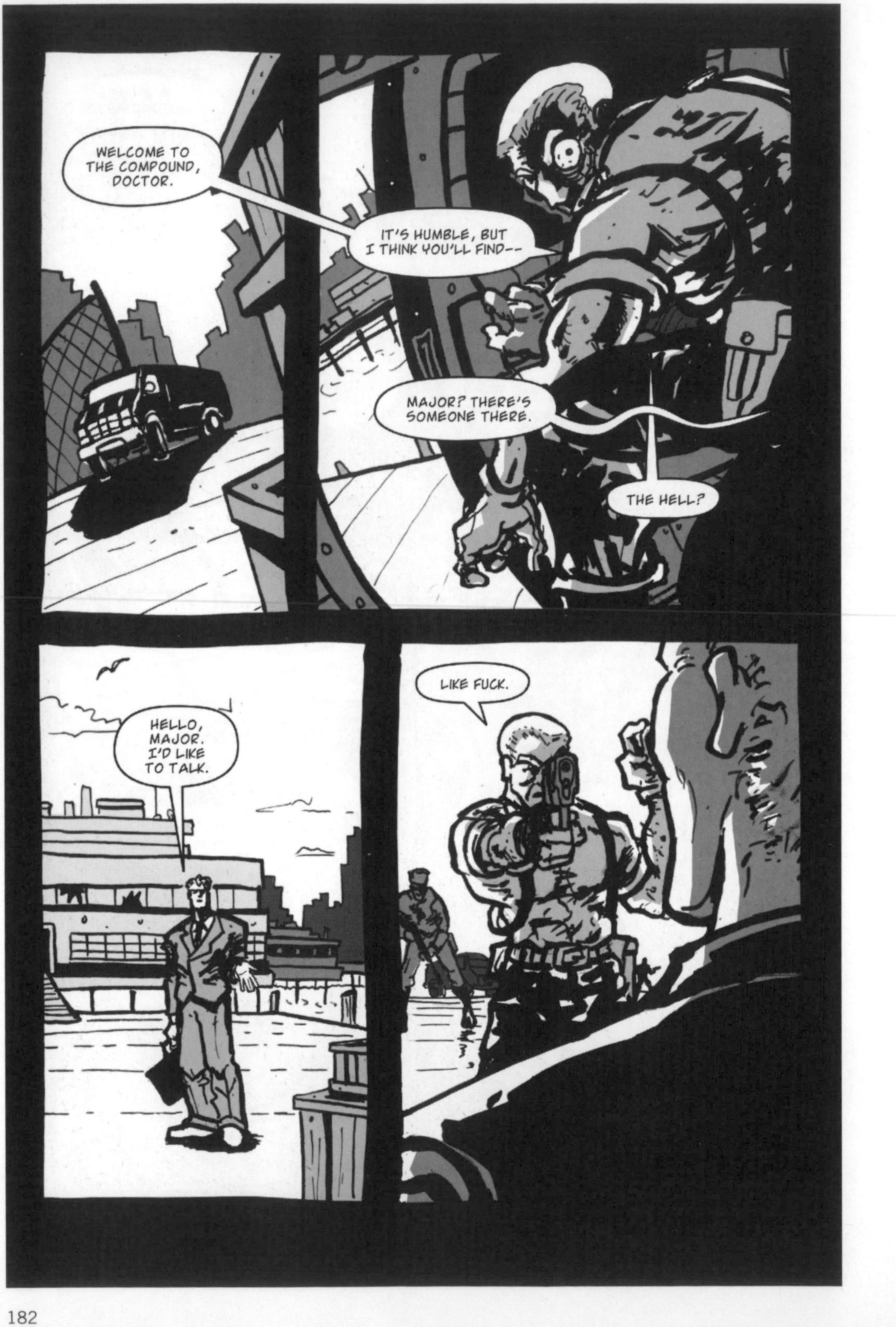
WELCOME TO THE COMPOUND, DOCTOR.
IT'S HUMBLE, BUT I THINK YOU'LL FIND--
MAJOR? THERE'S SOMEONE THERE.
THE HELL?
HELLO, MAJOR. I'D LIKE TO TALK.
LIKE FUCK.

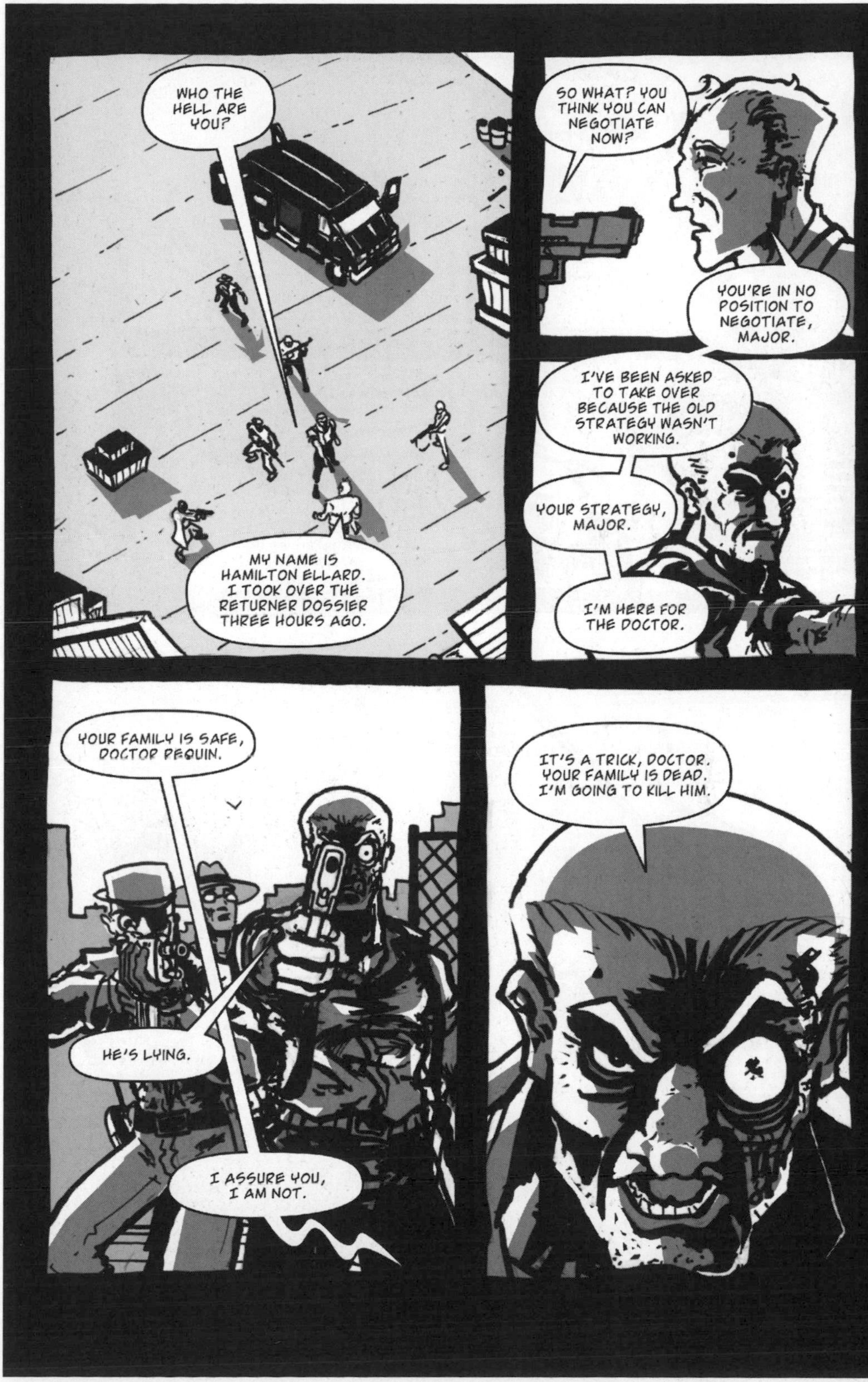
WHO THE HELL ARE YOU?
MY NAME IS HAMILTON ELLARD. I TOOK OVER THE RETURNER DOSSIER THREE HOURS AGO.
SO WHAT? YOU THINK YOU CAN NEGOTIATE NOW?
YOU'RE IN NO POSITION TO NEGOTIATE, MAJOR.
I'VE BEEN ASKED TO TAKE OVER BECAUSE THE OLD STRATEGY WASN'T WORKING.
YOUR STRATEGY, MAJOR.
I'M HERE FOR THE DOCTOR.
YOUR FAMILY IS SAFE, DOCTOR PEQUIN.
HE'S LYING.
I ASSURE YOU, I AM NOT.
IT'S A TRICK, DOCTOR. YOUR FAMILY IS DEAD. I'M GOING TO KILL HIM.

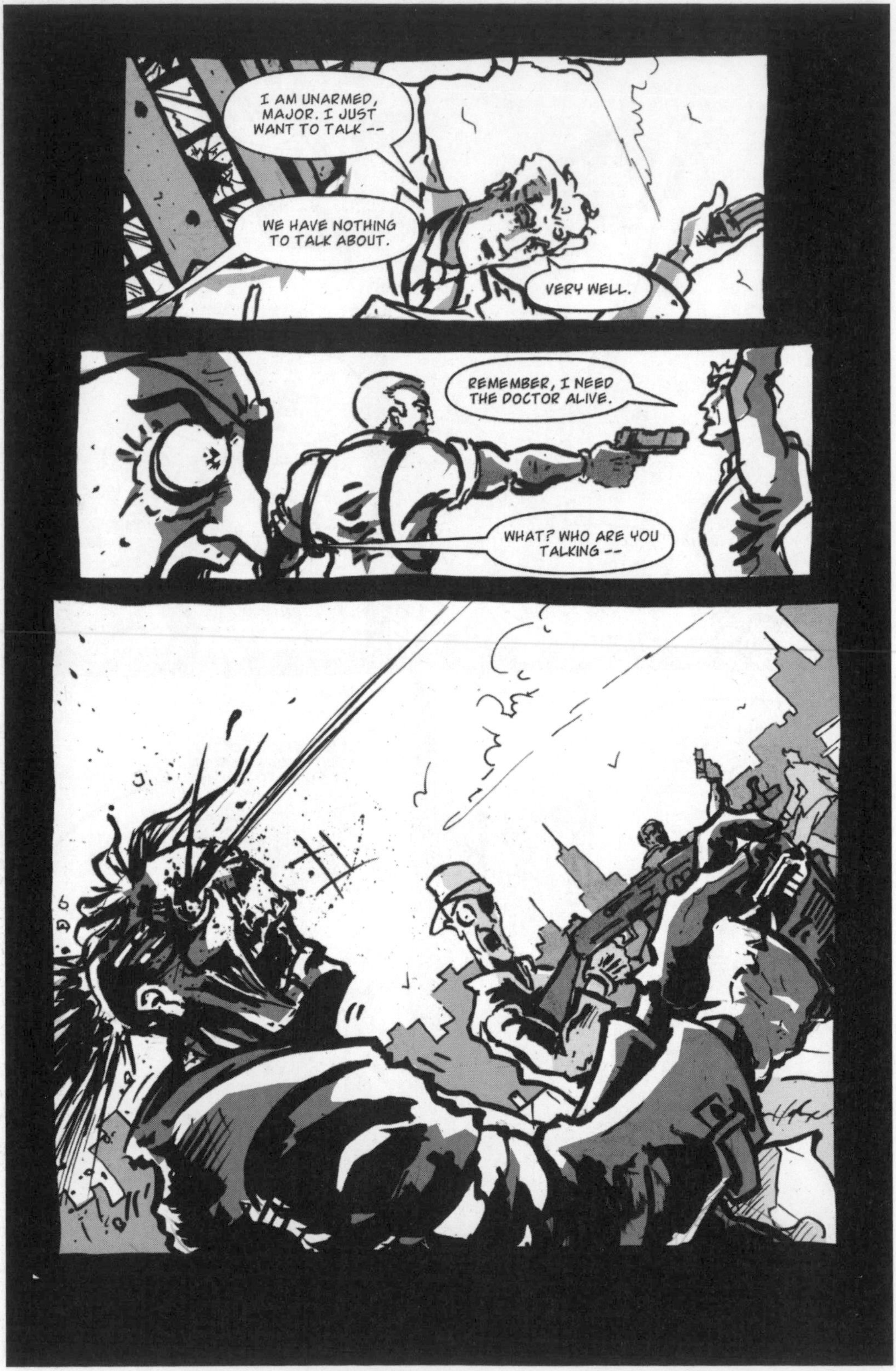
I AM UNARMED, MAJOR. I JUST WANT TO TALK --
WE HAVE NOTHING TO TALK ABOUT.
VERY WELL.
REMEMBER, I NEED THE DOCTOR ALIVE.
WHAT? WHO ARE YOU TALKING --

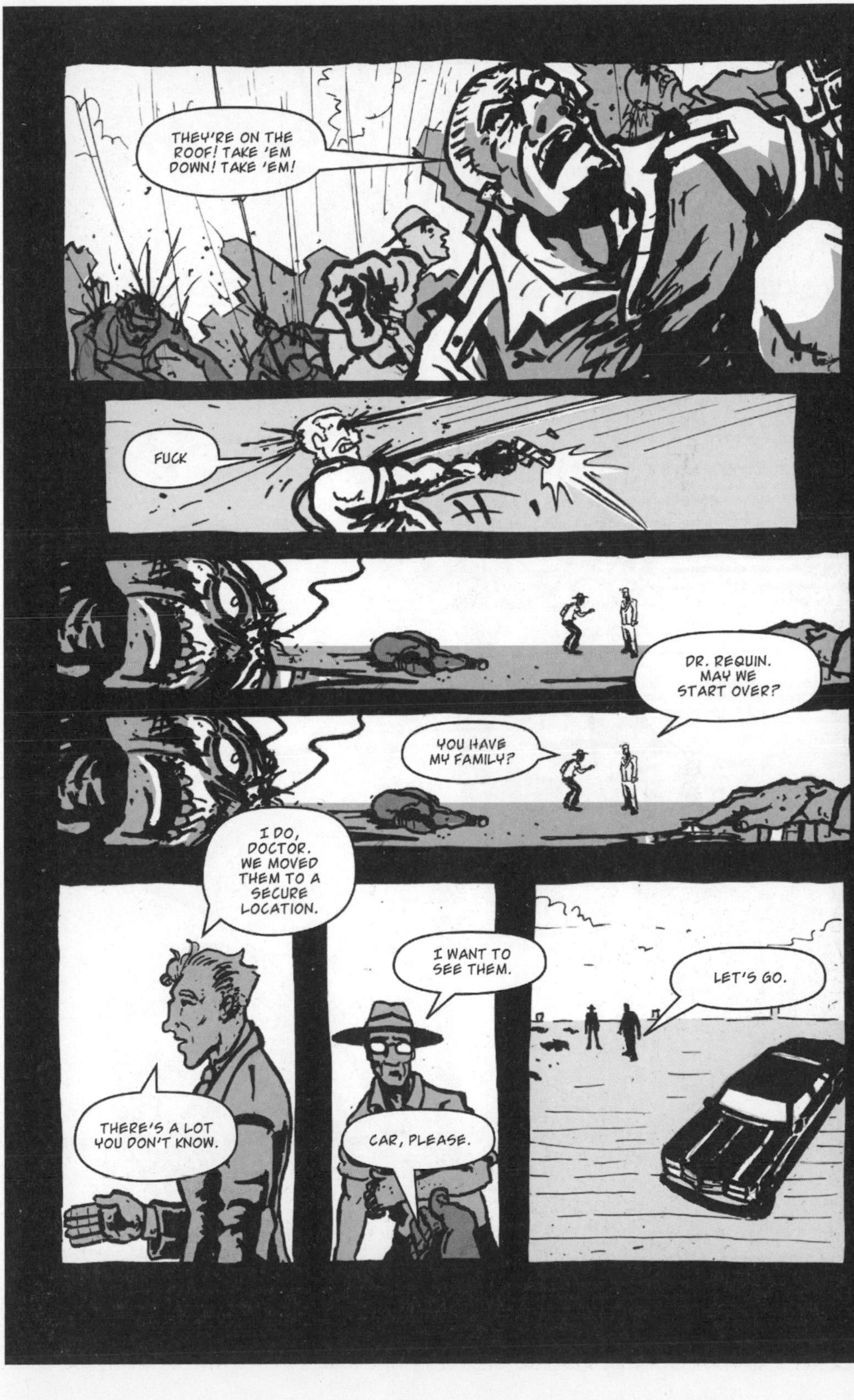
THEY'RE ON THE ROOF! TAKE 'EM DOWN! TAKE 'EM!
FUCK
DR. REQUIN. MAY WE START OVER?
YOU HAVE MY FAMILY?
I DO, DOCTOR. WE MOVED THEM TO A SECURE LOCATION.
THERE'S A LOT YOU DON'T KNOW.
I WANT TO SEE THEM.
CAR, PLEASE.
LET'S GO.

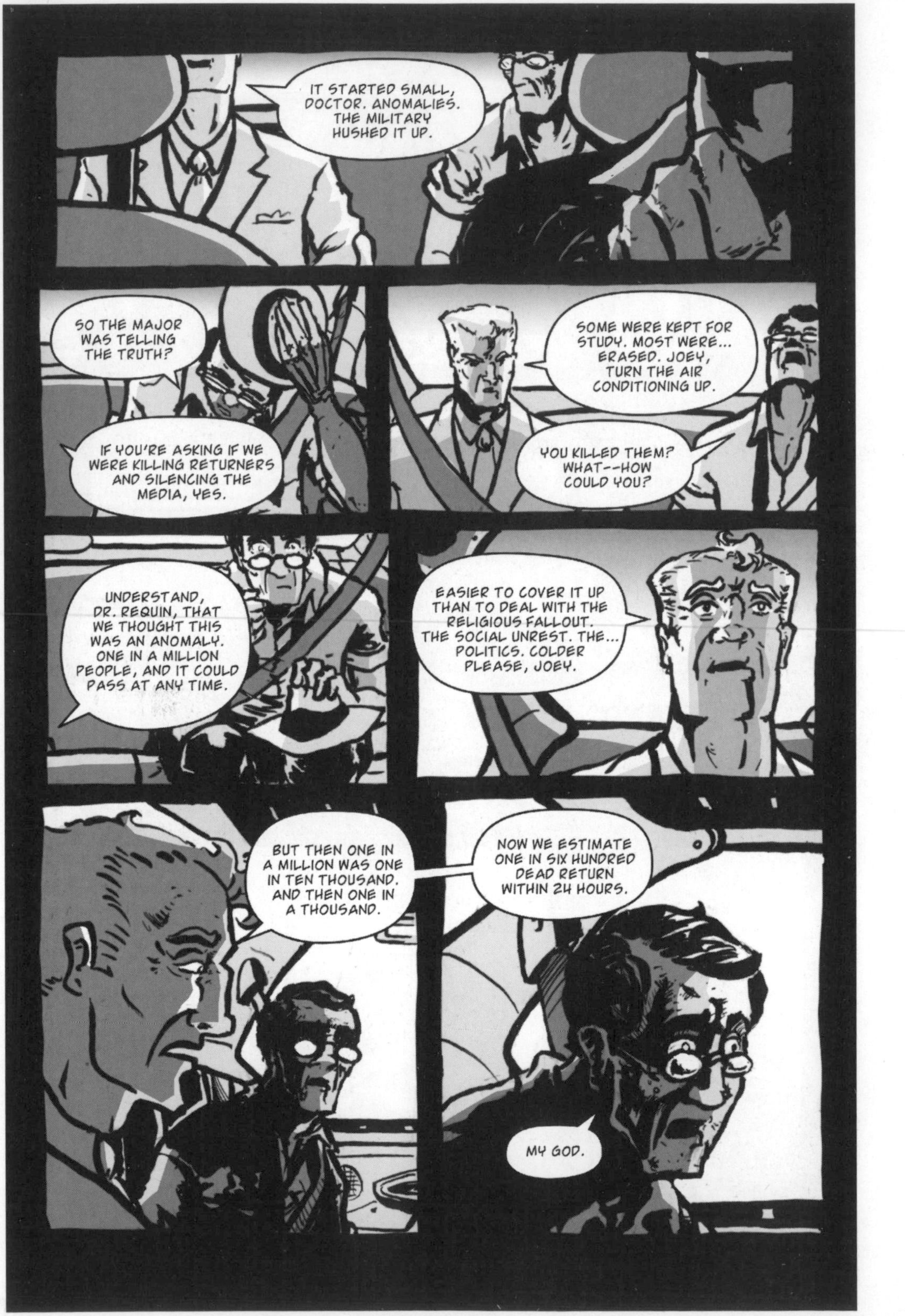
IT STARTED SMALL, DOCTOR. ANOMALIES. THE MILITARY HUSHED IT UP.
SO THE MAJOR WAS TELLING THE TRUTH?
IF YOU'RE ASKING IF WE WERE KILLING RETURNERS AND SILENCING THE MEDIA, YES.
SOME WERE KEPT FOR STUDY. MOST WERE... ERASED. JOEY, TURN THE AIR CONDITIONING UP.
YOU KILLED THEM? WHAT--HOW COULD YOU?
UNDERSTAND, DR. REQUIN, THAT WE THOUGHT THIS WAS AN ANOMALY. ONE IN A MILLION PEOPLE, AND IT COULD PASS AT ANY TIME.
EASIER TO COVER IT UP THAN TO DEAL WITH THE RELIGIOUS FALLOUT. THE SOCIAL UNREST. THE... POLITICS. COLDER PLEASE, JOEY.
BUT THEN ONE IN A MILLION WAS ONE IN TEN THOUSAND. AND THEN ONE IN A THOUSAND.
NOW WE ESTIMATE ONE IN SIX HUNDRED DEAD RETURN WITHIN 24 HOURS.
MY GOD.

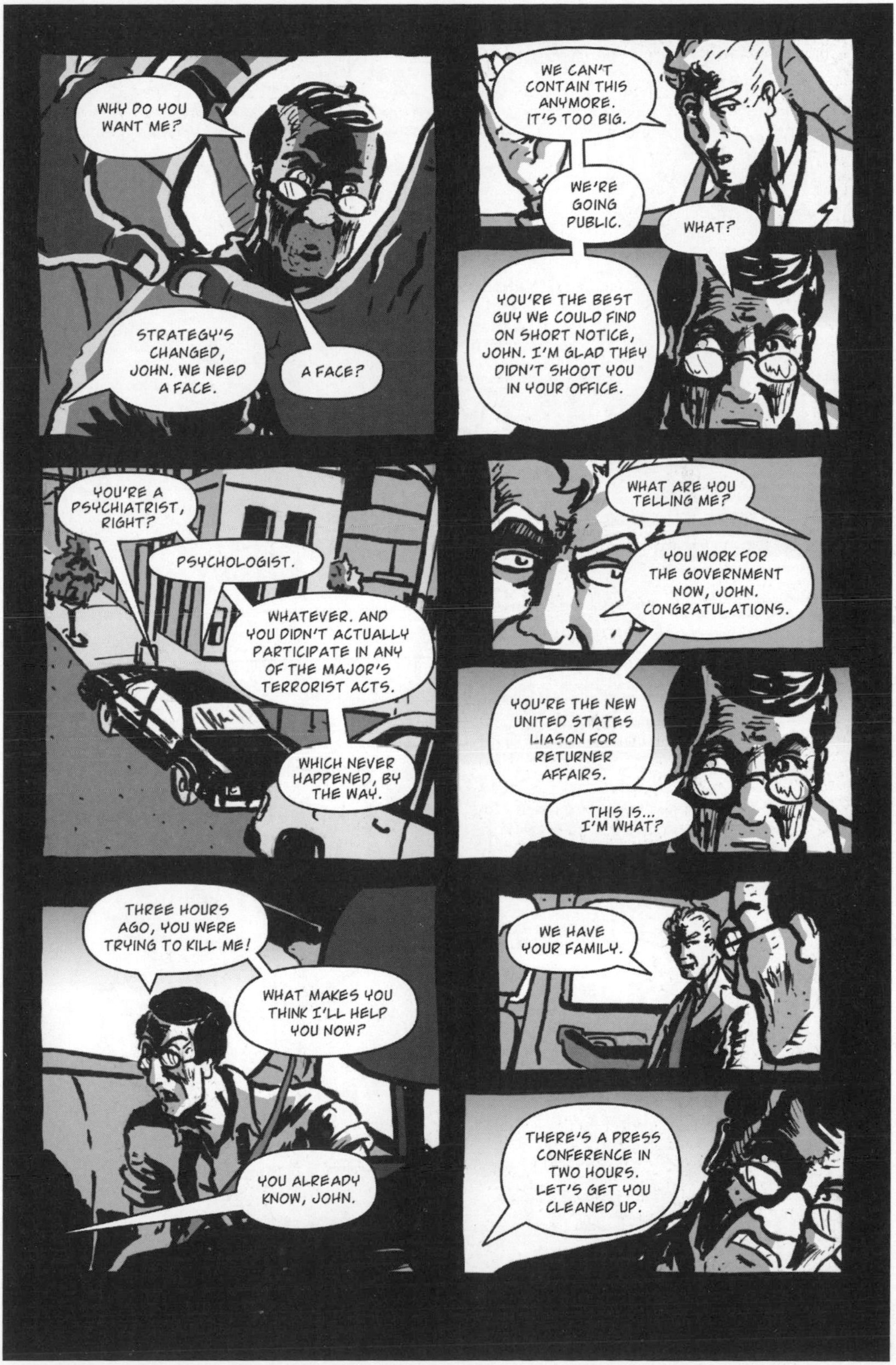
WHY DO YOU WANT ME?
STRATEGY'S CHANGED, JOHN. WE NEED A FACE.
A FACE?
WE CAN'T CONTAIN THIS ANYMORE. IT'S TOO BIG.
WE'RE GOING PUBLIC.
WHAT?
YOU'RE THE BEST GUY WE COULD FIND ON SHORT NOTICE, JOHN. I'M GLAD THEY DIDN'T SHOOT YOU IN YOUR OFFICE.
YOU'RE A PSYCHIATRIST, RIGHT?
PSYCHOLOGIST.
WHATEVER. AND YOU DIDN'T ACTUALLY PARTICIPATE IN ANY OF THE MAJOR'S TERRORIST ACTS.
WHICH NEVER HAPPENED, BY THE WAY.
WHAT ARE YOU TELLING ME?
YOU WORK FOR THE GOVERNMENT NOW, JOHN. CONGRATULATIONS.
YOU'RE THE NEW UNITED STATES LIASON FOR RETURNER AFFAIRS.
THIS IS... I'M WHAT?
THREE HOURS AGO, YOU WERE TRYING TO KILL ME!
WHAT MAKES YOU THINK I'LL HELP YOU NOW?
YOU ALREADY KNOW, JOHN.
WE HAVE YOUR FAMILY.
THERE'S A PRESS CONFERENCE IN TWO HOURS. LET'S GET YOU CLEANED UP.

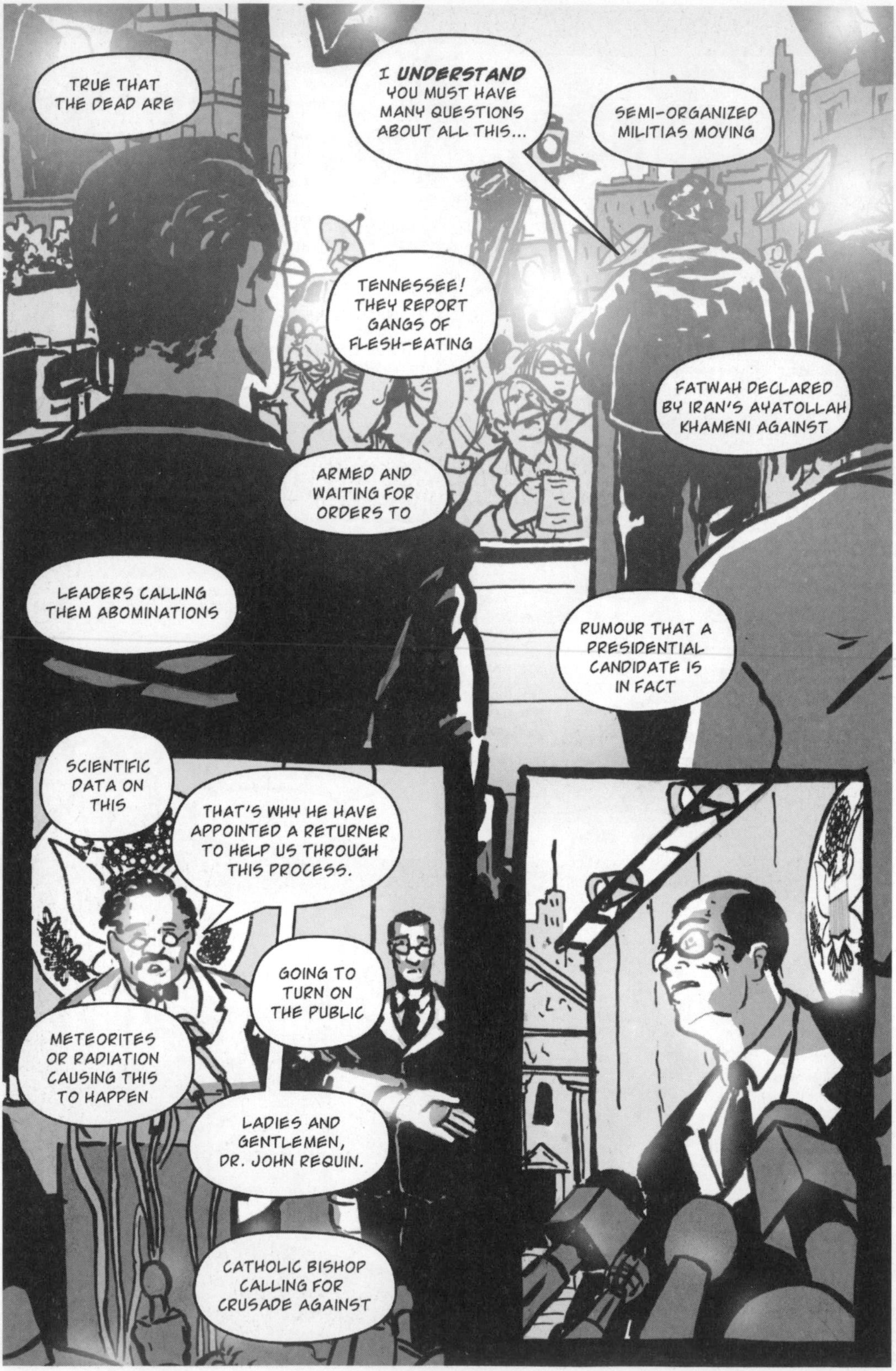

TRUE THAT THE DEAD ARE
I UNDERSTAND YOU MUST HAVE MANY QUESTIONS ABOUT ALL THIS...
SEMI-ORGANIZED MILITIAS MOVING
TENNESSEE! THEY REPORT GANGS OF FLESH-EATING
FATWAH DECLARED BY IRAN'S AYATOLLAH KHAMENI AGAINST
ARMED AND WAITING FOR ORDERS TO
LEADERS CALLING THEM ABOMINATIONS
RUMOUR THAT A PRESIDENTIAL CANDIDATE IS IN FACT
SCIENTIFIC DATA ON THIS
THAT'S WHY WE HAVE APPOINTED A RETURNER TO HELP US THROUGH THIS PROCESS.
GOING TO TURN ON THE PUBLIC
METEORITES OR RADIATION CAUSING THIS TO HAPPEN
LADIES AND GENTLEMEN, DR. JOHN REQUIN.
CATHOLIC BISHOP CALLING FOR CRUSADE AGAINST

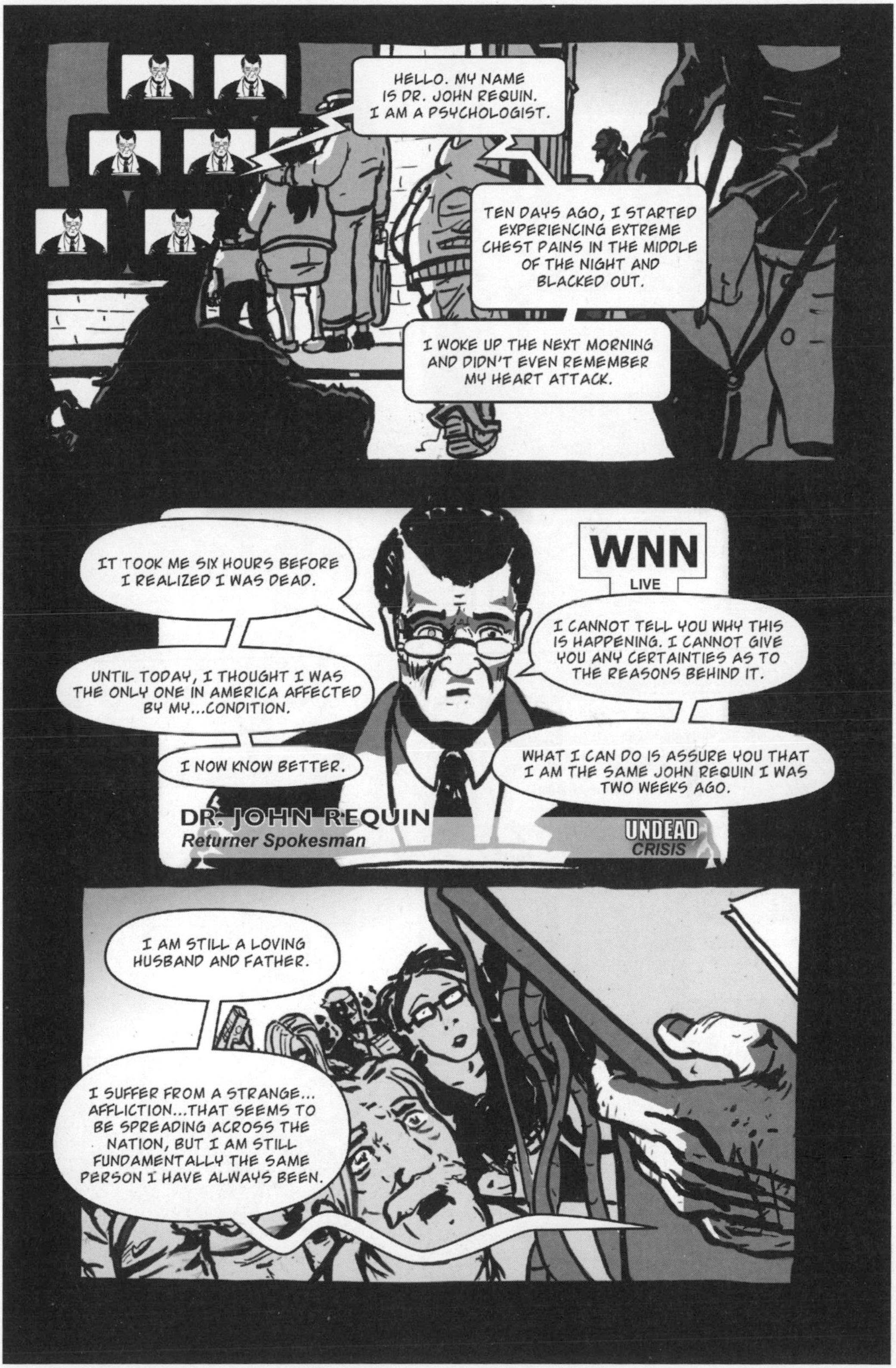
HELLO. MY NAME IS DR. JOHN REQUIN. I AM A PSYCHOLOGIST.
TEN DAYS AGO, I STARTED EXPERIENCING EXTREME CHEST PAINS IN THE MIDDLE OF THE NIGHT AND BLACKED OUT.
I WOKE UP THE NEXT MORNING AND DIDN'T EVEN REMEMBER MY HEART ATTACK.
WNN
LIVE
IT TOOK ME SIX HOURS BEFORE I REALIZED I WAS DEAD.
UNTIL TODAY, I THOUGHT I WAS THE ONLY ONE IN AMERICA AFFECTED BY MY...CONDITION.
I NOW KNOW BETTER.
I CANNOT TELL YOU WHY THIS IS HAPPENING. I CANNOT GIVE YOU ANY CERTAINTIES AS TO THE REASONS BEHIND IT.
WHAT I CAN DO IS ASSURE YOU THAT I AM THE SAME JOHN REQUIN I WAS TWO WEEKS AGO.
DR. JOHN REQUIN
Returner Spokesman
UNDEAD
CRISIS
I AM STILL A LOVING HUSBAND AND FATHER.
I SUFFER FROM A STRANGE... AFFLICTION...THAT SEEMS TO BE SPREADING ACROSS THE NATION, BUT I AM STILL FUNDAMENTALLY THE SAME PERSON I HAVE ALWAYS BEEN.

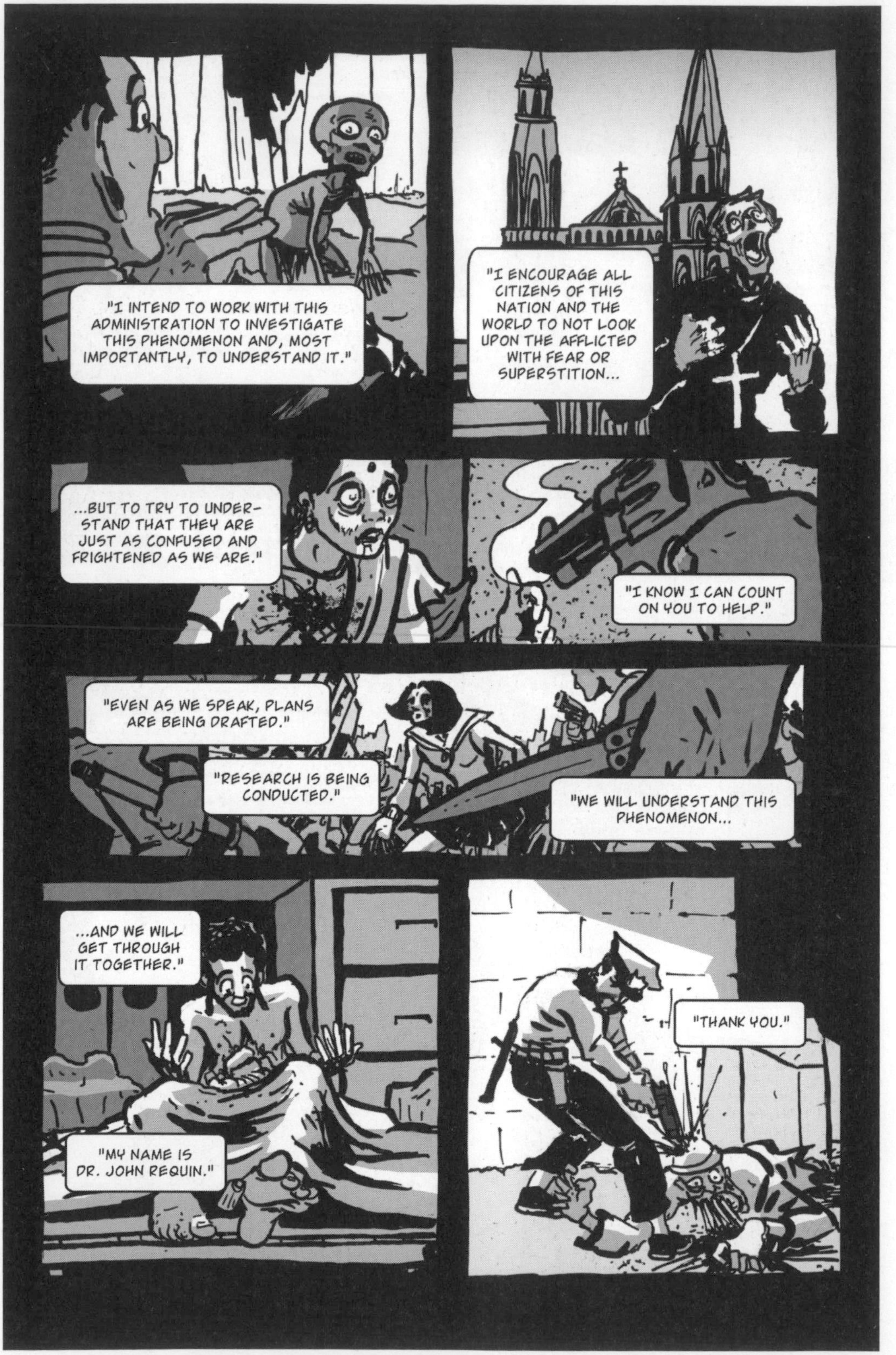
"I INTEND TO WORK WITH THIS ADMINISTRATION TO INVESTIGATE THIS PHENOMENON AND, MOST IMPORTANTLY, TO UNDERSTAND IT."
"I ENCOURAGE ALL CITIZENS OF THIS NATION AND THE WORLD TO NOT LOOK UPON THE AFFLICTED WITH FEAR OR SUPERSTITION...
...BUT TO TRY TO UNDERSTAND THAT THEY ARE JUST AS CONFUSED AND FRIGHTENED AS WE ARE."
"I KNOW I CAN COUNT ON YOU TO HELP."
"EVEN AS WE SPEAK, PLANS ARE BEING DRAFTED."
"RESEARCH IS BEING CONDUCTED."
"WE WILL UNDERSTAND THIS PHENOMENON...
...AND WE WILL GET THROUGH IT TOGETHER."
"MY NAME IS DR. JOHN REQUIN."
"THANK YOU."

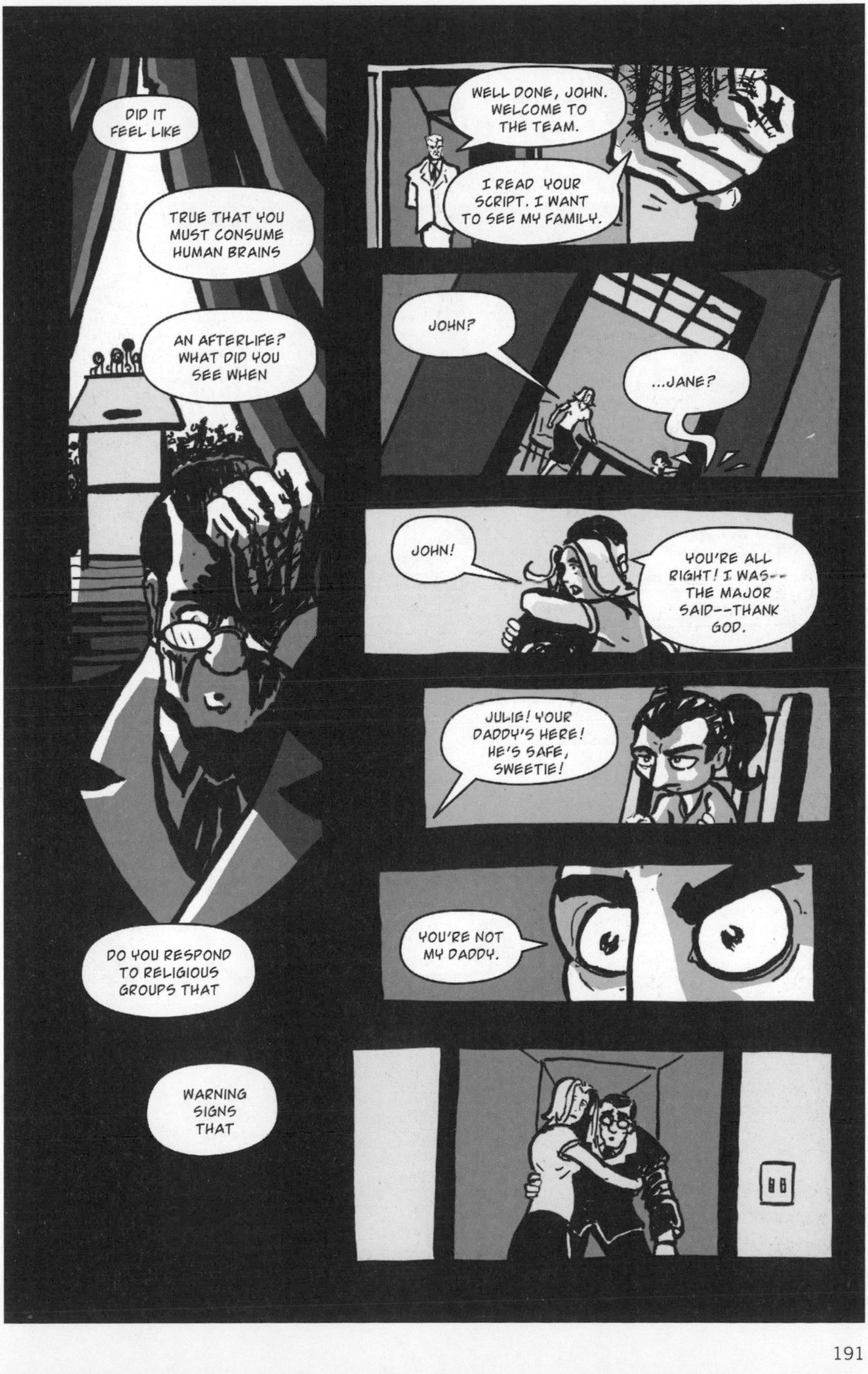
DID IT FEEL LIKE
TRUE THAT YOU MUST CONSUME HUMAN BRAINS
AN AFTERLIFE? WHAT DID YOU SEE WHEN
DO YOU RESPOND TO RELIGIOUS GROUPS THAT
WARNING SIGNS THAT
WELL DONE, JOHN. WELCOME TO THE TEAM.
I READ YOUR SCRIPT. I WANT TO SEE MY FAMILY.
JOHN?
...JANE?
JOHN!
YOU'RE ALL RIGHT! I WAS-- THE MAJOR SAID--THANK GOD.
JULIE! YOUR DADDY'S HERE! HE'S SAFE, SWEETIE!
YOU'RE NOT MY DADDY.

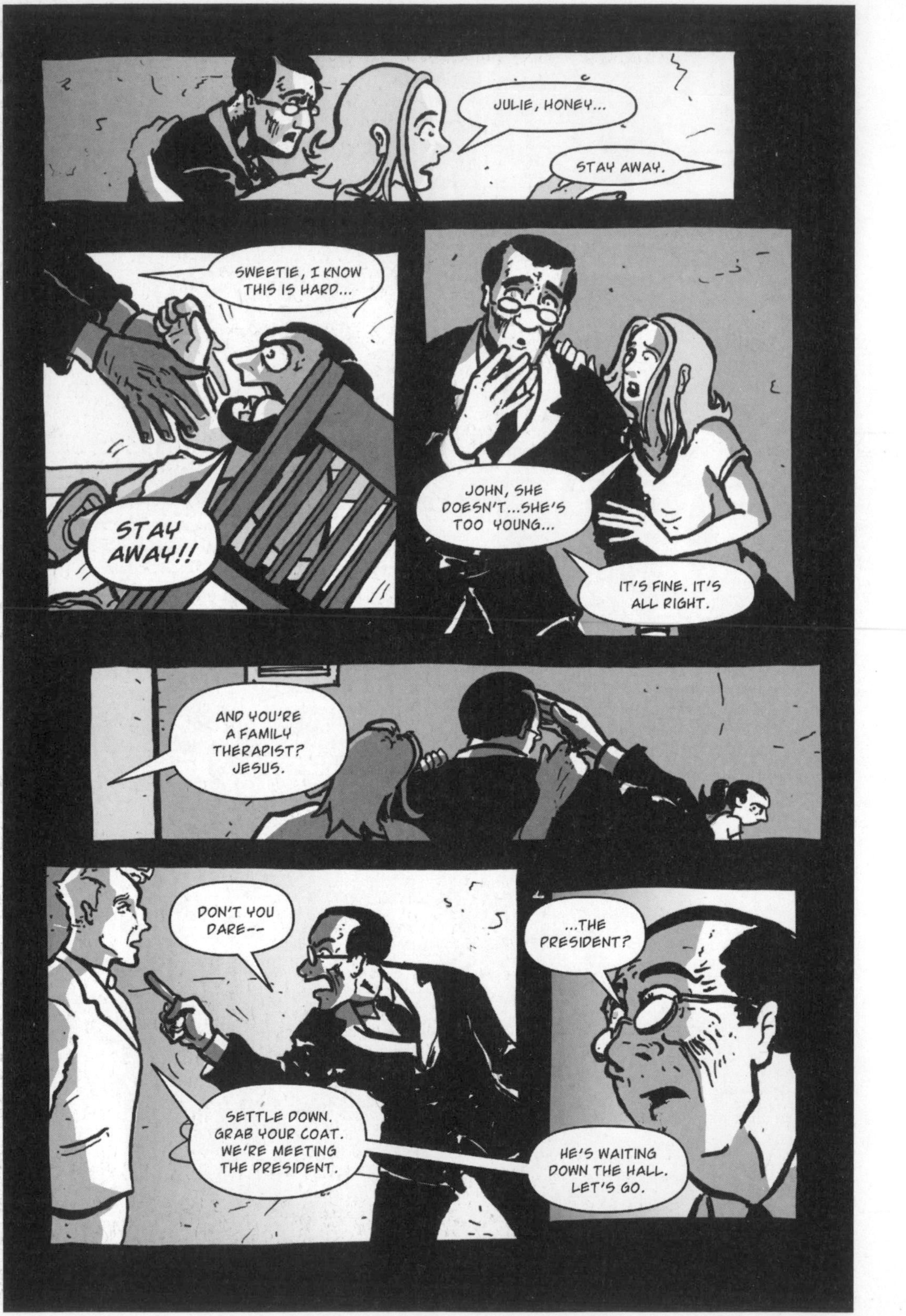
JULIE, HONEY...
STAY AWAY.
SWEETIE, I KNOW THIS IS HARD...
STAY AWAY!!
JOHN, SHE DOESN'T...SHE'S TOO YOUNG...
IT'S FINE. IT'S ALL RIGHT.
AND YOU'RE A FAMILY THERAPIST? JESUS.
DON'T YOU DARE--
SETTLE DOWN. GRAB YOUR COAT. WE'RE MEETING THE PRESIDENT.
...THE PRESIDENT?
HE'S WAITING DOWN THE HALL. LET'S GO.

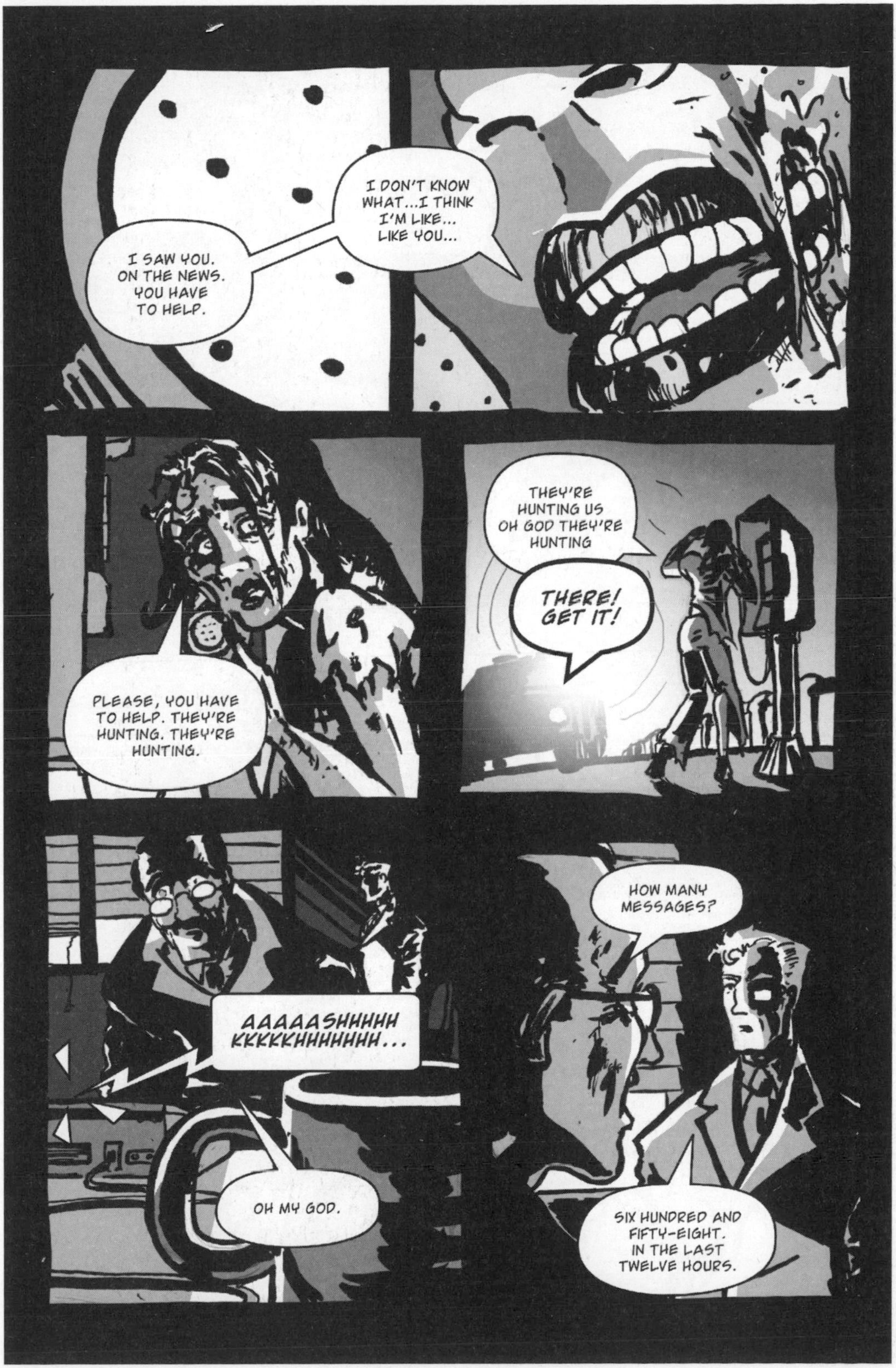
I SAW YOU. ON THE NEWS. YOU HAVE TO HELP.
I DON'T KNOW WHAT...I THINK I'M LIKE... LIKE YOU...
PLEASE, YOU HAVE TO HELP. THEY'RE HUNTING. THEY'RE HUNTING.
THEY'RE HUNTING US OH GOD THEY'RE HUNTING
THERE! GET IT!
AAAAASHHHHH KKKKKHHHHHHH...
OH MY GOD.
HOW MANY MESSAGES?
SIX HUNDRED AND FIFTY-EIGHT. IN THE LAST TWELVE HOURS.

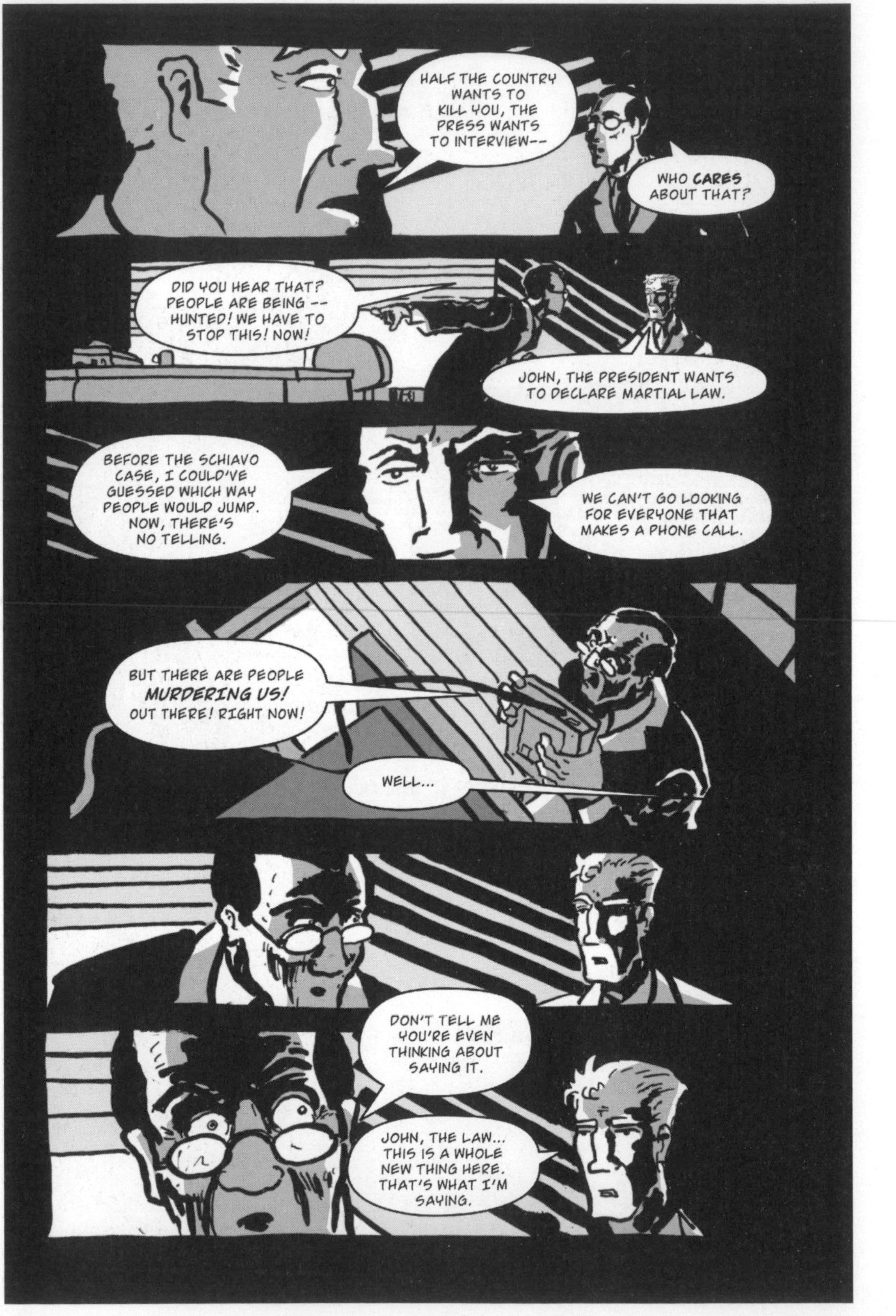
HALF THE COUNTRY WANTS TO KILL YOU, THE PRESS WANTS TO INTERVIEW--
WHO CARES ABOUT THAT?
DID YOU HEAR THAT? PEOPLE ARE BEING -- HUNTED! WE HAVE TO STOP THIS! NOW!
JOHN, THE PRESIDENT WANTS TO DECLARE MARTIAL LAW.
BEFORE THE SCHIAVO CASE, I COULD'VE GUESSED WHICH WAY PEOPLE WOULD JUMP. NOW, THERE'S NO TELLING.
WE CAN'T GO LOOKING FOR EVERYONE THAT MAKES A PHONE CALL.
BUT THERE ARE PEOPLE MURDERING US! OUT THERE! RIGHT NOW!
WELL...
DON'T TELL ME YOU'RE EVEN THINKING ABOUT SAYING IT.
JOHN, THE LAW... THIS IS A WHOLE NEW THING HERE. THAT'S WHAT I'M SAYING.

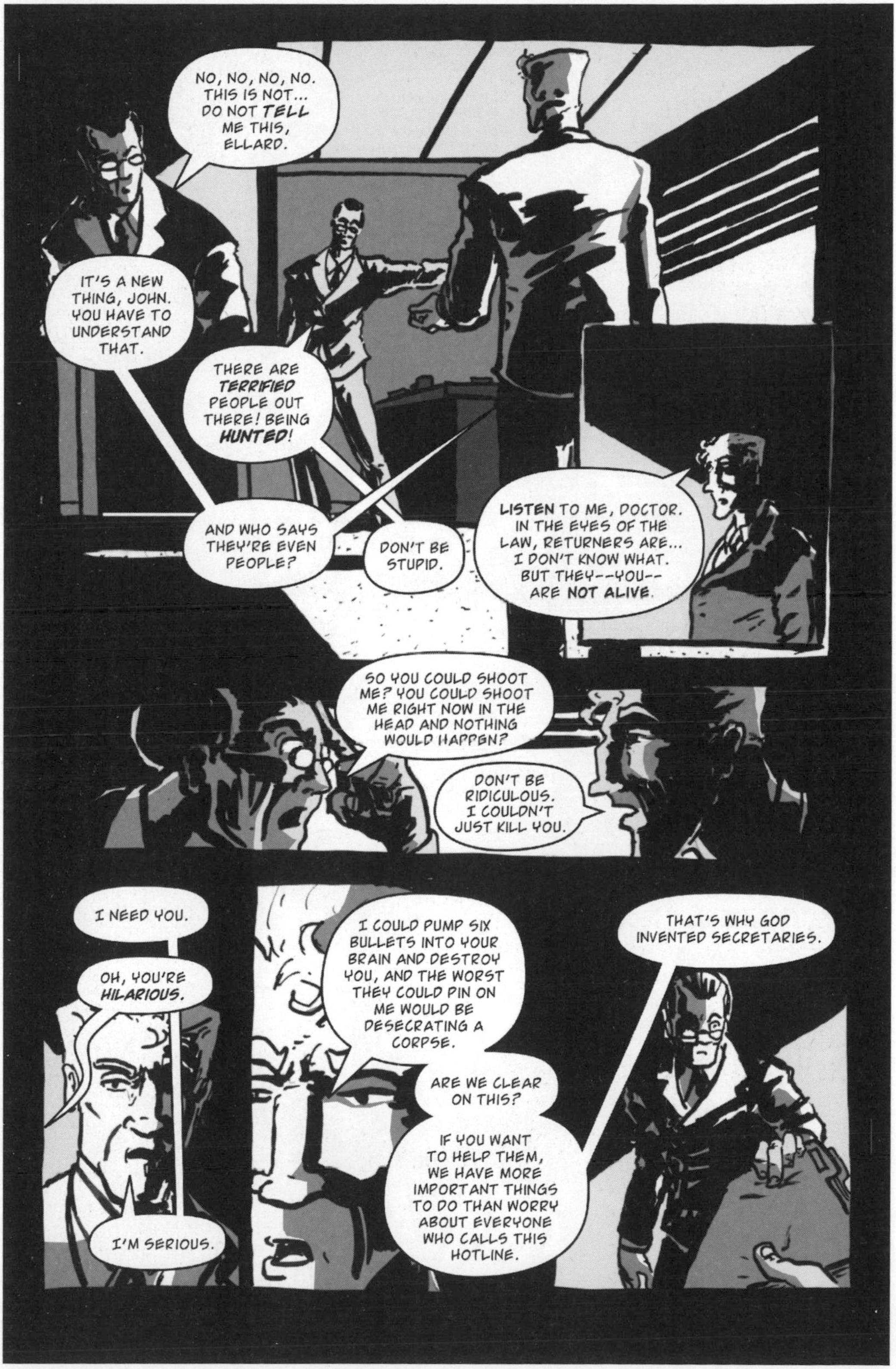
NO, NO, NO, NO. THIS IS NOT... DO NOT TELL ME THIS, ELLARD.
IT'S A NEW THING, JOHN. YOU HAVE TO UNDERSTAND THAT.
THERE ARE TERRIFIED PEOPLE OUT THERE! BEING HUNTED!
AND WHO SAYS THEY'RE EVEN PEOPLE?
DON'T BE STUPID.
LISTEN TO ME, DOCTOR. IN THE EYES OF THE LAW, RETURNERS ARE... I DON'T KNOW WHAT. BUT THEY--YOU-- ARE NOT ALIVE.
SO YOU COULD SHOOT ME? YOU COULD SHOOT ME RIGHT NOW IN THE HEAD AND NOTHING WOULD HAPPEN?
DON'T BE RIDICULOUS. I COULDN'T JUST KILL YOU.
I NEED YOU.
OH, YOU'RE HILARIOUS.
I'M SERIOUS.
I COULD PUMP SIX BULLETS INTO YOUR BRAIN AND DESTROY YOU, AND THE WORST THEY COULD PIN ON ME WOULD BE DESECRATING A CORPSE.
ARE WE CLEAR ON THIS?
IF YOU WANT TO HELP THEM, WE HAVE MORE IMPORTANT THINGS TO DO THAN WORRY ABOUT EVERYONE WHO CALLS THIS HOTLINE.
THAT'S WHY GOD INVENTED SECRETARIES.

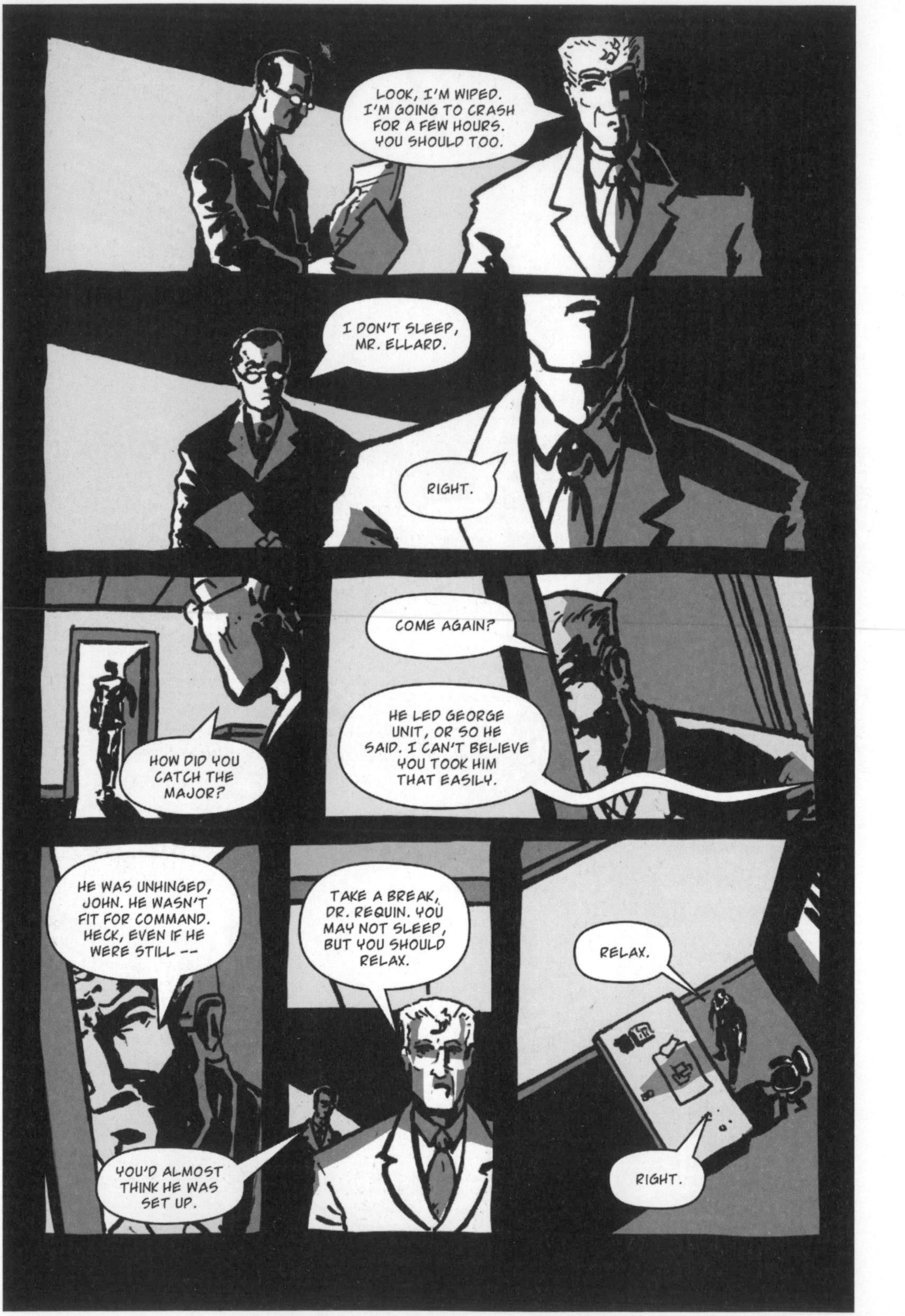
LOOK, I'M WIPED. I'M GOING TO CRASH FOR A FEW HOURS. YOU SHOULD TOO.
I DON'T SLEEP, MR. ELLARD.
RIGHT.
HOW DID YOU CATCH THE MAJOR?
COME AGAIN?
HE LED GEORGE UNIT, OR SO HE SAID. I CAN'T BELIEVE YOU TOOK HIM THAT EASILY.
HE WAS UNHINGED, JOHN. HE WASN'T FIT FOR COMMAND. HECK, EVEN IF HE WERE STILL --
YOU'D ALMOST THINK HE WAS SET UP.
TAKE A BREAK, DR. REQUIN. YOU MAY NOT SLEEP, BUT YOU SHOULD RELAX.
RELAX.
RIGHT.

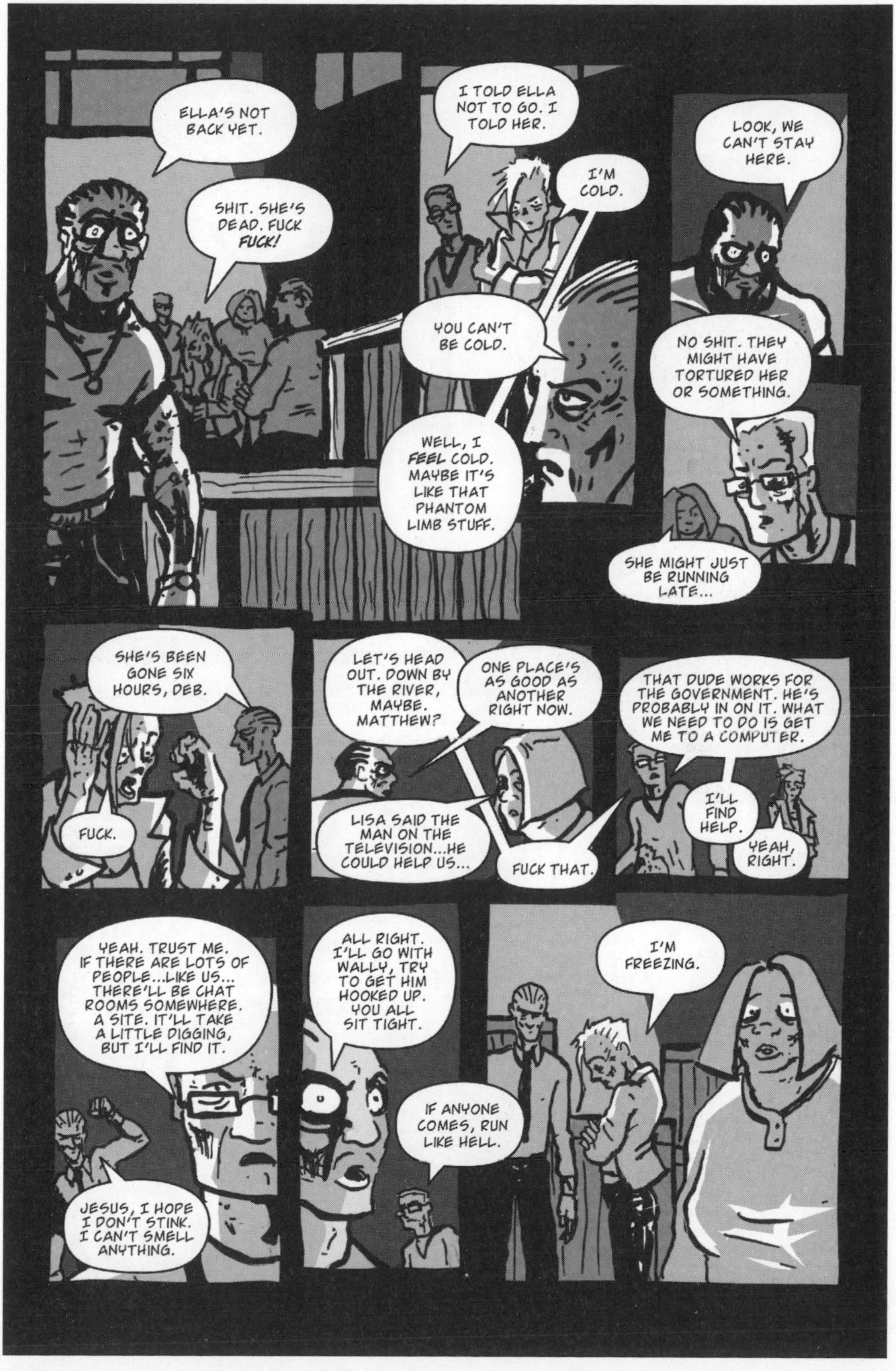
ELLA'S NOT BACK YET.
SHIT. SHE'S DEAD. FUCK FUCK!
I TOLD ELLA NOT TO GO. I TOLD HER.
I'M COLD.
YOU CAN'T BE COLD.
WELL, I FEEL COLD. MAYBE IT'S LIKE THAT PHANTOM LIMB STUFF.
LOOK, WE CAN'T STAY HERE.
NO SHIT. THEY MIGHT HAVE TORTURED HER OR SOMETHING.
SHE MIGHT JUST BE RUNNING LATE...
SHE'S BEEN GONE SIX HOURS, DEB.
FUCK.
LET'S HEAD OUT. DOWN BY THE RIVER, MAYBE. MATTHEW?
ONE PLACE'S AS GOOD AS ANOTHER RIGHT NOW.
LISA SAID THE MAN ON THE TELEVISION...HE COULD HELP US...
FUCK THAT.
THAT DUDE WORKS FOR THE GOVERNMENT. HE'S PROBABLY IN ON IT. WHAT WE NEED TO DO IS GET ME TO A COMPUTER.
I'LL FIND HELP.
YEAH, RIGHT.
YEAH. TRUST ME. IF THERE ARE LOTS OF PEOPLE...LIKE US... THERE'LL BE CHAT ROOMS SOMEWHERE. A SITE. IT'LL TAKE A LITTLE DIGGING, BUT I'LL FIND IT.
JESUS, I HOPE I DON'T STINK. I CAN'T SMELL ANYTHING.
ALL RIGHT. I'LL GO WITH WALLY, TRY TO GET HIM HOOKED UP. YOU ALL SIT TIGHT.
IF ANYONE COMES, RUN LIKE HELL.
I'M FREEZING.

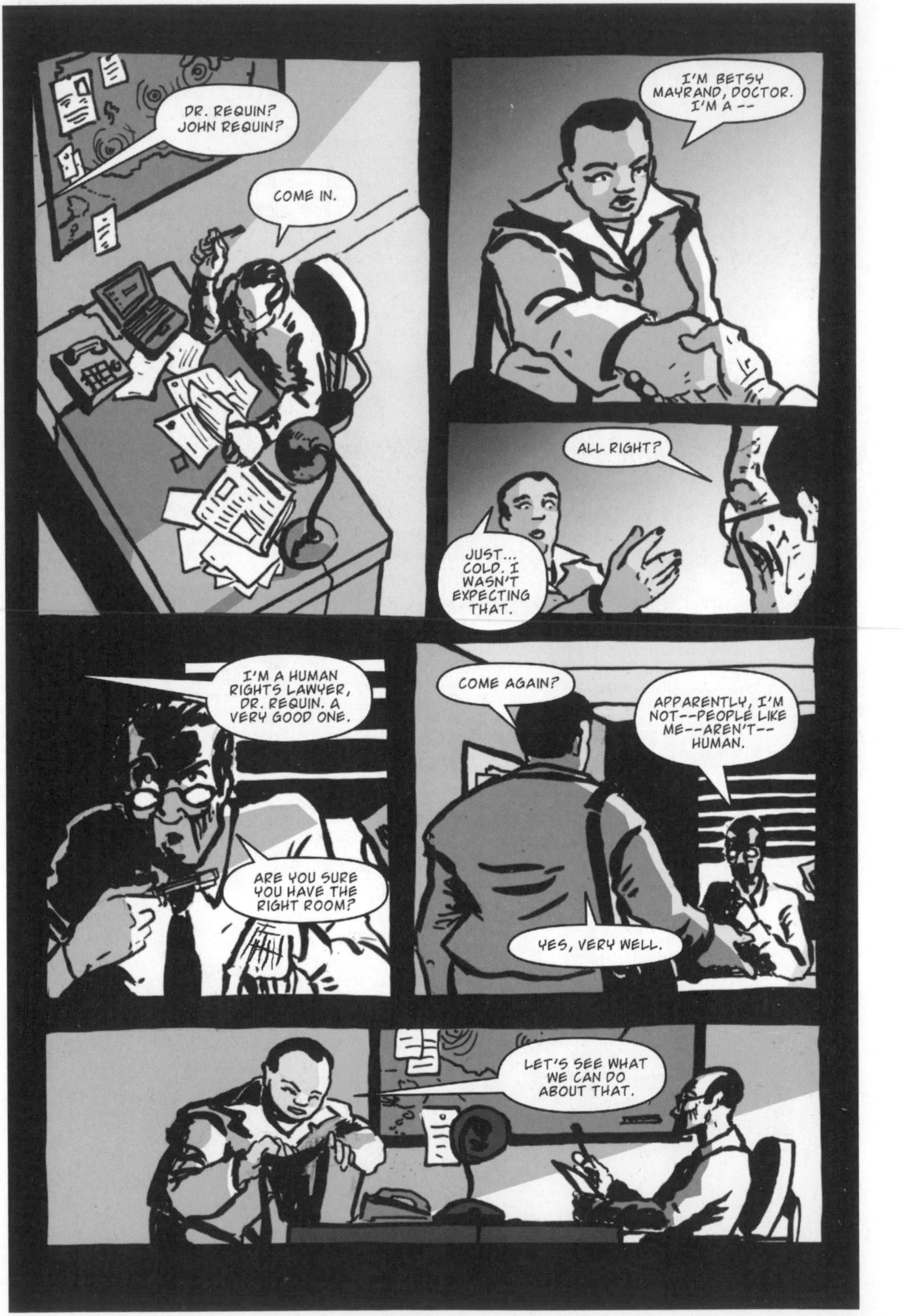
DR. REQUIN? JOHN REQUIN?
COME IN.
I'M BETSY MAYRAND, DOCTOR. I'M A --
ALL RIGHT?
JUST... COLD. I WASN'T EXPECTING THAT.
I'M A HUMAN RIGHTS LAWYER, DR. REQUIN. A VERY GOOD ONE.
ARE YOU SURE YOU HAVE THE RIGHT ROOM?
COME AGAIN?
APPARENTLY, I'M NOT--PEOPLE LIKE ME--AREN'T--HUMAN.
YES, VERY WELL.
LET'S SEE WHAT WE CAN DO ABOUT THAT.

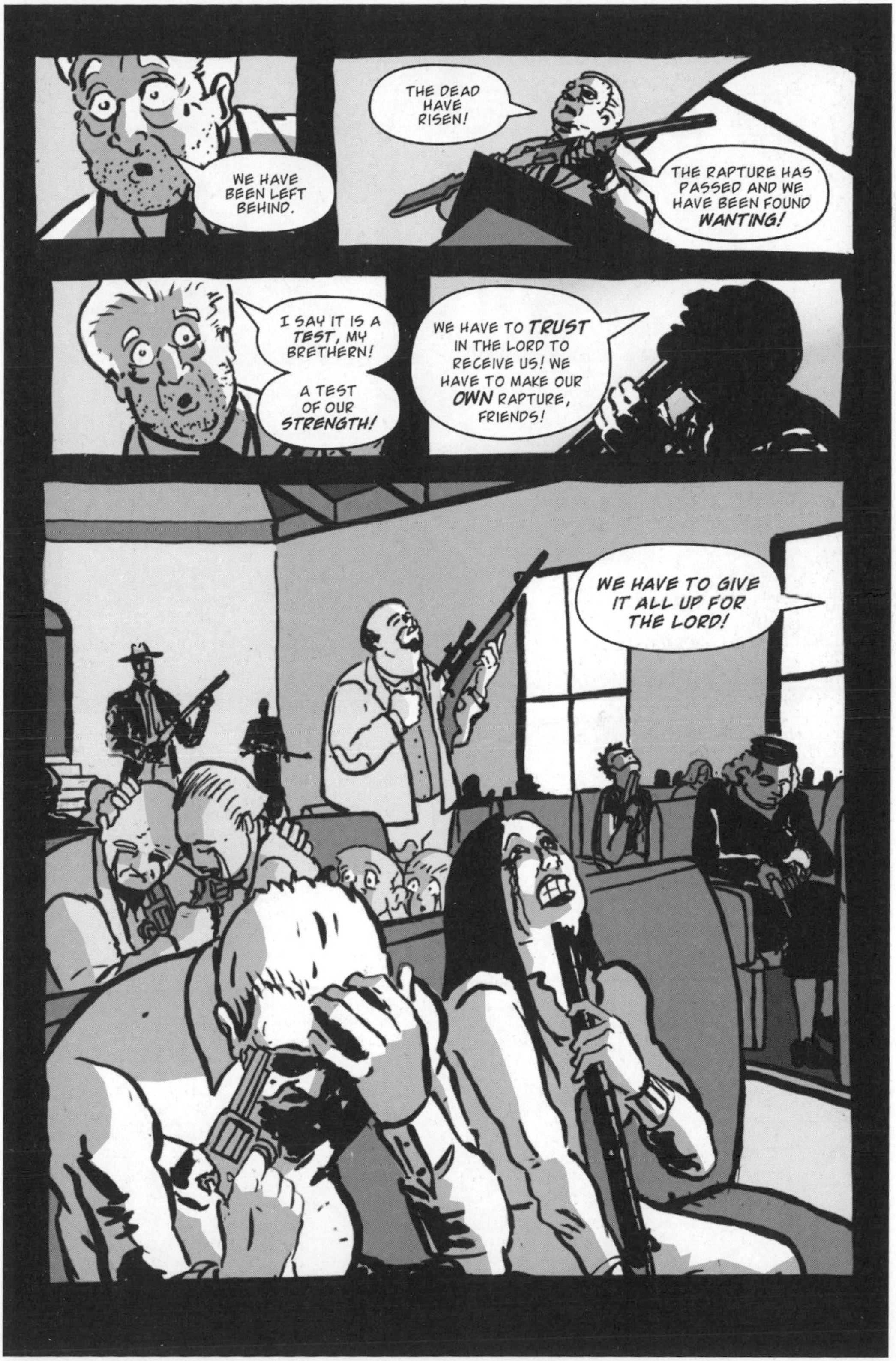
WE HAVE BEEN LEFT BEHIND.
THE DEAD HAVE RISEN!
THE RAPTURE HAS PASSED AND WE HAVE BEEN FOUND WANTING!
I SAY IT IS A TEST, MY BRETHERN!
A TEST OF OUR STRENGTH!
WE HAVE TO TRUST IN THE LORD TO RECEIVE US! WE HAVE TO MAKE OUR OWN RAPTURE, FRIENDS!
WE HAVE TO GIVE IT ALL UP FOR THE LORD!

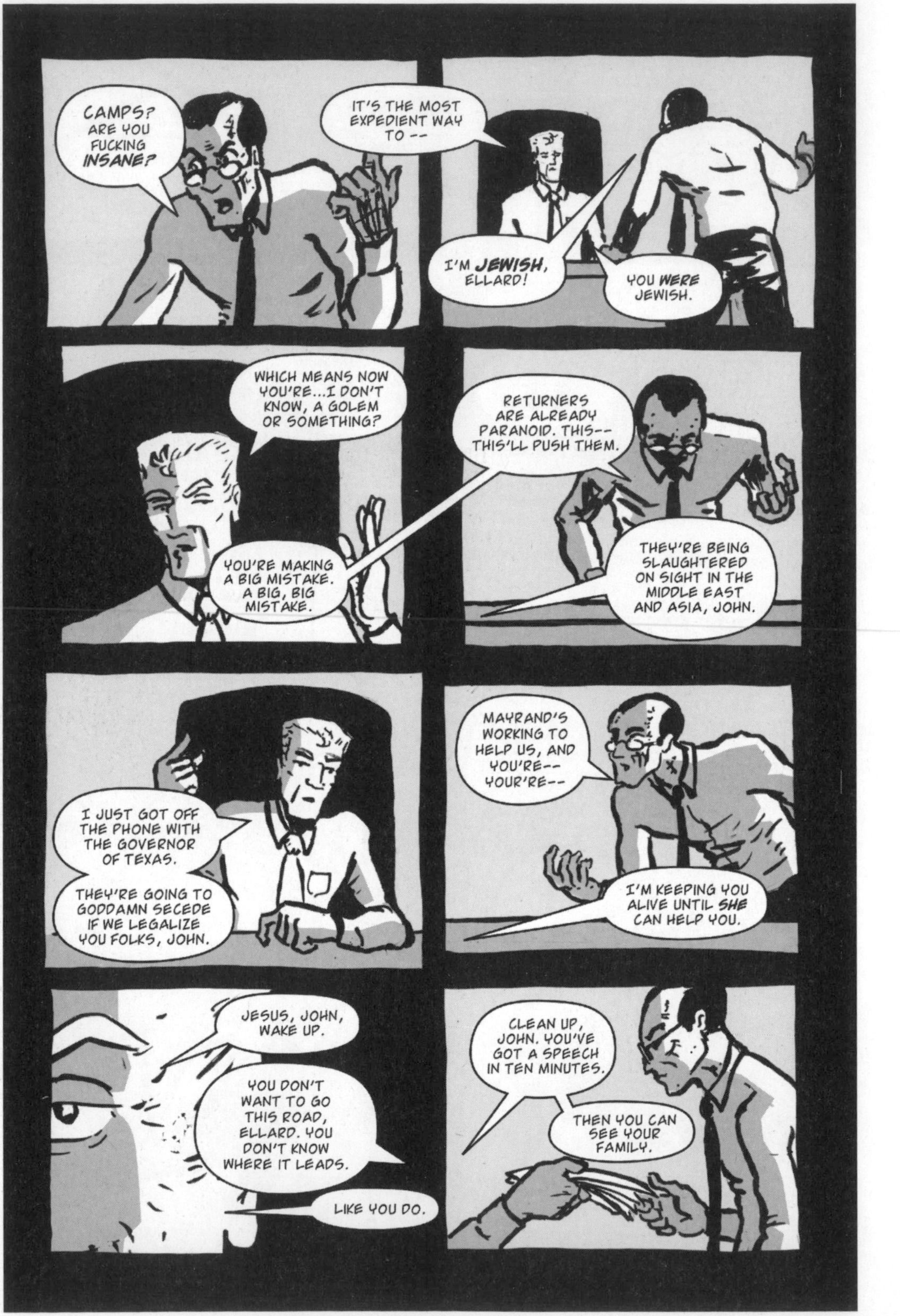

CAMPS? ARE YOU FUCKING INSANE?
IT'S THE MOST EXPEDIENT WAY TO --
I'M JEWISH, ELLARD!
YOU WERE JEWISH.
WHICH MEANS NOW YOU'RE...I DON'T KNOW, A GOLEM OR SOMETHING?
YOU'RE MAKING A BIG MISTAKE. A BIG, BIG MISTAKE.
RETURNERS ARE ALREADY PARANOID. THIS-- THIS'LL PUSH THEM.
THEY'RE BEING SLAUGHTERED ON SIGHT IN THE MIDDLE EAST AND ASIA, JOHN.
I JUST GOT OFF THE PHONE WITH THE GOVERNOR OF TEXAS.
THEY'RE GOING TO GODDAMN SECEDE IF WE LEGALIZE YOU FOLKS, JOHN.
MAYRAND'S WORKING TO HELP US, AND YOU'RE-- YOUR'RE--
I'M KEEPING YOU ALIVE UNTIL SHE CAN HELP YOU.
JESUS, JOHN, WAKE UP.
YOU DON'T WANT TO GO THIS ROAD, ELLARD. YOU DON'T KNOW WHERE IT LEADS.
LIKE YOU DO.
CLEAN UP, JOHN. YOU'VE GOT A SPEECH IN TEN MINUTES.
THEN YOU CAN SEE YOUR FAMILY.

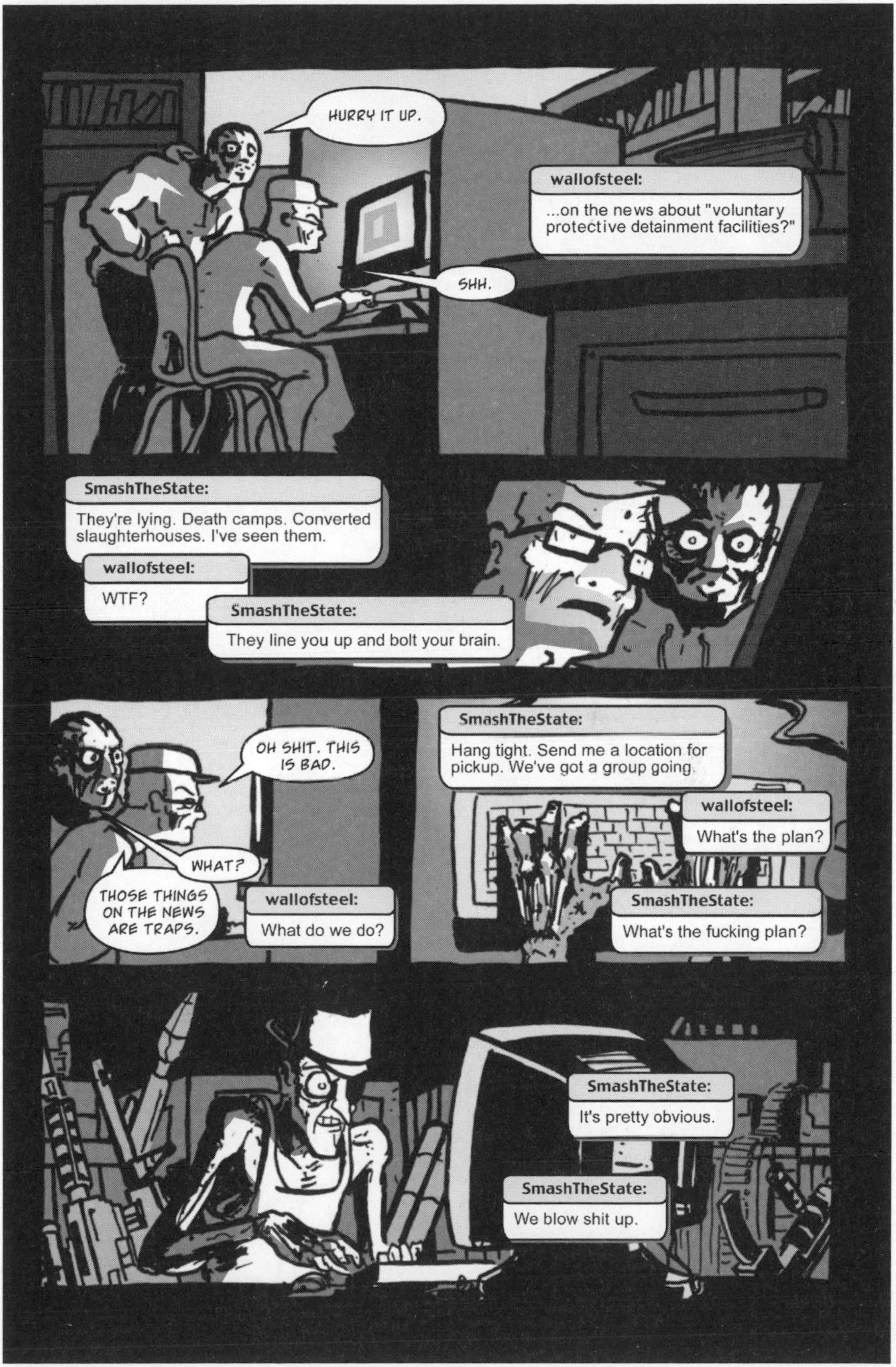
HURRY IT UP.
wallofsteel:
...on the news about "voluntary protective detainment facilities?"
SHH.
SmashTheState:
They're lying. Death camps. Converted slaughterhouses. I've seen them.
wallofsteel:
WTF?
SmashTheState:
They line you up and bolt your brain.
OH SHIT. THIS IS BAD.
WHAT?
THOSE THINGS ON THE NEWS ARE TRAPS.
wallofsteel:
What do we do?
SmashTheState:
Hang tight. Send me a location for pickup. We've got a group going.
wallofsteel:
What's the plan?
SmashTheState:
What's the fucking plan?
SmashTheState:
It's pretty obvious.
SmashTheState:
We blow shit up.

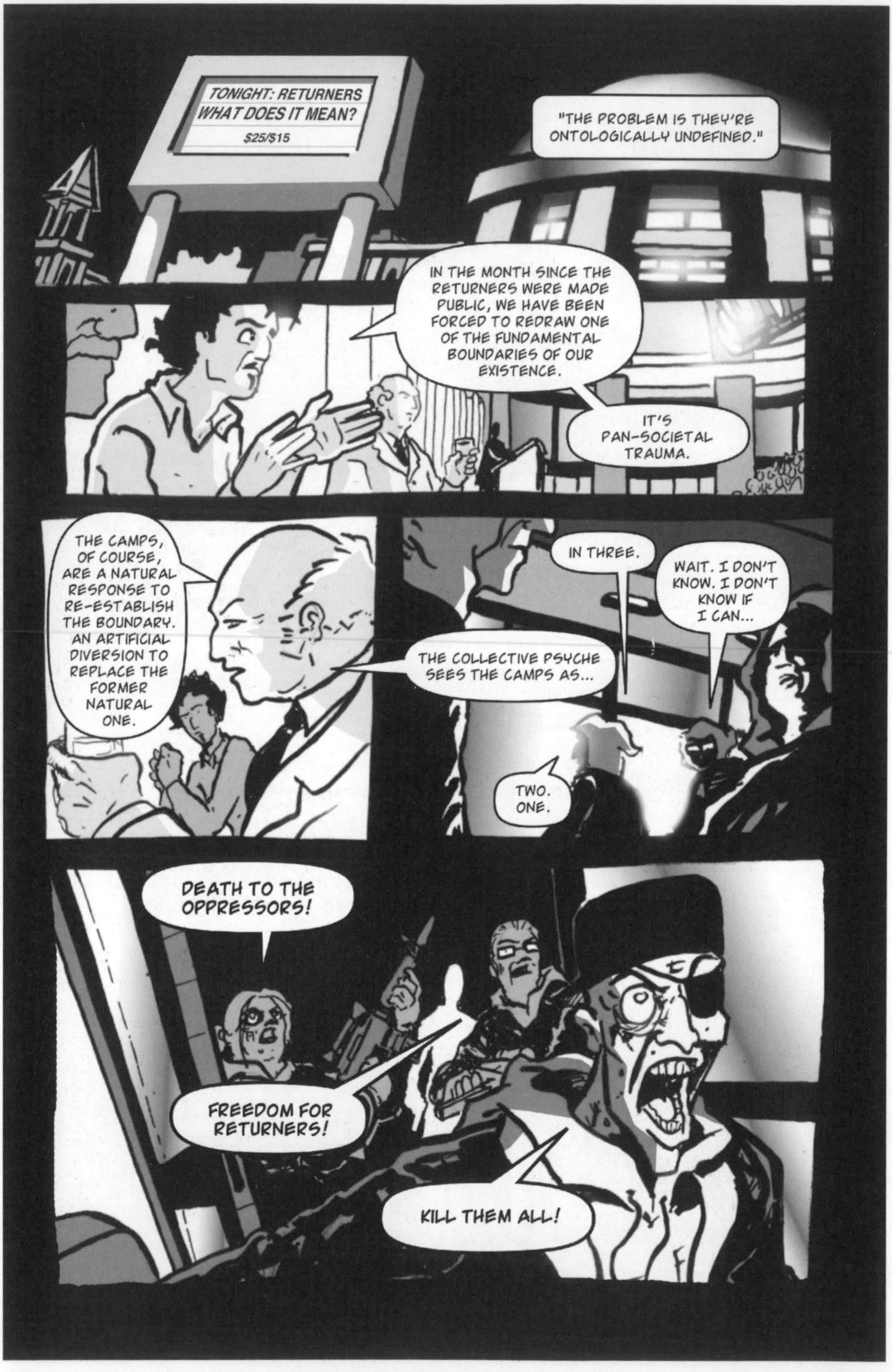
TONIGHT: RETURNERS
WHAT DOES IT MEAN?
$25/$15
"THE PROBLEM IS THEY'RE ONTOLOGICALLY UNDEFINED."
IN THE MONTH SINCE THE RETURNERS WERE MADE PUBLIC, WE HAVE BEEN FORCED TO REDRAW ONE OF THE FUNDAMENTAL BOUNDARIES OF OUR EXISTENCE.
IT'S PAN-SOCIETAL TRAUMA.
THE CAMPS, OF COURSE, ARE A NATURAL RESPONSE TO RE-ESTABLISH THE BOUNDARY. AN ARTIFICIAL DIVERSION TO REPLACE THE FORMER NATURAL ONE.
THE COLLECTIVE PSYCHE SEES THE CAMPS AS...
IN THREE.
WAIT. I DON'T KNOW. I DON'T KNOW IF I CAN...
TWO. ONE.
DEATH TO THE OPPRESSORS!
FREEDOM FOR RETURNERS!
KILL THEM ALL!

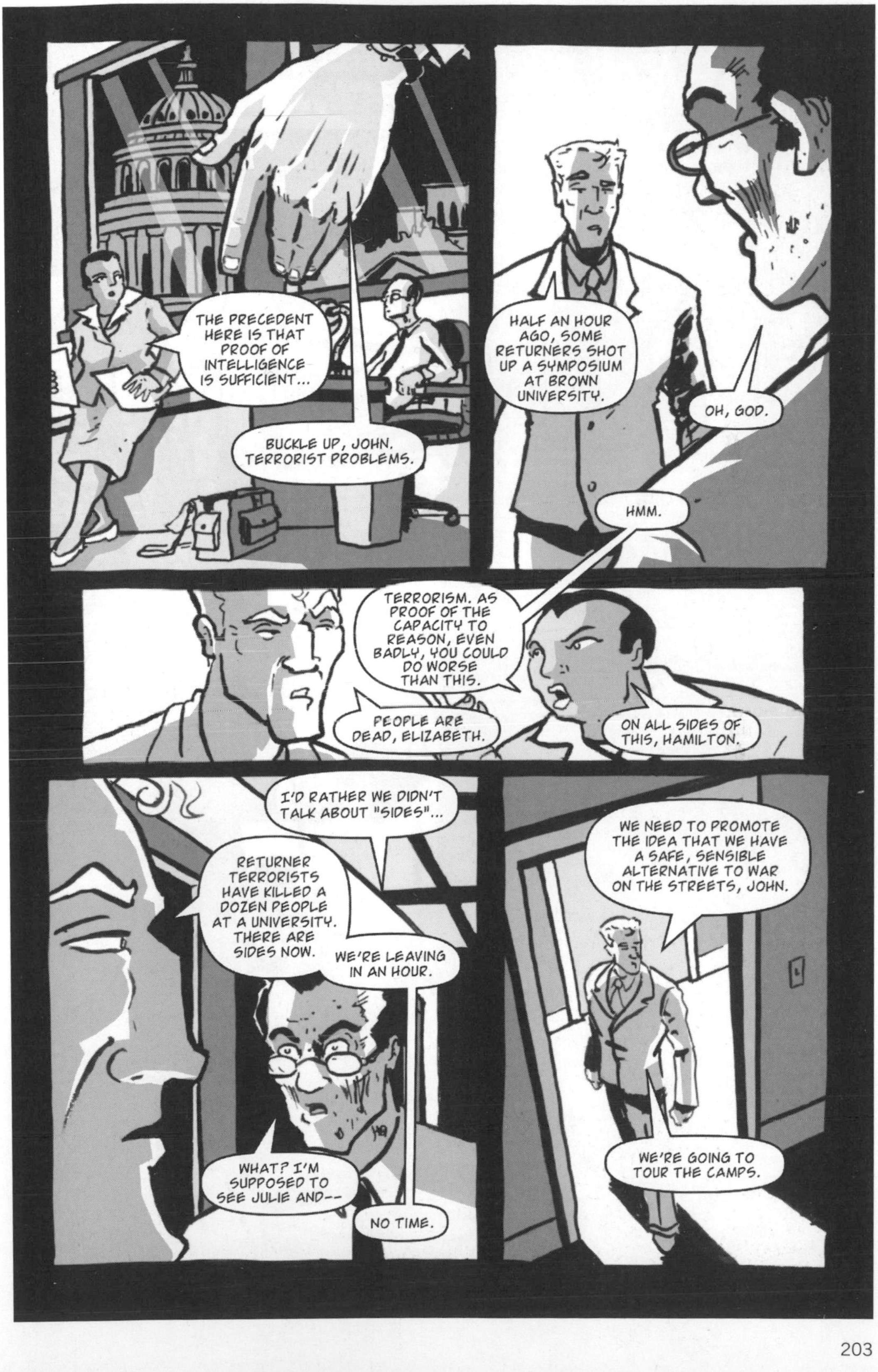
THE PRECEDENT HERE IS THAT PROOF OF INTELLIGENCE IS SUFFICIENT...
BUCKLE UP, JOHN. TERRORIST PROBLEMS.
HALF AN HOUR AGO, SOME RETURNERS SHOT UP A SYMPOSIUM AT BROWN UNIVERSITY.
OH, GOD.
HMM.
TERRORISM. AS PROOF OF THE CAPACITY TO REASON, EVEN BADLY, YOU COULD DO WORSE THAN THIS.
PEOPLE ARE DEAD, ELIZABETH.
ON ALL SIDES OF THIS, HAMILTON.
I'D RATHER WE DIDN'T TALK ABOUT "SIDES"...
RETURNER TERRORISTS HAVE KILLED A DOZEN PEOPLE AT A UNIVERSITY. THERE ARE SIDES NOW.
WE'RE LEAVING IN AN HOUR.
WHAT? I'M SUPPOSED TO SEE JULIE AND--
NO TIME.
WE NEED TO PROMOTE THE IDEA THAT WE HAVE A SAFE, SENSIBLE ALTERNATIVE TO WAR ON THE STREETS, JOHN.
WE'RE GOING TO TOUR THE CAMPS.

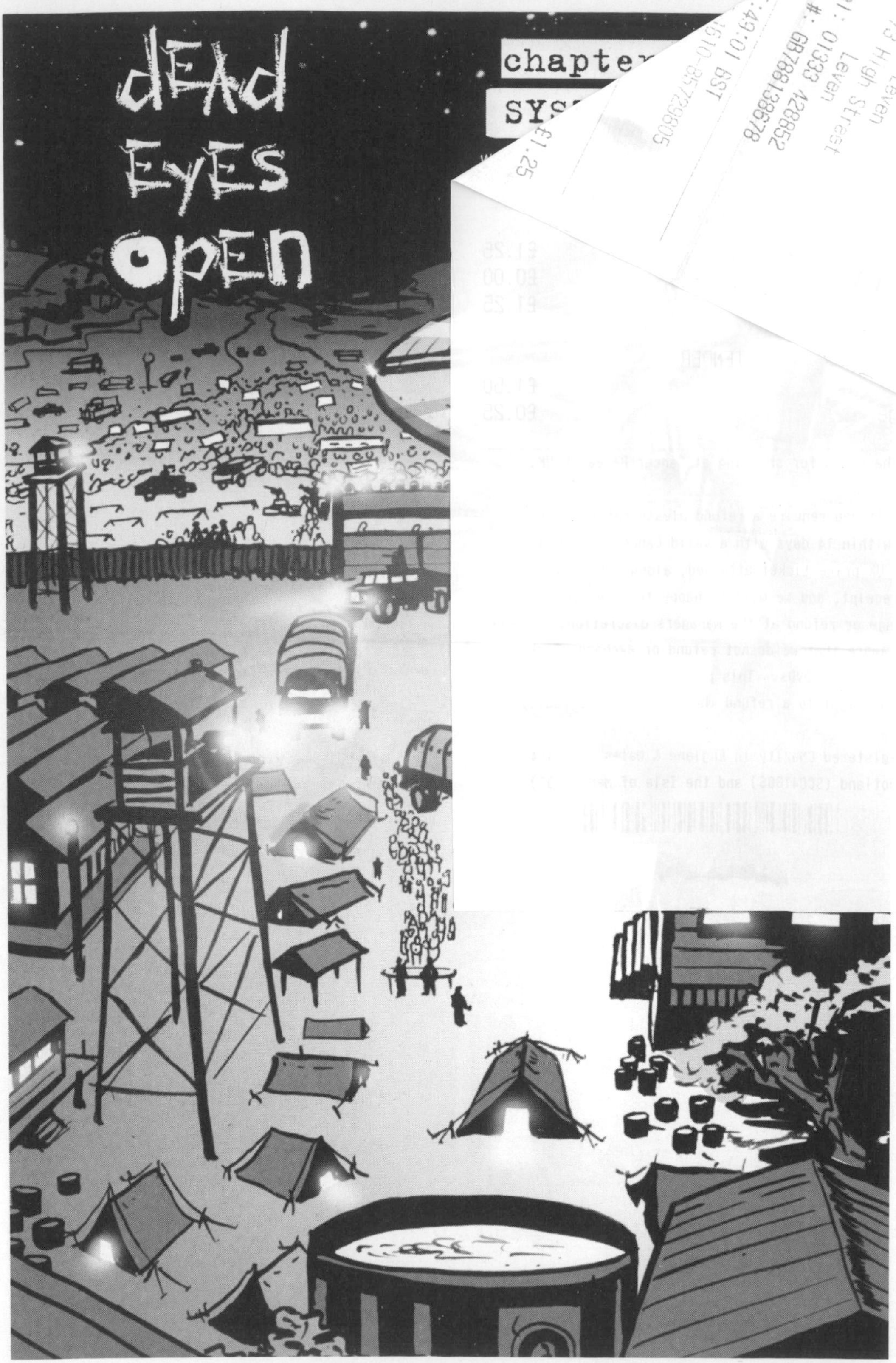
dEAd EYES open
chapter
SYS

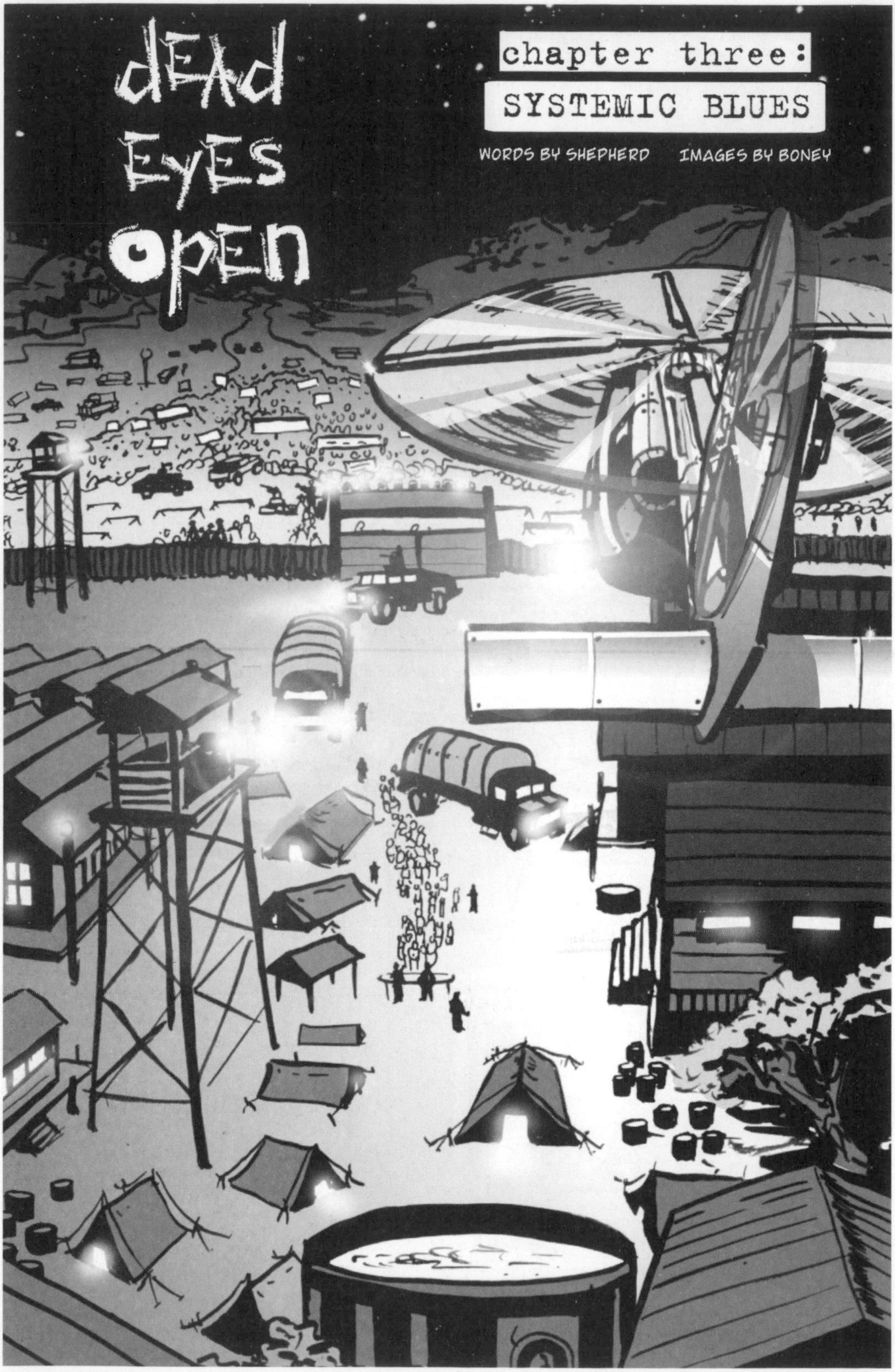
dEAd EyES opEn
chapter three:
SYSTEMIC BLUES
WORDS BY SHEPHERD IMAGES BY BONEY

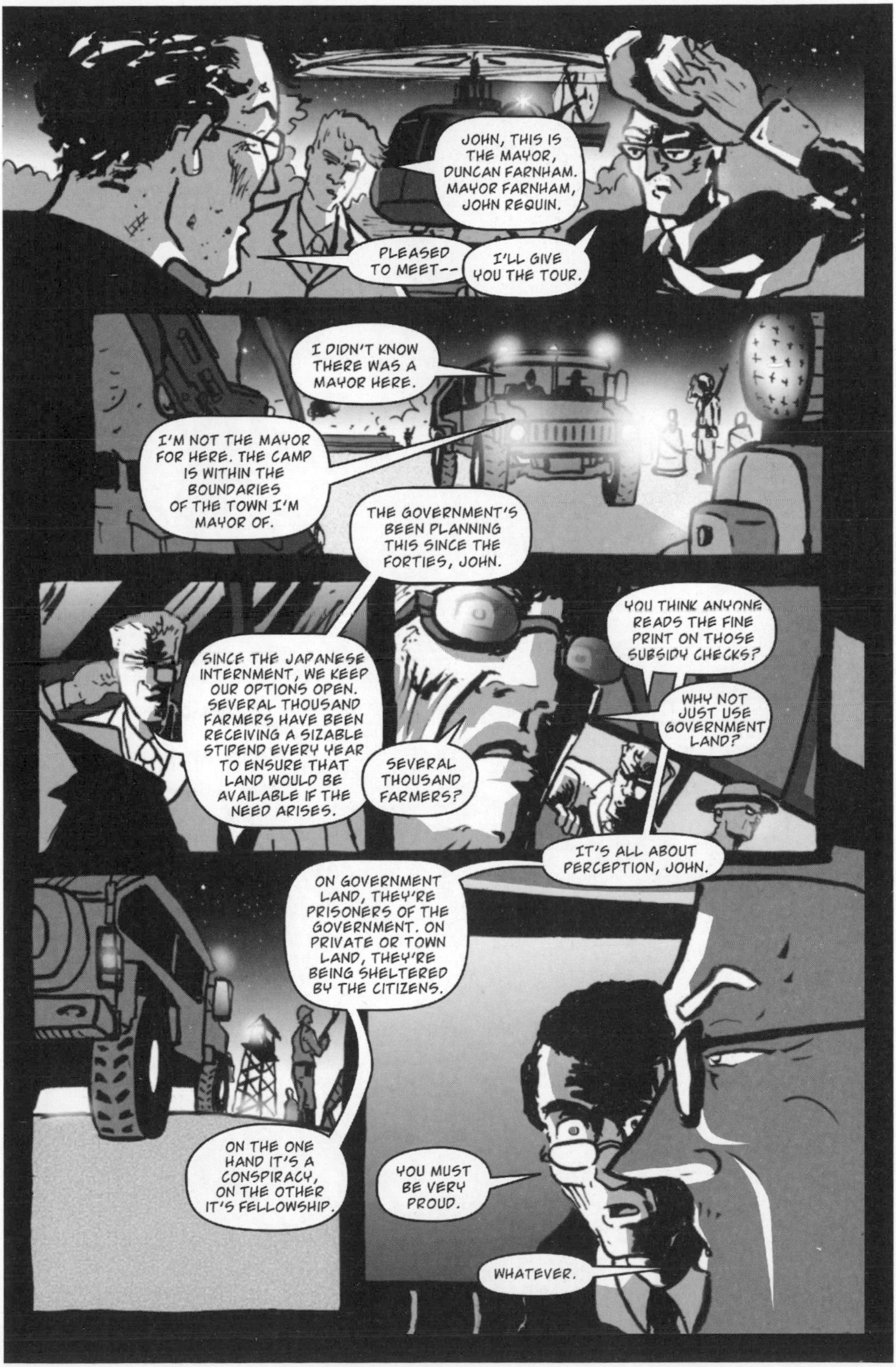
JOHN, THIS IS THE MAYOR, DUNCAN FARNHAM. MAYOR FARNHAM, JOHN REQUIN.
PLEASED TO MEET--
I'LL GIVE YOU THE TOUR.
I DIDN'T KNOW THERE WAS A MAYOR HERE.
I'M NOT THE MAYOR FOR HERE. THE CAMP IS WITHIN THE BOUNDARIES OF THE TOWN I'M MAYOR OF.
THE GOVERNMENT'S BEEN PLANNING THIS SINCE THE FORTIES, JOHN.
SINCE THE JAPANESE INTERNMENT, WE KEEP OUR OPTIONS OPEN. SEVERAL THOUSAND FARMERS HAVE BEEN RECEIVING A SIZABLE STIPEND EVERY YEAR TO ENSURE THAT LAND WOULD BE AVAILABLE IF THE NEED ARISES.
SEVERAL THOUSAND FARMERS?
YOU THINK ANYONE READS THE FINE PRINT ON THOSE SUBSIDY CHECKS?
WHY NOT JUST USE GOVERNMENT LAND?
IT'S ALL ABOUT PERCEPTION, JOHN.
ON GOVERNMENT LAND, THEY'RE PRISONERS OF THE GOVERNMENT. ON PRIVATE OR TOWN LAND, THEY'RE BEING SHELTERED BY THE CITIZENS.
ON THE ONE HAND IT'S A CONSPIRACY, ON THE OTHER IT'S FELLOWSHIP.
YOU MUST BE VERY PROUD.
WHATEVER.

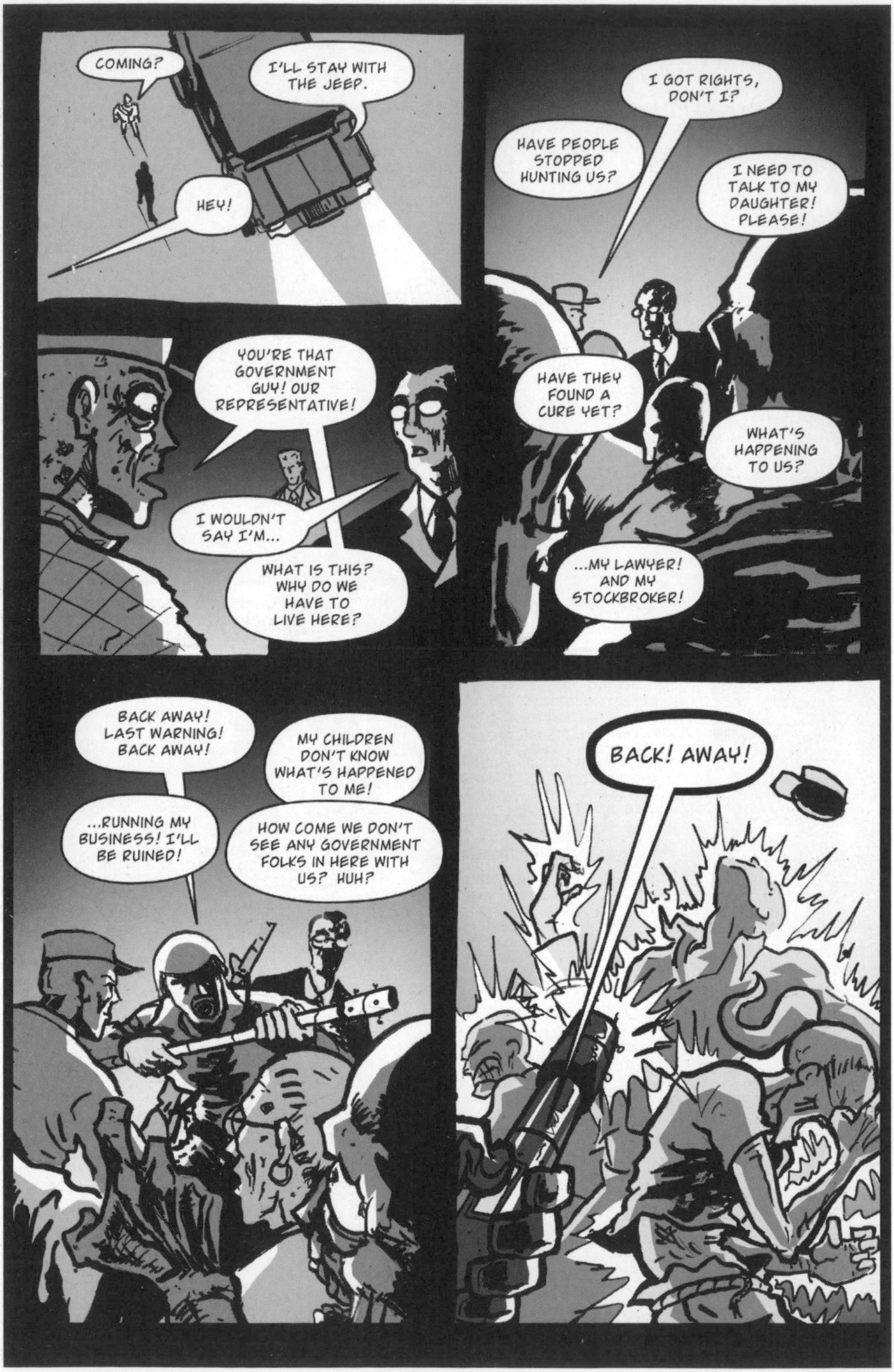
COMING?
I'LL STAY WITH THE JEEP.
HEY!
HAVE PEOPLE STOPPED HUNTING US?
I GOT RIGHTS, DON'T I?
I NEED TO TALK TO MY DAUGHTER! PLEASE!
YOU'RE THAT GOVERNMENT GUY! OUR REPRESENTATIVE!
I WOULDN'T SAY I'M...
WHAT IS THIS? WHY DO WE HAVE TO LIVE HERE?
HAVE THEY FOUND A CURE YET?
WHAT'S HAPPENING TO US?
...MY LAWYER! AND MY STOCKBROKER!
BACK AWAY! LAST WARNING! BACK AWAY!
MY CHILDREN DON'T KNOW WHAT'S HAPPENED TO ME!
...RUNNING MY BUSINESS! I'LL BE RUINED!
HOW COME WE DON'T SEE ANY GOVERNMENT FOLKS IN HERE WITH US? HUH?
BACK! AWAY!

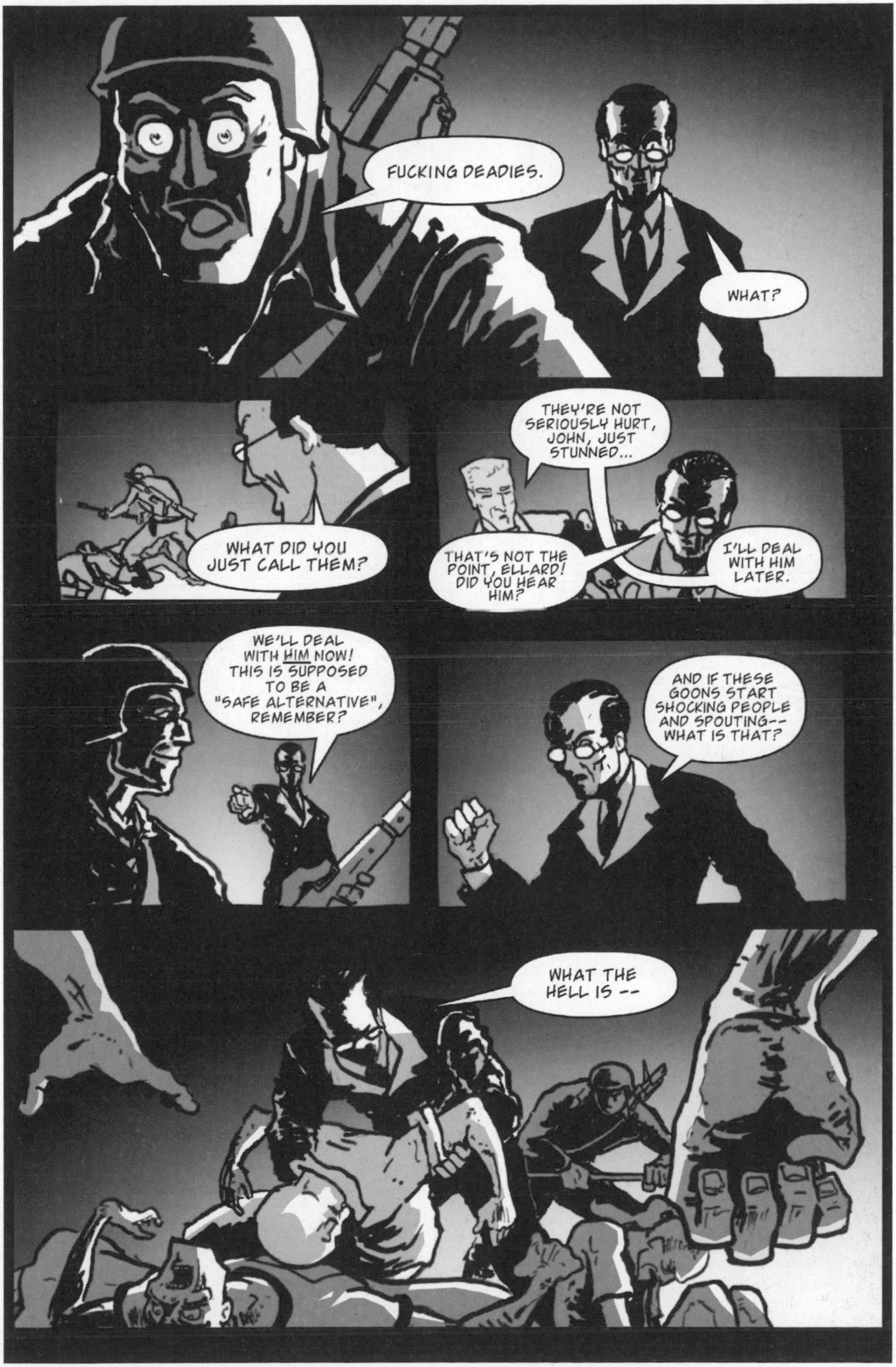
FUCKING DEADIES.
WHAT?
WHAT DID YOU JUST CALL THEM?
THEY'RE NOT SERIOUSLY HURT, JOHN, JUST STUNNED...
THAT'S NOT THE POINT, ELLARD! DID YOU HEAR HIM?
I'LL DEAL WITH HIM LATER.
WE'LL DEAL WITH HIM NOW! THIS IS SUPPOSED TO BE A "SAFE ALTERNATIVE", REMEMBER?
AND IF THESE GOONS START SHOCKING PEOPLE AND SPOUTING--WHAT IS THAT?
WHAT THE HELL IS --

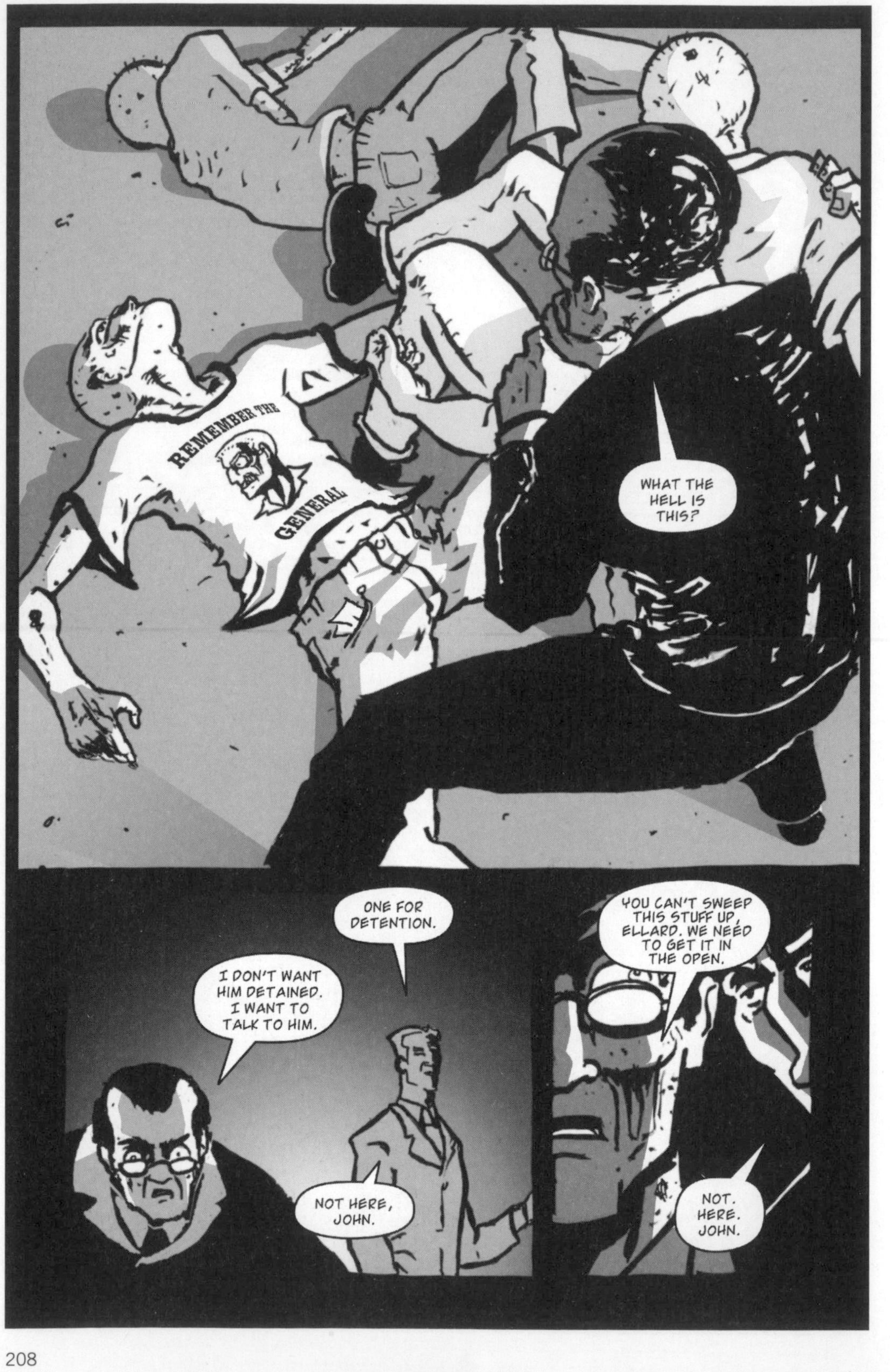
REMEMBER THE GENERAL
WHAT THE HELL IS THIS?
ONE FOR DETENTION.
I DON'T WANT HIM DETAINED. I WANT TO TALK TO HIM.
NOT HERE, JOHN.
YOU CAN'T SWEEP THIS STUFF UP, ELLARD. WE NEED TO GET IT IN THE OPEN.
NOT. HERE. JOHN.

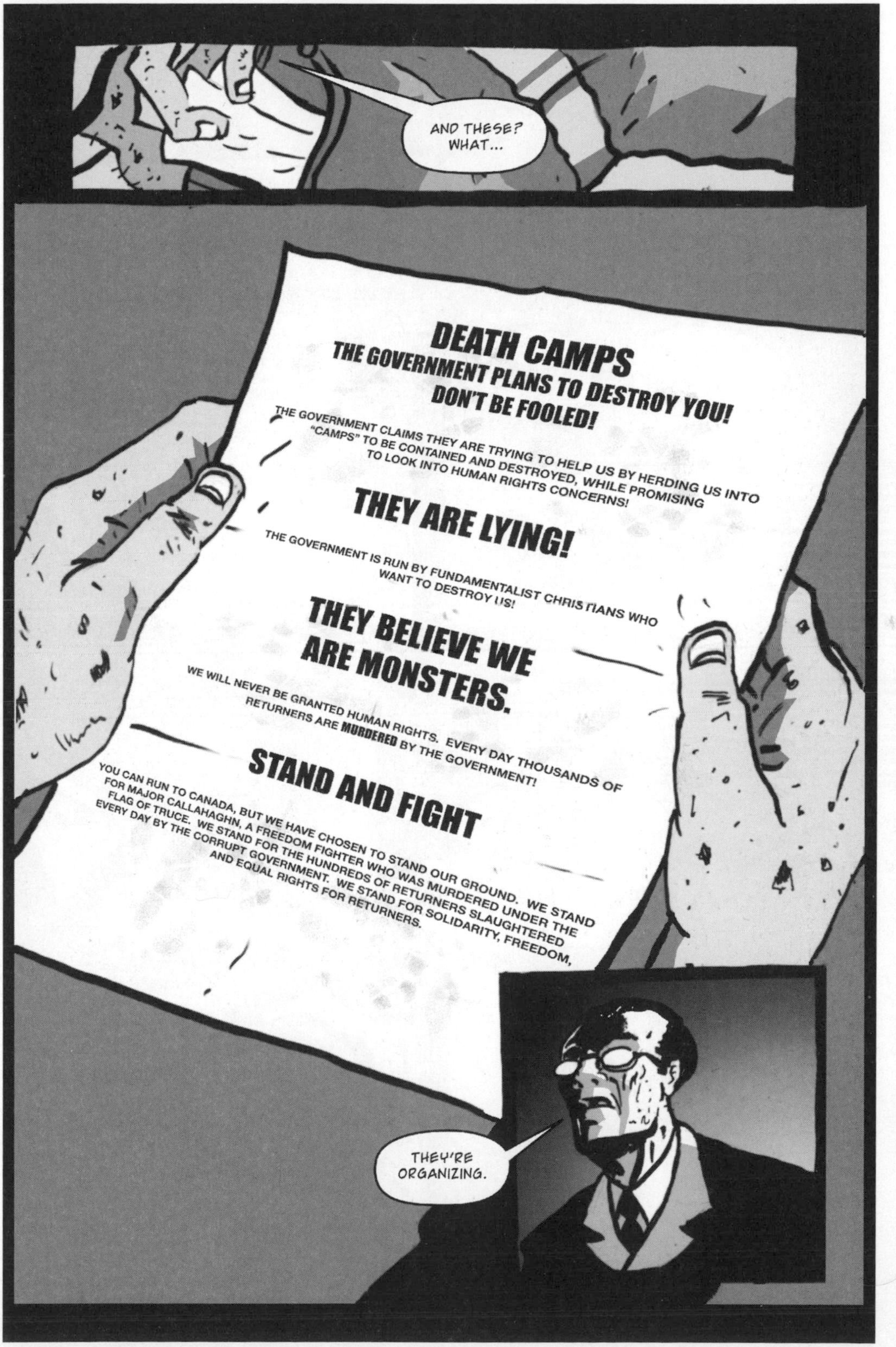
AND THESE? WHAT...
DEATH CAMPS
THE GOVERNMENT PLANS TO DESTROY YOU!
DON'T BE FOOLED!
THE GOVERNMENT CLAIMS THEY ARE TRYING TO HELP US BY HERDING US INTO "CAMPS" TO BE CONTAINED AND DESTROYED, WHILE PROMISING TO LOOK INTO HUMAN RIGHTS CONCERNS!
THEY ARE LYING!
THE GOVERNMENT IS RUN BY FUNDAMENTALIST CHRISTIANS WHO WANT TO DESTROY US!
THEY BELIEVE WE ARE MONSTERS.
WE WILL NEVER BE GRANTED HUMAN RIGHTS. EVERY DAY THOUSANDS OF RETURNERS ARE MURDERED BY THE GOVERNMENT!
STAND AND FIGHT
YOU CAN RUN TO CANADA, BUT WE HAVE CHOSEN TO STAND OUR GROUND. WE STAND FOR MAJOR CALLAHAGHN, A FREEDOM FIGHTER WHO WAS MURDERED UNDER THE FLAG OF TRUCE. WE STAND FOR THE HUNDREDS OF RETURNERS SLAUGHTERED EVERY DAY BY THE CORRUPT GOVERNMENT. WE STAND FOR SOLIDARITY, FREEDOM, AND EQUAL RIGHTS FOR RETURNERS.
THEY'RE ORGANIZING.

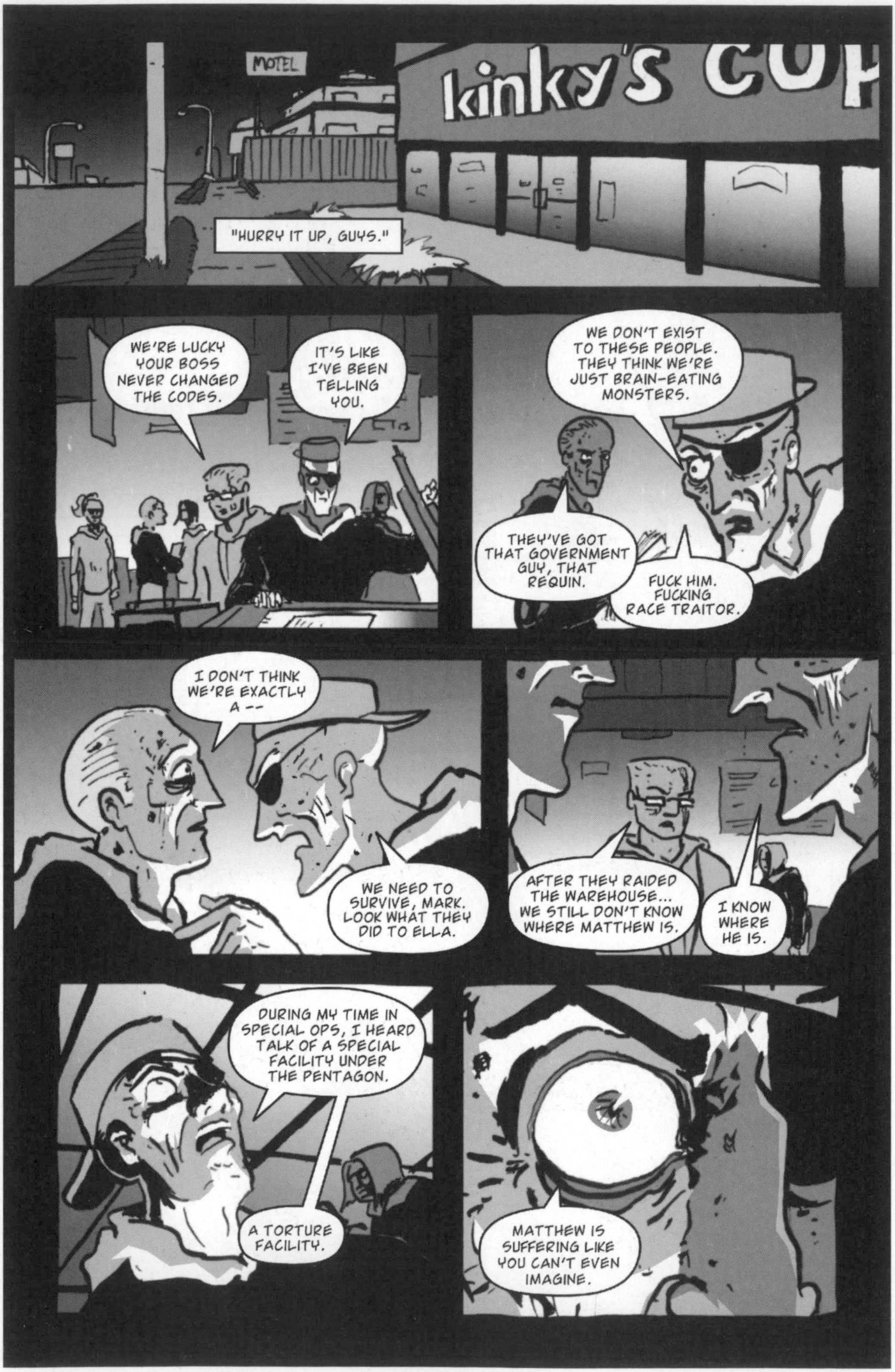

MOTEL
kinky's CUP
"HURRY IT UP, GUYS."
WE'RE LUCKY YOUR BOSS NEVER CHANGED THE CODES.
IT'S LIKE I'VE BEEN TELLING YOU.
WE DON'T EXIST TO THESE PEOPLE. THEY THINK WE'RE JUST BRAIN-EATING MONSTERS.
THEY'VE GOT THAT GOVERNMENT GUY, THAT REQUIN.
FUCK HIM. FUCKING RACE TRAITOR.
I DON'T THINK WE'RE EXACTLY A --
WE NEED TO SURVIVE, MARK. LOOK WHAT THEY DID TO ELLA.
AFTER THEY RAIDED THE WAREHOUSE... WE STILL DON'T KNOW WHERE MATTHEW IS.
I KNOW WHERE HE IS.
DURING MY TIME IN SPECIAL OPS, I HEARD TALK OF A SPECIAL FACILITY UNDER THE PENTAGON.
A TORTURE FACILITY.
MATTHEW IS SUFFERING LIKE YOU CAN'T EVEN IMAGINE.

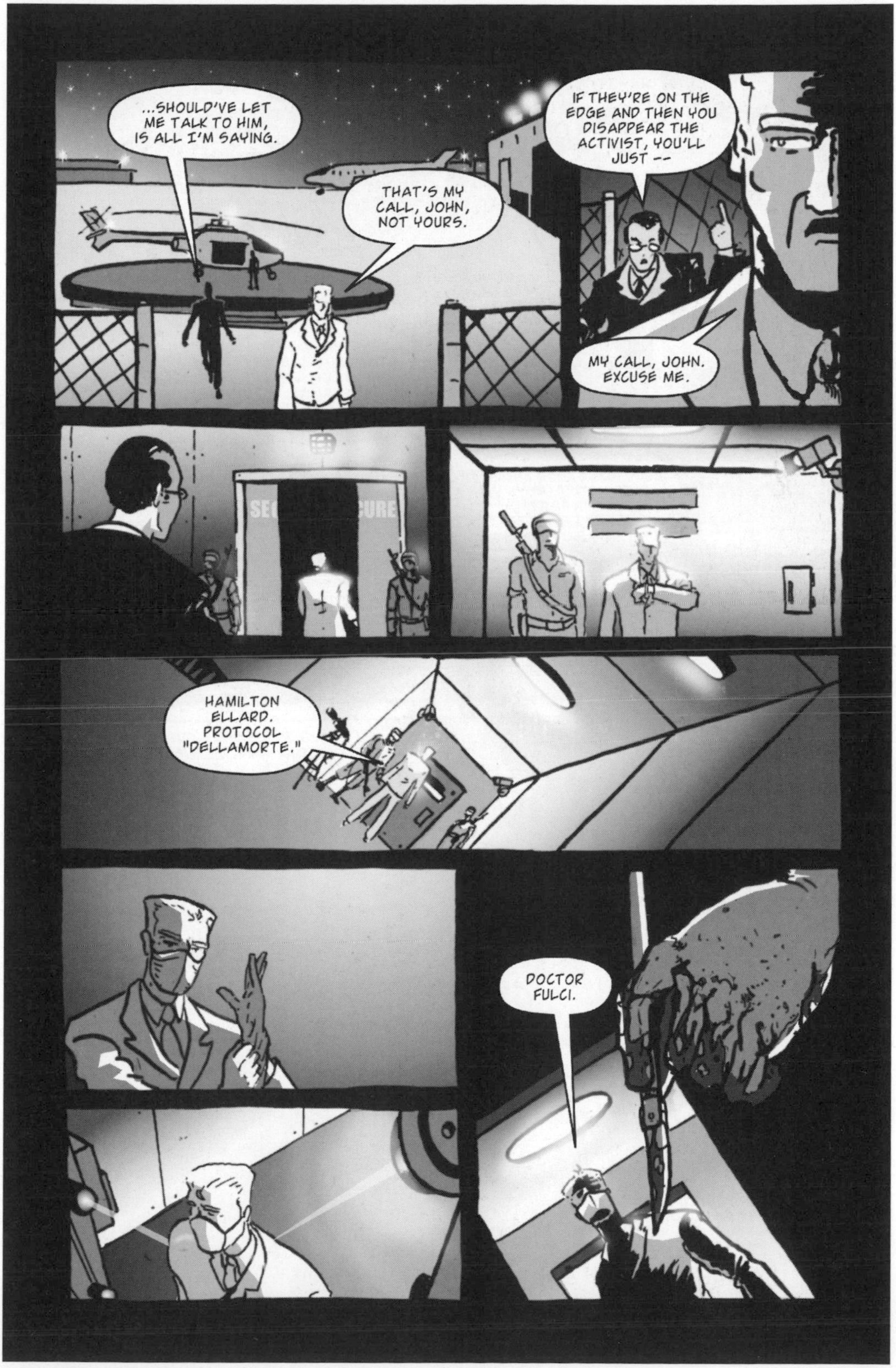
...SHOULD'VE LET ME TALK TO HIM, IS ALL I'M SAYING.
THAT'S MY CALL, JOHN, NOT YOURS.
IF THEY'RE ON THE EDGE AND THEN YOU DISAPPEAR THE ACTIVIST, YOU'LL JUST --
MY CALL, JOHN. EXCUSE ME.
HAMILTON ELLARD. PROTOCOL "DELLAMORTE."
DOCTOR FULCI.

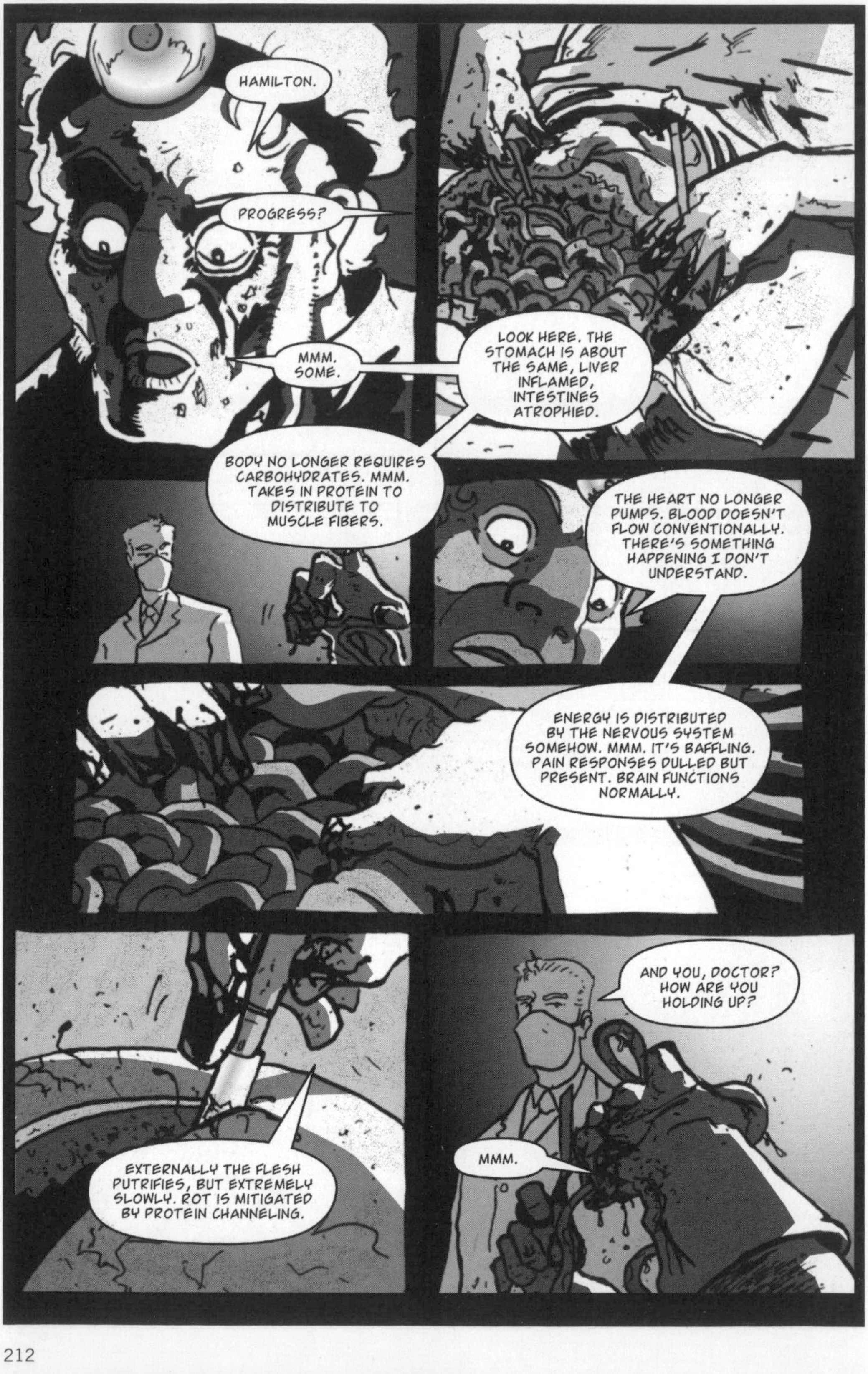
HAMILTON.
PROGRESS?
MMM. SOME.
LOOK HERE. THE STOMACH IS ABOUT THE SAME, LIVER INFLAMED, INTESTINES ATROPHIED.
BODY NO LONGER REQUIRES CARBOHYDRATES. MMM. TAKES IN PROTEIN TO DISTRIBUTE TO MUSCLE FIBERS.
THE HEART NO LONGER PUMPS. BLOOD DOESN'T FLOW CONVENTIONALLY. THERE'S SOMETHING HAPPENING I DON'T UNDERSTAND.
ENERGY IS DISTRIBUTED BY THE NERVOUS SYSTEM SOMEHOW. MMM. IT'S BAFFLING. PAIN RESPONSES DULLED BUT PRESENT. BRAIN FUNCTIONS NORMALLY.
EXTERNALLY THE FLESH PUTRIFIES, BUT EXTREMELY SLOWLY. ROT IS MITIGATED BY PROTEIN CHANNELING.
AND YOU, DOCTOR? HOW ARE YOU HOLDING UP?
MMM.

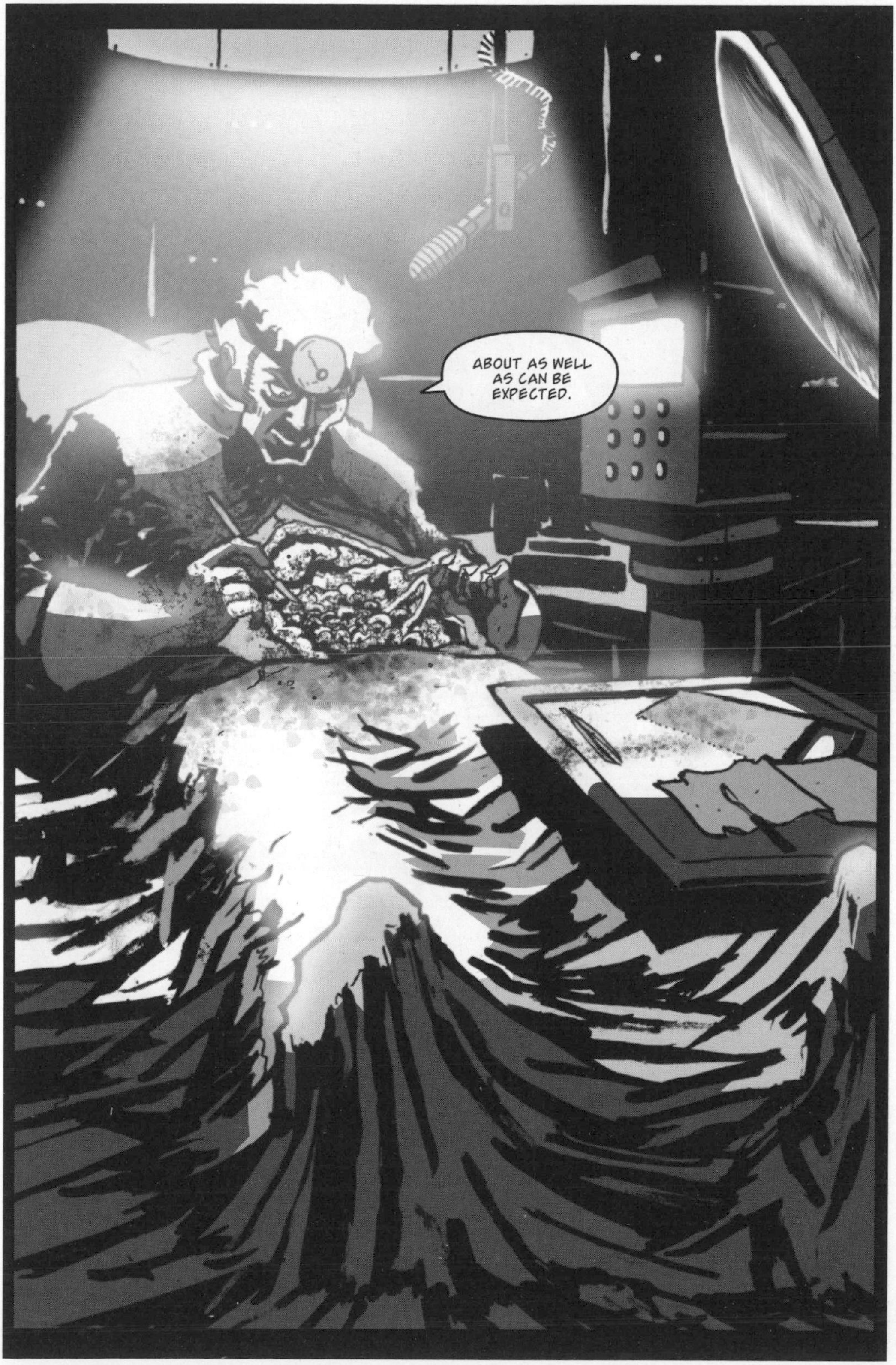
ABOUT AS WELL AS CAN BE EXPECTED.

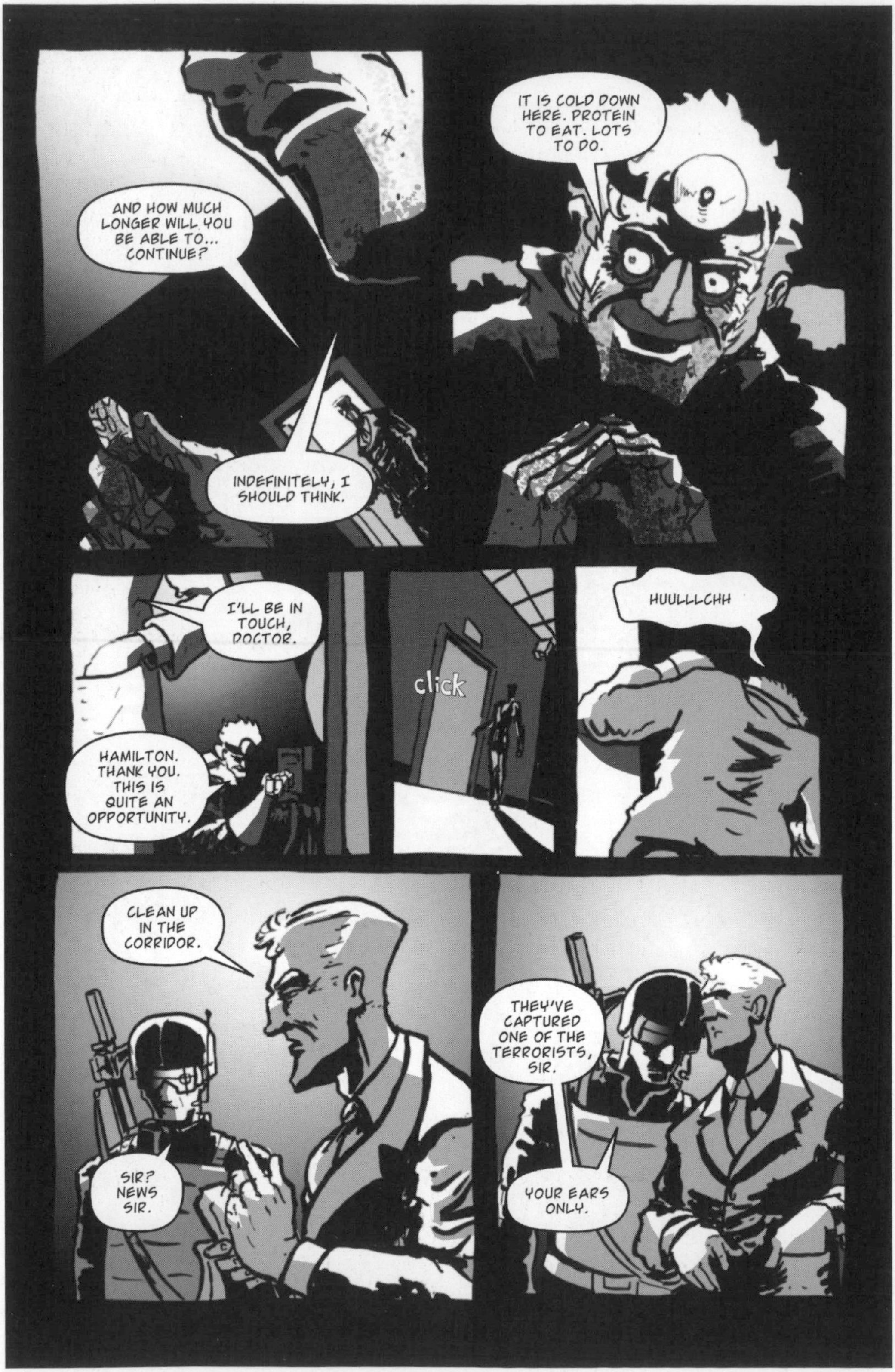
AND HOW MUCH LONGER WILL YOU BE ABLE TO... CONTINUE?
IT IS COLD DOWN HERE. PROTEIN TO EAT. LOTS TO DO.
INDEFINITELY, I SHOULD THINK.
I'LL BE IN TOUCH, DOCTOR.
HAMILTON. THANK YOU. THIS IS QUITE AN OPPORTUNITY.
click
HUULLLCHH
CLEAN UP IN THE CORRIDOR.
SIR? NEWS SIR.
THEY'VE CAPTURED ONE OF THE TERRORISTS, SIR.
YOUR EARS ONLY.

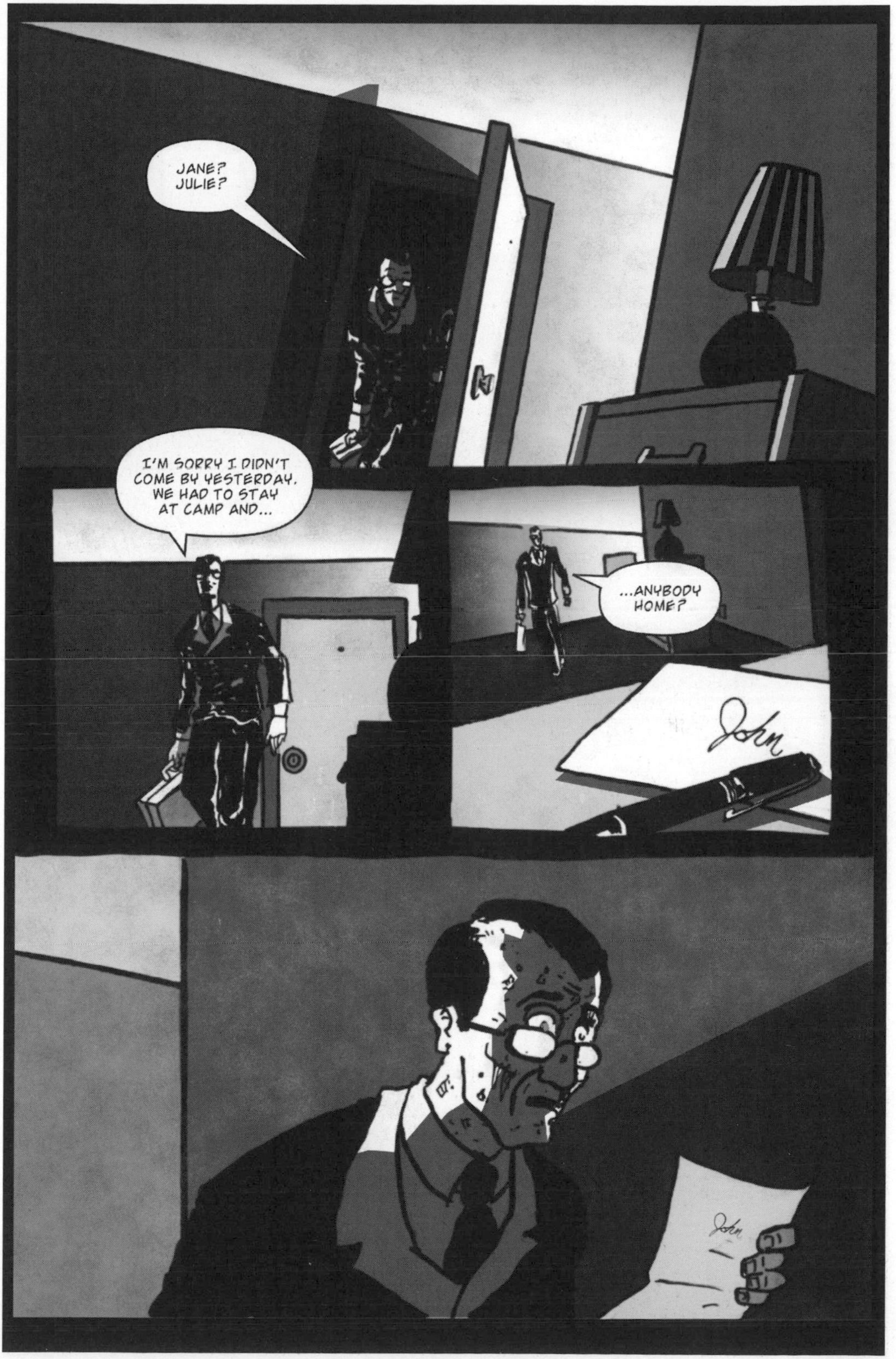
JANE? JULIE?
I'M SORRY I DIDN'T COME BY YESTERDAY. WE HAD TO STAY AT CAMP AND...
...ANYBODY HOME?
John
John

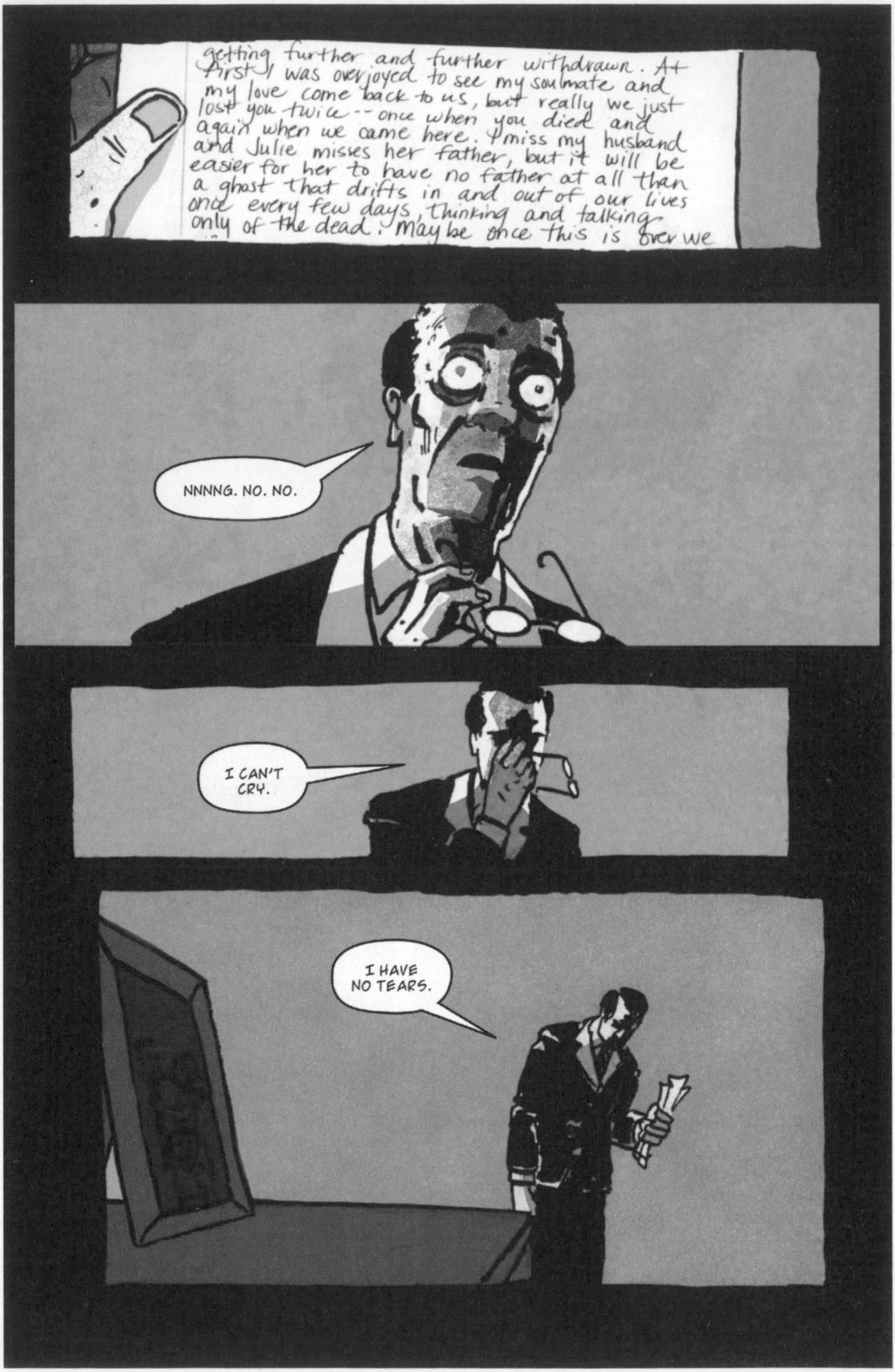
getting further and further withdrawn. At first I was overjoyed to see my soulmate and my love come back to us, but really we just lost you twice -- once when you died and again when we came here. I miss my husband and Julie misses her father, but it will be easier for her to have no father at all than a ghost that drifts in and out of our lives once every few days, thinking and talking only of the dead. Maybe once this is over we
NNNNG. NO. NO.
I CAN'T CRY.
I HAVE NO TEARS.

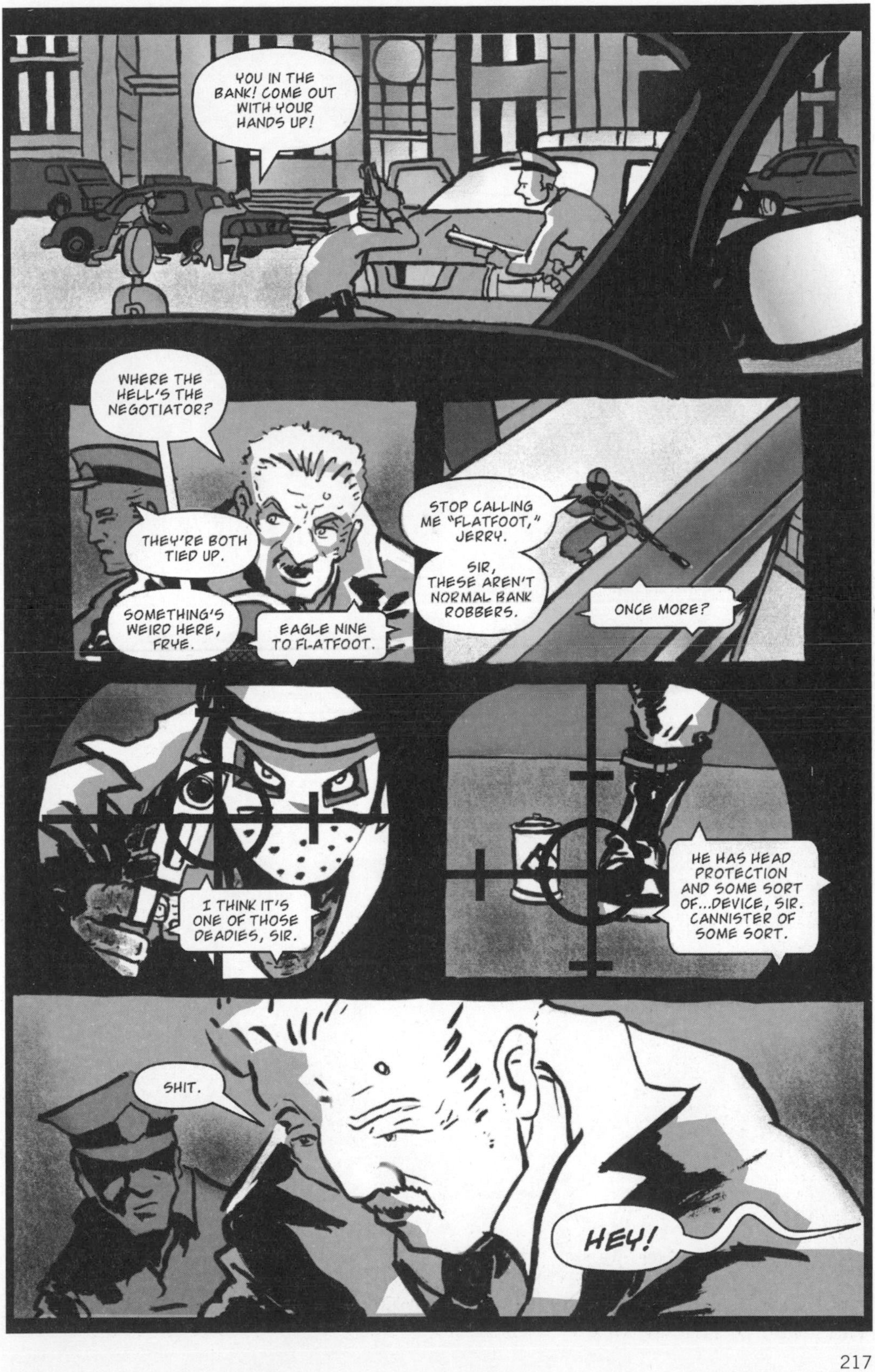
YOU IN THE BANK! COME OUT WITH YOUR HANDS UP!
WHERE THE HELL'S THE NEGOTIATOR?
THEY'RE BOTH TIED UP.
SOMETHING'S WEIRD HERE, FRYE.
EAGLE NINE TO FLATFOOT.
STOP CALLING ME "FLATFOOT," JERRY.
SIR, THESE AREN'T NORMAL BANK ROBBERS.
ONCE MORE?
I THINK IT'S ONE OF THOSE DEADIES, SIR.
HE HAS HEAD PROTECTION AND SOME SORT OF...DEVICE, SIR. CANNISTER OF SOME SORT.
SHIT.
HEY!

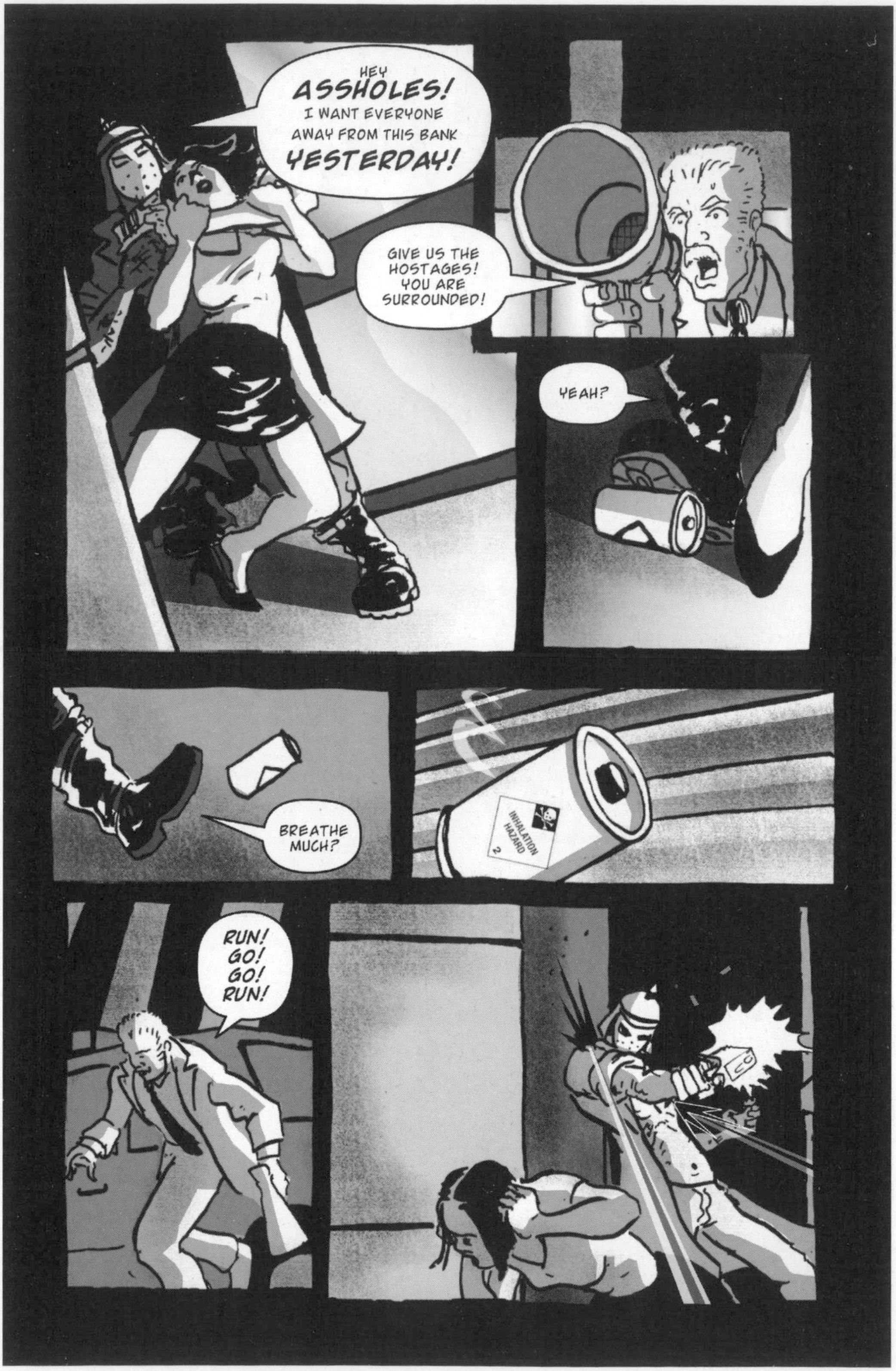
HEY ASSHOLES! I WANT EVERYONE AWAY FROM THIS BANK YESTERDAY!
GIVE US THE HOSTAGES! YOU ARE SURROUNDED!
YEAH?
BREATHE MUCH?
INHALATION HAZARD 2
RUN! GO! GO! RUN!

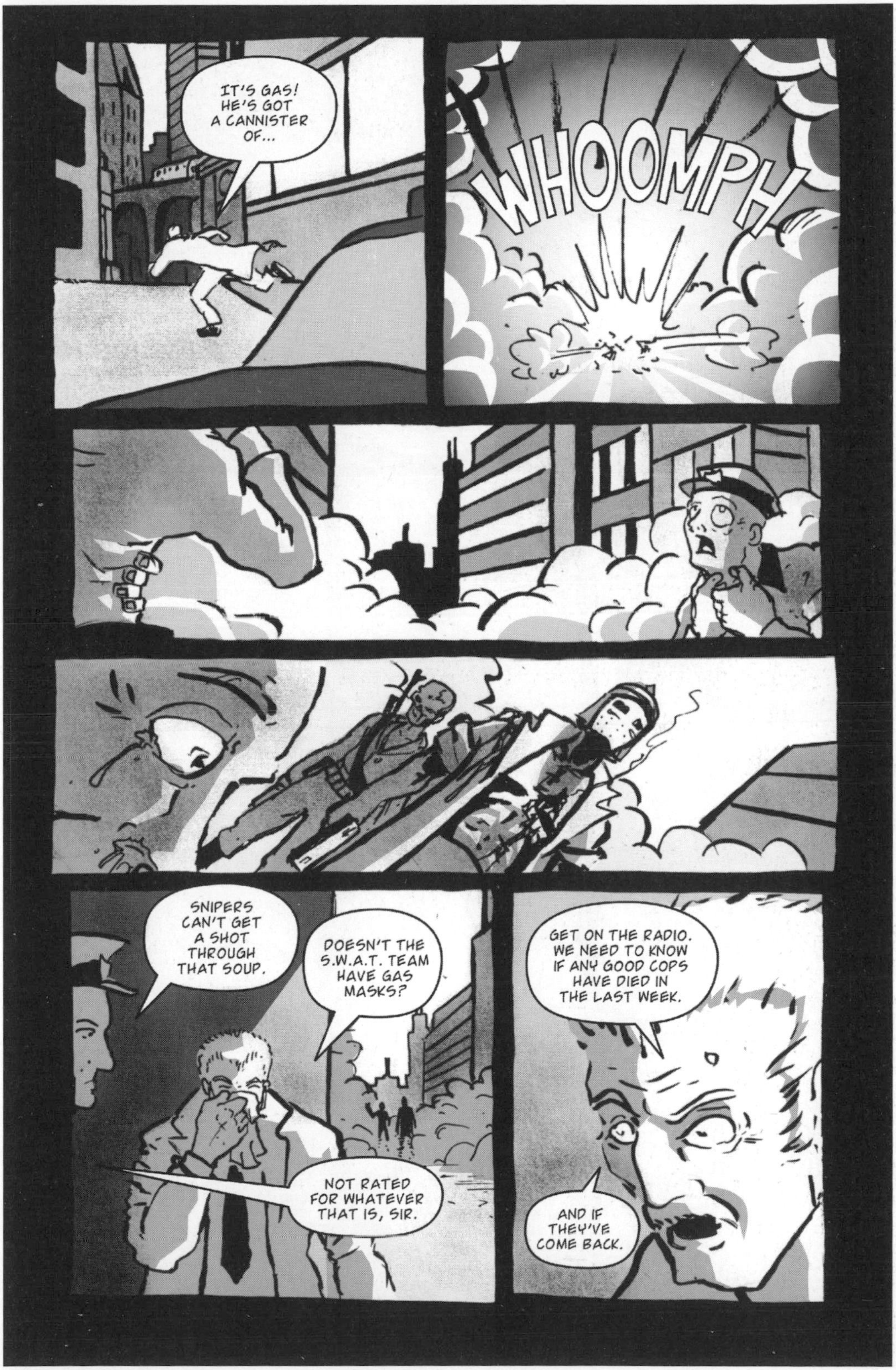
IT'S GAS! HE'S GOT A CANNISTER OF...
WHOOMPH
SNIPERS CAN'T GET A SHOT THROUGH THAT SOUP.
DOESN'T THE S.W.A.T. TEAM HAVE GAS MASKS?
NOT RATED FOR WHATEVER THAT IS, SIR.
GET ON THE RADIO. WE NEED TO KNOW IF ANY GOOD COPS HAVE DIED IN THE LAST WEEK.
AND IF THEY'VE COME BACK.

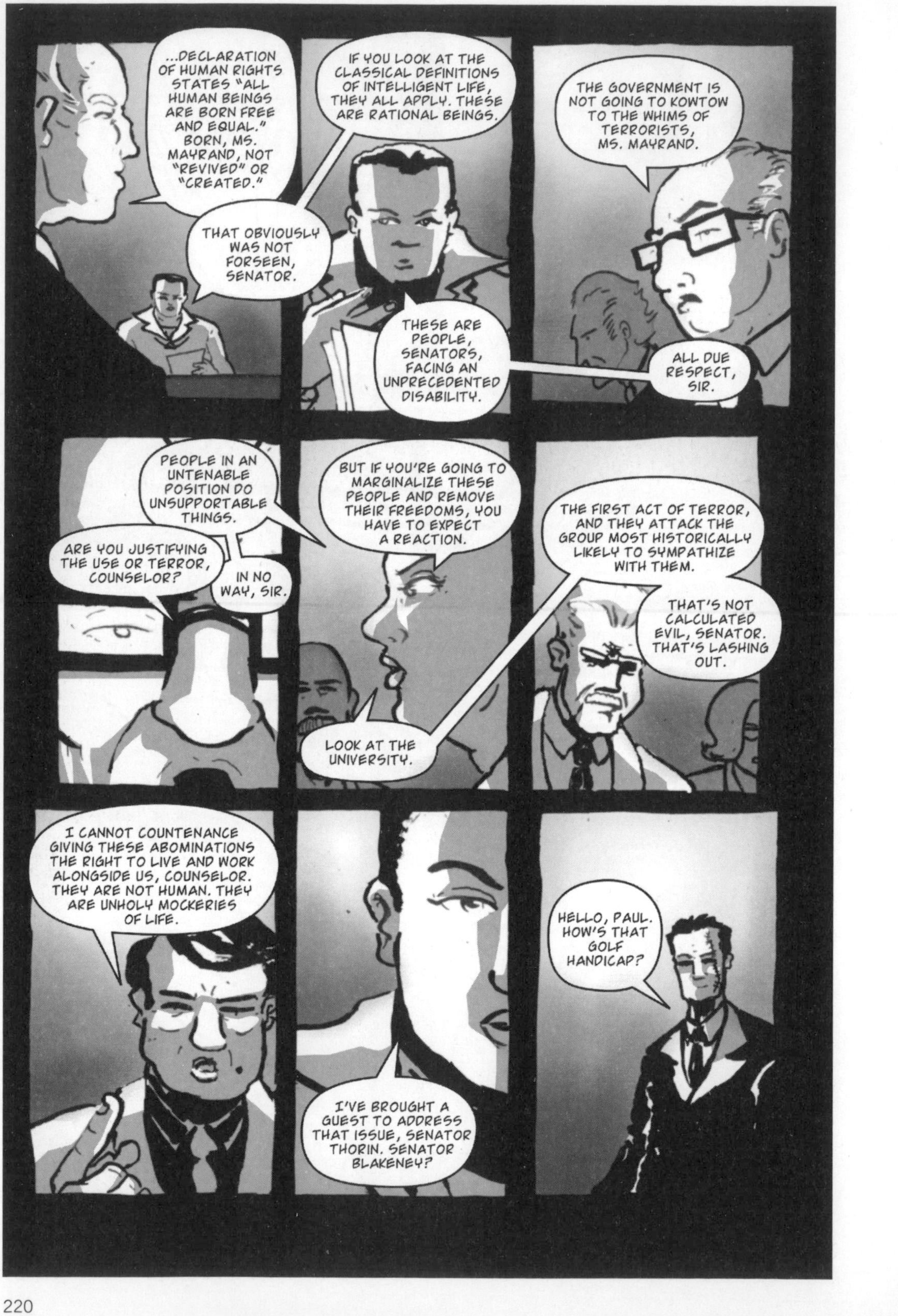
...DECLARATION OF HUMAN RIGHTS STATES "ALL HUMAN BEINGS ARE BORN FREE AND EQUAL." BORN, MS. MAYRAND, NOT "REVIVED" OR "CREATED."
THAT OBVIOUSLY WAS NOT FORSEEN, SENATOR.
IF YOU LOOK AT THE CLASSICAL DEFINITIONS OF INTELLIGENT LIFE, THEY ALL APPLY. THESE ARE RATIONAL BEINGS.
THESE ARE PEOPLE, SENATORS, FACING AN UNPRECEDENTED DISABILITY.
THE GOVERNMENT IS NOT GOING TO KOWTOW TO THE WHIMS OF TERRORISTS, MS. MAYRAND.
ALL DUE RESPECT, SIR.
PEOPLE IN AN UNTENABLE POSITION DO UNSUPPORTABLE THINGS.
ARE YOU JUSTIFYING THE USE OR TERROR, COUNSELOR?
IN NO WAY, SIR.
BUT IF YOU'RE GOING TO MARGINALIZE THESE PEOPLE AND REMOVE THEIR FREEDOMS, YOU HAVE TO EXPECT A REACTION.
LOOK AT THE UNIVERSITY.
THE FIRST ACT OF TERROR, AND THEY ATTACK THE GROUP MOST HISTORICALLY LIKELY TO SYMPATHIZE WITH THEM.
THAT'S NOT CALCULATED EVIL, SENATOR. THAT'S LASHING OUT.
I CANNOT COUNTENANCE GIVING THESE ABOMINATIONS THE RIGHT TO LIVE AND WORK ALONGSIDE US, COUNSELOR. THEY ARE NOT HUMAN. THEY ARE UNHOLY MOCKERIES OF LIFE.
I'VE BROUGHT A GUEST TO ADDRESS THAT ISSUE, SENATOR THORIN. SENATOR BLAKENEY?
HELLO, PAUL. HOW'S THAT GOLF HANDICAP?

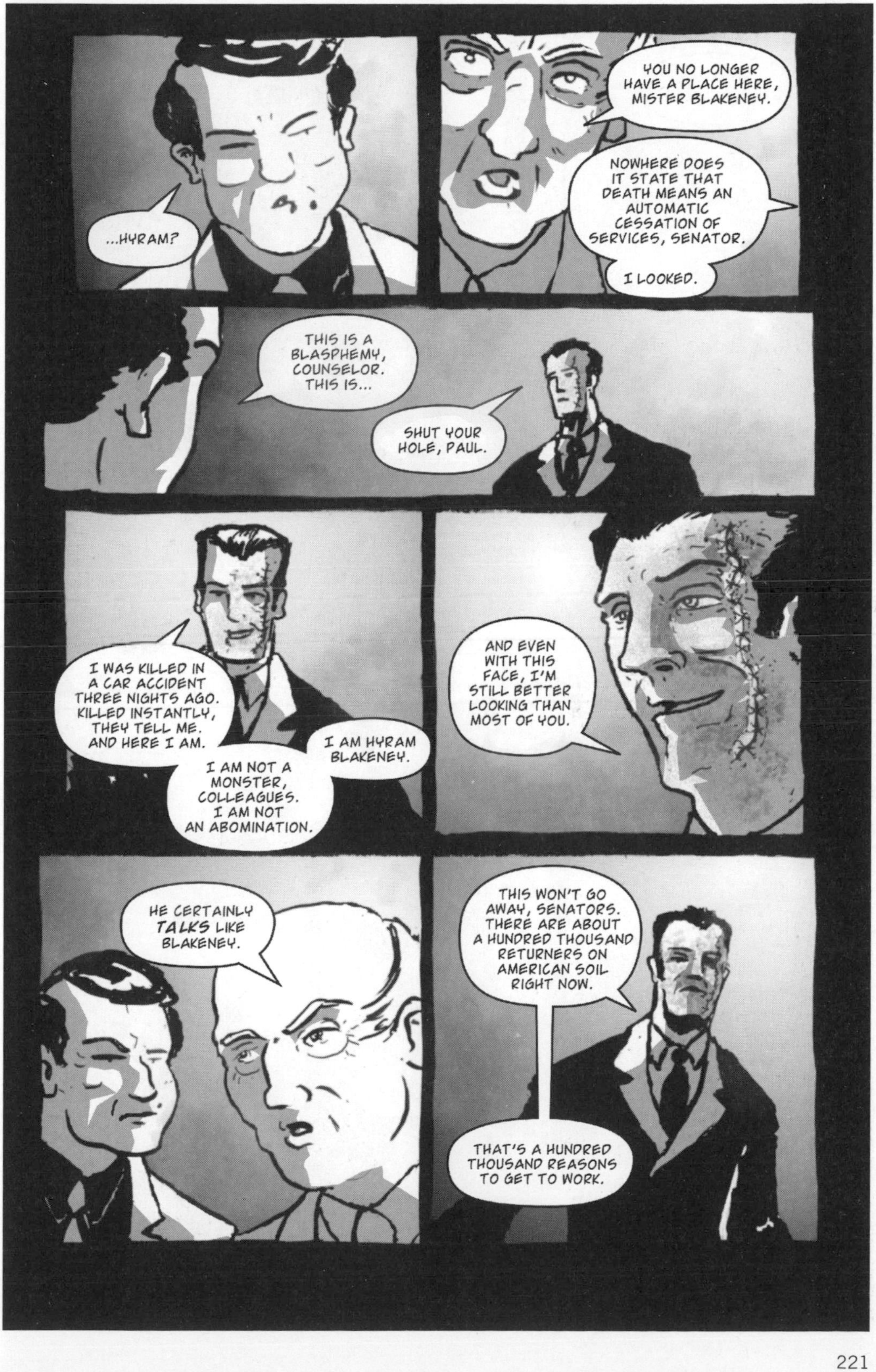
...HYRAM?
YOU NO LONGER HAVE A PLACE HERE, MISTER BLAKENEY.
NOWHERE DOES IT STATE THAT DEATH MEANS AN AUTOMATIC CESSATION OF SERVICES, SENATOR.
I LOOKED.
THIS IS A BLASPHEMY, COUNSELOR. THIS IS...
SHUT YOUR HOLE, PAUL.
I WAS KILLED IN A CAR ACCIDENT THREE NIGHTS AGO. KILLED INSTANTLY, THEY TELL ME. AND HERE I AM.
I AM HYRAM BLAKENEY.
I AM NOT A MONSTER, COLLEAGUES. I AM NOT AN ABOMINATION.
AND EVEN WITH THIS FACE, I'M STILL BETTER LOOKING THAN MOST OF YOU.
HE CERTAINLY TALKS LIKE BLAKENEY.
THIS WON'T GO AWAY, SENATORS. THERE ARE ABOUT A HUNDRED THOUSAND RETURNERS ON AMERICAN SOIL RIGHT NOW.
THAT'S A HUNDRED THOUSAND REASONS TO GET TO WORK.

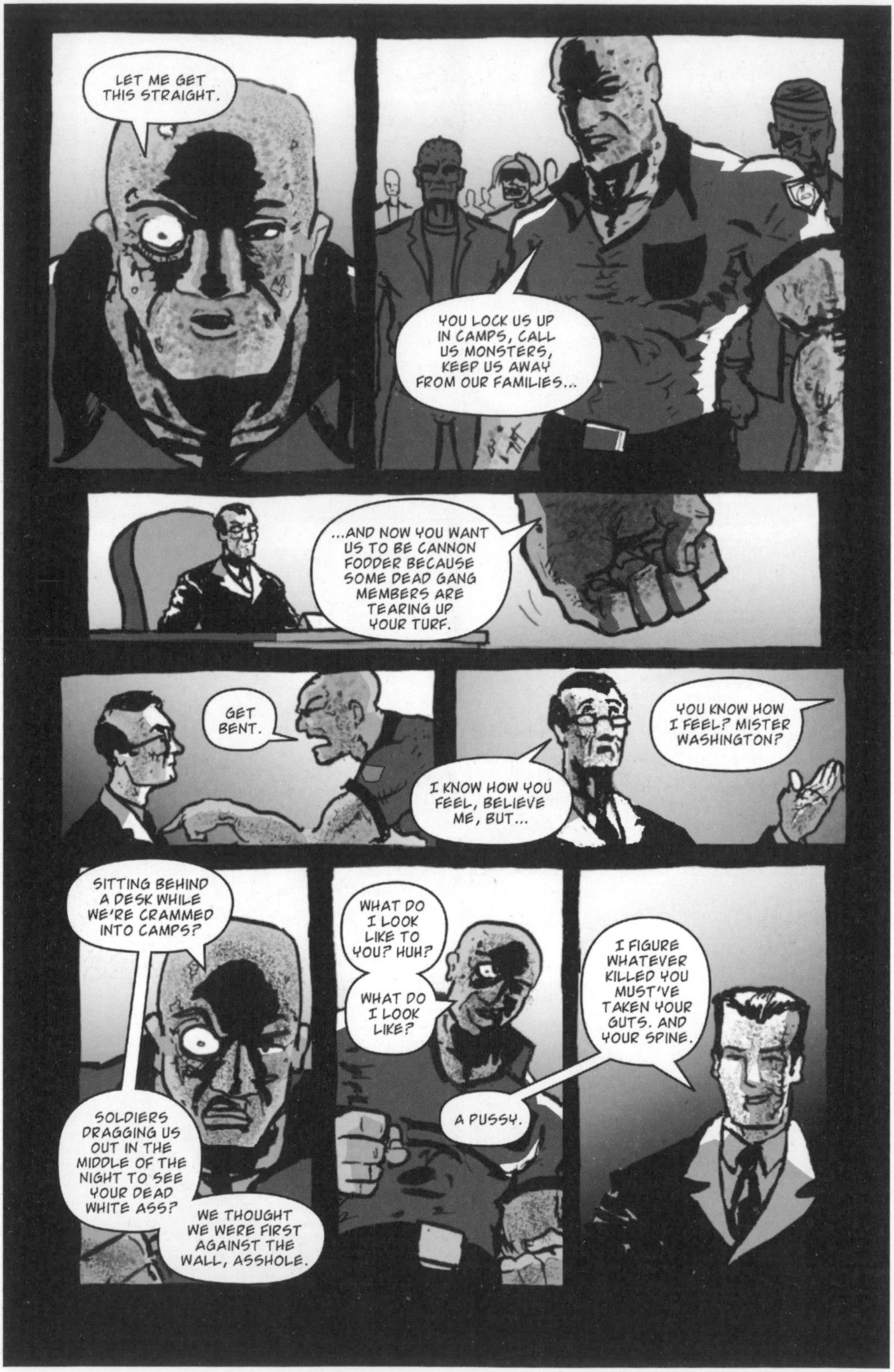
LET ME GET THIS STRAIGHT.
YOU LOCK US UP IN CAMPS, CALL US MONSTERS, KEEP US AWAY FROM OUR FAMILIES...
...AND NOW YOU WANT US TO BE CANNON FODDER BECAUSE SOME DEAD GANG MEMBERS ARE TEARING UP YOUR TURF.
GET BENT.
I KNOW HOW YOU FEEL, BELIEVE ME, BUT...
YOU KNOW HOW I FEEL? MISTER WASHINGTON?
SITTING BEHIND A DESK WHILE WE'RE CRAMMED INTO CAMPS?
SOLDIERS DRAGGING US OUT IN THE MIDDLE OF THE NIGHT TO SEE YOUR DEAD WHITE ASS?
WE THOUGHT WE WERE FIRST AGAINST THE WALL, ASSHOLE.
WHAT DO I LOOK LIKE TO YOU? HUH?
WHAT DO I LOOK LIKE?
I FIGURE WHATEVER KILLED YOU MUST'VE TAKEN YOUR GUTS. AND YOUR SPINE.
A PUSSY.

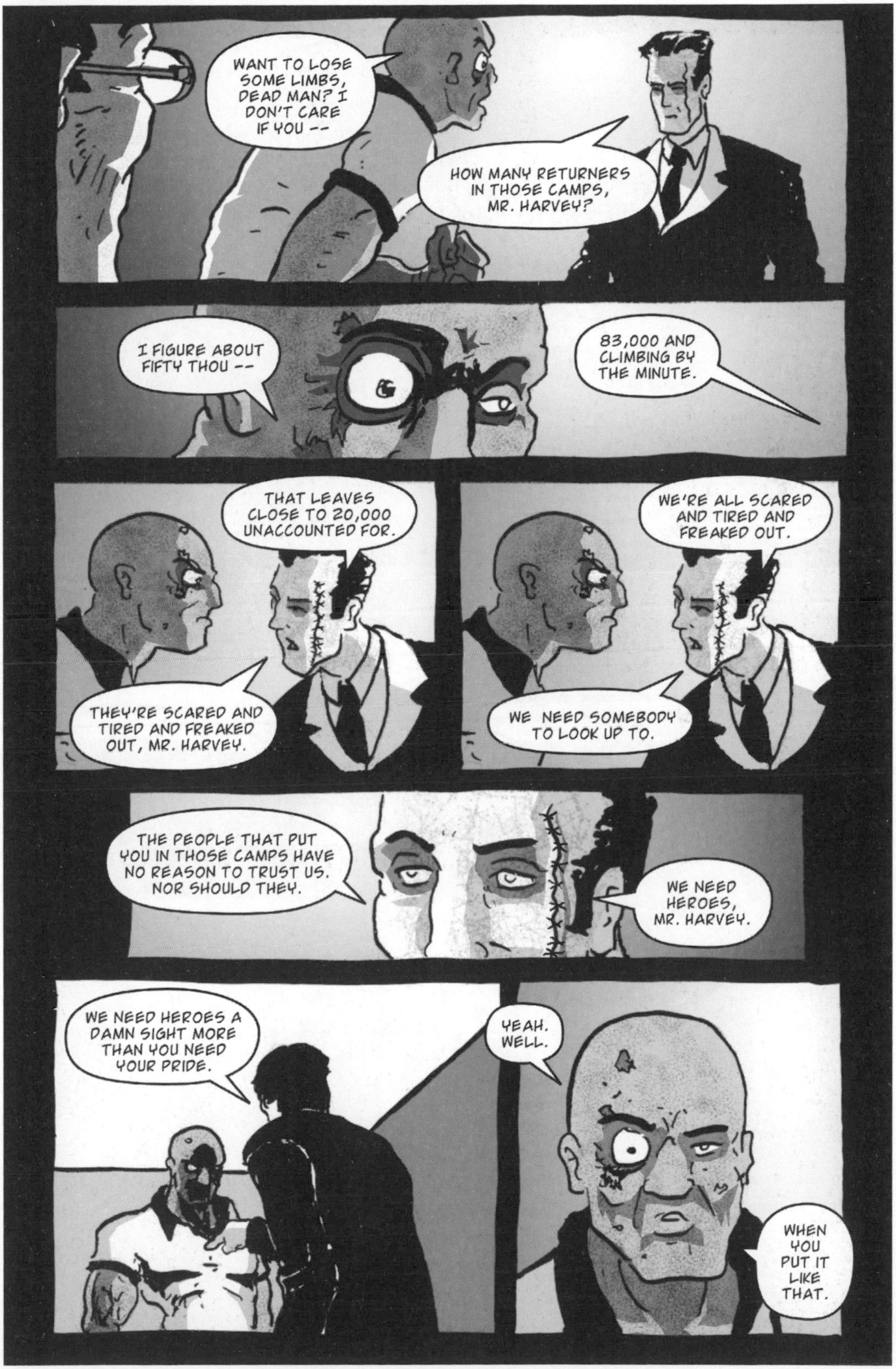
WANT TO LOSE SOME LIMBS, DEAD MAN? I DON'T CARE IF YOU --
HOW MANY RETURNERS IN THOSE CAMPS, MR. HARVEY?
I FIGURE ABOUT FIFTY THOU --
83,000 AND CLIMBING BY THE MINUTE.
THAT LEAVES CLOSE TO 20,000 UNACCOUNTED FOR.
THEY'RE SCARED AND TIRED AND FREAKED OUT, MR. HARVEY.
WE'RE ALL SCARED AND TIRED AND FREAKED OUT.
WE NEED SOMEBODY TO LOOK UP TO.
THE PEOPLE THAT PUT YOU IN THOSE CAMPS HAVE NO REASON TO TRUST US. NOR SHOULD THEY.
WE NEED HEROES, MR. HARVEY.
WE NEED HEROES A DAMN SIGHT MORE THAN YOU NEED YOUR PRIDE.
YEAH. WELL.
WHEN YOU PUT IT LIKE THAT.

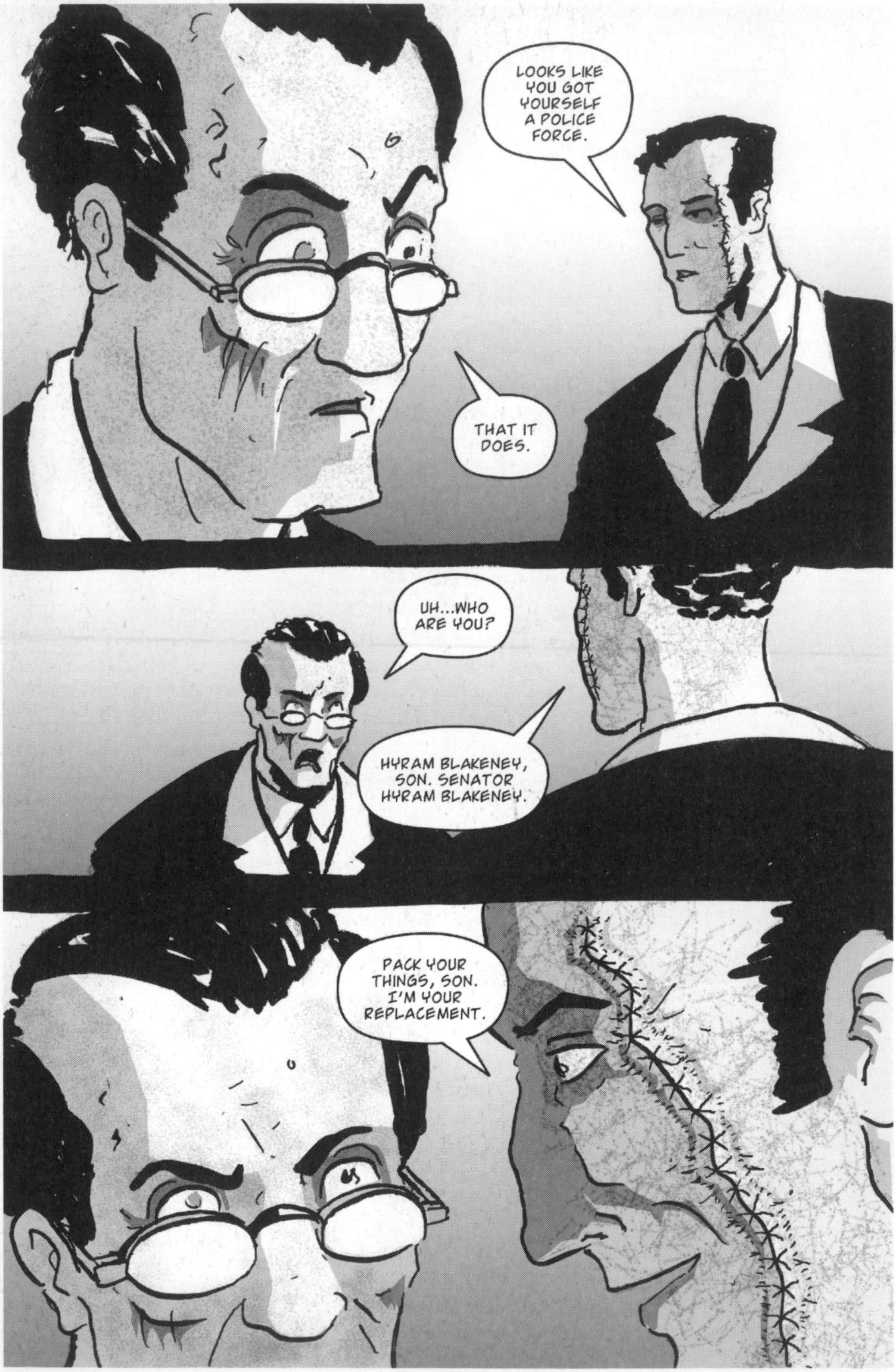
LOOKS LIKE YOU GOT YOURSELF A POLICE FORCE.
THAT IT DOES.
UH...WHO ARE YOU?
HYRAM BLAKENEY, SON. SENATOR HYRAM BLAKENEY.
PACK YOUR THINGS, SON. I'M YOUR REPLACEMENT.

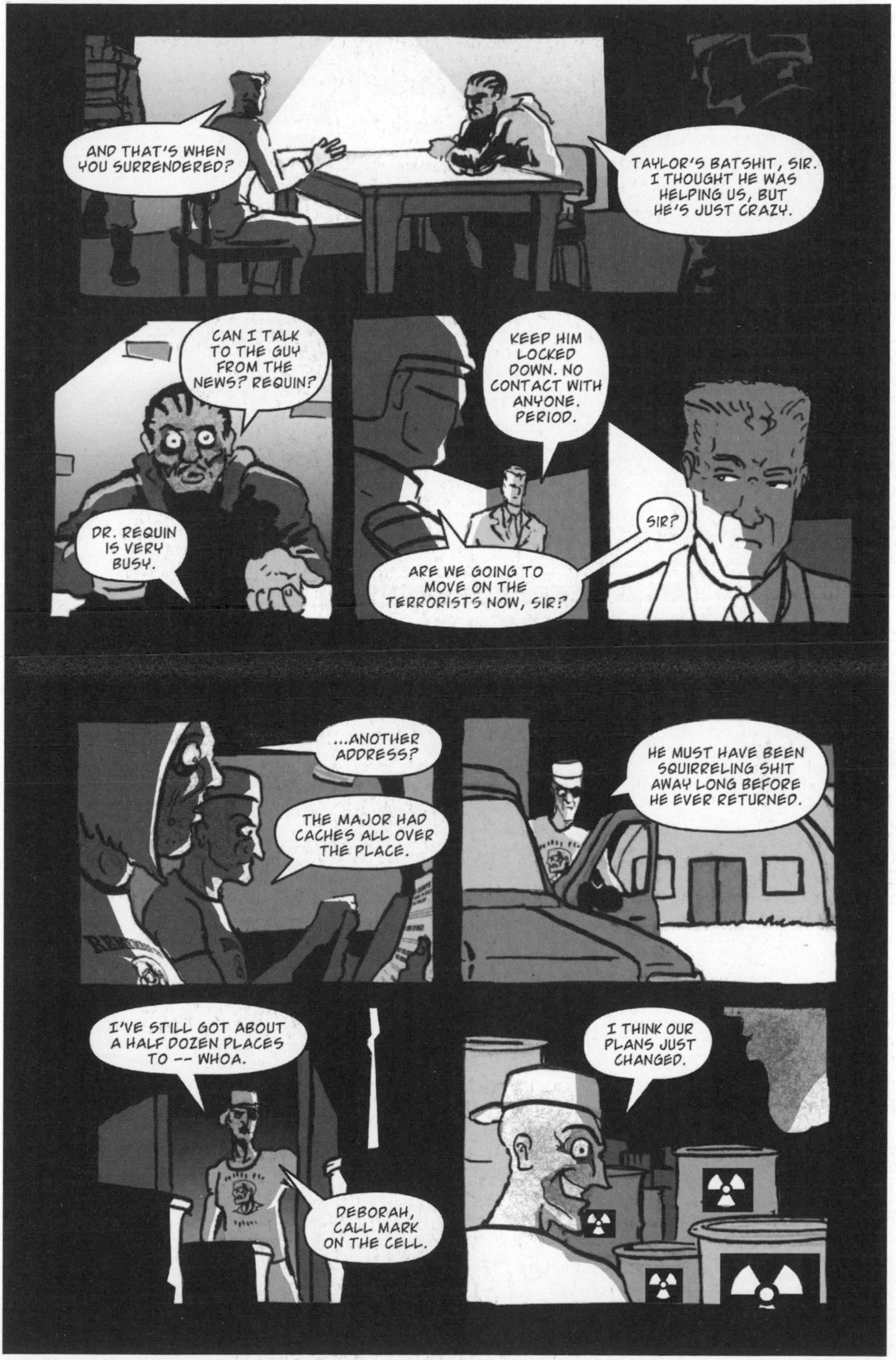
AND THAT'S WHEN YOU SURRENDERED?
TAYLOR'S BATSHIT, SIR. I THOUGHT HE WAS HELPING US, BUT HE'S JUST CRAZY.
CAN I TALK TO THE GUY FROM THE NEWS? REQUIN?
DR. REQUIN IS VERY BUSY.
KEEP HIM LOCKED DOWN. NO CONTACT WITH ANYONE. PERIOD.
ARE WE GOING TO MOVE ON THE TERRORISTS NOW, SIR?
SIR?
...ANOTHER ADDRESS?
THE MAJOR HAD CACHES ALL OVER THE PLACE.
HE MUST HAVE BEEN SQUIRRELING SHIT AWAY LONG BEFORE HE EVER RETURNED.
I'VE STILL GOT ABOUT A HALF DOZEN PLACES TO -- WHOA.
DEBORAH, CALL MARK ON THE CELL.
I THINK OUR PLANS JUST CHANGED.

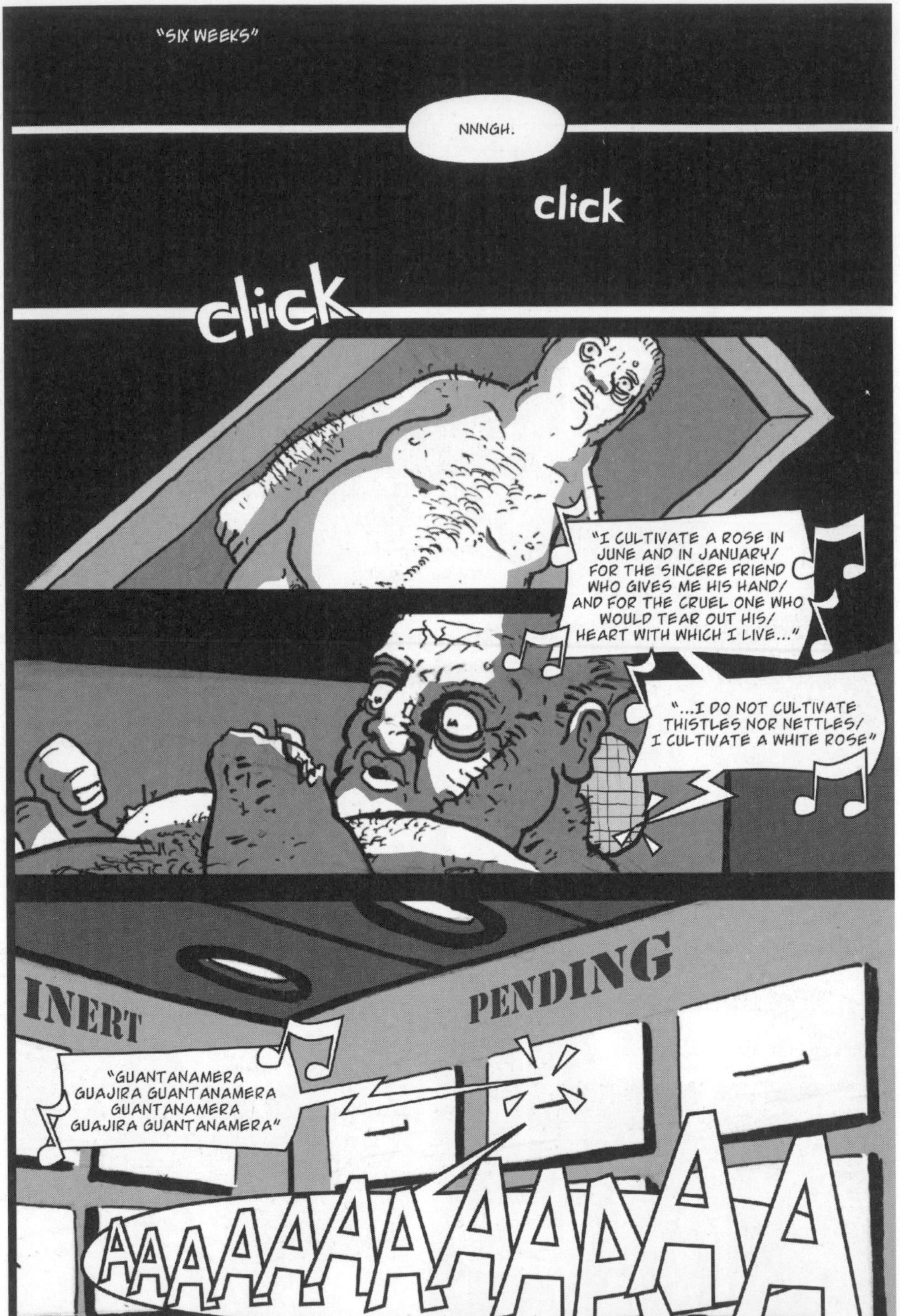
"SIX WEEKS"
NNNGH.
click
click
"I CULTIVATE A ROSE IN JUNE AND IN JANUARY/ FOR THE SINCERE FRIEND WHO GIVES ME HIS HAND/ AND FOR THE CRUEL ONE WHO WOULD TEAR OUT HIS/ HEART WITH WHICH I LIVE..."
"...I DO NOT CULTIVATE THISTLES NOR NETTLES/ I CULTIVATE A WHITE ROSE"
INERT
PENDING
"GUANTANAMERA GUAJIRA GUANTANAMERA GUANTANAMERA GUAJIRA GUANTANAMERA"
AAAAAAAAAAAAA

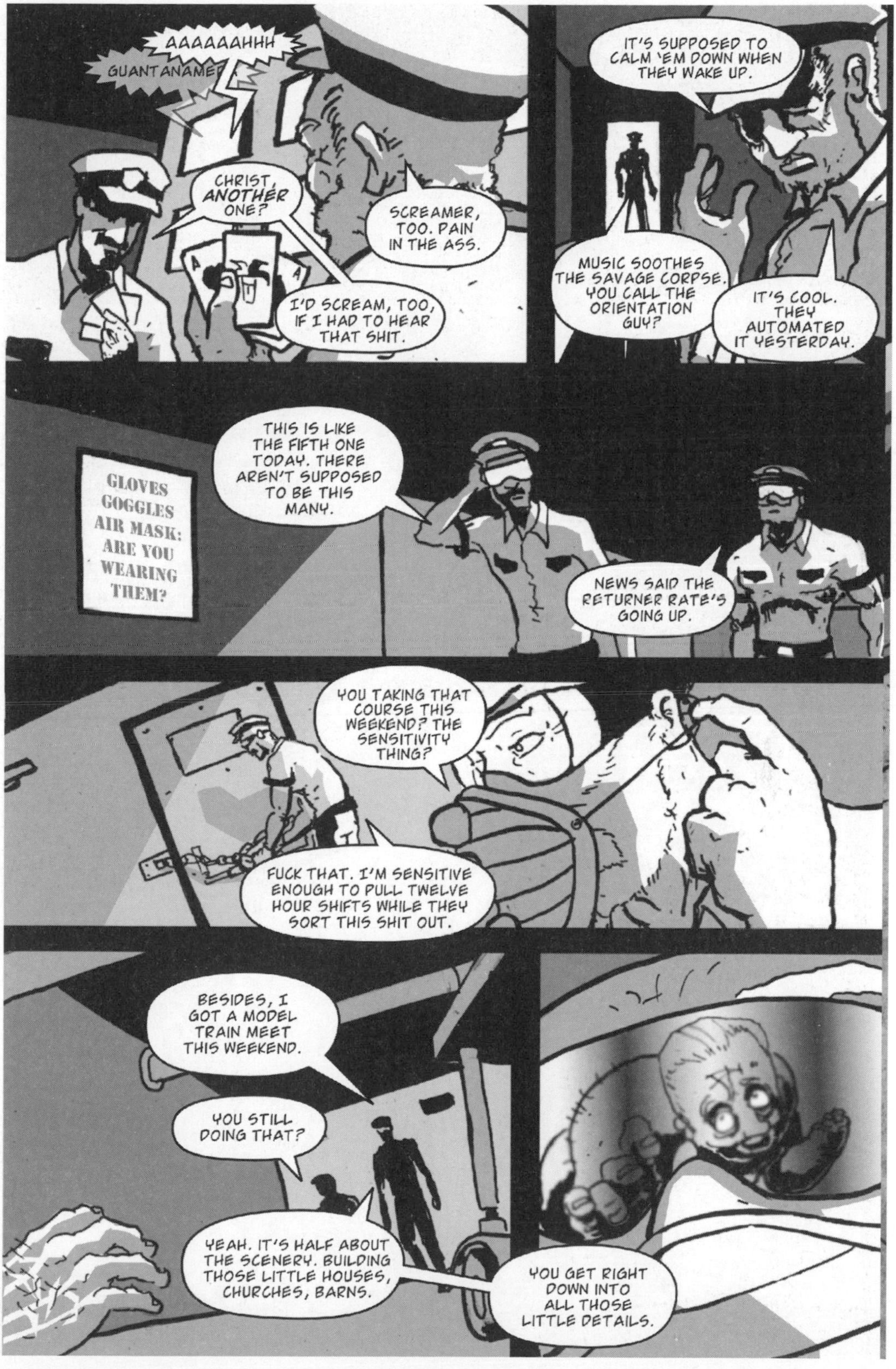
AAAAAAHHH
GUANTANAME
CHRIST, ANOTHER ONE?
SCREAMER, TOO. PAIN IN THE ASS.
I'D SCREAM, TOO, IF I HAD TO HEAR THAT SHIT.
IT'S SUPPOSED TO CALM 'EM DOWN WHEN THEY WAKE UP.
MUSIC SOOTHES THE SAVAGE CORPSE. YOU CALL THE ORIENTATION GUY?
IT'S COOL. THEY AUTOMATED IT YESTERDAY.
GLOVES GOGGLES AIR MASK: ARE YOU WEARING THEM?
THIS IS LIKE THE FIFTH ONE TODAY. THERE AREN'T SUPPOSED TO BE THIS MANY.
NEWS SAID THE RETURNER RATE'S GOING UP.
YOU TAKING THAT COURSE THIS WEEKEND? THE SENSITIVITY THING?
FUCK THAT. I'M SENSITIVE ENOUGH TO PULL TWELVE HOUR SHIFTS WHILE THEY SORT THIS SHIT OUT.
BESIDES, I GOT A MODEL TRAIN MEET THIS WEEKEND.
YOU STILL DOING THAT?
YEAH. IT'S HALF ABOUT THE SCENERY. BUILDING THOSE LITTLE HOUSES, CHURCHES, BARNS.
YOU GET RIGHT DOWN INTO ALL THOSE LITTLE DETAILS.

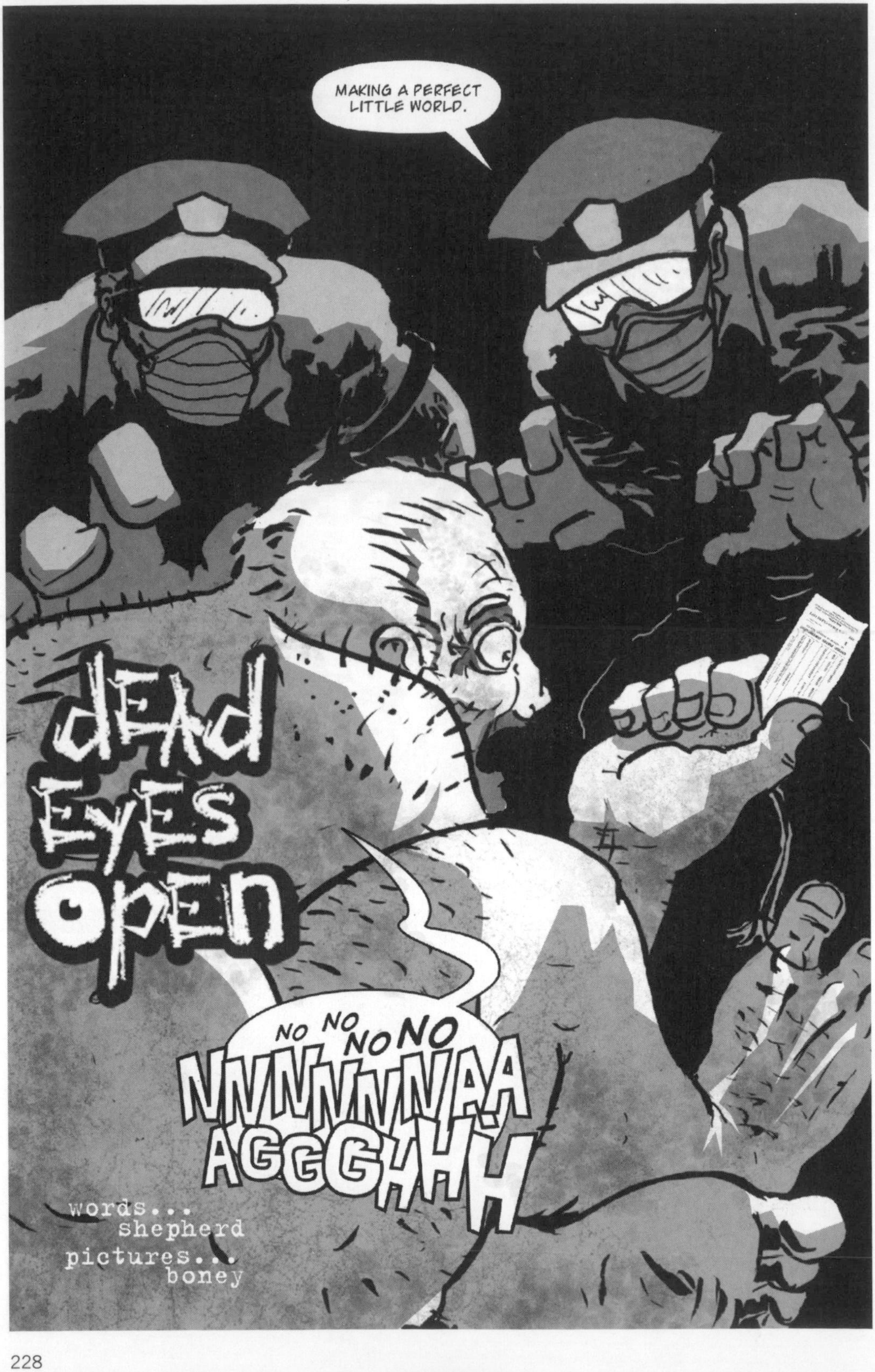
MAKING A PERFECT LITTLE WORLD.
dead eyes open
NO NO NO NO
NNNNNNNAA AGGGHHH
words... shepherd
pictures... boney

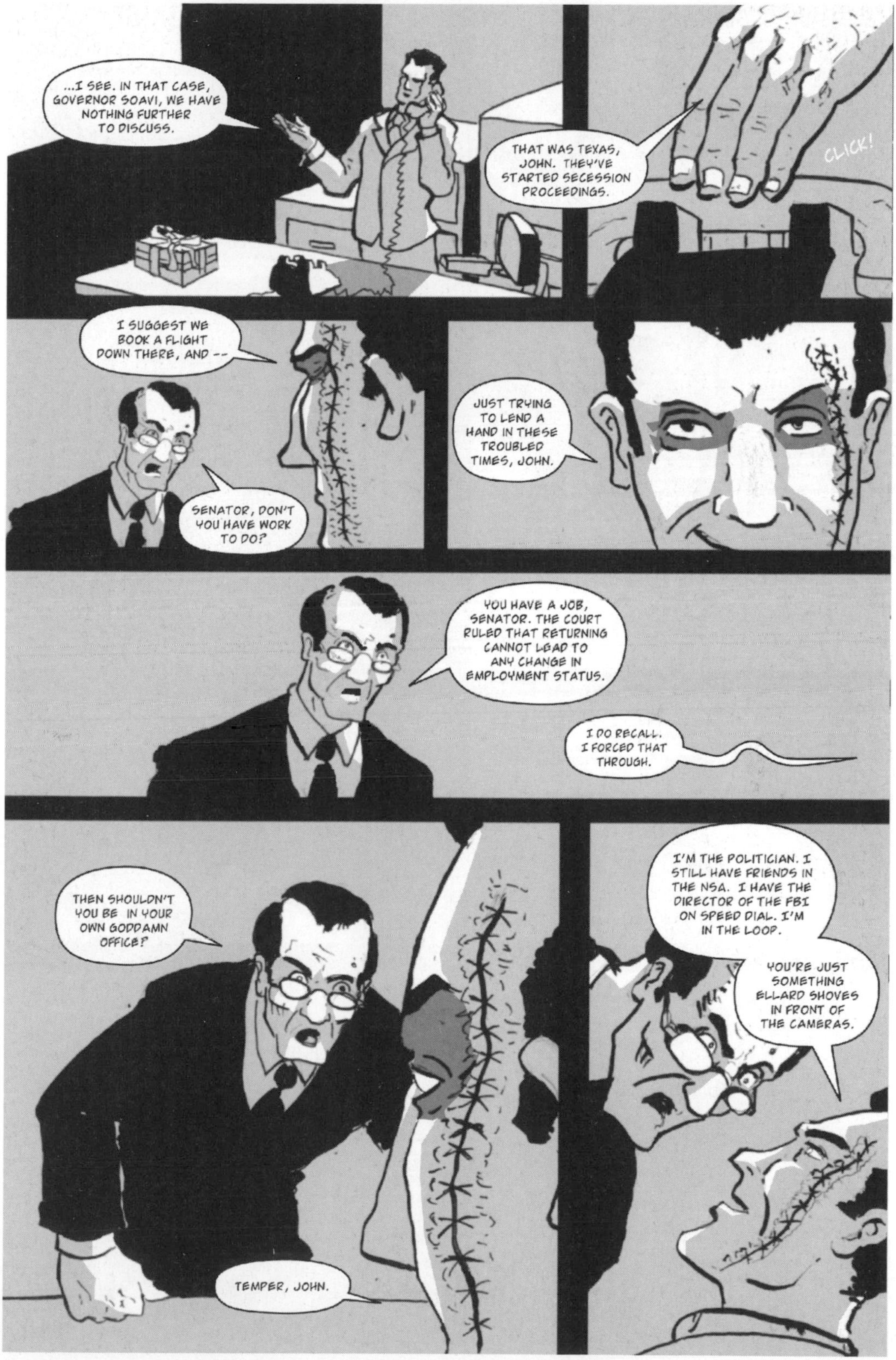
...I SEE. IN THAT CASE, GOVERNOR SOAVI, WE HAVE NOTHING FURTHER TO DISCUSS.
THAT WAS TEXAS, JOHN. THEY'VE STARTED SECESSION PROCEEDINGS.
CLICK!
I SUGGEST WE BOOK A FLIGHT DOWN THERE, AND --
SENATOR, DON'T YOU HAVE WORK TO DO?
JUST TRYING TO LEND A HAND IN THESE TROUBLED TIMES, JOHN.
YOU HAVE A JOB, SENATOR. THE COURT RULED THAT RETURNING CANNOT LEAD TO ANY CHANGE IN EMPLOYMENT STATUS.
I DO RECALL. I FORCED THAT THROUGH.
THEN SHOULDN'T YOU BE IN YOUR OWN GODDAMN OFFICE?
TEMPER, JOHN.
I'M THE POLITICIAN. I STILL HAVE FRIENDS IN THE NSA. I HAVE THE DIRECTOR OF THE FBI ON SPEED DIAL. I'M IN THE LOOP.
YOU'RE JUST SOMETHING ELLARD SHOVES IN FRONT OF THE CAMERAS.

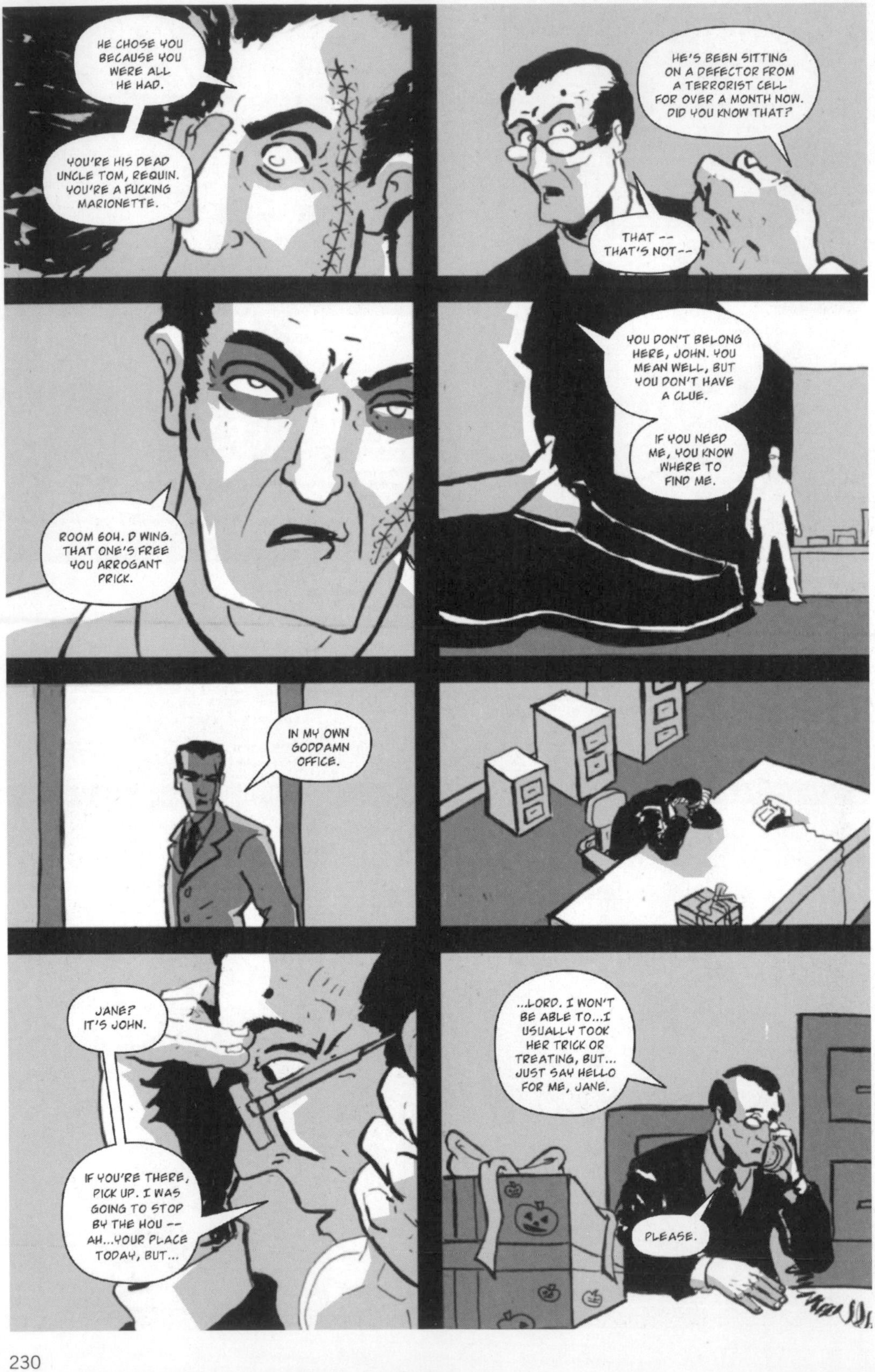
HE CHOSE YOU BECAUSE YOU WERE ALL HE HAD.
YOU'RE HIS DEAD UNCLE TOM, REQUIN. YOU'RE A FUCKING MARIONETTE.
HE'S BEEN SITTING ON A DEFECTOR FROM A TERRORIST CELL FOR OVER A MONTH NOW. DID YOU KNOW THAT?
THAT -- THAT'S NOT--
ROOM 604. D WING. THAT ONE'S FREE YOU ARROGANT PRICK.
YOU DON'T BELONG HERE, JOHN. YOU MEAN WELL, BUT YOU DON'T HAVE A CLUE.
IF YOU NEED ME, YOU KNOW WHERE TO FIND ME.
IN MY OWN GODDAMN OFFICE.
JANE? IT'S JOHN.
IF YOU'RE THERE, PICK UP. I WAS GOING TO STOP BY THE HOU -- AH...YOUR PLACE TODAY, BUT...
...LORD. I WON'T BE ABLE TO...I USUALLY TOOK HER TRICK OR TREATING, BUT... JUST SAY HELLO FOR ME, JANE.
PLEASE.

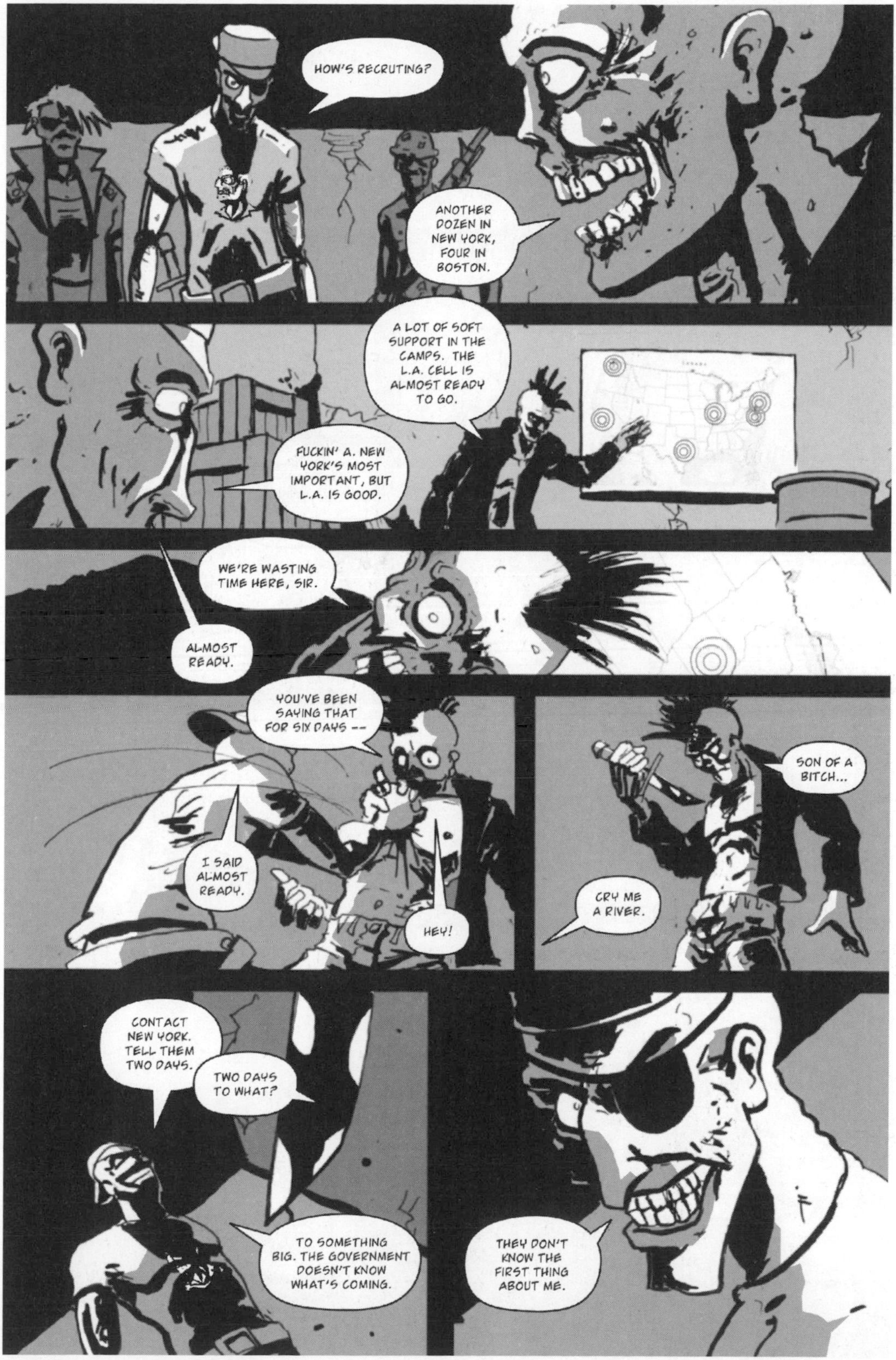
HOW'S RECRUTING?
ANOTHER DOZEN IN NEW YORK, FOUR IN BOSTON.
A LOT OF SOFT SUPPORT IN THE CAMPS. THE L.A. CELL IS ALMOST READY TO GO.
FUCKIN' A. NEW YORK'S MOST IMPORTANT, BUT L.A. IS GOOD.
WE'RE WASTING TIME HERE, SIR.
ALMOST READY.
YOU'VE BEEN SAYING THAT FOR SIX DAYS --
I SAID ALMOST READY.
HEY!
SON OF A BITCH...
CRY ME A RIVER.
CONTACT NEW YORK. TELL THEM TWO DAYS.
TWO DAYS TO WHAT?
TO SOMETHING BIG. THE GOVERNMENT DOESN'T KNOW WHAT'S COMING.
THEY DON'T KNOW THE FIRST THING ABOUT ME.

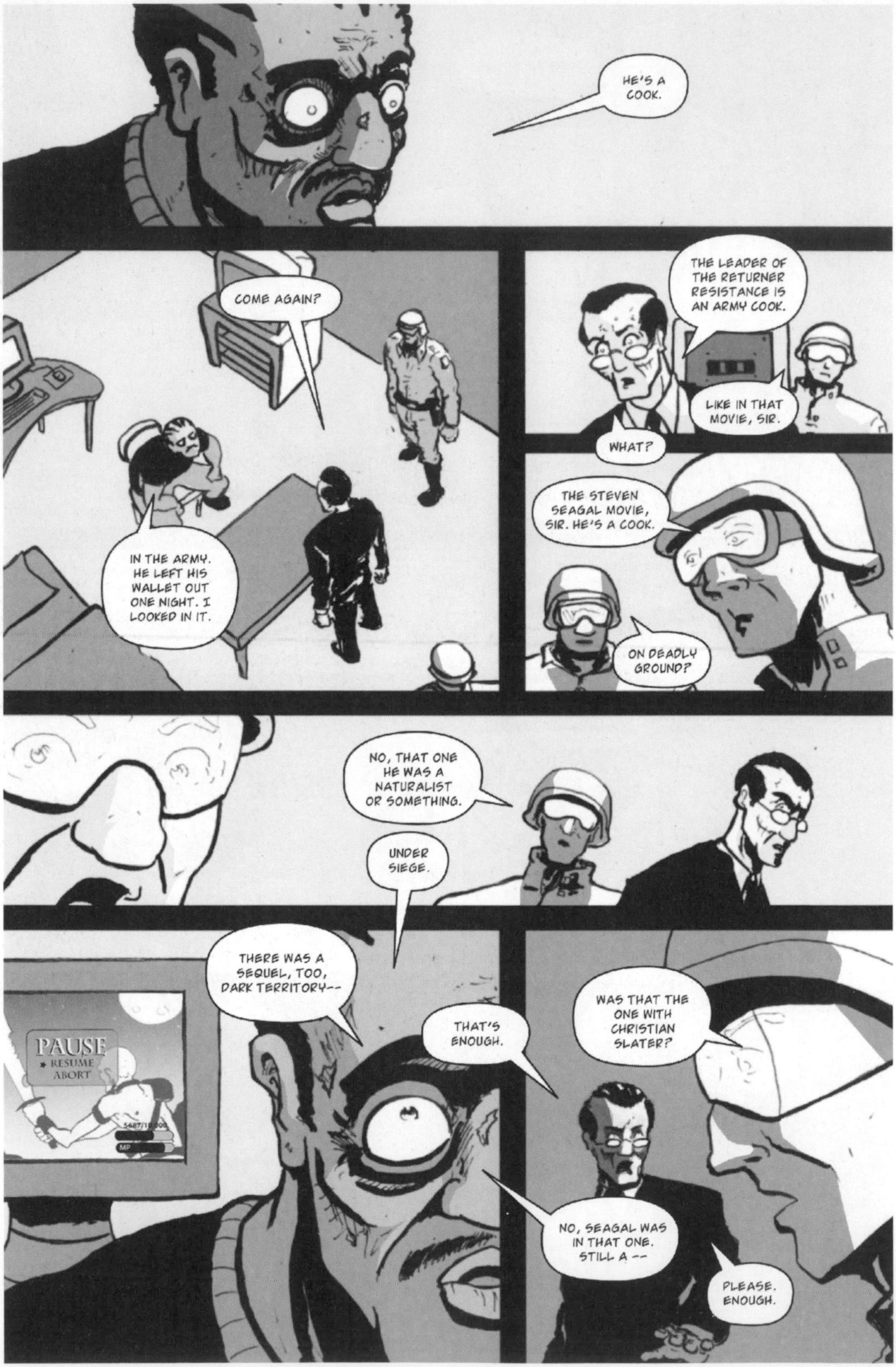
HE'S A COOK.
COME AGAIN?
IN THE ARMY. HE LEFT HIS WALLET OUT ONE NIGHT. I LOOKED IN IT.
THE LEADER OF THE RETURNER RESISTANCE IS AN ARMY COOK.
LIKE IN THAT MOVIE, SIR.
WHAT?
THE STEVEN SEAGAL MOVIE, SIR. HE'S A COOK.
ON DEADLY GROUND?
NO, THAT ONE HE WAS A NATURALIST OR SOMETHING.
UNDER SIEGE.
PAUSE
RESUME
ABORT
MP
THERE WAS A SEQUEL, TOO, DARK TERRITORY--
THAT'S ENOUGH.
WAS THAT THE ONE WITH CHRISTIAN SLATER?
NO, SEAGAL WAS IN THAT ONE. STILL A --
PLEASE. ENOUGH.

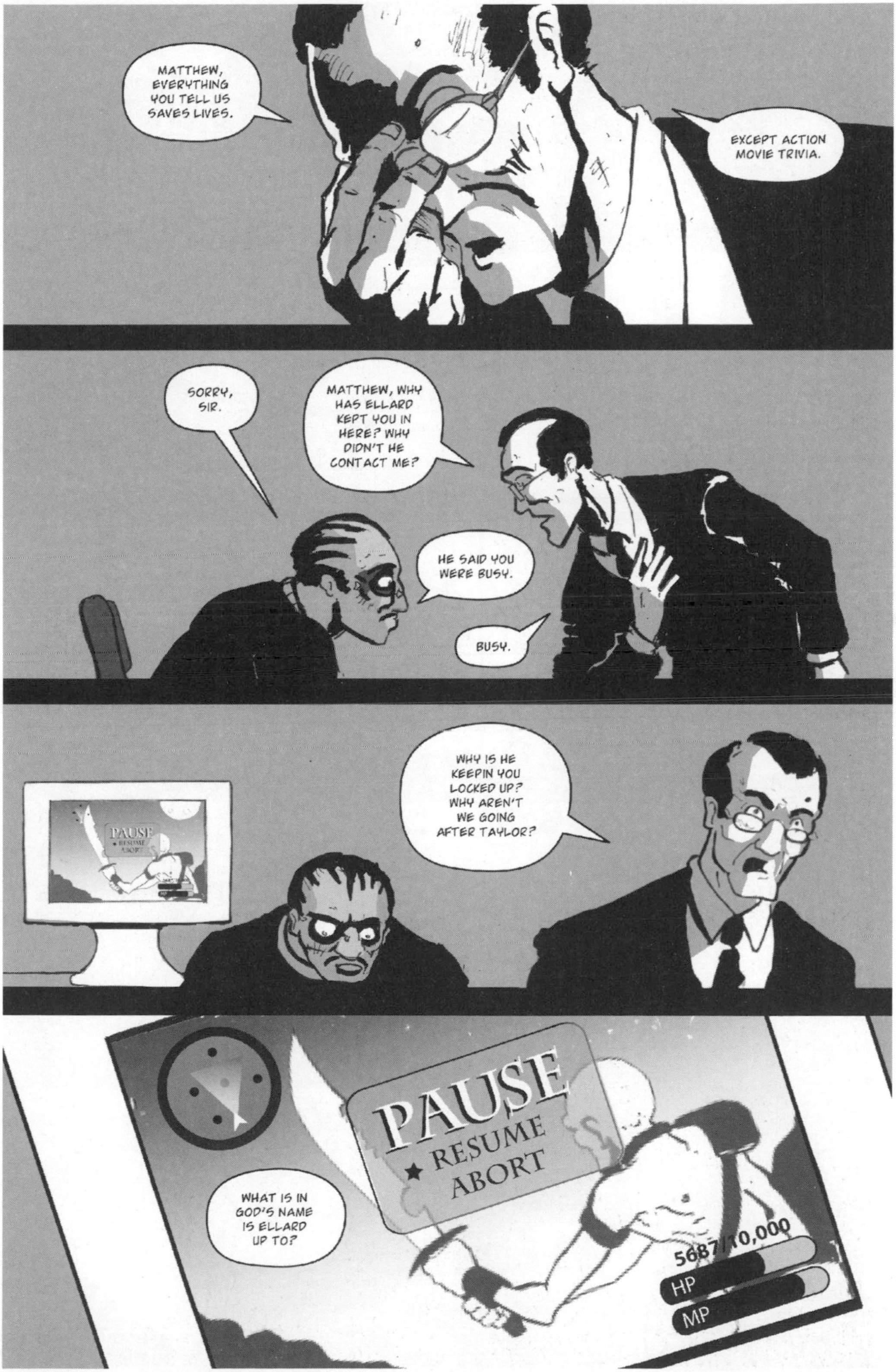
MATTHEW, EVERYTHING YOU TELL US SAVES LIVES.
EXCEPT ACTION MOVIE TRIVIA.
SORRY, SIR.
MATTHEW, WHY HAS ELLARD KEPT YOU IN HERE? WHY DIDN'T HE CONTACT ME?
HE SAID YOU WERE BUSY.
BUSY.
WHY IS HE KEEPIN YOU LOCKED UP? WHY AREN'T WE GOING AFTER TAYLOR?
PAUSE
RESUME
ABORT
WHAT IS IN GOD'S NAME IS ELLARD UP TO?
5687/10,000
HP
MP

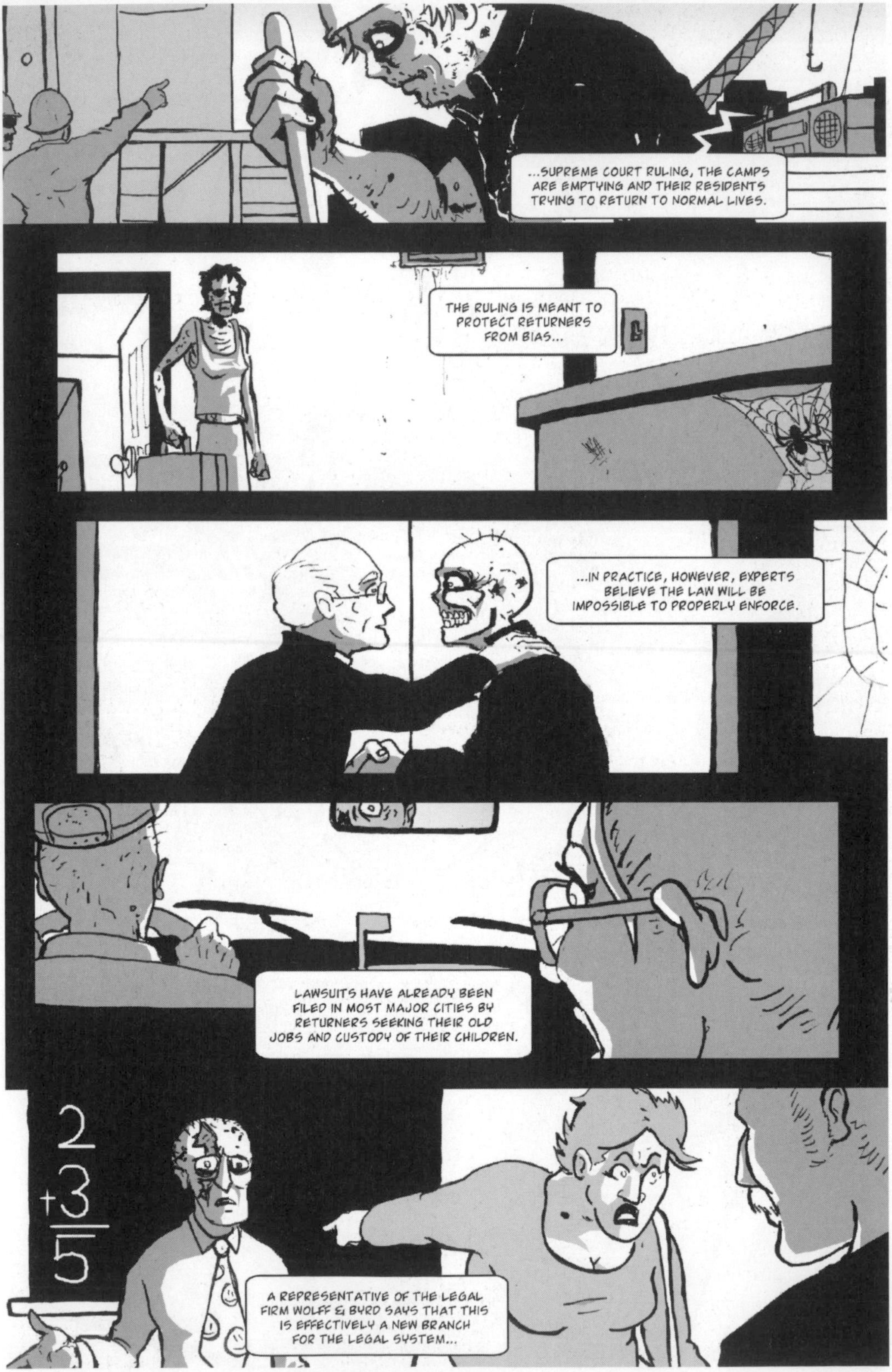
...SUPREME COURT RULING, THE CAMPS ARE EMPTYING AND THEIR RESIDENTS TRYING TO RETURN TO NORMAL LIVES.
THE RULING IS MEANT TO PROTECT RETURNERS FROM BIAS...
...IN PRACTICE, HOWEVER, EXPERTS BELIEVE THE LAW WILL BE IMPOSSIBLE TO PROPERLY ENFORCE.
LAWSUITS HAVE ALREADY BEEN FILED IN MOST MAJOR CITIES BY RETURNERS SEEKING THEIR OLD JOBS AND CUSTODY OF THEIR CHILDREN.
2
+3
5
A REPRESENTATIVE OF THE LEGAL FIRM WOLFF & BYRD SAYS THAT THIS IS EFFECTIVELY A NEW BRANCH FOR THE LEGAL SYSTEM...

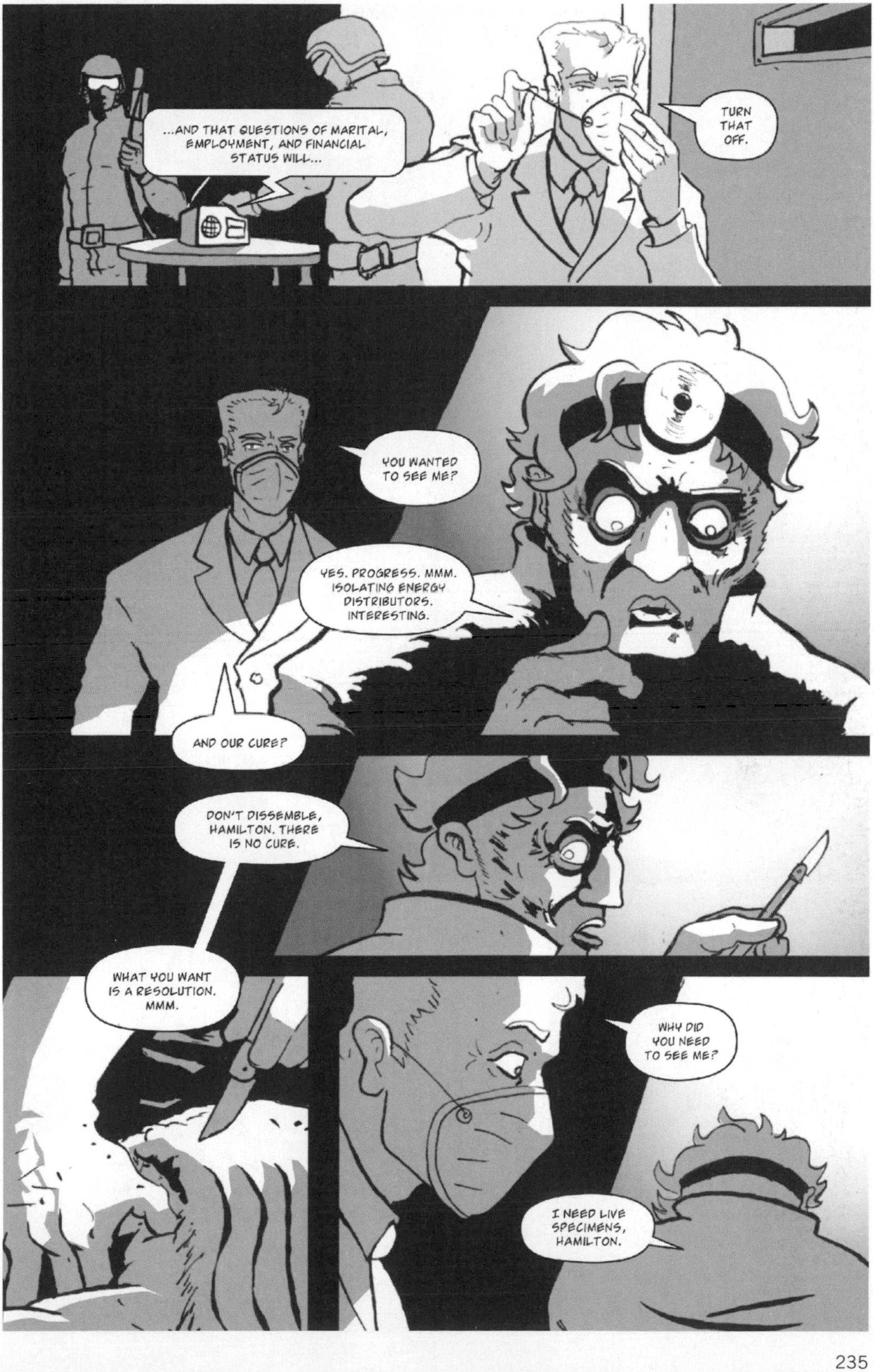
...AND THAT QUESTIONS OF MARITAL, EMPLOYMENT, AND FINANCIAL STATUS WILL...
TURN THAT OFF.
YOU WANTED TO SEE ME?
YES. PROGRESS. MMM. ISOLATING ENERGY DISTRIBUTORS. INTERESTING.
AND OUR CURE?
DON'T DISSEMBLE, HAMILTON. THERE IS NO CURE.
WHAT YOU WANT IS A RESOLUTION. MMM.
WHY DID YOU NEED TO SEE ME?
I NEED LIVE SPECIMENS, HAMILTON.

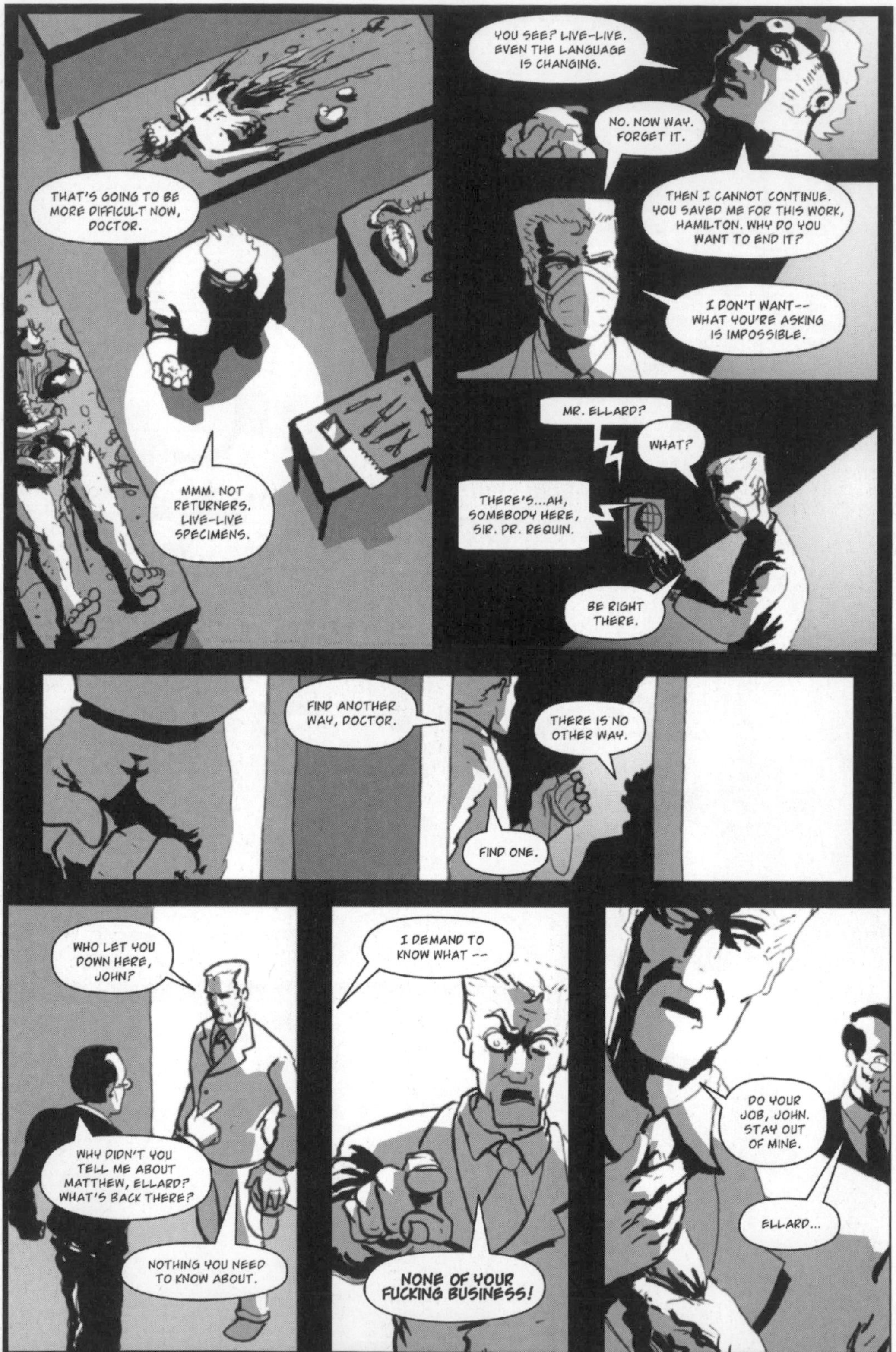

THAT'S GOING TO BE MORE DIFFICULT NOW, DOCTOR.
MMM. NOT RETURNERS. LIVE-LIVE SPECIMENS.
YOU SEE? LIVE-LIVE. EVEN THE LANGUAGE IS CHANGING.
NO. NOW WAY. FORGET IT.
THEN I CANNOT CONTINUE. YOU SAVED ME FOR THIS WORK, HAMILTON. WHY DO YOU WANT TO END IT?
I DON'T WANT-- WHAT YOU'RE ASKING IS IMPOSSIBLE.
MR. ELLARD?
WHAT?
THERE'S...AH, SOMEBODY HERE, SIR. DR. REQUIN.
BE RIGHT THERE.
FIND ANOTHER WAY, DOCTOR.
THERE IS NO OTHER WAY.
FIND ONE.
WHO LET YOU DOWN HERE, JOHN?
WHY DIDN'T YOU TELL ME ABOUT MATTHEW, ELLARD? WHAT'S BACK THERE?
NOTHING YOU NEED TO KNOW ABOUT.
I DEMAND TO KNOW WHAT --
NONE OF YOUR FUCKING BUSINESS!
DO YOUR JOB, JOHN. STAY OUT OF MINE.
ELLARD...

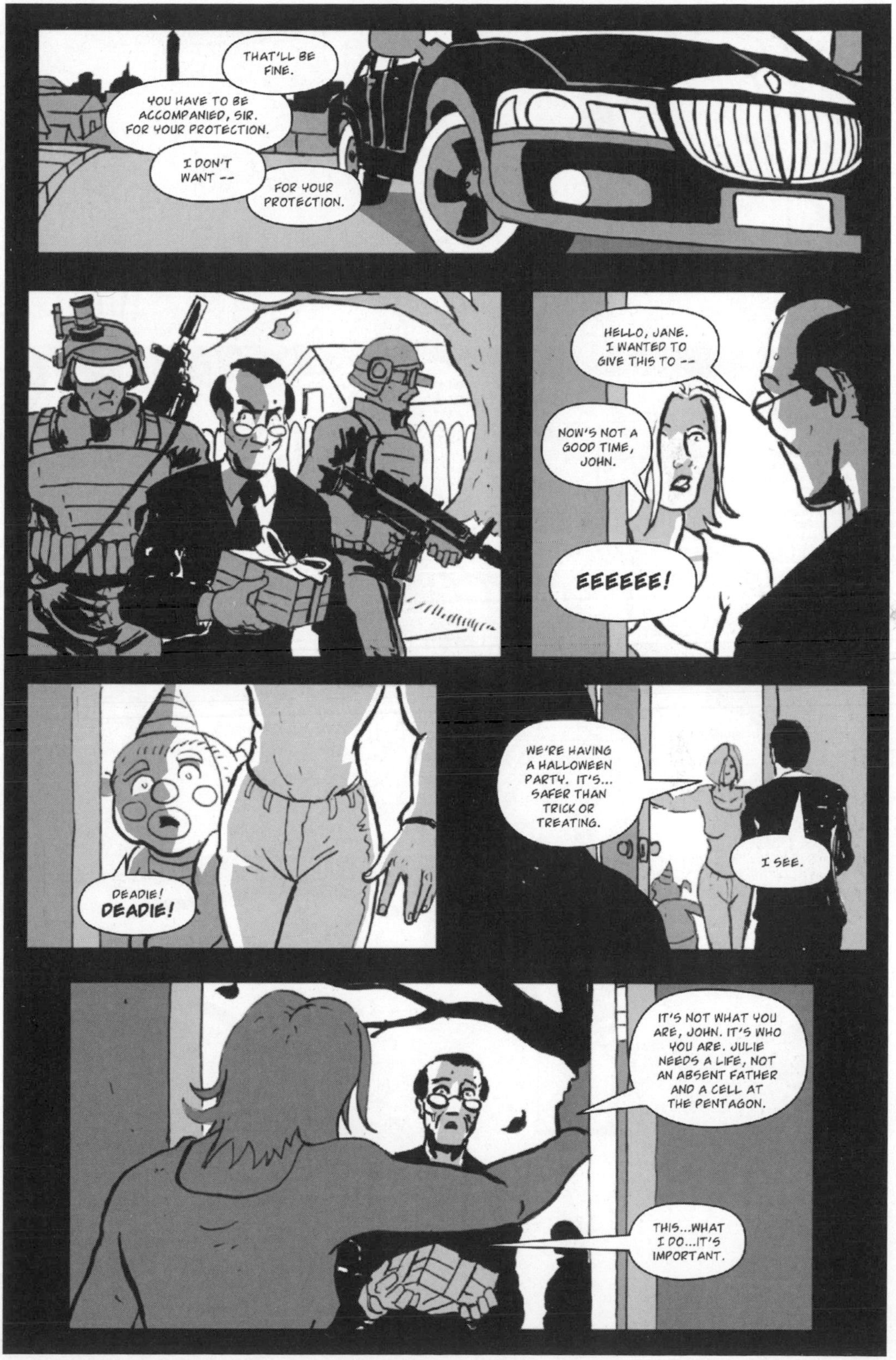
THAT'LL BE FINE.
YOU HAVE TO BE ACCOMPANIED, SIR. FOR YOUR PROTECTION.
I DON'T WANT --
FOR YOUR PROTECTION.
HELLO, JANE. I WANTED TO GIVE THIS TO --
NOW'S NOT A GOOD TIME, JOHN.
EEEEEE!
DEADIE! DEADIE!
WE'RE HAVING A HALLOWEEN PARTY. IT'S... SAFER THAN TRICK OR TREATING.
I SEE.
IT'S NOT WHAT YOU ARE, JOHN. IT'S WHO YOU ARE. JULIE NEEDS A LIFE, NOT AN ABSENT FATHER AND A CELL AT THE PENTAGON.
THIS...WHAT I DO...IT'S IMPORTANT.

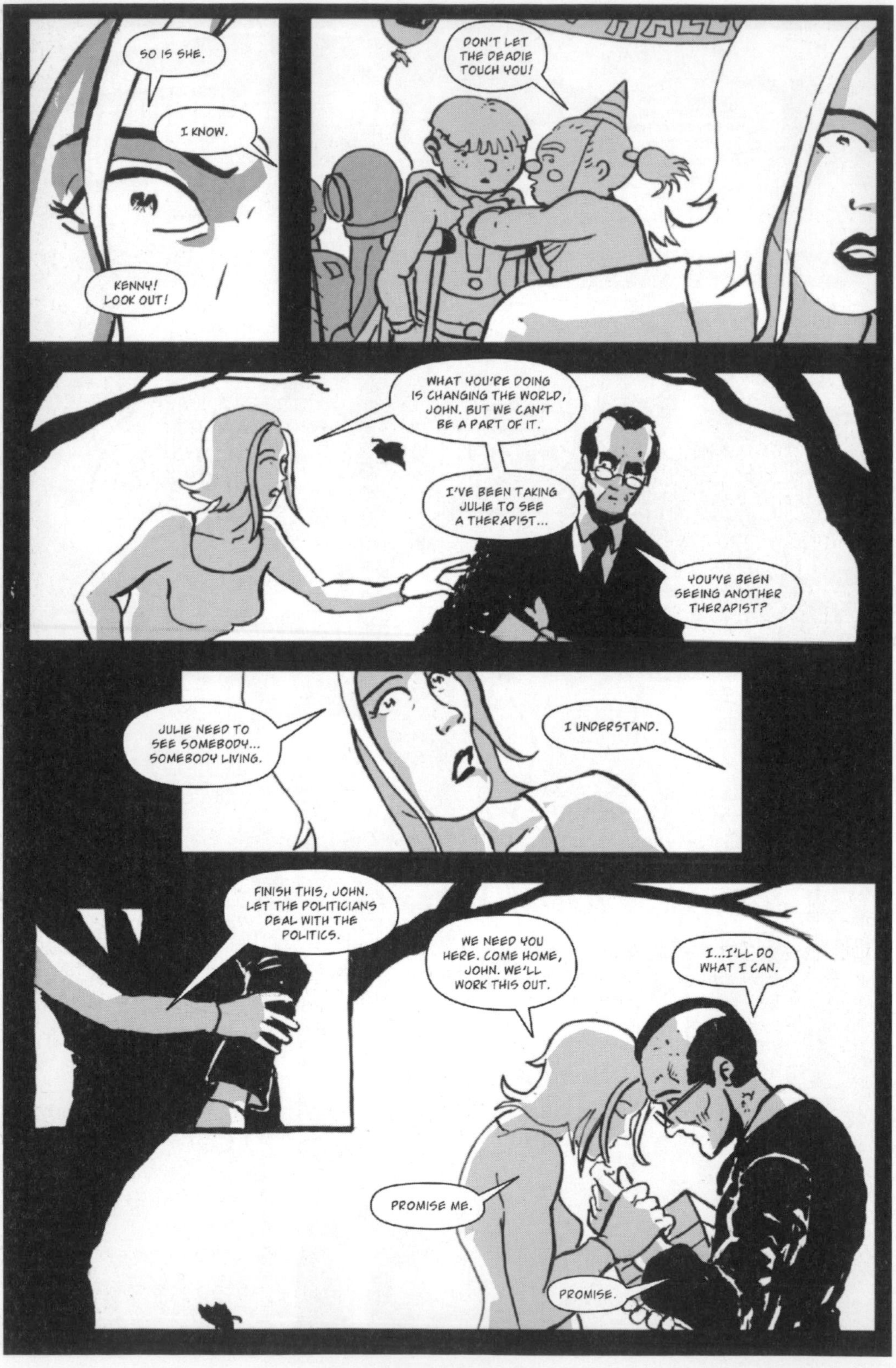
SO IS SHE.
I KNOW.
KENNY! LOOK OUT!
DON'T LET THE DEADIE TOUCH YOU!
WHAT YOU'RE DOING IS CHANGING THE WORLD, JOHN. BUT WE CAN'T BE A PART OF IT.
I'VE BEEN TAKING JULIE TO SEE A THERAPIST...
YOU'VE BEEN SEEING ANOTHER THERAPIST?
JULIE NEED TO SEE SOMEBODY... SOMEBODY LIVING.
I UNDERSTAND.
FINISH THIS, JOHN. LET THE POLITICIANS DEAL WITH THE POLITICS.
WE NEED YOU HERE. COME HOME, JOHN. WE'LL WORK THIS OUT.
I...I'LL DO WHAT I CAN.
PROMISE ME.
PROMISE.

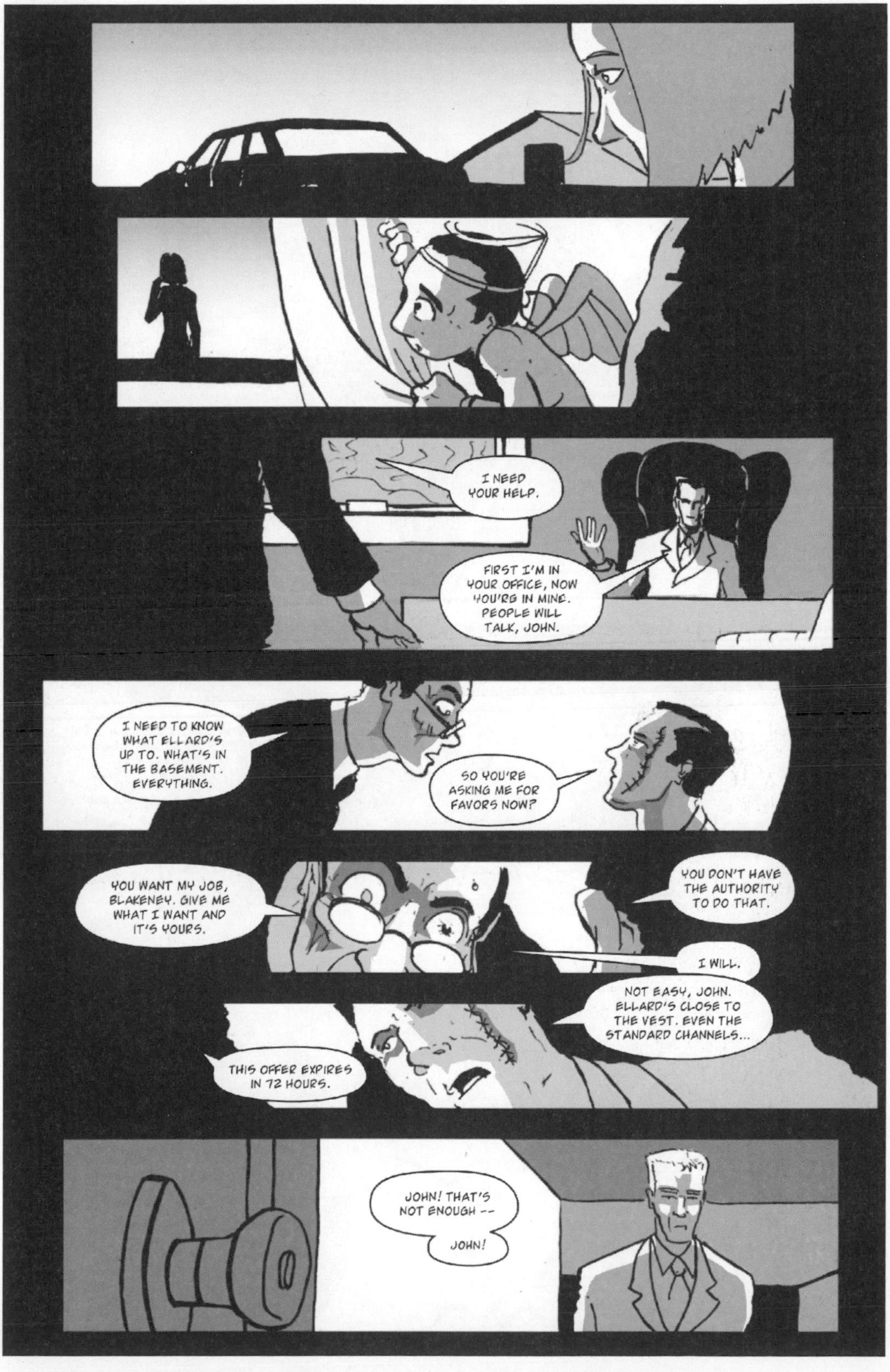
I NEED YOUR HELP.
FIRST I'M IN YOUR OFFICE, NOW YOU'RE IN MINE. PEOPLE WILL TALK, JOHN.
I NEED TO KNOW WHAT ELLARD'S UP TO. WHAT'S IN THE BASEMENT. EVERYTHING.
SO YOU'RE ASKING ME FOR FAVORS NOW?
YOU WANT MY JOB, BLAKENEY. GIVE ME WHAT I WANT AND IT'S YOURS.
YOU DON'T HAVE THE AUTHORITY TO DO THAT.
I WILL.
NOT EASY, JOHN. ELLARD'S CLOSE TO THE VEST. EVEN THE STANDARD CHANNELS...
THIS OFFER EXPIRES IN 72 HOURS.
JOHN! THAT'S NOT ENOUGH --
JOHN!

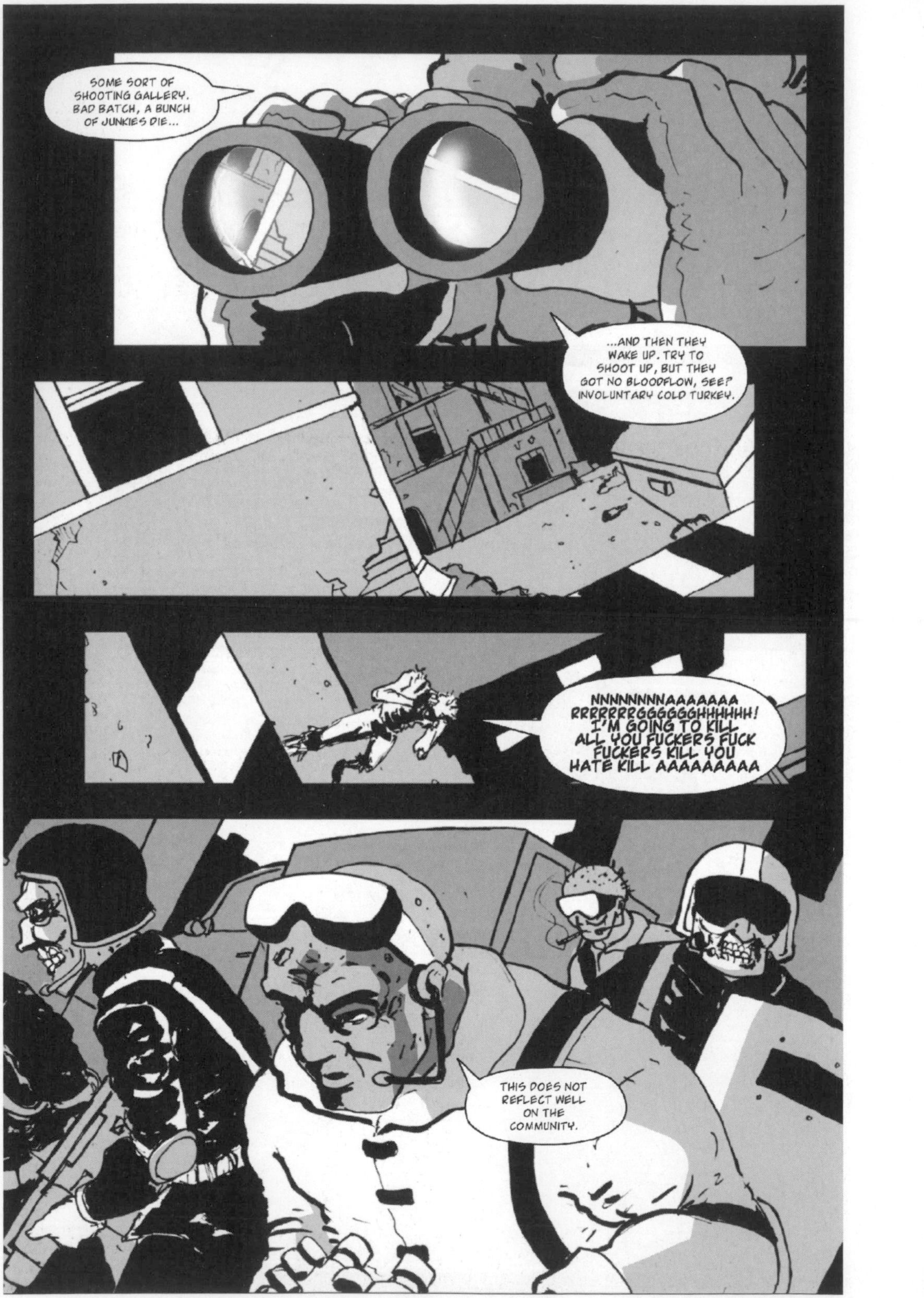
SOME SORT OF SHOOTING GALLERY. BAD BATCH, A BUNCH OF JUNKIES DIE...
...AND THEN THEY WAKE UP. TRY TO SHOOT UP, BUT THEY GOT NO BLOODFLOW, SEE? INVOLUNTARY COLD TURKEY.
NNNNNNNAAAAAAA RRRRRRRGGGGGGHHHHHH! I'M GOING TO KILL ALL YOU FUCKERS FUCK FUCKERS KILL YOU HATE KILL AAAAAAAAA
THIS DOES NOT REFLECT WELL ON THE COMMUNITY.

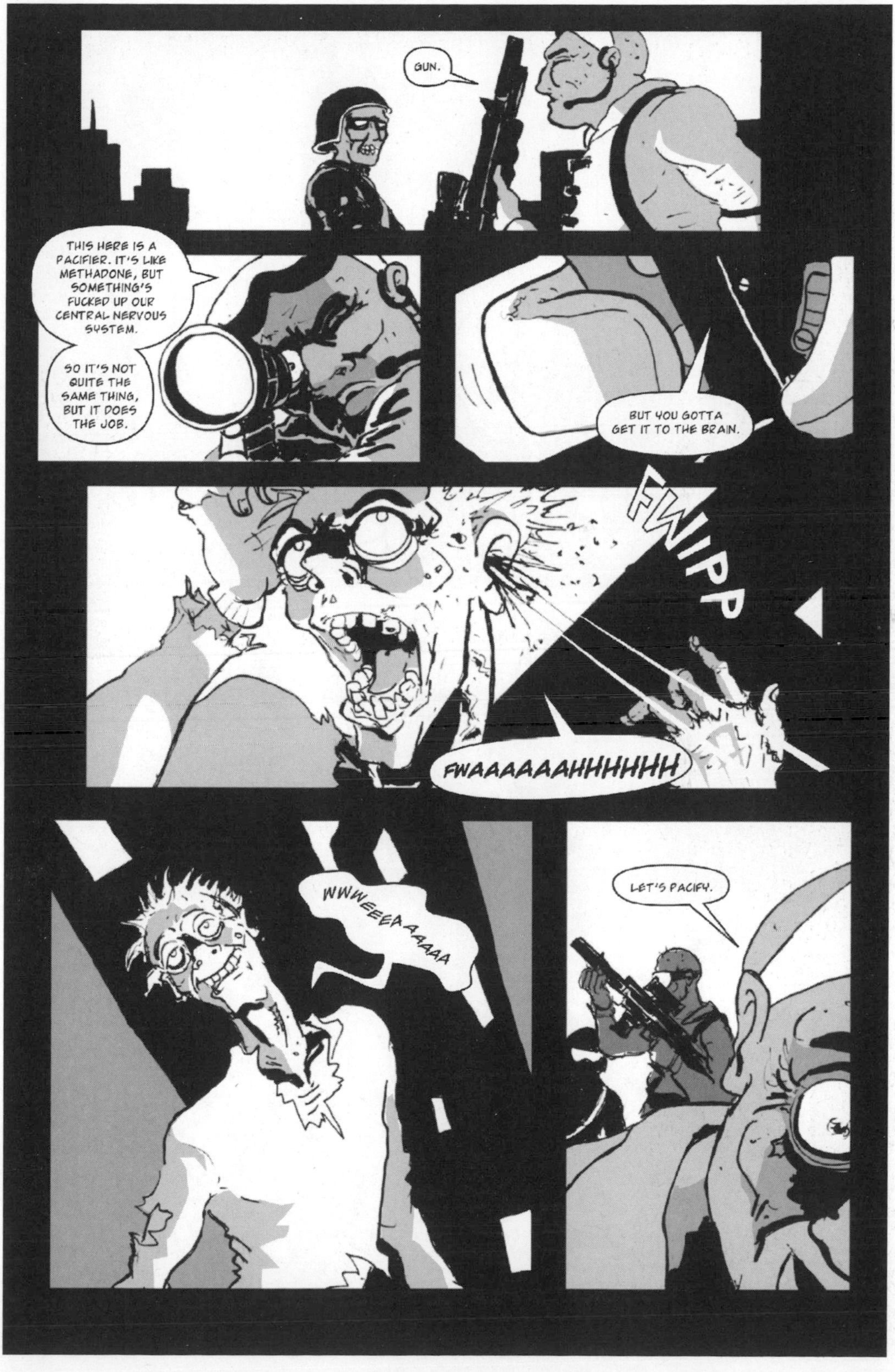
GUN.
THIS HERE IS A PACIFIER. IT'S LIKE METHADONE, BUT SOMETHING'S FUCKED UP OUR CENTRAL NERVOUS SYSTEM.
SO IT'S NOT QUITE THE SAME THING, BUT IT DOES THE JOB.
BUT YOU GOTTA GET IT TO THE BRAIN.
FWIPP
FWAAAAAAHHHHHHH
WWWEEEAAAAAA
LET'S PACIFY.

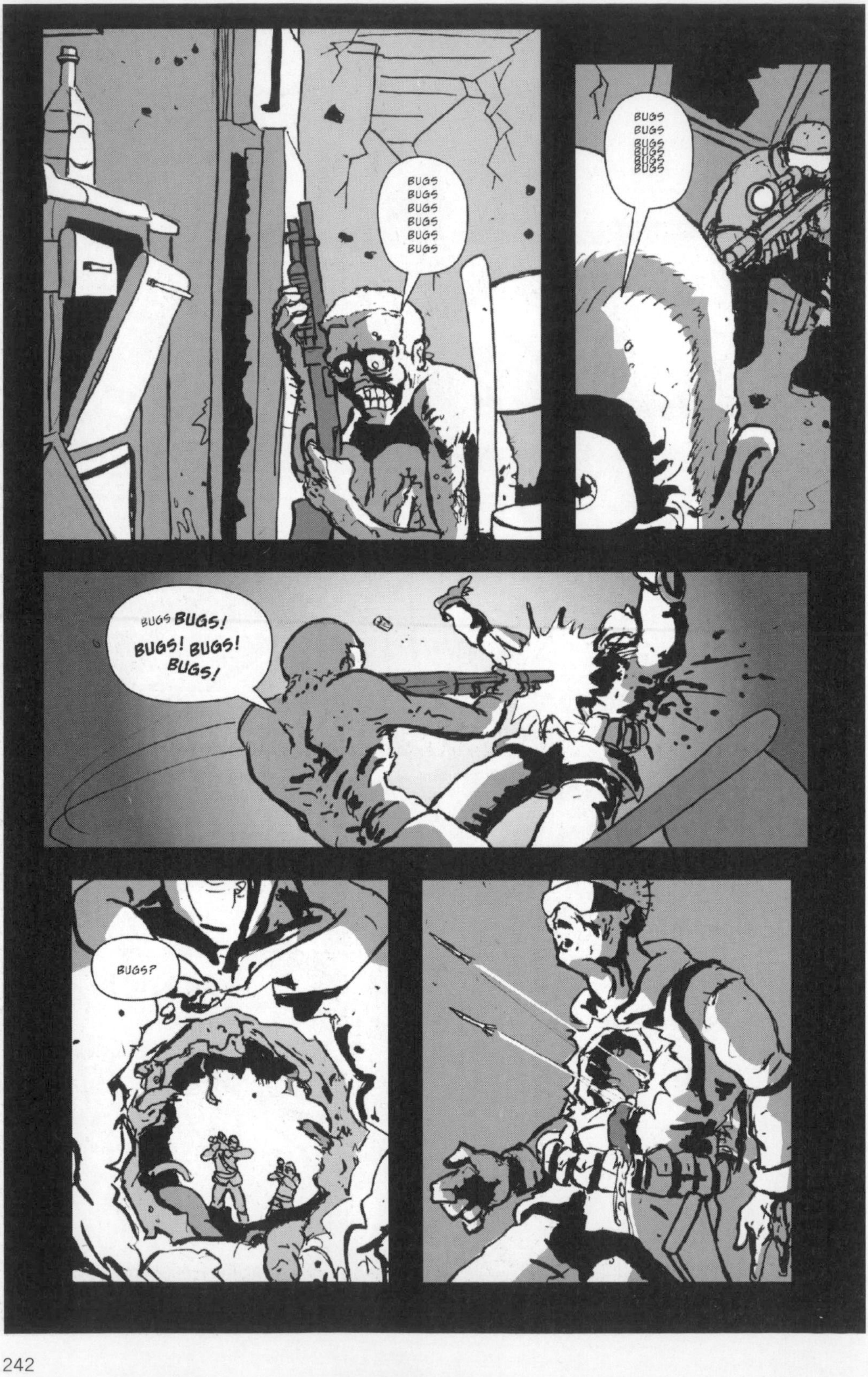
BUGS BUGS BUGS BUGS BUGS BUGS
BUGS BUGS BUGS BUGS BUGS BUGS
BUGS BUGS! BUGS! BUGS! BUGS!
BUGS?

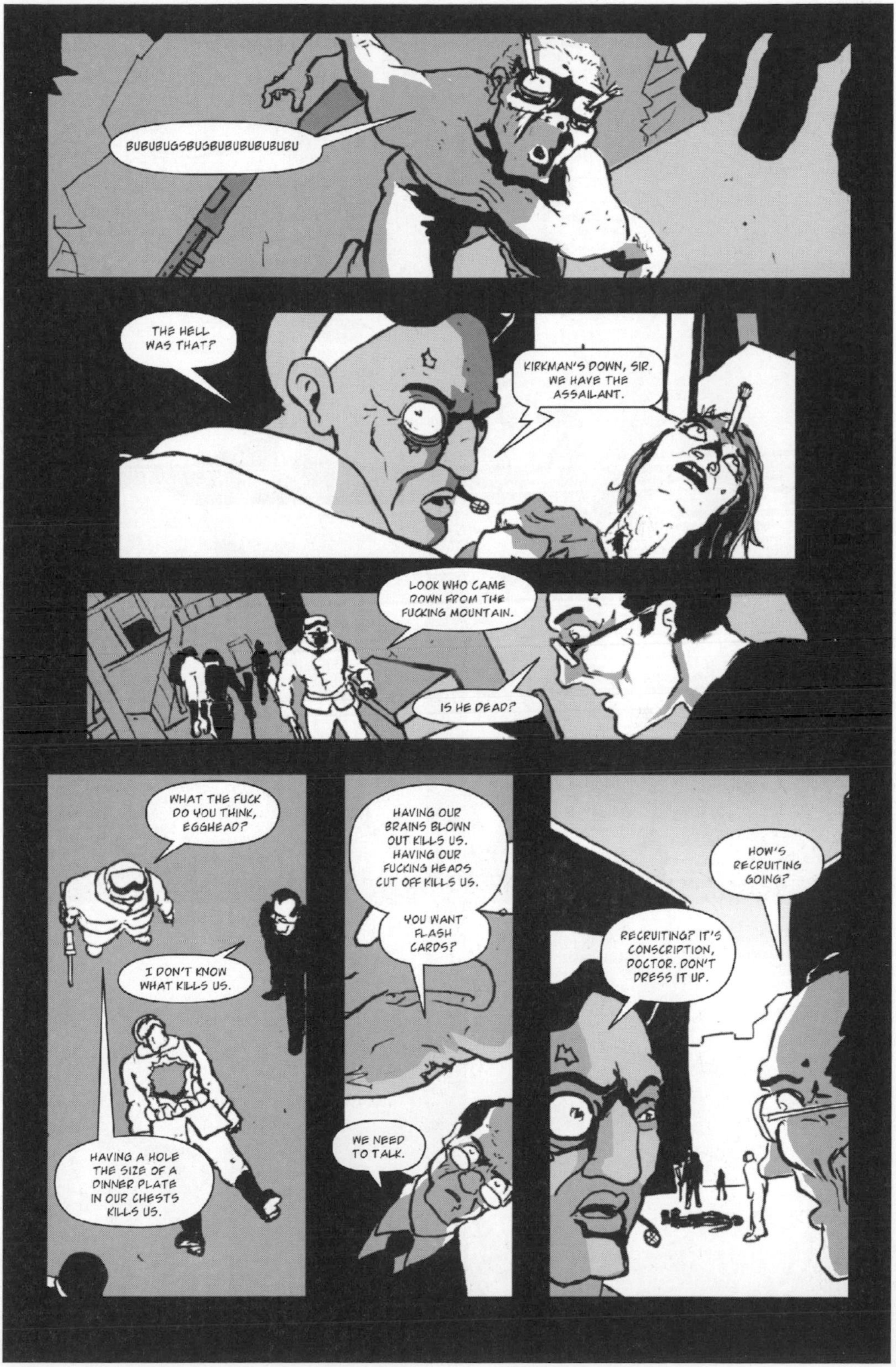
BUBUBUGSBUGBUBUBUBUBU
THE HELL WAS THAT?
KIRKMAN'S DOWN, SIR. WE HAVE THE ASSAILANT.
LOOK WHO CAME DOWN FROM THE FUCKING MOUNTAIN.
IS HE DEAD?
WHAT THE FUCK DO YOU THINK, EGGHEAD?
I DON'T KNOW WHAT KILLS US.
HAVING A HOLE THE SIZE OF A DINNER PLATE IN OUR CHESTS KILLS US.
HAVING OUR BRAINS BLOWN OUT KILLS US. HAVING OUR FUCKING HEADS CUT OFF KILLS US.
YOU WANT FLASH CARDS?
WE NEED TO TALK.
HOW'S RECRUITING GOING?
RECRUITING? IT'S CONSCRIPTION, DOCTOR. DON'T DRESS IT UP.

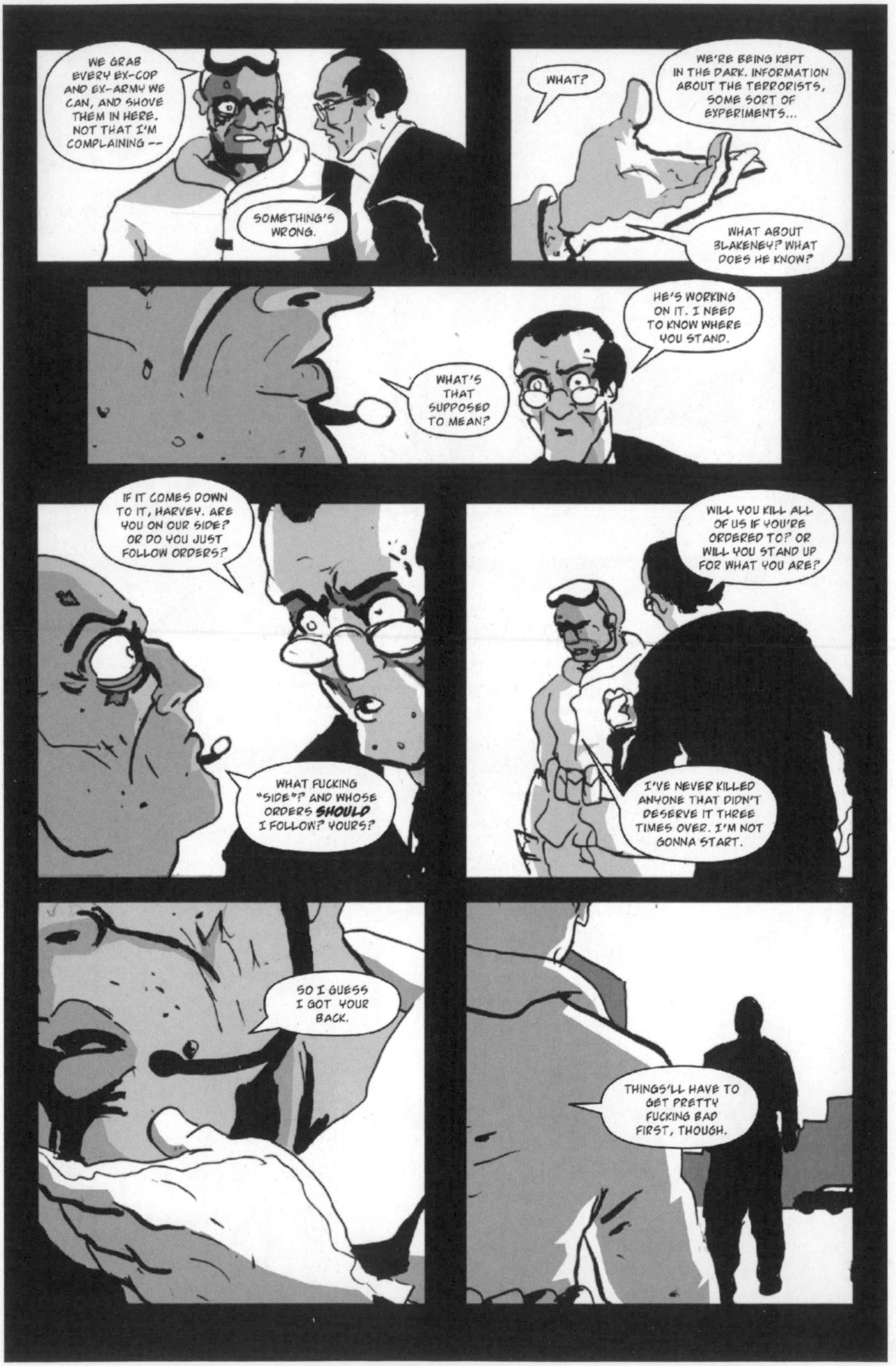
WE GRAB EVERY EX-COP AND EX-ARMY WE CAN, AND SHOVE THEM IN HERE. NOT THAT I'M COMPLAINING --
SOMETHING'S WRONG.
WHAT?
WE'RE BEING KEPT IN THE DARK. INFORMATION ABOUT THE TERRORISTS, SOME SORT OF EXPERIMENTS...
WHAT ABOUT BLAKENEY? WHAT DOES HE KNOW?
HE'S WORKING ON IT. I NEED TO KNOW WHERE YOU STAND.
WHAT'S THAT SUPPOSED TO MEAN?
IF IT COMES DOWN TO IT, HARVEY. ARE YOU ON OUR SIDE? OR DO YOU JUST FOLLOW ORDERS?
WHAT FUCKING "SIDE"? AND WHOSE ORDERS SHOULD I FOLLOW? YOURS?
WILL YOU KILL ALL OF US IF YOU'RE ORDERED TO? OR WILL YOU STAND UP FOR WHAT YOU ARE?
I'VE NEVER KILLED ANYONE THAT DIDN'T DESERVE IT THREE TIMES OVER. I'M NOT GONNA START.
SO I GUESS I GOT YOUR BACK.
THINGS'LL HAVE TO GET PRETTY FUCKING BAD FIRST, THOUGH.

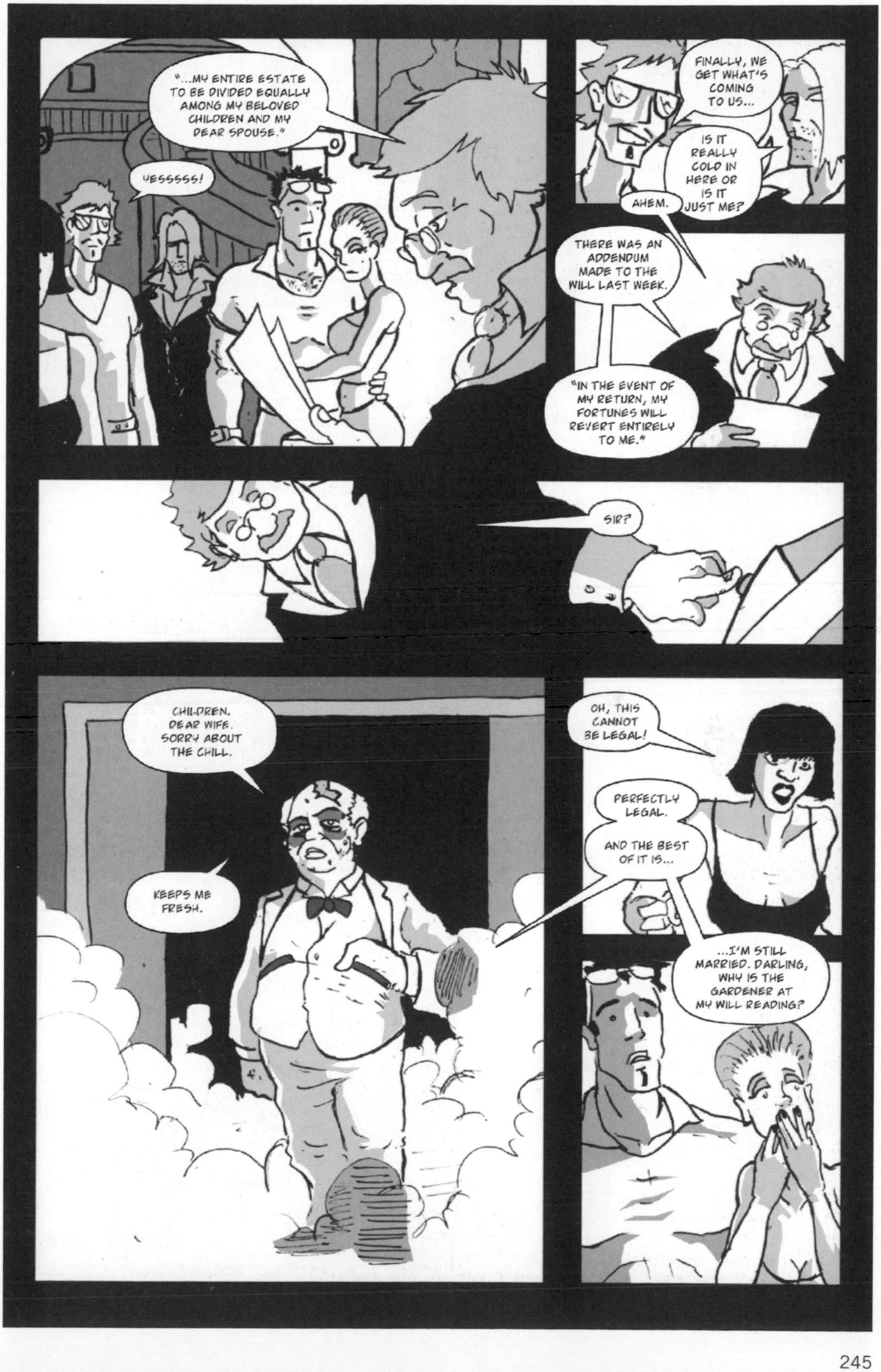
"...MY ENTIRE ESTATE TO BE DIVIDED EQUALLY AMONG MY BELOVED CHILDREN AND MY DEAR SPOUSE."
YESSSSS!
FINALLY, WE GET WHAT'S COMING TO US...
IS IT REALLY COLD IN HERE OR IS IT JUST ME?
AHEM.
THERE WAS AN ADDENDUM MADE TO THE WILL LAST WEEK.
"IN THE EVENT OF MY RETURN, MY FORTUNES WILL REVERT ENTIRELY TO ME."
SIR?
CHILDREN. DEAR WIFE. SORRY ABOUT THE CHILL.
KEEPS ME FRESH.
OH, THIS CANNOT BE LEGAL!
PERFECTLY LEGAL.
AND THE BEST OF IT IS...
...I'M STILL MARRIED. DARLING, WHY IS THE GARDENER AT MY WILL READING?

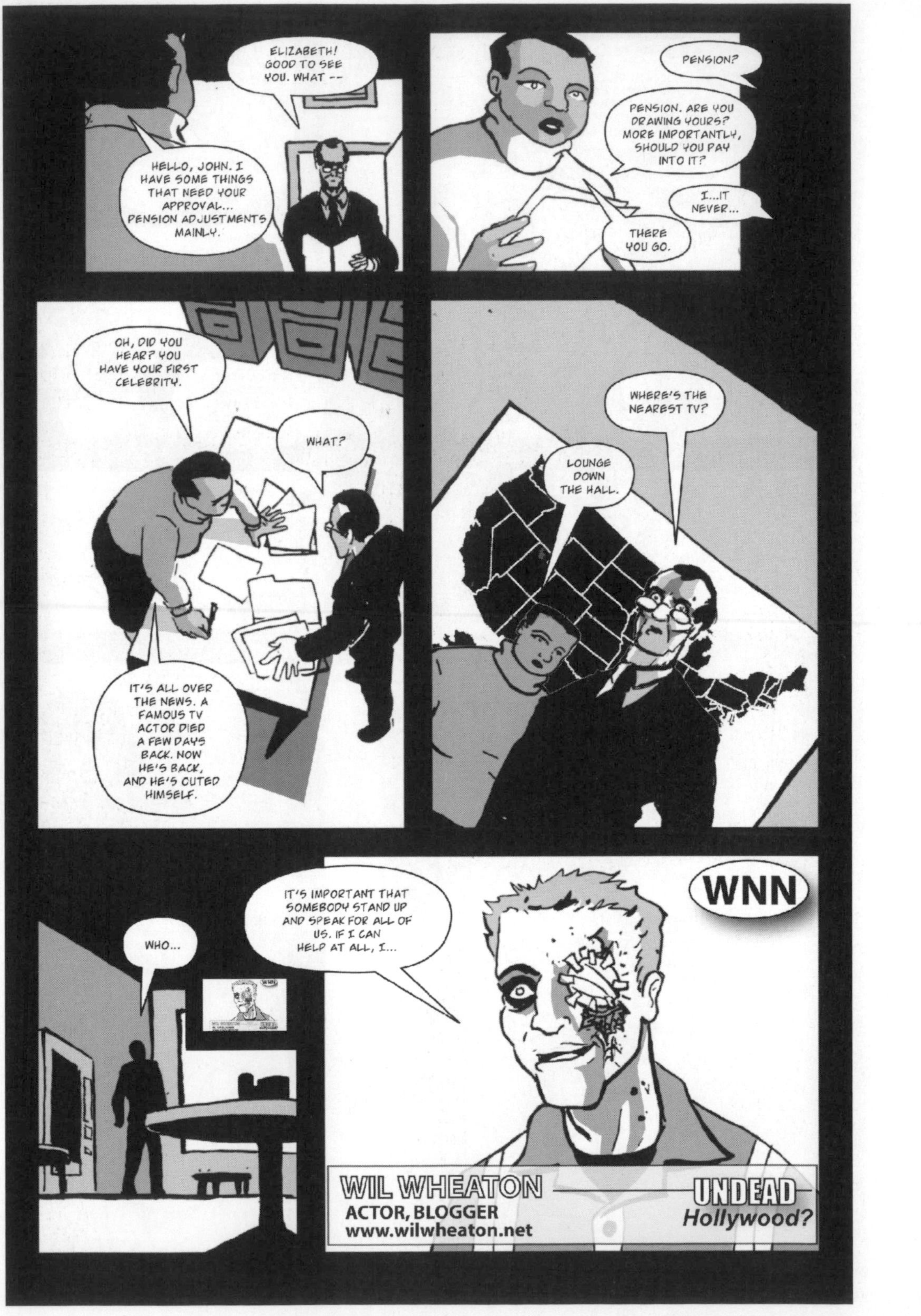
ELIZABETH! GOOD TO SEE YOU. WHAT --
HELLO, JOHN. I HAVE SOME THINGS THAT NEED YOUR APPROVAL... PENSION ADJUSTMENTS MAINLY.
PENSION?
PENSION. ARE YOU DRAWING YOURS? MORE IMPORTANTLY, SHOULD YOU PAY INTO IT?
I...IT NEVER...
THERE YOU GO.
OH, DID YOU HEAR? YOU HAVE YOUR FIRST CELEBRITY.
WHAT?
IT'S ALL OVER THE NEWS. A FAMOUS TV ACTOR DIED A FEW DAYS BACK. NOW HE'S BACK, AND HE'S OUTED HIMSELF.
WHERE'S THE NEAREST TV?
LOUNGE DOWN THE HALL.
WHO...
IT'S IMPORTANT THAT SOMEBODY STAND UP AND SPEAK FOR ALL OF US. IF I CAN HELP AT ALL, I...
WNN
WIL WHEATON
ACTOR, BLOGGER
www.wilwheaton.net
UNDEAD
Hollywood?

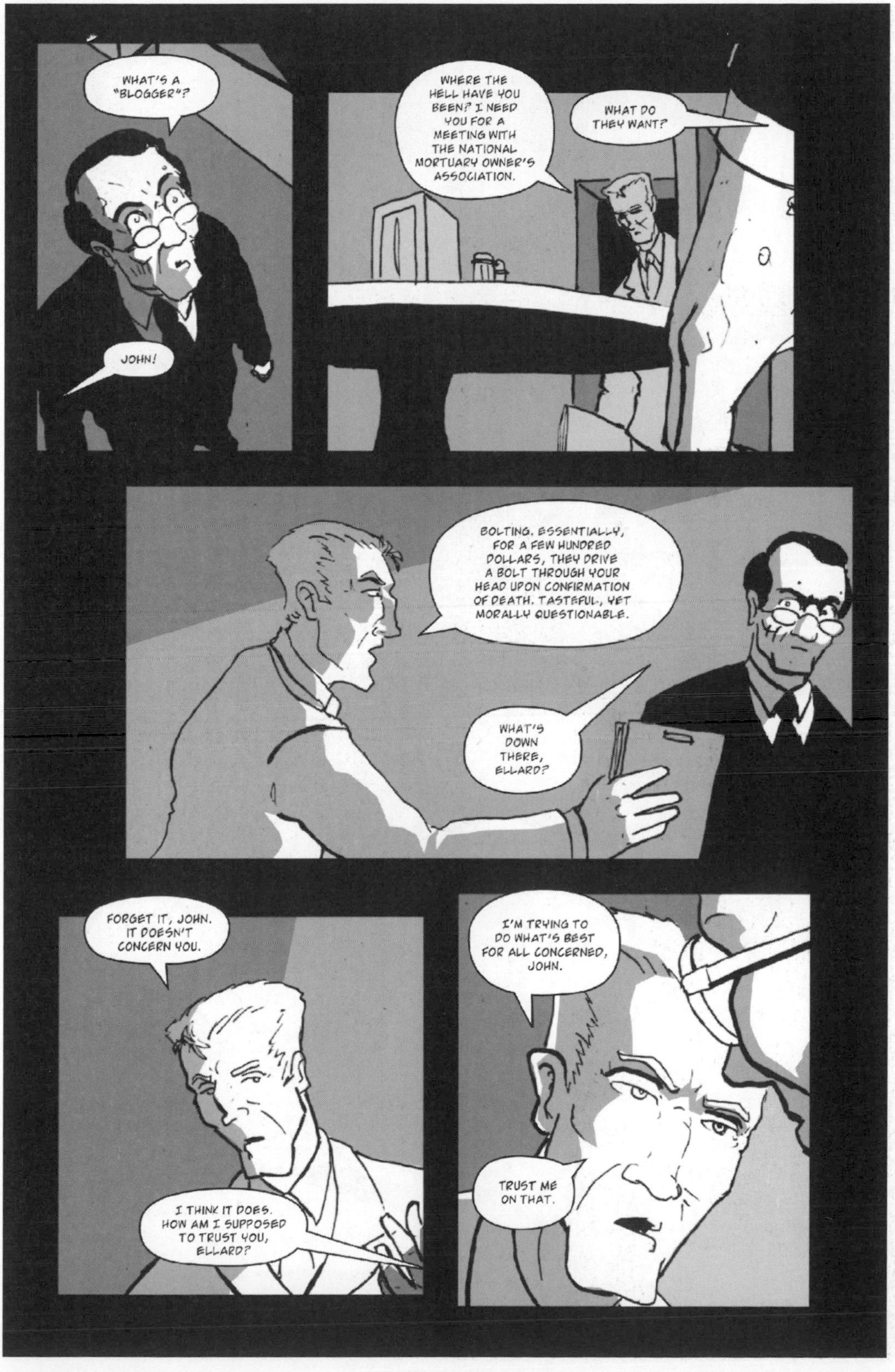
WHAT'S A "BLOGGER"?
JOHN!
WHERE THE HELL HAVE YOU BEEN? I NEED YOU FOR A MEETING WITH THE NATIONAL MORTUARY OWNER'S ASSOCIATION.
WHAT DO THEY WANT?
BOLTING. ESSENTIALLY, FOR A FEW HUNDRED DOLLARS, THEY DRIVE A BOLT THROUGH YOUR HEAD UPON CONFIRMATION OF DEATH. TASTEFUL, YET MORALLY QUESTIONABLE.
WHAT'S DOWN THERE, ELLARD?
FORGET IT, JOHN. IT DOESN'T CONCERN YOU.
I THINK IT DOES. HOW AM I SUPPOSED TO TRUST YOU, ELLARD?
I'M TRYING TO DO WHAT'S BEST FOR ALL CONCERNED, JOHN.
TRUST ME ON THAT.

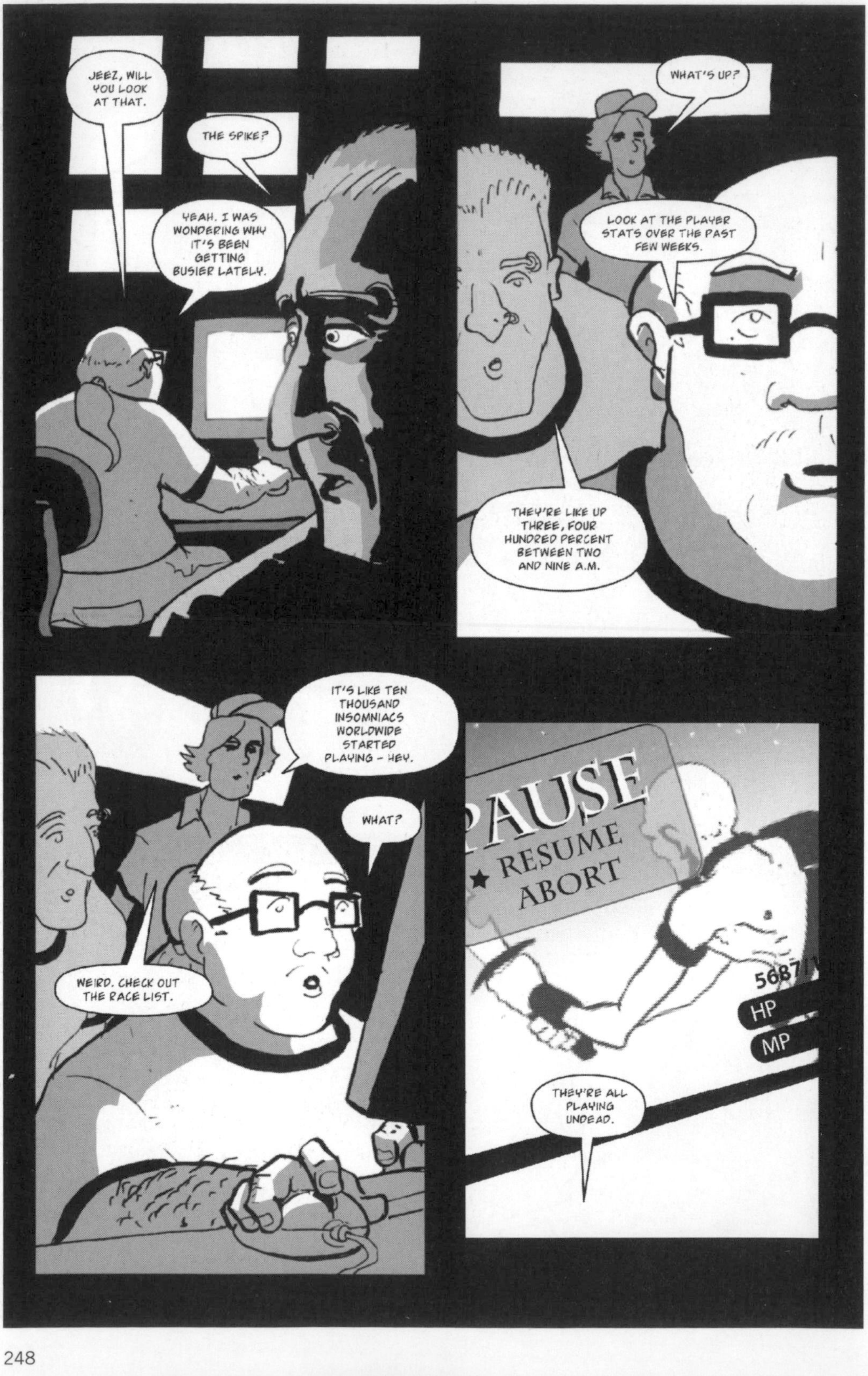
JEEZ, WILL YOU LOOK AT THAT.
THE SPIKE?
YEAH. I WAS WONDERING WHY IT'S BEEN GETTING BUSIER LATELY.
WHAT'S UP?
LOOK AT THE PLAYER STATS OVER THE PAST FEW WEEKS.
THEY'RE LIKE UP THREE, FOUR HUNDRED PERCENT BETWEEN TWO AND NINE A.M.
IT'S LIKE TEN THOUSAND INSOMNIACS WORLDWIDE STARTED PLAYING – HEY.
WHAT?
WEIRD. CHECK OUT THE RACE LIST.
PAUSE
★ RESUME
ABORT
HP
MP
THEY'RE ALL PLAYING UNDEAD.

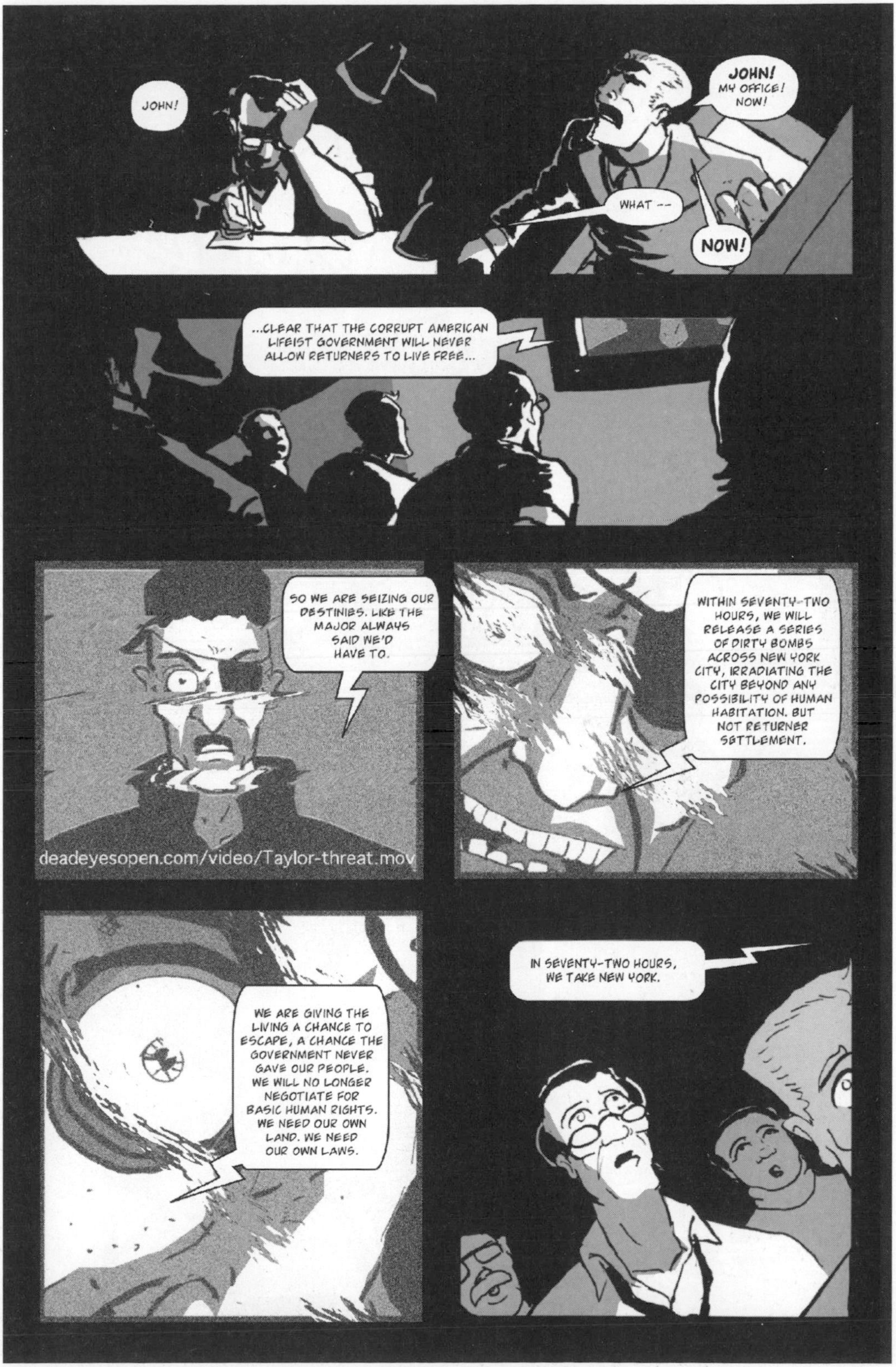
JOHN!
JOHN! MY OFFICE! NOW!
WHAT --
NOW!
...CLEAR THAT THE CORRUPT AMERICAN LIFEIST GOVERNMENT WILL NEVER ALLOW RETURNERS TO LIVE FREE...
SO WE ARE SEIZING OUR DESTINIES. LIKE THE MAJOR ALWAYS SAID WE'D HAVE TO.
deadeyesopen.com/video/Taylor-threat.mov
WITHIN SEVENTY-TWO HOURS, WE WILL RELEASE A SERIES OF DIRTY BOMBS ACROSS NEW YORK CITY, IRRADIATING THE CITY BEYOND ANY POSSIBILITY OF HUMAN HABITATION. BUT NOT RETURNER SETTLEMENT.
WE ARE GIVING THE LIVING A CHANCE TO ESCAPE, A CHANCE THE GOVERNMENT NEVER GAVE OUR PEOPLE. WE WILL NO LONGER NEGOTIATE FOR BASIC HUMAN RIGHTS. WE NEED OUR OWN LAND. WE NEED OUR OWN LAWS.
IN SEVENTY-TWO HOURS, WE TAKE NEW YORK.

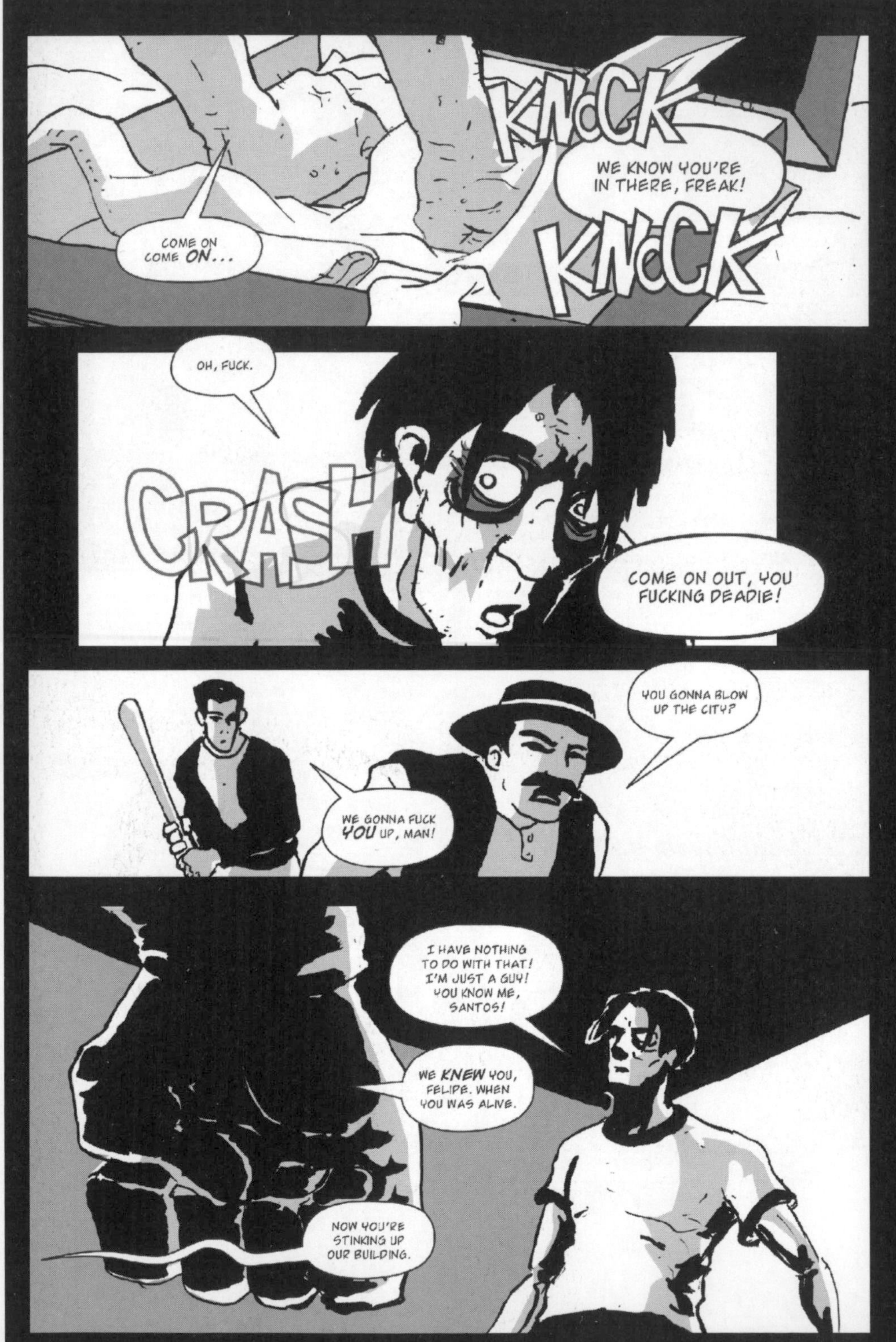
KNOCK
WE KNOW YOU'RE IN THERE, FREAK!
KNOCK
COME ON COME ON...
OH, FUCK.
CRASH
COME ON OUT, YOU FUCKING DEADIE!
YOU GONNA BLOW UP THE CITY?
WE GONNA FUCK YOU UP, MAN!
I HAVE NOTHING TO DO WITH THAT! I'M JUST A GUY! YOU KNOW ME, SANTOS!
WE KNEW YOU, FELIPE. WHEN YOU WAS ALIVE.
NOW YOU'RE STINKING UP OUR BUILDING.

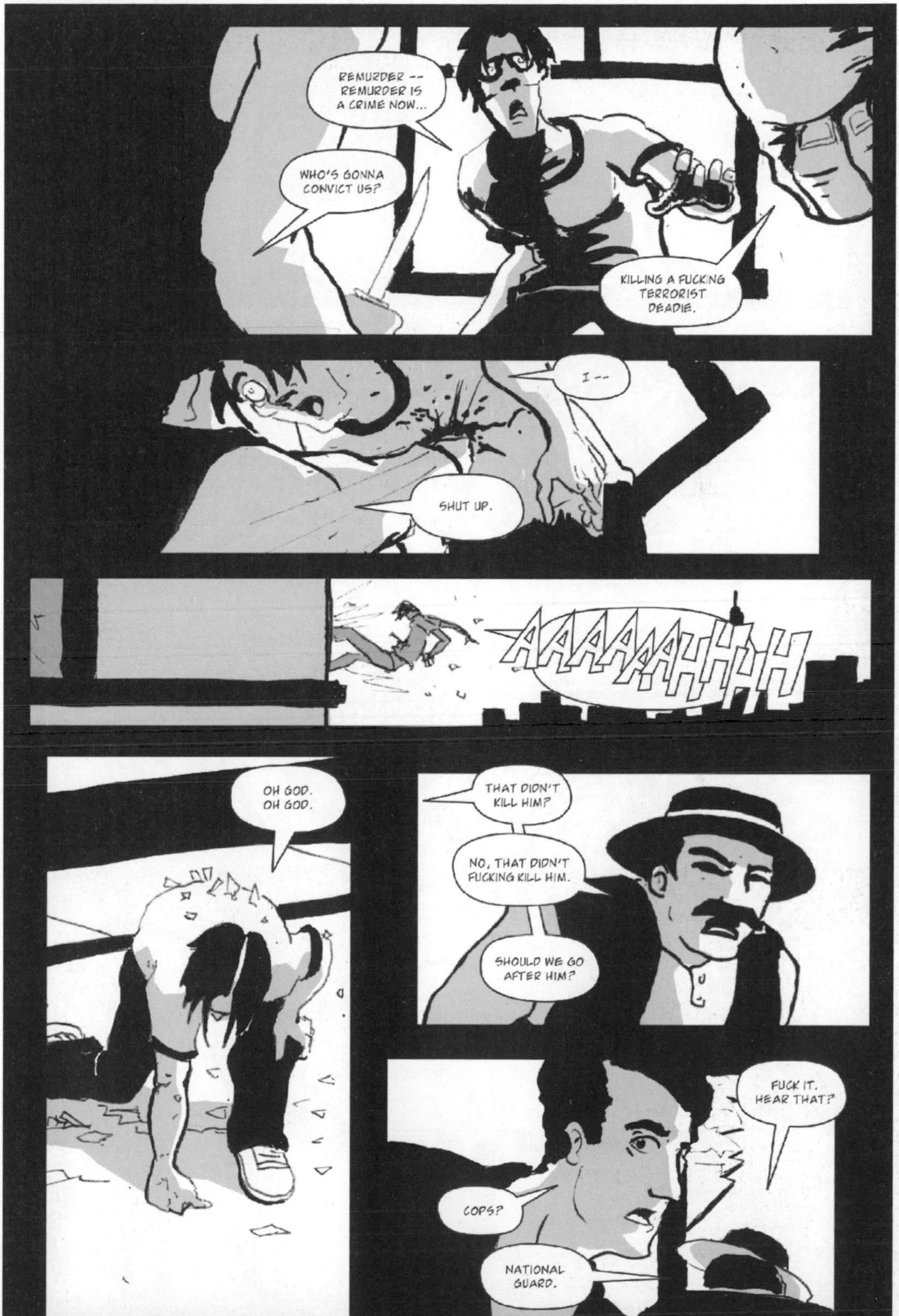
REMURDER -- REMURDER IS A CRIME NOW...
WHO'S GONNA CONVICT US?
KILLING A FUCKING TERRORIST DEADIE.
I --
SHUT UP.
AAAAAAHHHH
OH GOD. OH GOD.
THAT DIDN'T KILL HIM?
NO, THAT DIDN'T FUCKING KILL HIM.
SHOULD WE GO AFTER HIM?
FUCK IT. HEAR THAT?
COPS?
NATIONAL GUARD.

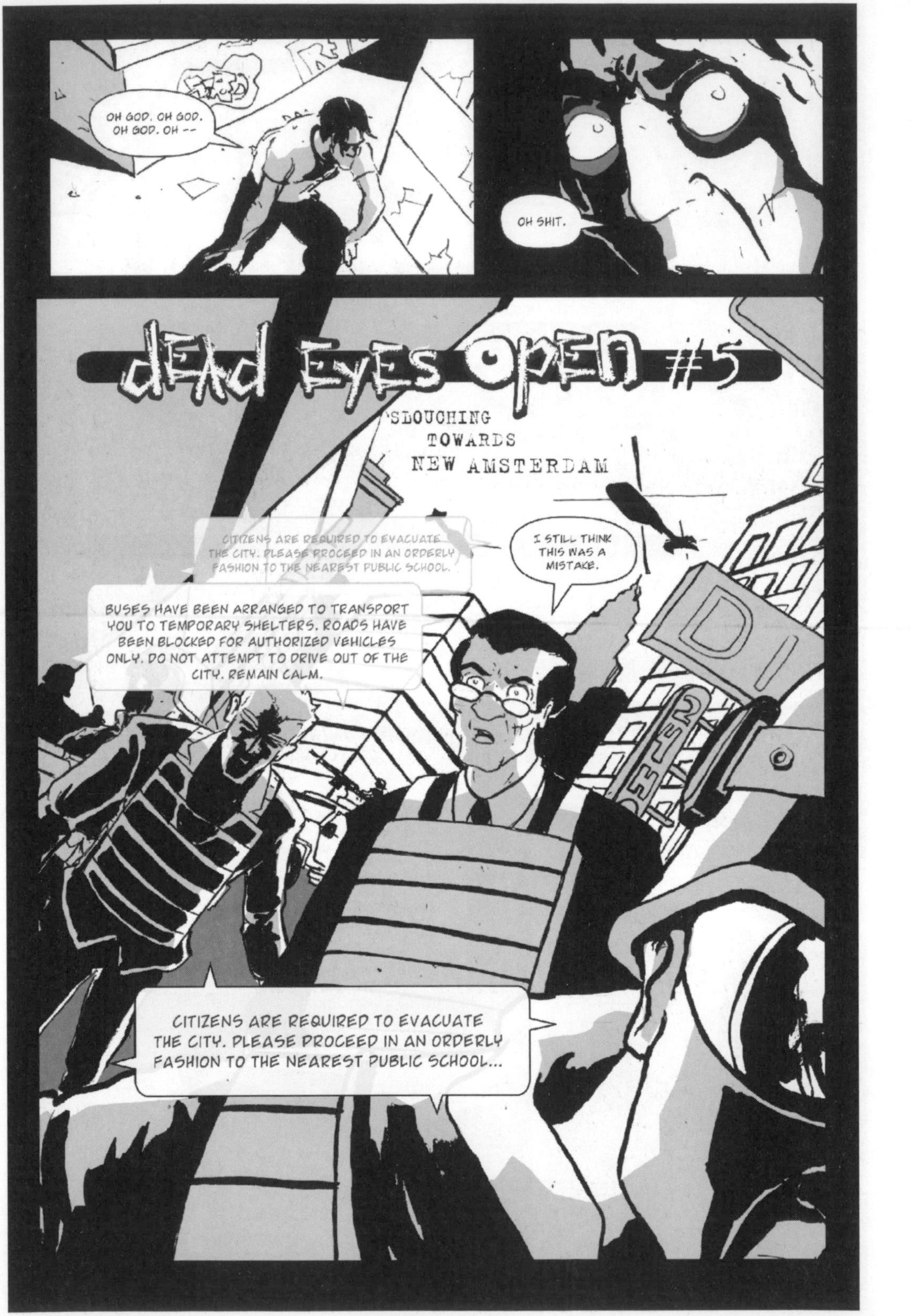
OH GOD. OH GOD. OH GOD. OH --
OH SHIT.
DEAD EYES OPEN #5
SLOUCHING TOWARDS NEW AMSTERDAM
CITIZENS ARE REQUIRED TO EVACUATE THE CITY. PLEASE PROCEED IN AN ORDERLY FASHION TO THE NEAREST PUBLIC SCHOOL.
I STILL THINK THIS WAS A MISTAKE.
BUSES HAVE BEEN ARRANGED TO TRANSPORT YOU TO TEMPORARY SHELTERS. ROADS HAVE BEEN BLOCKED FOR AUTHORIZED VEHICLES ONLY. DO NOT ATTEMPT TO DRIVE OUT OF THE CITY. REMAIN CALM.
CITIZENS ARE REQUIRED TO EVACUATE THE CITY. PLEASE PROCEED IN AN ORDERLY FASHION TO THE NEAREST PUBLIC SCHOOL...

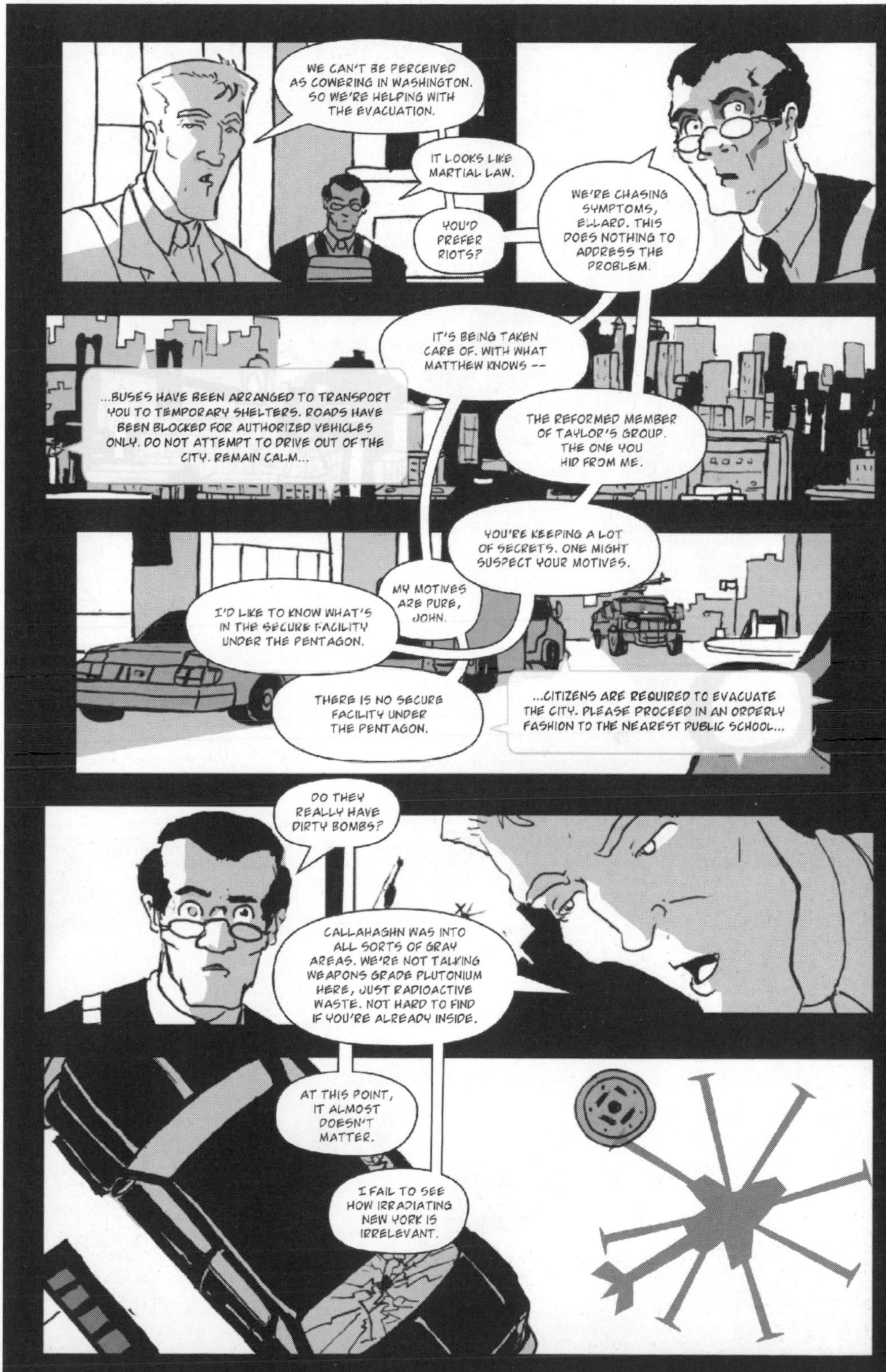
WE CAN'T BE PERCEIVED AS COWERING IN WASHINGTON. SO WE'RE HELPING WITH THE EVACUATION.
IT LOOKS LIKE MARTIAL LAW.
YOU'D PREFER RIOTS?
WE'RE CHASING SYMPTOMS, ELLARD. THIS DOES NOTHING TO ADDRESS THE PROBLEM.
...BUSES HAVE BEEN ARRANGED TO TRANSPORT YOU TO TEMPORARY SHELTERS. ROADS HAVE BEEN BLOCKED FOR AUTHORIZED VEHICLES ONLY. DO NOT ATTEMPT TO DRIVE OUT OF THE CITY. REMAIN CALM...
IT'S BEING TAKEN CARE OF. WITH WHAT MATTHEW KNOWS --
THE REFORMED MEMBER OF TAYLOR'S GROUP. THE ONE YOU HID FROM ME.
YOU'RE KEEPING A LOT OF SECRETS. ONE MIGHT SUSPECT YOUR MOTIVES.
MY MOTIVES ARE PURE, JOHN.
I'D LIKE TO KNOW WHAT'S IN THE SECURE FACILITY UNDER THE PENTAGON.
THERE IS NO SECURE FACILITY UNDER THE PENTAGON.
...CITIZENS ARE REQUIRED TO EVACUATE THE CITY. PLEASE PROCEED IN AN ORDERLY FASHION TO THE NEAREST PUBLIC SCHOOL...
DO THEY REALLY HAVE DIRTY BOMBS?
CALLAHAGHN WAS INTO ALL SORTS OF GRAY AREAS. WE'RE NOT TALKING WEAPONS GRADE PLUTONIUM HERE, JUST RADIOACTIVE WASTE. NOT HARD TO FIND IF YOU'RE ALREADY INSIDE.
AT THIS POINT, IT ALMOST DOESN'T MATTER.
I FAIL TO SEE HOW IRRADIATING NEW YORK IS IRRELEVANT.

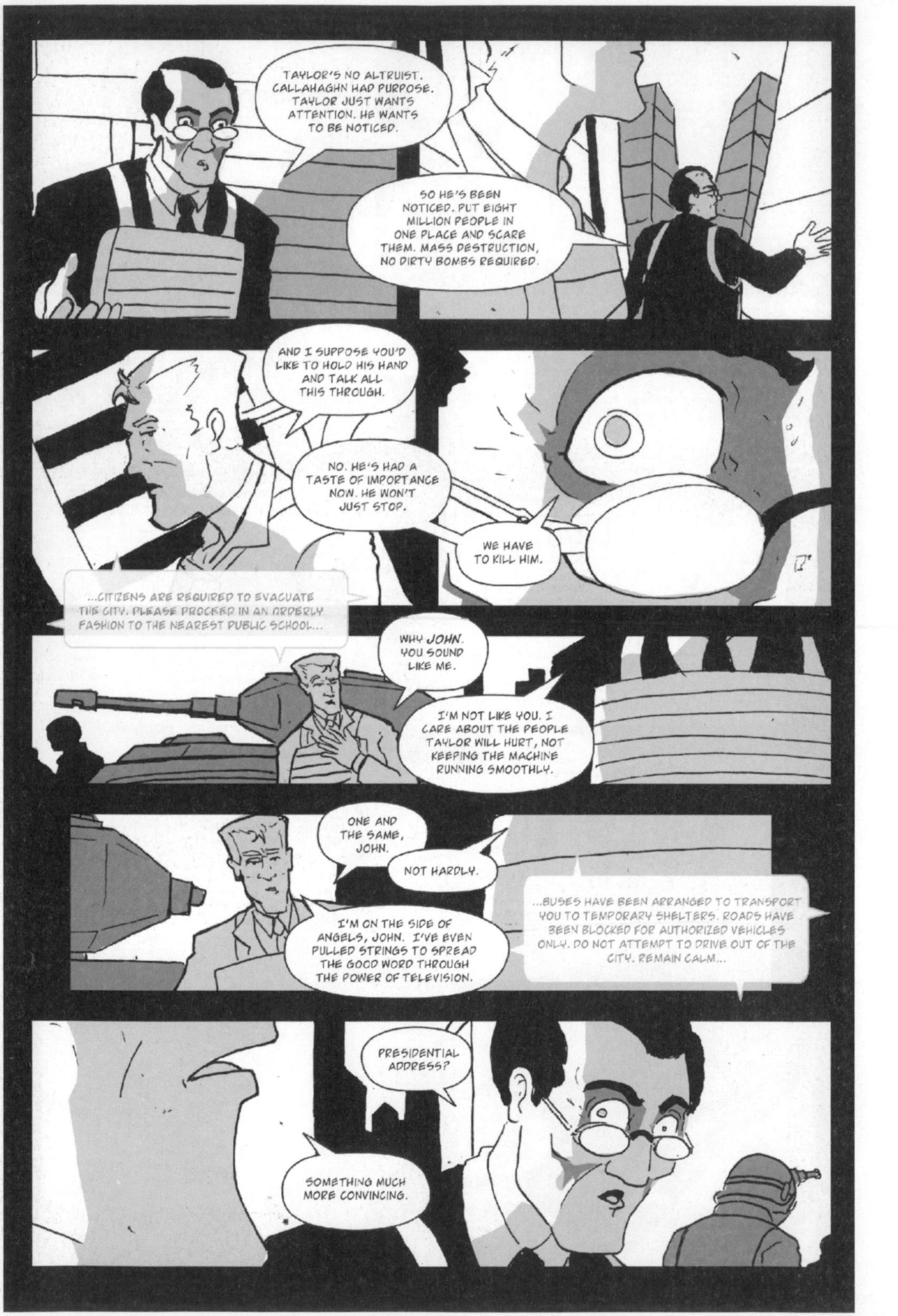

TAYLOR'S NO ALTRUIST. CALLAHAGHN HAD PURPOSE. TAYLOR JUST WANTS ATTENTION. HE WANTS TO BE NOTICED.
SO HE'S BEEN NOTICED. PUT EIGHT MILLION PEOPLE IN ONE PLACE AND SCARE THEM. MASS DESTRUCTION, NO DIRTY BOMBS REQUIRED.
AND I SUPPOSE YOU'D LIKE TO HOLD HIS HAND AND TALK ALL THIS THROUGH.
NO. HE'S HAD A TASTE OF IMPORTANCE NOW. HE WON'T JUST STOP.
WE HAVE TO KILL HIM.
...CITIZENS ARE REQUIRED TO EVACUATE THE CITY. PLEASE PROCEED IN AN ORDERLY FASHION TO THE NEAREST PUBLIC SCHOOL...
WHY JOHN. YOU SOUND LIKE ME.
I'M NOT LIKE YOU. I CARE ABOUT THE PEOPLE TAYLOR WILL HURT, NOT KEEPING THE MACHINE RUNNING SMOOTHLY.
ONE AND THE SAME, JOHN.
NOT HARDLY.
I'M ON THE SIDE OF ANGELS, JOHN. I'VE EVEN PULLED STRINGS TO SPREAD THE GOOD WORD THROUGH THE POWER OF TELEVISION.
...BUSES HAVE BEEN ARRANGED TO TRANSPORT YOU TO TEMPORARY SHELTERS. ROADS HAVE BEEN BLOCKED FOR AUTHORIZED VEHICLES ONLY. DO NOT ATTEMPT TO DRIVE OUT OF THE CITY. REMAIN CALM...
PRESIDENTIAL ADDRESS?
SOMETHING MUCH MORE CONVINCING.

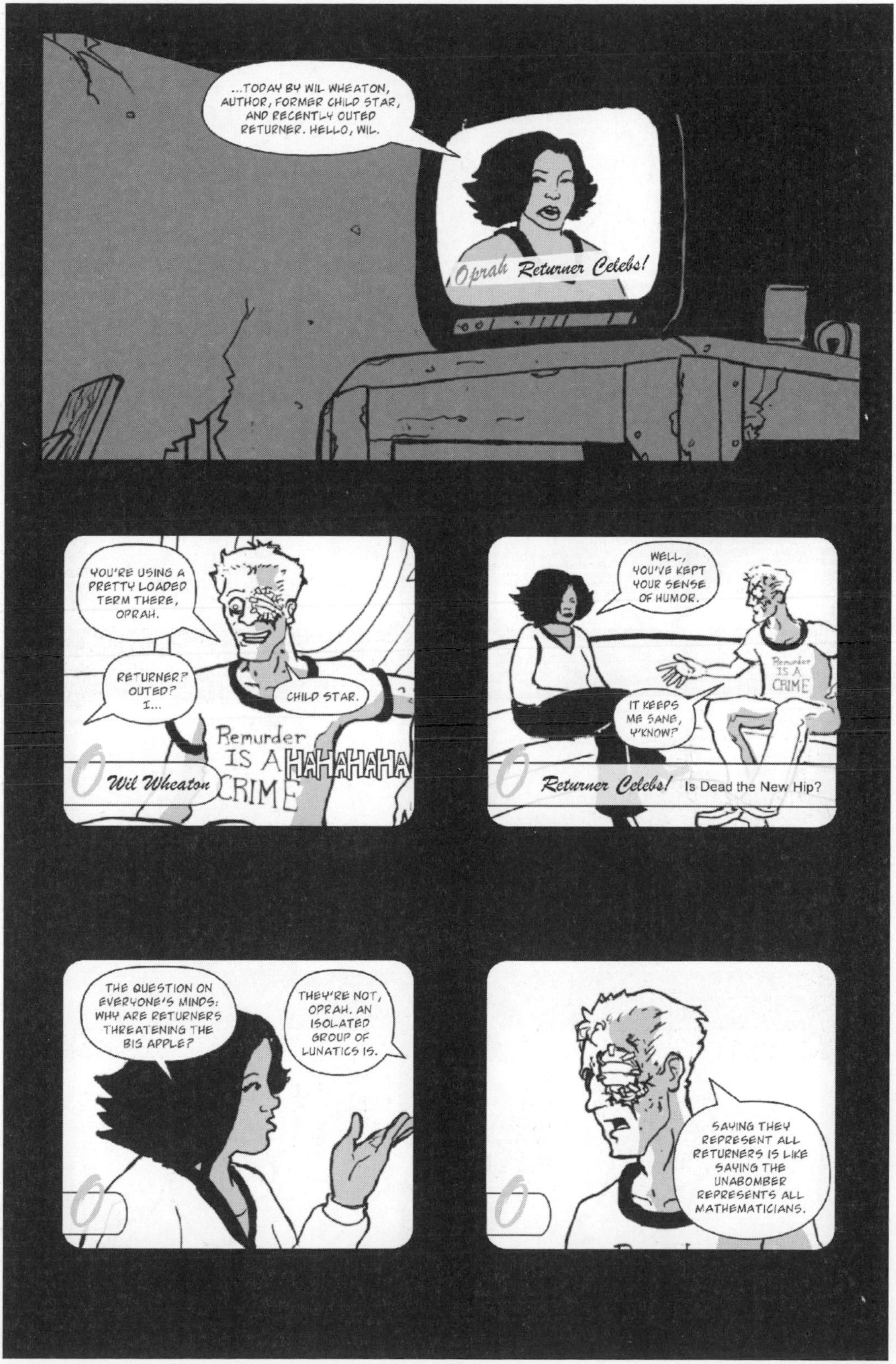
...TODAY BY WIL WHEATON, AUTHOR, FORMER CHILD STAR, AND RECENTLY OUTED RETURNER. HELLO, WIL.
Oprah Returner Celebs!
YOU'RE USING A PRETTY LOADED TERM THERE, OPRAH.
RETURNER? OUTED? I...
CHILD STAR.
Remurder IS A CRIME
HAHAHAHA
Wil Wheaton
WELL, YOU'VE KEPT YOUR SENSE OF HUMOR.
IT KEEPS ME SANE, Y'KNOW?
Remurder IS A CRIME
Returner Celebs! Is Dead the New Hip?
THE QUESTION ON EVERYONE'S MINDS: WHY ARE RETURNERS THREATENING THE BIG APPLE?
THEY'RE NOT, OPRAH. AN ISOLATED GROUP OF LUNATICS IS.
SAYING THEY REPRESENT ALL RETURNERS IS LIKE SAYING THE UNABOMBER REPRESENTS ALL MATHEMATICIANS.

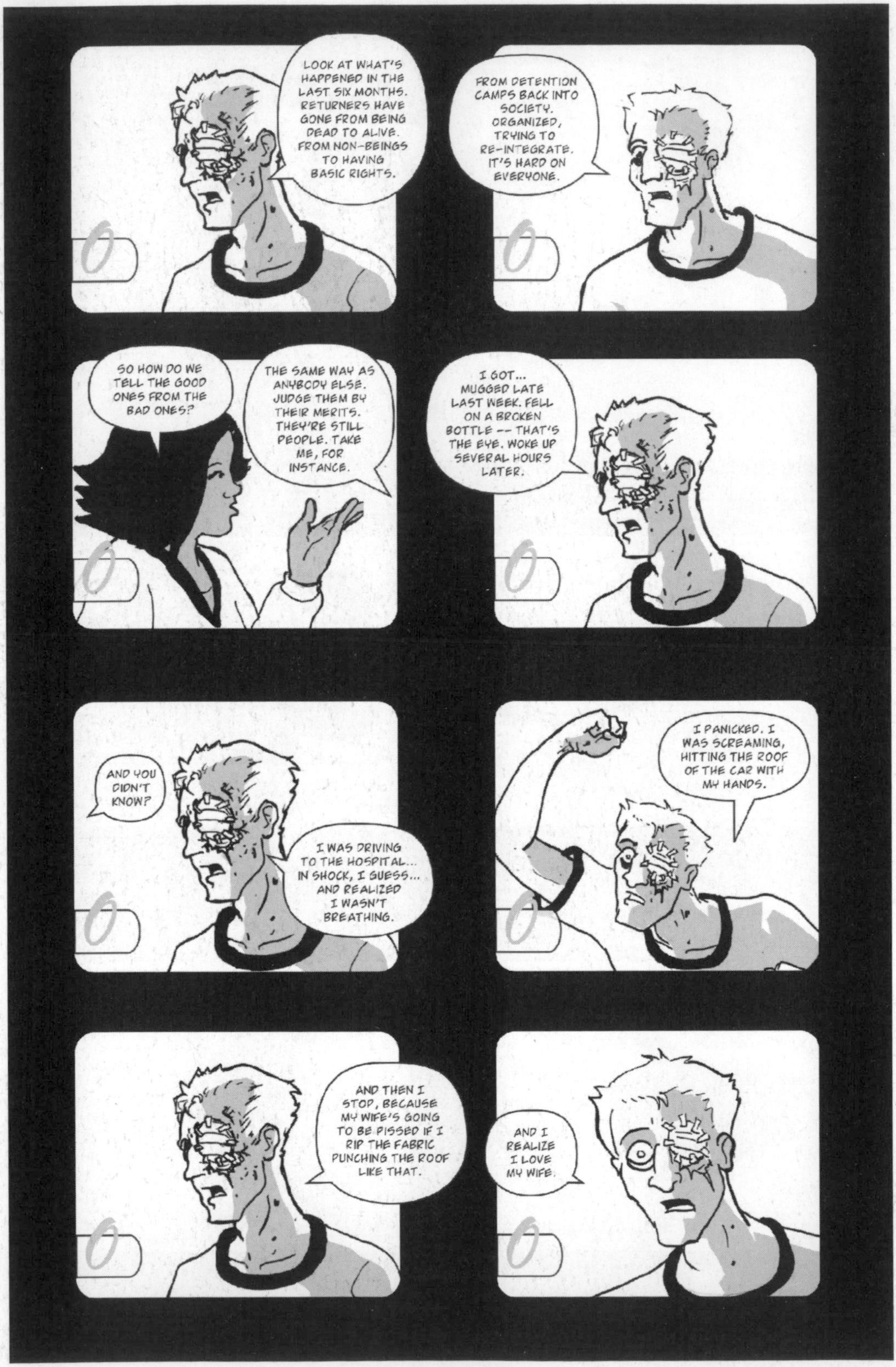
LOOK AT WHAT'S HAPPENED IN THE LAST SIX MONTHS. RETURNERS HAVE GONE FROM BEING DEAD TO ALIVE. FROM NON-BEINGS TO HAVING BASIC RIGHTS.
FROM DETENTION CAMPS BACK INTO SOCIETY. ORGANIZED, TRYING TO RE-INTEGRATE. IT'S HARD ON EVERYONE.
SO HOW DO WE TELL THE GOOD ONES FROM THE BAD ONES?
THE SAME WAY AS ANYBODY ELSE. JUDGE THEM BY THEIR MERITS. THEY'RE STILL PEOPLE. TAKE ME, FOR INSTANCE.
I GOT... MUGGED LATE LAST WEEK. FELL ON A BROKEN BOTTLE -- THAT'S THE EYE. WOKE UP SEVERAL HOURS LATER.
AND YOU DIDN'T KNOW?
I WAS DRIVING TO THE HOSPITAL... IN SHOCK, I GUESS... AND REALIZED I WASN'T BREATHING.
I PANICKED. I WAS SCREAMING, HITTING THE ROOF OF THE CAR WITH MY HANDS.
AND THEN I STOP, BECAUSE MY WIFE'S GOING TO BE PISSED IF I RIP THE FABRIC PUNCHING THE ROOF LIKE THAT.
AND I REALIZE I LOVE MY WIFE.

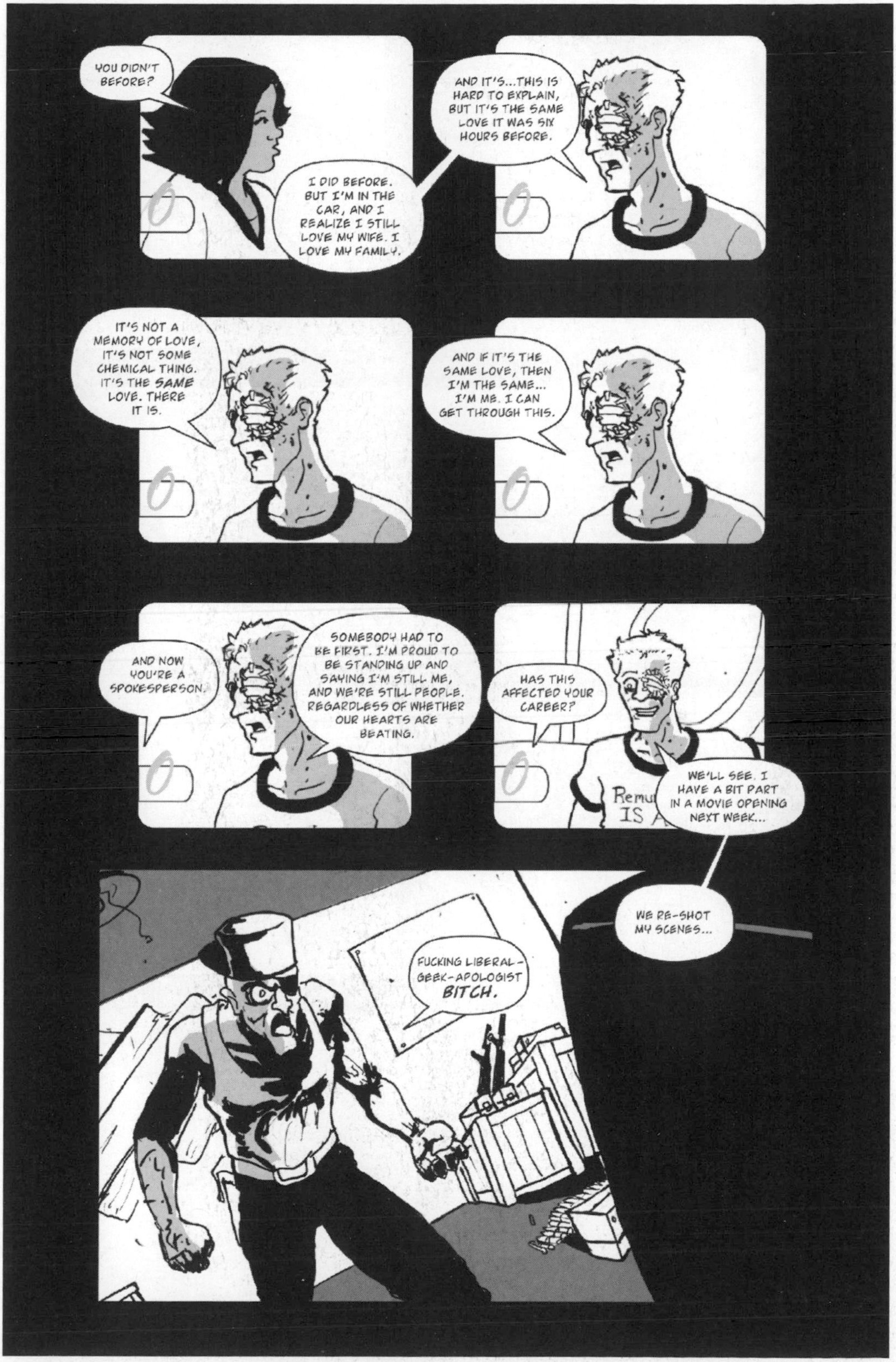
YOU DIDN'T BEFORE?
I DID BEFORE. BUT I'M IN THE CAR, AND I REALIZE I STILL LOVE MY WIFE. I LOVE MY FAMILY.
AND IT'S...THIS IS HARD TO EXPLAIN, BUT IT'S THE SAME LOVE IT WAS SIX HOURS BEFORE.
IT'S NOT A MEMORY OF LOVE, IT'S NOT SOME CHEMICAL THING. IT'S THE SAME LOVE. THERE IT IS.
AND IF IT'S THE SAME LOVE, THEN I'M THE SAME... I'M ME. I CAN GET THROUGH THIS.
AND NOW YOU'RE A SPOKESPERSON.
SOMEBODY HAD TO BE FIRST. I'M PROUD TO BE STANDING UP AND SAYING I'M STILL ME, AND WE'RE STILL PEOPLE. REGARDLESS OF WHETHER OUR HEARTS ARE BEATING.
HAS THIS AFFECTED YOUR CAREER?
WE'LL SEE. I HAVE A BIT PART IN A MOVIE OPENING NEXT WEEK...
WE RE-SHOT MY SCENES...
FUCKING LIBERAL-GEEK-APOLOGIST BITCH.

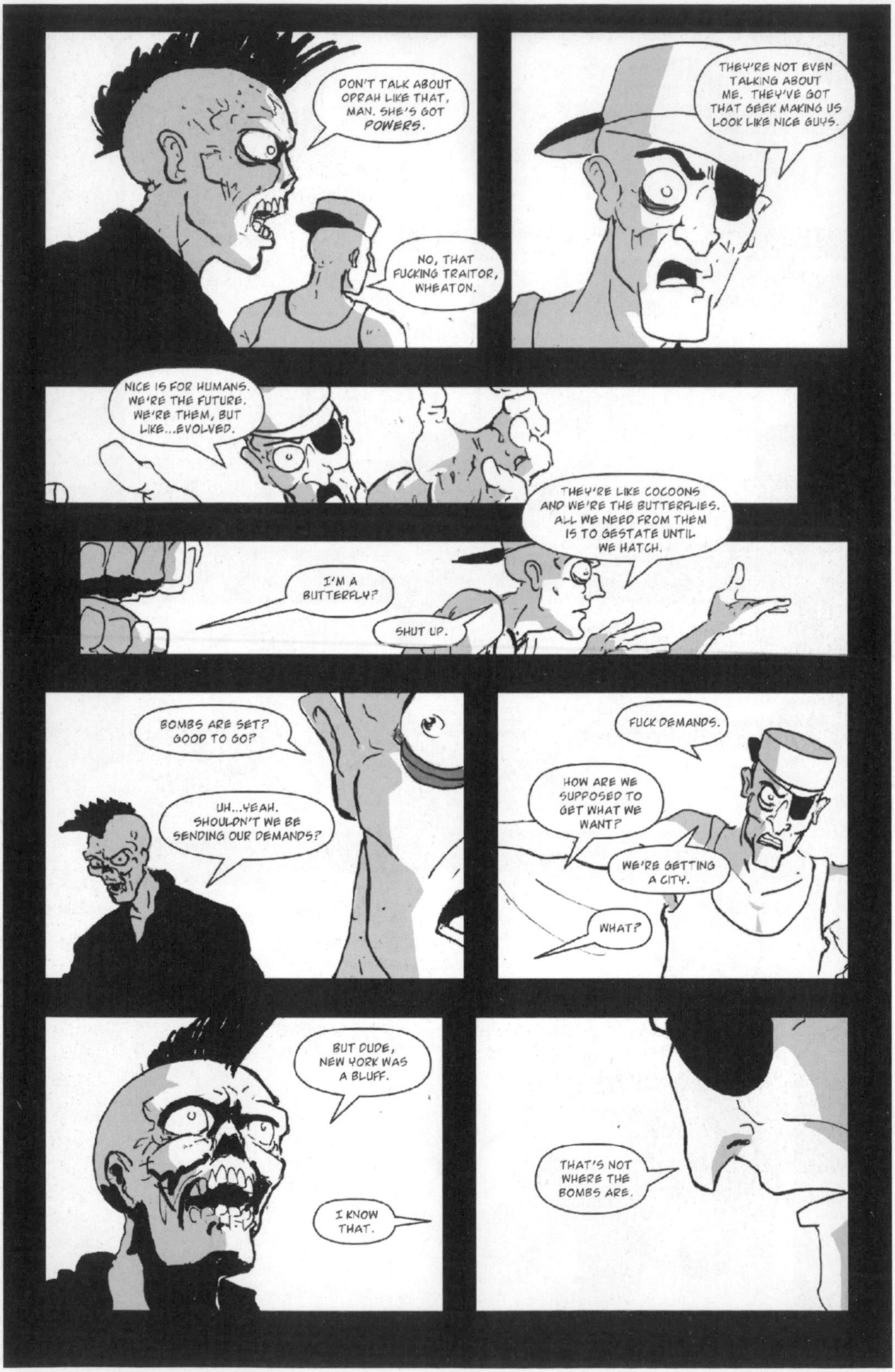
DON'T TALK ABOUT OPRAH LIKE THAT, MAN. SHE'S GOT POWERS.
NO, THAT FUCKING TRAITOR, WHEATON.
THEY'RE NOT EVEN TALKING ABOUT ME. THEY'VE GOT THAT GEEK MAKING US LOOK LIKE NICE GUYS.
NICE IS FOR HUMANS. WE'RE THE FUTURE. WE'RE THEM, BUT LIKE...EVOLVED.
THEY'RE LIKE COCOONS AND WE'RE THE BUTTERFLIES. ALL WE NEED FROM THEM IS TO GESTATE UNTIL WE HATCH.
I'M A BUTTERFLY?
SHUT UP.
BOMBS ARE SET? GOOD TO GO?
UH...YEAH. SHOULDN'T WE BE SENDING OUR DEMANDS?
FUCK DEMANDS.
HOW ARE WE SUPPOSED TO GET WHAT WE WANT?
WE'RE GETTING A CITY.
WHAT?
BUT DUDE, NEW YORK WAS A BLUFF.
I KNOW THAT.
THAT'S NOT WHERE THE BOMBS ARE.

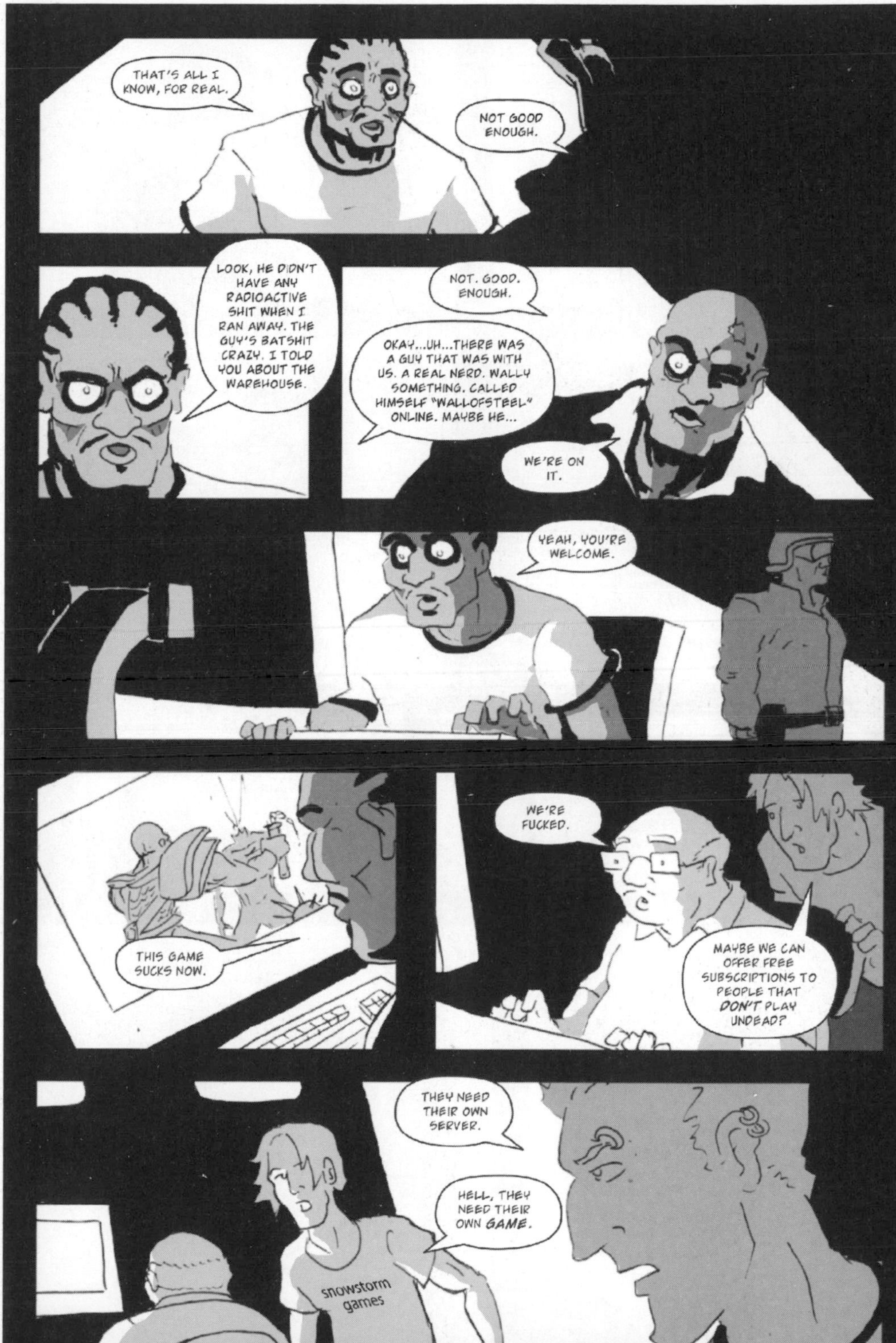
THAT'S ALL I KNOW, FOR REAL.
NOT GOOD ENOUGH.
LOOK, HE DIDN'T HAVE ANY RADIOACTIVE SHIT WHEN I RAN AWAY. THE GUY'S BATSHIT CRAZY. I TOLD YOU ABOUT THE WAREHOUSE.
NOT. GOOD. ENOUGH.
OKAY...UH...THERE WAS A GUY THAT WAS WITH US. A REAL NERD. WALLY SOMETHING. CALLED HIMSELF "WALLOFSTEEL" ONLINE. MAYBE HE...
WE'RE ON IT.
YEAH, YOU'RE WELCOME.
THIS GAME SUCKS NOW.
WE'RE FUCKED.
MAYBE WE CAN OFFER FREE SUBSCRIPTIONS TO PEOPLE THAT DON'T PLAY UNDEAD?
THEY NEED THEIR OWN SERVER.
HELL, THEY NEED THEIR OWN GAME.
snowstorm games

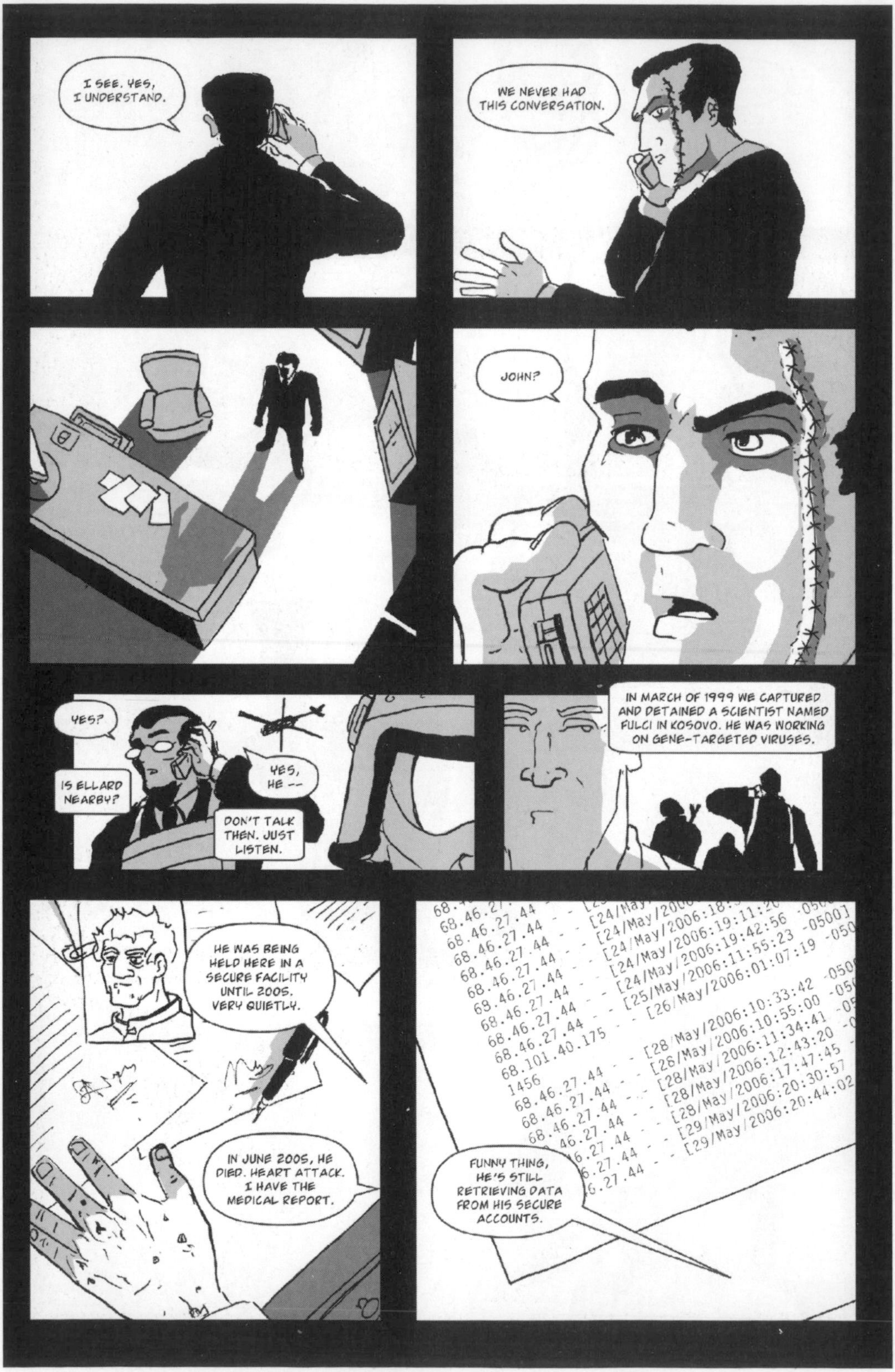
I SEE. YES, I UNDERSTAND.
WE NEVER HAD THIS CONVERSATION.
JOHN?
YES?
IS ELLARD NEARBY?
YES, HE --
DON'T TALK THEN. JUST LISTEN.
IN MARCH OF 1999 WE CAPTURED AND DETAINED A SCIENTIST NAMED FULCI IN KOSOVO. HE WAS WORKING ON GENE-TARGETED VIRUSES.
HE WAS BEING HELD HERE IN A SECURE FACILITY UNTIL 2005. VERY QUIETLY.
IN JUNE 2005, HE DIED. HEART ATTACK. I HAVE THE MEDICAL REPORT.
FUNNY THING, HE'S STILL RETRIEVING DATA FROM HIS SECURE ACCOUNTS.

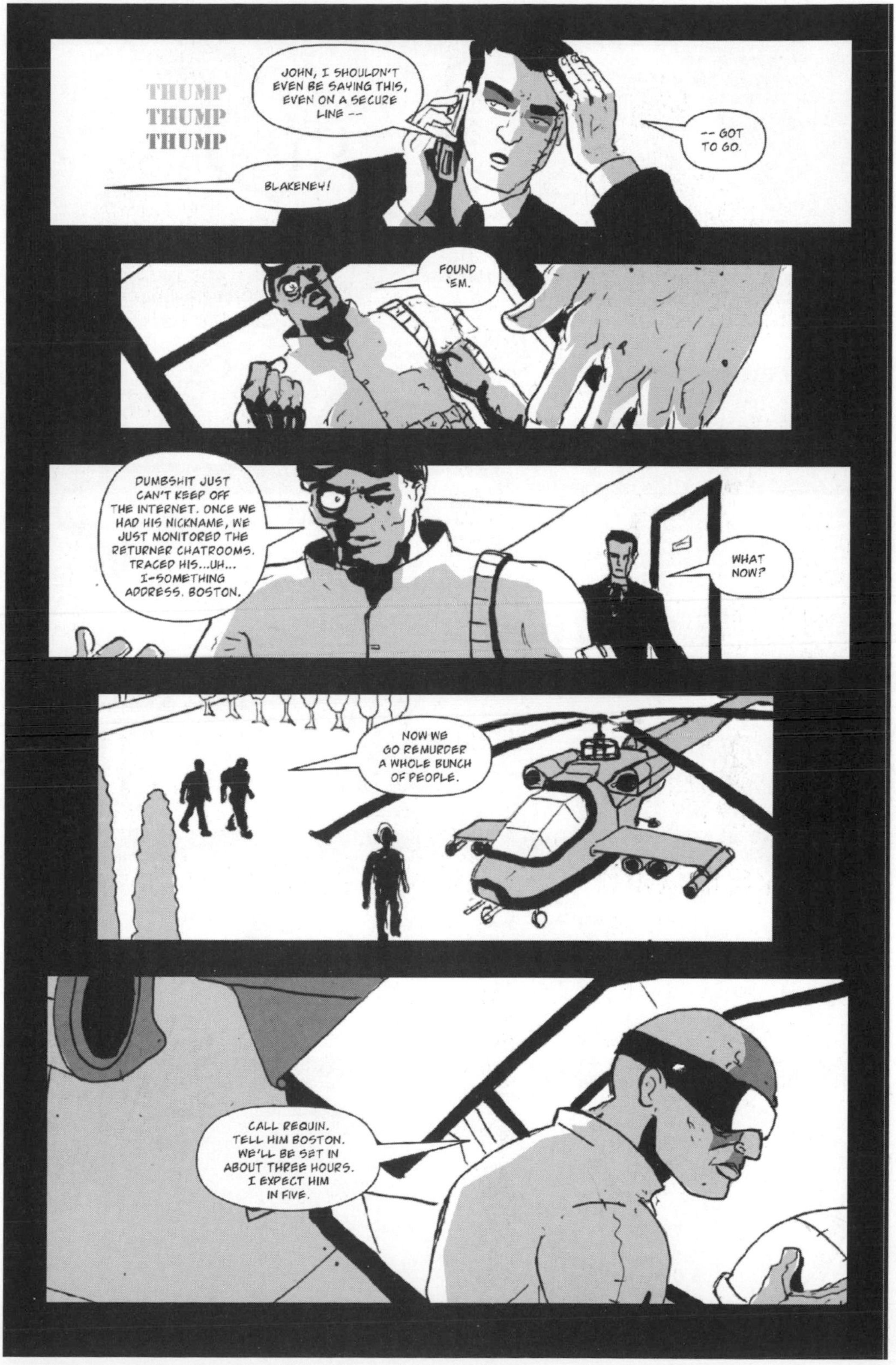
JOHN, I SHOULDN'T EVEN BE SAYING THIS, EVEN ON A SECURE LINE --
THUMP
THUMP
THUMP
BLAKENEY!
-- GOT TO GO.
FOUND 'EM.
DUMBSHIT JUST CAN'T KEEP OFF THE INTERNET. ONCE WE HAD HIS NICKNAME, WE JUST MONITORED THE RETURNER CHATROOMS. TRACED HIS...UH... I-SOMETHING ADDRESS. BOSTON.
WHAT NOW?
NOW WE GO REMURDER A WHOLE BUNCH OF PEOPLE.
CALL REQUIN. TELL HIM BOSTON. WE'LL BE SET IN ABOUT THREE HOURS. I EXPECT HIM IN FIVE.

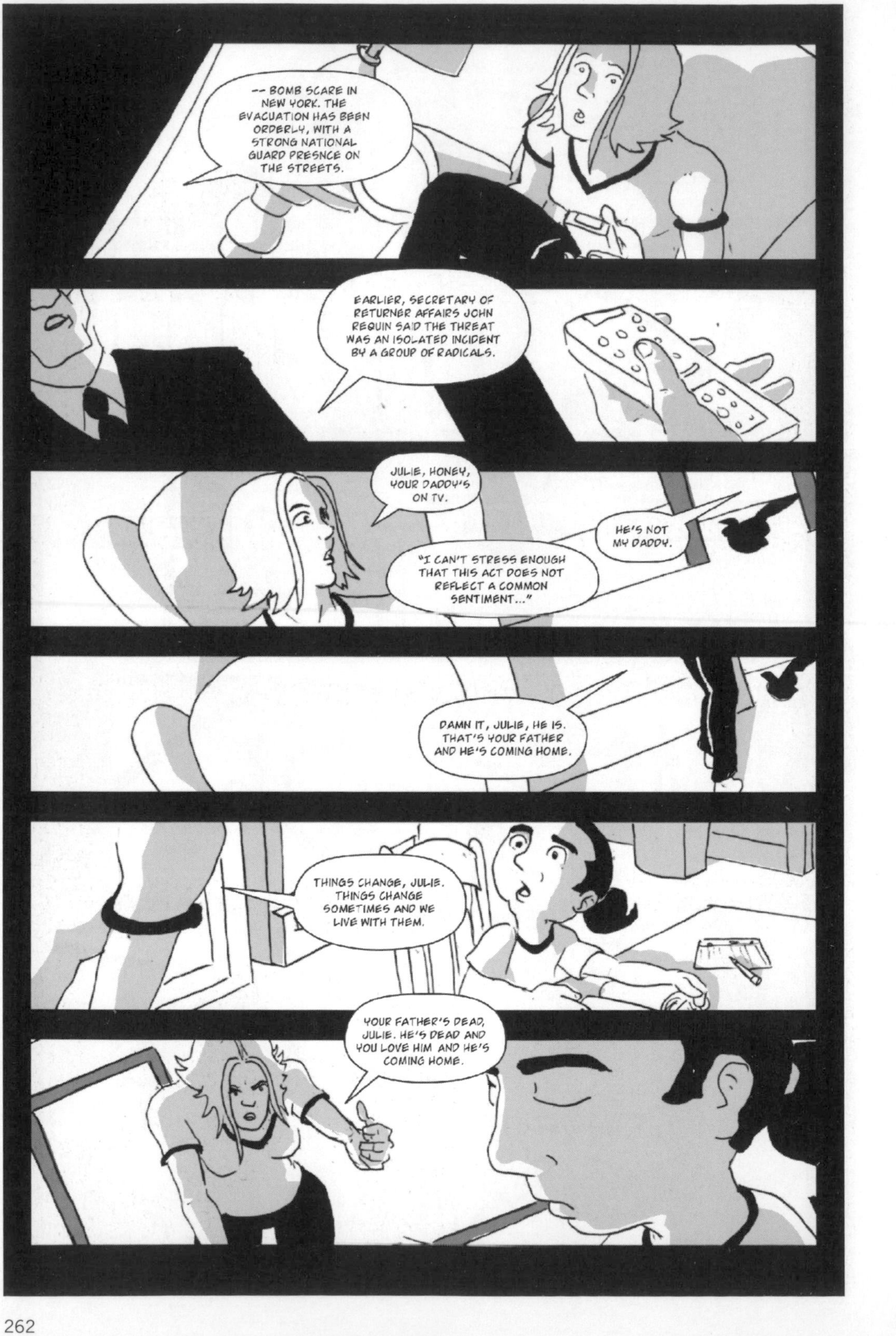
-- BOMB SCARE IN NEW YORK. THE EVACUATION HAS BEEN ORDERLY, WITH A STRONG NATIONAL GUARD PRESNCE ON THE STREETS.
EARLIER, SECRETARY OF RETURNER AFFAIRS JOHN REQUIN SAID THE THREAT WAS AN ISOLATED INCIDENT BY A GROUP OF RADICALS.
JULIE, HONEY, YOUR DADDY'S ON TV.
HE'S NOT MY DADDY.
"I CAN'T STRESS ENOUGH THAT THIS ACT DOES NOT REFLECT A COMMON SENTIMENT..."
DAMN IT, JULIE, HE IS. THAT'S YOUR FATHER AND HE'S COMING HOME.
THINGS CHANGE, JULIE. THINGS CHANGE SOMETIMES AND WE LIVE WITH THEM.
YOUR FATHER'S DEAD, JULIE. HE'S DEAD AND YOU LOVE HIM AND HE'S COMING HOME.

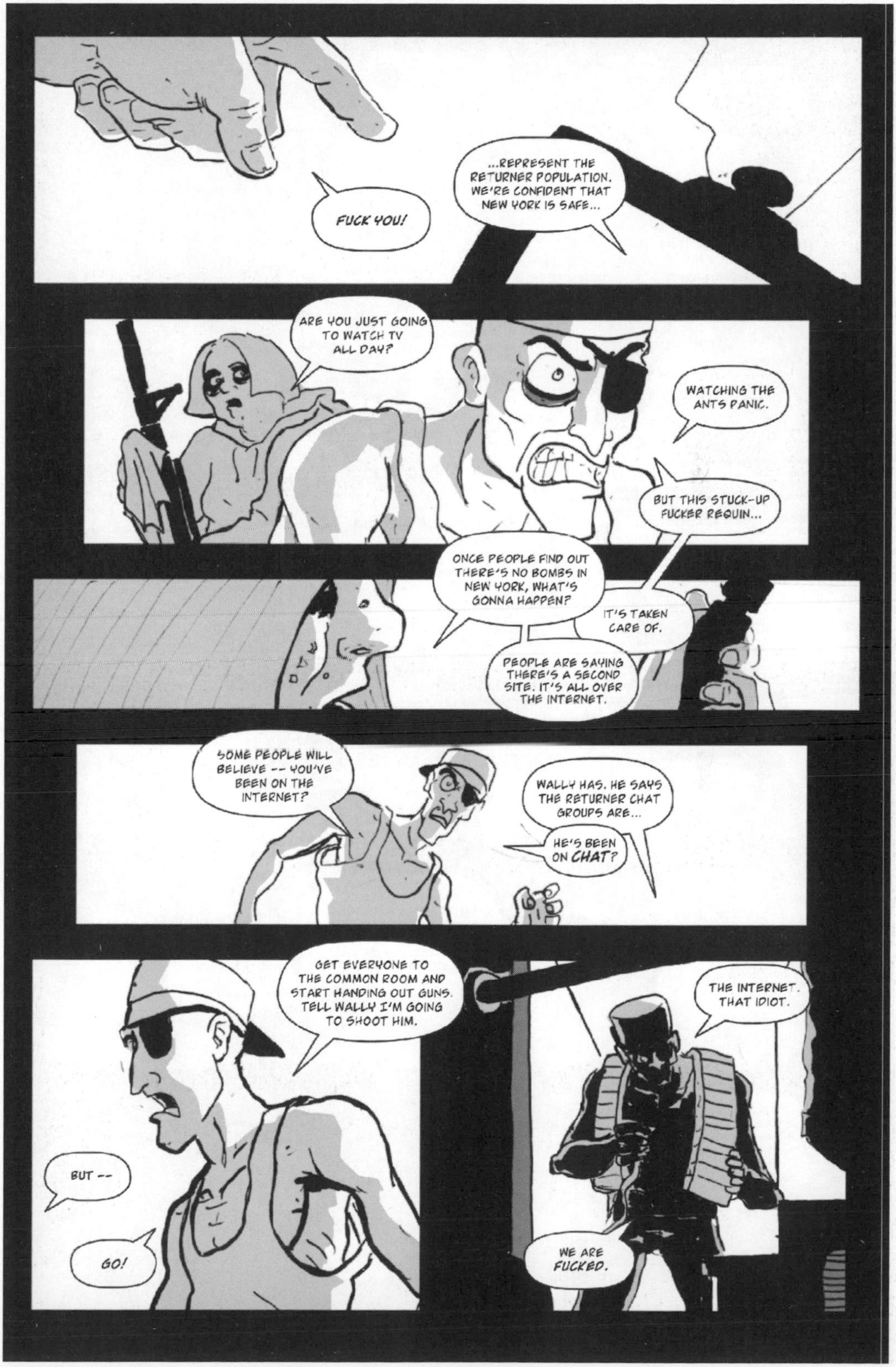
...REPRESENT THE RETURNER POPULATION. WE'RE CONFIDENT THAT NEW YORK IS SAFE...
FUCK YOU!
ARE YOU JUST GOING TO WATCH TV ALL DAY?
WATCHING THE ANTS PANIC.
BUT THIS STUCK-UP FUCKER REQUIN...
ONCE PEOPLE FIND OUT THERE'S NO BOMBS IN NEW YORK, WHAT'S GONNA HAPPEN?
IT'S TAKEN CARE OF.
PEOPLE ARE SAYING THERE'S A SECOND SITE. IT'S ALL OVER THE INTERNET.
SOME PEOPLE WILL BELIEVE -- YOU'VE BEEN ON THE INTERNET?
WALLY HAS. HE SAYS THE RETURNER CHAT GROUPS ARE...
HE'S BEEN ON CHAT?
GET EVERYONE TO THE COMMON ROOM AND START HANDING OUT GUNS. TELL WALLY I'M GOING TO SHOOT HIM.
BUT --
GO!
THE INTERNET. THAT IDIOT.
WE ARE FUCKED.

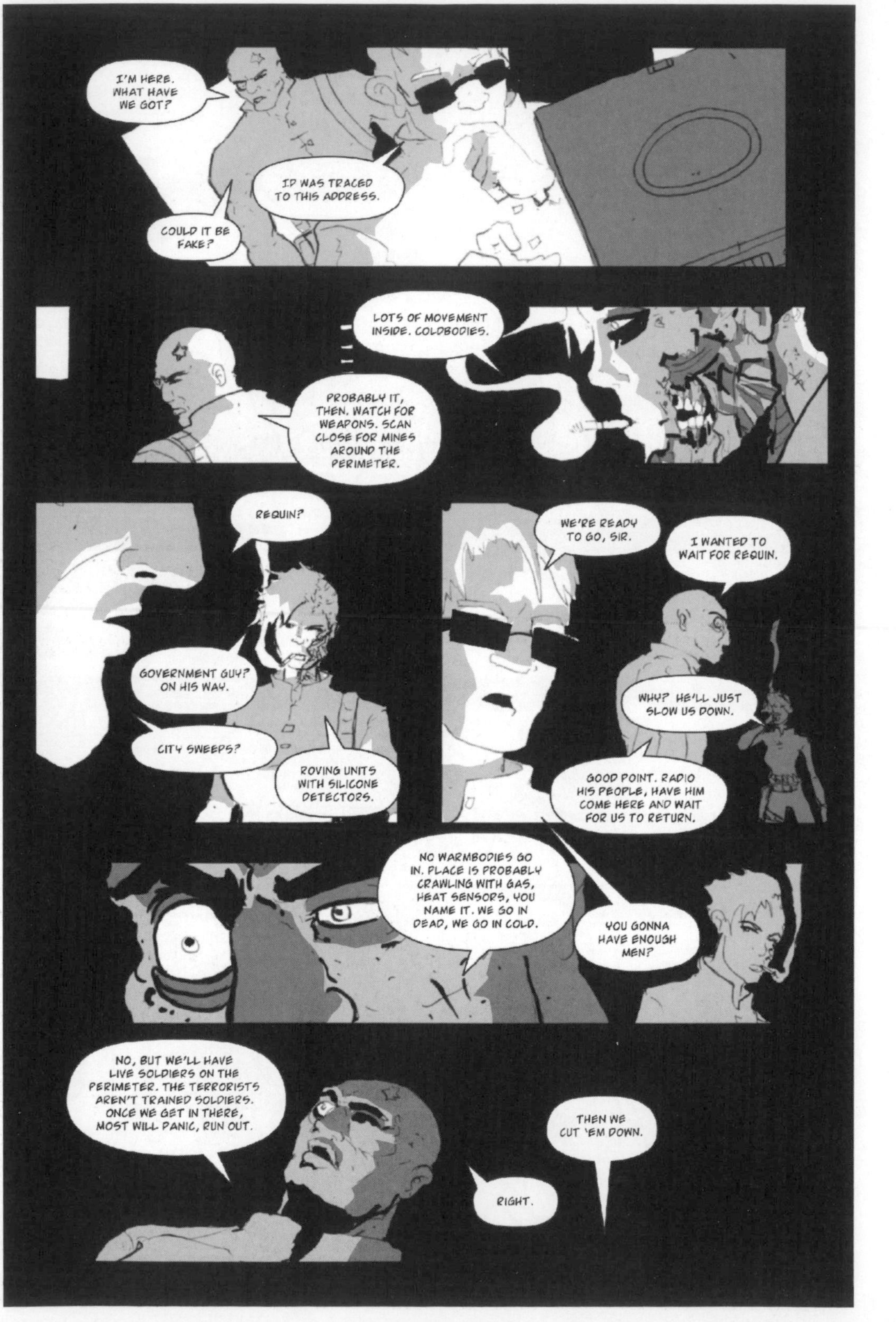
I'M HERE. WHAT HAVE WE GOT?
I.D WAS TRACED TO THIS ADDRESS.
COULD IT BE FAKE?
LOTS OF MOVEMENT INSIDE. COLDBODIES.
PROBABLY IT, THEN. WATCH FOR WEAPONS. SCAN CLOSE FOR MINES AROUND THE PERIMETER.
REQUIN?
GOVERNMENT GUY? ON HIS WAY.
CITY SWEEPS?
ROVING UNITS WITH SILICONE DETECTORS.
WE'RE READY TO GO, SIR.
I WANTED TO WAIT FOR REQUIN.
WHY? HE'LL JUST SLOW US DOWN.
GOOD POINT. RADIO HIS PEOPLE, HAVE HIM COME HERE AND WAIT FOR US TO RETURN.
NO WARMBODIES GO IN. PLACE IS PROBABLY CRAWLING WITH GAS, HEAT SENSORS, YOU NAME IT. WE GO IN DEAD, WE GO IN COLD.
YOU GONNA HAVE ENOUGH MEN?
NO, BUT WE'LL HAVE LIVE SOLDIERS ON THE PERIMETER. THE TERRORISTS AREN'T TRAINED SOLDIERS. ONCE WE GET IN THERE, MOST WILL PANIC, RUN OUT.
THEN WE CUT 'EM DOWN.
RIGHT.

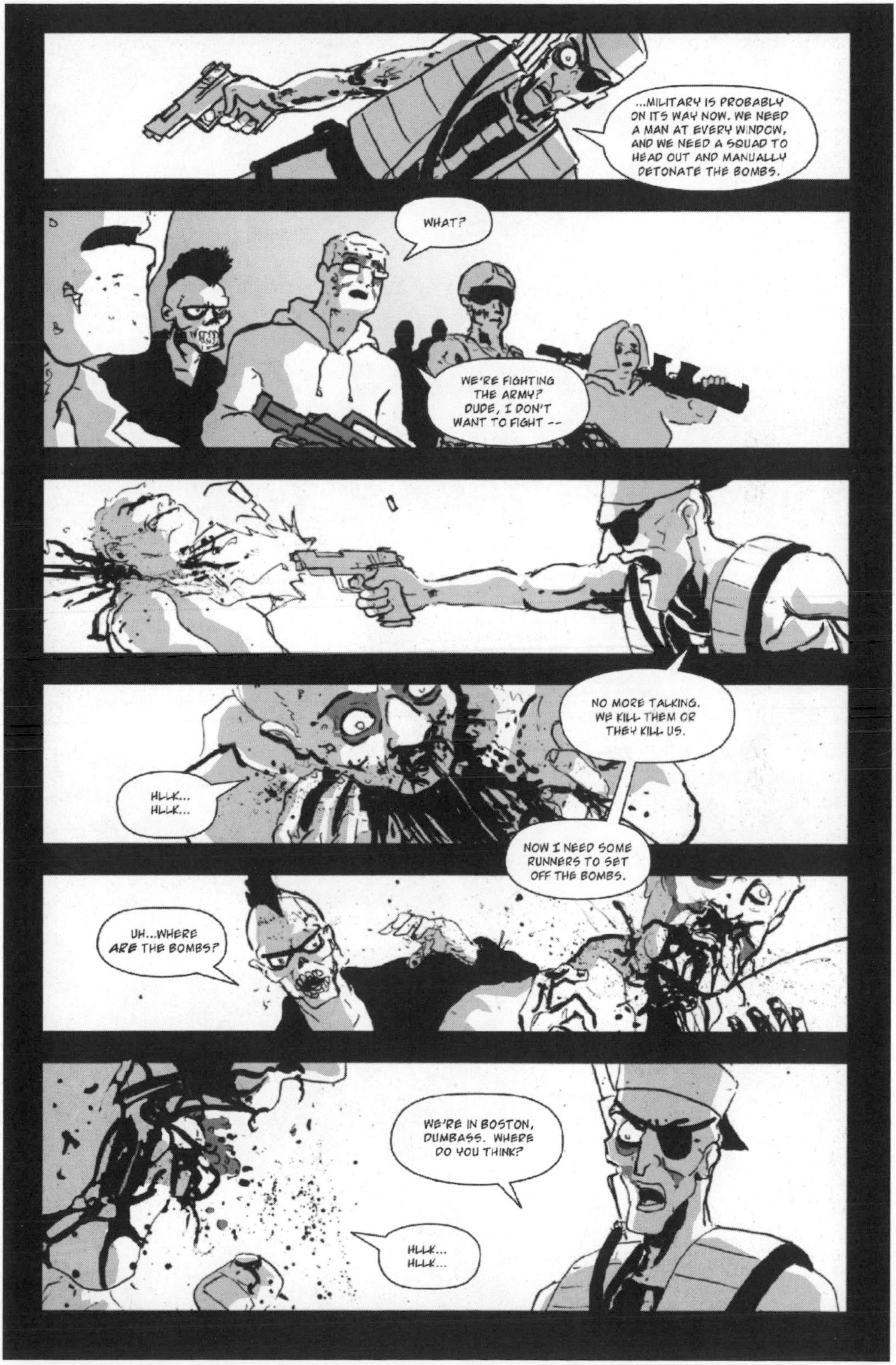
...MILITARY IS PROBABLY ON ITS WAY NOW. WE NEED A MAN AT EVERY WINDOW, AND WE NEED A SQUAD TO HEAD OUT AND MANUALLY DETONATE THE BOMBS.
WHAT?
WE'RE FIGHTING THE ARMY? DUDE, I DON'T WANT TO FIGHT --
NO MORE TALKING. WE KILL THEM OR THEY KILL US.
HLLK... HLLK...
NOW I NEED SOME RUNNERS TO SET OFF THE BOMBS.
UH...WHERE ARE THE BOMBS?
WE'RE IN BOSTON, DUMBASS. WHERE DO YOU THINK?
HLLK... HLLK...

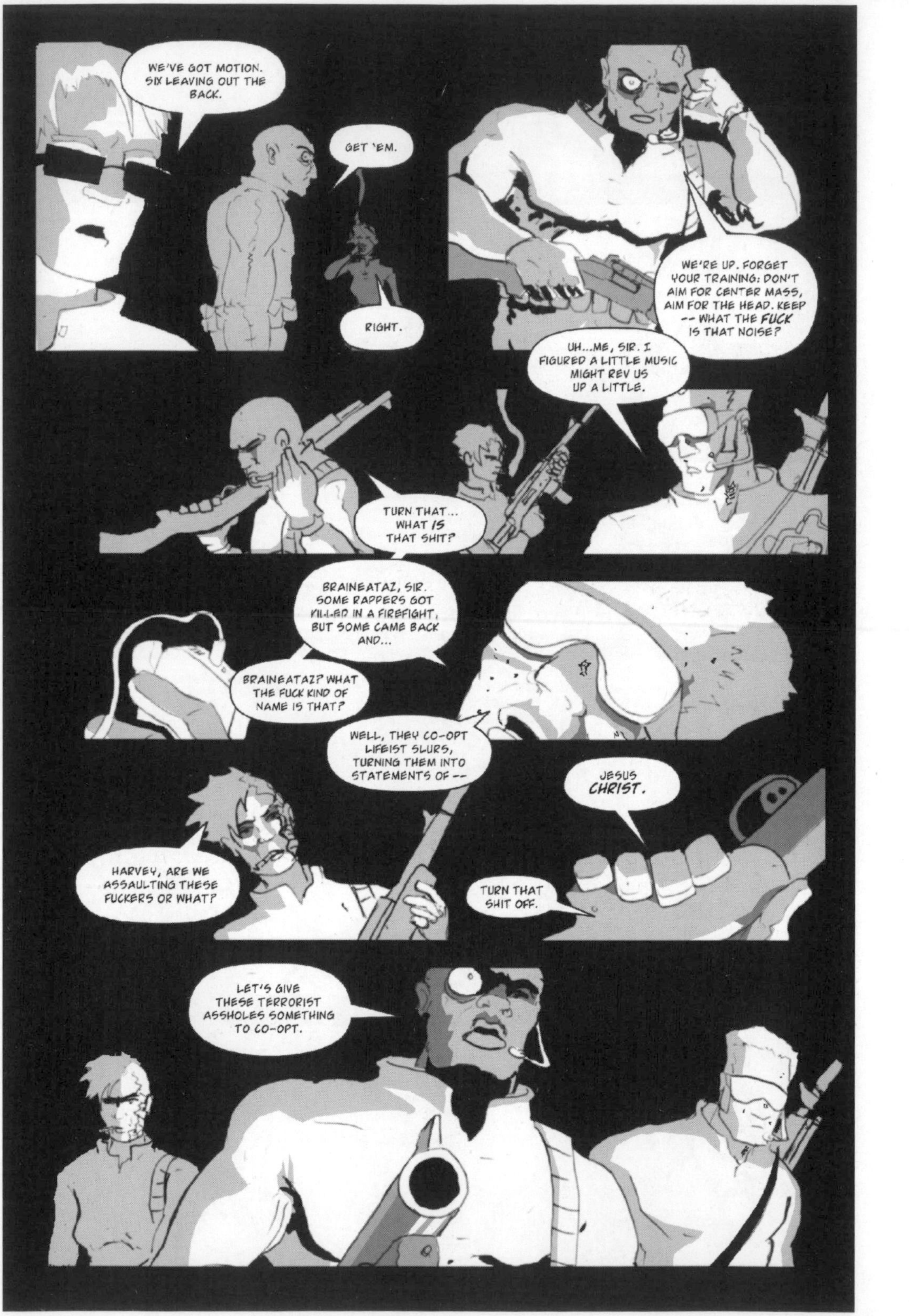
WE'VE GOT MOTION. SIX LEAVING OUT THE BACK.
GET 'EM.
RIGHT.
WE'RE UP. FORGET YOUR TRAINING: DON'T AIM FOR CENTER MASS, AIM FOR THE HEAD. KEEP -- WHAT THE FUCK IS THAT NOISE?
UH...ME, SIR. I FIGURED A LITTLE MUSIC MIGHT REV US UP A LITTLE.
TURN THAT... WHAT IS THAT SHIT?
BRAINEATAZ, SIR. SOME RAPPERS GOT KILLED IN A FIREFIGHT, BUT SOME CAME BACK AND...
BRAINEATAZ? WHAT THE FUCK KIND OF NAME IS THAT?
WELL, THEY CO-OPT LIFEIST SLURS, TURNING THEM INTO STATEMENTS OF --
HARVEY, ARE WE ASSAULTING THESE FUCKERS OR WHAT?
JESUS CHRIST.
TURN THAT SHIT OFF.
LET'S GIVE THESE TERRORIST ASSHOLES SOMETHING TO CO-OPT.

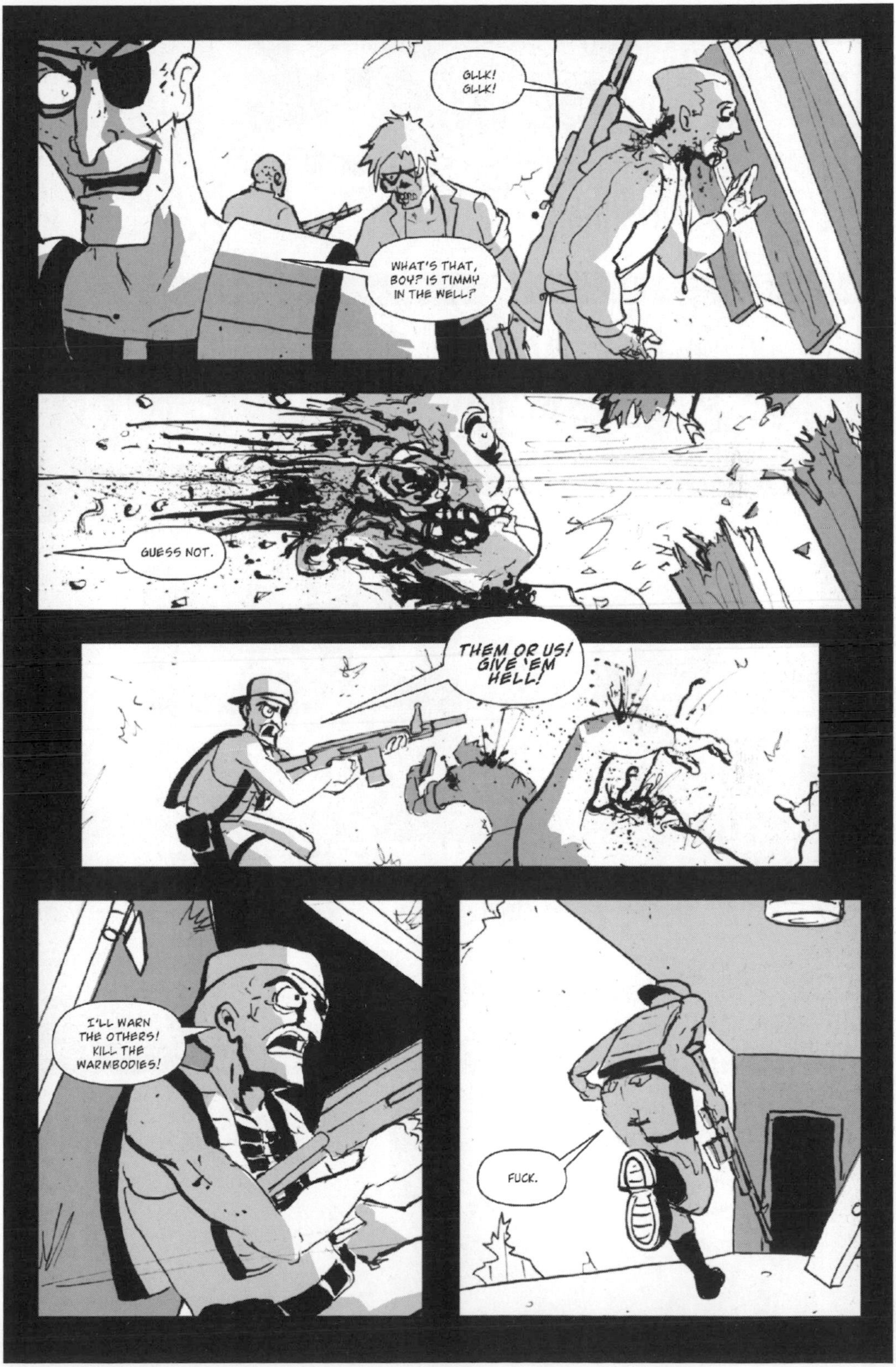
GLLK! GLLK!
WHAT'S THAT, BOY? IS TIMMY IN THE WELL?
GUESS NOT.
THEM OR US! GIVE 'EM HELL!
I'LL WARN THE OTHERS! KILL THE WARMBODIES!
FUCK.

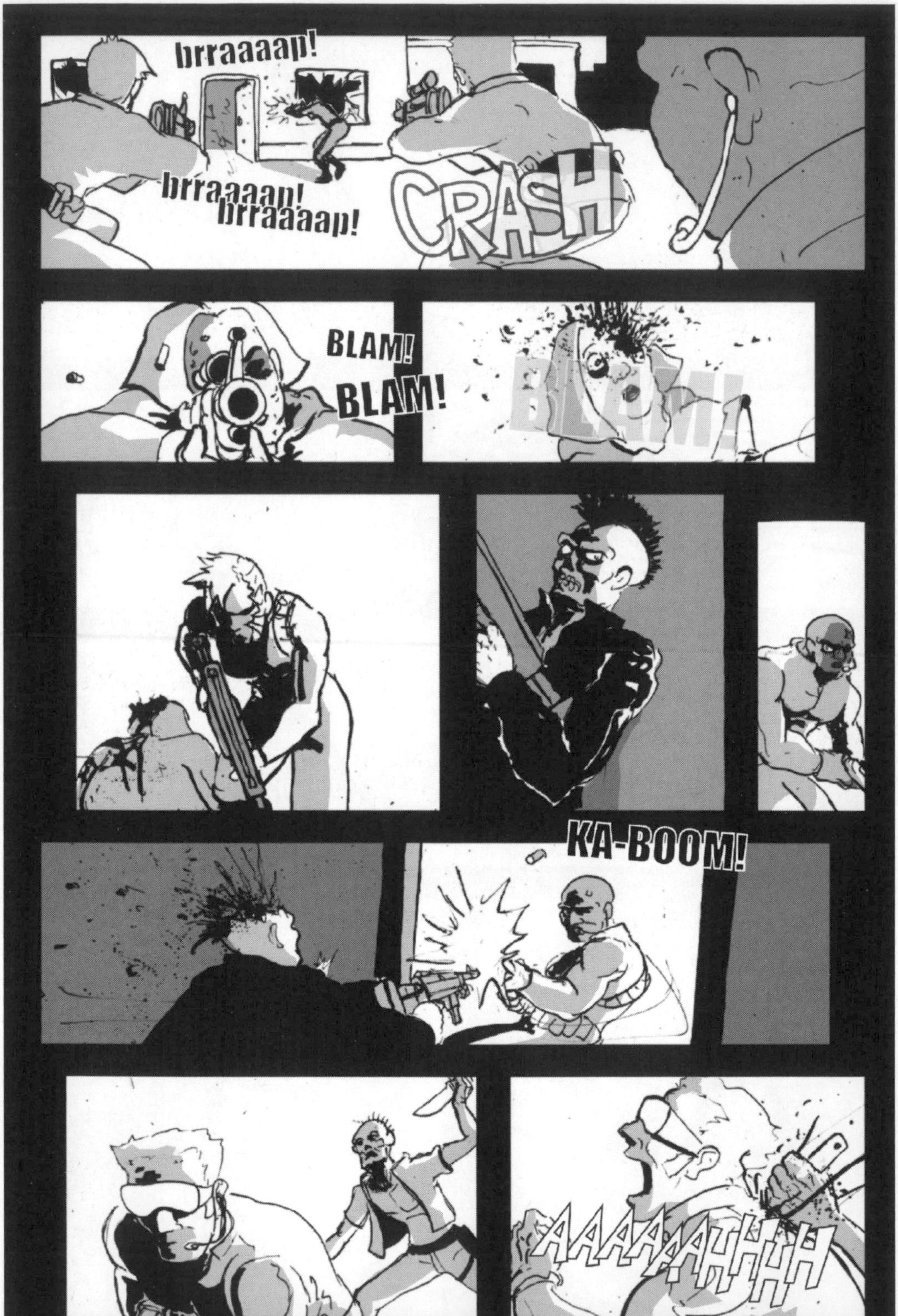
brraaaap!
brraaaap!
brraaaap!
CRASH
BLAM!
BLAM!
BLAM!
KA-BOOM!
AAAAAAHHHH

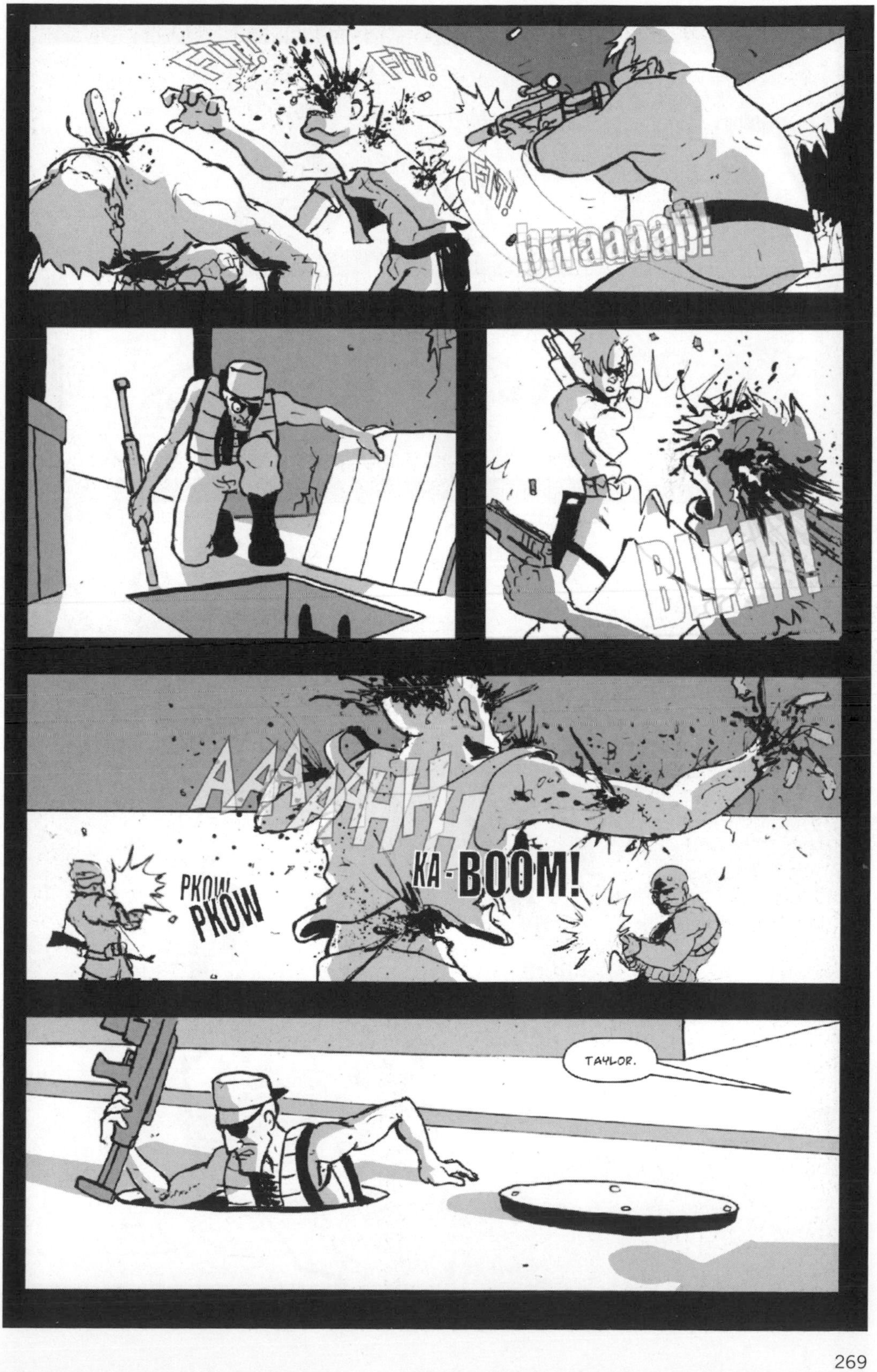
FIT!
FIT!
FIT!
brraaaap!
BLAM!
AAAAAHHH
PKOW PKOW
KA-BOOM!
TAYLOR.

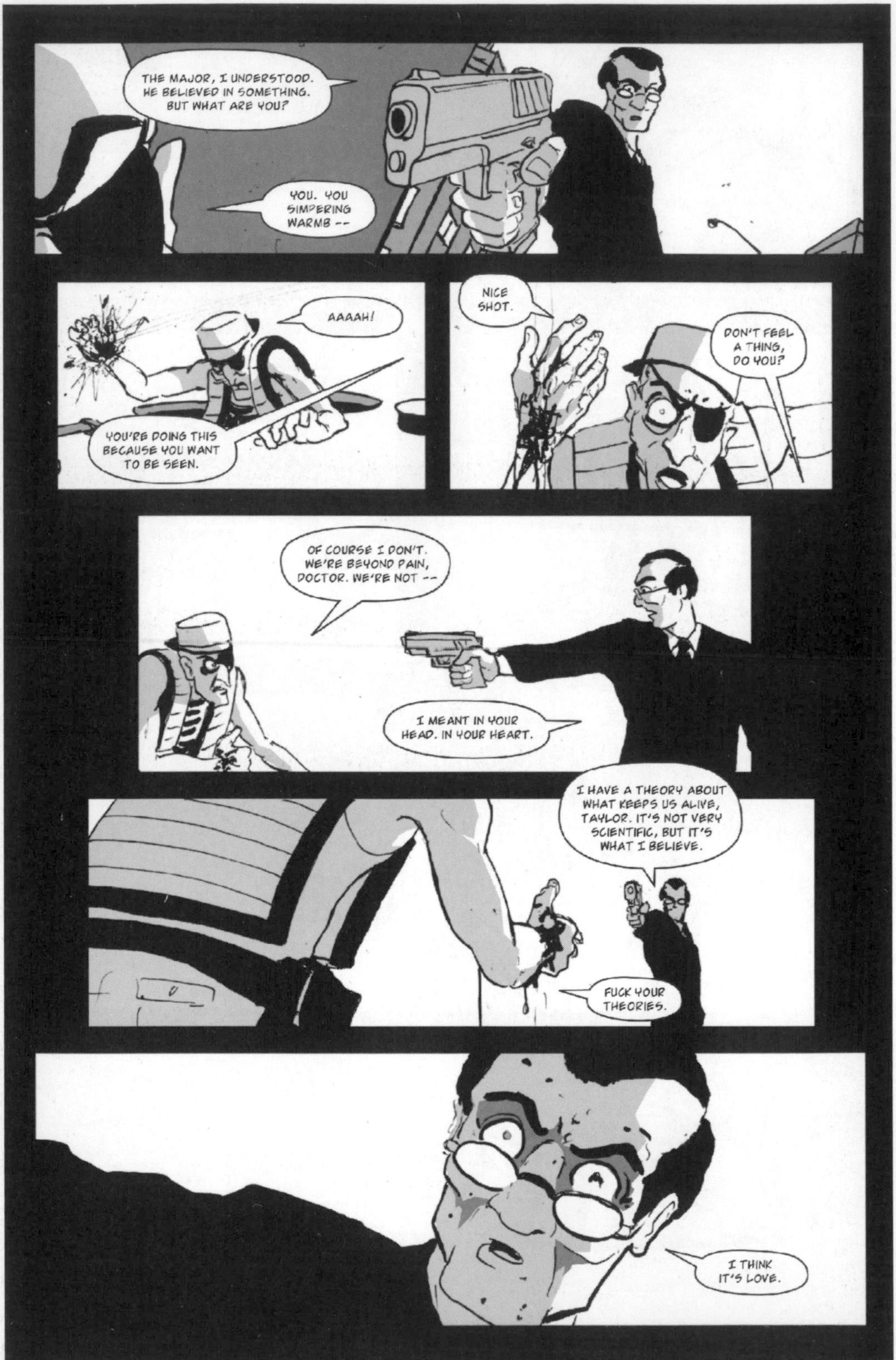
THE MAJOR, I UNDERSTOOD. HE BELIEVED IN SOMETHING. BUT WHAT ARE YOU?
YOU. YOU SIMPERING WARMB --
AAAAH!
YOU'RE DOING THIS BECAUSE YOU WANT TO BE SEEN.
NICE SHOT.
DON'T FEEL A THING, DO YOU?
OF COURSE I DON'T. WE'RE BEYOND PAIN, DOCTOR. WE'RE NOT --
I MEANT IN YOUR HEAD. IN YOUR HEART.
I HAVE A THEORY ABOUT WHAT KEEPS US ALIVE, TAYLOR. IT'S NOT VERY SCIENTIFIC, BUT IT'S WHAT I BELIEVE.
FUCK YOUR THEORIES.
I THINK IT'S LOVE.

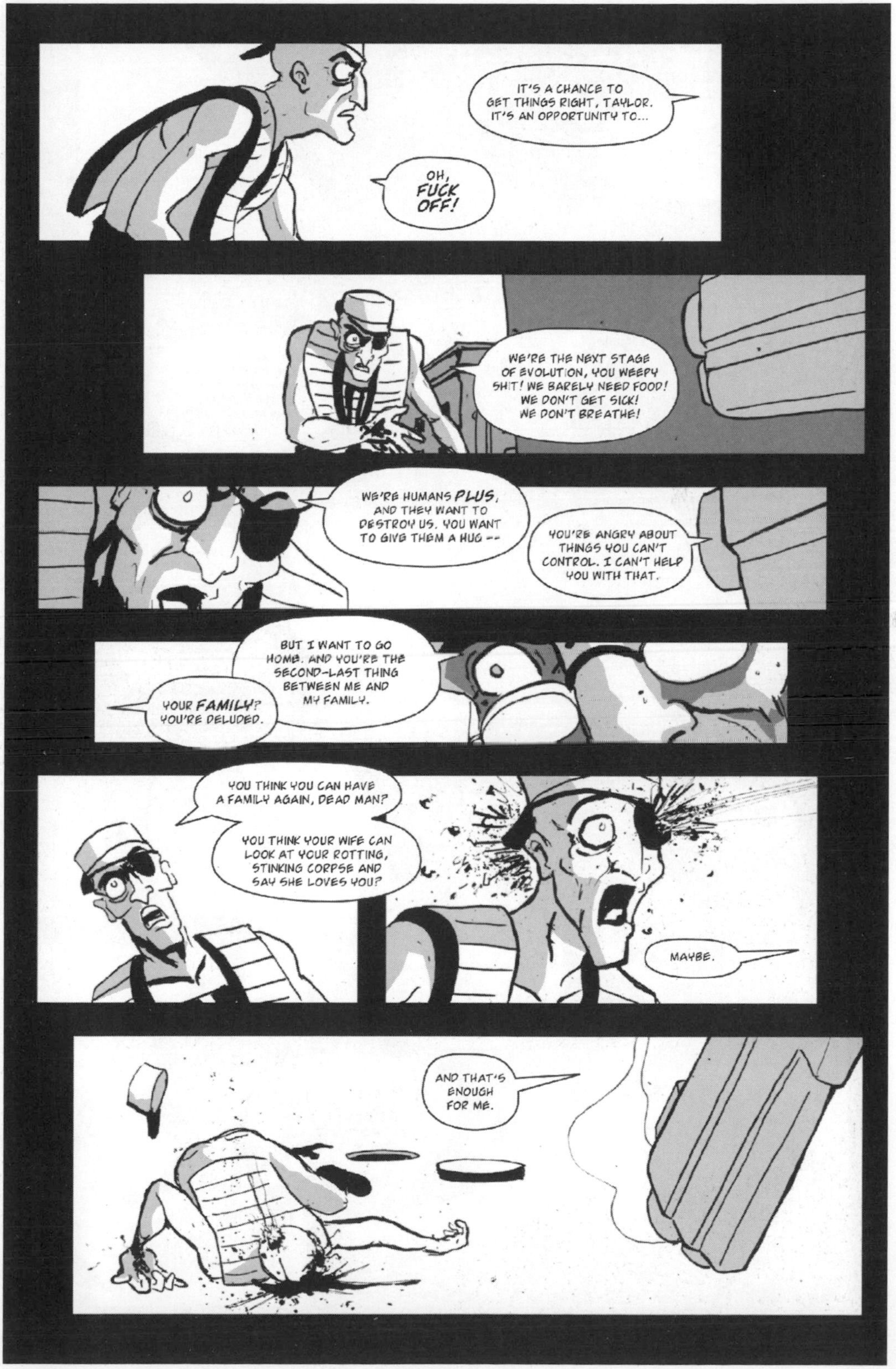
IT'S A CHANCE TO GET THINGS RIGHT, TAYLOR. IT'S AN OPPORTUNITY TO...
OH, FUCK OFF!
WE'RE THE NEXT STAGE OF EVOLUTION, YOU WEEPY SHIT! WE BARELY NEED FOOD! WE DON'T GET SICK! WE DON'T BREATHE!
WE'RE HUMANS PLUS, AND THEY WANT TO DESTROY US. YOU WANT TO GIVE THEM A HUG --
YOU'RE ANGRY ABOUT THINGS YOU CAN'T CONTROL. I CAN'T HELP YOU WITH THAT.
YOUR FAMILY? YOU'RE DELUDED.
BUT I WANT TO GO HOME. AND YOU'RE THE SECOND-LAST THING BETWEEN ME AND MY FAMILY.
YOU THINK YOU CAN HAVE A FAMILY AGAIN, DEAD MAN?
YOU THINK YOUR WIFE CAN LOOK AT YOUR ROTTING, STINKING CORPSE AND SAY SHE LOVES YOU?
MAYBE.
AND THAT'S ENOUGH FOR ME.

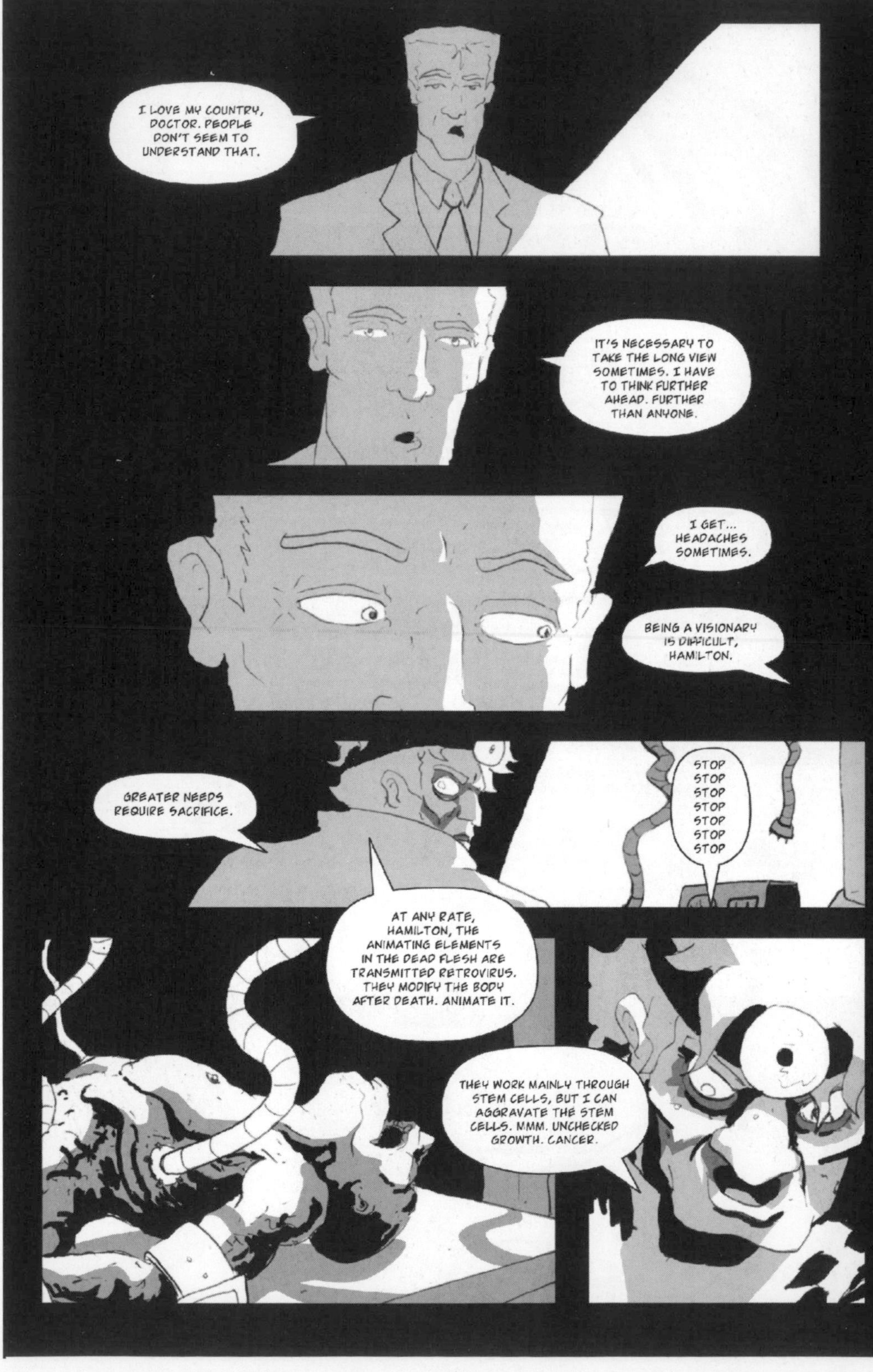
I LOVE MY COUNTRY, DOCTOR. PEOPLE DON'T SEEM TO UNDERSTAND THAT.
IT'S NECESSARY TO TAKE THE LONG VIEW SOMETIMES. I HAVE TO THINK FURTHER AHEAD. FURTHER THAN ANYONE.
I GET... HEADACHES SOMETIMES.
BEING A VISIONARY IS DIFFICULT, HAMILTON.
GREATER NEEDS REQUIRE SACRIFICE.
STOP STOP STOP STOP STOP STOP STOP
AT ANY RATE, HAMILTON, THE ANIMATING ELEMENTS IN THE DEAD FLESH ARE TRANSMITTED RETROVIRUS. THEY MODIFY THE BODY AFTER DEATH. ANIMATE IT.
THEY WORK MAINLY THROUGH STEM CELLS, BUT I CAN AGGRAVATE THE STEM CELLS. MMM. UNCHECKED GROWTH. CANCER.

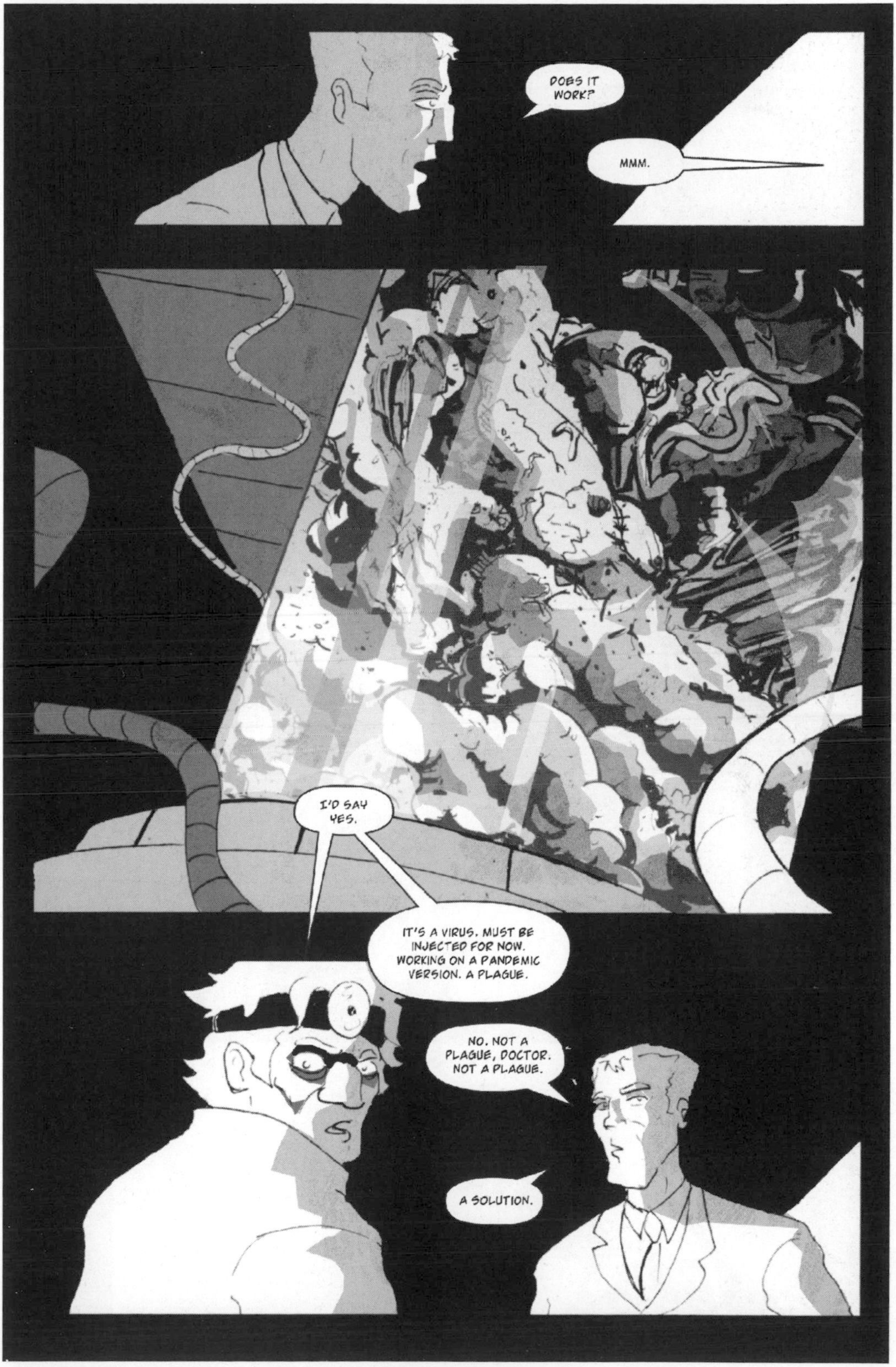
DOES IT WORK?
MMM.
I'D SAY YES.
IT'S A VIRUS. MUST BE INJECTED FOR NOW. WORKING ON A PANDEMIC VERSION. A PLAGUE.
NO. NOT A PLAGUE, DOCTOR. NOT A PLAGUE.
A SOLUTION.

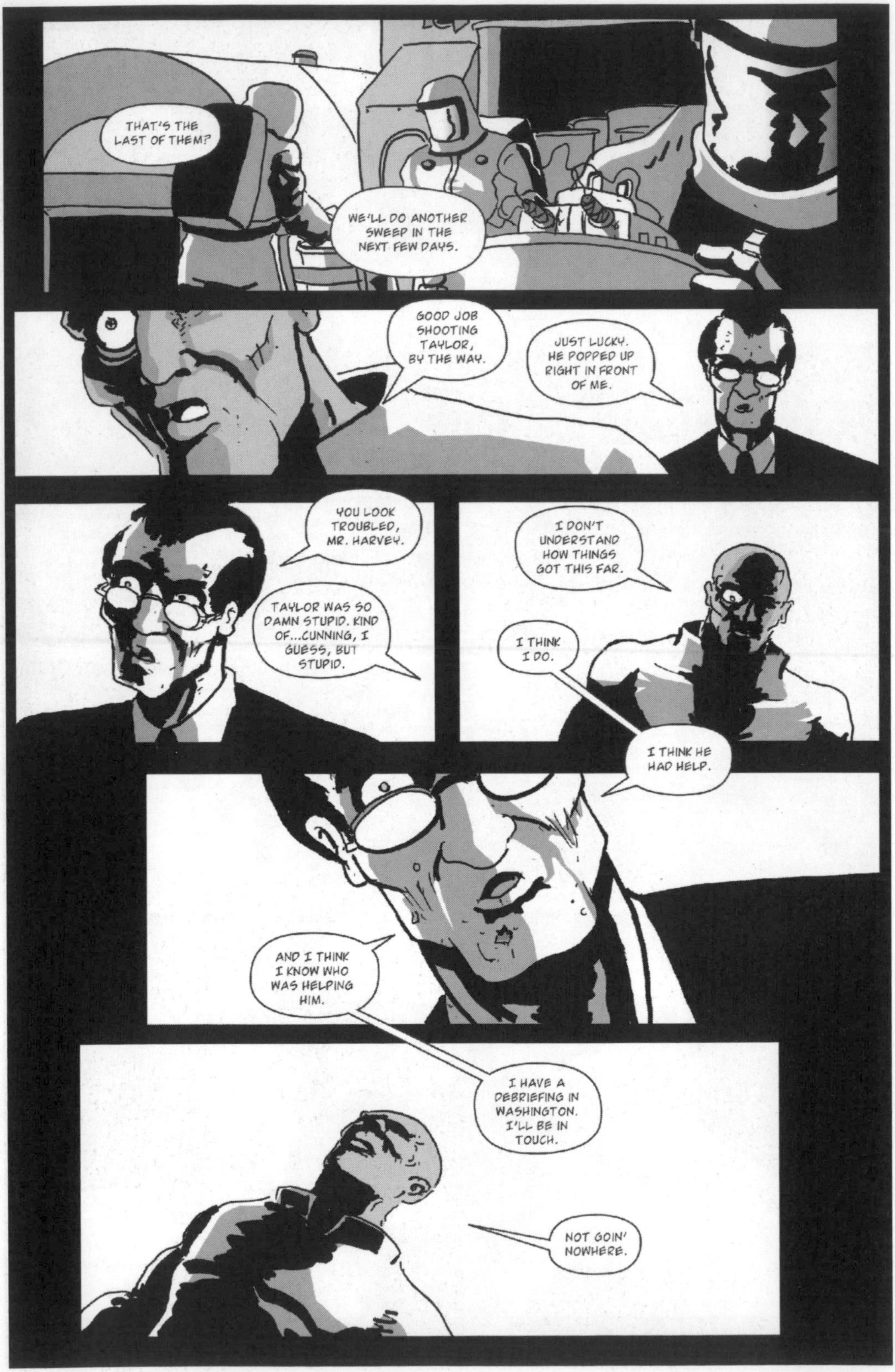
THAT'S THE LAST OF THEM?
WE'LL DO ANOTHER SWEEP IN THE NEXT FEW DAYS.
GOOD JOB SHOOTING TAYLOR, BY THE WAY.
JUST LUCKY. HE POPPED UP RIGHT IN FRONT OF ME.
YOU LOOK TROUBLED, MR. HARVEY.
TAYLOR WAS SO DAMN STUPID. KIND OF...CUNNING, I GUESS, BUT STUPID.
I DON'T UNDERSTAND HOW THINGS GOT THIS FAR.
I THINK I DO.
I THINK HE HAD HELP.
AND I THINK I KNOW WHO WAS HELPING HIM.
I HAVE A DEBRIEFING IN WASHINGTON. I'LL BE IN TOUCH.
NOT GOIN' NOWHERE.

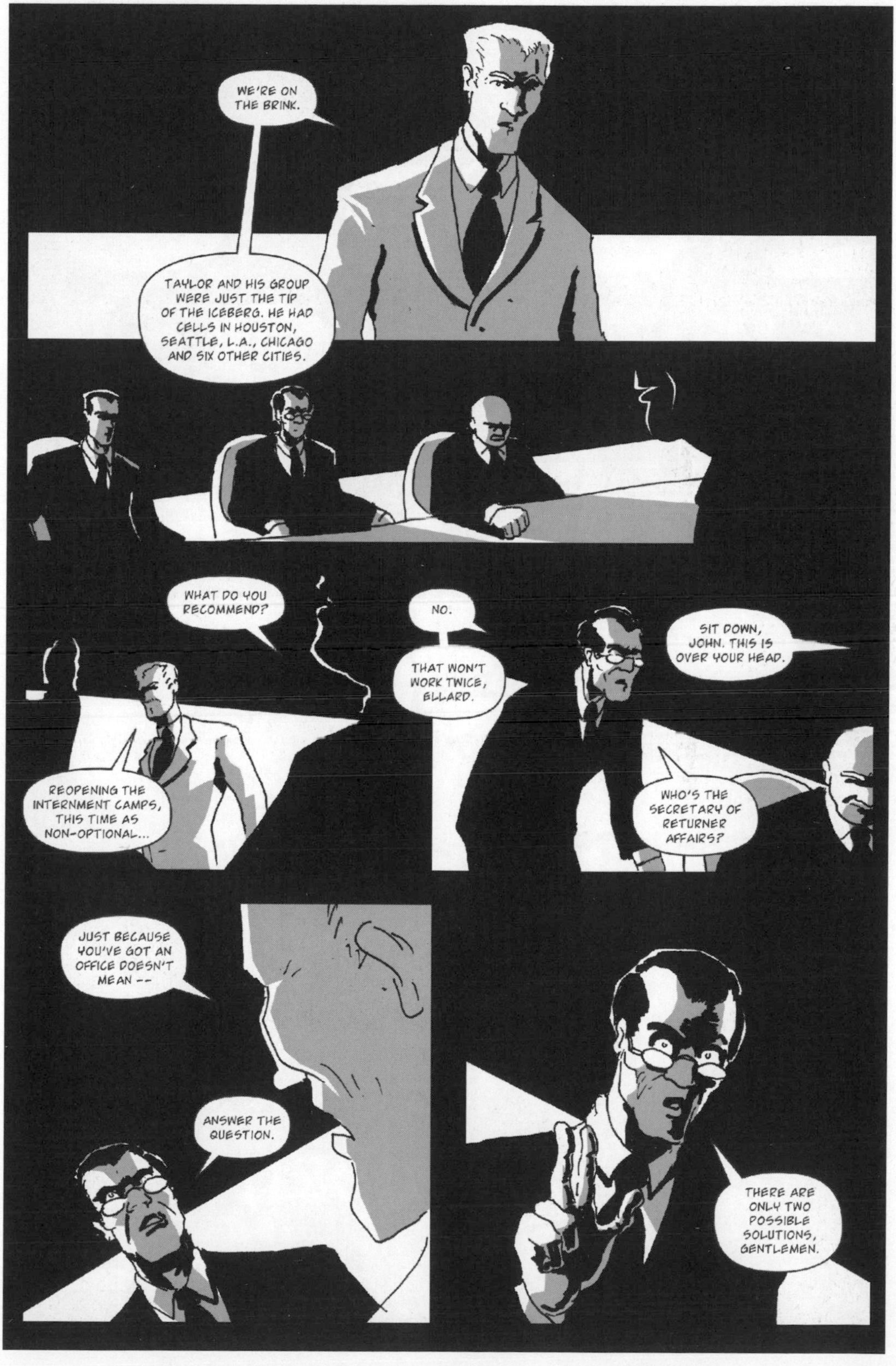
WE'RE ON THE BRINK.
TAYLOR AND HIS GROUP WERE JUST THE TIP OF THE ICEBERG. HE HAD CELLS IN HOUSTON, SEATTLE, L.A., CHICAGO AND SIX OTHER CITIES.
WHAT DO YOU RECOMMEND?
REOPENING THE INTERNMENT CAMPS, THIS TIME AS NON-OPTIONAL...
NO.
THAT WON'T WORK TWICE, ELLARD.
SIT DOWN, JOHN. THIS IS OVER YOUR HEAD.
WHO'S THE SECRETARY OF RETURNER AFFAIRS?
JUST BECAUSE YOU'VE GOT AN OFFICE DOESN'T MEAN --
ANSWER THE QUESTION.
THERE ARE ONLY TWO POSSIBLE SOLUTIONS, GENTLEMEN.

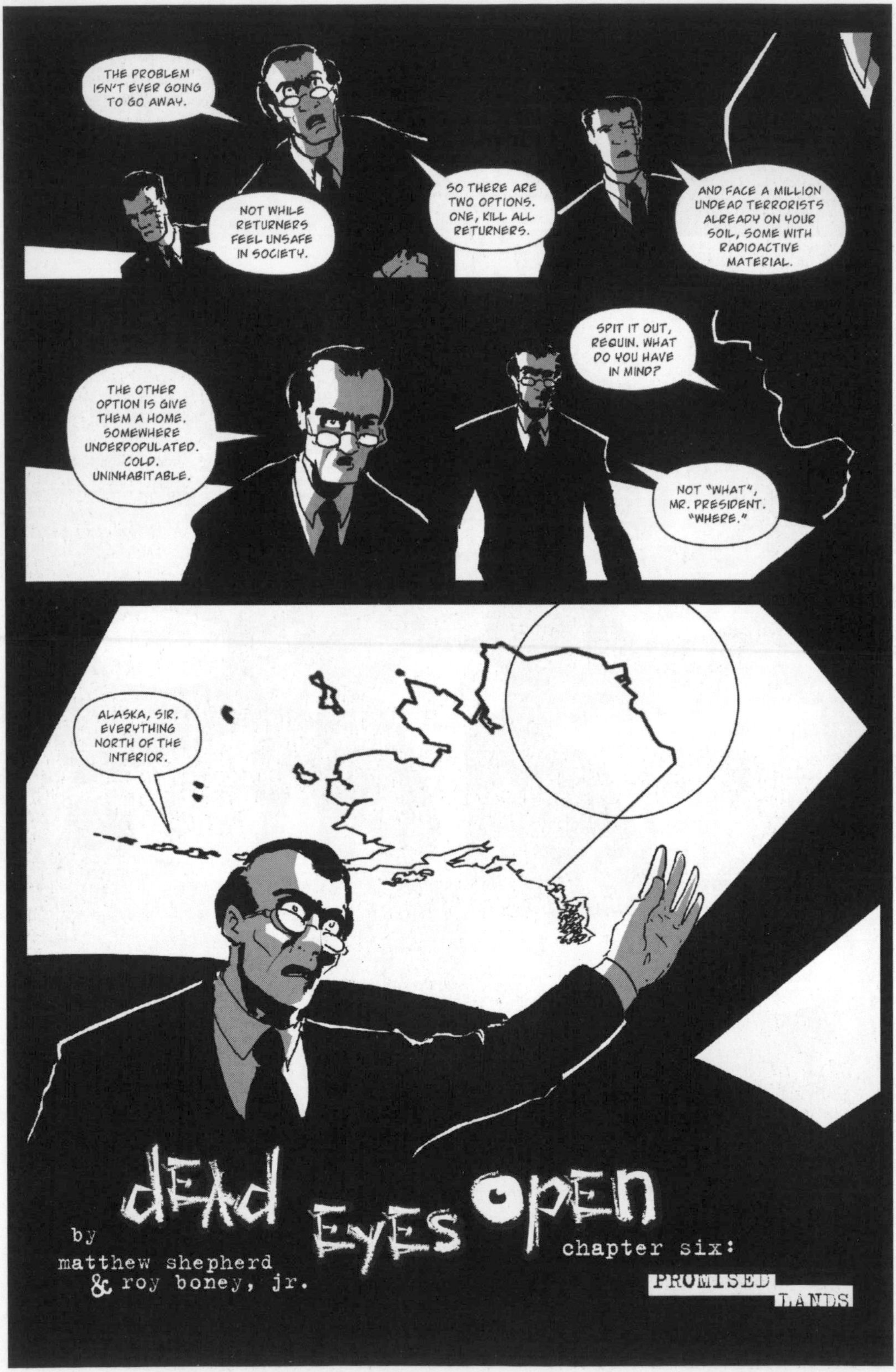
THE PROBLEM ISN'T EVER GOING TO GO AWAY.
NOT WHILE RETURNERS FEEL UNSAFE IN SOCIETY.
SO THERE ARE TWO OPTIONS. ONE, KILL ALL RETURNERS.
AND FACE A MILLION UNDEAD TERRORISTS ALREADY ON YOUR SOIL, SOME WITH RADIOACTIVE MATERIAL.
THE OTHER OPTION IS GIVE THEM A HOME. SOMEWHERE UNDERPOPULATED. COLD. UNINHABITABLE.
SPIT IT OUT, REQUIN. WHAT DO YOU HAVE IN MIND?
NOT "WHAT", MR. PRESIDENT. "WHERE."
ALASKA, SIR. EVERYTHING NORTH OF THE INTERIOR.
dEAd EYES OPEN
by
matthew shepherd
& roy boney, jr.
chapter six:
PROMISED LANDS

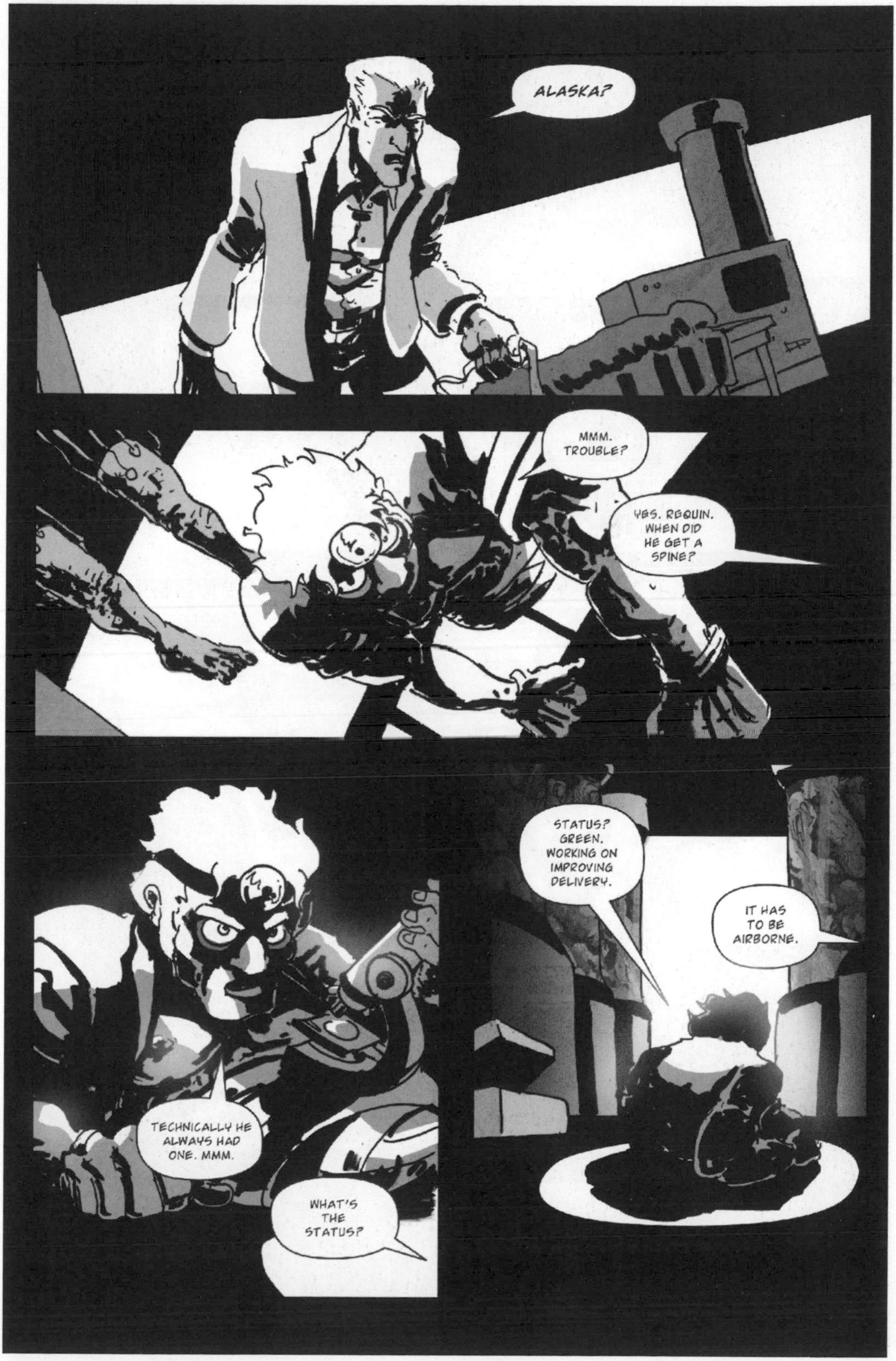
ALASKA?
MMM. TROUBLE?
YES. REQUIN. WHEN DID HE GET A SPINE?
TECHNICALLY HE ALWAYS HAD ONE. MMM.
WHAT'S THE STATUS?
STATUS? GREEN. WORKING ON IMPROVING DELIVERY.
IT HAS TO BE AIRBORNE.

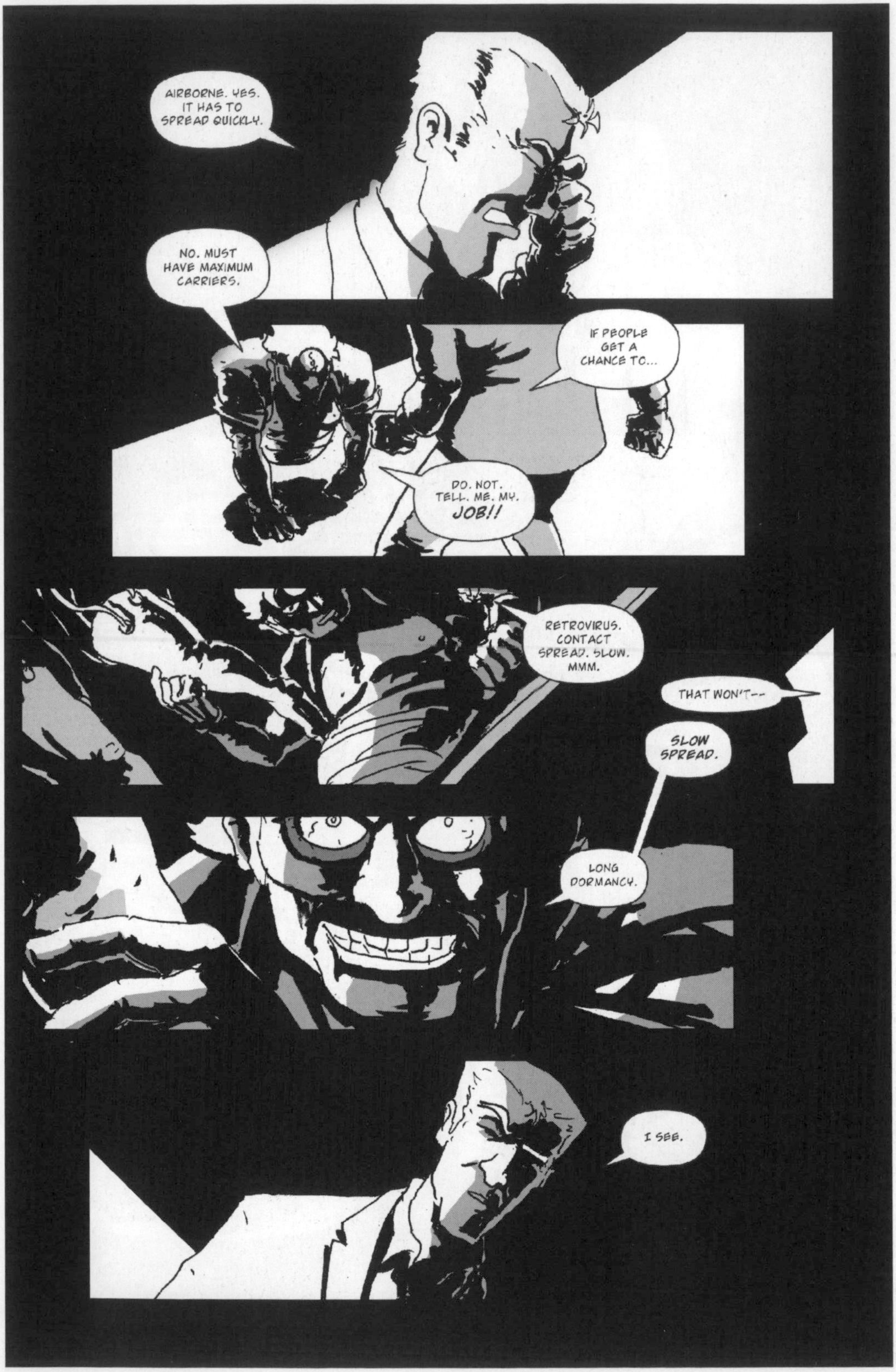
AIRBORNE. YES. IT HAS TO SPREAD QUICKLY.
NO. MUST HAVE MAXIMUM CARRIERS.
IF PEOPLE GET A CHANCE TO...
DO. NOT. TELL. ME. MY. JOB!!
RETROVIRUS. CONTACT SPREAD. SLOW. MMM.
THAT WON'T--
SLOW SPREAD.
LONG DORMANCY.
I SEE.

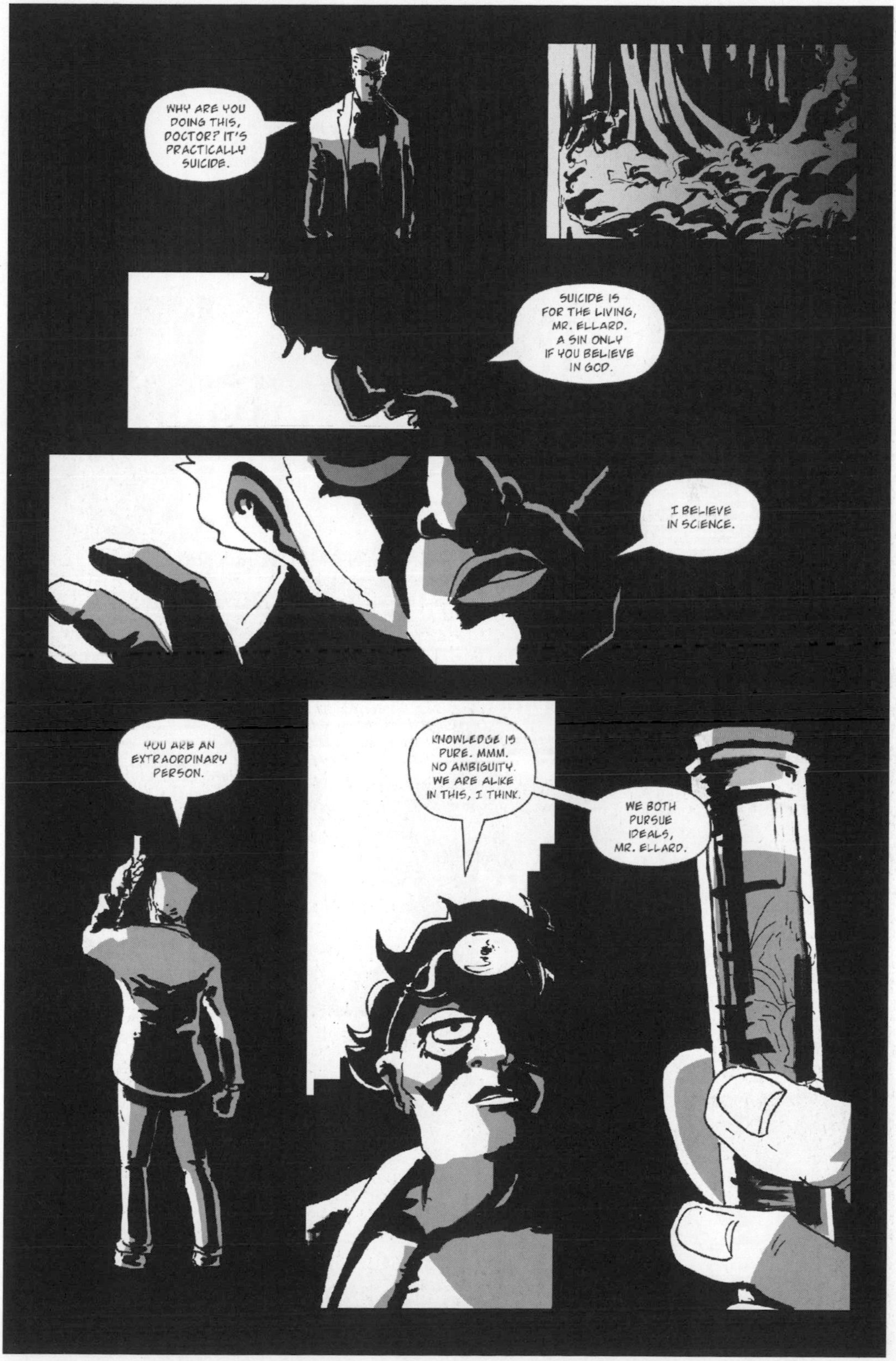
WHY ARE YOU DOING THIS, DOCTOR? IT'S PRACTICALLY SUICIDE.
SUICIDE IS FOR THE LIVING, MR. ELLARD. A SIN ONLY IF YOU BELIEVE IN GOD.
I BELIEVE IN SCIENCE.
YOU ARE AN EXTRAORDINARY PERSON.
KNOWLEDGE IS PURE. MMM. NO AMBIGUITY. WE ARE ALIKE IN THIS, I THINK.
WE BOTH PURSUE IDEALS, MR. ELLARD.

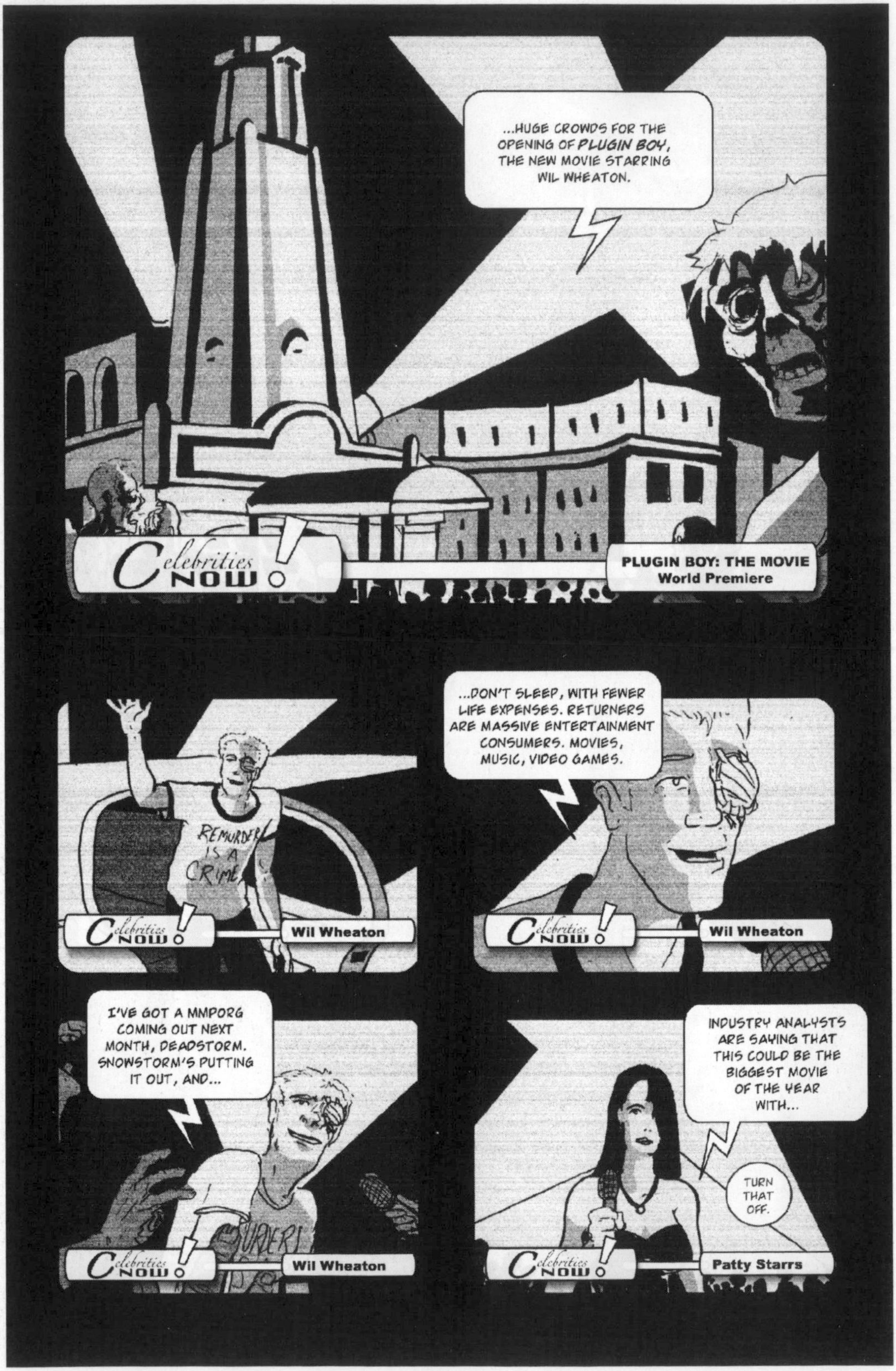
...HUGE CROWDS FOR THE OPENING OF PLUGIN BOY, THE NEW MOVIE STARRING WIL WHEATON.
Celebrities NOW!
PLUGIN BOY: THE MOVIE
World Premiere
REMURDER IS A CRIME
Celebrities NOW!
Wil Wheaton
...DON'T SLEEP, WITH FEWER LIFE EXPENSES. RETURNERS ARE MASSIVE ENTERTAINMENT CONSUMERS. MOVIES, MUSIC, VIDEO GAMES.
Celebrities NOW!
Wil Wheaton
I'VE GOT A MMPORG COMING OUT NEXT MONTH, DEADSTORM. SNOWSTORM'S PUTTING IT OUT, AND...
Celebrities NOW!
Wil Wheaton
INDUSTRY ANALYSTS ARE SAYING THAT THIS COULD BE THE BIGGEST MOVIE OF THE YEAR WITH...
TURN THAT OFF.
Celebrities NOW!
Patty Starrs

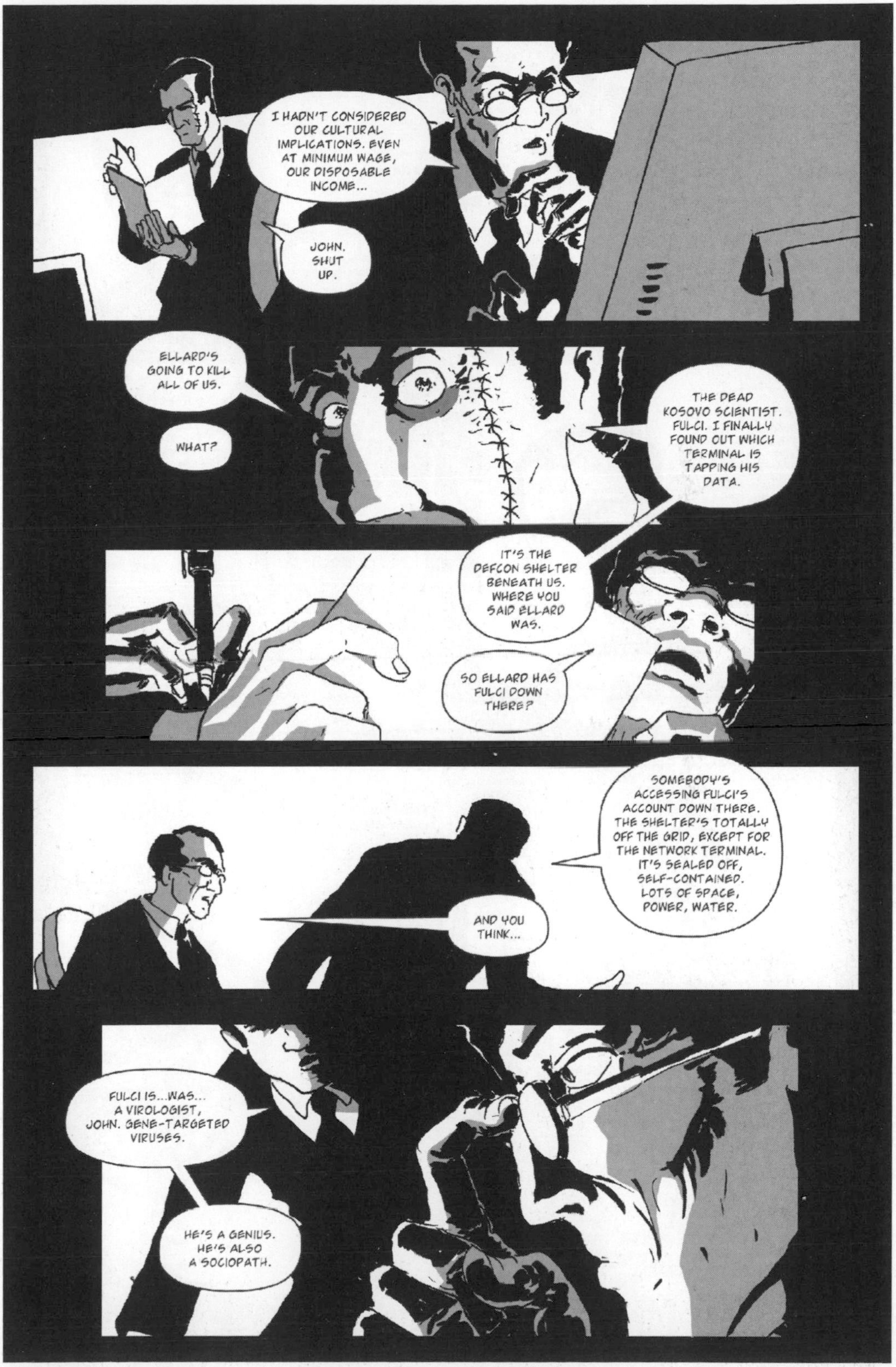
I HADN'T CONSIDERED OUR CULTURAL IMPLICATIONS. EVEN AT MINIMUM WAGE, OUR DISPOSABLE INCOME...
JOHN. SHUT UP.
ELLARD'S GOING TO KILL ALL OF US.
WHAT?
THE DEAD KOSOVO SCIENTIST. FULCI. I FINALLY FOUND OUT WHICH TERMINAL IS TAPPING HIS DATA.
IT'S THE DEFCON SHELTER BENEATH US. WHERE YOU SAID ELLARD WAS.
SO ELLARD HAS FULCI DOWN THERE?
SOMEBODY'S ACCESSING FULCI'S ACCOUNT DOWN THERE. THE SHELTER'S TOTALLY OFF THE GRID, EXCEPT FOR THE NETWORK TERMINAL. IT'S SEALED OFF, SELF-CONTAINED. LOTS OF SPACE, POWER, WATER.
AND YOU THINK...
FULCI IS...WAS... A VIROLOGIST, JOHN. GENE-TARGETED VIRUSES.
HE'S A GENIUS. HE'S ALSO A SOCIOPATH.

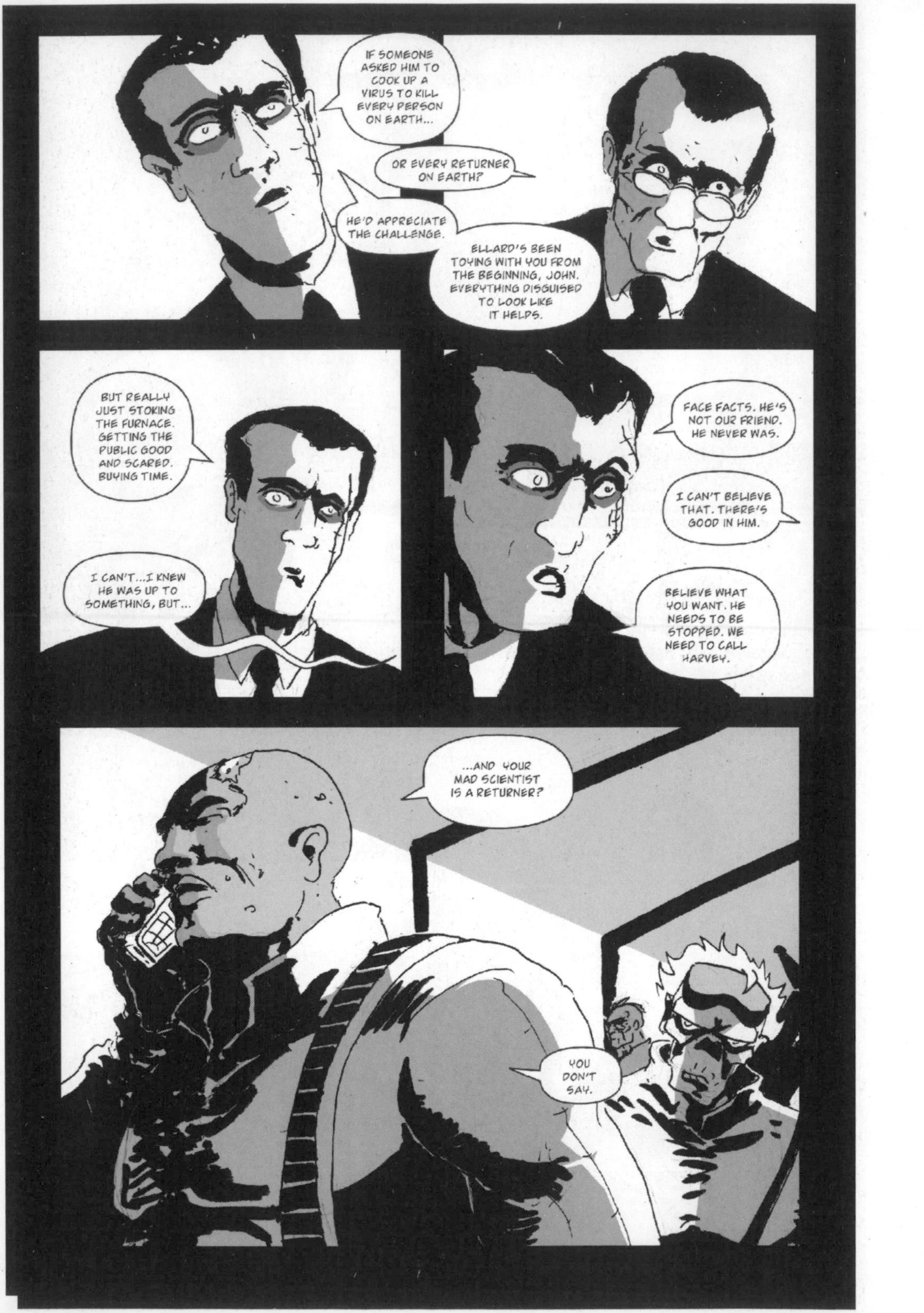
IF SOMEONE ASKED HIM TO COOK UP A VIRUS TO KILL EVERY PERSON ON EARTH...
OR EVERY RETURNER ON EARTH?
HE'D APPRECIATE THE CHALLENGE.
ELLARD'S BEEN TOYING WITH YOU FROM THE BEGINNING, JOHN. EVERYTHING DISGUISED TO LOOK LIKE IT HELPS.
BUT REALLY JUST STOKING THE FURNACE. GETTING THE PUBLIC GOOD AND SCARED. BUYING TIME.
I CAN'T...I KNEW HE WAS UP TO SOMETHING, BUT...
FACE FACTS. HE'S NOT OUR FRIEND. HE NEVER WAS.
I CAN'T BELIEVE THAT. THERE'S GOOD IN HIM.
BELIEVE WHAT YOU WANT. HE NEEDS TO BE STOPPED. WE NEED TO CALL HARVEY.
...AND YOUR MAD SCIENTIST IS A RETURNER?
YOU DON'T SAY.

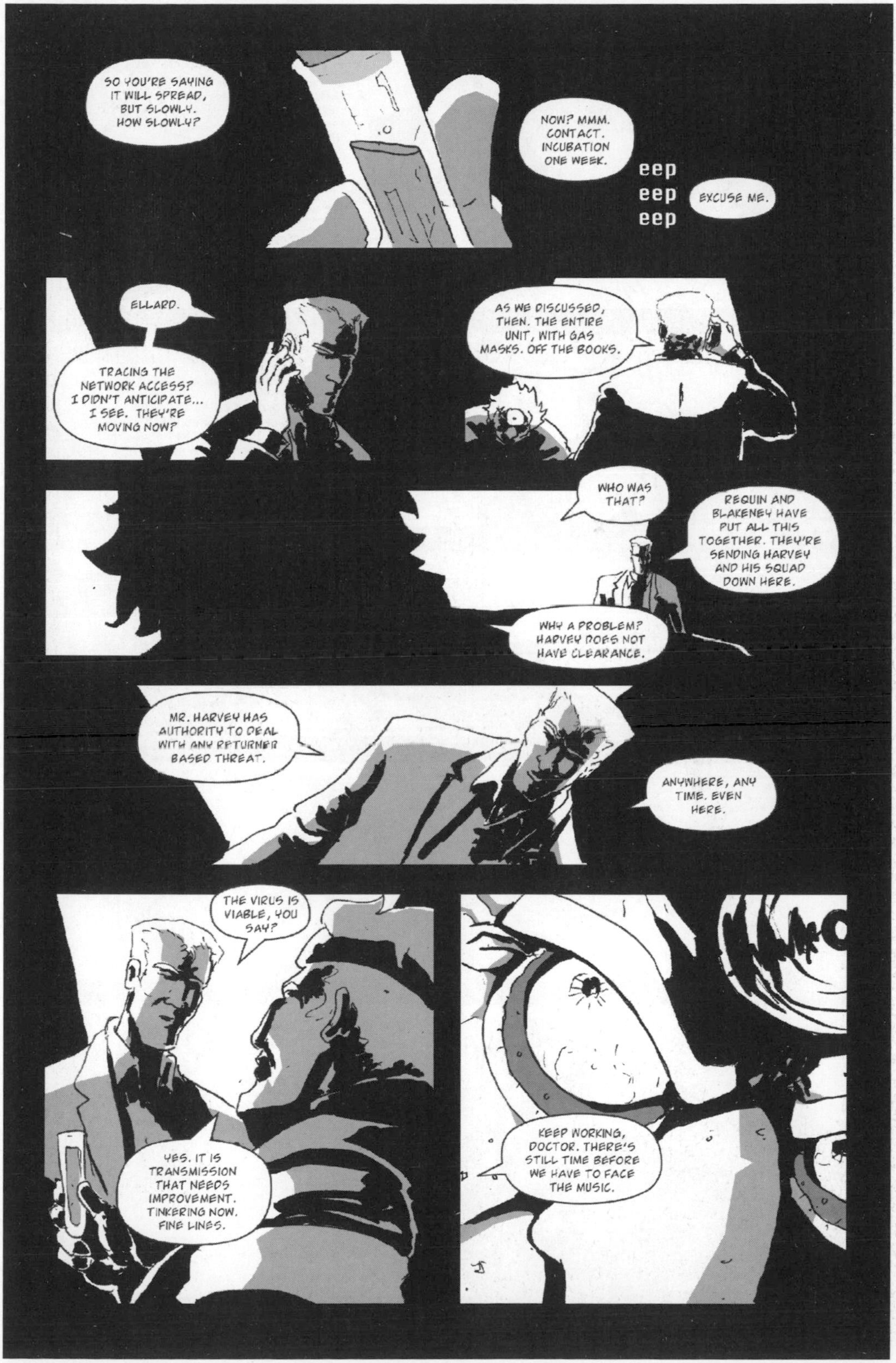
SO YOU'RE SAYING IT WILL SPREAD, BUT SLOWLY. HOW SLOWLY?
NOW? MMM. CONTACT. INCUBATION ONE WEEK.
eep eep eep
EXCUSE ME.
ELLARD.
TRACING THE NETWORK ACCESS? I DIDN'T ANTICIPATE... I SEE. THEY'RE MOVING NOW?
AS WE DISCUSSED, THEN. THE ENTIRE UNIT, WITH GAS MASKS. OFF THE BOOKS.
WHO WAS THAT?
REQUIN AND BLAKENEY HAVE PUT ALL THIS TOGETHER. THEY'RE SENDING HARVEY AND HIS SQUAD DOWN HERE.
WHY A PROBLEM? HARVEY DOES NOT HAVE CLEARANCE.
MR. HARVEY HAS AUTHORITY TO DEAL WITH ANY RETURNER BASED THREAT.
ANYWHERE, ANY TIME. EVEN HERE.
THE VIRUS IS VIABLE, YOU SAY?
YES. IT IS TRANSMISSION THAT NEEDS IMPROVEMENT. TINKERING NOW. FINE LINES.
KEEP WORKING, DOCTOR. THERE'S STILL TIME BEFORE WE HAVE TO FACE THE MUSIC.

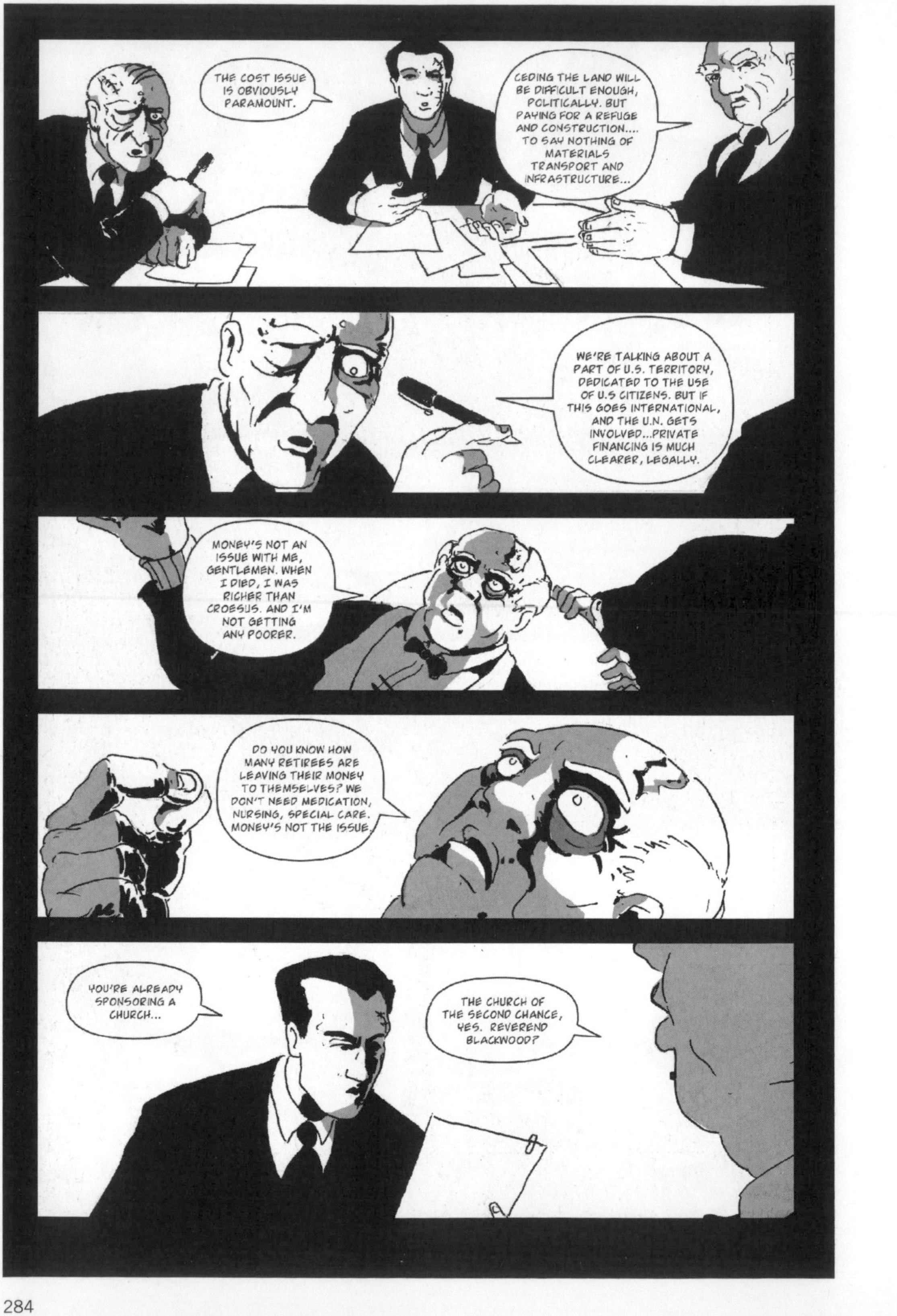
THE COST ISSUE IS OBVIOUSLY PARAMOUNT.
CEDING THE LAND WILL BE DIFFICULT ENOUGH, POLITICALLY. BUT PAYING FOR A REFUGE AND CONSTRUCTION.... TO SAY NOTHING OF MATERIALS TRANSPORT AND INFRASTRUCTURE...
WE'RE TALKING ABOUT A PART OF U.S. TERRITORY, DEDICATED TO THE USE OF U.S CITIZENS. BUT IF THIS GOES INTERNATIONAL, AND THE U.N. GETS INVOLVED...PRIVATE FINANCING IS MUCH CLEARER, LEGALLY.
MONEY'S NOT AN ISSUE WITH ME, GENTLEMEN. WHEN I DIED, I WAS RICHER THAN CROESUS. AND I'M NOT GETTING ANY POORER.
DO YOU KNOW HOW MANY RETIREES ARE LEAVING THEIR MONEY TO THEMSELVES? WE DON'T NEED MEDICATION, NURSING, SPECIAL CARE. MONEY'S NOT THE ISSUE.
YOU'RE ALREADY SPONSORING A CHURCH...
THE CHURCH OF THE SECOND CHANCE, YES. REVEREND BLACKWOOD?

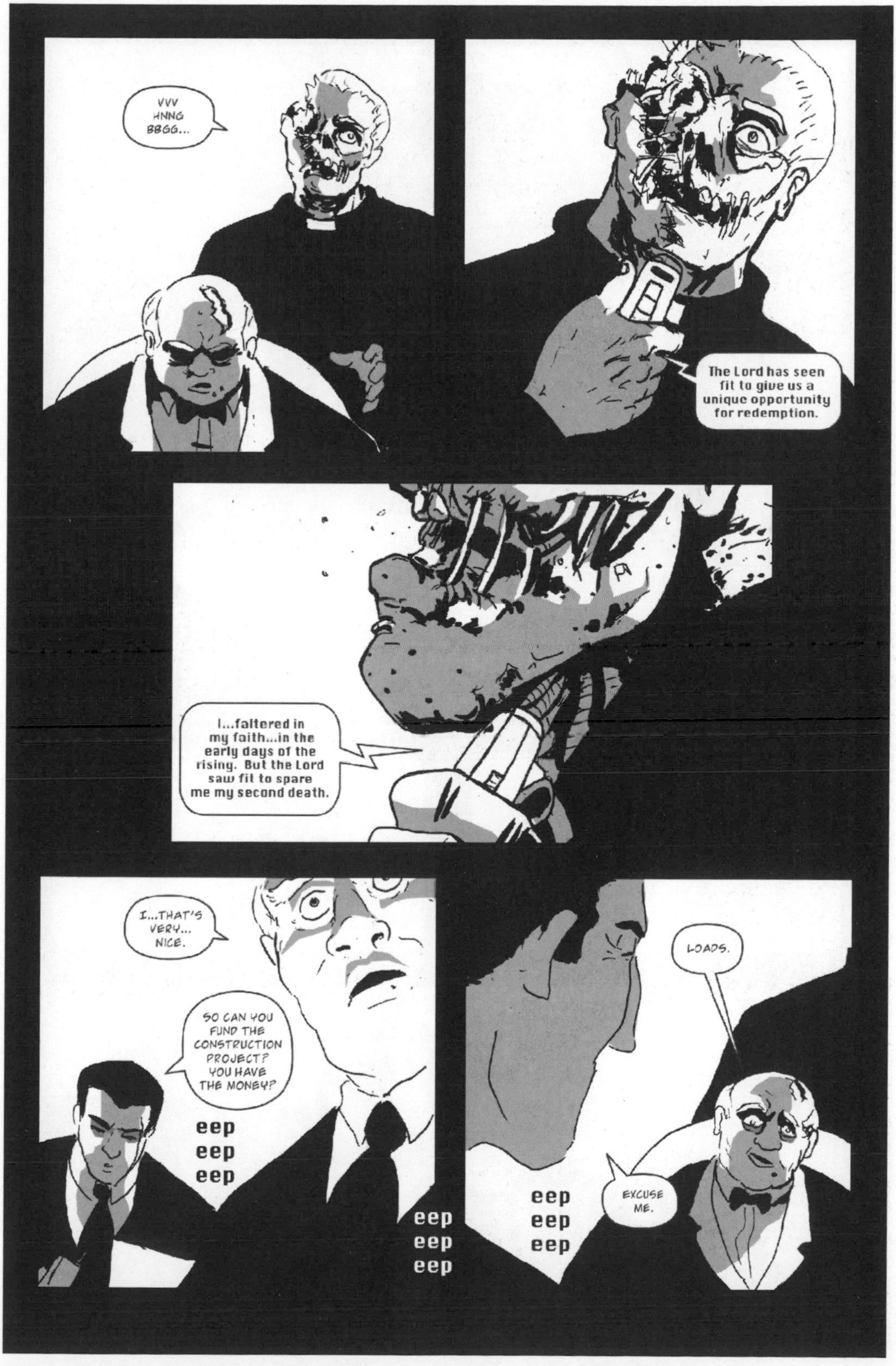
VVV
HNNG
BBGG...
The Lord has seen fit to give us a unique opportunity for redemption.
I...faltered in my faith...in the early days of the rising. But the Lord saw fit to spare me my second death.
I...THAT'S VERY... NICE.
SO CAN YOU FUND THE CONSTRUCTION PROJECT? YOU HAVE THE MONEY?
eep
eep
eep
eep
eep
eep
LOADS.
eep
eep
eep
EXCUSE ME.

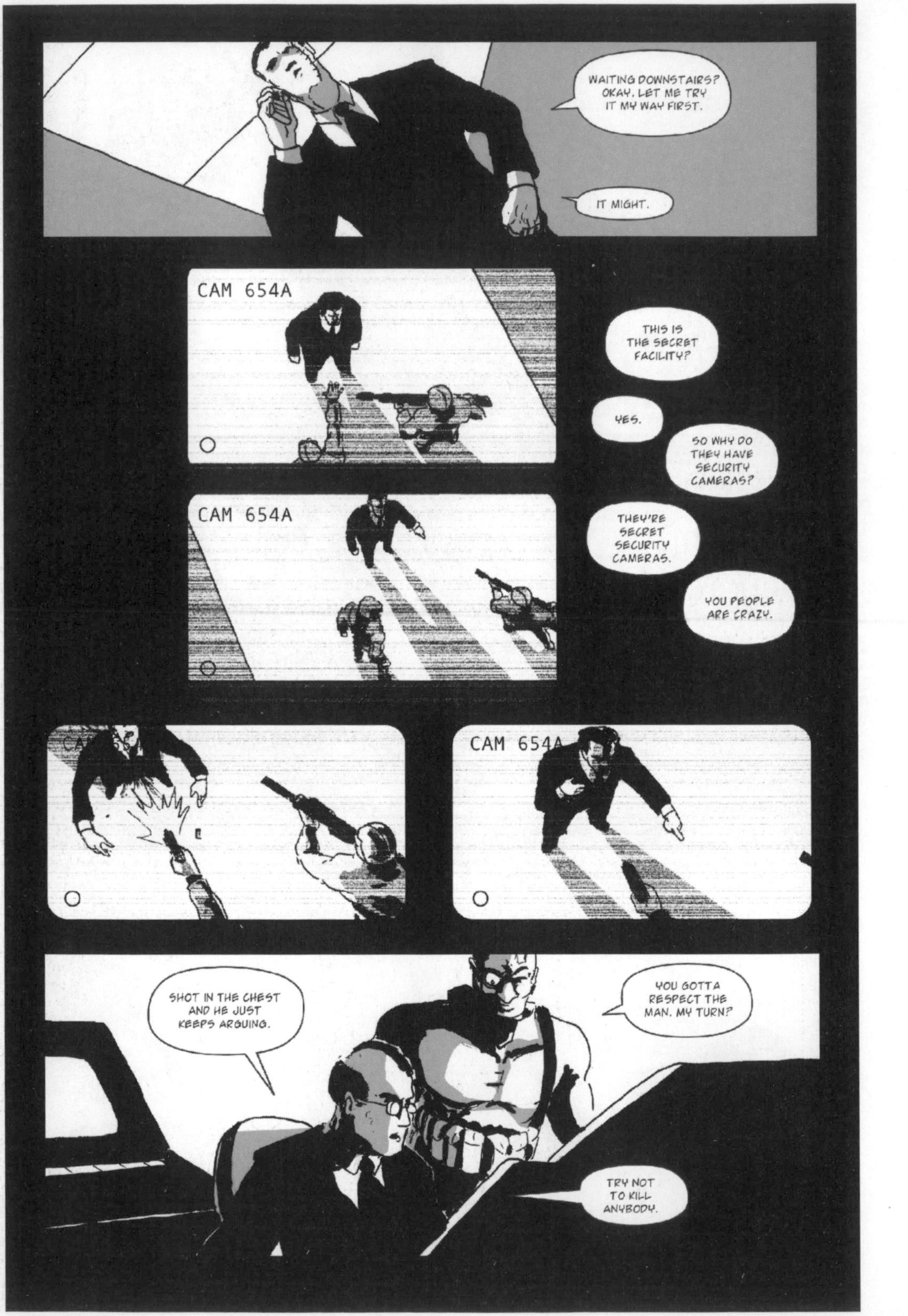
WAITING DOWNSTAIRS? OKAY. LET ME TRY IT MY WAY FIRST.
IT MIGHT.
CAM 654A
THIS IS THE SECRET FACILITY?
YES.
SO WHY DO THEY HAVE SECURITY CAMERAS?
CAM 654A
THEY'RE SECRET SECURITY CAMERAS.
YOU PEOPLE ARE CRAZY.
CAM 654A
SHOT IN THE CHEST AND HE JUST KEEPS ARGUING.
YOU GOTTA RESPECT THE MAN. MY TURN?
TRY NOT TO KILL ANYBODY.

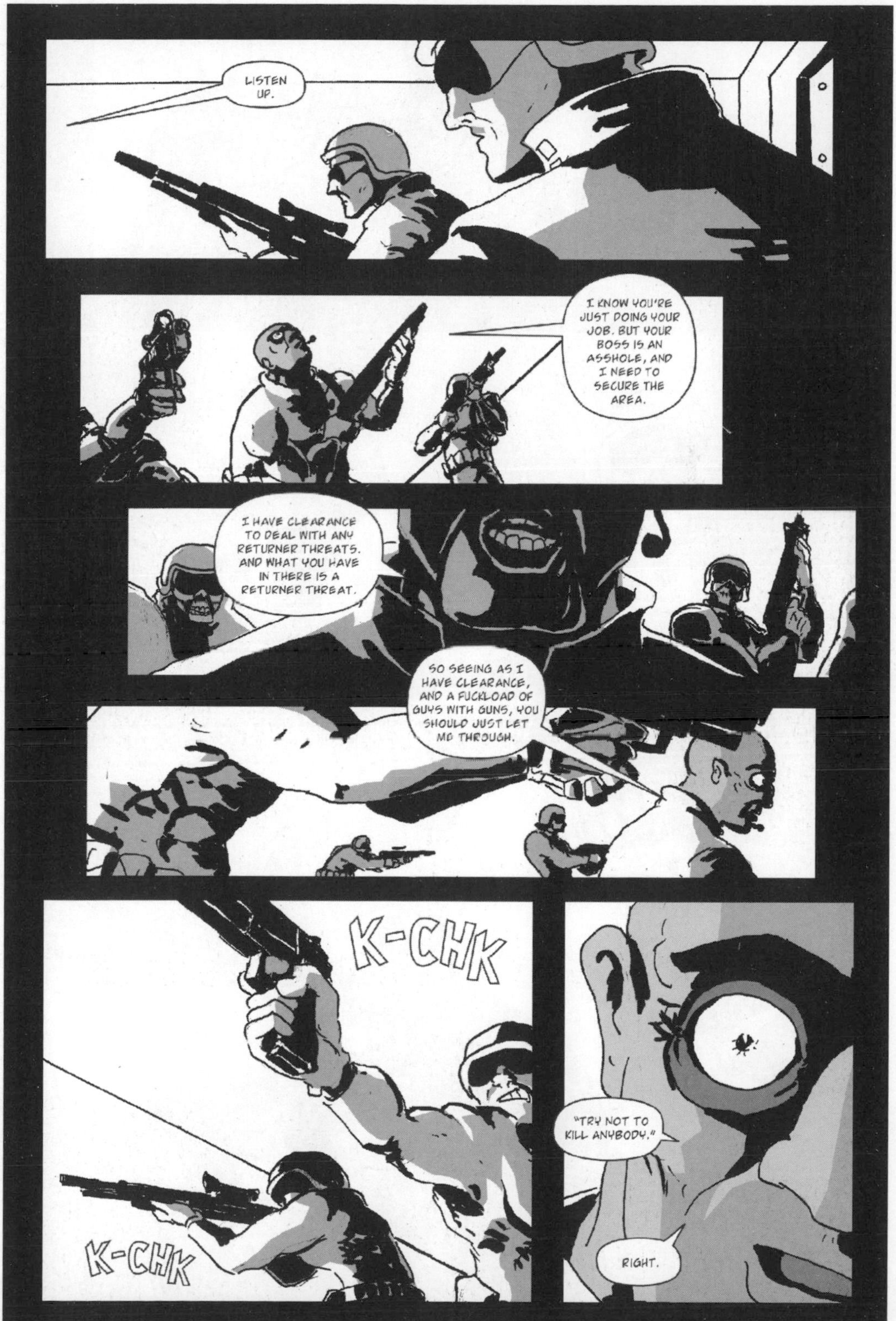
LISTEN UP.
I KNOW YOU'RE JUST DOING YOUR JOB. BUT YOUR BOSS IS AN ASSHOLE, AND I NEED TO SECURE THE AREA.
I HAVE CLEARANCE TO DEAL WITH ANY RETURNER THREATS. AND WHAT YOU HAVE IN THERE IS A RETURNER THREAT.
SO SEEING AS I HAVE CLEARANCE, AND A FUCKLOAD OF GUYS WITH GUNS, YOU SHOULD JUST LET ME THROUGH.
K-CHK
K-CHK
"TRY NOT TO KILL ANYBODY."
RIGHT.

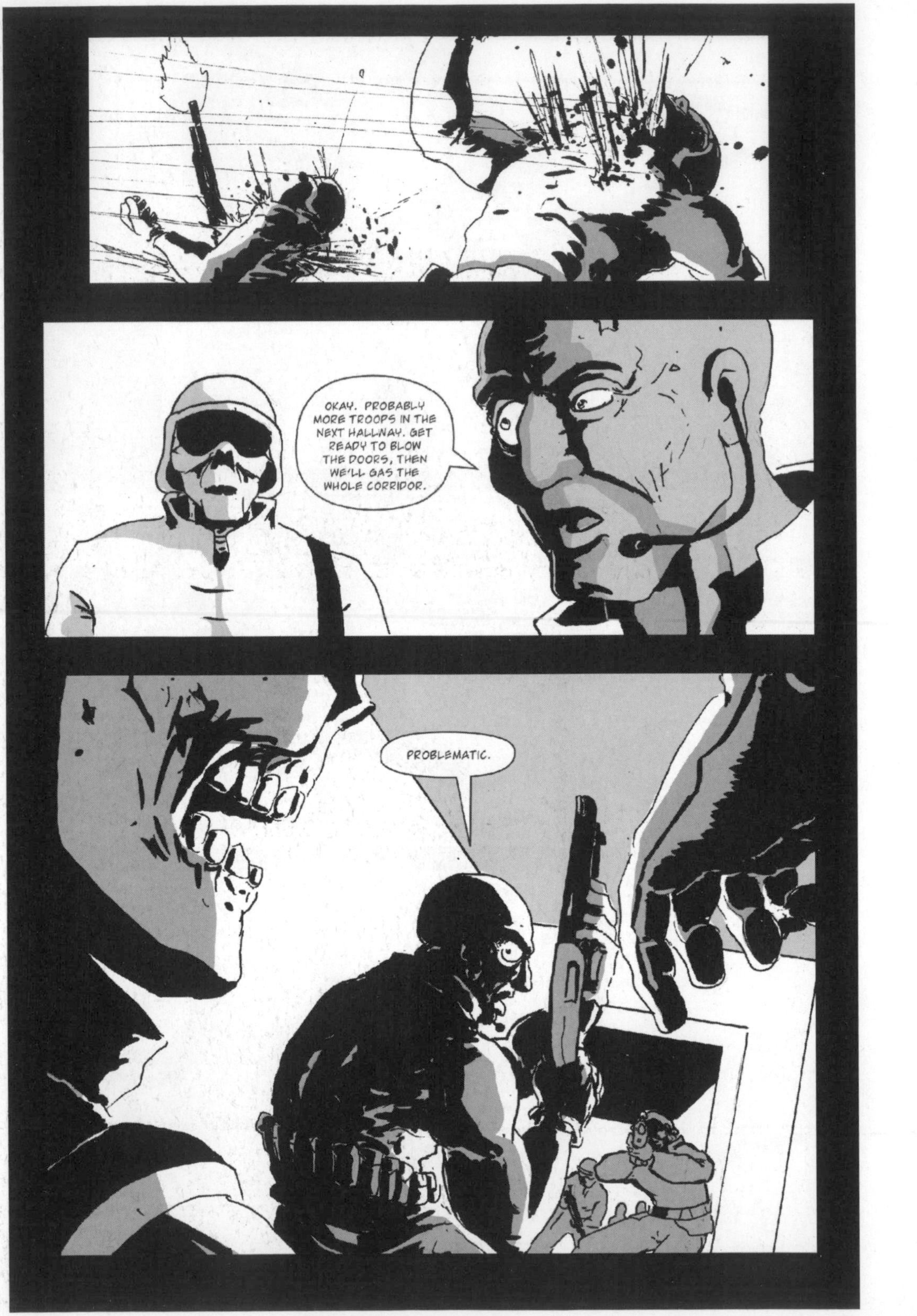
OKAY. PROBABLY MORE TROOPS IN THE NEXT HALLWAY. GET READY TO BLOW THE DOORS, THEN WE'LL GAS THE WHOLE CORRIDOR.
PROBLEMATIC.

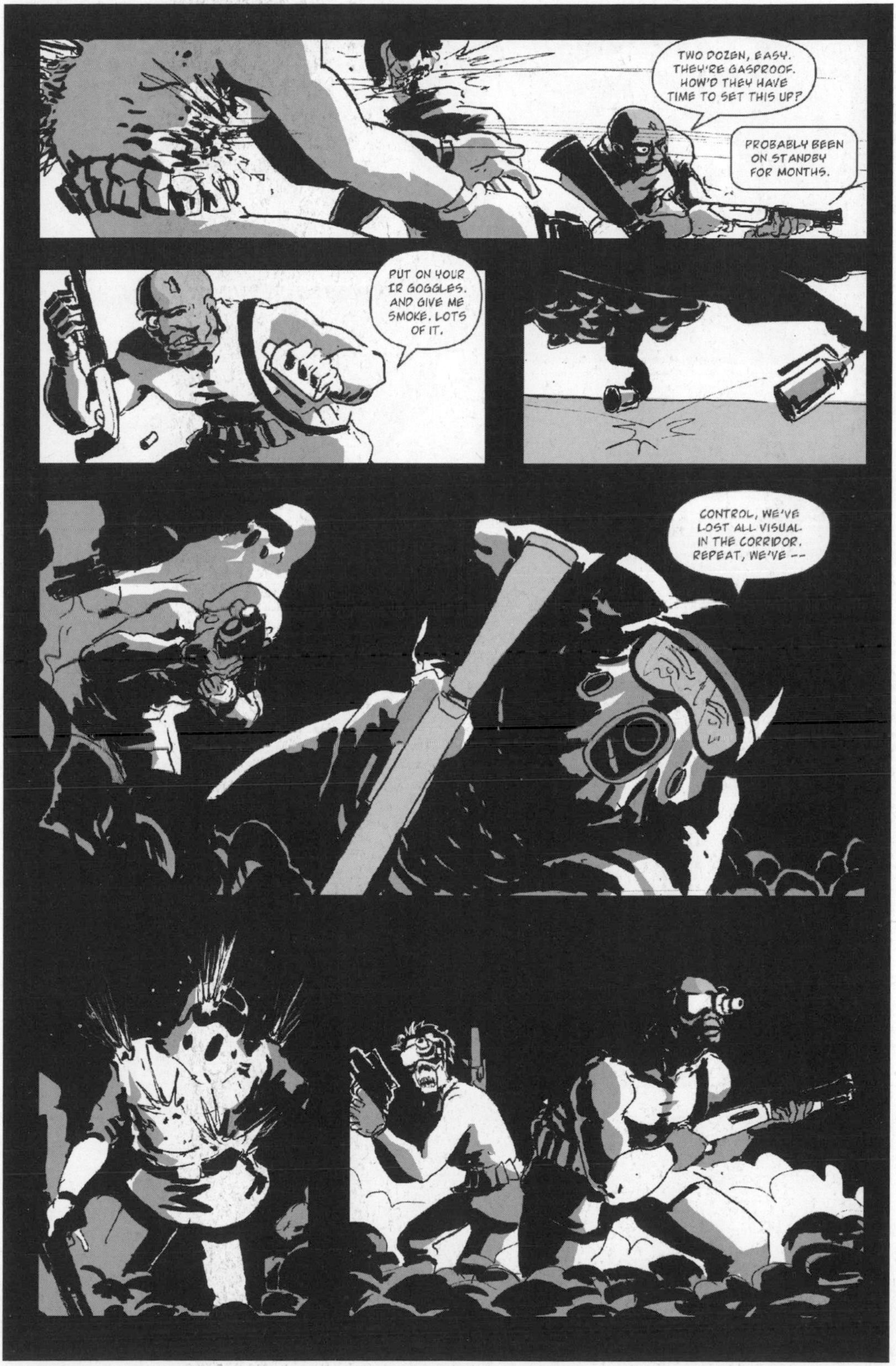
TWO DOZEN, EASY. THEY'RE GASPROOF. HOW'D THEY HAVE TIME TO SET THIS UP?
PROBABLY BEEN ON STANDBY FOR MONTHS.
PUT ON YOUR IR GOGGLES. AND GIVE ME SMOKE. LOTS OF IT.
CONTROL, WE'VE LOST ALL VISUAL IN THE CORRIDOR. REPEAT, WE'VE --

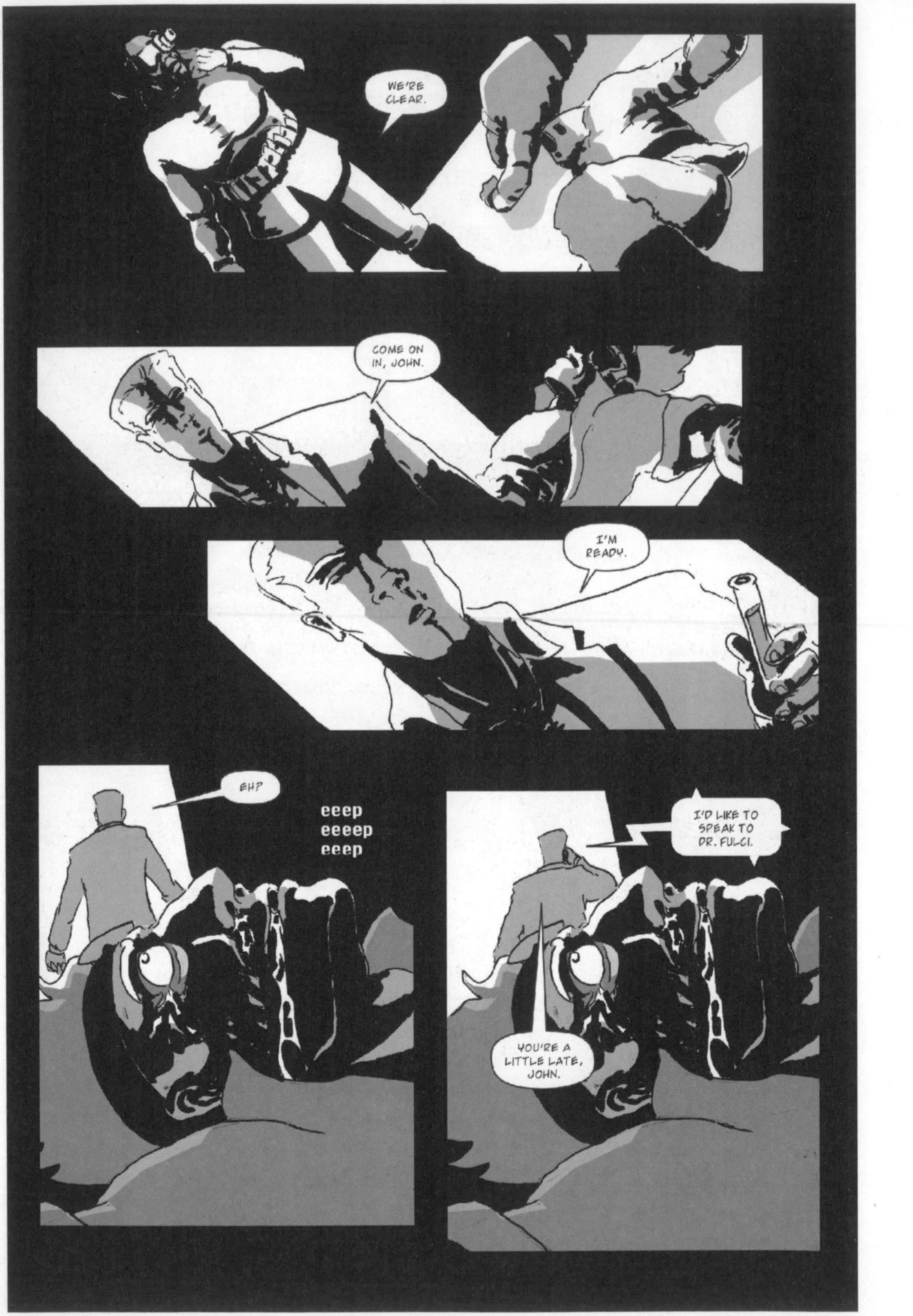
WE'RE CLEAR.
COME ON IN, JOHN.
I'M READY.
EH?
eeep
eeeep
eeep
I'D LIKE TO SPEAK TO DR. FULCI.
YOU'RE A LITTLE LATE, JOHN.

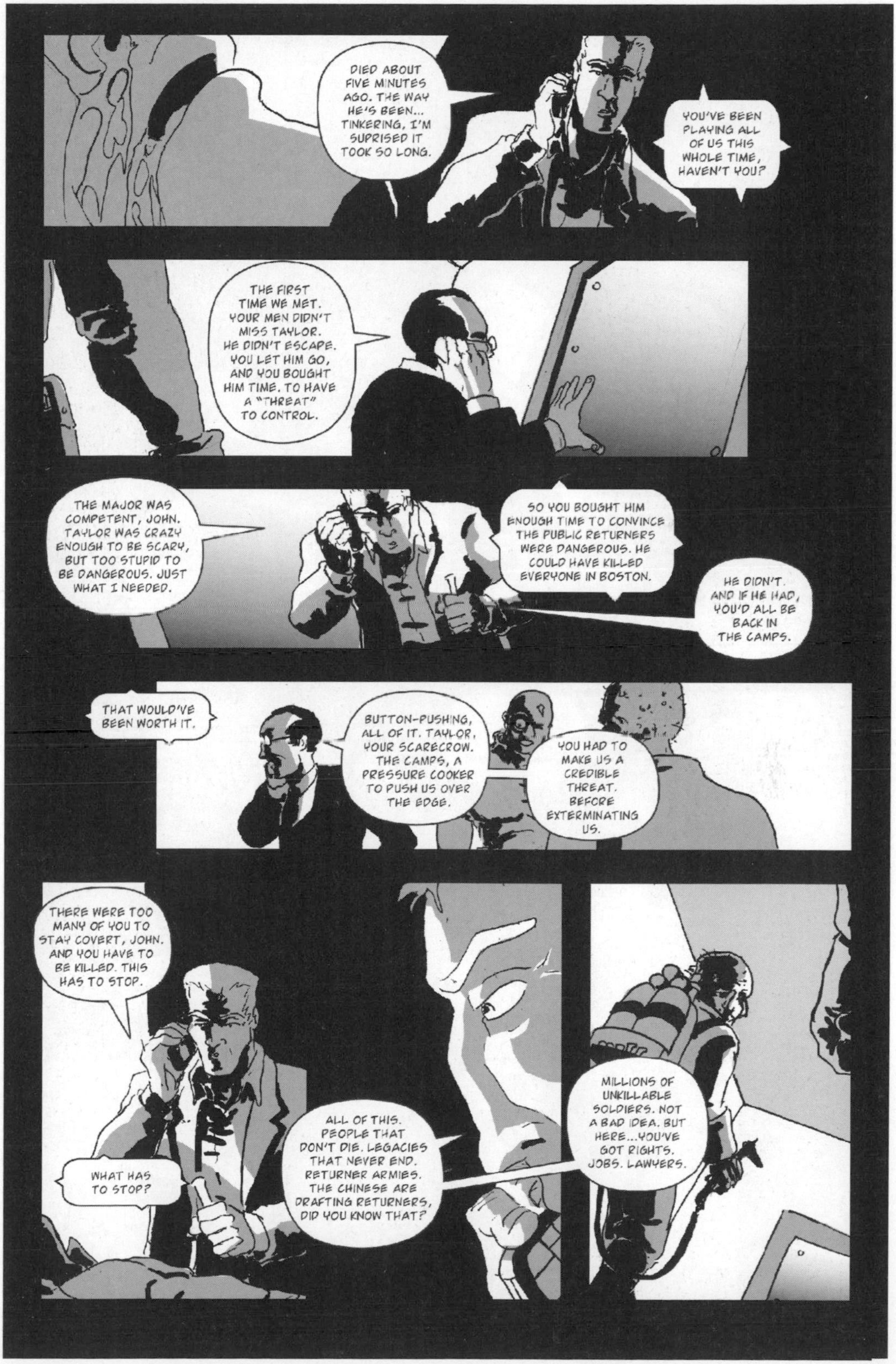
DIED ABOUT FIVE MINUTES AGO. THE WAY HE'S BEEN... TINKERING, I'M SUPRISED IT TOOK SO LONG.
YOU'VE BEEN PLAYING ALL OF US THIS WHOLE TIME, HAVEN'T YOU?
THE FIRST TIME WE MET. YOUR MEN DIDN'T MISS TAYLOR. HE DIDN'T ESCAPE. YOU LET HIM GO, AND YOU BOUGHT HIM TIME. TO HAVE A "THREAT" TO CONTROL.
THE MAJOR WAS COMPETENT, JOHN. TAYLOR WAS CRAZY ENOUGH TO BE SCARY, BUT TOO STUPID TO BE DANGEROUS. JUST WHAT I NEEDED.
SO YOU BOUGHT HIM ENOUGH TIME TO CONVINCE THE PUBLIC RETURNERS WERE DANGEROUS. HE COULD HAVE KILLED EVERYONE IN BOSTON.
HE DIDN'T. AND IF HE HAD, YOU'D ALL BE BACK IN THE CAMPS.
THAT WOULD'VE BEEN WORTH IT.
BUTTON-PUSHING, ALL OF IT. TAYLOR, YOUR SCARECROW. THE CAMPS, A PRESSURE COOKER TO PUSH US OVER THE EDGE.
YOU HAD TO MAKE US A CREDIBLE THREAT. BEFORE EXTERMINATING US.
THERE WERE TOO MANY OF YOU TO STAY COVERT, JOHN. AND YOU HAVE TO BE KILLED. THIS HAS TO STOP.
WHAT HAS TO STOP?
ALL OF THIS. PEOPLE THAT DON'T DIE. LEGACIES THAT NEVER END. RETURNER ARMIES. THE CHINESE ARE DRAFTING RETURNERS, DID YOU KNOW THAT?
MILLIONS OF UNKILLABLE SOLDIERS. NOT A BAD IDEA. BUT HERE...YOU'VE GOT RIGHTS. JOBS. LAWYERS.

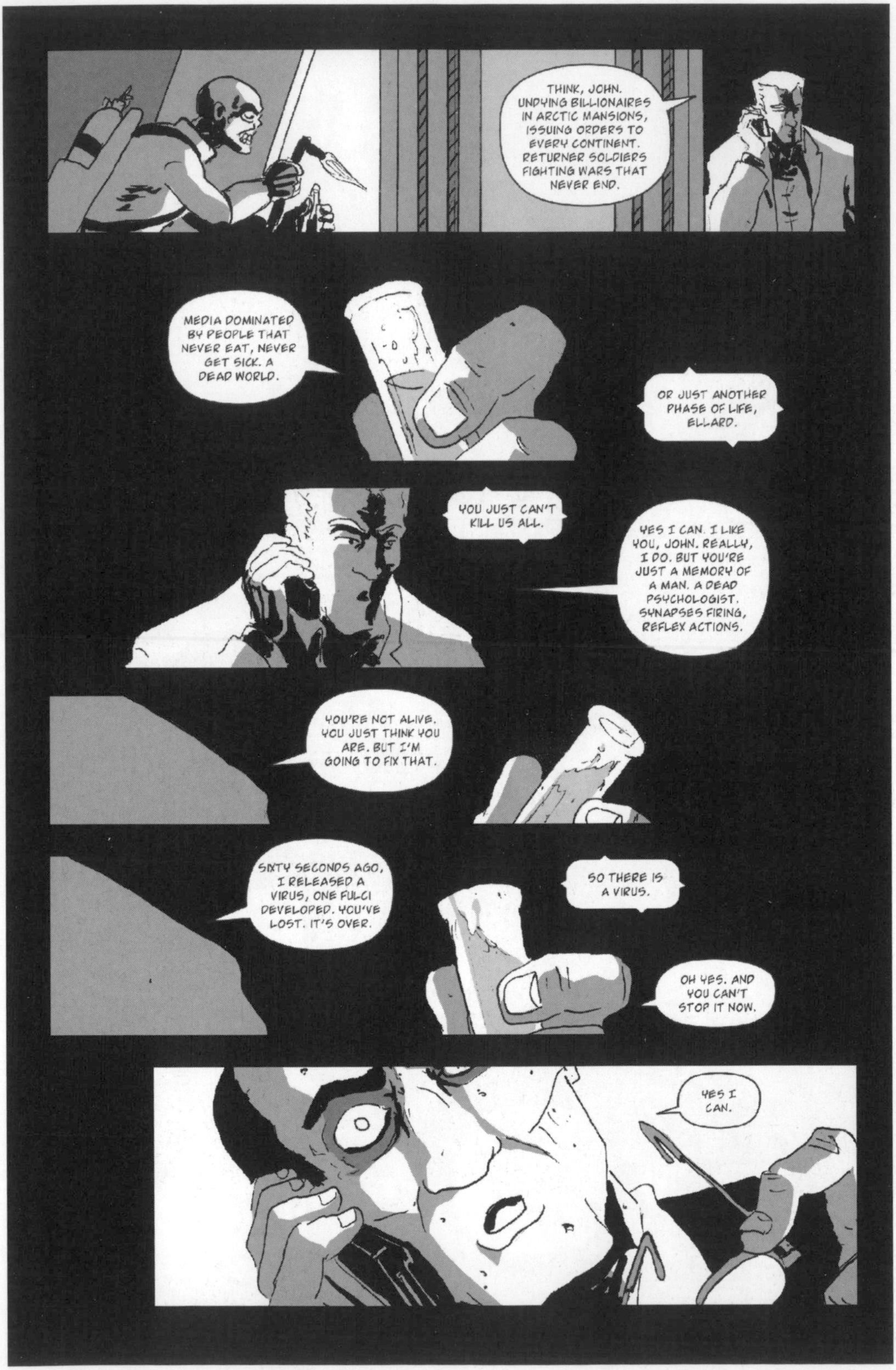
THINK, JOHN. UNDYING BILLIONAIRES IN ARCTIC MANSIONS, ISSUING ORDERS TO EVERY CONTINENT. RETURNER SOLDIERS FIGHTING WARS THAT NEVER END.
MEDIA DOMINATED BY PEOPLE THAT NEVER EAT, NEVER GET SICK. A DEAD WORLD.
OR JUST ANOTHER PHASE OF LIFE, ELLARD.
YOU JUST CAN'T KILL US ALL.
YES I CAN. I LIKE YOU, JOHN. REALLY, I DO. BUT YOU'RE JUST A MEMORY OF A MAN. A DEAD PSYCHOLOGIST. SYNAPSES FIRING, REFLEX ACTIONS.
YOU'RE NOT ALIVE. YOU JUST THINK YOU ARE. BUT I'M GOING TO FIX THAT.
SIXTY SECONDS AGO, I RELEASED A VIRUS, ONE FULCI DEVELOPED. YOU'VE LOST. IT'S OVER.
SO THERE IS A VIRUS.
OH YES. AND YOU CAN'T STOP IT NOW.
YES I CAN.

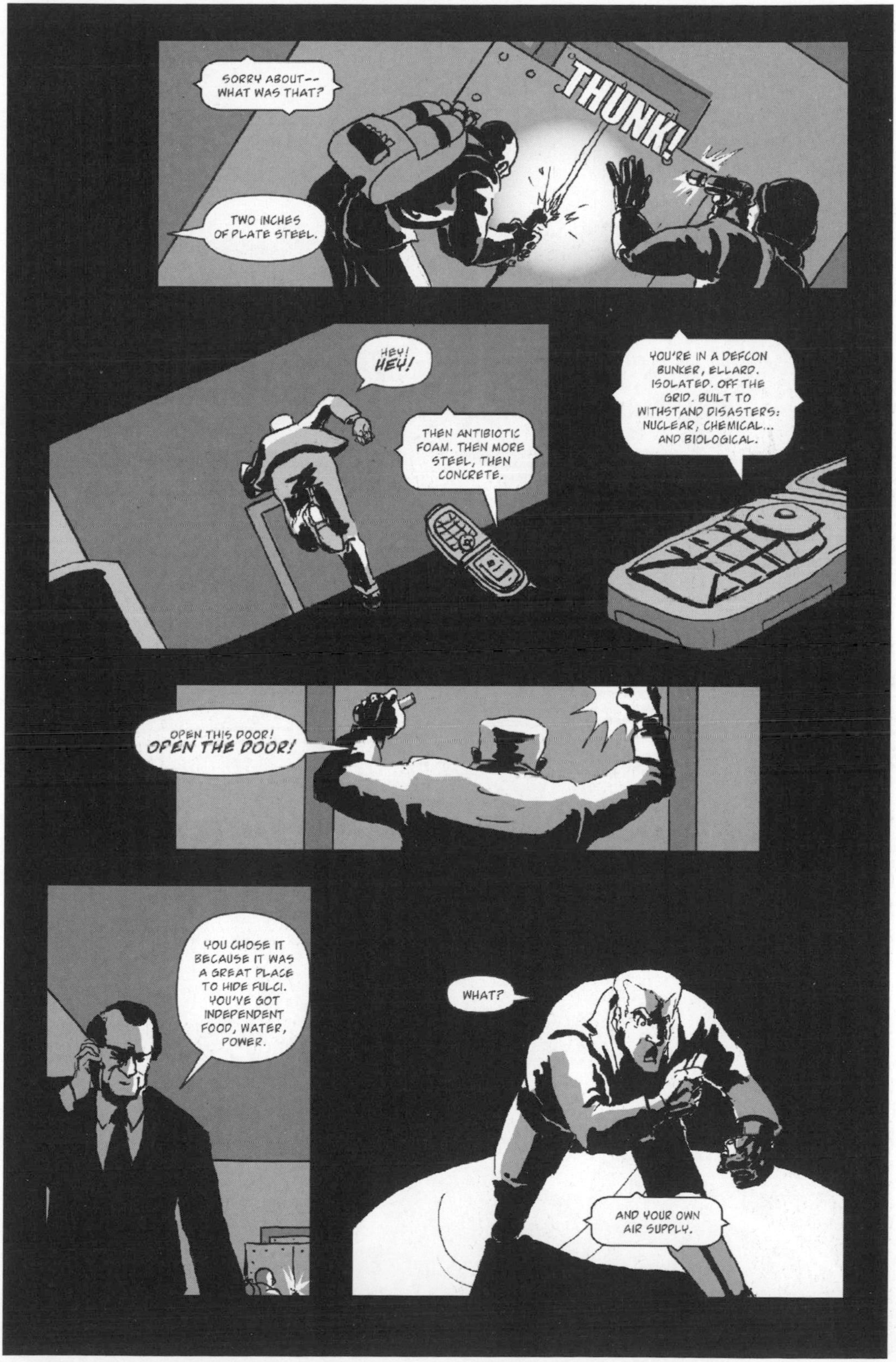
SORRY ABOUT-- WHAT WAS THAT?
THUNK!
TWO INCHES OF PLATE STEEL.
HEY! HEY!
THEN ANTIBIOTIC FOAM. THEN MORE STEEL, THEN CONCRETE.
YOU'RE IN A DEFCON BUNKER, ELLARD. ISOLATED. OFF THE GRID. BUILT TO WITHSTAND DISASTERS: NUCLEAR, CHEMICAL... AND BIOLOGICAL.
OPEN THIS DOOR! OPEN THE DOOR!
YOU CHOSE IT BECAUSE IT WAS A GREAT PLACE TO HIDE FULCI. YOU'VE GOT INDEPENDENT FOOD, WATER, POWER.
WHAT?
AND YOUR OWN AIR SUPPLY.

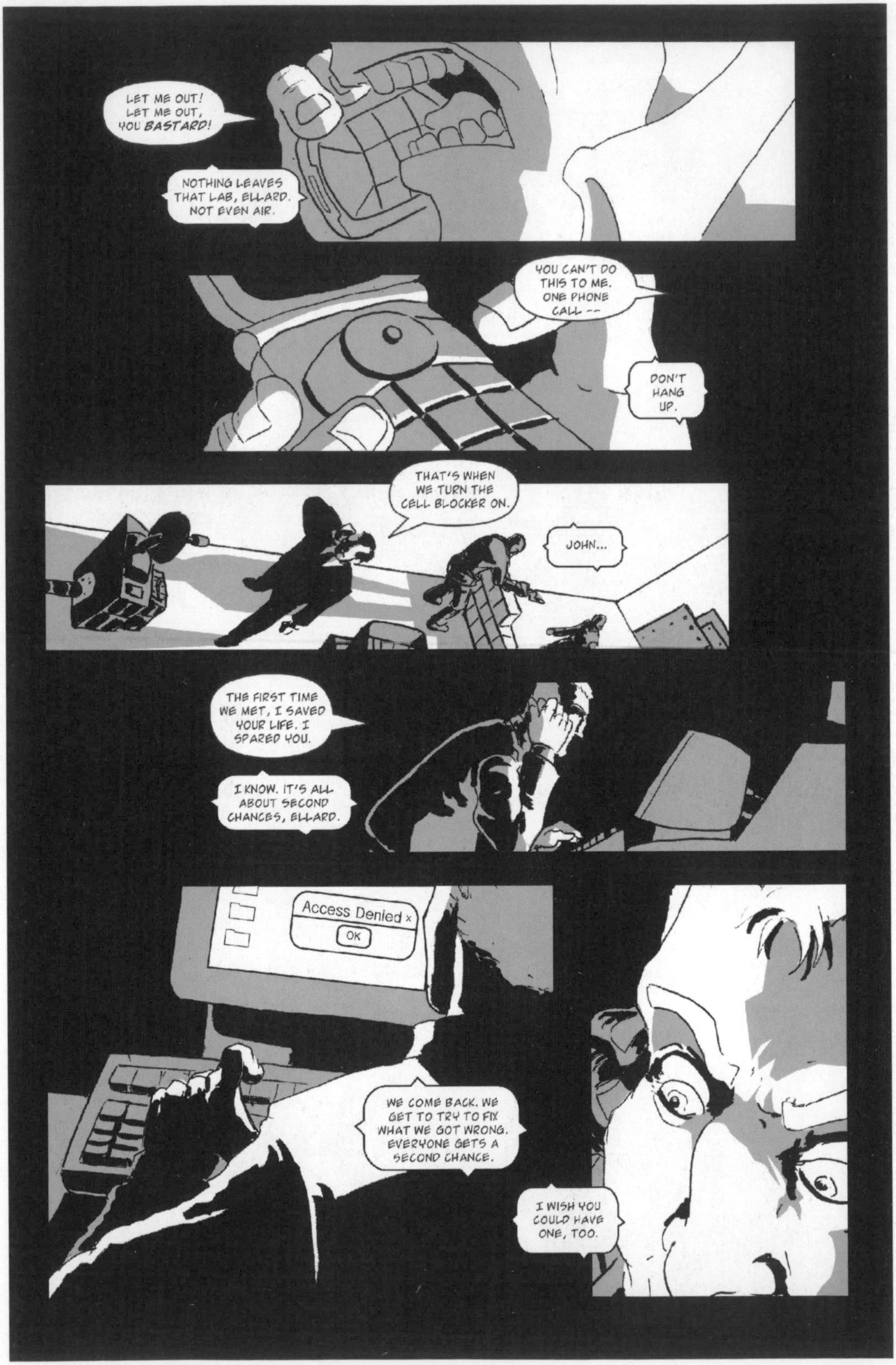
LET ME OUT! LET ME OUT, YOU BASTARD!
NOTHING LEAVES THAT LAB, ELLARD. NOT EVEN AIR.
YOU CAN'T DO THIS TO ME. ONE PHONE CALL --
DON'T HANG UP.
THAT'S WHEN WE TURN THE CELL BLOCKER ON.
JOHN...
THE FIRST TIME WE MET, I SAVED YOUR LIFE. I SPARED YOU.
I KNOW. IT'S ALL ABOUT SECOND CHANCES, ELLARD.
Access Denied x
OK
WE COME BACK. WE GET TO TRY TO FIX WHAT WE GOT WRONG. EVERYONE GETS A SECOND CHANCE.
I WISH YOU COULD HAVE ONE, TOO.

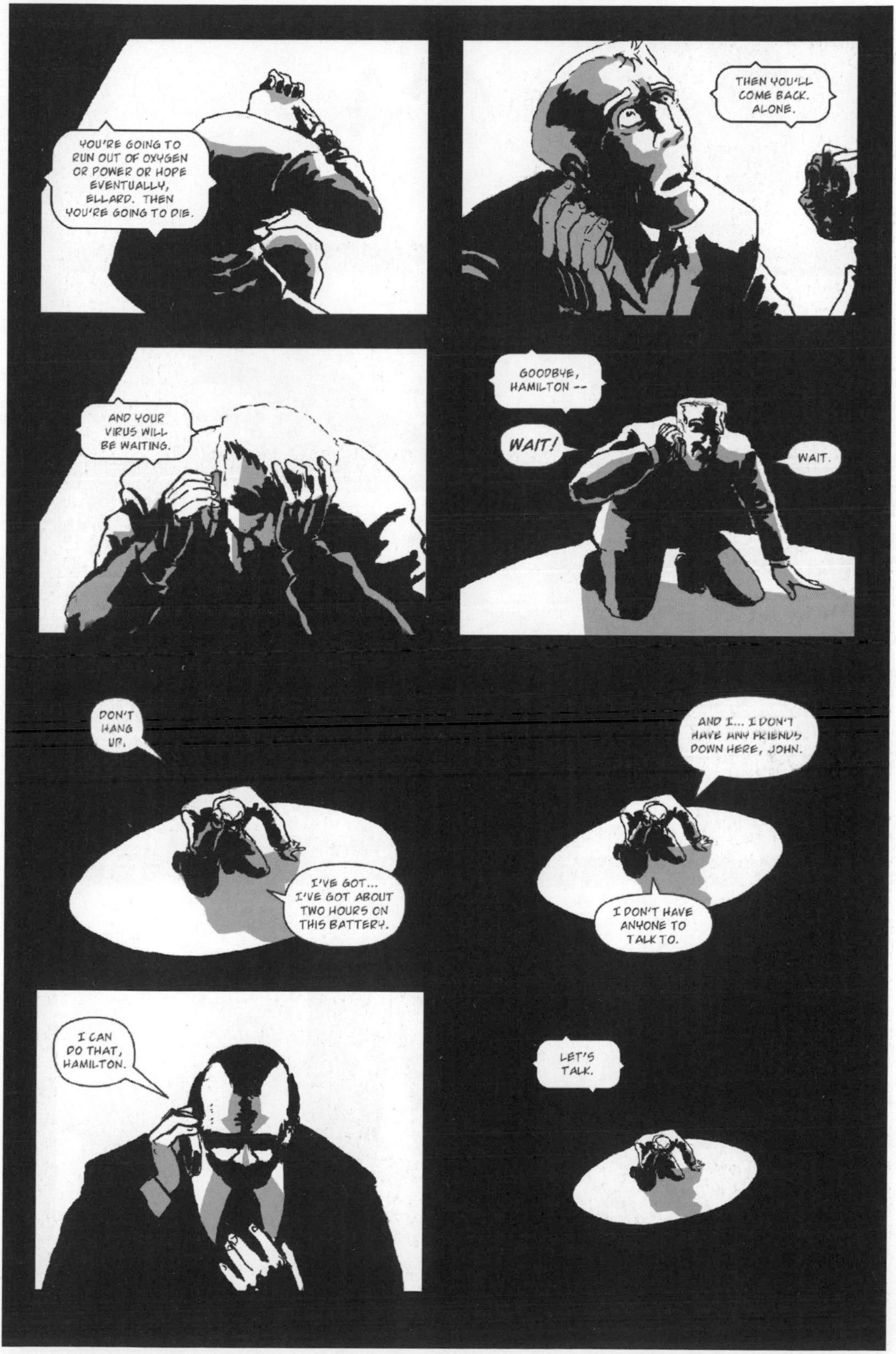
YOU'RE GOING TO RUN OUT OF OXYGEN OR POWER OR HOPE EVENTUALLY, ELLARD. THEN YOU'RE GOING TO DIE.
THEN YOU'LL COME BACK. ALONE.
AND YOUR VIRUS WILL BE WAITING.
GOODBYE, HAMILTON --
WAIT!
WAIT.
DON'T HANG UP.
I'VE GOT... I'VE GOT ABOUT TWO HOURS ON THIS BATTERY.
AND I... I DON'T HAVE ANY FRIENDS DOWN HERE, JOHN.
I DON'T HAVE ANYONE TO TALK TO.
I CAN DO THAT, HAMILTON.
LET'S TALK.

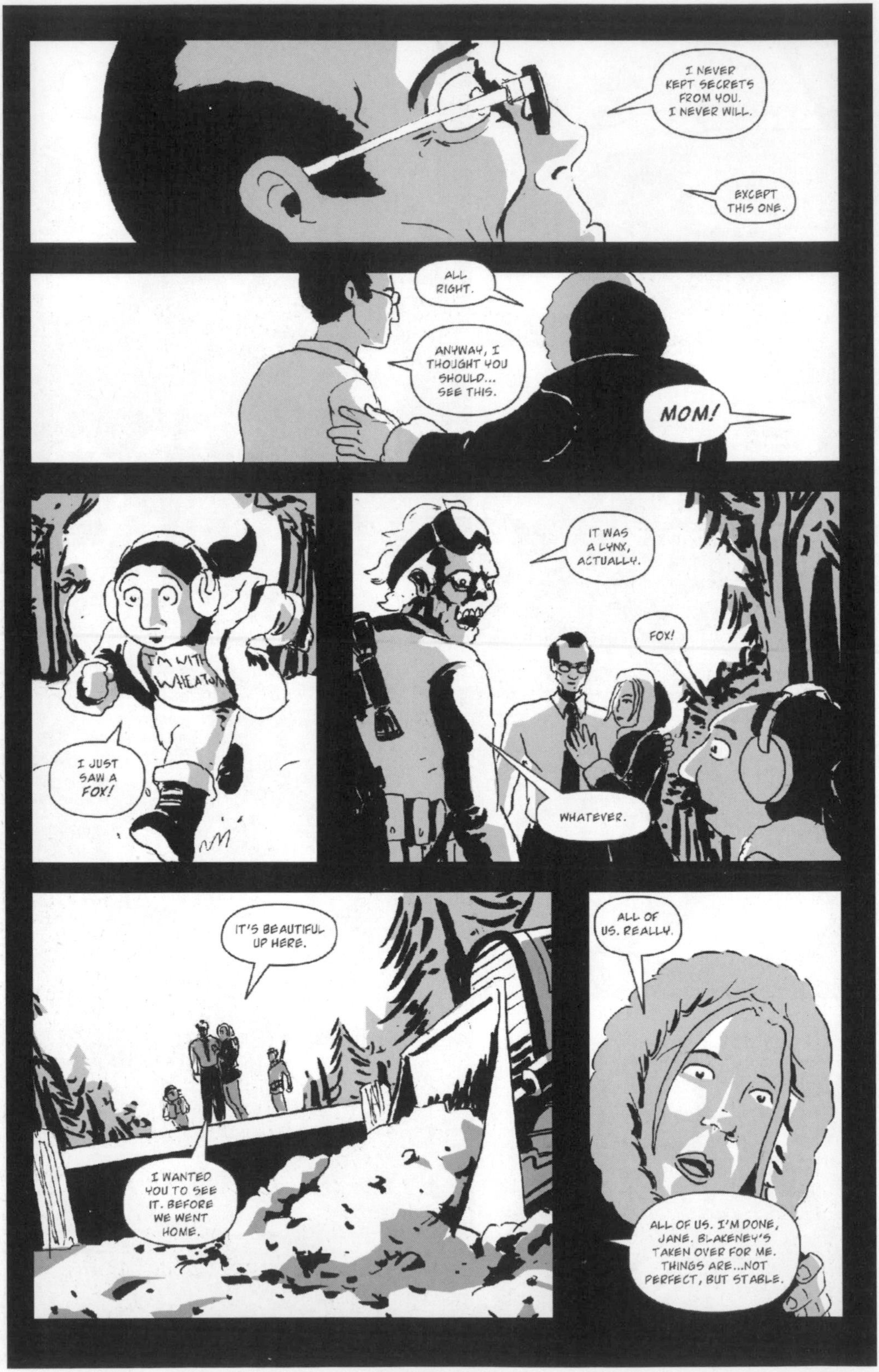
I NEVER KEPT SECRETS FROM YOU. I NEVER WILL.
EXCEPT THIS ONE.
ALL RIGHT.
ANYWAY, I THOUGHT YOU SHOULD... SEE THIS.
MOM!
I'M WITH WHEATON
I JUST SAW A FOX!
IT WAS A LYNX, ACTUALLY.
FOX!
WHATEVER.
IT'S BEAUTIFUL UP HERE.
I WANTED YOU TO SEE IT. BEFORE WE WENT HOME.
ALL OF US. REALLY.
ALL OF US. I'M DONE, JANE. BLAKENEY'S TAKEN OVER FOR ME. THINGS ARE...NOT PERFECT, BUT STABLE.

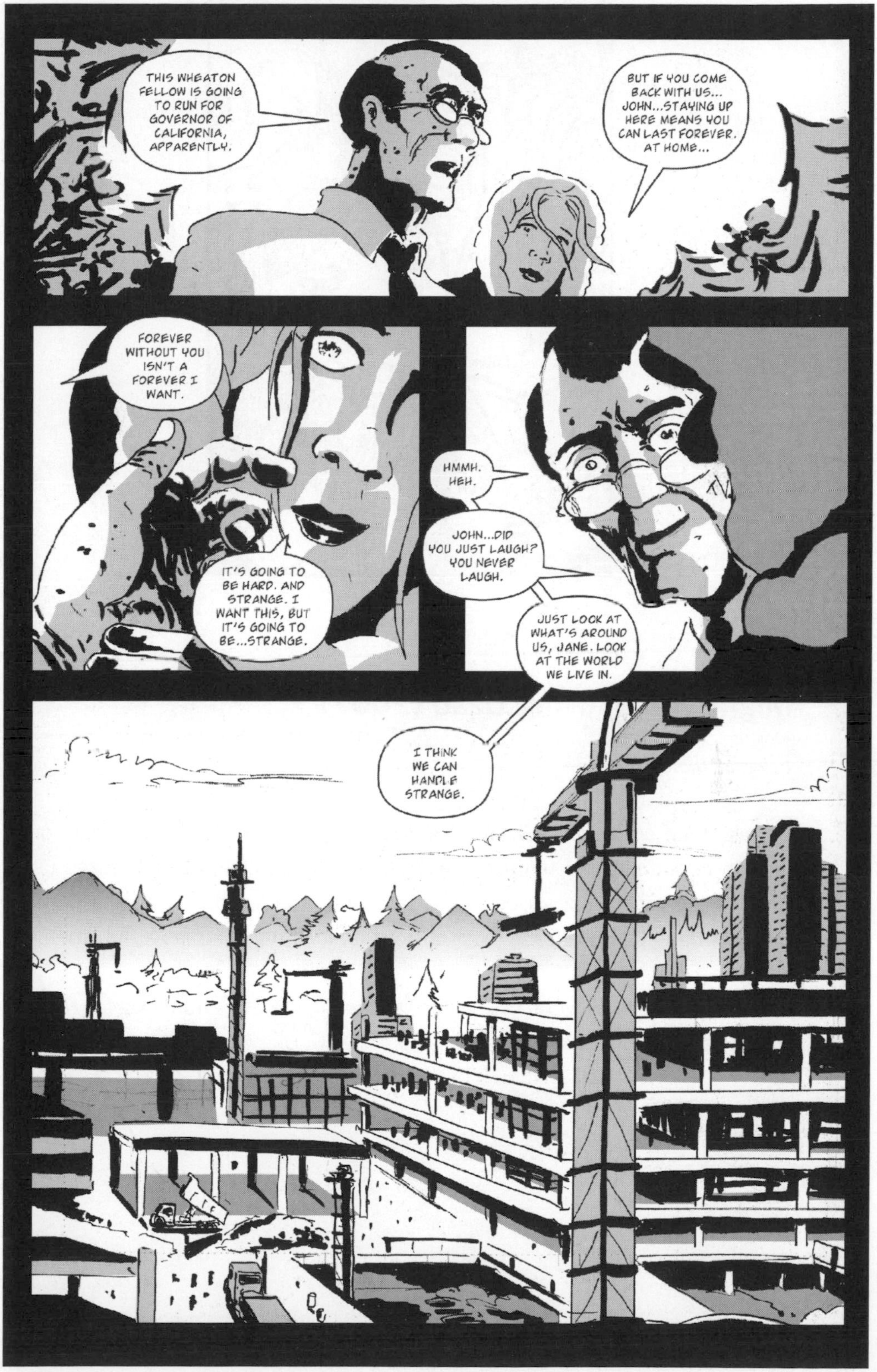
THIS WHEATON FELLOW IS GOING TO RUN FOR GOVERNOR OF CALIFORNIA, APPARENTLY.
BUT IF YOU COME BACK WITH US... JOHN...STAYING UP HERE MEANS YOU CAN LAST FOREVER. AT HOME...
FOREVER WITHOUT YOU ISN'T A FOREVER I WANT.
IT'S GOING TO BE HARD. AND STRANGE. I WANT THIS, BUT IT'S GOING TO BE...STRANGE.
HMMH. HEH.
JOHN...DID YOU JUST LAUGH? YOU NEVER LAUGH.
JUST LOOK AT WHAT'S AROUND US, JANE. LOOK AT THE WORLD WE LIVE IN.
I THINK WE CAN HANDLE STRANGE.

Might of the Living Dead (2007)

Creator: Indio

So just what are zombies about? Do they represent our innermost fears or just an opportunity for nihilistic fun? "Might of the Living Dead" takes us through the various scenarios, whilst lamenting that both comics and films lack the thing that would be most obvious on meeting zombies – the smell.

Indio has produced several scripts for *Dogbreath*, the Strontium Dog fanzine, as well as the 2000AD fanzine, *Zarjaz*.

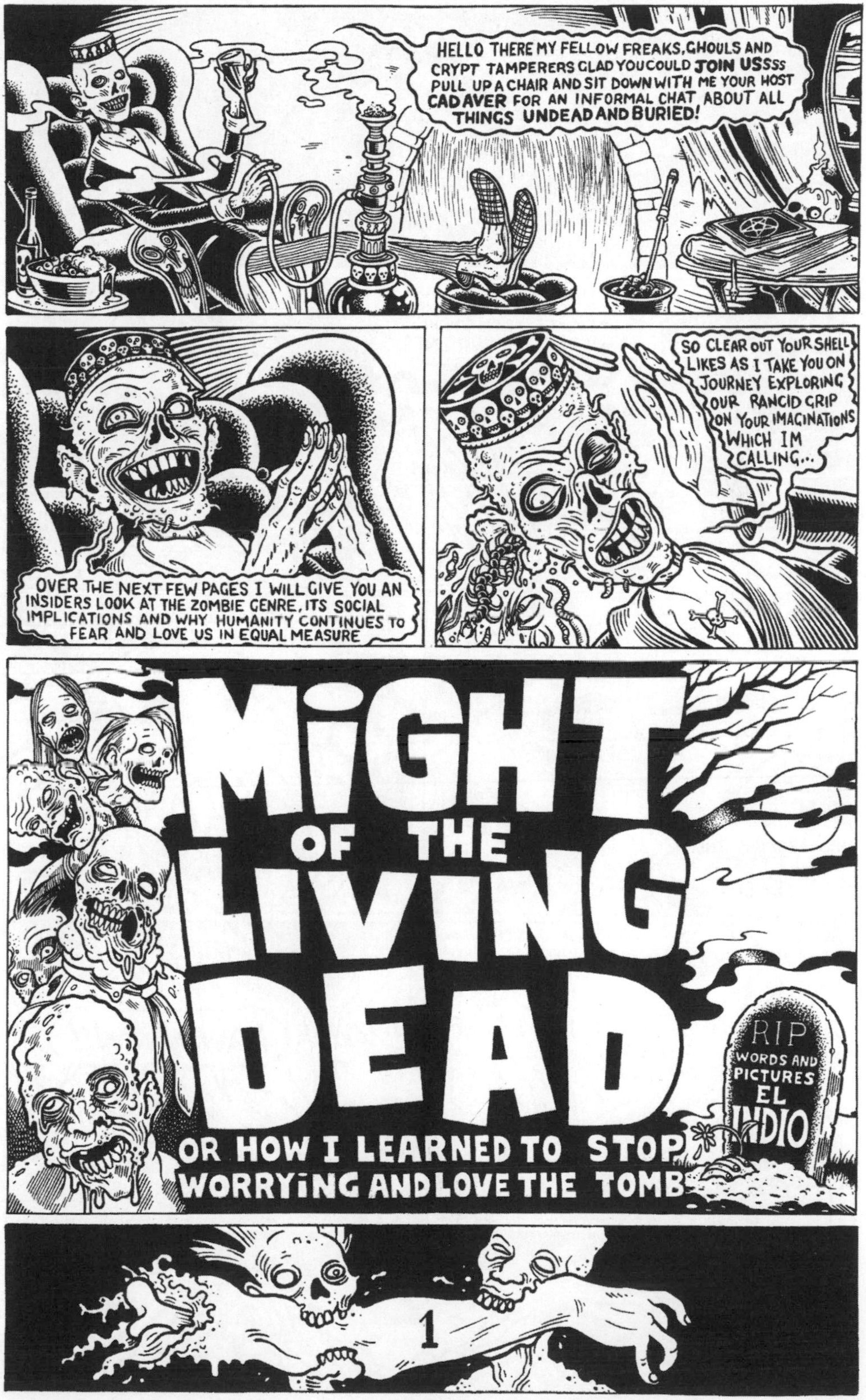
HELLO THERE MY FELLOW FREAKS, GHOULS AND CRYPT TAMPERERS GLAD YOU COULD JOIN USSSS PULL UP A CHAIR AND SIT DOWN WITH ME YOUR HOST CADAVER FOR AN INFORMAL CHAT ABOUT ALL THINGS UNDEAD AND BURIED!
OVER THE NEXT FEW PAGES I WILL GIVE YOU AN INSIDERS LOOK AT THE ZOMBIE GENRE, ITS SOCIAL IMPLICATIONS AND WHY HUMANITY CONTINUES TO FEAR AND LOVE US IN EQUAL MEASURE
SO CLEAR OUT YOUR SHELL LIKES AS I TAKE YOU ON JOURNEY EXPLORING OUR RANCID GRIP ON YOUR IMAGINATIONS WHICH IM CALLING...
MiGHT OF THE LiViNG DEAD
RIP
WORDS AND PICTURES EL INDIO
OR HOW I LEARNED TO STOP WORRYiNG AND LOVE THE TOMB
1

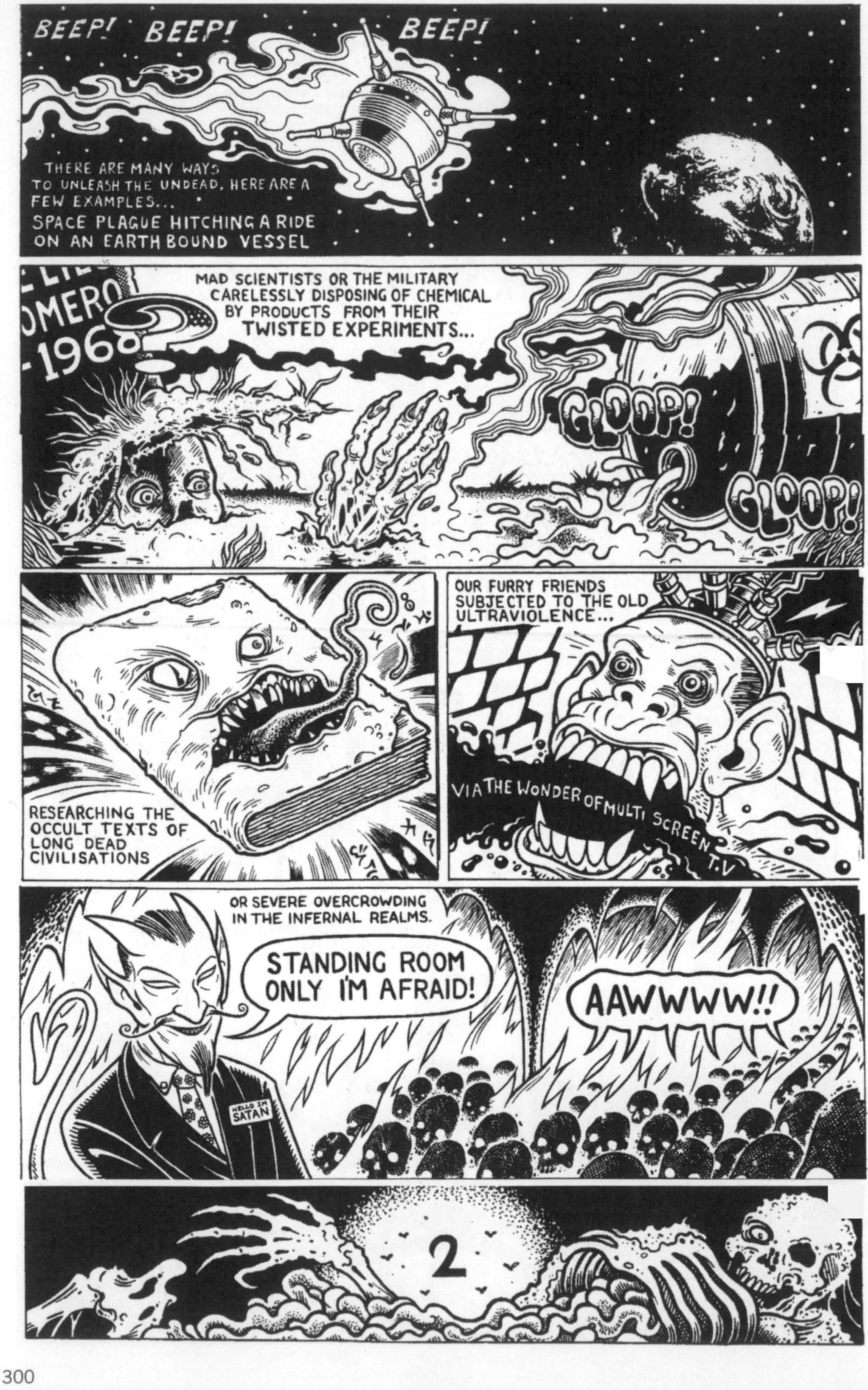
BEEP! BEEP! BEEP!
THERE ARE MANY WAYS TO UNLEASH THE UNDEAD, HERE ARE A FEW EXAMPLES...
SPACE PLAGUE HITCHING A RIDE ON AN EARTH BOUND VESSEL
MAD SCIENTISTS OR THE MILITARY CARELESSLY DISPOSING OF CHEMICAL BY PRODUCTS FROM THEIR TWISTED EXPERIMENTS...
GLOOP!
GLOOP!
RESEARCHING THE OCCULT TEXTS OF LONG DEAD CIVILISATIONS
OUR FURRY FRIENDS SUBJECTED TO THE OLD ULTRAVIOLENCE...
VIA THE WONDER OF MULTI SCREEN T.V
OR SEVERE OVERCROWDING IN THE INFERNAL REALMS.
STANDING ROOM ONLY I'M AFRAID!
AAWWWW!!
HELLO I'M SATAN
2

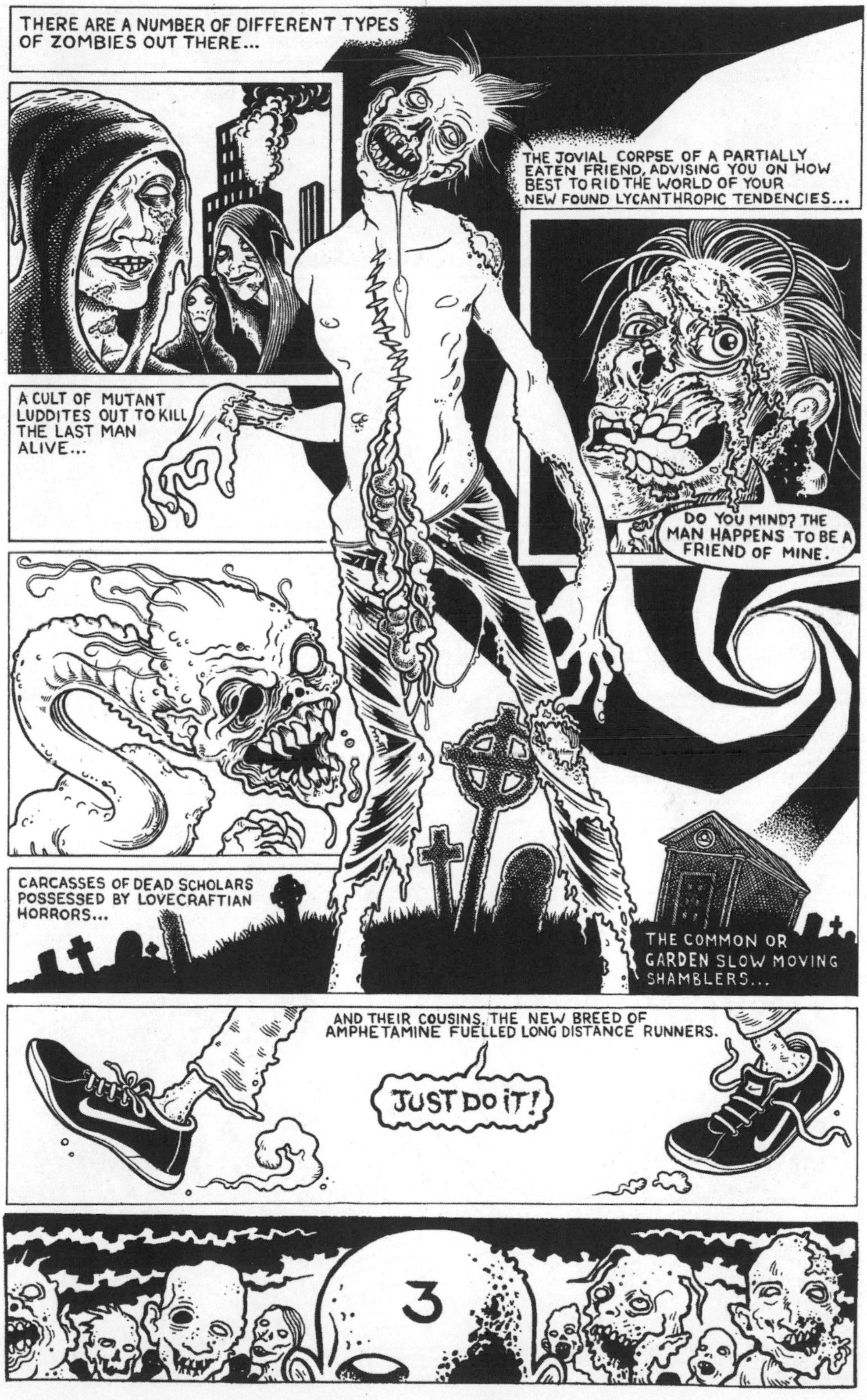
THERE ARE A NUMBER OF DIFFERENT TYPES OF ZOMBIES OUT THERE...
A CULT OF MUTANT LUDDITES OUT TO KILL THE LAST MAN ALIVE...
THE JOVIAL CORPSE OF A PARTIALLY EATEN FRIEND, ADVISING YOU ON HOW BEST TO RID THE WORLD OF YOUR NEW FOUND LYCANTHROPIC TENDENCIES...
DO YOU MIND? THE MAN HAPPENS TO BE A FRIEND OF MINE.
CARCASSES OF DEAD SCHOLARS POSSESSED BY LOVECRAFTIAN HORRORS...
THE COMMON OR GARDEN SLOW MOVING SHAMBLERS...
AND THEIR COUSINS, THE NEW BREED OF AMPHETAMINE FUELLED LONG DISTANCE RUNNERS.
JUST DO IT!
3

AAAAAAA!! AND WITH MORE MOVIES, BOOKS AND COMICS BEING PRODUCED WORLDWIDE THAN EVER BEFORE OUR REIGN OF TERROR SHOWS NO SIGN OF ABATING WITH NEW MEDIUMS TO BE EXPLORED AND EXPLOITED THE YOUNG CONSOLE ZOMBIE SLAYERS OF TODAY ARE TOMORROWS WRITERS, ARTISTS AND DIRECTORS WHO WILL INSPIRE A WHOLE NEW GENERATION OF FANS.

BLAM!
GWOOARGH!
TAP!
TAP!
TAP!
TAP!

DOES OUR APPEAL HARK BACK TO THE PLAYGROUND AS THOUGH YOU WISH FOR A FAR DARKER GAME OF TAG IN ADULTHOOD?

HAHAHA YOUR IT!
OHHHH... SHEE-IT!!

ONE THING NOTABLE BY ITS ABSENCE IS THE DISTINCT AROMA WE ZOMBIES PRIDE OURSELVES ON, IT SEEMS STRANGE THAT WE NEVER SEE THIS...

GAHD THEY STINK!!
BWORP!
ALIVE!
HEL ALIVE
ALIVE INSIDE!
URP!
YOP!

..OR THIS...
RRRRRRR!
PUT!
PUT!
GROOBY!

PERHAPS FULL ON OLFACTORY TERROR WILL TAKE PLACE IN SOME YET TO BE INVENTED INTERACTIVE MEDIUM.

SHOOT 'EM IN THE HEAD!
BLAM!
GRNF?

DOES THE IDEA OF VIOLENTLY DESPATCHING OTHER HUMAN BEINGS WITHOUT RECOURSE TO THE LAW OR HAVING TO DEAL WITH THE TWIN KILL JOYS OF MORALITY OR ETHICS THRILL YOU?

4

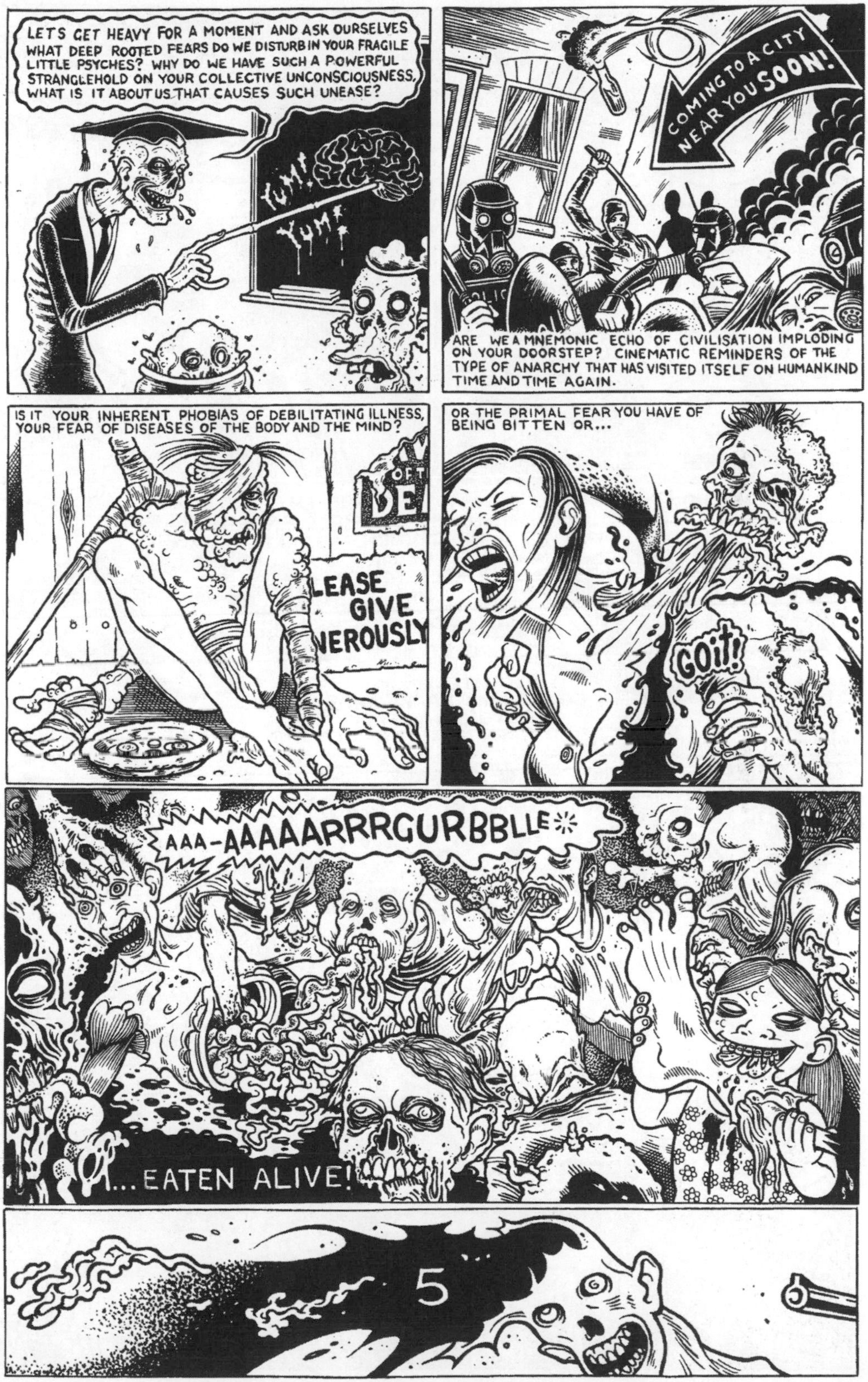
LETS GET HEAVY FOR A MOMENT AND ASK OURSELVES WHAT DEEP ROOTED FEARS DO WE DISTURB IN YOUR FRAGILE LITTLE PSYCHES? WHY DO WE HAVE SUCH A POWERFUL STRANGLEHOLD ON YOUR COLLECTIVE UNCONSCIOUSNESS. WHAT IS IT ABOUT US THAT CAUSES SUCH UNEASE?
YUM! YUM!
COMING TO A CITY NEAR YOU SOON!
ARE WE A MNEMONIC ECHO OF CIVILISATION IMPLODING ON YOUR DOORSTEP? CINEMATIC REMINDERS OF THE TYPE OF ANARCHY THAT HAS VISITED ITSELF ON HUMANKIND TIME AND TIME AGAIN.
IS IT YOUR INHERENT PHOBIAS OF DEBILITATING ILLNESS, YOUR FEAR OF DISEASES OF THE BODY AND THE MIND?
LEASE GIVE NEROUSLY
OR THE PRIMAL FEAR YOU HAVE OF BEING BITTEN OR...
GOIT!
AAA-AAAAARRRGURBBLLE
... EATEN ALIVE!
5

SOME WOULD SAY THAT ZOMBIES ARE ALREADY AMONG YOU, JUST TAKE A LOOK AT SOME OF THE PEOPLE STAGGERING AROUND YOUR LOCAL AMENITIES NEXT TIME YOU USE THEM!
AND ISNT A TWIGHLIGHT HALF LIFE SPENT PURSUING THE SMORGASBORD THAT WOULD BE THE REMNANTS OF HUMANITY PREFERABLE...
AAAAAHH!!!
HALP!
..TO THE ETERNAL SILENCE OF THE GRAVE OR BEING INCINERATED AND PUMPED INTO THE SKIES NO MORE THAN A HANDFUL OF ASH?
...EVEN MY ENEMIES AND MY FOES COME UPON ME TO DEVOUR ME... EARTH TO EARTH, ASHES TO ASHES.. DUST TO DUST.
AND HERE'S A PARADOX FOR YOU, THERE ARE PHYSICISTS WHO CLAIM THAT WHEN THE UNIVERSE ENDS THERE MAY BE A BIG CRUNCH AND THAT AS SPACE BEGINS TO RETRACT TOWARD AN INFINITESIMALLY SMALL POINT OF ULTIMATE DENSITY TIME COULD RUN BACKWARDS AND IF IT DOES RETURNING FROM THE GRAVE WILL BE EASIER THAN FALLING OUT OF A TREE!
KORTCH!
NOW THAT REALLY IS FOOD FOR THOUGHT UNTIL NEXT TIME MY FIENDS BON APPETIT!
the END.
6

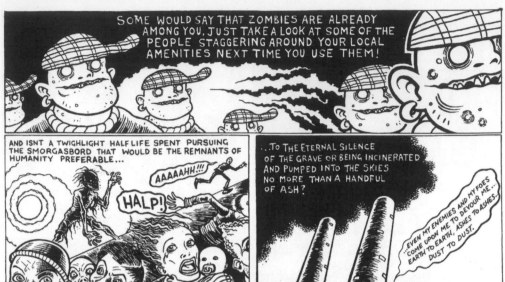

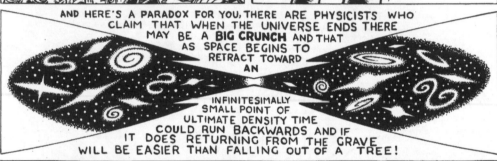

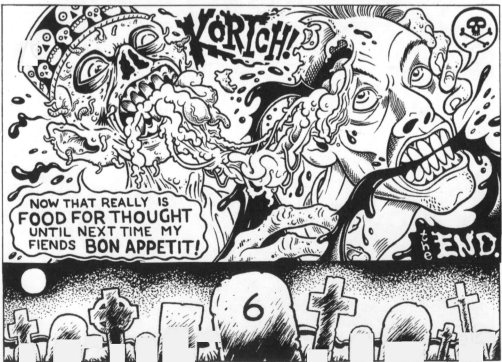

Job Satisfaction (2007)

Creator: Gary Crutchley

When zombies take over the world most people are running fast to make sure they're not the next victims. "Job Satisfaction" shows that, however dark the situation, someone somewhere always finds a silver lining.

Gary Crutchley's work has appeared in horror anthologies such as the infamous *Shriek* and *Gore Shriek*, as well as *2000AD*, and *Revolver*.

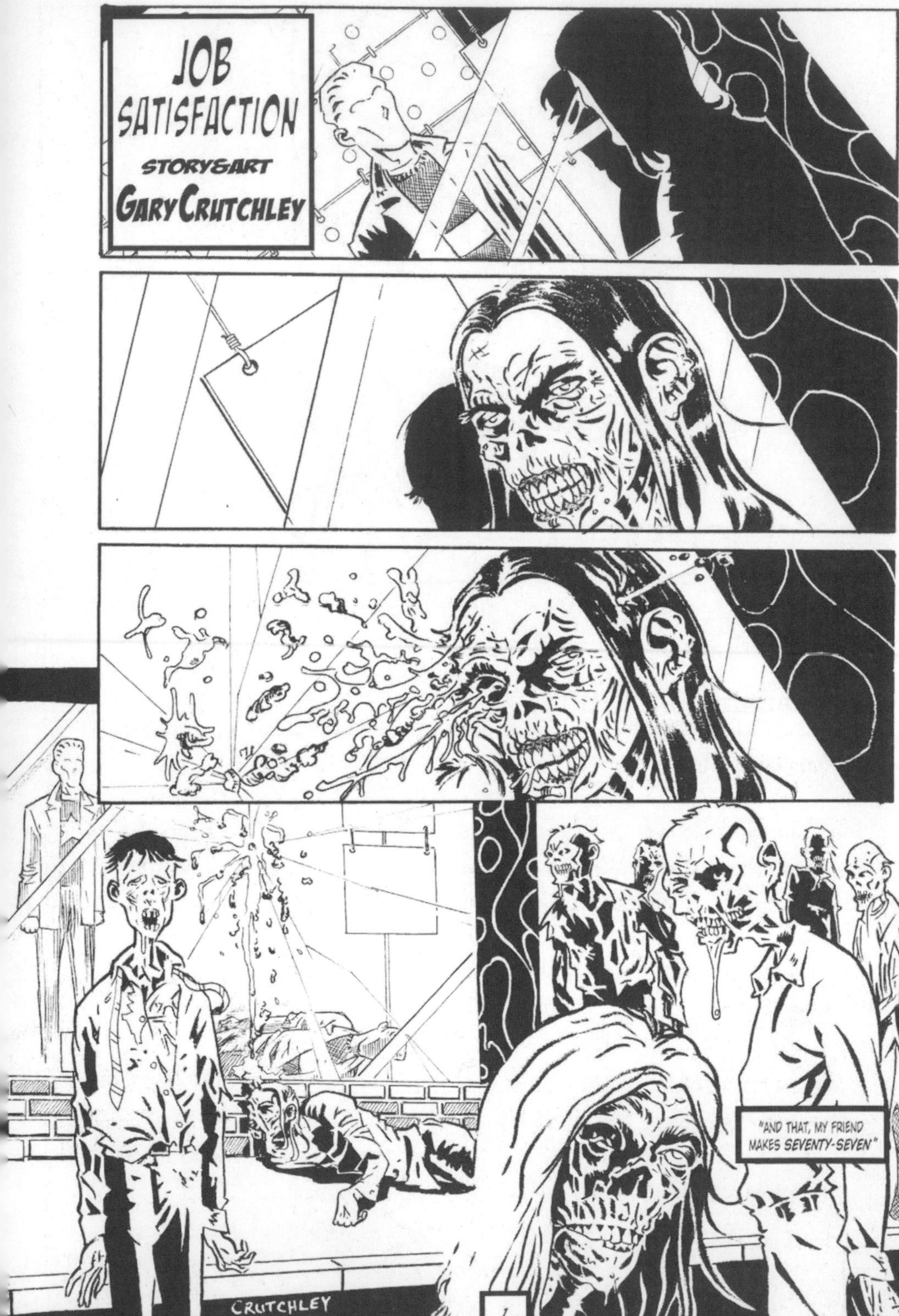
JOB SATISFACTION
STORY&ART
GARY CRUTCHLEY
"AND THAT, MY FRIEND MAKES SEVENTY-SEVEN"
CRUTCHLEY
7

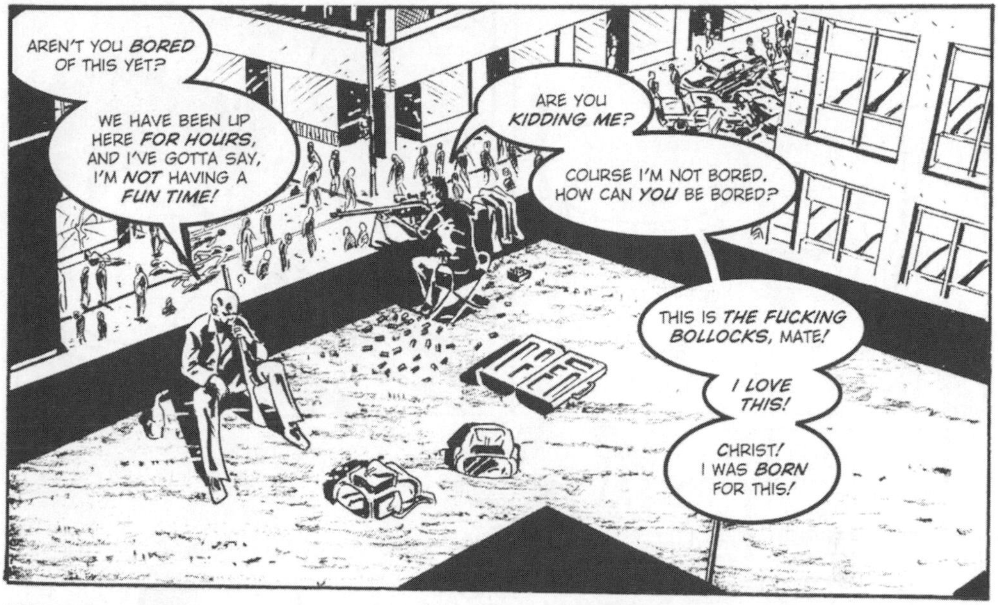
AREN'T YOU BORED OF THIS YET?
WE HAVE BEEN UP HERE FOR HOURS, AND I'VE GOTTA SAY, I'M NOT HAVING A FUN TIME!
ARE YOU KIDDING ME?
COURSE I'M NOT BORED. HOW CAN YOU BE BORED?
THIS IS THE FUCKING BOLLOCKS, MATE!
I LOVE THIS!
CHRIST! I WAS BORN FOR THIS!

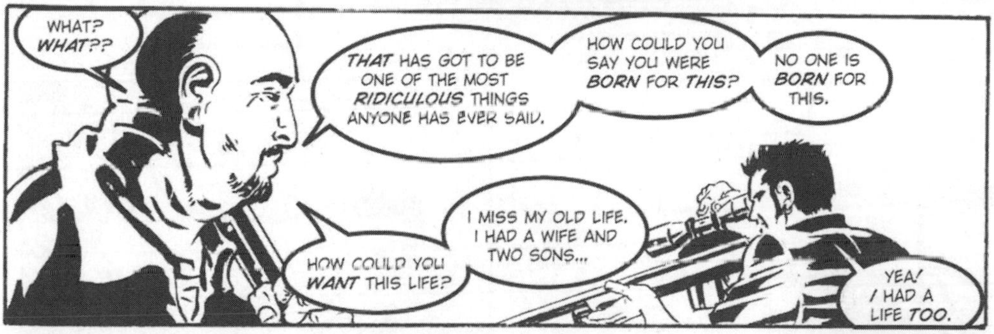
WHAT? WHAT??
THAT HAS GOT TO BE ONE OF THE MOST RIDICULOUS THINGS ANYONE HAS EVER SAID.
HOW COULD YOU SAY YOU WERE BORN FOR THIS?
NO ONE IS BORN FOR THIS.
HOW COULD YOU WANT THIS LIFE?
I MISS MY OLD LIFE. I HAD A WIFE AND TWO SONS...
YEA! I HAD A LIFE TOO.

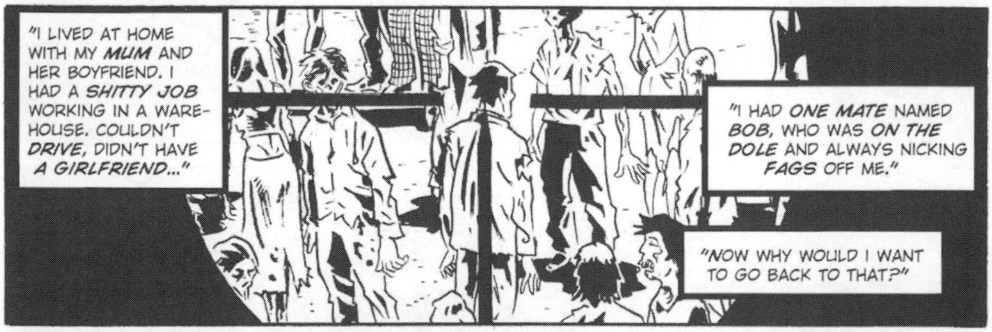
"I LIVED AT HOME WITH MY MUM AND HER BOYFRIEND. I HAD A SHITTY JOB WORKING IN A WAREHOUSE. COULDN'T DRIVE, DIDN'T HAVE A GIRLFRIEND..."
"I HAD ONE MATE NAMED BOB, WHO WAS ON THE DOLE AND ALWAYS NICKING FAGS OFF ME."
"NOW WHY WOULD I WANT TO GO BACK TO THAT?"

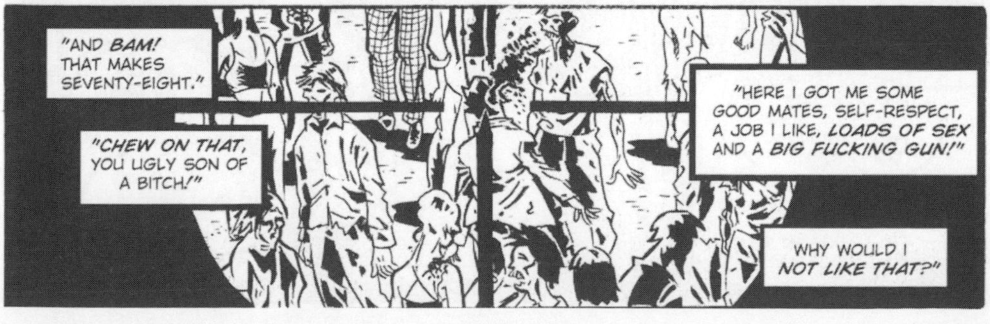
"AND BAM! THAT MAKES SEVENTY-EIGHT."
"CHEW ON THAT, YOU UGLY SON OF A BITCH!"
"HERE I GOT ME SOME GOOD MATES, SELF-RESPECT, A JOB I LIKE, LOADS OF SEX AND A BIG FUCKING GUN!"
WHY WOULD I NOT LIKE THAT?"

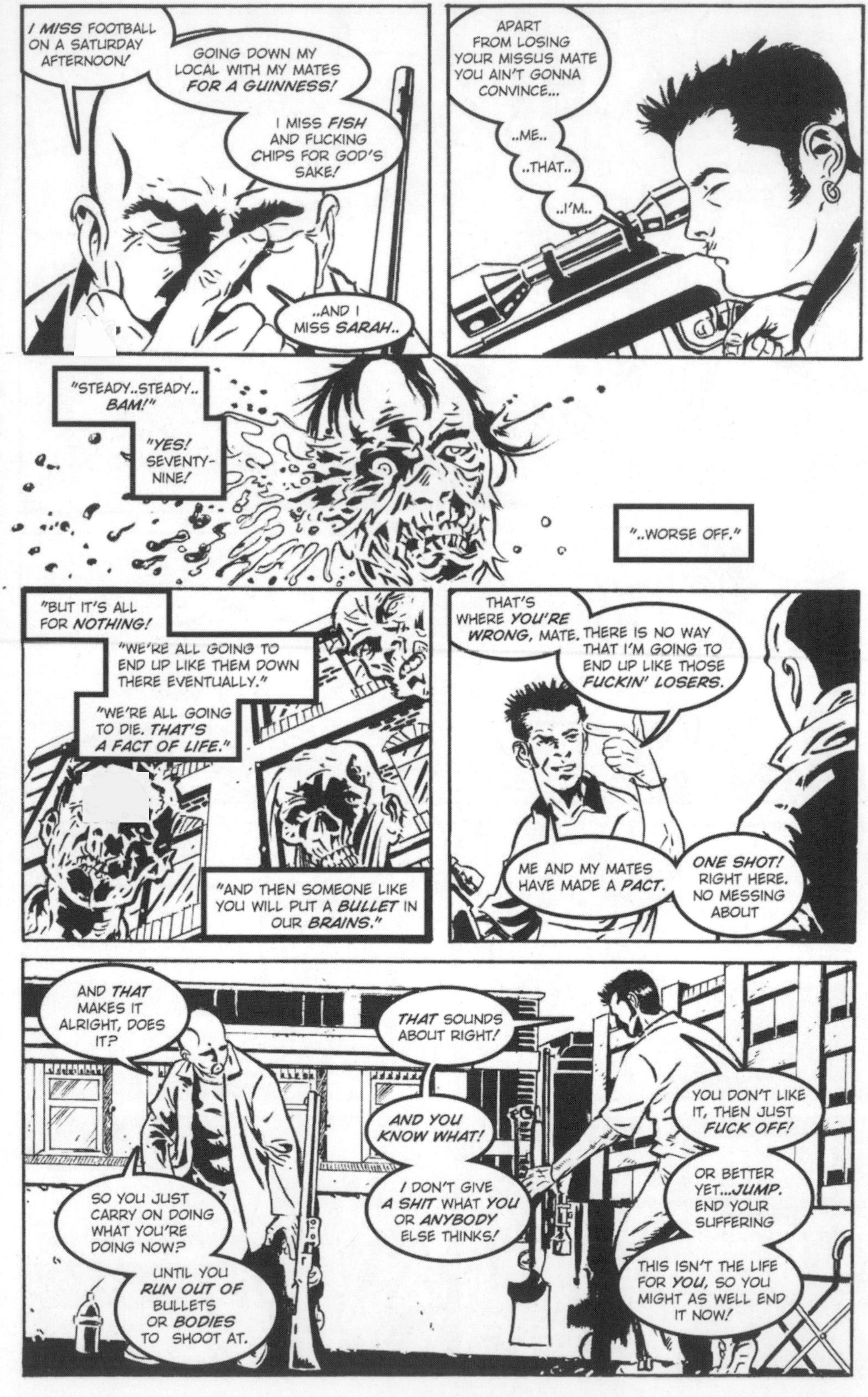
I MISS FOOTBALL ON A SATURDAY AFTERNOON!
GOING DOWN MY LOCAL WITH MY MATES FOR A GUINNESS!
I MISS FISH AND FUCKING CHIPS FOR GOD'S SAKE!
..AND I MISS SARAH..
APART FROM LOSING YOUR MISSUS MATE YOU AIN'T GONNA CONVINCE...
..ME..
..THAT..
..I'M..
"STEADY..STEADY.. BAM!"
"YES! SEVENTY-NINE!
"..WORSE OFF."
"BUT IT'S ALL FOR NOTHING!
"WE'RE ALL GOING TO END UP LIKE THEM DOWN THERE EVENTUALLY."
"WE'RE ALL GOING TO DIE. THAT'S A FACT OF LIFE."
"AND THEN SOMEONE LIKE YOU WILL PUT A BULLET IN OUR BRAINS."
THAT'S WHERE YOU'RE WRONG, MATE.
THERE IS NO WAY THAT I'M GOING TO END UP LIKE THOSE FUCKIN' LOSERS.
ME AND MY MATES HAVE MADE A PACT.
ONE SHOT! RIGHT HERE. NO MESSING ABOUT
AND THAT MAKES IT ALRIGHT, DOES IT?
SO YOU JUST CARRY ON DOING WHAT YOU'RE DOING NOW?
UNTIL YOU RUN OUT OF BULLETS OR BODIES TO SHOOT AT.
THAT SOUNDS ABOUT RIGHT!
AND YOU KNOW WHAT!
I DON'T GIVE A SHIT WHAT YOU OR ANYBODY ELSE THINKS!
YOU DON'T LIKE IT, THEN JUST FUCK OFF!
OR BETTER YET...JUMP. END YOUR SUFFERING
THIS ISN'T THE LIFE FOR YOU, SO YOU MIGHT AS WELL END IT NOW!

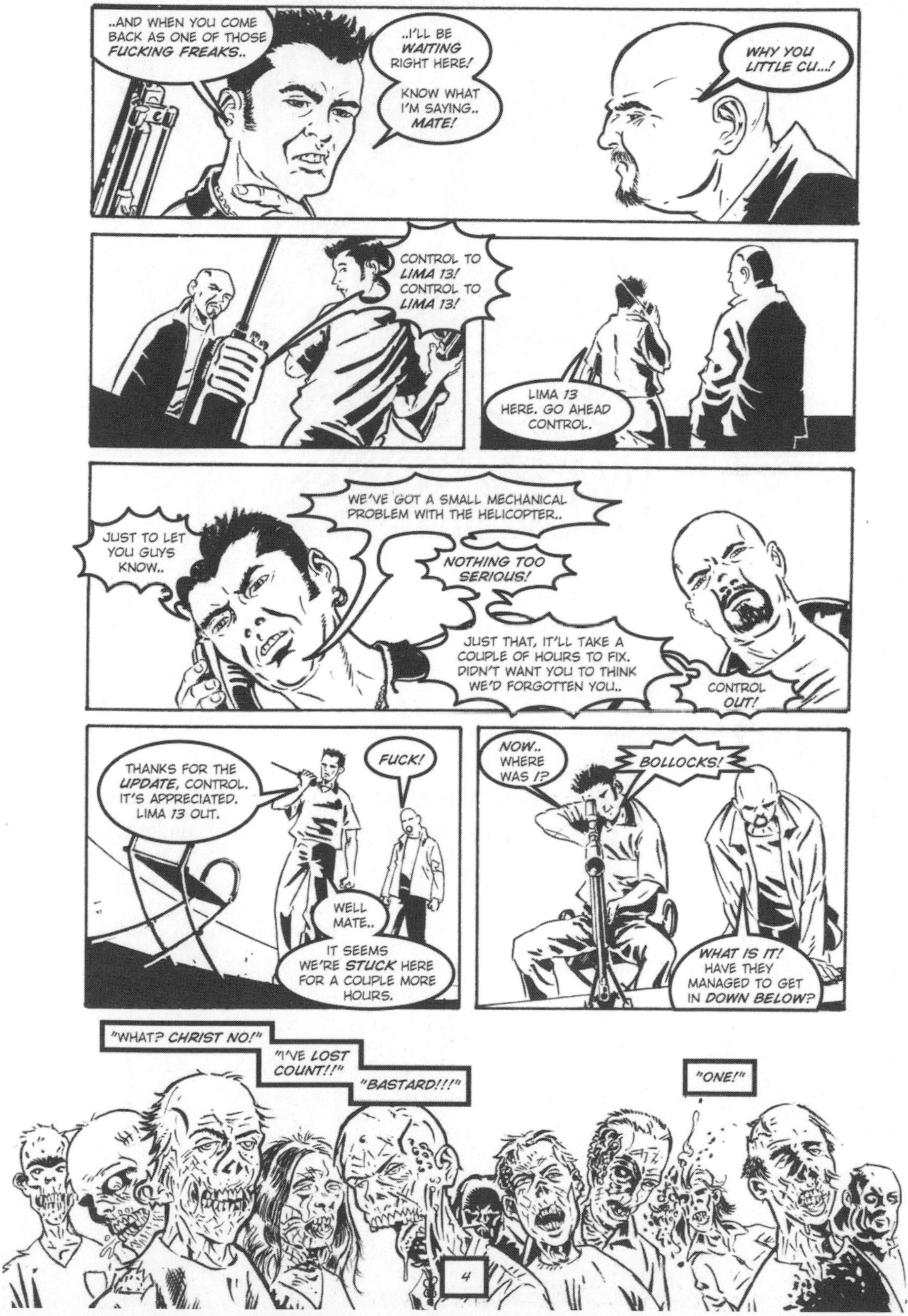
..AND WHEN YOU COME BACK AS ONE OF THOSE *FUCKING FREAKS*..
..I'LL BE *WAITING* RIGHT HERE!
KNOW WHAT I'M SAYING.. *MATE!*
WHY YOU LITTLE CU...!
CONTROL TO *LIMA 13!* CONTROL TO *LIMA 13!*
LIMA 13 HERE. GO AHEAD CONTROL.
JUST TO LET YOU GUYS KNOW..
WE'VE GOT A SMALL MECHANICAL PROBLEM WITH THE HELICOPTER..
NOTHING TOO SERIOUS!
JUST THAT, IT'LL TAKE A COUPLE OF HOURS TO FIX. DIDN'T WANT YOU TO THINK WE'D FORGOTTEN YOU..
CONTROL *OUT!*
THANKS FOR THE *UPDATE*, CONTROL. IT'S APPRECIATED. LIMA 13 OUT.
FUCK!
WELL MATE..
IT SEEMS WE'RE *STUCK* HERE FOR A COUPLE MORE HOURS.
NOW.. WHERE WAS *I?*
BOLLOCKS!
WHAT IS IT! HAVE THEY MANAGED TO GET IN *DOWN BELOW?*
"WHAT? *CHRIST NO!*"
"I'VE *LOST COUNT!!*"
"*BASTARD!!!*"
"*ONE!*"
4

The Corpse (2008)

Creator: Askold Akishin.

Based on an old Russian folk tale, "The Corpse" gives us the staples of such stories – a threat, and a task for the hero – but there is also an underlying sadness to it, which outlasts its brevity.

Askold Akishin is one of the most prolific comic creators in Russia. He has completed graphic novel versions of Erich Maria Remarque's *All Quiet On the Western Front*, as well as stories by H P Lovecraft, and Ray Bradbury.

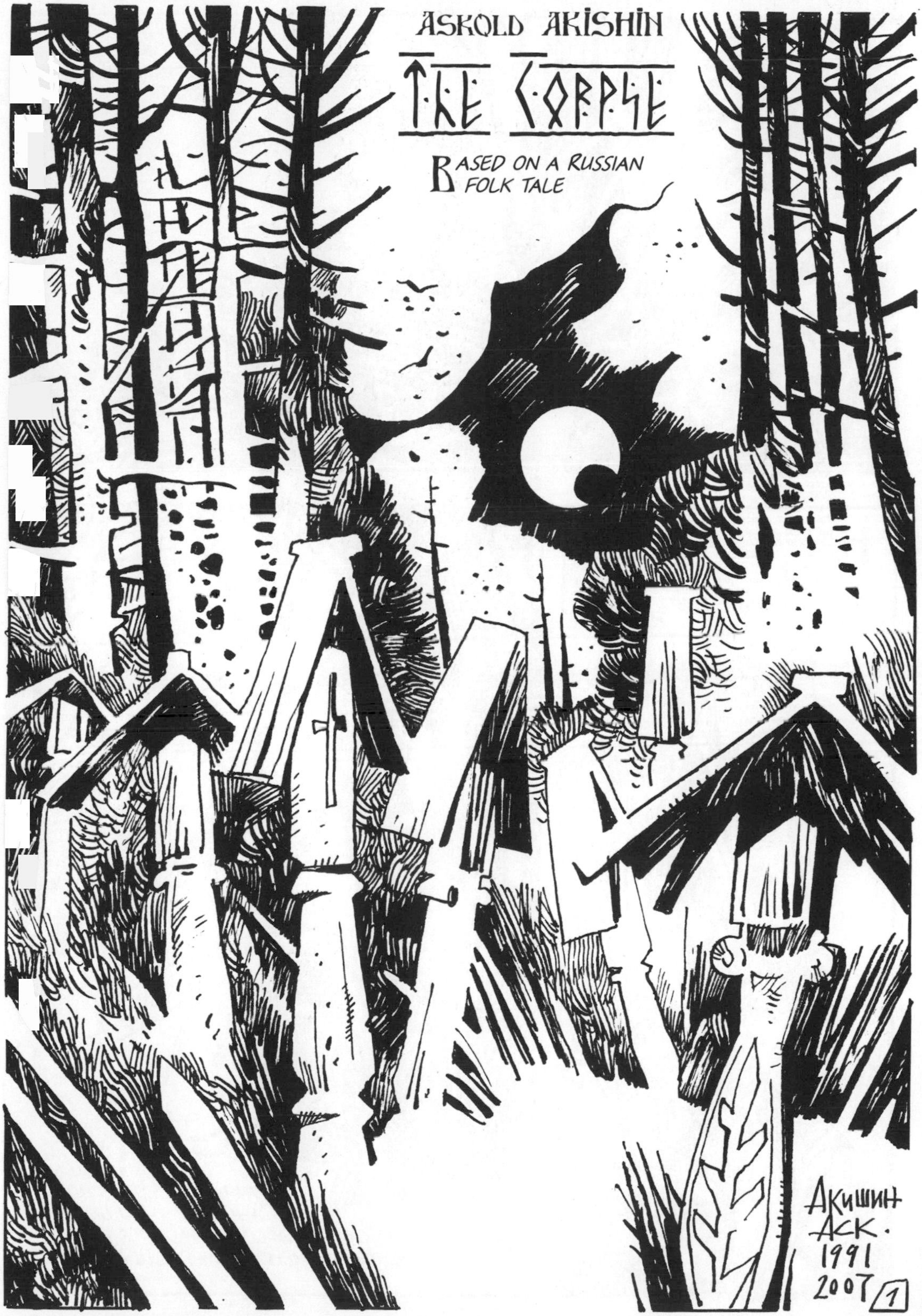
ASKOLD AKISHIN
THE CORPSE
BASED ON A RUSSIAN FOLK TALE
Акишин
Аск.
1991
2007
1

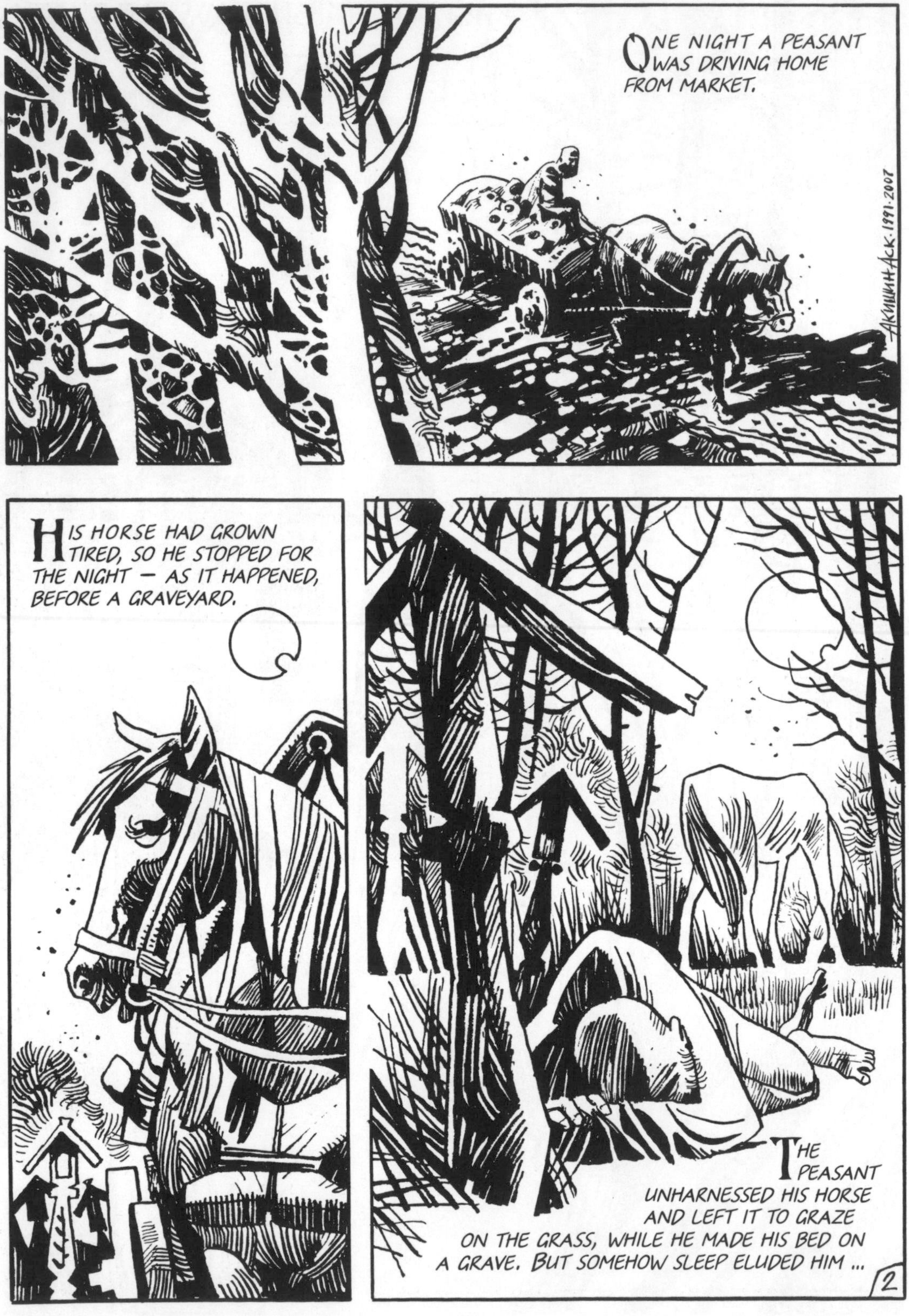
ONE NIGHT A PEASANT WAS DRIVING HOME FROM MARKET.
HIS HORSE HAD GROWN TIRED, SO HE STOPPED FOR THE NIGHT — AS IT HAPPENED, BEFORE A GRAVEYARD.
THE PEASANT UNHARNESSED HIS HORSE AND LEFT IT TO GRAZE ON THE GRASS, WHILE HE MADE HIS BED ON A GRAVE. BUT SOMEHOW SLEEP ELUDED HIM ...
2

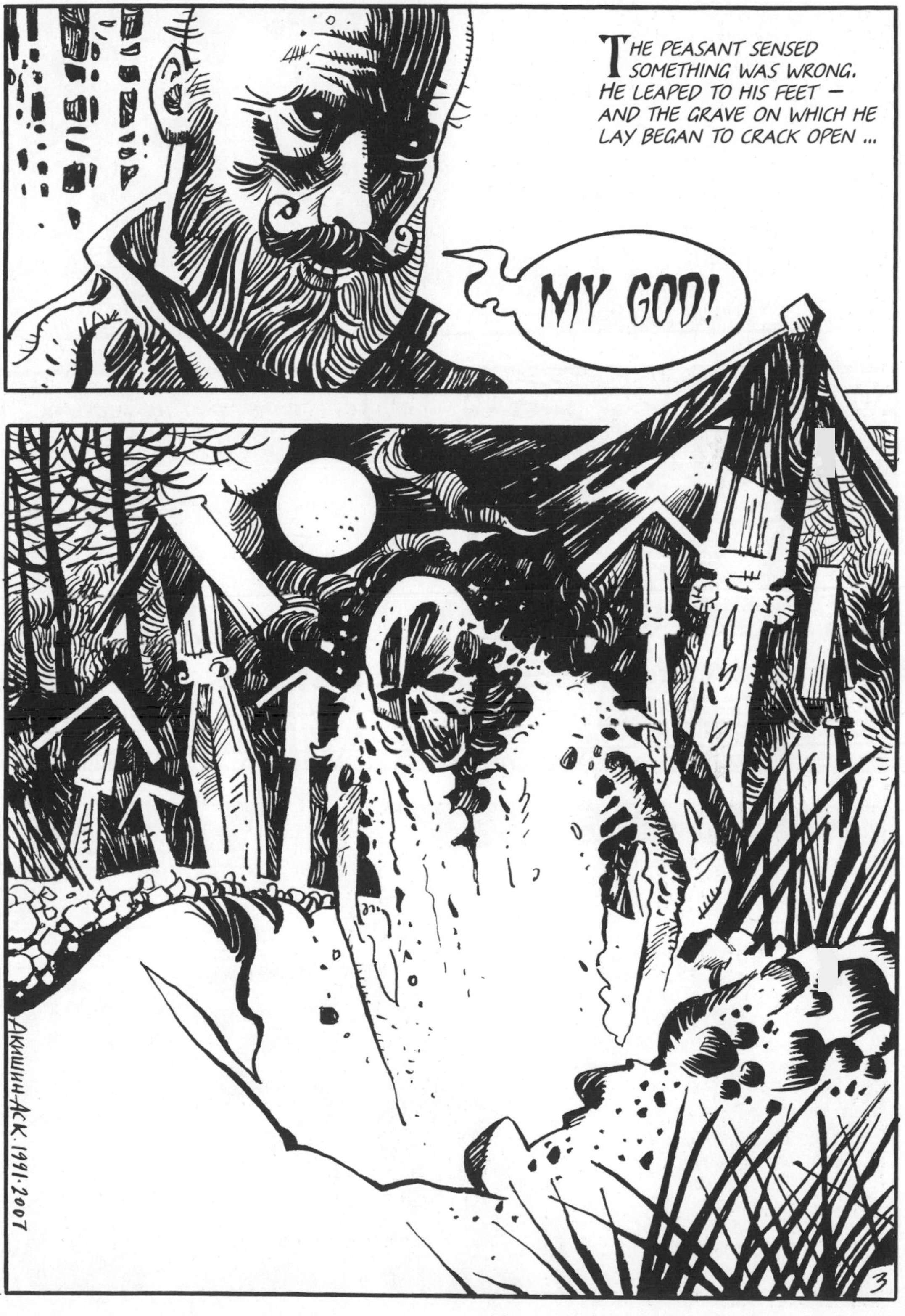
THE PEASANT SENSED SOMETHING WAS WRONG. HE LEAPED TO HIS FEET — AND THE GRAVE ON WHICH HE LAY BEGAN TO CRACK OPEN ...
MY GOD!
АКИШИН-АСК. 1991-2007
3

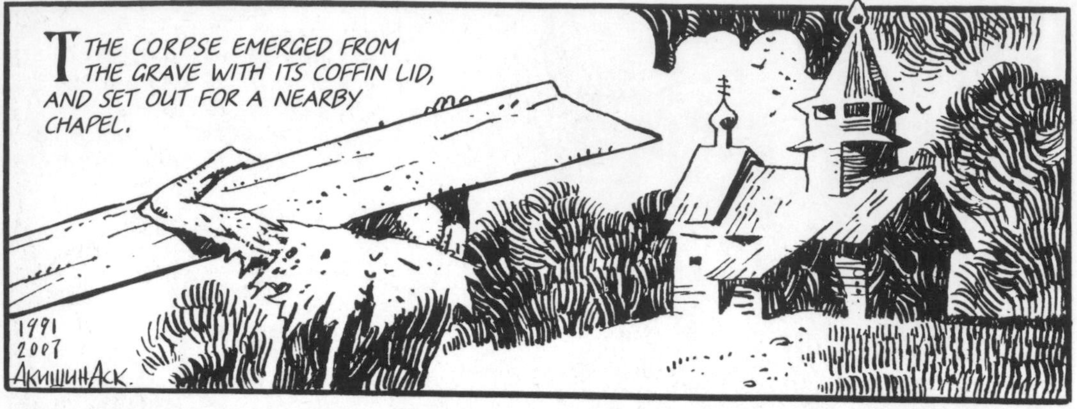
T THE CORPSE EMERGED FROM THE GRAVE WITH ITS COFFIN LID, AND SET OUT FOR A NEARBY CHAPEL.
1991
2007
АкишинАск.

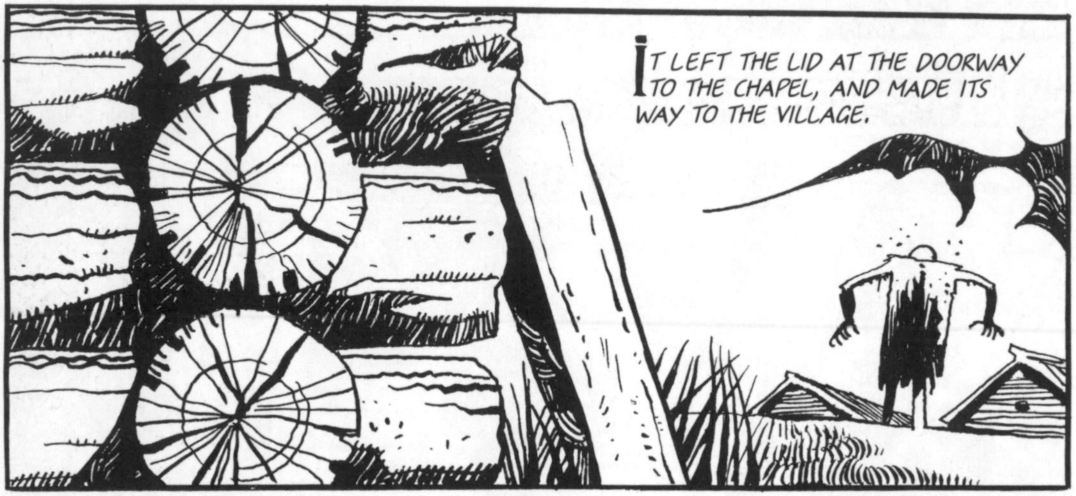
IT LEFT THE LID AT THE DOORWAY TO THE CHAPEL, AND MADE ITS WAY TO THE VILLAGE.

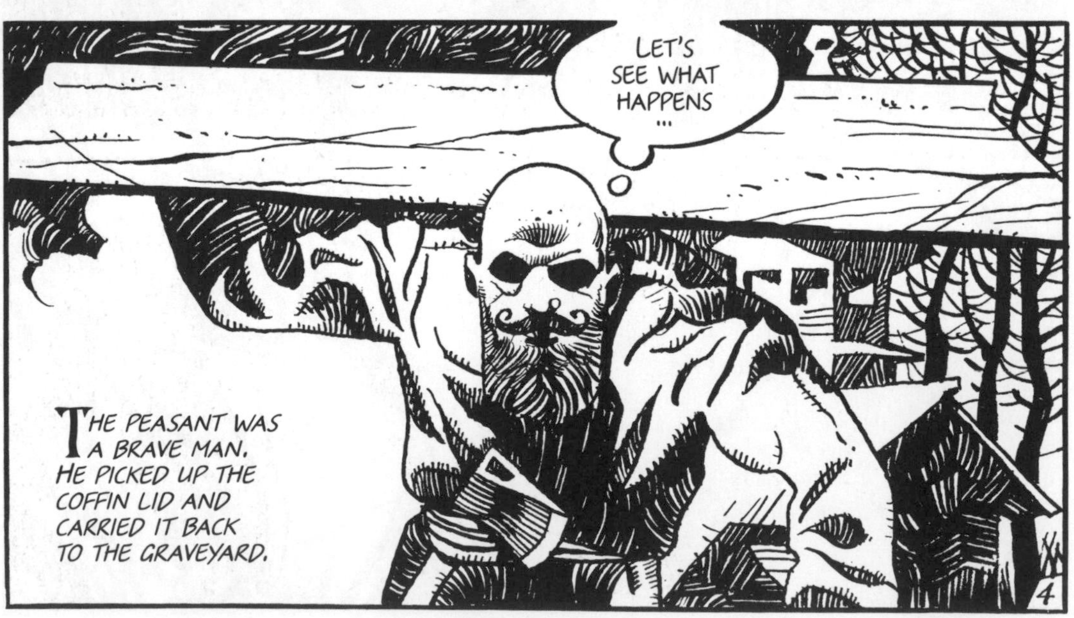
LET'S SEE WHAT HAPPENS ...
THE PEASANT WAS A BRAVE MAN. HE PICKED UP THE COFFIN LID AND CARRIED IT BACK TO THE GRAVEYARD.
4

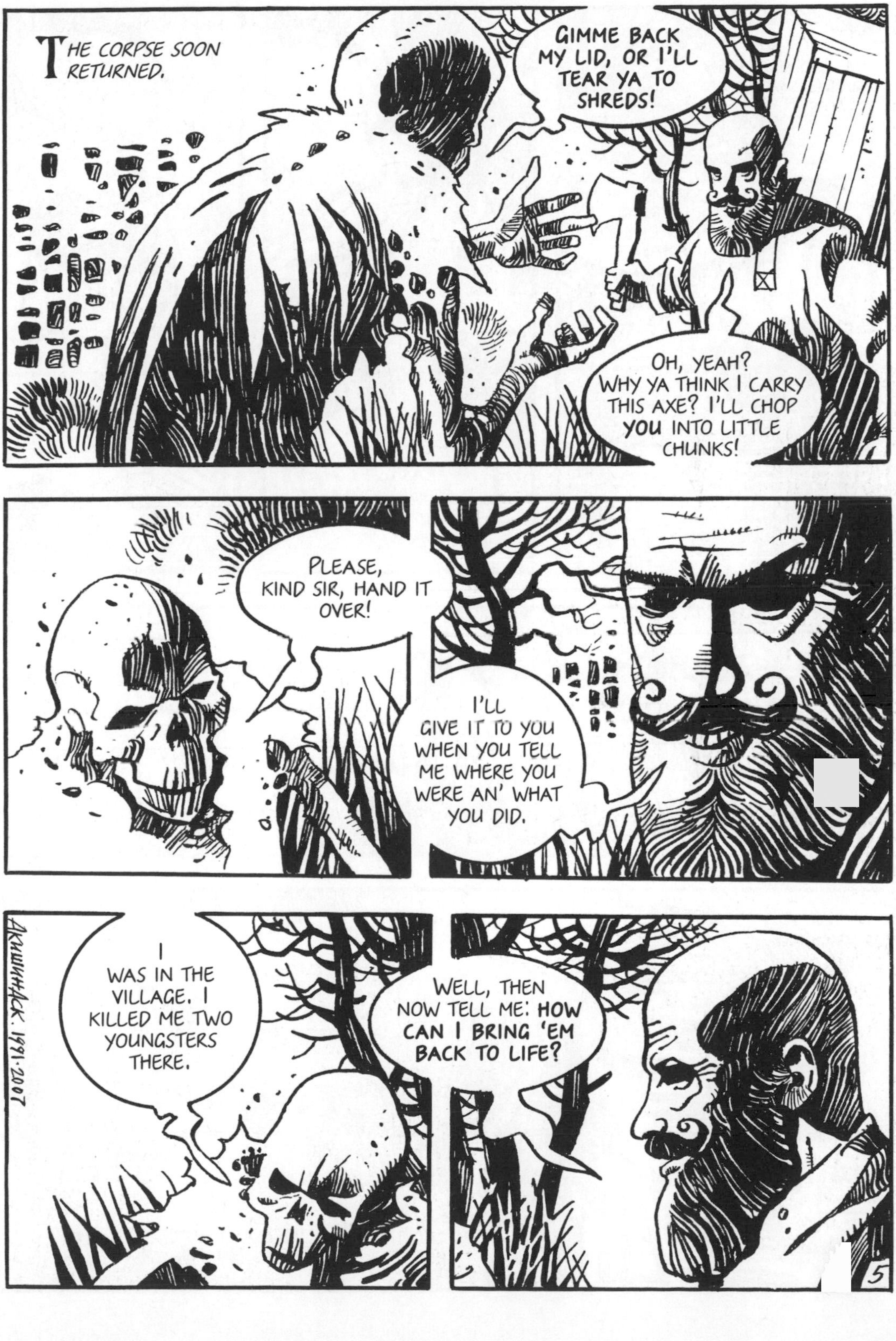
THE CORPSE SOON RETURNED.
GIMME BACK MY LID, OR I'LL TEAR YA TO SHREDS!
OH, YEAH? WHY YA THINK I CARRY THIS AXE? I'LL CHOP **YOU** INTO LITTLE CHUNKS!
PLEASE, KIND SIR, HAND IT OVER!
I'LL GIVE IT TO YOU WHEN YOU TELL ME WHERE YOU WERE AN' WHAT YOU DID.
I WAS IN THE VILLAGE. I KILLED ME TWO YOUNGSTERS THERE.
1991-2007
WELL, THEN NOW TELL ME: **HOW CAN I BRING 'EM BACK TO LIFE?**
5

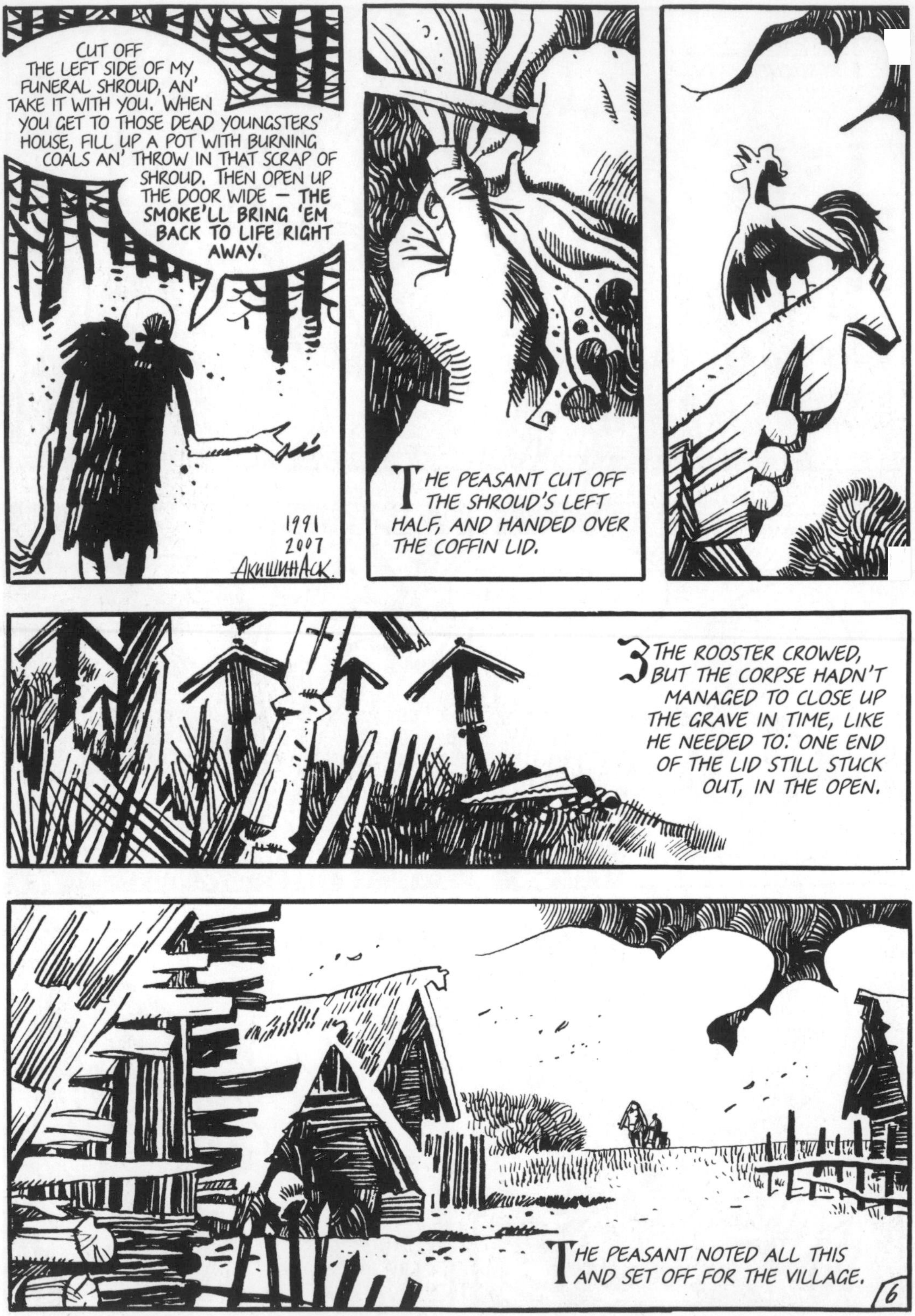
CUT OFF THE LEFT SIDE OF MY FUNERAL SHROUD, AN' TAKE IT WITH YOU. WHEN YOU GET TO THOSE DEAD YOUNGSTERS' HOUSE, FILL UP A POT WITH BURNING COALS AN' THROW IN THAT SCRAP OF SHROUD. THEN OPEN UP THE DOOR WIDE — THE SMOKE'LL BRING 'EM BACK TO LIFE RIGHT AWAY.
1991
2007
АКИШИНАСК.
THE PEASANT CUT OFF THE SHROUD'S LEFT HALF, AND HANDED OVER THE COFFIN LID.
THE ROOSTER CROWED, BUT THE CORPSE HADN'T MANAGED TO CLOSE UP THE GRAVE IN TIME, LIKE HE NEEDED TO: ONE END OF THE LID STILL STUCK OUT, IN THE OPEN.
THE PEASANT NOTED ALL THIS AND SET OFF FOR THE VILLAGE.
6

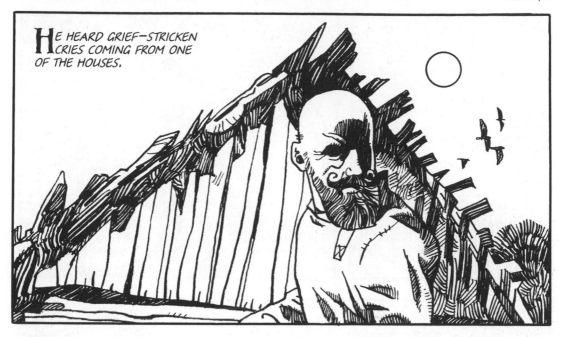

He heard grief-stricken cries coming from one of the houses.

Don't cry! I can bring 'em back to life.

Do it, son — bring 'em back! We'll give ya half'a everything we got!

7

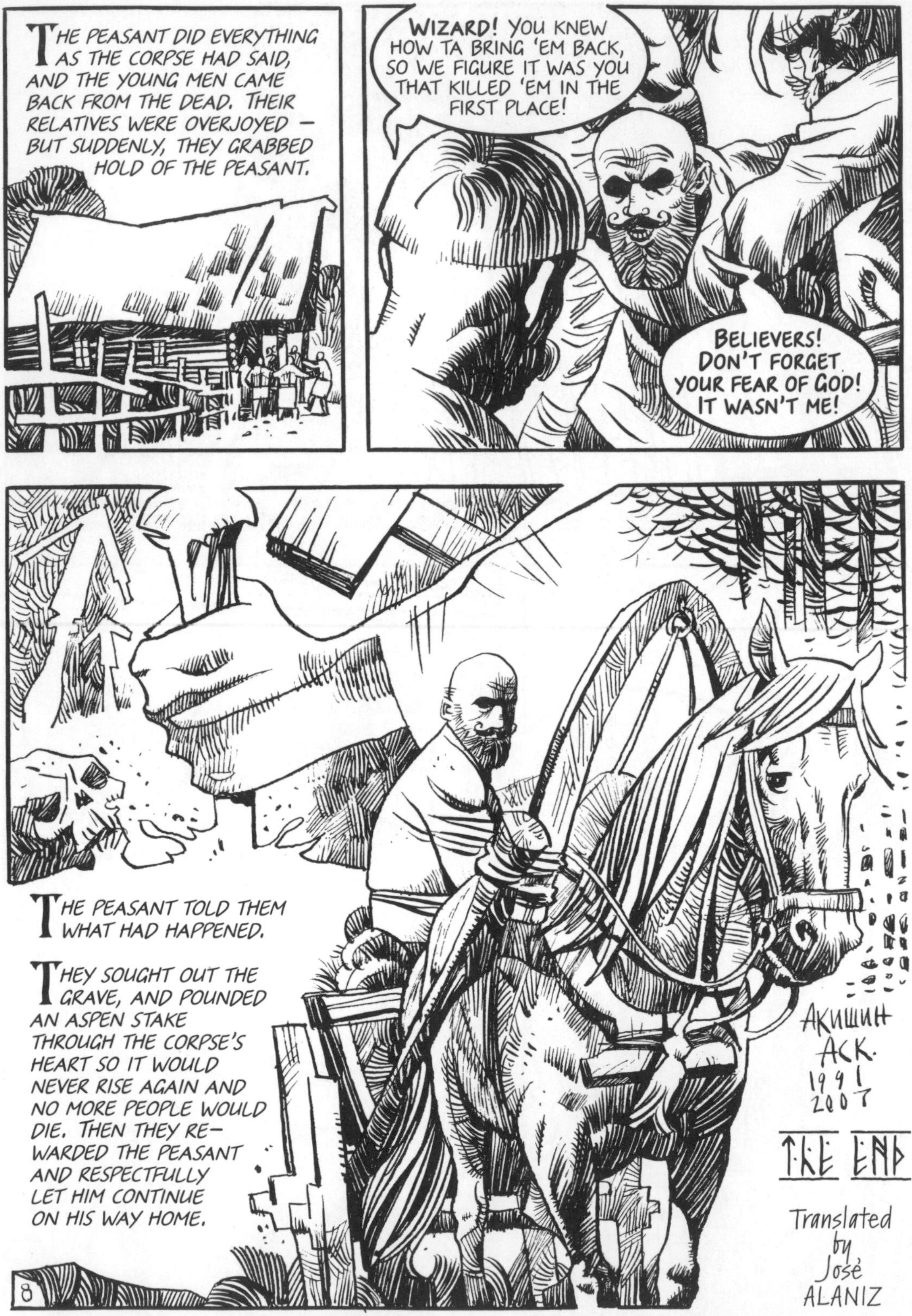
THE PEASANT DID EVERYTHING AS THE CORPSE HAD SAID, AND THE YOUNG MEN CAME BACK FROM THE DEAD. THEIR RELATIVES WERE OVERJOYED – BUT SUDDENLY, THEY GRABBED HOLD OF THE PEASANT.
WIZARD! YOU KNEW HOW TA BRING 'EM BACK, SO WE FIGURE IT WAS YOU THAT KILLED 'EM IN THE FIRST PLACE!
BELIEVERS! DON'T FORGET YOUR FEAR OF GOD! IT WASN'T ME!
THE PEASANT TOLD THEM WHAT HAD HAPPENED.
THEY SOUGHT OUT THE GRAVE, AND POUNDED AN ASPEN STAKE THROUGH THE CORPSE'S HEART SO IT WOULD NEVER RISE AGAIN AND NO MORE PEOPLE WOULD DIE. THEN THEY REWARDED THE PEASANT AND RESPECTFULLY LET HIM CONTINUE ON HIS WAY HOME.
АКИШИН
АСК.
1991
2007
THE END
Translated by José ALANIZ
8

The Haunted Ship (2008)

Creator: Askold Akishin

Survivors from a shipwreck are delighted to find an empty boat floating near them. They quickly realize that this boat is haunted by its crew who are bizarrely nailed to the planks and masthead. Now why would that be?

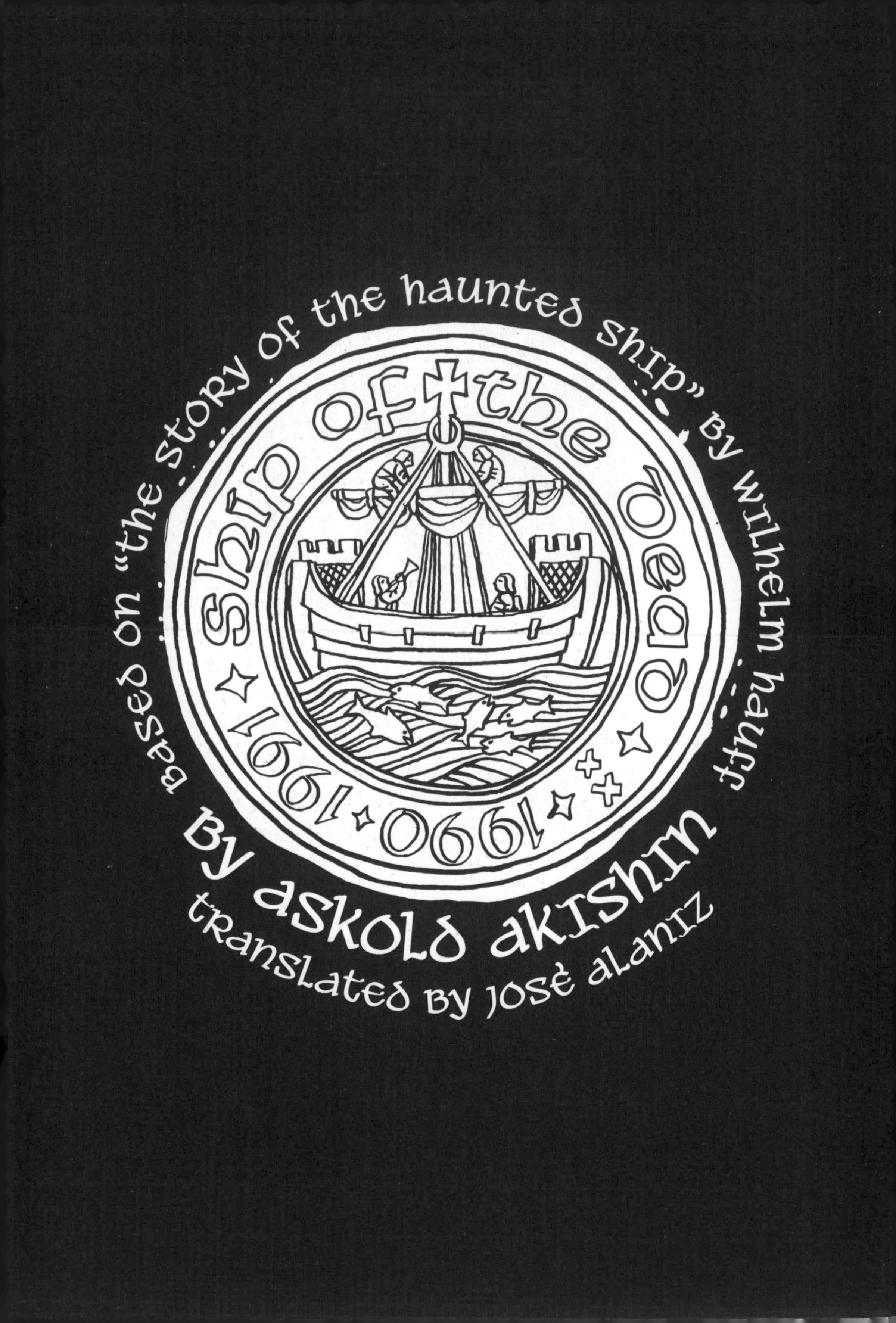
Ship of the Dead
1990·1991

based on "the story of the haunted ship" by Wilhelm Hauff

By Askold Akishin

translated by José Alaniz

When the storm died down, we spied an unknown vessel where our ship-wreck had been.

АКИШИН АСК.90.

AHOY! IS ANYONE ALIVE THERE?

No matter how long we hailed them, no one answered. The absence of life on the ship filled us with dread. But this was our only chance of survival.

2

OH, HORRORS!

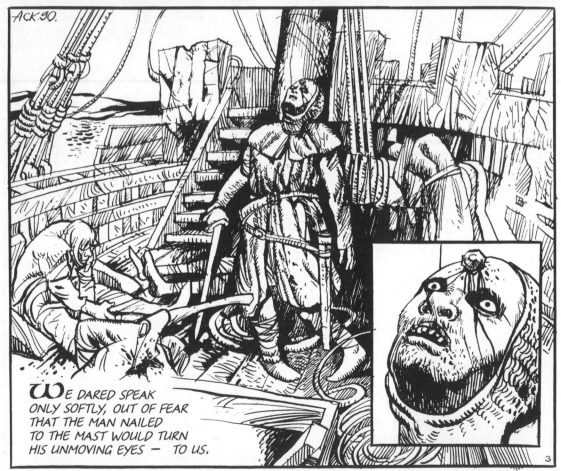

ACK.90.

WE DARED SPEAK ONLY SOFTLY, OUT OF FEAR THAT THE MAN NAILED TO THE MAST WOULD TURN HIS UNMOVING EYES — TO US.

3

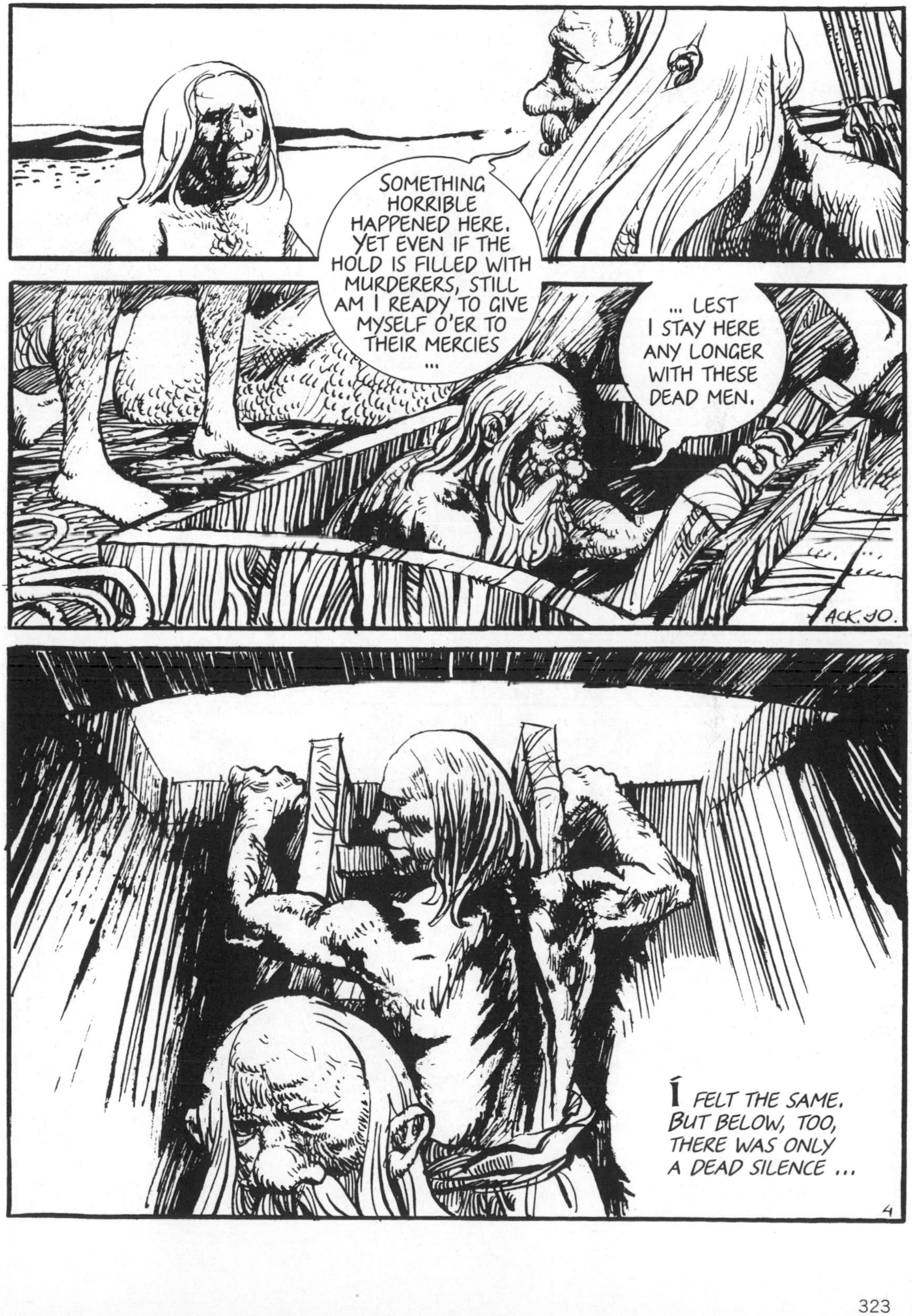
SOMETHING HORRIBLE HAPPENED HERE. YET EVEN IF THE HOLD IS FILLED WITH MURDERERS, STILL AM I READY TO GIVE MYSELF O'ER TO THEIR MERCIES ...
... LEST I STAY HERE ANY LONGER WITH THESE DEAD MEN.
ACK. JO.
I FELT THE SAME. BUT BELOW, TOO, THERE WAS ONLY A DEAD SILENCE ...
4

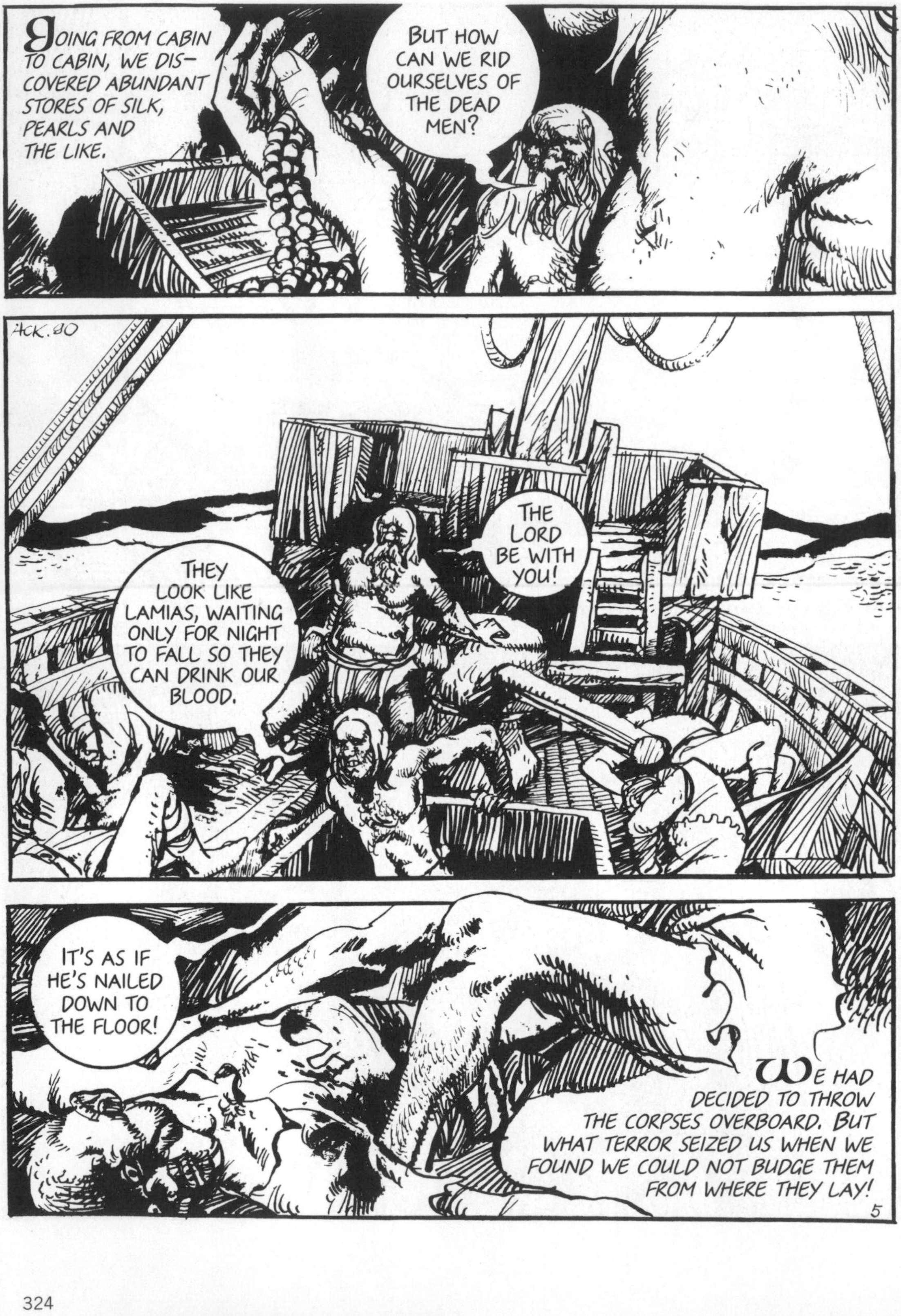
GOING FROM CABIN TO CABIN, WE DIS-COVERED ABUNDANT STORES OF SILK, PEARLS AND THE LIKE.
BUT HOW CAN WE RID OURSELVES OF THE DEAD MEN?
ACK. 80
THEY LOOK LIKE LAMIAS, WAITING ONLY FOR NIGHT TO FALL SO THEY CAN DRINK OUR BLOOD.
THE LORD BE WITH YOU!
IT'S AS IF HE'S NAILED DOWN TO THE FLOOR!
WE HAD DECIDED TO THROW THE CORPSES OVERBOARD. BUT WHAT TERROR SEIZED US WHEN WE FOUND WE COULD NOT BUDGE THEM FROM WHERE THEY LAY!
5

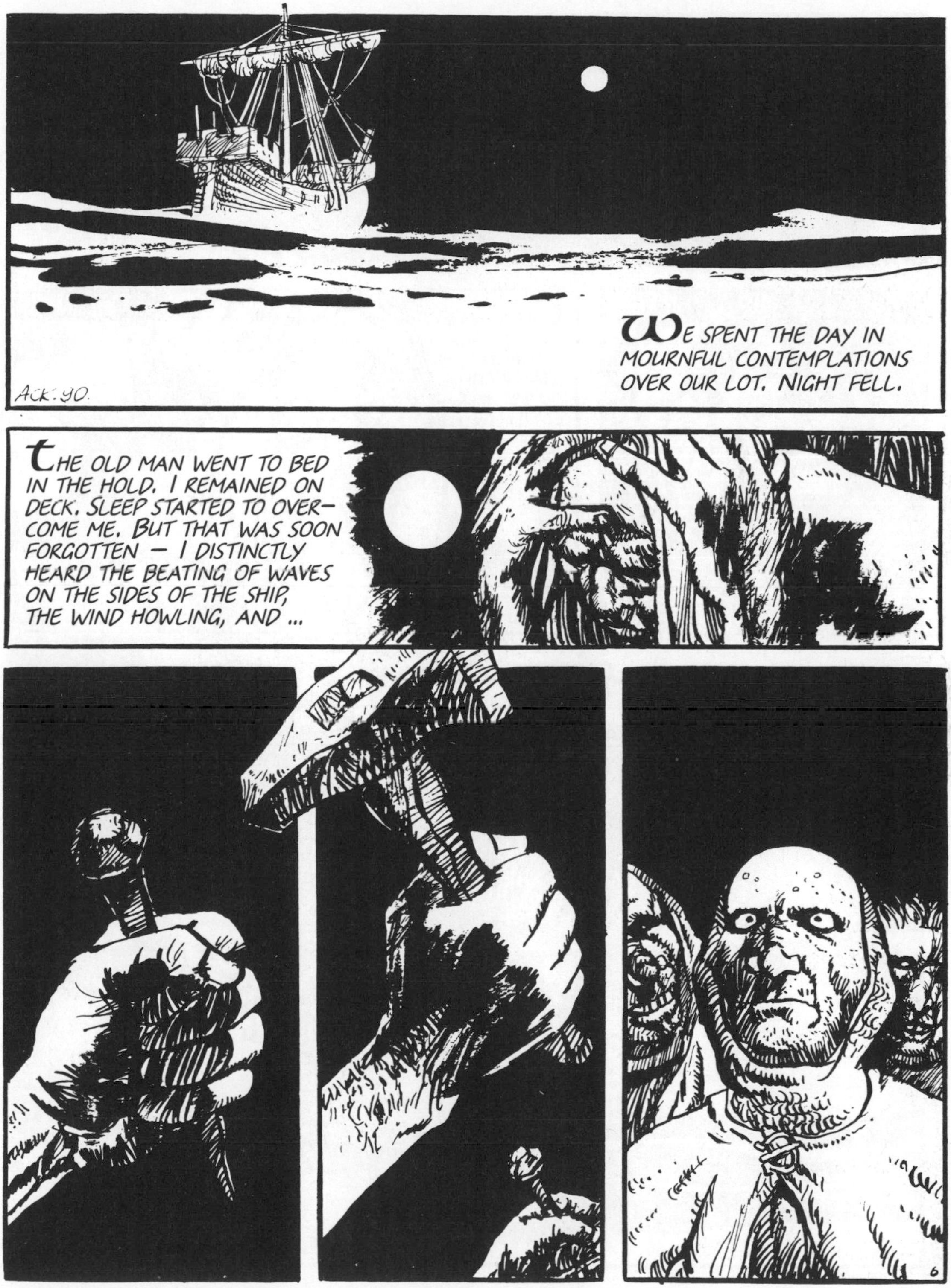
WE SPENT THE DAY IN MOURNFUL CONTEMPLATIONS OVER OUR LOT. NIGHT FELL.
ACK:90.
THE OLD MAN WENT TO BED IN THE HOLD. I REMAINED ON DECK. SLEEP STARTED TO OVER-COME ME. BUT THAT WAS SOON FORGOTTEN — I DISTINCTLY HEARD THE BEATING OF WAVES ON THE SIDES OF THE SHIP, THE WIND HOWLING, AND ...
6

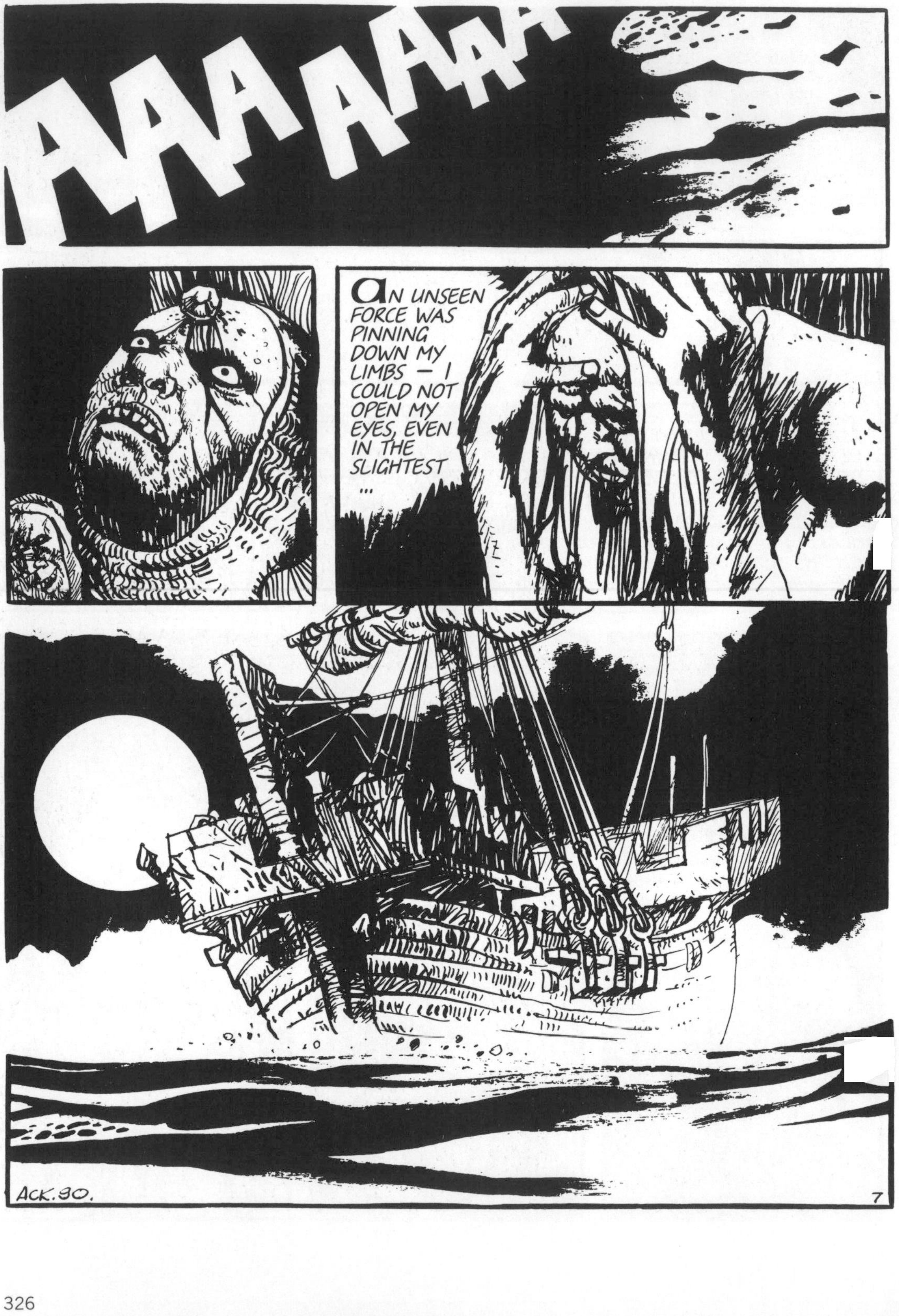
AAAAAAA
AN UNSEEN FORCE WAS PINNING DOWN MY LIMBS — I COULD NOT OPEN MY EYES, EVEN IN THE SLIGHTEST ...
ACK. 80.
7

THIS WAS NO DREAM. I TOO HEARD THE SCREAMS.
WHEN WE LAND WE'LL PUT UP A CROSS.
ACK.90.
THE SHIP SAILED NORTH, WHERE BY OUR CALCULATIONS THERE MUST BE LAND. BUT A STRANGE THING HAPPENED: OVER THE COURSE OF THE DAY THE SHIP WOULD TRAVERSE THE EXPECTED DISTANCE – BUT AT NIGHT IT REVERSED ITSELF, SO THAT BY SUNRISE WE ALWAYS TURNED UP AT OUR OLD POSITION.
TO PREVENT THIS, BEFORE NIGHTFALL WE TIED UP THE SAIL AND SAID EVENING PRAYERS.
8

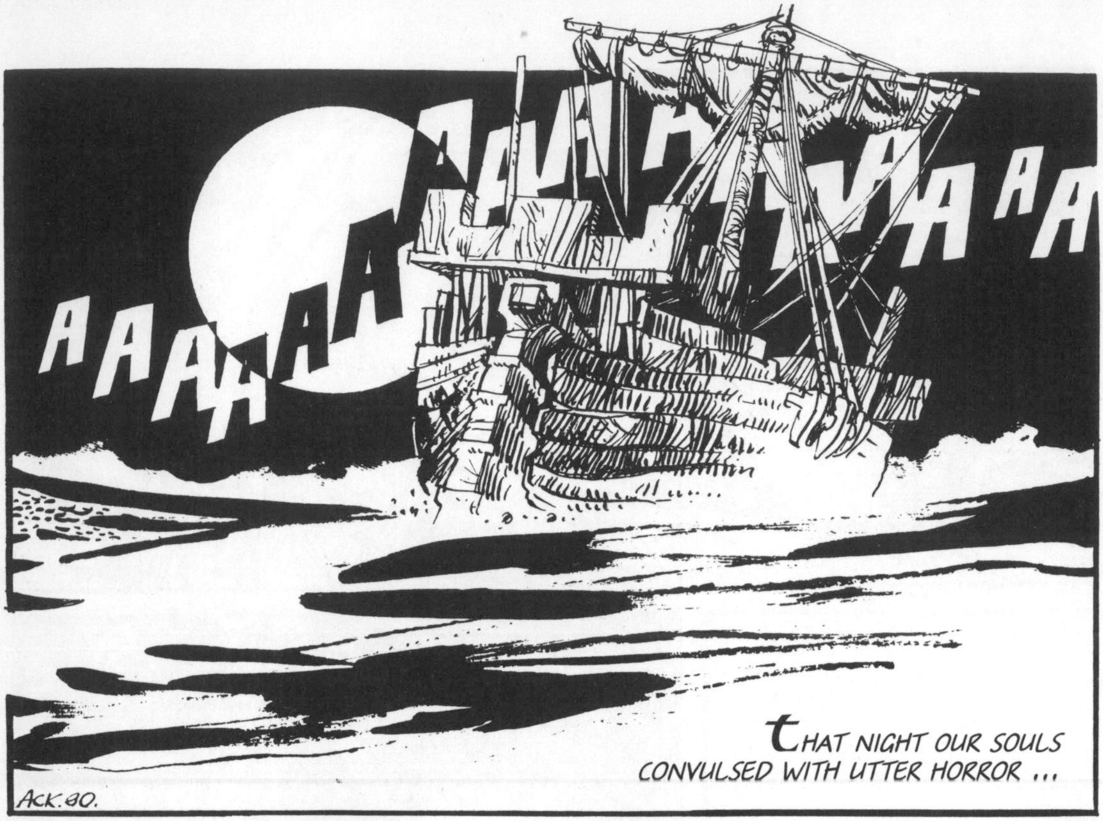
AAAAAAAAAAAAAAAAAA
THAT NIGHT OUR SOULS CONVULSED WITH UTTER HORROR ...
ACK.80.

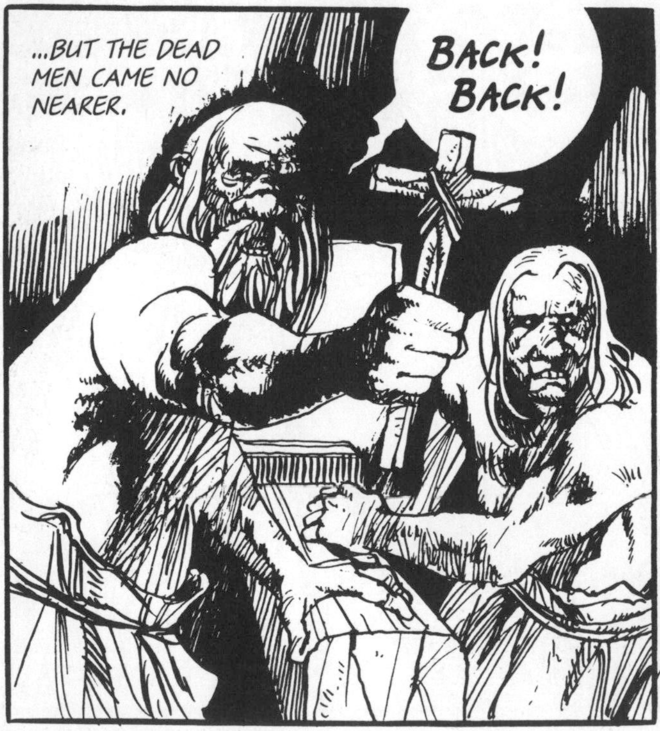
...BUT THE DEAD MEN CAME NO NEARER.
BACK! BACK!

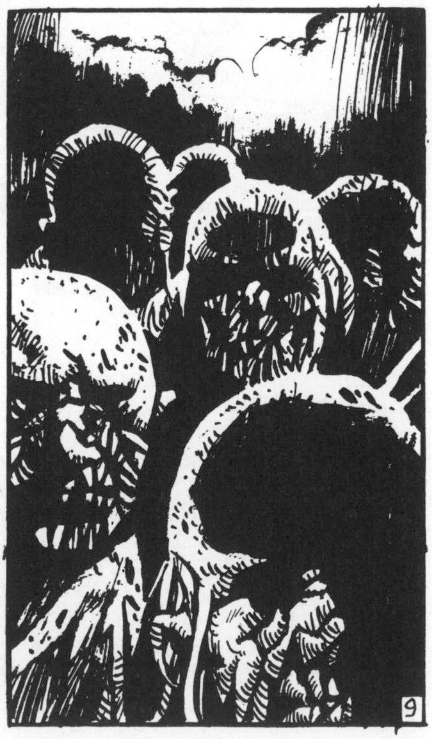
9

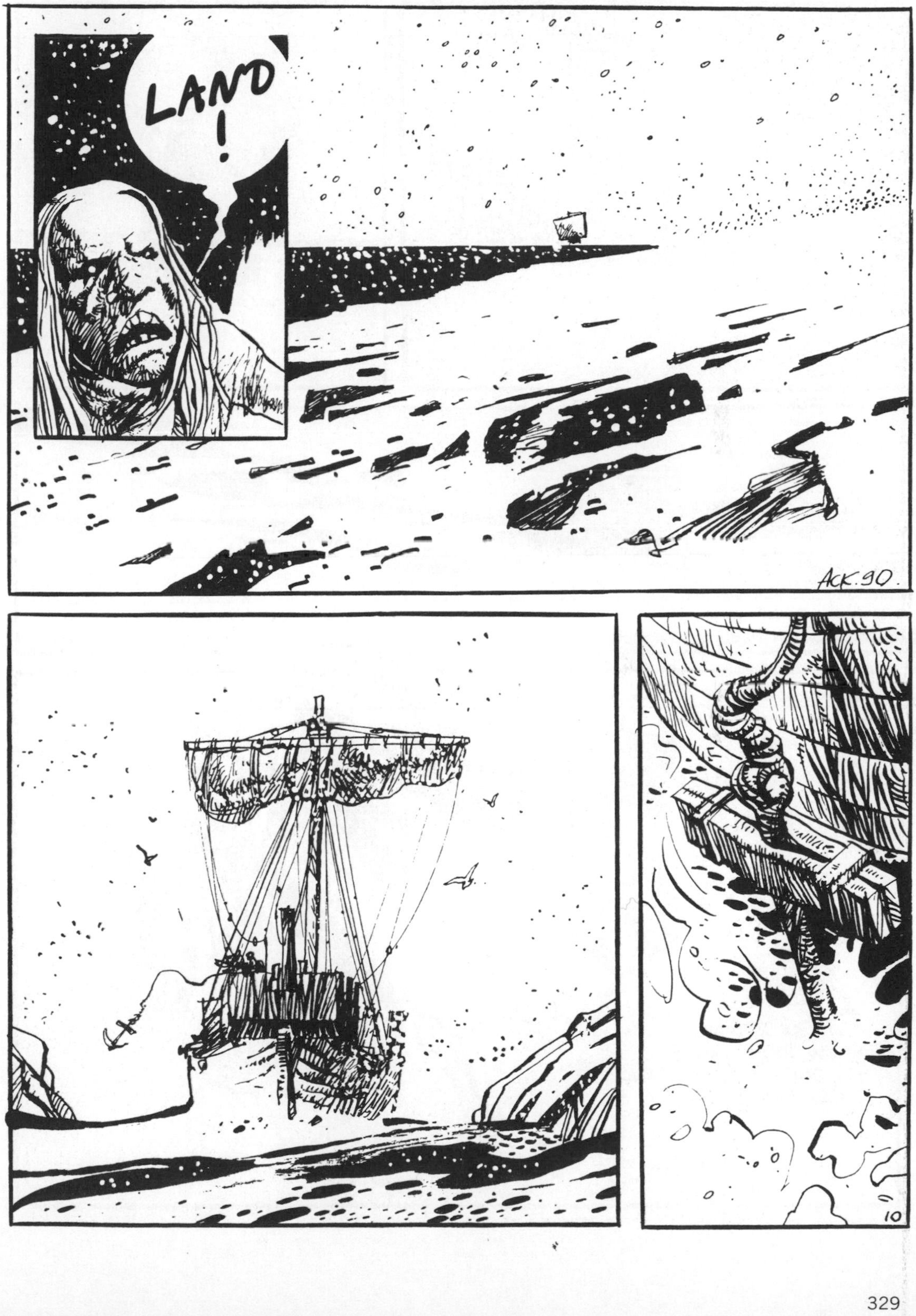
LAND!
ACK.90
10

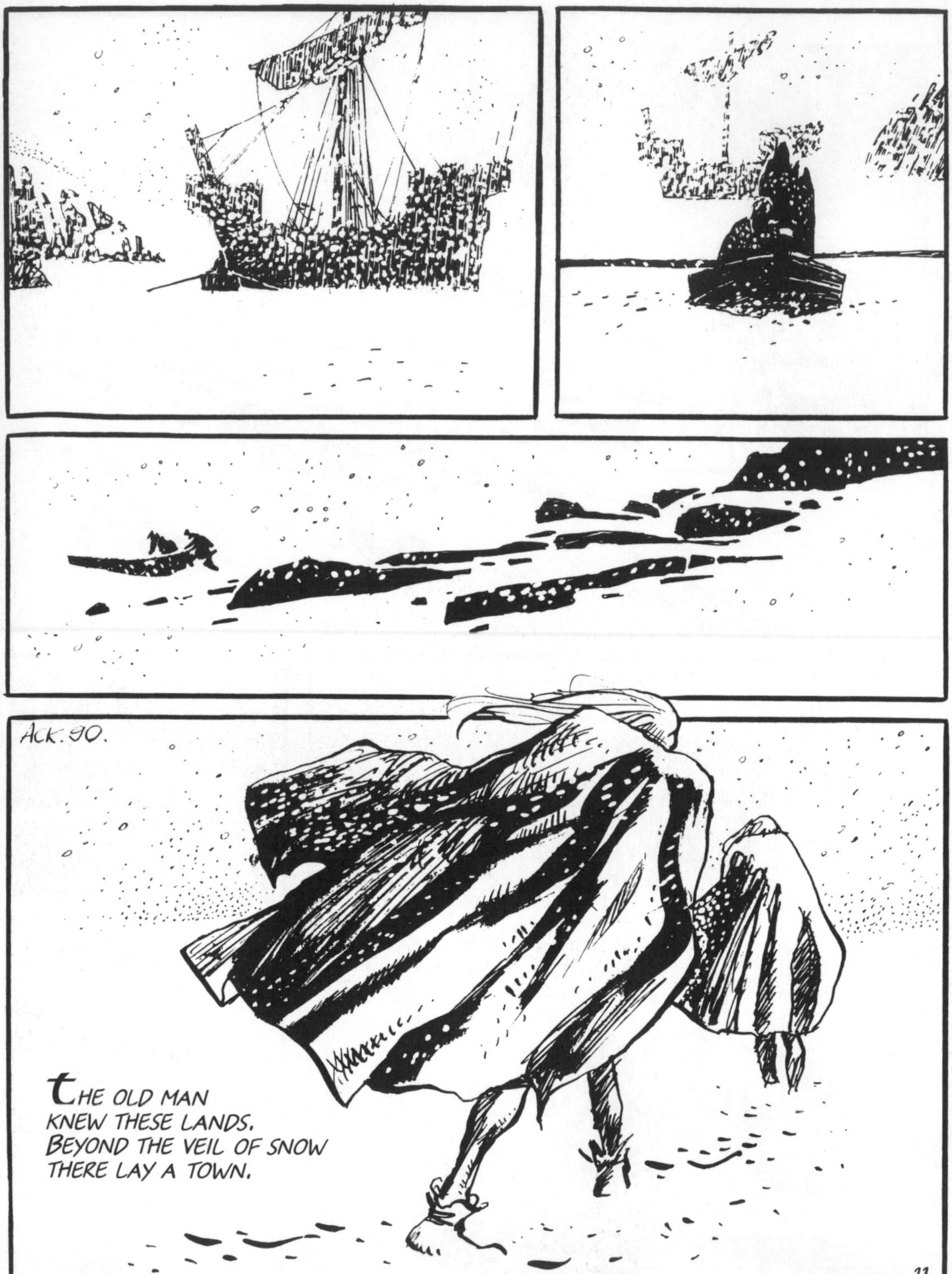

ACK. 90.
THE OLD MAN
KNEW THESE LANDS.
BEYOND THE VEIL OF SNOW
THERE LAY A TOWN.
11

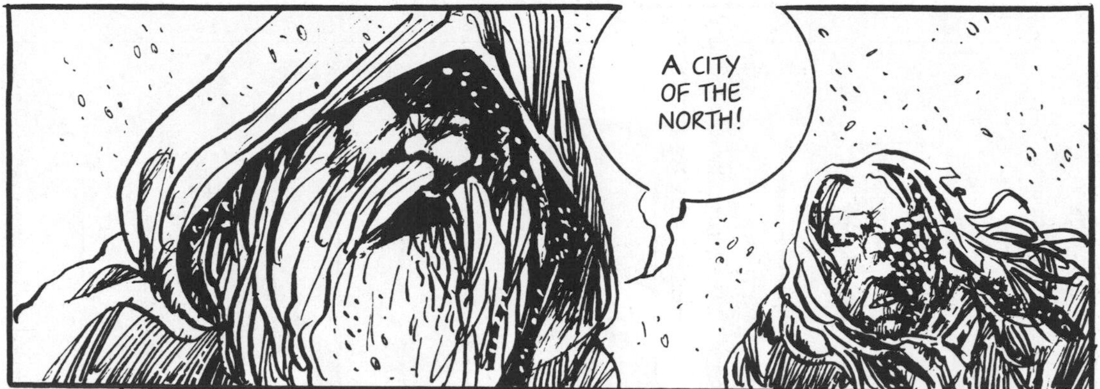
A CITY OF THE NORTH!

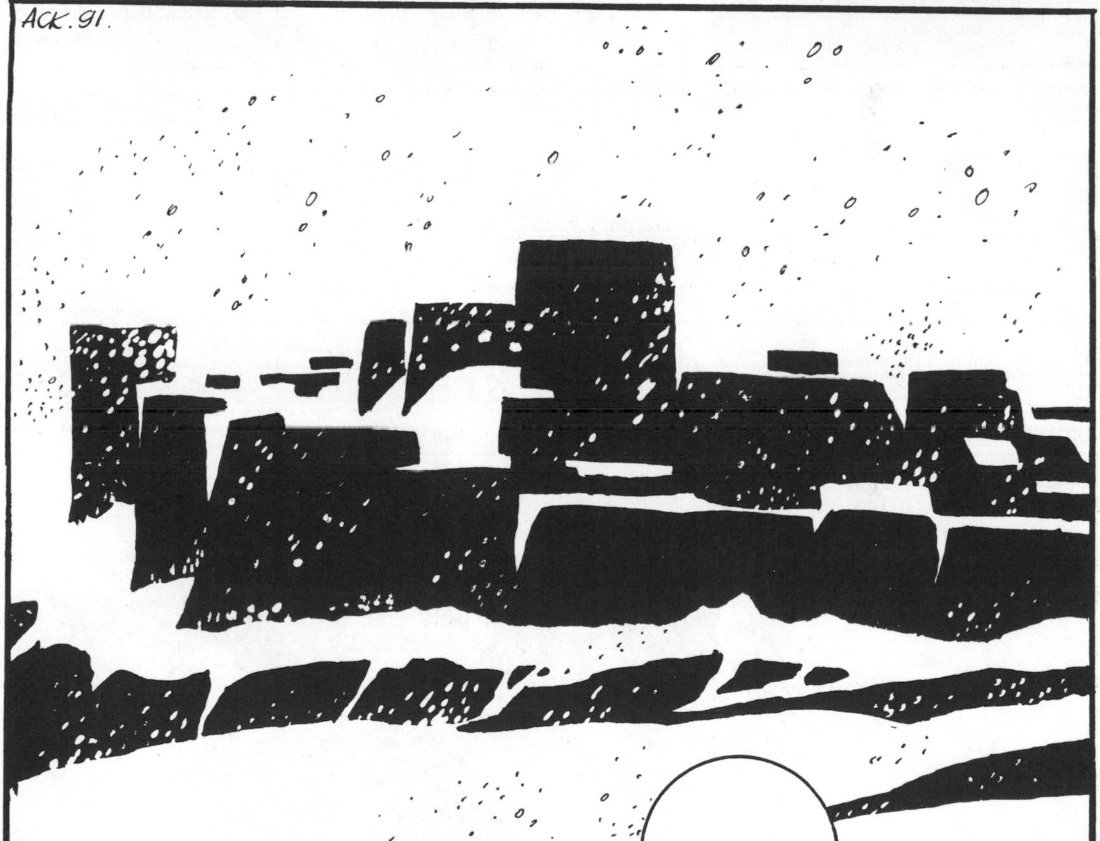
ACK. 91.
ONWARD!
12

ACK.91.

LET US SEE THE STONEMASON. THE CROSS MUST BE OF STONE!

THE TOWN LOOKS DESERTED.

WE SOUGHT OUT THE STONEMASON, AND BOUGHT THE CROSS, BUT ...

TAKE YE CARE THIS NIGHT. IT IS AT THIS VERY TIME, EVERY MONTH, THAT SEA PIRATES FALL UPON THIS TOWN!

IT IS SAID THAT THEY COME FROM THE OTHER WORLD ... ALL WHO LIVE HAVE ALREADY FLED!

13

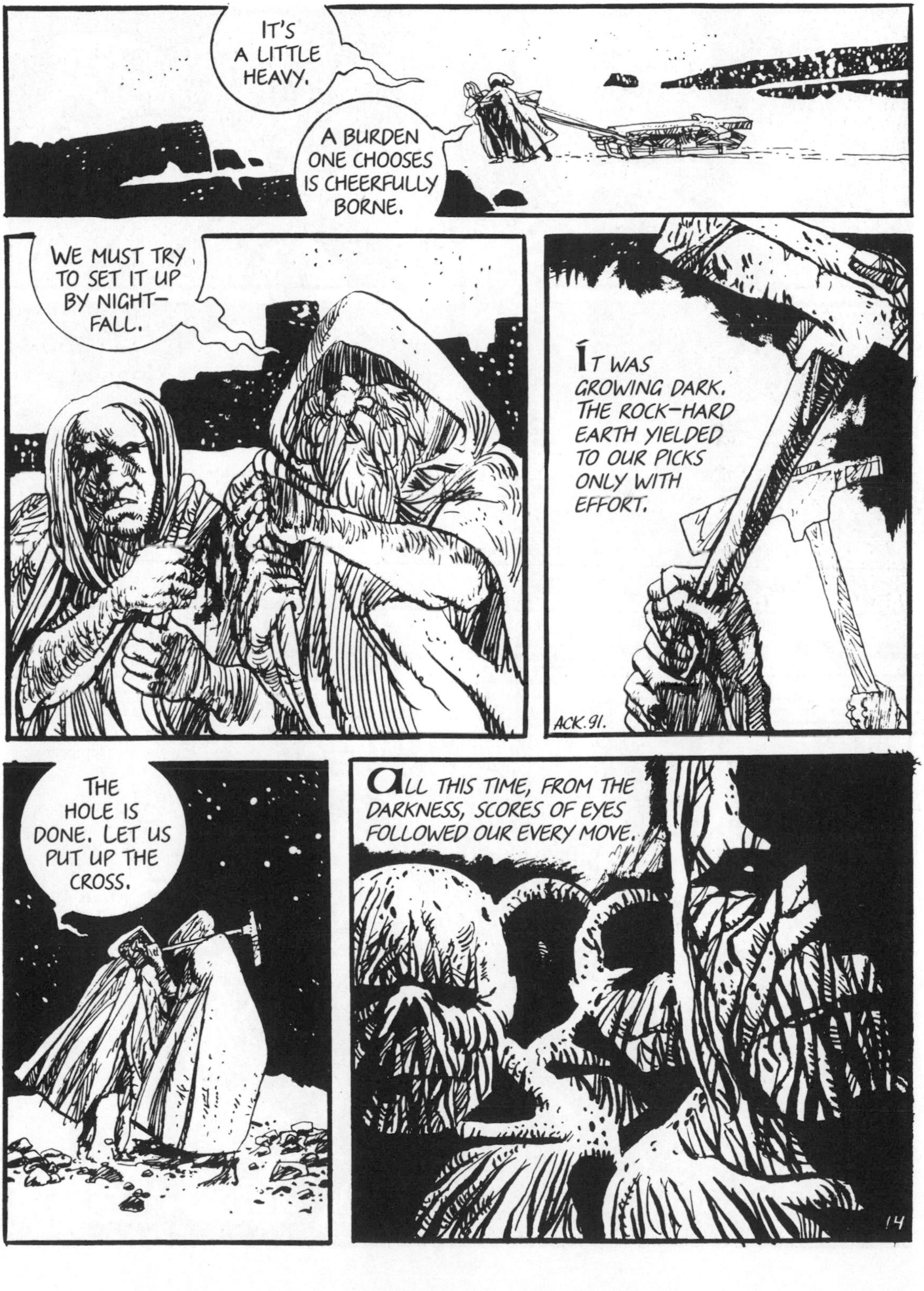
IT'S A LITTLE HEAVY.
A BURDEN ONE CHOOSES IS CHEERFULLY BORNE.
WE MUST TRY TO SET IT UP BY NIGHT-FALL.
IT WAS GROWING DARK. THE ROCK-HARD EARTH YIELDED TO OUR PICKS ONLY WITH EFFORT.
ACK.91.
THE HOLE IS DONE. LET US PUT UP THE CROSS.
ALL THIS TIME, FROM THE DARKNESS, SCORES OF EYES FOLLOWED OUR EVERY MOVE.
14

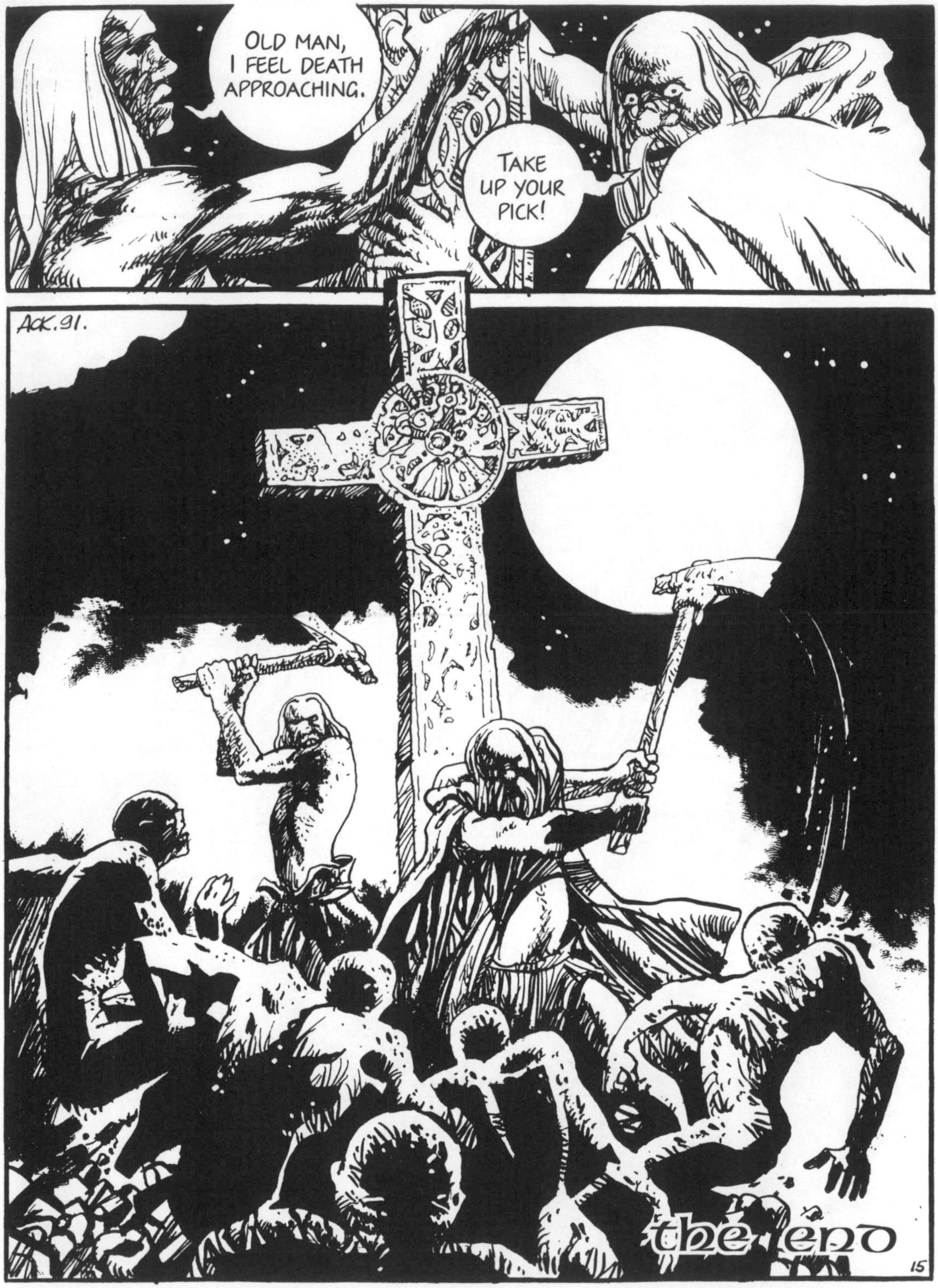

OLD MAN, I FEEL DEATH APPROACHING.
TAKE UP YOUR PICK!
ACK.91.
THE END
15

The Zombie (2008)

Creator: Askold Akishin.

When zombies first entered the horror cast list at the beginning of the last century they would always be linked to voodoo and slave plantations. Hardly any of those stories made it into comic form and so that makes this story particularly interesting.

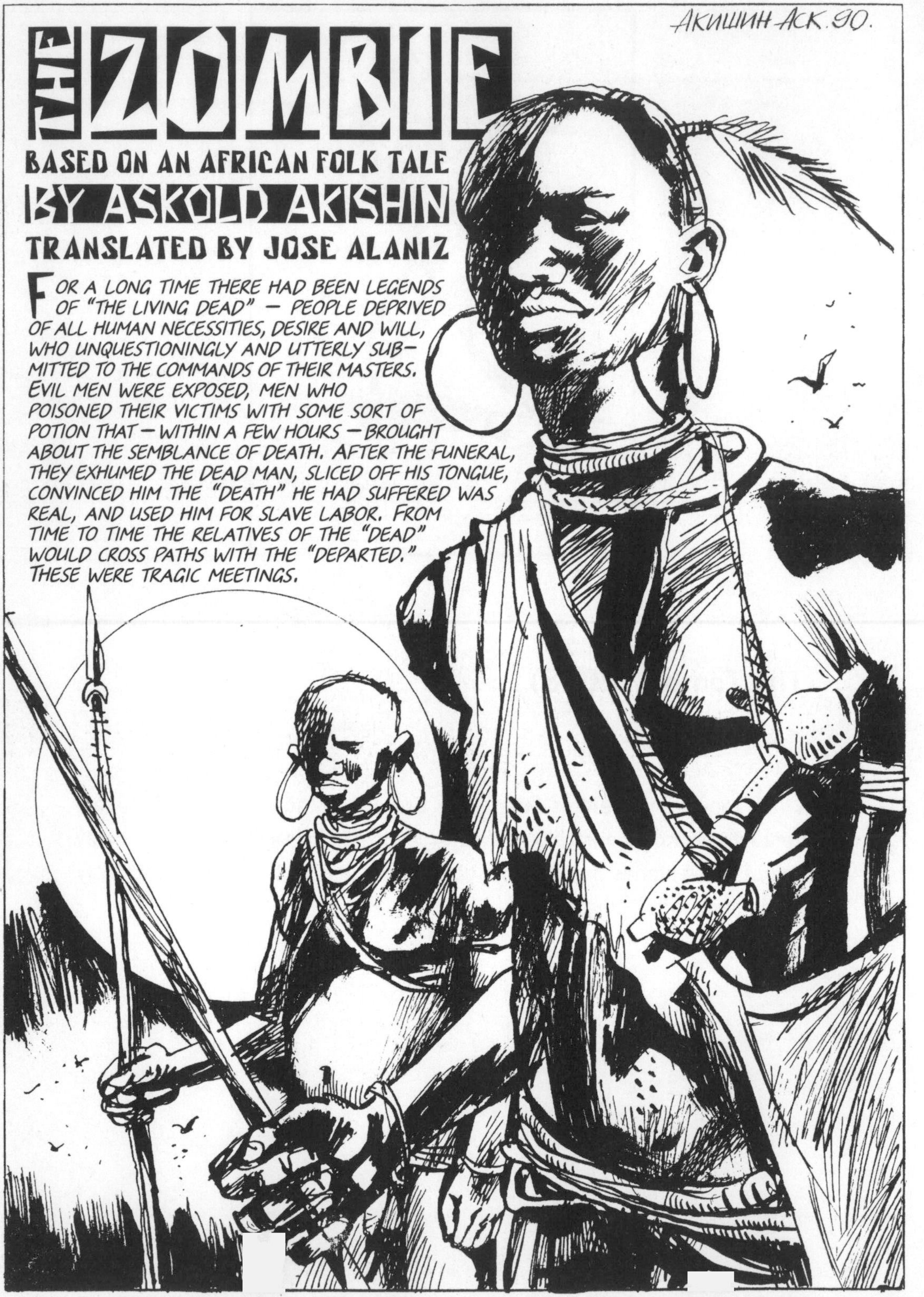
АКИШИН АСК. 90.
THE ZOMBIE
BASED ON AN AFRICAN FOLK TALE
BY ASKOLD AKISHIN
TRANSLATED BY JOSE ALANIZ
FOR A LONG TIME THERE HAD BEEN LEGENDS OF "THE LIVING DEAD" — PEOPLE DEPRIVED OF ALL HUMAN NECESSITIES, DESIRE AND WILL, WHO UNQUESTIONINGLY AND UTTERLY SUBMITTED TO THE COMMANDS OF THEIR MASTERS. EVIL MEN WERE EXPOSED, MEN WHO POISONED THEIR VICTIMS WITH SOME SORT OF POTION THAT — WITHIN A FEW HOURS — BROUGHT ABOUT THE SEMBLANCE OF DEATH. AFTER THE FUNERAL, THEY EXHUMED THE DEAD MAN, SLICED OFF HIS TONGUE, CONVINCED HIM THE "DEATH" HE HAD SUFFERED WAS REAL, AND USED HIM FOR SLAVE LABOR. FROM TIME TO TIME THE RELATIVES OF THE "DEAD" WOULD CROSS PATHS WITH THE "DEPARTED." THESE WERE TRAGIC MEETINGS.

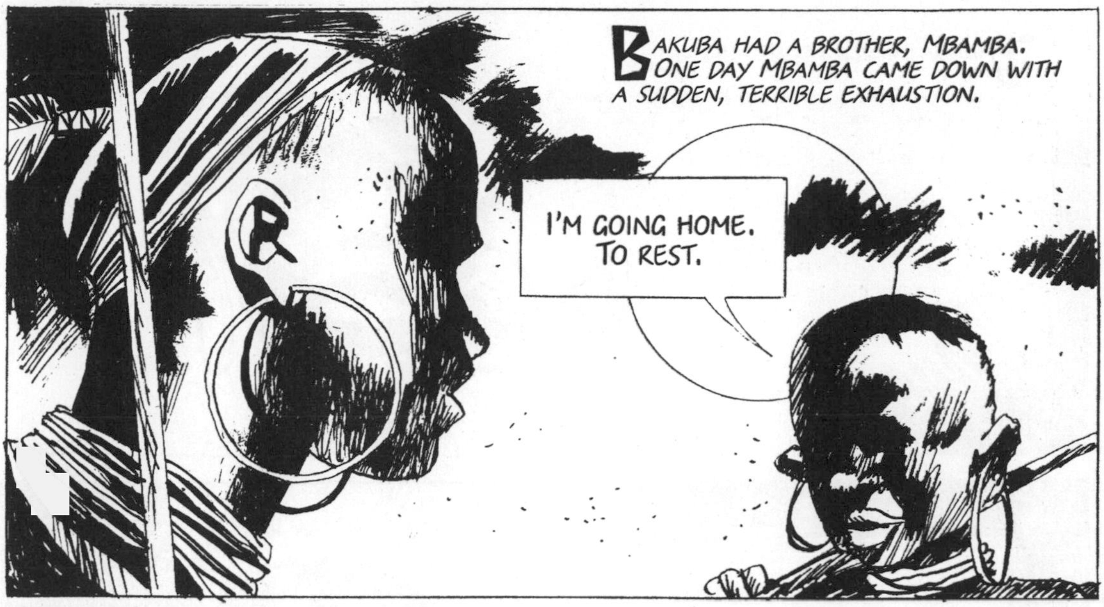
BAKUBA HAD A BROTHER, MBAMBA. ONE DAY MBAMBA CAME DOWN WITH A SUDDEN, TERRIBLE EXHAUSTION.
I'M GOING HOME. TO REST.

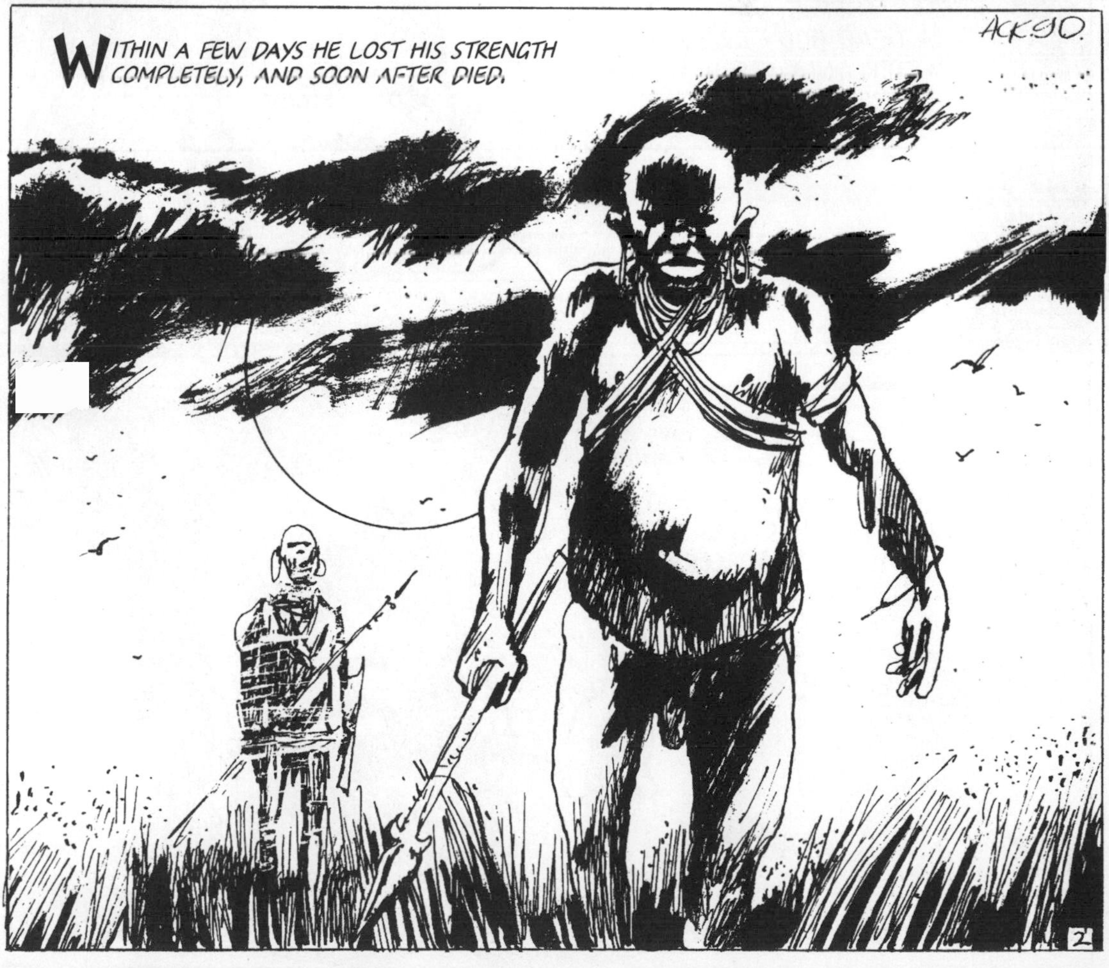
WITHIN A FEW DAYS HE LOST HIS STRENGTH COMPLETELY, AND SOON AFTER DIED.
ACK 90.
2

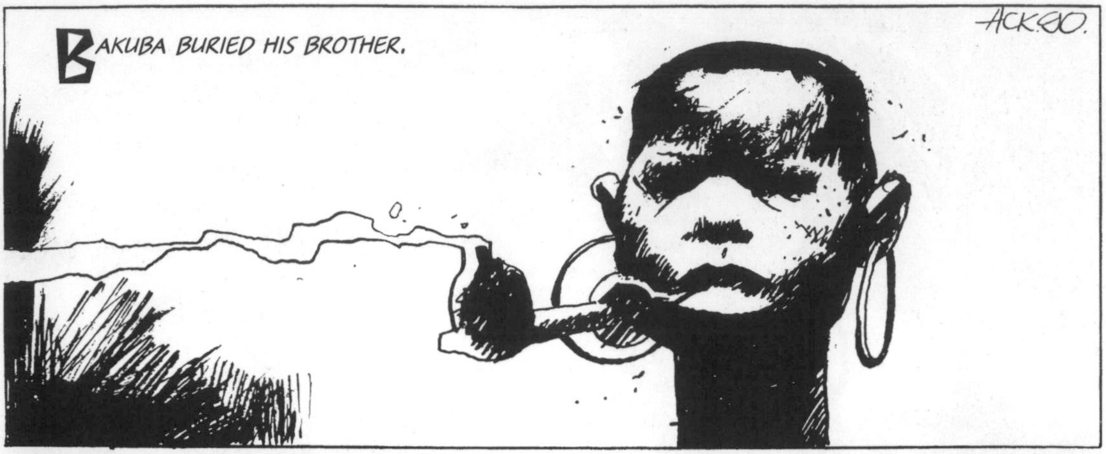
ACK.90.
BAKUBA BURIED HIS BROTHER.

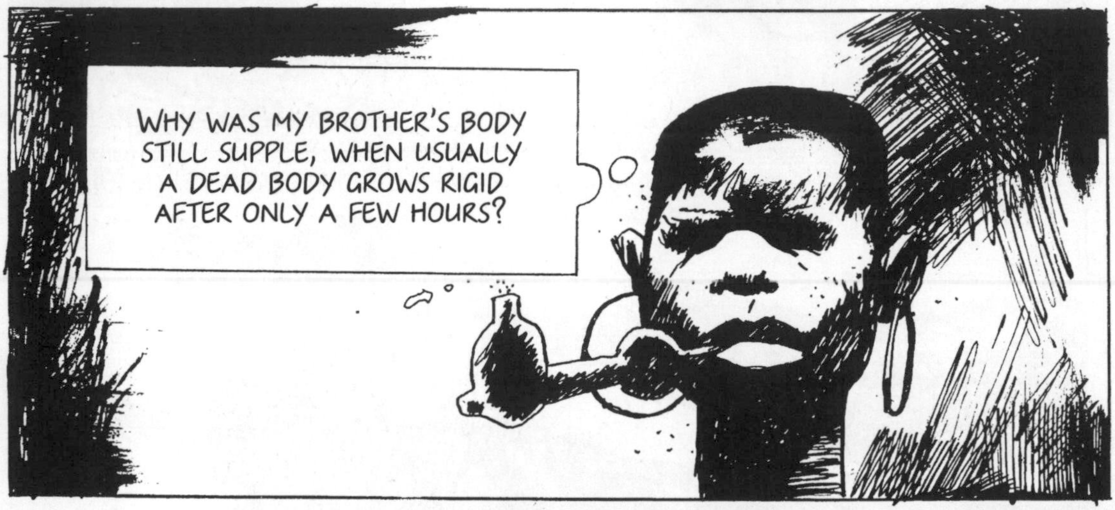
WHY WAS MY BROTHER'S BODY STILL SUPPLE, WHEN USUALLY A DEAD BODY GROWS RIGID AFTER ONLY A FEW HOURS?

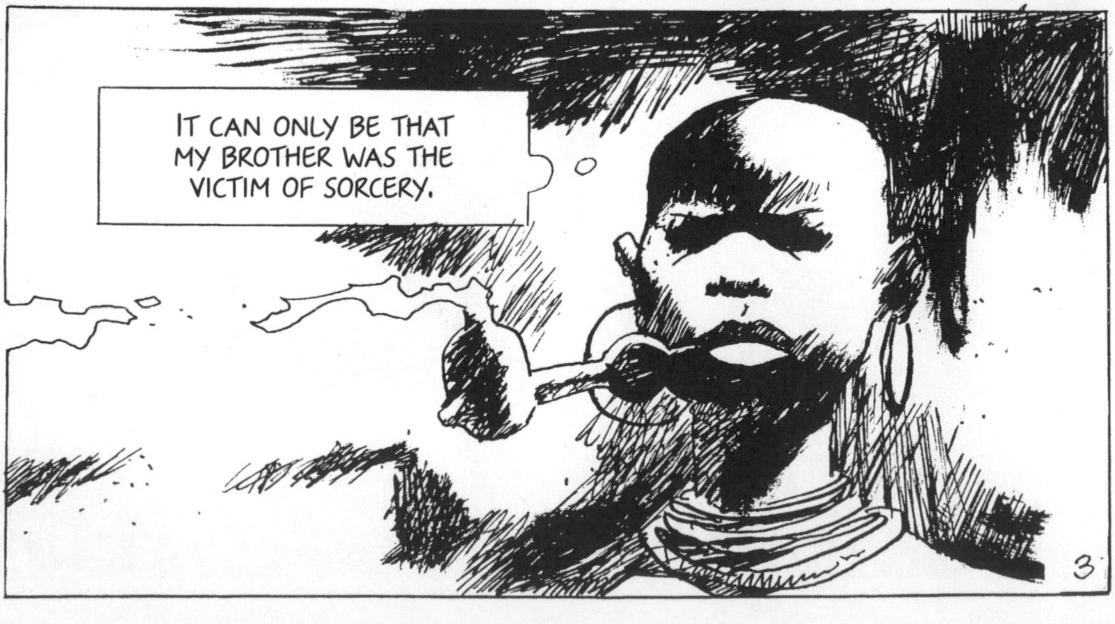
IT CAN ONLY BE THAT MY BROTHER WAS THE VICTIM OF SORCERY.
3

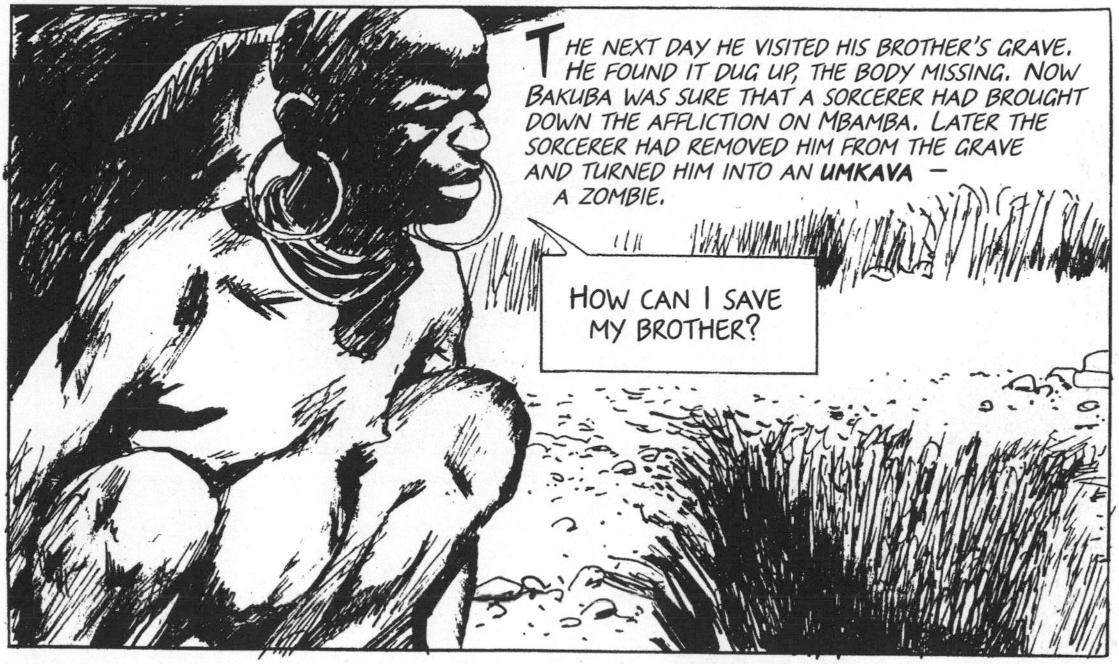
THE NEXT DAY HE VISITED HIS BROTHER'S GRAVE. HE FOUND IT DUG UP, THE BODY MISSING. NOW BAKUBA WAS SURE THAT A SORCERER HAD BROUGHT DOWN THE AFFLICTION ON MBAMBA. LATER THE SORCERER HAD REMOVED HIM FROM THE GRAVE AND TURNED HIM INTO AN **UMKAVA** — A ZOMBIE.
HOW CAN I SAVE MY BROTHER?

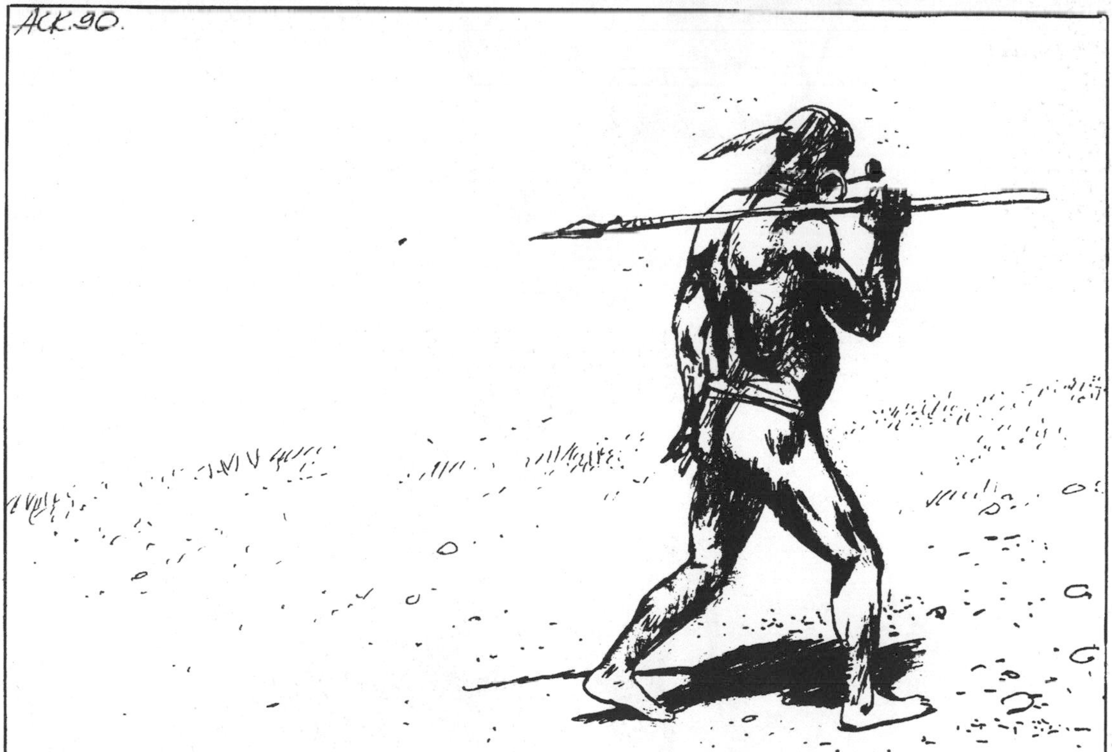
ACK.90.
BAKUBA MADE UP HIS MIND TO GO OFF IN SEARCH OF HIM.
4

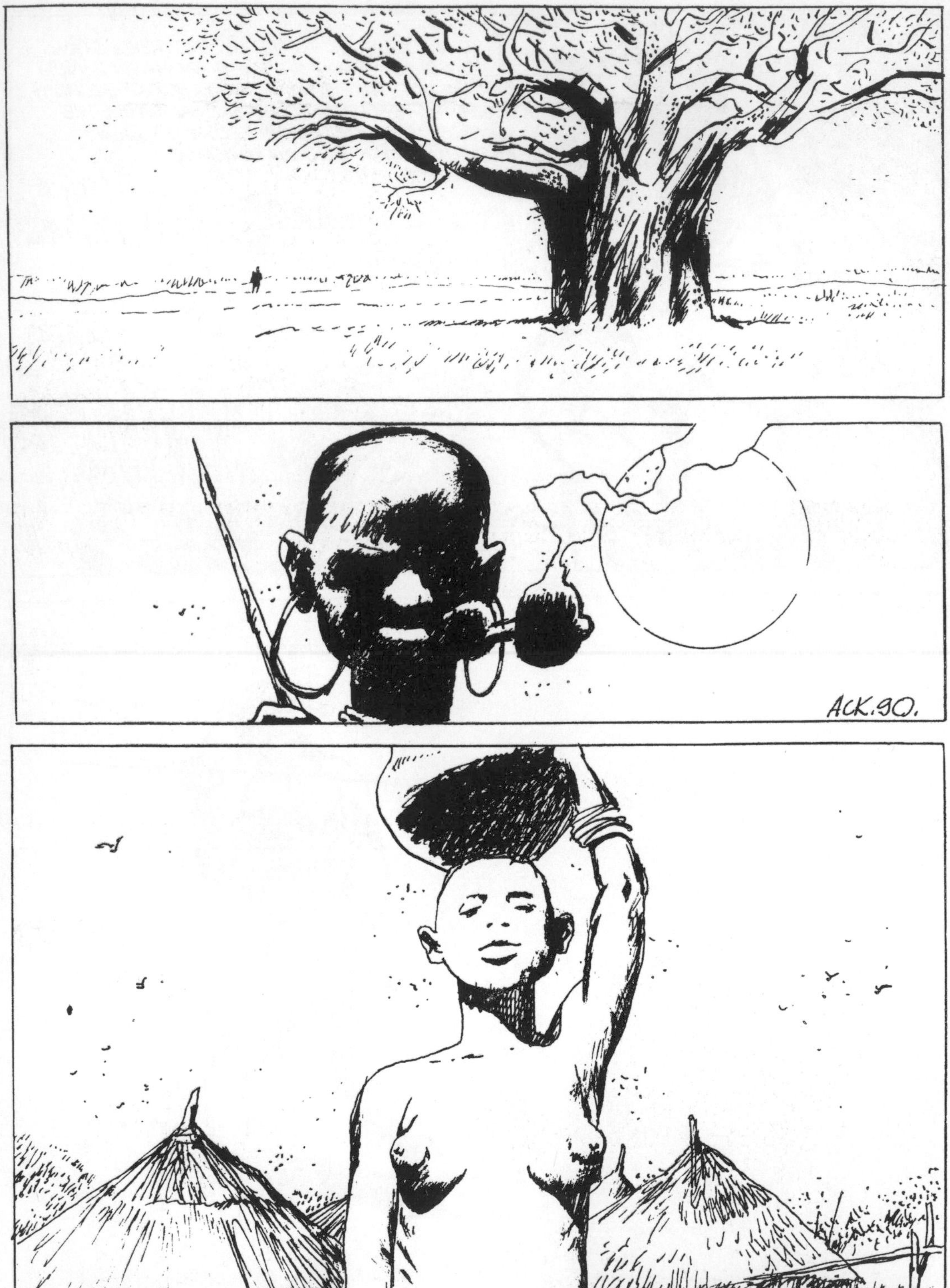
ACK.90.
5

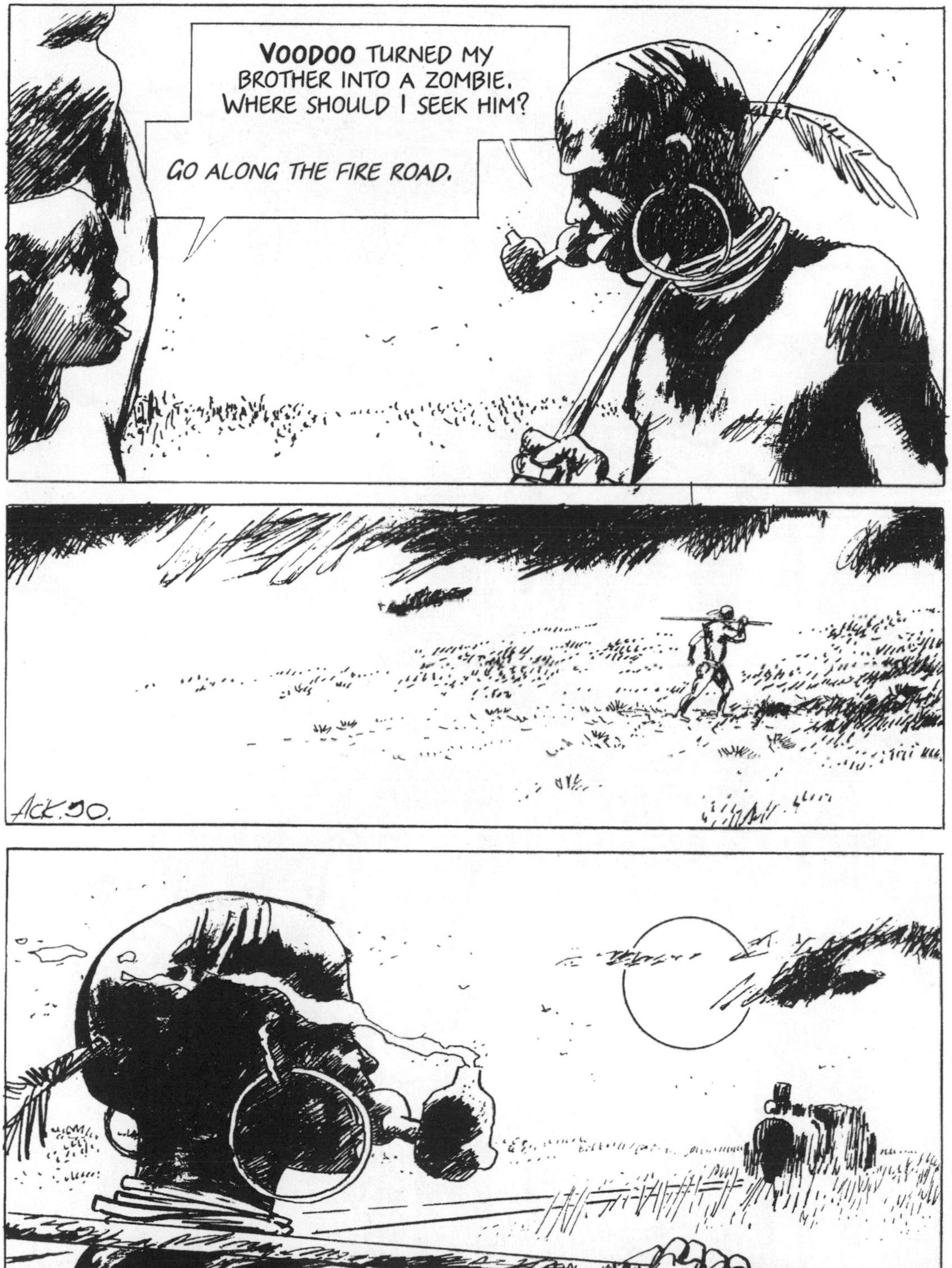
VOODOO TURNED MY BROTHER INTO A ZOMBIE. WHERE SHOULD I SEEK HIM?
GO ALONG THE FIRE ROAD.
ACK.90.
6

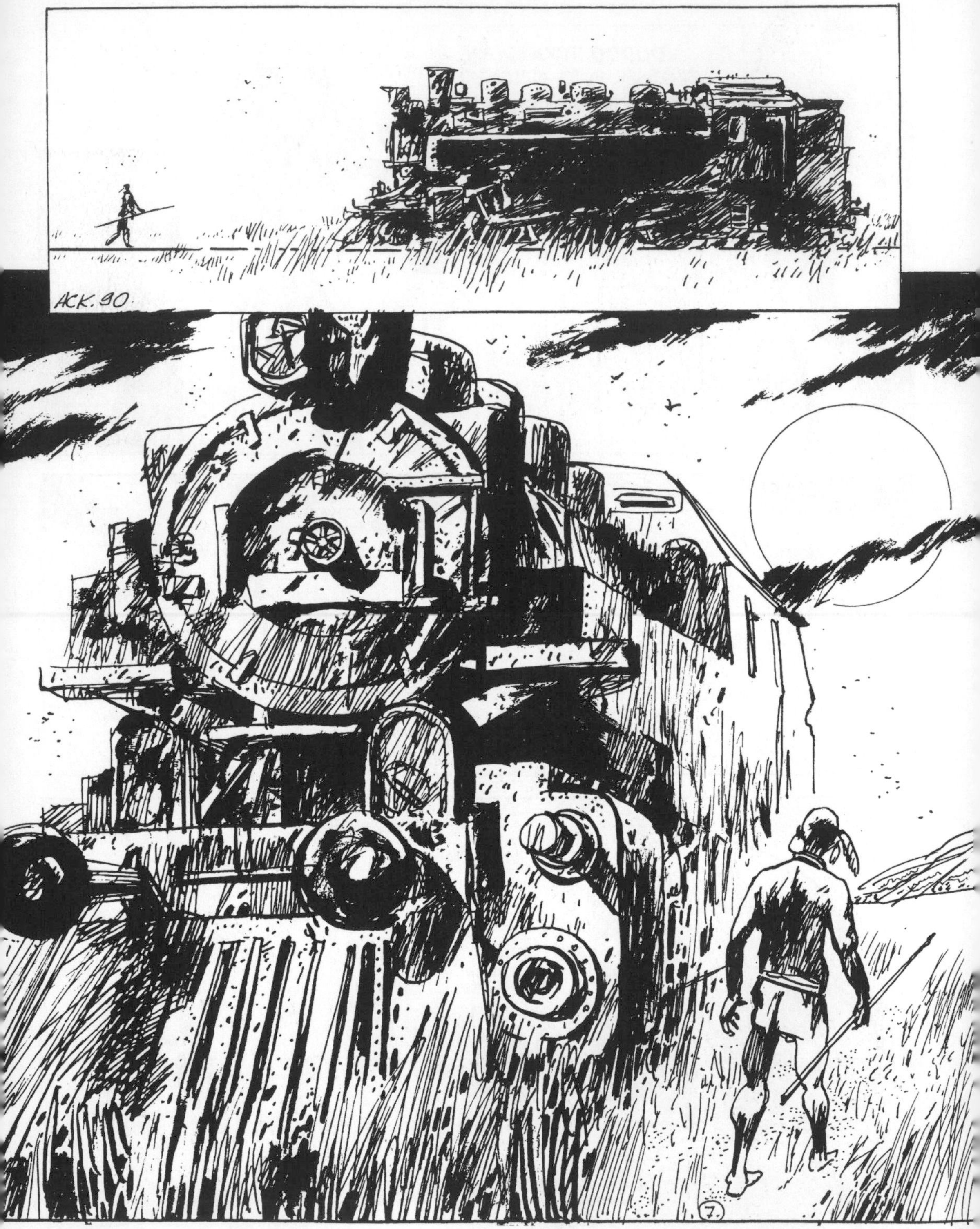
ACK. 90
7.

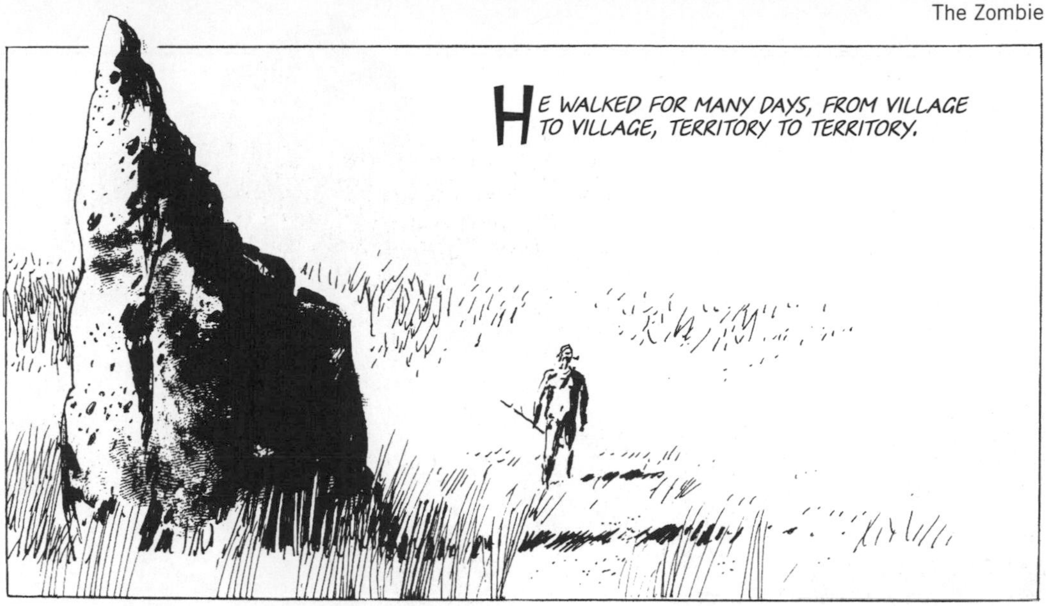
HE WALKED FOR MANY DAYS, FROM VILLAGE TO VILLAGE, TERRITORY TO TERRITORY.

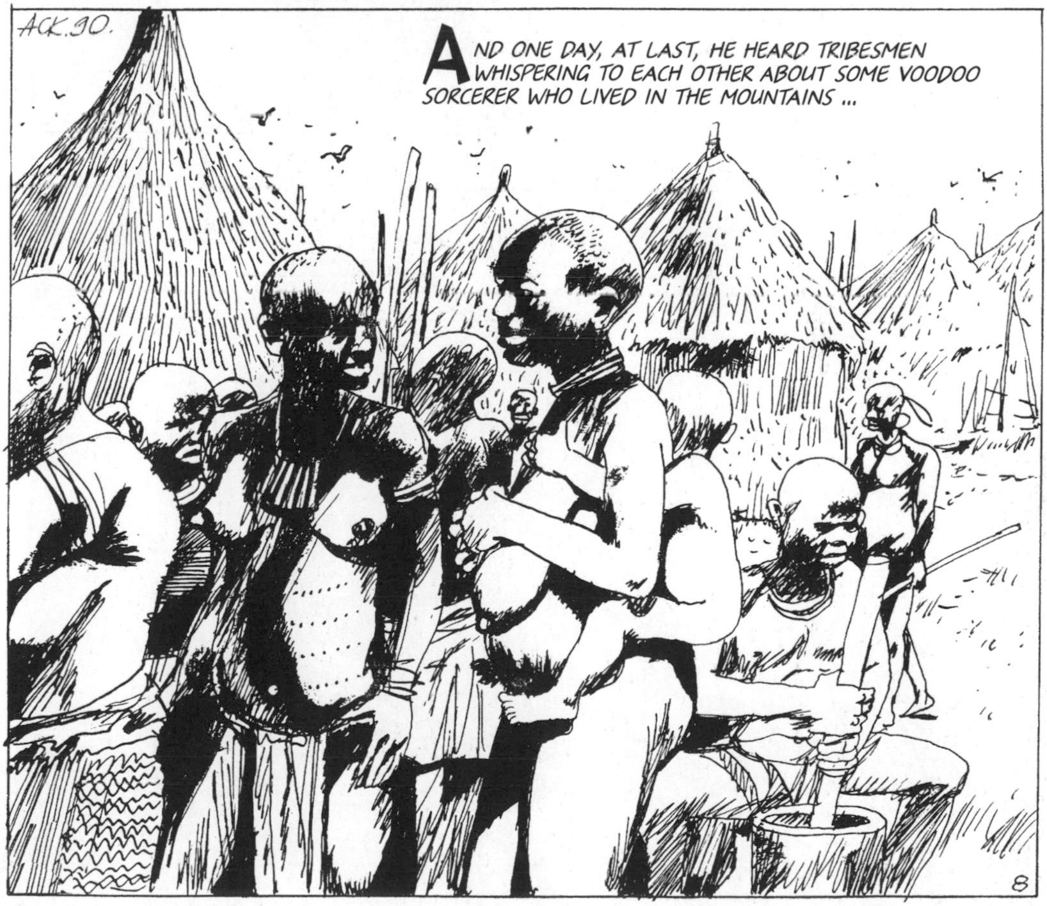
ACK.90.
AND ONE DAY, AT LAST, HE HEARD TRIBESMEN WHISPERING TO EACH OTHER ABOUT SOME VOODOO SORCERER WHO LIVED IN THE MOUNTAINS ...
8

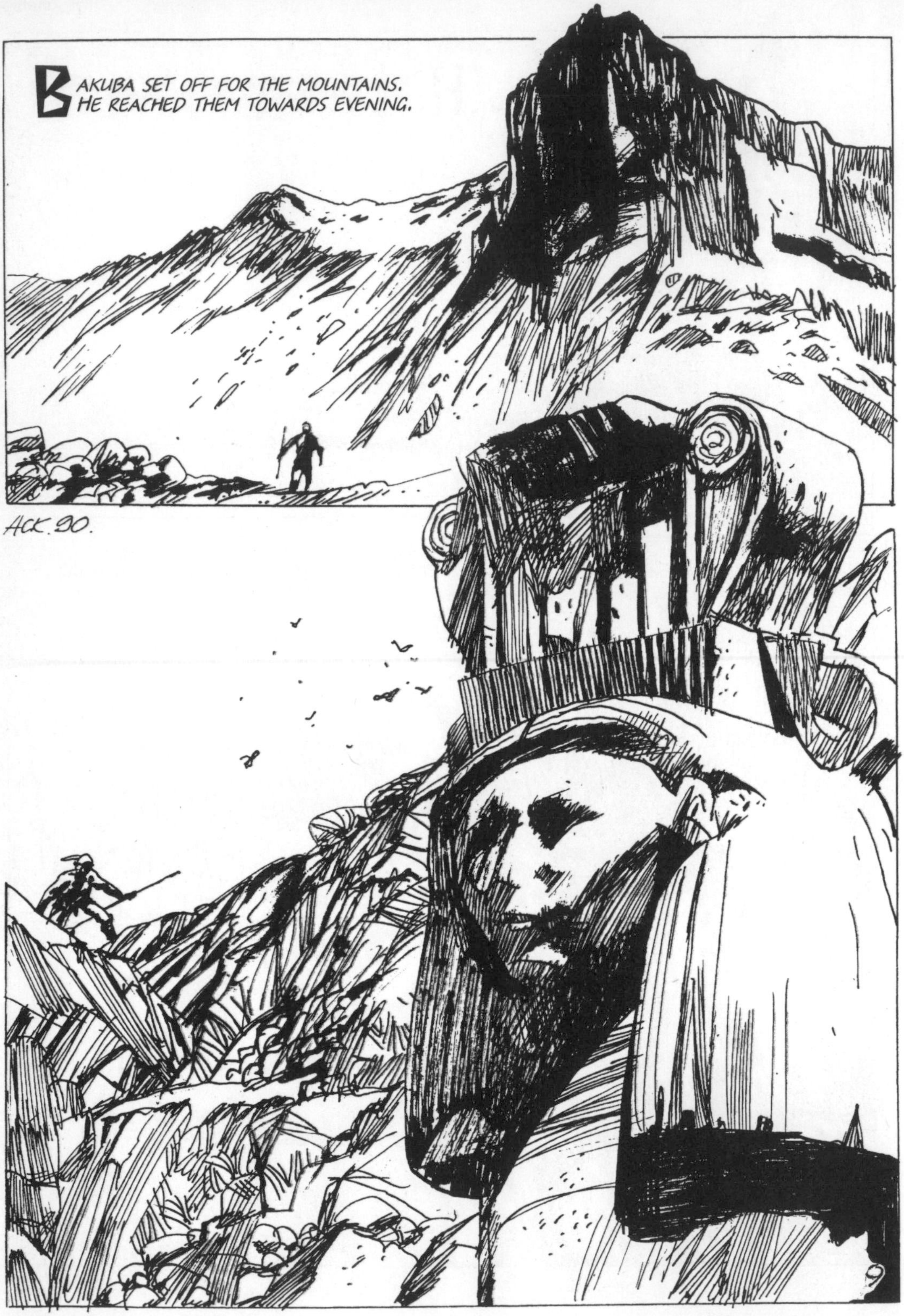
BAKUBA SET OFF FOR THE MOUNTAINS. HE REACHED THEM TOWARDS EVENING.
ACK. 90.

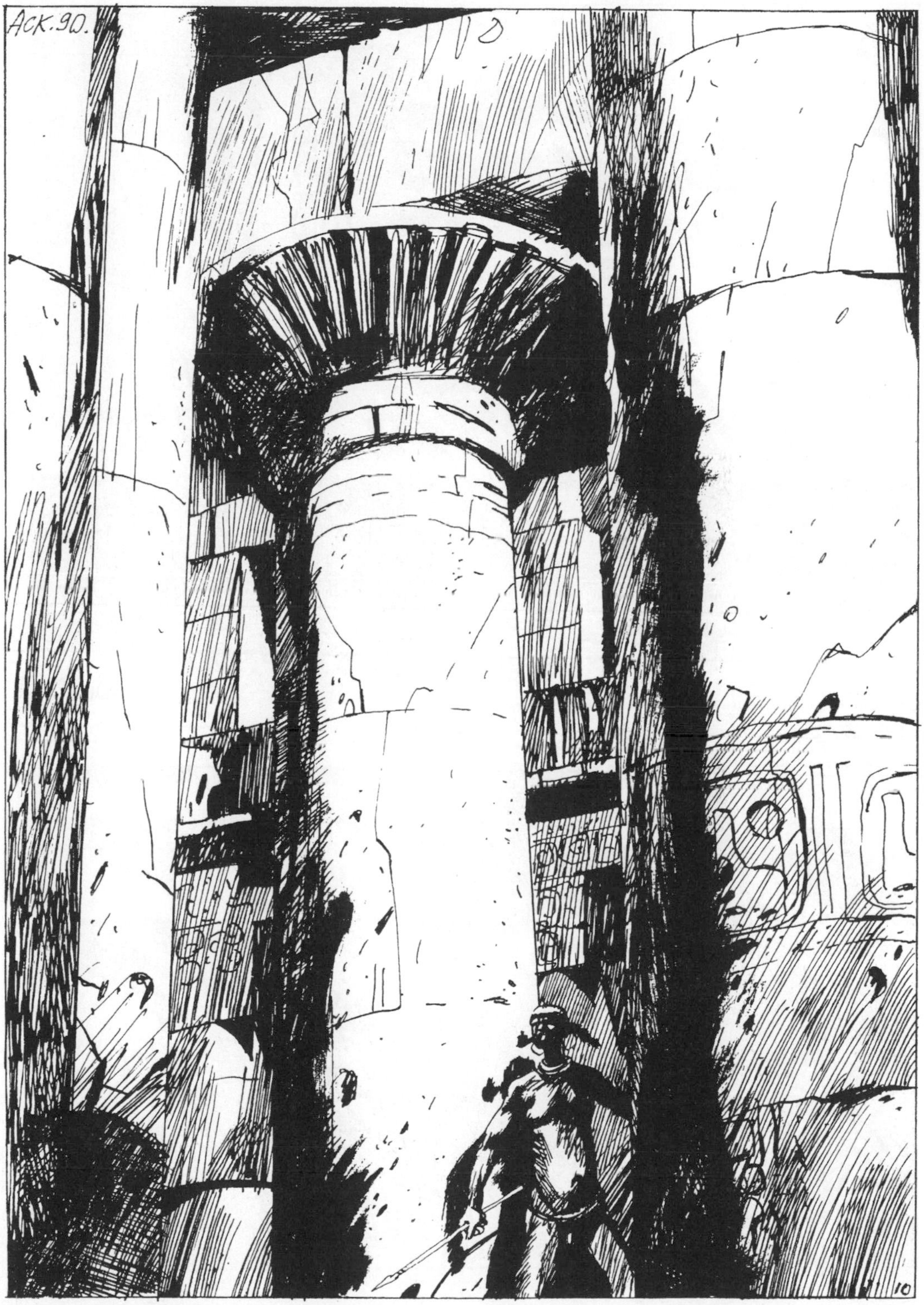
ACK.90.
10

A STRANGE SIGHT APPEARED BEFORE HIS EYES.

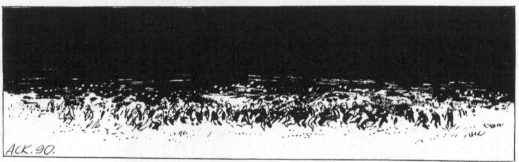

ACK. 90.

THESE PEOPLE CHOSE AN ODD TIME TO PLANT MAIZE. BUT ARE THEY ALIVE, OR FLESHLESS SHADES?

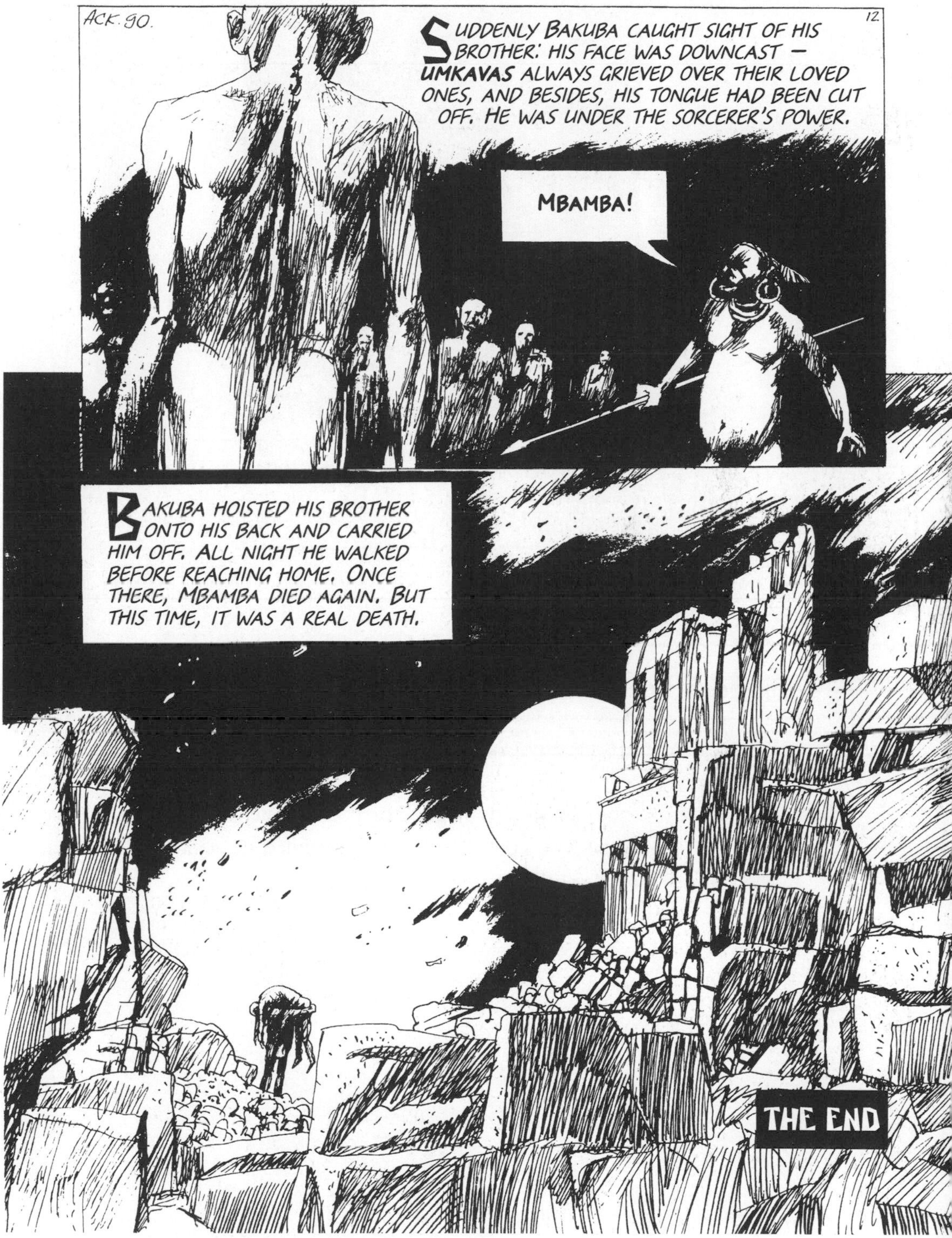
ACK. 90.
12.
SUDDENLY BAKUBA CAUGHT SIGHT OF HIS BROTHER: HIS FACE WAS DOWNCAST — **UMKAVAS** ALWAYS GRIEVED OVER THEIR LOVED ONES, AND BESIDES, HIS TONGUE HAD BEEN CUT OFF. HE WAS UNDER THE SORCERER'S POWER.
MBAMBA!
BAKUBA HOISTED HIS BROTHER ONTO HIS BACK AND CARRIED HIM OFF. ALL NIGHT HE WALKED BEFORE REACHING HOME. ONCE THERE, MBAMBA DIED AGAIN. BUT THIS TIME, IT WAS A REAL DEATH.
THE END

Pigeons From Hell

Creators Robert E Howard (original story), Scott Hampton (adaptation and art)

This slice of southern gothic was inspired by the folk tales Howard was told as a child. They reach back into the days of slavery and give us what Stephen King called "one of the finest horror stories of the twentieth century".

Along with his brother Bo, Scott Hampton studied with Will Eisner in the 1970s. His published work includes the Batman titles: Night Cries, and Gotham County, and Spookhouse.

I. THE WHISTLER IN THE DARK

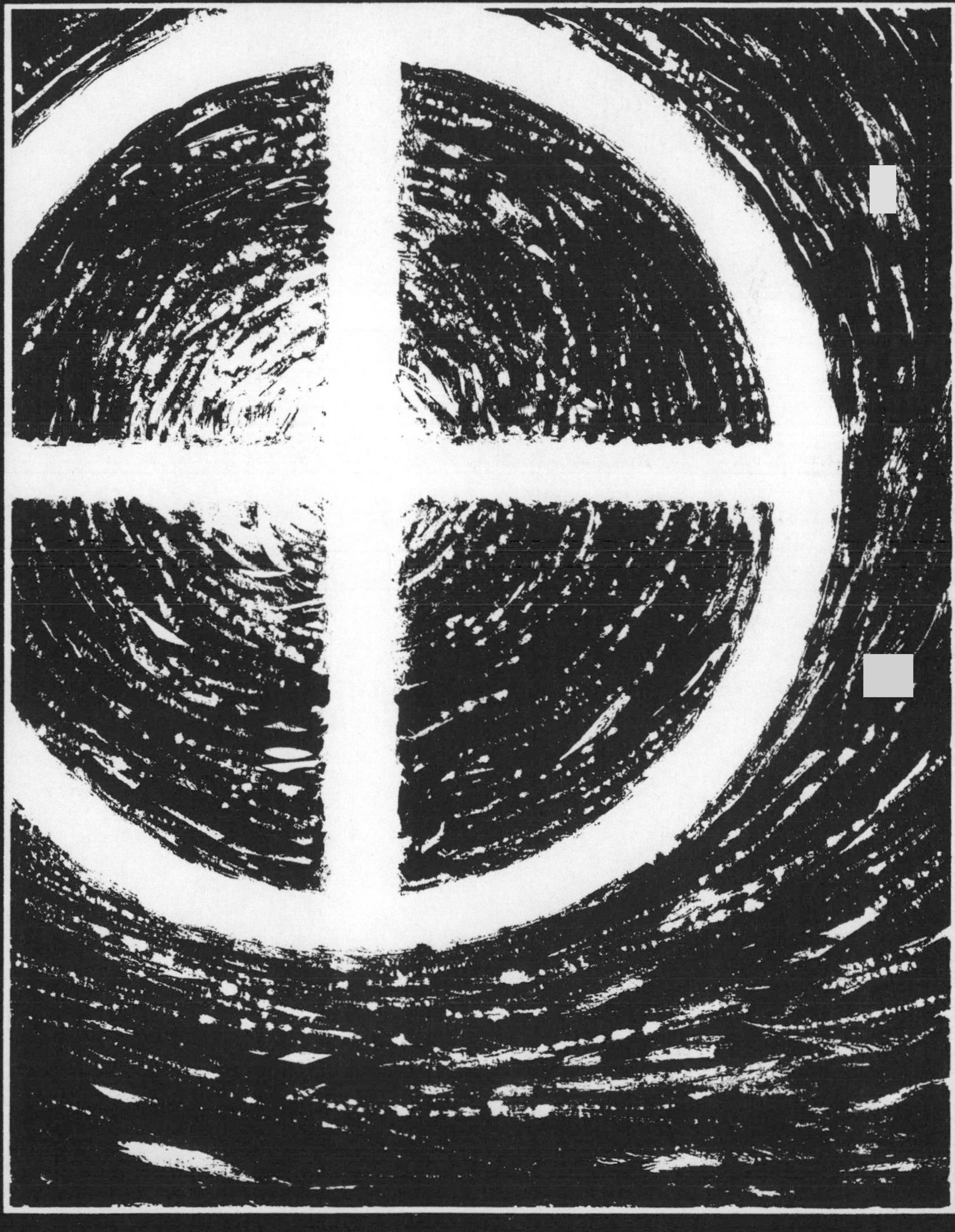

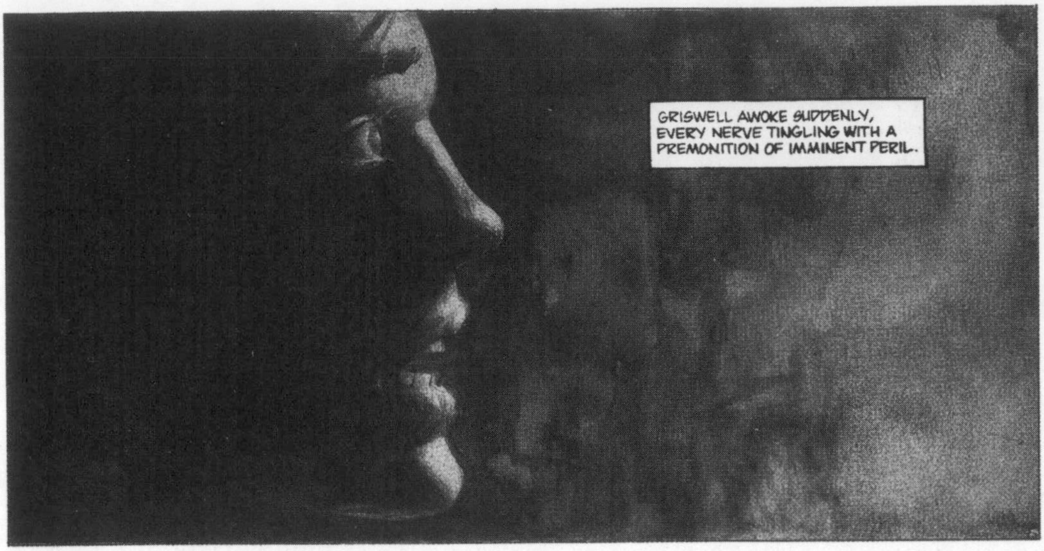
GRISWELL AWOKE SUDDENLY, EVERY NERVE TINGLING WITH A PREMONITION OF IMMINENT PERIL.

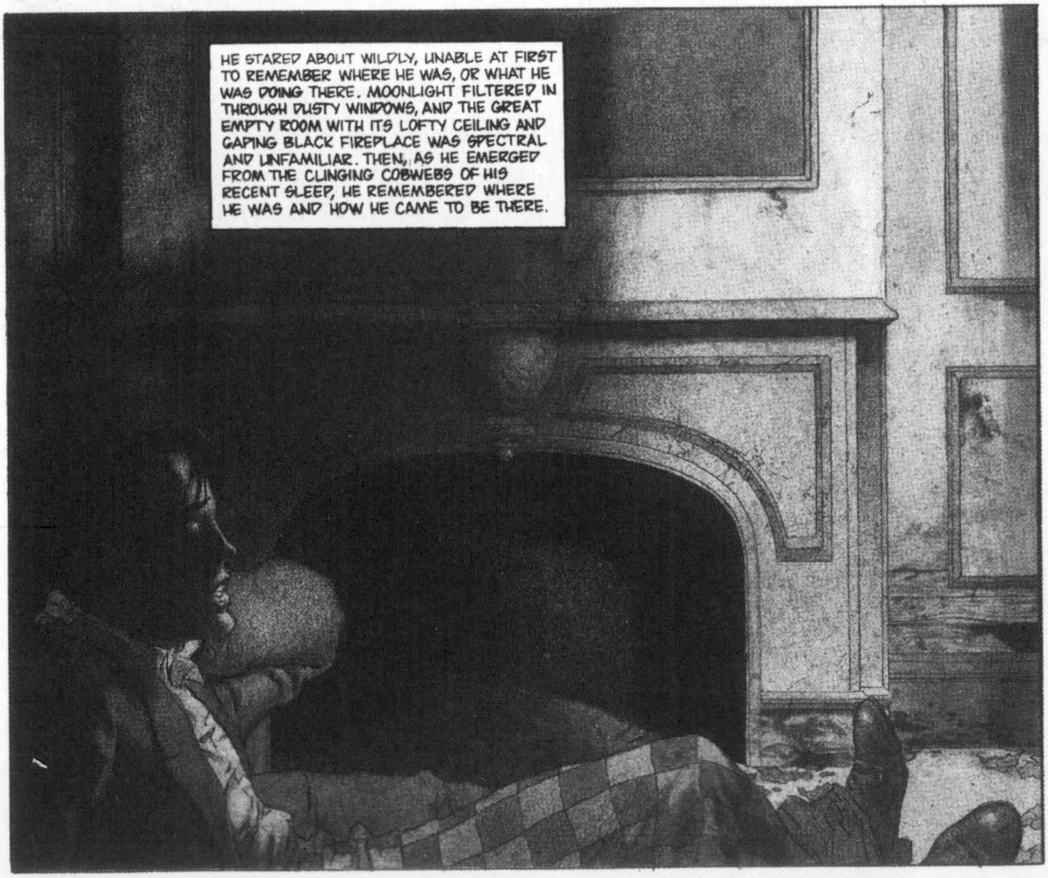
HE STARED ABOUT WILDLY, UNABLE AT FIRST TO REMEMBER WHERE HE WAS, OR WHAT HE WAS DOING THERE. MOONLIGHT FILTERED IN THROUGH DUSTY WINDOWS, AND THE GREAT EMPTY ROOM WITH ITS LOFTY CEILING AND GAPING BLACK FIREPLACE WAS SPECTRAL AND UNFAMILIAR. THEN, AS HE EMERGED FROM THE CLINGING COBWEBS OF HIS RECENT SLEEP, HE REMEMBERED WHERE HE WAS AND HOW HE CAME TO BE THERE.

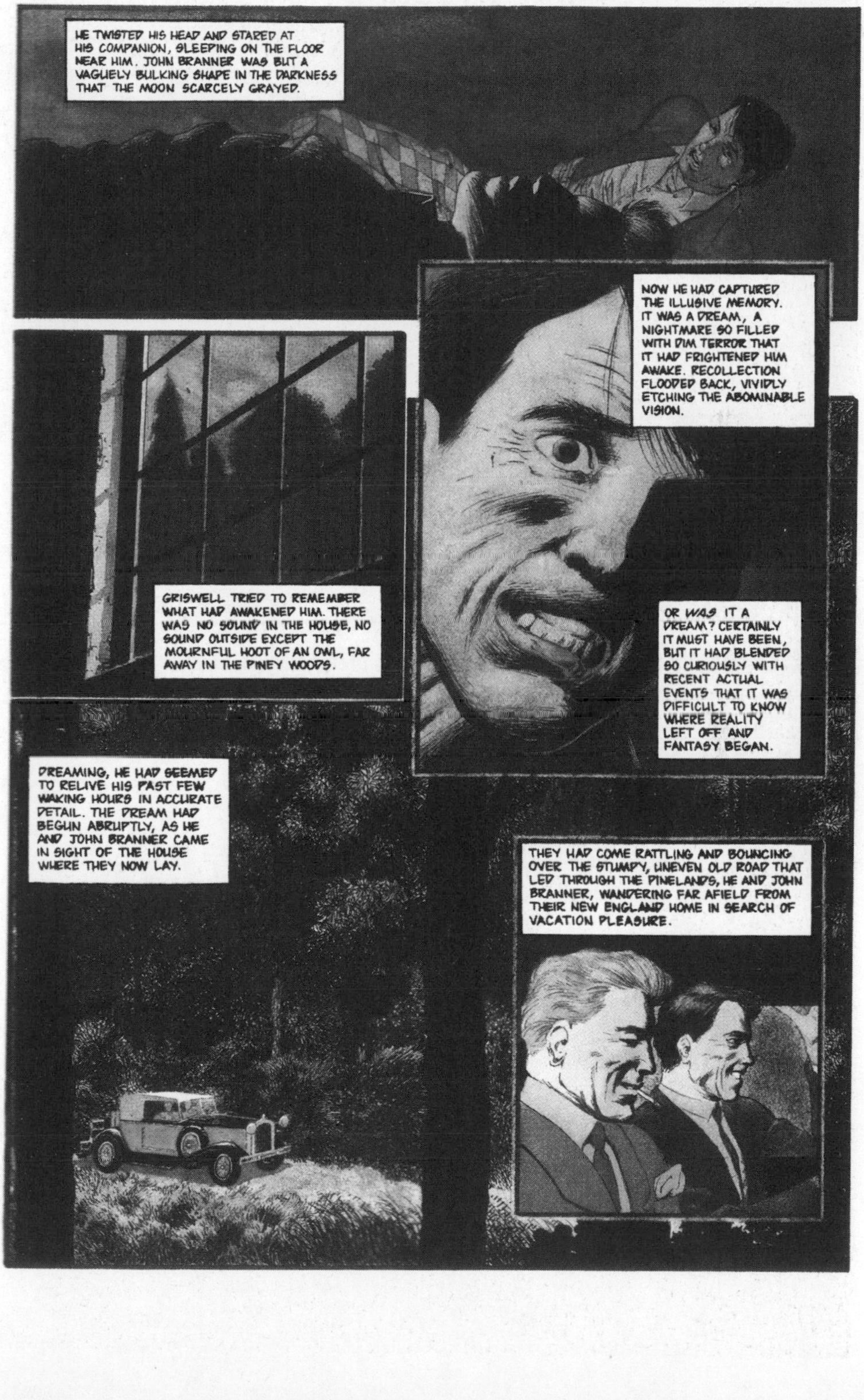
HE TWISTED HIS HEAD AND STARED AT HIS COMPANION, SLEEPING ON THE FLOOR NEAR HIM. JOHN BRANNER WAS BUT A VAGUELY BULKING SHAPE IN THE DARKNESS THAT THE MOON SCARCELY GRAYED.
GRISWELL TRIED TO REMEMBER WHAT HAD AWAKENED HIM. THERE WAS NO SOUND IN THE HOUSE, NO SOUND OUTSIDE EXCEPT THE MOURNFUL HOOT OF AN OWL, FAR AWAY IN THE PINEY WOODS.
NOW HE HAD CAPTURED THE ILLUSIVE MEMORY. IT WAS A DREAM, A NIGHTMARE SO FILLED WITH DIM TERROR THAT IT HAD FRIGHTENED HIM AWAKE. RECOLLECTION FLOODED BACK, VIVIDLY ETCHING THE ABOMINABLE VISION.
OR *WAS* IT A DREAM? CERTAINLY IT MUST HAVE BEEN, BUT IT HAD BLENDED SO CURIOUSLY WITH RECENT ACTUAL EVENTS THAT IT WAS DIFFICULT TO KNOW WHERE REALITY LEFT OFF AND FANTASY BEGAN.
DREAMING, HE HAD SEEMED TO RELIVE HIS PAST FEW WAKING HOURS IN ACCURATE DETAIL. THE DREAM HAD BEGUN ABRUPTLY, AS HE AND JOHN BRANNER CAME IN SIGHT OF THE HOUSE WHERE THEY NOW LAY.
THEY HAD COME RATTLING AND BOUNCING OVER THE STUMPY, UNEVEN OLD ROAD THAT LED THROUGH THE PINELANDS, HE AND JOHN BRANNER, WANDERING FAR AFIELD FROM THEIR NEW ENGLAND HOME IN SEARCH OF VACATION PLEASURE.

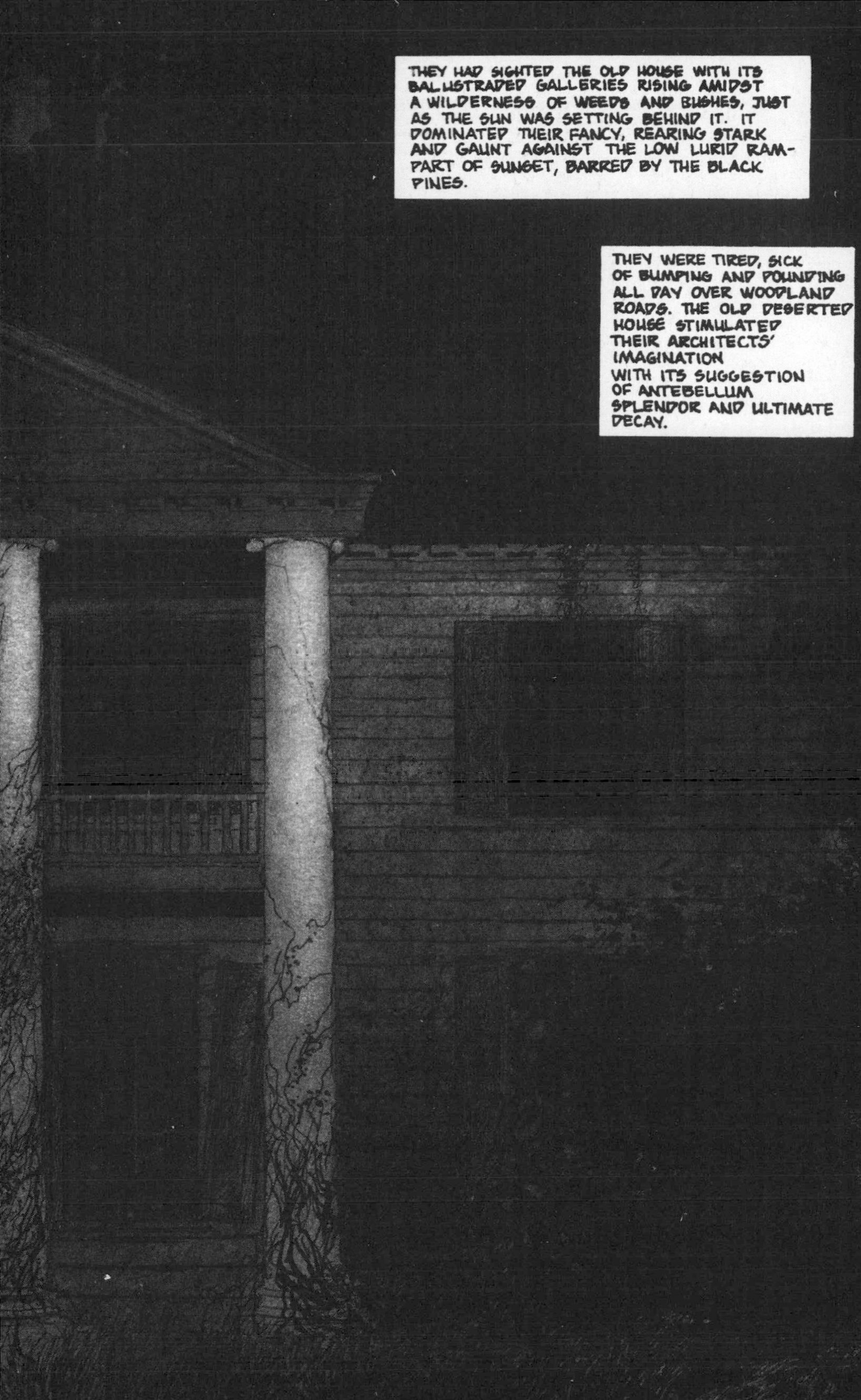
THEY HAD SIGHTED THE OLD HOUSE WITH ITS BALUSTRADED GALLERIES RISING AMIDST A WILDERNESS OF WEEDS AND BUSHES, JUST AS THE SUN WAS SETTING BEHIND IT. IT DOMINATED THEIR FANCY, REARING STARK AND GAUNT AGAINST THE LOW LURID RAMPART OF SUNSET, BARRED BY THE BLACK PINES.
THEY WERE TIRED, SICK OF BUMPING AND POUNDING ALL DAY OVER WOODLAND ROADS. THE OLD DESERTED HOUSE STIMULATED THEIR ARCHITECTS' IMAGINATION WITH ITS SUGGESTION OF ANTEBELLUM SPLENDOR AND ULTIMATE DECAY.

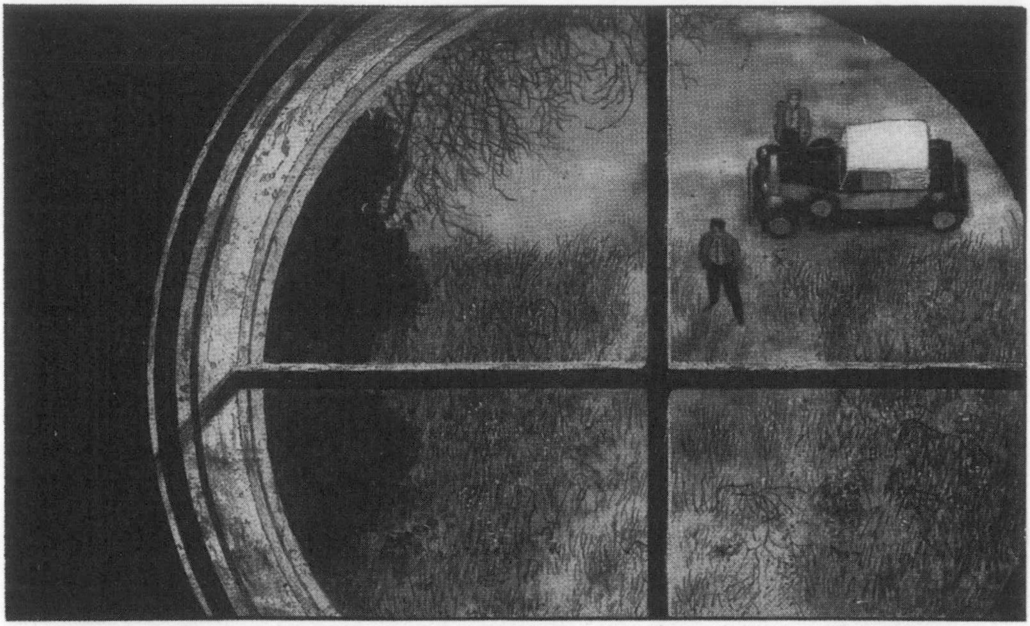

THEY LEFT THE AUTOMOBILE BESIDE THE RUTTY ROAD, AND AS THEY WENT UP THE WALK OF CRUMBLING BRICKS, ALMOST LOST IN THE TANGLE OF RANK GROWTH, PIGEONS ROSE FROM THE BALUSTRADES IN A FLUTTERING, FEATHERY CROWD AND SWEPT AWAY WITH A LOW THUNDER OF BEATING WINGS.

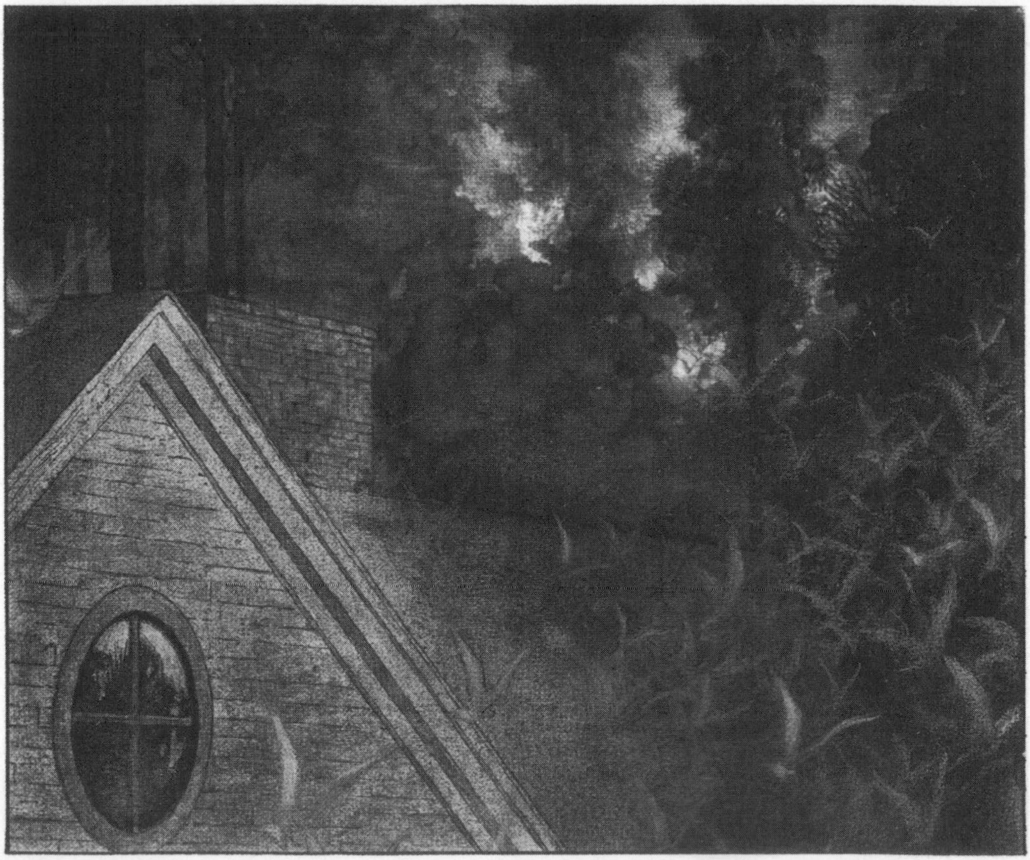

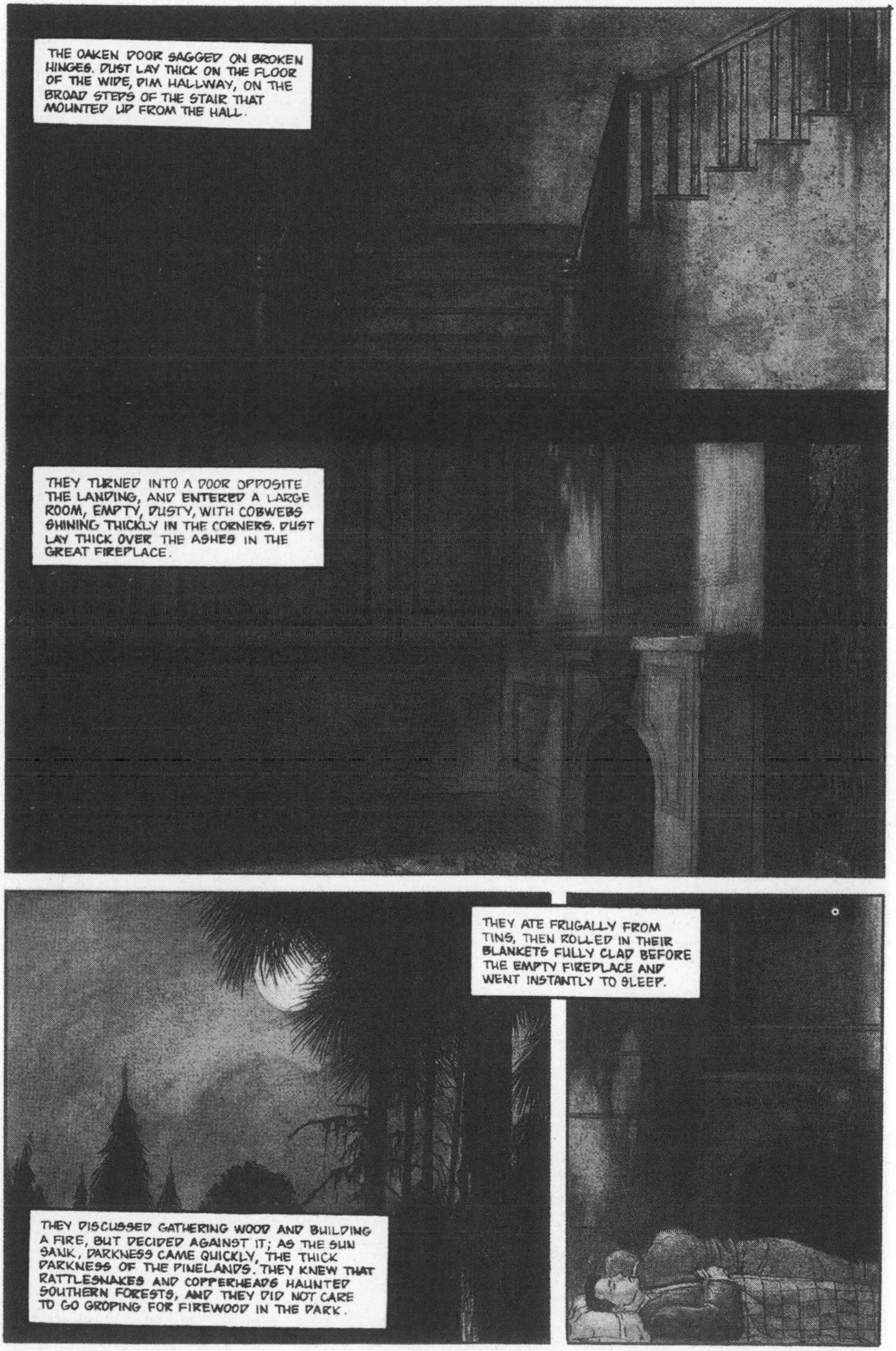
THE OAKEN DOOR SAGGED ON BROKEN HINGES. DUST LAY THICK ON THE FLOOR OF THE WIDE, DIM HALLWAY, ON THE BROAD STEPS OF THE STAIR THAT MOUNTED UP FROM THE HALL.
THEY TURNED INTO A DOOR OPPOSITE THE LANDING, AND ENTERED A LARGE ROOM, EMPTY, DUSTY, WITH COBWEBS SHINING THICKLY IN THE CORNERS. DUST LAY THICK OVER THE ASHES IN THE GREAT FIREPLACE.
THEY DISCUSSED GATHERING WOOD AND BUILDING A FIRE, BUT DECIDED AGAINST IT; AS THE SUN SANK, DARKNESS CAME QUICKLY, THE THICK DARKNESS OF THE PINELANDS. THEY KNEW THAT RATTLESNAKES AND COPPERHEADS HAUNTED SOUTHERN FORESTS, AND THEY DID NOT CARE TO GO GROPING FOR FIREWOOD IN THE DARK.
THEY ATE FRUGALLY FROM TINS, THEN ROLLED IN THEIR BLANKETS FULLY CLAD BEFORE THE EMPTY FIREPLACE AND WENT INSTANTLY TO SLEEP.

THIS, IN PART, WAS WHAT GRISWELL HAD DREAMED. HE SAW AGAIN THE GAUNT HOUSE LOOMING STARK AGAINST THE CRIMSON SUNSET, SAW THE FLIGHT OF THE PIGEONS AS HE AND BRANNER CAME UP THE SHATTERED WALK. HE SAW THE DIM ROOM IN WHICH THEY PRESENTLY LAY, AND THE TWO FORMS THAT WERE HIMSELF AND HIS COMPANION LYING WRAPPED IN THEIR BLANKETS. THEN, FROM THAT POINT, HIS DREAM ALTERED SUBTLY, PASSED OUT OF THE REALM OF THE COMMONPLACE AND BECAME TINGED WITH FEAR.

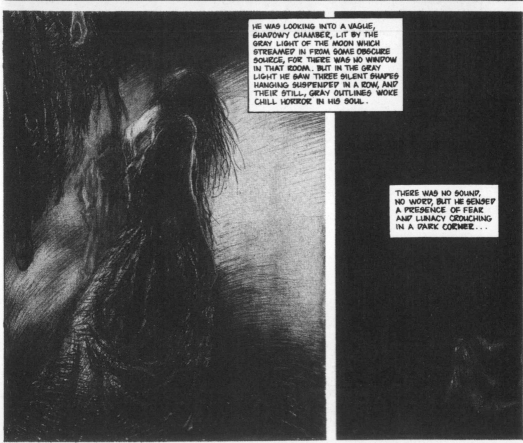

HE WAS LOOKING INTO A VAGUE, SHADOWY CHAMBER, LIT BY THE GRAY LIGHT OF THE MOON WHICH STREAMED IN FROM SOME OBSCURE SOURCE, FOR THERE WAS NO WINDOW IN THAT ROOM. BUT IN THE GRAY LIGHT HE SAW THREE SILENT SHAPES HANGING SUSPENDED IN A ROW, AND THEIR STILL, GRAY OUTLINES WOKE CHILL HORROR IN HIS SOUL.

THERE WAS NO SOUND, NO WORD, BUT HE SENSED A PRESENCE OF FEAR AND LUNACY CROUCHING IN A DARK CORNER...

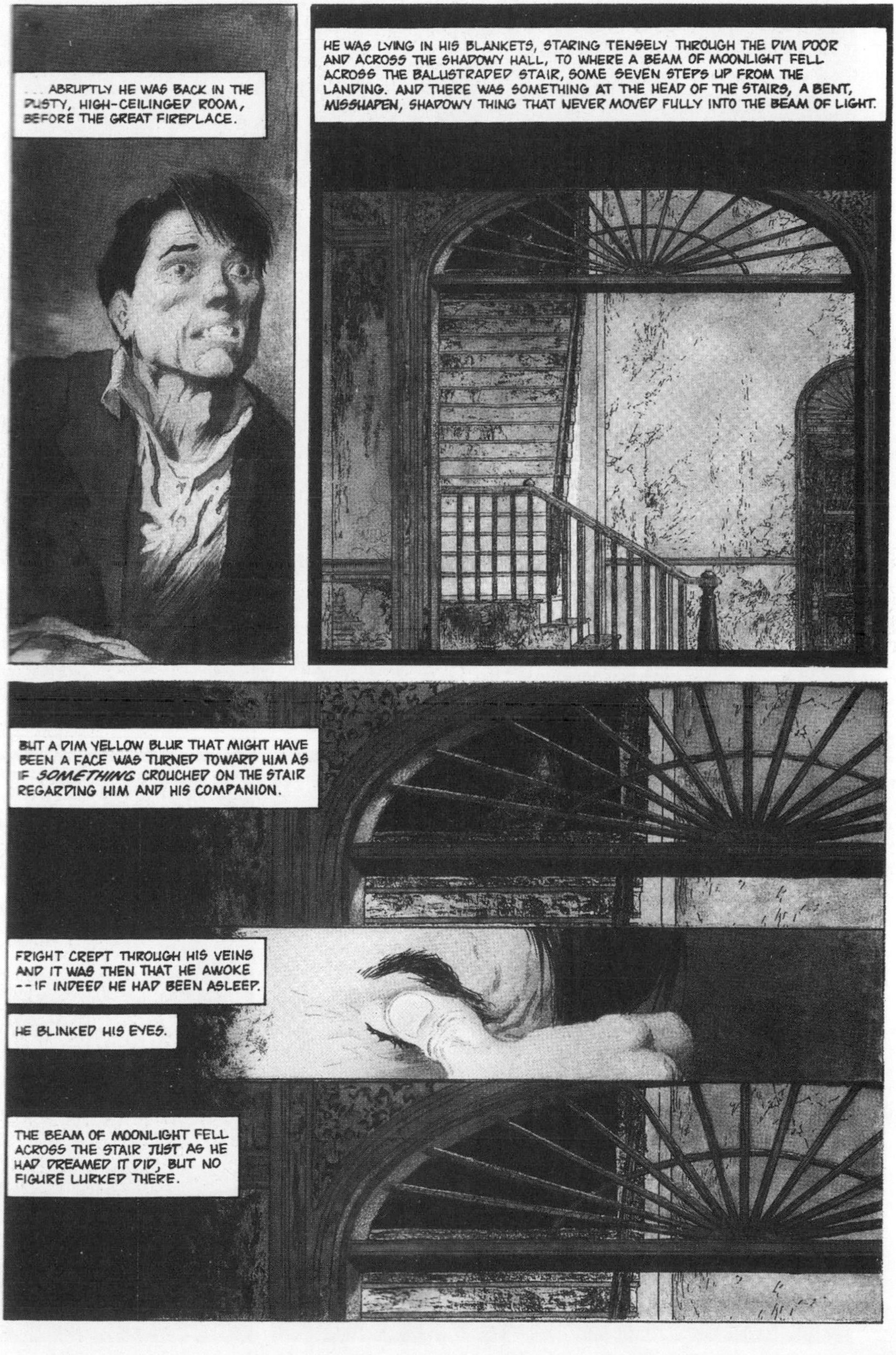
. . . ABRUPTLY HE WAS BACK IN THE DUSTY, HIGH-CEILINGED ROOM, BEFORE THE GREAT FIREPLACE.
HE WAS LYING IN HIS BLANKETS, STARING TENSELY THROUGH THE DIM DOOR AND ACROSS THE SHADOWY HALL, TO WHERE A BEAM OF MOONLIGHT FELL ACROSS THE BALUSTRADED STAIR, SOME SEVEN STEPS UP FROM THE LANDING. AND THERE WAS SOMETHING AT THE HEAD OF THE STAIRS, A BENT, MISSHAPEN, SHADOWY THING THAT NEVER MOVED FULLY INTO THE BEAM OF LIGHT.
BUT A DIM YELLOW BLUR THAT MIGHT HAVE BEEN A FACE WAS TURNED TOWARD HIM AS IF SOMETHING CROUCHED ON THE STAIR REGARDING HIM AND HIS COMPANION.
FRIGHT CREPT THROUGH HIS VEINS AND IT WAS THEN THAT HE AWOKE --IF INDEED HE HAD BEEN ASLEEP.
HE BLINKED HIS EYES.
THE BEAM OF MOONLIGHT FELL ACROSS THE STAIR JUST AS HE HAD DREAMED IT DID, BUT NO FIGURE LURKED THERE.

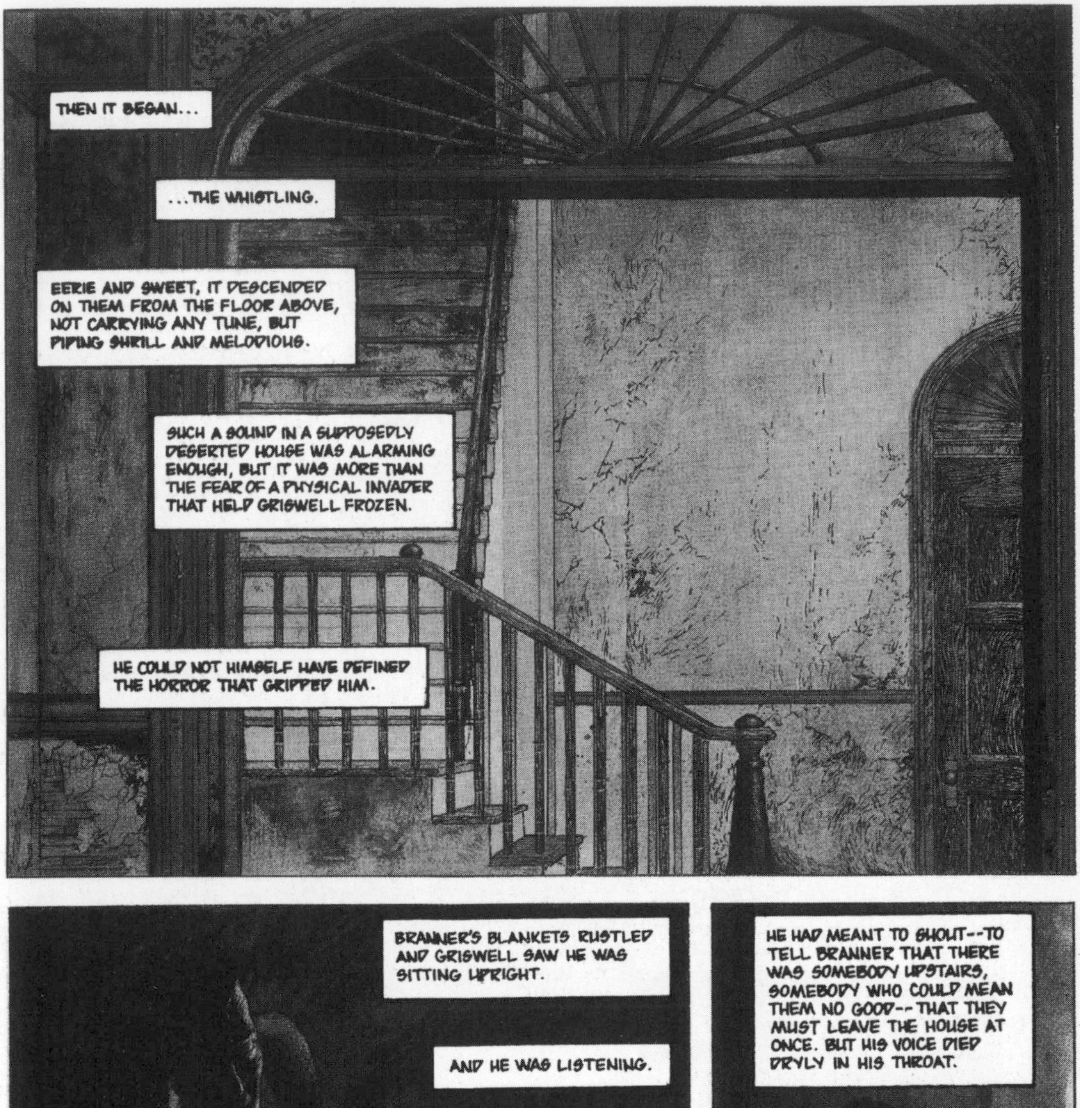
THEN IT BEGAN...
...THE WHISTLING.
EERIE AND SWEET, IT DESCENDED ON THEM FROM THE FLOOR ABOVE, NOT CARRYING ANY TUNE, BUT PIPING SHRILL AND MELODIOUS.
SUCH A SOUND IN A SUPPOSEDLY DESERTED HOUSE WAS ALARMING ENOUGH, BUT IT WAS MORE THAN THE FEAR OF A PHYSICAL INVADER THAT HELD GRISWELL FROZEN.
HE COULD NOT HIMSELF HAVE DEFINED THE HORROR THAT GRIPPED HIM.
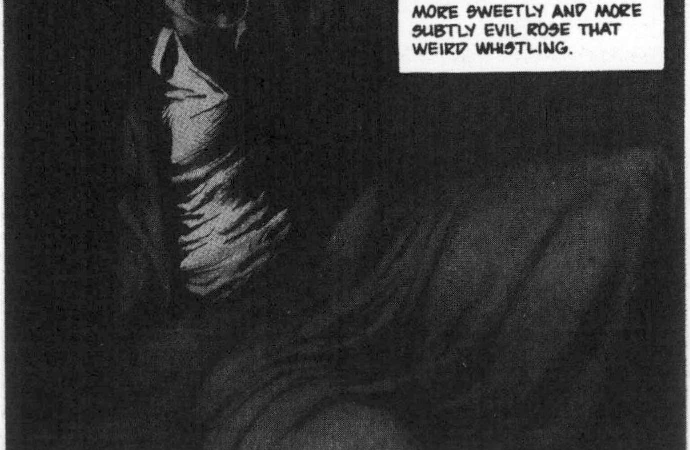
BRANNER'S BLANKETS RUSTLED AND GRISWELL SAW HE WAS SITTING UPRIGHT.
AND HE WAS LISTENING.
MORE SWEETLY AND MORE SUBTLY EVIL ROSE THAT WEIRD WHISTLING.
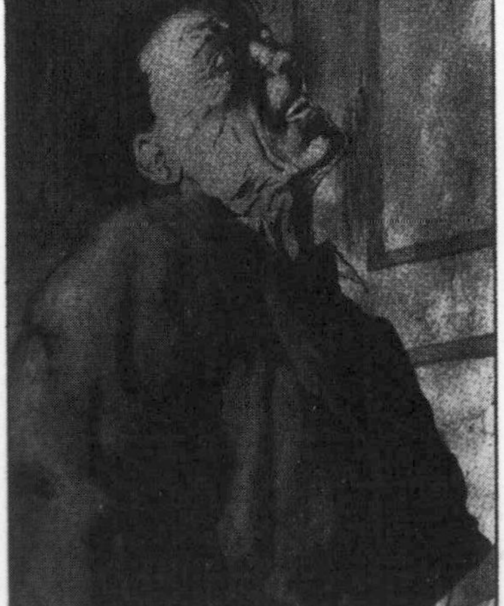
HE HAD MEANT TO SHOUT--TO TELL BRANNER THAT THERE WAS SOMEBODY UPSTAIRS, SOMEBODY WHO COULD MEAN THEM NO GOOD--THAT THEY MUST LEAVE THE HOUSE AT ONCE. BUT HIS VOICE DIED DRYLY IN HIS THROAT.

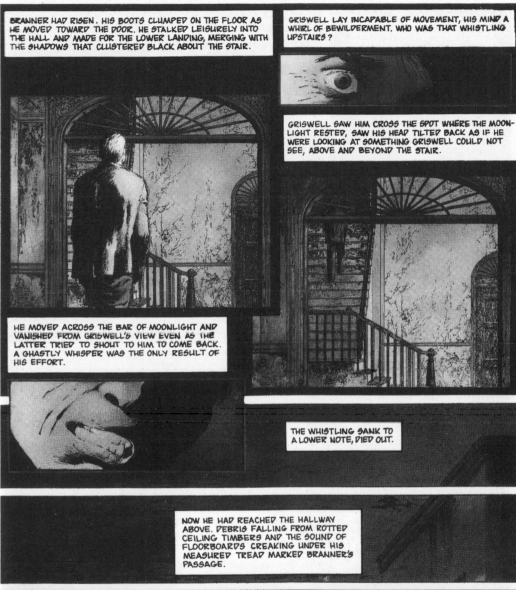

BRANNER HAD RISEN. HIS BOOTS CLUMPED ON THE FLOOR AS HE MOVED TOWARD THE DOOR. HE STALKED LEISURELY INTO THE HALL AND MADE FOR THE LOWER LANDING, MERGING WITH THE SHADOWS THAT CLUSTERED BLACK ABOUT THE STAIR.

GRISWELL LAY INCAPABLE OF MOVEMENT, HIS MIND A WHIRL OF BEWILDERMENT. WHO WAS THAT WHISTLING UPSTAIRS?

GRISWELL SAW HIM CROSS THE SPOT WHERE THE MOON-LIGHT RESTED, SAW HIS HEAD TILTED BACK AS IF HE WERE LOOKING AT SOMETHING GRISWELL COULD NOT SEE, ABOVE AND BEYOND THE STAIR.

HE MOVED ACROSS THE BAR OF MOONLIGHT AND VANISHED FROM GRISWELL'S VIEW EVEN AS THE LATTER TRIED TO SHOUT TO HIM TO COME BACK. A GHASTLY WHISPER WAS THE ONLY RESULT OF HIS EFFORT.

THE WHISTLING SANK TO A LOWER NOTE, DIED OUT.

NOW HE HAD REACHED THE HALLWAY ABOVE. DEBRIS FALLING FROM ROTTED CEILING TIMBERS AND THE SOUND OF FLOORBOARDS CREAKING UNDER HIS MEASURED TREAD MARKED BRANNER'S PASSAGE.

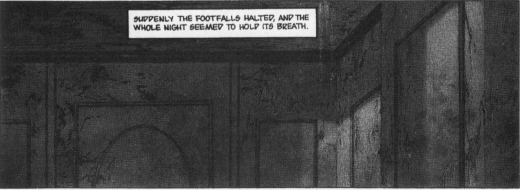

SUDDENLY THE FOOTFALLS HALTED, AND THE WHOLE NIGHT SEEMED TO HOLD ITS BREATH.

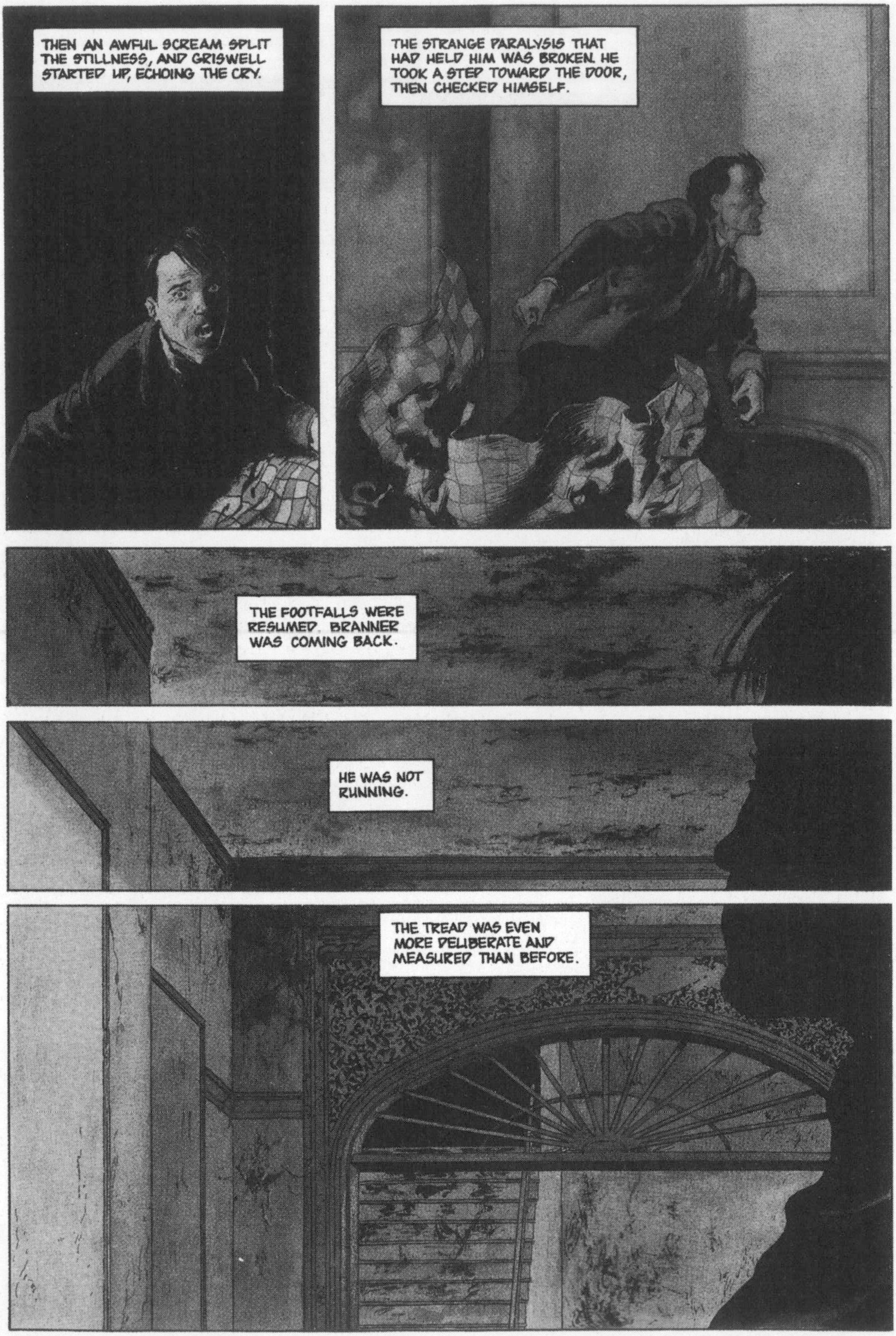
THEN AN AWFUL SCREAM SPLIT THE STILLNESS, AND GRISWELL STARTED UP, ECHOING THE CRY.
THE STRANGE PARALYSIS THAT HAD HELD HIM WAS BROKEN. HE TOOK A STEP TOWARD THE DOOR, THEN CHECKED HIMSELF.
THE FOOTFALLS WERE RESUMED. BRANNER WAS COMING BACK.
HE WAS NOT RUNNING.
THE TREAD WAS EVEN MORE DELIBERATE AND MEASURED THAN BEFORE.

NOW THE STAIRS BEGAN TO CREAK AGAIN. A GROPING HAND, MOVING ALONG THE BALUSTRADE, CAME INTO THE BAR OF MOONLIGHT;

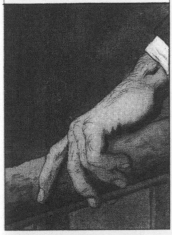

THEN ANOTHER, AND A GHASTLY THRILL WENT THROUGH GRISWELL AS HE SAW THAT THE OTHER HAND GRIPPED A HATCHET --

--A HATCHET WHICH DRIPPED BLACKLY. *WAS* THAT BRANNER WHO WAS COMING DOWN THE STAIR?

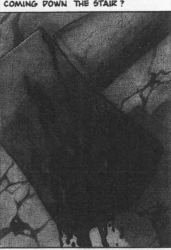

YES! THE FIGURE HAD MOVED INTO THE BAR OF MOONLIGHT NOW, AND GRISWELL RECOGNIZED IT. THEN HE SAW BRANNER'S FACE, AND A SHRIEK BURST FROM GRISWELL'S LIPS. BRANNER'S FACE WAS BLOODLESS, CORPSE-LIKE; GOUTS OF BLOOD DRIPPED DARKLY DOWN IT; HIS EYES WERE GLASSY AND WET, AND BLOOD OOZED FROM THE GREAT GASH...

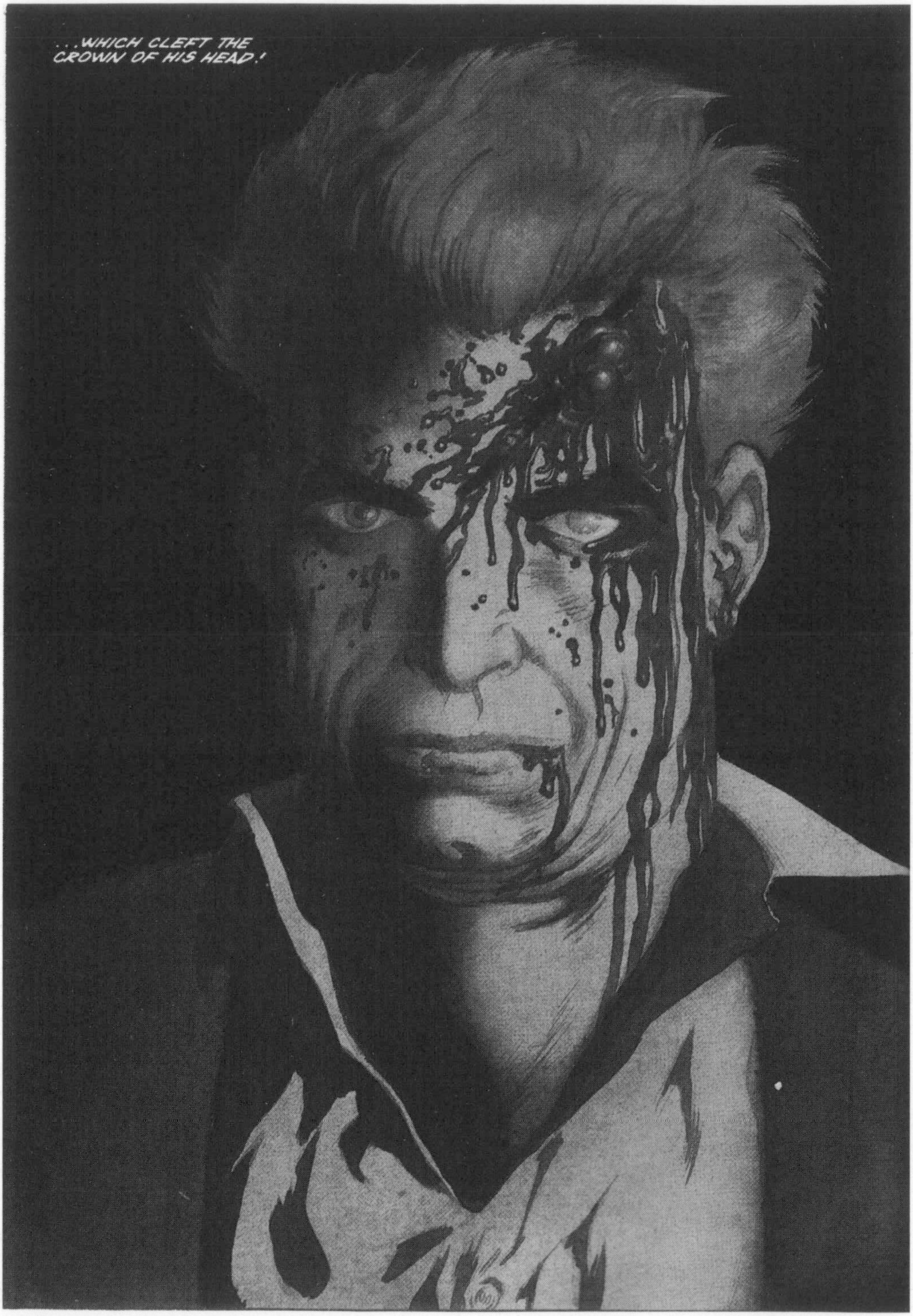
...WHICH CLEFT THE CROWN OF HIS HEAD!

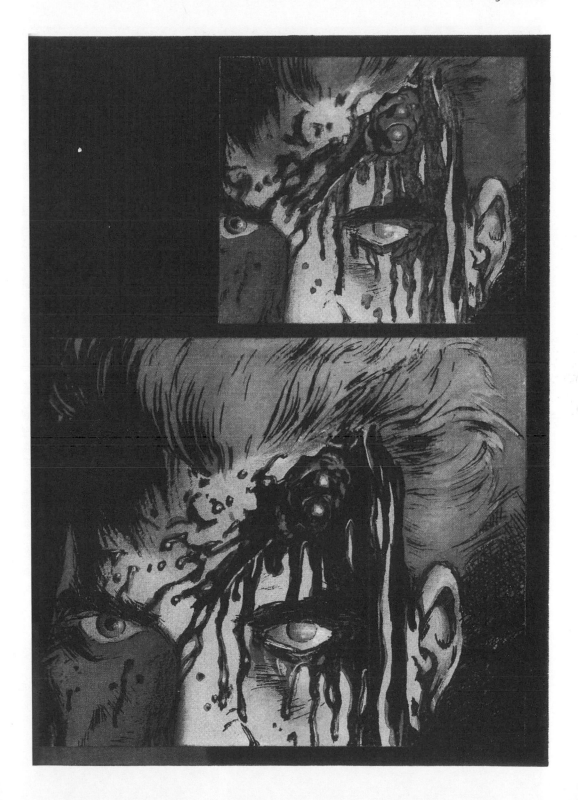

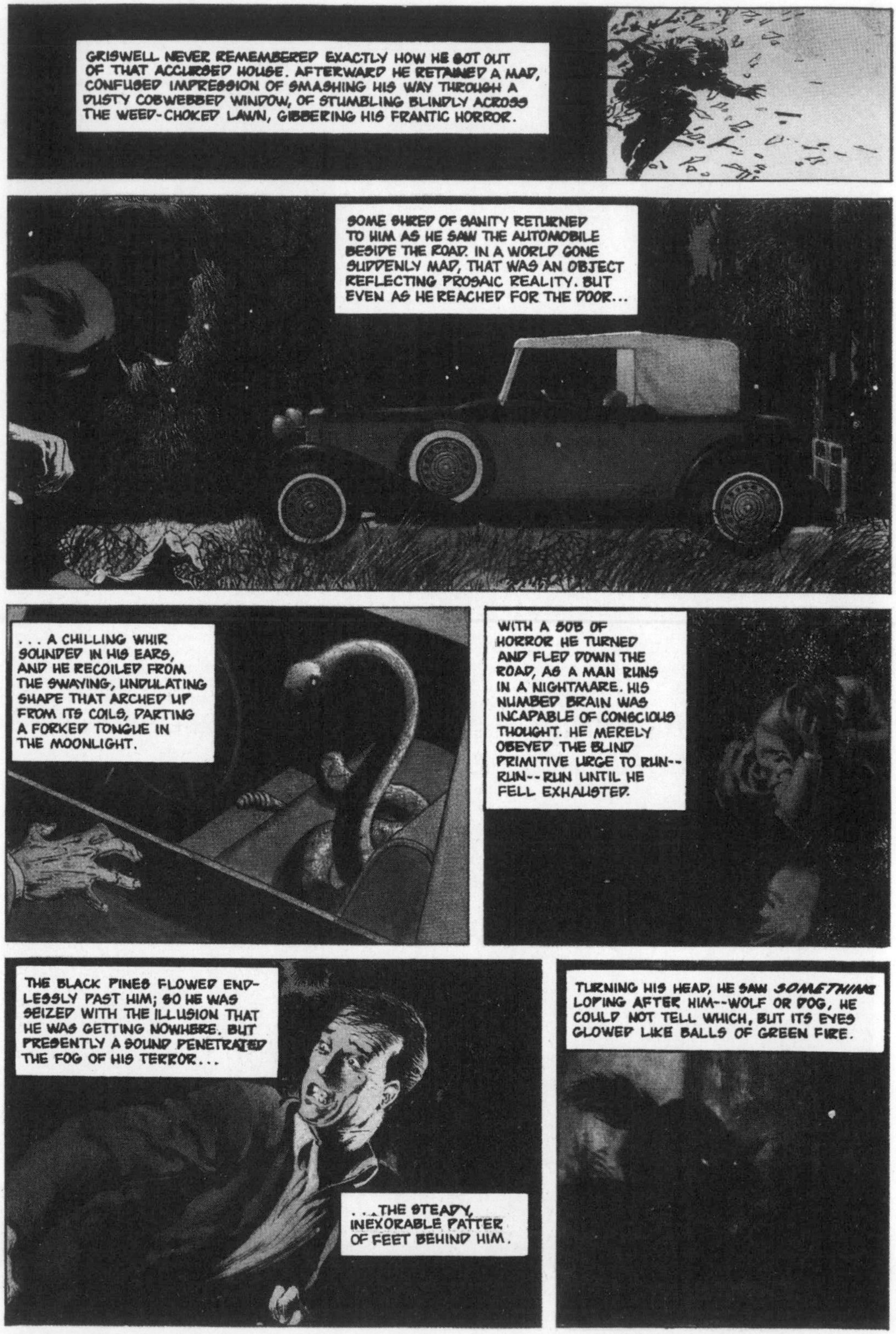
GRISWELL NEVER REMEMBERED EXACTLY HOW HE GOT OUT OF THAT ACCURSED HOUSE. AFTERWARD HE RETAINED A MAD, CONFUSED IMPRESSION OF SMASHING HIS WAY THROUGH A DUSTY COBWEBBED WINDOW, OF STUMBLING BLINDLY ACROSS THE WEED-CHOKED LAWN, GIBBERING HIS FRANTIC HORROR.
SOME SHRED OF SANITY RETURNED TO HIM AS HE SAW THE AUTOMOBILE BESIDE THE ROAD. IN A WORLD GONE SUDDENLY MAD, THAT WAS AN OBJECT REFLECTING PROSAIC REALITY. BUT EVEN AS HE REACHED FOR THE DOOR...
... A CHILLING WHIR SOUNDED IN HIS EARS, AND HE RECOILED FROM THE SWAYING, UNDULATING SHAPE THAT ARCHED UP FROM ITS COILS, DARTING A FORKED TONGUE IN THE MOONLIGHT.
WITH A SOB OF HORROR HE TURNED AND FLED DOWN THE ROAD, AS A MAN RUNS IN A NIGHTMARE. HIS NUMBED BRAIN WAS INCAPABLE OF CONSCIOUS THOUGHT. HE MERELY OBEYED THE BLIND PRIMITIVE URGE TO RUN-- RUN-- RUN UNTIL HE FELL EXHAUSTED.
THE BLACK PINES FLOWED ENDLESSLY PAST HIM; SO HE WAS SEIZED WITH THE ILLUSION THAT HE WAS GETTING NOWHERE. BUT PRESENTLY A SOUND PENETRATED THE FOG OF HIS TERROR...
...THE STEADY, INEXORABLE PATTER OF FEET BEHIND HIM.
TURNING HIS HEAD, HE SAW SOMETHING LOPING AFTER HIM--WOLF OR DOG, HE COULD NOT TELL WHICH, BUT ITS EYES GLOWED LIKE BALLS OF GREEN FIRE.

WITH A GASP HE INCREASED HIS SPEED, REELED AROUND A BEND IN THE ROAD, AND HEARD A HORSE SNORT, SAW IT REAR AND HEARD ITS RIDER CURSE, SAW THE GLEAM OF BLUE STEEL IN THE MAN'S LIFTED HAND.

FOR GOD'S SAKE, HELP ME! THE THING! IT KILLED BRANNER--IT'S COMING AFTER ME!!

LOOK!!

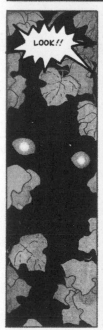

BLAM! BLAM! BLAM!

SON OF A ...

BLAM! BLAM!

BLAM! CLICK!

CLICK!

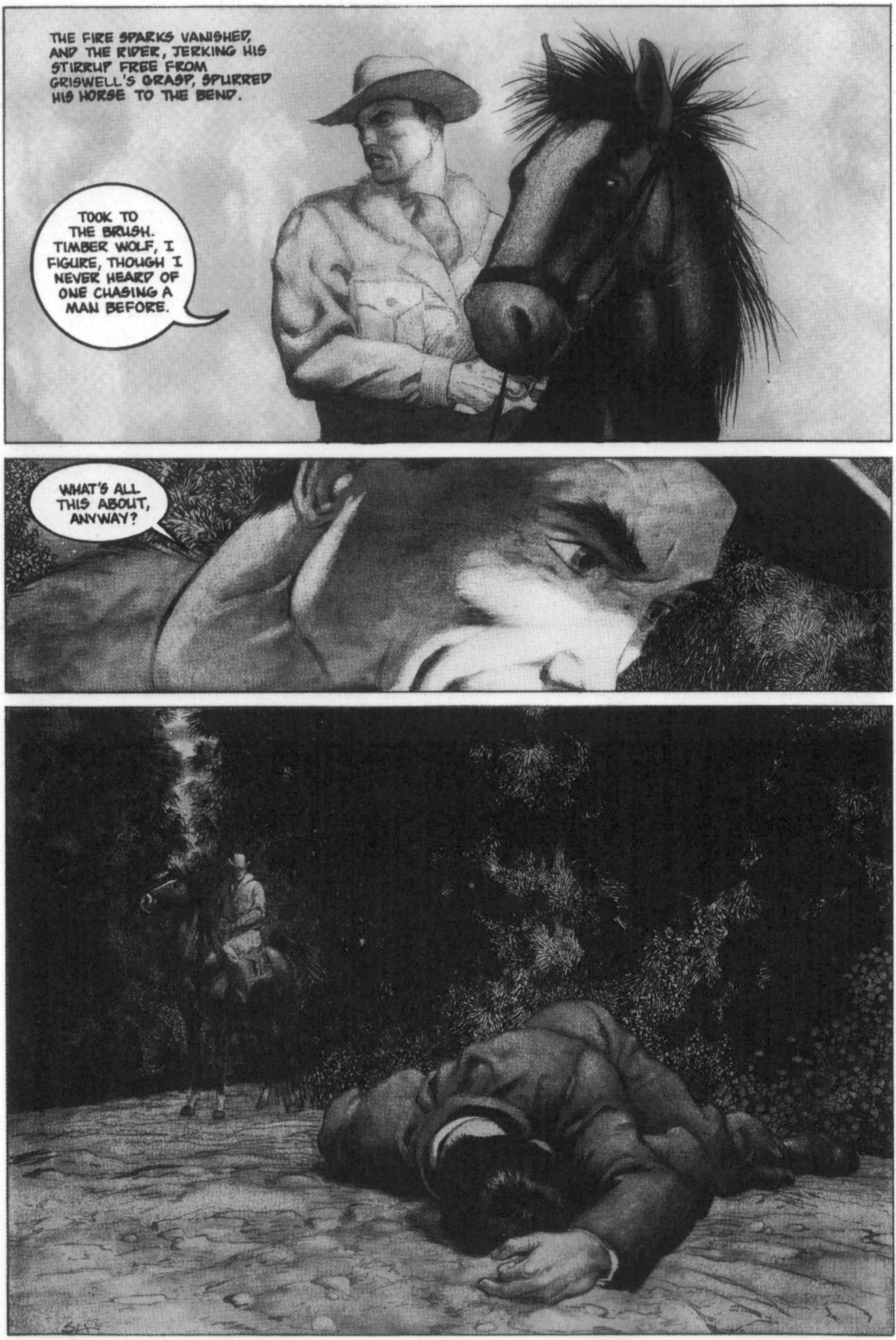
THE FIRE SPARKS VANISHED, AND THE RIDER, JERKING HIS STIRRUP FREE FROM GRISWELL'S GRASP, SPURRED HIS HORSE TO THE BEND.
TOOK TO THE BRUSH. TIMBER WOLF, I FIGURE, THOUGH I NEVER HEARD OF ONE CHASING A MAN BEFORE.
WHAT'S ALL THIS ABOUT, ANYWAY?

2. RETURN

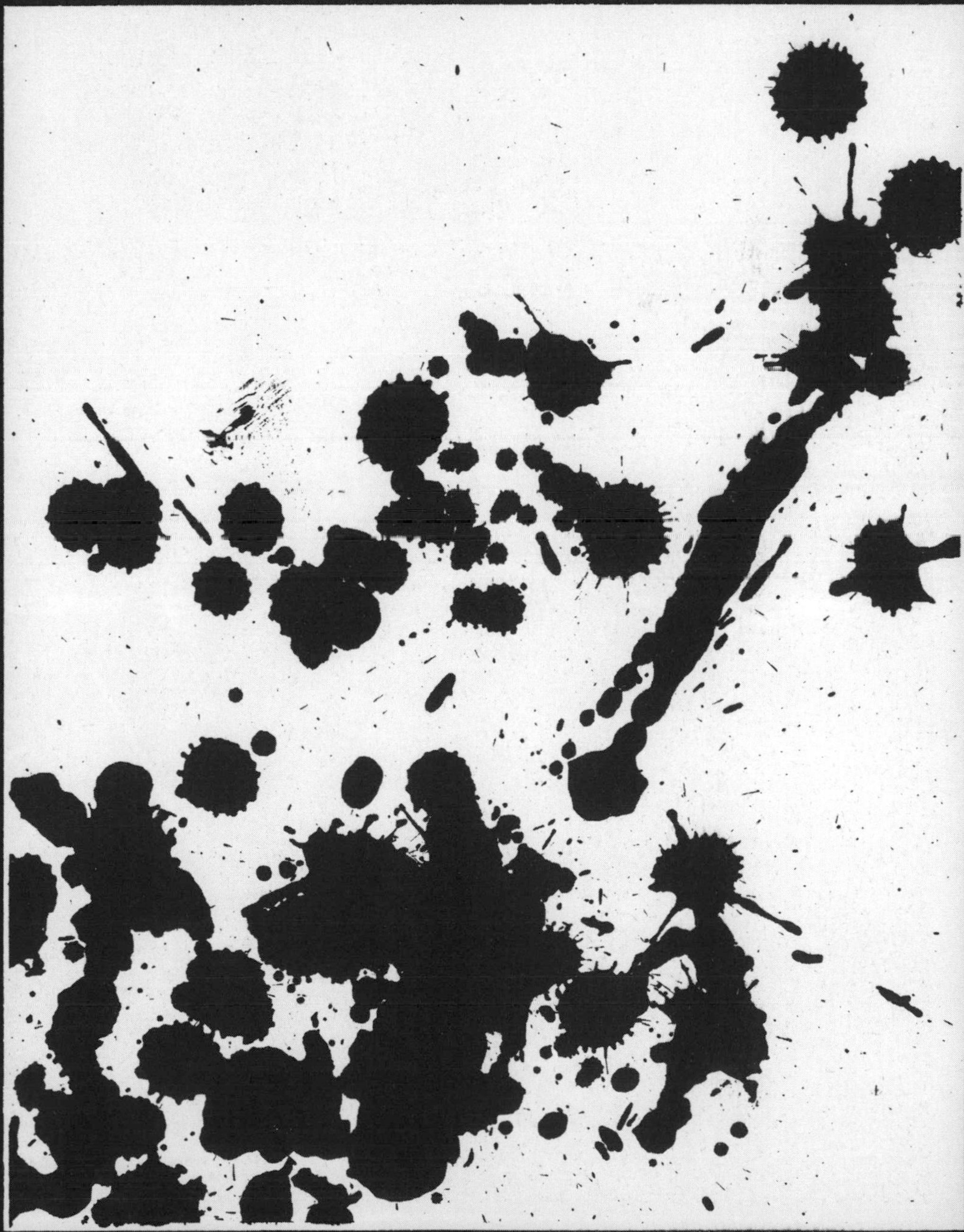

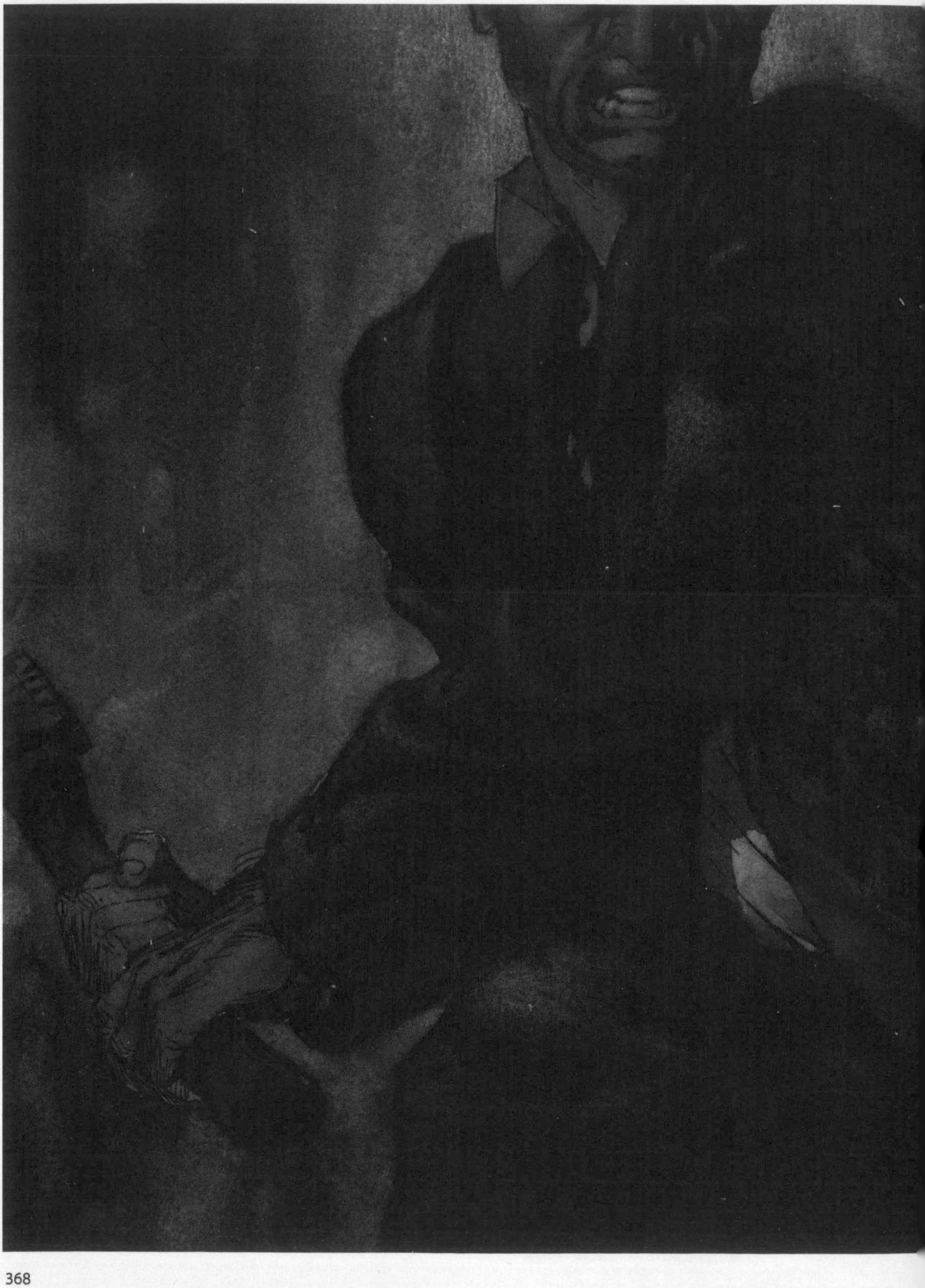

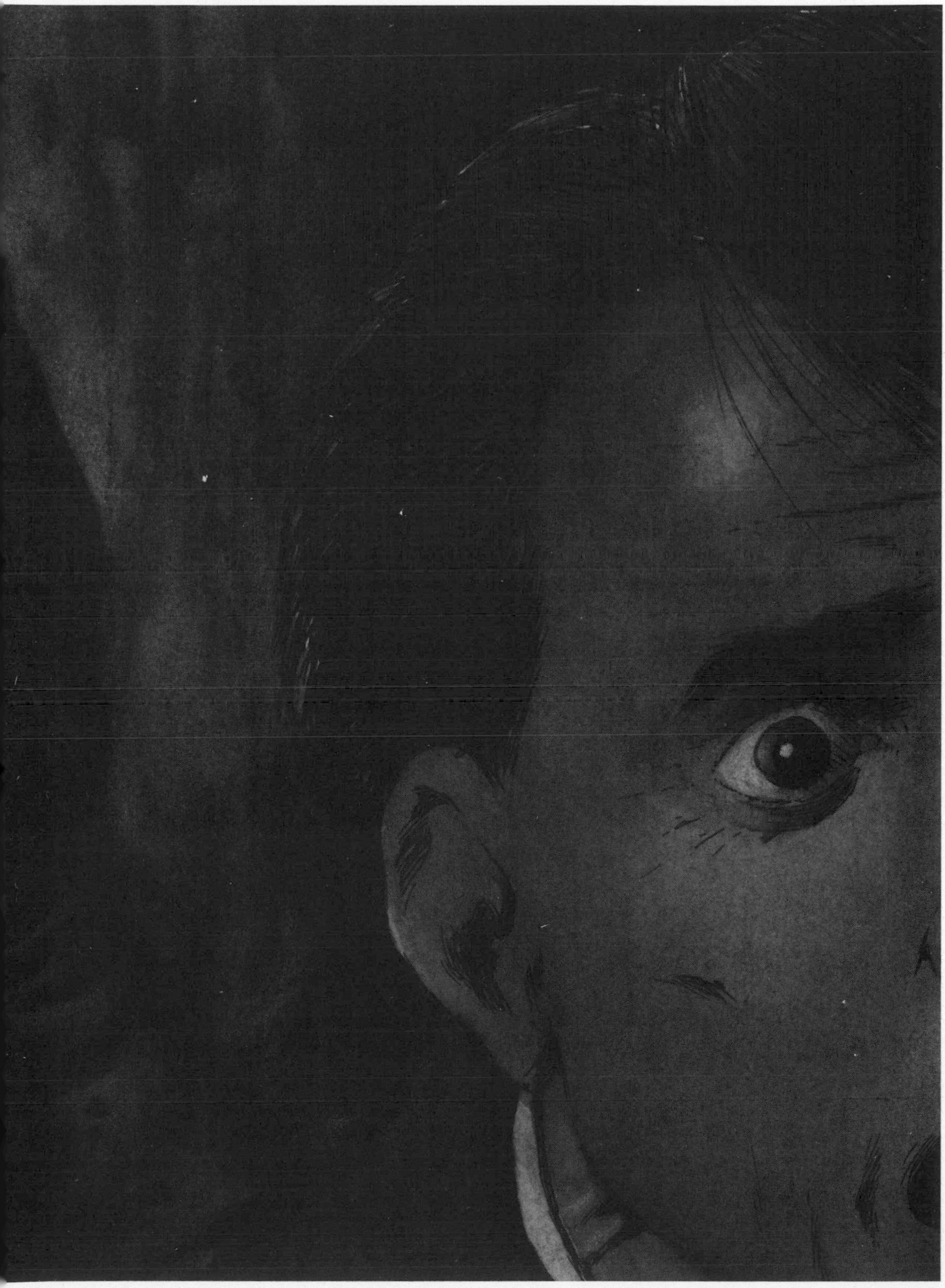

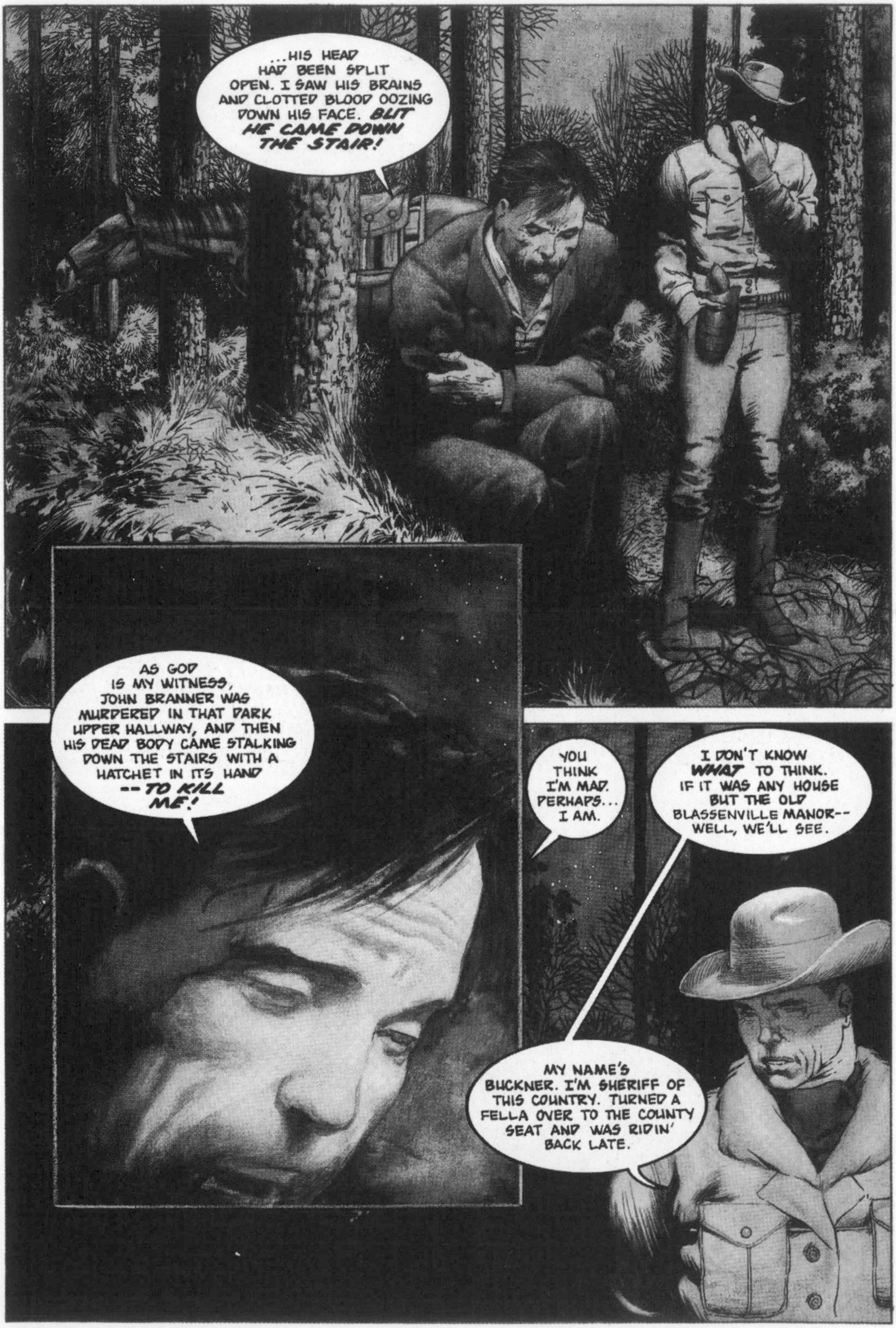
...HIS HEAD HAD BEEN SPLIT OPEN. I SAW HIS BRAINS AND CLOTTED BLOOD OOZING DOWN HIS FACE. BUT HE CAME DOWN THE STAIR!
AS GOD IS MY WITNESS, JOHN BRANNER WAS MURDERED IN THAT DARK UPPER HALLWAY, AND THEN HIS DEAD BODY CAME STALKING DOWN THE STAIRS WITH A HATCHET IN ITS HAND --TO KILL ME!
YOU THINK I'M MAD. PERHAPS... I AM.
I DON'T KNOW WHAT TO THINK. IF IT WAS ANY HOUSE BUT THE OLD BLASSENVILLE MANOR-- WELL, WE'LL SEE.
MY NAME'S BUCKNER. I'M SHERIFF OF THIS COUNTRY. TURNED A FELLA OVER TO THE COUNTY SEAT AND WAS RIDIN' BACK LATE.

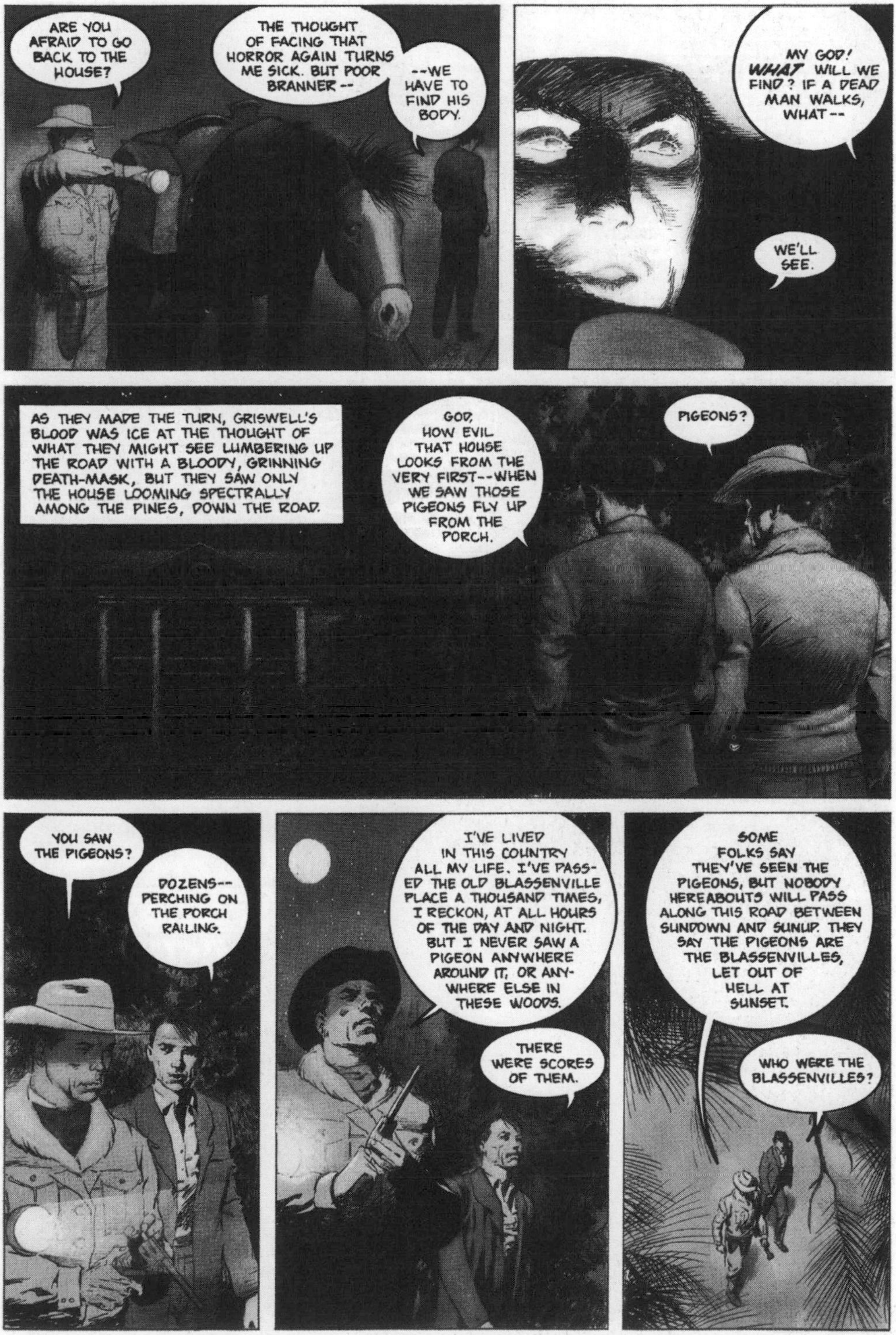
ARE YOU AFRAID TO GO BACK TO THE HOUSE?
THE THOUGHT OF FACING THAT HORROR AGAIN TURNS ME SICK. BUT POOR BRANNER --
--WE HAVE TO FIND HIS BODY.
MY GOD! WHAT WILL WE FIND? IF A DEAD MAN WALKS, WHAT --
WE'LL SEE.
AS THEY MADE THE TURN, GRISWELL'S BLOOD WAS ICE AT THE THOUGHT OF WHAT THEY MIGHT SEE LUMBERING UP THE ROAD WITH A BLOODY, GRINNING DEATH-MASK, BUT THEY SAW ONLY THE HOUSE LOOMING SPECTRALLY AMONG THE PINES, DOWN THE ROAD.
GOD, HOW EVIL THAT HOUSE LOOKS FROM THE VERY FIRST--WHEN WE SAW THOSE PIGEONS FLY UP FROM THE PORCH.
PIGEONS?
YOU SAW THE PIGEONS?
DOZENS-- PERCHING ON THE PORCH RAILING.
I'VE LIVED IN THIS COUNTRY ALL MY LIFE. I'VE PASSED THE OLD BLASSENVILLE PLACE A THOUSAND TIMES, I RECKON, AT ALL HOURS OF THE DAY AND NIGHT. BUT I NEVER SAW A PIGEON ANYWHERE AROUND IT, OR ANYWHERE ELSE IN THESE WOODS.
THERE WERE SCORES OF THEM.
SOME FOLKS SAY THEY'VE SEEN THE PIGEONS, BUT NOBODY HEREABOUTS WILL PASS ALONG THIS ROAD BETWEEN SUNDOWN AND SUNUP. THEY SAY THE PIGEONS ARE THE BLASSENVILLES, LET OUT OF HELL AT SUNSET.
WHO WERE THE BLASSENVILLES?

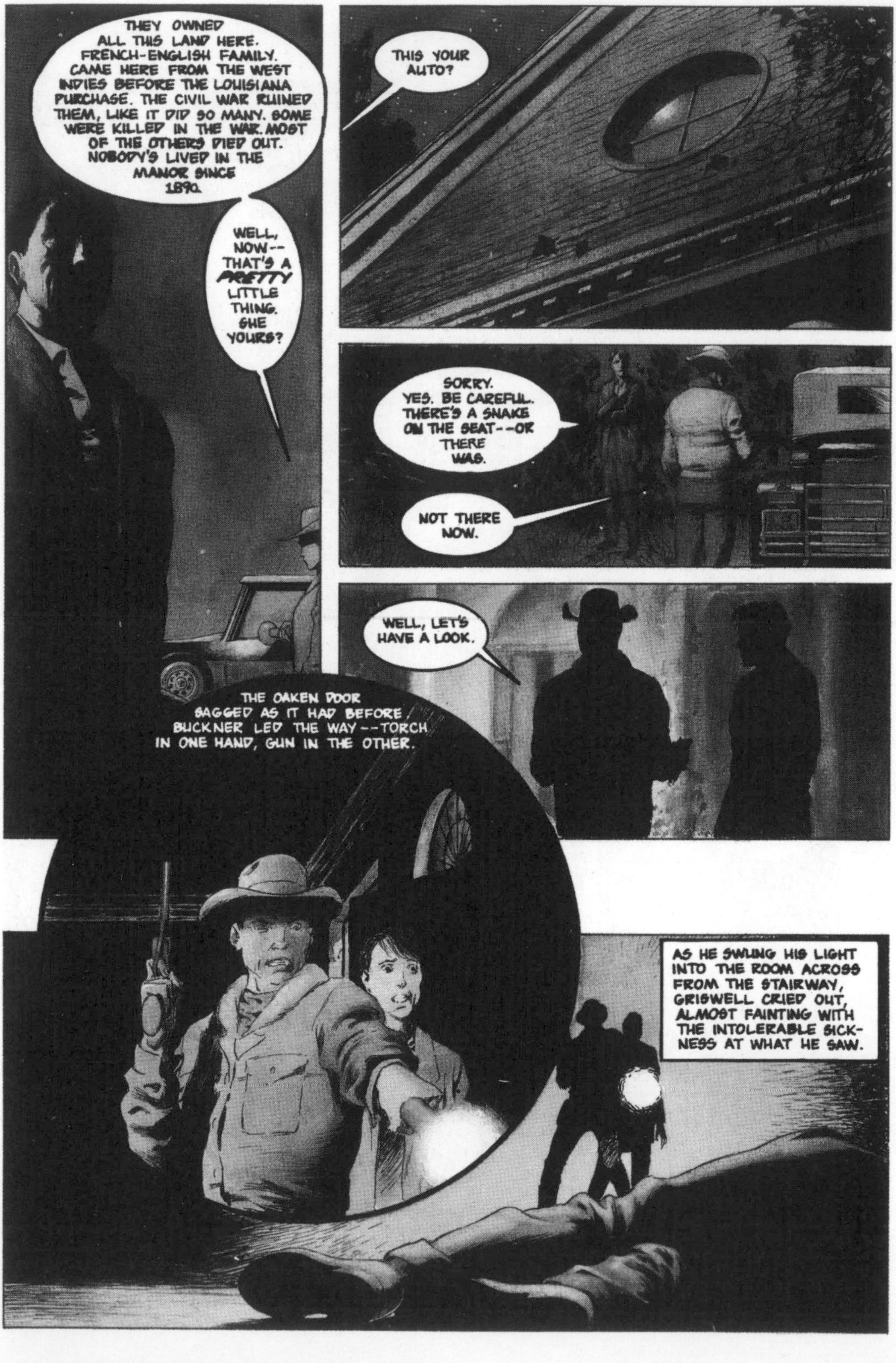
THEY OWNED ALL THIS LAND HERE. FRENCH-ENGLISH FAMILY. CAME HERE FROM THE WEST INDIES BEFORE THE LOUISIANA PURCHASE. THE CIVIL WAR RUINED THEM, LIKE IT DID SO MANY. SOME WERE KILLED IN THE WAR. MOST OF THE OTHERS DIED OUT. NOBODY'S LIVED IN THE MANOR SINCE 1890.
WELL, NOW-- THAT'S A PRETTY LITTLE THING. SHE YOURS?
THIS YOUR AUTO?
SORRY. YES. BE CAREFUL. THERE'S A SNAKE ON THE SEAT--OR THERE WAS.
NOT THERE NOW.
WELL, LET'S HAVE A LOOK.
THE OAKEN DOOR SAGGED AS IT HAD BEFORE. BUCKNER LED THE WAY--TORCH IN ONE HAND, GUN IN THE OTHER.
AS HE SWUNG HIS LIGHT INTO THE ROOM ACROSS FROM THE STAIRWAY, GRISWELL CRIED OUT, ALMOST FAINTING WITH THE INTOLERABLE SICKNESS AT WHAT HE SAW.

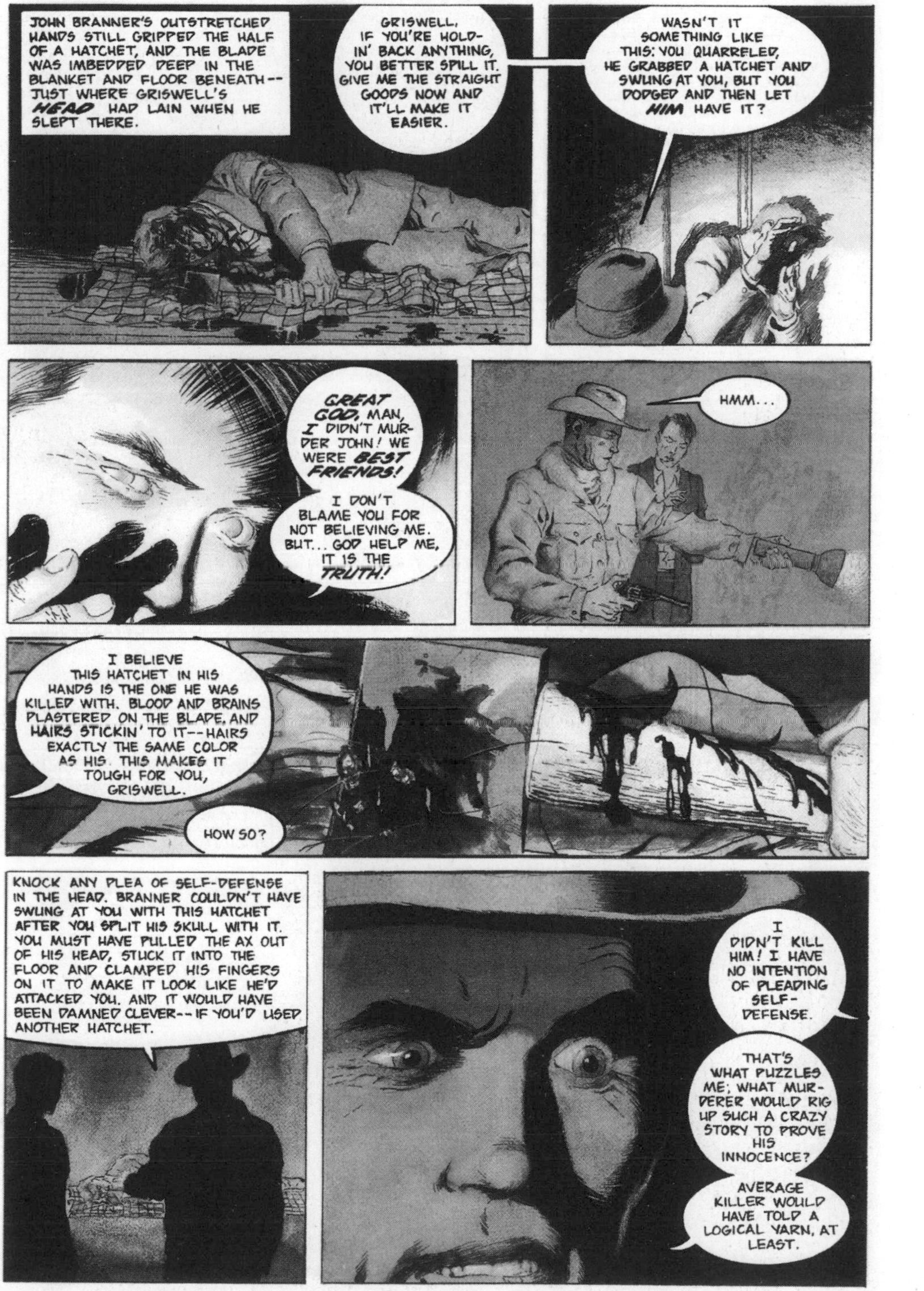
JOHN BRANNER'S OUTSTRETCHED HANDS STILL GRIPPED THE HALF OF A HATCHET, AND THE BLADE WAS IMBEDDED DEEP IN THE BLANKET AND FLOOR BENEATH -- JUST WHERE GRISWELL'S HEAD HAD LAIN WHEN HE SLEPT THERE.
GRISWELL, IF YOU'RE HOLD-IN' BACK ANYTHING, YOU BETTER SPILL IT. GIVE ME THE STRAIGHT GOODS NOW AND IT'LL MAKE IT EASIER.
WASN'T IT SOMETHING LIKE THIS: YOU QUARRELED, HE GRABBED A HATCHET AND SWUNG AT YOU, BUT YOU DODGED AND THEN LET HIM HAVE IT?
GREAT GOD, MAN, I DIDN'T MUR-DER JOHN! WE WERE BEST FRIENDS!
I DON'T BLAME YOU FOR NOT BELIEVING ME. BUT... GOD HELP ME, IT IS THE TRUTH!
HMM...
I BELIEVE THIS HATCHET IN HIS HANDS IS THE ONE HE WAS KILLED WITH. BLOOD AND BRAINS PLASTERED ON THE BLADE, AND HAIRS STICKIN' TO IT--HAIRS EXACTLY THE SAME COLOR AS HIS. THIS MAKES IT TOUGH FOR YOU, GRISWELL.
HOW SO?
KNOCK ANY PLEA OF SELF-DEFENSE IN THE HEAD. BRANNER COULDN'T HAVE SWUNG AT YOU WITH THIS HATCHET AFTER YOU SPLIT HIS SKULL WITH IT. YOU MUST HAVE PULLED THE AX OUT OF HIS HEAD, STUCK IT INTO THE FLOOR AND CLAMPED HIS FINGERS ON IT TO MAKE IT LOOK LIKE HE'D ATTACKED YOU. AND IT WOULD HAVE BEEN DAMNED CLEVER-- IF YOU'D USED ANOTHER HATCHET.
I DIDN'T KILL HIM! I HAVE NO INTENTION OF PLEADING SELF-DEFENSE.
THAT'S WHAT PUZZLES ME; WHAT MUR-DERER WOULD RIG UP SUCH A CRAZY STORY TO PROVE HIS INNOCENCE?
AVERAGE KILLER WOULD HAVE TOLD A LOGICAL YARN, AT LEAST.

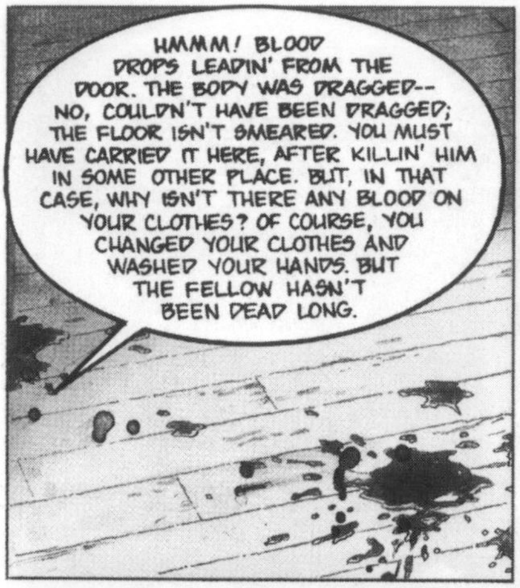
HMMM! BLOOD DROPS LEADIN' FROM THE DOOR. THE BODY WAS DRAGGED-- NO, COULDN'T HAVE BEEN DRAGGED; THE FLOOR ISN'T SMEARED. YOU MUST HAVE CARRIED IT HERE, AFTER KILLIN' HIM IN SOME OTHER PLACE. BUT, IN THAT CASE, WHY ISN'T THERE ANY BLOOD ON YOUR CLOTHES? OF COURSE, YOU CHANGED YOUR CLOTHES AND WASHED YOUR HANDS. BUT THE FELLOW HASN'T BEEN DEAD LONG.

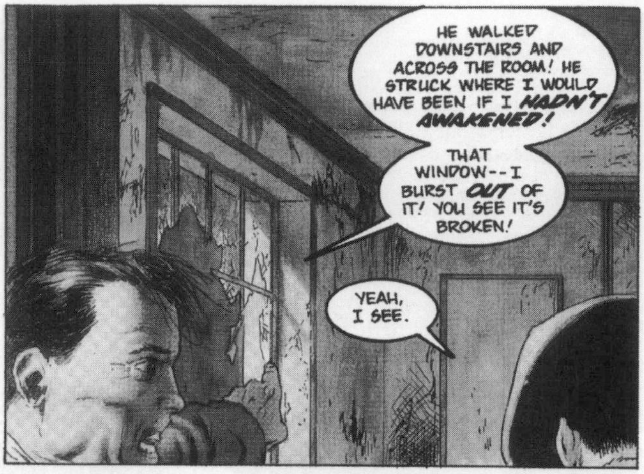
HE WALKED DOWNSTAIRS AND ACROSS THE ROOM! HE STRUCK WHERE I WOULD HAVE BEEN IF I HADN'T AWAKENED!
THAT WINDOW--I BURST OUT OF IT! YOU SEE IT'S BROKEN!
YEAH, I SEE.

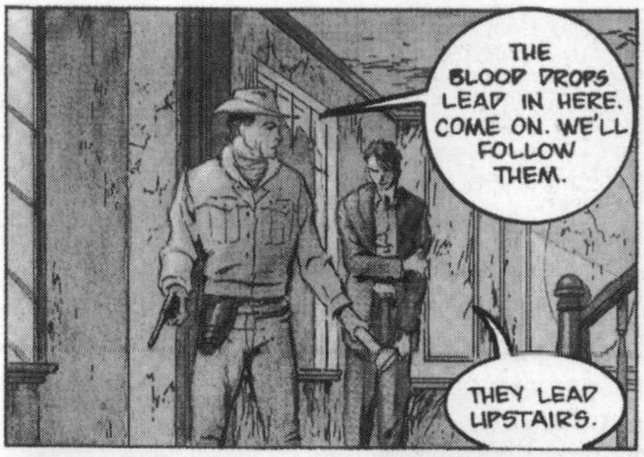
THE BLOOD DROPS LEAD IN HERE. COME ON. WE'LL FOLLOW THEM.
THEY LEAD UPSTAIRS.

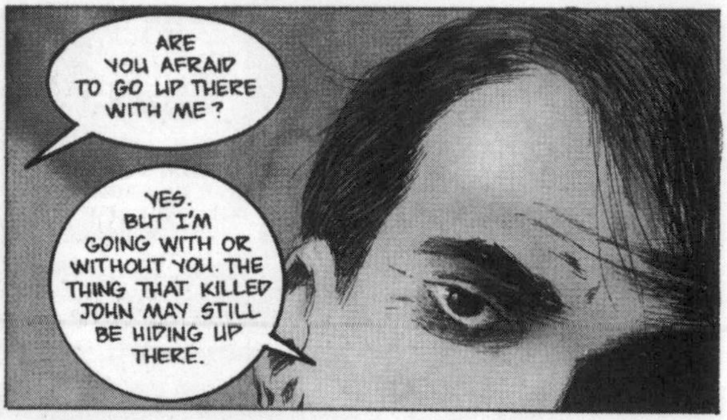
ARE YOU AFRAID TO GO UP THERE WITH ME?
YES. BUT I'M GOING WITH OR WITHOUT YOU. THE THING THAT KILLED JOHN MAY STILL BE HIDING UP THERE.

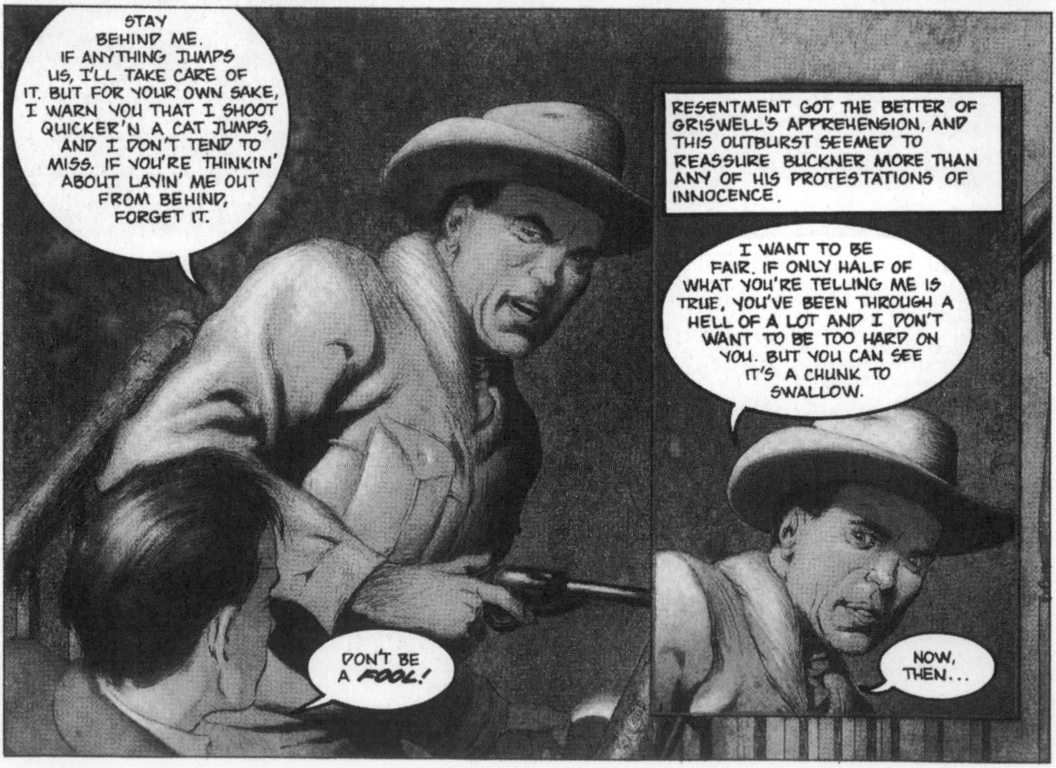
STAY BEHIND ME. IF ANYTHING JUMPS US, I'LL TAKE CARE OF IT. BUT FOR YOUR OWN SAKE, I WARN YOU THAT I SHOOT QUICKER'N A CAT JUMPS, AND I DON'T TEND TO MISS. IF YOU'RE THINKIN' ABOUT LAYIN' ME OUT FROM BEHIND, FORGET IT.
DON'T BE A FOOL!
RESENTMENT GOT THE BETTER OF GRISWELL'S APPREHENSION, AND THIS OUTBURST SEEMED TO REASSURE BUCKNER MORE THAN ANY OF HIS PROTESTATIONS OF INNOCENCE.
I WANT TO BE FAIR. IF ONLY HALF OF WHAT YOU'RE TELLING ME IS TRUE, YOU'VE BEEN THROUGH A HELL OF A LOT AND I DON'T WANT TO BE TOO HARD ON YOU. BUT YOU CAN SEE IT'S A CHUNK TO SWALLOW.
NOW, THEN...

MAN'S TRACKS IN THE DUST. ONE SET GOIN' UP. ONE COMIN' DOWN.

SAME MAN. NOT YOUR TRACKS. BRANNER WAS A BIGGER MAN THAN YOU ARE.

BLOOD ON THE BANNISTERS LIKE A MAN HAD LAID HIS BLOODY HAND THERE-- A SMEAR OF STUFF THAT LOOKS-- *BRAINS!*

OKAY. LET'S SEE WHAT'S UPSTAIRS.

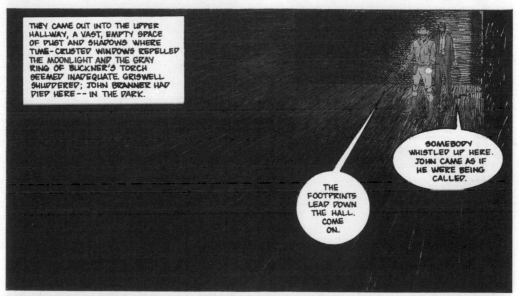

THEY CAME OUT INTO THE UPPER HALLWAY, A VAST, EMPTY SPACE OF DUST AND SHADOWS WHERE TIME-CRUSTED WINDOWS REPELLED THE MOONLIGHT AND THE GRAY RING OF BUCKNER'S TORCH SEEMED INADEQUATE. GRISWELL SHUDDERED; JOHN BRANNER HAD DIED HERE-- IN THE DARK.

SOMEBODY WHISTLED UP HERE. JOHN CAME AS IF HE WERE BEING CALLED.

THE FOOTPRINTS LEAD DOWN THE HALL. COME ON.

SAME AS ON THE STAIR-- ONE SET GOIN', ONE COMIN'. SAME PRINTS.

JESUS!

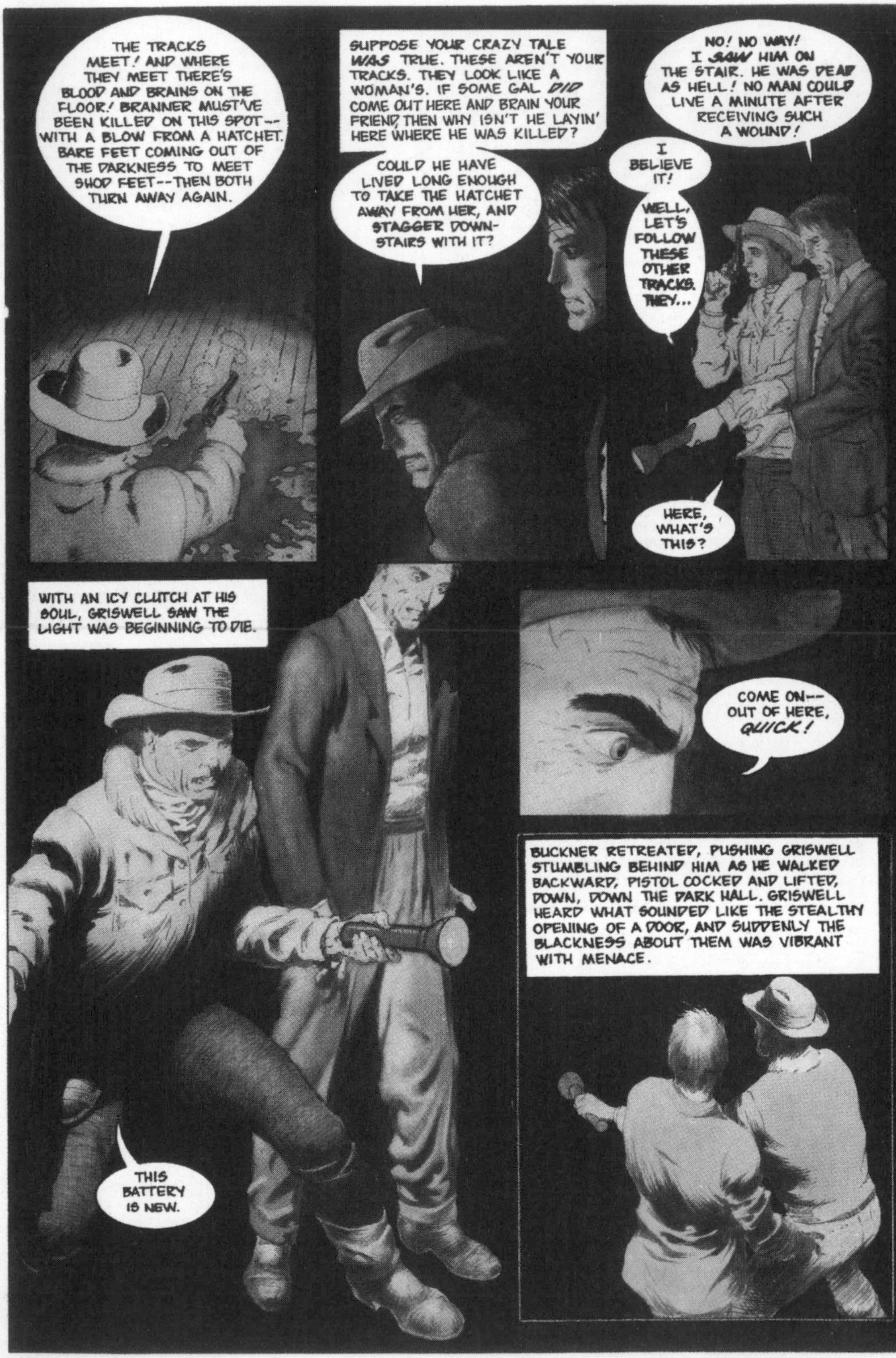
THE TRACKS MEET! AND WHERE THEY MEET THERE'S BLOOD AND BRAINS ON THE FLOOR! BRANNER MUST'VE BEEN KILLED ON THIS SPOT-- WITH A BLOW FROM A HATCHET. BARE FEET COMING OUT OF THE DARKNESS TO MEET SHOD FEET--THEN BOTH TURN AWAY AGAIN.
SUPPOSE YOUR CRAZY TALE WAS TRUE. THESE AREN'T YOUR TRACKS. THEY LOOK LIKE A WOMAN'S. IF SOME GAL DID COME OUT HERE AND BRAIN YOUR FRIEND, THEN WHY ISN'T HE LAYIN' HERE WHERE HE WAS KILLED?
COULD HE HAVE LIVED LONG ENOUGH TO TAKE THE HATCHET AWAY FROM HER, AND STAGGER DOWN-STAIRS WITH IT?
NO! NO WAY! I SAW HIM ON THE STAIR. HE WAS DEAD AS HELL! NO MAN COULD LIVE A MINUTE AFTER RECEIVING SUCH A WOUND!
I BELIEVE IT!
WELL, LET'S FOLLOW THESE OTHER TRACKS. THEY...
HERE, WHAT'S THIS?
WITH AN ICY CLUTCH AT HIS SOUL, GRISWELL SAW THE LIGHT WAS BEGINNING TO DIE.
THIS BATTERY IS NEW.
COME ON-- OUT OF HERE, QUICK!
BUCKNER RETREATED, PUSHING GRISWELL STUMBLING BEHIND HIM AS HE WALKED BACKWARD, PISTOL COCKED AND LIFTED, DOWN, DOWN THE DARK HALL. GRISWELL HEARD WHAT SOUNDED LIKE THE STEALTHY OPENING OF A DOOR, AND SUDDENLY THE BLACKNESS ABOUT THEM WAS VIBRANT WITH MENACE.

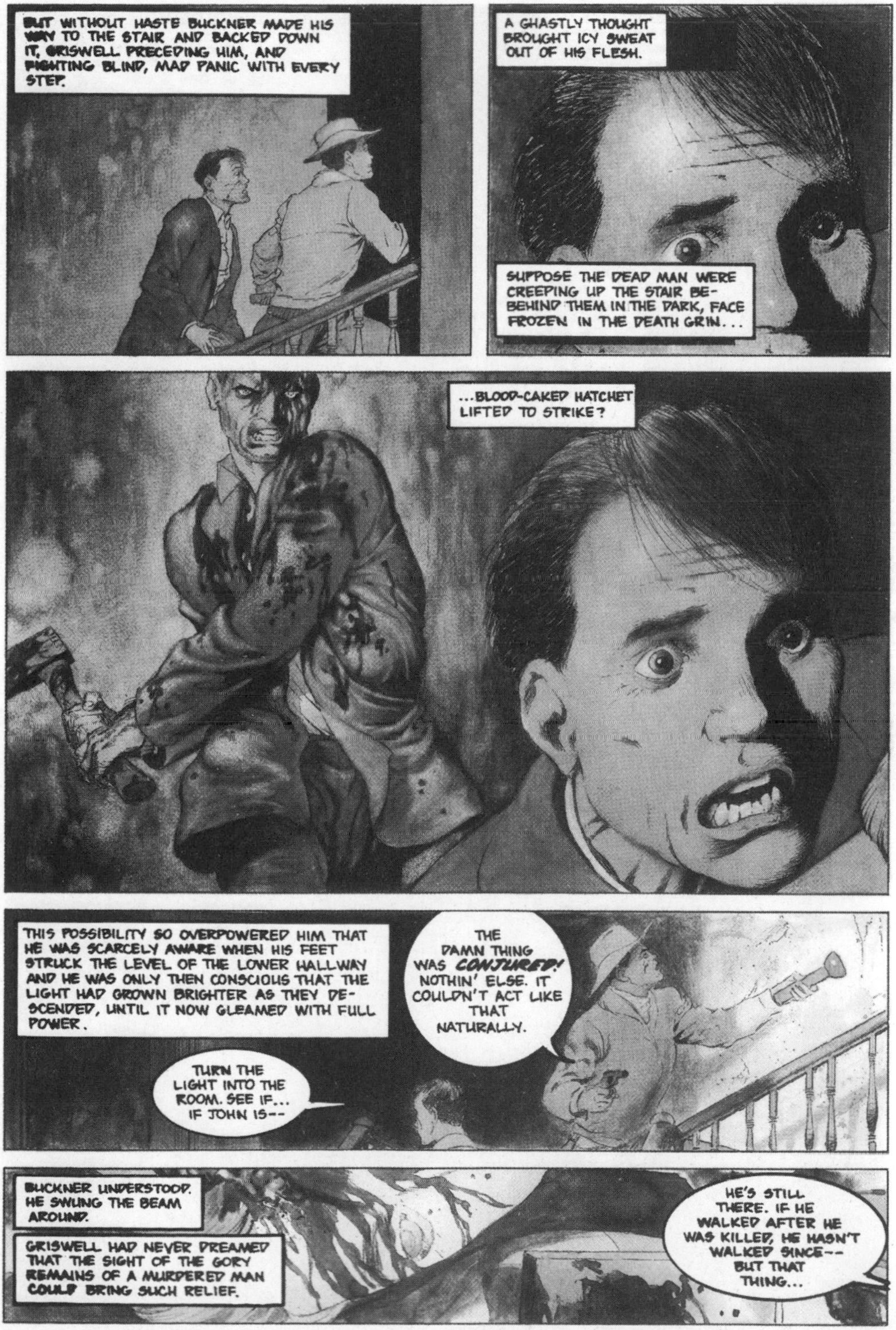
BUT WITHOUT HASTE BUCKNER MADE HIS WAY TO THE STAIR AND BACKED DOWN IT, GRISWELL PRECEDING HIM, AND FIGHTING BLIND, MAD PANIC WITH EVERY STEP.
A GHASTLY THOUGHT BROUGHT ICY SWEAT OUT OF HIS FLESH.
SUPPOSE THE DEAD MAN WERE CREEPING UP THE STAIR BE-BEHIND THEM IN THE DARK, FACE FROZEN IN THE DEATH GRIN...
...BLOOD-CAKED HATCHET LIFTED TO STRIKE?
THIS POSSIBILITY SO OVERPOWERED HIM THAT HE WAS SCARCELY AWARE WHEN HIS FEET STRUCK THE LEVEL OF THE LOWER HALLWAY AND HE WAS ONLY THEN CONSCIOUS THAT THE LIGHT HAD GROWN BRIGHTER AS THEY DE-SCENDED, UNTIL IT NOW GLEAMED WITH FULL POWER.
THE DAMN THING WAS CONJURED! NOTHIN' ELSE. IT COULDN'T ACT LIKE THAT NATURALLY.
TURN THE LIGHT INTO THE ROOM. SEE IF... IF JOHN IS--
BUCKNER UNDERSTOOD. HE SWUNG THE BEAM AROUND.
GRISWELL HAD NEVER DREAMED THAT THE SIGHT OF THE GORY REMAINS OF A MURDERED MAN COULD BRING SUCH RELIEF.
HE'S STILL THERE. IF HE WALKED AFTER HE WAS KILLED, HE HASN'T WALKED SINCE-- BUT THAT THING...

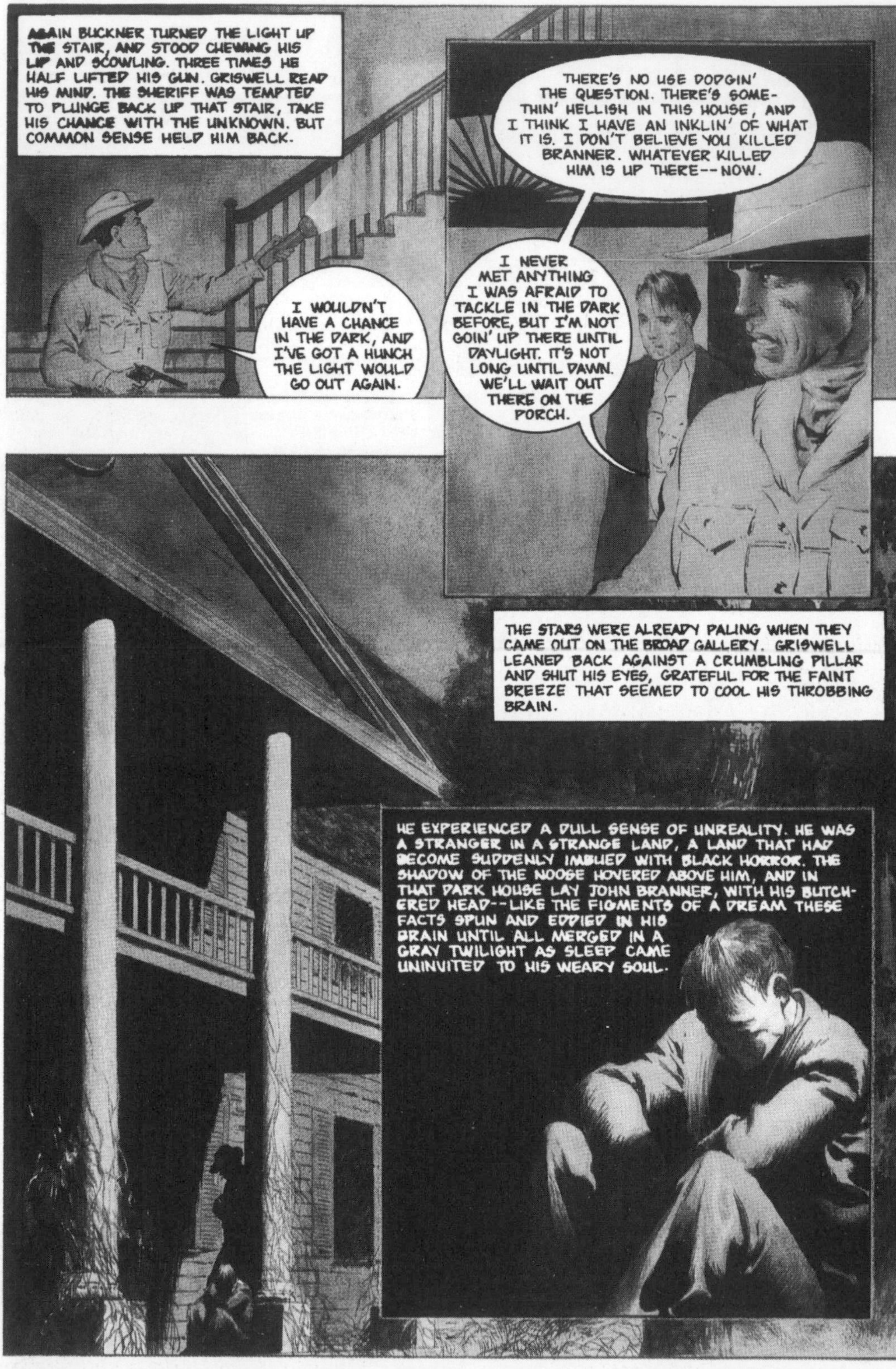
AGAIN BUCKNER TURNED THE LIGHT UP THE STAIR, AND STOOD CHEWING HIS LIP AND SCOWLING. THREE TIMES HE HALF LIFTED HIS GUN. GRISWELL READ HIS MIND. THE SHERIFF WAS TEMPTED TO PLUNGE BACK UP THAT STAIR, TAKE HIS CHANCE WITH THE UNKNOWN. BUT COMMON SENSE HELD HIM BACK.
I WOULDN'T HAVE A CHANCE IN THE DARK, AND I'VE GOT A HUNCH THE LIGHT WOULD GO OUT AGAIN.
THERE'S NO USE DODGIN' THE QUESTION. THERE'S SOME-THIN' HELLISH IN THIS HOUSE, AND I THINK I HAVE AN INKLIN' OF WHAT IT IS. I DON'T BELIEVE YOU KILLED BRANNER. WHATEVER KILLED HIM IS UP THERE--NOW.
I NEVER MET ANYTHING I WAS AFRAID TO TACKLE IN THE DARK BEFORE, BUT I'M NOT GOIN' UP THERE UNTIL DAYLIGHT. IT'S NOT LONG UNTIL DAWN. WE'LL WAIT OUT THERE ON THE PORCH.
THE STARS WERE ALREADY PALING WHEN THEY CAME OUT ON THE BROAD GALLERY. GRISWELL LEANED BACK AGAINST A CRUMBLING PILLAR AND SHUT HIS EYES, GRATEFUL FOR THE FAINT BREEZE THAT SEEMED TO COOL HIS THROBBING BRAIN.
HE EXPERIENCED A DULL SENSE OF UNREALITY. HE WAS A STRANGER IN A STRANGE LAND, A LAND THAT HAD BECOME SUDDENLY IMBUED WITH BLACK HORROR. THE SHADOW OF THE NOOSE HOVERED ABOVE HIM, AND IN THAT DARK HOUSE LAY JOHN BRANNER, WITH HIS BUTCH-ERED HEAD--LIKE THE FIGMENTS OF A DREAM THESE FACTS SPUN AND EDDIED IN HIS BRAIN UNTIL ALL MERGED IN A GRAY TWILIGHT AS SLEEP CAME UNINVITED TO HIS WEARY SOUL.

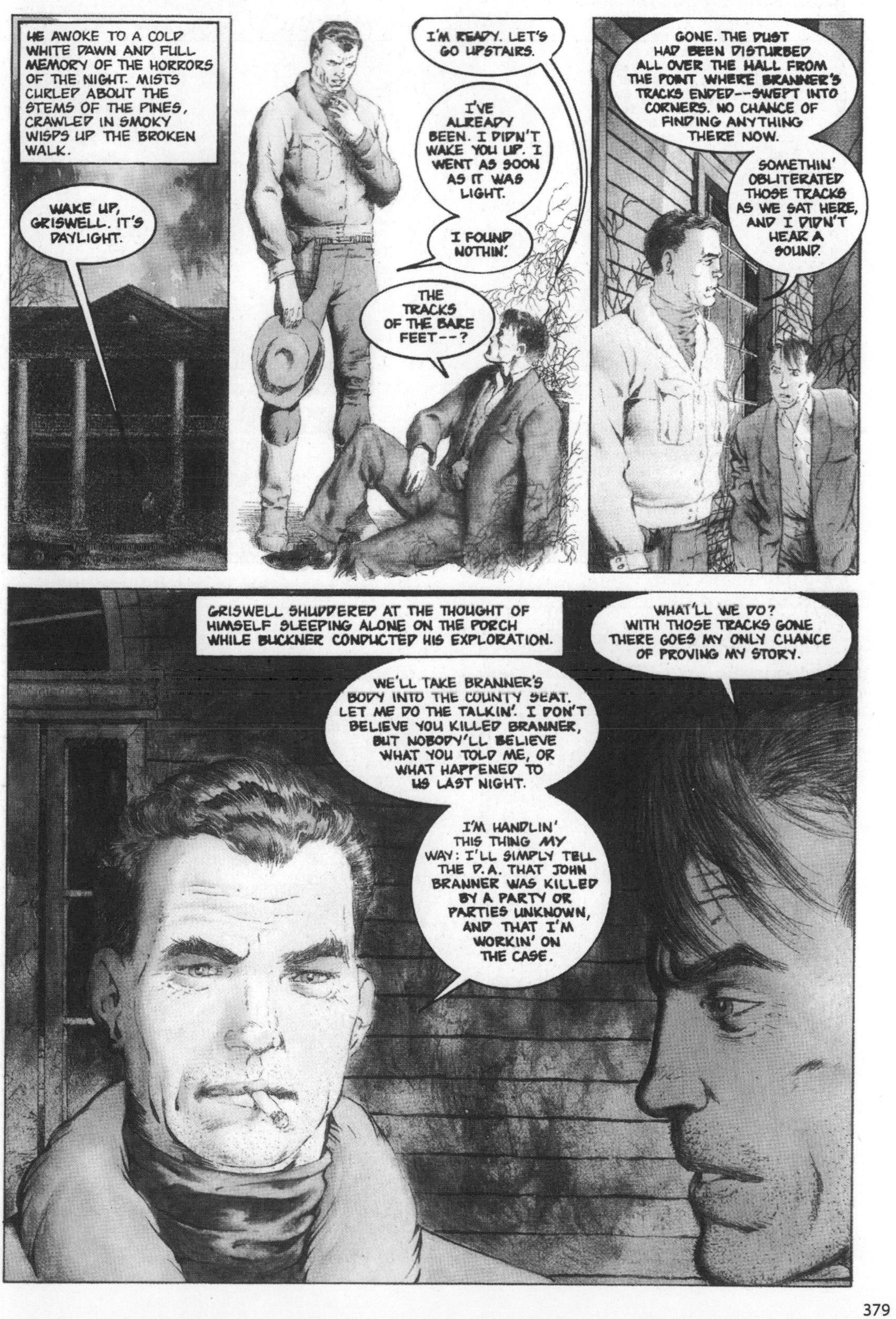
HE AWOKE TO A COLD WHITE DAWN AND FULL MEMORY OF THE HORRORS OF THE NIGHT. MISTS CURLED ABOUT THE STEMS OF THE PINES, CRAWLED IN SMOKY WISPS UP THE BROKEN WALK.
WAKE UP, GRISWELL. IT'S DAYLIGHT.
I'M READY. LET'S GO UPSTAIRS.
I'VE ALREADY BEEN. I DIDN'T WAKE YOU UP. I WENT AS SOON AS IT WAS LIGHT.
I FOUND NOTHIN'.
THE TRACKS OF THE BARE FEET--?
GONE. THE DUST HAD BEEN DISTURBED ALL OVER THE HALL FROM THE POINT WHERE BRANNER'S TRACKS ENDED--SWEPT INTO CORNERS. NO CHANCE OF FINDING ANYTHING THERE NOW.
SOMETHIN' OBLITERATED THOSE TRACKS AS WE SAT HERE, AND I DIDN'T HEAR A SOUND.
GRISWELL SHUDDERED AT THE THOUGHT OF HIMSELF SLEEPING ALONE ON THE PORCH WHILE BUCKNER CONDUCTED HIS EXPLORATION.
WHAT'LL WE DO? WITH THOSE TRACKS GONE THERE GOES MY ONLY CHANCE OF PROVING MY STORY.
WE'LL TAKE BRANNER'S BODY INTO THE COUNTY SEAT. LET ME DO THE TALKIN'. I DON'T BELIEVE YOU KILLED BRANNER, BUT NOBODY'LL BELIEVE WHAT YOU TOLD ME, OR WHAT HAPPENED TO US LAST NIGHT.
I'M HANDLIN' THIS THING MY WAY: I'LL SIMPLY TELL THE D.A. THAT JOHN BRANNER WAS KILLED BY A PARTY OR PARTIES UNKNOWN, AND THAT I'M WORKIN' ON THE CASE.

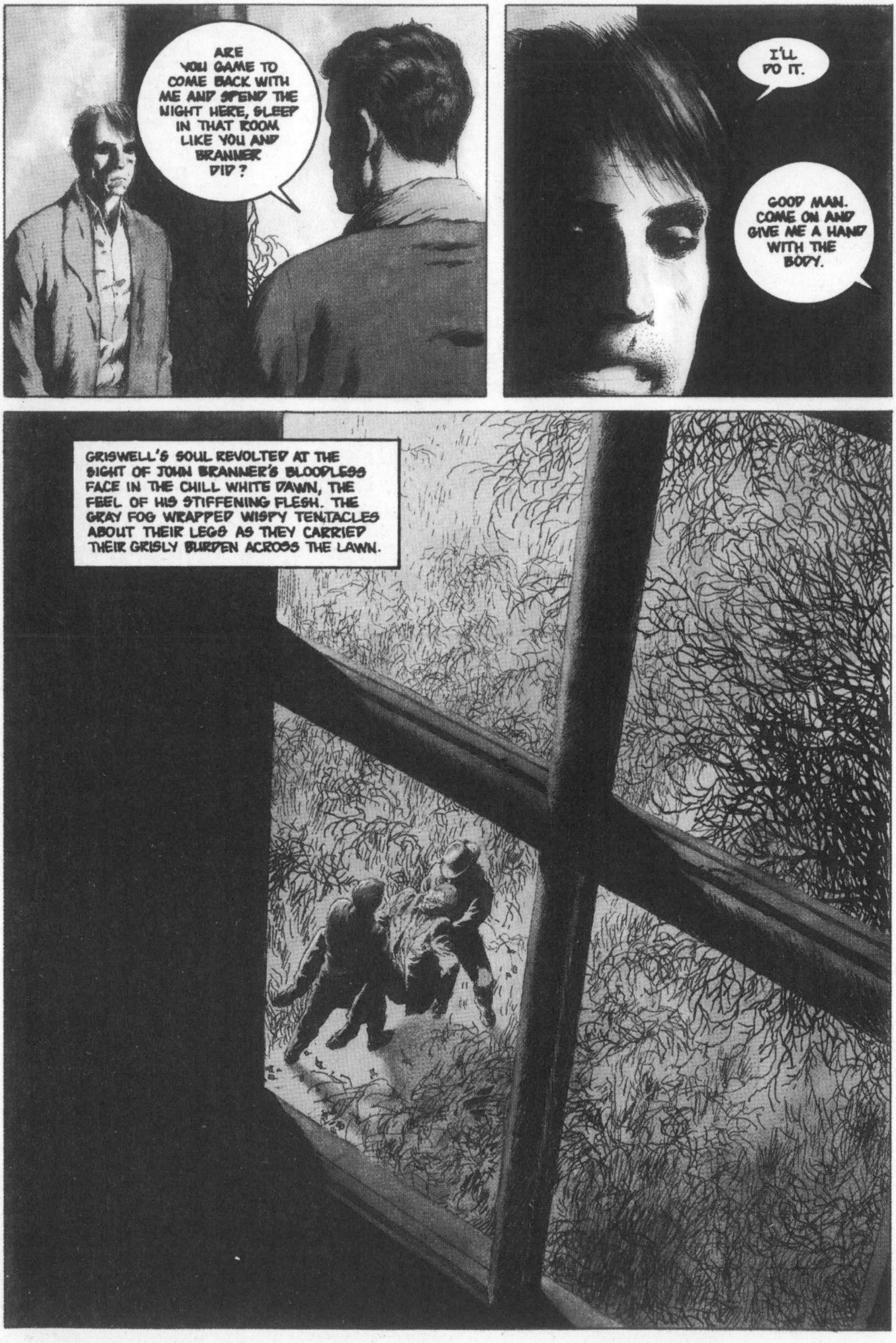
ARE YOU GAME TO COME BACK WITH ME AND SPEND THE NIGHT HERE, SLEEP IN THAT ROOM LIKE YOU AND BRANNER DID?
I'LL DO IT.
GOOD MAN. COME ON AND GIVE ME A HAND WITH THE BODY.
GRISWELL'S SOUL REVOLTED AT THE SIGHT OF JOHN BRANNER'S BLOODLESS FACE IN THE CHILL WHITE DAWN, THE FEEL OF HIS STIFFENING FLESH. THE GRAY FOG WRAPPED WISPY TENTACLES ABOUT THEIR LEGS AS THEY CARRIED THEIR GRISLY BURDEN ACROSS THE LAWN.

7. THE SNAKE'S BROTHER

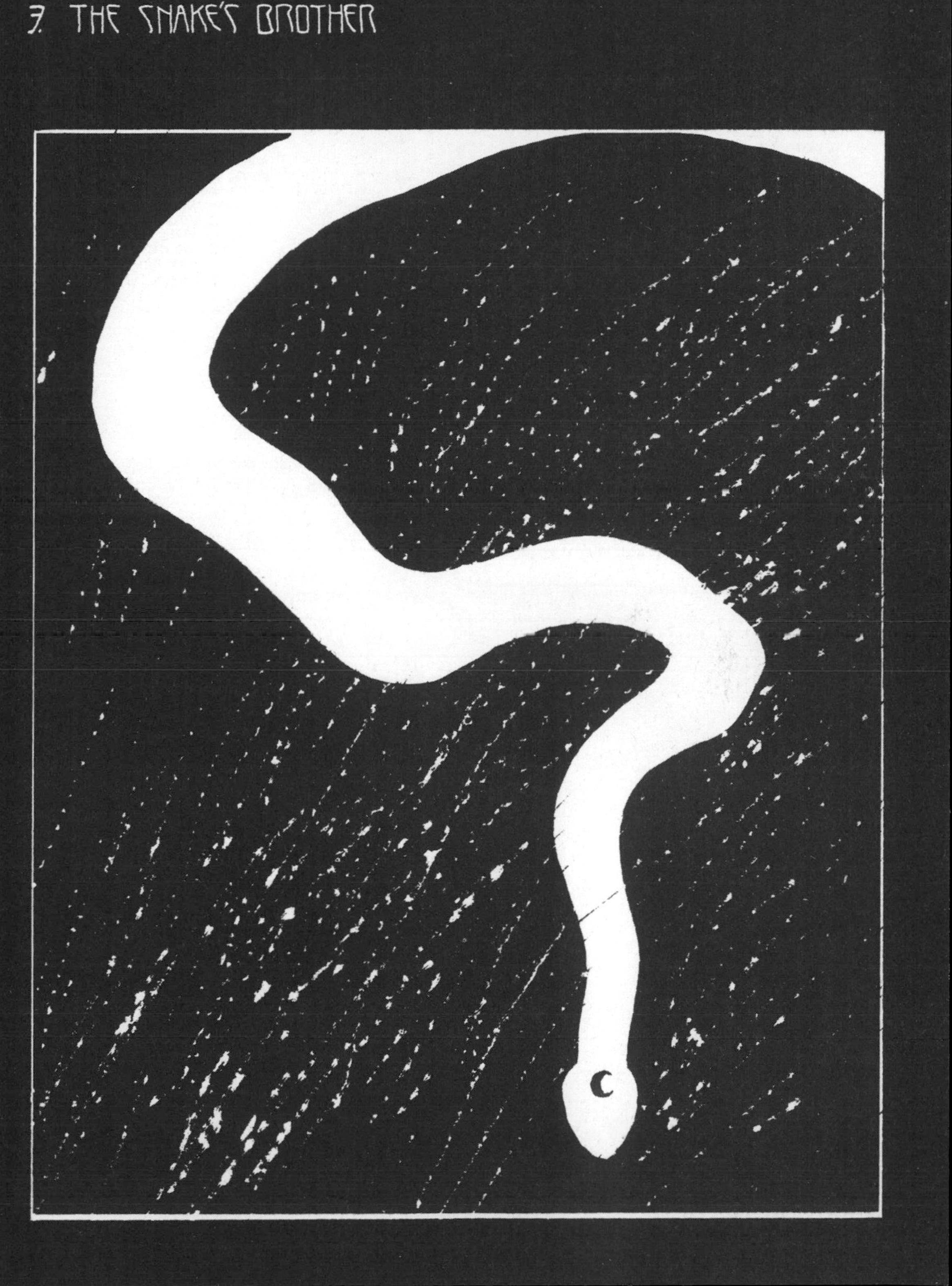

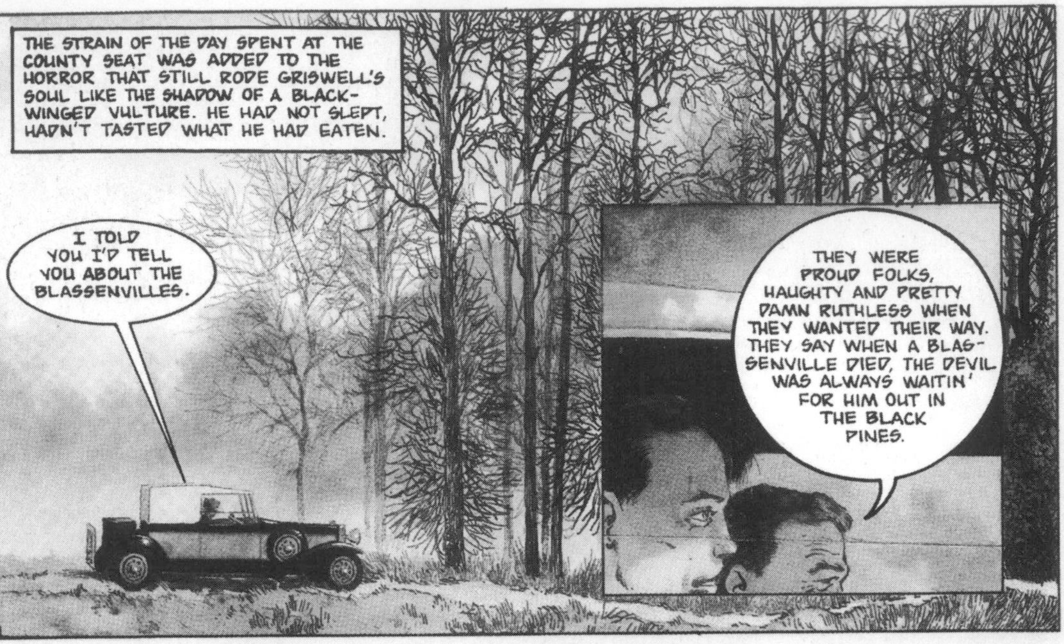
THE STRAIN OF THE DAY SPENT AT THE COUNTY SEAT WAS ADDED TO THE HORROR THAT STILL RODE GRISWELL'S SOUL LIKE THE SHADOW OF A BLACK-WINGED VULTURE. HE HAD NOT SLEPT, HADN'T TASTED WHAT HE HAD EATEN.
I TOLD YOU I'D TELL YOU ABOUT THE BLASSENVILLES.
THEY WERE PROUD FOLKS, HAUGHTY AND PRETTY DAMN RUTHLESS WHEN THEY WANTED THEIR WAY. THEY SAY WHEN A BLASSENVILLE DIED, THE DEVIL WAS ALWAYS WAITIN' FOR HIM OUT IN THE BLACK PINES.

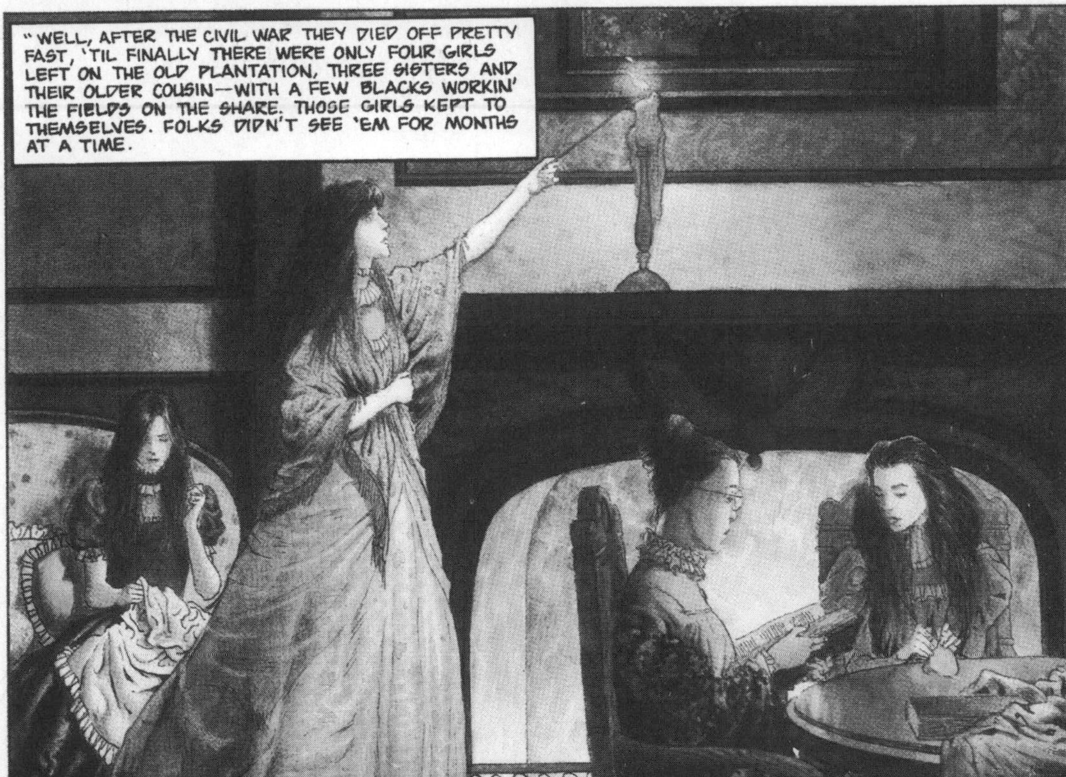
"WELL, AFTER THE CIVIL WAR THEY DIED OFF PRETTY FAST, 'TIL FINALLY THERE WERE ONLY FOUR GIRLS LEFT ON THE OLD PLANTATION, THREE SISTERS AND THEIR OLDER COUSIN—WITH A FEW BLACKS WORKIN' THE FIELDS ON THE SHARE. THOSE GIRLS KEPT TO THEMSELVES. FOLKS DIDN'T SEE 'EM FOR MONTHS AT A TIME.

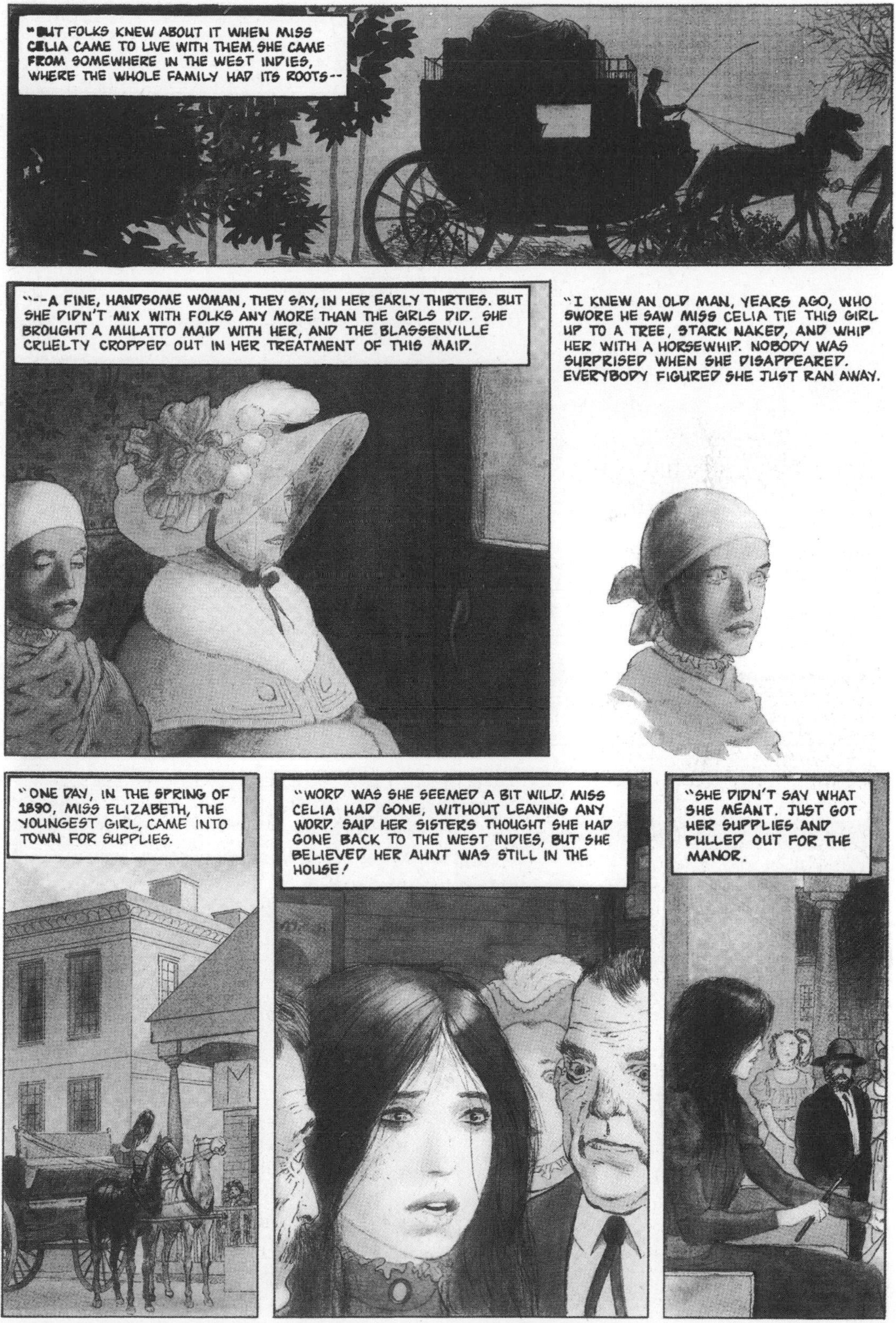
"BUT FOLKS KNEW ABOUT IT WHEN MISS CELIA CAME TO LIVE WITH THEM. SHE CAME FROM SOMEWHERE IN THE WEST INDIES, WHERE THE WHOLE FAMILY HAD ITS ROOTS--
"--A FINE, HANDSOME WOMAN, THEY SAY, IN HER EARLY THIRTIES. BUT SHE DIDN'T MIX WITH FOLKS ANY MORE THAN THE GIRLS DID. SHE BROUGHT A MULATTO MAID WITH HER, AND THE BLASSENVILLE CRUELTY CROPPED OUT IN HER TREATMENT OF THIS MAID.
"I KNEW AN OLD MAN, YEARS AGO, WHO SWORE HE SAW MISS CELIA TIE THIS GIRL UP TO A TREE, STARK NAKED, AND WHIP HER WITH A HORSEWHIP. NOBODY WAS SURPRISED WHEN SHE DISAPPEARED. EVERYBODY FIGURED SHE JUST RAN AWAY.
"ONE DAY, IN THE SPRING OF 1890, MISS ELIZABETH, THE YOUNGEST GIRL, CAME INTO TOWN FOR SUPPLIES.
"WORD WAS SHE SEEMED A BIT WILD. MISS CELIA HAD GONE, WITHOUT LEAVING ANY WORD. SAID HER SISTERS THOUGHT SHE HAD GONE BACK TO THE WEST INDIES, BUT SHE BELIEVED HER AUNT WAS STILL IN THE HOUSE!
"SHE DIDN'T SAY WHAT SHE MEANT. JUST GOT HER SUPPLIES AND PULLED OUT FOR THE MANOR.

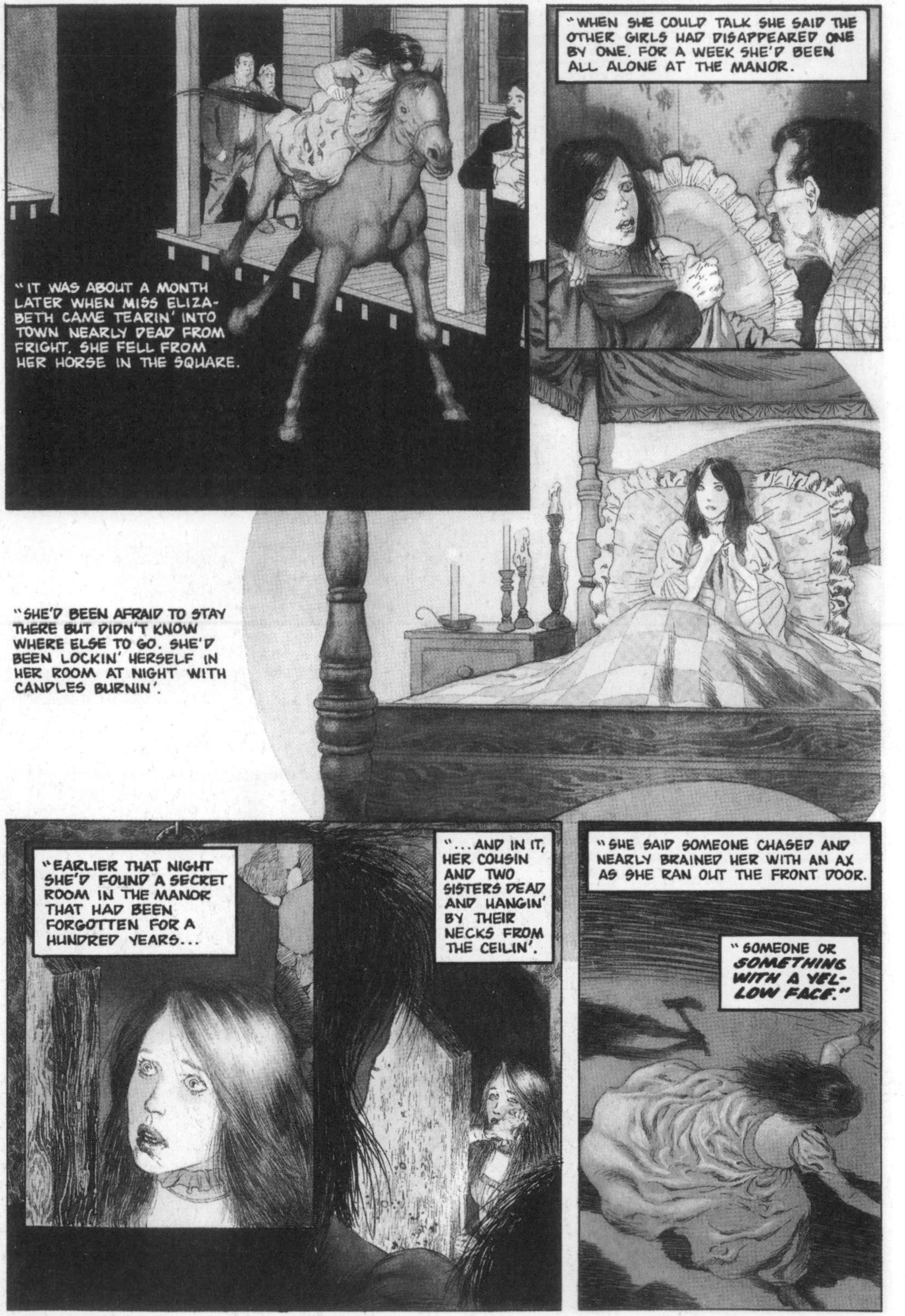
"IT WAS ABOUT A MONTH LATER WHEN MISS ELIZABETH CAME TEARIN' INTO TOWN NEARLY DEAD FROM FRIGHT. SHE FELL FROM HER HORSE IN THE SQUARE.
"WHEN SHE COULD TALK SHE SAID THE OTHER GIRLS HAD DISAPPEARED ONE BY ONE. FOR A WEEK SHE'D BEEN ALL ALONE AT THE MANOR.
"SHE'D BEEN AFRAID TO STAY THERE BUT DIDN'T KNOW WHERE ELSE TO GO. SHE'D BEEN LOCKIN' HERSELF IN HER ROOM AT NIGHT WITH CANDLES BURNIN'.
"EARLIER THAT NIGHT SHE'D FOUND A SECRET ROOM IN THE MANOR THAT HAD BEEN FORGOTTEN FOR A HUNDRED YEARS...
"...AND IN IT, HER COUSIN AND TWO SISTERS DEAD AND HANGIN' BY THEIR NECKS FROM THE CEILIN'.
"SHE SAID SOMEONE CHASED AND NEARLY BRAINED HER WITH AN AX AS SHE RAN OUT THE FRONT DOOR.
"SOMEONE OR SOMETHING WITH A YELLOW FACE."

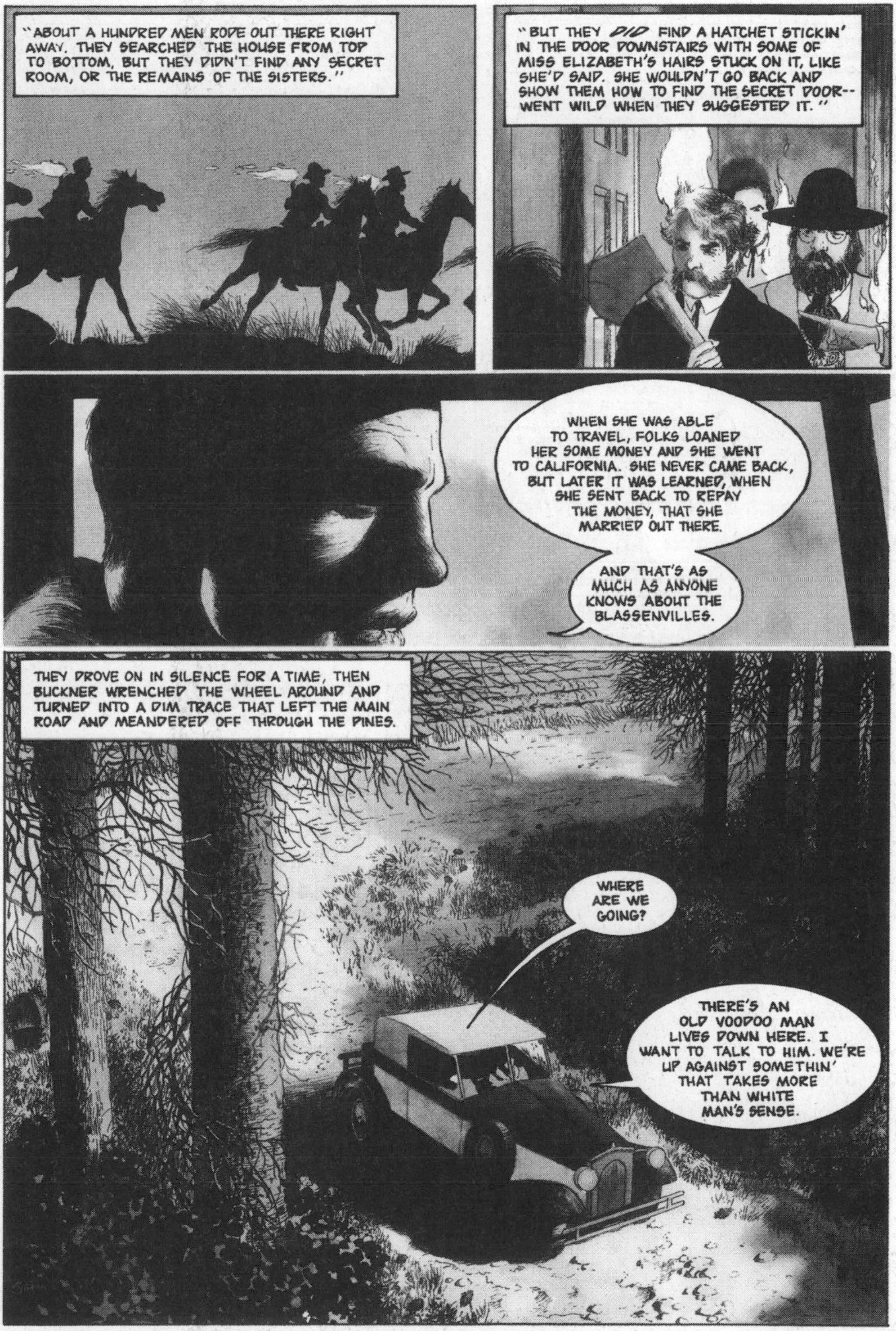
"ABOUT A HUNDRED MEN RODE OUT THERE RIGHT AWAY. THEY SEARCHED THE HOUSE FROM TOP TO BOTTOM, BUT THEY DIDN'T FIND ANY SECRET ROOM, OR THE REMAINS OF THE SISTERS."
"BUT THEY DID FIND A HATCHET STICKIN' IN THE DOOR DOWNSTAIRS WITH SOME OF MISS ELIZABETH'S HAIRS STUCK ON IT, LIKE SHE'D SAID. SHE WOULDN'T GO BACK AND SHOW THEM HOW TO FIND THE SECRET DOOR-- WENT WILD WHEN THEY SUGGESTED IT."
WHEN SHE WAS ABLE TO TRAVEL, FOLKS LOANED HER SOME MONEY AND SHE WENT TO CALIFORNIA. SHE NEVER CAME BACK, BUT LATER IT WAS LEARNED, WHEN SHE SENT BACK TO REPAY THE MONEY, THAT SHE MARRIED OUT THERE.
AND THAT'S AS MUCH AS ANYONE KNOWS ABOUT THE BLASSENVILLES.
THEY DROVE ON IN SILENCE FOR A TIME, THEN BUCKNER WRENCHED THE WHEEL AROUND AND TURNED INTO A DIM TRACE THAT LEFT THE MAIN ROAD AND MEANDERED OFF THROUGH THE PINES.
WHERE ARE WE GOING?
THERE'S AN OLD VOODOO MAN LIVES DOWN HERE. I WANT TO TALK TO HIM. WE'RE UP AGAINST SOMETHIN' THAT TAKES MORE THAN WHITE MAN'S SENSE.

BUCKNER BROUGHT THE AUTOMOBILE TO A HALT IN A CLEARING WHERE THE ONLY EVIDENCE OF HUMAN HABITATION, A SMALL CABIN, SQUATTED IN THE SHADE OF HUGE OAKS AND CYPRESSES.

THERE HE IS. COME ON.

AN OLD MAN SAT SEPARATING MUSHROOMS AT THE FRINGE OF THE CLEARING. HE LOOKED UP AS THEY APPROACHED, BUT DID NOT RISE.

TIME'S COME FOR YOU TO TALK, JACOB.

YOU KNOW THE SECRET OF BLASSENVILLE MANOR. NOW, A MAN WAS MURDERED THERE LAST NIGHT AND THIS MAN HERE COULD HANG FOR IT UNLESS YOU TELL ME WHAT *HAUNTS* THAT OLD HOUSE.

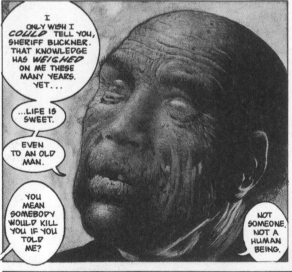

I ONLY WISH I *COULD* TELL YOU, SHERIFF BUCKNER. THAT KNOWLEDGE HAS *WEIGHED* ON ME THESE MANY YEARS. YET...

...LIFE IS SWEET.

EVEN TO AN OLD MAN.

YOU MEAN SOMEBODY WOULD KILL YOU IF YOU TOLD ME?

NOT SOMEONE. NOT A HUMAN BEING.

THE BIG SERPENT, THE BLACK GOD OF THE SWAMPS, GUARDS MY SECRET.

HE WOULD SEND A LITTLE BROTHER TO KISS ME WITH HIS COLD LIPS.

A LITTLE BROTHER WITH A WHITE CRESCENT MOON ON HIS HEAD.

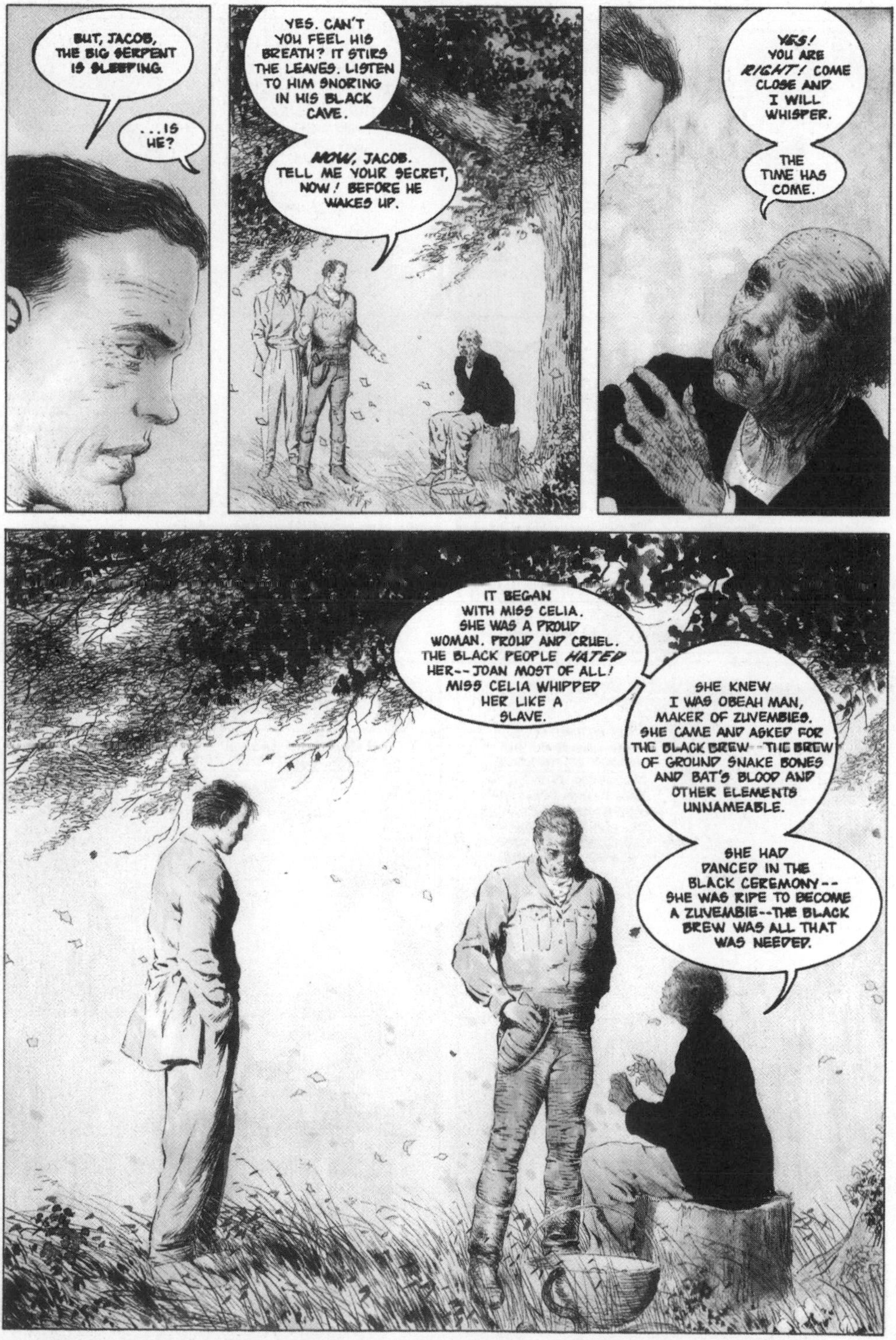
BUT, JACOB, THE BIG SERPENT IS SLEEPING.
...IS HE?
YES. CAN'T YOU FEEL HIS BREATH? IT STIRS THE LEAVES. LISTEN TO HIM SNORING IN HIS BLACK CAVE.
NOW, JACOB. TELL ME YOUR SECRET, NOW! BEFORE HE WAKES UP.
YES! YOU ARE RIGHT! COME CLOSE AND I WILL WHISPER.
THE TIME HAS COME.
IT BEGAN WITH MISS CELIA. SHE WAS A PROUD WOMAN. PROUD AND CRUEL. THE BLACK PEOPLE HATED HER--JOAN MOST OF ALL! MISS CELIA WHIPPED HER LIKE A SLAVE.
SHE KNEW I WAS OBEAH MAN, MAKER OF ZUVEMBIES. SHE CAME AND ASKED FOR THE BLACK BREW--THE BREW OF GROUND SNAKE BONES AND BAT'S BLOOD AND OTHER ELEMENTS UNNAMEABLE.
SHE HAD DANCED IN THE BLACK CEREMONY--SHE WAS RIPE TO BECOME A ZUVEMBIE--THE BLACK BREW WAS ALL THAT WAS NEEDED.

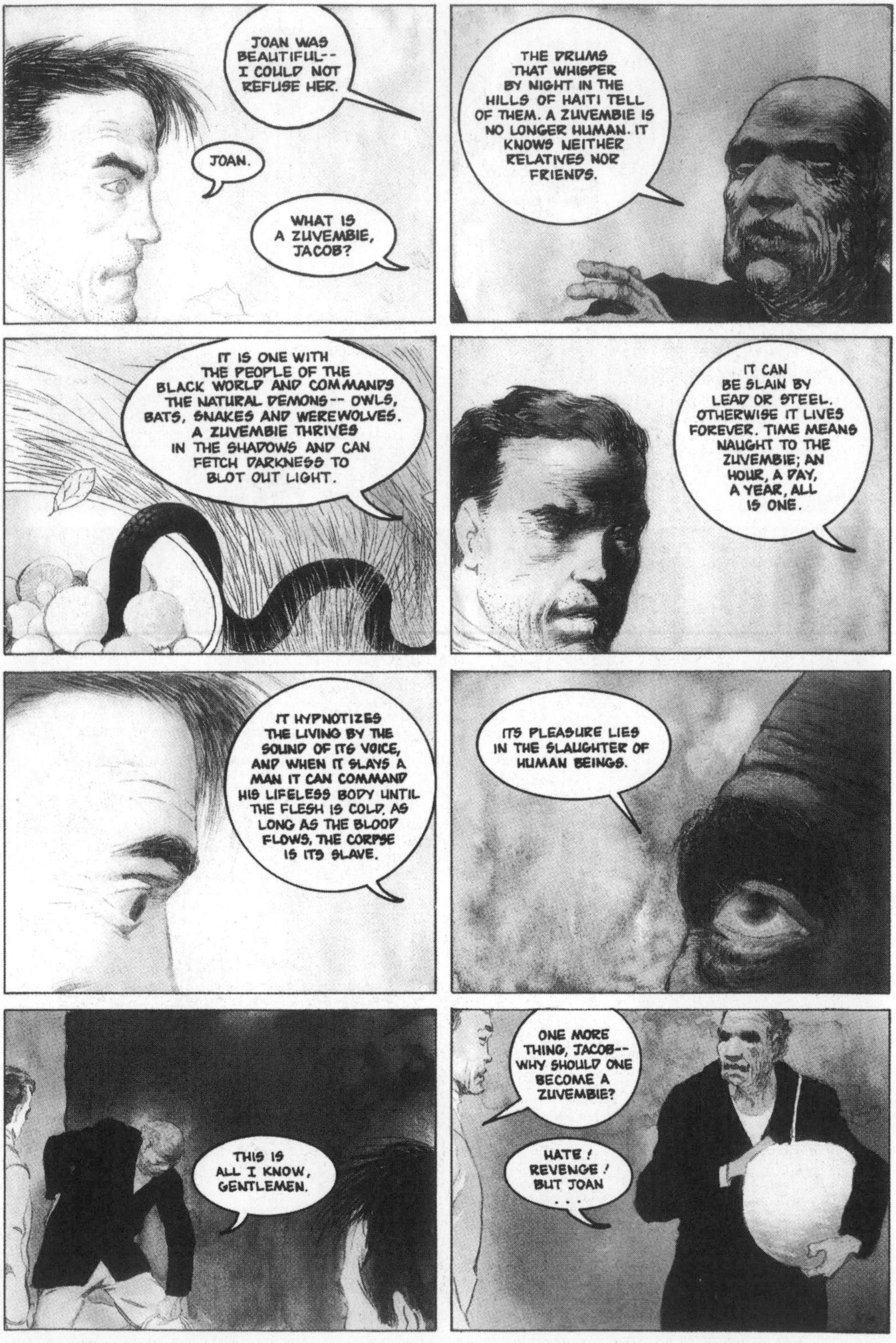
JOAN WAS BEAUTIFUL-- I COULD NOT REFUSE HER.
JOAN.
WHAT IS A ZUVEMBIE, JACOB?
THE DRUMS THAT WHISPER BY NIGHT IN THE HILLS OF HAITI TELL OF THEM. A ZUVEMBIE IS NO LONGER HUMAN. IT KNOWS NEITHER RELATIVES NOR FRIENDS.
IT IS ONE WITH THE PEOPLE OF THE BLACK WORLD AND COMMANDS THE NATURAL DEMONS-- OWLS, BATS, SNAKES AND WEREWOLVES. A ZUVEMBIE THRIVES IN THE SHADOWS AND CAN FETCH DARKNESS TO BLOT OUT LIGHT.
IT CAN BE SLAIN BY LEAD OR STEEL. OTHERWISE IT LIVES FOREVER. TIME MEANS NAUGHT TO THE ZUVEMBIE; AN HOUR, A DAY, A YEAR, ALL IS ONE.
IT HYPNOTIZES THE LIVING BY THE SOUND OF ITS VOICE, AND WHEN IT SLAYS A MAN IT CAN COMMAND HIS LIFELESS BODY UNTIL THE FLESH IS COLD. AS LONG AS THE BLOOD FLOWS, THE CORPSE IS ITS SLAVE.
ITS PLEASURE LIES IN THE SLAUGHTER OF HUMAN BEINGS.
THIS IS ALL I KNOW, GENTLEMEN.
ONE MORE THING, JACOB-- WHY SHOULD ONE BECOME A ZUVEMBIE?
HATE! REVENGE! BUT JOAN . . .

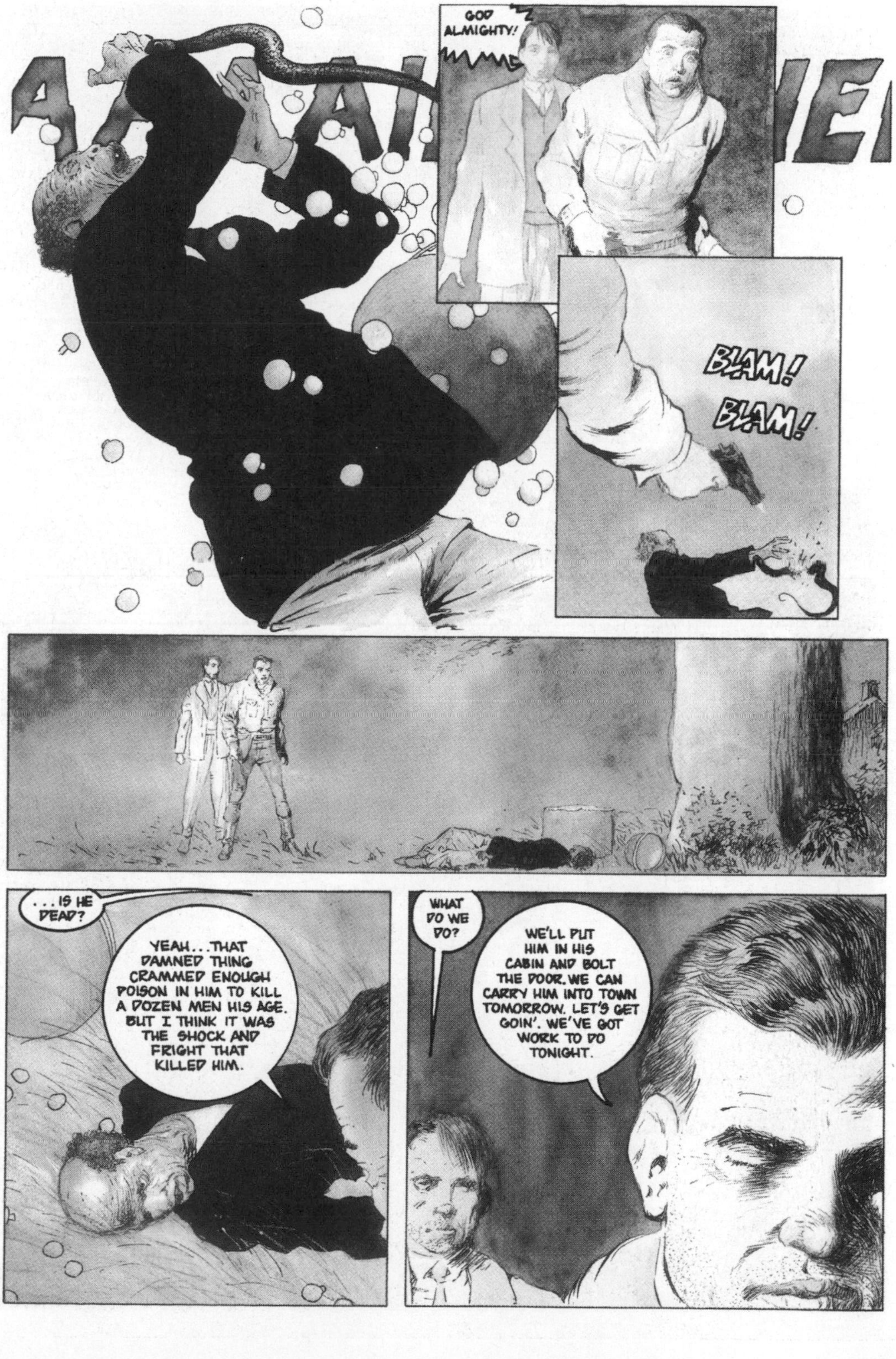
GOD ALMIGHTY!
BLAM! BLAM!
...IS HE DEAD?
YEAH...THAT DAMNED THING CRAMMED ENOUGH POISON IN HIM TO KILL A DOZEN MEN HIS AGE. BUT I THINK IT WAS THE SHOCK AND FRIGHT THAT KILLED HIM.
WHAT DO WE DO?
WE'LL PUT HIM IN HIS CABIN AND BOLT THE DOOR. WE CAN CARRY HIM INTO TOWN TOMORROW. LET'S GET GOIN'. WE'VE GOT WORK TO DO TONIGHT.

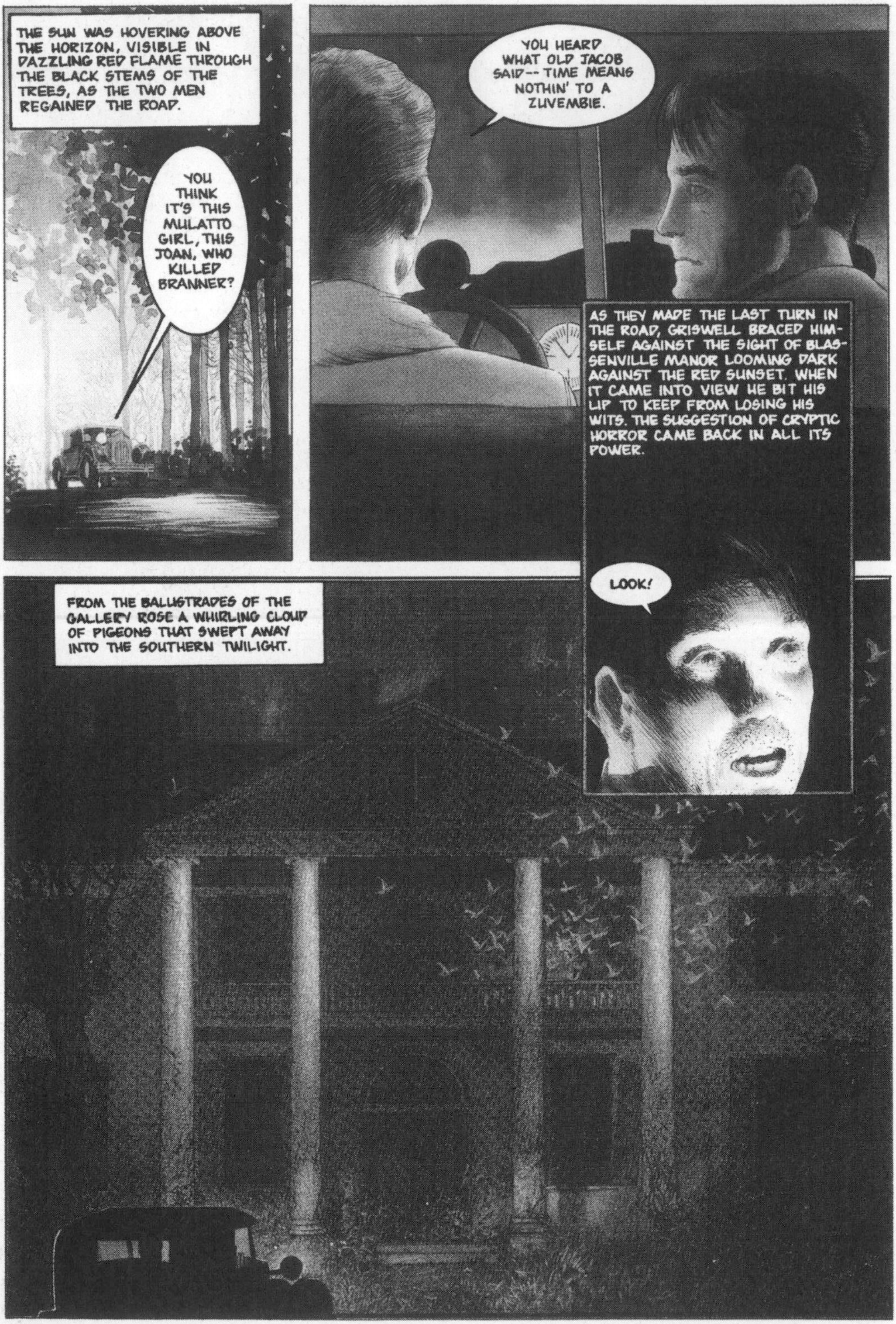
THE SUN WAS HOVERING ABOVE THE HORIZON, VISIBLE IN DAZZLING RED FLAME THROUGH THE BLACK STEMS OF THE TREES, AS THE TWO MEN REGAINED THE ROAD.
YOU THINK IT'S THIS MULATTO GIRL, THIS JOAN, WHO KILLED BRANNER?
YOU HEARD WHAT OLD JACOB SAID-- TIME MEANS NOTHIN' TO A ZUVEMBIE.
AS THEY MADE THE LAST TURN IN THE ROAD, GRISWELL BRACED HIMSELF AGAINST THE SIGHT OF BLASSENVILLE MANOR LOOMING DARK AGAINST THE RED SUNSET. WHEN IT CAME INTO VIEW HE BIT HIS LIP TO KEEP FROM LOSING HIS WITS. THE SUGGESTION OF CRYPTIC HORROR CAME BACK IN ALL ITS POWER.
LOOK!
FROM THE BALLUSTRADES OF THE GALLERY ROSE A WHIRLING CLOUD OF PIGEONS THAT SWEPT AWAY INTO THE SOUTHERN TWILIGHT.

4. THE CALL OF ZUVEMBIE

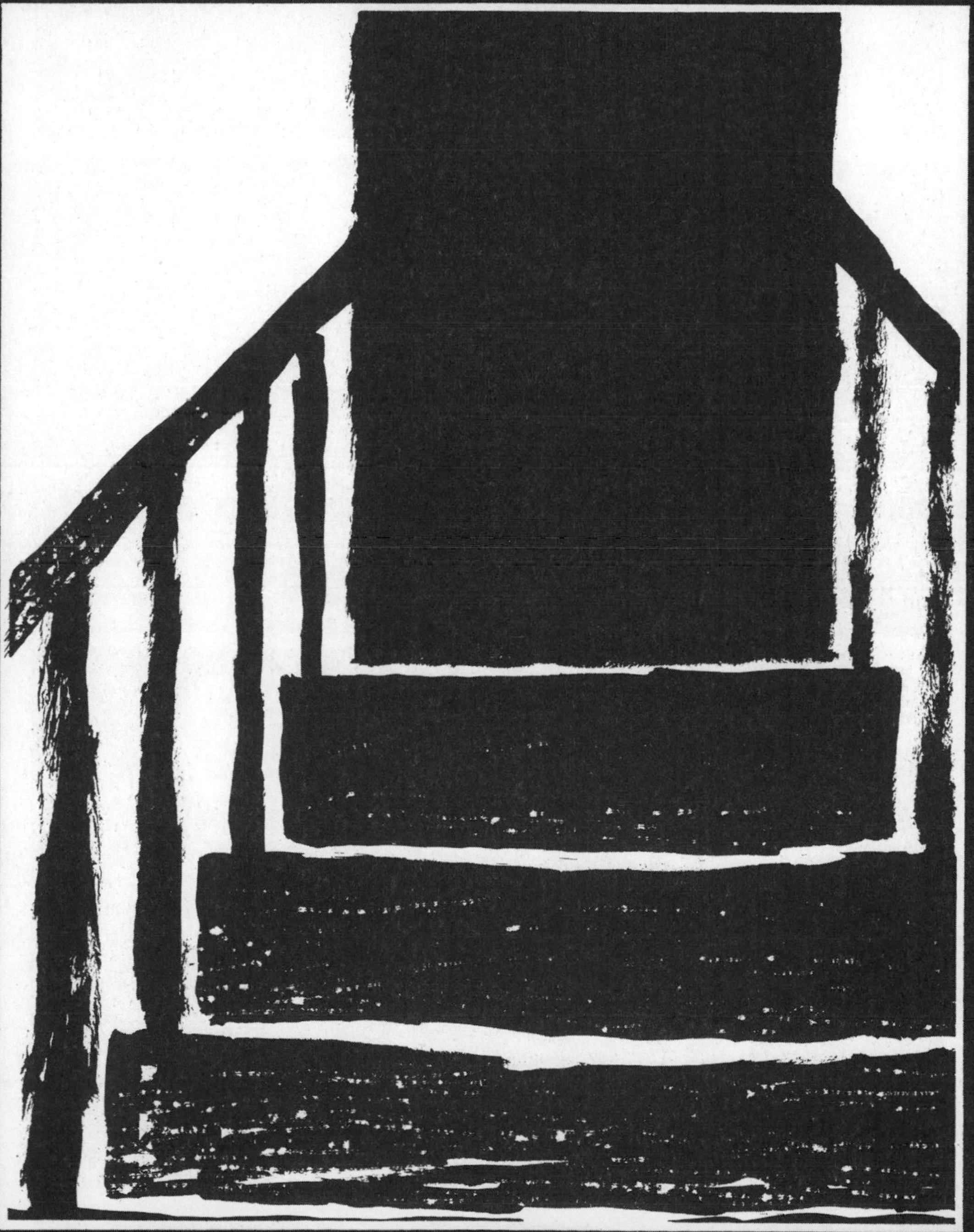

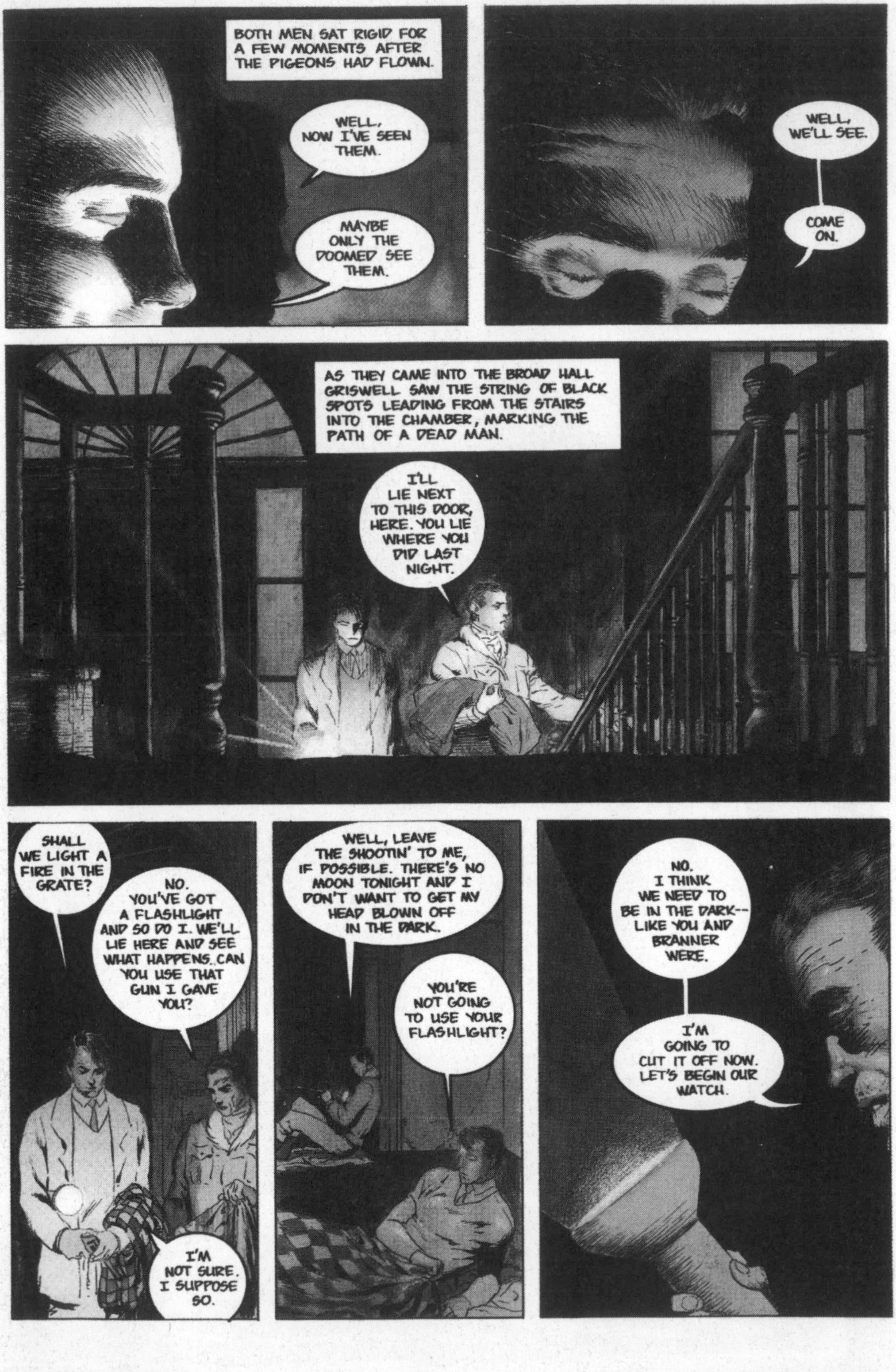
BOTH MEN SAT RIGID FOR A FEW MOMENTS AFTER THE PIGEONS HAD FLOWN.
WELL, NOW I'VE SEEN THEM.
MAYBE ONLY THE DOOMED SEE THEM.
WELL, WE'LL SEE.
COME ON.
AS THEY CAME INTO THE BROAD HALL GRISWELL SAW THE STRING OF BLACK SPOTS LEADING FROM THE STAIRS INTO THE CHAMBER, MARKING THE PATH OF A DEAD MAN.
I'LL LIE NEXT TO THIS DOOR, HERE. YOU LIE WHERE YOU DID LAST NIGHT.
SHALL WE LIGHT A FIRE IN THE GRATE?
NO. YOU'VE GOT A FLASHLIGHT AND SO DO I. WE'LL LIE HERE AND SEE WHAT HAPPENS. CAN YOU USE THAT GUN I GAVE YOU?
I'M NOT SURE. I SUPPOSE SO.
WELL, LEAVE THE SHOOTIN' TO ME, IF POSSIBLE. THERE'S NO MOON TONIGHT AND I DON'T WANT TO GET MY HEAD BLOWN OFF IN THE DARK.
YOU'RE NOT GOING TO USE YOUR FLASHLIGHT?
NO. I THINK WE NEED TO BE IN THE DARK-- LIKE YOU AND BRANNER WERE.
I'M GOING TO CUT IT OFF NOW. LET'S BEGIN OUR WATCH.

FEAR LIKE A PHYSICAL SICKNESS ASSAILED GRISWELL WHEN THE ROOM WAS PLUNGED IN DARKNESS. HE LAY TREMBLING AND HIS HEART BEAT SO HEAVILY HE FELT AS IF HE WOULD SUFFOCATE. TIME SEEMED AT A STANDSTILL. THE EFFORT HE MADE TO CONTROL HIS CRUMBLING NERVES BATHED HIS LIMBS IN SWEAT. HE CLENCHED HIS TEETH UNTIL HIS JAWS ACHED AND ALMOST LOCKED, AND THE NAILS OF HIS FINGERS BIT DEEPLY INTO HIS PALMS.

HE DID NOT KNOW WHAT HE WAS EXPECTING. THE FIEND WOULD STRIKE AGAIN -- BUT HOW? WOULD IT BE A HORRIBLE, SWEET WHISTLING, BARE FEET STEALING DOWN THE CREAKING STEPS, OR A SUDDEN HATCHET-STROKE IN THE DARK? WOULD IT CHOOSE HIM OR BUCKNER? WAS BUCKNER *ALREADY DEAD?* HE COULD SEE NOTHING IN THE BLACKNESS, BUT HE HEARD THE MAN'S STEADY BREATHING.

OR *WAS* THAT BUCKNER BREATHING BESIDE HIM, SEPARATED BY A NARROW STRIP OF DARKNESS? HAD THE FIEND ALREADY STRUCK IN SILENCE, AND TAKEN THE SHERIFF'S PLACE, THERE TO LIE IN GHOULISH GLEE UNTIL IT WAS READY TO STRIKE? -- A THOUSAND HIDEOUS FANCIES ASSAILED GRISWELL TOOTH AND CLAW.

HE BEGAN TO FEEL THAT HE WOULD GO MAD IF HE DIDN'T LEAP TO HIS FEET, SCREAMING, AND BURST FRENZIEDLY OUT OF THAT ACCURSED HOUSE -- NOT EVEN THE FEAR OF THE GALLOWS COULD KEEP HIM LYING THERE IN THE DARKNESS ANY LONGER! THE RHYTHM OF BUCKNER'S BREATHING WAS SUDDENLY BROKEN, AND GRISWELL FELT AS IF A BUCKET OF ICE-WATER HAD BEEN POURED OVER HIM. FROM SOMEWHERE ABOVE THEM ROSE A SOUND OF WEIRD, SWEET WHISTLING...

GRISWELL'S CONTROL SNAPPED, PLUNGING HIS BRAIN INTO DARKNESS DEEPER THAN THE PHYSICAL BLACKNESS WHICH ENGULFED HIM.

THERE WAS A PERIOD OF ABSOLUTE BLACKNESS, IN WHICH A REALIZATION OF *MOTION* WAS HIS FIRST SENSATION OF AWAKENING CONSCIOUSNESS.

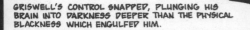

HE WAS RUNNING, MADLY, STUMBLING OVER AN INCREDIBLY ROUGH ROAD. ALL WAS DARKNESS ABOUT HIM, AND HE RAN BLINDLY. VAGUELY HE REALIZED THAT HE MUST HAVE BOLTED FROM THE HOUSE, AND FLED FOR PERHAPS MILES BEFORE HIS OVERWROUGHT BRAIN BEGAN TO FUNCTION. HE DID NOT CARE; DYING ON THE GALLOWS FOR A CRIME HE NEVER COMMITTED DID NOT TERRIFY HIM HALF AS MUCH AS THE THOUGHT OF RETURNING TO THAT HOUSE OF HORROR. HE WAS OVERPOWERED BY THE URGE TO RUN--RUN--RUN AS HE WAS RUNNING NOW, BLINDLY, UNTIL HE REACHED THE END OF HIS ENDURANCE.

THE MIST HAD NOT YET FULLY LIFTED FROM HIS BRAIN, BUT HE WAS AWARE THAT HE COULDN'T SEE THE STARS THROUGH THE BLACK BRANCHES. HE WISHED VAGUELY THAT HE COULD SEE WHERE HE WAS GOING. HE BELIEVED HE MUST BE CLIMBING A HILL, AND THAT WAS STRANGE, SINCE HE KNEW THERE WERE NO HILLS WITHIN MILES OF THE MANOR.

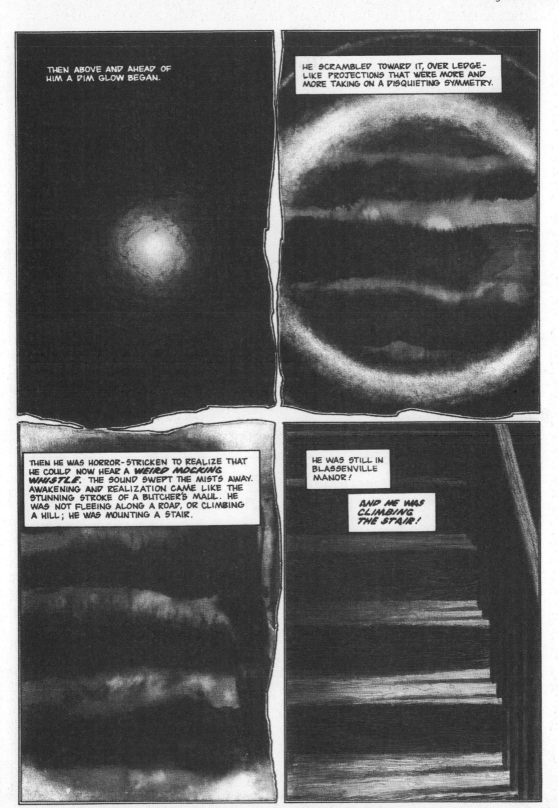

THEN ABOVE AND AHEAD OF HIM A DIM GLOW BEGAN.

HE SCRAMBLED TOWARD IT, OVER LEDGE-LIKE PROJECTIONS THAT WERE MORE AND MORE TAKING ON A DISQUIETING SYMMETRY.

THEN HE WAS HORROR-STRICKEN TO REALIZE THAT HE COULD NOW HEAR A *WEIRD MOCKING WHISTLE.* THE SOUND SWEPT THE MISTS AWAY. AWAKENING AND REALIZATION CAME LIKE THE STUNNING STROKE OF A BUTCHER'S MAUL. HE WAS NOT FLEEING ALONG A ROAD, OR CLIMBING A HILL; HE WAS MOUNTING A STAIR.

HE WAS STILL IN BLASSENVILLE MANOR!

AND HE WAS CLIMBING THE STAIR!

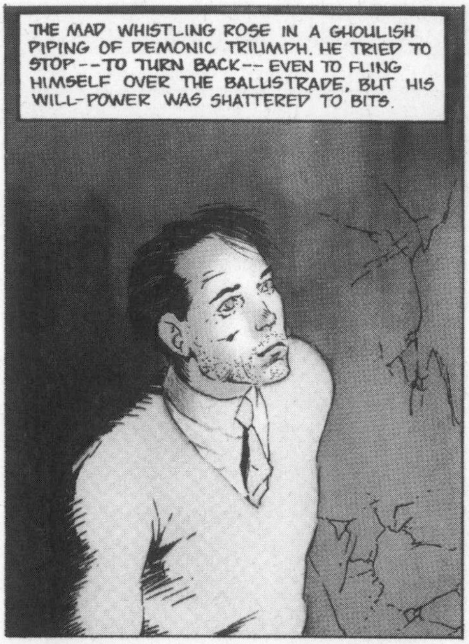
THE MAD WHISTLING ROSE IN A GHOULISH PIPING OF DEMONIC TRIUMPH. HE TRIED TO STOP--TO TURN BACK-- EVEN TO FLING HIMSELF OVER THE BALUSTRADE, BUT HIS WILL-POWER WAS SHATTERED TO BITS.
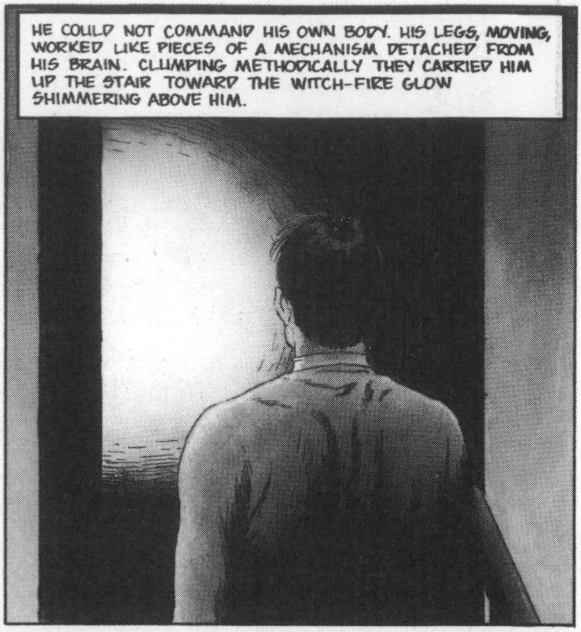
HE COULD NOT COMMAND HIS OWN BODY. HIS LEGS, MOVING, WORKED LIKE PIECES OF A MECHANISM DETACHED FROM HIS BRAIN. CLUMPING METHODICALLY THEY CARRIED HIM UP THE STAIR TOWARD THE WITCH-FIRE GLOW SHIMMERING ABOVE HIM.
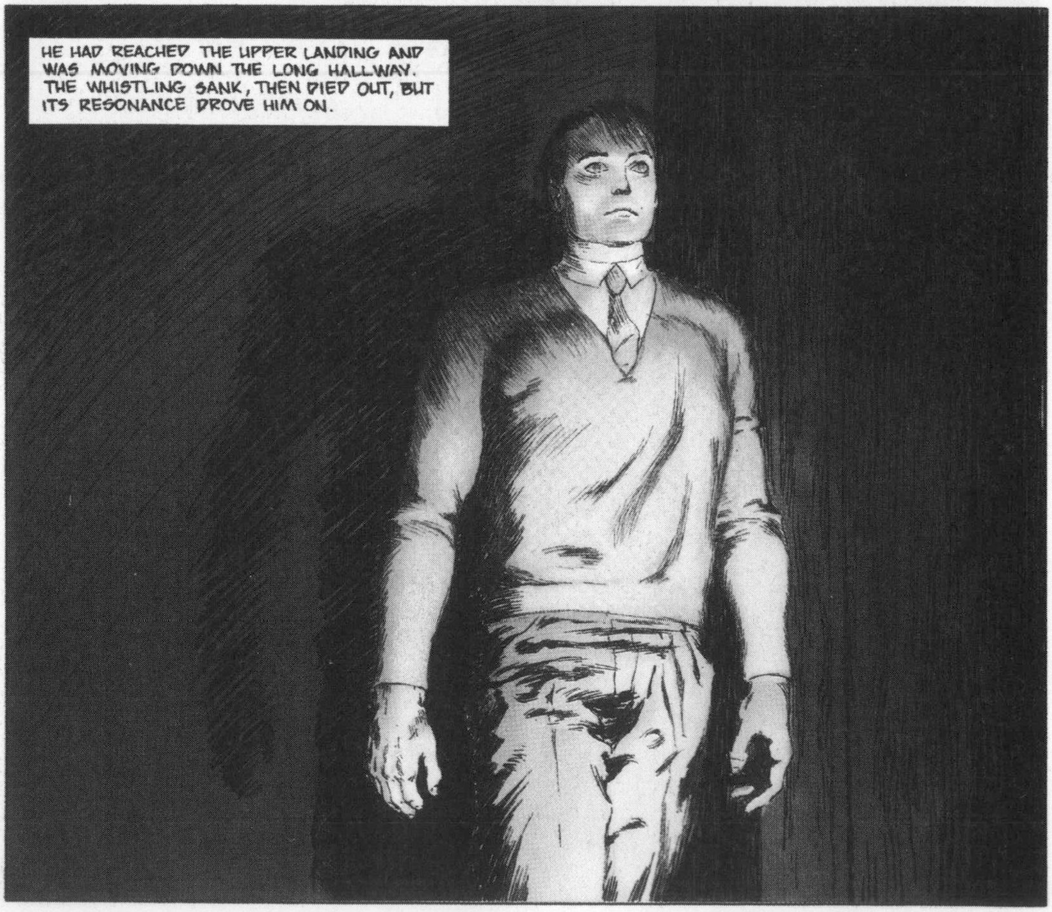
HE HAD REACHED THE UPPER LANDING AND WAS MOVING DOWN THE LONG HALLWAY. THE WHISTLING SANK, THEN DIED OUT, BUT ITS RESONANCE DROVE HIM ON.

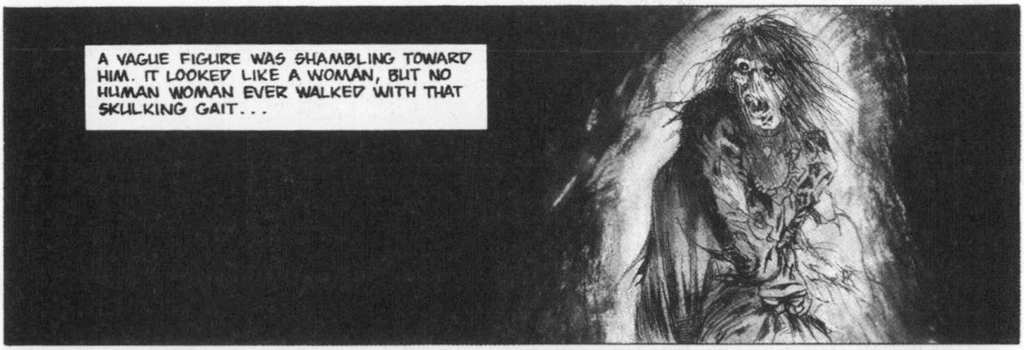
A VAGUE FIGURE WAS SHAMBLING TOWARD HIM. IT LOOKED LIKE A WOMAN, BUT NO HUMAN WOMAN EVER WALKED WITH THAT SKULKING GAIT...

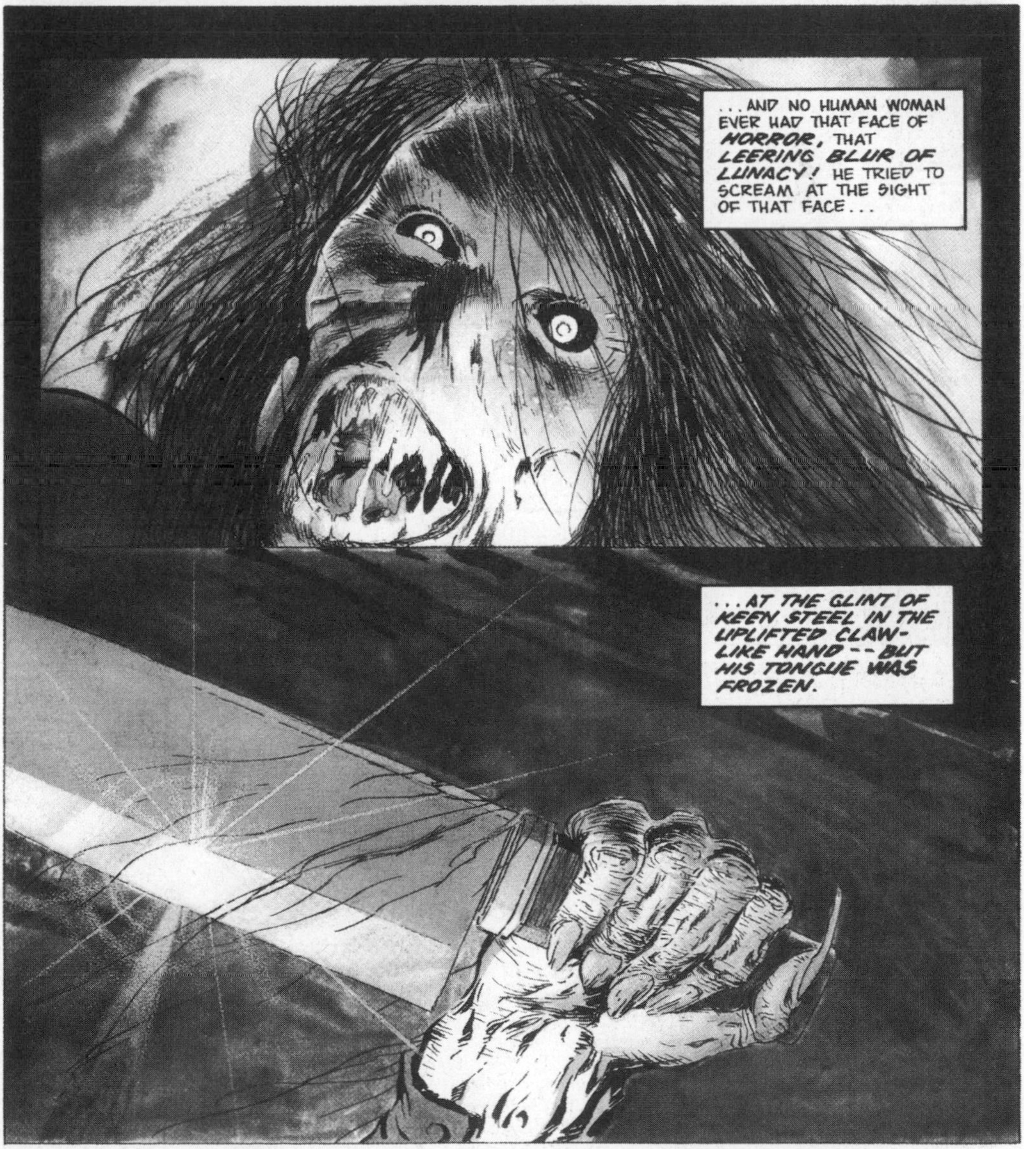
...AND NO HUMAN WOMAN EVER HAD THAT FACE OF HORROR, THAT LEERING BLUR OF LUNACY! HE TRIED TO SCREAM AT THE SIGHT OF THAT FACE...
...AT THE GLINT OF KEEN STEEL IN THE UPLIFTED CLAW-LIKE HAND -- BUT HIS TONGUE WAS FROZEN.

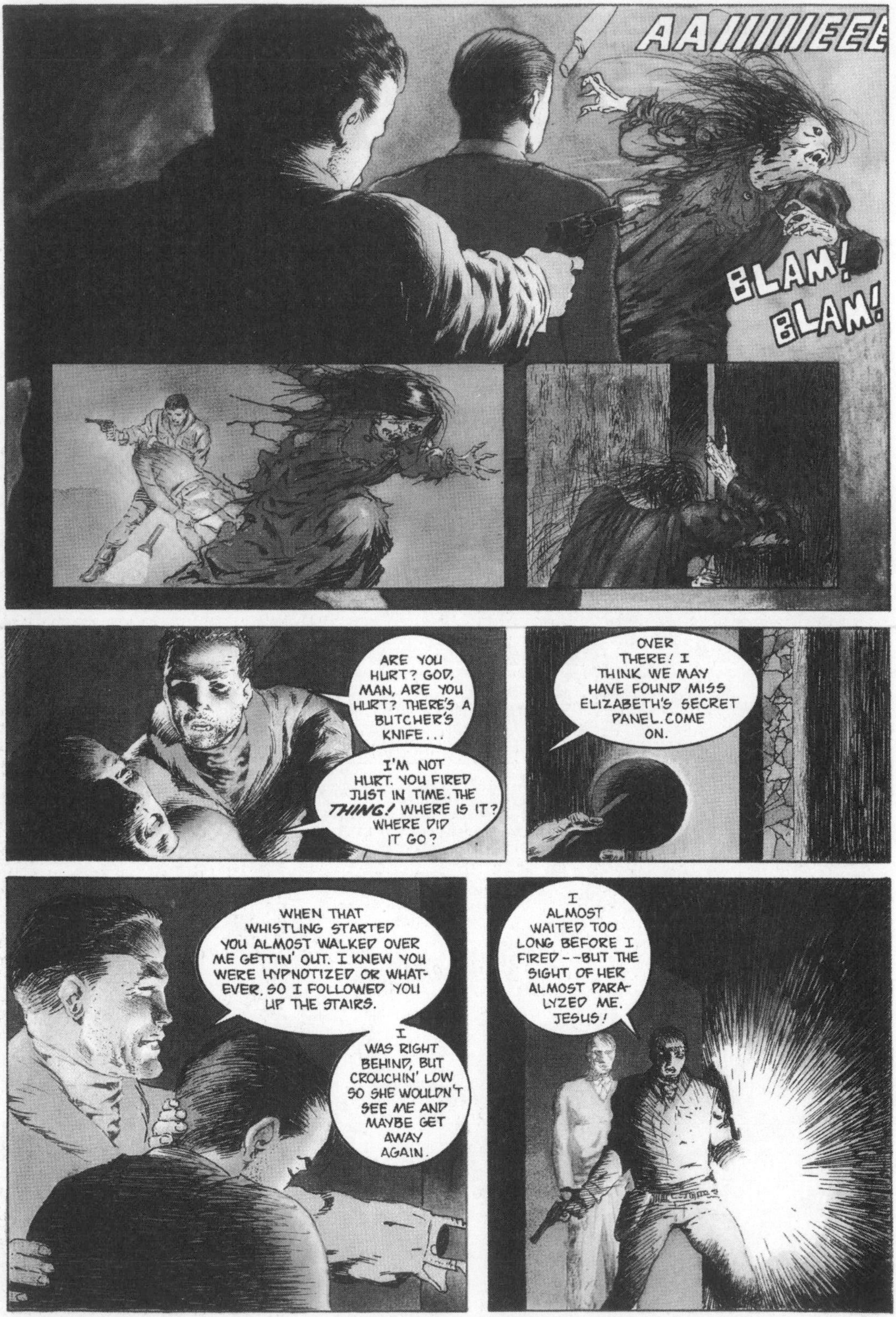
AAIIIIIIEEE
BLAM! BLAM!
ARE YOU HURT? GOD, MAN, ARE YOU HURT? THERE'S A BUTCHER'S KNIFE...
I'M NOT HURT. YOU FIRED JUST IN TIME. THE THING! WHERE IS IT? WHERE DID IT GO?
OVER THERE! I THINK WE MAY HAVE FOUND MISS ELIZABETH'S SECRET PANEL. COME ON.
WHEN THAT WHISTLING STARTED YOU ALMOST WALKED OVER ME GETTIN' OUT. I KNEW YOU WERE HYPNOTIZED OR WHAT-EVER. SO I FOLLOWED YOU UP THE STAIRS.
I WAS RIGHT BEHIND, BUT CROUCHIN' LOW SO SHE WOULDN'T SEE ME AND MAYBE GET AWAY AGAIN.
I ALMOST WAITED TOO LONG BEFORE I FIRED--BUT THE SIGHT OF HER ALMOST PARA-LYZED ME. JESUS!

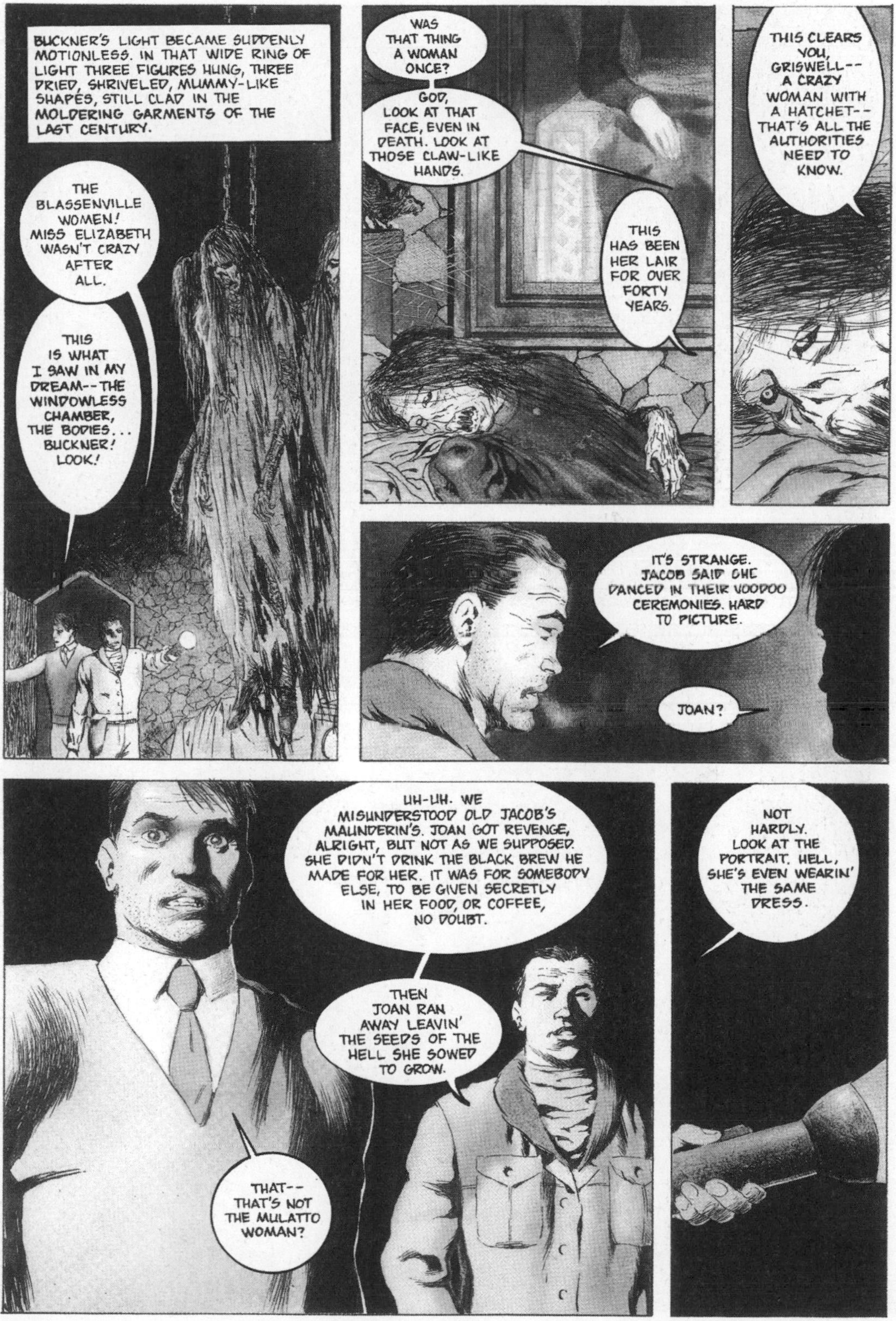
BUCKNER'S LIGHT BECAME SUDDENLY MOTIONLESS. IN THAT WIDE RING OF LIGHT THREE FIGURES HUNG, THREE DRIED, SHRIVELED, MUMMY-LIKE SHAPES, STILL CLAD IN THE MOLDERING GARMENTS OF THE LAST CENTURY.
THE BLASSENVILLE WOMEN! MISS ELIZABETH WASN'T CRAZY AFTER ALL.
THIS IS WHAT I SAW IN MY DREAM--THE WINDOWLESS CHAMBER, THE BODIES... BUCKNER! LOOK!
WAS THAT THING A WOMAN ONCE?
GOD, LOOK AT THAT FACE, EVEN IN DEATH. LOOK AT THOSE CLAW-LIKE HANDS.
THIS HAS BEEN HER LAIR FOR OVER FORTY YEARS.
THIS CLEARS YOU, GRISWELL--A CRAZY WOMAN WITH A HATCHET--THAT'S ALL THE AUTHORITIES NEED TO KNOW.
IT'S STRANGE. JACOB SAID SHE DANCED IN THEIR VOODOO CEREMONIES. HARD TO PICTURE.
JOAN?
UH-UH. WE MISUNDERSTOOD OLD JACOB'S MAUNDERIN'S. JOAN GOT REVENGE, ALRIGHT, BUT NOT AS WE SUPPOSED. SHE DIDN'T DRINK THE BLACK BREW HE MADE FOR HER. IT WAS FOR SOMEBODY ELSE, TO BE GIVEN SECRETLY IN HER FOOD, OR COFFEE, NO DOUBT.
THEN JOAN RAN AWAY LEAVIN' THE SEEDS OF THE HELL SHE SOWED TO GROW.
THAT--THAT'S NOT THE MULATTO WOMAN?
NOT HARDLY. LOOK AT THE PORTRAIT. HELL, SHE'S EVEN WEARIN' THE SAME DRESS.

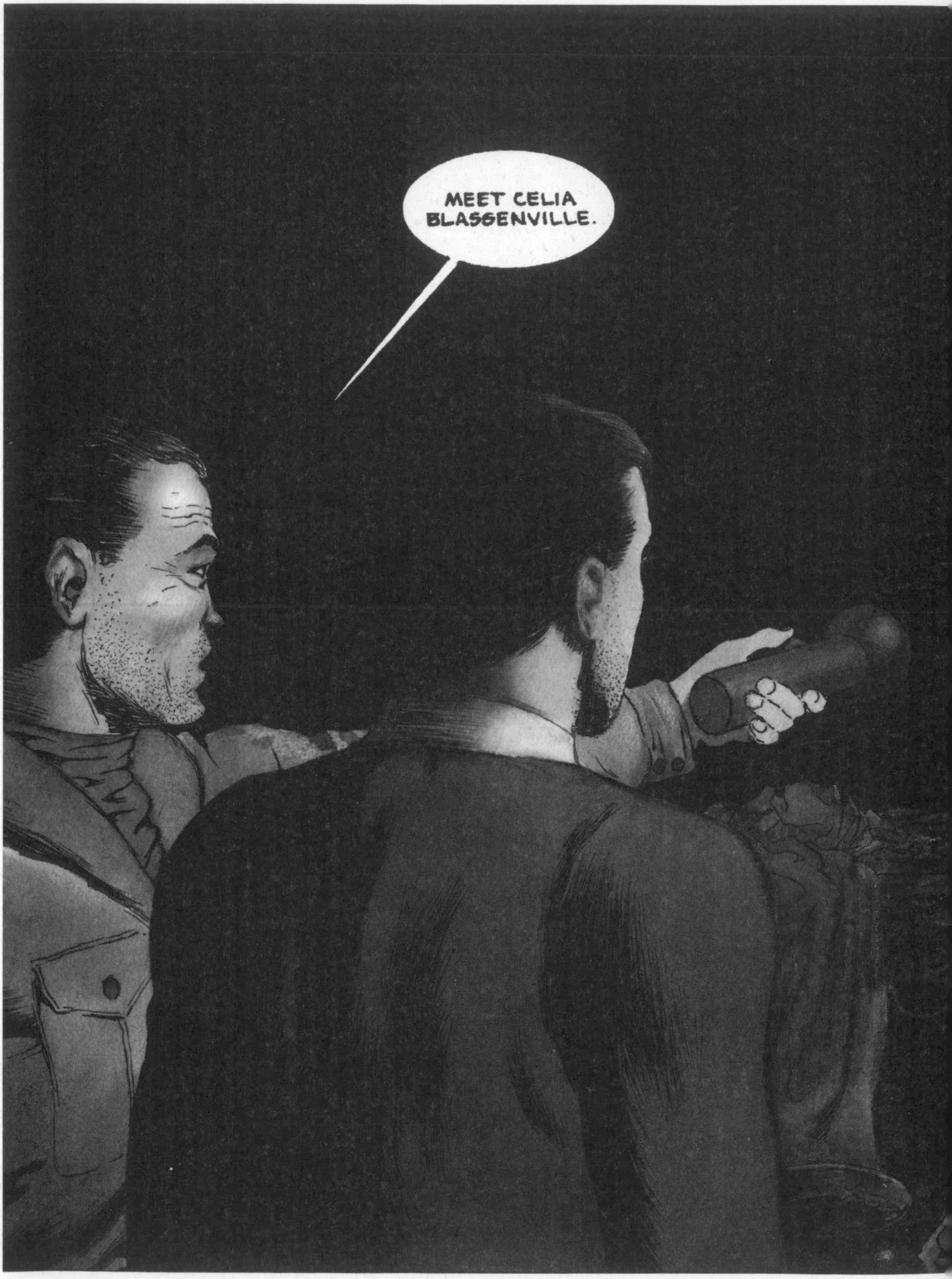
MEET CELIA BLASSENVILLE.

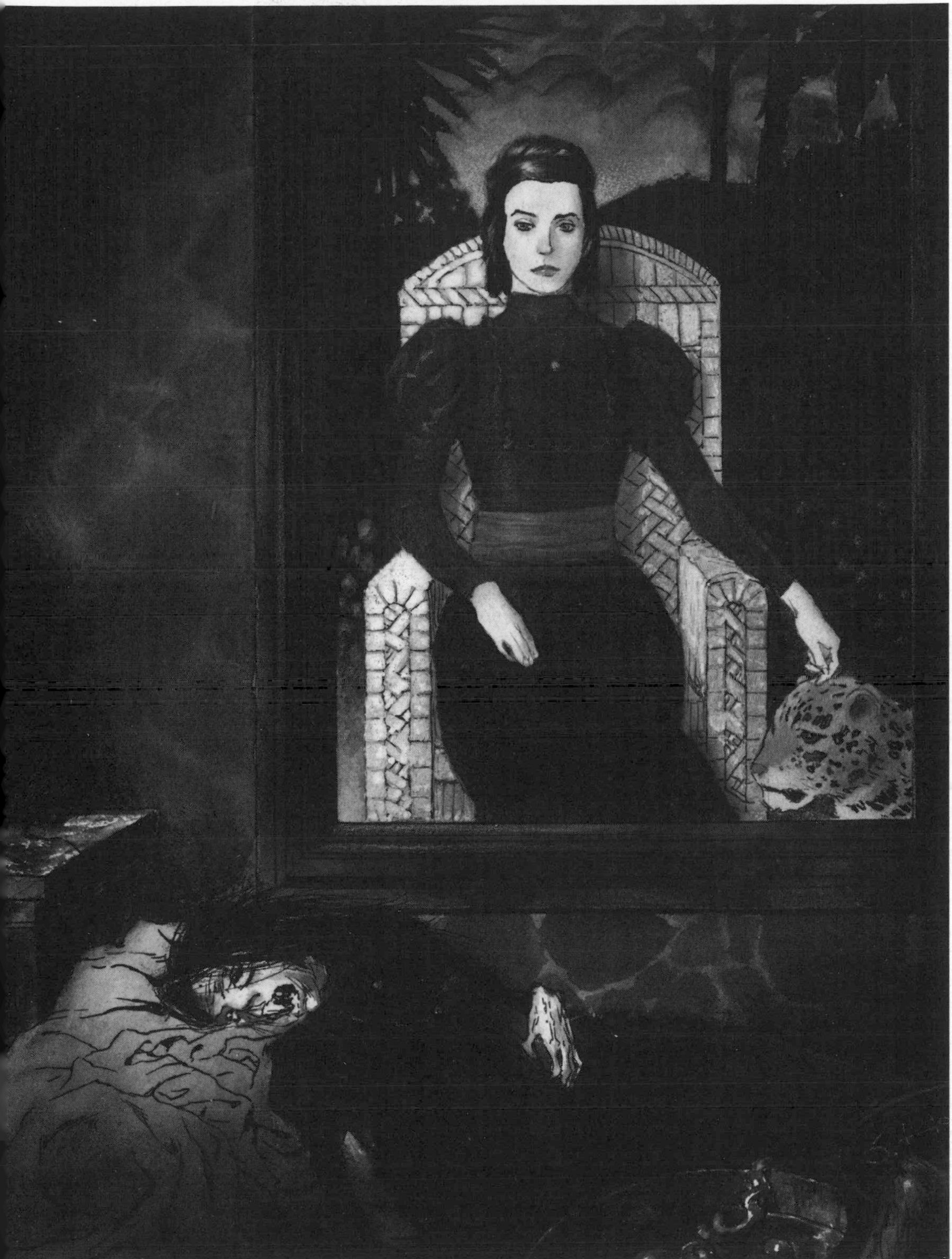

DARK HORSE COMICS
ZOMBIE WORLD
ZOMBIE WORLD
1 OF 2
$2.95 US
$4.15 CAN
DEAD END
7734-NI
STEPHEN BLUE

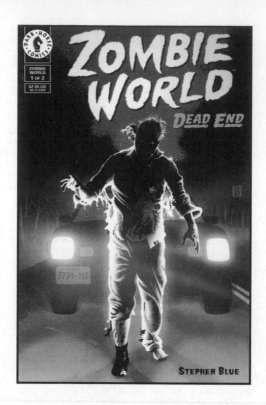

Zombie World: Dead End (1988)

***Creator:** Stephen Blue*

"Dead End" shows what a bad idea it would be to walk home alone from a fancy dress party dressed like an angel. Particularly on the night when the dead come back to life. And especially if the house where you took sanctuary had two very strange occupants.

As well as having stories in the horror anthology *Taboo*, Stephen Blue created the horror mini series *The Awakening*, and the graphic novel *Red River*.

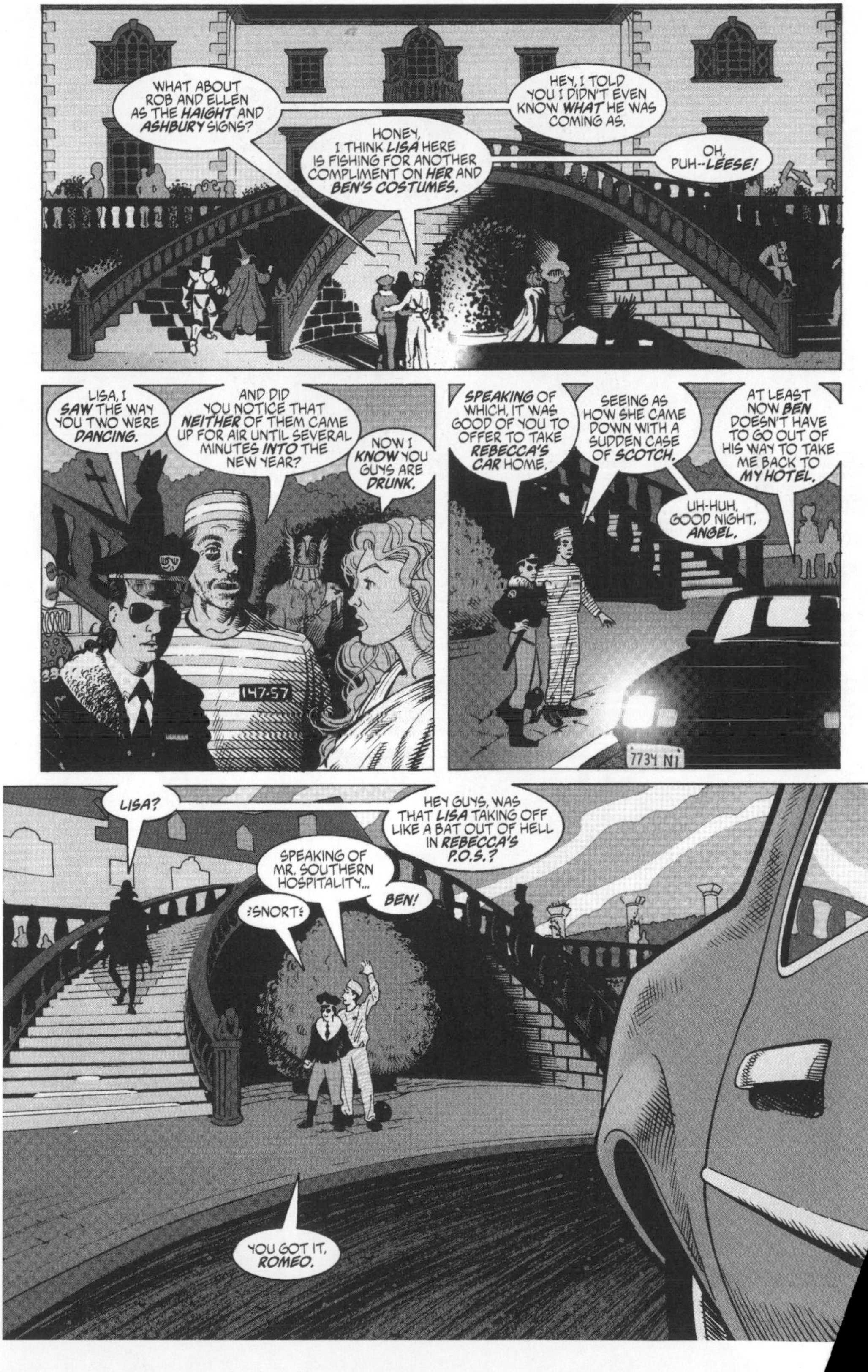
WHAT ABOUT ROB AND ELLEN AS THE HAIGHT AND ASHBURY SIGNS?
HEY, I TOLD YOU I DIDN'T EVEN KNOW WHAT HE WAS COMING AS.
HONEY, I THINK LISA HERE IS FISHING FOR ANOTHER COMPLIMENT ON HER AND BEN'S COSTUMES.
OH, PUH--LEESE!
LISA, I SAW THE WAY YOU TWO WERE DANCING.
AND DID YOU NOTICE THAT NEITHER OF THEM CAME UP FOR AIR UNTIL SEVERAL MINUTES INTO THE NEW YEAR?
NOW I KNOW YOU GUYS ARE DRUNK.
147-57
SPEAKING OF WHICH, IT WAS GOOD OF YOU TO OFFER TO TAKE REBECCA'S CAR HOME,
SEEING AS HOW SHE CAME DOWN WITH A SUDDEN CASE OF SCOTCH.
AT LEAST NOW BEN DOESN'T HAVE TO GO OUT OF HIS WAY TO TAKE ME BACK TO MY HOTEL.
UH-HUH, GOOD NIGHT, ANGEL.
7734 NI
LISA?
HEY GUYS, WAS THAT LISA TAKING OFF LIKE A BAT OUT OF HELL IN REBECCA'S P.O.S.?
SPEAKING OF MR. SOUTHERN HOSPITALITY...
:SNORT:
BEN!
YOU GOT IT, ROMEO.

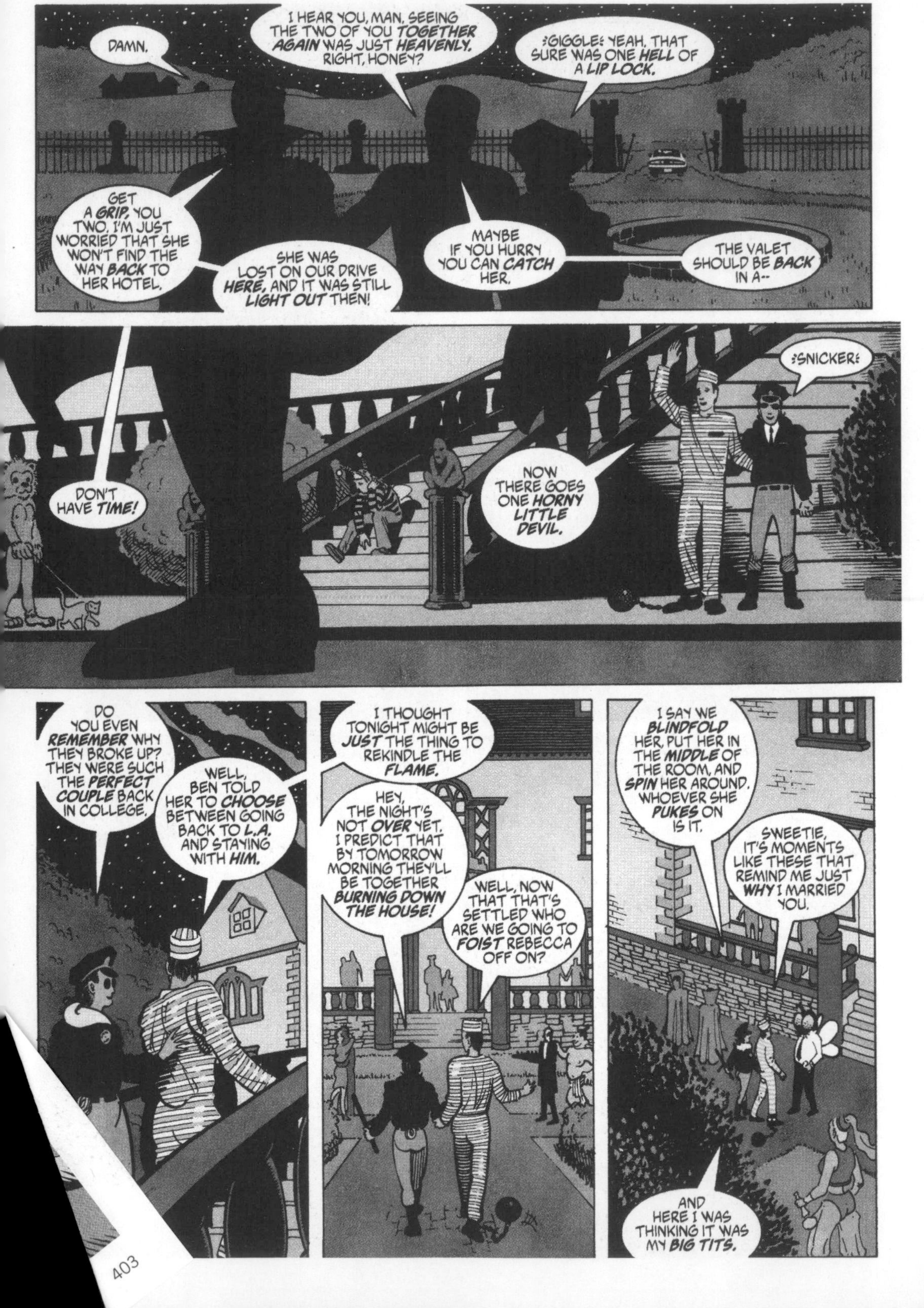
DAMN.
I HEAR YOU, MAN. SEEING THE TWO OF YOU TOGETHER AGAIN WAS JUST HEAVENLY. RIGHT, HONEY?
:GIGGLE: YEAH. THAT SURE WAS ONE HELL OF A LIP LOCK.
GET A GRIP, YOU TWO. I'M JUST WORRIED THAT SHE WON'T FIND THE WAY BACK TO HER HOTEL.
SHE WAS LOST ON OUR DRIVE HERE, AND IT WAS STILL LIGHT OUT THEN!
MAYBE IF YOU HURRY YOU CAN CATCH HER.
THE VALET SHOULD BE BACK IN A--
DON'T HAVE TIME!
NOW THERE GOES ONE HORNY LITTLE DEVIL.
:SNICKER:
DO YOU EVEN REMEMBER WHY THEY BROKE UP? THEY WERE SUCH THE PERFECT COUPLE BACK IN COLLEGE.
WELL, BEN TOLD HER TO CHOOSE BETWEEN GOING BACK TO L.A. AND STAYING WITH HIM.
I THOUGHT TONIGHT MIGHT BE JUST THE THING TO REKINDLE THE FLAME.
HEY, THE NIGHT'S NOT OVER YET. I PREDICT THAT BY TOMORROW MORNING THEY'LL BE TOGETHER BURNING DOWN THE HOUSE!
WELL, NOW THAT THAT'S SETTLED WHO ARE WE GOING TO FOIST REBECCA OFF ON?
I SAY WE BLINDFOLD HER, PUT HER IN THE MIDDLE OF THE ROOM, AND SPIN HER AROUND. WHOEVER SHE PUKES ON IS IT.
SWEETIE, IT'S MOMENTS LIKE THESE THAT REMIND ME JUST WHY I MARRIED YOU.
AND HERE I WAS THINKING IT WAS MY BIG TITS.

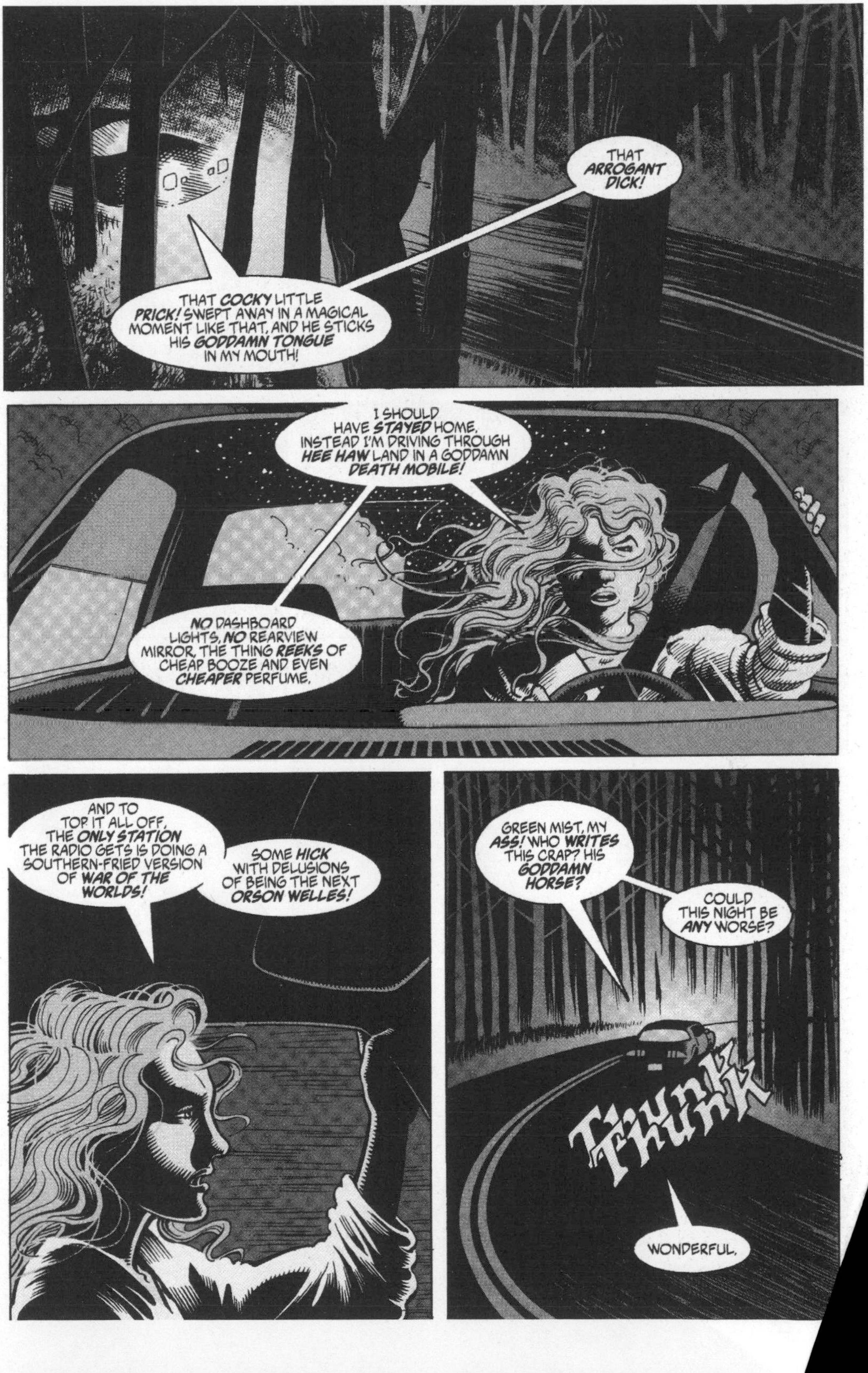
THAT ARROGANT DICK!
THAT COCKY LITTLE PRICK! SWEPT AWAY IN A MAGICAL MOMENT LIKE THAT, AND HE STICKS HIS GODDAMN TONGUE IN MY MOUTH!
I SHOULD HAVE STAYED HOME. INSTEAD I'M DRIVING THROUGH HEE HAW LAND IN A GODDAMN DEATH MOBILE!
NO DASHBOARD LIGHTS, NO REARVIEW MIRROR, THE THING REEKS OF CHEAP BOOZE AND EVEN CHEAPER PERFUME.
AND TO TOP IT ALL OFF, THE ONLY STATION THE RADIO GETS IS DOING A SOUTHERN-FRIED VERSION OF WAR OF THE WORLDS!
SOME HICK WITH DELUSIONS OF BEING THE NEXT ORSON WELLES!
GREEN MIST, MY ASS! WHO WRITES THIS CRAP? HIS GODDAMN HORSE?
COULD THIS NIGHT BE ANY WORSE?
THUNK THUNK
WONDERFUL.

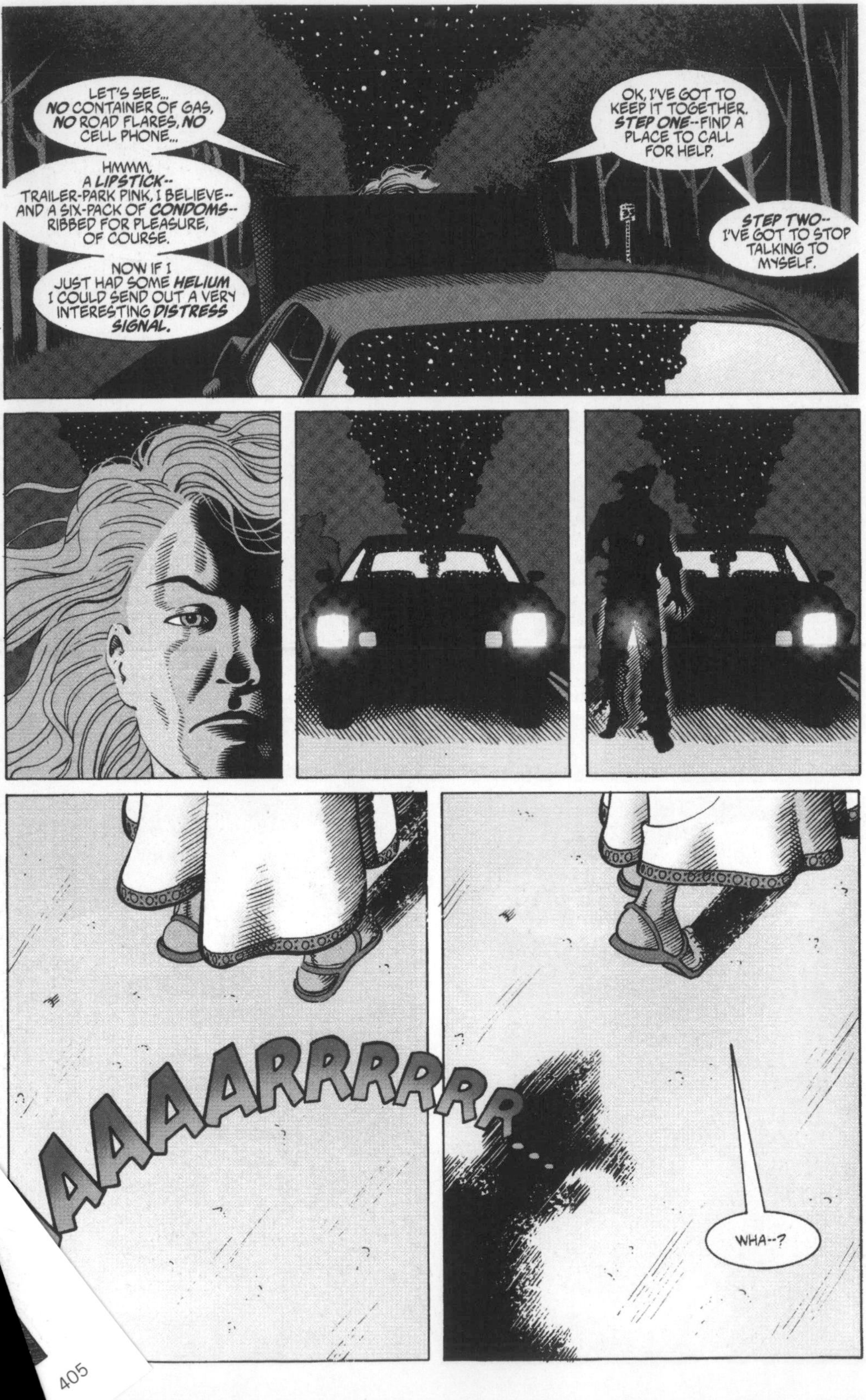
LET'S SEE... NO CONTAINER OF GAS, NO ROAD FLARES, NO CELL PHONE...
HMMM, A LIPSTICK-- TRAILER-PARK PINK, I BELIEVE-- AND A SIX-PACK OF CONDOMS-- RIBBED FOR PLEASURE, OF COURSE.
NOW IF I JUST HAD SOME HELIUM I COULD SEND OUT A VERY INTERESTING DISTRESS SIGNAL.
OK, I'VE GOT TO KEEP IT TOGETHER. STEP ONE--FIND A PLACE TO CALL FOR HELP.
STEP TWO-- I'VE GOT TO STOP TALKING TO MYSELF.
AAAARRRRRRR...
WHA--?

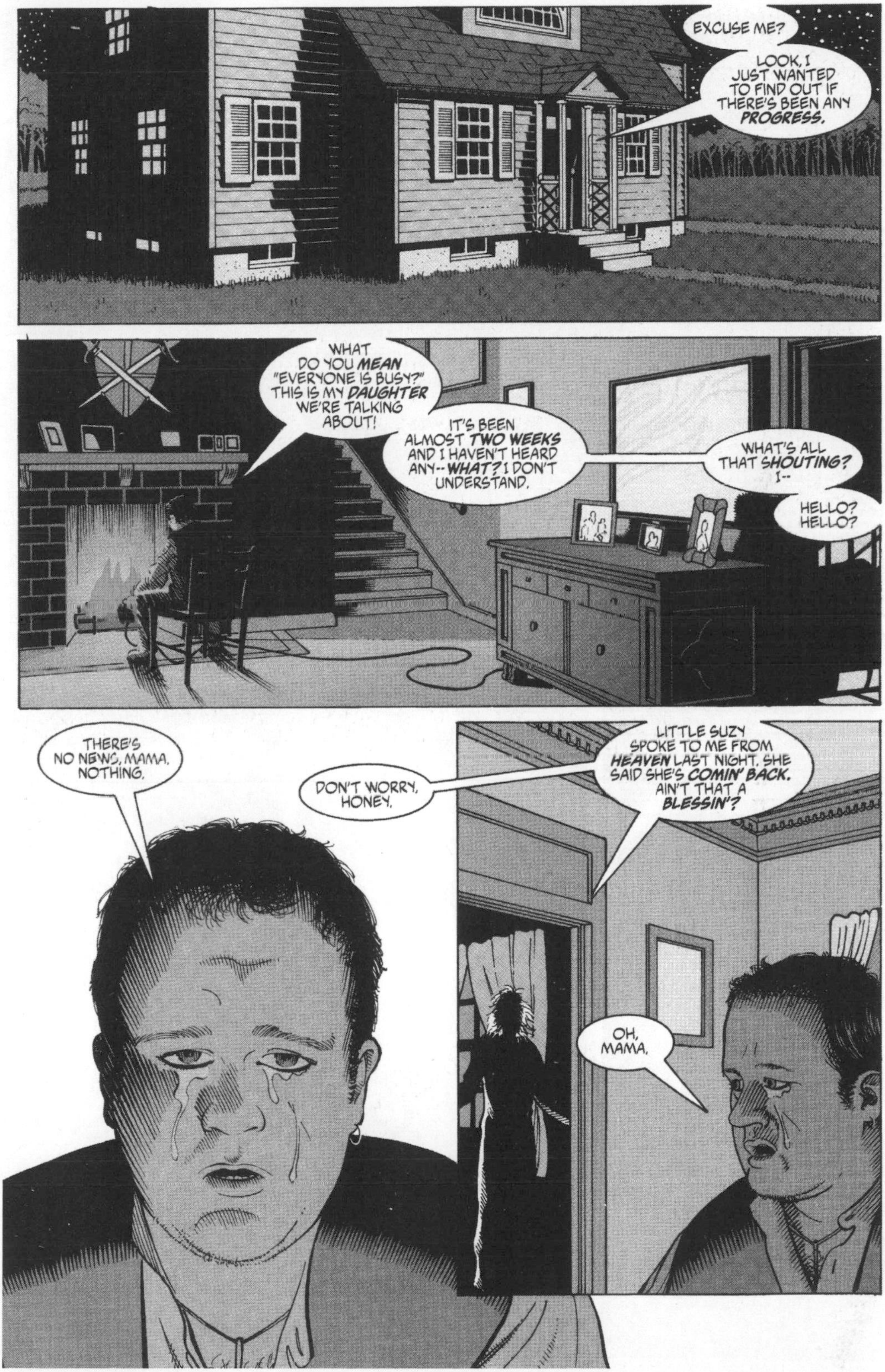
EXCUSE ME?
LOOK, I JUST WANTED TO FIND OUT IF THERE'S BEEN ANY PROGRESS.
WHAT DO YOU MEAN "EVERYONE IS BUSY?" THIS IS MY DAUGHTER WE'RE TALKING ABOUT!
IT'S BEEN ALMOST TWO WEEKS AND I HAVEN'T HEARD ANY-- WHAT? I DON'T UNDERSTAND.
WHAT'S ALL THAT SHOUTING? I--
HELLO? HELLO?
THERE'S NO NEWS, MAMA. NOTHING.
DON'T WORRY, HONEY.
LITTLE SUZY SPOKE TO ME FROM HEAVEN LAST NIGHT. SHE SAID SHE'S COMIN' BACK. AIN'T THAT A BLESSIN'?
OH, MAMA.

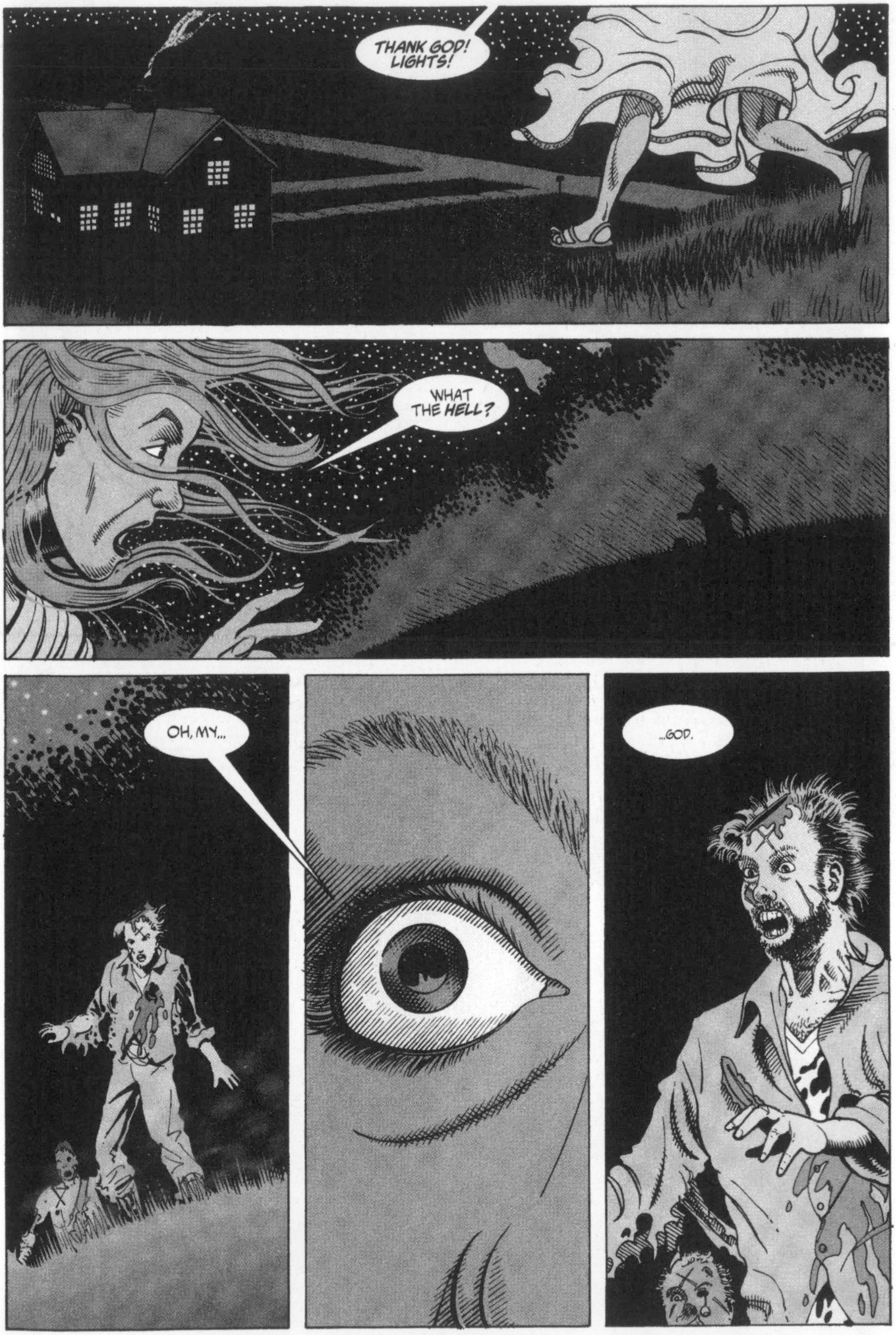
THANK GOD! LIGHTS!
WHAT THE HELL?
OH, MY...
...GOD.

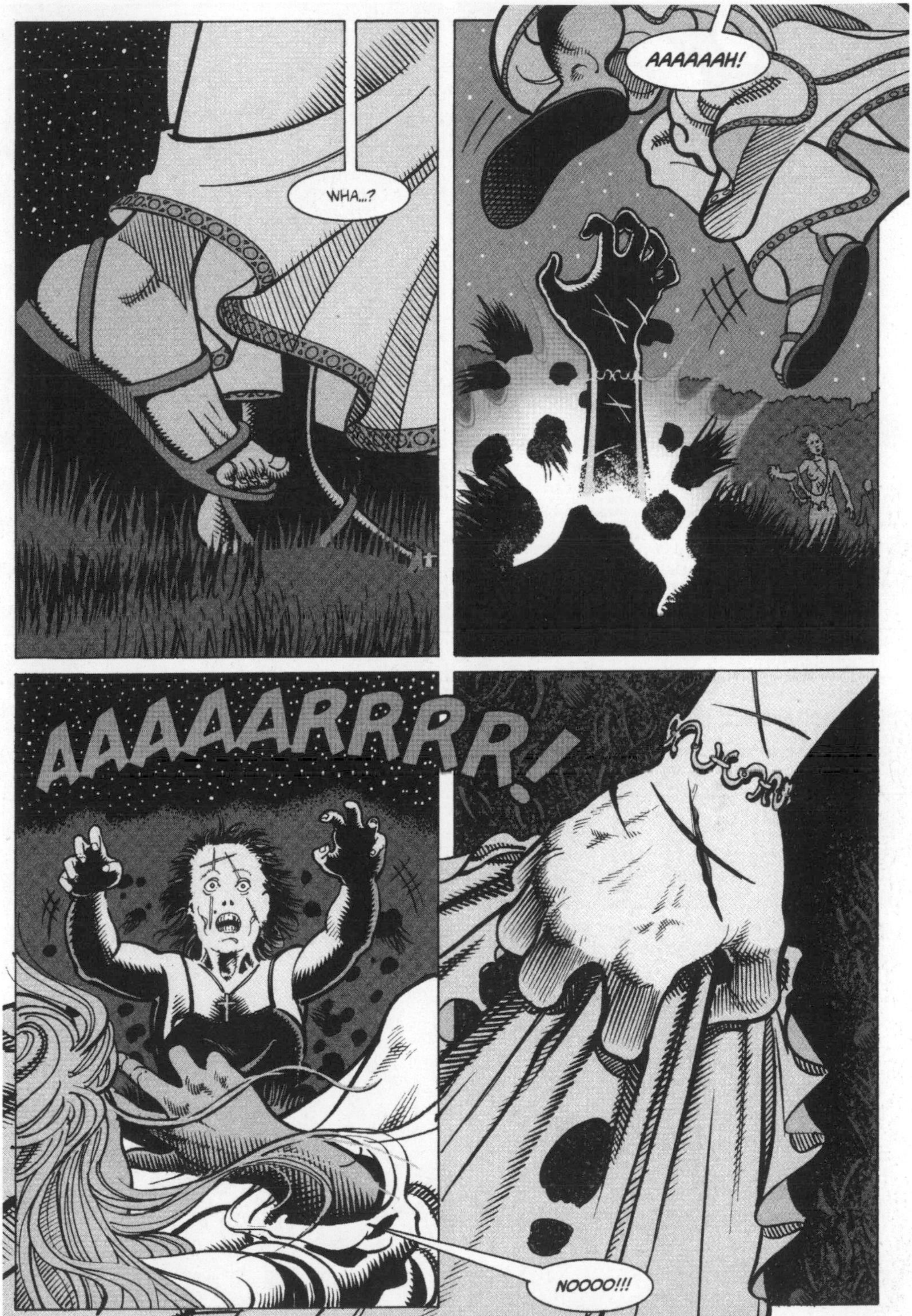
WHA...?
AAAAAAH!
AAAAARRRR!
NOOOO!!!

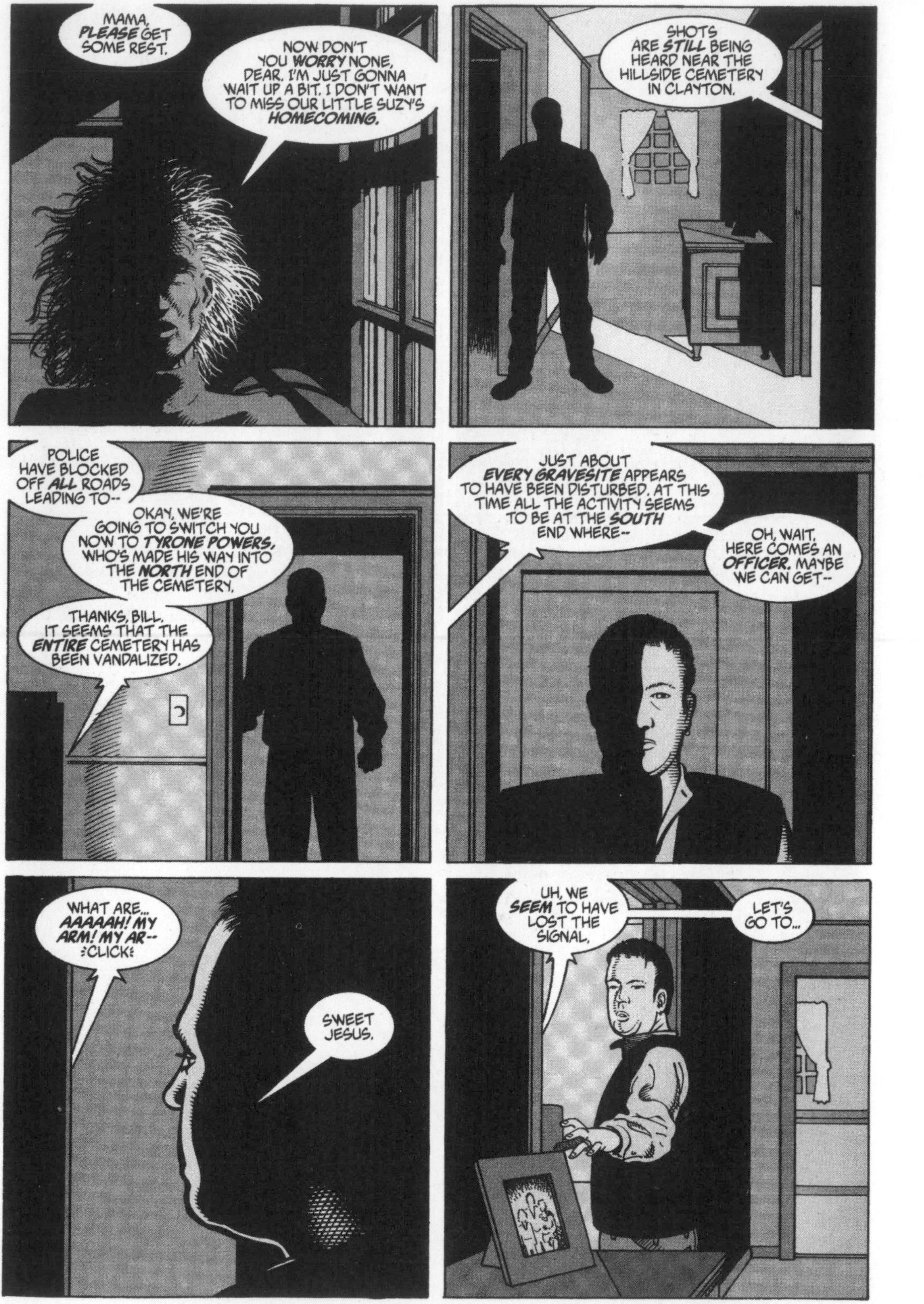
MAMA, PLEASE GET SOME REST.
NOW DON'T YOU WORRY NONE, DEAR. I'M JUST GONNA WAIT UP A BIT. I DON'T WANT TO MISS OUR LITTLE SUZY'S HOMECOMING.
SHOTS ARE STILL BEING HEARD NEAR THE HILLSIDE CEMETERY IN CLAYTON.
POLICE HAVE BLOCKED OFF ALL ROADS LEADING TO--
OKAY, WE'RE GOING TO SWITCH YOU NOW TO TYRONE POWERS, WHO'S MADE HIS WAY INTO THE NORTH END OF THE CEMETERY.
THANKS, BILL. IT SEEMS THAT THE ENTIRE CEMETERY HAS BEEN VANDALIZED.
JUST ABOUT EVERY GRAVESITE APPEARS TO HAVE BEEN DISTURBED. AT THIS TIME ALL THE ACTIVITY SEEMS TO BE AT THE SOUTH END WHERE--
OH, WAIT, HERE COMES AN OFFICER. MAYBE WE CAN GET--
WHAT ARE... AAAAAH! MY ARM! MY AR-- *CLICK*
SWEET JESUS.
UH, WE SEEM TO HAVE LOST THE SIGNAL.
LET'S GO TO...

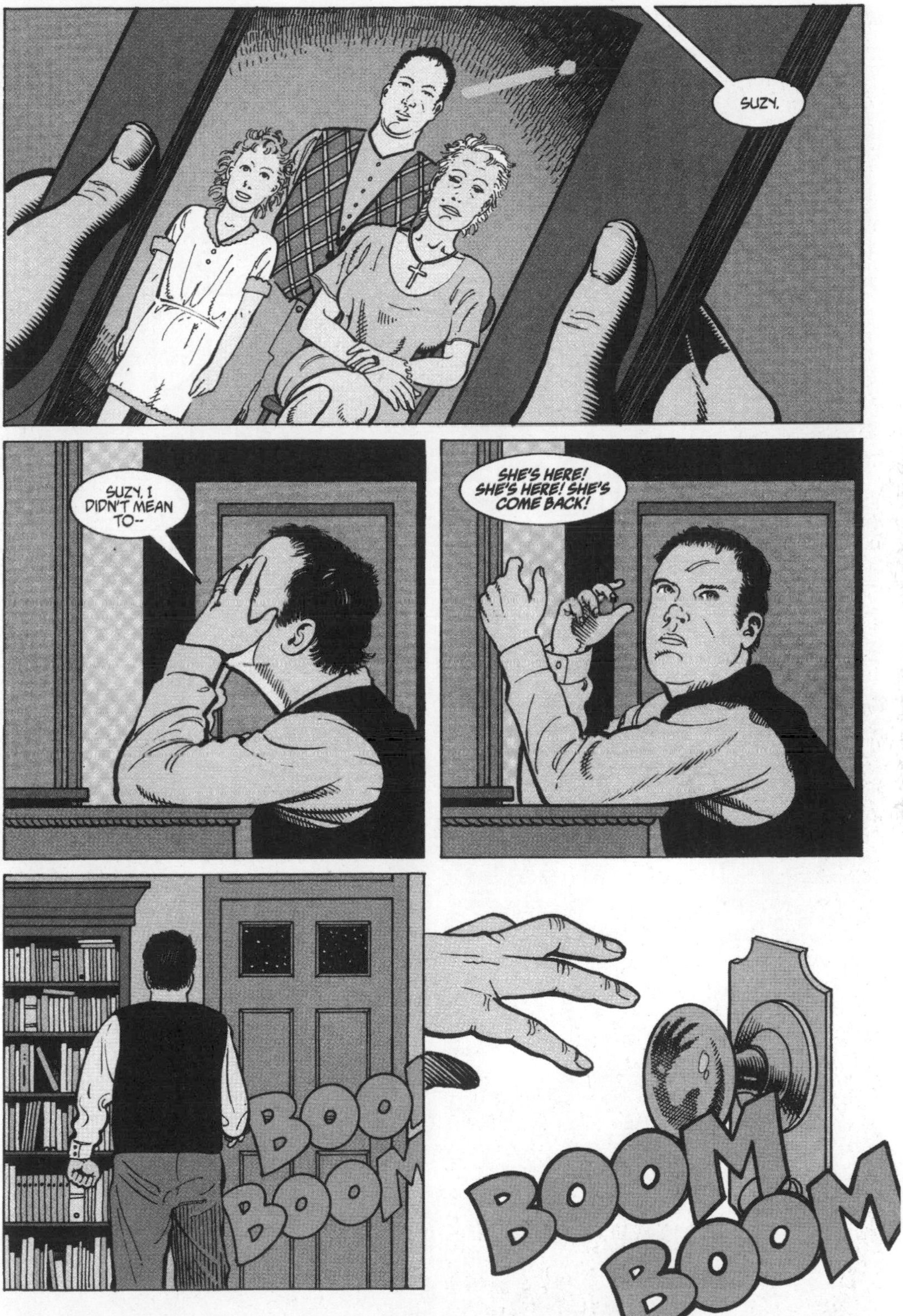
SUZY.
SUZY, I DIDN'T MEAN TO--
SHE'S HERE! SHE'S HERE! SHE'S COME BACK!
BOOM BOOM
BOOM BOOM

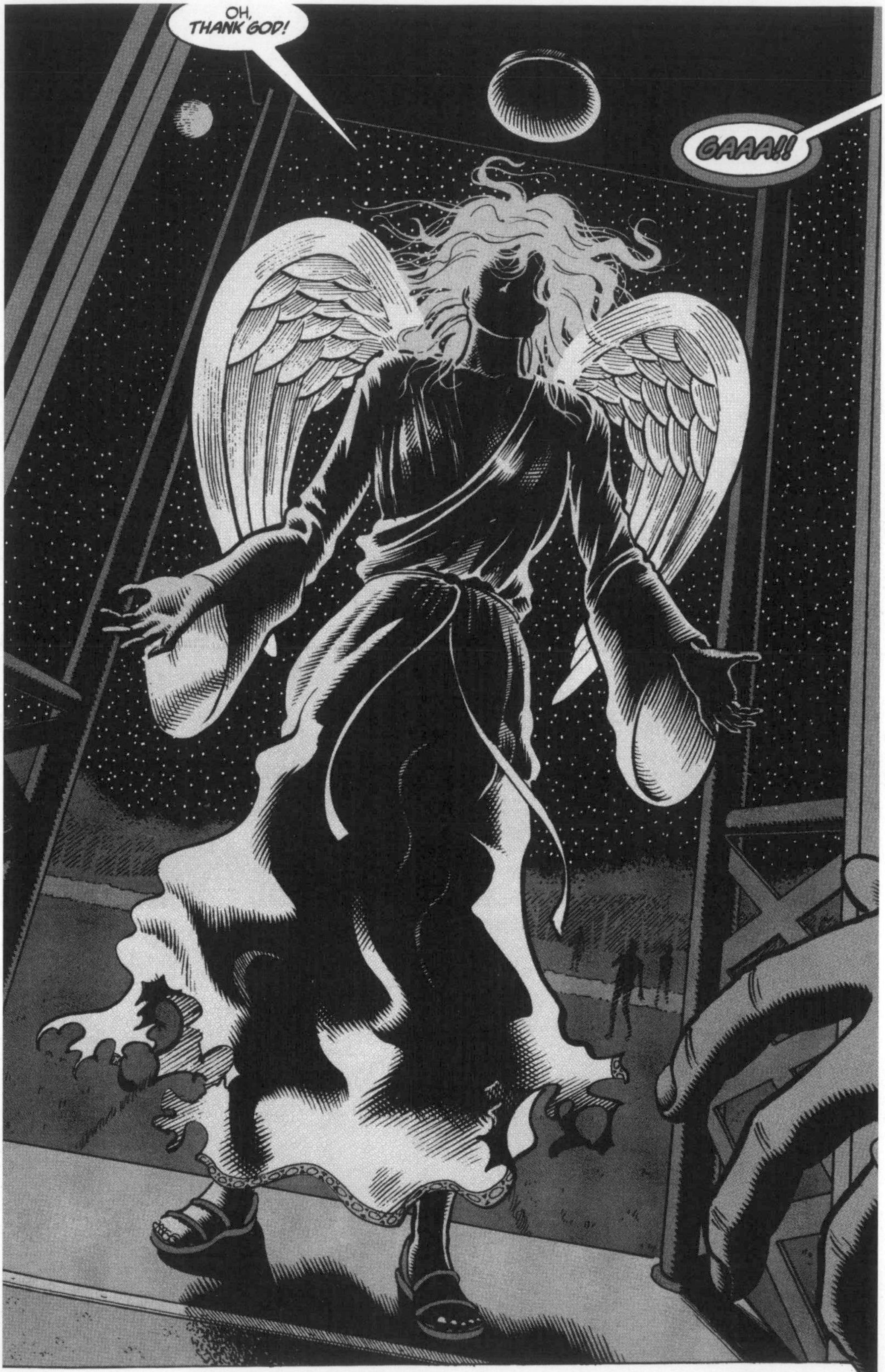
OH, THANK GOD!
GAAA!!

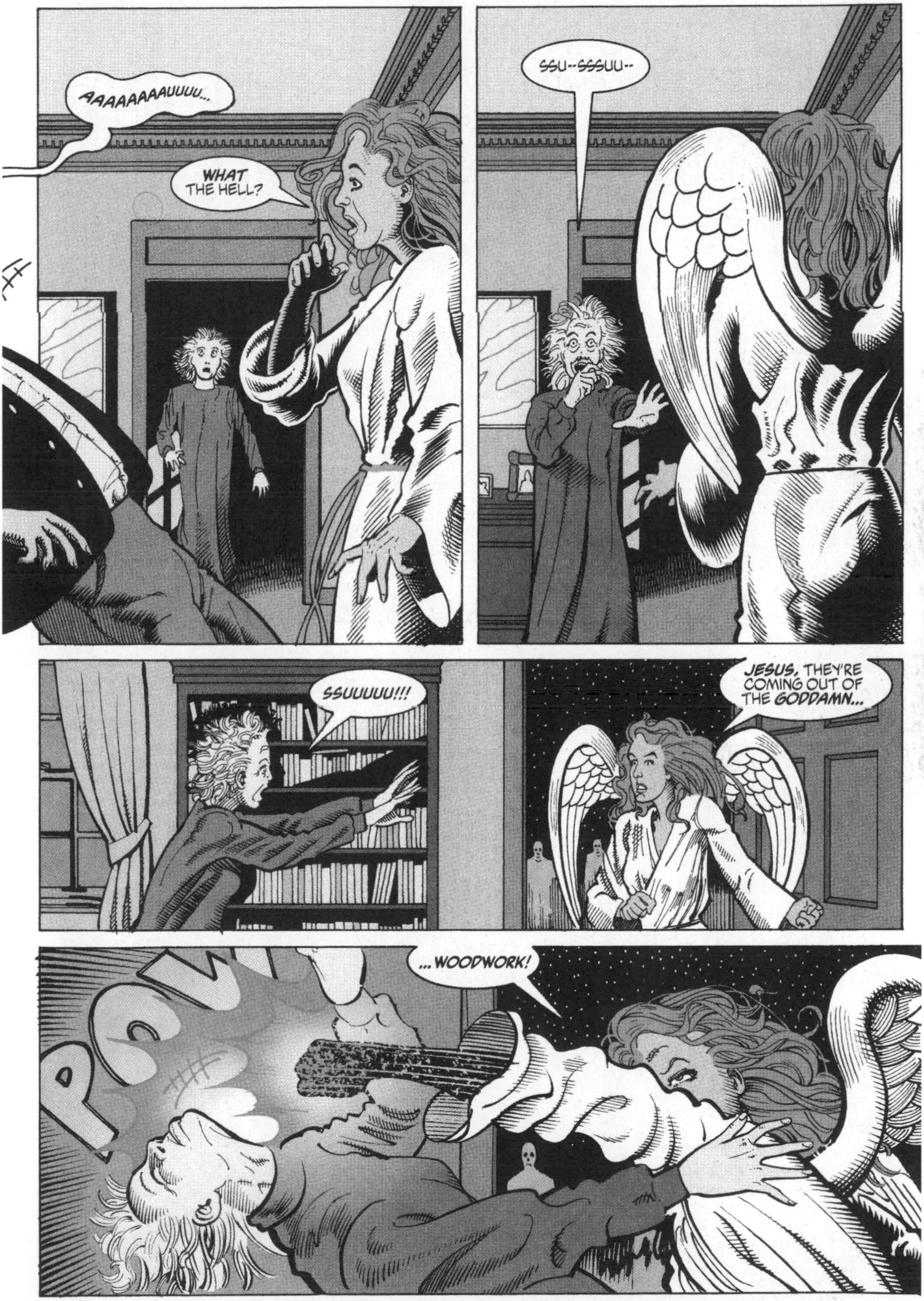
AAAAAAAAUUUU...
WHAT THE HELL?
SSU--SSSUU--
SSUUUUU!!!
JESUS, THEY'RE COMING OUT OF THE GODDAMN...
...WOODWORK!

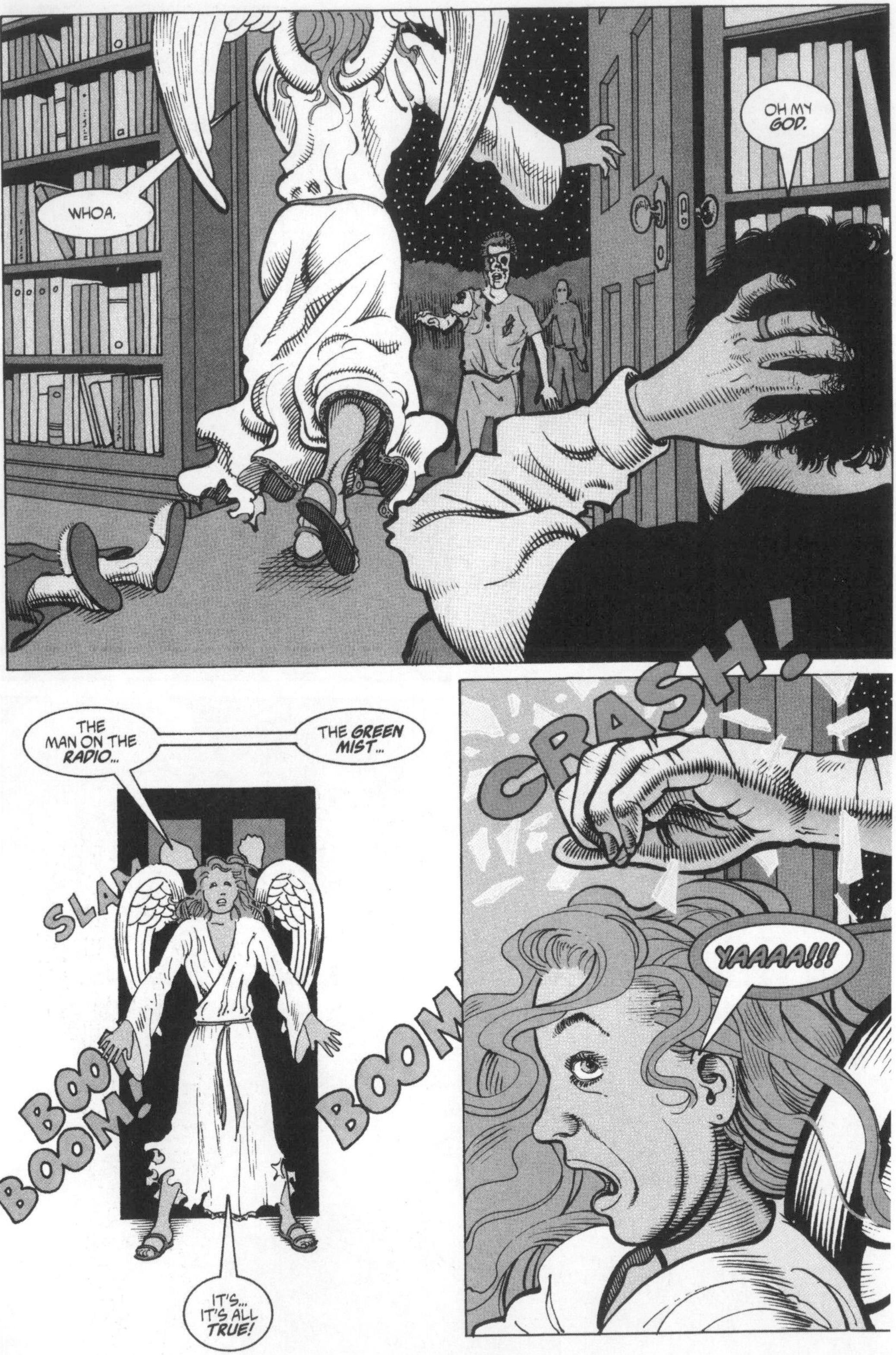
WHOA.
OH MY GOD.
THE MAN ON THE RADIO...
THE GREEN MIST...
BOOM!
IT'S... IT'S ALL TRUE!
CRASH!
YAAAA!!!

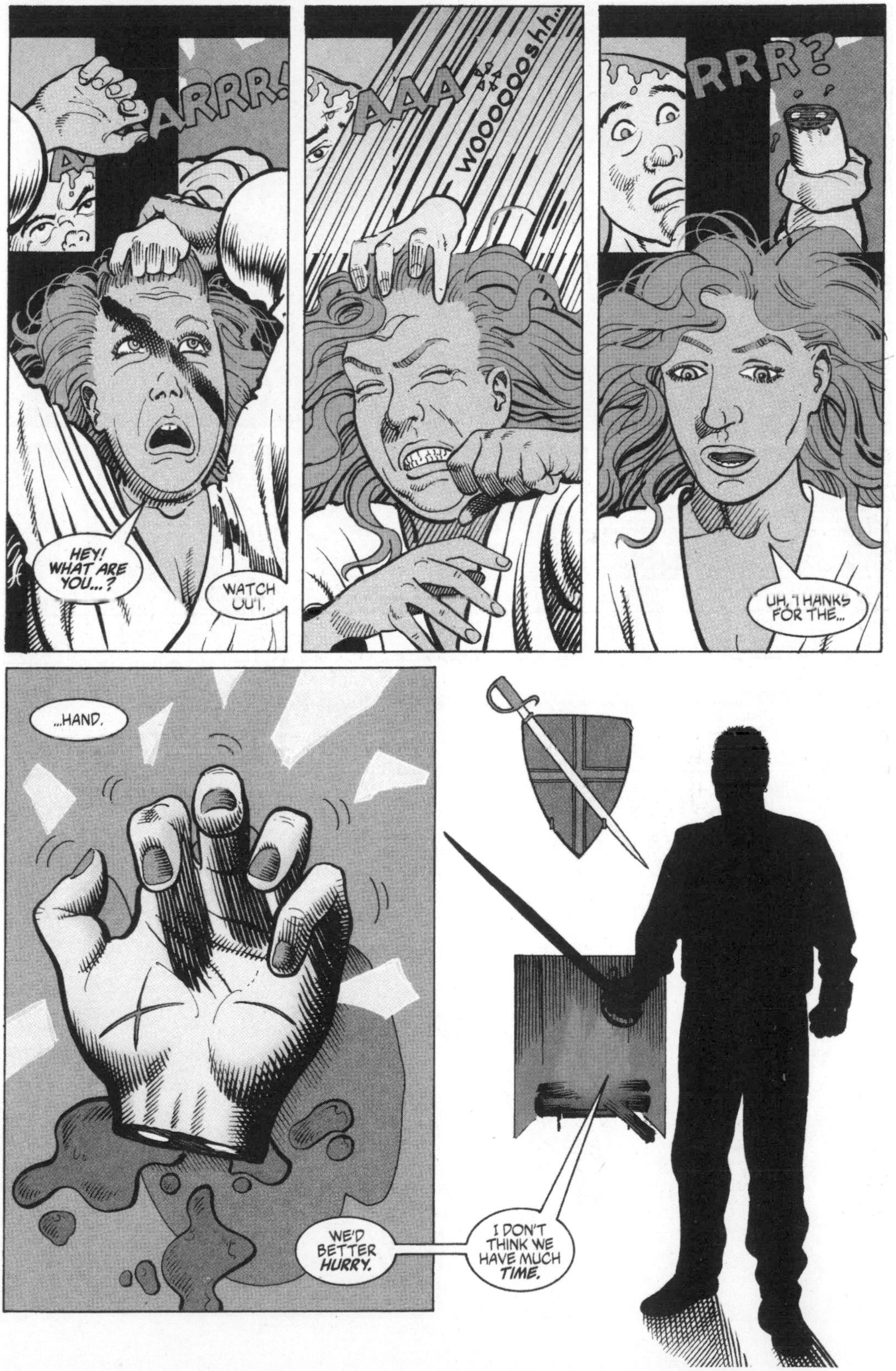
ARRR!
HEY! WHAT ARE YOU...?
WATCH OUT.
AAA
WOOOOOOSHH...
RRR?
UH, THANKS FOR THE...
...HAND.
WE'D BETTER HURRY.
I DON'T THINK WE HAVE MUCH TIME.

HOLY BIBLE
ANTIQUES
THIRD REICH
CHARLES DICKENS
ART THROUGH THE AGES
ANGST & SOCIETY
TED BUNDY
GREY'S ANATOMY
BABY
DO YOU NEED ANY--?
I HAVE HER.

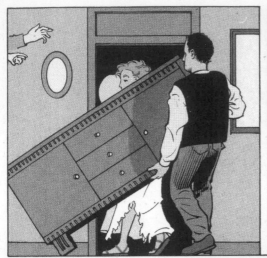

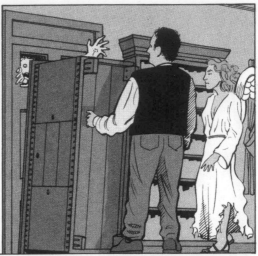

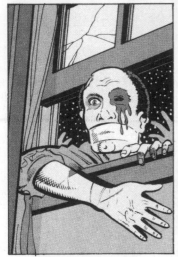

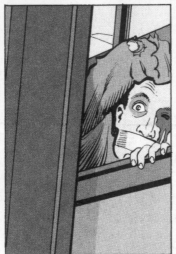

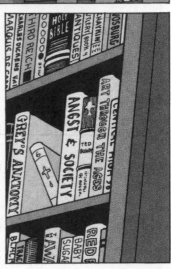

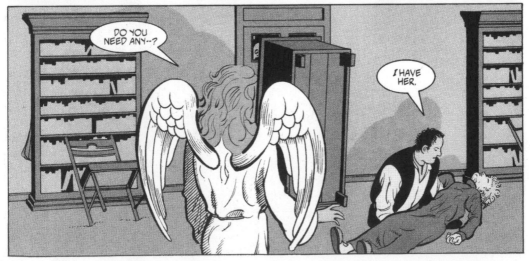

...AND WHEN JESUS CAME *OUT* OF THAT CAVE MARY MAGDALENE DIDN'T *RECOGNIZE* HIM.

YES, I KNOW, MAMA.

THE APOSTLES MADE HIM SHOW HIS *SCARS.* HIS *CRUCIFIXION* SCARS. HIS...

STIGMATA.

HIS *STIGMATA.*

SHE SPOKE TO ME FROM *ABOVE,* ARTHUR. SHE SAID SHE'D *RETURN* AND SHE *HAS!*

I... I *KNOW,* MAMA.

BUT LITTLE SUZY DOESN'T HAVE NO *SCARS.*

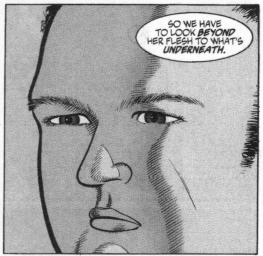

SO WE HAVE TO LOOK *BEYOND* HER FLESH TO WHAT'S *UNDERNEATH.*

I'M SORRY ABOUT YOUR *MOTHER.* I THOUGHT SHE WAS ONE OF THOSE... ZOMBIES.

GOD, I CAN'T BELIEVE I'M USING THAT *WORD.*

MY DAD USED TO CALL HER HIS *"LITTLE PECAN."*

A REAL *SOUTHERN NUT.* FUNNY, SAY...

THAT'S MY *WIFE* AND *DAUGHTER.*

WHERE...?

MY WIFE *LEFT* ME. AND SUZY...

417

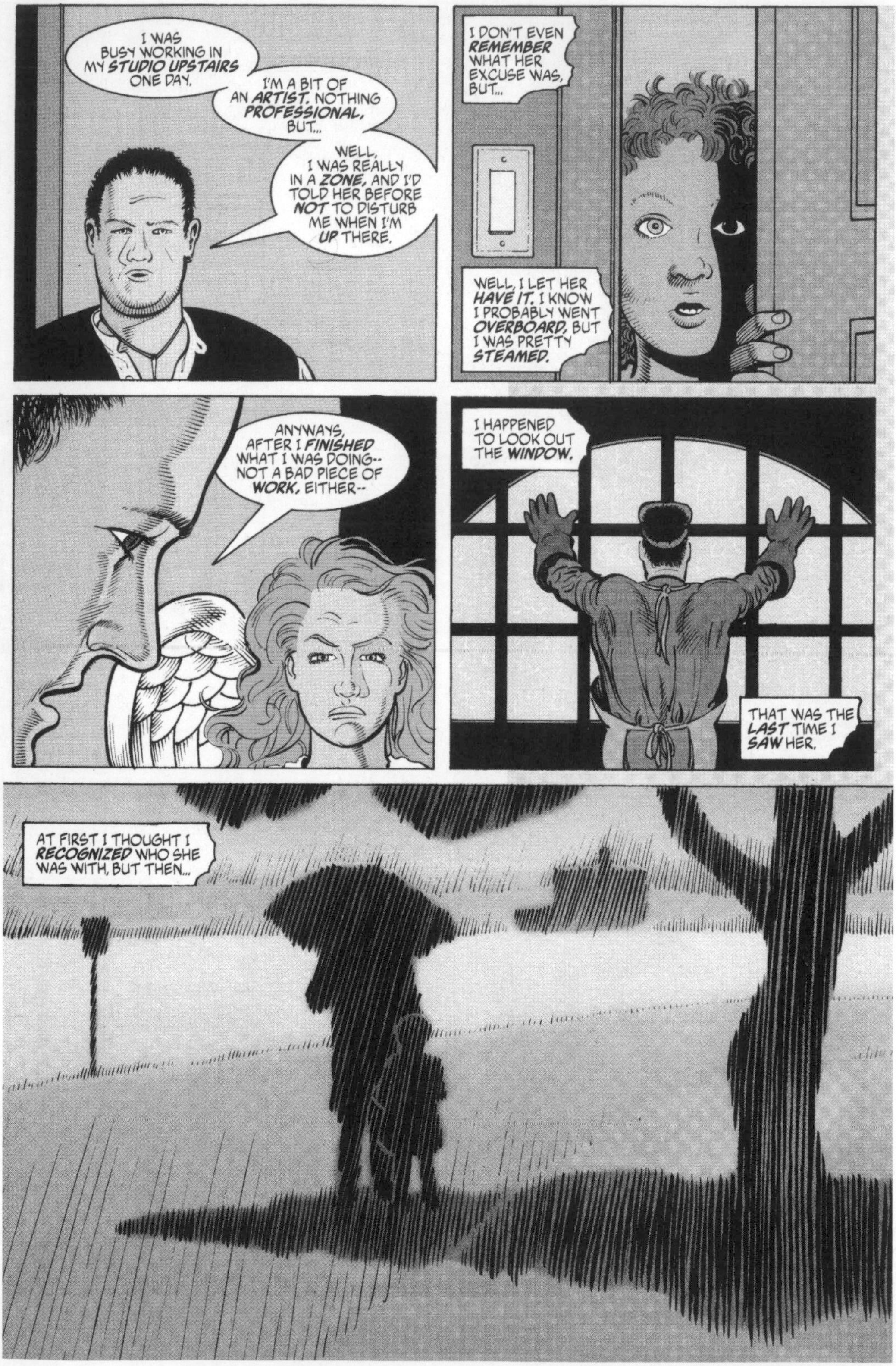
I WAS BUSY WORKING IN MY STUDIO UPSTAIRS ONE DAY.
I'M A BIT OF AN ARTIST. NOTHING PROFESSIONAL, BUT...
WELL, I WAS REALLY IN A ZONE, AND I'D TOLD HER BEFORE NOT TO DISTURB ME WHEN I'M UP THERE.
I DON'T EVEN REMEMBER WHAT HER EXCUSE WAS, BUT...
WELL, I LET HER HAVE IT. I KNOW I PROBABLY WENT OVERBOARD, BUT I WAS PRETTY STEAMED.
ANYWAYS, AFTER I FINISHED WHAT I WAS DOING-- NOT A BAD PIECE OF WORK, EITHER--
I HAPPENED TO LOOK OUT THE WINDOW.
THAT WAS THE LAST TIME I SAW HER.
AT FIRST I THOUGHT I RECOGNIZED WHO SHE WAS WITH, BUT THEN...

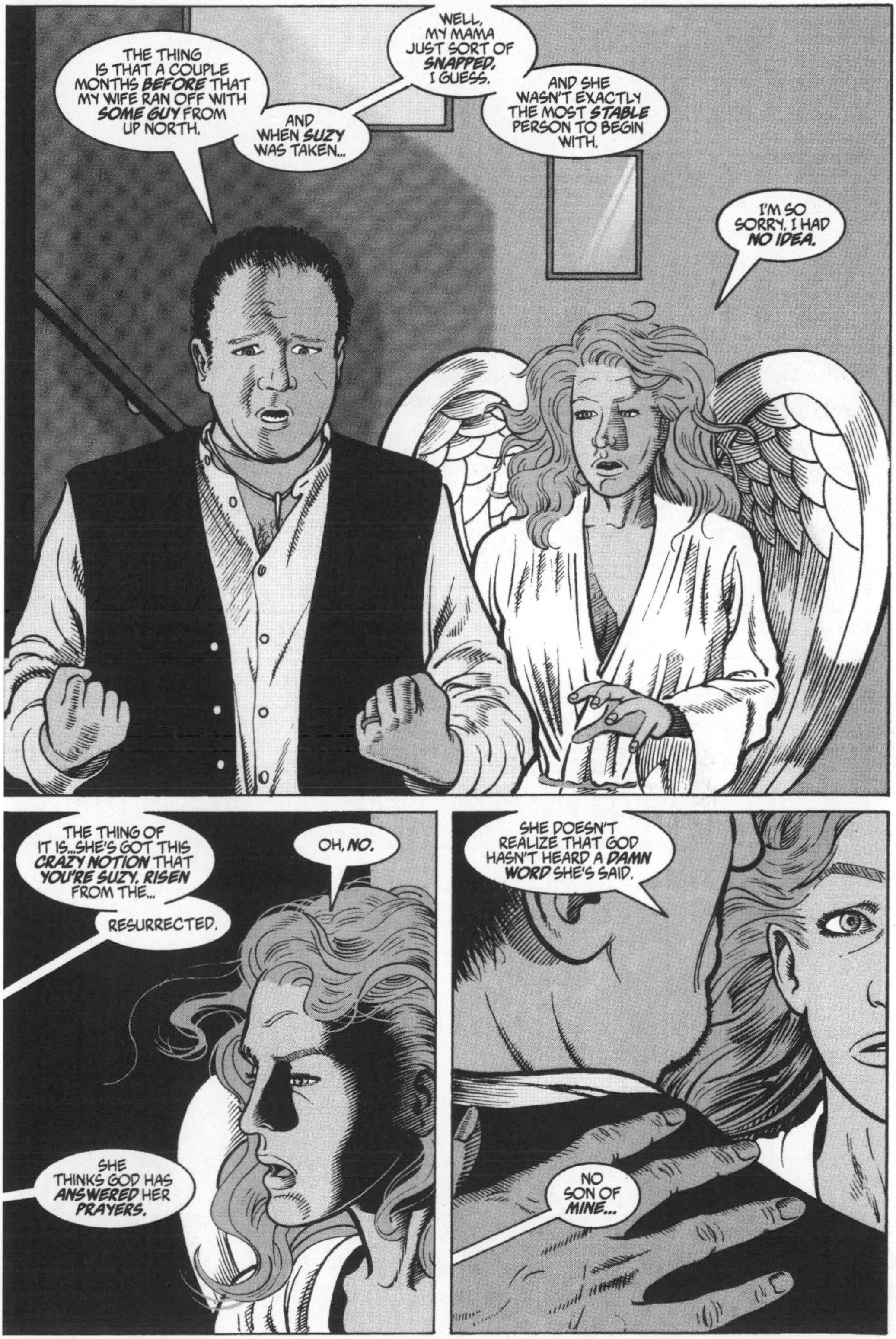
THE THING IS THAT A COUPLE MONTHS BEFORE THAT MY WIFE RAN OFF WITH SOME GUY FROM UP NORTH.
AND WHEN SUZY WAS TAKEN...
WELL, MY MAMA JUST SORT OF SNAPPED, I GUESS.
AND SHE WASN'T EXACTLY THE MOST STABLE PERSON TO BEGIN WITH.
I'M SO SORRY. I HAD NO IDEA.
THE THING OF IT IS...SHE'S GOT THIS CRAZY NOTION THAT YOU'RE SUZY, RISEN FROM THE...
OH, NO.
RESURRECTED.
SHE THINKS GOD HAS ANSWERED HER PRAYERS.
SHE DOESN'T REALIZE THAT GOD HASN'T HEARD A DAMN WORD SHE'S SAID.
NO SON OF MINE...

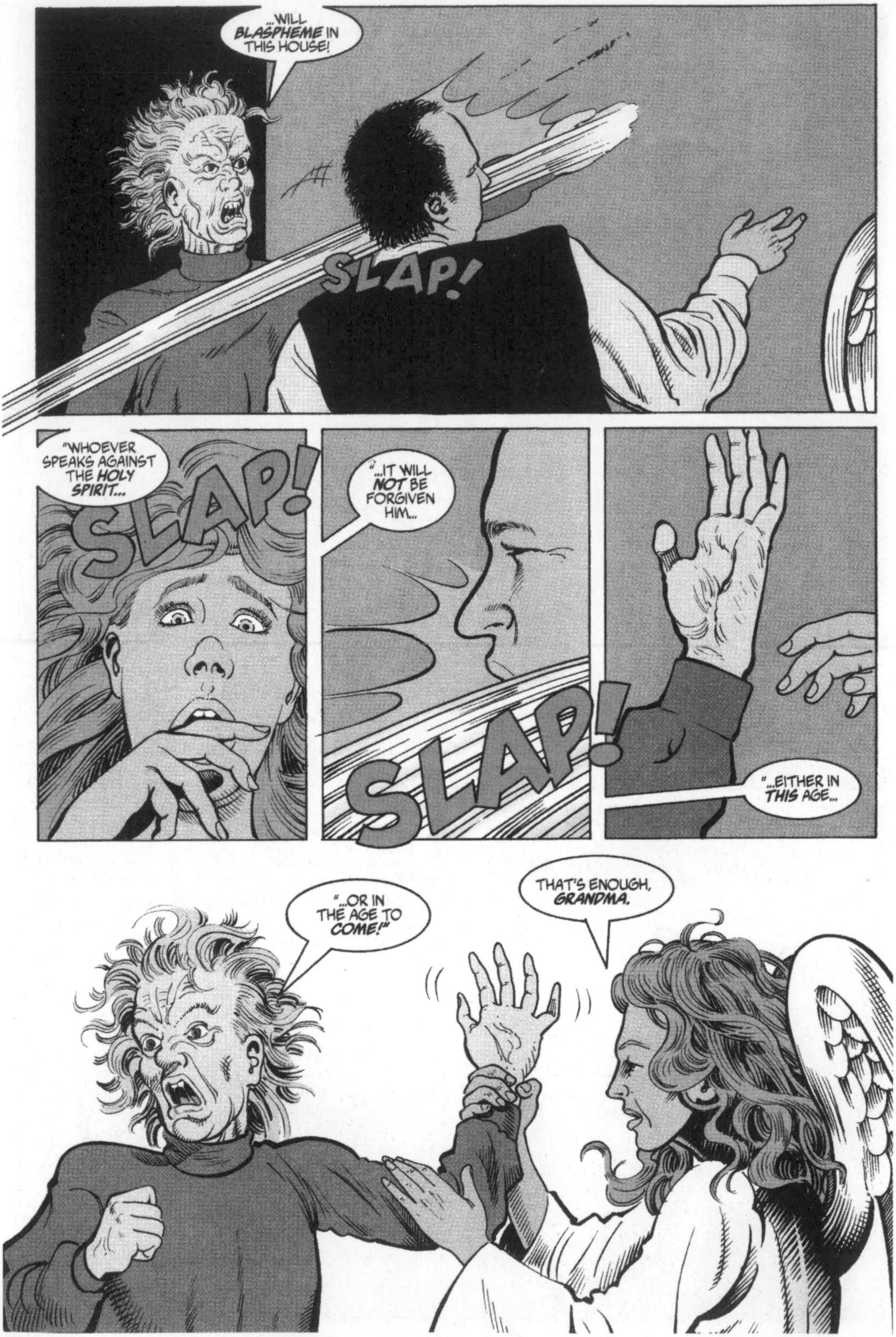
...WILL BLASPHEME IN THIS HOUSE!
SLAP!
"WHOEVER SPEAKS AGAINST THE HOLY SPIRIT...
SLAP!
"...IT WILL NOT BE FORGIVEN HIM...
SLAP!
"...EITHER IN THIS AGE...
"...OR IN THE AGE TO COME!"
THAT'S ENOUGH, GRANDMA.

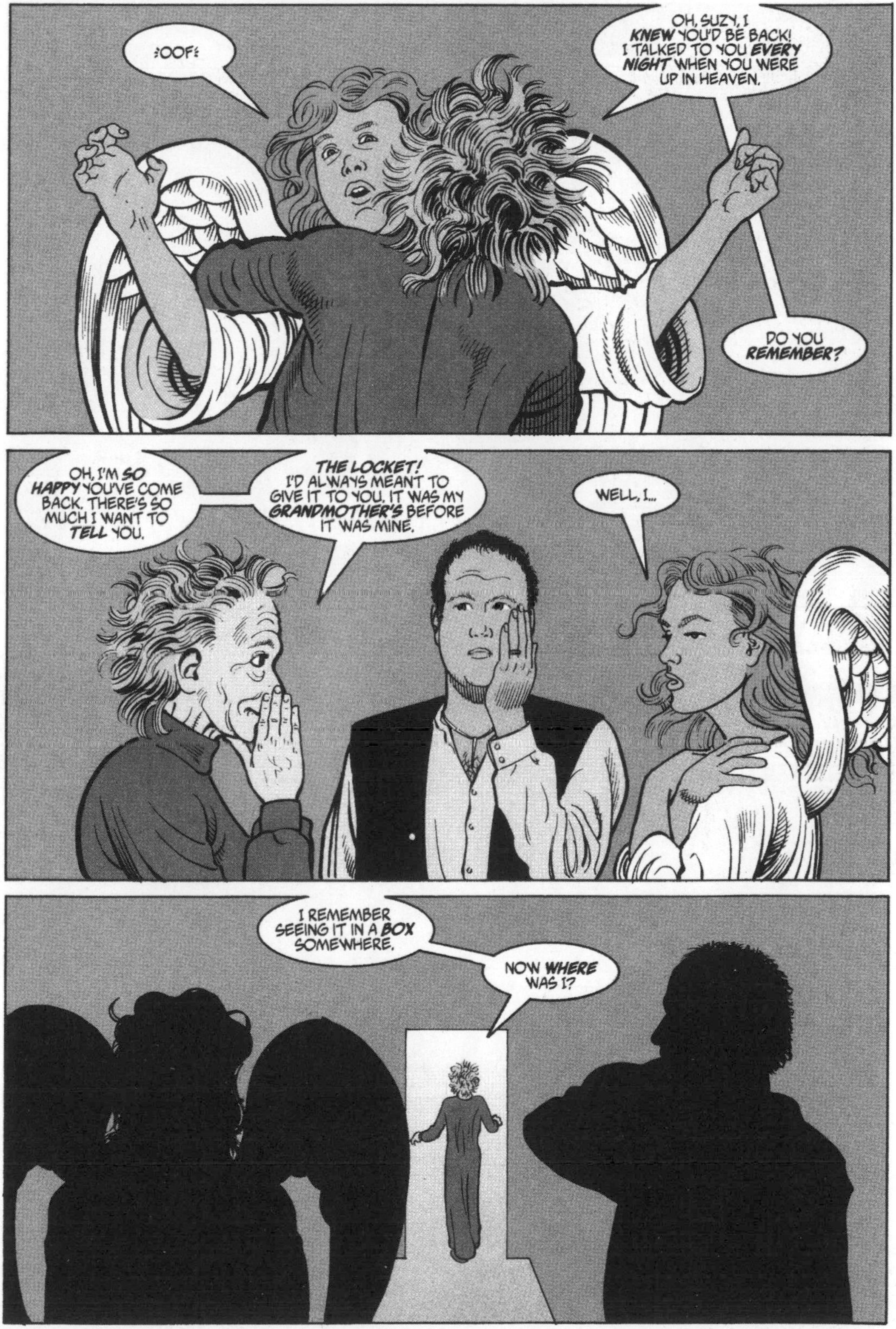
:OOF:
OH, SUZY, I KNEW YOU'D BE BACK! I TALKED TO YOU EVERY NIGHT WHEN YOU WERE UP IN HEAVEN.
DO YOU REMEMBER?
OH, I'M SO HAPPY YOU'VE COME BACK. THERE'S SO MUCH I WANT TO TELL YOU.
THE LOCKET! I'D ALWAYS MEANT TO GIVE IT TO YOU. IT WAS MY GRANDMOTHER'S BEFORE IT WAS MINE.
WELL, I...
I REMEMBER SEEING IT IN A BOX SOMEWHERE.
NOW WHERE WAS I?

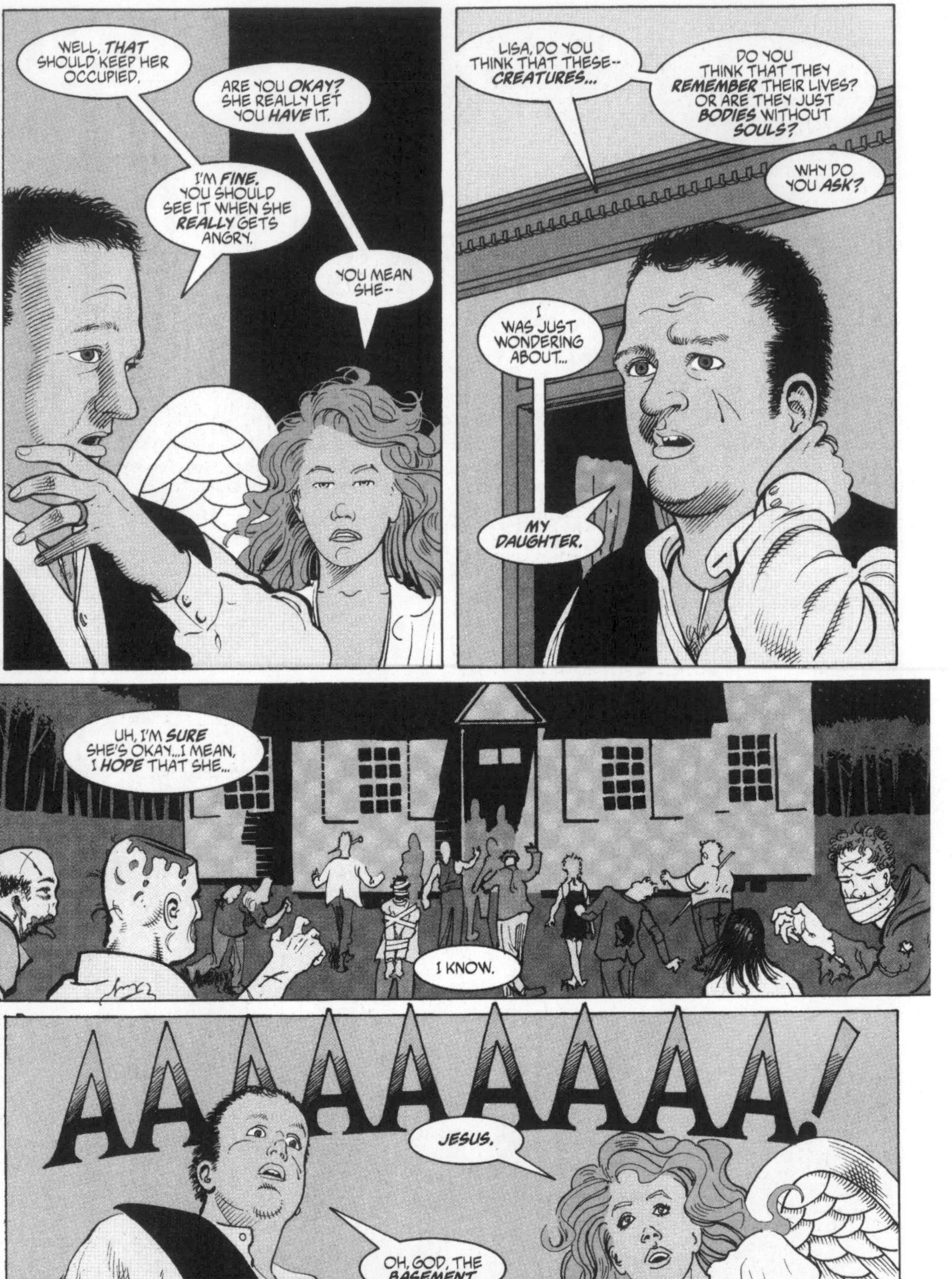
WELL, THAT SHOULD KEEP HER OCCUPIED.
ARE YOU OKAY? SHE REALLY LET YOU HAVE IT.
I'M FINE. YOU SHOULD SEE IT WHEN SHE REALLY GETS ANGRY.
YOU MEAN SHE--
LISA, DO YOU THINK THAT THESE--CREATURES...
DO YOU THINK THAT THEY REMEMBER THEIR LIVES? OR ARE THEY JUST BODIES WITHOUT SOULS?
WHY DO YOU ASK?
I WAS JUST WONDERING ABOUT...
MY DAUGHTER.
UH, I'M SURE SHE'S OKAY...I MEAN, I HOPE THAT SHE...
I KNOW.
AAAAAAAA!
JESUS.
OH, GOD, THE BASEMENT.

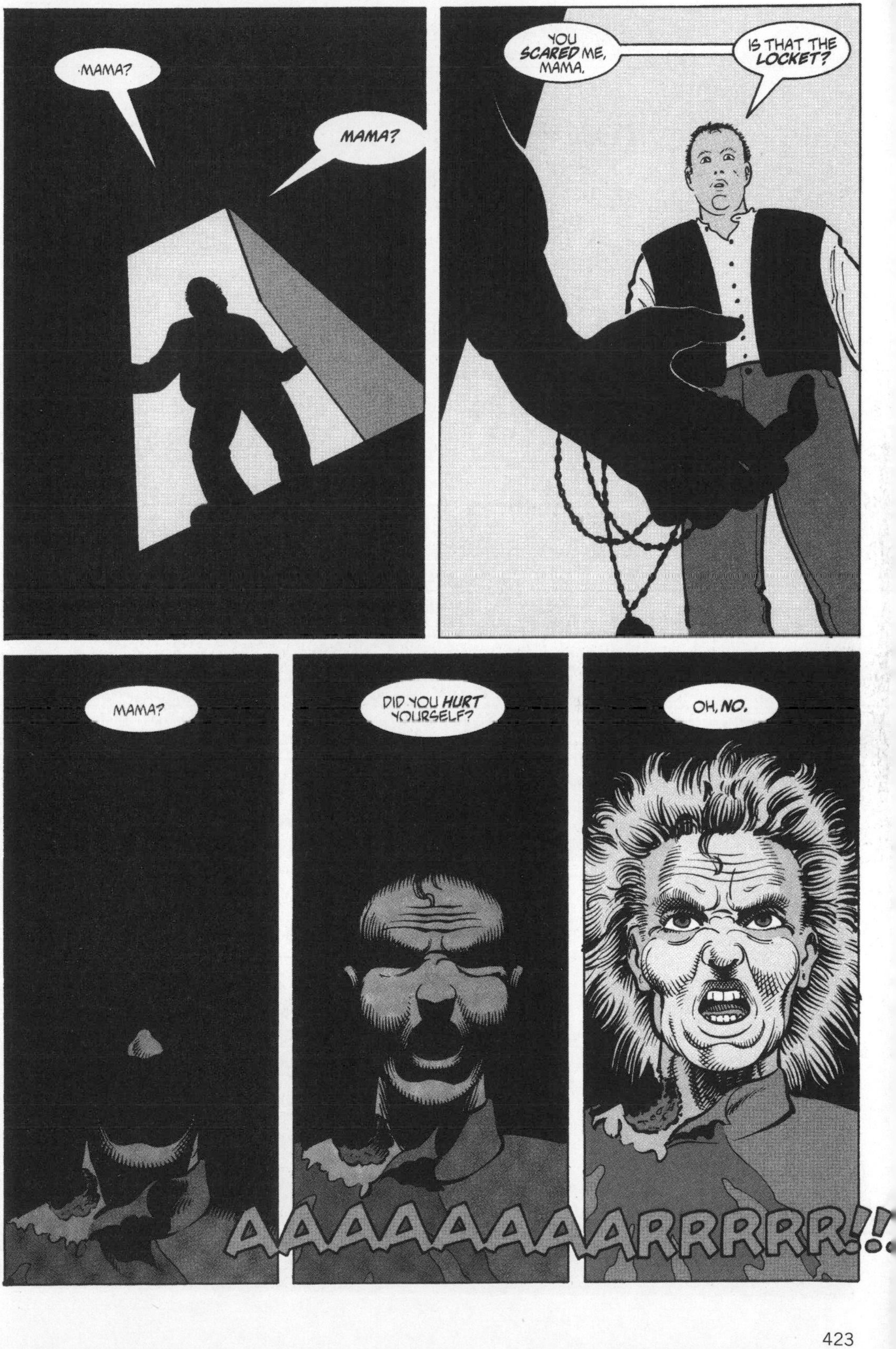
MAMA?
MAMA?
YOU SCARED ME, MAMA.
IS THAT THE LOCKET?
MAMA?
DID YOU HURT YOURSELF?
OH, NO.
AAAAAAAAARRRRR!!

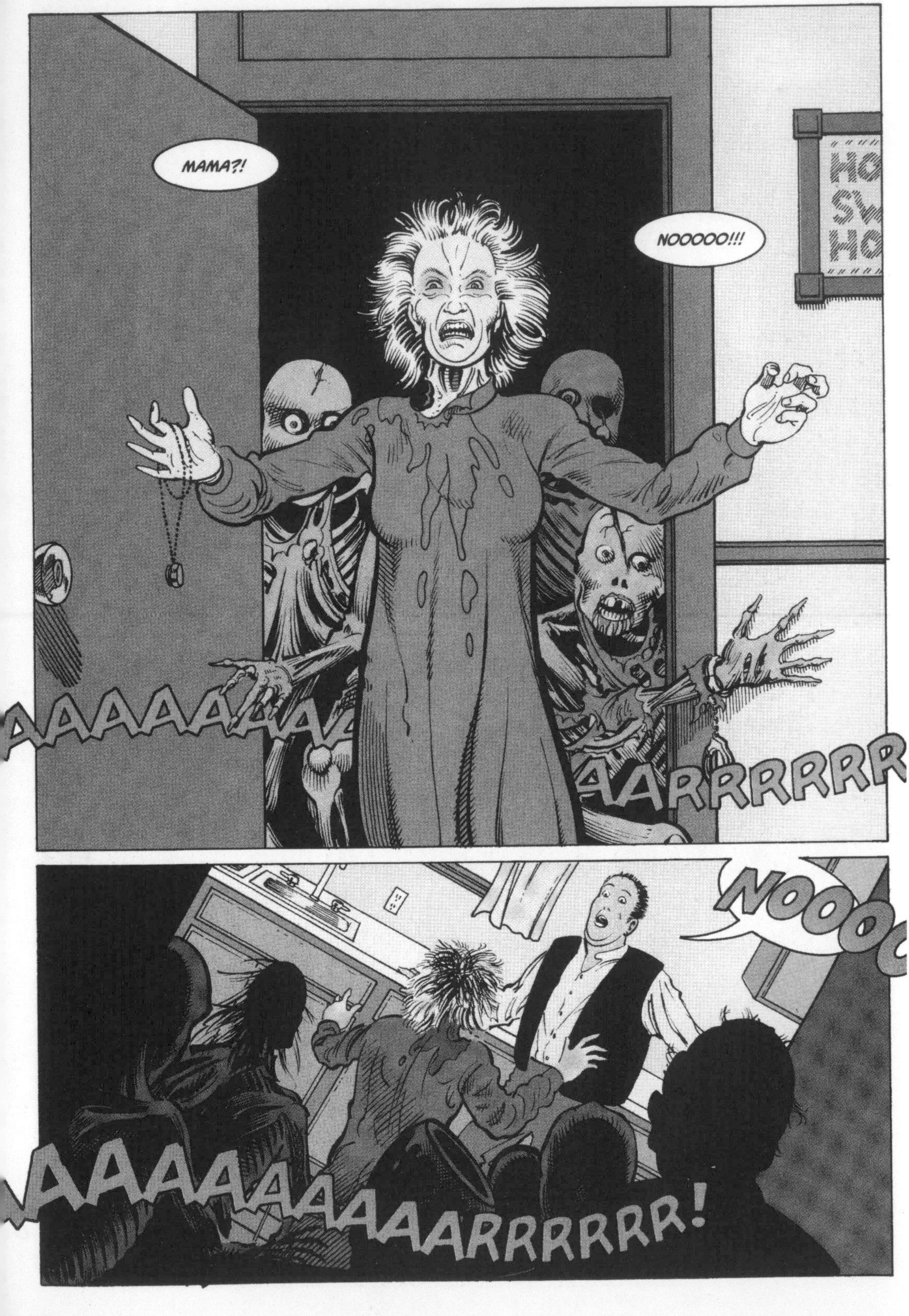
MAMA?!
NOOOOO!!!
AAAAAAA
AARRRRRR
NOOOO
AAAAAAAAAAARRRRRRR!

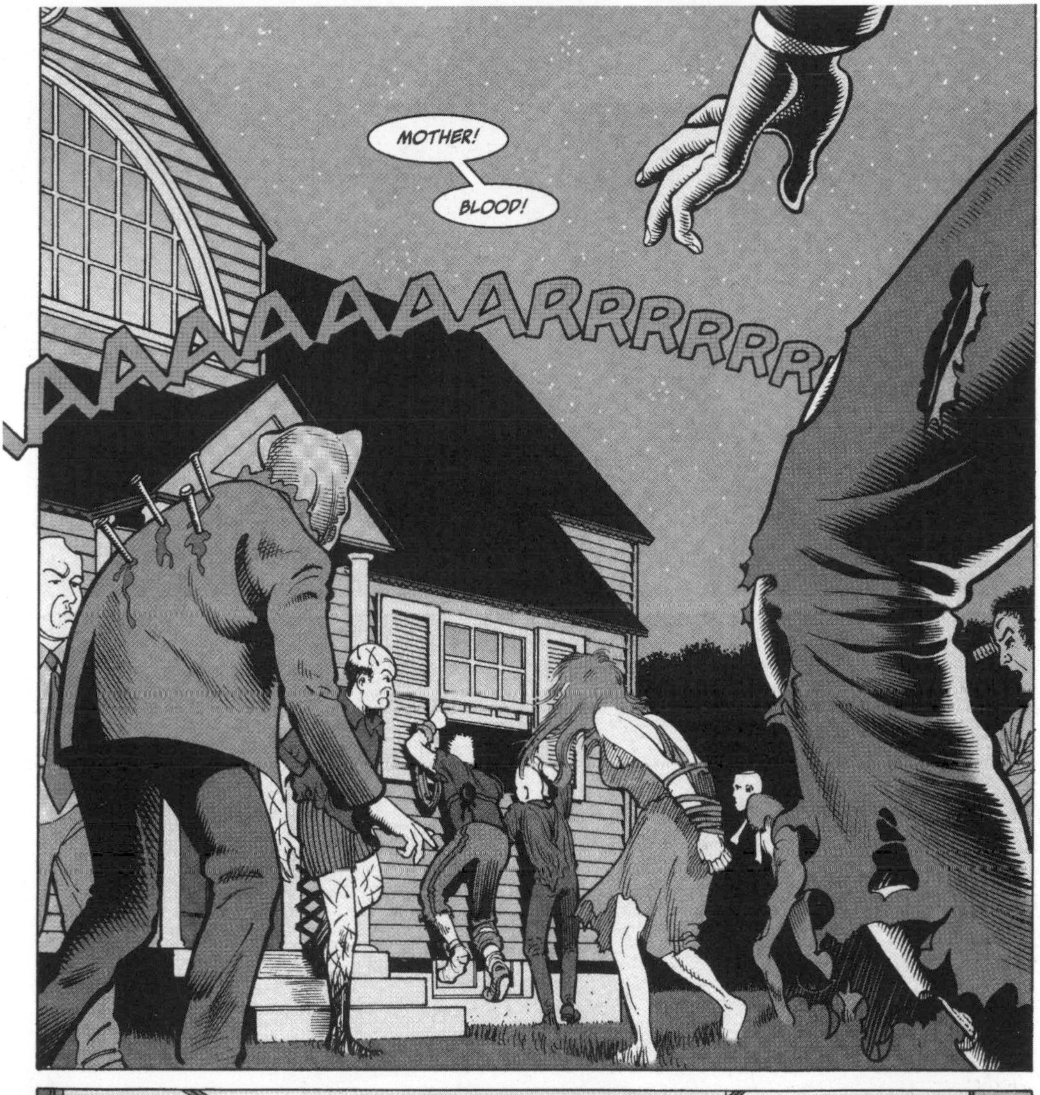
MOTHER!
BLOOD!
AAAAAAAARRRRRRR

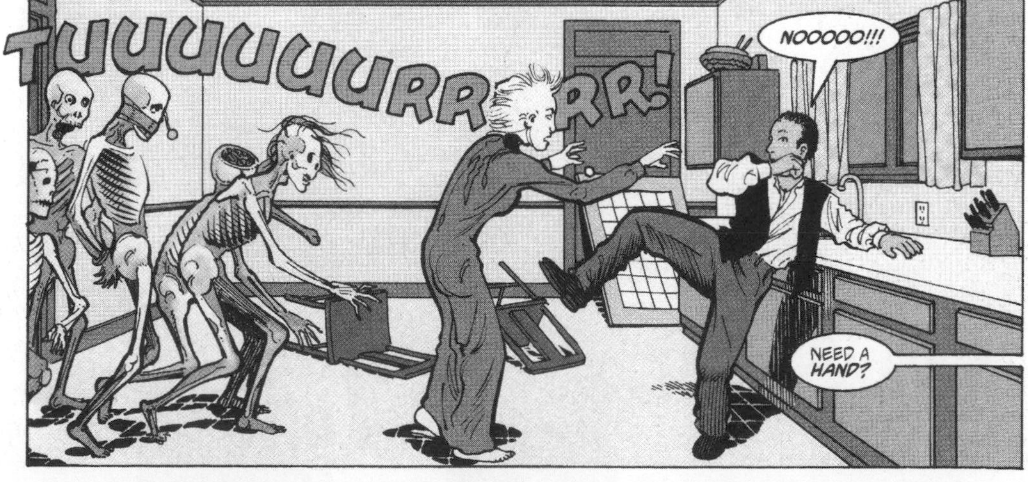
TUUUUUURRRRR!
NOOOOO!!!
NEED A HAND?

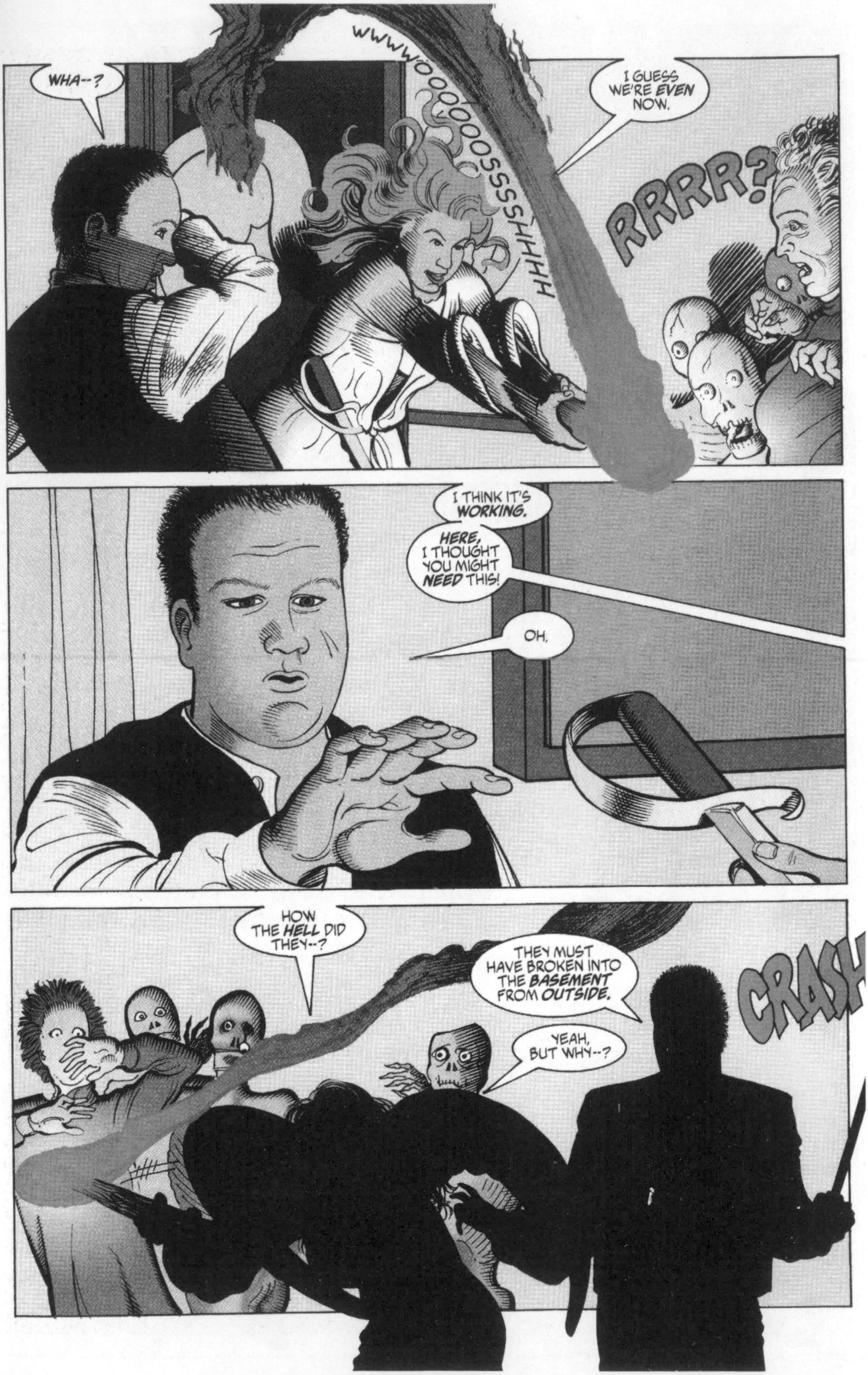
WWWWOOOOOOOOOOOSSSSHHHH
WHA--?
I GUESS WE'RE EVEN NOW.
RRRR?
I THINK IT'S WORKING.
HERE, I THOUGHT YOU MIGHT NEED THIS!
OH.
HOW THE HELL DID THEY--?
THEY MUST HAVE BROKEN INTO THE BASEMENT FROM OUTSIDE.
YEAH, BUT WHY--?
CRASH

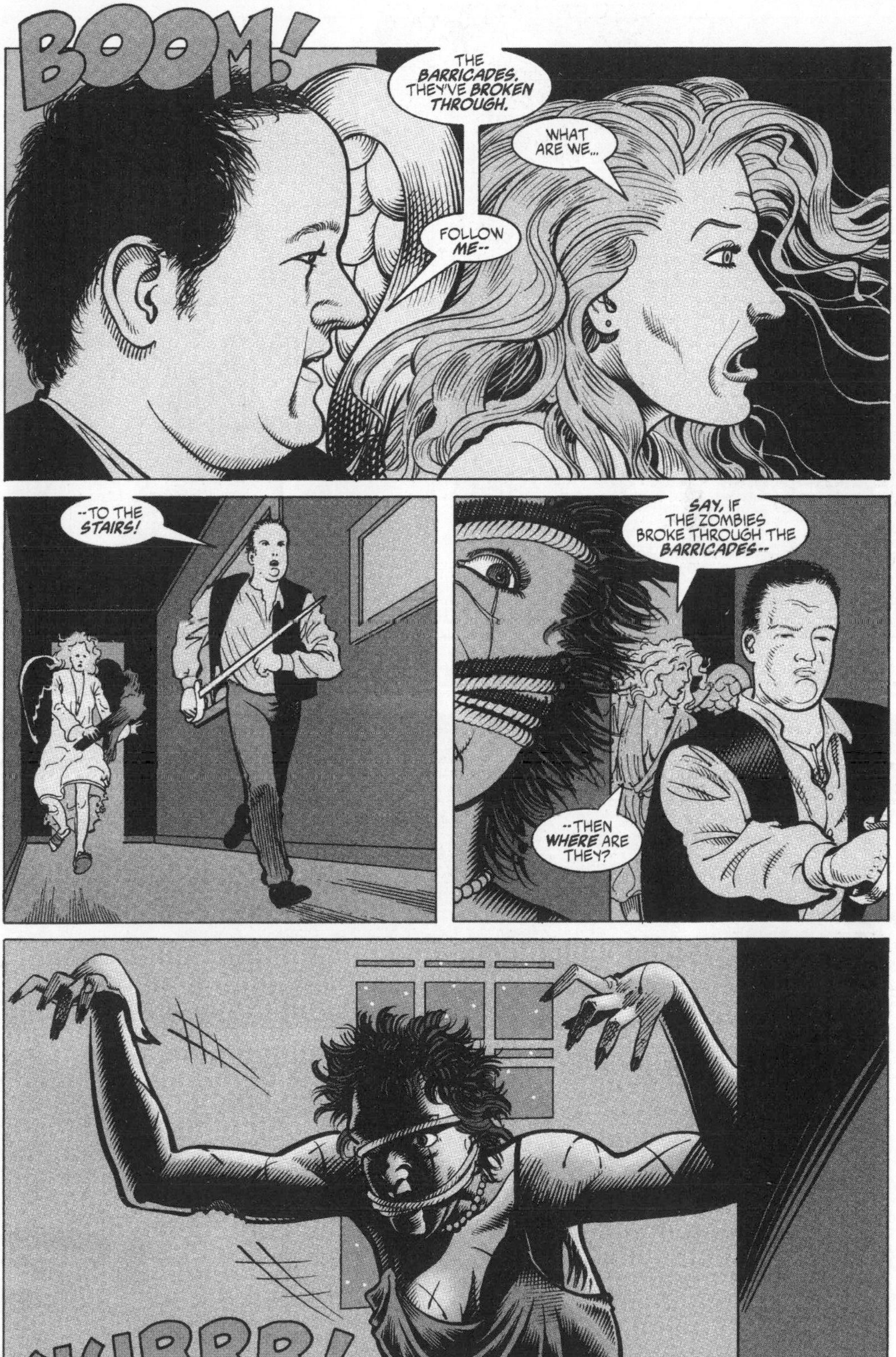
BOOM!
THE BARRICADES. THEY'VE BROKEN THROUGH.
WHAT ARE WE...
FOLLOW ME--
--TO THE STAIRS!
SAY, IF THE ZOMBIES BROKE THROUGH THE BARRICADES--
--THEN WHERE ARE THEY?
UURRR!

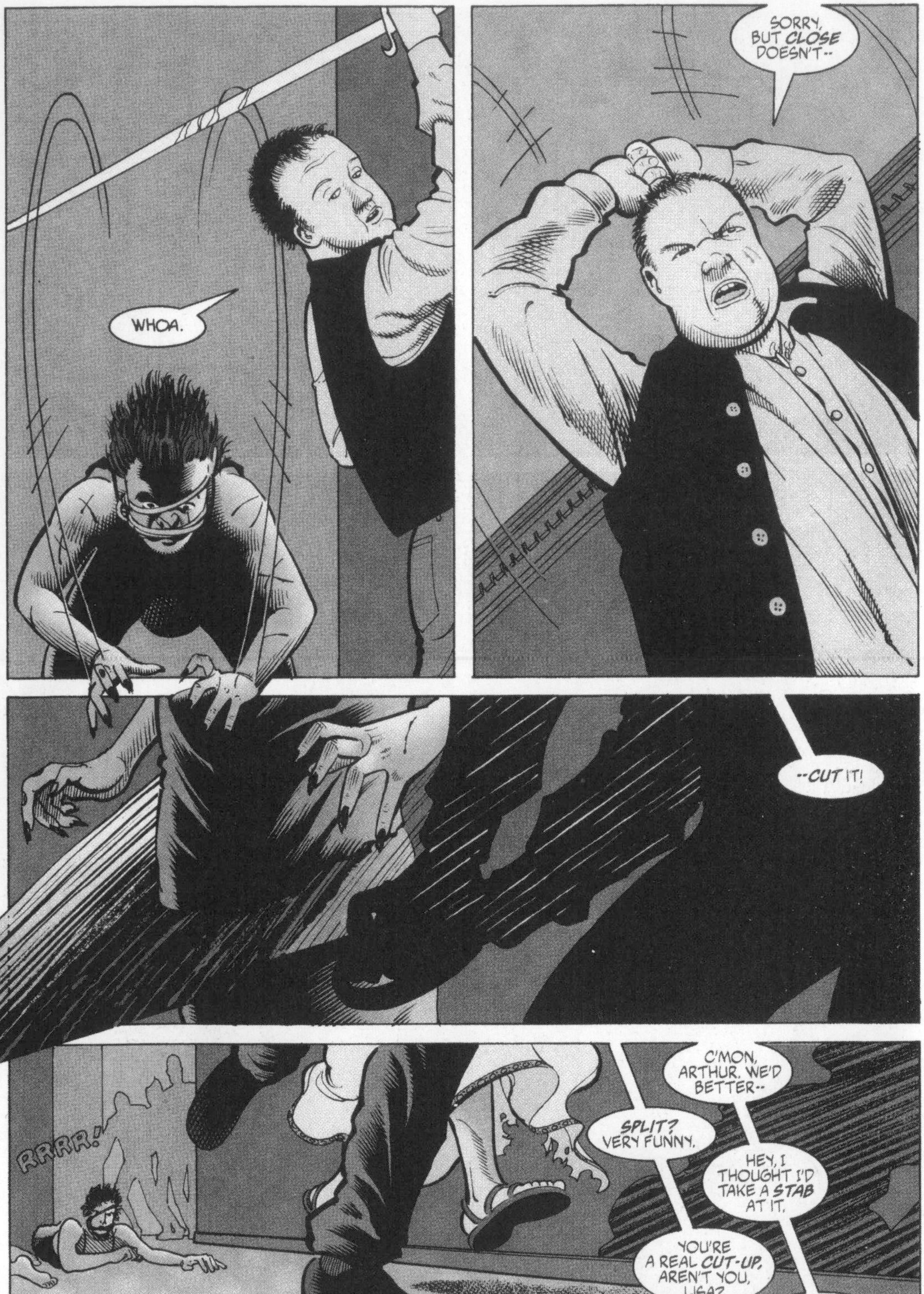
WHOA.
SORRY, BUT CLOSE DOESN'T--
--CUT IT!
RRRR!
C'MON, ARTHUR. WE'D BETTER--
SPLIT? VERY FUNNY.
HEY, I THOUGHT I'D TAKE A STAB AT IT.
YOU'RE A REAL CUT-UP, AREN'T YOU, LISA?
LOOK WHO'S TALKING.

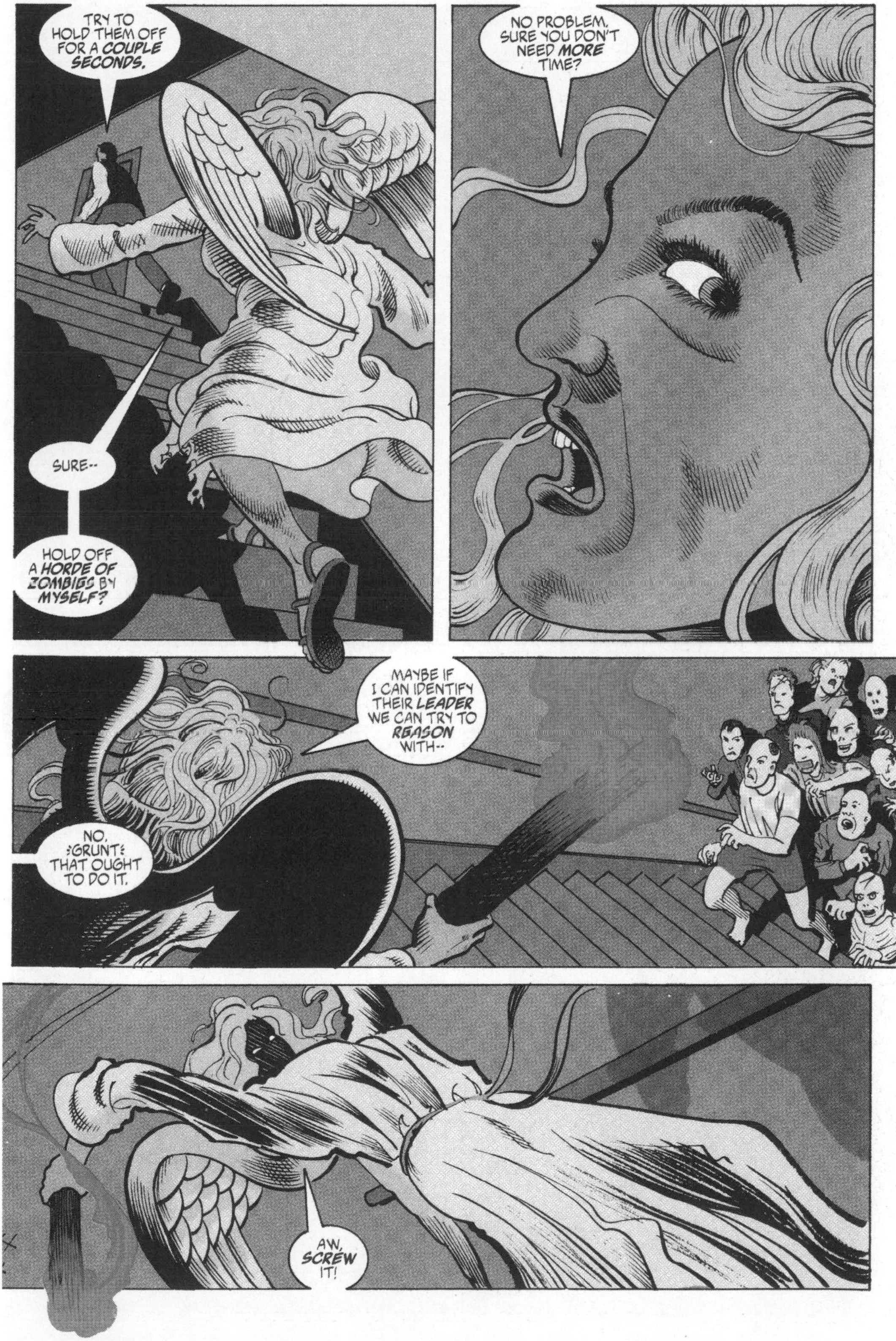
TRY TO HOLD THEM OFF FOR A COUPLE SECONDS.
SURE--
HOLD OFF A HORDE OF ZOMBIES BY MYSELF?
NO PROBLEM. SURE YOU DON'T NEED MORE TIME?
MAYBE IF I CAN IDENTIFY THEIR LEADER WE CAN TRY TO REASON WITH--
NO. GRUNT THAT OUGHT TO DO IT.
AW, SCREW IT!

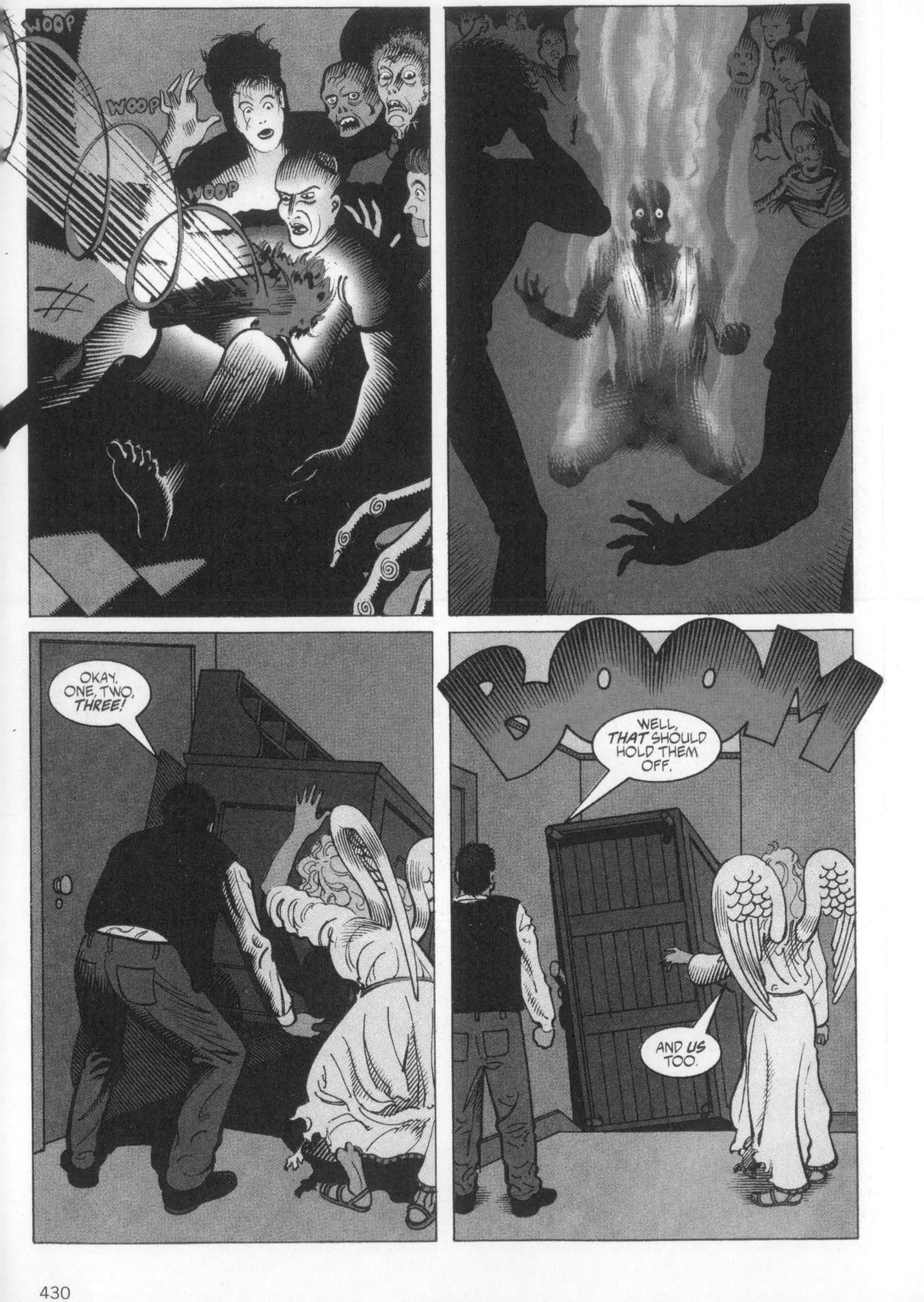
WOOP
WOOP
WOOP
OKAY, ONE, TWO, THREE!
BOOM
WELL, THAT SHOULD HOLD THEM OFF.
AND US TOO.

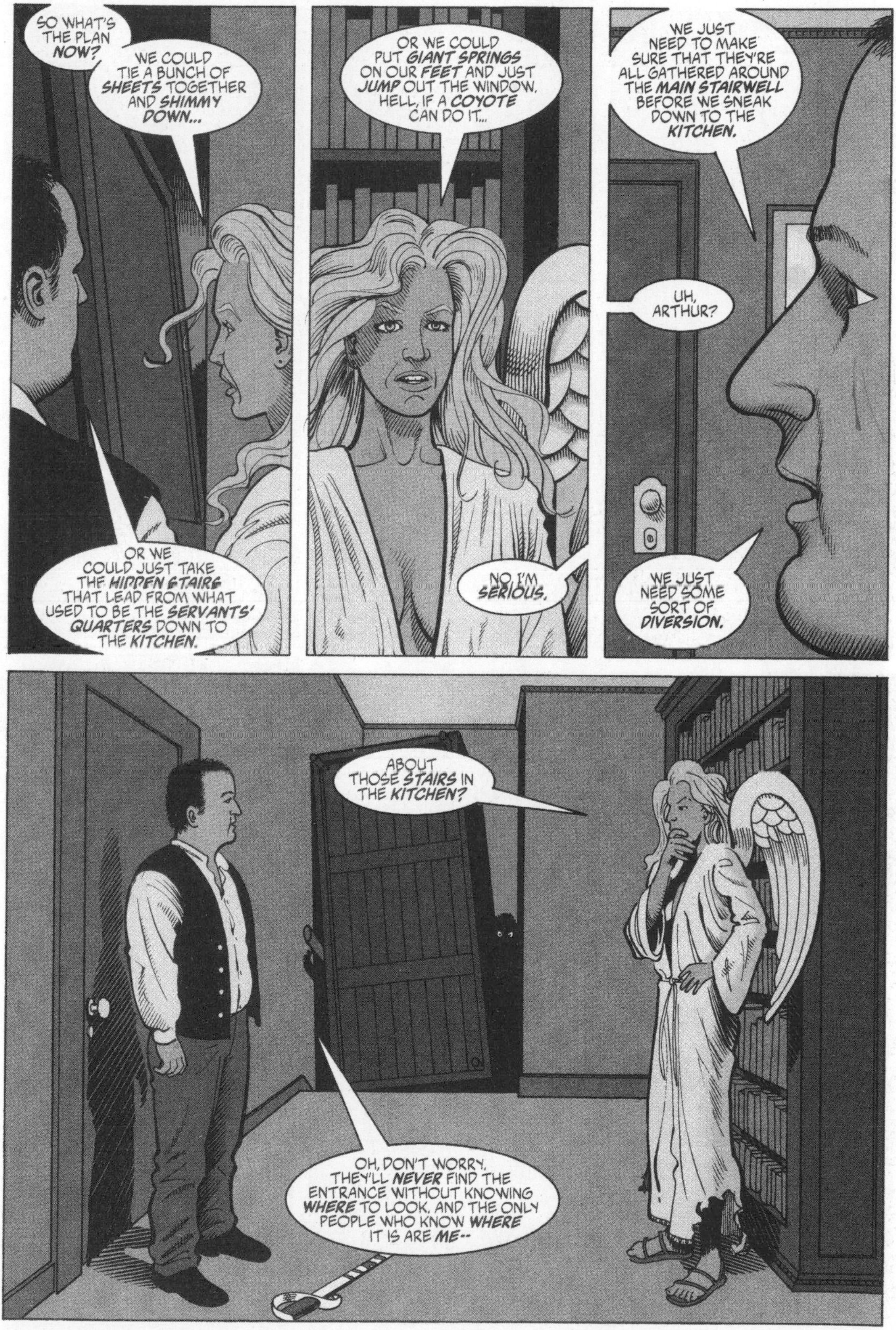
SO WHAT'S THE PLAN NOW?
WE COULD TIE A BUNCH OF SHEETS TOGETHER AND SHIMMY DOWN...
OR WE COULD JUST TAKE THE HIDDEN STAIRS THAT LEAD FROM WHAT USED TO BE THE SERVANTS' QUARTERS DOWN TO THE KITCHEN.
OR WE COULD PUT GIANT SPRINGS ON OUR FEET AND JUST JUMP OUT THE WINDOW. HELL, IF A COYOTE CAN DO IT...
NO, I'M SERIOUS.
WE JUST NEED TO MAKE SURE THAT THEY'RE ALL GATHERED AROUND THE MAIN STAIRWELL BEFORE WE SNEAK DOWN TO THE KITCHEN.
UH, ARTHUR?
WE JUST NEED SOME SORT OF DIVERSION.
ABOUT THOSE STAIRS IN THE KITCHEN?
OH, DON'T WORRY. THEY'LL NEVER FIND THE ENTRANCE WITHOUT KNOWING WHERE TO LOOK. AND THE ONLY PEOPLE WHO KNOW WHERE IT IS ARE ME--

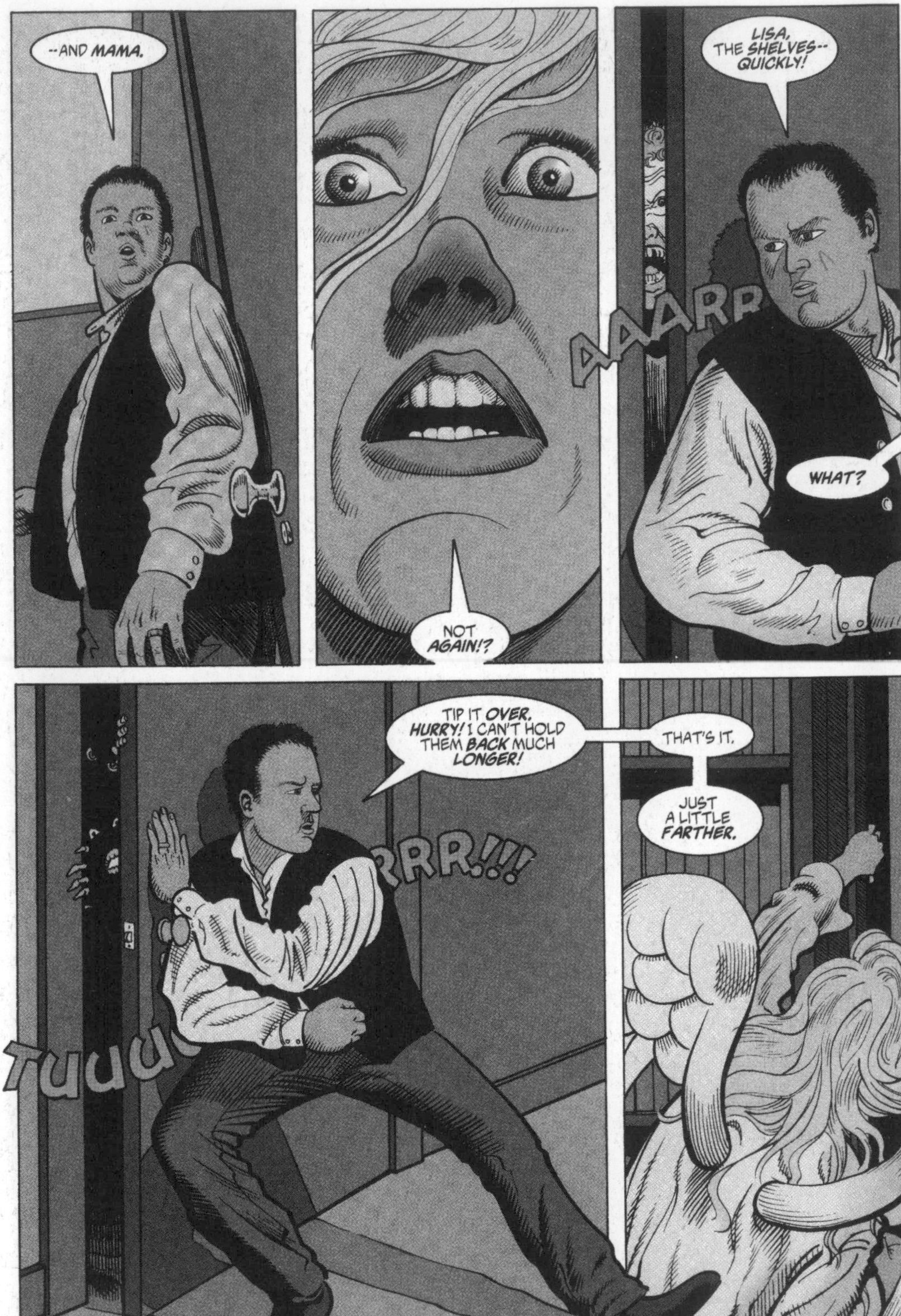
--AND MAMA.
NOT AGAIN!?
LISA, THE SHELVES-- QUICKLY!
AAARR
WHAT?
TUUU
RRR!!!
TIP IT OVER. HURRY! I CAN'T HOLD THEM BACK MUCH LONGER!
THAT'S IT.
JUST A LITTLE FARTHER.

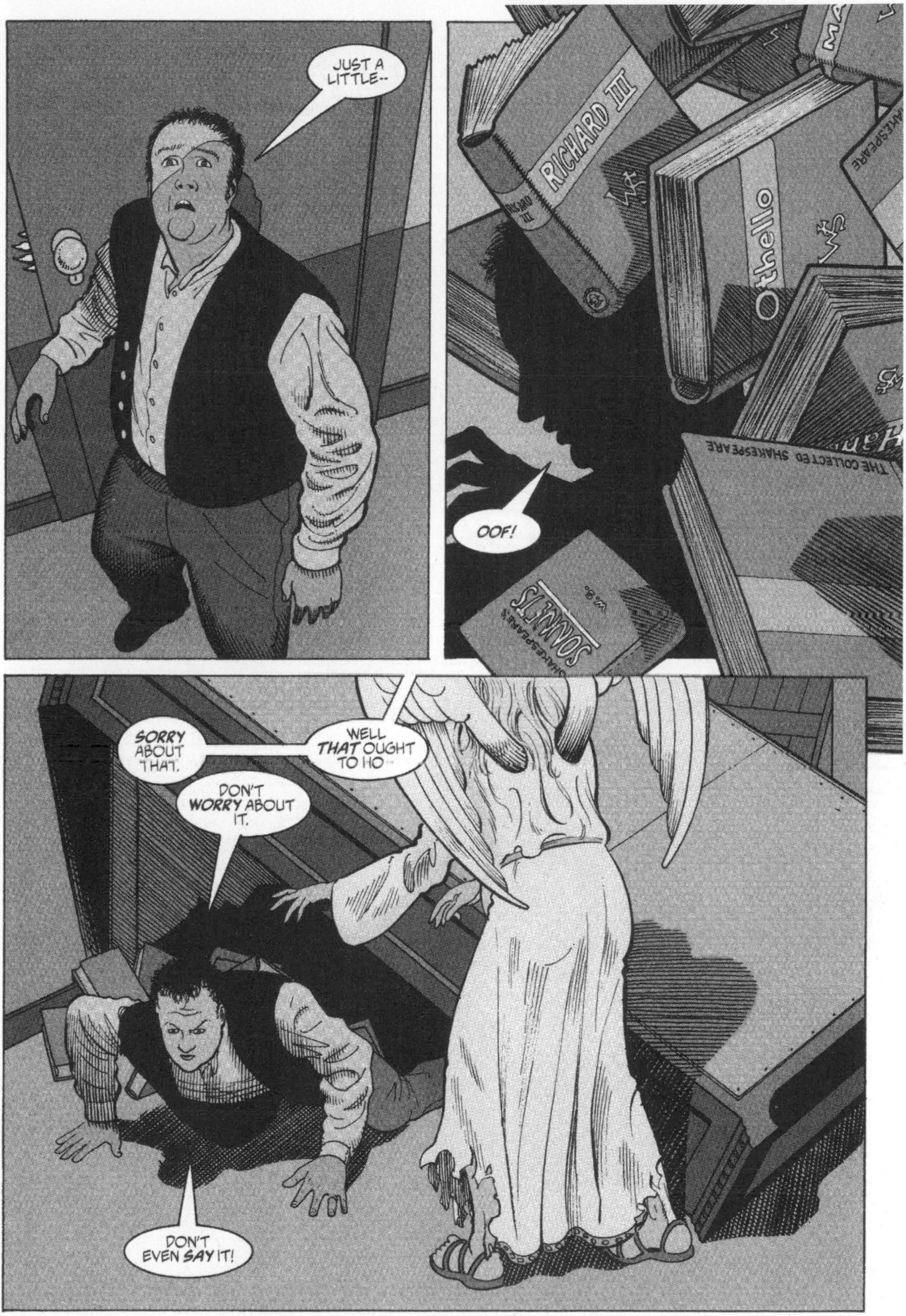
JUST A LITTLE--
RICHARD III
Othello
SHAKESPEARE
THE COLLECTED SHAKESPEARE
OOF!
SHAKESPEARE'S SONNETS
WELL THAT OUGHT TO HO--
SORRY ABOUT THAT.
DON'T WORRY ABOUT IT.
DON'T EVEN SAY IT!

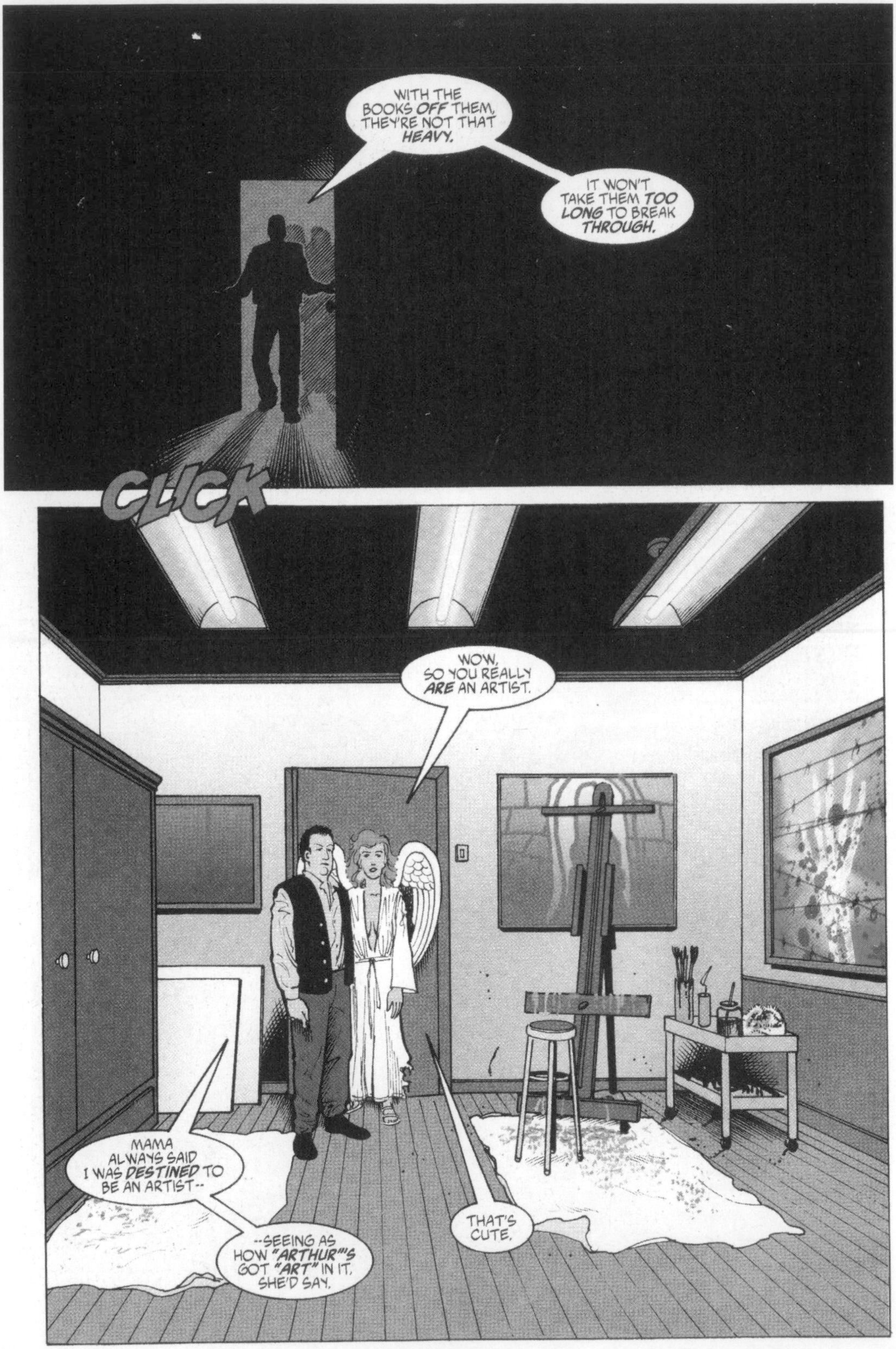
WITH THE BOOKS OFF THEM, THEY'RE NOT THAT HEAVY.
IT WON'T TAKE THEM TOO LONG TO BREAK THROUGH.
CLICK
WOW, SO YOU REALLY ARE AN ARTIST.
MAMA ALWAYS SAID I WAS DESTINED TO BE AN ARTIST--
--SEEING AS HOW "ARTHUR"'S GOT "ART" IN IT, SHE'D SAY.
THAT'S CUTE.

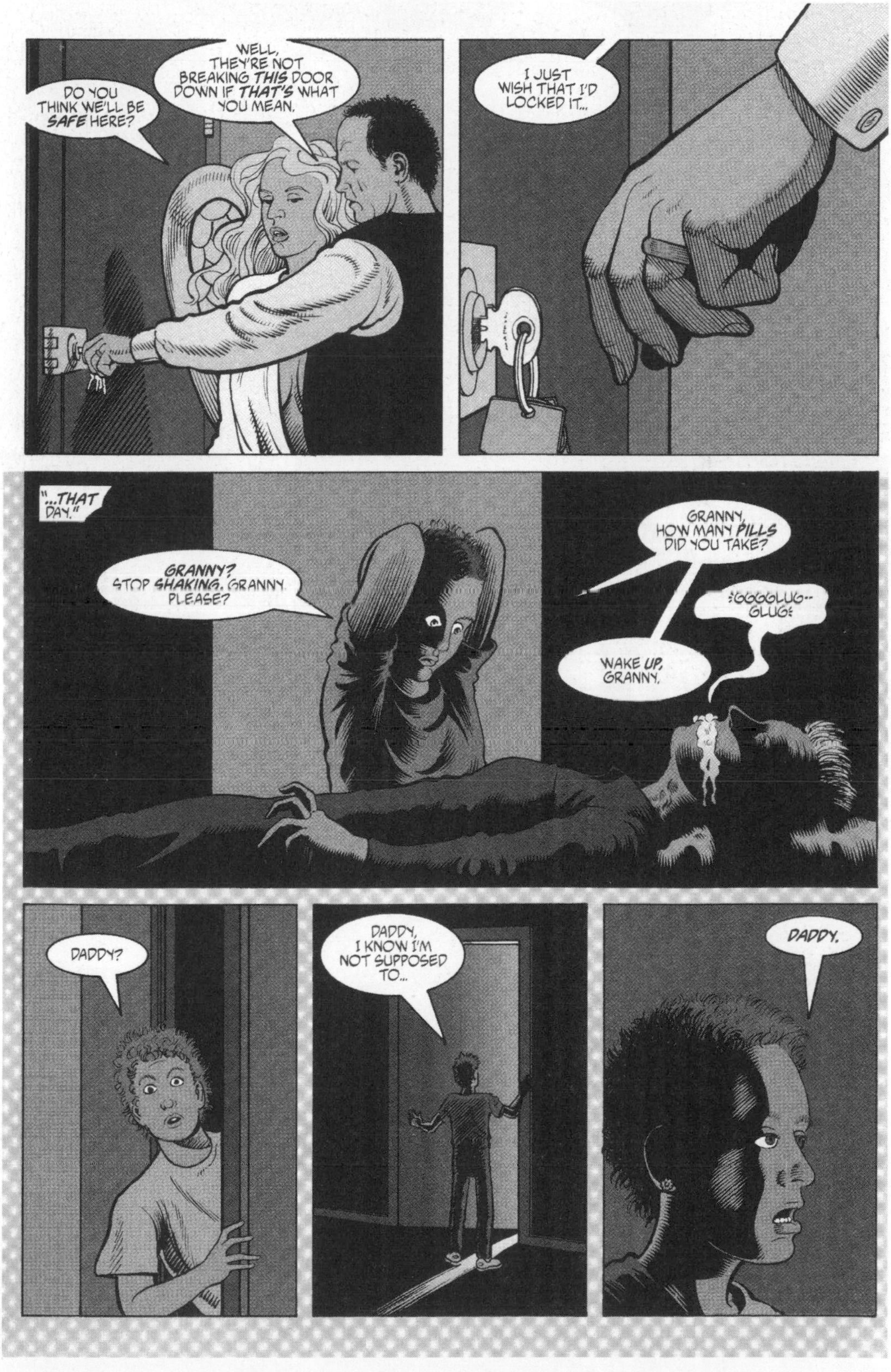
DO YOU THINK WE'LL BE SAFE HERE?
WELL, THEY'RE NOT BREAKING THIS DOOR DOWN IF THAT'S WHAT YOU MEAN.
I JUST WISH THAT I'D LOCKED IT...
"...THAT DAY."
GRANNY? STOP SHAKING, GRANNY. PLEASE?
GRANNY, HOW MANY PILLS DID YOU TAKE?
GGGGLUG-- GLUG
WAKE UP, GRANNY.
DADDY?
DADDY, I KNOW I'M NOT SUPPOSED TO...
DADDY.

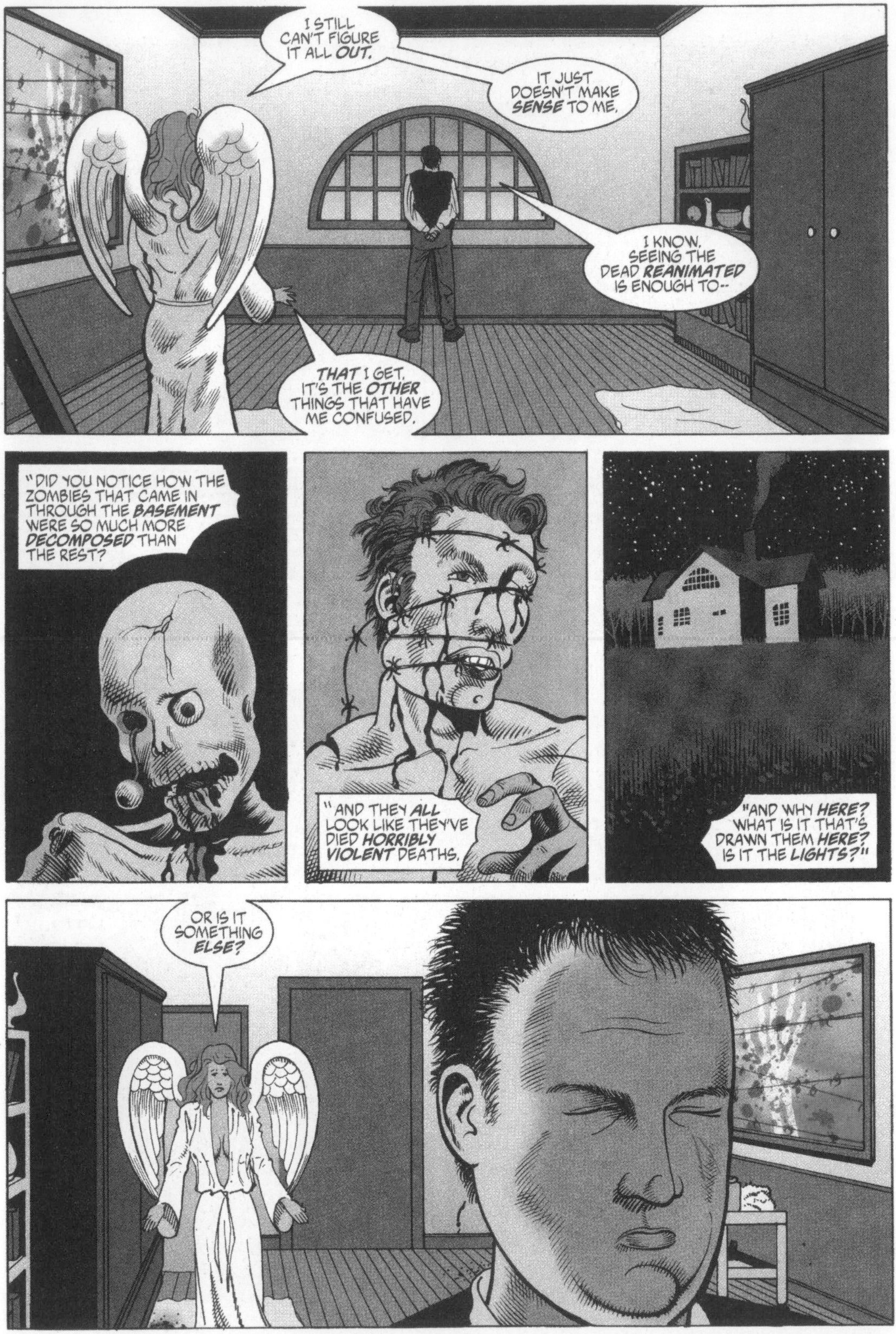
I STILL CAN'T FIGURE IT ALL OUT.
IT JUST DOESN'T MAKE SENSE TO ME.
I KNOW. SEEING THE DEAD REANIMATED IS ENOUGH TO--
THAT I GET. IT'S THE OTHER THINGS THAT HAVE ME CONFUSED.
"DID YOU NOTICE HOW THE ZOMBIES THAT CAME IN THROUGH THE BASEMENT WERE SO MUCH MORE DECOMPOSED THAN THE REST?
"AND THEY ALL LOOK LIKE THEY'VE DIED HORRIBLY VIOLENT DEATHS.
"AND WHY HERE? WHAT IS IT THAT'S DRAWN THEM HERE? IS IT THE LIGHTS?"
OR IS IT SOMETHING ELSE?

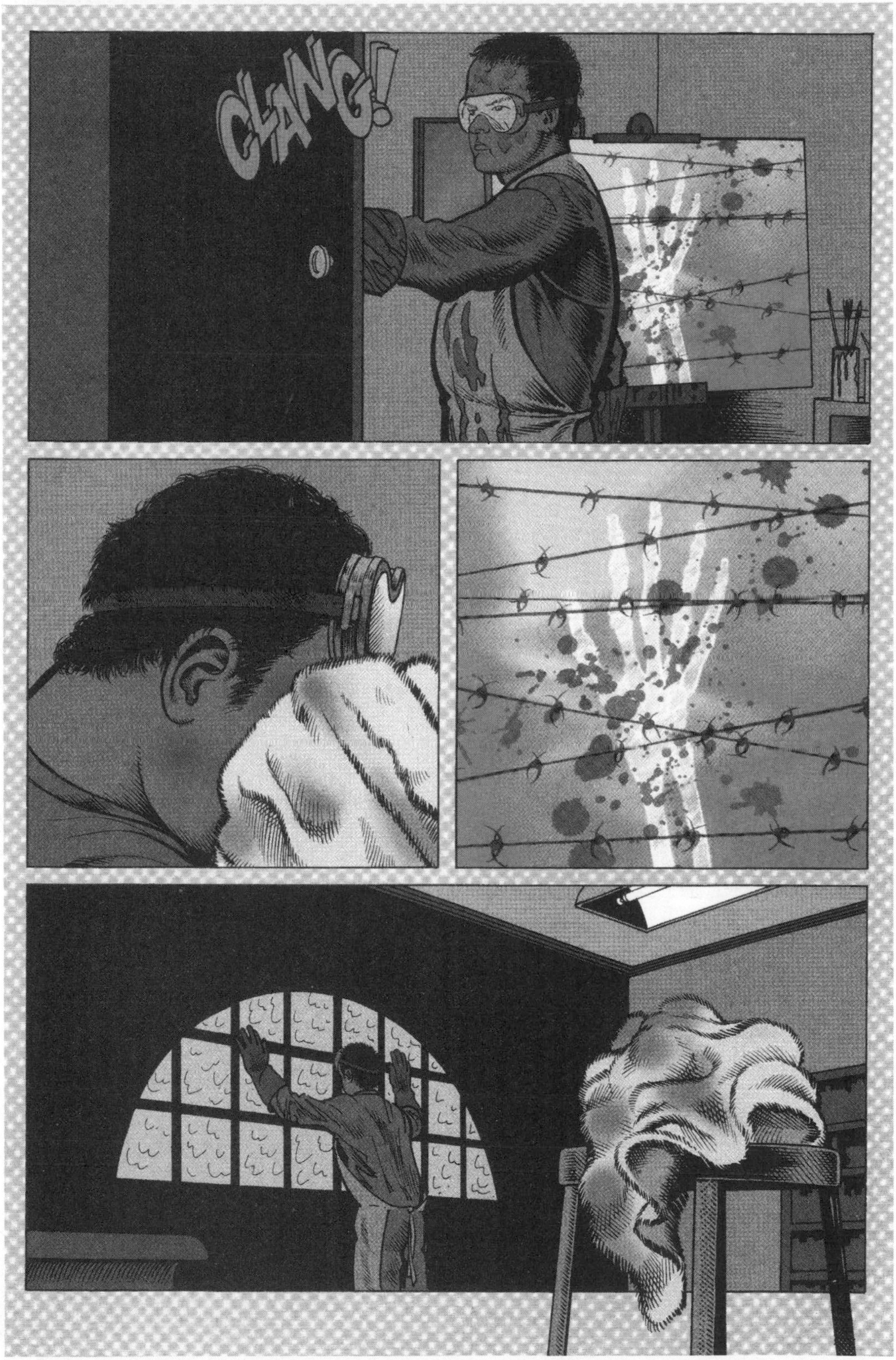
CLANG!

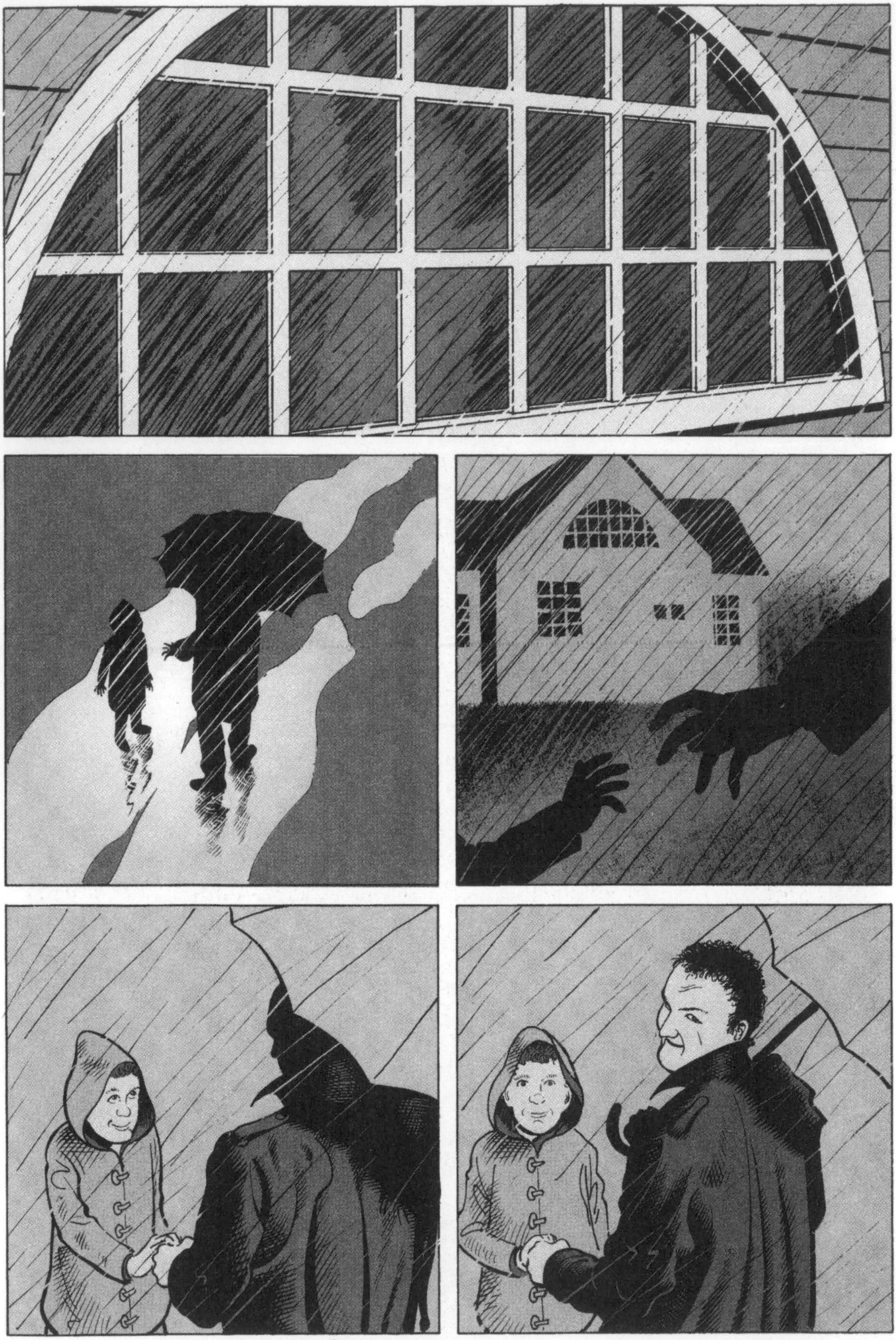

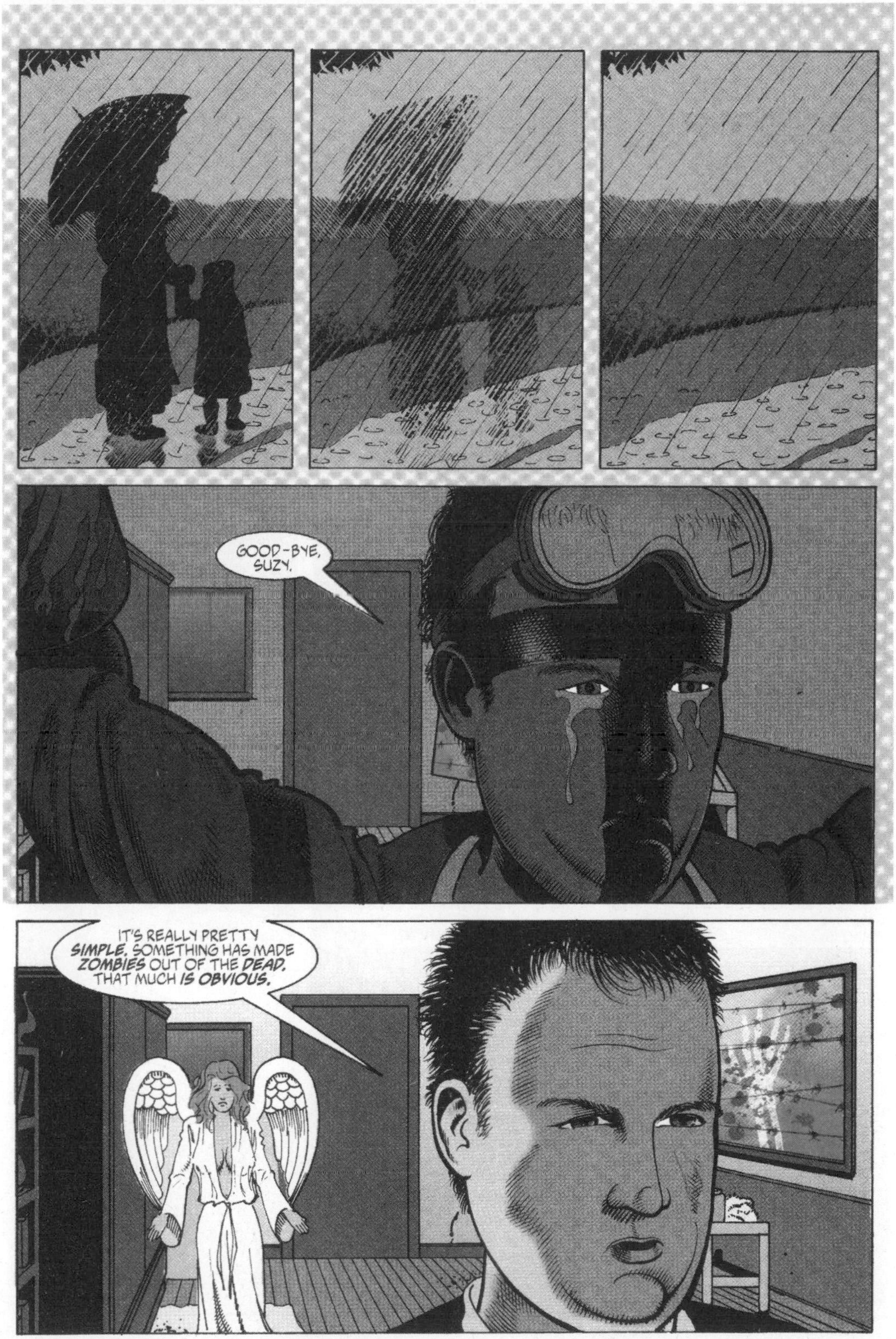
GOOD-BYE, SUZY.
IT'S REALLY PRETTY SIMPLE. SOMETHING HAS MADE ZOMBIES OUT OF THE DEAD. THAT MUCH IS OBVIOUS.

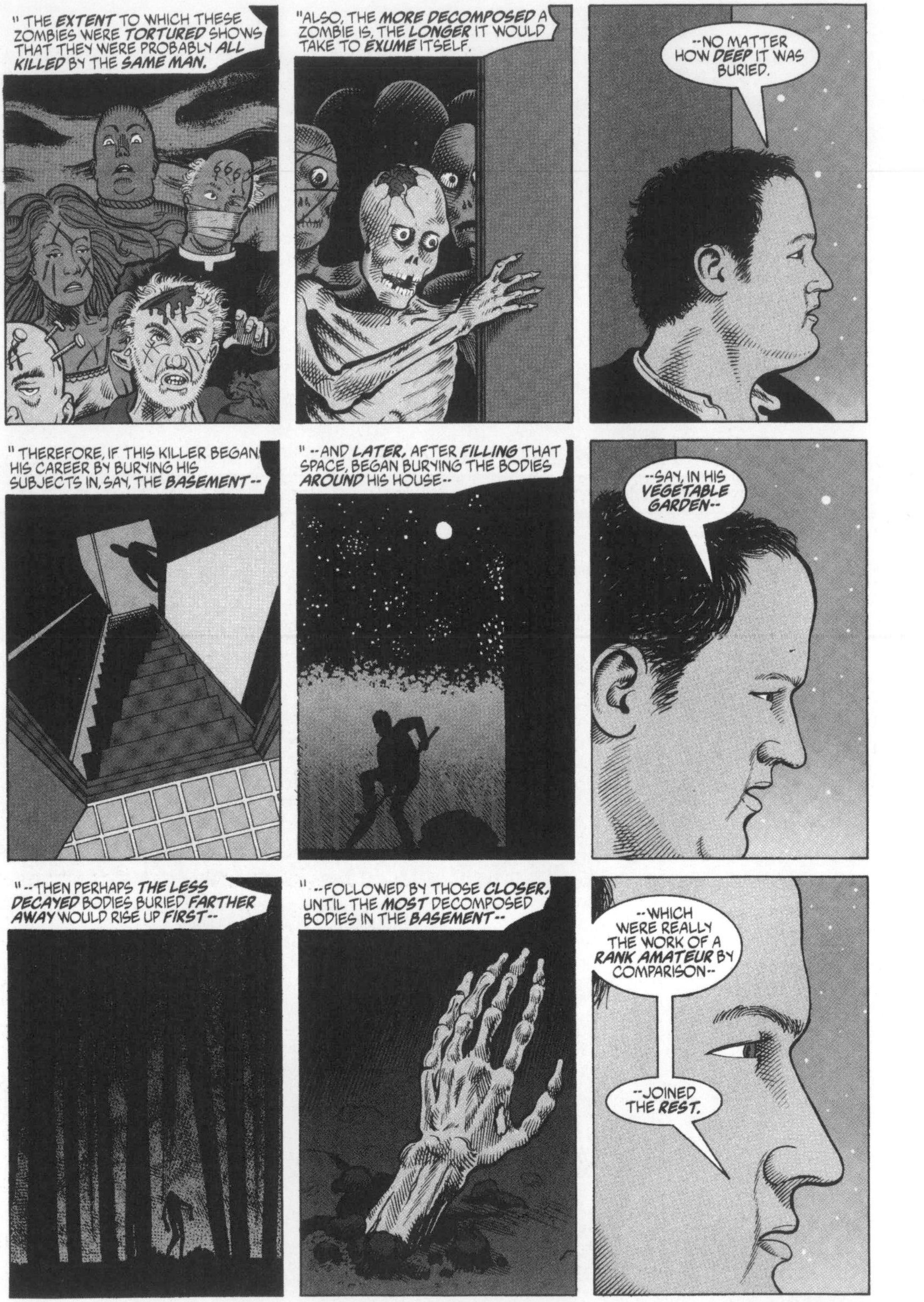
"THE EXTENT TO WHICH THESE ZOMBIES WERE TORTURED SHOWS THAT THEY WERE PROBABLY ALL KILLED BY THE SAME MAN.
"ALSO, THE MORE DECOMPOSED A ZOMBIE IS, THE LONGER IT WOULD TAKE TO EXUME ITSELF.
--NO MATTER HOW DEEP IT WAS BURIED.
"THEREFORE, IF THIS KILLER BEGAN HIS CAREER BY BURYING HIS SUBJECTS IN, SAY, THE BASEMENT--
"--AND LATER, AFTER FILLING THAT SPACE, BEGAN BURYING THE BODIES AROUND HIS HOUSE--
--SAY, IN HIS VEGETABLE GARDEN--
"--THEN PERHAPS THE LESS DECAYED BODIES BURIED FARTHER AWAY WOULD RISE UP FIRST--
"--FOLLOWED BY THOSE CLOSER, UNTIL THE MOST DECOMPOSED BODIES IN THE BASEMENT--
--WHICH WERE REALLY THE WORK OF A RANK AMATEUR BY COMPARISON--
--JOINED THE REST.

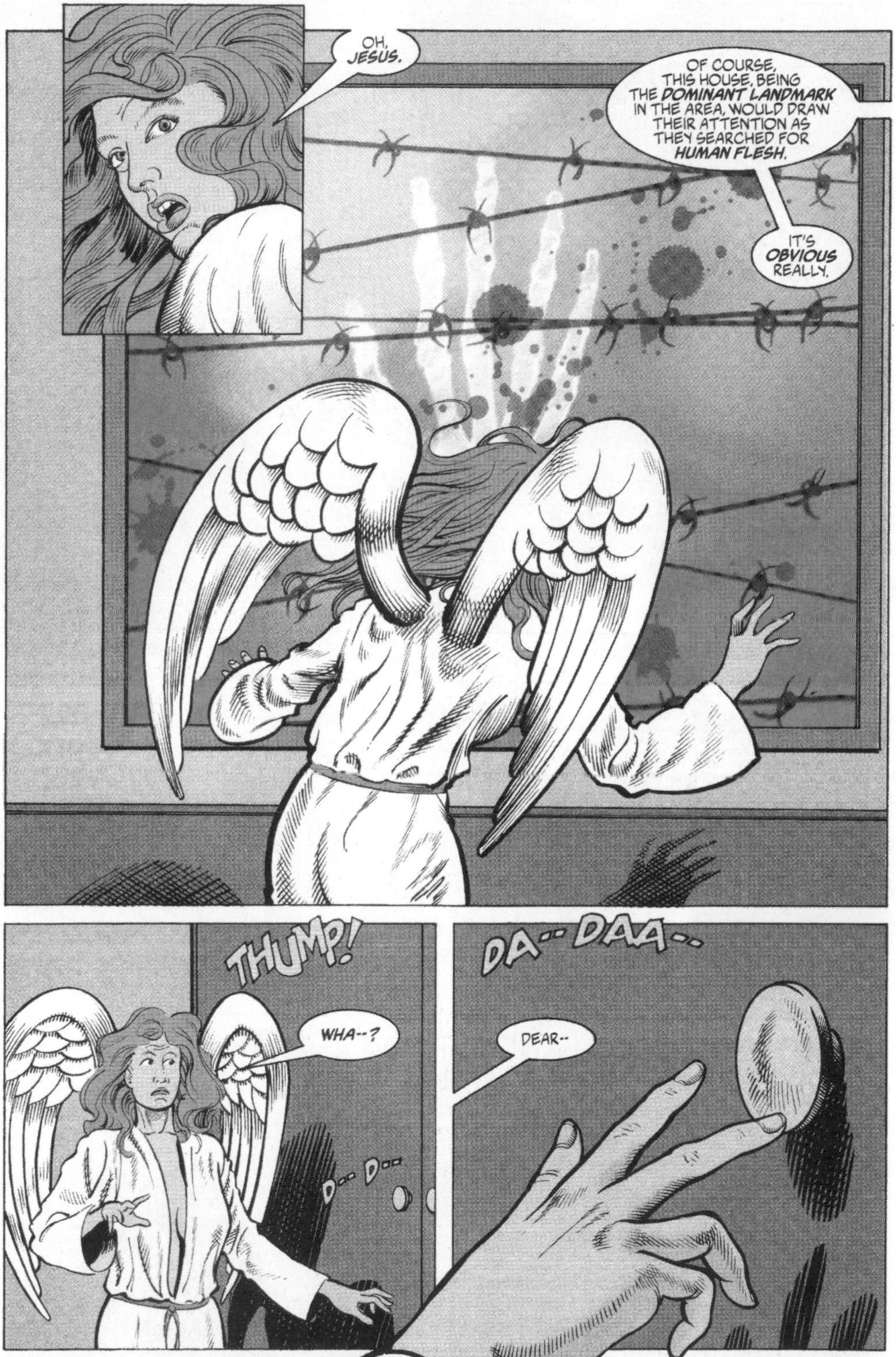
OH, JESUS.
OF COURSE, THIS HOUSE, BEING THE DOMINANT LANDMARK IN THE AREA, WOULD DRAW THEIR ATTENTION AS THEY SEARCHED FOR HUMAN FLESH.
IT'S OBVIOUS REALLY.
THUMP!
WHA--?
D-- D--
DA-- DAA--
DEAR--

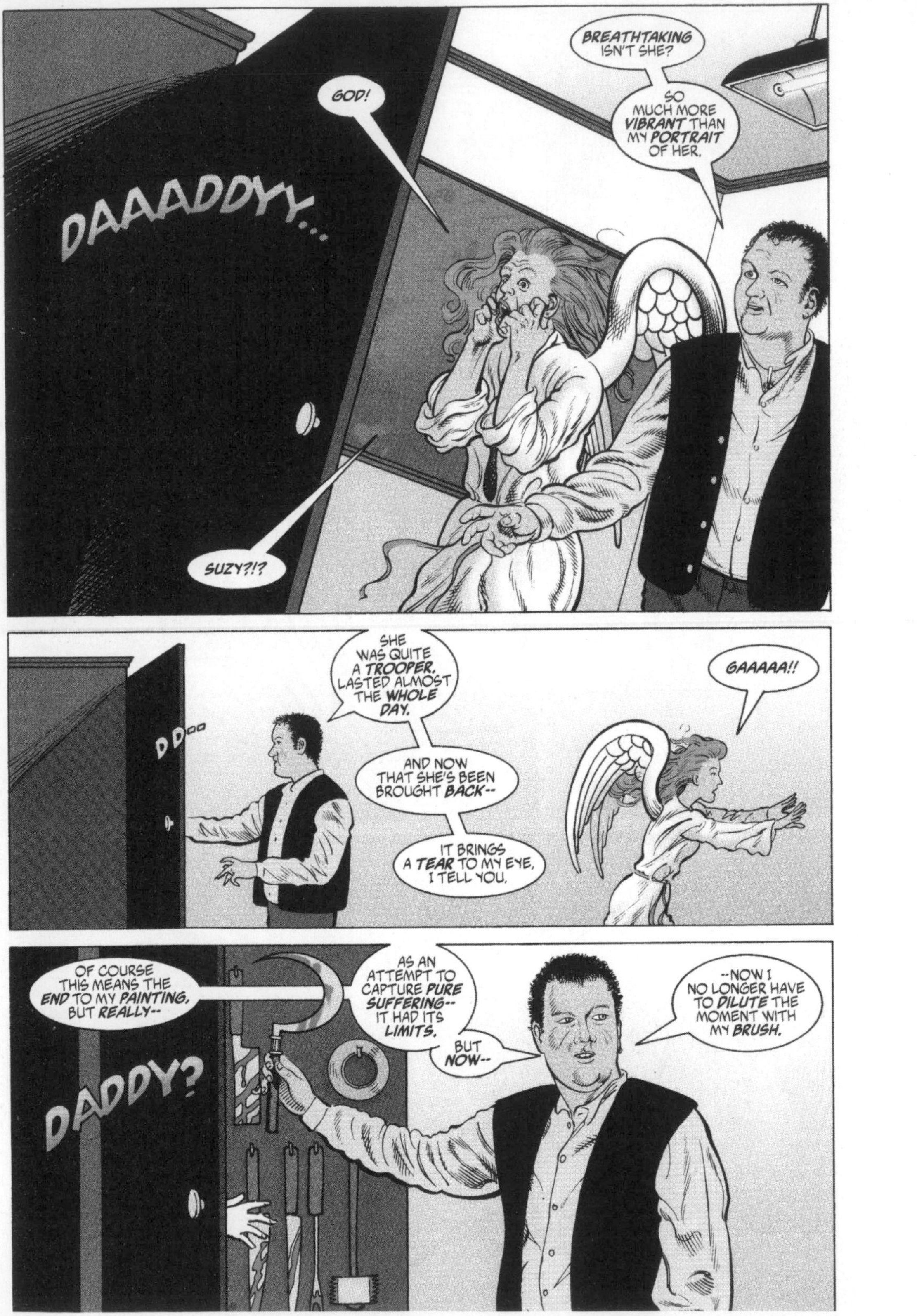

DAAADDYY...
GOD!
SUZY?!?
BREATHTAKING ISN'T SHE?
SO MUCH MORE VIBRANT THAN MY PORTRAIT OF HER.
D D...
SHE WAS QUITE A TROOPER. LASTED ALMOST THE WHOLE DAY.
AND NOW THAT SHE'S BEEN BROUGHT BACK--
IT BRINGS A TEAR TO MY EYE, I TELL YOU.
GAAAAA!!
OF COURSE THIS MEANS THE END TO MY PAINTING, BUT REALLY--
DADDY?
AS AN ATTEMPT TO CAPTURE PURE SUFFERING-- IT HAD ITS LIMITS.
BUT NOW--
--NOW I NO LONGER HAVE TO DILUTE THE MOMENT WITH MY BRUSH.

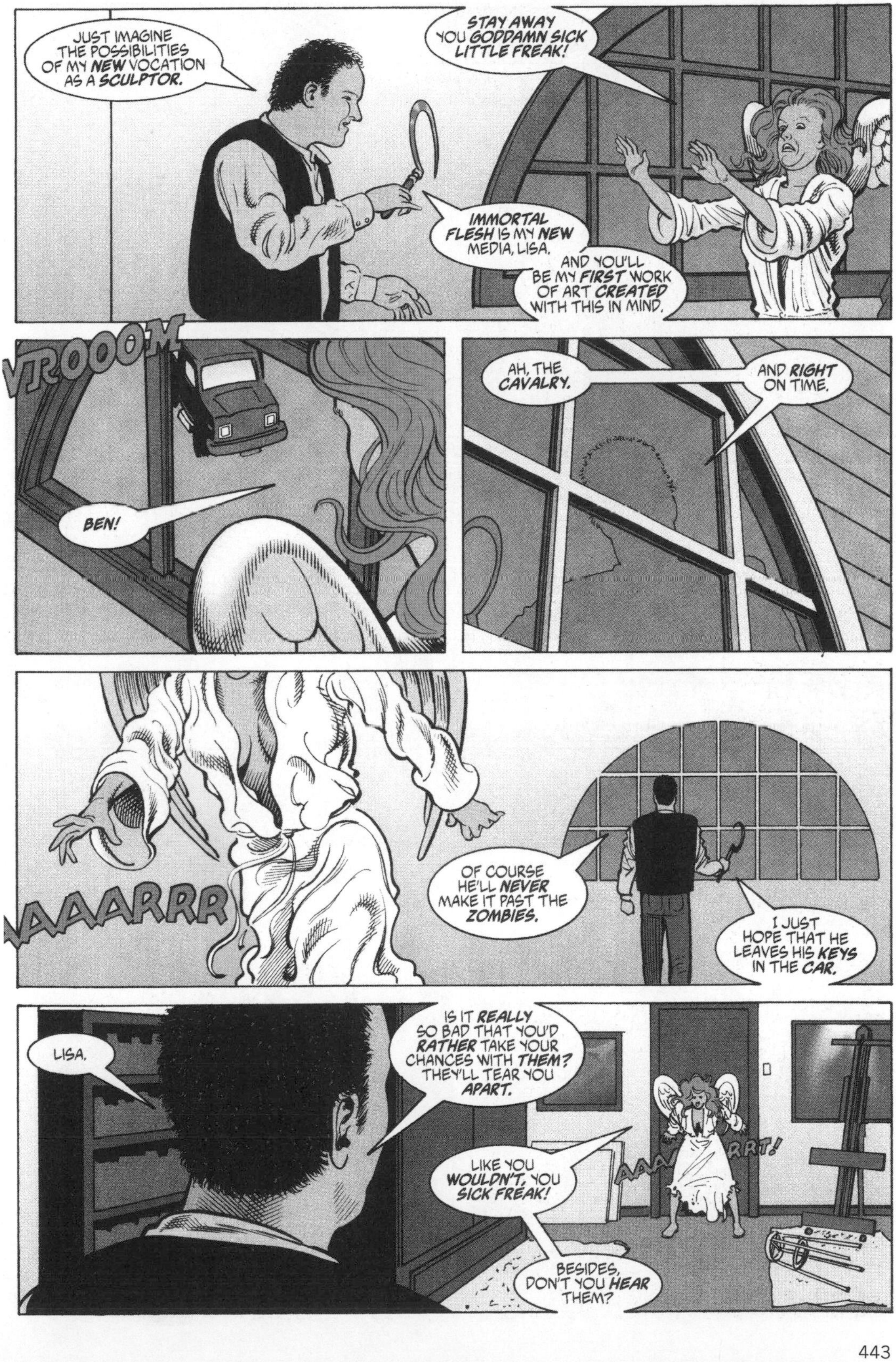
JUST IMAGINE THE POSSIBILITIES OF MY NEW VOCATION AS A SCULPTOR.
STAY AWAY YOU GODDAMN SICK LITTLE FREAK!
IMMORTAL FLESH IS MY NEW MEDIA, LISA.
AND YOU'LL BE MY FIRST WORK OF ART CREATED WITH THIS IN MIND.
VROOOM
BEN!
AH, THE CAVALRY.
AND RIGHT ON TIME.
AAAARRR
OF COURSE HE'LL NEVER MAKE IT PAST THE ZOMBIES.
I JUST HOPE THAT HE LEAVES HIS KEYS IN THE CAR.
LISA.
IS IT REALLY SO BAD THAT YOU'D RATHER TAKE YOUR CHANCES WITH THEM? THEY'LL TEAR YOU APART.
AAAA RRRT!
LIKE YOU WOULDN'T, YOU SICK FREAK!
BESIDES, DON'T YOU HEAR THEM?

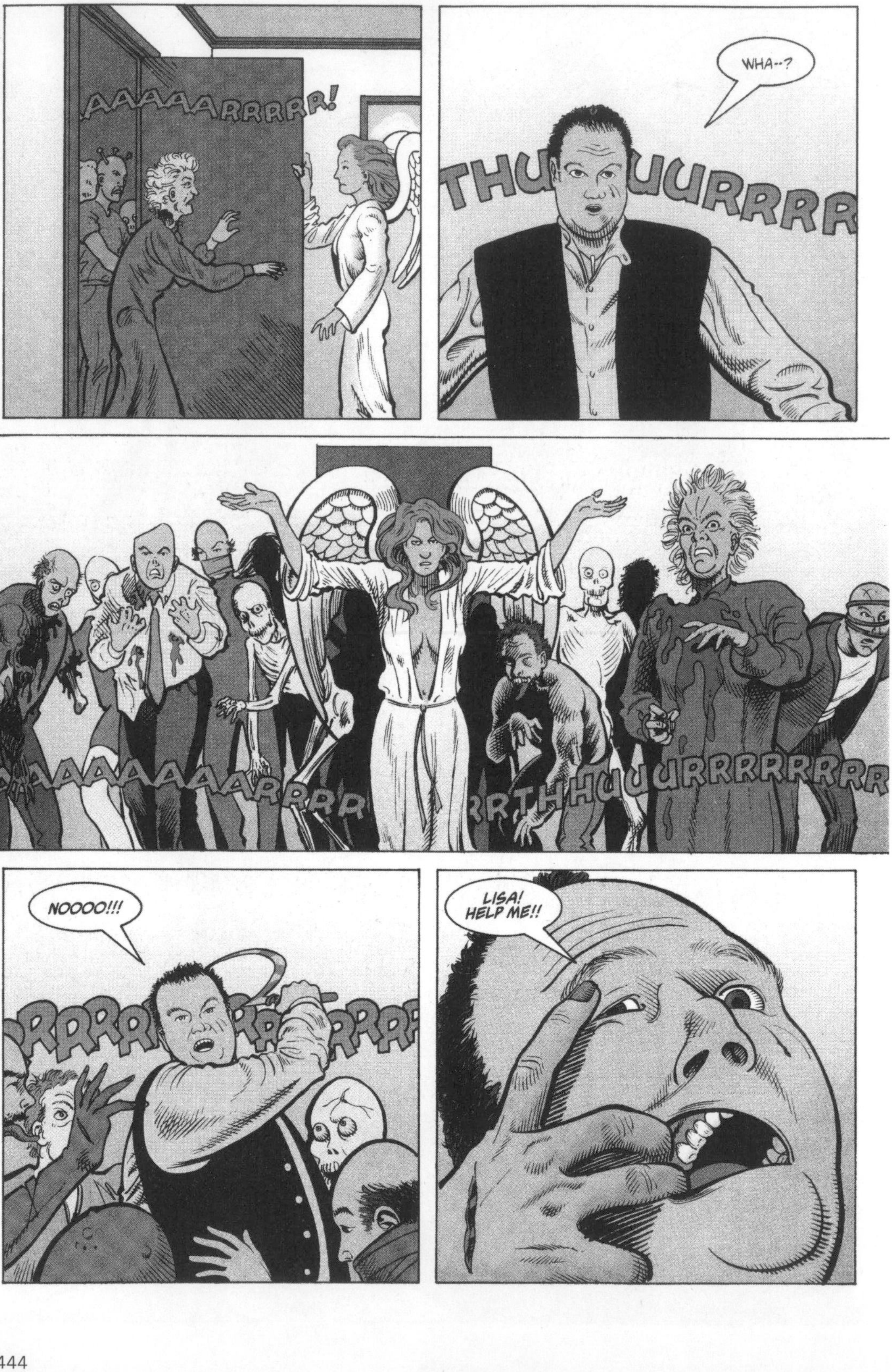
AAAAARRRRR!
WHA--?
THU
UURRRRR
AAAAAAAAAAAARRRR
RRTHHUUURRRRRRRRR
NOOOO!!!
LISA! HELP ME!!

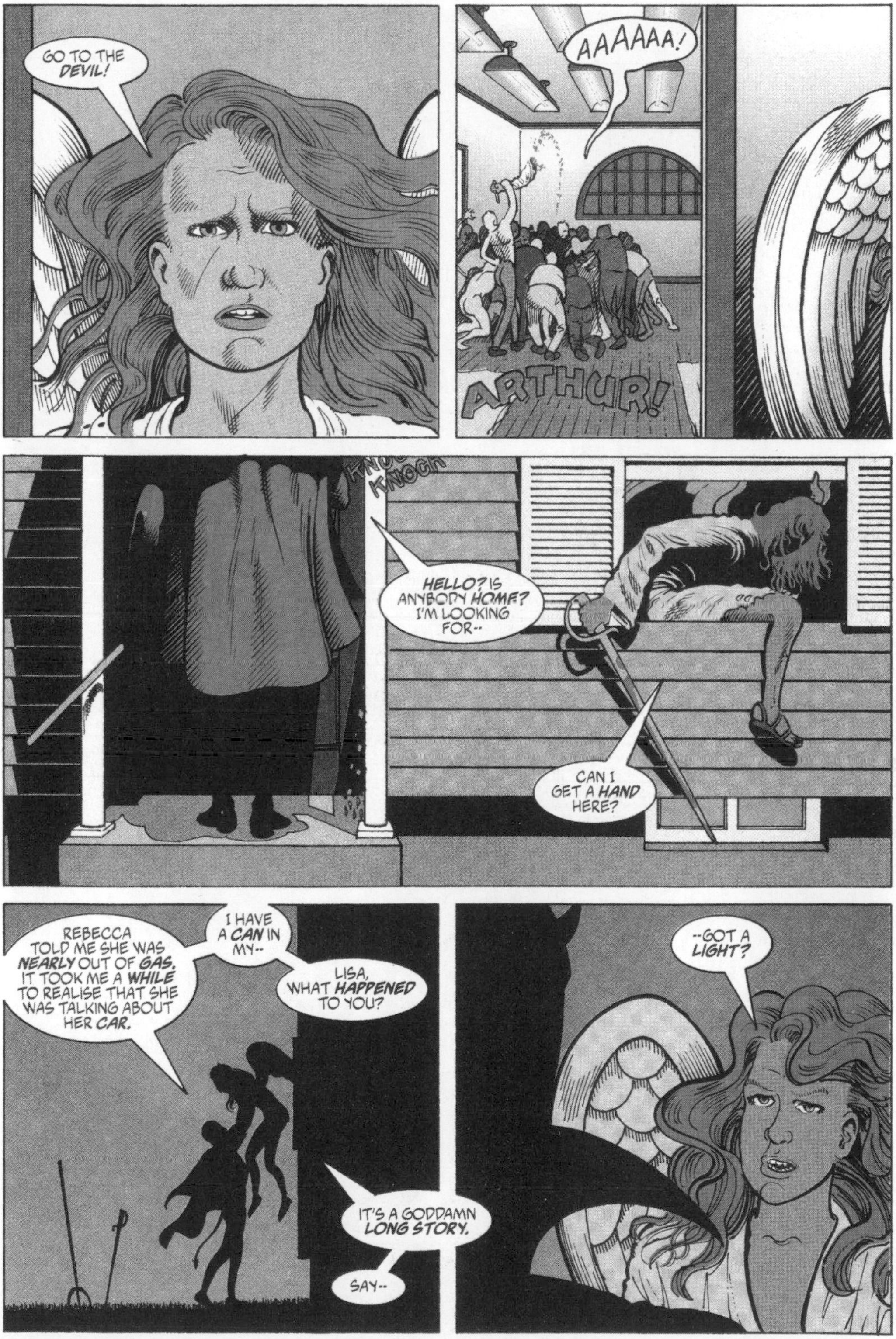
GO TO THE DEVIL!
AAAAAA!
ARTHUR!
KNOCK KNOCK
HELLO? IS ANYBODY HOME? I'M LOOKING FOR--
CAN I GET A HAND HERE?
REBECCA TOLD ME SHE WAS NEARLY OUT OF GAS. IT TOOK ME A WHILE TO REALISE THAT SHE WAS TALKING ABOUT HER CAR.
I HAVE A CAN IN MY--
LISA, WHAT HAPPENED TO YOU?
IT'S A GODDAMN LONG STORY.
SAY--
--GOT A LIGHT?

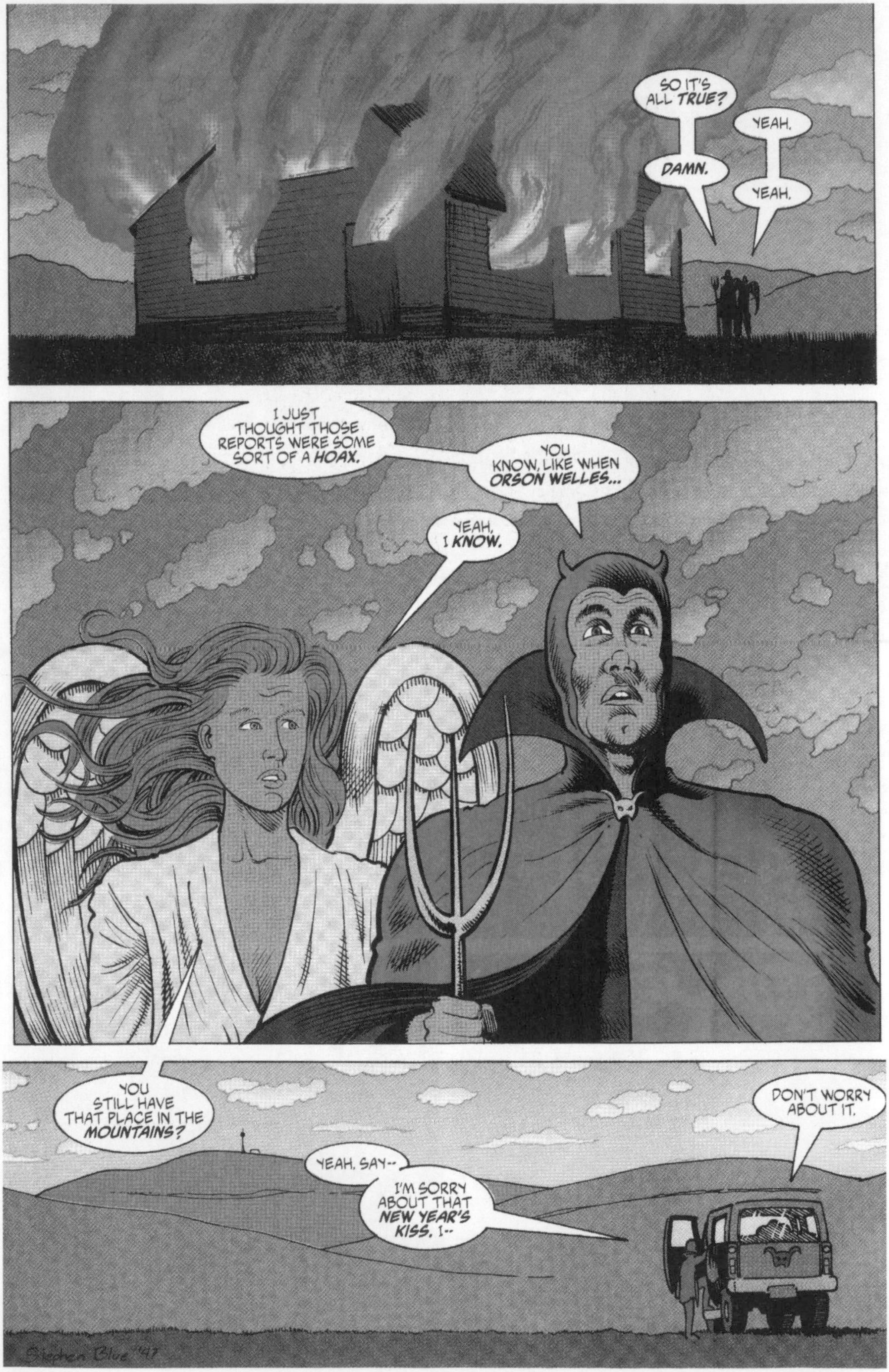
SO IT'S ALL TRUE?
YEAH.
DAMN.
YEAH.
I JUST THOUGHT THOSE REPORTS WERE SOME SORT OF A HOAX.
YOU KNOW, LIKE WHEN ORSON WELLES...
YEAH, I KNOW.
YOU STILL HAVE THAT PLACE IN THE MOUNTAINS?
DON'T WORRY ABOUT IT.
YEAH. SAY--
I'M SORRY ABOUT THAT NEW YEAR'S KISS. I--
Stephen Blue '97

"Zombies" (2007)

Creators: Kieron Gillen (script) Andy Bloor (art)

Just what would you do to try to survive? "Zombies" takes the premise that in a world where zombies rule you had better fit in.

Kieron Gillen is the writer of *Phonogram* (Image Comics), Andy Bloor's artwork appears in several anthologies by Accent UK and others.

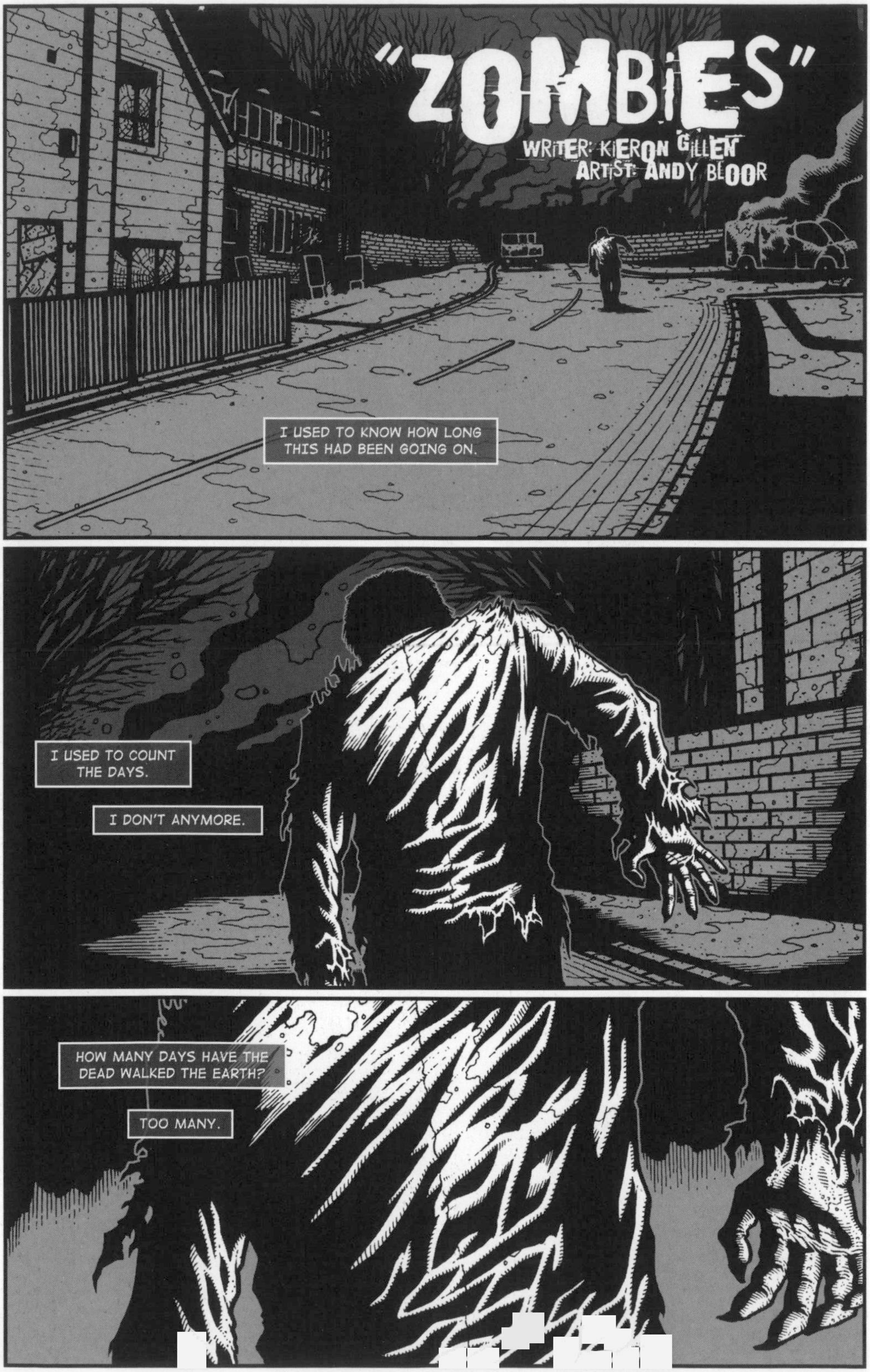
"ZOMBIES"
WRITER: KIERON GILLEN
ARTIST: ANDY BLOOR
I USED TO KNOW HOW LONG THIS HAD BEEN GOING ON.
I USED TO COUNT THE DAYS.
I DON'T ANYMORE.
HOW MANY DAYS HAVE THE DEAD WALKED THE EARTH?
TOO MANY.

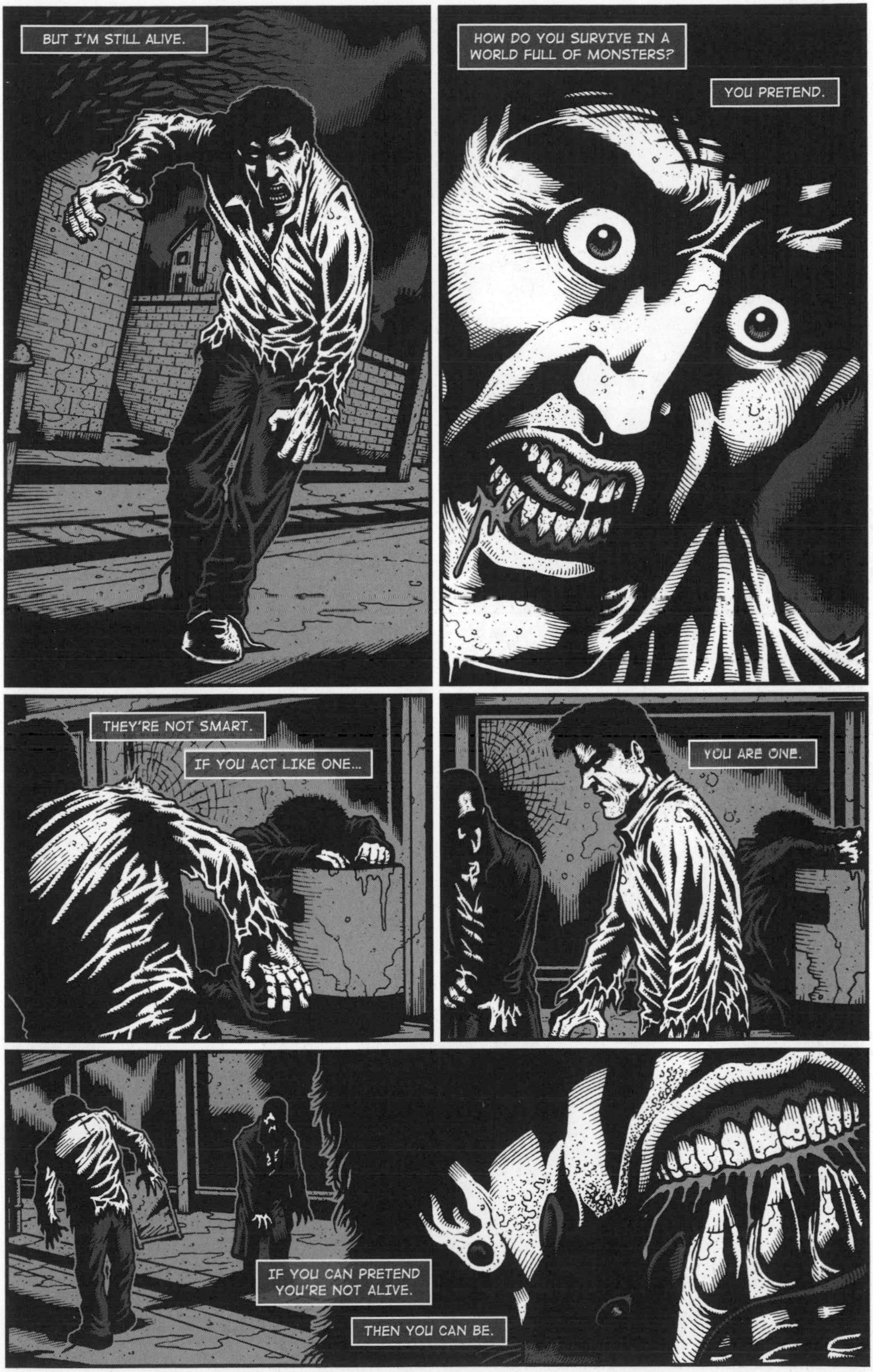
BUT I'M STILL ALIVE.
HOW DO YOU SURVIVE IN A WORLD FULL OF MONSTERS?
YOU PRETEND.
THEY'RE NOT SMART.
IF YOU ACT LIKE ONE...
YOU ARE ONE.
IF YOU CAN PRETEND YOU'RE NOT ALIVE.
THEN YOU CAN BE.

SO YOU WALK LIKE YOU WERE BROKEN AT THE ANKLE.

AND YOU DROOL.

LET YOUR CLOTHES FALL APART.

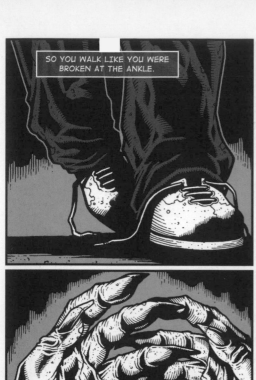

YOU SMEAR YOURSELF IN... EVERYTHING.

EVERY-FUCKING-THING.

YOU BUMP INTO DOORS.

UHHH.

WITHOUT SAYING "OW".

I STILL CLEAN MY TEETH.

CAN'T HELP IT.

BUT BEFORE I SHAMBLE OUT, I PREPARE MYSELF.

EVERY DAY, ALL I CAN TASTE IS OLD MEAT.

I'M NOT SURE WHETHER I'M MORE SCARED OF RUNNING OUT OF FOOD...

OR RUNNING OUT OF TOOTHPASTE.

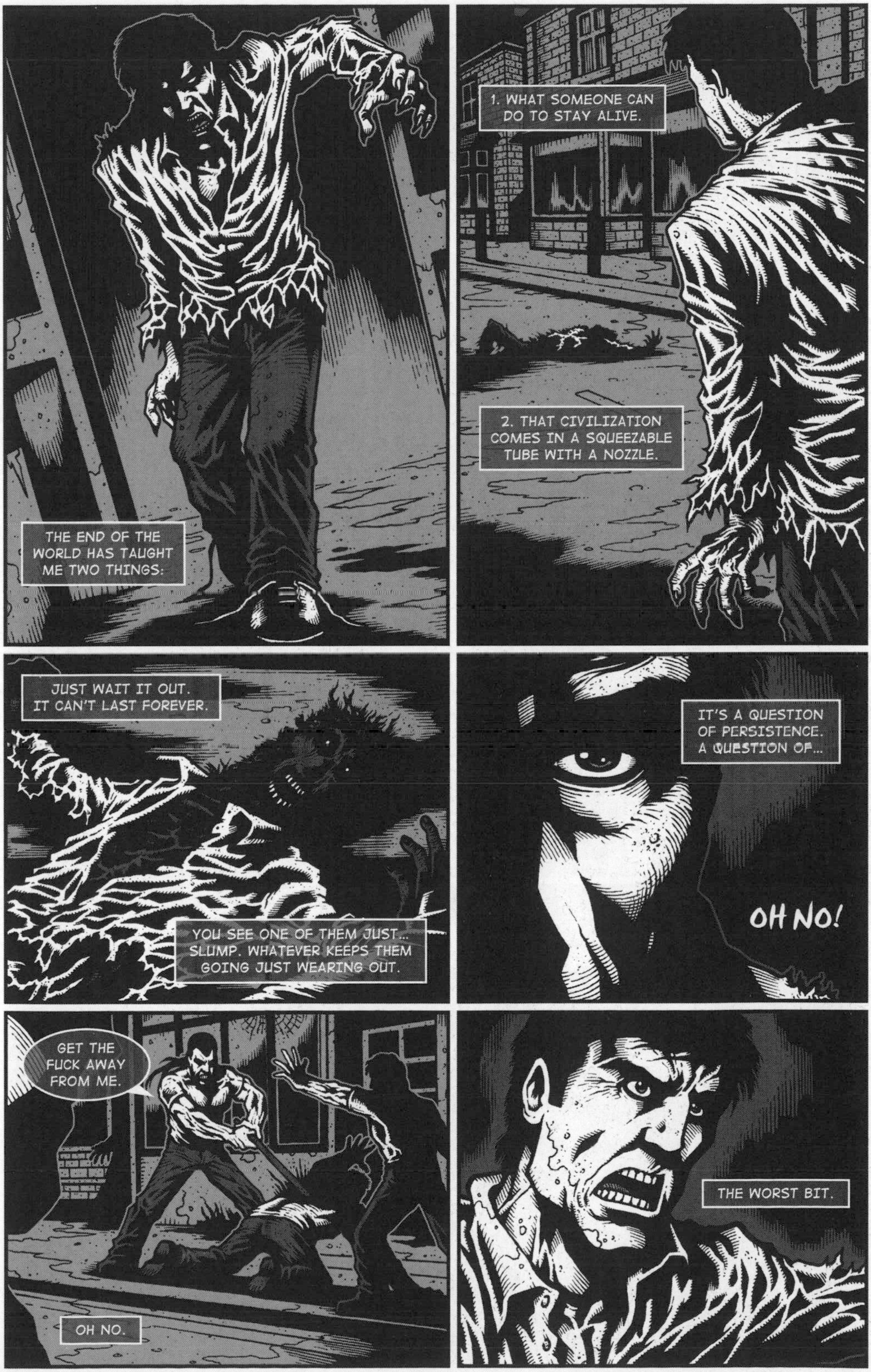
THE END OF THE WORLD HAS TAUGHT ME TWO THINGS:
1. WHAT SOMEONE CAN DO TO STAY ALIVE.
2. THAT CIVILIZATION COMES IN A SQUEEZABLE TUBE WITH A NOZZLE.
JUST WAIT IT OUT. IT CAN'T LAST FOREVER.
YOU SEE ONE OF THEM JUST... SLUMP. WHATEVER KEEPS THEM GOING JUST WEARING OUT.
IT'S A QUESTION OF PERSISTENCE. A QUESTION OF...
OH NO!
GET THE FUCK AWAY FROM ME.
OH NO.
THE WORST BIT.

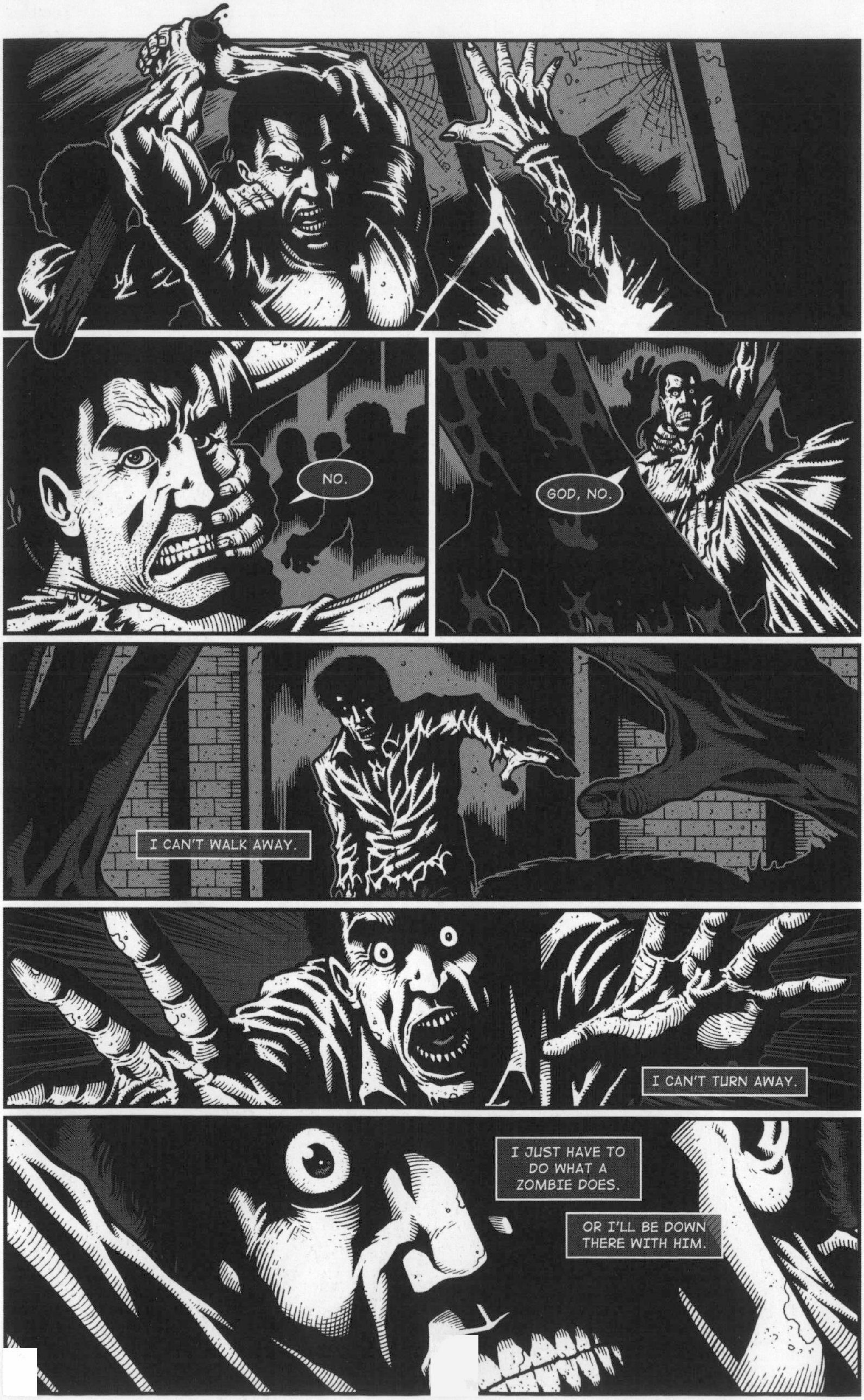
NO.
GOD, NO.
I CAN'T WALK AWAY.
I CAN'T TURN AWAY.
I JUST HAVE TO DO WHAT A ZOMBIE DOES.
OR I'LL BE DOWN THERE WITH HIM.

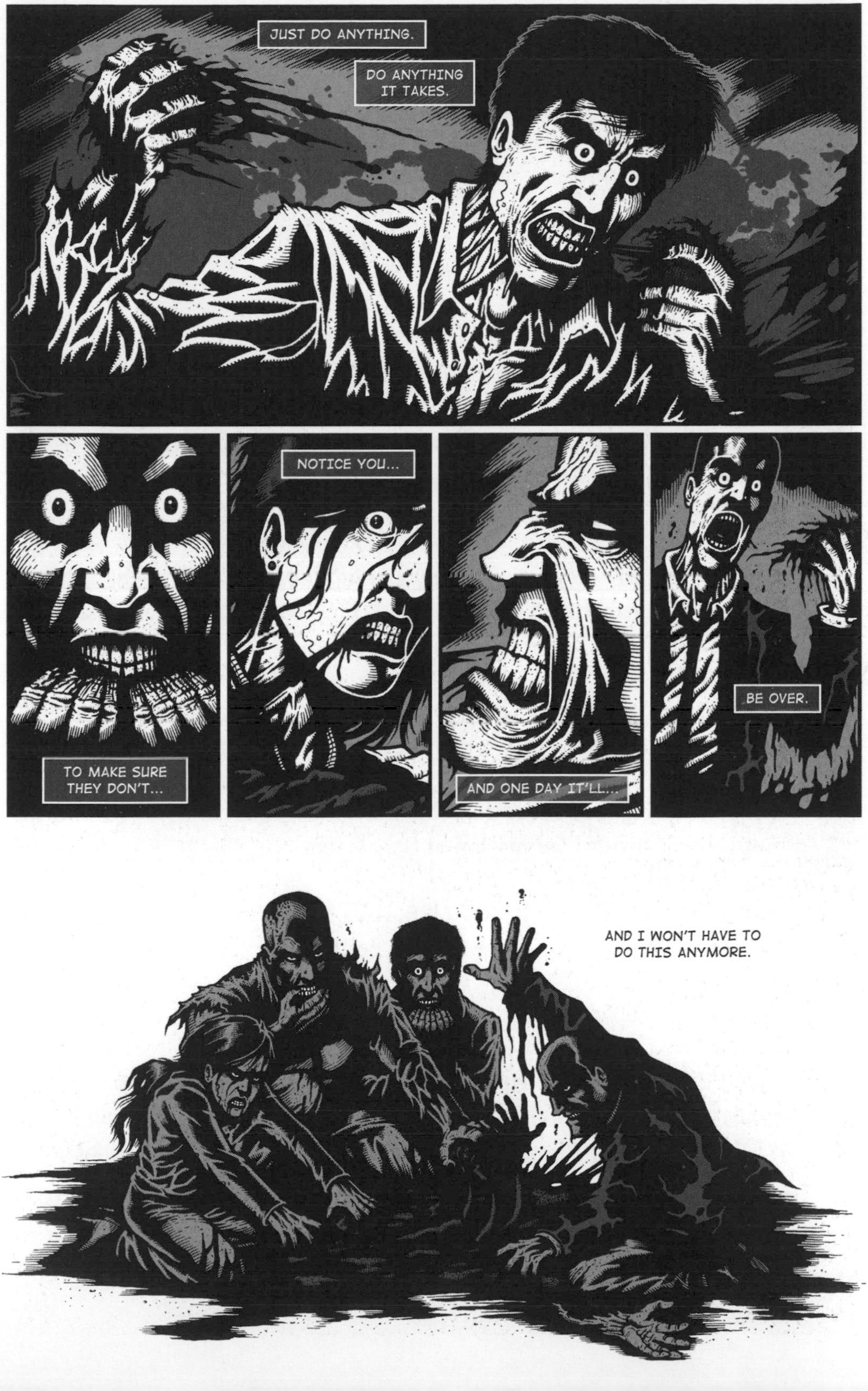
JUST DO ANYTHING.
DO ANYTHING IT TAKES.
TO MAKE SURE THEY DON'T...
NOTICE YOU...
AND ONE DAY IT'LL...
BE OVER.
AND I WON'T HAVE TO DO THIS ANYMORE.

Acknowledgments

"Making Amends" , copyright © 2004 by Steve Niles, Josh Medors, and Idea + Design Works. Originally published in Horrorcide, 2004. Reprinted by permission of the writer and artist, and IDW.

"Pariah" , copyright © 2007 by Jon Ayre & One Neck. Originally published in *Zombies*, 2007. Reprinted by permission of the writer and the artist.

"In Sickness", copyright © 2007 by Jon Ayre & Stephen Hill.

"Necrotic: Dead Flesh On A Living Body" , copyright © 2001 by Buddy Scalera. Originally published by After Hours Press, 2001. Reprinted by permission of the author.

"The Immortals" , copyright © by Darko Macan & Edvin Biukovic. Originally published in *Negative Burn*, 2005. Reprinted by permission of the writer, and the artist's estate.

"Flight From Earth" , copyright © 2005 by Publishing House Forward Press. Reprinted by permission of Publishing House Forward Press.

"Amy" , copyright © 1988 Gary Reed. Originally published by Calibre Press. Reprinted by permission of Gary Reed.

"Black Sabbath", copyright © 1986, Gary Reed. Originally published by Calibre Press, 1986. Reprinted by permission of Gary Reed.

"M*A*S*H" copyright © 2007 by Andrew Davies & Laura Watton.

"Dead Eyes Open", copyright © 2005 by Mathew Shepherd, Roy Boney & SLG Publishing. Originally published by SLG Publishing 2005-6. Reprinted by permission of the writer and artist, and SLG Publishing.

"Might of the Living Dead" , copyright © 2007 by Indio. Originally published in *Zombies*, 2007. Reprinted by permission of the author.

New and Forthcoming
Mammoth Comic Titles...

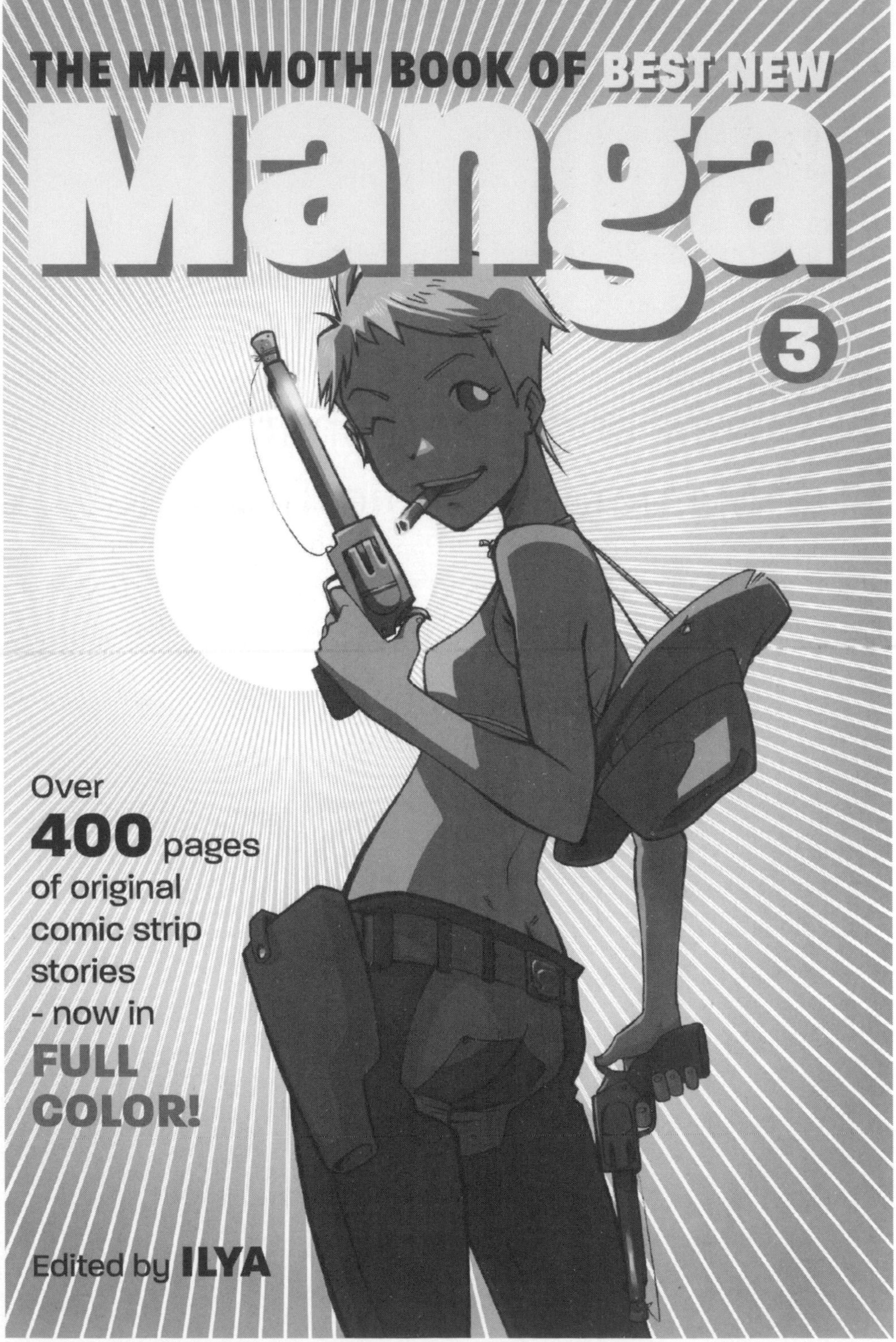
THE MAMMOTH BOOK OF BEST NEW
Manga
3
Over
400 pages
of original
comic strip
stories
- now in
FULL
COLOR!
Edited by ILYA

The Mammoth Book of Best New Manga 3

Edited by Ilya

£9.99 (UK); $15.95 (US); $17.00 (CAN)
978-1-84529-827-2 (UK); 978-0-76243-399-5 (US)

The new must-have collection of manga genius!

The essential collection for every manga fan, this latest volume of **Best New Manga** brings you two dozen self-contained comic strip stories from the superstars of tomorrow – for you to enjoy today!

Dystopic visions, wild aerial action, troubled romance, rueful robots, monster mayhem, ghosts, gourmets, and goofball humor – the manga world in all its colorful variety and every genre you can think of. Storytellers from East and West come together as equals, entire generations dancing to the beat of Japanese comics and animation. Unmissable!

'Visually stunning … spans the genres in every way you can imagine … a must for all anime fans.'—*Big Issue*

'An excellent collection, both for the quality and the diversity. Unreservedly recommended.'—*Manga Life*

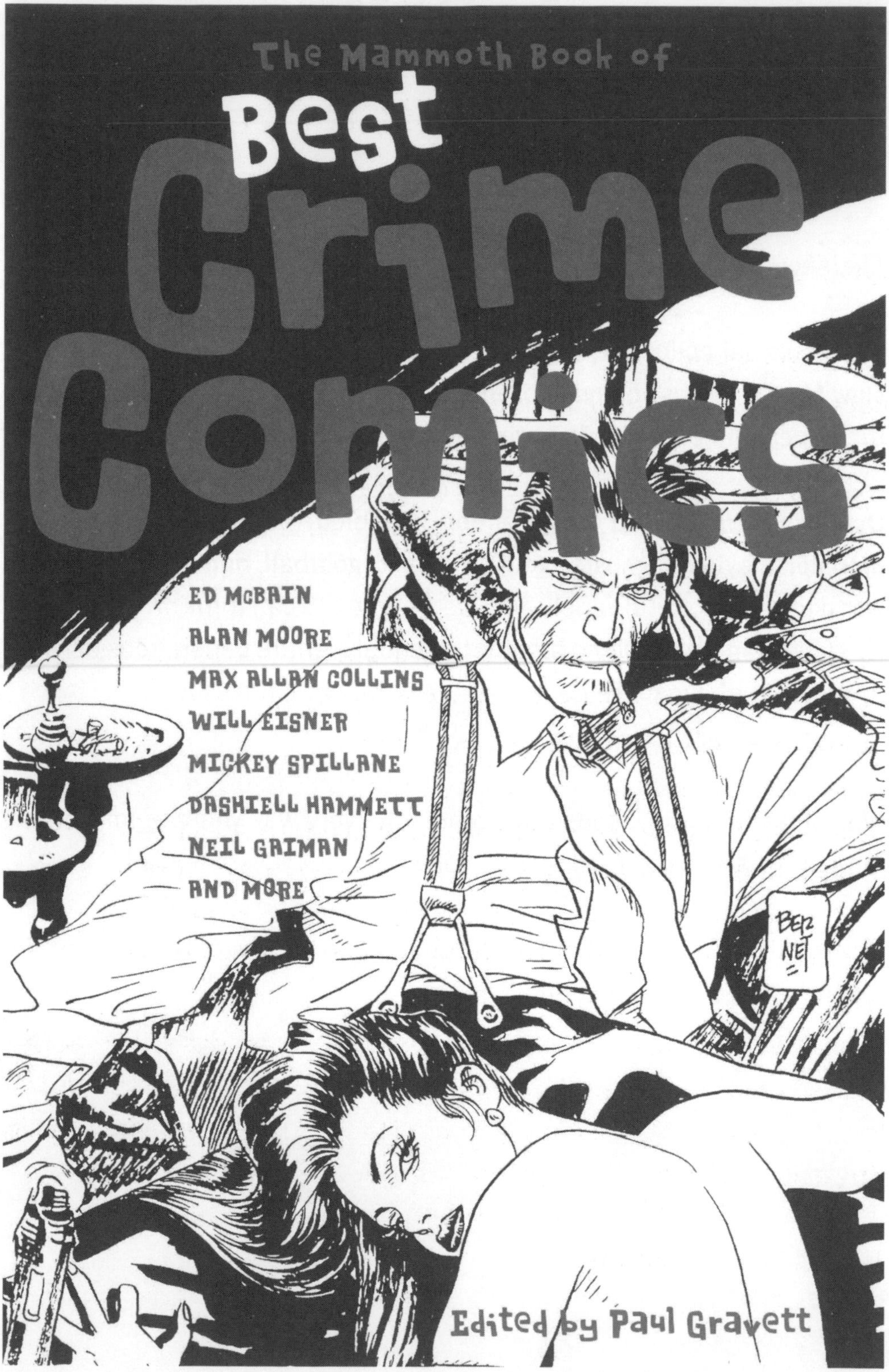
The Mammoth Book of
Best
Crime
Comics
ED McBAIN
ALAN MOORE
MAX ALLAN COLLINS
WILL EISNER
MICKEY SPILLANE
DASHIELL HAMMETT
NEIL GAIMAN
AND MORE
BERNET
Edited by Paul Gravett

The Mammoth Book of Best New Crime Comics

Edited by Paul Gravett

£12.99 (UK); $17.95 (US); $19.50 (CAN)
978-1-84529-710-7 (UK); 978-0-76243-394-0 (US)

24 of the greatest crime comics ever

These are some of the slickest, moodiest, graphic short stories ever collected, from the mean streets and sin cities of crime. They range from America's classic newspaper-strip serials and notorious uncensored comic books to modern graphic-novel masterpieces.

The gallery includes:

- **Dashiell Hammett & Alex Raymond**'s operator Secret Agent X-9
- **Will Eisner**'s masked man of mystery The Spirit
- **Mickey Spillane**'s tough-guy Mike Hammer
- **Ed McBain**'s streetwise police squad of 87th Precinct
- **José Muñoz & Carlos Sampayo**'s brooding ex-cop Alack Sinner
- **Max Allan Collins & Terry Beatty**'s femme fatale Ms. Tree
- **Enrique Sánchez Abuli & Jordi Bernet**'s venal hitman Torpedo
- **Charles Burns**'s wrestler and defective detective El Borbah

Spanning all shades of noir, this must-have collection is fully loaded with some of the greatest writers and artists in comics: Alan Moore, Neil Gaiman, Joe Simon, Jack Kirby, Johnny Craig, Alex Toth, Bernie Krigstein, Jack Cole, Jacques Tardi, Gianni De Luca and Paul Grist.

This, for sure, is one offer you can't refuse!

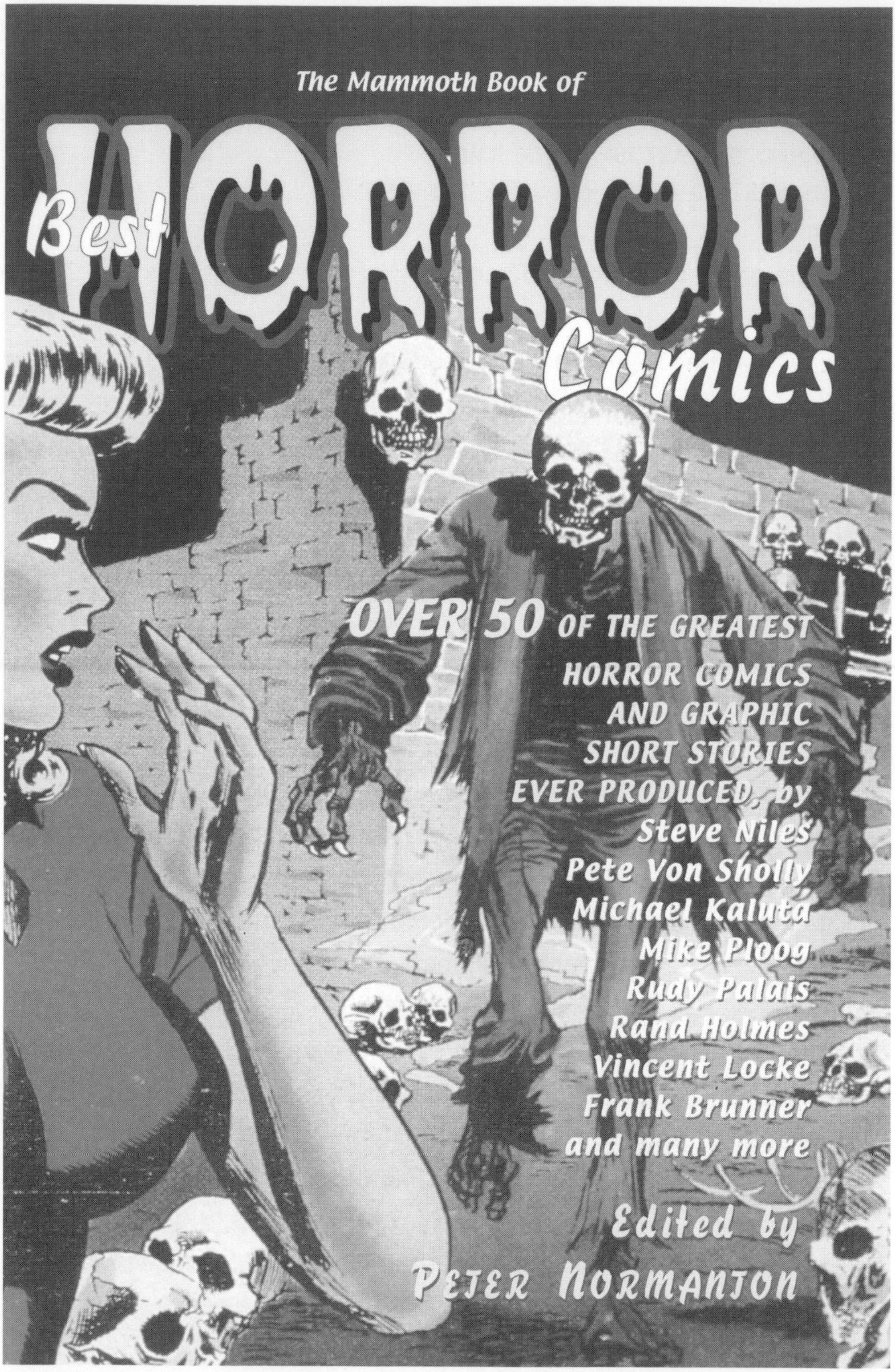

The Mammoth Book of
Best HORROR Comics
OVER 50 OF THE GREATEST HORROR COMICS AND GRAPHIC SHORT STORIES EVER PRODUCED, by
Steve Niles
Pete Von Sholly
Michael Kaluta
Mike Ploog
Rudy Palais
Rand Holmes
Vincent Locke
Frank Brunner
and many more
Edited by
Peter Normanton

The Mammoth Book of Best Horror Comics

Edited by Peter Normanton

£12.99 (UK); $17.95 (US); $21.50 (CAN)
978-1-84529-641-4 (UK); 978-0-78672-072-9 (US)

OVER 50 of the greatest horror comics of all time

Bringing together the finest names in comic book horror, here is a feast of graphic terror from the early decades of the pre-Code macabre—including the likes of Dark Mysteries, Chamber of Chills, Weird Terror and Journey into Fear—to the darkest fantasies of modern times.

Some of these stories from the 1950s were believed to have driven American youth into a frenzy, resulting in legislation to censor gruesome content. But the zombies, werewolves, and vampires refused to die and in recent decades, the damned and the dead have taken on even darker powers.

- One of these Days, from DEADWORLD — one of the finest zombie comics ever
- Steve Niles's CAL MCDONALD — modern horror with the noir of the 1950s
- Dreamsnake, from ROBERT E. HOWARD: MYTHMAKER — adaptation of the giant of fantasy horror
- Jerry Grandenetti's The Secret Files of Dr. Drew — a classic, in the style of Will Eisner
- Now Another Maniac, from Skywald's PSYCHO — uncompromising darkness